THE VICTORIA HISTORY
OF THE
COUNTIES OF ENGLAND

—

A HISTORY OF
MIDDLESEX

VOLUME V

THE VICTORIA HISTORY
OF THE
COUNTIES OF ENGLAND

EDITED BY R. B. PUGH, D. LIT.

THE UNIVERSITY OF LONDON
INSTITUTE OF
HISTORICAL RESEARCH

Oxford University Press

OXFORD LONDON GLASGOW NEW YORK
TORONTO MELBOURNE WELLINGTON CAPE TOWN
IBADAN NAIROBI DAR ES SALAAM LUSAKA ADDIS ABABA
KUALA LUMPUR SINGAPORE JAKARTA HONG KONG TOKYO
DELHI BOMBAY CALCUTTA MADRAS KARACHI

ISBN 0 19 722742 2

PRINTED IN GREAT BRITAIN BY
ROBERT MACLEHOSE AND CO. LTD
PRINTERS TO THE UNIVERSITY OF GLASGOW

INSCRIBED TO THE
MEMORY OF HER LATE MAJESTY
QUEEN VICTORIA
WHO GRACIOUSLY GAVE THE TITLE TO
AND ACCEPTED THE DEDICATION
OF THIS HISTORY

LITTLE STANMORE: THE INTERIOR OF ST. LAWRENCE'S CHURCH
Decorative painting of *c.* 1715 attributed to Francesco Sleter, Gaetano Brunetti, and Louis Laguerre

A HISTORY OF the County of

MIDDLESEX

EDITED BY T. F. T. BAKER

VOLUME V

PUBLISHED FOR

THE INSTITUTE OF HISTORICAL RESEARCH

BY

OXFORD UNIVERSITY PRESS

1976

Distributed by Oxford University Press until 1 January 1979
thereafter by Dawsons of Pall Mall

CONTENTS OF VOLUME FIVE

LIST OF ILLUSTRATIONS

For permission to reproduce material in their possession and for the loan of prints thanks are rendered to: City of London, Guildhall Library; *Country Life*; the Greater London Council Photographic Library; the Hamlyn Group Picture Library; London Borough of Enfield, Central Library and Edmonton Library; London Borough of Haringey, Bruce Castle Museum; the National Monuments Record (N.M.R.) of the Royal Commission on Historical Monuments (England), Crown Copyright; the Royal Small Arms Factory, Enfield Lock. The coats of arms were drawn by C. W. Scott-Giles and H. Ellis Tomlinson.

LIST OF ILLUSTRATIONS

LIST OF MAPS

All the maps were drawn by K. J. Wass of the Department of Geography, University College, London, from drafts prepared by Eileen P. Scarff, Diane K. Bolton, T. F. T. Baker, and G. C. Tyack. Thanks are rendered to the Warden and Fellows of All Souls College, Oxford, for making material available for the map of Kingsbury, to the Marquess of Salisbury for material used in the map of Edmonton parish, and to the Master and Fellows of Trinity College, Cambridge, for material used in the map of Enfield parish. The development maps are based upon the Ordnance Survey, with the sanction of the Controller of H. M. Stationery Office, Crown Copyright reserved.

EDITORIAL NOTE

THE revival of the *Victoria History of Middlesex* in 1955 is described in the Editorial Note to Volume III, and later modifications of the arrangements in that to Volume I. The University of London again records its true appreciation of the generous grants made by the Local Authorities. The membership of the Middlesex *Victoria County History* Council in 1975 is set out below. Mr. G. C. Tyack, appointed Assistant County Editor in 1969, resigned at the end of 1971 and was succeeded by Miss E. P. Bailey (now Mrs. Scarff). Miss Bailey resigned in 1974, when she was succeeded by Mr. (now Dr.) M. A. Hicks.

The present volume is the fifth to be published in the Middlesex set and broadly follows the usual scheme of 'topographical' volumes of the *Victoria History*. It was begun in 1969, when work was still proceeding on Volume IV. The structure and aims of the *Victoria History* series as a whole are outlined in the *General Introduction* to the *History*.

Many people have helped in the compilation of the volume by providing information or by reading and commenting on parts of the text. Those who have read the drafts of individual parish articles are named in the footnotes. The co-operation of the town clerks, education officers, and librarians of the various Local Authorities is gratefully acknowledged, together with that of their respective staffs. Special thanks are due to the Marquess of Salisbury, for allowing access to material at Hatfield House, to Mr. H. V. Borley, for help with the passages on railways, and to the staff of the Greater London Record Office (Middlesex Records).

LIST OF CLASSES OF DOCUMENTS
IN THE PUBLIC RECORD OFFICE

USED IN THIS VOLUME
WITH THEIR CLASS NUMBERS

Chancery

		Proceedings	
C	1	Early	
C	2	Series I	
C	3	Series II	
C	5	Six Clerks Series,	Bridges
C	6		Collins
C	7		Hamilton
C	8		Mitford
C	9		Reynardson
C	10		Whittington
C	47	Miscellanea	
C	54	Close Rolls	
C	56	Confirmation Rolls	
C	60	Fine Rolls	
C	66	Patent Rolls	
C	78	Decree Rolls	
C	93	Proceedings of Commissioners of Charitable Uses, Inquisitions, and Decrees	
		Inquisitions post mortem	
C	132	Series I, Hen. III	
C	133	Edw. I	
C	134	Edw. II	
C	135	Edw. III	
C	136	Ric. II	
C	137	Hen. IV	
C	138	Hen. V	
C	139	Hen. VI	
C	140	Edw. IV	
C	142	Series II	

Court of Common Pleas

	Feet of Fines	
C.P. 25(1)	Series I
C.P. 25(2)	Series II
C.P. 40	Plea Rolls
C.P. 43	Recovery Rolls

Duchy of Lancaster

D.L. 1	Pleadings
D.L. 3	Depositions and Examinations, Series I
D.L. 25	Deeds, Series L
D.L. 30	Court Rolls
D.L. 31	Maps and Plans
D.L. 36	Cartae Miscellaneae
D.L. 41	Miscellanea
D.L. 42	Miscellaneous Books
D.L. 43	Rentals and Surveys
D.L. 44	Special Commissions and Returns
D.L. 46	Coroners' Inquests and Returns

Exchequer, Treasury of Receipt

	Ancient Deeds	
E 40	Series A
E 42	Series AS

Exchequer, King's Remembrancer

E 133	Depositions taken before the Barons of the Exchequer
E 134	Depositions taken by Commission
E 164	Miscellaneous Books, Series I
E 178	Special Commissions of Inquiry
E 179	Subsidy Rolls, etc.
E 210	Ancient Deeds, Series D
E 214	Modern Deeds

Exchequer, Augmentation Office

E 301	Certificates of Colleges and Chantries
E 303	Conventual Leases
E 305	Deeds of Purchase and Exchange
E 309	Enrolments of Leases
E 310	Particulars for Leases
E 315	Miscellaneous Books
E 317	Parliamentary Surveys
E 318	Particulars for Grants of Crown Lands
E 320	Particulars for the Sale of the Estates of Charles I
E 321	Proceedings of the Court of Augmentations
E 326	Ancient Deeds, Series B

Exchequer, Lord Treasurer's Remembrancer's and Pipe Offices

E 351	Declared Accounts
E 364	Rolls of Foreign Accounts
E 367	Particulars and Warrants for Leases
E 368	Memoranda Rolls

Ministry of Education

Ed. 7	Public Elementary Schools, Preliminary Statements

Registry of Friendly Societies

F.S. 1	Rules and Amendments, Series I

LIST OF CLASSES OF DOCUMENTS IN THE PUBLIC RECORD OFFICE

Home Office
  H.O. 67   Acreage Returns
  H.O. 107   Population Returns
  H.O. 129   Ecclesiastical Returns

Justices Itinerant, Assize and Gaol Delivery Justices, etc.
  J.I. 1   Eyre Rolls, Assize Rolls, etc.
  J.I. 3   Gaol Delivery Rolls

Court of King's Bench, Crown Side
  K.B. 9   Ancient Indictments
  K.B. 29   Controlment Rolls

Court of King's Bench, Plea Side
  K.B. 122   Plea or Judgement Rolls

Exchequer, Office of the Auditors of the Land Revenue
  L.R.   Miscellaneous Books

Ministry of Agriculture, Fisheries, and Food
  M.A.F. 9   Deeds and Awards of Enfranchisement
  M.A.F. 20   Manor Files
  M.A.F. 68   Agricultural Returns: Parish Summaries

Maps and Plans
  M.P.C. ⎫   (documents with the call-marks
  M.P.H. ⎬   M.P.C., M.P.H., and M.R. belong
  M.R.   ⎭   to various classes)

Prerogative Court of Canterbury
  Prob. 11   Registered Copies of Wills proved in P.C.C.

Court of Requests
  Req. 2   Proceedings
  Req. 3   Miscellaneous Proceedings

Special Collections
  S.C. 2   Court Rolls
  S.C. 6   Ministers' and Receivers' Accounts Rentals and Surveys
  S.C. 11   Rolls
  S.C. 12   Portfolios

State Paper Office
               State Papers Domestic
  S.P. 12   Eliz. I
  S.P. 17   Chas. I

Court of Star Chamber
  Sta. Cha. 3 Proceedings, Edw. VI

Court of Wards and Liveries
  Wards 5   Feodaries' Surveys

War Office
  W.O. 30   Miscellanea

SELECT LIST OF CLASSES OF DOCUMENTS IN THE GREATER LONDON RECORD OFFICE (MIDDLESEX RECORDS)

USED IN THIS VOLUME
WITH THEIR CLASS NUMBERS

Deposited Records

Acc. 174	Manor of Hendon		
Acc. 262	Stowe Collection		
Acc. 349	Delme Radcliffe Collection		
Acc. 695	Manors of Tottenham and Edmonton		
Acc. 727			
Acc. 903	Enfield Parochial Charities		
Acc. 1016	Archives of Messrs Couchman of Tottenham		
Cal. Mdx. Sess. Bks.	Calendar of Sessions Books, 1638–1752		

D.R.O. 4 — Diocesan Records, Enfield Parish Records

D.R.O. 5 — Diocesan Records, South Mimms Parish Records

D.R.O. 14 — Diocesan Records, Great Stanmore Parish Records

D.R.O. 17 — Diocesan Records, Monken Hadley Parish Records

F — Facsimile

MR/TH — Hearth Tax Assessments

L.V. — Licensed Victuallers' Lists

TA — Tithe Awards

NOTE ON ABBREVIATIONS

Among the abbreviations and short titles used the following may require elucidation:

B.M.	British Museum (used in references to documents which in 1973 were transferred to the new British Library)
B.T.C.	British Transport Commission
Brewer, *Beauties of Eng. and Wales*, x (5)	J. N. Brewer, vol. x (1816) of *The Beauties of England and Wales* (1810–16), ed. E. W. Brayley and J. Britton. The part of the work cited is alternatively known either as the fifth part, or as the second part of vol. iv, of *London and Middlesex*, which is itself vol. x of *The Beauties*
Davenport MSS.	Notes and transcripts by P. Davenport in the possession of the London and Middlesex Archaeological Society
Educ. Enquiry Abstract	*Education Enquiry Abstract*, H.C. 62 (1835), xli
Educ. of Poor Digest	*Digest of Returns to the Select Committee on Education of the Poor*, H.C. 224 (1819), ix (1)
Ft. of F. Lond. & Mdx.	*Calendar to the Feet of Fines for London and Middlesex*, ed. W. J. Hardy and W. Page (2 vols. 1892–3)
Foot, *Agric. of Middlesex*	P. Foot, *General View of the Agriculture of the County of Middlesex* (1794)
Freshfield, *Communion Plate*	E. Freshfield, *The Communion Plate of the Parish Churches in the County of Middlesex* (1897)
Guildhall MSS.	City of London, Guildhall Library. The collection includes bishops' registers (MS. 9531), diocesan administrative records (MSS. 9532–60), and records of bishops' estates (MSS. 10234–51)
Hennessy, *Novum Repertorium*	G. Hennessy, *Novum Repertorium Ecclesiasticum Parochiale Londinense* (1898)
Hist. Mon. Com. *Mdx.*	Royal Commission on Historical Monuments, *An Inventory of the Historical Monuments in Middlesex* (H.M.S.O. 1937)
Kelly's Dir. Mdx.	The Post Office *Directories*. The directories for Middlesex between 1845 and 1863 are published as part of the *Home Counties Directory*
Lond. Dioc. Bk.	*Yearbook* of the diocese of London (1940 to date)
Lysons, *Environs*	D. Lysons, *The Environs of London* (1792–6), vols. ii and iii (1795)
Lysons, *Mdx. Pars.*	D. Lysons, *An Historical Account of those Parishes in the County of Middlesex which are not described in the Environs of London* (1800)
M.L.R.	Middlesex Land Registry. The enrolments and indexes are at the Greater London Record Office (Middlesex Records), the volumes are at the Greater London Record Office
M.R.O.	Middlesex Record Office. On the incorporation of Middlesex within Greater London on 1 April 1965 the office became known as the Greater London Record Office (Middlesex Records)
Mdx. Cnty. Recs.	*Middlesex County Records* [1550–1688], ed. J. C. Jeaffreson (4 vols. 1886–92)
Mdx. Cnty. Recs. Sess. Bks. 1689–1709	*Middlesex County Records, Calendar of the Sessions Books 1689 to 1709*, ed. W. J. Hardy (1905)
Mdx. Sess. Recs.	*Calendar to the Sessions Records* [1612–18] ed. W. le Hardy (4 vols. 1935–41)
Middleton, *View*	J. Middleton, *View of the Agriculture of Middlesex* (1798)
Mudie-Smith, *Rel. Life*	R. Mudie-Smith, *The Religious Life of London* (1904)

NOTE ON ABBREVIATIONS

Newcourt, *Repertorium*	R. Newcourt, *Repertorium Ecclesiasticum Parochiale Londinense* (2 vols. 1708–10)
P.N. Mdx. (E.P.N.S.)	*The Place-Names of Middlesex* (English Place-Name Society, vol. xviii, 1942)
Poor Law Com. 1st Rep.	*First Report of the Poor Law Commission,* H.C. 500 (1835), xxxv
Pevsner, *Mdx.*	N. Pevsner, *The Buildings of England, Middlesex* (1951)
Rep. on Bridges in Mdx.	*Report of the Committee of Magistrates appointed to make Enquiry respecting the Public Bridges in the County of Middlesex* (1826) *penes* M.R.O.
Rep. Com. Eccl. Revenues	*Report of the Commissioners Appointed to Inquire into the Ecclesiastical Revenues of England and Wales* [67], H.C. (1835), xxii
Rep. Cttee. on Rets. by Overseers, 1776	*Report of the Select Committee on Returns by Overseers of the Poor 1776,* H.C., 1st ser. ix
9th Rep. Com. Char.	*9th Report of the Commissioners Appointed to Enquire Concerning Charities* (Lord Brougham's Commission), H.C. 258 (1823), ix
Robbins, *Mdx.*	M. Robbins, *Middlesex* (1953)
Thorne, *Environs*	J. Thorne, *Handbook to the Environs of London* [alphabetically arranged in two parts] (1876)
T.L.M.A.S.	*Transactions of the London and Middlesex Archaeological Society* (1856 to date). Consecutive numbers are used for the whole series, although vols. vii–xvii (1905–54) appeared as N.S. i–xi
W.A.M.	Westminster Abbey Muniments

GORE HUNDRED

(continued)

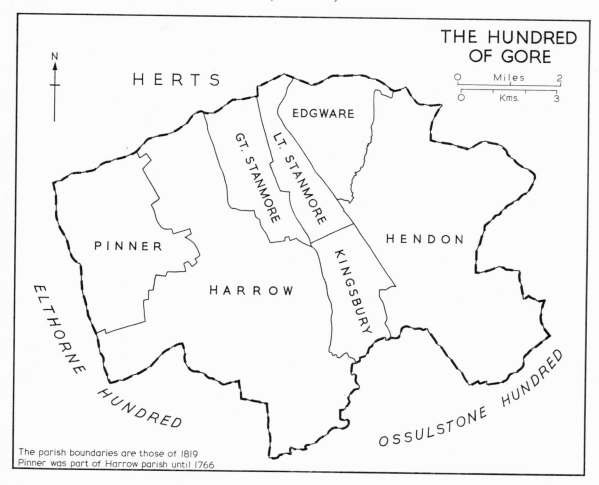

THE HUNDRED OF GORE

HERTS

EDGWARE

GT. STANMORE

LT. STANMORE

HENDON

PINNER

KINGSBURY

HARROW

ELTHORNE HUNDRED

OSSULSTONE HUNDRED

N

Miles 0 — 2
Kms. 0 — 3

The parish boundaries are those of 1819
Pinner was part of Harrow parish until 1766

HENDON

HENDON,[1] the third largest parish in Middlesex, totalled 8,290 a. in 1831[2] and measured approximately seven miles from north to south and four miles from east to west at its widest points.[3] Several modern suburbs, including Mill Hill, which is 10 miles from London, Golders Green, Childs Hill, part of Cricklewood, and the greater part of Hampstead Garden Suburb, lie within the ancient parish. It was bounded to the north and north-east by Elstree and Arkley (Herts.) and Totteridge (Herts., later Barnet L.B.), to the east by Finchley, to the south by Hampstead, to the south-west by Willesden, and to the west by Kingsbury, Little Stanmore, and Edgware. The eastern boundary, after following Dollis and Mutton brooks, ran across fields to a point some 300 yards north-west of the Spaniards inn (on the borders of Hampstead and Finchley), where it turned south-west to meet Watling Street (Edgware Road), south of Cricklewood. The western boundary followed the road for almost five miles north-westward to Edgware bridge, except between Brent bridge and the Hyde where it turned west along the Brent and then north to rejoin the road. From Edgware bridge the boundary ran north-east along Dean's brook and across fields to Hertfordshire. The boundaries were largely fixed by the

---

[1] The article was written in 1970. Any references to later years are dated. The help of Miss M. McDerby, Mrs. J. M. Corden, and Miss M. Brown in commenting on the article is gratefully acknowledged. Some preliminary work was done by Mr. G. R. Thomas.

[2] *Census*, 1831.
[3] Except where otherwise stated, the rest of the para. is based on O.S. Maps 6″, Mdx. VI; XI. NW., NE., SE. (1894–8 edns.).

late 10th century, the northern one being that of an estate called *Lotheresleage* and the southern that of another estate called Blechenham.[4] The parish corresponded to Hendon U.D., created in 1895, before Edgware was added from Hendon R.D. in 1931. The urban district was incorporated in 1932 and became part of Barnet L.B. in 1965.[5]

The soil is predominantly London Clay but there is a small outcrop of pebble gravel north of Highwood Hill, while the Mill Hill ridge and the northern slopes of Hampstead Heath are topped by Claygate Beds. There is a large area of glacial gravel around Church End in the centre of the parish, a smaller one north of Golders Green, and a patch of Taplow Gravel near Brent Underground station.[6] Alluvium lies along Silk stream and Dollis brook. Topography and settlement were strongly influenced by ridges and their intervening valleys. The highest point, 443 ft., is in the north, where Highwood Hill marks the junction of two ridges, one stretching east to Totteridge and the other south-east through Holcombe Hill to Mill Hill and Bittacy Hill. West of the second ridge the land slopes down to the Hale and Edgware Road; it also slopes to the south, before rising to the hill where Church End stands. South, east, and west of Church End the land descends to the Brent and its tributaries, but in the south-east it rises again to the heights of Hampstead Heath, at Childs Hill and Golders Hill.

The main river is the Brent, which cuts across the parish from west to east. Silk stream, a tributary, runs parallel to Edgware Road and is formed by the confluence of Dean's brook, known in the Middle Ages as the Heybourne (*Yburnan*),[7] with Edgware brook south-east of Edgware bridge. The Brent itself splits at Mutton bridge, the northern portion becoming Dollis brook and the eastern Mutton brook. For much of its distance the boundary between Hendon and Totteridge (Herts.) follows a headstream of the Brent which was called the Tatbourne as late as 1574.[8] In 1835–9 the Brent and Silk stream were dammed to construct Brent reservoir (the Welsh Harp), in order to supply the Paddington Canal at Harlesden.[9] The reservoir, which lay within Hendon, Kingsbury, and Willesden, was enlarged between 1851 and 1853,[10] to cover 350 a. In 1921 the part of the northern arm which reached north-east of Edgware Road was reclaimed and a culvert was built to carry Silk stream under the road.[11] The courses of the southern end of Silk stream and of the river Brent were straightened at about the same time.

Prominent residents not mentioned elsewhere included Henry Joynes (d. 1754), mason-architect and comptroller of the works at Blenheim Palace, who lived at Golders Green and was buried in Hendon churchyard;[12] Jeremy Bentham, who lodged at Dollis Farm in the early 19th century;[13] and Sir Richard Hoare (1648–1718), banker, who died at a house in the parish. Later inhabitants included Granville George Leveson-Gower, Earl Granville (1815–91), Liberal statesman, who occupied Golders Green, or Hodford, Farm;[14] Thomas Tilling (1825–93), founder of the London omnibus firm, who was born at Gutters Hedge Farm,[15] and Sir Francis Pettit Smith (1808–74), inventor of the screw propeller for ships, who lived at the same farm in the mid 19th century;[16] Thomas Woolner (1825–92), sculptor and poet;[17] James Willing (1818–1906), inventor of bill-posting, who lived at Rockhall, Cricklewood;[18] Thomas Cobden-Sanderson (1840–1922), book-binder and printer, who lived from 1885 at Goodyers, Brent Street;[19] and Sir John Blundell Maple, Bt. (1845–1903), sportsman and chairman of the London furnishing firm, who lived at Orange Hill House.[20] Mr. Harold Wilson (b. 1916) moved to no. 10 Southway, Hampstead Garden Suburb, in 1948 and to no. 12 Southway in 1953, where he lived until becoming Prime Minister in 1964.[21]

COMMUNICATIONS. The Roman Watling Street, part of it later known as Edgware Road, passed over the Brent and Silk stream, and, at the northernmost extremity, crossed Edgware brook at Edgware bridge.[22] There was a grant of pavage in 1389 to six persons, including John atte Hegge of Hendon, to repair the road.[23] In 1621 Brent and Silk bridges were so decayed as to form a serious danger to wayfarers[24] but the first was rebuilt in 1770, 1788, and 1818,[25] and the second, then very old and ruinous, in 1821.[26] Brent bridge was known as Harp bridge in 1826[27] because of its proximity to the Welsh Harp inn, but later it reverted to its original name. Both bridges were rebuilt with the construction of Brent reservoir and they effectively disappeared in the 1920s, when the rivers were made to pass under the road in culverts. The Hendon section of Edgware Road was turnpiked in 1711.[28] Part of another Roman road was discovered in Copthall Fields in 1967[29] but its significance is uncertain.

The second important route, from London via Hampstead, entered the parish at Golders Hill and joined Edgware Road north of the Hyde, after passing through Golders Green and Brent Street to the Burroughs, whence it bore north-west along Colindeep Lane. The route, part of it called Hendon path ('wante'), was said in 1593 to be an 'ancient highway now unaccustomed',[30] suggesting that it had formerly been preferred to Edgware

[4] *P.N. Mdx.* (E.P.N.S.), 219–21; see below, p. 6.
[5] See p. 31.
[6] Geol. Surv. Map 1″, drift, sheet 256 (1951 edn.); *V.C.H. Mdx.* i. 2, 4–5.
[7] *P.N. Mdx.* (E.P.N.S.), 3.
[8] Ibid.
[9] A. J. Garrett, 'Hist. Geog. of Upper Brent' (Lond. Univ. M.A. thesis, 1935), 97.
[10] *Home Cnties. Mag.* i. 177; J. Hopkins, *Hist. Hendon*, 87.
[11] Howard Farrow Ltd., *Work in Progress*, 42.
[12] M.L.R. 1755/2/484; Lysons, *Environs*, iii. 12.
[13] Mill Hill Hist. Soc., Add. Items 59.
[14] *D.N.B.*
[15] Mill Hill Hist. Soc., Add. Items 61.   [16] Ibid. 3.
[17] *D.N.B.*; Robbins, *Mdx.* 290.
[18] Mill Hill Hist. Soc., Add. Items 57; *D.N.B.*

[19] *D.N.B.*; Hopkins, *Hendon*, 91.
[20] *D.N.B.*; A. G. Clarke, *Story of Goldbeaters and Watling*, 19.
[21] Ex inf. the Rt. Hon. J. H. Wilson.
[22] Edgware bridge is discussed in *V.C.H. Mdx.* iv. 151. In 1814 the lord of the manor of Hendon was liable for one quarter of the cost of repairs.
[23] *Cal. Pat.* 1388–92, 123.
[24] *Mdx. Cnty. Recs.* ii. 236.
[25] *Rep. on Bridges in Mdx.* 202.
[26] Ibid. 205.   [27] Ibid. 202.
[28] *V.C.H. Mdx.* iv. 152, where the subsequent hist. of the road is discussed.
[29] *T.L.M.A.S.* xxii(2), 55.
[30] John Norden, *Speculum Britanniae* (1723 edn.), 15. Norden probably lived at Hendon Ho., Brent Street; see below, p. 6.

Road; part of Colindeep Lane was known as late as 1863 as Ancient Street.[31] The road crossed the river Brent by Brent Street bridge at the foot of Brent Street; parishioners were indicted for failing to repair the bridge in 1623[32] but a new one of brick and stone with three arches was built by subscription in 1782.[33] At Colin Deep there was a ford across Silk stream and, in 1826, a footbridge.[34] A permanent bridge for vehicles was built later.

A network of minor roads included Parson Street, the northward continuation of Brent Street, which by 1321[35] was presumably part of the main route to the north of the parish. The road led via Holders Hill to Bittacy Hill, at the top of which it became the Ridgeway, so called by 1471.[36] The Ridgeway followed the high ground north-westward to Highwood Hill, where it met a road which ran north-eastward across the parish from a point south of Edgware bridge to Totteridge, passing through the Hale and known in its western portion as Deans Lane, in the centre as Selvage Lane, and in the east as Marsh Lane. Farther east Hendon Wood Lane left Highwood Hill to run north to the county boundary at Barnet Gate.[37] A second northerly route in 1594[38] left Parson Street and followed Ashley Lane, Dole Street, and Milespit Hill, to join the Ridgeway at Mill Hill. A third ran from the parish church along the present Hall Lane, Page Street, Featherstone Hill, and Wise Lane, to join the Ridgeway by the Three Hammers.[39] Bunns Lane left Page Street by Copt Hall and led in a north-westerly direction along Hale Lane to the Hale and thence to Edgware. The northern hamlets and farms were linked by several minor roads, including Lawrence (or Gladwin) Street, which in the early 18th century joined Bunns Lane with Holcombe Hill.[40]

Several routes in the less populous southern part were no more than winding tracks. In 1754 they included Burroughs Lane (later Station Road), from the Burroughs to Edgware Road south of Silk bridge, Finchley Lane, from Church End to Finchley, Cowhouse Green (later Cricklewood Lane), which linked Cricklewood with Childs Hill and continued along a road later known as Childs Hill Lane and Hermitage Lane to West Heath, Hampstead, and Bell Lane, which ran south-east from Brent Street to Temple Fortune, crossing the Brent at Mutton bridge.[41] In 1826 the bridge was of brick, with one arch over the river and another three arches over an adjoining decoy;[42] it was frequently drawn by artists, including Constable,[43] but was rebuilt in 1931.[44] West of Edgware Road, Kingsbury Road and Cool Oak Lane linked Hendon with Kingsbury.[45]

The first major addition to the old road structure was Finchley Road, running from Childs Hill through Golders Green to Finchley, and, like other additions, intended to improve access to the west end of London.[46] It was established by an Act of 1826 under the control of the Marylebone and Finchley turnpike trust, with toll-gates at Childs Hill and Golders Green, and was opened to traffic in 1830.[47] It later came, like Edgware Road, under the control of the commissioners for the metropolitan turnpike roads. No further significant alterations were made until 1924, when a large scheme began with the construction of the North Circular Road along the Brent valley from a point south of Brent bridge to one adjacent to Mutton bridge.[48] In the same year work began on Hendon Way, which leaves Finchley Road at Childs Hill and runs north to Hendon Central Underground station. The northern section of the road, called Watford Way, continues to Northway Circus at the end of Selvage Lane, where Barnet Way heads north to the Hertfordshire border at Stirling Corner and Edgware Way takes a westerly course across Dean's brook into Edgware. The North Circular Road and Watford Way were finished in 1927 and connected by Great North Way, which was built in 1926. No more new roads were built until 1967, when the M1 motorway was extended south through the parish to a junction with Watford Way near its bridge over Bunns Lane; a short extension to Five Ways Corner at the northern end of Great North Way, where a fly-over was built, was opened in 1970. A stretch of the motorway farther south to the North Circular Road was near completion in 1974. Access to the motorway was improved by a large 3-tier fly-over built in 1965 at Brent Cross, where Hendon Way crosses the North Circular Road.[49]

Coaches travelled from Hendon to the Old Bell, Holborn, via Hampstead at the end of the 17th century.[50] In 1839 there was a daily coach to London from the Bell, while one carrier operated from Hendon and another from Mill Hill;[51] a coach for Hendon and Mill Hill left the Blue Post, Tottenham Court Road, every afternoon.[52] The centre of the parish remained relatively inaccessible until an omnibus began to run from Church End to Hendon station after the building of the Midland Railway in 1868. Infrequent omnibus services, some of them short-lived, were later introduced to Swiss Cottage Metropolitan Railway station and Marble Arch.[53] By 1904, when a tramway was built along Edgware Road from Cricklewood to Edgware, road transport in most parts of Hendon was still poor, although omnibuses ran along Finchley Road to Finchley through Golders Green and from Cricklewood to Oxford Circus.[54] Eight trams an hour in each direction ran between Cricklewood and Edgware but London-bound passengers had to

[31] O.S. Map 1/2,500, Mdx. XI. 6 (1863 edn.).
[32] Mdx. Cnty. Recs. ii. 237.
[33] Rep. on Bridges in Mdx. 207.   [34] Ibid. 204.
[35] T.L.M.A.S. xii. 581.
[36] Cal. Close, 1468–76, 166.
[37] The roads are shown on J. Ogilby, Map of Mdx. (c. 1677).
[38] All Souls Coll., Hovenden maps, portfolio II, no. 17.
[39] Except where otherwise stated, the rest of the para. and the foll. para. are based on B.M. Add. MS. 9839. The map was made by Isaac Messeder in 1754; there are copies in Hendon Libr. and at the Bodleian, the former accompanied by a ref. bk., MS. L. 1703.
[40] Bodl. MS. Rawl. B. 389 b.
[41] O.S. Map 6″, Mdx. XI. NE. (1894–6 edn.).

[42] Rep. on Bridges in Mdx. 201.
[43] Victoria & Albert Mus., 271–1888.
[44] Hopkins, Hendon, 70.
[45] O.S. Map 6″, Mdx. XI. NW., SW. (1938 edn.).
[46] M.R.O., Acc. 262/4/47.
[47] M.R.O., LA. HW., Tp. 18, 19.
[48] Except where otherwise stated, the rest of the para. is based on Hopkins, Hendon, 70.
[49] Ex inf. Barnet L.B., Planning Offices. See plate facing p. 64.
[50] Mdx. & Herts. N. & Q. iv. 104.
[51] Robson's Com. Dir. (1839).
[52] Pigot's Lond. Dir. (1839).
[53] Hendon & Finchley Times, 25 July 1958.
[54] Garrett, 'Upper Brent Valley', 130–4.

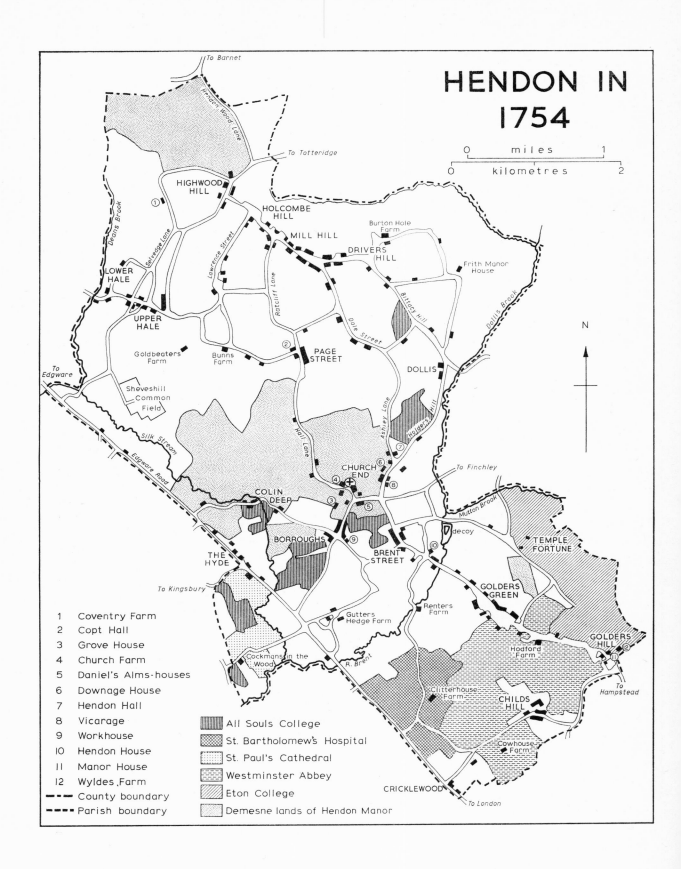

HENDON IN 1754

1 Coventry Farm
2 Copt Hall
3 Grove House
4 Church Farm
5 Daniel's Alms-houses
6 Downage House
7 Hendon Hall
8 Vicarage
9 Workhouse
10 Hendon House
11 Manor House
12 Wyldes Farm
--- County boundary
--- Parish boundary

All Souls College
St. Bartholomew's Hospital
St. Paul's Cathedral
Westminster Abbey
Eton College
Demesne lands of Hendon Manor

change at Cricklewood.[55] Another tramway was opened in 1909 by the Metropolitan Electric Tramways Co., from Finchley along Finchley Road to Hampstead, and a link was opened from the Castle inn, Childs Hill, to Cricklewood along Cricklewood Lane; all routes were converted for trolley-buses in 1936 but in 1970 they were being served by motor-buses.[56] By 1903 an omnibus service, at 15-minute intervals, had started between Hendon and Oxford Circus along Finchley Road[57] and by 1912 another service, between the Bell and London Bridge, had been introduced. In the north motor-buses did not run regularly until after the First World War; they linked Golders Green station with Harrow via Mill Hill by 1923[58] and the building of the Underground railway to Edgware had given rise to a network of connecting routes in all parts by the early 1930s.[59]

The first railway was the G.N.R.'s branch line from Finsbury Park to Edgware, which was opened in 1867 and entered the parish by an impressive 13-arched viaduct over Dollis brook; Mill Hill East station was opened, as Mill Hill, in the same year. From 1868 trains ran from Edgware to Ludgate Hill and Loughborough Junction (Surr.) but in 1869 they were diverted to Moorgate; in 1872, with the building of the branch from Finchley to High Barnet, through services were withdrawn from the Edgware line and a shuttle service was instituted from Edgware to Finchley. A station was opened near the Hale, in Bunns Lane, in 1906[60] but the line later suffered from road competition and was closed to passenger traffic in 1939. A proposal under the 1935–40 New Works Programme to link it to London Transport's Underground system was not carried out in full; the eastern end of the branch, from Finchley Central to Mill Hill East, was electrified in 1941 to serve the near-by barracks, while frequent Underground trains began running to the west end of London, the City, and Morden (Surr.) over the Northern line.[61] In 1970 the rest of the railway lay derelict.

The main line of the Midland Railway from Bedford to London was opened for goods traffic in 1867 and for passengers in 1868;[62] it ran south through Hendon, crossing the Brent by a viaduct west of Edgware Road. Passenger stations were opened in 1868 in Bunns Lane (later Mill Hill Broadway), at the foot of Burroughs Lane, and in Cricklewood Lane; another station called Welsh Harp was opened near the inn of that name to cater for excursion traffic in 1870[63] but was closed in 1903.[64] Stopping trains were infrequent and there were several complaints about the slowness of journeys to St. Pancras or Moorgate.[65] A through service from Hendon to Victoria via Moorgate, Ludgate Hill, and Loughborough Junction was instituted in 1875[66] but was discontinued in 1908.[67]

Services from Mill Hill, Hendon, and Cricklewood to St. Pancras and Moorgate remained poor until 1960, when steam trains were replaced by a diesel service, running hourly throughout the day and more frequently at rush hours. An important feature of the Midland Railway's installations in Hendon was the Brent sidings and marshalling yard for goods and coal traffic, which covered a large area north of Childs Hill (later Cricklewood) station.[68] To connect the yard with the G.W.R. and the L.S.W.R., the Midland & South Western Junction Railway opened a line to Acton in 1875. A passenger service was later provided by the Midland, from 1878 to 1880 forming part of its 'Super Outer Circle' from St. Pancras to Earl's Court, but Childs Hill never became an important passenger junction. The line carried only an intermittent shuttle service to Gunnersbury from 1894 and was closed to passengers in 1902,[69] although the 'Dudding Hill Loop', as it was known, was still open to goods traffic in 1970. Short-lived services were also provided from Childs Hill to Richmond in 1875 and to Dudding Hill and Stonebridge Park in 1880.[70]

The inadequacy of the services provided by the G.N.R. and the Midland led to several fruitless proposals for new railways, including a plan put forward by the Metropolitan Railway for a line from Wembley, which was thwarted by the price asked by the Ecclesiastical Commissioners for their land.[71] In 1902, however, the Underground Electric Railway Co. obtained powers to extend to Golders Green its proposed line from Charing Cross to Hampstead tube, and in the same year the Edgware & Hampstead Railway Co., promoted by the Underground Group, was empowered to extend the line across Hendon to Edgware.[72] The line was opened in 1907 as far as Golders Green, where a surface station was built; after delays caused by the First World War the extension to Hendon Central was opened in 1923, although trains did not run through to Edgware until 1924.[73] From Golders Green the railway ran above the surface, apart from a tunnel at the Burroughs north of Hendon Central station, and a viaduct was built over the river Brent; four intermediate stations, Brent, Hendon Central, Colindale, and Burnt Oak, were opened. The underground railway, providing Hendon for the first time with a fast and frequent train service to London, greatly stimulated suburban development.[74] In 1924 rush-hour trains ran as often as every 8 minutes from Edgware to Moorgate and every 4 minutes from Golders Green to Charing Cross;[75] in 1970 intervals were nominally similar but many trains ran south to Morden, either via the Bank or via Charing Cross. Since 1937, four years after its acquisition by the London Passenger Transport Board and after several changes of name, the railway has formed part of the Northern line.[76]

[55] Rep. Com. on Lond. Traffic [Cd. 2744], diagram 37, H.C.(1906), xxxiii.
[56] Hopkins, Hendon, 62.
[57] Rep. Com. on Lond. Traffic [Cd. 2752], pp. 136–7, H.C.(1906), xxviii.
[58] Hopkins, Hendon, 63.
[59] Garrett, 'Upper Brent Valley', 138.
[60] Rly. Mag. xlv. 2, 3, 6.
[61] C. E. Lee, Sixty Years of the Northern, 25–6.
[62] C. E. Stretton, Hist. of Midland Rly. 186.
[63] Hopkins, Hendon, 54.   [64] Mdx. Monthly, ii. 6.
[65] Hendon Libr., DD. MHS. 539.

[66] Stretton, Midland Rly. 189.
[67] Ex inf. Mr. H. V. Borley.
[68] Stretton, Midland Rly. 187; see below, p. 26.
[69] Rly. Mag. lxxxix. 89.
[70] Ex inf. Mr. H. V. Borley.
[71] Rep. Com. on Lond. Traffic [Cd. 2751], p. 711, H.C.(1906), xl.
[72] Lee, op. cit. 13.
[73] Ibid. 16, 22.
[74] See pp. 13–14.
[75] Rly. Mag. lv. 305–7.
[76] Lee, op. cit. 24–5.

GROWTH BEFORE 1850. There is no firm evidence of pre-Roman settlement in the parish, which has yielded many Romano-British finds.[77] Hendon was first mentioned in a charter purporting to date from 972–8,[78] by which time a settlement had presumably grown up at Church End, on a well-watered eminence[79] where the parish church, with its Norman font, is situated. The same charter mentions land in the north of the parish called *Lotheresleage*,[80] whose name had disappeared by the end of the Middle Ages, as had that of Blechenham, an estate to the south which was first mentioned in a charter reputedly dating from 959.[81] In 1321 trees still covered many slopes. There were woods called Highpark and Downage, the latter near Church End,[82] while Cricklewood and Highwood Hill, first recorded then, gave their names to later hamlets.[83] The survival of some early-14th-century names in those of later fields[84] indicates that the common fields lay north of Church End. Parts of the parish may never have had a common-field system; the presence of large areas of woodland in the 16th century, both in compact 'groves' and in hedgerows, suggests that small fields were assarted in the south.[85]

Most of the cultivated land seems to have been inclosed by 1574, when there were common fields called Sheveshill, Shoelands, Dinge, and Forty near the Hale.[86] The last to survive was Sheveshill, near the site of Burnt Oak Underground station, which disappeared between 1828[87] and 1843.[88] There were no large commons or heaths, although in 1754 manorial waste at Golders Green stretched for some distance on either side of the main road from Hampstead;[89] the name, apparently derived from that of a local family, the Goodyers, was first recorded in 1612.[90] In 1754 there were also greens at Lower Hale and at Gibbs Green near by; at Holcombe Hill, Mill Hill, and Drivers Hill; near Burton Hole farm; at the Hyde; at Temple Fortune; in Cricklewood Lane (Cowhouse Green); and at Golders Hill.[91] As early as 1711 the lord's quit-rents were increasing each year through new admissions to the waste[92] and by the early 19th century the amount of common land had declined considerably,[93] while Golders Green was inclosed for villas. As a result animals were often grazed on the roads and in 1835 they broke down the fences at Clitterhouse.[94]

An attempt in 1878 to sell Brent Green, the last piece of manorial waste in southern Hendon, was defeated by local residents, and the land was bought by the parish as an open space.[95]

Most of the early inhabitants lived in hamlets on the gravel-topped hills. Until the late 19th century the low-lying and poorly drained western part of the parish contained little but isolated farm-houses.[96] There were two small settlements on Edgware Road: the Hyde, recorded in 1281,[97] and Cricklewood, mentioned in 1294.[98] The Hale, in the north-west corner (*healh*) of the parish, was an element in a personal name in 1294.[99] The Burroughs, named after the hill on which it stands, was recorded in 1316,[1] Highwood Hill in 1321,[2] Mill Hill in 1374,[3] and Childs Hill in 1593.[4] The hamlet of Golders Green originated, like Mill Hill and the Hyde, as a group of cottages on waste ground on each side of a main road; Brent Street, recorded in 1613, was similarly situated.[5] There was an inn c. 1274[6] but its location is unknown.

Hendon's proximity to London made it a favoured site for country houses, although few that were built before the 18th century have survived. The abbots of Westminster had a house there by 1285.[7] John Norden (1548–1625), the topographer, who is believed to have lived at Hendon House, Brent Street,[8] said that Sir John Fortescue (d. 1607), Chancellor of the Exchequer, often stayed at Hendon Place, the Herberts' manor-house.[9] Hendon House, Brent Street, a gabled building probably of the 16th century, had 16 hearths in 1664.[10] It was the residence of Sir William Rawlinson (1640–1703), a Commissioner of the Great Seal, from 1691[11] and afterwards of his daughter, whose second husband was Giles Earle (?1678–1759), the politician.[12] The house was rebuilt in the early 19th century and demolished in 1909.[13] Copt Hall, Page Street, was rebuilt between 1624 and 1637, as the seat of a branch of the Nicholl (Nicoll) family, and a building of similar date at Mill Hill may have been Cookes farm-house, which also belonged to the Nicholls.[14] Several other farm-houses were rebuilt in the 16th and 17th centuries. The sole survival is Church Farm House, Church End, a gabled brick building dating probably from the early 17th century and one of the most complete examples of Middlesex vernacular architecture of its time. It was bought by

[77] V.C.H. Mdx. i. 72; T.L.M.A.S. xxii(2), 53–5.
[78] Cart. Sax. ed. Birch, iii, pp. 604–5.
[79] 'Rep. on Church End Farm Excavation' (1961), TS. penes Hendon Libr.
[80] P.N. Mdx. (E.P.N.S.), 219–21, where the Hendon charters are discussed.
[81] Cart. Sax. ed. Birch, iii, p. 264.
[82] T.L.M.A.S. xii. 582 sqq. The original survey is in Cambridge Univ. Libr.
[83] P.N. Mdx. (E.P.N.S.), 58–9.
[84] e.g. le Brache (Breach), Boterwyk (Buttericks), Derefeld (Deer Field): P.N. Mdx. (E.P.N.S.), 210. See below, p. 24.
[85] St. Barts. Hosp., Hc 19/1/1; All Souls Coll., Hovenden Maps, II, nos. 16, 17.
[86] T.L.M.A.S. xiii. 54.
[87] F. Whishaw, Map of Hendon and ref. bk.
[88] M.R.O., TA/HEN.
[89] B.M. Add. MS. 9839.
[90] P.N. Mdx. (E.P.N.S.), 58.
[91] B.M. Add. MS. 9839.
[92] Nat. Libr. of Wales, Powis MS. 19802.
[93] Cooke, Map of Hendon (1796); Whishaw, Map of Hendon (1828).
[94] St. Barts. Hosp., Hc 9/3, ff. 164–5.

[95] Hendon Libr., DD. MHS. 441.
[96] Thorne, Environs, ii. 366.
[97] P.N. Mdx. (E.P.N.S.), 59. See below, p. 53.
[98] P.N. Mdx. (E.P.N.S.), 58.
[99] Ibid. 59.
[1] T.L.M.A.S. xiii. 67.
[2] P.N. Mdx. (E.P.N.S.), 59.
[3] W.A.M. 32589.
[4] Norden, Speculum Britanniae, map facing p. 8.
[5] P.N. Mdx. (E.P.N.S.), 60.
[6] J.I. 1/539 m. 16d.
[7] See p. 18.
[8] Lysons, Environs, iii. 7; Home Cnties. Mag. xi. 89.
[9] Norden, Speculum Britanniae, 21. For Hendon Place, see p. 18.
[10] M.R.O., MR/TH/5; Hopkins, Hendon, plate facing p. 33.
[11] D.N.B.; N. G. Brett-James, Story of Hendon, 78.
[12] D.N.B.; Home Cnties. Mag. xi. 84.
[13] Home Cnties. Mag. xi. 90. The new house was built before 1816 but contained parts of the old building: Brewer, Beauties of Eng. & Wales, x(5), 690.
[14] See p. 22.

Hendon U.D. in 1944 and restored in 1954 for use as a local history museum.[15] Farm-houses of similar date included Dole Street, a weatherboarded building demolished in 1937,[16] and Clitterhouse.[17]

In 1754 the chief hamlets in the north part were the Hale, Highwood Hill, and Mill Hill, the smallest being the Hale. At Lower Hale, on the Edgware border, there were no more than six houses,[18] of which the most prominent was Lower Hale or Hale Grove farm-house, a substantial building with an early-18th-century frontage which survived into the early 20th century[19] and may have been a capital messuage belonging to Edward Nicholl in 1732.[20] Upper Hale, a short distance to the south-east, was a larger collection of buildings at the junction of Deans, Hale, and Selvage lanes; it included Hale farm-house and the Green Man, which was first recorded in 1751.[21] The Hale remained a distinct hamlet until the 1920s.[22] The largest farm-houses near by were Stoneyfields, Shakerham, Goldbeaters, Bunns, and Coventry. All had disappeared by 1970, except for some of the Coventry farm buildings, which formed part of Mill Hill golf club.

In contrast to the Hale, a purely agricultural community, the Mill Hill ridge was occupied by fashionable houses, many of them built for London merchants. By 1814 Mill Hill was a considerable village and, like Highwood Hill, boasted many 'respectable family residences' in extensive grounds.[23] Some of the houses, like Littleberries and Ridgeway House, had been built in the 17th and early 18th centuries but most of them dated from c. 1800, when the area's popularity reached a peak, on account of its woods, its views, and its proximity to London.[24] The first notable resident was Rachel, Lady Russell (1636–1723), a friend of Queen Anne, who lived on or near the site of the later Highwood House, after the execution of her husband William, Lord Russell, in 1683.[25] Another well-known early resident was the actress Mary Porter (d. 1765), who moved to Highwood Hill after her retirement in 1745.[26]

The survival of several large houses at Mill Hill has helped to preserve an opulent and spacious air. At Highwood Hill the largest is Highwood House, a classical building of brick and stucco, with slightly projecting wings and a semicircular Ionic porch. It was built shortly before 1817 for William Anderson,[27] bought by Sir Stamford Raffles, founder of Singapore, in 1825, and inhabited by his widow from 1826

until 1858.[28] In 1954 it was restored for use as a nursing home.[29] The grounds contained Lady Russell's well, whose water was compared favourably in 1807 with that issuing from the Cheltenham springs.[30] To the east, at the other side of Nan Clarke's Lane, Hendon Park stood with an adjoining farm-house in 1756.[31] To its north-west the site of an old earthwork, described in 1756 as a proper place to build on, had been levelled to make way for a farm-house by 1764[32] and replaced by Moat Mount House by 1796.[33] The only other large house north of Highwood Hill was Hyver Hall, in existence by 1863.[34] Two smaller late-18th- or early-19th-century villas survived in 1970: Highwood Ash, a stuccoed house which contains parts of a timber-framed building, and Highwood Lodge, with bargeboarded gables, Tudor windows, and a battlemented wing. They stood, with some cottages, around the junction of Marsh Lane and the road leading to the Ridgeway. Of the two inns at Highwood Hill licensed in 1751[35] the Rising Sun survived, much rebuilt, in 1970 but the Three Crowns, an 18th-century bow-fronted building, had been demolished in 1937.[36]

South of Highwood Hill lies Holcombe Hill, where a forge, mentioned in 1839,[37] and some weatherboarded cottages form a group at the northern end of Lawrence Street. The Plough, a small weatherboarded inn which existed in 1751,[38] was demolished in 1931.[39] A large green at Holcombe Hill in 1754[40] disappeared, like much of the waste on either side of the Ridgeway, between 1754 and 1828.[41] Of the two farms at the foot of Lawrence Street, mentioned in 1796,[42] Uphill, an early-19th-century building, was demolished in 1931[43] but Lawrence Street farm-house, a large red-brick building of the early 18th century, survives among the semi-detached villas of Goodwyn Avenue.

On the Ridgeway itself Holcombe Hill marked the beginning of a line of buildings which by 1754,[44] stretched intermittently on either side of the road for about a mile to Drivers Hill. The area became known as Mill Hill village, to distinguish it from the 20th-century suburb called Mill Hill Broadway.[45] South-east of Holcombe Hill is Holcombe House, a stuccoed villa designed in 1775 by John Johnson for John William Anderson (d. 1813), afterwards Lord Mayor of London and a baronet. The interior contains some elaborate late-18th-century plaster work and a staircase with a wrought-iron balustrade. A domed Grecian temple in the grounds was

[15] Barnet L.B., *Guide to Church Farm Ho.* (1968).
[16] Hendon Libr., Prints L. 2903–5.   [17] See p. 20.
[18] Accounts of the hamlets in 1754 are based on J. Rocque, *Map of Mdx.* (1754) and on the more detailed B.M. Add. MS. 9839. Later dates are from Cooke, *Map of Hendon* (1796); Whishaw, *Map of Hendon* (1828); and M.R.O., TA/HEN (1843).
[19] The photographs were taken in 1931: Hendon Libr., DD. MHS. 1/145–6. The house is also illus. in M. Briggs, *Mdx. Old and New* (1934), 140.
[20] M.R.O., Acc. 351/759.
[21] M.R.O., L.V. 7/1.
[22] Cf. O.S. Map 1/2,500, Mdx. VI. 13 (1913 edn.); Hendon Libr., DD. MHS. 1/21; Briggs, *Mdx. Old and New*, 135.
[23] Brewer, *Beauties of Eng. & Wales*, x(5), 687–8.
[24] J. Hassell, *Picturesque Rides and Walks . . . around the Metropolis*, i (1817), 186.
[25] D.N.B.; Lysons, *Environs*, iii. 8.
[26] D.N.B.; Hendon Libr., MS. L.1703.
[27] Hassell, op. cit. i. 186–7; *Mdx. Quarterly*, N.S. xiii. 4.

[28] C. E. Wurtzburg, *Raffles of the Eastern Isles*, 718–42.
[29] *Mdx. Quarterly*, N.S. xiii. 5.
[30] *Ambulator* (10th edn.), 160.
[31] *Cat. of the Demesne Lands of the Earl of Powis* (1756) penes Hendon Libr.; M.L.R. 1757/2/124–6; see below, p. 23.
[32] M.L.R. 1764/3/47–9.
[33] Cooke, *Map of Hendon* (1796); *Mdx. Quarterly*, N.S. xiii. 4; see below, p. 23.
[34] O.S. Map 1/2,500, Mdx. VI. 6. (1863 edn.).
[35] M.R.O., L.V. 7/1.
[36] Hopkins, *Hendon*, 101.
[37] Robson, *Com. Dir.* (1839).
[38] M.R.O., L.V. 7/1.
[39] Hendon Libr., DD. MHS. 1/97–8.
[40] B.M. Add. MS. 9839.
[41] Whishaw, *Map of Hendon* (1828).
[42] Lysons, *Environs*, iii. 1.
[43] Hopkins, *Hendon*, 71.
[44] B.M. Add. MS. 9839.
[45] See p. 16.

demolished soon after the Second World War.[46] In 1970 Holcombe House was surrounded by the buildings of St. Mary's abbey, of which it had formed a part since 1881.[47] Almost opposite, on the north-east side of the Ridgeway, stood the late-18th-century Belmont House.[48] To the south-east Ridgeway House, an early-18th-century building,[49] was the home in 1754 of Peter Collinson (1694–1768), naturalist and antiquary,[50] and c. 1802 of the botanist Richard Anthony Salisbury (1761–1829).[51] It was taken over by Mill Hill school on its formation in 1807 but was demolished in 1825, although the garden, visited by Linnaeus, survived for another ten years.[52] In 1970 a wall-plaque marked the site of the house.

The site of Ridgeway House is occupied by the main block of Mill Hill school, which was built in 1825–7 to the designs of William Tite.[53] The two-storeyed building presents a severe aspect to the Ridgeway but the main front, facing south across playing fields, has a bold Ionic portico. The sanatorium, a plain gabled building designed by T. Roger Smith, was built c. 1877. Further additions to the school were made at the end of the 19th century: the red-brick chapel in the basilican style was built to the designs of Basil Champneys in 1898 and a group of buildings including the tuck shop and the Murray scriptorium, named after the lexicographer J. A. H. Murray (d. 1915), a master at the school from 1870 to 1875,[54] was begun in 1902 to the designs of T. E. Colcutt. The Winterstoke library, adjoining the scriptorium, was built before 1912 to Colcutt's designs[55] and the McClure music school was designed by Martin Briggs, a native of Mill Hill.[56] The style of both buildings, with their steeply-pitched roofs and mixture of vernacular and classical motifs, resembles that employed at the same time in Hampstead Garden Suburb.[57] The war memorial gateway on the Ridgeway front was designed by Stanley Hamp, Colcutt's partner, in 1919.[58] The boarding houses of the school are in Wills Grove, some of them dating from the early 20th century and others, like Hamp's neo-Georgian Burton Bank,[59] from a later period.

Two large houses stood in 1754 near the junction of the Ridgeway and Milespit Hill.[60] The Clock House[61] occupied the site of the residence later known as the Priory, while opposite was Littleberries, a large and plain brick building probably built by George Littlebury, who bought the site in 1691.[62] A pedimented Ionic temple, with baroque plasterwork inside, was later built in the grounds and alterations and additions to the house were carried out by J. F. Pawson before 1850.[63] After its purchase by a religious community in 1885 some elaborate fittings were sold[64] but in 1970 a mid-18th-century wrought iron staircase and an early plaster ceiling in the Gilt Room remained *in situ*. Littleberries, like Holcombe House, became surrounded by later buildings. A smaller 18th-century house called Jeanettes occupied an adjacent site until the early 1930s, when it made way for an extension to the convent's vegetable garden.[65] At the south-eastern end of the Ridgeway, at the top of Bittacy Hill, stood Bittacy House, a plain stuccoed villa described as modern in 1828.[66] It was demolished in 1950[67] and replaced by Watchtower House.[68]

Between the mansions of Mill Hill many smaller villas and groups of cottages survive. One group stands at the corner of Hammers Lane and the Ridgeway, and in Hammers Lane itself there are two stuccoed villas of c. 1800, called West Grove and Sunnyside. The Three Hammers was mentioned in 1751[69] but the old weatherboarded building was replaced soon after 1925.[70] Opposite Belmont there is a pair of brick and weatherboarded cottages, one of them containing a shop and post office. To the east, the King's Head, a three-storeyed brick building[71] mentioned in 1751,[72] was demolished in 1949, when the site was incorporated in the playing-fields of Belmont school.[73] Farther east Church Cottages, with St. Paul's church and school, survive from the 1830s. More weatherboarded houses face Mill Hill school and include the Grove, with features of c. 1700, which was restored in 1912 as a residence for masters at the school,[74] and Rosebank, the meeting-place of late-17th-century Quakers.[75] A larger cluster of buildings by the village pond and green, where Milespit Hill meets the Ridgeway, includes Nicholl's alms-houses and some modern houses on the site of the Angel, an inn mentioned in 1751.[76] Shops, cottages, and a Methodist chapel were built north of the pond in the 19th century on an inclosed part of the green. The weatherboarded Adam and Eve stood at the junction of the Ridgeway and Burton Hole Lane in 1751 but was replaced soon after 1915.[77] It served the small hamlet of Drivers Hill, which consisted in 1754 of a few cottages around a green, all of which have disappeared. Burton Hole Lane, recorded in 1754,[78] leads downhill from the Ridgeway to Burton Hole farm-house, a small 18th-century weatherboarded building.[79]

Several small groups of cottages and farm-houses stood on the southern slopes of the Mill Hill ridge. In Page Street, mentioned in 1588,[80] the cottages

[46] TS. notes *penes* St. Mary's abbey, Holcombe Hill; G.E.C. *Baronetage*, v. 324.
[47] See p. 38.
[48] See p. 22.
[49] Drawing reproduced in Brett-James, *Hendon*, 81.
[50] *D.N.B.*; Hendon Libr., MS. L. 1703.
[51] *D.N.B.*
[52] Brett-James, *Hendon*, 81–5.
[53] Brett-James, *Hist. of Mill Hill Sch.*; Pevsner, *Mdx.* 125.
[54] *D.N.B.*
[55] *Arch. Rev.* xxxi. 40–1.
[56] *Builder*, cii. 573–4.
[57] See p. 14.
[58] *Arch. Rev.* xlvi. 165.
[59] Robbins, *Mdx.* 310; *Builder*, clv. 529.
[60] B.M. Add. MS. 9839.
[61] So called in Cooke, *Map of Hendon* (1796).
[62] Brett-James, *Hendon*, 69.
[63] Keane, *Beauties of Mdx.* 263.
[64] Evans, *Hendon*, 258. See p. 38.
[65] *Hendon & Finchley Times*, 15 Feb. 1957.
[66] Whishaw, *Map of Hendon* and ref. bk.
[67] Hopkins, *Hendon*, 104.
[68] See p. 43.
[69] M.R.O., L.V. 7/1.
[70] Hendon Libr., DD. MHS. 1/108.
[71] Hendon Libr., DD. MHS. 1/346.
[72] M.R.O., L.V. 7/1.
[73] *Hendon & Finchley Times*, 7 Sept. 1956.
[74] *Country Life*, xxxii, 7*.
[75] Plaque on house; see p. 40.
[76] M.R.O., L.V. 7/1.
[77] Hendon Libr., DD. MHS. 1/109.
[78] B.M. Add. MS. 9839.
[79] Hendon Libr., DD. MHS. 1/137.
[80] *P.N. Mdx.* (E.P.N.S.), 60 n.

which stood near Copt Hall at the junction with Bunns Lane in 1754[81] have all disappeared. Among them was Old Goodhews farm-house, a large 18th-century brick building with a mansard roof, demolished soon after 1928.[82] At the foot of Bittacy Hill the hamlet of Dollis, mentioned in 1574,[83] consisted in 1754[84] of two groups of farm buildings, together with the Harrow, an inn recorded in 1751[85] but converted before 1796[86] into a private house. Dollis Farm was demolished in 1932.[87] Near-by farm-houses in 1754 included the later Dole Street, Elm (or Rose), and Sanders Lane (or Devonshire) farms, all west of Bittacy Hill, while east of the road stood Bittacy, Frith, and Partingdale (Pattengale) farms. The last forms the nucleus of the house in Partingdale Lane known as Partingdale Manor, a substantial brick building, mostly early-19th-century. Residences south of Mill Hill include Featherstone House, in Wise Lane, a small brick building refronted in the 18th century, and Chase Lodge, formerly Page Street House, of brick and stucco with a projecting Ionic porch, built by 1802.[88] Arrandene, in Wise Lane, a cottage with barge-boarded gables much altered in the later 19th century,[89] was probably built soon after 1800.

The high ground in the centre of the parish was occupied by the three hamlets of the Burroughs, Church End, and Brent Street. By 1597 there was a cross-roads at the Burroughs,[90] where the work-house and other buildings later stood around a pond at a point where the ground sloped steeply to the south, north, and west. Houses which survived the construction of Watford Way through the cross-roads in 1927 were nos. 9–15, an early-18th-century group in brick, no. 42 (Burroughs House), a larger brick building, and early-19th-century terraced cottages stretching along the road towards Church End. The White Bear, mentioned in 1751,[91] was rebuilt in 1932.[92] Burroughs Lodge, west of the cross-roads, was gabled and probably once a farm-house, with early-19th-century alterations; its site is occupied by Richmond Gardens.[93] Grove House, one of the largest seats in the parish, stood in extensive grounds to the north of the Burroughs by 1753.[94] It was a stuccoed building, altered in the early 19th century and demolished in 1934, when the grounds became a public park.[95] Burroughs, or Grove, Farm, also demolished, was a small weather-boarded building at the cross-roads.[96]

Church End consisted in 1754[97] of a cluster of small buildings around St. Mary's church, including Church End Farm (later called Hinge's and the Model Dairy farms), Church Farm,[98] the weather-boarded Greyhound inn on the site of the old church house,[99] and several weatherboarded cottages. The hamlet, away from main roads, retains something of its rural character among acres of suburban housing. To the south were Daniel's alms-houses and Ravensfield House, a stuccoed building of c. 1800, which made way for a bus garage in 1912.[1]

Some substantial houses were built in Parson Street, near Hendon Place and the Vicarage,[2] in the 18th century. The largest was Hendon Hall, at the corner of Ashley Lane, described as new in 1756.[3] Its body is a plain brick three-storeyed block with a six-bay front and moulded wooden window-surrounds; the most notable feature, however, is a massive portico extending the whole height and almost the whole width of the house, with a pediment supported by four Corinthian columns of brick. The portico is said to have been added by Brian Scotney, the occupier in 1796,[4] and to have been brought from Wanstead House (Essex), sold for demolition in 1823.[5] The house was altered in the mid-19th century, when the front to Parson Street was given its Renaissance aspect, and refitted for C. F. Hancock, a London jeweller, in 1889.[6] It was later leased as a school and became a hotel in 1912, receiving large neo-Tudor extensions before the Second World War.[7] A ceiling painting by Tiepolo, supposedly a study for the painting of Olympia and the Four Continents in the Residenz, Würzburg (Germany), was discovered in 1954 and sold to an American; two other large ceiling paintings, in the drawing room and the red room, by unknown artists, are still *in situ*.[8] Hendon Hall is said to have belonged for a time to David Garrick, lord of the manor 1765–79, but there is no evidence that he lived there.[9] The grounds contained an octagonal brick temple and many other ornaments celebrating his connexion with the theatre.[10] The only surviving monuments are small obelisks in the hotel courtyard, inscribed with poems in praise of Garrick and Shakespeare, taken from a larger monument which stood until c. 1957 in Manor Hall Road.[11]

South of Hendon Hall was Downage House, or Downage Wood House, an 18th-century brick building occupied in 1754 by Lady Torrington;[12] it was altered in the 19th century[13] and demolished in 1928.[14] Down House, a neighbouring late-18th-century stuccoed building, was demolished in 1876.[15] Parson Street and its northern continuation, Holders Hill, on account of the wooded, undulating

[81] B.M. Add. MS. 9839.
[82] F. Hitchin-Kemp, 'Notes on a Survey' (TS. *penes* Hendon Libr.), 90–1; illus. in Briggs, *Mdx. Old and New*, 130.
[83] *P.N. Mdx.* (E.P.N.S.), 58.
[84] B.M. Add. MS. 9839.
[85] M.R.O., L.V. 7/1.
[86] Cooke, *Map of Hendon*.
[87] Hendon Libr., Print L. 6196.
[88] M.L.R. 1802/5/139; early-19th-cent. watercolour in B.M. K. xxx. 32.
[89] Hendon Libr., DD. MHS. 1/16.
[90] All Souls Coll., Hovenden Maps, II, no. 16.
[91] M.R.O., L.V. 7/1.
[92] Hopkins, *Hendon*, 99.
[93] Hendon Libr., Prints L. 3314–5.
[94] Hendon Libr., MS. L. 260.
[95] Hendon Libr., Print L. 4010; Hopkins, *Hendon*, 100.
[96] Hendon Libr., DD. MHS. 561.
[97] B.M. Add. MS. 9839.   [98] See above.

[99] See p. 29. It was rebuilt in 1896.
[1] Hendon Libr., Print L. 1005.
[2] See pp. 18, 34.
[3] *Cat. of Demesne Lands* (1756) *penes* Hendon Libr.
[4] Cooke, *Map of Hendon* and ref. bk.
[5] Pevsner, *Mdx.* 109; *V.C.H. Essex*, vi. 326. There is no evidence for the belief that it was brought to Wanstead from Canons, in Little Stanmore.
[6] Evans, *Hendon*, 237–8; *Hendon & Finchley Times*, 30 Jan. 1925.
[7] Ex inf. the gen. manager, Hendon Hall hotel.
[8] *Mdx. Quarterly*, iv. 14; ex inf. the gen. manager.
[9] C. Oman, *David Garrick*, 396. From 1754 Garrick's home was at Hampton: *V.C.H. Mdx.* ii. 321.
[10] Evans, *Hendon*, 240–5.
[11] N.M.R. photo. coll.
[12] *Cat. of Demesne Lands penes* Hendon Libr.
[13] Evans, *Hendon*, 249–50.
[14] Hitchin-Kemp, 'Notes on a Survey', 8.
[15] Hendon Libr., Print L. 2217.

countryside, attracted many villas. Among them was Holders Hill House, a *cottage orné* built to the designs of Robert Lugar before 1811[16] and pulled down later in the century.[17]

South-east of Church End lay a settlement at Brent Street, which in 1754[18] stretched south along the road of that name towards the Brent. It was the largest hamlet in the 18th century and retained its identity until the late 19th, when building linked it with Church End and the Burroughs. Brent Street, while lacking the grandeur of Mill Hill, was noted for handsome dwellings,[19] the largest of which was Hendon House.[20] Fosters and Brent Lodge were two 18th-century brick houses at the corner of Butchers Lane, later Queen's Road; the first became a Christian Science reading room in 1930 and the second, enlarged in the early 19th century and re-named St. Peter's Ouvroir, was demolished in 1957.[21] Goodyers, near by, was built in 1774.[22] At the foot of Brent Street another group of substantial houses included, on the north bank, Brent Bridge House, an 18th-century stuccoed building, later the seat of the Whishaws, part of which survives as the Brent Bridge hotel. Brook Lodge, south of the river, was an 18th-century farm-house converted by Charles Whishaw into a gentleman's residence shortly before 1828[23] and demolished in 1935, after serving as an annexe to the hotel.[24] Among other houses near Brent Bridge in 1754 were those later known as Bridge House, Holmebush, and Decoy House (so named after a decoy on the Brent).[25] In the lane leading to Renters Farm, Shire Hall was mentioned in 1712,[26] rebuilt in the Renaissance manner *c.* 1850, and demolished *c.* 1920.[27] Many cottages and shops clustered about the junction of Brent Street and Bell Lane, including the Bell, mentioned in 1751[28] and considerably altered by 1970. Villas built between Bell Lane and Parson Street in the early 19th century,[29] almost linking the hamlet of Brent Street with Church End, have all been demolished.

Two small hamlets lay among rich grassland west of the high ground at the centre of the parish: Colin Deep, by a ford over Silk stream, and the Hyde, on Edgware Road at its junction with Kingsbury Road. The former consisted in 1594 of only four houses[30] and was always very small. The Hyde, divided between Hendon and Kingsbury, contained about a dozen cottages and farm-houses in 1597.[31] It had not grown much by the mid 18th century,[32] but some villas with small gardens were built *c.* 1800, including Cowleaze House, Rose Cottage, and Hyde Cottage.[33] In 1863 the Hendon part of the Hyde

also contained Hyde, Manor, and Rookery farms.[34] A weatherboarded ale-house called the George was mentioned in 1756, when it also served as Daniel Weedon's farm-house.[35] The Hyde was the sole hamlet along Edgware Road between Cricklewood, at the southern extremity of the parish, and Edgware bridge at the north. Two isolated inns stood along the road: the Bowl and Pin near Edgware bridge existed in 1751[36] but by 1803 had been replaced by the Bald Faced Stag, farther south,[37] while the Welsh Harp near Brent bridge, mentioned in 1803, seems to have been the Harp and Horn recorded in 1751.[38] The Old Welsh Harp, so named to distinguish it from the Upper Welsh Harp built farther north in the 19th century, came to be much frequented by day trippers from London;[39] it was rebuilt in 1937.[40] Scattered farm-houses along the Brent valley, away from the main centres of population, included Decoy Farm, demolished in 1935,[41] Renters Farm, Upper and Lower Guttershedge farms, and Cockmans in the Wood, in Cool Oak Lane, on the Kingsbury border. The last, a farm in 1754,[42] later became known as Woodfield House; it was occupied from 1852 to 1858 by Passionist fathers and was demolished in 1940.[43]

The largest hamlet south of the river Brent in 1754 was Childs Hill, where small houses and cottages stood together on the northern slopes of Hampstead Heath. Few wealthy residents lived there, many of the inhabitants being brick-makers.[44] No inn was recorded before the Castle, mentioned in 1796[45] and rebuilt in the late 19th century. After 1828 Finchley Road ran through Childs Hill, intersecting Cricklewood Lane by the Castle inn, where several houses were built in the years before 1850.[46] Among the very few villas built near by in the early 19th century, the Hermitage, a small house in the Tudor manner on the road to Golders Hill, is the only survivor.

Cricklewood, a small hamlet in the extreme south-west, lay partly in Willesden parish and consisted in 1754[47] of a group of farm buildings near the Crown inn at the corner of Edgware Road and the road to Childs Hill. The Crown, mentioned in 1751,[48] was rebuilt in 1889. Some early-19th-century villas along Edgware Road[49] included Cricklewood House, the residence before 1798 of William Huntington (1745–1813), Calvinistic divine and author.[50] Neighbouring farms were Clitterhouse,[51] to the north, and Cowhouse and Westcroft, south of Cowhouse Green, a stretch of waste near the modern Cricklewood tavern.[52]

By 1754 there were about 16 houses with small

[16] R. Lugar, *Plans and Views of Buildings* (1811), 24.
[17] It seems to have been on the site occupied by the house called Ravensfield in 1970.
[18] B.M. Add. MS. 9839.
[19] Brewer, *Beauties of Eng. & Wales*, x(5), 690.
[20] See above.
[21] Hendon Libr., DD. MHS. 505–7.
[22] Hitchin-Kemp, 'Notes on a Survey', 139.
[23] Whishaw, *Map of Hendon* and ref. bk.
[24] Hendon Libr., Print L. 2759.
[25] B.M. Add. MS. 9839.   [26] M.L.R. 1712/5/140.
[27] Hendon Libr., Print L.1006.
[28] M.R.O., L.V. 7/1.
[29] O.S. Map 1/2,500, Mdx. XI. 7 (1863 edn.).
[30] All Souls Coll., Hovenden Maps, II, no. 17.
[31] Ibid. no. 9.   [32] B.M. Add. MS. 9839.
[33] Cooke, *Map of Hendon* (1796); Whishaw, *Map of Hendon* (1828); O.S. Map 1/2,500, Mdx. XI. 6 (1863 edn.).
[34] O.S. Map 1/2,500, Mdx. XI. 6 (1863 edn.).

[35] *Cat. of Demesne Lands penes* Hendon Libr.
[36] M.R.O., L.V. 7/1.
[37] Ibid. 10/113. The modern inn was built in 1927–8: Hitchin-Kemp, 'Notes on a Survey', 107.
[38] M.R.O., L.V. 7/1.
[39] See p. 28.
[40] H. P. Clunn, *Face of London* (1957 edn.), 451.
[41] Hopkins, *Hendon*, 71.
[42] B.M. Add. MS. 9839.
[43] Ex inf. Father Sylvester Palmer, C.P.; see p. 38.
[44] See pp. 25–6.
[45] Cooke, *Map of Hendon*.
[46] Whishaw, *Map of Hendon* (1828); M.R.O., TA/HEN.
[47] B.M. Add. MS. 9839.
[48] M.R.O., L.V. 7/1.
[49] Whishaw, *Map of Hendon* (1828).
[50] *D.N.B.*; F. Hitchin-Kemp, 'Notes on a Survey', 69–70.
[51] See p. 20.
[52] Whishaw, *Map of Hendon* (1828).

gardens at Golders Green, near the later site of the Underground station,[53] most of them on small inclosures from the waste. In 1814 Golders Green contained 'many ornamental villas and cottages, surrounded with plantations',[54] and in 1828 detached houses spread on both sides of the road as far as Brent bridge.[55] The green, already much attenuated, was finally inclosed in 1873-4.[56] The villas in their wooded grounds, which gave Golders Green its special character, disappeared rapidly with the growth of suburban housing after the extension of the Underground; they included Alba Lodge, Golders Lodge, Gloucester Lodge, the Oaks, and Grove House.[57] Woodstock House, an early-19th-century stuccoed building, served as a dormitory for La Sagesse convent in 1970.[58] It was formerly known as Rose Cottage and was occupied from 1816 to 1835 by Sir Felix Booth (1775-1850), head of Booth and Co., distillers.[59] In 1751 there were two inns at Golders Green: the Hoop, commemorated in Hoop Lane, and the White Swan,[60] much altered by 1970. North-east of Golders Green the hamlet of Temple Fortune grew up after the construction of Finchley Road, when the Royal Oak was built;[61] some terraces of cottages had appeared near by by 1863.[62] Temple Fortune was a solitary farm-house when first mentioned in 1754; it stood at the intersection of two minor roads, by a small green which itself had disappeared by 1863.[63]

South of Golders Green, where Hodford Farm once stood, the Hampstead road, later North End Road, rose to Golders Hill, a hamlet bestriding the boundary.[64] In 1754[65] common land lined the road but several encroachments had been made to provide sites for large houses. In a house, later called the Manor House,[66] belonging to the politician Jeremiah Dyson (1722-76), Mark Akenside (1721-70) the poet and physician[67] recuperated in 1758. There he wrote a much quoted ode on his recovery in which 'Golder's Hill' is apostrophized.[68] Opposite Dyson's house, Golders Hill House was built between 1754 and 1796[69] in grounds of 27 a.[70] The house was enlarged in 1875 to the designs of E. F. Clarke[71] for Sir Thomas Spencer Wells, Bt. (1818-97), surgeon to the queen's household.[72] It was acquired by the L.C.C. in 1898[73] and destroyed during the Second World War[74] but the grounds were preserved as Golders Hill park. Immediately to the north an early-19th-century villa, Ivy House, was the home from 1857 of C. R. Cockerell (1788-1863), the

architect.[75] From 1913 it was occupied intermittently by Anna Pavlova (d. 1930), the ballet dancer, who made some alterations in 1929, before it became a school of drama.[76] Wyldes Farm, a little east of Golders Hill on the slopes of Hampstead Heath, is a small weatherboarded building with a large weatherboarded barn and outbuildings attached. The house, known in the 19th century as Collins's Farm or Heath Farm, was occupied by the painter John Linnell (1792-1882), who is said to have entertained William Blake there and added a room in 1826,[77] by Charles Dickens as a young man,[78] and by Sir Raymond Unwin, co-planner of the Hampstead Garden Suburb, from 1906 until his death in 1940.[79]

There were 400 communicants in the parish in 1547,[80] and 344 persons took the protestation oath in 1642.[81] Of 228 persons assessed for hearth-tax in 1664, 5 lived in houses with ten or more hearths.[82] In 1801 the total population was 1,955 and there were 373 houses. The population was 3,110 in 1831 and had reached 3,333 by 1851, when there were 585 houses.[83]

GROWTH AFTER 1850. Despite a rising population in the late 19th century, largely around Childs Hill and Brent Street, much of Hendon was unchanged until the Hampstead tube reached Golders Green in 1907 and Edgware in 1924.[84] Growth after 1850 therefore took place in two stages: the first, before the coming of the Underground, saw the expansion of some of the old hamlets and the creation of railway settlements, while the second saw most of the parish covered by suburban housing.

Brent Street, a 'genteel hamlet' in 1876,[85] became the leading shopping district in the late 19th century.[86] New Brent Street, with its terraced and semi-detached houses, was built between 1843 and 1863, and included a post office, a police station, and a school opposite the junction with Bell Lane.[87] The area around Church Road, which connected Brent Street with Church End, was also covered with houses after Hendon station was opened in 1868. Fuller Street was built before 1874[88] and nearby terraces, including Heading Street and Prince of Wales Road, were built at about that time.[89] The northern limit of housing was marked by Sunningfields Road, Sunny Gardens Road, and Sunningfields Crescent, the last of which was laid out in 1882 and built up at the end of the century.[90] East of Brent

[53] B.M. Add. MS. 9839.
[54] Brewer, *Beauties of Eng. & Wales*, x(5), 690. Engravings in Guildhall Libr., Pr. V HEN.
[55] Whishaw, *Map of Hendon*.
[56] Thorne, *Environs*, i. 233.
[57] O.S. Map 1/2,500, Mdx. XI. 11 (1863 edn.).
[58] *Hendon & Finchley Times*, 21 Sept. 1956. See p. 39.
[59] *D.N.B.*; Hendon Libr., DD. MHS. 534.
[60] M.R.O., L.V. 7/1.
[61] Evans, *Hendon*, 308.
[62] O.S. Map 1/2,500, Mdx. XI. 7 (1863 edn.).
[63] B.M. Add. MS. 9839; O.S. Map 1/2,500, Mdx. XI. 7 (1863 edn.).
[64] The Hampstead part was called North End by the mid 18th cent.: *P.N. Mdx.* (E.P.N.S.), 113.
[65] B.M. Add. MS. 9839.
[66] See p. 18.   [67] *D.N.B.*
[68] Thorne, *Environs*, i. 233.
[69] B.M. Add. MS. 9839; Cooke, *Map of Hendon*; M.L.R. 1807/5/219.
[70] Guildhall Libr., Pr. V HEN.; Keane, *Beauties of Mdx.* (1850), 174-6.
[71] *Architect*, xiv. 160.

[72] *D.N.B.*
[73] *Hampstead Annual* (1898), 53.
[74] Mill Hill Hist. Soc., Add. Items 147.
[75] *Trans. Hampstead Antiq. & Hist. Soc.* (1904-5), pp. 49-50.
[76] Mill Hill Hist. Soc., Add. Items 65.
[77] *Hampstead Annual* (1903), 131; Thorne, *Environs*, i. 291.
[78] *Hampstead Annual* (1903), 132.
[79] *D.N.B.*; plaque in house.
[80] E 301/34 m. 28.
[81] Hse. of Lords, Mdx. Protestation Rets.
[82] M.R.O., MR/TH/5.   [83] *Census*, 1801-51.
[84] Cf. *Mdx. Monthly*, ii. 14-16; Mill Hill Hist. Soc., Add. Items 24.
[85] Thorne, *Environs*, i. 338.
[86] *Hendon & Finchley Times*, 30 Jan. 1925, p. 6; *Kelly's Dirs. Mdx.* (1874, 1886, 1896).
[87] M.R.O., TA/HEN; O.S. Map 1/2,500, Mdx. XI. 7 (1863 edn.).
[88] *Kelly's Dir. Mdx.* (1874).
[89] *Hendon & Finchley Times*, 30 Jan. 1925, p. 6.
[90] Hopkins, *Hendon*, 90.

Street, small houses lined Victoria, Stratford, and Belle Vue roads by 1899.[91] A statement in 1876 that Hendon had recently come to look like any other suburban or railway village[92] applied to Church Road, Brent Street, and Finchley Lane, rather than to Church End, whose remoteness from the main roads allowed it to remain relatively unchanged until the 1960s.

North of Brent Street, large houses continued to be built in and around Parson Street.[93] Many of them, hidden by high walls and plantations and presenting a marked contrast to the humbler terraces lower down the hill, were built on the Hendon Place estate during the occupancy of a Mr. Somerville, who laid out Waverley Grove and Tenterden Grove after 1863.[94] Thirty-five acres of the estate were bought by C. F. Hancock of Hendon Hall, who built several houses,[95] as did a Mr. Prachitt, who came to live in Fuller Street in 1877.[96] Down House and other 18th-century houses made way for the new buildings, several of which were themselves later replaced by smaller dwellings and luxury flats. Those houses which survived in 1970 gave the area its character of tree-shaded Victorian opulence: among them were Westhorpe, an Italianate brick building in a derelict state, Nazareth House, known in 1902 as St. Swithins, a large brick house with a crenellated tower, extended c. 1900 to the designs of George Hornblower,[97] and the Towers, formerly Ivy Tower,[98] adorned with gables and turrets.

Away from Brent Street the fastest growth in the mid 19th century took place at Childs Hill, which was linked with near-by Hampstead. Terraces of artisans' houses sprang up along Cricklewood Lane near the Red Lion, in the Mead (later Granville Road), and near the Castle inn.[99] By 1863 a school and All Saints church had been built in the village and other streets, including the Ridge (later Ridge Road), had been laid out; the population of the parish of All Saints rose from 906 in 1861 to 2,138 in 1871 and 5,525 in 1891.[1] To the east, around West Heath Road on the slopes of Hampstead Heath, some large houses were built between 1863 and 1897,[2] several of which were standing in 1970. North of Childs Hill, however, open country survived the coming of the Underground in 1907, when Lyndale Avenue[3] and other roads were built on land belonging to the Ecclesiastical Commissioners.[4]

The growth of modern Cricklewood began after the opening of Childs Hill (later Cricklewood) station in 1868, when the 'railway village', terraced cottages for Midland railway employees, was built between the railway and Edgware Road.[5] After a pause small houses spread north from Kilburn and Brondesbury, until by 1897 they had been built in Elm Grove,

Yew Grove, and Ash Grove, south of Cricklewood Lane; St. Peter's church and school were opened at about that time, when housing began to creep up Cricklewood Lane towards Cowhouse Green and Childs Hill.[6] Rockhall Terrace, large houses in Edgware Road dating from before 1863,[7] was demolished in 1905, and the shopping centre of Cricklewood Broadway was built near the terminus for trams from the west end of London.[8] In 1908 the Hendon part of Cricklewood was much less built up than the area west of Edgware Road. Thorverton, Caddington, and Dersingham roads were laid out in 1907[9] but much of the land remained empty along Cricklewood Lane, leading to Childs Hill, until after the First World War.[10] Cowhouse Farm survived until 1932.[11]

The Midland Railway made its greatest impact on the western part of the parish, where, apart from Cricklewood, the only hamlets were at the Hyde, Colindeep, and the Hale. A small group of houses at Burnt Oak was under construction in 1863, presumably to serve the new Redhill workhouse; the houses occupied North, South, and East roads, which formed a square with Edgware Road.[12] A school and a church were built near by at the end of the 19th century but the area remained rural until the L.C.C.'s Watling estate was laid out in 1924–7.[13] To the south a new suburb called West Hendon grew up near Hendon station, opened in 1868 amid fields at the foot of Burroughs Lane (later Station Road). Streets of terraced houses stretching west from Edgware Road to Brent reservoir had been partially completed by 1897, while Herbert, Wilberforce, and Algernon roads were laid out to the east.[14] West Hendon expanded after the opening of Schweppes's mineral water factory in 1895. Deerfield Cottages were built for Schweppes's employees[15] and by 1914 small houses had spread up the hill towards the Burroughs on the Neeld family's estate,[16] in and around Vivian Avenue, Audley Road, and Graham Road.[17] Building also spread north to the Hyde and to Colindale, a suburban outpost near the old hamlet of Colindeep, where terraces were built in Colindale and Annesley avenues between 1897 and 1914,[18] presumably because of the near-by hospital, Public Health laboratory, and tramway depot. Open country, however, stretched south from West Hendon to Cricklewood railway sidings in 1914, while the badly drained ground on the Kingsbury border never attracted housing; Reets Farm survived in 1929,[19] and the area was occupied by a park, playing fields, a nursery, and allotment gardens in 1970.

The railway did little to affect Mill Hill, whose ward had a population of only 4,414 in 1911, com-

[91] O.S. Maps 6″, Mdx. XI. NE. (1897 edn.).
[92] Thorne, *Environs*, i. 336–7.
[93] O.S. Map 1/2,500, Mdx. XI. 7 (1863 edn.); Evans, *Hendon*, 233–7.
[94] Evans, *Hendon*, 233. For the estate, see below, p. 18.
[95] Mill Hill Hist. Soc., Add. Items 20; see above.
[96] Map (1874) *penes* Hendon Libr.
[97] *Building News*, lxxxiii. 255. It belonged in 1970 to the Sisters of Nazareth.
[98] O.S. Map 6″, Mdx. XI. NE. (1920 edn.).
[99] *Hendon & Finchley Times*, 30 Jan. 1925, p. 9; O.S. Map 1/2,500, Mdx. XI. 15 (1863 edn.).
[1] *Census*, 1861, 1871, 1891.
[2] O.S. Map. 1/2,500, Mdx. XI. 15 (1863 edn.); ibid. 6″, Mdx. XI. SE. (1897 edn.).
[3] See p. 19.
[4] Church Com. file. 83730.

[5] B. W. Dexter, *Cricklewood* [1908], 38.
[6] O.S. Map 6″, Mdx. XI. SE. (1897 edn.).
[7] O.S. Map 1/2,500, Mdx. XI. 15 (1863 edn.).
[8] Dexter, *Cricklewood*, 38. [9] Ibid. 53.
[10] O.S. Map 6″, Mdx. XI. SE. (1915 edn.).
[11] See p. 20.
[12] *Kelly's Dir. Mdx.* (1855); O.S. Maps. 1/2,500, Mdx. XI. 1, 2, 6, 10, 15 (1863 edn.).
[13] See pp. 15–16.
[14] O.S. Map 6″, Mdx. XI. SW. (1897 edn.).
[15] Hitchin-Kemp, 'Notes on a Survey', 3.
[16] *T L.M.A.S.* xii. 683; see below, p. 24.
[17] O.S. Map 1/2,500, Mdx. XI. 6 (1914 edn.).
[18] O.S. Map 6″, Mdx. XI. NW. (1897 edn.); 1/2,500, Mdx. XI. 2 (1914 edn.).
[19] Hitchin-Kemp, 'Notes on a Survey', 117.

pared with Central ward's 17,776 and Childs Hill's 16,616.[20] After the opening of the G.N.R.'s Mill Hill station (later Mill Hill East) in 1867 a few terraced cottages and a public house grew up near the gas-works at the foot of Bittacy Hill, but the poor train service failed to attract commuters. The Midland, too, seemed uninterested in suburban growth: fields stretched around its station (later called Mill Hill Broadway) until well into the 20th century, although between 1897 and 1913 some new streets, including Langley Park, Sylvan Avenue, and Brockenhurst Gardens, were laid out near by[21] and the nucleus of the shopping centre in Mill Hill Broadway (then still known as Lawrence Street) was built c. 1910.[22] Abortive plans were made in 1910 for a village, resembling Hampstead Garden Suburb, on 50 a. north-west of the Midland Railway station.[23] Some large villas were built along Hale Lane in the late 19th century,[24] but the Hale itself remained apart until the 1920s. The one early attempt at large-scale building failed, probably because of inadequate public transport. In 1878 the Birkbeck Building Society and the Birkbeck Freehold Land Society laid out plots for 500 small houses in the angle between Daws Lane and Hammers Lane.[25] The first houses were built in Tennyson Road in 1879 but buyers hung back and the society finally collapsed in 1910.[26] There were many vacant plots on the estate in 1897[27] and some as late as 1954.[28]

Religious communities first reached the old village of Mill Hill in 1871, when St. Joseph's college was opened near the top of Lawrence Street.[29] Other institutions followed and Mill Hill school began to expand at the end of the century, but the area remained free of dense housing. Residences at the tops of Bittacy Hill and Milespit Hill included the Priory and another house, possibly Parkfield, both built c. 1875 to designs by T. E. Colcutt in the tile-hung Norman Shaw manner,[30] and Wentworth House, west of Bittacy House, a gabled building with a cupola designed by W. E. and F. Brown c. 1891.[31] In the 1890s James C. Marshall established, in conjunction with the Linen and Woollen Drapers' Institution, a Cottage Home for retired members of the drapery trade. At first the home comprised 61 dwellings but after extensions in 1927 and 1961 it provided accommodation and full medical facilities for 250 people on both sides of Hammers Lane.[32] The original cottages, designed by George Hornblower and dating from 1898, form three sides of a courtyard; the central block, in the Jacobean manner, contains a hall with an open timber roof and is surmounted by a cupola.[33] Shortly before 1910 the Inglis barracks replaced Bittacy farm, although the farm-house survived in 1936.[34]

The barracks were occupied in 1970 by the Royal Engineers, for whom large extensions had been carried out in 1968.[35] In Frith Lane farther to the east Nether Court, the largest Victorian house in Hendon, was built to the neo-Jacobean designs of Percy Stone in 1883.[36] Most 20th-century buildings along the Ridgeway, including Watchtower House and cottages built on the site of the Angel and Crown, are of modest height, although the neo-Georgian headquarters of the National Institute of Medical Research, designed by Maxwell Ayrton and opened in 1950,[37] is an exception.

The Underground gave rise to two distinct kinds of housing, the one idealistic in conception and care-fully planned, the other commercially inspired and similar to scores of other suburban developments. The first kind is instanced in Hampstead Garden Suburb, built on part of Eton College's estate[38] to the east of Finchley Road. In 1905 a committee was formed at the instigation of Henrietta, afterwards Dame Henrietta, Barnett (1851–1936), the social reformer, to buy 80 a. as an extension to Hampstead Heath; later in that year, in expectation of the coming of the railway, the rest of the estate, totalling 243 a. east of Finchley Road and north of Golders Hill, was bought by the Hampstead Garden Suburb Trust for development on lines laid down by Mrs. Barnett.[39] Building was begun in 1907, near Asmuns Hill, by independent groups,[40] although the Hampstead Garden Suburb Act of 1906[41] enabled the character of the area to be determined by the trustees and their architects, Raymond Unwin and R. B. Parker, with Sir Edwin Lutyens as consultant. There were directions on the density of housing, the width of the streets, and the use of trees and building materials. The first major con-tractors included the Garden Suburb Development Co. and the Improved Industrial Dwellings Co. but many smaller houses were built by Hampstead Tenants Ltd. and Second Hampstead Tenants Ltd., collective enterprises financed by tenants' shares and outside contributions, which, it was hoped, would extend house-ownership to persons of smaller means.[42] The trustees themselves built the institute in Central Square and some cottages. In 1911 another 411 a., extending into Finchley, were leased from the Ecclesiastical Commissioners.[43] That part of the Suburb was built after the First World War, with J. C. S. Soutar as chief planner, while Hampstead Heath Extension Tenants Ltd., Oakwood Tenants Ltd., and other bodies joined the original con-tractors.[44]

The lay-out of the Suburb is similar to that employed by Parker and Unwin at Letchworth (Herts.) some ten years earlier, with winding roads,

[20] Census, 1911.
[21] O.S. Map 6″, Mdx. VI. SW. (1897 edn.); ibid. 1/2,500, Mdx. VII. 14 (1913 edn.).
[22] Date on building.
[23] British Architect, lxxiv. 384, 410.
[24] O.S. Maps 1/2,500, Mdx. VI. 14 (1863 edn.); ibid. 6″, Mdx. VI. SW. (1897 edn.).
[25] Mill Hill Hist. Soc., Add. Items 55.
[26] Hendon & Finchley Times, 28 Jan. 1955.
[27] O.S. Map 6″, Mdx. VI. SW. (1897 edn.).
[28] Hendon & Finchley Times, 14 May 1954.
[29] See p. 38.   [30] Building News, xxviii. 656, 686.
[31] Ibid. lxi. 716.   [32] Ex inf. the sec.
[33] Pevsner, Mdx. 126; Building News, lxxiv. 635.
[34] Kelly's Dirs. Mdx. (1906, 1910); O.S. Map 1/2,500, Mdx. XI. 7 (1936 edn.).

[35] Architect and Building News, ccxxxiii. 322.
[36] Architect, xxx. 177.
[37] Robbins, Mdx. 310; The Times, 21 Apr. 1950, 6 May 1950.
[38] See p. 21.
[39] Robbins, Mdx. 258–9; Country Life, lxxx. 410; Pevsner, Mdx. 59–62.
[40] Except where otherwise stated, the rest of the para. and the two foll. paras. are based on Builder, ciii. 250–6; Pevsner, Mdx. 59–64; and A. A. Jackson, Semi-detached Lond. 78–82.
[41] 6 Edw. VII, c. 192 (Local Act).
[42] E.B., Co-Partnership in Housing, foreword by Raymond Unwin, p. 4.   [43] Ibid. 10–11.
[44] H. Barnett, Story of Hampstead Garden Suburb 1907–1928, pp. 25–6.

many trees, and a diversity of styles and materials. The focal point, Central Square, occupies a hill and consists of large brick neo-Georgian houses around an open space containing the church of St. Jude-on-the-Hill, the Free church, and, between them, the institute, all designed by Lutyens.[45] Henrietta Barnett lived in no. 1 South Square from 1915 until her death.[46] Most of the houses elsewhere are terraced or semi-detached and many are grouped in closes. Other buildings included artisans' flats in Addison Way and a quadrangle of houses for the aged, called the Orchard, both designed by Unwin, and a quadrangle of flats for single working women called Waterlow Court, designed by Baillie Scott in 1909. On the edge of the estate, at Temple Fortune, two impressive blocks of shops and flats, of Germanic appearance, with steeply-pitched roofs and towers, were designed by Unwin, who also designed the club house in Willifield Way, destroyed in the Second World War. Several architects, including W. Curtis Green, E. Guy Dawber, C. M. Crickmer, and Geoffrey Lucas, were employed but at first there was a prevailing style, derived from vernacular building and emphasizing the choice of materials. Neo-Georgian designs, however, were chosen by Lutyens, C. Cowles Voysey, and others c. 1912 and became usual for larger houses after the First World War. Since the part of the Suburb which lay in Hendon was substantially complete by 1914, most later building took place beyond the boundary, where the eastern extension was served by a shopping centre in Lyttelton Way, Finchley.

Hampstead Garden Suburb was planned for people of widely varying incomes and in that respect differed both from earlier ventures like Bournville[47] or Port Sunlight, originally the products of industrial paternalism, and from later council estates. Idealism produced buildings which ranged from large detached houses overlooking the Heath Extension to small cottages and flats near Temple Fortune in the north. In practice, however, manual workers were forced out by rising prices and rents, until the suburb became middle-class. Central Square provided facilities of an improving nature but atrophied as a result of the banishment of all shops, public houses, and amusements to the fringes of the estate, at Temple Fortune and Finchley. Despite its failure as a social experiment the Suburb embodied one of the most influential housing schemes of its time in England and contrasted strongly with the rest of 20th-century Hendon.

At Golders Green, a straggling hamlet in 1901,[48] new houses were built at the corner of Wentworth Road and Hoop Lane in 1905. Two years later the arrival of the Underground started a building boom in houses whose rustic appearance was to set a trend for suburban exteriors over the next three decades. Growth continued until after the First World War: the new Golders Green ward, covering an area with a population of 4,465 in 1911, had 7,518 people by 1921 and 17,837 by 1931.[49] Work began on 85½ a. near Woodstock House in 1906[50] and the Finchley Road and Golders Green Syndicate began to build an estate south of Temple Fortune, including Templars Avenue and Wentworth Road, in 1907.[51] In the same year work started on the Ecclesiastical Commissioners' land south of Golders Green station, and Rodborough and Hodford roads were laid out,[52] whereupon housing spread south towards Childs Hill. Prominent among those responsible was Sir Edwin Evans, 'the Napoleon of suburban development', who worked on the Woodstock estate and elsewhere in conjunction with local firms, like those of Ernest Owers and Farrow and Howkins.[53] The old villas in their large gardens disappeared: in 1909 Golders Lodge was demolished and Golders Gardens, Gainsborough Gardens, and Powis Gardens were built on its site.[54] At Golders Green cross-roads, near the Underground station, rows of shops were under construction in 1911–12[55] on a site which in 1904 had been deserted;[56] churches, chapels, a theatre, a cinema, and a large shopping centre followed. After the First World War, most of the remaining villas in Golders Green Road were replaced by semi-detached houses and large blocks of luxury flats, such as Brook Lodge and Riverside Drive.[57] Houses were also built north and west of Temple Fortune, work beginning on Eastfield Crescent, Cranbourne Gardens, and Park Way in 1924.[58] Many of the new houses at Golders Green were bought by middle-class Jews, who opened their first synagogue in 1922[59] and became the forerunners of a large Jewish population.

Change in the agricultural north-west began in 1910, when Claude Grahame-White acquired a field near Colindale from which Louis Paulhan had set off for the first flight from London to Manchester in one day.[60] The field became part of Hendon Aerodrome which soon covered 207 a. In 1912 Grahame-White moved into Orange Hill House, a short distance to the north,[61] and by 1914 had made Hendon by skilful advertising one of the four leading airfields in the country and a major centre for the training of pilots. He also attracted thousands of visitors, for whom were provided a club-house, a 30-bedroomed hotel, and five enclosures for viewing.[62] Hendon witnessed several landmarks in the history of British aviation: an experimental aerial postal service was inaugurated there in 1911 and the first aerial Derby was held in 1912.[63] In 1914 the airfield was requisitioned for training by the Royal Naval Air Service and aircraft production was increased, but with the coming of peace Grahame-White resumed the development of its recreational side. The R.A.F. staged its first pageant there in 1920 and took the airport over completely

[45] See plate facing p. 65.
[46] Plaque on house.
[47] V.C.H. Warws. vii. 50, 55.
[48] Except where otherwise stated, the para. is based on F. Howkins, Story of Golders Grn. and its Remarkable Development, 20 and map facing p. 23, and Jackson, Semi-det. Lond. 70–77, 82–9.
[49] Census, 1911–31; the ward was reduced from 960 a. to 805 a. after 1921.
[50] Howard Farrow Ltd., Work in Progress, 27–8, 31.
[51] Hendon & Finchley Times, 20 Aug. 1954.
[52] Church Com. file 10113/3.
[53] Work in Progress, 27, 30, 35.

[54] Hopkins, Hendon, 60, 94.
[55] Church Com. file 83446; Builder, civ. 59.
[56] Lee, Sixty Years of the Northern, photographs facing p. 10.
[57] Hopkins, Hendon, 98, 99, 101.
[58] Hendon Libr., U.D.C. min. bk. (1924), 97.
[59] See p. 43.
[60] R. D. Brett, Hist. of British Aviation 1910–14, p. 41; G. Wallace, Claude Grahame-White, 47, 131; Hopkins, Hendon, 83.
[61] Wallace, Grahame-White, 174.
[62] Wallace, Grahame-White, 137, 163–8; see pp. 28–9.
[63] Hopkins, Hendon, 84.

in 1922. As a military airport[64] Hendon continued to draw large crowds in the period between the two World Wars. During the Second World War fighter aircraft were stationed at Hendon until 1940, after which the airport was used solely for transport and training. It was closed to flying in 1957, when the R.A.F. metropolitan communications squadron was transferred to Northolt, but remained in use by ground units.[65] In 1973 an R.A.F. museum opened on part of the site.[66]

In 1917 Claude Grahame-White planned housing for 300 employees, in the vain belief that Hendon would become 'the Charing Cross of our international air routes'. Simple terraced cottages, designed by Henry Matthews, were built around a square called Aeroville and some were occupied by 1919.[67] Handley Page established an airport at Claremont Road, Cricklewood, in 1912.[68] It was used by Handley Page Transport from 1919, and later also by Imperial Airways, for passenger flights to the Continent. Surrounding building so restricted expansion that the airfield was closed in 1929, whereupon the site was rapidly covered with houses or converted to playing fields.[69]

Aircraft production during the First World War hastened the growth of Colindale and the Hyde. Rows of small terraced and semi-detached houses continued to be built between the airport and Edgware Road after the factories had turned over to peacetime production.[70] Industry, restricted by Hendon U.D.C's determination not to offend owner-occupiers,[71] spread south along either side of Edgware Road towards Cricklewood after parts of the Brent reservoir had been reclaimed in 1921. The beginning of work on the North Circular Road in 1924 acted as a further impetus, until by the Second World War factories, second-hand car depots, and rubbish dumps, interspersed with blocks of flats, small shops, and houses, stretched from Cricklewood almost to Burnt Oak and Edgware. The British Museum's newspaper repository was opened in a new building in Colindale Avenue in 1932.[72]

Growth east of Edgware Road awaited the extension of the Underground through Hendon Central to Edgware and the building of arterial roads. All the new stations, except Colindale, were in open country[73] but the Underground group at once advertised 'little palaces' at Colindale,[74] and in 1923 the large Moat Mount estate in the north was said to be ready for development.[75] Hendon Way and the North Circular Road helped to open up the land west of Golders Green. At the southern end of Hendon Way, at Childs Hill, three large blocks of private flats, called Vernon Court, Wendover Court, and Moreland Court, with mock-Tudor timbering, were erected after the opening of the road in 1927.[76] Farther north the Vale, which ran from near Cricklewood to Golders Green, was being laid out in 1924, as was Renters Avenue, near Brent Underground station.[77] Houses were still being built in Shirehall Lane and neighbouring streets near the river Brent in 1928 by Messrs. Haymills, who were responsible for several estates in the area.[78] Council houses were built in 1924 on the Brent Farm estate around Sturgess Avenue,[79] and a larger estate was under construction at the Hyde in 1927.[80]

A roundabout and roads were constructed near Hendon Central station in 1923, where Watford Way crossed Queen's Road (formerly Butcher's Lane). As at Golders Green, motor-bus routes terminated in the station forecourt, close to a new shopping centre. Shops were spreading from Central Circus to the Burroughs in 1928[81] and some semi-detached houses were built near Watford Way, although the land west of the road was covered by the Hendon Aerodrome. Building was approved on part of the Hancock estate, near Sunny Gardens Road, in 1924[82] and was also about to begin on the site of Ashley Farm, west of Holders Hill Road, in 1929.[83] Holders Hill Road itself was lined with expensive houses and blocks of flats.[84] Beyond Great North Way, however, Copthall playing field, Hendon golf course, and Hendon Park cemetery together constituted a large open tract which, with the airfield, still separated the north of the parish from the south in 1970. Houses covered all the remaining spaces in the south before 1935,[85] apart from some low-lying land near the Brent, which included the area south of the old U.D.C. sewage works by the North Circular Road.[86] The Ecclesiastical Commissioners refused to allow building at Cowhouse Farm because of bad drainage and it was sold to University College school as a sports ground.[87]

North of Hendon Central the railway passed through Colindale, which served the factories along Edgware Road, to Burnt Oak, which was surrounded by farm-land in 1924.[88] Here the L.C.C. purchased 390 a., including Goldbeaters farm, for their Watling estate. The first residents arrived in 1927 and the estate was completed by 1931, when there were 4,021 houses and flats.[89] In 1937 its population, drawn mainly from Islington and St. Pancras, was 19,012, compared with a population of 1,016 in Burnt Oak ward in 1921.[90] The estate was designed by G. Topham Forrest,[91] architect to the L.C.C., who relied much on the design of earlier garden suburbs: houses of tarred weatherboarding, roughcast or brick, many of them sheltered by older trees, formed winding streets and closes, inter-

[64] See plate facing p. 337.
[65] *The Times*, 5 Nov. 1957.
[66] Ex inf. Hendon Libr.
[67] Wallace, *Grahame-White*, 212; *Builder*, cxvi. 458.
[68] See p. 26.　　　[69] Hopkins, *Hendon*, 85, 96.
[70] *Kelly's Dir. Mdx.* (1922).
[71] D. H. Smith, 'Recent Industrialization of Northern and Western Sectors of Greater Lond.' (Lond. Univ. Ph.D. thesis, 1932), 111.
[72] Hopkins, *Hendon*, 99.
[73] Hendon Libr., DD. MHS. 1/297–300.
[74] Robbins, *Mdx.* 185.
[75] Hendon Libr., DD. MHS. 1/628.
[76] H. P. Clunn, *Face of London*, 452.
[77] Hendon Libr., DD. MHS. 1/50–1.

[78] Hendon Libr., U.D.C. min. bk. (1927–8), 284.
[79] Ibid. (1924), 44.　　　[80] Ibid. (1929), 130.
[81] Hendon Libr., DD. MHS. 1/52–3, /297.
[82] Hendon Libr., U.D.C. min. bk. (1924), 77.
[83] Hitchin-Kemp, 'Notes on a Survey', 10.
[84] Hendon Libr., U.D.C. min. bks. (1927–8), 58; (1936), 96.
[85] O.S. Maps 1/2,500, Mdx. XI. 7, 10, 11, 12, 15 (1935–6 edn.).
[86] See p. 32.
[87] Hendon Libr., U.D.C. min. bk. (1935), 374.
[88] Hendon Libr., DD. MHS. 1/298.
[89] Clarke, *Story of Goldbeaters and Watling*, 3–4.
[90] R. Durant, *Watling* (1939), p. 2; *Census*, 1931.
[91] Pevsner, *Mdx.* 109.

spersed with small parks. Watling Avenue, leading to Burnt Oak station, became the chief shopping centre of the estate, and a market was built off Barnfield Road.

North and west of the Watling estate the remaining farm-land was slowly covered by private semi-detached houses in the 1920s and 1930s. Building was stimulated not only by the Underground but also by the opening of Watford Way and the Barnet and Edgware by-pass roads in 1927. The Stoney-fields estate, north of the Hale, was sold for building in 1924[92] and Upper and Lower Hale farms were sold in 1925,[93] when Hale and Selvage lanes were widened.[94] Fewer than 400 houses had been built by 1928, when the Elmgate Gardens estate was planned, although roads which included Downhurst Avenue and Sunbury Gardens had been laid out.[95] Shops at the Hale were also planned in 1928, when firms intended to build on nearly all the land near by;[96] they included Upper Hale Estates and Streather Estates.[97] In 1932 John Groom's Crippleage, founded in Clerkenwell in 1866, moved to new premises for 120 crippled women in Edgware Way.[98] By 1935[99] continuous building had spread as far north as the Moat Mount golf course.[1]

East of the former Midland Railway's main line suburban growth was slower than at the Hale, chiefly because of the distance from Underground stations. The Broadway, near Mill Hill Broadway station, became a major shopping centre between the two World Wars: in 1930 the site of Bunn's Farm was being built upon and there were plans for the area around Lawrence Street.[2] Large detached houses were erected in Uphill Road and Tretawn Gardens in 1924[3] and covered much of the area south of Marsh Lane by 1935.[4] The streets farther north did not appear until after the Second World War and a large tract of open land survived south of Mill Hill Broadway in 1935.[5] A council estate, including flats, was built near Mill Hill East station, at the foot of Bittacy Hill c. 1924.[6] A scheme by Mill Hill Homesteads Ltd. to build on Devonshire farm, south of the station, was approved in 1928,[7] although the farm was not sold until 1933.[8] An estate centred on Lullington Garth on the Finchley border was built c. 1932.[9] On the southern slopes of the Mill Hill ridge Engel Park, Bittacy Rise, and the avenues around Pursley Road were not completed until immediately before and after the Second World War; Dole Street farm survived until 1937, when the farm-house was replaced by a council estate.[10]

Hendon changed little in appearance between 1945 and 1970. The extreme north, from Mill Hill and Highwood Hill to the boundary, became part of the Green Belt. Elsewhere development was largely concerned with replacing older houses and making use of their grounds; new buildings of note included multi-storey flats east of Brent Street and a block of private flats, designed by Owen Luder, which had been built next to Hendon Hall by 1966.[11] There were sharp contrasts in 1970: between the open north and the shopping centres around the stations or the factories along Edgware Road, and between the expensive dwellings on the Mill Hill ridge or at Hampstead Garden Suburb and the avenues of semi-detached houses which covered most of the parish.

The population rose steadily from 4,544 in 1861 to 22,450 in 1901 and, more steeply, to 38,806 in 1911. Between 1921 and 1931 numbers nearly doubled, from 56,013 to 110,331. The rate slowed down to 40·2 per cent between 1931 and 1951, after which the population fell slightly to 151,843 by 1961. Mill Hill retained its low density in 1961, when there were 9 persons to the acre in Mill Hill ward, 26 in Childs Hill, and 34 in Burnt Oak.[12]

MANORS. In 957 King Edwy is said to have granted 9 hides at *Lotheresleage* and Tunworth to his thegn Lyfing.[13] Tunworth was in Kingsbury but the other estate was probably the 6 measures of land (*mansas*) in Hendon said to have been granted in 959 by King Edgar and Dunstan, as bishop of London, to the abbey of Westminster.[14] The estate seems to have consisted of that part of the parish which lay north and west of a line from Burnt Oak to Highwood Hill.[15] The grant of 959 also mentioned land called Blechenham, which lay south of the river Brent.[16] According to a charter of St. Dunstan, said to date from 963–75,[17] the archbishop purchased a total of 20 hides in Hendon for the abbey. A forged charter, claiming to originate from Edward the Confessor in 1066, confirmed grants of land in Hendon to Westminster by earlier kings;[18] Blechenham and *Lotheresleage* were mentioned, with another district of unknown location called *Codenhlaewe*. None of the names was recorded in Domesday, when the manor of *HENDON*, held by the abbot, was assessed at 20 hides, 10 of which were in demesne.[19]

A late-11th-century grant of the manor in fee farm by Abbot Gilbert Crispin to Gunter and his heir[20] was confirmed c. 1136, after the succession of Gunter's son Gilbert.[21] In 1224 Abbot Richard of Barking, attempting to recover the lands alienated by

[92] Hendon Libr., sales parts.
[93] Ibid.
[94] Hendon Libr., U.D.C. min. bk. (1925), 435.
[95] Hendon Libr., sales parts.
[96] Hendon Libr., DD. MHS. 1/21.
[97] Hendon Libr., U.D.C. min. bks. (1925), 435; (1928), 554.
[98] There was accommodation for 170 in 1969: ex inf. the sec.
[99] O.S. Map 1/2,500, Mdx. VI. 10 (1935 edn.).
[1] Hendon Libr., sales parts.
[2] *Mill Hill Times & Guardian*, 22 Aug. 1930.
[3] Hendon Libr., DD. MHS. 642.
[4] O.S. Map 1/2,500, Mdx. VI. 10 (1935 edn.).
[5] Garrett, 'Upper Brent Valley', 152; O.S. Map 1/2,500, Mdx. VI. 3, 15 (1936 edn.).
[6] Hendon Libr., U.D.C. min. bk. (1924), 46.
[7] Ibid. (1927–8), 104.

[8] Hendon Libr., DD. MHS. 1/11.
[9] Hendon Libr., U.D.C. min. bks. (1931–2), 842; (1932), 96, 200, 368.
[10] Mill Hill Hist. Soc., Add. Items 21.
[11] Ian Nairn, *Nairn's London*, 224.
[12] *Census*, 1861–1961.
[13] *Cart. Sax.* ed. Birch, iii, p. 188. The document is a 12th-cent. copy but the text may be authentic: Sawyer, *Anglo-Saxon Charters*, 219.
[14] *Cart. Sax.* ed. Birch, iii, p. 264. The charter is forged: Sawyer, op. cit. 374.
[15] *P.N. Mdx.* (E.P.N.S.), 219–20.
[16] Ibid. 220–1.
[17] Westm. Domesday, f. 121.
[18] B.M. Cott. Ch. vi. 2.   [19] *V.C.H. Mdx.* i. 123.
[20] Westm. Domesday, f. 124.
[21] Ibid.; *Regesta Regum Anglo-Normannorum*, iii, ed. H. A. Cronne and R. H. C. Davis, 337.

his predecessors, was involved in a law-suit with Gilbert of Hendon, the tenant of the manor and possibly a descendant of the earlier Gilbert, concerning a house and 3 carucates in Hendon.[22] In 1226 the land was granted to Gilbert for life[23] and the abbot was to receive rent and free hospitality at Hendon for two days and a part of a third every year. Gilbert had an interest in the manor in 1228[24] but by 1268 it had passed into the hands of Geoffrey le Rous.[25] In 1312 the abbot took the manor into his own hands, granting Richard le Rous the manor of Hodford and £100 in exchange.[26] Thereafter Hendon manor was retained by the abbey until the Dissolution, although it was leased in 1422[27] and 1505.[28]

In 1541 the king granted the manor to Thomas Thirlby, bishop of Westminster.[29] With the suppression of the bishopric it reverted to the Crown but was granted in 1550 first to Thomas, Lord Wentworth,[30] and afterwards to Sir William Herbert,[31] created earl of Pembroke in 1551.[32] Pembroke settled it in 1569 on his second son Sir Edward (d. 1595),[33] from whom it passed to Edward's eldest son William Herbert (d. 1656), created Lord Powis in 1629.[34] The manor, settled on Powis's eldest son Percy,[35] a recusant and royalist,[36] was sequestrated in 1650 and conveyed by Parliamentary trustees to Charles Whitmore of Balmes House, Shoreditch, two years later;[37] in 1654 Rhys Vaughan was holding manorial courts.[38] Percy Herbert, Lord Powis, regained possession at the Restoration and died in 1667.[39] His son William, who succeeded him, was made earl of Powis in 1674 and marquess of Powis in 1687, but fled the country in 1688 and forfeited his estates in the following year.[40] From 1690 until 1692 courts were held in the name of his brother-in-law Henry Somerset, duke of Beaufort, and others.[41] In 1692 and again in 1694 William Herbert, Viscount Montgomery, eldest son of Lord Powis, vainly petitioned to be admitted to the manor on the grounds that it had been settled on him.[42] Hendon was granted in 1696 to William Zuylestein, earl of Rochford, to be held at a small rent,[43] but the grant did not take effect because of a settlement on the marchioness of Powis before her husband's attainder.[44] The exiled marquess, who

received a dukedom from James II, was succeeded in 1696 by his eldest son, who was outlawed in that year but for whom courts were being held in 1698.[45] Lord Powis was committed to the Tower from 1715 until 1722, when his marquessate was restored,[46] and mortgaged the manor in 1721.[47] As the result of a further mortgage,[48] to Guy's hospital, Southwark, courts were held for the hospital from 1727,[49] although by 1733 they were again being held in the name of Lord Powis.[50] He died, still in debt, in 1745, having vested the manor in trustees;[51] in 1747 it was in the hands of John Hitchings.[52] Lord Powis's only son William died unmarried in 1748, devising his estates to a distant relative Henry Arthur Herbert, Lord Herbert of Cherbury, who was then created earl of Powis.[53]

In 1754 the earl was empowered to sell the manor and estate[54] and in 1757 the lordship was purchased by James Clutterbuck,[55] who conveyed it in 1765 to his friend David Garrick, the actor.[56] Garrick died in 1779, leaving the manor in trust for his nephew Carrington Garrick,[57] later vicar of Hendon, on whose death in 1787 it was again put up for sale.[58] It was in the hands of Charles Pratt, Earl Camden, and Albany Wallis in 1790[59] and was purchased later in that year by John Bond,[60] who died in 1801. Bond's executors[61] unsuccessfully attempted to sell the manor in 1802,[62] after which it passed into the hands of his mortgagee, Richard Lowndes, who held it under a direction of the Court of Chancery in 1816.[63] It was finally sold in 1825 to Samuel Dendy, who was succeeded in 1845 by his son Arthur Hyde Dendy. In 1889 it was held by Arthur Dendy's widow, Eliza,[64] on whose death it was conveyed to Sir John Carteret Hyde Seale, Bt., Mrs. Russell Simpson, and Major H. Dendy, who were joint lords in 1923.[65]

In 1754 the manor was conterminous with the parish[66] and two years later the demesne lands totalled 1,226 a.,[67] in two large blocks.[68] They were divided at auction in that year and several new estates were thereby formed.[69]

The abbots of Westminster also held the rectory estate, which was managed separately. The rectory was valued at £20 in 1291[70] and was leased to John Lamb, the farmer of Frith manor, in 1487.[71] It was

[22] *Cur. Reg. R.* xi, p. 296.
[23] C.P. 25(1)/146/7/10.
[24] *Cur. Reg. R.* xiii, p. 143.
[25] E 368/42 m. 20.
[26] C.P. 25(1)/149/42/88; C 143/89/8. For the manor of Hodford, see below.
[27] W.A.M. 4746.
[28] Ibid. 4744.
[29] Ibid. 6484A; *L. & P. Hen. VIII*, xvi, pp. 243–4.
[30] W.A.M. 6484B.
[31] *Cal. Pat.* 1550–53, 7.
[32] *Complete Peerage*, x. 406–7.
[33] B.M. Harl. MS. 760; *Complete Peerage*, x. 643; C 142/242/107.
[34] *Mdx. Sess. Recs.* ii. 94, 206, 285; *Complete Peerage*, x. 643.
[35] *Cal. Cttee. for Compounding*, i(3), 2197.
[36] *Complete Peerage*, x. 645.
[37] C 54/3673/16; C 54/3684/19.
[38] *Cal. Cttee. for Compounding*, i(2), 1628.
[39] *L.J.* xi. 36, 95, 96.
[40] *Complete Peerage*, x. 647.
[41] M.R.O., Acc. 174/1, ff. 13 sqq.
[42] *Cal. S.P. Dom.* 1691–2, 324–5, 544–5; *Cal. Treas. Bks.* 1693–6, 575.
[43] *Cal. Treas. Bks.* 1696–7, 92; Nat. Libr. of Wales, Powis MS. 1150.
[44] Lysons, *Environs*, iii. 3 n.

[45] M.R.O., Acc. 174/1, f. 39.
[46] Nat. Libr. of Wales, Powis MS. 14229.
[47] Ibid. 12838, 14229.
[48] Ibid. 14229.
[49] M.R.O., Acc. 174/3, f. 39.
[50] M.R.O., Acc. 174/4, f. 9.
[51] Nat. Libr. of Wales, Powis MSS. 14229, 15754.
[52] C.P. 43/656/309.
[53] *Complete Peerage*, x. 650–1.
[54] *L.J.* xxviii. 181, 211–12.
[55] Nat. Libr. of Wales, Powis MS. 12976.
[56] M.R.O., Acc. 174/10, f. 40; K.B. 122/332. The lands were divided: see below.
[57] Evans, *Hendon*, 47–8.
[58] Evans, *Hendon*, 49.
[59] C.P. 25(2)/1364(2)/30 Geo. III Trin., no. 343.
[60] Lysons, *Environs*, iii. 3.
[61] Evans, *Hendon*, 49.
[62] M.R.O., Acc. 790/62.
[63] Brewer, *Beauties of Eng. and Wales*, x(5), pp. 685–6.
[64] Evans, *Hendon*, 49.
[65] Howkins, *Golders Green*, 9.
[66] B.M. Add. MS. 9839.
[67] *Cat. of Demesne Lands* (1756).
[68] See p. 25.
[69] See below.
[70] *Tax. Eccl.* (Rec. Com.), 123.
[71] W.A.M. 4748. For Frith manor, see below.

worth £34 6s. 8d. in 1535, when it included lands near Silk stream and Colin Deep Lane and between Parson Street and Dollis brook, together with a park of 21 a.[72] At the Dissolution it passed to the Herbert family but by c. 1640 it was in the hands of the Crown and called the manor of *HENDON PLACE*.[73] It was then a compact block of lands bordered by Parson Street, Finchley Lane, and Dollis brook, together with some fields in Finchley, and contained 132 a. William Nicholl died seised of the property in 1645, by which date it had ceased to be called a manor,[74] and Paul Nicholl was in possession in 1664.[75] In 1721 it was conveyed, with the house called Hendon Place, to John Edwards, a London merchant.[76] He devised it to his daughter Susanna, wife of William Sneyd of Bishton (Staffs.), who conveyed it in 1730 to Thomas Snow, a London goldsmith[77] later resident at Littleberries. In 1808 George Snow of Langton (Dors.) sold the estate to James Ware, who conveyed it in 1811 to John Carbonell, from whom it was bought in 1824 by the Lord Chief Justice Sir Charles Abbott,[78] later Lord Tenterden of Hendon (d. 1832).[79] The Hendon Place estate, 75 a. in 1828,[80] was sold by Lord Tenterden's son in 1862[81] and afterwards divided for building.[82] The rectorial tithes, retained by the Herberts, were worth £200 in 1690[83] and £679 by 1755, the year before their sale to eleven purchasers.[84]

The abbot of Westminster owned a house in Hendon in 1285.[85] Soon after the manor came under the direct management of the abbey, a new country house was built in Parson Street; it was known at first as the parsonage but was later called Hendon Place. The house, which was finished in 1326, was built by Westminster workmen[86] and in 1540 contained a chapel on the ground floor.[87] Cardinal Wolsey stayed there on his way to the north of England in 1530[88] and Queen Elizabeth I was a visitor in 1566, 1571, and 1576, when the Herberts were in possession, and again in 1594, when Sir John Fortescue was the tenant.[89] In 1593 the building was called Hendon House and styled the manor-house.[90] It was described as pleasantly situated on a slope and large enough to entertain the king c. 1640[91] and had 23 hearths in 1664.[92] It was leased by the Nicholls in the late 17th century to the earl of Northampton, and then to John Aislabie (1670–1742), Chancellor of the Exchequer,[93]

who spent large sums on both house and grounds and on a bridge to connect them with Finchley. Thomas Snow built a new Palladian mansion,[94] pedimented and with wings;[95] by 1816, when the house was unoccupied, a large ballroom had been added.[96] Alterations were made by John Abbott, Lord Tenterden of Hendon (d. 1870), in the 19th century, when the house became known as Tenterden Hall.[97] After serving as a school, it was demolished in 1936.[98]

John Bond, lord of the manor after Garrick's death, lived from 1792 to 1797[99] in a house at Golders Hill, which was known from 1796 as the Manor House.[1] It seems to have been the building occupied from 1753 to 1763[2] by Jeremiah Dyson,[3] although his house has sometimes erroneously been identified as Golders Hill House, a later building on the opposite side of North End Road. The Manor House, an unpretentious stuccoed building, was considerably enlarged in the late 18th century, perhaps by John Bond,[4] but after its sale in 1797 to Robert Ward, the occupier in 1833,[5] it ceased to be the residence of a lord of the manor. It became the administrative and residential quarters of the Manor House hospital in 1917 and was demolished in 1962.[6]

The nucleus of the manor later known as *HODFORD and COWHOUSE* was a house and a carucate granted by Henry of Wymondley and Mabel his wife to Nicholas de Lisle and his wife Emme in 1278.[7] After Nicholas's death Emme conveyed the lands to Edward I, who in 1295 granted them to the abbey of Westminster for the soul of Queen Eleanor.[8] The estate was called the manor of Hodford in 1296, when royal officers were ordered not to take goods there belonging to the abbey.[9] In 1312 the abbot and Richard le Rous exchanged their respective manors of Hodford and Hendon, Richard becoming lord of Hodford.[10] The manor was held of Hendon manor and in 1321 a rent of 1d. was paid for it.[11] Richard le Rous and his wife Maud conveyed the manor in 1317 to Henry le Scrope,[12] lawyer and adherent of Edward II. Henry was already in possession of an estate at Blechenham, which he held of Westminster in 1312 by a quit rent,[13] and had acquired property from Thomas of Blechenham in 1315.[14] His lands in the south of the parish thereafter formed part of the Hodford estate. Henry le Scrope died in 1336,[15] leaving the

[72] *Valor Eccl.* (Rec. Com.), i. 411; W.A.M. 4742.
[73] S.P. 17/H ff. 608–10.
[74] C 142/707/51.
[75] M.R.O., MR/TH/5.
[76] M.R.O., Acc. 262/7/26.
[77] M.L.R. 1730/4/63.
[78] M.L.R. 1808/8/379; 1811/8/82; 1824/12/109.
[79] *Complete Peerage*, xii(1), 673.
[80] Whishaw, *Map of Hendon* and ref. bk.
[81] Evans, *Hendon*, 233; map (1862) *penes* Hendon Libr.
[82] See p. 12.
[83] E 178/6806.
[84] *Cat. of Grt. Tithes . . . of Man. of Hendon.*
[85] W.A.M. 28805.
[86] *T.L.M.A.S.* xxi. 158–9.
[87] *Mdx. & Herts. N. & Q.* i. 116–19.
[88] *D.N.B.*; *V.C.H. Mdx.* ii. 29.
[89] Brett-James, *Hendon*, 51–2; *T.L.M.A.S.* xiii. 235–6. The Herberts were last recorded as living in Hendon in 1583: S.P. 12/168/25(2).
[90] Norden, *Speculum Britanniae*, 21.
[91] S.P. 17/H ff. 608–9.
[92] M.R.O., MR/TH/5.

[93] Brett-James, *Hendon*, 78–9.
[94] Lysons, *Environs*, iii. 4.
[95] Guildhall Libr., illus. edn. of Lysons, *Environs*, ii, pt. 3, anon. watercolour c. 1800 facing p. 3.
[96] Brewer, *Beauties of Eng. and Wales*, x(5), pp. 688–9.
[97] Evans, *Hendon*, 233.
[98] *T.L.M.A.S.* xiii. 500–1.
[99] M.R.O., Acc. 839/24–7.
[1] Cooke, *Map of Hendon* (1796) and ref. bk.
[2] M.R.O., Acc. 839/1–6.
[3] See p. 11.
[4] Mill Hill Hist. Soc., Add. Items 147.
[5] M.R.O., Acc. 839/27–34.
[6] Ex inf. Manor House hosp.
[7] C.P. 25(1)/148/27/54.
[8] *Cal. Chart. R.* 1257–1300, 461; W.A.M. 17012–13.
[9] *Cal. Close*, 1296–1302, 8–9.
[10] *Cal. Pat.* 1307–13, 438.
[11] *T.L.M.A.S.* xii. 584.
[12] *D.N.B.*; C.P. 25(1)/149/48/229b; C.P. 25(1)/149/49/263.
[13] Westm. Domesday, f. 125.
[14] C.P. 25(1)/149/44/143.
[15] *Cal. Inq. p.m.* viii, p. 17.

manor to his wife Margaret, who later married Hugh Mortimer and died in 1358.[16] It then passed to her son Sir Richard le Scrope (?1327–1403), later Lord Scrope of Bolton and Lord Chancellor.[17] In 1399 Scrope granted the manor, then called Hodford and Cowhouse, to the king,[18] who immediately regranted it to the abbey of Westminster.[19] In 1542 it was granted to the chapter of the new cathedral of Westminster,[20] in 1556 to the restored monastery,[21] and in 1560 to the newly-founded collegiate church of St. Peter, Westminster,[22] whose chapter conveyed the estate to the Ecclesiastical Commissioners in 1855.[23] When the lord of Hendon was attempting to assert rights over the estate in 1870, it was claimed that its manorial status had lapsed after the Civil War.[24] The Church Commissioners sold the leaseholds of most of their houses in Hendon during the 1950s.[25]

The Hodford and Cowhouse estate consisted of a compact block of lands stretching from the Hampstead border to a point north of Golders Green Underground station and from Cricklewood to Golders Hill.[26] Westminster leased it out at all periods, although until the late 17th century it remained in direct control of the woodlands called Hodford wood and Beecham grove.[27] The estate totalled 434 a. in 1855[28] and was split into three farms known in 1889 as Hodford (or Golders) Green, Cowhouse (or Avenue),[29] and Westcroft farms. There is no record of a manor-house, although one was formerly thought to have stood on or near the site of the 18th-century Golders Hill House.[30] A chapel on the abbot of Westminster's manor of Hodford existed in 1321, when services were licensed by the bishop of London, but was not subsequently recorded.[31]

The third medieval manor in Hendon owned by Westminster was that of *FRITH and NEWHALL*. It was first mentioned by name as a manor in 1500[32] but the estate probably included lands in Hendon granted to the abbey c. 1222–46 by Walter del Frith and Ernald, son of Roger del Frith.[33] Gilbert of Hendon made another grant to the abbey c. 1226–8 of 2 crofts formerly held by Viel, stretching from the lands of Ernald del Frith to the river Brent.[34] A rent was paid to Westminster for Newhall in 1374.[35] From 1500 until the Dissolution, the manor of Frith and Newhall was farmed by John Lamb.[36] It was granted in 1541 to the see of

Westminster[37] and, on its suppression, to Thomas Thirlby, who became bishop of Norwich.[38] He conveyed it to his brother Thomas, of East Dereham (Norf.), who, on his death c. 1566 settled it on his eldest son Henry.[39] Henry Thirlby sold it c. 1585 to Richard Wickes of Hampstead,[40] by whom it was conveyed in 1608 to William Peacock.[41] In 1613 Robert Smythe and others conveyed it to Francis Townley[42] and in 1711 it was in the possession of James Walker of Stratford-le-Bow.[43] It was held in 1737 by Thomas, son of James Walker, and Sir John Lade, Bt.,[44] to whom a share had been conveyed in 1719 by Barbara, widow of Michael Grigg of St. Giles-in-the-Fields.[45] Sir John died in 1740, leaving his estates to a great-nephew John Inskip, who took the name Lade but was not created a baronet until 1758.[46] He died in 1759 and was succeeded by his son and namesake,[47] who, deeply in debt, conveyed the estate to Sir Charles Blake and others,[48] perhaps as trustees for T. G. Fentham, who was owner in 1810.[49] Manorial rights soon afterwards lapsed.

The lands of Frith and Newhall lay in the northwest of the parish adjoining the Finchley border, bounded on one side by Dollis brook; they consisted in 1754 of Dollis, Frith, and Partingdale farms, containing 69 a., 153 a., and 54 a., respectively, and of another 100 a.[50] The estate was split up after 1809;[51] in 1828 Partingdale farm was held by R. Franks, Frith farm by Thomas Fentham, and Dollis farm by Sir Charles Flower of Belmont, Mill Hill.[52] In 1893 Frith Manor farm, as it was then called, was in the hands of John Heal and T. M. Merriman, who conveyed it to Frank Head.[53] Frith Manor House, near the junction of Frith Lane, Partingdale Lane, and Lullington Garth, was built in 1790,[54] when the adjoining Frith farmhouse was converted into offices and servants' rooms.[55] The manor-house, a stuccoed building with wings, was said to contain a 16th-century stone fireplace and linen-fold panelling brought from elsewhere.[56] In 1889 it was occupied by Magwitch Davidson.[57] It was sold in 1951 to Maj.-Gen. Robb and gutted by fire in 1957.[58]

The nucleus of the manor of *CLITTERHOUSE* was a house and one carucate held by John de Langton in 1321[59] and by his younger son Robert in 1335.[60] Robert's son and namesake held it in 1361, when it was called the manor of Hendon, and

[16] Ibid. x, p. 339.
[17] *D.N.B.*
[18] W.A.M. 17015.
[19] Ibid. 17016; *Cal. Chart. R.* 1341–1417, 375.
[20] *L. & P. Hen. VIII*, xvii, p. 392.
[21] *Cal. Pat.* 1555–7, 348–9.
[22] Ibid. 1558–60, 397.
[23] Church Com. C.C.1, ff. 139–51.
[24] Church Com. file 10113/1.
[25] Church Com. C.C.1, ff. 161–208; ex inf. Church Com.
[26] Whishaw, *Map of Hendon* (1828) and ref. bk.
[27] Req. 2/92/49.
[28] Church Com. C.C.1, ff. 139–51.
[29] Evans, *Hendon*, 56–7.
[30] Evans, *Hendon*, 57–8.
[31] W.A.M. 17014.
[32] W.A.M. 57487.
[33] Westm. Domesday, ff. 374–5.
[34] Ibid. f. 122b.
[35] W.A.M. 32589.
[36] Ibid. 4847, 4855, 57487.
[37] *L. & P. Hen. VIII*, xvi, pp. 243–4.
[38] Lysons, *Environs*, iii. 5; *D.N.B.*

[39] Req. 2/64/1.
[40] Ibid.; C 3/230/17.
[41] C.P. 25(2)/323/6 James I East.
[42] C.P. 25(2)/324/10 James I Hil.
[43] E 214/1200.
[44] Nat. Libr. of Wales, Powis MS. 15747.
[45] M.L.R. 1719/1/12, /13.
[46] G.E.C. *Baronetage*, v. 69.
[47] Ibid. 109–10.
[48] Hendon Libr., MS. L. 3606.
[49] Evans, *Hendon*, 59.
[50] Hendon Libr., MS. L. 1703.
[51] M.L.R. 1811/3/474; Hendon Libr., MS. L. 3606.
[52] Whishaw, *Map of Hendon* and ref. bk.; for Flower's estate, see below.
[53] Hendon Libr., MS. L. 3592.
[54] Date on porch; Mill Hill Hist. Soc., Add. Items 96.
[55] Hendon Libr., MS. L. 3606.
[56] Hist. Mon. Com. *Mdx.* 72.
[57] Evans, *Hendon*, 60.
[58] Mill Hill Hist. Soc., Add. Items 53.
[59] *T.L.M.A.S.* xii. 582.
[60] St. Barts. Hosp., med. deeds 1027; C.P. 25(1)/286/38/
171.

successfully defended his tenure against Ralph de Langton, his uncle.[61] In 1371 Robert de Langton conveyed it to Adam de Walton and his daughter Joan,[62] who married Robert Derby of Liverpool. The estate was conveyed to Joan and Robert in 1382[63] and by them to Richard of Foxton, clerk, and Walter Norman, chandler,[64] who in 1383 granted it to Hugh Winkburn and Isabel his wife.[65] Isabel afterwards married Henry Lynch and granted it in 1403 to John Winkburn, her son, Thomas Ardynton, John Carter, and others.[66] John Winkburn quitclaimed his interest to Ardynton and Carter in 1408,[67] the others already having done so,[68] and after Ardynton's death in the same year John Carter granted the estate to William Loveney and other feoffees.[69] They granted it in 1428 to Robert Warner, citizen of London,[70] who conveyed it in 1429 to Thomas Pynchon, Henry Frowyk, and others,[71] from whom the manor was acquired in 1439 by St. Bartholomew's hospital.[72] The hospital's property in Hendon was augmented in 1446 by two near-by estates granted by Henry Frowyk and William Cleeve, master of the king's works.[73] The first, called Vynces, lay north of the Clitterhouse estate and the second, Rockholts, lay south of the road to Childs Hill. The manor was held of Westminster abbey[74] and was retained by St. Bartholomew's in 1547, when the hospital was vested in the Corporation of London.[75] Manorial rights had lapsed by 1771.[76] The estate, diminished by the encroachments of the Midland Railway's Cricklewood carriage-sidings in 1868,[77] remained the property of St. Bartholomew's hospital until 1921, when it was sold to the War Department;[78] it was later split up among private developers.

In 1584 the estate was managed as one farm, called Clitterhouse, consisting of 118 a. of arable and pasture and 80 a. of wood, in a compact block in the south-west of the parish by Edgware Road near Cricklewood.[79] It remained intact until the mid 19th century. The farm-house, near the modern Hendon football club grounds in Claremont Road, was shown in 1715[80] as a large timber-framed building of two storeys, with three gables and a jettied first storey. It occupied one side of a courtyard, on the other sides of which were weather-boarded barns of the standard Middlesex type, with steeply pitched roofs, and stables. Alterations were carried out after 1794[81] and by 1838 another farm-house had been built on the site.[82] The 19th-century building had been converted into flats by 1974.[83]

The priory of St. Bartholomew, Smithfield, owned an estate at Hendon in the Middle Ages. Its later name, the manor of *RENTERS*, may derive from a house and a carucate held in 1309 by John of Islington of Geoffrey le Renter and Joan, widow of John le Renter.[84] Geoffrey le Renter held a freehold estate of that size in 1321, along with Bourncroft,[85] perhaps identifiable with Bone Croft, which in 1754 lay a short distance north of Renters farm-house.[86] In 1359 the abbot of Westminster licensed Hugh de la Mare, chaplain, to alienate to the convent of St. Bartholomew a house and lands in Hendon, together with property in Great Stanmore, to be held of the abbot at a small annual rent.[87] The priory's Hendon estate consisted *c.* 1538 of 15 fields, crofts, and meadows, and some woodland, north of the Clitterhouse estate.[88] The manor, called Renters or Romers, was granted by the king in 1543, along with the manor of Edgware Boys, to Sir John Williams and Antony Stringer.[89] They in turn granted it in 1548, together with a barn, 30 a. of arable land, 40 a. of meadow, 60 a. of pasture, and 26 a. of wood, to Sir Roger Cholmley, the judge,[90] who in 1565 left it to his servant and clerk Jasper Cholmley.[91] In 1682 the manor was alienated by William Cholmley of Teddington, Jasper's descendant, to Jerome Newbolt, great-grandfather of J. M. Newbolt, prebendary of Winchester, who held it in 1795.[92] Manorial rights had already been extinguished and in 1796 Newbolt's estate, no longer described as a manor, consisted of 12 fields.[93]

The estate was tenanted in 1795 by P. Rundell, a London goldsmith, and after his death in 1827 by his great-nephew Joseph Neeld,[94] a solicitor, who had married the eldest daughter of John Bond[95] and had bought houses and land in Brent Street and Burroughs Lane from Joseph Crosse Crooke in 1809.[96] In 1874 Joseph's son Sir John Neeld, Bt., owned 668 a. in Middlesex[97] and by the beginning of the 20th century he had acquired a large block of land in Hendon stretching south from the Burroughs to Park Road and including part of the old Renters property. His land was developed for housing by Sir Audley Dallas Neeld, Bt., grandson of Joseph Neeld, who succeeded in 1900, and several of the streets in the neighbourhood were named after members of the family.[98] No trace remains of the farm-house called Renters, which in 1828 occupied a site near the point where Shire Hall Lane crossed the Brent,[99] on the site of the present Brent Cross road junction.

[61] St. Barts. Hosp., med. deeds 2039.
[62] Ibid. 1027, 205.
[63] Ibid. 982.
[64] Ibid. 970B.
[65] Ibid. 970A.
[66] Ibid. 666.
[67] Ibid. 670.
[68] Ibid. 667, 668.
[69] Ibid. 669.
[70] Ibid. 673.
[71] Ibid. 675.   [72] C 143/448/26.
[73] St. Barts. Hosp., med. deeds 185, 196, 203; *Cal. Pat.* 1441–6, pp. 416–17.
[74] St. Barts. Hosp., Ha 19/1/1, f. 16.
[75] *L. & P. Hen. VIII*, xxi(2), p. 415.
[76] St. Barts. Hosp., Hc 9/2, pp. 140–1.
[77] St. Barts. Hosp., Ha 1/23, p. 216.
[78] Ibid. /29, p. 550.
[79] St. Barts. Hosp., Hc 10/22; 19/1/1.
[80] St. Barts. Hosp., Hc 19/6B/19; M. W. Barley, *English Farmhouse and Cottage*, plate VIIIb.

[81] St. Barts. Hosp., Ha 1/15, pp. 290–1.
[82] Ibid. Hc 9/3, pp. 253–4.
[83] Ex inf. Hendon Libr.
[84] C.P. 25(1)/149/40/30.
[85] *T.L.M.A.S.* xii. 584.
[86] *P.N. Mdx.* (E.P.N.S.), 210; B.M. Add. MS. 9839.
[87] Westm. Domesday, f. 128; Liber Niger, f. 108; *Cal. Pat.* 1358–61, 185. See below, p. 96.
[88] S.C. 6/Hen. VIII/2396 m. 121; E 318/1227 m. 26.
[89] *L. & P. Hen. VIII*, xviii (1), pp. 130–1.
[90] *Cal. Pat.* 1547–8, 327; *D.N.B.*
[91] *I.P.M. Lond.* ii. 43.
[92] Lysons, *Environs*, iii. 6.
[93] Cooke, *Map of Hendon* (1796).
[94] Evans, *Hendon*, 64.
[95] *Burke's Peerage* (1931).   [96] M.L.R. 1810/2/227.
[97] *Return of Owners of Land in each Co.* [C. 1097], p. 12, H.C. (1874), lxxii(1).
[98] Cf. Neeld Crescent, Rundell Crescent, Audley Road: Mill Hill Hist. Soc., Add. Items 80.
[99] Whishaw, *Map of Hendon*.

OTHER ESTATES. The Knights Templar had two estates in Hendon, originating in grants of 80 a. by Matthew of Ditton and Hamon son of Roger in 1243.[1] One was held in 1359 by the Knights Hospitaller[2] who presumably had received it on the dissolution of the Templars. It formed part of the manor of Freren in Kingsbury and passed with Freren in 1544 to the chapter of St. Paul's;[3] the lands lay west of Edgware Road on the Kingsbury border. The estate, which consisted in 1828 of 110 a.,[4] was leased to the duke of Chandos (d. 1744) and his descendants[5] and was vested in the Ecclesiastical Commissioners in 1872.[6] Most of it was sold to Hendon U.D.C. in 1919 for use as playing fields and a park.[7] The second estate, which was granted to the Hospitallers in 1331,[8] was situated north of the Hale on the Edgware border and in 1528 formed part of the manor of Edgware Boys,[9] with which it later descended.[10] In 1754 it was in the possession of Lord Coventry and consisted of 127 a., part of which lay in Edgware.[11] The estate was later called Coventry farm and had passed by 1923 into the hands of the Cox family of Moat Mount.[12]

Eton College's estate, which consisted in 1828 of 315 a.,[13] originated in grants of land by Bela, widow of Austin the mercer, in 1259[14] and by William de Pavely and Millicent his wife in 1273[15] to the hospital of St. James, Westminster, which in 1321 held 124 a. of land and wood in the parish.[16] After 1449, when custody of the hospital was granted to the newly founded Eton College,[17] the college took possession of the Hendon estate, which was called 'the Wylde' in 1480–1.[18] Eton surrendered St. James's hospital to the Crown in 1531[19] but retained the Wyldes estate until 1907, when it was sold to the Hampstead Garden Suburb trust, which had acquired some property from the college in 1906, and to the trustees of the Hampstead Heath Extension.[20] In the 18th century it was leased to the Earle family of Hendon House, the freehold owners in 1754 of Decoy farm, which consisted of 99 a. north and west of Temple Fortune;[21] in 1828 the Wyldes estate was leased to Thomas Clark, who also owned Decoy farm.[22] The college lands, which stretched northward from the Hampstead border to Mutton brook, were divided in 1903 into three farms, called Temple Fortune, Tooley's (or Wildwood), and Home (or Heath) farms.[23]

The Goldbeaters estate, comprising 312 a. in 1828,[24] may have originated in a grant of land and rent by John le Bret to William of Aldenham, goldbeater of London, in 1308.[25] John Goldbeater held a house and some land of the manor of Hendon in 1321.[26] The Goldbeaters estate was held by John and Eve Clerk in 1434.[27] By the early 18th century it had passed to Joseph Marsh, whose daughter and heir married Thomas Beech of London,[28] the holder of 130 a. in the north of Hendon parish in 1754.[29] After Beech's death in 1772 some of the property was conveyed to John Raymond and later to Richard Capper.[30] In 1802 Mary Capper of Bushey (Herts.) and Robert Capper sold the whole of Goldbeaters to William Smith of Mayfair, who bought two closes called Staines and Shoelands, adjoining the farm, from John Nicholl of the Inner Temple in 1803 and a house, later the Bald Faced Stag, and four fields at Redhill from William Geeves in 1807. William Smith bought part of the near-by Shoelands farm from John Nicholl of the Hyde in 1812 and purchased the rest from Jasper Holmes of Blackheath in 1821.[31] In 1859 John Smith sold Goldbeaters and Shoelands and Stagg fields, adjoining the Bald Faced Stag, which together totalled 253 a., to James Marshall, co-founder of Marshall and Snelgrove's drapery store in Oxford Street, London. Marshall in 1867 also bought the neighbouring Bunns farm, totalling 77 a., from the five coheirs of Robert Randall, a Fleet Street wine-merchant. After Marshall's death in 1893 his son James C. Marshall sold Goldbeaters and Bunns farms to A. O. Crooke, a Hendon brewer,[32] who sold them in 1900 to Sir John Blundell Maple, Bt., of Orange Hill House.[33] In 1924 the property, totalling 200 a., was bought by the L.C.C. as a site for the Watling housing estate.[34]

All Souls College, Oxford, owned several scattered parcels, including Arnold's lands, granted by Richard Arnold to William Page of Edgware in 1311,[35] and Piricroft, granted by John of Morden to Page in 1309.[36] William Page held 2 houses and lands including Arnoledeshawe and Piricroft in 1321.[37] The lands, with others in Edgware and Kingsbury, were conveyed in 1384 by William Page of Kingsbury and Christine his wife to John Raven.[38] In 1442 they were granted, with the manor of Kingsbury, to All Souls College,[39] which retained them until the 20th century. The college's estate consisted in 1597 of fields at Bittacy Hill, Holders Hill, the Burroughs, and Colin Deep, and on the Kingsbury border.[40] In 1828 it totalled 224 a.[41]

John Fortescue and others granted a house and

[1] C.P. 25(1)/147/204, /205.
[2] Cal. Pat. 1358–61, 167; C 143/329/3.
[3] See p. 60.
[4] Whishaw, Map of Hendon (1828) and ref. bk.
[5] M.R.O., Acc. 262/71/2, /72/1, /50/9.
[6] Church Com. file 51708.
[7] Ibid. 87928.
[8] B.M. Cott. MS. Nero C. vi, f. 77.
[9] Ibid. Claud. E. vi, ff. 218–9.
[10] For the descent, see V.C.H. Mdx. iv. 157.
[11] Hendon Libr., MS. L. 1703.
[12] See above.
[13] Whishaw, Map of Hendon and ref. bk.
[14] C.P. 25(1)/147/21/408.
[15] C.P. 25(1)/148/25/1.
[16] T.L.M.A.S. xii. 586.   [17] V.C.H. Lond. i. 545.
[18] Eton Coll. Recs., St. James 3, m. 1d.
[19] L. & P. Hen. VIII, v, pp. 201, 276.
[20] Eton Coll. Recs., lease bk. 1891–1912, ff. 394–5, 409–24, 447–53.
[21] Hendon Libr., MS. L. 1703.

[22] Whishaw, Map of Hendon and ref. bk.
[23] A. Whishaw, 'Wyldes and its Story', Hampstead Annual (1903), 129–32.
[24] Whishaw, Map of Hendon and ref. bk.
[25] C.P. 25(1)/149/39/9.   [26] T.L.M.A.S. xii. 588.
[27] Clarke, Story of Goldbeaters, 7, quoting deed in possession of N. G. Brett-James.
[28] M.R.O., Acc. 351/748.
[29] Hendon Libr., MS. L. 1703.
[30] M.R.O., Acc. 174/10, ff. 122–3.
[31] M.L.R. 1802/6/625–6; 1803/3/103; 1807/7/750; 1812/4/604; 1821/6/195.
[32] Clarke, Story of Goldbeaters, 13–14, 16, 19.
[33] See p. 2.
[34] Clarke, Story of Goldbeaters, 20; see above, p. 15.
[35] Bodl. MS. D.D. All Souls c76/96.
[36] Ibid. /107.
[37] T.L.M.A.S. xii. 596.
[38] Bodl. MS. D.D. All Souls c75/25.   [39] See p. 56.
[40] All Souls Coll., Hovenden Maps, II, nos. 17–18.
[41] Whishaw, Map of Hendon and ref. bk.

43 a. of meadow and pasture in Hendon to the hospital of St. Mary within Cripplegate, London, commonly called Elsyng Spital,[42] in 1457.[43] The estate was granted in 1543 to Hugh Losse and Thomas Boucher,[44] who alienated it in the same year to Thomas Nicholl of Highwood Hill.[45] Nicholl conveyed it in 1551 to William Copwood and John Snow,[46] and in 1617 it was held by Thomas Marsh;[47] the land later formed part of Stoneyfields farm, near the Hale, totalling 110 a., which was held in 1828 by Francis Dollman.[48]

Kilburn priory held a small amount of unspecified land in Hendon at the Dissolution, worth 2s. and leased to John Brent.[49] The later history of the estate is unknown.

The estate of the Nicholls of Copt Hall originated in lands belonging in 1574 to Richard Nicholl of the Ridgeway, who held a tenement called Goodhews and 20 fields and crofts around Mill Hill, both freehold and copyhold.[50] In 1585 he surrendered six fields to his son Thomas[51] and in 1602 two of them, called Burdens, were conveyed to Richard Nicholl of Milespit Hill,[52] who bought the adjacent house called Copt Hall from John Storer, a London banker, in 1603;[53] Richard Nicholl later rebuilt the house.[54] John Brent conveyed another 10 a. called Slatton, formerly belonging to William Marsh of Drivers Hill,[55] to Richard Nicholl in 1612 and Henry Nicholl of the Ridgeway conveyed two closes called Widmores to Randall, Richard's son, in 1623.[56] Randall Nicholl held 36 a. of copyhold property in 1651[57] and his heirs added to the estate until in 1754 Dr. James Ingram, who enjoyed a life-interest after the death of John Nicholl in 1753,[58] held 286 a. divided into four farms, one of them called Cookes, together with a further 83 a. leased from All Souls College.[59] Dr. Ingram died in 1755, when the estate passed to another John Nicholl.[60] In 1828 Mrs. Susanna Nicholl held 234 a. around Page Street,[61] including the farm later known as Old Goodhews. On the death of Thomas Nicholl in 1859 the land passed to his widow Emma, who died in 1882, and then to their daughter, Mary, who married C. R. P. Hodgson. Their son Charles Bertram Hodgson Nicholl sold the estate in 1925.[62] Copt Hall, Page Street, was rebuilt between 1624 and 1637 by Richard Nicholl. It had a front of seven bays, crowned by shaped gables,[63] but was greatly altered in the mid 19th century;[64] after conversion into flats, it was demolished in 1959.[65]

Cooke's farm-house may have been a building at Mill Hill which was pulled down soon after 1814, when it was said to date from the reign of Charles I and to contain murals of religious subjects.[66]

Another branch of the Nicholl family held a small estate near Dole Street in 1480.[67] Somewhat enlarged, it descended to Margaret, daughter of John Nicholl of Minchenden, Southgate, and wife of James Brydges, marquess of Carnarvon and later duke of Chandos (d. 1789),[68] and in 1828 it totalled 81 a.[69] It was conveyed in 1839 by Richard Temple-Nugent - Brydges - Chandos - Grenville, duke of Buckingham and Chandos, to Jason Smith, the owner of Goldbeaters farm.[70]

Peter Hamond (d. 1794) bought the lands around Belmont House, Mill Hill, which were later known as Belmont farm, in piecemeal lots between 1768 and 1792.[71] He devised them to his daughter Anne, the wife of Somerset Davies,[72] who in 1801 conveyed 83 a. to Robert Anderson.[73] On Anderson's bankruptcy in 1803 the estate was bought by Captain Robert Williams,[74] whose devisees and trustees conveyed it in 1812 to David Prior[75] from whose widow it was acquired in 1820 by Sir Charles Flower, Bt., mill-owner and former lord mayor of London.[76] Sir Charles bought more land near Lawrence Street from Robert Finch and Michael Coomes in 1821 and 1826,[77] until his property stretched from the Hale to the Totteridge boundary and included Lawrence Street, Uphill, and Bittacy farms, the last of which had formed part of the Frith manor estate;[78] his estate in Hendon totalled 441 a. in 1828.[79] Sir Charles died in 1835 and was succeeded by his son James, who died in 1850; by 1889 the estate had been split among several persons, including C. H. Martyn, rector of Long Melford (Suff.).[80] Belmont House, built for Peter Hamond to the designs of James Paine the younger,[81] was occupied as a preparatory school in 1970, when it contained some original plaster ceilings. A Gothic dairy, 'of unique elegance and splendidly decorated', was built in the grounds by Robert Williams.[82]

Some large estates were formed out of the demesne of Hendon manor sold in 1756. In 1828[83] owners of former demesne lands in the centre of the parish included Mrs. Broadhead, who held 359 a. including Church farm, W. J. Johnson, who held Church End farm with 111 a., Thomas Ryder, who held 123 a. west of Parson Street, and J. R. Wheeler, who held 135 a. near the Hyde. Farther north former demesne

[42] V.C.H. Lond. i. 535.
[43] C 143/452/7; Cal. Pat. 1452–61, 473.
[44] L. & P. Hen. VIII, i(1), p. 364.
[45] Ibid. p. 447.
[46] Cal. Pat. 1550–3, 84.
[47] C 142/362/160.
[48] Whishaw, Map of Hendon and ref. bk.
[49] S.C. 6/Hen. VIII/2345 m. 12.
[50] T.L.M.A.S. xiii. 44, 52.
[51] M.R.O., Acc. 790/1.
[52] Ibid. /4.
[53] Ibid. /5.
[54] See p. 6.
[55] M.R.O., Acc. 790/11, /12A.
[56] Ibid. /9.
[57] Ibid. /16.
[58] M.R.O., Acc. 174/8, ff. 119–20.
[59] Hendon Libr., MS. L. 1703.
[60] M.R.O., Acc. 174/8, f. 156.
[61] Whishaw, Map of Hendon and ref. bk.
[62] M.R.O., Acc. 790/79.
[63] Hopkins, Hendon, plate facing p. 32.

[64] Hist. Mon. Com. Mdx. 72; photographs in Hendon Libr., DD. MHS. 796–8.
[65] Hendon & Finchley Times, 23 Jan. 1959.
[66] Brewer, Beauties of Eng. and Wales, x(5), 687; T.L.M.A.S. xiii. 43.
[67] M.R.O., Acc. 262/7/3.
[68] M.R.O., Acc. 262/50/9; Complete Peerage, iii. 132.
[69] Whishaw, Map of Hendon and ref. bk.
[70] Hendon Libr., MS. L. 2452.
[71] M.R.O., Acc. 460/4, /5, /22, /23, /32, /33, /42–6, /58; B.M. Add. MS. 9840.
[72] M.R.O., Acc. 460/80.
[73] Ibid. /82, /83.
[74] Ibid. /87, /88
[75] Ibid. /97, /98.
[76] Ibid. /102, /103; Brett-James, Hendon, 93.
[77] M.L.R. 1821/5/711.
[78] M.R.O., Acc. 460/402.
[79] Whishaw, Map of Hendon and ref. bk.
[80] Evans, Hendon, 270–2.
[81] B.M. Add. MS. 31323 A3; Add. MS. 9839.
[82] Brewer, Beauties of Eng. and Wales, x(5), 687.
[83] Whishaw, Map of Hendon and ref. bk.

lands were held in 1828 by R. Jennings, of Hyvers Hill Wood farm, and the philanthropist William Wilberforce, who bought Hendon Park and the surrounding estate of 122 a. in 1825 as a retreat 'beyond the disk of the metropolis' and lived there until 1831.[84] Hendon Park, a substantial brick building in 1756,[85] was rebuilt and stuccoed in the early 19th century;[86] it had fallen into neglect by 1951 and had been replaced by three houses and Crown Close by 1961.[87] The neighbouring Moat Mount estate, also former demesne, was held in 1828 by Richard Jackson, who owned 139 a. in Hendon, including Barnet Gate farm.[88] The estate was greatly enlarged by the Cox family, until in 1874 Edward William Cox (1809–79), serjeant-at-law,[89] held 209 a. in Middlesex.[90] In 1923, when the lands were put up for sale, the executors of Irwin Cox held 1,090 a. in Hendon and Edgware, including Barnet Gate, Coventry, Stoneyfields, and Uphill farms.[91] Moat Mount House, a stuccoed villa, was rebuilt by Edward William Cox in the Renaissance manner, to include a large main block with a carriage-porch,[92] and survived in 1970.

ECONOMIC HISTORY.

AGRICULTURE. In 1086 there was land for 16 ploughs on the manor of Hendon, which was assessed at 20 hides; the lord had three ploughs on his 10 demesne hides and the villeins had another eight, but it was said that the land could support five more. There was also meadow for two oxen, as well as woodland for 1,000 pigs, which yielded 10s. The estate, worth £8 in 1086, had been valued at £12 T.R.E.[93] A series of farm accounts for the manor begins in 1316,[94] four years after Westminster abbey resumed direct control,[95] and a survey was carried out in 1321.[96] The demesne consisted in 1321 of 469 a. of arable land, 35 a. of meadow, and an unspecified amount of wood,[97] while the freehold lands amounted to at least four carucates and 759 a. and the copyhold to a further 1,043 a.[98] The manor of Hodford was not included in the calculations.

In 1318 the chief crops on the demesne were wheat (133 qr.) and oats (102 qr.), while smaller crops included beans and peas.[99] Rye was grown in 1324.[1] Animal and dairy farming was less important than arable farming: in 1317 there were 51 cattle and 126 sheep on the demesne, apart from oxen and draught-beasts.[2] In 1373–4 Westminster made £18 from the sale of corn and malt and £11 from the sale of milk.[3] There were two fruit gardens in 1321[4] and an orchard on All Souls College's estate near Parson Street in 1584.[5] A pound existed c. 1550 and survived in 1831 at the corner of Brent Street and Finchley Lane.[6]

As elsewhere in northern Middlesex Hendon later specialized in hay-farming for the London market. The proportion of arable land had declined by the 17th century, although many rents were still paid in wheat and oats in 1574;[7] in 1630 there were only 40 a. of arable on All Souls College's estate of 219 a.,[8] while on Westminster's Hodford and Cowhouse estate of 423 a. only 20 per cent was arable.[9] Hodford and Cowhouse farms were both largely given over to hay in 1760[10] and Wyldes farm produced only hay in 1800.[11] By 1798 there were about 300 a. of arable in the parish to 7,700 a. of grass and about 120 a. of wood.[12] The arable was divided in 1801 between 116 a. sown with beans, 98 a. with wheat, 54 a. with oats, 15 a. with rye, and 13 a. with potatoes.[13] Local farmers were noted for making compost,[14] with the result that Hendon's bent grass was thought to be the best in Middlesex.[15] Although a return to arable farming was advocated in 1801,[16] the amount of arable continued to dwindle until by 1843 it accounted for only 3 per cent of the whole.[17] Wheat was still being grown c. 1880, however, in Sunny Hill fields and at Wild Hatch near Golders Green.[18]

In the early and mid 19th century farm-rents were progressively reduced with the price of hay,[19] which fell by some 40 per cent between 1845 and 1849.[20] As suburban building approached, the southern part of Hendon became conveniently placed for dairy farming;[21] in 1868 there were two substantial dairy farms, Lord Granville's (Hodford) at Golders Green and Mr. Sumpton's nearer Church End.[22] The farmer at Clitterhouse sent milk to London twice daily in 1879[23] and his farm was wholly given over to dairying in 1881,[24] although by 1887 it was used for breeding cattle and for hay.[25] Horses were raised on the near-by Cowhouse farm[26] and in 1890 their breeding and training was widespread; there were several dairy farms and others where sheep were fed for the London market.[27]

[84] R. and S. Wilberforce, *Life of Wm. Wilberforce*, v (1838), 248, 325.
[85] *Cat. of the Demesne Lands of the Earl of Powis* (1756), *penes* Hendon Libr.; M.L.R. 1757/2/124–6.
[86] Hendon Libr., DD. MHS. 681.
[87] Pevsner, *Mdx.* 125; ex inf. Hendon Libr.
[88] Whishaw, *Map of Hendon* and ref. bk.
[89] *D.N.B.*; Evans, *Hendon*, 262.
[90] *Return of Owners of Land in each Co.* [C. 1097], p. 5, H.C. (1874), lxxii(1).
[91] Whishaw, *Map of Hendon* and ref. bk.
[92] Hendon Libr., DD. MHS. 1/185–8.
[93] *V.C.H. Mdx.* i. 123.   [94] W.A.M. 32532–32589.
[95] See p. 17.
[96] *T.L.M.A.S.* xii. 580 sqq.
[97] Ibid. 582–3.
[98] Ibid. 582–627. The figures are low, since the acreage of some of the estates is not given.
[99] W.A.M. 32533. The amounts are set out in *T.L.M.A.S.* xii. 626–7.
[1] W.A.M. 32541.
[2] Ibid. 32532.
[3] Ibid. 32589.
[4] *T.L.M.A.S.* xii. 580–1.
[5] Bodl. MS. D.D. All Souls c243/25.

[6] M.R.O., Acc. 174/28; Hendon Libr. MS. L. 130.
[7] *T.L.M.A.S.* xiii. 36 and *passim*.
[8] Bodl. MS. D.D. All Souls c243/29. There were 58 a. of pasture and 114 a. of wood.
[9] C 56/3469, quoted in Garrett, 'Upper Brent Valley', 76; pasture accounted for 71 per cent and wood for 9 per cent. The figures exclude Hodford wood, which was farmed separately.
[10] Church Com. deed 145886, f. 94.
[11] Eton Coll. Recs. 49/19.
[12] Middleton, *View*, 560.   [13] H.O. 67/16.
[14] Middleton, *View*, 314.
[15] Garrett, 'Upper Brent Valley', 84.   [16] H.O. 67/16.
[17] Garrett, 'Upper Brent Valley', 78.
[18] *Hendon & Finchley Times*, 30 Jan. 1925, p. 8.
[19] M. Rees, 'Extra-Metropolitan Mdx.' (Lond. Univ. M.Sc. thesis, 1953), 139, 171–3, 185.
[20] St. Barts. Hosp., Hc 9/4, pp. 171–3, 185.
[21] Garrett, 'Upper Brent Valley', 123.
[22] Rees, 'Extra-Metropolitan Mdx.', 157.
[23] St. Barts. Hosp., EO 8/6, f. 168.
[24] Rees, 'Extra-Metropolitan Mdx.', 166.
[25] St. Barts. Hosp., EO 8/6, f. 272.
[26] Evans, *Hendon*, 56–7.
[27] Ibid. 331.

Upper Guttershedge farm, sometimes called Brent farm, was being used for growing mushrooms in 1902.[28] Economic distress caused a procession of the unemployed to march from the parish pump in Brent Street to the local board offices in the Burroughs in 1887, when a soup kitchen was opened in Hendon House and the vicar provided free meals for the poor.[29] The spread of housing soon afterwards affected the agricultural value of land in southern Hendon. In 1894 the Ecclesiastical Commissioners were forced to accept a lower rent for their estate west of Edgware Road, after the tenant had complained of a drop in the price of hay and of trespassing by visitors to the Welsh Harp.[30] In 1905 Clitterhouse farm was said to be on the immediate north-western outskirts of London and to be growing less desirable as a dairy farm, since the public broke down fences, although its building value was steadily rising.[31] It was finally sold in 1921,[32] and the last farm in the area, Cowhouse or Avenue farm, in 1931.[33]

Farther north good quality hay remained the staple product of the Mill Hill area until at least 1900.[34] At the end of the 19th century all the available local men helped to harvest the hay, which was taken daily to Cumberland Market. Extra labourers came from Bedfordshire and Ireland, some 75 being engaged at Moat Mount and the farmer at Lawrence Street undertaking to bring a shipload of Irish men and women to Mill Hill each year. Workers congregated at the Three Hammers, which opened at 6.30 a.m. At Church End a model dairy farm existed near Hinge's farm from 1888, although both had gone by 1970.[35] Goodhews and Dollis farms were dairy farms in 1925[36] but Goodhews was up for auction in 1928 and was later sold for building. The Express Dairy Co. took over Tithe farm, which had become a centre for the distribution of milk by 1931,[37] and Frith Manor farm, which was being used in 1958 as a rest-home for horses.[38] Most of the countryside in north Hendon had given way to suburban streets by the Second World War[39] but the imposition of the Green Belt prevented them from reaching the northern boundary; fields survived north of Mill Hill and Highwood Hill in 1970, including those of Hendon Park farm, which had become a dairy farm by 1937.[40] In 1956 there was a total of 1,509 a. under crops and grass in the borough of Hendon, including Edgware, of which 851 a. supported grass and 219 a. wheat. Other

crops were barley and oats and there were also 576 cattle and 1,374 pigs.[41]

Even allowing for the exclusion of the manor of Hodford, it is clear that large areas were not under cultivation in 1321. Several fields were of considerable size: there were 121 a. of arable and 15 a. of meadow belonging to the demesne alone in Hillesden, 59 a. of arable and 10 a. of meadow in 'le Brache', and 99 a. of arable and 5 a. of meadow in Broadmead.[42] Much of the parish was woodland, of which evidence has survived in names like Highwood Hill, Hendon Wood Lane, Cricklewood, and Frith (wooded country).[43] There was a woodward in 1321, when the lord was entitled to profits from the 'hedgerows' or groves around the fields in the manor,[44] and hedgerows were still substantial in the 16th century,[45] suggesting that many fields had been assarted before the first survey. Westminster made considerable profits from the sale of wood: 2,300 faggots were sold in 1321[46] and in 1374 the profits were greater than from any other single source apart from rents.[47] Some wood was reserved by the abbey for its own use and £42 was spent in 1374 on the carriage of logs from Hendon to Westminster;[48] timber from Hendon may have been used in work on the abbey in the 14th century,[49] as it undoubtedly was for the building of Hendon Place.[50] The abbey paid John Nicholl of Highwood Hill in the early 16th century for making laths in Hendon wood[51] but payments for hedging suggest that other woodland was being cleared at that time.[52] Over half of All Souls College's estate in Hendon was woodland[53] and its scattered parcels may well have been bought for their trees; woodland was reserved in leases of 1567[54] and 1634[55] but in the second grant it was stated that large areas, including Hamonds Land grove, west of Burroughs Lane, and Bush grove, south of Colindeep Lane, were about to be grubbed up. Hodford wood and Beecham grove, which belonged to Westminster, had disappeared by 1649[56] but in 1690 the lord still held 100 a. of wood in demesne, which he leased out,[57] and in 1754 there were two large blocks on the demesne land north of Highwood Hill, called Hyvers Hill and Grimsgate woods.[58] Frith woods amounted to about 30 a. in 1711 but had dwindled by 1754 and had disappeared by 1796.[59] Some of the woodland which had formed much of the Clitterhouse estate in the 16th century[60] survived until 1756, when Clitterhouse wood, north of the farm-house, was to be felled and the land incorporated into neighbouring fields,[61] but Older-

[28] Kelly's Dir. Mdx. (1902).
[29] F. M. Gravatt, And We Their Deeds Record: Baptists in Hendon 1832–1970, 25.
[30] Church Com. file 51708/1.
[31] St. Barts. Hosp., EO 8/7, f. 468.
[32] See p. 20.   [33] Church Com. file 9882.
[34] Section based on transcript of lecture by C. Lee Davies (Hendon Libr., DD. MHS. 437) and the reminiscences of Bert. Wallis of Coventry Farm (Mill Hill Hist. Soc., Add. Items 24).
[35] Ex inf. Hendon Libr.; Hopkins, Hendon, 91, dates the model dairy farm 1889.
[36] Hitchin-Kemp, 'Notes on a Survey', 65, 90–1.
[37] Mill Hill Hist. Soc., Add. Items 135.
[38] Ibid. 53.
[39] O.S. Maps 1/2,500, Mdx. VI. 10, 14; XI. 1, 6–7 (1938 edn.).
[40] Kelly's Dir. Mdx. (1937).   [41] M.A.F. 68/4465.
[42] T.L.M.A.S. xii. 582–3.
[43] See p. 6.
[44] T.L.M.A.S. xii. 582–3.

[45] St. Barts. Hosp., Hc 19/1/1; All Souls Coll., Hovenden Maps, II, nos. 16, 17.
[46] W.A.M. 32532.
[47] Ibid. 32589. The abbot received £18 from sales of corn and malt, £11 for milk, and £19 for commuted labour services.
[48] W.A.M. 32589.
[49] E. Lloyd, 'Farm Accts. of the Man. of Hendon, 1316–1416', T.L.M.A.S. xxi. 158.
[50] See p. 18.   [51] W.A.M. 32273.
[52] Ibid. 32044 C.
[53] All Souls Coll., Hovenden Maps, II, nos. 16, 17.
[54] Bodl. MS. D.D. All Souls c79/20.
[55] Ibid. /38.   [56] W.A.M. 17049.
[57] C 5/176/22.   [58] B.M. Add. MS. 9839.
[59] E 214/1200; B.M. Add. MS. 9839; Cooke, Map of Hendon (1796).
[60] St. Barts. Hosp., Hc 19/1/1. The largest blocks were Clitterhouse Grove, south-east of the farm-house, and Prayle Grove, by Edgware Road.
[61] St. Barts. Hosp., Ha 1/12, f. 553.

hills, one of the woods belonging to All Souls College, survived until after 1798,[62] when there was about 120 a. of woodland left in the parish.[63] Part of Westminster's woodland served as a deer-park of 20 a. in 1517, when its formation had not destroyed any arable land or dispossessed any person.[64] The location of the park is unknown.

In 1086 the demesne of Hendon manor consisted of 10 hides; there were three villein holdings of ½ hide each, seven of a virgate each, and 16 of ½ virgate each, while 12 bordars had holdings amounting together to ½ hide.[65] The demesne served as a home farm for Westminster from 1312 and was managed by a serjeant or reeve.[66] At the time of the Black Death Hendon seems to have become a refuge for monks and cattle from abbey manors in the London area.[67] In 1321 money rents amounted to £44 4s. 4d.[68] and dues were also paid in wheat, oats, and malt.[69] Customary labour services were owed at the great reap, the second reap, and the dry reap (*drue bedrip*);[70] they included ploughing, harrowing, scything, threshing, and haymaking.[71] Several of the services had already been commuted, the abbey in 1320 having made 31s. 4d. from the sale of works.[72] From 1374 until 1416 the demesne, with its meadow, pastures, and customary services, was leased to John atte Hegge.[73] It was also being leased in 1446[74] and again in 1501 when the farmer, Christopher Roper, was imprisoned for non-payment of his arrears of rent,[75] having prevented the abbot's officers from resuming possession.[76] A new farmer was appointed in 1505.[77] The demesne lands had been split up among at least 10 tenants by 1655[78] and 17 tenants were recorded in 1690.[79]

When auctioned in 1756 the demesne lands totalled 1,226 a.[80] and consisted of two large blocks, one stretching from the Hyde to Parson Street and the other from Highwood Hill to the Hertfordshire border. There were also two isolated fields near Temple Fortune. The lands were divided in 1753 into six large farms, including those later known as Church, Church End, Tithe, and Manor farms, and the demesne in the northern part of the parish, which included the later Barnet Gate farm and the Hendon Park estate, was leased to one man, Abel Brown. The Hendon manorial estate was described by the surveyor, Thomas Browne, as the completest and best in Middlesex;[81] four of its farms were thought to be well managed and only one poorly, while three of the farm-houses were fit for gentlemen to live in. The location of the demesne lands of the four smaller manors is unknown, although the

demesne of Frith and Newhall was mentioned in 1711.[82]

There were 52 freeholders and 77 copyholders of the manor of Hendon in 1321.[83] By 1574 there were 84 copyhold tenants and 31 holding in free socage; at least 57 were head tenants but there were also some 'under-setters', who rented their lands from the head tenants.[84] There were 39 head tenants in 1685,[85] some of them holding two or more tenements and many belonging to the Nicholl and Marsh families. Most of the copyhold land was in the north of the parish, where modest farm-houses were grouped together in Page Street, Drivers Hill, Mill Hill, Highwood Hill, the southern end of Lawrence Street, and the Hale.[86] Substantial blocks were formed out of copyhold land during the 18th century[87] but in some areas, particularly around the Hale, the earlier system persisted in a confusion of small holdings,[88] in sharp contrast to the large consolidated estates farther south.

MILLS. A windmill worth 12s. a year existed in 1321[89] and may have given its name to 'melnehel' (Mill Hill), mentioned in 1374.[90] The mill at Mill Hill survived in 1685, when it was held by Robert Crane.[91] It had disappeared by 1754 but its name was perpetuated by Mill field,[92] in 1970 a recreation ground on the south side of the Ridgeway. Another windmill, called Goldherd's mill, is said to have stood in the 15th century between Clitterhouse and Cowhouse farms.[93] The existence of a third mill at some date is suggested by another Mill field south of the Bald Faced Stag on Edgware Road, adjoining Silk stream.[94]

MARKETS AND FAIRS. A fair was reputed to have been held at the Burroughs during Whitsun week in 1697[95] but it never obtained a charter. A small fair was still held at the same place c. 1720,[96] and had degenerated by the end of the 18th century into an occasion for rural sports.[97]

TRADE AND INDUSTRY. In 1318 116 qr. of malt were made on the demesne and in 1319 a malt-house was recorded.[98] A brewhouse existed at the Burroughs c. 1530[99] and charcoal was made at Clitterhouse grove in 1558.[1] In 1753 bricks were being made on the waste near Church End Farm and an abandoned brick-kiln stood north of Highwood Hill.[2] Another brick-kiln, at Golders Green, was shown in a map of 1754[3] and at Childs Hill yellow clay was being used for brick-making and

[62] Bodl. MS. D.D. All Souls c245/34 m.
[63] Middleton, *View*, 560. The figure probably includes the grounds of Hendon Place, Copt Hall, and other mansions.
[64] *V.C.H. Mdx.* ii. 89.
[65] Ibid. i. 123.
[66] *T.L.M.A.S.* xxi. 158.
[67] Ibid. 162–3.
[68] *T.L.M.A.S.* xii. 626–7.
[69] Ibid. 628–9.
[70] Ibid. 614–15, 631.
[71] W.A.M. 32536.
[72] Ibid. 32534.
[73] *T.L.M.A.S.* xxi. 159.
[74] W.A.M. 32619.
[75] Ibid. 32623.
[76] Req. 2/3/238.   [77] W.A.M. 4744.
[78] Nat. Libr. of Wales, Powis MS. 12184.
[79] E 178/6806.
[80] *Cat. of Demesne Lands* (1756).

[81] Hendon Libr., DD. MHS. 830.
[82] E 214/1200.
[83] *T.L.M.A.S.* xii. 632.
[84] *T.L.M.A.S.* xiii. 35–6 and *passim*.
[85] Ibid. 546 sqq.
[86] B.M. Add. MS. 9839.
[87] See p. 22.
[88] Cf. Whishaw, *Map of Hendon* (1828) and ref. bk.
[89] *T.L.M.A.S.* xii. 580–1.
[90] W.A.M. 32589.
[91] *T.L.M.A.S.* xiii. 557.   [92] B.M. Add. MS. 9839.
[93] *Trans. Mill Hill Hist. Soc.* (1932), 4.
[94] B.M. Add. MS. 9839.
[95] *Mdx. Cnty. Recs. Sess. Bks. 1689–1709*, 170.
[96] Bodl. MS. Rawl. B. 389b, f. 80.
[97] Evans, *Hendon*, 287.
[98] W.A.M. 32533, 32534.   [99] C 1/629/23.
[1] St. Barts. Hosp., Ha 1/1, f. 172v.
[2] Hendon Libr., DD. MHS. 830.
[3] B.M. Add. MS. 9839.

blue clay for tile-making and pottery in the early 19th century.[4] There were 16 brick-makers in Hendon in 1851[5] and the Hendon & Finchley Brick & Tile Works was manufacturing in Finchley Lane in 1866,[6] although the industry died out soon afterwards.

Retail trades in the early 19th century catered for a predominantly rural population; in 1796 there were four carpenters' shops, three blacksmiths', wheelwrights', and butchers', a plumber's, a baker's, and a collar-maker's.[7] By 1828 a chair-maker had started a business south of the Crown inn at Cricklewood, where a successor was producing 'rustic chairs' in 1855;[8] a brick-layer owned a shed in 1828 at the corner of Brent Street and Shirehall Lane.[9] In 1831 162 families were engaged in agriculture and 163 in trade or manufacturing; 177 persons were employed in retail trade or handicraft out of a population of 3,110.[10] In 1839 there were 53 retail shops and small businesses, including a hairdresser's, a dressmaker's, an auctioneer's, a corn dealer's, and several builders, carpenters, painters and glaziers, while a watch-maker had opened a shop at Golders Green.[11] In 1855 the 22 retailers in Brent Street, the largest shopping centre, included a tobacconist, an undertaker, a draper, an ironmonger, and a toy dealer.[12] There were also smaller groups of shops at the Hyde, Mill Hill, Childs Hill, Church End, the Burroughs, and Golders Green. A nurseryman and a seedsman had started business in Brent Street by 1862[13] and in 1863 there were also two nurseries at Mill Hill and one at Childs Hill.[14] A large brewery at the Hyde, later known at Hendon Brewery, was first recorded in 1862[15] and there was another brewery at Highwood Hill in 1870, which closed soon afterwards.[16] The Hendon Co-Operative Society was founded in 1874 and had 1,944 members in 1914; it was transferred to the London Co-Operative Society in 1925.[17] By 1886 there were 11 laundries at Childs Hill,[18] presumably catering for Hampstead, where several small-scale domestic concerns were still open in 1935.[19]

The opening of the Midland Railway's main line to St. Pancras in 1868 did little to stimulate industry until shortly before the First World War. At the marshalling yard of Brent sidings goods from the north were sorted,[20] Childs Hill engine-shed was used in 1897 for repairing engines,[21] and carriage sidings were later built near by. In 1970 the marshalling yard lay derelict but a depot for diesel trains occupied part of the site. The Express Dairy Co. opened a bottling factory in Claremont Road, adjoining Cricklewood station, in the late 19th century[22] and was still there in 1970.

The Pyramid Night Light Works was established at Childs Hill by 1886.[23] The Courier Co., steam printers, were operating in Brent Street in 1890.[24] Schweppes began to make soft drinks at West Hendon in 1896, on a site chosen near an artesian well and because of its proximity to Edgware Road and the Midland Railway;[25] in 1970 the factory, one of the largest of its kind, held almost 700 employees. By 1902 Best & Co., portmanteaux manufacturers, had opened in Brent Street and the Normal Powder and Ammunition Co. in Guttershedge Lane.[26] The Phoenix Telephone Co. leased land for a factory in Cricklewood Lane in 1911[27] and an optical works, occupied in 1970 by U.K. Optical Bausch & Lomb, was opened at the top of Bittacy Hill in 1912.[28] Johnson's of Hendon, manufacturers of photographic chemicals, opened a factory, which later adjoined Hendon Way, in 1913.[29] By 1914 Colindale possessed a trunk factory in Colindale Avenue, an engineering works in Colindeep Lane, a 'linaline works' in Booth Road, and two laundries.[30]

The building trade received an impetus from the extension of the Underground railway to Golders Green. Farrow and Howkins, a firm of contractors founded at Childs Hill in 1908, were prominent builders near the station and became one of the largest local companies.[31] Work was carried out before the First World War on roads and sewers in Hendon and on speculative estates elsewhere in Middlesex. In 1920 premises were opened in Highfield Road, which later became the head offices, in 1926 the firm was reconstituted as Howard Farrow Construction Ltd., and by 1970 there were 1,200 employees. Another major building firm was John Laing & Son Ltd., which moved its headquarters from Carlisle to Mill Hill in 1926 and built new head offices in 1956.[32]

Aircraft were first made in Hendon by Everett, Edgcumbe and Co. of Colindale soon after 1900 and were flown from a field later bought by Claude Grahame-White, which became the nucleus of Hendon Aerodrome.[33] They were later made in factories adjoining the airfield after its opening in 1911. Production was stimulated by the outbreak of the First World War: 1,000 men were employed in 1915, a new factory was completed in 1916, and by 1917 the buildings covered 50 a. After the war Grahame-White turned to motor-cars and furniture, until the government took over the airfield and the adjoining factory in 1922, when the manufacture of aircraft was resumed.[34] In 1912 Handley Page Ltd. established an aircraft factory at Cricklewood after moving from Barking (Essex).[35] Pioneer military aircraft were built there during the First World War and flown from the company's adjacent air-

[4] Park, Topog. of Hampstead (1818), 42.
[5] Census, 1851.
[6] Kelly's Dir. Mdx. (1866).
[7] Cooke, Map of Hendon (1796) and ref. bk.
[8] Kelly's Dir. Home Cnties. (1855).
[9] Whishaw, Map of Hendon (1828) and ref. bk.
[10] Census, 1831.
[11] Robson's Com. Dir. (1839).
[12] Kelly's Dir. Home Cnties. (1853).
[13] Kelly's Dir. Mdx. (1862).
[14] O.S. Maps 1/2,500, Mdx. VI. 15; XI. 15 (1863 edn.).
[15] Kelly's Dir. Mdx. (1862).
[16] Ibid. (1870).
[17] Rees, 'Extra-Metropolitan Mdx.', 608-10.
[18] Kelly's Dir. Mdx. (1886).
[19] Garrett, 'Upper Brent Valley', 171.
[20] Stretton, Midland Rly., 187.
[21] O.S. Map 6", Mdx. XI. SE. (1897 edn.).
[22] Garrett, 'Upper Brent Valley', 160.
[23] Kelly's Dir. Mdx. (1886).
[24] Ibid. (1890).
[25] Ex inf. Schweppes Ltd.
[26] Kelly's Dir. Mdx. (1902).
[27] Church Com. file 13196.
[28] Mill Hill Hist. Soc., Add. Items 100.
[29] Advt. in Boro. of Hendon, Official Guide [1961].
[30] O.S. Map 1/2,500, Mdx. XI. 6 (1914 edn.).
[31] Ex inf. Howard Farrow Ltd.
[32] Builder, cxci. 388; ex inf. John Laing and Son Ltd.
[33] Hopkins, Hendon, 83.
[34] Wallace, Grahame-White, 192, 207-11, 217-19, 227.
[35] Handley Page Ltd., Forty Years On, 13.

field. In 1929 the airfield was closed and a new one built at Radlett (Herts.); the construction of aircraft at Cricklewood continued until after 1964,[36] when the premises were sold to become the Cricklewood trading estate.

In 1914 the government opened several factories for munitions and aircraft components at Colindale and the Hyde. Their sale in 1920 led to a great expansion of industry,[37] which was encouraged by extensive road-building,[38] and the number of large factories rose from six in 1911 to 16 in 1921 and to 65 in 1931.[39] By 1931 13,570 persons worked in Hendon factories, nearly half of them near Cricklewood and the North Circular Road and about a third at Colindale and the Hyde on Edgware Road. Smaller concentrations were at West Hendon and Mill Hill. The largest single employers were motor firms,[40] although manufacturers of foodstuffs, furniture, electrical equipment, machinery, paper products, and aircraft all employed over 500 persons.[41] By the Second World War factories lined both sides of the road from Cricklewood to Burnt Oak, their products including shampoos, speedometers, motor bodies, ball bearings, tennis racquets, radiators, organs, cellulose lacquers, potato peelers, hair curlers, and sheet metal.[42] Elsewhere industry was much more thinly spread; in 1937, however, in addition to the laundries in Childs Hill, factories making wallpaper, tires, neon signs, and other products were scattered along Hendon Way.

Smith's Potato Crisps opened their first factory in two garages in Crown Yard, Cricklewood, with 12 employees in 1920. They moved in 1921 to a disused canteen for aircraft workers in Somerton Road and in 1938[43] left for a new factory on the North Circular Road, outside the parish. The Duple Group moved to the Hyde in 1925 and produced public service vehicles on a site which eventually covered 12½ a., including the former Cowleaze farm-house; the factory was sold to Messrs. Ronald Lyons in 1968 but the head offices of the organization remained at Hendon. The labour force, which was 30 in 1925, rose to 1,000 in the Second World War and subsequently fell to about 650.[44] A branch of the Car Mart Ltd., later Kenning Car Mart Ltd., motor distributors and repairers, was founded in 1938 on land reclaimed from Brent reservoir in 1924–5. During the Second World War the depot was taken over by the de Havilland Aircraft Co. for the production of pioneer jet engines but in 1946 the premises reverted to their normal use and in 1970 the labour force was 150.[45] Clang Ltd. was founded in 1932 by Curt Lange in the premises in Crown Yard formerly owned by Smith's Potato Crisps; the firm made domestic electrical accessories

but extended its range after 1946 to include commercial weather-proof electrical fittings and motor trailer electrical connexions. In 1940–1 Clang took over no. 108 Cricklewood Lane, which had previously housed eight separate trades, including the building of car bodies, and in 1943 it expanded to no. 110 Cricklewood Lane, formerly occupied by a refrigerator manufacturer. Both factories were later improved and in 1970 the labour force was 220.[46] Other firms which have remained since before 1939 include Rawlplug in Hale Lane, Titanine in Sheaveshill Avenue, Franco Traffic Signs in Aerodrome Road,[47] and Spurling Motor Bodies in Rookery Way.[48]

Several concerns have moved to Hendon since 1945. Among them is the National Cash Register Co., which built a large three-storeyed block by the North Circular Road in 1956 as a service engineers' training school and a repair depot for cash registers.[49] In 1966 the firm also acquired a large factory on the Willesden boundary, at the junction of Edgware and the North Circular roads, which had formerly been used by Scribbons-Kemp, biscuit makers.[50] Keyswitch Relays took over a factory in Cricklewood Lane in 1963 and built a new office block in front of it. The firm, which employed some 300 persons in 1970, produced electro-magnetic relays for industry and telecommunications and also occupied a block in the Cricklewood trading estate.[51] Other firms on that estate in 1970 included Phonographic Equipment Distributors, Associated Leisure, Les Leston, steering-wheel manufacturers, and Victor International Plastics.

SOCIAL LIFE. There was a may-pole at Drivers Hill in 1734.[52] Rural sports were held at the Bell in 1801, possibly connected with the fair at the Burroughs,[53] and outside the King's Head, Mill Hill, on Whit Tuesdays in the 19th century.[54] Cockfighting at the Burroughs during the 1820s had the tacit approval of the vicar, Theodore Williams, whom Methodists called the 'cock-fighting parson';[55] it persisted in 1865 at Childs Hill, where drunkenness and vice were said to be rife.[56] Ploughing teams met c. 1875 at the Bald Faced Stag on May Day[57] and mummers still performed at the large houses at Christmas in 1900,[58] when an observer at Highwood House found their performance 'sophisticated and debased'.[59]

By 1751 there were 20 licensed houses in the parish.[60] Tea-gardens adjoined the White Bear in 1828[61] and a bowling green adjoining the Crown at Cricklewood in 1842[62] may have been the forerunner of a pleasure-ground which was called the

[36] Hopkins, Hendon, 85.
[37] Smith, 'Recent Industrialization', 93.
[38] See p. 15.
[39] Smith, 'Recent Industrialization', 110. The figures include some factories over the borders of Kingsbury and Willesden.
[40] Smith, 'Recent Industrialization', 113.
[41] Ibid. 113–14.
[42] Kelly's Dir. Mdx. (1937).
[43] Mill Hill Hist. Soc., Add. Items 135; Mdx. Monthly, i (1953), 2.
[44] Ex inf. Duple Group Sales Ltd.
[45] Ex inf. Kenning Car Mart Ltd.
[46] Ex inf. the managing dir., Clang Ltd.
[47] O.S. Maps 1/2,500, Mdx. XI. 3 (1936 edn.); VI. 14 (1935 edn.); XI. 6 (1935 edn.).

[48] Kelly's Dir. Mdx. (1937).
[49] Builder, cxci. 388.
[50] Ex inf. National Cash Register Co. The factory is just within the parish of Willesden.
[51] Ex inf. Keyswitch Relays Ltd.
[52] M.R.O., Acc. 174/5.
[53] Mill Hill Hist. Soc., Add. Items 44. For the fair, see above.
[54] Brett-James, Hist. of Mill Hill Sch. 30.
[55] Mill Hill Hist. Soc., Add. Items 36, 43.
[56] Gravatt, And We Their Deeds Record, 14.
[57] Hendon & Finchley Times, 30 Jan. 1925, p. 8.
[58] Ibid. 2, 10.
[59] Home Cnties. Mag. iii. 246.   [60] M.R.O., L.V. 7/1.
[61] Whishaw, Map of Hendon (1828) and ref. bk.
[62] M.R.O., TA/HEN.

Abode of Bliss in 1877.[63] The White Swan had tea-gardens for summer visitors to Golders Green in 1882.[64] The Green Man at the Hale was a favourite meeting-place of boxers and other sportsmen,[65] until after the building of Brent reservoir the Old Welsh Harp was preferred.[66] The Welsh Harp also attracted a much wider *clientèle* on bank holidays, when the Midland Railway provided special trains.[67] In 1891 attractions there included rifle galleries and an abortive balloon ascent.[68] Pigeon-shooters[69] and anglers also came,[70] as well as skaters, who first held a championship on the frozen reservoir in 1880.[71] Jack Selby, a celebrated whip, is said to have driven a coach and four across the ice in the 1890s.[72]

Thomas Spalding of Shire Hall, founder of the Congregational church, gave magic-lantern lectures in the 1850s, apparently the only organized entertainments at that time.[73] The Band of Hope extended its activities to Hendon after 1876 under the patronage of Stephen Shirley, a prominent Baptist, and parades from Kentish Town to the Burroughs were enlivened by fireworks. In 1878 Shirley also built a Temperance hall in Finchley Lane, which was immediately let to the Baptists as a temporary church.[74] A church institute, opened at All Saints, Childs Hill, in 1896, was intended as a social centre and contained a library.[75] A new church-house was also opened in 1896 opposite St. Mary's parish church; it included a reading room, and was used by the Young Men's Friendly Society and similar organizations.[76]

The Court Buckingham of Foresters was founded in 1861 and the Hendon Flower of Oddfellows in 1865; they survived in 1925,[77] while the Pride of Mill Hill Court of Foresters followed in 1875 and lasted until 1913.[78] Brass and silver bands flourished at the end of the 19th century,[79] when dances and concerts were held at the Hendon institute,[80] opened in Brent Street in 1875[81] and later a Post Office sorting office. A debating society, where theology was excluded, lasted from 1879 until 1919, attracting well-known speakers.[82] A rate-payers' association and a horticultural society existed in 1883[83] and 'penny readings' were held in St. Mary's school until *c.* 1900, causing inn-keepers to complain of loss of custom.[84] A branch of the Primrose League was opened in 1886,[85] followed by political organizations[86] which included a Social Democratic club for Schweppes's employees[87] and Mill Hill Constitutional Club, which existed in

1902.[88] The *Hendon & Finchley Times* was founded in 1875[89] and was still published in 1970, with offices in Church Road.

Hendon's only theatre, the Golders Green Hippodrome, was opened in 1914[90] but was no longer in regular use in 1970. The near-by Ionic cinema, so named because of its pedimented frontage to Finchley Road, existed by 1922, as did the Hendon electric theatre in Brent Street and the Mill Hill cinema in Lawrence Street (afterwards the Broadway).[91] Later cinemas included the Ambassador (later the Classic), Hendon Central, opened in 1932, the Capitol, Mill Hill, opened in 1932 and demolished after the Second World War, and the Odeon, at the corner of Church Road and Parson Street, opened in 1939.[92] The Cricklewood electric palace stood beside a dance-hall and skating rink in 1937.[93]

At Hampstead Garden Suburb[94] several societies used the club house and the institute.[95] Other local groups[96] included Mill Hill (later Mill Hill and Hendon) Historical Society, from 1928, and Mill Hill Preservation Society, founded in 1949.[97] An association was formed on the Watling estate in 1928, to allay the hostility of neighbouring owner-occupiers, and published a news-sheet called the *Watling Resident*.[98] In 1933 a community centre was opened in Orange Hill Road on the edge of the estate, where gatherings were also held in two church halls and a Labour hall.[99]

A rifle range was opened at Childs Hill in 1860.[1] In 1906 the Middlesex Gun Club, which had 120 members, owned 7 a. adjoining the Welsh Harp railway station[2] and in 1915 there were several ranges between Cricklewood Lane and the Brent.[3] Horse races were held at the Burroughs from 1864 but caused offence in 1882[4] and were discontinued soon afterwards. The first mechanical hare, invented by a Mr. Geary, was tried out near the Welsh Harp in 1876.[5] Hendon Greyhound Stadium was opened by the North Circular Road in the early 1930s and enlarged to hold 5,000 persons in 1970.[6]

From 1911 Claude Grahame-White attracted large crowds by carefully managed flying displays,[7] spectators in that year including the Prime Minister and members of the royal family. Regular shows were started in 1912, when the millionth visitor was said to have entered Hendon Aerodrome. In 1913 51 race-meetings, two aerial fêtes, eleven demonstrations of street-flying and five of illuminated

[63] Rees, 'Extra-Metropolitan Mdx.', 237.
[64] Walford, *Greater Lond.* i. 280.
[65] Hitchin-Kemp, 'Notes on a Survey', 29.
[66] *Mdx. Quarterly*, i (1953), 18.
[67] *Hendon & Finchley Times*, 30 Jan. 1925, p. 6.
[68] Hopkins, *Hendon*, 55.
[69] St. Barts. Hosp., EO 8/2, ff. 213–15.
[70] *Mdx. Quarterly*, i. 18.
[71] Hopkins, *Hendon*, 90.
[72] *Hendon & Finchley Times*, 30 Jan. 1925, p. 8.
[73] Walker, *Hendon 1851–1951*, p. 7.
[74] Gravatt, *And We Their Deeds Record*, 18–19.
[75] Dexter, *Cricklewood*, 68.
[76] *Kelly's Dir. Mdx.* (1906).
[77] *Hendon & Finchley Times*, 30 Jan. 1925, p. 2.
[78] Mill Hill Hist. Soc., Add. Items 67.
[79] *Hendon & Finchley Times*, 30 Jan. 1925, p. 2; Hopkins, *Hendon*, 92.
[80] Walker, *Hendon 1851–1951*, p. 7; Mill Hill Hist. Soc., Add. Items 2.
[81] *Hendon & Finchley Times*, 30 Jan. 1925, p. 6.
[82] Walker, *Hendon 1851–1951*, p. 8. [83] Ibid.
[84] Mill Hill Hist. Soc., Add. Items 27.

[85] Hopkins, *Hendon*, 91.
[86] *Hendon & Finchley Times*, 30 Jan. 1925, p. 2.
[87] Hitchin-Kemp, 'Notes on a Survey', 3–4.
[88] *Kelly's Dir. Mdx.* (1902).
[89] Hopkins, *Hendon*, 64.
[90] Ibid. See below, plate facing p. 336.
[91] *Kelly's Dir. Mdx.* (1922).
[92] Hopkins, *Hendon*, 99, 100, 102.
[93] *Kelly's Dir. Mdx.* (1937).
[94] Residents' Assoc., *Hist. of Hampstead Gdn. Suburb* (1954), 18–21.
[95] See p. 14.
[96] Hopkins, *Hendon*, 96, 103.
[97] Ibid. 98, 103.
[98] Durant, *Watling* (1939), 22.
[99] Ibid. 92, 97–8, 108, 126.
[1] Evans, *Hendon*, 342.   [2] *Kelly's Dir. Mdx.* (1906).
[3] O.S. Maps 1/2,500, Mdx. XI. 11 (1915 edn.).
[4] Walford, *Greater Lond.* i. 280.
[5] *Mdx. Quarterly*, N.S. xix (1959), 5.
[6] Ex inf. Hackney & Hendon Greyhounds Ltd.
[7] R. D. Brett, *Hist. of Brit. Aviation*, 331–2; see above, p. 14.

night-flying were held there.[8] After the First World War Grahame-White founded the London Flying Club, 'the last word in luxurious London life',[9] but from 1920 pageants were staged by the R.A.F.[10] and in 1934 the club's building became the headquarters of the Metropolitan Police College.[11]

Hendon cricket club played near the later Brampton Grove from 1852 to 1892[12] and Mill Hill cricket club was founded in 1881.[13] Clubs for hockey were recorded in the 1880s, when Hampstead Town football club played in Cricklewood Lane,[14] and for tennis in 1890.[15] Hendon golf club was founded in 1903 on land which had formed part of Holders Hill farm;[16] the 18-hole course was remodelled after the First World War and a new club house in Devonshire Road was completed in 1965. Mill Hill golf club was founded as Moat Mount golf club in 1927;[17] the course, of 18 holes, was remodelled in 1931 and covered 160 a. in 1970, when 450 members[18] used a club house which had formed part of Coventry farm. In 1970 Finchley golf club occupied a large course in the former Nether Court estate east of Frith Lane. Mill Hill rugby football club was founded in 1937 but had no ground in the parish until 1958, when one was opened in Copthall playing fields.[19] Hendon association football club, which won the F.A. Amateur Cup in 1960 and the Athenian League championship in 1961,[20] played in Claremont Road in 1970.

Volunteers were raised in Hendon in 1798 but were disbanded in 1813.[21] A troop was again formed in 1885 as part of the 3rd Middlesex Rifle Volunteers with headquarters in Burroughs House, whence they moved in 1889 to the former Wesleyan chapel in Chapel Walk.[22] A detachment of the Hertfordshire Yeomanry Cavalry was also active in 1889[23] and a drill hall was opened in Algernon Road in 1900.[24]

LOCAL GOVERNMENT. Courts for the abbot of Westminster's manor of Hendon were held four times a year from 1316 until 1374.[25] In 1574 courts leet and baron were held twice a year, on the Tuesday before Whitsun and on the Tuesday before the feast of St. Catherine.[26] They exercised the view of frankpledge and the assizes of bread and ale but by the early 17th century they had ceased to deal with minor criminal offences.[27] Court rolls survive from 1461 to 1474 and, with gaps in the mid 17th century, from 1518.[28] In the 18th century courts were held yearly at the White Bear,[29] where they

last met in 1916. Special courts baron were also held. Stocks stood at the corner of Brent Street and Bell Lane in 1828[30] and there was also a lock-up in Bell Lane, which was sold in 1883.[31]

There was a reeve in 1316 and a bailiff in 1318, who was replaced c. 1370 by a beadle or rent-collector.[32] Beadles, headboroughs, constables, ale-tasters, and carcass-inspectors (caronet') were recorded. There were no ale-tasters after c. 1634[33] and by 1688 the manorial officials were a reeve or 'collector', two constables, and four headboroughs, whose functions were divided between the north and south ends of the parish.[34] Constables and headboroughs continued to be appointed by the manorial courts until 1843,[35] although constables sometimes received expenses from the vestry and took orders from it, as in 1798, when they were ordered to eject Mrs. Love from one of the parish houses which had been turned into a brothel.[36] There were beadles at Mill Hill in the 19th century.[37]

Churchwardens' accounts survive from 1656 to 1893[38] and minutes of the vestry, which was first recorded in 1658,[39] from 1707 to 1913.[40] By 1596 a church house, adjoining the churchyard, had replaced an older building near by.[41] It was rebuilt after a fire in 1676[42] and was the meeting-place of the vestry by 1678, continuing as such after becoming the Greyhound inn until in 1876 meetings were transferred to the National schools;[43] a new church house was built opposite the Greyhound in 1896.[44] The vestry usually met monthly from the early 18th century and 36 parishioners promised to pay fines for non-attendance in 1736.[45] Attendance varied during the 18th and early 19th centuries from three to twenty, when meetings were dominated by a group of regular attenders, most of them tenant farmers. Efforts were made to control the parish officers: in 1658 the churchwardens were fined for making assessments without the consent of the parishioners, in 1663 no unauthorized pensions were to be paid to the poor, and in 1695 the churchwardens were condemned for extravagance during public celebrations.[46]

Overseers of the poor were recorded in 1663.[47] Until the end of the 18th century there was usually one overseer for each end of the parish and on relinquishing office the overseers automatically became the next year's churchwardens. There were five overseers for each end of the parish in 1787 but sometimes there were only three.[48] In 1833 they were independent gentlemen, although farmers or tradesmen were sometimes appointed.[49] Surveyors

[8] C. C. Turner, Old Flying Days, 46.
[9] G. Wallace, Claude Grahame-White, 222.
[10] See p. 14.
[11] Kelly's Dir. Mdx. (1937); Hopkins, Hendon, 84.
[12] Walker, Hendon 1851–1951, p. 8.
[13] Hopkins, Hendon, 90.
[14] Hendon & Finchley Times, 30 Jan. 1925, p. 2.
[15] Kelly's Dir. Mdx. (1890).
[16] Hendon golf club, Official Handbk. (1968).
[17] Mill Hill golf club, Official Handbk. (1969).
[18] Ex inf. the sec.
[19] Hendon Libr., DD. MHS. 544.
[20] Boro. of Hendon, Official Guide [1961].
[21] Evans, Hendon, 336–7.
[22] Ibid. 341–4.   [23] Ibid. 337–8.
[24] Hopkins, Hendon, 93.   [25] W.A.M. 32532–89.
[26] T.L.M.A.S. xiv. 35.   [27] M.R.O., Acc. 174/28.
[28] Schedule in M.R.O., Acc. 174/33. Court rolls and bks. 1688–1934 are M.R.O., Acc. 174/1–27; rolls from 1461 are indexed, ibid. /28.

[29] M.R.O., Acc. 174/28.
[30] Whishaw, Map of Hendon (1828) and ref. bk.
[31] Hopkins, Hendon, 90.
[32] W.A.M. 32532, 33264; T.L.M.A.S. xiii. 568.
[33] M.R.O., Acc. 174/28.
[34] The south end included Church End and the area to the south.
[35] M.R.O., Acc. 174/29–32.
[36] Hendon Libr., MS. L. 128.
[37] Brett-James, Hendon, 96.
[38] Hendon Libr., MSS. L. 86–9.
[39] Ibid. L. 86.   [40] Ibid. L. 126–32.
[41] Ibid. L. 2.   [42] Ibid. L. 86.
[43] Walker, Hendon 1851–1951, p. 17.
[44] Kelly's Dir. Mdx. (1906).
[45] Hendon Libr., MS. L. 126.
[46] Ibid. L. 86.
[47] Ibid.
[48] Ibid. L. 127.
[49] Rep. Poor Law Com. App. B(2), pp. 102 sqq.

of the highways were mentioned in 1700[50] and were usually appointed annually during the 18th century; by 1795 there were five for each end of the parish.[51] The surveyors were chosen by the vestry and in 1801 it was laid down that they must be substantial landowners in the parish.[52] A salaried assistant surveyor was proposed in 1824[53] and was finally appointed in 1837.[54] A highway rate was imposed in 1702[55] and intermittently during the 18th and early 19th centuries.[56] Repair of the roads was usually financed by a composition in lieu of statute duty, varying in 1736 from 9s. for gentlemen to 2s. for labourers,[57] but in 1822 every parishioner liable to more than six days' duty was required to perform a sixth of the work in kind.[58] A salaried vestry clerk was mentioned in 1796[59] and received larger payments from 1813, on account of an increase in parish business.[60]

Vestry meetings in the 18th century were usually presided over by prominent laymen, the vicar attending only when he was directly concerned. In 1800 the assistant curate, Mr. Barton, was thanked for his devotion to the parish and was requested to attend vestries as often as he could[61] but Theodore Williams, vicar 1812–75, fought several battles over tithes and burial fees.[62] Angered by the vestry's proposal to raise his rating assessment, Williams appealed to quarter sessions in 1823, when a special committee was formed to work out the rateable value of lands in the parish.[63] Soon afterwards he began to preside over the meetings regularly, until in 1836 four men arrived early and claimed to constitute a vestry, abusing the vicar when he declared their meeting invalid.[64] All four were cited in the consistory court for brawling on consecrated ground, the boundary of which was indicated by a beam on the ceiling of the parlour of the Greyhound, beyond which the vicar took care to place himself. The defendants, who had only recently bought land in the parish, were convicted of attempting to monopolize the proceedings and were fined. A proposal to create a select vestry in 1822 was easily defeated.[65]

In 1729 the vestry resolved to pay for the prosecution of thieves[66] and in 1777 four men were to be paid for apprehending thieves and highwaymen.[67]

The parish rate brought in £515 in 1776, of which £411 was spent on the poor,[68] and £905 in 1803, when £607 was spent on the poor.[69] Income from the rates was distributed by the vestry to the overseers for the north and south ends of the parish, who presented their accounts separately every month.

A workhouse near Ridgeway House, Mill Hill, was mentioned in 1712[70] but was presumably superseded by one built at the Burroughs in 1735,[71] in gardens adjoining six cottages which had been acquired by the parish soon after 1731. The cottages, sometimes called alms-houses, were inhabited by paupers and later annexed to the workhouse.[72] They survived until 1934 and in 1970 their site was occupied by a block of flats.[73] More cottages were built on an adjacent site in 1787 and allotted by the vestry.[74] Most of the inhabitants of the workhouse in 1751 were children, who were employed in spinning flax and weaving thread into sheeting.[75] The workhouse lacked a suitable master in 1757[76] but its administration had improved by the end of the 18th century, when unmarried males and females were separated.[77] The diet was thought in 1797 to be monotonous, though not unwholesome,[78] and it improved in the early 19th century,[79] perhaps because of a return to the system of farming the poor, which had first been instituted in 1767.[80] The practice had been revived in 1793, with the contractor being paid to manage all the poor, both within and outside the workhouse,[81] given a rent-free house, and made subject to inspection by a committee of the vestry. In 1800 the parish resumed direct control but the new master was dismissed soon afterwards for embezzling materials.[82] Farming began again in 1802 and continued until 1825; the contractor also ran a school for workhouse children, with the aid of a schoolmistress who was paid 1s. a week. Numbers in the workhouse fluctuated between 17 and 47 in the late 18th and early 19th centuries.[83] In 1834 most inmates were children and old people, on whom an average of 4s. 6d. a head was spent each week. Able-bodied labourers, when no work was available on the land or on the roads, were required to pick oakum in the workhouse during the day.[84]

The parish also owned several houses which it let cheaply to paupers. A house was mentioned in 1663 and a cottage at the Hale belonged to the parish in 1701.[85] Property in 1753 consisted of the cottage at the Hale, another at Highwood Hill, two tenements at Church End, the church house, the parish clerk's house, the workhouse, the charity school at the Burroughs[86] and Nicholl's alms-houses at Mill Hill.[87] Rents from some of the properties, notably the church house, were devoted to poor-relief and contributed £100 towards building the workhouse in 1735.[88] The parish houses at Church End and the Hale were sold in 1837.[89] Hospital fees were some-

[50] Hendon Libr., MS. L. 126.
[51] Ibid. L. 128.
[52] Ibid. L. 129.
[53] Ibid. L. 130.
[54] Ibid. L. 131.
[55] *Trans. Mill Hill Hist. Soc.* ii. 9.
[56] Hendon Libr., MS. L. 129.
[57] Ibid. L. 126.
[58] Ibid. L. 130.
[59] Ibid. L. 128.
[60] Ibid. L. 129.
[61] Ibid.
[62] See p. 34.
[63] Hendon Libr., MS. L. 130.
[64] Section based on Evans, *Hendon*, 191–3.
[65] Hendon Libr., MS. L. 130.
[66] Ibid. L. 126.   [67] Ibid. L. 189.
[68] *Rep. Cttee. on Rets. by Overseers, 1776*, 396.
[69] *Returns on Expense and Maintenance of Poor* [175], pp. 296–7, H.C. (1803–4), xiii.
[70] M.R.O., Acc. 174/2.   [71] Hendon Libr., MS. L. 87.

[72] Ibid. L. 470[1].
[73] Hopkins, *Hendon*, 100.
[74] Hendon Libr., MS. L. 128.
[75] T. H. G. Giles, 'Relief of Poor in Hendon', TS. *penes* Hendon Libr. 24.
[76] Hendon Libr., MS. L. 127.
[77] H. Ward, 'Admin. of Poor Laws in Hendon 1795–1834', TS. *penes* Hendon Libr. 34.
[78] Eden, *State of the Poor* (1797), i. 470.
[79] Ward, 'Admin. of Poor Laws', 35.
[80] Hendon Libr., MS. L. 189.
[81] Ibid. L. 128.
[82] Ibid. L. 129.
[83] Ward, 'Admin. of Poor Laws', 32.
[84] *Rep. Com. Poor Laws* [44], H.C., pp. 102g and h (1834), xxxv(1).
[85] Hendon Libr., MS. L. 286.   [86] See p. 44.
[87] The alms-houses were administered by the vestry; see p. 48.
[88] Hendon Libr., MS. L. 287.
[89] Ibid. L. 131.

times paid by the parish and in 1738 a parish physician was appointed,[90] with a salary which had doubled by 1793.[91]

At the end of the 18th century special efforts were made to satisfy a growing demand for outdoor relief. Thirteen inhabitants of the south end of the parish resolved in 1795 to help relieve men who lacked work because of the onset of winter; bread, potatoes, and coal were also provided or sold cheaply in periods of frost.[92] A more comprehensive system was introduced in 1800, whereby bread was distributed according to the size of a family; at the same time all money in hand for charitable purposes was delivered to the workhouse committee and subscriptions for poor-relief were solicited.[93] Out of £607 spent on the poor in 1803, £354 was devoted to outdoor relief; the sum was divided between 15 adults and 40 children on permanent relief and 40 recipients of occasional relief.[94] In 1825 Sir Stamford Raffles considered the local poor to be unchecked by any authority and to be in a degraded state.[95] By 1834 over 50 persons received outdoor relief, as well as 14 able-bodied men, mostly unemployed farm labourers, who were set to work on the roads.[96]

Hendon poor law union was formed in 1835, to comprise the parishes of Hendon, Harrow, Pinner, Edgware, Kingsbury, Great and Little Stanmore, and Willesden.[97] A red-brick workhouse in the Tudor style was built at Redhill, Edgware Road, in 1835 to hold 350 inmates; a union school for 150 children was erected near by in 1859 and the workhouse itself was extended in 1889.[98] Old people's flats were built on the site of the union workhouse in 1971.[99]

In 1863 Hendon was put under the jurisdiction of the new Edgware highway board, to which it elected two waywardens.[1] After complaints about the drainage in the southern part of the parish, Childs Hill special drainage district was formed in 1871[2] but in 1875 it was merged with Edgware rural sanitary authority,[3] of which body the parish of Hendon became a part under the Public Health Act of 1872.[4] The name was changed to Hendon rural sanitary authority in 1877[5] but in 1879 the area was divided and the old parish of Hendon became an urban sanitary authority, under a local board.[6] Hendon rural sanitary authority thereafter comprised the districts of Pinner, Harrow Weald, Great and Little Stanmore, Kingsbury, and Edgware. The authority met in the workhouse at Redhill in 1890,[7] becoming Hendon R.D.C. in 1895 and transferring its meetings to Stanmore by 1910.[8]

Hendon local board consisted of 12 members, who were elected for the three wards of Hendon, Mill Hill, and Childs Hill. Membership was increased to 15 in 1895, when the board became Hendon U.D.C.[9] The number of wards was increased to six in 1915 and to nine in 1931, when there were 33 councillors.[10] A proposal in 1906 to add Kingsbury was successfully resisted: both the drainage system and the roads of Hendon U.D. were praised at an inquiry and it was felt that the inclusion of Kingsbury, which was notoriously mismanaged and highly rated, would benefit only the landowners of that parish.[11] Hendon U.D. was enlarged by the addition of Edgware in 1931 and was incorporated as the borough of Hendon in 1932.[12] A small part of the old parish, containing Finchley golf course in Frith Lane, was transferred to Finchley U.D. in 1934.[13] The borough was merged with Finchley, Barnet, East Barnet, and Friern Barnet to become part of Barnet L.B. in 1965.[14] Hendon B.C. from the outset was dominated by opponents of the Labour party, who stood as Conservatives from 1938. The council of Barnet L.B., similarly, has always had a Conservative majority.[15]

BOROUGH OF HENDON. *Azure, a paschal lamb proper standing upon a grassy mount; on a chief or two windmill sails sable*
[Granted 1932]

LONDON BOROUGH OF BARNET. *Azure, a paschal lamb proper standing upon a grassy mount; on a chief per pale argent and gules a Saxon crown or between two roses counterchanged barbed and seeded proper*

[Granted 1965]

Hendon local board met at first in the Hendon institute, Brent Street,[16] and by 1890 in the old workhouse at the Burroughs.[17] In 1901 new offices were opened in an ornate building to the east, designed by T. H. Watson,[18] which became the town hall in 1932. It was enlarged in 1934[19] and housed the town clerk's and treasurer's departments of Barnet L.B. in 1967.[20]

PUBLIC SERVICES. A fire-brigade, formed in 1855,[21] was refounded as Hendon volunteer fire

[90] Ibid. L. 126.
[91] Ibid. L. 128.
[92] Ibid.
[93] Ibid. L. 129.
[94] *Returns on Expense and Maintenance of Poor* [175], pp. 296–7, H.C. (1803–4), xiii.
[95] Wurtzburg, *Raffles of the Eastern Isles*, 723.
[96] *Rep. Com. Poor Laws*, H.C. 44, p. 102h (1834), xxxv(1).
[97] *Poor Law Com. 1st Rep.* 251.
[98] *Kelly's Dir. Mdx.* (1890).   [99] Ex inf. Hendon Libr.
[1] *Lond. Gaz.* 13 Mar. 1863, p. 1480.
[2] Church Com. file 10113/1.
[3] 38 & 39 Vic. c.10.
[4] 35 & 36 Vic. c.79; Evans, *Hendon*, 325.
[5] Hopkins, *Hendon*, 90.
[6] Ibid.

[7] *Kelly's Dir. Mdx.* (1890).
[8] Ibid. (1910).
[9] Hopkins, *Hendon*, 92.
[10] Ibid. 95, 99.
[11] M.R.O., *Reps. of Local Inqs.* (1906), 37–40.
[12] Hopkins, *Hendon*, 99.
[13] Briggs, *Mdx. Old and New*, 132; *Kelly's Dir. Mdx.* (1937).
[14] London Govt. Act (1963), c.33.
[15] Election results in *The Times*, e.g. 2 Nov. 1933, 1 Nov. 1938, 9 May 1964.
[16] *Hendon & Finchley Times*, 30 Jan. 1925, p. 8. For the institute, see p. 14.
[17] *Kelly's Dir. Mdx.* (1890).   [18] *Builder*, lxxxvii. 492.
[19] Boro. of Hendon, *Official Guide* [1961].
[20] Barnet L.B., *Official Guide* [1967].
[21] Hopkins, *Hendon*, 87.

brigade in 1866 and kept a manual engine in a building, later used as a garage, opposite St. Mary's church.[22] Subsidiary fire stations were opened at Mill Hill in 1889 and at Childs Hill in 1895. In 1899 the brigade was taken over by Hendon U.D.C., which opened sub-stations at Burnt Oak, West Hendon, and Golders Green in 1900. The engine-house opposite the church was replaced by a fire station in the Burroughs in 1914 and the sub-stations at West Hendon and Golders Green were closed in 1922 and 1927 respectively.[23]

The parish of Hendon was added to the Metropolitan Police District in 1840.[24] In 1863 the police station was in Brent Street, opposite the junction with Bell Lane.[25] It was replaced in 1884 by a building north of the junction of Brent Street with Brampton Grove.[26]

Until 1866, when the West Middlesex Water-works Co. was empowered to provide piped water,[27] the southern part of Hendon was supplied from the parish pump at the junction of Brent Street and Bell Lane[28] and, at Childs Hill, from a stream and a spring at the Leg of Mutton pond on Hampstead Heath.[29] In 1873 the Colne Valley Water Co. obtained powers to supply Mill Hill, which previously had relied on wells.[30]

Gas street-lighting was introduced to parts of Hendon, including Childs Hill, in 1871.[31] In 1890 gas was provided by the Gas Light and Coke Co. and from works of the North Middlesex Gas Co.,[32] opened near the later Mill Hill East railway station between 1862 and 1866,[33] although Mill Hill itself was still lit by oil lamps in the early 20th century.[34] An electric lighting order for Hendon U.D. was granted to a private company in 1899 but powers were transferred to the U.D.C. in the same year.[35]

In the 1860s sewage from Childs Hill ran through open ditches to the Brent reservoir, causing complaints which led to the formation of Childs Hill special drainage district.[36] An outfall works to serve the whole parish was built near Renters farm in 1886 and a main drainage works, visited by W. E. Gladstone, was built in 1887.[37] Parts of Childs Hill were still without drains in 1894, when offence was caused by cesspools and over-flowing ditches,[38] and areas in the Hyde and Mill Hill had no drains until the end of the 19th century.[39] In 1895, however, 80 per cent of Hendon's houses drained into sewers and by 1900 the figure had risen to 98 per cent.[40] Hendon U.D.C. bought 13 a. of Clitterhouse farm for extensions to the sewage farm in 1905,[41] and a new sewage disposal works was being built in 1914.[42] Hendon became part of the West Middlesex Drainage Scheme in 1931, four years before its sewage farm was superseded by the new works at Mogden.[43]

There was a private lunatic asylum for ladies run by Miss Dence at Hendon House, Brent Street, in 1861.[44] The Metropolitan Convalescent Institution accommodated 40 young girls at Burroughs House c. 1874[45] and Dr. Henry Hicks had an asylum at Grove House in the Burroughs from 1879 to 1899.[46] A small isolation hospital was built south of Kingsbury Road in 1890[47] and was controlled by Hendon U.D.C. in 1901, when there were five patients.[48] The last of several additions was made in 1922 and the building was replaced in 1929 by the new Hendon isolation hospital in Goldsmith Avenue, with 86 beds. Two ward blocks were built between 1929 and 1940 but by 1970, when there were 103 beds, the institution had become a geriatric hospital. Its grounds contained the Northgate clinic, opened in 1968 by the North West Metropolitan regional hospital board for the treatment of 25 psychopaths. Colindale hospital was opened in 1912, on land given by Sir Audley Neeld,[49] and had 50 beds in 1925. Additions included an operating theatre in 1923, a new wing with 20 beds in 1934, and a physiotherapy department in 1966. Hendon cottage hospital was opened in 1913 near the later junction of Hendon Way and Elliot Road; it was extended in 1925 and again in 1933.[50] Manor House hospital was founded in 1917 by the Allied Hospital Benevolent Society to care for war victims;[51] its administrative block occupied John Bond's manor-house at Golders Hill, while patients were treated in temporary huts. The hospital was transferred to the Industrial Orthopaedic Society in 1919 and thereafter catered largely for victims of industrial accidents. Two permanent wards were opened in 1931 and further extensions were made in 1938 and after the Second World War. A four-storeyed wing was opened in 1969, containing 52 beds and a twin operating theatre. Redhill hospital was opened by Hendon board of guardians in 1927 in a new building to replace the former workhouse infirmary which had been built in 1865.[52] It was occupied in 1970 by Edgware general hospital, which, like the former isolation hospital and Colindale hospital, was administered by Hendon group hospital management committee.

The first public park in Hendon was Golders Hill park, formerly the grounds of Golders Hill House, which were bought by the L.C.C. in 1899.[53] The L.C.C. also took over the upkeep of the Hampstead Heath Extension after its purchase by trustees from

[22] Walker, *Hendon 1851–1951*, p. 7.
[23] Hopkins, *Hendon*, 64, 91–7.
[24] *Lond. Gaz.* 13 Oct. 1840, p. 2250.
[25] O.S. Map 1/2,500, Mdx. XI. 7 (1863 edn.).
[26] Ex inf. Hendon Libr.
[27] Hopkins, *Hendon*, 57.
[28] Whishaw, *Map of Hendon* (1828) and ref. bk.; Mill Hill Hist. Soc., Add. Items 2.
[29] *Hendon & Finchley Times*, 30 Jan. 1926, p. 9.
[30] Hopkins, *Hendon*, 57; Mill Hill Hist. Soc., Add. Items 2.
[31] Hopkins, *Hendon*, 57.
[32] *Kelly's Dir. Mdx.* (1890).   [33] Ibid. (1862, 1866).
[34] *Mdx. Monthly*, ii (1953), 14.
[35] Hopkins, *Hendon*, 57.
[36] Church Com. file 10113; see p. 31.
[37] Hopkins, *Hendon*, 91; O.S. Map 6″, Mdx. XI. NW. (1897 edn.).

[38] Church Com. file 10113/2.
[39] Hopkins, *Hendon*, 56.
[40] M. Rees, 'Extra-Metrop. Mdx.', 39.
[41] St. Barts. Hosp., EO 8/7, f. 468.
[42] Howard Farrow Ltd. *Work in Progress*, 38.
[43] Rees, 'Extra-Metrop. Mdx.', 393 n.
[44] *Census*, 1861; ex inf. Hendon Libr.
[45] *Kelly's Dir. Mdx.* (1874); Evans, *Hendon*, 282.
[46] Ex inf. Hendon Libr.
[47] Section based on inf. supplied by deputy hosp. sec., Edgware gen. hosp. geriatric sub-group.
[48] *Census*, 1901.
[49] Section based on inf. supplied by hosp. sec.
[50] Hopkins, *Hendon*, 64, 97, 100.
[51] Section based on inf. supplied by gen. sec. Manor Ho. hosp.
[52] Wembley Hist. Soc., Acc. 346.
[53] Dexter, *Cricklewood*, 83.

Eton College in 1907.[54] Hendon public park, 30 a. between Queens Road (formerly Butchers Lane) and Shire Hall Lane, was opened by Hendon U.D.C. in 1903[55] and other parks were opened by the council after the First World War, including Sunny Hill park (50 a.) c. 1922[56] and Mill Hill park (39 a.) in 1924.[57] In 1932 Hendon B.C. owned 793½ a. of open spaces in Hendon and Edgware,[58] including Moat Mount open space (67 a.),[59] Arrandene park (57 a.), Watling park (46 a.), Montrose playing fields (30 a.), Copthall park (146 a.), West Hendon playing fields (62 a.), Woodfield park (40 a.), and Clitterhouse playing fields (50 a.).

The U.D.C.'s first housing estate, consisting of 50 houses, was laid out at Childs Hill in 1914.[60] By 1932 Hendon had erected 1,012 council houses, including a large estate at the Hyde,[61] but none was as big as the L.C.C.'s Watling estate, on which work began in 1927.[62] By 1961 there were about 4,500 houses owned by the borough of Hendon.[63]

An open-air swimming pool was built at the Hyde in 1922, and another in Daws Lane, Mill Hill, in 1935. Slipper baths were opened at Childs Hill and West Hendon in 1930.[64]

Hendon central library was opened in 1929 in a brick neo-Georgian building with a cupola, designed by T. M. Wilson, next to the town hall.[65] Branch libraries were opened at Golders Green in 1935, in Hartley Avenue, Mill Hill, in 1937,[66] and at Childs Hill in 1962.[67] At Burnt Oak a temporary building opened in 1954 was replaced by a permanent library in 1968.[68]

Golders Green crematorium, Hoop Lane, was opened in 1902 by Sir Henry Thompson, founder of the Cremation Society of England.[69] It was designed by Sir Ernest George and A. B. Yeates as a range of red-brick buildings in a 'Lombardic' style, dominated by a chapel. A columbarium for the receipt of ashes was completed in 1911, the cloister in 1914, and a second columbarium in 1916.[70] A second chapel, to the designs of Mitchell and Bridgewater, was added in 1938.[71] Paddington B.C. opened a large cemetery east of Milespit Hill before 1937.[72]

Land opposite the site of the crematorium was bought for a cemetery by Sephardi Jews and the West London Reform synagogue. They erected a building of red brick with stone dressings, containing two halls for their respective burial services, and in 1897 the first interment took place.[73] In 1974 the north-eastern part of the cemetery was still reserved for Sephardi burials, marked by prostrate slabs, and the south-western for members of the West London synagogue, who were commemorated by erect monuments.[74]

CHURCHES. There was a priest at Hendon in 1086.[75] A church was mentioned in 1157[76] and was valued with a chapelry at Hampstead in the mid 13th century.[77] The chapelry was still annexed to Hendon rectory in 1476[78] but it became the separate parish of Hampstead in 1549.[79] Several new churches were founded in the 19th and 20th centuries, until in 1970 there were 14 ecclesiastical parishes and two mission chapels within the old parish.

There is no mention of the church at Hendon in early grants of the manor to Westminster[80] but in 1157 Pope Adrian IV confirmed that the abbey held the advowson,[81] as was subsequently reaffirmed by the bishop of London.[82] In 1258 the abbey retained the advowson when it granted the church to the bishop of London.[83] Except in 1262 and when the king acted as patron sede vacante in 1349, the abbey presented all the rectors until 1476,[84] when it appropriated the church.[85] In 1550 the Herberts became lay rectors.[86]

A vicarage was ordained before 1244.[87] Vicars were appointed by the rectors from 1329 to 1477, when the bishop of London collated by lapse, and from 1478 until the Dissolution by the abbot of Westminster.[88] The advowson of the vicarage passed in 1541 to the new diocese of Westminster[89] and in 1550 to the Herberts,[90] who, as recusants, appear to have leased it; J. Askew and William Lambert presented in 1557, Sir Francis Walsingham in 1582, John Goldesborough in 1606, Thomas Staresmere in 1662, John Herne in 1679, and John Wand and John Wright in 1707 and 1726.[91] The advowson was sold after the death of John Bond in 1801 to the Revd. C. L. Eldridge, who presented in 1812.[92] Edward Bailey presented in 1876[93] but by 1890 the living was in the hands of Lady Howard de Walden.[94] Lord Howard de Walden was patron in 1940 and the bishop of London in 1947.[95]

The vicarage was valued at five marks c. 1244, out of which two marks a year were paid to the sacristy of Westminster abbey[96] until the Dissolution.[97] In 1535 the vicarage was worth £15[98] and by 1650 its value had risen to £55, which was augmented

[54] Howkins, Golders Green, 21–2.
[55] Hopkins, Hendon, 93.
[56] Hitchin-Kemp, 'Notes on a Survey', 7.
[57] Hopkins, Hendon, 96.
[58] Mill Hill Times & Guardian, 30 Sept. 1932, p. 20.
[59] Leased to Mill Hill golf club. See p. 29.
[60] Hendon & Finchley Times, 30 Jan. 1925, p. 9.
[61] Boro. Incorp. Booklet penes Hendon Libr.
[62] See p. 15.
[63] Boro. of Hendon, Official Guide [1961]. The figure includes Edgware.
[64] Hopkins, Hendon, 72, 98.
[65] Pevsner, Mdx. 108.
[66] Hopkins, Hendon, 71.
[67] Ibid. 73.
[68] Ex inf. Hendon Libr.
[69] Barnet L.B., Official Guide [1967].
[70] Building News, lxxxiii. 788–9; c. 698; cvi. 401; cx. 44.
[71] Pevsner, Mdx. 57.
[72] Kelly's Dir. Mdx. (1937).
[73] Inscription on tombstone of Frances Salaman.
[74] Ex inf. Mr. E. M. Marmorstein.
[75] V.C.H. Mdx. i. 123.
[76] Westm. Domesday, f. 3b. See below.

[77] St. Paul's MS. W.D.9, f. 85.
[78] Cal. Pat. 1467–77, 601. Reserved for treatment under Hampstead.
[79] Park, Topog. of Hampstead, 212–13.
[80] See p. 16.
[81] Westm. Domesday, f. 3b.
[82] Ibid. f. 627.
[83] St. Paul's MS. 1453.
[84] Hennessy, Novum Repertorium, 214–15.
[85] Cal. Pat. 1467–77, 601.
[86] Cal. Pat. 1550–3, 7.
[87] St. Paul's MS. W.D.9, f. 85.
[88] Hennessy, Novum Repertorium, 215.
[89] L. & P. Hen. VIII, xvi, pp. 243–4.
[90] Cal. Pat. 1550–3, 7.
[91] Hennessy, Novum Repertorium, 215.
[92] Evans, Hendon, 88.
[93] Hennessy, Novum Repertorium, 216.
[94] Kelly's Dir. Mdx. (1890).   [95] Crockford (1940, 1947).
[96] St. Paul's MS. W.D.9, f. 85.
[97] Newcourt, Repertorium, i. 642.
[98] Valor Eccl. (Rec. Com.), i. 433.

by £37 from the profits of the rectory.[99] The vicar's stipend was increased by £100 in 1694, after the attainder of Lord Powis,[1] but the grant was revoked after the manor had returned to the Herberts.[2] The endowment was chiefly drawn c. 1705 from the small tithes, including 6d. for each new-born lamb and 1d. for every barren ewe; pigs, geese, ducks, honey, wool, and other articles were also taken.[3] Apart from the profits from the lambs the tithes were not worth more than £10 but except when lambs failed the vicar thought his income 'generally considerable'. In 1706 the vestry offered him £80 out of the church rates in lieu of tithes, in return for which he was to preach twice each Sunday and read Mattins twice a week during the summer.[4] The arrangement excluded the lucrative burial fees for non-parishioners, which were divided between the vicar and the parish. In 1814 the vicar, Theodore Williams, who maintained that the parish's share of the money was wasted at vestry meetings,[5] refused to bury non-parishioners, but the vestry won its suit in the consistory court.[6] In 1835 the gross income of the vicarage was £1,300, out of which was paid an assistant curate's annual stipend of £100 and other sums amounting to £20.[7] In 1843 the vicar was given an annual rent-charge of £850 in lieu of small tithes.[8] The vicarial glebe amounted in 1640 to 4 a. of pasture adjoining the vicarage house[9] and remained intact until the 1930s, when it was sold for the building of Glebe Crescent and the Quadrant.[10] The vicarage house in Parson Street is an early-19th-century stuccoed villa, in whose garden Theodore Williams kept a noted collection of potted coniferous trees.[11]

A chantry priest in 1547 was paid £8 a year for a term of twenty years out of the profits of houses and lands in Hendon to sing masses for the soul of Allen Brent.[12] An obit was founded in 1492 under the will of John Atwood, who left 6s. 8d. a year for prayers to be said by the parish clerk and for a candle before the Easter Sepulchre each year.[13] The profits of a tenement and three closes were devoted in 1547 to an obit established by Richard Brent.[14]

Several of the pre-Reformation vicars were pluralists; Robert Shether, for instance, held two other benefices in 1535.[15] In 1586 the vicar was non-resident and his curate was absent at the time of the diocesan examination in the Scriptures,[16] whereas in 1640 a 'very able' minister preached twice each Sunday.[17] Francis Warham, appointed by Parliament in 1643, was a lecturer at the church of St. Mary Magdalen, Milk Street, London, and was said to serve the cure diligently[18] but was ejected in 1662.[19] During the 18th century services were held twice on Sundays, with Holy Communion monthly and at festivals.[20] In 1778 there was an average of fifty communicants[21] but by 1810 the number had dropped to ten.[22] With the exception of Hugh Bailey, 1787–90, all 18th- and 19th-century vicars seem to have resided.[23] There was a charity sermon at Hendon church in the 18th century and in 1795 Robert Johnson endowed a sermon to be preached there before officials of the Stationers' Company of London on the text: 'The Life of man is a bubble'.[24] William Wilberforce wrote in 1830 on the wretched spiritual state of the parish,[25] while his neighbour Sir Stamford Raffles noted in 1826[26] how Theodore Williams had antagonized most of his parishioners; in 1823, during the dispute over burial fees, the vicar had demolished a new tomb in the churchyard and scattered the materials in the road outside.[27] Although the vestry thought that the vicar's attitude promoted secession, church attendances increased: in 1851 an average of 500 to 700 worshippers attended morning service at the parish church, as well as 250 in the afternoon and 300 to 600 in the evening, while some 25 attended a Sunday evening cottage lecture.[28] The vicar was indicted in 1906, along with the vicar of St. John's, West Hendon, for High Church practices, which included the use of eucharistic vestments, candles on the high altar, and the daily celebration of communion.[29] The Anglo-Catholic tradition has since been maintained in several churches, including the old parish church and St. Jude-on-the-Hill.[30]

Among those who held the benefice in the Middle Ages was William Dudley (d. 1483), rector from 1466, who became bishop of Durham in 1476 and chancellor of Oxford University in 1483.[31] Richard Rawlins (d. 1536) became vicar in 1504, warden of Merton College, Oxford, from 1508 to 1521 and bishop of St. Davids in 1523.[32] James Townley, 1768–77, was the author of several farces,[33] while his curate, Henry Bate, later Sir Henry Bate Dudley, Bt., became a noted journalist. Bate, known as 'the fighting parson',[34] was a friend of David Garrick, the patron of the living.[35] F. H. A. Scrivener, who succeeded Theodore Williams in 1875, was a noted classical scholar.[36]

The parish church of ST. MARY is built of flint rubble and pudding-stone with Reigate stone dressings; the tower is of ragstone, while the modern south aisle is of Portland and Weldon stone.[37] Excavations during restoration in 1929–31 are said

[99] Home Cnties. Mag. i. 320–1.
[1] Cal. Treas. Bks. 1693–6, 530.
[2] Lysons, Environs, iii. 14.
[3] Lambeth Palace, MS. 1298.
[4] Hendon Libr., MS. L. 126.
[5] Ibid. L. 129.
[6] Evans, Hendon, 173.
[7] Rep. Com. Eccl. Revenues, 651.
[8] M.R.O., TA/HEN. [9] Home Cnties. Mag. i. 320–1.
[10] F. Hitchin-Kemp, 'Notes on Hist. of Hendon' (TS. penes Hendon Libr.).
[11] Gardeners' Mag. xiv (1838), 220–232.
[12] E 301/34 m. 28.
[13] Hitchin-Kemp, 'Notes on Hist. of Hendon Ch.' (TS. penes Hendon Libr.).
[14] E 301/34 m. 28.
[15] L. & P. Hen. VIII, ix, p. 309.
[16] Guildhall MS. 9537/6. [17] S.P. 17/H, f. 609.
[18] Home Cnties. Mag. i. 320–1.
[19] Calamy Revised, ed. Matthews, 510.
[20] Guildhall MS. 9550.
[21] Ibid. 9557.
[22] Ibid. 9558, f. 449.
[23] Ibid. 9550, 9557. [24] Evans, Hendon, 120–1.
[25] R. and S. Wilberforce, Life of Wilberforce, v. 310.
[26] Wurtzburg, Raffles of the Eastern Isles, 724.
[27] Hendon Libr., MS. L. 130.
[28] H.O. 129/134/4/1/2–3.
[29] Rep. Cttee. on Eccl. Discipline [C. 3069], pp. 144–5, H.C. (1906), xxxiii.
[30] See below.
[31] D.N.B.
[32] Ibid.
[33] Ibid.
[34] Robbins, Mdx. 155.
[35] Evans, Hendon, 85–7; D.N.B. [36] D.N.B.
[37] Except where otherwise stated, the foll. account is based on Hist. Mon. Com. Mdx. 71–2, and F. C. Eeles, Parish Ch. of St. Mary, Hendon (1931). See also below, plate facing p. 81.

to have revealed the foundations of the 12th-century chancel. The church was rebuilt and enlarged in the 13th, 15th, and early 16th centuries. There were restorations in 1783 and 1827 and in 1915 the building was doubled in size, giving it an almost square plan. The east wall of the chancel contains 13th-century arcading, springing from foliated capitals, and fragments of contemporary wall-paintings were discovered near by between 1929 and 1931. The east window of three lights was added in 1408 under the will of John Ware, canon of St. Stephen's, Westminster.[38] Aisles were added to the nave in the 13th century, and the existing three-bay south nave arcade, supported on low octagonal piers, dates from that time. The north nave arcade, also of three bays, was rebuilt in the 15th century, when the clerestory and flat-pitched wooden nave roof were also built. The clerestory windows, which have no tracery, date from the 18th century. The embattled western tower, of three storeys, was built during the 15th century and repaired in 1783.[39] The chapel north of the chancel, lit by two three-light windows, was added in the early 16th century.

The interior was considerably altered after the Reformation by the addition of galleries, of which there were two by 1691, belonging to Sir William Rawlinson and to John Nicholl of Hendon Place.[40] Another gallery was added at the west end in 1788 to hold the charity school children.[41] Extensive repairs were carried out in 1827 by T. H. Taylor, after a scheme to demolish the old nave and build a new one of brick had been quashed by the vestry;[42] work included the construction of more galleries and of the chancel arch and wide arches in the chancel walls. With the ritualistic changes of the later 19th century the three-decker pulpit was removed, the chancel floor tiled, and the north chapel transformed by the removal of a gallery and the insertion of an altar to the designs of G. F. Bodley. In 1915 the south aisle was replaced by a new nave, south aisle, and south porch, designed by Temple Moore in a restrained late Gothic style; the new nave and south aisle were equal in height and separated by an arcade of seven bays, the columns of which were without capitals. The effect was to produce a light and spacious appearance, which was enhanced in 1929-31, when some 19th-century features were removed from the older part of the church and the walls were plastered.

The church contains a mid- to late-12th-century font and three small brasses, of which the earliest, to John Downer, is dated 1515. Monuments include a large black marble floor slab of 1677 to Sir Jeremy Whichcote of Hendon House, a large wall monument to Sir William Rawlinson erected in 1705, with a life-sized reclining effigy, a draped marble tablet dated 1714 to Edward Fowler (1632–1714), bishop of Gloucester, and wall monuments to Sir Charles Colman by the younger Flaxman, dated 1795, and

to Giles Earle by J. Smith, dated 1811. In the south aisle there is a painting of the Flight into Egypt by a member of the school of the Bassani. The plate includes a silver-gilt cup and paten-cover dated 1607, a silver-gilt paten probably of the late 17th century, and a silver-gilt flagon dated 1730. There are also two chalices, two patens, and two cruets, designed by G. F. Bodley in 1890.[43] There are six bells: (i) and (vi) Lester and Pack, 1759; (ii) Brian Eldridge, 1637; (iii) Ellis Knight, 1638; (iv) Thomas Mears, 1802; (v) James Bartlett, 1690.[44] The registers are complete from 1653. Among those buried in the churchyard are: Charles Johnson (1679–1748), dramatist; Sir Joseph Ayloffe, Bt. (1709–81), antiquary; Nathaniel Hone (1718–84), portrait painter; George Carter (1737–94), painter; and Benjamin Travers (1783–1858), eye surgeon.[45]

A rise in the population of Mill Hill led to many proposals in the early 19th century to build a church there. Arrangements were said by the vestry to be well advanced in 1826[46] but nothing had been done by 1828, when William Wilberforce proposed to build a chapel near his house at Highwood Hill, with the aid of private contributions.[47] After remonstrances by Theodore Williams he agreed to locate it farther south, on the Ridgeway, but the vicar replied with a pamphlet attributing mercenary motives to Wilberforce and maintaining that any chapel would be injurious to religion and private property.[48] Williams refused to allow a district to be allotted to the chapel, the building of which began in 1829 and, despite support for it from both the bishop of London and the Ecclesiastical Commissioners, the consecration of the chapel of ST. PAUL, Mill Hill, was delayed until a few days after Wilberforce's death in 1833.[49] As the main benefactor, Wilberforce appointed the first minister, although Williams continued to claim the patronage; in 1838 the case was still being argued[50] but by 1855 the vicar had become patron and St. Paul's, described as a district chapel, was served by a curate of the parish church.[51] The patronage passed later to the Revd. E. C. Lethbridge, who transferred it in 1896 to the bishop of London, with whom it remained in 1970.[52] The church, which was erected on land given by Sir Charles Flower,[53] was designed by Samuel Hood Page[54] in a plain Gothic style. It is built of brick, later stuccoed and painted, and has a short chancel and a nave with a west gallery supported on slender cast-iron columns. In addition to private monuments the interior houses several memorials and banners relating to the Middlesex Regiment.

The district chapelry of ALL SAINTS, Childs Hill, was formed in 1857 out of the southern part of St. Mary's parish, services having formerly been held in a laundry belonging to Mrs. Hipwell.[55] It was served by a perpetual curate, appointed by the vicar of Hendon,[56] but by 1878 the living was described as a vicarage, in the gift of trustees.[57] The

[38] Prob. 11/2A (P.C.C. 20 Marche).
[39] Rainwater heads.   [40] Hendon Libr., MS. L. 286.
[41] Ibid. L. 128.
[42] Ibid. L. 130.   [43] Freshfield, *Communion Plate*, 31.
[44] *T.L.M.A.S.* xvii. 144.
[45] *D.N.B.*; Lysons, *Environs*, iii. 12, 17–19.
[46] Hendon Libr., MS. L. 130.
[47] *Life of Wilberforce*, v. 299.
[48] *Correspondence of Bp. of Lond. and Revd. Theodore Williams* (1829), 2, *penes* Hendon Libr.

[49] *Life of Wilberforce*, v. 303–11.
[50] Ibid. 312.
[51] *Kelly's Dir. Home Cnties.* (1855).
[52] *47th Rep. Eccl. Com.* [C. 8391], p. 52, H.C. (1897), xxiv.
[53] Evans, *Hendon*, 176.   [54] M.R.O., Acc. 516.
[55] *Returns of Districts assigned to Churches, 1856–61* [C. 267], p. 10, H.C. (1862), xli; TS. notes on the church *penes* the vicar.
[56] *Kelly's Dir. Mdx.* (1862).   [57] Ibid. (1878).

patronage was transferred in 1908 by Sir Samuel Hoare, Bt., and others to the bishop of London, with whom it remained in 1970.[58] The church, which was consecrated in 1856,[59] was designed, like the adjacent red-brick vicarage, by Thomas Talbot Bury. It is built of ragstone in the 'middle pointed' style and had originally only a short aisled chancel and a nave, although it was probably intended to be enlarged later; the north aisle and transept were added in 1878[60] and the south aisle and transept in 1884. The church was badly damaged by fire in 1940 and restored in 1952.

CHRIST CHURCH, Brent Street, was built in 1881 to the designs of S. Salter as a chapel-of-ease served by the clergy of Hendon parish church.[61] It became the centre of a new parish, formed out of St. Mary's in 1923, and in 1970 the patronage was held by the bishop of London.[62] The church, a small and plain ragstone building in an early Decorated style, consists of an aisled and clerestoried nave, north porch, and chancel. The rood screen was designed by Temple Moore in 1896.[63]

Services for Anglicans in the Cricklewood area were held from 1882 in a combined mission church and schoolroom in Cricklewood Lane designed by Ewan Christian.[64] The permanent church of ST. PETER, Cricklewood, on a site given by the Ecclesiastical Commissioners,[65] was dedicated in 1891 and became in 1892 the centre of a district chapelry formed out of the parishes of St. Mary, Hendon, and All Saints, Childs Hill.[66] The patronage was held by the vicar of All Saints but was transferred in 1910 to the bishop of London, who held it in 1970.[67] The church, a large building in a plain French Gothic style, was designed by T. H. Watson.[68] It is of uncoursed Burgate stone and has a clerestoried nave, with aisles and small transepts, and a south-eastern chapel. A Perpendicular chancel and Lady Chapel were added in 1911 and the nave was extended to the west in 1912.[69] The church was closed in 1971 and awaited demolition in 1972, when services were held in the neighbouring parish hall and at the chapel of Little St. Peter, Claremont Way.[70]

A temporary iron church was built in Edgware Road in 1866 to serve Anglicans in West Hendon.[71] Services were later held in another building, in Milton Road, shared with St. John's school.[72] The permanent church of ST. JOHN, West Hendon, in Algernon Road, was consecrated in 1896 and in the same year became the centre of a district chapelry formed out of the parish of St. Mary, Hendon; the advowson was vested in the bishop of London.[73] The church, which was designed by Temple Moore in a late Gothic style, is a spacious

and lofty building of yellow brick and has an undivided chancel and nave, with the south aisle continued as a south chapel. A north arcade was provided for an aisle but this and the belfry were not built. Among the fittings are some panelling from two of Wren's London churches, St. George, Botolph Lane (demolished 1904), and St. Bartholomew-by-the-Exchange (demolished 1902), a font and cover of the same date, and a mid-18th-century pulpit from St. Michael Bassishaw (demolished 1900).[74]

The first Anglican worshippers in Hampstead Garden Suburb met from 1908 in a wooden hut.[75] In 1909 services were transferred to the Institute and in 1911 the church of ST. JUDE-on-the-HILL was consecrated, as the centre of a new district chapelry taken from the parish of St. Mary, the patron being the bishop of London. The Lady Chapel had been consecrated in 1910 but the church was not completed until 1935.[76] The architect was Sir Edwin Lutyens, whose building, with its lofty spire and steeply-pitched roof covering both nave and aisles and extending nearly to ground level, is a prominent landmark. The plan is cruciform, with aisles to both nave and chancel and chapels to north-east and south-east. The style shows a mixture of influences from Byzantine to English 18th-century. Apart from the west window the nave is lit only by square-headed dormers set on the aisle walls and the dimness is emphasized by the woodwork and bare brick.

At Golders Green services were held from 1910 in an iron church in Golders Green Road, which occupied the site of the church hall of ST. MICHAEL.[77] The church was begun in 1914, when its parish was taken from that of St. Mary, Hendon. In 1970 the living was in the gift of the bishop of London.[78] The original church, designed by J. T. Lee of Tufnell Park and not orientated, is a large Gothic building of buff brick with an aisled, galleried, and clerestoried chancel, an east chancel chapel, and an aisled and clerestoried nave of three bays.[79] Two more bays were added to the nave in 1925 by Caroë and Passmore and a low north-western tower, surmounted by a classical cupola, was added in 1960. From 1970 the church was shared with a Greek Orthodox community, which had used Christ Church, Brent Street, in 1968,[80] and part of the light and spacious interior was furnished for Orthodox worship.

The church of ST. ALBAN, Golders Green, was built as a chapel-of-ease to All Saints', Childs Hill, in 1910.[81] It became the centre of a new parish taken from that of All Saints in 1922: in 1970 the patron of the living was the bishop of London.[82]

[58] 61st Rep. Eccl. Com. [Cd. 4541], p. 67, H.C. (1909), xvi; Lond. Dioc. Bk. (1970).
[59] Except where otherwise stated, the foll. account is based on TS. notes penes the vicar.
[60] Evans, Hendon, 179.
[61] Ibid. 182.
[62] Lond. Dioc. Bk. (1970).
[63] Ex inf. the vicar.
[64] Evans, Hendon, 179. For the school see below, p. 45.
[65] Dexter, Cricklewood, 51.
[66] Return of Parishes Divided, 1891–6, H.C. 302, p. 10 (1897), lxvii (6).
[67] 62nd Rep. Eccl. Com. [Cd. 5551], p. 67, H.C. (1911), xv; Lond. Dioc. Bk. (1970).
[68] T.L.M.A.S. xviii(2), no. 111.
[69] Kelly's Dir. Mdx. (1937).

[70] Ex inf. the vicar; see p. 37.
[71] Evans, Hendon, 182.
[72] Nat. Soc. files.
[73] Return of Parishes Divided, 1891–6, H.C. 302, p. 14 (1897), lxvii (6); Lond. Dioc. Bk. (1970).
[74] T.L.M.A.S. xviii(2), no. 106; Building News, lxxiii. 365. Architectural drawings of 1894–5 are at the vicarage.
[75] Section based on inf. supplied by the vicar.
[76] Lond. Dioc. Bk. (1970).
[77] Except where otherwise stated, the section is based on inf. supplied by the vice-chairman of the par. ch. council and on T.L.M.A.S. xviii(2), no. 108.
[78] Lond. Dioc. Bk. (1970).   [79] Architect, xiv. 321–2.
[80] Barnet L.B., List of Religious Orgs. (1968).
[81] Section based on inf. supplied by Mr. V. C. Cordingley.
[82] Lond. Dioc. Bk. (1970).

The original church, a simple brick building, became the parish hall in 1933, when another church was built adjacent to it. The second church was by Sir Giles Gilbert Scott, who also designed most of the fittings, and in a Gothic-inspired style. It is of dark red brick with stone dressings and has a cruciform plan with a massive central tower surmounted by a short spire.

Temple Fortune was served from the 1890s by a mission under the control of St. Mary's, Hendon, which conducted services at no. 24 Hendon Park Row.[83] In 1915 its functions were taken over by a London Diocesan Home Mission dedicated to the Holy Name, which held services in a temporary building in Cranbourne Gardens, serving also as a church hall. The mission district became the consolidated chapelry of *ST. BARNABAS*, Temple Fortune, in 1923, taken from the parishes of St. Mary, Hendon, and St. Mary, Finchley. In 1970 the living was described as a vicarage in the gift of the bishop of London.[84] The original church of 1915, which was aligned north to south, was designed by J. S. Alder and had a nave with apsidal sanctuary, south porch, and east vestries. The chancel, part of the nave and the Lady Chapel of a new church designed by E. C. Sherman were built at its north end in 1932–4 but it was not until 1962 that a new aisled nave, replacing that of J. S. Alder, was dedicated. The architect was R. B. Craze and although the building is much plainer than had been intended in 1932 it matches the north end in scale, the colour of the brickwork, and the simple Gothic-inspired design.[85]

A brick church in Flower Lane, serving the area around the Midland Railway station at Mill Hill, was consecrated in 1909.[86] It became the church hall in 1922, when the chancel and two bays of the nave of the permanent church of *ST. MICHAEL and ALL ANGELS*, Mill Hill, were consecrated on an adjacent site. This church became the centre of a new parish, taken out of that of St. Paul, Mill Hill, in 1926, and in 1970 the bishop of London was patron of the living.[87] The church is built of uncoursed ashlar in a 15th-century Gothic style, with some rich interior detail; the architects were W. D. Caroë and Passmore.[88] The sanctuary was consecrated in 1932 and the church was finally completed in 1957, when the end bays of the aisled nave, a chapel, baptistry, vestries, and porches were added.

A mission church in East Road, Burnt Oak, dedicated to St. Paul and served from St. John, West Hendon, was consecrated in 1904; the building, which was of corrugated iron, had formerly been occupied by Burnt Oak National school.[89] It ceased to be used for worship in 1927, when the church of *ST. ALPHAGE*, Burnt Oak, was built in Montrose Avenue, as the centre of a new parish

which covered the Watling estate; in 1970 the living was in the gift of the bishop of London.[90] The architect of the church, a plain brick building with a basilican plan in the Early Christian style, was J. E. Dixon-Spain; the church was restored in 1952 after war-damage.[91]

The ecclesiastical district of *JOHN KEBLE* church, Mill Hill, was created in 1932 to serve the area around the Hale. A parish was created out of St. Michael, Mill Hill, and St. Alphage, Burnt Oak, in 1937,[92] and in 1970 the patron of the living, a vicarage, was the bishop of London.[93] The congregation worshipped for the first six months of 1932 in a wooden hut in Deans Lane, before moving to a dual-purpose hall and church, later the parish hall.[94] A permanent church was consecrated in 1936. It was designed by D. F. Martin-Smith and ranked as one of the more notable modern churches in Middlesex. Built of brick around a reinforced concrete frame, it has a square plan with a flat coffered ceiling and a spacious interior unencumbered with columns. The altar is set in a recess in the east wall and there is a west gallery and tower.[95]

There was a mission church at Colindale in 1905, dedicated to St. Mellitus and served by clergy from St. John's, West Hendon.[96] With the building of St. Alphage's, Burnt Oak, in 1927, the mission church became a parish hall.[97] In 1934 the mission district of *ST. MATTHIAS*, Colindale, was formed out of the parishes of St. John, West Hendon, and St. Alphage.[98] Services were held in a dual-purpose church and hall in Rushgrove Avenue which had been given in that year by Christ Church, Lancaster Gate (Paddington). The district became a parish in 1951 and in 1970 the benefice was a vicarage in the gift of the bishop of London.[99] In 1972 work was started on a permanent church, behind the dual-purpose building, designed by R. W. Hurst.

In 1934 the mission church of St. Mary Magdalen, Holders Hill Road, was opened as a chapel-of-ease to St. Mary's parish church.[1] The church is a plain wooden hut. In 1958 the mission chapel of Little St. Peter, Claremont Way, was founded as a chapel-of-ease to St. Peter, Cricklewood, and was served in 1970 by a deaconess.[2]

ROMAN CATHOLICISM.[3] In 1577 a resident of Hendon, Thomas Devell, was a recusant member of Staple Inn[4] and in 1583 one Vicars, possibly a Roman Catholic priest educated at Lincoln College, Oxford, was teaching Sir Edward Herbert's children in Hendon.[5] There were no recusants in the parish in 1593, after the Herberts had moved,[6] but William Everingham was indicted in 1610 and his wife in 1612.[7] No indictments for recusancy were recorded after 1625[8] and in 1676 there were no papists in the

[83] Golden Jubilee Commem. Booklet (1964) *penes* the vicar, St. Barnabas.   [84] *Lond. Dioc. Bk.* (1970).
[85] E. H. Bustard, *St. Barnabas Ch. Temple Fortune: 1915–65.*   [86] Section based on inf. supplied by the vicar.
[87] *Lond. Dioc. Bk.* (1970).
[88] *T.L.M.A.S.* xviii(2), no. 109.
[89] Nat. Soc. files.   [90] *Lond. Dioc. Bk.* (1970).
[91] *T.L.M.A.S.* xviii(2), no. 113.
[92] Pamphlet *penes* Hendon Libr.
[93] *Lond. Dioc. Bk.* (1970).
[94] Pamphlet *penes* Hendon Libr.
[95] *T.L.M.A.S.* xviii(2), no. 103.
[96] *Hendon Dir. and Local Compendium* (1905).

[97] *Kelly's Dir. Mdx.* (1933).
[98] Section based on inf. supplied by the vicar.
[99] *Lond. Dioc. Bk.* (1970).
[1] Ex inf. the priest-in-charge.
[2] *Lond. Dioc. Bk.* (1970).
[3] Much material for the sections on Roman Catholicism and Protestant Nonconformity was collected by Mr. G. R. Thomas.
[4] *Miscellanea* (Cath. Rec. Soc. xii), 108.
[5] S.P. 12/168/25(2); *London Recusant*, i. 9.
[6] *Recusants' Rolls* (Cath. Rec. Soc. xviii), *passim.*
[7] M.R.O., Cal. Reg. Bk. of Indictments, i. 2, 18.
[8] *Mdx. Cnty. Recs.* iii. 5 and *passim.*

parish.[9] Edward Herbert of Gray's Inn, a Roman Catholic resident in 1706, was probably a distant relative of the absentee lord of the manor.[10]

In 1849 Passionist fathers from Poplar House, West End Lane, Hampstead, set up a temporary chapel at the Hyde to serve a substantial local congregation.[11] Later in that year the Passionists left Hampstead for a house in Hyde Lane (probably the modern Kingsbury Road), where the billiard-room was converted into a chapel dedicated to St. Joseph. In 1851 50 persons attended services there.[12] In 1852 the building, which was demolished in 1934, was exchanged for the larger Woodfield House in Cool Oak Lane,[13] which was renamed St. Joseph's Retreat. From there the fathers directed missions in north-west London, Middlesex, and the Barnet area. Foundations were laid in the grounds for a large monastery[14] but from lack of funds work was limited to extending the house and the temporary chapel. In 1858 the Passionists moved to Highgate Hill, where they remained in 1970.

The Passionists established a chapel in a wooden hut near the Burroughs in 1850, which became the centre of Roman Catholic worship in Hendon after the departure of the community.[15] In 1863 the hut was replaced by a church of ragstone in the Early English style, dedicated to Our Lady of Dolours; it was reconstructed as a low cruciform building with an aisled nave in 1927, to the designs of T. H. B. Scott, but was not finally consecrated until 1966. St. John's hall, West Hendon, acquired by the church c. 1962 and renamed St. Patrick's hall, was registered for worship in 1964[16] and was served by its own priest in 1969.

The church of St. Agnes, Cricklewood Lane, opened in 1883 as an iron building,[17] which was replaced by another temporary structure in Gillingham Road in 1920.[18] A permanent church in Cricklewood Lane was consecrated in 1929.[19] It is a large plain brick building in the Early Christian manner, with nave, narrow aisles, and an apsidal chancel.

The chapel of St. Vincent's convent, the Ridgeway, served Mill Hill after its opening in 1887[20] and a mission was later begun by Vincentians in Flower Lane, near the Midland Railway station.[21] In 1923 a permanent church, dedicated to the Sacred Heart and Mary Immaculate, was opened in Flower Lane and in 1968 a parish centre was added.[22] The church is of brick with stone dressings, in the Byzantine manner, and has a basilican plan.

A mission was established at Golders Green shortly before 1909[23] and the permanent church of St. Edward the Confessor, Finchley Road, was opened in 1915.[24] The church was designed by A. Young[25] as a cruciform building of brick in the Perpendicular style, surmounted by a prominent central lantern tower.

Services on the Watling estate were first held in 1928 in a hut in Thirleby Road. The permanent church of the Annunciation, financed by an anonymous benefactor, was opened in 1929.[26]

Hendon is notable for its large number of Roman Catholic institutions. Apart from the Passionists the earliest was St. Joseph's Society for Foreign Missions, which moved into Holcombe House in 1866[27] and provided the first systematic training for Roman Catholic missionaries in England. In 1871 a brick building to house 72 students, designed by Goldie and Child in a 'freely treated style' was opened in Lawrence Street on part of the same estate; a large apsidal chapel in the French Gothic style, occupying one side of a courtyard, was opened in 1873.[28] The college, which was extended in 1896, 1923, and 1929, is dominated by the tower of the chapel, which is surmounted by a gilded statue of St. Joseph. Cardinal Vaughan (d. 1903), who helped to establish the society at Mill Hill, is buried in the grounds. In 1969 there were 61 student missionaries at St. Joseph's college, which was the headquarters of the society and the residence of its superior general. It was served by nuns of the Pontifical Society of the Franciscan Missionaries of St. Joseph, whose first members took their vows at Mill Hill in 1880.

In 1881 Holcombe House was acquired at Vaughan's instigation by a recently-founded congregation of Franciscan nuns of the Regular Third Order, who renamed it St. Mary's abbey.[29] A convent wing was added in 1883 and in 1889 the wooden chapel was replaced by a large brick cruciform building in a plain early Gothic style, with a central tower surmounted by a short pyramid spire. The nuns began missions in the 1880s and established several local schools.[30] In 1952 a separate missionary congregation was established and in 1969 the sisters at Mill Hill were engaged only in education, although the abbey also served as their administrative centre and housed the regional superior.

The British Province of the Sisters of Charity of St. Vincent de Paul purchased Littleberries and its adjoining 40 a. in 1885.[31] A seminary block was begun in 1886 and in 1887 a large stone chapel, designed in the Perpendicular style by F. W. Tasker, was opened; it was rebuilt after a fire in 1935. Other additions have included a retreat block. In 1969 the convent was the administrative and training centre for the 1,200 sisters in the British province; it also supervised a school for deprived children, a nursery for abandoned babies, and a college for children's nurses on an adjoining site.

Sisters of St. Joseph, or Poor Handmaids of Jesus Christ, were established in Ravensfield House, Church End, in 1887.[32] In 1889 the community, whose work has always been chiefly educational,

[9] William Salt Libr. Stafford, Salt MS. 33 p. 40.
[10] Guildhall MS. 9800.
[11] Section based on inf. supplied by Father Sylvester Palmer, C.P.
[12] H.O. 129/135/4/1/7.   [13] For the house, see p. 10.
[14] Hendon Libr., Print L. 330.
[15] Section based on inf. supplied by the par. priest, Our Lady of Dolours.
[16] G.R.O. Worship Reg. no. 69775.
[17] Ex inf. the par. priest.
[18] G.R.O. Worship Reg. no. 47923.
[19] Ibid. 51820.
[20] Ibid. 30515. For the religious community, see below.
[21] Westminster Yr. Bk. (1969).
[22] Ex inf. the parish priest.
[23] Westminster Yr. Bk. (1969).
[24] G.R.O. Worship Reg. no. 46658.
[25] Ex inf. the par. priest.   [26] Ex inf. the par. priest.
[27] Section based on inf. supplied by the archivist, St. Joseph's coll.
[28] Builder, xxix. 964.
[29] Section based on inf. supplied by Sister Mary Gabriel.
[30] See p. 47.
[31] Section based on inf. supplied by the sec., St. Vincent's convent.
[32] Ex inf. the par. priest, Our Lady of Dolours.

moved to Norden Court, near the Burroughs, which was renamed St. Joseph's convent and greatly enlarged.[33] A school was attached to the convent in 1970.

Sisters of La Sagesse, known also as the Montfort sisters, settled in Cricklewood in 1903 after their expulsion from France. They engaged in social and educational work[34] and in 1909 moved to Woodstock House, Golders Green,[35] which was renamed La Sagesse convent. An adjoining school was built and in 1970 was served by 15 resident sisters.

Discalced Carmelite nuns of the Primitive Rule,[36] from Fulham, moved into a new convent in Bridge Lane in 1908. The community, an enclosed contemplative order, comprised 21 sisters in 1969.

Dominican sisters were established in 1930 in St. Rose's convent, Orange Hill Road.[37] A school was subsequently built in the grounds and served by the nuns.

The Poor Sisters of Nazareth, a charitable order founded in Hammersmith in 1851, purchased St. Swithins, Parson Street, in 1932 as a training centre and renamed it Nazareth House.[38] It served as an orphanage during the Second World War but later reverted to its original use; in 1969 the average number of residents was 25.

A congregation of St. Ottilien of the Benedictine Missionary Fathers, a German community, took over a house in Ashley Lane in the mid 1930s and renamed it St. Augustine's mission house.[39] Their chapel was in use before 1940.[40]

In 1967 the Society of the Catholic Apostolate, or Pallottine fathers, bought a house in Armitage Road, Golders Green, as the residence of the provincial. Three priests were living there in 1969.[41]

Religious communities which stayed only briefly in Hendon included the Society of the Holy Child Jesus, at Ravensfield in 1878,[42] and Franciscans who occupied a house in Hermitage Villas, Childs Hill, in 1890 but had left by 1902.[43] In 1937 some sisters of St. Peter's Community were at Brent Lodge, which had been renamed St. Peter's Ouvroir,[44] but they left the parish when the building was demolished. In 1969 a mission-house of the Catholic Missionary Society in West Heath Road, Golders Green, was served by Franciscan nuns.[45]

PROTESTANT NONCONFORMITY. Francis Warham, the vicar ejected in 1662,[46] was licensed as a Congregationalist in 1672,[47] when he was living at Upper Hale.[48] Richard Swift, ejected from Edgware in 1660,[49] was imprisoned on several occasions for holding conventicles in his house, Jeanettes, at Mill Hill.[50] The Independents who registered Samuel Everard's house at Childs Hill as a place of worship in 1672[51] may have been the dissenters who registered Mary Everett's house there in 1690.[52]

The Quakers were the most active of the early sectaries.[53] George Fox conducted a well-attended meeting in 1677 and returned in 1678. By the early 1680s there were regular meetings at Guttershedge and Mill Hill, supervised by a separate monthly meeting. Attendance at Mill Hill declined during the later 1680s, revived during the following decade, and was again declining by 1707. Thereafter numbers at both Mill Hill and Guttershedge continued to fall, until in 1729 the Hendon meetings were merged with the Peel meeting at Clerkenwell. After an abortive revival at Guttershedge in the 1730s both meeting-houses were sold, although several notable Quakers continued to live in Hendon.

Presbyterianism may have contributed to the Quakers' decline. In 1730 Mary Nicholl's house at Highwood Hill was registered by seven Presbyterians, led by Celia Fiennes, who owned the property.[54] By the end of the 18th century, however, it was claimed that there were no dissenters in the parish.[55]

Independents took a lead in the general revival of nonconformity, establishing places of worship at Highwood Hill in 1797[56] and in Parson Street in 1799.[57] In 1807 Independents founded Mill Hill school, whose chapel, used by local people,[58] was said in 1816 to be the only dissenters' meeting-place but to be thinly attended.[59] Independents began to meet in a cottage at Holcombe Hill in 1822[60] and at the Hyde in 1836,[61] but in 1851 Mill Hill school chapel was their sole place of worship, with an average morning attendance of 200.[62]

Wesleyan Methodism was introduced by Henry Burden, whose open-air preaching at the Burroughs was violently opposed.[63] His house in Brent Street was registered for worship in 1821, another house was registered in 1824,[64] and in 1827 a permanent chapel opened in Chapel Walk.[65]

Baptists used a house at Childs Hill in 1823,[66] registered a house at the Burroughs in 1831,[67] and built a small chapel in Brent Street in 1832. After 1843 the chapel served as a warehouse[68] until it was taken over in 1845 by the Shouldham Street Baptist chapel, St. Marylebone, which share it with

---

[33] Hitchin-Kemp, 'Notes on a Survey', *penes* Hendon Libr. 113.
[34] Section based on inf. supplied by the superior, La Sagesse convent.   [35] See p. 11.
[36] Section based on inf. supplied by Sister Ann Fitzherbert.
[37] Ex inf. the par. priest, the Annunciation, Burnt Oak.
[38] Section based on inf. supplied by the Sisters of Nazareth. For St. Swithins house, see p. 12.
[39] *Catholic Dir.* (1937).
[40] G.R.O. Worship Reg. no. 59426.
[41] Ex inf. the bursar.
[42] *Kelly's Dir. Mdx.* (1878).   [43] Ibid. (1890, 1902).
[44] Ibid. (1937); for the house, see p. 10.
[45] *Westminster Year Bk.* (1969).   [46] See p. 34.
[47] G. Nuttall, *Visible Saints*, 116.
[48] *Trans. Congreg. Hist. Soc.* xvi. 33.
[49] *V.C.H. Mdx.* iv. 164.
[50] A. G. Matthews, *Calamy Revised*, 472; *Mdx. Cnty. Recs.* iii. 343; *Trans. Congreg. Hist. Soc.* xvi. 35.
[51] *Cal. S.P. Dom.* 1671–2, 309, 606.
[52] *Mdx. Cnty. Recs. Sess. Bks. 1689–1709*, 11; Brett-James, *Hendon*, 76.
[53] See below, p. 40.
[54] M.R.O., Acc. 96.
[55] Guildhall MSS. 9557, 9558.
[56] Guildhall MS. 9580/1.
[57] Ibid. /2.
[58] *Trans. Congreg. Hist. Soc.* xvi. 33. For the school, see *V.C.H. Mdx.* i. 307.
[59] Brewer, *Beauties of Eng. and Wales*, x(5), 687.
[60] Guildhall MS. 9580/5.
[61] Ibid. /7.
[62] H.O. 129/135/4/1/5.
[63] Mill Hill Hist. Soc., Add. Items 2.
[64] Guildhall MS. 9580/5.
[65] See below.
[66] Guildhall MS. 9580/5.
[67] Ibid. /7/28.
[68] F. M. Gravatt, *And We Their Deeds Record*, 9 sqq.

Congregationalists.[69] In 1851 there were 30 worshippers[70] but attendance dwindled after the opening of Hendon Congregational church and in 1857 services ceased.[71] Another Baptist church, founded at the Hyde in 1843, had closed by 1857.[72]

The late 19th century saw the permanent establishment of the major sects.[73] Congregationalists opened a chapel in Brent Street in 1855 and, after several setbacks, Baptists followed suit in Finchley Lane in 1878. Both groups owed much to local families, the Spaldings of Shire Hall and the Smarts of Brent Street, and both produced offshoots at the Hyde and Mill Hill. The Salvation Army appeared in 1881 and the Wesleyans moved to a larger chapel in 1891. On one Sunday in 1903 over two-fifths of the 7,823 worshippers were nonconformists, while Anglicans accounted for 2,932 and Roman Catholics for 1,391. Baptists constituted by far the largest sect, with an attendance of 1,277, while Wesleyan and Primitive Methodists together totalled 768.[74]

In the 20th century the older denominations erected small churches on the housing estates, while new sects arrived, many of them from the U.S.A. Two of the newcomers, the Pillar of Fire Society in 1926 and Jehovah's Witnesses in 1959, chose Hendon for their national headquarters. The inter-denominational church built in Hampstead Garden Suburb in 1910 was said at the time of opening to be unique in England.

SOCIETY OF FRIENDS. In 1678, the year after George Fox conducted a successful meeting at Ann Hayly's house at Guttershedge,[75] Quakers leased a low weatherboarded building in Mill Hill; the building was enlarged in 1693 and survived in 1970, when it was called Rosebank.[76] During the 1690s, after regular meetings had been established at Guttershedge and Mill Hill,[77] some local Quakers were distrained for their tithes.[78] The Mill Hill meeting, after a brief decline, registered new premises in 1692, acquired better ones by 1695, and erected a new meeting-house in 1701.[79] In 1707, however, falling attendance caused Apphia Nicholl to seek support from the London quarterly meeting. In 1709 meetings at both Mill Hill and Guttershedge were held once every two months,[80] by 1719 there were doubts about retaining a separate meeting for the Hendon area,[81] and in 1729 a merger was effected with the Peel meeting at Clerkenwell.[82] In 1733 an attempt was made to revive the meetings at

Guttershedge but within 6 years they had ceased.[83] The meeting-house was later sold, although the burial ground was reserved for Quakers,[84] and in 1739 the Mill Hill meeting-house also was sold.[85] Despite the cessation of regular worship, later Quaker residents included Michael Russell, Peter and Michael Collinson, and Richard Salisbury, all of whom lived at Ridgeway House, which became the nucleus of Mill Hill school.[86]

In the early 20th century Quakers at Hampstead Garden Suburb attended the services that preceded the establishment of the Free Church, before hiring their own room in the Club House, Willifield Green, in 1910. Largely as a result of the initiative of J. B. (later Sir John) Braithwaite, a permanent red-brick meeting-house, designed by Frederick Rowntree, was opened in Central Square in 1913.[87]

METHODISTS.[88] Hendon Methodist (W) church was built in Chapel Walk in 1827, six years after Henry Burden, the vicar's gardener, registered a house in Brent Street. The chapel originally accommodated 100 worshippers[89] but was extended in 1871.[90] A new church in the Burroughs was registered in 1891, as Hendon Methodist chapel,[91] and replaced in 1937 by a modernistic building of red brick, designed by Welch and Lander.[92] The Methodist institute was opened at the rear in 1910 and modernized and renamed the Henry Burden hall in 1964.[93]

Finchley Road (P) chapel had been built by 1895 for a group which had met at Childs Hill at least since 1882.[94] In 1915 the chapel was being used by the Salvation Army.[95]

Ridgeway Methodist (W) church originated in the late 1880s, when a Wesleyan mission was opened in a temporary iron hall in Mill Hill.[96] In 1893 a red-brick chapel in the Perpendicular style was built by the village pond.[97] At first Ridgeway Methodist church was under the control of Hendon Methodist church, but in 1970 it was linked with Goodwyn Avenue Methodist church.[98]

Booth Road (W) church was opened in Booth Road, Colindale, in 1908.[99] It survived in 1961[1] but had been closed by 1970.

Golders Green (W) church stood by 1915 at the corner of Armitage Road.[2] In 1922 it was replaced by a brick church in Hodford Road, built in the Byzantine style, with a square plan and four corner towers.[3]

[69] W. T. Whitley, *Baptists of Lond.* 171.
[70] H.O. 129/135/4/1/6.
[71] Whitley, *Baptists of Lond.* 171.   [72] Ibid. 167.
[73] The hist. of each chapel is given below.
[74] Mudie-Smith, *Rel. Life*, 419.
[75] *Short Jnl. and Itinerary Jnls. of Geo. Fox*, ed. N. Penney, 232, 270.
[76] W. Beck and T. F. Ball, *Lond. Friends' Meetings*, 309; *Trans. Congreg. Hist. Soc.* xvi. 37.
[77] Beck and Ball, op. cit. 71, 96, 290. The meeting, known as the Hendon 'monthly meeting', appears later to have supervised a meeting at South Mimms.
[78] Friends' Ho. MS. 59. Hubbersty was a Quaker preacher from Glos. who had settled in Hendon: *Jnl. of Geo. Fox*, i. 406.
[79] M.R.O., MR/R05/27; *Jnl. Friends Hist. Soc.* li. 181, 183, 187.
[80] Friends' Ho. Lond. Quarterly Meeting min. bk. 1703–13, ff. 127, 158–9.
[81] Beck and Ball, op. cit. 309.
[82] Friends' Ho. Peel min. bk. 1729–36.
[83] Ibid. 1736–44.
[84] Beck and Ball, *Lond. Friends' Meetings*, 308.

[85] *Jnl. Friends Hist. Soc.* li. 187.
[86] *Trans. Congreg. Hist. Soc.* xvi. 36.
[87] Ex inf. Miss M. E. Sullivan; G.R.O. Worship Reg. no. 45980; *Ill. Hist. of Hampstead Garden Suburb* (1954), 17.
[88] In the following accounts the letters (W) and (P) denote former Wesleyan and Primitive Methodist chs.
[89] Guildhall MS. 9580/5, 30 Sept. 1824; H.O. 129/135/4/1/4.
[90] Evans, *Hendon*, 187.
[91] G.R.O. Worship Reg. no. 32621.
[92] Hopkins, *Hendon*, 101; Robbins, *Mdx.* 289.
[93] Ex inf. the trust sec., Hendon Meth. ch.
[94] *Ret. of churches, chapels . . .* H.C. 401, p. 172 (1882), i; O.S. Map 1/2,500, Mdx. XI. 5 (1896 edn.).
[95] O.S. Map 1/2,500, Mdx. XI. 5 (1915 edn.).
[96] Evans, *Hendon*, 188.
[97] G.R.O. Worship Reg. no. 33640.
[98] See below.
[99] G.R.O. Worship Reg. no. 43295.
[1] Hendon, *Official Guide* [1961].
[2] O.S. Map 1/2,500, Mdx. XI. 11 (1915 edn.).
[3] G.R.O. Worship Reg. no. 48643.

Goodwyn Avenue (W) church, a brick building in the Perpendicular style, was opened in Mill Hill in 1930.[4] After the Second World War a hall was added at the rear.

CONGREGATIONALISTS. Hendon Congregational church[5] was opened in Brent Street in 1855. It was an aisleless building of Kentish ragstone in the Decorated style, designed by W. G. and E. Habershon.[6] In 1876 a gallery increased the number of seats to 500 and in 1901 a hall named after Thomas Spalding, one of the founders of the church, was opened. In 1950 the building was reopened after bomb damage and given stained glass windows from Avenue Road Congregational church, Swiss Cottage, which had closed in 1941. There was seating for 250 in 1972.[7]

The Hyde church originated in services in a hut in Edgware Road opposite Manor Farm in 1873.[8] Members became affiliated to Hendon Congregational church in 1900, at about the time when they built a permanent church. In 1909 Hendon Congregational church ceased to exercise responsibility and shortly afterwards the church at the Hyde closed for about four years.[9] It was reopened as a mission by Cricklewood Congregational church,[10] whose daughter church it had become by 1931.[11] The congregation transferred c. 1930 to a hall in Colin Close and became independent in 1936.[12] A new red-brick church, facing Edgware Road, was opened in 1956, when the building in Colin Close became a church hall.[13] The church built c. 1900 was used as a motor-car showroom in 1969.

Union church[14] was established by Congregationalists after the expansion of Mill Hill school had deprived them of the use of the school chapel. A small iron hall in Tennyson Road on the Birkbeck estate, formerly used by Baptists, was rented in 1908 and vacated in 1911, when services were started in a temporary building at the foot of Lawrence Street, later the Broadway. The church was renamed Union church in 1918 and a hall was built in 1927. The temporary church was replaced in 1936 by a cruciform building of red brick in a plain Gothic style, with an open timber roof and a low western tower, designed by Arnold Harwood and Martin Briggs.

Watling church was opened in Eversfield Gardens, on the edge of the Watling estate, in 1938.[15] It was dependent on Union church, until in 1942 it acquired its own minister.[16] The church was a plain brick hall, used also for social activities in 1970.[17]

Mill Hill East Free church began when members of Union church started a Sunday school in a hall in 1944, seven years before a permanent church was opened in Salcombe Gardens.[18] At first it was supervised by the minister of Watling church, with help from Union church, until in 1956 a full-time minister was appointed.[19] A new church, with a west wall of glass bricks and a pyramid-shaped roof, was opened in 1963, when the original brick building was converted into a church hall.[20]

BAPTISTS. Hendon Baptist church[21] was formed in 1873 by a group led by E. J. Smart, a Brent Street ironmonger, which had been meeting since c. 1869 in the former Hendon charity school in Church Road. In 1878 the congregation moved to an iron hall in Finchley Lane, built by Stephen Shirley as a temperance hall. A permanent church, seating 600, was opened in 1886 on a sloping site 80 yards to the west. It was designed by J. E. Sears in an individualistic version of 13th-century Gothic, and is an aisled cruciform building, whose crypt serves as a church hall.

West Hendon Baptist church arose from a Sunday school which was meeting in private premises in Pollard Road in 1884. Through the efforts of E. J. Smart, a mission hall, used also as a day school, was built in Edgware Road in 1885; the building survived behind a shop in 1970.[22] Members began meeting in new premises on the corner of Wilberforce and Station roads in 1898[23] and shared a minister with Hendon Baptist church until 1901.[24] A church of brick and pebble-dash was built in 1930.[25] It had seating for 250 in 1970,[26] when the old church was used as a hall.

Childs Hill Baptist chapel originated in open-air meetings which were held in a cock-pit at the Old Mead in 1865 and were transferred to a laundry in Granville Road in 1866,[27] shortly before the foundation of the chapel. In 1875 new premises in Granville Road, erected at the expense of Heath Street church, Hampstead, were registered for worship.[28] The church was built of brick in a partially Byzantine style and a hall of similar design was added later. The seating capacity was 400 in 1972.[29]

Claremont Baptist Free church originated in a mission started by Childs Hill Baptists in Claremont Road, Cricklewood, by 1928.[30] A separate church was formed in 1931,[31] when brick premises, registered in 1935, were erected between Claremont Road and Cheviot Gardens. A brick hall was added in 1958.[32] There was seating for 350 worshippers in 1972.[33]

Tennyson Road mission arose from a Baptist

---

[4] Ibid. 52487.
[5] The para. is based on Hendon Congreg. Ch. *Centenary Booklet* (1954).
[6] See plate facing p. 321.
[7] *Congreg. Yr. Bk.* (1971–2).
[8] O.S. Map 1/2,500, Mdx. XI. 6 (1896 edn.).
[9] Hendon Congreg. Ch. *Centenary Booklet* (1954); *Congreg. Yr. Bk.* (1906), 328; (1913), 280.
[10] *Congreg. Yr. Bk.* (1918), 238.
[11] Ibid. (1932), 322; O.S. Map 1/2,500, Mdx. XI. 6 (1937 edn.).
[12] *Congreg. Yr. Bk.* (1936), 380; (1938), 386.
[13] G.R.O. Worship Reg. no. 65652; *Congreg. Yr. Bk.* (1971–2).
[14] The para. is based on Union Ch. *Golden Jubilee Booklet* (1958).
[15] G.R.O. Worship Reg. no. 58438.
[16] *Congreg. Yr. Bk.* (1943), 144.
[17] Ex inf. the minister.

[18] Union Ch. *Golden Jubilee Booklet*.
[19] *Congreg. Yr. Bk.* (1952), 205; (1957), 207; (1967–8), 218.
[20] G.R.O. Worship Reg. no. 69284.
[21] The para. is based on Gravatt, *And We Their Deeds Record*.
[22] Gravatt, op. cit. 21–2.
[23] O.S. Map 1/2,500, Mdx. XI. 10 (1914 edn.).
[24] Whitley, *Baptists of Lond.* 215, 247.
[25] Date on church.
[26] *Baptist Handbk.* (1970).
[27] Gravatt, op. cit. 14.
[28] G.R.O. Worship Reg. no. 22498; ex inf. the pastor.
[29] *Baptist Handbk.* (1972).
[30] Whitley, op. cit. 221.
[31] *Baptist Handbk.* (1933).
[32] G.R.O. Worship Reg. no. 56399; dates on church and hall.
[33] *Baptist Handbk.* (1933).

group which was flourishing at Mill Hill in 1881.[34] A chapel was built in Tennyson Road between 1894 and 1896 but by 1906 had been leased to the Brethren.[35] In 1908 the building became the first meeting-place of Union Congregational church.

STRICT BAPTISTS. In 1938 a long-established chapel in Christchurch Passage, Hampstead, was compulsorily purchased, whereupon the congregation took over a building in Bridge Lane, Temple Fortune,[36] which was registered as Ebenezer Strict Baptist chapel later that year.[37] In 1972 the congregation was affiliated to the 'Gospel Standard' section of Strict Baptists.

THE SALVATION ARMY. Meetings began in a wooden hall behind premises on the west side of Brent Street in 1881,[38] where General William Booth attended the laying of the foundation stone of a permanent building in 1884.[39] The hall was burned down in 1935 and replaced in 1937 by a red-brick building.[40] A second brick building facing Brampton Grove was registered in 1957 and in 1970 formed the headquarters of the Hendon corps, although the earlier hall was still in use.[41]

At Childs Hill Salvationists were meeting in the former Primitive Methodist chapel in Finchley Road by 1915.[42] The premises were registered in 1931[43] and in 1970 were used as the Army's North London divisional headquarters.

At Burnt Oak a hall was opened in Barnfield Road, to serve the Watling estate, in 1934.[44] Services were held there in 1969.

At West Hendon a hall in Borthwick Road was registered for worship in 1944.[45] It survived in 1961 but had disappeared by 1970.[46]

INTERDENOMINATIONAL.[47] Hampstead Garden Suburb Free church originated in services which were transferred from a wooden hut in Hampstead Way to the newly-opened institute in 1909. A United Free church, designed to serve all nonconformist denominations, was established in 1910 under the auspices of the London Baptist Association, after the Baptists had conceded that membership would be on the widest possible basis. The church building, occupying a prominent site in Central Square provided by the Garden Suburb Trust, was opened in 1911, although it was not completed until after the Second World War. It was designed by Sir Edwin Lutyens, who also designed the manse, to complement his Anglican church of St. Jude at the opposite side of the square. The Free church is a large domed structure of brick, with a steep tiled roof; it is cruciform in plan and has a severely classical interior, with a tunnel-

vaulted nave separated from the aisles by Doric columns. In 1969 it was served by both Baptist and Congregationalist ministers.

OTHER DENOMINATIONS. The Presbyterian Church of England formed a congregation at Golders Green, probably in 1910.[48] Premises on the corner of Helenslea Avenue and Finchley Road were opened for worship in 1911 and, as St. Ninian's church, registered for marriages in 1912. The church, a red-brick building in the Perpendicular style, was designed by T. Phillips Figgis. The foundation stone of a church hall, which replaced a wooden hut, was laid in 1925.

Unitarians opened All Souls church in Hoop Lane, Golders Green, in 1925, after moving from Weech Road, Hampstead.[49] The building, a small basilican red-brick structure in the Early Christian style, was designed by G. R. Farrow and J. R. Turner.[50]

The Pillar of Fire Society established a chapel in Brent Street in 1926 and named it after the society's American founder, Alma White, as part of a complex of buildings which included a Bible college and a school.[51] The society still held evangelistic services and ran a kindergarten school at the college in 1971.[52]

The Elim Foursquare Gospel Alliance registered Elim tabernacle, Somerset Road, in 1928.[53] It was later replaced by premises in near-by Ravenshurst Avenue, which were used by the Alliance in 1968.

Christian Brethren opened a hall on the corner of Gervase Road and Watling Avenue in 1928. It was later named Woodcroft Evangelical church and was still in use in 1968.[54]

The Christian Science Society[55] began meeting in Highfields, Golders Green Road, in 1930. Later in that year it purchased Fosters, overlooking Brent Green, which it immediately registered as the First Church of Christ Scientist, Hendon. In 1961 a new church was built between Brent Green and Fosters.[56] The building is octagonal, with a copper roof surmounted by a spire, and has a brickwork relieved by stepped slit windows and a glazed porch.

Assemblies of God met on the first floor of premises in West Hendon Broadway in 1943.[57] By 1956 the group apparently was linked with the Hendon Brotherhood Movement, which met in its own brick and concrete building in the Broadway.[58] The Hendon Sanctuary and Truth Centre, a room on the ground floor of no. 96 Finchley Lane, was registered in 1959 by a group of unspecified worshippers,[59] who had ceased using it by 1968.

Jehovah's Witnesses opened a new national headquarters at Watchtower House, on the site of Bittacy House, Mill Hill, in 1959. Part of the premises was registered for worship,[60] although

[34] Gravatt, op. cit. 21.
[35] Whitley, op. cit. 242.
[36] Ex inf. the deacon. The chapel had been founded in 1825 after a split among Strict Baptists at Hollybush Hill, Hampstead.
[37] G.R.O. Worship Reg. no. 58344.
[38] Gravatt, op. cit. 21.
[39] Evans, *Hendon*, 190.
[40] Inscription on building.
[41] G.R.O. Worship Reg. no. 66699.
[42] O.S. Map 1/2,500, Mdx. XI. 15 (1915 edn.).
[43] G.R.O. Worship Reg. no. 53281.
[44] Ibid. 55015.
[45] Ibid. 60967.
[46] Hendon, *Official Guide* [1961].

[47] The para. is based on *Fifty Years of Witness* (Free Ch. Golden Jubilee Booklet, 1960).
[48] The para. is based on inf. supplied by the session clerk.
[49] G.R.O. Worship Reg. no. 50019; ex inf. the chairman.
[50] Robbins, *Mdx.* 255.
[51] G.R.O. Worship Reg. no. 50416.
[52] *Pillar of Fire*, lxi (11).
[53] G.R.O. Worship Reg. no. 51137.
[54] Ibid. 51185.
[55] The para. is based on inf. supplied by Mrs. G. G. Newman.
[56] The house continued in use as a Sunday sch.
[57] G.R.O. Worship Reg. no. 60456.
[58] Ibid. 65694.
[59] Ibid. 67114.
[60] Ibid. 67428.

regular meetings were not held there. Watchtower House contained a large printing works, extended in 1965, and a training school for ministers.[61] It was designed by Keith Roberts as a Z-shaped building, of red brick with some glass curtain-walling.[62]

Christadelphians worshipped in the Co-operative hall at West Hendon in 1962 and continued to meet there in 1969.[63] Christian Spiritualists registered the Golders Green Sanctuary of the Spirit, in Finchley Road, in 1951 but apparently no longer used it in 1969.[64]

JUDAISM. Jews apparently arrived soon after the opening of the Underground station at Golders Green. Their numbers increased after the extension of the line to Edgware, until in 1959 it was claimed that one quarter of the population of the borough was Jewish.[65]

All the various synagogue organizations are represented in the area. The United Synagogue came first with Golders Green synagogue,[66] opened in Dunstan Road in 1922, and Hendon synagogue, opposite the Brent Bridge hotel, in 1928.[67] In Golders Green Jews had previously used St. Alban's hall, West Heath Drive, and several had been members of Brondesbury synagogue in 1914,[68] while in central Hendon worshippers had met in a private house in Alderton Crescent from 1925 and rented a near-by hall for festivals. In 1935 Hendon synagogue moved to a new building in Raleigh Close. A later constituent of the United Synagogue was Mill Hill and District Hebrew congregation, which began meeting in Sylvan Avenue in 1950, became Mill Hill District synagogue in 1960, and had erected a hall by 1969.

A new phase followed Hitler's rise to power, which resulted in a steady influx of middle-class immigrants. Not altogether satisfied with the main-stream of traditional Judaism in England, rep-resented by the United Synagogue, some of them sought help from other organizations in setting up branches.[69] Thus with aid from the West London synagogue a Reform synagogue was founded in 1933 in a private house in Hampstead Garden Suburb. Members later hired a hall in Bridge Lane and the larger hall of the Free Church and in 1936 a permanent building in Alyth Gardens near the Jews' cemetery, the North Western Reform syna-gogue, was opened.[70] A more significant event, however, was the foundation of Golders Green Beth Hamedrash synagogue in the Lincoln institute, Broadwalk Lane, in 1934. Although it was aided by the Adath Ysroel synagogue in Stamford Hill, with which it continued to co-operate for a number of religious purposes, it has retained its independence in the Ridings, where it moved in 1959. The Federation of Synagogues opened a Golders Green branch in Woodstock Avenue in 1935 and moved in

1959 to another building in the same road, which was renamed Sinai synagogue in 1960. Hendon Reform synagogue was established in 1949, meeting in Egerton Gardens and from 1955 in Danescroft Gardens.

A third phase began when after the bombing of east London people moved thence into Hendon. This led to the proliferation of small orthodox synagogues, some transferred and others the result of the newcomers' initiative. Those that survived were variously reorganized. In 1974 the leading synagogue in the group was Beth Shmuel, at no. 171 Golders Green Road. Most of them were connected with one another through membership of the Union of Orthodox Hebrew Congregations, which in 1974 had the following constituent members: the North Western Sephardish synagogue, which met at no. 15 Russell Parade, Temple Fortune, in 1940 and moved very soon afterwards to no. 4 Highfield Avenue, Golders Green; Finchley Road synagogue, founded in 1941 and meeting by 1969 at no. 843 Finchley Road; Hendon Adath Ysroel synagogue, which held services in the Central hall, Queen's Road, in 1945, opened a community centre in Shirehall Lane in 1947, and moved to the bottom of Brent Street in 1948; Bridge Lane Beth Hamedrash, founded in 1947 and at no. 85 Bridge Lane from 1948; North Hendon Adath synagogue, founded in 1948 and moving in 1950 from Ravensfield to the N. B. Walters centre in Holders Hill Road; Beth Abraham syna-gogue, in Woodstock Road from 1951 until its move to the Ridgeway in 1958; and Sunny Hills Adath Ysroel synagogue, on the corner of South-fields and Watford Way from 1958.

In 1957 the North West London Talmudical college was founded at no. 861 Finchley Road and in 1968 the Tree of Life college was transferred from the east end of London to no. 85 Bridge Lane. Golders Green and its neighbourhood thus came to be second only to Stoke Newington as a centre of orthodox Judaism in London.

The transfer of power in India prompted certain old families of oriental Jews to come to Britain. Those who settled in Hendon were attached to the Baghdadi rite and retained it in their prayers at the Lincoln institute, which they took over from Golders Green Beth Hamedrash synagogue in 1959 and named Ohel David Eastern synagogue.

EDUCATION. It is doubtful whether a school-master recorded in 1586[71] was connected with Hendon charity school, which existed by 1685. A second charity school, with branches at Church End and Mill Hill, was founded by John Bennett in 1766 and merged with the older school in 1788.[72] The poor in 1819 were said to be without the means of education:[73] the branch at Mill Hill had been closed after 1802[74] and up to 100 children there had needed instruction in 1816.[75] An infants' school was

[61] Ex inf. Watch Tower Soc.
[62] I. Nairn, *Modern Buildings in Lond.* 80–1.
[63] G.R.O. Worship Reg. no. 68694.   [64] Ibid. 63207.
[65] V. D. Lipman, 'Rise of Jewish Suburbia', *Trans. Jewish Hist. Soc.* xxi. 90; Hopkins, *Hendon*, 72.
[66] V. D. Lipman, *Social Hist. of Jews in Eng. 1850–1950*, 176.
[67] Except where otherwise stated, the rest of the section is based on inf. supplied by Mr. E. M. Marmorstein, the ministers of the congregations, and *Jewish Yr. Bk.* (1940 and later edns.).

[68] *Trans. Jewish Hist. Soc.* xxi. 90.
[69] Lipman, *Social Hist. of Jews*, 167, 170; A. Cohen, 'Structure of Anglo-Jewry Today', *Three Cents. of Anglo-Jewish Hist.* ed. V. D. Lipman, 178.
[70] *Short Hist. of North-Western Reform Synagogue* (1958).
[71] Guildhall MS. 9537/6.
[72] See below.
[73] *Educ. of Poor Digest*, 538.
[74] *Rules for govt. of Charity Schs. at Hendon* (1802) *penes* Hendon Libr.
[75] Hendon Libr., L. 282.

established opposite the King's Head by 1828[76] but it was not until 1835 that complaints led to the opening of a permanent, National, school at Mill Hill.[77] The southern part of the parish was served c. 1830 by a dame school at Childs Hill, which moved to a building at Cowhouse Green, said to form part of the later no. 17 Cricklewood Lane.[78] In 1856 the pupils were transferred to the new National school at Childs Hill.[79]

Methodists began a night school in 1827,[80] Congregationalists opened New Brent Street British school in 1856, and another British school followed at Childs Hill in 1870. The first Roman Catholic elementary school was opened at Mill Hill in 1873 and the second at the Burroughs in 1896. Anglican opposition delayed until 1897 the establishment of a school board;[81] in 1884 the vicar wrote that Hendon was the only parish in the area without a board and that it hoped to remain so.[82] Areas of expanding population suffered from lack of funds for building. At West Hendon nonconformists contributed to the Anglican school built in 1889, after seeing shoeless children walking the 1½ mile to Church End,[83] and in 1889 the Hendon schools emergency committee was set up to give grants to elementary schools, regardless of their affiliations.[84]

By 1898 parliamentary grants were received by 12 schools, six of them Anglican, three Roman Catholic and three, all formerly nonconformist, run by the school board.[85] Four new schools were built by the board in 1901 before its supersession by Hendon U.D., a Part III authority under the Education Act of 1902.[86] The U.D.C. provided several central, secondary modern, and primary schools between the two World Wars to cater for the new housing estates, until in 1938 it controlled 28 schools, two of them in the old parish of Edgware.[87] Under the 1944 Education Act Hendon became an excepted district under the supreme control of the education committee of Middlesex C.C.[88] In 1965 responsibility for education passed to Barnet L.B.; in 1969 there were 25 primary, 3 secondary modern, 3 bilateral, and 5 grammar schools, as well as one special school, within the old parish.[89] Woodcroft, St. David's, Copthall, and Hendon grammar schools were reorganized under comprehensive plans in 1970.[90]

Elementary schools founded before 1903.[91] Hendon charity school in 1685 was being managed by

trustees, who held half a house and half an orchard at the Burroughs.[92] A house at the Burroughs was purchased by the parish in 1707[93] and in 1709 the vestry ordered that the school dames be paid for giving the children religious instruction, as well as for teaching them in their horn books and primers.[94] Twenty boys and 10 girls attended in 1710, when the school was supported by voluntary subscriptions which amounted to £20 a year, by gifts worth £100, and by offertory collections.[95] In 1727 it was endowed under the will of Nicholas Bradshaw with the interest on £300.[96]

A second charity school was founded in 1766 by John Bennett, who built a school-house on waste ground given by David Garrick at Church End, adjoining Daniel's alms-houses.[97] Bennett left the school £100 and in 1772 John Crosse endowed it with £250 stock; it was also supported by voluntary subscriptions, gifts, and annual charity sermons, a treasurer and sub-treasurer being appointed annually by the subscribers.[98] In 1788 65 boys and girls were educated under the charity, 30 of them at Hendon and the rest at a branch at Mill Hill, the date of whose foundation is not known. There was one schoolmaster at each school and 20 children received free clothing.[99]

Bennett's schools and the charity school merged in 1788 as Hendon charity school, which took over Bennett's building at Church End, where another schoolroom was added. The teachers were examined annually by the subscribers and in 1789 the schoolmaster and his wife, 'too imbecile and full of engagements', were dismissed.[1] Bell's monitorial system was being used in 1816.[2] By 1819 the number of pupils had risen to 109 and the yearly income was £160, of which £60 came from endowments.[3] The school was united with the National Society in 1828 and was later called St. Mary's National school.[4] In 1851 accommodation was too small for the 175 pupils[5] and in 1857 they moved to a red-brick building in Church Walk, paid for by Lord Tenterden.[6] The buildings at Church End, which had acquired a neo-Tudor façade in the early 19th century, were later used by Hendon Baptist church[7] and as a working mens' club;[8] they were demolished in 1937.[9] The new school buildings were extended in 1860,[10] 1881,[11] and 1915,[12] and in 1938 they contained 221 senior boys and girls and 249 juniors. The seniors moved to the new St. Mary's secondary modern school in 1960,[13] leaving

76 Whishaw, *Map of Hendon* and ref. bk.
77 Hendon Libr., L. 282. For individual schs., see below.
78 Evans, *Hendon*, 180; Mill Hill Hist. Soc., Add. Items 127.
79 Evans, *Hendon*, 180; see below.
80 Mill Hill Hist. Soc., Add. Items 43.
81 Hopkins, *Hendon*, 92.   82 Nat. Soc. files.
83 Ibid.   84 Evans, *Hendon*, 127.
85 *Schs. in receipt of Parl. Grants, 1898* [C. 9454], p. 169, H.C. (1899), lxxiv.
86 Mdx. C.C., *Primary and Secondary Educ. in Mdx. 1900–1965*, 26.
87 Bd. of Educ., *List 21* (H.M.S.O. 1938), 284–5.
88 *Primary and Secondary Educ. in Mdx.* 41.
89 Barnet L.B., List of Schools. Two of the grammar schs., Henrietta Barnett and Hasmonean boys', were Voluntary Aided.
90 Ex inf. the headmasters and headmistresses.
91 Attendance figs. for 1906 are from *Public Elem. Schs. 1906* [Cd. 3510], p. 456, H.C. (1907), lxiii, those for 1919 and 1938 from *Bd. of Educ., List 21* (H.M.S.O. 1919, 1938), and those for 1969–74 from the headmaster or headmistress.

92 *T.L.M.A.S.* xiv. 571.
93 Lambeth Palace, MS. 1298.
94 Hendon Libr., L. 126.
95 *Account of Charity Schs. lately Erected in Great Britain and Ireland* (1710), 10.
96 *4th Rep. Com. Char.* H.C. 312, p. 167 (1820), v.
97 Brewer, *Beauties of Eng. & Wales*, x(5), 693.
98 *4th Rep. Com. Char.* 167.
99 Hendon Libr., L. 282.
1 Ibid.
2 Brewer, *Beauties of Eng. & Wales*, x(5), 694.
3 *Educ. of Poor Digest*, 538.
4 Hendon Libr., L. 282; *19th Annual Rep. of Nat. Soc.* (1830), appendix vi.
5 Ed. 7/87.   6 Nat. Soc. files.
7 See p. 41.
8 Evans, *Hendon*, 126–7.
9 [T. Constantiniotes], *Story of St. Mary's C. of E. Schs.* 16.
10 Nat. Soc. files.
11 Evans, *Hendon*, 127.
12 Nat. Soc. files.
13 See below.

the juniors to form St. Mary's primary school, whose pupils in 1973 moved to Prothero Gardens.

St. Paul's school, Mill Hill, opened in 1835 in a stuccoed building adjoining the church, on land given by Sir James Flower.[14] It began as a branch of St. Mary's National school but from 1849 it was managed independently, although still assisted by subscribers to the school at Church End.[15] There were 105 pupils in 1836[16] and 143 in 1893.[17] Extensions were carried out in 1874[18] and again in 1969. St. Paul's, a Voluntary Aided school, had 185 juniors and infants in 1974.

All Saints' school, Childs Hill, opened in 1856 in a new building with three rooms in Childs Walk.[19] There were 54 pupils in the first year[20] and 485 by 1906. Extensions were carried out between 1870 and 1890[21] and again, after an adverse report, in 1922. A new building was erected in 1962 and extended in 1968.[22] The school was Voluntary Aided in 1974, when there were 226 pupils on the roll.

New Brent Street British school opened for girls in 1856 and for boys in 1858 in a building leased from Thomas Spalding and others and consisting of separate rooms for boys, girls, and infants.[23] It was financed at first by Spalding and other local Congregationalists.[24] There were 111 pupils in 1868[25] but rising numbers necessitated rebuilding in the 1880s,[26] and in 1893 there were 249 pupils.[27] The school was placed under Hendon school board in 1898[28] and closed in 1901, when pupils were transferred to the central board school.

Childs Hill British school opened in 1870 in a new building adjoining the Baptist chapel in the Mead, containing two schoolrooms and a classroom.[29] In its first year the school had an average attendance of 26 girls and 40 infants, taught by one mistress,[30] but by 1898, when it was transferred to the school board, attendance had risen to 242.[31] The school was closed in 1901, when pupils moved to Childs Hill board school.

St. Michael's Roman Catholic school, Mill Hill, was founded by the Franciscan nuns of St. Mary's abbey in 1873 and superseded by St. Vincent's school in 1896. The cottage occupied by St. Michael's was later used as a science room by St. Mary's Abbey school.[32]

St. Peter's school, Cricklewood, opened in 1883 in a two-roomed building which was also used for Sunday evening services.[33] There was an average attendance of 25 infants in the first year and of 108 in 1893.[34] The school closed in 1917.[35]

Burnt Oak Church of England school opened in 1884 in a corrugated-iron building, provided by the

vicar of Hendon and also used for Sunday services.[36] At first there was an average attendance of 34 girls, who were taught in one schoolroom.[37] In 1901 the school was replaced by Burnt Oak board school. The buildings thereafter served as a mission church,[38] although in 1927 and 1928 they housed some pupils from Burnt Oak council school.[39]

West Hendon Free Church school opened in 1885 on a site in Edgware Road belonging to Hendon Baptist chapel. It was supported by voluntary contributions and in 1897 had 77 children taught in one schoolroom.[40] The school passed to Hendon school board in 1898[41] and was closed in 1901, when its pupils moved to Algernon Road.

St. John's school, West Hendon, opened in 1889 in Milton Road, on a site purchased out of the Bishop of London's Fund, and at first accommodated only girls and infants in a schoolroom and a classroom.[42] In 1893 there were 126 pupils, when the building was enlarged;[43] and in 1896, with the completion of St. John's church, a separate boys' department was opened in the old temporary church, to cater for the children of workers at the new Schweppes's factory.[44] There were 359 pupils in 1906. In 1974 St. John's, a Voluntary Aided school, had 157 infants and 260 juniors in adjoining buildings in Prothero Gardens.

Hendon Roman Catholic school, later known as St. Mary's and, from 1967, as St. Joseph's R.C. primary school, opened in 1889. During the first year an average of 65 boys and girls attended a schoolroom and classroom in Chapel Walk, off Egerton Gardens, where they were taught by sisters from St. Joseph's convent.[45] There were 125 pupils in 1938. In 1967 the school moved to new premises with accommodation for 500 children in Watford Way, whereupon the old buildings were turned into a social centre for the parish of Our Lady of Dolours.[46] There were 234 infants and 305 juniors on the roll in 1974.

St. Vincent's Roman Catholic school was opened in 1896 by the Sisters of Charity of St. Vincent de Paul on a site adjoining Littleberries, replacing St. Michael's school.[47] St. Vincent's contained one room for junior boys and girls and another for infants.[48] There were 62 pupils in 1898[49] and 137 by 1938. In 1969 the school contained junior mixed and infants' departments, and was separate from the adjoining boarding school, which was founded by the sisters as an orphanage in 1887 and catered in 1969 for 80 deprived boys and girls.[50] There were 242 juniors and infants on the roll in 1974.

The Good Shepherd Roman Catholic school, from

---

[14] Nat. Soc. files.
[15] Char. Com. files.
[16] Hendon Libr., L. 282.
[17] *Returns of Schs. 1893* [C. 7529], p. 422, H.C. (1894), lxv.
[18] Nat. Soc. files.
[19] Evans, *Hendon*, 180.
[20] Ed. 7/88.
[21] Ed. 7/88; Nat. Soc. files.
[22] Nat. Soc. files.
[23] Ed. 7/87.
[24] Evans, *Hendon*, 185.
[25] Ed. 7/87.
[26] Evans, *Hendon*, 185.
[27] *Returns of Schs. 1893*, p. 422.
[28] *Schs. in receipt of Parl. Grants, 1898*, p. 169.
[29] Ed. 7/88.
[30] Ibid.
[31] *Schs. in receipt of Parl. Grants, 1898*, p. 169.
[32] Ex inf. the mother superior, St. Mary's abbey.

[33] Ed. 7/88. See p. 36.
[34] *Returns of Schs. 1893*, p. 422.
[35] Nat. Soc. files.
[36] Ibid. See p. 37.
[37] Ed. 7/88.
[38] See p. 37.
[39] Ed. 7/88.
[40] Ibid.
[41] *Schs. in receipt of Parl. Grants, 1898*, p. 169.
[42] Ed. 7/88.
[43] *Returns of Schs. 1893*, p. 422.
[44] Nat. Soc. files.
[45] *Kelly's Dir. Mdx.* (1890); Ed. 7/88.
[46] Ex inf. the par. priest, Our Lady of Dolours.
[47] Ex inf. the mother superior, St. Mary's abbey.
[48] Ed. 7/88.
[49] *Schs. in receipt of Parl. Grants, 1898*, p. 169.
[50] Ex inf. the Sisters of Charity. For the boarding sch. see below.

1906 St. Agnes's Roman Catholic primary school, opened in Gillingham Road, Childs Hill, in 1895. It consisted of a single schoolroom, where an average of 25 boys and girls was taught in the first year. A new building was erected in 1906[51] and greatly extended in 1939. There were 400 children on the roll in 1970.[52]

Childs Hill board school opened in Granville Road in 1899 and moved to a permanent building in Dersingham Road in 1901, when it replaced Childs Hill British school.[53] There was accommodation for 1,007 in 1906, when the attendance was 918, and for 800 in 1938. In 1974 the premises were occupied by Childs Hill junior mixed and infants' school, which had 348 children on the roll.

Hendon central board school, Bell Lane, opened in 1901.[54] There was accommodation for 684 in 1906, when the attendance was 466, for 948 in 1919, and for 710 in 1938. In 1974 Bell Lane junior mixed and infants' school, on the same site, had 386 children on the roll.

Algernon Road board school, opened in 1901,[55] had accommodation for 1,010 in 1906 and 1919 and for 816 in 1938. In 1974 there were adjoining schools, with 286 juniors and 206 infants on their respective rolls.

Burnt Oak board school opened in 1901.[56] There was accommodation for 296 in 1906 and 1919 and for 360 in 1938. The school closed between 1937 and 1957.[57]

Elementary schools founded between 1903 and 1945.[58] The Hyde school, opened in 1909, accommodated 848 pupils in 1919 and 860 in 1938. Separate schools occupied the site in 1974, with 226 juniors and 219 infants on their respective rolls.

Garden Suburb school opened in 1909 and moved from the institute to a new building in Childs Way in 1913. There was accommodation for 990 in 1919, when the attendance was 599, and for 870 in 1938. In 1974 there was a junior school, with 388 children enrolled, and an infants', with 298.

Wessex Gardens school, Golders Green, opened in 1920 and accommodated 940 in 1938. In 1970 there were 300 children in the junior school and 184 in the infants'.

Colindale infants' school opened in Colindeep Lane in 1921 and moved to a new building for juniors and infants in Woodfield Avenue in 1933, when it was attended by 236 children. In 1938 there was accommodation for 500 and the attendance was 482. In 1970 it had 490 children on the roll.

Woodcroft school, Goldbeaters Grove, opened in 1928. There was accommodation for 1,304 in 1938, when the attendance was 1,042. In 1968 a separate senior school was erected in Page Street, which in 1970 was attended by 520 girls. Woodcroft junior school in 1970 had 590 children on the roll.

Barnfield school, Silkstream Road, opened in 1928. There was accommodation for 1,264 in 1938, when the attendance was 902. In 1964 the secondary boys moved to extended premises at St. David's

Place, Park Road. In 1970 Barnfield junior mixed and infants' school had 240 children on the roll.

The Meads school, Burnt Oak, opened in 1930. There was accommodation for 360 in 1938, when it was attended by 228 children. It closed between 1964 and 1969.

Deansbrook school, Hale Drive, opened in 1931. There was accommodation for 800 in 1938, when the attendance was 624. In 1974 there was a junior school, with 376 children, and an infants', with 286.

Goldbeaters school, Thirleby Road, opened in 1931. There was accommodation for 1,512 in 1938, when attendance was only 1,017. In 1974 it was a junior mixed and infants' school, with 273 children on the roll.

The Annunciation Roman Catholic school, Thirleby Road, opened in 1931. There was accommodation for 336 in 1938, when it was attended by 268 children. In 1974 the school was Voluntary Aided. It has an annexe in North Road and 525 juniors and infants on the roll.

Clitterhouse school, Claremont Road, opened in 1934 and accommodated 400 in 1938. In 1974 there was a junior school, with 238 children enrolled, and an infants', with 166.

Sunnyfields school, Sunningfields Road, existed by 1938, when it accommodated 300 infants. Juniors were admitted from 1971 and there were 204 children on the roll in 1974.

Dollis school, Pursley Road, opened in 1939. In 1974 there was a junior school, with 400 children enrolled, and an infants', with 338.

Frith Manor school, Lullington Garth, opened in 1939 and in 1970 was attended by 149 infants and 244 juniors.

Primary schools founded after 1945. The Fairway school, Mill Hill, opened in 1952. Hutted classrooms were added in 1955 and there were 180 juniors and infants on the roll in 1970.

Courtland school, Courtland Avenue, Mill Hill, opened in 1954 and had 330 juniors and infants on the roll in 1970.

Secondary and senior schools. Henrietta Barnett school was founded as a girls' grammar school in 1909 in the Garden Suburb institute. In 1969, when the school was Voluntary Aided, there were 600 pupils.

Hendon county, later Hendon grammar, school opened in Golders Rise in 1914. A gymnasium and new wing were added in 1930 and further extensions were carried out in 1960. There were 636 boys and girls on the roll in 1970. After comprehensive reorganization, the premises in Golders Rise housed Hendon senior high school, while St. David's Place in Park Road housed Hendon junior high school.

Orange Hill central schools opened in 1932 in Abbots Road, accommodating 720 boys and girls in 1938. The schools became grammar schools in 1948, when they were extended. In 1970 there were 478 girls in Hamonde Close, whither they had moved in 1965, and 550 boys at Abbots Road. In 1974 the former girls' premises were occupied by

[51] Ed. 7/88.
[52] Ex inf. the headmaster.
[53] Ed. 7/88.
[54] Ibid.
[55] Ibid.
[56] Ibid.

[57] *Bd. of Educ., List 21* (H.M.S.O. 1938), 284; Mdx. C.C., *List of Schools* (1957).
[58] The foll. four sections are based on Ed. 7/88; *Bd. of Educ., List 21* (H.M.S.O. 1919–1938); and on inf. supplied by the headmasters and headmistresses.

Orange Hill junior high school and the boys' by Orange Hill senior high school.

St. James's Roman Catholic, later St. James's bilateral, school opened in 1934 in the grounds of St. Rose's convent and afterwards took over the convent's school. There was accommodation for 320 boys and girls in 1938. St. James's was Voluntary Aided in 1974, when there were 1,452 children enrolled.

Copthall grammar school for girls opened in Page Street in 1936. A science block was later added and in 1970 there were 566 children enrolled.

Brent secondary modern school opened in Sturgess Avenue in 1936 and accommodated 400 pupils in 1938. They moved to a new building in St. David's Place in 1964, together with senior boys from Barnfield school, to form St. David's secondary school. There were 500 boys enrolled in 1970, before the premises were taken over for Hendon junior high school.

The Hasmonean grammar school was founded in 1945 as a co-educational school in the Drive, Golders Green, by Rabbi S. Schonfeld, principal of the Jewish Secondary Schools Movement. In 1947 the boys moved to Ravensfield, which was later extended and had 465 pupils in 1969, when the school was Voluntary Aided. In 1952 the girls left Golders Green for Downhurst, a former private school in Parson Street, which was later extended and had 289 pupils in 1974.

Moat Mount secondary modern, later bilateral, school opened in Worcester Crescent in 1957. It was extended in 1969 and had 730 boys and girls on the roll in 1970.

St. Mary's Church of England secondary modern school was built in Downage on land bought by the diocesan authorities. Senior boys and girls from the old National school moved there in 1960. St. Mary's, which was Voluntary Aided, had 580 pupils in 1974.

Whitefield bilateral school, Claremont Road, was opened in 1964 and extended in 1969. There were 1,000 boys and girls on the roll in 1970.

Secondary departments also existed at Barnfield (boys), Woodcroft (girls), Goldbeaters, and the Hyde (mixed) schools.

Special school. Northway school, the Fairway, opened in 1967 for slow-learning boys and girls from the northern and western parts of Barnet L.B. There were 83 pupils, aged from 5 to 14, in 1970.

Hampstead Garden Suburb Institute,[59] the first centre of adult and further education in Hendon, opened in a neo-Georgian building designed by Sir Edwin Lutyens in 1909. It was at first used for lectures and meetings on social problems but later housed the Henrietta Barnett school, as well as adult-education classes. The original building, the Old Institute hall, has become the north wing; the Queen Mary hall was opened as a south wing in 1918 and the connecting block, Crewe hall, in 1935. A temporary annexe was built in 1955. In 1970 the institute housed, besides the school, an

arts establishment, a department of English for foreign students, and a local centre for the Extra-Mural Department of London University. There were 2,934 students on the roll.

Hendon College of Technology,[60] in the Burroughs, was designed in the neo-Georgian style by H. W. Burchett and opened in 1939. In 1955 there were minor extensions and in 1969 a new refectory block and an engineering block were being built. By 1969 there were 1,700 evening students, 1,380 students taking short full-time or part-time day courses, and 1,350 on full-time or sandwich courses. From 1973 the college formed part of Middlesex Polytechnic.[61]

Private schools. In 1660 Richard Swift (d. 1701), the ejected curate of Edgware, started a small but short-lived boarding academy, possibly for Quakers, at Mill Hill.[62] In 1788 the old charity school premises at the Burroughs was taken over by the vestry clerk as a private school for day-boys and boarders which lasted until 1819, when the building was turned into cottages.[63] By 1835 there were 12 private schools in the parish,[64] where many more were later established in large houses: Brent Bridge House was a boys' preparatory school in 1872,[65] Hendon Hall served as a school for 'daughters of gentlemen' in 1902,[66] Belmont House became a boys' preparatory school in 1912,[67] and Tenterden Hall, formerly Hendon Place, was a boys' school in 1930.[68] Some schools were established as a result of the opening of Mill Hill school in 1807, while others followed the building of large Roman Catholic convents. In the 20th century several private schools, including the Hasmonean boys' and girls' grammar schools, have catered for Jewish immigrants. The more notable surviving private and Voluntary Aided schools are described below.

St. George's school, a small and select boarding establishment for girls, was opened by the Franciscan nuns at Holcombe House[69] in 1879. In 1902 it took over a building to the south, which from 1876 had been the home of St. Margaret's industrial school for 100 pauper girls, and was renamed St. Mary's Abbey school. There were 48 boarders, many of them foreign, and 69 day girls in 1969. A preparatory department, St. Anthony's school, opened in 1911 and later moved to Hale Lane, Mill Hill, where in 1969 it was run on Montessori lines.

La Sagesse Convent school originated in classes held by the Daughters of Wisdom at Woodstock House, Golders Green, soon after their move there in 1909. Later they opened an independent day and boarding school for girls of all ages, extending the premises in 1926-7 and 1932. From 1965 the school catered for backward children, of whom there were 86 on the roll in 1969.[70]

Belmont school was founded in 1912 in Belmont House by Rooker Roberts, a master at Mill Hill school. It opened as a junior house of Mill Hill but became a separate preparatory school after the First World War, when it was extended. In 1969 there

---

[59] Section based on inf. supplied by the vice-principal.
[60] Section based on inf. supplied by the principal.
[61] Ex inf. Hendon Libr.
[62] A. G. Matthews, *Calamy Revised*, 472; *V.C.H. Mdx.* iv. 164.
[63] Hendon Libr., L. 130.

[64] *Educ. Enquiry Abstract*, 564.
[65] F. J. Bisson, *Our Schools and Colleges* (1872), 274.
[66] *Hampton's Scholastic Dir.* (1902-3).
[67] See below.   [68] See p. 18.
[69] Ex inf. the mother superior, St. Mary's abbey.
[70] Ex inf. the superior.

were 190 pupils, 80 of them day boys, aged between 7 and 13.[71]

King Alfred school, a 'rational school' founded in Hampstead in 1898, moved in 1919 to Manor Wood, North End Road. Alterations at the rear of the school were carried out in a modernistic style in 1934–6 to the designs of F. C. Kaufmann.[72] In 1969 there were 350 boys and girls aged between 4 and 20.[73]

The Mount school,[74] a girls' boarding school founded by Mary Macgregor in Highgate in 1925, moved in 1935 to the Mount, Milespit Hill. Extensions were carried out in 1946 and in the 1950s. There were 200 girls aged 8 to 18 on the roll in 1969.[75]

CHARITIES FOR THE POOR.[76] By will proved 1670 Edward Nicholl of Knightsland, South Mimms, left £10 a year with interest to the poor of Hendon. In 1687 his son John was ordered in Chancery to pay the money[77] but the charity seems to have lapsed soon afterwards.

In 1696 Thomas Nicholl of Hendon erected a single-storeyed brick alms-house at the junction of Milespit Hill and the Ridgeway, Mill Hill.[78] He did not endow the premises, which accommodated 6 pauper residents of Hendon at a nominal rent, and the parish was forced to undertake repairs. Consequently the building was generally called the parish alms-house, although it was later known as Nicholl's alms-house. Trustees were appointed in 1863, under a Scheme for the charities of the parish, but by 1881 the only income was the weekly rent of 6d. paid by each inmate. In 1892 the executors of Eliza Holm, the widow of a former resident of Mill Hill, gave £2,700 stock to provide each alms-person with a small weekly pension.[79] Her endowment was administered separately until in 1910 a Scheme established the Nicholl and Holm charity, whose income was administered with that of the Daniel and Holm charity.

By will proved 1682, Robert Daniel, a London merchant, instructed his executors to spend £2,000 on land and after ten years to use the accumulated revenue to build an alms-house within ten miles of the City for 6 men and 4 women of at least fifty years of age. Thereafter the income was to provide each resident with a grey cloth gown, lined with orange baize, every two years, a shilling loaf at Christmas, and a weekly pension of 3s.[80] In 1686 the executors purchased 110 a. at North Aston (Oxon.) and by 1727 their plans to establish an alms-house at Hendon had been approved in Chancery. The building was opened in 1729[81] and sometimes held more women than men, despite Daniel's stipulations. The women's pensions were increased to 4s. a week in 1806 and the men's in 1818. The trustees had run short of funds when Eliza Holm, by will dated 1890, left some £30,000 to such charitable institutions as her executor thought fit. In 1892 Daniel's alms-houses became the first beneficiaries and were endowed with £6,100

stock, after the premises had been repaired at the cost of the Holm estate. The Daniel and Holm charities were consolidated under a new Scheme of 1910, whereby the Daniel and Holm and the Nicholl and Holm charities, while retaining their separate names, jointly contributed towards alms-houses for 16 poor persons who had resided in Hendon for not less than five years and towards weekly pensions for the inmates and other parishioners. A detached portion of Daniel's endowment at Stoke Lyne (Oxon.) was sold in 1935 and the rest of the Oxfordshire land in 1959. By 1965 the total investment income of £775 a year was spent mainly on the alms-houses and on medical services for the residents. The alms-houses, a gaunt brick building with a pedimented centrepiece, were largely rebuilt c. 1800 and extensively repaired in 1854 and the late 1950s.

Elizabeth Parsons of the parish of St. Anne, Westminster, by will proved 1758, bequeathed £100, the income to be used to maintain the family vault at Hendon and to benefit poor unrelieved parishioners.[82] After the death of her sister Martha, who bequeathed £100 on similar terms, the money was invested in stock. By 1843 the income amounted to £6 6s., which was spent in bread.[83] In 1966, when the charity was administered jointly with the Neeld charity, £5 10s. was distributed in bread.

An early-19th-century lord of the manor of Hendon gave a piece of land at Temple Fortune to compensate the parish for loss of rights on some recently inclosed waste. The vestry directed that the land should be sold and some of the proceeds spent on a stove for the church. The remainder was invested in stock and by 1854 the annual income of £5 1s. was distributed as bread at Christmas. From 1863 the charity was no longer administered separately.

By will proved 1856, Joseph Neeld bequeathed £500 to be invested in stock; the income was to maintain Neeld's tomb and benefit two aged unrelieved parishioners. In 1902 the commissioners declared the former purpose invalid and that henceforth all the income was to benefit the poor. In 1966 each beneficiary received £7 10s.

Elizabeth Bragg Shaw of Dorking (Surr.), by will proved 1874, bequeathed £100 to be invested, the interest to supply the inmates of the alms-houses at Mill Hill, and other old people, with tea and sugar at Christmas. In 1961 the annual income of £2 13s. 8d. was devoted to the sick and the poor of the parish.

By will proved in 1874 Anne Prince left £200, which was to be invested and used for the poor as the vicar of Hendon thought fit. In 1966 the income of £5 9s. was passed to the vicar for distribution to the poor. Mary Elizabeth Partridge, by will proved 1902, bequeathed £200 to provide coal for aged men and women in Hendon or the Hale. In 1965 the income of £5 9s. was distributed by the vicar. George Sneath, by will proved 1922, left £200 to be invested on behalf of aged parishioners. By 1965 the capital had grown to £311 stock and the vicar received £7 2s. to be given to the poor.

[71] Ex inf. the master.
[72] Pevsner, *Mdx.* 57.
[73] Ex inf. the headmaster.
[74] *V.C.H. Mdx.* i. 289.
[75] Ex inf. the headmistress.
[76] Except where otherwise stated the section is based on Char. Com. files and *4th Rep. Com. Char.* H.C. 312, pp. 164–7 (1820), v.
[77] C 93/42/39.
[78] Hist. Mon. Com. *Mdx.* 72; plaque on building.
[79] *Hendon and Finchley Times*, 11 Nov. 1892.
[80] Prob. 11/370 (P.C.C. 96 Cottle).
[81] Inscription on building.
[82] Prob. 11/838 (P.C.C. 163 Hutton).
[83] *Char. to be Distrib. to Poor*, H.C. 436, p. 161 (1843), xviii.

In 1895 Mrs. Eliza Burgess opened a day nursery at Devonshire Place, Childs Hill. In 1922, after her death, it was endowed with three houses (one of which was to be sold) and £2,236 stock. The nursery had a regular daily attendance of more than a dozen until it became redundant during the later 1930s. In 1942 a new Scheme established the Mrs. Burgess fund for children, to benefit children under school age in Hendon and its neighbourhood by helping mothers and by providing remedial assistance and appliances.

An Air Raid distress fund, established in 1941,[84] appears to have been perpetuated after the war as the mayor's benevolent fund. Registered as a charity in 1963, its objects are the relief of poverty and other such works as will benefit the community of Hendon. It has an annual income of about £2,000, apparently derived from investments. The Hampstead Garden Suburb charitable trust was incorporated in 1968, to apply money raised for general charitable purposes within the Garden Suburb. In 1972 the income exceeded £100.

KINGSBURY

KINGSBURY[1] was a small parish, estimated in 1831 as 1,700 a.,[2] which lay west of Edgware Road, about 6 miles from London. The river Brent formed its southern boundary with Willesden and it was separated from Harrow on the west by the Lydding brook and Honeypot Lane. The eastern boundary, with Hendon, was formed by Edgware Road as far as the Hyde, where it turned west along Kingsbury Road and then south along field boundaries and a road to the Brent. The northern boundary, with Little Stanmore, does not seem to have been fixed until after 1276–7, when Colmans Dean was regarded as part of Stanmore Chenduit manor.[3] In 1536 the inhabitants of Kingsbury were presented at the manor court for not having any marked boundaries.[4]

The civil parish of Kingsbury formed part of Wembley U.D. from 1894 until 1900, when it became Kingsbury U.D. In 1934 Kingsbury (then 1,829 a.) and Wembley were again combined in Wembley U.D., later a municipal borough, and minor changes were made in the boundaries with Harrow and Willesden; there were further adjustments in 1938 when the course of the river Brent was altered.[5] In 1965, under the London Government Act of 1963, Wembley merged with Willesden in the London Borough of Brent, of which Queensbury, Kingsbury, and Chalkhill wards covered approximately the area of the former parish of Kingsbury.[6]

Almost the whole of Kingsbury is composed of London Clay. There are small deposits of Boyn Hill Gravel at St. Andrew's church and Blackbird Hill, just north of Kingsbury bridge, and of glacial gravel on the Hendon border, north of Wood Lane. There are strips of alluvium along the course of the river Brent and Lydding brook, and some Taplow Gravel where they meet in the south-west corner of Kingsbury.[7] The London Clay gives most of Kingsbury an undulating landscape of between 100 ft. and 200 ft. Barn Hill in Wembley Park (Harrow parish) sends two tongues of higher land

into western Kingsbury, at Hill Farm and just north of Forty Lane. There are hills near Bush Farm, Wood Lane, Redhill, and Wakemans Hill Avenue in central Kingsbury where the land rises to its highest point, 302 ft.[8]

In north Kingsbury tributaries of the Lydding brook flow westward while tributaries of the Silk stream flow to the east. Southern Kingsbury is drained by two tributaries of the river Brent. One flowed from Kingsbury Green and entered the river to the east of St. Andrew's church; the other rose near Hill Farm and followed Salmon Street, joining the river to the west of the church.[9] Flooding was always a problem in the south especially after the building of Brent reservoir in 1835–9.[10] There were serious floods in 1841,[11] and as late as 1932 Salmon Street and the surrounding fields were under water.[12]

Among those who lived in Kingsbury were two servants of Elizabeth I and James I. Thomas Scudamore (d. 1626), described in 1596 as one of the queen's yeomen,[13] lived in Brasiers at Kingsbury Green. John Bull (d. 1621), gentleman of the poultry, probably lived at Roe Green. Both men were buried in St. Andrew's church.[14] A contemporary, John Chalkhill (fl. 1600), the poet and friend of Edmund Spenser, may have lived at Chalkhill House.[15] The head of Chalkhill House at the time was called Jon or Eyan Chalkhill (d. 1605), and he was succeeded by a son of the same name,[16] but there was a John Chalkhill of Kingsbury in 1606[17] and it is possible that the poet was a younger son or that the later generation which published his work misinterpreted the name Jon. The most famous of Kingsbury's residents was Oliver Goldsmith, who from 1771 to 1774 lodged at Hyde farm-house, where he wrote *She Stoops to Conquer* and where he was visited by Reynolds, Johnson, Boswell, and Mickle, the translator of the *Lusiad*.[18] Just as his walks 'about the hedges' inspired Goldsmith to write his *Animated Nature*,[19] so did James Harting,

[84] Hopkins, *Hendon*, 102.
[1] The article was written in 1970. Any references to later years are dated. The help of Mr. G. Hewlett in making material available and commenting on the article is gratefully acknowledged.   [2] *Census*, 1831.
[3] S.C. 11/439.   [4] Bodl. MS. D.D. All Souls c38/13.
[5] *Census*, 1901–51.
[6] Lond. Govt. Act, 1963, c. 33; *Brent Civic Revue*, July 1965.
[7] Geol. Surv. Map 6″, Mdx. XI. NW. (1920 edn.).
[8] O.S. Maps 1/25,000, TQ 28 (1948 edn.); TQ 29 (1949 edn.); TQ 19 (1950 edn.), 51 18 (1951 edn.).
[9] Geol. Surv. Map 6″, Mdx. XI. NW. (1920 edn.).
[10] See p. 2.

[11] S. Potter, *Old Kingsbury Church*, 26–7.
[12] Wemb. Hist. Soc., Acc. 517/2; Wemb. Hist. Soc., Photographical Collection, Acc. 333/33.
[13] Davenport MSS., Com. Ct. Lond., Reg. xviii, f. 377.
[14] Bodl. MS. Rawl. B. 389 b, ff. 85–86; see p. 85.
[15] *D.N.B.*; *N. & Q.* 4th ser. iv. 93; 5th ser. iii. 365; 8th ser. xii. 441–2.
[16] E 179/253/2; Bodl. MS. D.D. All Souls b1/19; All Souls Coll., Hovenden maps, portfolio II, no. 14.
[17] Prob. 11/109 (P.C.C. 2 Huddleston, will of Wm. Chalkhill).
[18] *D.N.B.*; J. Prior, *Life of Goldsmith*, ii. 328 sqq.; *Boswell's Life of Johnson*, ed. G. B. Hill, ii. 182.
[19] Cf. letter quoted in Prior, op. cit. ii. 328.

the naturalist who lived at St. Mary's Lodge *c.* 1851–1876, find most of the material for his *Birds of Middlesex* in Kingsbury's countryside and especially at Brent reservoir.[20] Field-Marshal Lord Roberts of Kandahar lived at Grove Park from 1893 until 1895.[21] Capt. Bertram Mills raised horses at Redhill farm in the early 1920s.[22] John Logie Baird (d. 1946), the television pioneer, rented the coach-house and stables at Kingsbury Manor in 1928 and a year later received there the first television signals from Berlin.[23]

Kingsbury lay between two ancient north–south routes, Watling Street or Edgware Road and Honeypot Lane, earlier called Old Street[24] or Hell Lane. Edgware Road remained important throughout Kingsbury's history[25] but Honeypot Lane disappeared as a road between 1597 and 1729–38,[26] although part of it remained as a footpath.[27] The other roads in Kingsbury were access roads linking the scattered farms and cottages and mostly converging on Kingsbury Green. One early road ran northward from Roe Green to Little Stanmore church. Its name, Bacon Lane, may have been derived from the Bucointe family, whose estates lay in Little Stanmore and northern Kingsbury in the 12th and 13th centuries,[28] or from John Bacun, a tenant of Edgware manor in 1284.[29] Between 1729–38 and 1754 the middle portion of Bacon Lane fell into disuse, leaving a short road, the present Bacon Lane, and a northern road beginning in Kingsbury and continuing into Little Stanmore.[30] By 1819 the Kingsbury portion of the latter had disappeared altogether.[31]

Kingsbury was linked to Harrow by Forty Lane, known in 1597 as Wembley Lane,[32] and by Gore or Kenton Lane. John Lyon (d. 1592), whose lands bordered the latter, left a bequest for the repair of the road which he described as between Goreland Gate and Hyde House;[33] payments of £2 for that purpose were still being made by Harrow School to the highway board in the later 19th century.[34] The payments were inadequate, however, and in the 1770s Oliver Goldsmith lost his shoes 'stuck fast in a slough' there, on his way to visit his friend, Hugh Boyd, at Kenton.[35] Kenton Lane was

widened in the 1880s[36] but its condition was very bad at the beginning of the 20th century, mainly because of the activities of Dr. Arthur Calcutta White and his lessee at Gore Farm.[37] The road was covered with tarmac in 1912[38] and widened and straightened as Kingsbury Road in the 1920s.[39]

In 1597 many roads converged on Kingsbury Green. One, originally called Ox Street or London Lane[40] and later Kingsbury Road, ran eastward to the Hyde; Buck Lane, earlier known as Stonepits or Postle Lane,[41] ran northward from Kingsbury Green to join Hay Lane, a road mentioned in the 13th century.[42] Another early road in northern Kingsbury was Tunworth or Stag Lane, which ran from Redhill to Roe Green.[43] Church Lane, in 1563 called Northland Lane,[44] ran southward from Kingsbury Green to the church and Green Lane[45] joined the green to Townsend Lane, known as North Dean Lane in 1394 and 1503.[46] On the west Gibbs or Piggs Lane[47] joined Kingsbury Green to Slough Lane or Sloe Street, as it was called in 1428.[48] The southward extension of Slough Lane, Salmon Street, was called Dorman Stone Lane in the 15th and 16th centuries.[49] The portion of road between the Brent and the junction of Salmon Street and Forty Lane, now called Blackbird Hill, was usually known as Kingsbury Lane.[50] There was an east–west road joining Hill and Freren farms to Hendon. The portion between Church Lane and Salmon Street, called Freren Lane in 1379,[51] had disappeared by the early 18th century.[52] That between Townsend Lane and Hendon, known as Wadlifs Lane in 1574,[53] survives as Wood Lane.

Green Lane, Gibbs Lane, and Freren Lane, as well as Honeypot Lane, fell into disuse between 1597 and 1729–38,[54] as did part of Bacon Lane soon afterwards. Thereafter for almost two centuries there was little change, in spite of frequent complaints that there were too many miles of road for a small population to keep in repair.[55] The very bad state even of Edgware Road is reflected in the bequests for repairs made by 16th-century parishioners[56] and in the name Deadman Slough, which was applied to the central portion of the road in 1597.[57] In 1851 it was pointed out that the church was isolated by dirty and sometimes

[20] Thorne, *Environs*, i. 395; H.O. 107/1700/135/2, ff. 310–28; Bodl. MS., D.D. All Souls c53, ct. bk. 1861–1914; *Kelly's Dirs. Lond.* (1860, 1872).
[21] Kingsbury U.D.C., Min. Bk. (1903–15), 429; Wemb. Hist. Soc., Acc. 28.
[22] Kingsbury U.D.C., Min. Bk. (1915–22), 366.
[23] Wemb. Hist. Soc., Acc. 907/11; Acc. 950/2; Wemb. Hist. Soc., *Jnl.* i(4), 26–31.
[24] *V.C.H. Mdx.* iv. 150, 187.
[25] For Edgware Rd., see p. 111.
[26] All Souls Coll. Oxford, Hovenden maps, portfolio II, nos. 10, 12, 14; M.R.O., Acc. 262/72/1–2. On the possible early course of Honeypot Lane, see C. F. Baylis, *Edgware and the Stanmores.*
[27] O.S. Maps 1/2,500, Mdx. XI. 5, 9 (1873, 1914 edns.).
[28] Baylis, op. cit. 7.
[29] S.C. 12/188/54.
[30] M.R.O., Acc. 262/72/1; J. Rocque, *Map of Mdx.* (1754).
[31] M.R.O., Acc. 262/30.
[32] All Souls Coll., Hovenden map, portfolio II, no. 14.
[33] Wemb. Hist. Soc., Acc. 713.
[34] M.R.O., LA. HW., Edgware Highway Bd., Par. Ledger (1863–79).
[35] J. Prior, *Life of Goldsmith,* ii. 334.
[36] M.R.O., LA. HW., Hendon Rural Sanitary Authority, Gen. Ledger (1882–91), f. 162.

[37] Kingsbury U.D.C., Wks. & Finance Cttee. Mins. (1900–2), 13; Rep. on Kingsbury U.D. 1906, *Reps. of Local Inqs.* (1895–1907), 13 *penes* M.R.O.
[38] Kingsbury U.D.C., Min. Bk. (1903–15), 364.
[39] Mdx. Educ. Cttee., *Schools Gaz.* iv(5), 73 sqq.
[40] Bodl. MS. All Souls c37/10; c79/18; c243/27.
[41] Ibid. c37/7(1); c38/13; c39/18; c78/187b.
[42] D.L. 25/159.
[43] D.L. 25/160; Bodl. MS. D.D. All Souls c37/10.
[44] Bodl. MS. D.D. All Souls c243/33.
[45] Mentioned in 1435: Bodl. MS. D.D. All Souls c37/7(1).
[46] Bodl. MS. D.D. All Souls c37/5, /10.
[47] Ibid. c37/9 (1469); c38/16 (1553); c52, ct. bk. (1616–49), s.v. 1626; c52, ct. bk., f. 57d.
[48] Ibid. c37/7(1).   [49] Ibid. c37/9; c243/33.
[50] *Kelly's Dir. Hendon* (1926).
[51] Bodl. MS. D.D. All Souls c37/4.
[52] M.R.O., Acc. 262/72/1.
[53] Bodl. MS. D.D. All Souls c243/27.
[54] All Souls Coll., Hovenden maps, portfolio II, nos. 9–15; M.R.O., Acc. 262/72/1.
[55] Kingsbury U.D.C., *San Rep.* (1906); Hendon Rural Sanitary District, Inq. 1894, *Reps. of Local Inqs.* (1889–94), 11 sqq. *penes* M.R.O.
[56] C 1/239/25; C 3/255/12; B.M. Harl. MS. 2211, ff. 23–32; Bodl. MS. D.D. All Souls c38/13.
[57] All Souls Coll., Hovenden maps, portfolio II, no. 11.

flooded roads,[58] a problem still much in evidence during the heavy storms of 1903.[59] Heavy traffic along Stag Lane in connexion with the aircraft industry led to an improvement in the road there in 1917.[60] The most important factor, however, in the transformation of Kingsbury's quiet country lanes into wide and busy thoroughfares was the opening of the British Empire Exhibition at Wembley Park in 1924. To provide access to it Blackbird Hill, Forty Lane, Kenton Lane, and Church Lane were widened and straightened.[61] In 1926 work began on a new north–south road to follow the route of the ancient Honeypot Lane.[62] By 1935 Kingsbury had been covered by a network of suburban roads, although most of the old roads survived.[63]

From ancient times the river Brent had probably been crossed at Blackbird Hill, the point where Salmon Street crosses the river. The road and bridge were mentioned in 1531 and in 1596 there was said to have been a footbridge there from time immemorial. Responsibility for its repair was divided between the lords of Kingsbury and Neasden manors. There was a ford next to the bridge for horses and carts, except when the river was in flood when the footbridge might be used by horses. Jon Chalkhill's water-mill[64] caused the formation of a large pool which submerged the ford. All Souls College built a bridge strong enough to take horses and carts and agreed with Chalkhill that he would repair it as long as he retained his mill.[65] Responsibility probably reverted to the college during the 17th century,[66] and in 1824 Kingsbury vestry asked it to repair or rebuild the bridge.[67] It is not known whether the bridge was repaired then but in 1826 it was described as wooden and 11 ft. wide, spanning a river 33 ft. wide and 6 ft. deep.[68] A new bridge was built in 1922 as part of the changes connected with the British Empire Exhibition.[69]

The bad state of the roads kept Kingsbury comparatively isolated although coach services passed along Edgware Road.[70] Trams ran along Edgware Road in 1904[71] but bad roads prevented the opening of a motor-bus service from Golders Green to Harrow along Kingsbury Road in 1920.[72] Week-end services along Kingsbury Road, Kingsbury Lane, and Forty Lane were introduced by the London General Omnibus Co. Ltd. in 1925, mainly as a result of the British Empire Exhibition.[73] More buses followed the improvement of roads and suburban building development until by 1934 most of Kingsbury was adequately served.[74]

The railway came late to Kingsbury. The Metropolitan Railway line was built across the south-western corner in 1880 and a station was opened at Wembley Park near the Wembley-Kingsbury border in 1894 but it had little effect upon the parish until the 1920s.[75] In 1932 the Stanmore branch of the Metropolitan line, which in 1939 became part of the Bakerloo line, was built across western Kingsbury and stations were opened at Kingsbury in 1932 and at Queensbury in 1934.[76]

It is possible that Kingsbury was settled before the Anglo-Saxon period. Bronze-age cinerary vessels have been reported from Brent reservoir[77] but they could have been washed some distance by streams. Roman bricks and hypocaust tiles in the fabric of old St. Andrew's church and alongside Salmon Street probably came from somewhere in the close vicinity. Roman pottery has been found inside the churchyard and in Old Church Lane; although bricks and tiles might have been brought some distance it is improbable that small sherds of pottery would have been of interest to the builders of the church.[78] William Stukeley's identification of Kingsbury churchyard with Caesar's camp[79] is entirely fanciful, possibly based upon the configuration formed by rubble from a disused sand-pit.[80]

Settlers probably reached Kingsbury along the valley of the Brent and by Watling Street. Early settlement was on the two outcrops of Boyn Hill Gravel in southern Kingsbury, which provided well-drained but water-bearing sites of light vegetation in the midst of the dense forest cover of the London Clay. Kingsbury, unlike neighbouring Harrow, was never an area of nucleated villages; the forest was probably gradually cleared from isolated farms, one of the earliest of which was Tunworth or Tuna's farm at Redhill.[81]

The settlement pattern in the Middle Ages was probably even more scattered than it was later. Most of the 21 tenements or messuages held from Edgware manor in 1426[82] were in existence in the 13th and 14th centuries.[83] A northern group included Groves in Stag Lane, Seakins, and Roes on either side of Hay Lane, and Hillhouse at Roe Green. There was a group around Kingsbury Green — Randolfs, Gardiners, Masons, Wilkin Johns, and Jack Johns. Hamonds, on the site of the later Hyde farm-house, and Perrys at Townsend Lane were in the east, and there was another group along the northern part of Salmon Street. There was a house called Lewgars at Slough Lane from the 13th century until c. 1952.[84] Dibbels probably stood opposite it, on the south side of Slough Lane. On the west side of Salmon Street stood Richards, Warrens, Edwins, and Dermans.

There were at least 12 holdings of Kingsbury

[58] H.O. 129/135/2/4/4.
[59] Kingsbury U.D.C., Min. Bk. (1903–15), 11.
[60] Ibid. (1915–22), 105.
[61] Church Com. file 51708; S4 surveys; Mdx. Educ. Cttee., Schools Gaz. iv(5), 73 sqq.
[62] A. J. Garrett, 'Hist. Geog. of Upper Brent Valley' (Lond. Univ. M.A. thesis, 1935), 140.
[63] O.S. Maps 1/2,500, Mdx. XI. 2, 5, 6, 9, 10, 13 (1935 edn.); 1 (1938 edn.).
[64] See p. 77.
[65] Bodl. MS. D.D. All Souls c77/179a.   [66] See p. 61.
[67] Kingsbury Vestry Min. Bk. (1802–34) penes Brent Cent. Ref. Libr.
[68] Rep. on Bridges in Mdx. 210.
[69] Potter, Old Kingsbury Church, 41.
[70] V.C.H. Mdx. iv. 152.

[71] See p. 3.
[72] Kingsbury U.D.C., Min. Bk. (1915–22), 323, 328.
[73] Ibid. (1922–6), 108, 233.
[74] Garrett, 'Upper Brent Valley', map and pp. 136 sqq.
[75] V.C.H. Mdx. iv. 198; Hendon Rural Sanitary District, Inq. 1894, Reps. of Local Inqs. (1889–94), 11 sqq. penes M.R.O.
[76] Robbins, Mdx. 306; V.C.H. Mdx. iv. 199.
[77] V.C.H. Mdx. i. 44–45.   [78] Ex inf. Mr. P. S. Ventner.
[79] W. Stukeley, Itinerarium Curiosum (1776 edn.), ii. 2 and plate 62.2d.
[80] S. Holliday, Hist. of Kingsbury [pamphlet, 1934].
[81] P.N. Mdx. (E.P.N.S.), 62–3.
[82] Bodl. MS. D.D. All Souls c56/2.
[83] See below sub other estates.
[84] S.C. 2/188/54; see below.

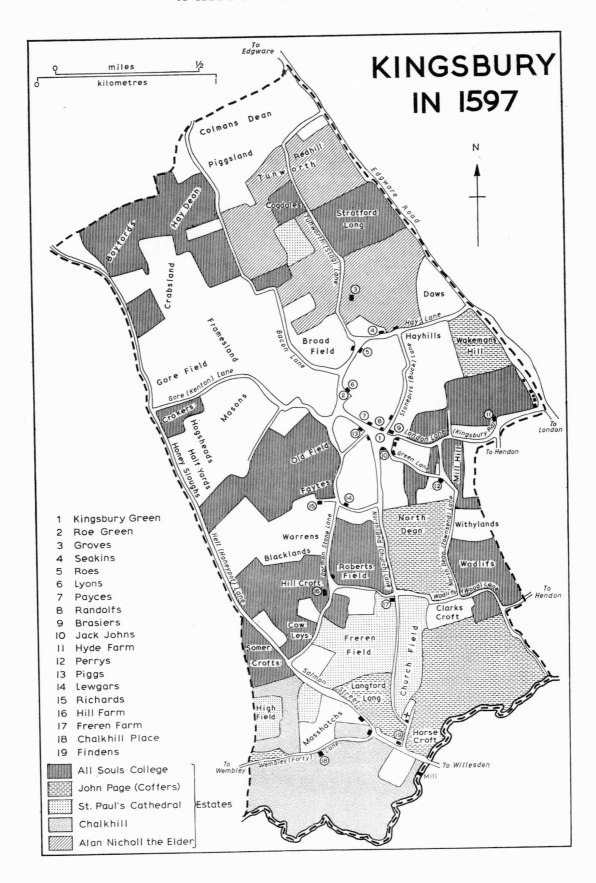

KINGSBURY
IN 1597

miles

kilometres

To
Edgware

Colmans Dean

Piggsland

Redhill

Tunworth

Coggales

Stratford
Long

Boxfords

Hay Dean

Crabsland

Framesland

Daws

Bacon Lane

Broad
Field

Hayhills

Wakemans
Hill

Hay Lane

Gore Field

Gore (Kenton) Lane

Crokers

Hogsheads

Masons

Half Yards

Stonepits (Buck) Lane

Hell (Honeypot) Lane

Honey Sloughs

Old Field

Faytes

London Lane

(Kingsbury Rd)

Green Lane

Mill Hill

To
London

To Hendon

Warrens

Blacklands

Hill Croft

Roberts
Field

North
Dean

Withylands

Wadlfs

Dorman Stone Lane

Northland (Church) Lane

North Dean (Townsend) Lane

Wadlfs

Kwool Lane

To
Hendon

Clarks
Croft

Cow
Leys

Somer
Crofts

Freren
Field

Church
Field

Salmon Street Lane

Langford
Long

High
Field

Mosshatchs

Lane

Horse
Croft

To
Wembley

Wembley (Forty)

To Willesden

Mill

1   Kingsbury Green
2   Roe Green
3   Groves
4   Seakins
5   Roes
6   Lyons
7   Payces
8   Randolfs
9   Brasiers
10 Jack Johns
11 Hyde Farm
12 Perrys
13 Piggs
14 Lewgars
15 Richards
16 Hill Farm
17 Freren Farm
18 Chalkhill Place
19 Findens

All Souls College
John Page (Coffers)
St. Paul's Cathedral   }Estates
Chalkhill
Alan Nicholl the Elder

manor, to most of which a messuage was attached in the 13th and early 14th centuries.[85] Most of these houses probably lay between Chalkhill Place and Kingsbury church.[86] The settlement was decimated by the Black Death. In 1350 the deaths of at least 13 people 'at the time of the pestilence' were presented at Kingsbury manor court after which the property became concentrated in the hands of survivors, leaving the houses to decay.[87] Elsewhere the disaster probably caused the abandonment of most of the tenements in Salmon Street. Presentments for not repairing dilapidated houses, 'for fear of disease', continued throughout the next two centuries.[88] Although Kingsbury recovered, the pattern of settlement was never the same again. Southern Kingsbury shrank from a village to a church and one or two farms. The most populous area was Kingsbury Green, which grew as new houses were built there during the 15th and 16th centuries.

The Hyde, another area of settlement, first appears as a surname in the 13th century,[89] although there is no evidence of any dwellings there before the 16th century. Edgware Road, bordered by dense woods infested with brigands and the scene of frequent violence during the 13th century,[90] was not likely to attract settlement. The first cottage was built on the waste at the Hyde in 1556–7. Another was built next to it in 1574–7 and a third in 1590–1.[91]

By 1597 there were 5 cottages at the Hyde and 26 houses in the rest of Kingsbury, although there may also have been labourers' cottages attached to some of the larger farms.[92] Fifty-two houses were listed under Kingsbury for the hearth-tax assessment of 1664.[93] In 1801 there were 45 inhabited and 5 uninhabited houses.[94] Maps show few topographical changes between 1597 and 1800.[95] Pasture had increased at the expense of arable and much woodland had been cleared but thick hedges still conveyed a wooded appearance. There had been little change in the pattern of settlement beyond the growth of the Hyde, where new houses and cottages had been built in 1675, 1684, and 1752,[96] one of them probably Shell Cottage at no. 44 Kingsbury Road, which was still there in 1971.[97]

Kingsbury's growth during the 19th century was erratic. The population trebled between 1801 and 1851 and the number of inhabited houses increased from 45 to 102. By 1881 there were 142 houses, yet in 1901 there were only 140 inhabited houses.[98] The pattern of settlement remained much the same.

Apart from the scattered farms and their attendant labourers' cottages, most housing was concentrated around the two ancient greens, Kingsbury Green and Roe Green, and the Hyde. A new centre was Pipers Green, situated to the west of Kingsbury Green at the junction of Kenton Lane with Slough Lane. The name, which may have been derived from John Lyon, piper, who was mentioned in 1422,[99] was taken from a close called Pipers. A building, probably Pipers Farm, was erected next to Slough Lane between 1597[1] and 1729–38.[2] Between 1839[3] and 1865[4] the Green Man and another house were erected to the west and the National school was built to the north; a smithy and a small group of terraced houses, probably Uxbridge Terrace,[5] were built on Kenton Lane to the west of Pipers Green. The house on the site of Pipers Farm was, from 1851 until 1880, called Rose Villa.[6] Another house at Pipers Green was in 1860 called Kingsland Villa.[7] The villas may have been rebuilt during the late 19th century, and from 1894[8] until after the Second World War they were known as Fern Dene, the Glen, and Oakfields.[9]

Kingsbury unlike its neighbours Harrow and Hendon, was never the home of many wealthy or influential people, but each of its hamlets possessed some large villa-residences. In 1816[10] there were 'a few residences of an ornamental character' at Kingsbury Green and in 1850 such villas included Kingsbury House and Mount Pleasant, as well as Grove Park, a 'distinguished seat'.[11] Kingsbury House, situated to the east of Kingsbury Green on the site of the medieval tenement of Wilkin John,[12] was probably rebuilt in the mid 19th century[13] and demolished c. 1930.[14] Mount Pleasant, which stood in Hay Lane on the site occupied in 1597 by Hopcock's cottage,[15] was demolished in 1926.[16]

Other houses at Kingsbury Green included St. Mary's Lodge, erected on the site of Piggs tenement between 1839[17] and 1851[18] and demolished c. 1949,[19] and Eden Lodge, erected on the site of Collins tenement by 1865[20] and demolished in 1967 when the new synagogue was built.[21] At Roe Green in 1887 Roe Green House and Haydon House were 'pleasant little mansions half-buried in their surrounding foliage'.[22] Larger houses along Edgware Road included Springfield House, Grove House or Elm Lea, erected between 1839 and 1851[23] and, in the north, Redhill House, erected between

[85] Bodl. MS. D.D. All Souls c37/7(1).
[86] Ibid. c75/39.
[87] Ibid. c37/2.
[88] Ibid. c37/3, /6, /7(1); c38/13.
[89] Ibid. c76/113–4, /140.
[90] S.C. 2/188/54; Garrett, 'Upper Brent Valley', 54.
[91] Bodl. MS. All Souls c52, ct. bk. f. 49.
[92] Pictorial representation used makes it difficult to distinguish attached cottages from barns or wings of houses: All Souls Coll., Hovenden maps, portfolio II, nos. 9–15.
[93] M.R.O., MR/TH/5.   [94] Census, 1801.
[95] M.R.O., Acc. 262/72/1; J. Rocque, Map of Mdx. (1754); Milne, Plan of Lond. etc. (1800).
[96] Bodl. MS. D.D. All Souls c245/34z.
[97] Ex inf. Mr. G. Hewlett.   [98] Census, 1801–1901.
[99] So called to distinguish him from his namesake, a mason: Bodl. MS. D.D. All Souls c37/6. See p. 65.
[1] All Souls Coll., Hovenden maps, portfolio II, no. 12.
[2] M.R.O., Acc. 262/72/1.
[3] M.R.O., TA/KIN.
[4] O.S. Map 1/2,500, Mdx. XI. 5 (1873 edn.).

[5] H.O. 107/1700/135/2, ff. 310–28.
[6] Ibid.; Kelly's Dir. Lond. (1880), 206.
[7] Ibid. (1860), 66.   [8] Ibid. (1894), 364.
[9] Age of Bldgs. map penes Brent L.B., Planning and Research Dept.
[10] Brewer, Beauties of Eng. and Wales, x(5), 681.
[11] Wemb. Hist. Soc., Jnl. N.S. i(8), 18–19. For Grove Park, see p. 68.
[12] All Souls Coll., Hovenden maps, portfolio II, no. 13.
[13] M.R.O., TA/KIN; O.S. Map 1/2,500, Mdx. XI. 6 (1873 edn.).
[14] Ex inf. British Leyland (Austin–Morris) Ltd. (1969).
[15] All Souls Coll., Hovenden maps, portfolio II, no. 13.
[16] Hendon Libr., Print L.4249.   [17] M.R.O., TA/KIN.
[18] H.O. 107/1700/135/2, ff. 310–28; Kelly's Dir. Lond. (1860), 66.
[19] Ex inf. Mr. G. Hewlett.
[20] O.S. Map 1/2,500, Mdx. XI. 6 (1873 edn.).
[21] See p. 87.
[22] H. J. Foley, Our Lanes and Meadow Paths, 43; see below, p. 67.
[23] M.R.O., TA/KIN; H.O. 107/1700/135/2, ff. 310–28.

1819[24] and 1839, which from 1851 was called Oak Cottage or Lodge.[25]

One of the most striking of the 19th-century houses was Lewgars in Slough Lane. A house stood on the site probably from the 13th century. It was rebuilt in the 18th or early 19th century and enlarged in 1872 with a west wing in a fantastic castellated and ecclesiastical Gothic style by its new owner, Edward Nelson Haxell, a churchwarden and enthusiastic antiquary, who used materials from St. Andrew's church which had been discarded during the restoration of 1870. Lewgars was demolished *c.* 1952.[26] In 1899 a large, half-timbered house, designed by W. West Neve, was erected east of Valley Farm for Mary, dowager duchess of Sutherland, the wife of Sir Albert Kaye Rollit, M.P. Called the Cottage, Manor House and, after 1929, Kingsbury Manor, it was acquired by Middlesex C.C. in 1938 and used as an old people's home.[27]

Until the First World War and, in many parts of the parish, until the 1930s,[28] Kingsbury impressed outsiders by its totally rural appearance. Oliver Goldsmith wrote in 1771 of his sojourn at Hyde House as being in the country, where he had been strolling about the hedges, and in 1837 his biographer described the prospect from the farm-house of the wooded, undulating country towards Hendon.[29] A view of the Hyde in 1799 shows a cluster of probably weatherboarded cottages and a wide, rut-marked road with well-wooded verges.[30] In 1860 the view from Kingsbury church was rural in every direction,[31] and in 1887 praise was lavished upon Kingsbury's winding lanes overhung by luxuriant foliage, its hayfields and its buildings with their old world look.[32] Many writers[33] eulogized southern Kingsbury and Brent reservoir for the wealth of wild life found there.

The reality for most of the inhabitants must have been different, for the parish at that period was characterized by neglect. Its hedges were unkempt because cheap coal had replaced hedge-wood as fuel.[34] Its many winding lanes, difficult to maintain and a burden on the rates, were frequently uncared for and almost impassable in winter.[35] Its beautiful reservoir brought destruction to farm-land and death to injudicious bathers.[36] The small population meant that rates, though high, could not finance essential services and insanitary conditions and ill-health were prevalent. Perhaps the most important cause of neglect was the system of leasing. Almost all the picturesque farms and cottages were held on short leases and often sub-let, which meant that

they were rarely in good repair and were frequently overcrowded and squalid.[37] The building of Holy Innocents church in 1884 was a belated recognition that the main area of settlement was central Kingsbury. From the two new farms, Gore and Valley farms, in the west, houses stretched through Kingsbury Manor, Pipers and Kingsbury greens and the terraced cottages built in Buck Lane in 1843[38] to those which were creeping westward along Kingsbury Road from the Hyde; tall, narrow buildings known locally as the windjammers,[39] they were described in 1934 as 'the ugliest thing in rural Middlesex'.[40] In contrast, there was little development along Edgware Road itself between 1839 and the First World War, largely because of the difficulties of sewerage and inadequate public transport.[41]

The First World War and the siting of the British Empire Exhibition at Wembley Park hastened development. The number of houses rose from 140 to 1901 to 440 in 1921, 3,937 in 1931, and 11,776 in 1951.[42] Work started before the war in Stag Lane, near Edgware Road, where 20 houses were built in 1909–10 and 16 more by 1919.[43] The 1914–18 war brought the aircraft industry to north-east Kingsbury and in 1916 the Office of Works commissioned Frank Baines to design Roe Green Village for employees of the Aircraft Manufacturing Co. Ltd. He was to build 250 houses on a 24-acre site north-west of Roe Green, between Bacon Lane and Stag Lane; 150 had been built by 1919 but the slump following the war left about 75–90 houses unoccupied in 1920.[44]

The Metropolitan Railway Co. Estates Ltd., which was largely responsible for the development of Wembley, bought most of the Chalkhill estate in 1919. By 1924 large, detached houses had been built around the new Chalkhill and Barnhill roads.[45] The widening of Forty Lane and Blackbird Hill to give access to the British Empire Exhibition opened up the whole of southern Kingsbury to the builders and roads and houses to the east of Salmon Street, between Queens Walk and Old Church Lane, were constructed during the early 1920s.[46] During that period industry was established in Edgware Road and at Kingsbury Works in Kingsbury Road,[47] and 37 council houses were built at High Meadow Crescent near Kingsbury Green.[48]

Most development, however, took place in the late 1920s and early 1930s. From 1931 until 1933 houses were being erected at a rate of over 1,000 a year, mostly by private firms,[49] some of which, like Kingsbury Estates Ltd. (1925),[50] Salmon Estate

[24] M.R.O., Acc. 262/30.
[25] M.R.O., TA/KIN; H.O. 107/1700/135/2, ff. 310–28.
[26] Potter, *Old Kingsbury Church*, 10–11, 27; Wemb. Hist. Soc., Photo. Coll., Acc. 412/6; Acc. 464.
[27] *The Times*, 21 Dec. 1937; Wemb. Hist. Soc., Acc. 950/2; Wemb. Hist. Soc., *Jnl.* i(4), 26–31; *Kelly's Dir. Lond.* (1900), 304; *Building News*, lxxvii. 229.
[28] e.g. Pipers Green in 1930: Wemb. Hist. Soc., Acc. 388/3, 7 and 10.
[29] J. Prior, *Life of Goldsmith*, ii. 328–30, 332.
[30] B.M. King's Coll. xxx. 4.
[31] Quoted in Elsley, *Wembley*, 180.
[32] Foley, *Lanes and Meadow Paths*, 34–43.
[33] Thorne, *Environs*, i. 395.
[34] G. B. G. Bull, 'Changing Landscape of Rural Mdx. 1500–1850' (Lond. Univ. Ph.D. thesis, 1958), 78.
[35] Hendon rural sanitary dist., Inq. 1894, *Reps. of Local Inqs.* (1889–94), 11 *penes* M.R.O.; Kingsbury U.D.C., *San. Rep.* (1906).

[36] Potter, *Old Kingsbury Ch.* 39.
[37] M.O.H., *Reps. on San. Conditions of Wembley U.D.C.* (1895–1901); Kingsbury U.D.C., *San. Reps.* (1901–9).
[38] Bodl. MS. D.D. All Souls c151/F/4.
[39] Ex inf. Brent L.B., Planning and Research Dept. (1971).
[40] M. S. Briggs, *Mdx. Old and New*, 156.
[41] M.R.O., TA/KIN; O.S. Maps 1/2,500, Mdx. XI. 6 (1873, 1896, and 1914 edns.). [42] *Census*, 1901–51.
[43] Kingsbury U.D.C., Min. Bk. (1915–22), 205.
[44] Ibid. 26, 156, 205, 231; Kingsbury U.D.C., *M.O.H. Ann. Rep.* (1919); *Builder*, cxiv. 5–6.
[45] Kingsbury U.D.C., Min. Bk. (1915–22), 228, 252, 297; Kingsbury U.D.C., *M.O.H. Ann. Reps.* (1920, 1922) Wemb. Hist. Soc., Acc. 761/2.
[46] M.R.O., Acc. 954; *Kelly's Dir. Hendon* (1926).
[47] See p. 78.
[48] Ex inf. Brent L.B., Housing Dept. (1970).
[49] Kingsbury U.D.C., *M.O.H. Ann Rep.* (1933).
[50] M.R.O., Acc. 954.

(Kingsbury) Ltd. (1928),[51] Kingsbury Development Co. Ltd. (1934),[52] and Woodfields Development Co. Ltd. (1936),[53] were set up expressly to develop Kingsbury. Most of the housing in the area enclosed by Edgware Road, Stag Lane, and Roe Green was built after 1926 and complete by 1935.[54] In the south planning permission was granted for building near Wood Lane in 1926;[55] 108 houses were being built on Townsend Park estate in 1926, the council built 63 houses in Elthorne Road and Way in 1927–31,[56] and plans were submitted for 116 houses on Fryent Farm estate in 1928.[57] Shop sites and building land in Church Lane were being offered for sale in 1933[58] and building was taking place along Salmon Street in 1934.[59] By 1935 houses filled the area east of Salmon Street and south of Lavender Avenue, and much of that between Forty Lane on the south and Salmon Street on the north-east.[60] The farm-lands of Gore farm and Hungry Down were sold in 1928[61] and 1931[62] respectively but growth in north-west Kingsbury really began with the construction of the Underground railway and opening of stations at Kingsbury and Queensbury in 1932 and 1934 and with the widening of Kingsbury Road in the 1920s and building of Honeypot Lane in 1934.[63] In 1932 development extended on either side of Kingsbury Road, along Valley Drive and some of its side streets to the south, and northward as far as Girton Avenue and Fairway Avenue.[64] Stag Lane airfield formed a gap in the advancing housing until it was sold to developers in 1933, after which building spread northward until by 1940 northern Kingsbury was entirely covered by roads, houses, schools, and small factories.[65]

There were few large areas left for building after the Second World War. All Souls sold the portion of Hill Farm east of Salmon Street and north of Lavender Avenue in 1948[66] and 154 houses were built there by the council in 1949–51.[67] By 1951 Pilgrims Way had appeared to the south-west of Fryent Way[68] and the council built 91 houses and flats on either side of the northern part of Fryent Way between 1949 and 1952.[69] Most post-war development, however, was of small sites, farm-houses or large houses like Valley, Hill, and both Bush farm-houses, Chalkhill House, Lewgars, and Grove Park. There was rebuilding, mainly by the council, at Kingsbury and Pipers greens while Chalkhill was transformed from an area of low-density detached houses to one of high-density flats.[70]

By 1970, apart from old St. Andrew's church, a few 19th-century cottages and one or two larger buildings at the Hyde, nothing remained of old Kingsbury. Its identity as a parish had long since disappeared and Kingsbury Green, once the focal point of many lanes and the centre of the village, had been destroyed by the straightening of Kingsbury Road and subsequent building. No farmhouses remain. Instead continuous suburban housing obliterates all distinction between Kingsbury, Harrow, and Stanmore. Southern Kingsbury, with Brent reservoir and Fryent open space, and its detached houses around the two churches of St. Andrew, retains traces of its former quiet, wooded appearance. The factories and shopping centres are concentrated in the north,[71] as are most of the churches and schools. Although it had lost some of its houses and trees, Roe Green Village, which had been made a conservation area in 1968, retained something of the atmosphere of a village green. In Slough Lane and Buck Lane there are some timbered, thatched houses, built between 1921 and 1930 by Ernest George Trobridge, aptly described as 'artificial old-world creations heavy with thatch and make-up'.[72] Also in Buck Lane are some striking castellated and turreted brick and stone houses and flats. Most of the area, however, is covered by the more conventional semi-detached brick houses characteristic of the period between the two World Wars, interspersed with some more modern-looking small blocks of flats.

There were 98 communicants in Kingsbury in 1547[73] and 210 conformists and 1 nonconformist in 1676.[74] Far from increasing, the population may even have declined during the next 125 years: the number of houses, 52, was the same in 1795[75] as in 1664.[76] The population in 1801 was 209. It rose to 606 in 1851 but decreased to 509 in 1861 because some cottages had been converted into larger houses and a boarding-school had closed. It rose to 759 in 1881 but remained stationary at the end of the century and was still only 821 in 1911. It more than doubled in the next decade, to 1,856 in 1921, and thereafter increased rapidly, to 16,636 in 1931 and 41,905 in 1951. After some inhabitants had been moved to new towns like Hemel Hempstead, the numbers fell to 38,687 in 1961.[77]

MANORS. The early English kings had parted with their manor of Kingsbury long before the Conquest.[78] An estate called Tunworth,[79] in the

[51] Church Com., S4 surveys, p. 530A.
[52] *The Times*, 21 Aug. 1934.
[53] Tithe-rent redemption certs. A9/20–60 *penes* Holy Innocents church, Kingsbury.
[54] Kingsbury U.D.C., Min. Bk. (1922–6), 138, 341, 371; (1926–9), 106, 126, 129; O.S. Map 1/2,500, Mdx. XI. 2, 6 (1935 edn.); Land Util. Survey Map 1″, sheet 106 (1935 edn.).
[55] Kingsbury U.D.C., Min. Bk. (1926–9), 4.
[56] Ex inf. Brent L.B., Housing Dept.
[57] Kingsbury U.D.C., Min. Bk. (1926–9), 43, 307.
[58] Hendon Libr., MS. R.L.942. 1911.
[59] Holliday, *Hist. Kingsbury*.
[60] Land Util. Survey Map 1″, sheet 106 (1935 edn.).
[61] Kingsbury U.D.C., Min. Bk. (1926–9), 307.
[62] Ex inf. Daniel Smith, Briant and Done (land agents for All Souls Coll.).
[63] Holliday, *Hist. Kingsbury*.
[64] O.S. Map 1/2,500, Mdx. XI. 5 (1932 edn.).
[65] Ibid. (1940 edn.).

[66] Ex inf. Daniel Smith, Briant and Done.
[67] Ex inf. Brent L.B., Housing Dept.
[68] O.S. Map 1/25,000, 51 18 (1951 edn.). The site is being dismantled and will be absorbed in Fryent open space; ex inf. Brent L.B., Planning and Research Dept. (1971).
[69] Ex inf. Brent L.B., Housing Dept. (1970).
[70] Age of Bldgs. map *penes* Brent L.B., Planning and Research Dept.; ex inf. Brent L.B., Housing Dept. (1970). For the post-war growth of Chalkhill, see *V.C.H. Mdx.* iv. 202.
[71] See pp. 77–8.
[72] Robbins, *Mdx.* 307.
[73] E 301/34 m. 32.
[74] William Salt Libr., Stafford, Salt MS. 33, p. 40.
[75] Lysons, *Environs*, iii. 235.
[76] M.R.O., MR/TH/5.
[77] *Census*, 1801–1961.
[78] *P.N. Mdx.* (E.P.N.S.), 61.
[79] *Pace P.N. Mdx.* 219–20. Tunworth was an identifiable locality around Tunworth, later Stag, Lane: see map on p. 52.

northern part of Kingsbury parish, was granted by Edwy to his thegn Lyfing in 957.[80] By 1066 it probably formed part of the manor of Kingsbury (7½ hides), which was then held by Wlward White, a thegn of the Confessor, and passed from him to Ernulf of Hesdin.[81] Ernulf died in 1097 and his lands passed to the ancestors of the earls of Salisbury, probably through the marriage of his granddaughter Sibyl with Walter of Salisbury. Thereafter the overlordship of Kingsbury descended with Edgware manor.[82]

By 1086 Ernulf's manor in Kingsbury had been subinfeudated to Albold.[83] It was not mentioned again until 1317, when, under the name of the manor of *KINGSBURY*, it belonged to Baldwin Poleyn of Tebworth (Beds.)[84] into whose hands it seems to have come from John Poleyn (*c* 1300)[85] and to him from Gilbert of Tebworth (fl. *c.* 1202–27).[86] Between 1329 and 1331 Baldwin Poleyn sold the manor[87] to Walter Saling who died not later than 1340, when the manor was divided between three daughters, Alice, Maud, and Isabel,[88] one of whom may have married Thomas Page of Little Stanmore or sold the manor to him.[89] Thomas's son William married Christine Raven, his guardian's daughter, and from 1358, when he came of age, William held the manor jointly with his wife.[90] The Pages had two daughters, Elizabeth, who died unmarried, and Margaret, who married William Bury but died before her husband and father.[91] A trust was formed for the benefit of William and Margaret Bury with remainder, in default of heirs to Margaret, to William Page's heirs general. In 1410 the trustees granted the manor to William Bury and his second wife Joan.[92]

In 1425 John Penne, a London grocer, William Page's heir, recovered the manor from William Bury.[93] Penne mortgaged it in 1434 to Richard Clopton, a London draper[94] who foreclosed the mortgage in 1436. Clopton at once conveyed the property to Richard Barnett *alias* Somry and Robert Wight, clerks, possibly as trustees or mortgagees.[95] After various changes, presumably in trusteeship,[96] Thomas Chichele, archdeacon of Canterbury, and another granted the manor in 1441 to Henry VI,[97] who granted it in 1442 to All Souls College, Oxford,[98] still the owners of some property in Kingsbury in 1970.[99] In 1597 All Souls College owned 418 a. scattered through Kingsbury.[1] The

two ploughs in demesne held by Albold in 1086[2] and the demesne land attached to Kingsbury manor, first mentioned in 1325,[3] were probably located in south-western Kingsbury near the later Hill Farm. Other lands acquired by the owners of the manor became merged in the demesne lands. Of these the Page lands and Hamonds and Collins were the largest.

The Page family began to build up an estate in Kingsbury before acquiring the manor in the mid 14th century. In 1295 William Page, then described as of Little Stanmore, exchanged property with William Pypard, also of Little Stanmore, son of one of the heiresses of William Paris.[4] In exchange for land in Stanmore, Page received land in Edgware and Kingsbury, which was held by charter from the earl of Lincoln.[5] The portion in Kingsbury consisted of strips in Tunworth and Colmans Dean and Mays Field, an 11-acre field to the west of Bacon Lane.[6]

Faytisland was acquired in 1300. Among property held by free tenants of Edgware manor in 1276–7 was one carucate held by Hamon Constantine and two virgates held by John of Westmelne.[7] These can probably be identified with the lands and tenements in Kingsbury which Michael Constantine and John of Westmelne granted to Roger de Fleg, who conveyed them to Henry de Affeyte (La Feyte) and Alice, daughter of Millicent of Pelyndon and their daughters, Joan and Cecily.[8] Cecily sold the estate to William Page, then described as of Edgware, in 1300.[9] In 1316 Page settled on himself and his wife, Margaret Roos (La Rous), property in Stanmore, Edgware, and Kingsbury, of which the Kingsbury portion was described as a messuage, 140 a. of arable, 2 a. of meadow, and 5s. 1d. rent which he had acquired from William Aunsel and Cecily, daughter of Henry La Feyte.[10] Faytes, a 7-acre meadow lying west of Slough Lane, was presumably part of this estate.[11]

At the beginning of the 14th century Richard, son of Simon the elder of Kingsbury, who had held 3 quartrons of customary land in 1276–7,[12] sold 6½ a. of land and meadow in strips in Apsfurlong, Sneteleshale, and Old Haw, all in the region of Hay Lane, to William Page.[13] In 1306 Page exchanged 3 a. in Sneteleshale for 3¾ a. in Street Furlong, Old Haw, and Arneyshaw with the daughters of Michael atte Hyde, Alice, who was unmarried, Isabel, Mariot, and

[80] *Cart. Sax.* ed. Birch, iii, p. 188.
[81] *V.C.H. Mdx.* i. 126.
[82] *Complete Peerage*, s.v. Salisbury. For the subsequent descent, see *V.C.H. Mdx.* iv. 155.
[83] *V.C.H. Mdx.* i. 126.
[84] Bodl. MS. D.D. All Souls c75/1.
[85] D.L. 25/160.
[86] Bodl. MS. D.D. All Souls c76/114. Gilbert did not belong (*pace* Mr. S. C. Holliday) to the Poleyn family, but he came from the same village in Bedfordshire: Marian K. Dale, *Court Roll of Chalgrave Manor, 1278–1313* (Beds. Hist. Rec. Soc. xxviii), pp. xxviii–xxix, 53; *Beds. Hist. Rec. Soc.* x. 139–40, 218.
[87] Bodl. MSS. D.D. All Souls c75/4, /6–7; C.P. 25(1)/150/54.
[88] Bodl. MS. D.D. All Souls c75/10.
[89] Ibid. c37/2; c240/10.
[90] Ibid. c75/12, /15–16. Wm. Page (aged 13 in 1350) was the ward of the prior of St. Bartholomew's, Smithfield, his overlord in Stanmore. The prior granted the wardship and marriage to Ric. Raven, who engineered the marriage and joint settlement.
[91] Bodl. MSS. D.D. All Souls c75/19; c240/10.
[92] Ibid. c75/18–19, /27–31, /33, /35.

[93] Ibid. /35.
[94] Ibid. c76/50, /52–53, /59–60.
[95] Ibid. /72–73, /75.
[96] Ibid. /67, /77, /79, /83–4, /86–7.
[97] Ibid. /89–90; c139/7.
[98] Ibid. c76/91; *Cal. Pat.* 1441–6, 20, 99.
[99] Ex inf. Daniel Smith, Briant and Done (land agents for All Souls College).
[1] All Souls Coll., Hovenden maps, portfolio II, nos. 9–15.
[2] *V.C.H. Mdx.* i. 126.
[3] Bodl. MS. D.D. All Souls c75/2.
[4] C. F. Baylis, *Edgware and the Stanmores*, 16; J.I. 1/543 m. 49.
[5] Held for 1 lb. of cumin at Easter and suit at the hundred and county cts.
[6] Bodl. MS. D.D. All Souls c76/133; All Souls Coll., Hovenden map, portfolio II, no. 10.
[7] S.C. 11/439.
[8] Bodl. MS. D.D. All Souls c76/134.   [9] Ibid. /135.
[10] Ibid. /143–4; C.P. 25(1)/149/47/208.
[11] All Souls Coll., Hovenden map, portfolio II, no. 12.
[12] S.C. 11/439.
[13] Bodl. MS. D.D. All Souls, c76/136. Richard's son, Richard, quitclaimed to Page in 1306: ibid./137.

Helen, and their husbands, Simon Taylor of Hendon, William Shepherd, and Richard, son of Reynold Smith.[14] These transactions were presumably the origin of the two demesne fields (32 a.) of Stratford Long.[15]

In 1316 Alice, Helen, and Isabel granted Page 6 a. in the Hay Dean (Thaydene).[16] Like other land in northern Kingsbury — Hay Lane, Haydon Mead, Haydon Shots, and Hay Hills — it was probably originally part of Hayland, the estate owned by the de la Haye family. Possibly identifiable with the Lincolnshire family which was connected by marriage with William Longespée and which also had property in Bedfordshire,[17] the de la Hayes held land in Kingsbury during the 13th century.[18] Agnes, widow of Roger de la Haye (atte Haye) leased her dower-land to William Page in 1305–6[19] and Roger's daughter and heir, Christine, and her husband, William Aunsel of Kenton, sold 17 a. of Hayland to Page in 1310.[20]

William Page died between 1325 and 1329[21] and his property passed to his son, Thomas, of Edgware,[22] and, between 1346 and 1350, to his grandson, William.[23] Other land which became merged in the demesne lands of Kingsbury manor included the rest of Haydon Mead, formerly part of a 180-acre estate in north Kingsbury, Hendon, and Edgware, which had been conveyed by Walter and Isabel of Watford to William Bereford in 1285–6.[24] John Bereford of Hendon conveyed the Haydon Mead portion in 1381 to William de Stanton, chaplain of Little Stanmore,[25] who in 1387 conveyed it to John Raven and others.[26]

Although all William Page's lands were included in a survey made of the manorial demesne in 1438–9,[27] a distinction between the original demesne and other lands was still sufficiently recognized in 1485 for it to be necessary for All Souls College to make a grant of £1 13s. 4d. for 36 years to Richard Bury to relinquish all title to William Bury's lands, identifiable as all the Page lands in northern Kingsbury.[28]

The lands of Kingsbury manor acquired two copyhold estates in the 1450s. These were the lands held from Kingsbury manor by Lucy Dorman (Derman) and John Head, identifiable with Dormans Mead and other land mingled with the demesne lands west of Salmon Street.[29]

Hyde Farm, or Hamonds and Collins, which in the earliest extant terrier (1574)[30] consisted of 87 a. in eastern Kingsbury and Hendon, originated in an estate built up by Edmund Stevens and conveyed by him to All Souls College in 1503.[31] The farm-house itself, situated north of Kingsbury Road

in the centre of land stretching from Edgware Road almost to Kingsbury Green (27 a. in 1597),[32] can be identified with Lorchons, described in 1426 as a tenement and ½ virgate.[33] It had been held by Richard Page alias Lorchon (fl. 1359), whose widow died seised of it in 1393.[34] The property passed to Page's daughter and heir, Sarah, wife of John Smith, and to their daughters and coheirs, Joan, wife of Edward Collins, and Margaret, married successively to John Cox, John Gardiner, and John Hamond,[35] although only Hamond appears as the holder on the rental of 1426.[36] In 1471 Hamond's son, Richard, conveyed the property to John Canon, who surrendered it in 1486 to John Pinner, tallow-chandler of London, from whom it passed in 1488 to Sir Thomas Brian, chief justice of the King's Bench. Brian must have surrendered the property to Edmund Stevens before 1495, when John Canon quitclaimed his interest, and in 1499 Stevens bought out the interest of George Collins, son of Joan, the other coheir. Stevens's purchase from Brian included Mill Hill, 12 a. south of Kingsbury Road, which John Pinner had acquired from Henry Mosshatch in 1488.[37] Part of the property held by the Grove family in the early 15th century,[38] it had passed to John Lyon by 1441,[39] and to Robert Mosshatch in 1466.[40] Other near-by property acquired by Edmund Stevens included Wadlifs, Spencers, and Longcrofts (19 a. in 1597), land held in 1426 by Alice Clerk, whence it passed to the Mosshatch family and to Hugh Morland, who conveyed it to Stevens in 1492.[41] Simonds (9 a. in 1597), in 1426 a tenement and three quartrons, was sold by Richard Simond's executors to Stevens in 1493.[42] The name 'Hamonds' was extended from its original description of Lorchons to the whole of Edmund Stevens's estate in eastern Kingsbury.

The 'Collins' portion of the estate consisted of freehold lands in western Hendon which were conveyed in 1312 by Simon King and his wife Mariot to their daughter, Mabel, and her husband, John Collins. Their daughter, the wife of William atte Hegge, inherited the property, which was divided between her daughters and coheirs, the wives of Thomas Freville of Laleham and Roger Smith of Hendon. Freville's portion had passed to Thomas Forster of Laleham before 1395 when Forster conveyed it to John Fremley, also of Laleham.[43] In 1495 Henry Fremley, husbandman of Laleham, conveyed it to Edmund Stevens.[44] Roger Smith's portion remained in the hands of the Smiths of Hendon until 1496, when John Smith and others conveyed it to Edmund Stevens and others.[45]

[14] Ibid. /138.
[15] All Souls Coll., Hovenden map, portfolio II, no. 11.
[16] Bodl. MS. D.D. All Souls c76/140–2. Alice was still unmarried and Helen was the widow of Richard atte Hyde.
[17] I. J. Sanders, *English Baronies*, 109; W. Austin, *Hist. of Luton*, ii. 252.
[18] D.L. 25/159–61; Bodl. M.S. D.D. All Souls c76/113–14.
[19] Bodl. MS. D.D. All Souls c76/116.
[20] Ibid. /117; C.P. 25(1)/149/40; see above.
[21] Bodl. MS. D.D. All Souls c75/2, /4.
[22] Ibid. c76/147.
[23] Ibid. c75/11–12.
[24] C.P. 25(1)/148/31.
[25] Bodl. MS. D.D. All Souls c76/118.
[26] Ibid. /119.
[27] Ibid. c78/186.
[28] Ibid. c37/10.

[29] All Souls Coll., Hovenden map, portfolio II, no. 12; Davenport MSS.: Bursars' Accts.; Bodl. MS. D.D. All Souls c56/11–12.
[30] Bodl. MS. D.D. All Souls c243/27.
[31] Ibid. c37/10; c52.
[32] All Souls Coll., Hovenden map, portfolio II, no. 13.
[33] Bodl. MS. D.D. All Souls c56/2.
[34] Ibid. c37/3, /5.
[35] Ibid. /10.
[36] Ibid. c56/2.
[37] Ibid. c37/10.   [38] See p. 67
[39] Bodl. MS. D.D. All Souls c37/8.
[40] Ibid. /9.
[41] Ibid. /6, /8, /10; c56/2.
[42] Ibid. c37/10; c56/2.
[43] Ibid. c76/120–1, /124; c77/162.
[44] Ibid. c76/126.
[45] Ibid. /127–8; c77/162; C 1/26/237.

Stevens received £80 from All Souls College in 1498 for all his copyhold lands in Kingsbury and for Collins in Hendon,[46] although the conveyance was not entered in the court rolls until 1503,[47] and with others he granted Collins in 1504 to Thomas Judde and others who in 1515 granted it to William Broke and others.[48] The college was certainly in possession of both Hamonds and Collins by 1533–6.[49] Wheat Croft, 4 a. lying east of Salmon Street, which was acquired from Thomas Wilkins by Edmund Stevens in 1489 and conveyed by him to All Souls with his other property, became absorbed into Kingsbury manor farm.[50]

William Mowbray (fl. 1521)[51] surrendered a customary close held from the manor of Kingsbury, then 6 a. and later 9 a., lying to the west of Stag Lane in north Kingsbury to All Souls College to be held for life by William Cogdale (Cockdale) and after his death to be sold for charitable purposes. Cogdale, who was the holder by 1528–9,[52] held the close, which took his name, for 30 years, after which it was seized by the college and absorbed into its estate. In spite of a protest made in 1610, profits from the close were never used for charity.[53] In 1591 Thomas Shepherd conveyed a cottage, Vassetts, which lay east of Salmon Street, almost opposite Hill Farm, and other copyhold land of the manor of Kingsbury to All Souls College.[54]

Purchases and exchanges during the 19th century extended and consolidated the All Souls College estate. Threshbeings Acre (4 a.) in north Kingsbury was bought in 1842 from Nicholl's estate.[55] In 1843 the college acquired Little Bush farm (44 a.), which joined and intermingled with the farm-land of Kingsbury manor, and in 1845 it bought Old Haws (5½ a.) adjoining Old Field, all from Francis Stubbs's estate.[56] In an exchange with William Field in 1858 it relinquished 7 a. to the west of Townsend Lane for 14 a. on the east, giving it the whole of the area between Kingsbury Road and Wood Lane.[57] Between 1868 and 1879, 20 a. on the border with Wembley south of Kingsbury manor farm-lands were bought from John W. Prout.[58] By an exchange with the Ecclesiastical Commissioners in 1890, All Souls acquired 34 a., of which 18½ a. joined the lands recently bought from Prout, and the rest lay near Hyde farm-house and in the north. In return, the college surrendered 35 a., mostly the original Collins land in Hendon.[59]

Before the First World War All Souls College[60] sold some land, including the site of the maternity hospital at Honeypot Lane and part of Stratford Long or Shoelands adjoining Edgware Road, which was developed for industry. The rest of Shoelands

and Hungry Down in north-west Kingsbury was sold for building in 1931. The site for Wembley town hall in Forty Lane was sold to Wembley U.D.C. and the southern part of Hyde farm at Kinloch Avenue for building in 1933. The land north of it, Jubilee park (36 a.), was bought by Wembley U.D.C. in 1936. Most of Kingsbury manor or Hill farm-lands and Little Bush farm (160 a.) was sold in 1938 to Middlesex C.C. and Wembley B.C. for use as open space. In 1967, as Fryent regional open space, it was grassland leased by the Greater London Council to the London Borough of Brent.[61] In 1948 19 a. of Hill farm-land east of Salmon Street was sold to Wembley. The rest of the estate, comprising Crokers, land on the border with Wembley, some land east of Salmon Street, and Hyde farm-lands north of Kingsbury Road, was retained by the college, let on building leases for houses and shops. The home farm of the Kingsbury manor estate was situated to the west of Salmon Street. Buildings (domibus) were attached to the estate in 1325 and a 'messuage' was first specified in 1331.[62] It was called a manor c. 1438–9[63] and from 1445–6 repairs to Kingsbury Manor appear as a regular item in the accounts of the bursar of All Souls College.[64] In 1951 15th-century hammers were found when a barn collapsed at Hill Farm.[65] From 1574 the house and its lands were called the Hill farm.[66] The farm-house was depicted in 1597 as a house facing Salmon Street with a complex of buildings around a courtyard behind it, a kitchen-garden, orchard, and two ponds.[67] The house was assessed for 6 hearths in 1664.[68] From 1700 the house became the centre of one of the four farms into which the estate was divided by leasing.[69]

The southern part of Kingsbury was freehold land which may have originated in the woodland held in common by freeholders, which was mentioned in early documents.[70] In 1276–7 Hamon Constantine held a carucate and John of Westmelne held two virgates of freehold land.[71] Most of this property seems to have passed by the 1290s to Thomas of Brancaster, who was building up an estate in Kingsbury and Hendon at the end of the 13th century.[72] It was held in 1325 by Geoffrey le Scrope, possibly as a lessee from the Brancasters or as a reward for his support of Edward II.[73] The estate reverted to the Brancasters, probably after Edward II's fall. In 1333 it was held by Gilbert, son of Alan Brancaster, a former citizen of London, who, in association with Gillian le Joigneur, jeweller of London, leased an estate in south-east Kingsbury to Henry and Christine Page.[74]

[46] Bodl. MS. D.D. All Souls c76/130.
[47] Ibid. c37/10.
[48] Bodl. MS. D.D. All Souls c76/129, /131.
[49] Ibid. c268/225.
[50] Ibid. c37/10; All Souls Coll., Hovenden maps, portfolio II, no. 14.
[51] Bodl. MS. D.D. All Souls c56/12. [52] Ibid. /11.
[53] B.M. Harl. MS. 2211, ff. 23–32; see p. 50.
[54] Bodl. MS. D.D. All Souls c76/149; c56/11.
[55] Ibid. c151/G/4.
[56] Ibid. c151/F/5; /H/15–16, /42, /128. See p. 63.
[57] Bodl. MS. D.D. All Souls c77/149c; see p. 64.
[58] Bodl. MS. D.D. All Souls c53; ct. bk. 1861–1914; c85/138, /142.
[59] Church Com., S4 surveys, p. 537.
[60] Unless otherwise stated, the foll. two paras. are based upon inf. supplied by Messrs. Daniel Smith, Briant & Done (1970).

[61] Background to Brent (Rep. by Brent L.B., Planning and Research Dept., 1967), 90.
[62] Bodl. MS. D.D. All Souls c75/6.
[63] Ibid. c78/186.
[64] Davenport MSS.
[65] Wemb. Hist. Soc., Acc. 907/8.
[66] Bodl. MS. D.D. All Souls c243/27.
[67] All Souls Coll., Hovenden maps, portfolio II, no. 14.
[68] M.R.O., MR/TH/5.
[69] See below.
[70] F. E. Harmer, Anglo-Saxon Writs, 345; Rot. Cur. Reg. (Rec. Com.), 95.
[71] S.C. 11/439. Some became part of Kingsbury manor: see above.
[72] C.P. 25(1)/148/29; S.C. 2/188/54; D.L. 25/162; Cat. Anct. D. iv, A 6861.
[73] W.A.M. 27844–5.
[74] B.M. Cott. MS. Nero E. vi(1), f. 75.

The Brancaster estate, which may confusingly have been called Kingsbury manor, consisted of a moated manor-house and an estate in Kingsbury of about 300 a. stretching from Salmon Street to Townsend Lane and southward to the Brent.[75] It probably extended southward over the Brent into Willesden and eastward into Hendon as far as Edgware Road.[76] It was held by knight service from Edgware manor, a tenure commuted to a pair of gold spurs or 6d. a year.[77]

The largest portion of Gilbert Brancaster's estate passed to his daughter Katharine, wife of John Farnborough (fl. c. 1362–c. 1384),[78] a basket-maker or cofferer, from whom the manor of *COFFERS, COFFERERS* or *COFFERHOUSE* took its name.[79] In 1400 Joan, widow of John Farnborough the elder, and her second husband John Mosshatch lost an action for dower against her stepson, John Farnborough the younger, stockfishmonger of London, for one third of a messuage, 132 a. of arable, 3 a. of meadow, 18 a. of wood and appurtenances in Kingsbury, Hendon, and Willesden.[80] The younger John Farnborough and his wife Gillian conveyed the estate, presumably as a settlement or mortgage, to Thomas Haseley, Clerk of the Crown of Chancery, and to John Frank, Keeper of the Rolls of Chancery, in 1424–5,[81] and Thomas Haseley was listed as the owner in 1426.[82]

Haseley (d. c. 1450) conveyed the premises, described as the manor of Kingsbury in Kingsbury, Hendon, and Willesden, to the use of himself and his wife for life, and in 1451 his widow, Agnes, leased them to Henry Waver and his wife, Christine, probably Agnes's daughter.[83] Henry and Christine enjoyed full possession of the manor after Agnes's death, and in 1476 Christine, whose second husband was Thomas Cook, won her action against her son, Henry Waver, for possession of the manor.[84] Henry predeceased Christine, who died in 1479, whereupon the estate, described as a messuage and 240 a. called Coffers, worth £7 3s. 4d. a year, passed to her granddaughter, Christine Waver. All Souls College, as the lord of Kingsbury (*recte* Edgware) manor, was granted the wardship of the younger Christine, then a minor. The college was neglectful, however, and in August 1479 William Edward, yeoman of Kingsbury, forcibly entered the premises. When he died the following February, his wife, Margaret, continued to take the profits from the estate. In 1481 the escheator declared that the manor was held in chief and Margaret Edward gave her husband's goods and chattels to the king

in compensation, although she apparently remained in possession.[85]

Christine Waver seems to have recovered the manor at her majority and she and her two husbands, William Brown and Sir Humphrey Dymock, held it during the early 16th century. A dispute between John Brown, Christine's son by her first husband, and Humphrey and Christine Dymock was decided in 1540 in favour of the latter.[86] Christine was dead by 1550 when Dymock sold Coffers to Humphrey White,[87] who sold it to Henry Page of Wembley in 1555.[88] In 1556 the estate was described as a messuage, the site of a water-mill, 390 a., free fishing in the Brent at Brent bridge, and 10s. rent in Kingsbury, Hendon, and Willesden.[89] Much of the land in Hendon and Willesden had been acquired during the 15th century, but all the land in Kingsbury seems to have belonged to the original Brancaster holding.

In 1597 John Page had about 167 a. in Kingsbury, mostly in the south-east.[90] His family, while retaining possession of the bulk of Coffers until the 18th century, began to break up the estate in the 17th century. Richard Page of Uxendon sold Wakemans Hill (20 a.) and 20 a. in Hendon to Thomas Marsh of the Hyde in 1632, and another 14 a. in Hendon to Edward Franklin of Willesden in 1633.[91] North Dean was already being treated separately in 1636,[92] and it was not included in the conveyance of Coffers by Richard Page of St. Giles-in-the-Fields (Holborn) to Henry Cope of Dublin in 1716.[93] Cope and his wife, Mary, sold Coffers to James Brydges in 1720.[94] Henry Brydges, duke of Chandos, sold the manor in 1757 to Benjamin Hays of Wimbledon[95] and in 1836 it was apparently held by Trebe Hele Hays of Delamere (Devon), who sold 9 a. next to the Brent to the Grand Junction Canal Co.[96] William Praed, who was the owner in 1839 of an estate there totalling 107 a.,[97] was still in possession in 1870.[98] By 1927 the estate was in the hands of Kingsbury Estates Ltd.[99] Building had begun at Langford Long as early as 1924,[1] but a large area in the south-east was still open space, as a cemetery and recreation ground, in 1970.

Thomas Marsh of Roe Green devised Wakemans Hill, by will proved 1695,[2] to Thomas Nicholl, who sold two of the three fields there to John Cranmer of Eccleshall (Staffs.) in 1710.[3] Cranmer's son John conveyed them to Francis Newman in 1735,[4] and Newman mortgaged and in 1749 sold them to William Harrison of Hendon.[5] In 1782, after Harrison's death, the two fields were sold by

[75] W.A.M. 27844–5; D.L. 25/162.
[76] B.M. Cott. MS. Nero E. vi(1), f. 75.
[77] Bodl. MS. D.D. All Souls c56/2, /5, /11. The escheator of 1481, who asserted that the manor was held in chief, was almost certainly mistaken: C 1/60/76.
[78] Bodl. MS. D.D. All Souls c37/5; *Ft. of F. Lond. & Mdx.* i. 139, 146, 159.
[79] John Farnborough was probably John Cofrer, who witnessed a deed in Kingsbury in 1384: Bodl. MS. D.D. All Souls c75/25.
[80] C 260/137/4. Joan was presumably the second wife of John Farnborough the cofferer.
[81] C.P. 25(1)/152/88.
[82] Bodl. MS. D.D. All Souls c56/2.
[83] *Cal. Close, 1447–54*, 135, 285–6.
[84] C 1/48/305; C.P. 25(1)/152/98.
[85] Bodl. MS. D.D. All Souls c77/171; C 1/60/76.
[86] C 3/43/44.
[87] M.R.O., Acc. 727/2.

[88] Ibid. /4–5.
[89] C.P. 25(2)/74/630/10.
[90] All Souls Coll., Hovenden maps, portfolio II, nos. 9, 12–15; only the outline is marked. The acreage is taken from the maps of 1819 and 1839: M.R.O., Acc. 262/30; TA/KIN.
[91] Bodl. MS. D.D. All Souls c52, ct. bk. 1616–49.
[92] M.R.O., Acc. 210/37.
[93] M.L.R. 1716/5/168–9.   [94] Ibid. 1720/3/305.
[95] Ibid. 1757/4/52.
[96] Ibid. 1836/5/694.
[97] M.R.O., TA/KIN award and map.
[98] M.R.O., Acc. 262/27 (1).
[99] Kingsbury U.D.C., Min. Bk. (1926–9), p. 202.
[1] Ibid. (1922–6), p. 80.
[2] Davenport MSS.: Com. Ct. Lond. f. 53; C 8/640/5.
[3] Hendon Libr. MS. L. 1705.
[4] M.L.R. 1735/5/615–17.
[5] Ibid. 1747/2/89; 1749/3/446–7.

devisees under his will to George Marsh of Black-heath (Kent).[6] In 1819 one field at Wakemans Hill was held by John Nicholl and the other two by Arthur Cuthbert Marsh.[7] Elizabeth Vidler and George Wheeler were the holders in 1839[8] and 1870.[9] The area was developed for building in 1927.[10]

North Dean (45 a.) was in the hands of Samuel Nicholl c. 1729–38.[11] John Nicholl of York sold it in 1769 to Frederick Reynolds of Pall Mall (Westminster), upon whose death in 1799 it passed to Anne Marie Reynolds, his sister, who devised it by will dated 1801 to James Royer of Eastbourne. It was sold in 1810, under the terms of Royer's will, to Charles Pieschall of Sise Lane (London).[12] Between 1822 and 1839 North Dean passed from Pieschall to Henry Hoffman,[13] who was still in possession in 1870.[14]

A manor-house was attached to Geoffrey le Scrope's estate in 1325, although its site is not known. Accounts mention the lord's chamber, a kitchen, larder and malt-kiln, and a surrounding moat with its bridges.[15] A tenement with curtilage was included in the lease of 1333.[16] The 'Coffer-house' was mentioned in the 1550s.[17] If that house still existed in 1597 it must have been situated in one of the areas not marked on the map. The centre of the Coffers estate in Kingsbury was, probably from the 17th or 18th century, Blackbird farm-house, which was built south of the junction of Blackbird Hill with Old Church Lane.[18] At the beginning of the 20th century it was a two-storeyed brick building with a tiled roof, possibly dating from the 18th century.[19] The farm-house was demolished in 1936 to make way for shops.[20]

Part of Gilbert of Brancaster's estate was conveyed by him to Gillian le Joigneur, who may have been his daughter, and who can be identified with Gillian, wife of Guy of Hoddesdon, fishmonger of London. Before 1351 Guy and Gillian conveyed to the knights of St. John of Jerusalem 40 a. of land and 4 a. of meadow in Kingsbury worth 10s. 4d., which was held from Edgware manor for 1½d. rent, 6 a. of wood in Hendon worth 3s., which was held from Westminster abbey for a clove of garlic, and 6s. 8d. rent from free tenants in Kingsbury and Hendon. The estate is identifiable with Church field, 32 a., lying west of Church Lane, and Kingsbury Hill, 6 a. in the corner between Townsend Lane and Wood Lane.[21]

The Hoddesdon grant was not the only source of *FREREN* or *FRYENT* manor, as the estate belonging to the Knights Hospitallers was called. Kingsbury church was appropriated to the Hospitallers by c. 1244–8[22] and land in Tokyngton was owned by them in the late 13th century.[23] In the 1330s the prior of St. John of Jerusalem seems to have owned land in south-western Kingsbury.[24] Property in Kingsbury was included in an extent made of the knights' possessions in 1338.[25] When the Hospitallers' property in Tokyngton was surveyed in 1511–12, it consisted of 23 a. in strips and parcels of land interspersed with the estates of Tokyngton and Wembley manors.[26] It had disappeared by the middle of the 16th century, probably through exchange.[27] The Freren lands in Tokyngton were absorbed into Tokyngton and Wembley manors while their property in Kingsbury, as two blocks of land — High field or Nomansland (18½ a.) on the border with Harrow — became part of the Freren estate.[28]

By 1597 two fields in north Kingsbury belonged to Freren manor.[29] Bowes (Boys or Bouse), otherwise Hyde Hill field or Mayden croft, near Hyde Farm, was held from Kingsbury manor for 1s. rent[30] and may be identifiable with Nelesfield, originally part of the Brancaster estate, for which Geoffrey le Scrope paid 1s. rent to William Page in 1326.[31] Freren field, to the west of Stag Lane, was mentioned in 1426, although it was then apparently a common field.[32] By 1597 it belonged exclusively to the demesne of Freren manor.[33] Although only the outline of the Freren estate was marked on the map of 1597,[34] there is sufficient information to suggest that its area was essentially that of c. 1729–38[35] and 1839,[36] consisting of 120 a., concentrated mostly in southern Kingsbury.

The estate remained in the hands of the Knights Hospitallers until the Order was suppressed in 1540.[37] The king received the rents[38] until 1544 when he granted the estate to the dean and chapter of St. Paul's cathedral.[39] With the exception of a brief period during the Interregnum when Freren manor, then described as 186 a. in Kingsbury and Hendon, was sold by Parliamentary trustees to Richard Gibbs, goldsmith of London,[40] St. Paul's retained the estate until it was vested in the Ecclesiastical Commissioners in 1872.[41]

Tithes, great and small, formed part of the Freren or rectory estate. By c. 1668, except for those

[6] M.L.R. 1779/1/234; 1782/3/329.
[7] M.R.O., Acc. 262/30.
[8] M.R.O., TA/KIN.   [9] M.R.O., Acc. 262/27(1).
[10] Kingsbury U.D.C., Min. Bk. (1926–9), 129.
[11] M.R.O., Acc. 262/72/1–2.
[12] M.L.R. 1769/6/176–7; 1810/4/22.
[13] M.R.O., Acc. 262/27(1); TA/KIN.
[14] M.R.O., Acc. 262/27(1).   [15] W.A.M. 27844–5.
[16] B.M. Cott. MS. Nero E. vi(1), f. 75.
[17] Req. 3/25/157.
[18] O.S. Map 1/2,500, Mdx. XI. 13 (1914 edn.); O.S. Map 6″, Mdx. XI. SW. (1873 edn.).
[19] Wemb. Hist. Soc., Photo. Coll., Acc. 412/8.
[20] O.S. Map 1/2,500, Mdx. XI. 14 (1936 edn.).
[21] B.M. Cott. MS. Nero E. vi(1), ff. 75–77; C 143/329/3; Cal. Pat. 1358–61, 167. The conveyance was complicated by transactions with Richard Seler, citizen of London, and Roger Boudon, Robert Stokes, and John Wroxston, clerks, but mortgages and uses may have been involved.
[22] St. Paul's MS., W.D. 9.
[23] B.M. Cott. MS. Nero E. vi(2), f. 287v.
[24] e.g. trespass against Richard Edwin in 1334: Bodl. MS. D.D. All Souls c37/1. For Edwins, see p. 62.

[25] V.C.H. Mdx. i. 199.
[26] S.C. 2/191/45; Cal. Close, 1399–1402, 293–7.
[27] M.R.O., Acc. 76/222a; Acc. 1052.
[28] M.R.O., Acc. 262/72/1–2; Acc. 262/30.
[29] All Souls Coll., Hovenden maps, portfolio II, nos. 11, 13.
[30] Bodl. MS. D.D. All Souls c37/7(1), /10, /13; c56/11–12; c243/27; M.R.O., Acc. 262/72/1; TA/KIN.
[31] W.A.M. 27845. Cf. B.M. Cott. MS. Nero E. vi(1), f. 75. Possibly named from Robert Nel, who paid 1s. rent to William of Westmelne c. 1230: Cat. Anct. D. iv, A 6861.
[32] Bodl. MS. D.D. All Souls c56/2.
[33] All Souls Coll., Hovenden map, portfolio II, no. 11.
[34] Ibid. nos. 9, 11, 13–15.
[35] M.R.O., Acc. 262/72/1–2.
[36] M.R.O., TA/KIN.
[37] V.C.H. Mdx. i. 196.
[38] S.C. 6/Hen. VIII/2402 m. 9d.
[39] L. & P. Hen. VIII, xix(1), p. 495.
[40] C 54/3556 no. 24, mm. 10 sqq.
[41] Lond. Gaz. 13 Aug. 1872, p. 3587.

paid by three or four parishioners, all tithes had been compounded for £60, although the parishioners estimated their worth as £110.[42] Composition for tithes was £420 in 1822[43] and in 1839 they were commuted for an annual rent-charge of £500, when the joint owners were said to be the chapter of St. Paul's and their lessee, the duke of Buckingham.[44] All tithe rent-charges were redeemed between 1878 and 1936.[45]

Modifications were made to consolidate the estate in the 19th century. Between 1858 and 1866 Kingsbury Hill (9 a.) was exchanged with William Field of Townsends for Rolf crofts, 10 a. in the angle of Salmon Street.[46] In 1890 34 a., consisting of Freren field, Nomansland, and Hyde Hill field, were surrendered to All Souls College in exchange for 35 a. in western Hendon.[47]

The Ecclesiastical Commissioners sold most of the estate, 80 a. around Fryent Farm, between 1928 and 1931. The property was divided into building lots, of which the largest purchasers were Campbell & Heath and Salmon Estate (Kingsbury) Ltd., each of which purchased 26 a., and F. G. Parsons, who bought 21 a.[48]

Freren or Fryent farm-house was situated to the west of Church Lane near its junction with Wood Lane. In 1597 it was a modest house facing Church Lane, flanked on the north and south by barns.[49] In 1837 the farm-house had two storeys and attics.[50] By 1889 it was called the Old House and described as 'slightly built in the first place'. The walls were cracked and held together with iron ties and the house was damp and 'scarcely fit for habitation'. After a fire in 1914, the Ecclesiastical Commissioners granted £1,000 for building, mostly in connexion with a dairy business. The farm buildings, which were sold to Frederick Lavender in 1929,[51] were still used as a dairy farm in 1937[52] but were demolished after the Second World War.[53]

OTHER ESTATES. In 1044–51 Edward the Confessor confirmed a grant made by his housecarl Thurstan to Westminster abbey of land and rights at Chalkhill, including the third tree and third pig of pannage from the wood belonging to Kingsbury, which had been held in common since ancient times.[54] A writ, probably spurious, purporting to be a confirmation made in 1071–5 by William I of Thurstan's grant, mentioned that the Chalkhill lands and rights of sake and soke, toll, team, infangthief and flymenafyrmth, were for a supplement to the monks' diet (ad subsidium victuale).[55] The estate was probably subinfeudated or farmed out from an early date. Alwin Horne, one of Edward the Confessor's thegns, held it in pledge from 'a certain man of St. Peter's' and in 1086 William the Chamberlain held it under Westminster abbey.[56]

A tenement belonging to the abbot of Westminster, which was mentioned as an abutment of land in south-east Harrow in 1236, was probably part of the Chalkhill estate,[57] but its subsequent history is obscure. A 15th-century gloss in the Westminster Domesday noted that a servant of the infirmary received an annual stipend of 5s. from Chalkhill.[58] Although the grant made by Abbot Gervase (1138–57) to his mother Dameta is now thought to refer to Chelsea rather than to Chalkhill,[59] it is possible that a similar grant was made. As at neighbouring Hendon, one or more mesne estates probably developed, while the Westminster overlordship became more and more attenuated until it disappeared completely.

One mesne estate which developed was probably that held by the Chalkhill family, which was active in Kingsbury from the late 12th until the 17th century.[60] The core of the later Chalkhill estate, however, was a capital messuage and 40 a. of freehold land, called in 1350 'le Chalkhulland', which was held in socage from Kingsbury manor. Richard Page died seised of it and in 1350 his heir was his kinsman, John, son of William Page, an infant two years old, for whom guardians, Roger and Agnes Cheeseman, were appointed. At the same time John Page inherited three messuages and three half-virgates of bondland, Blakehaw, Bootland, and one unnamed, of which Robert, William, and John Page respectively had died seised.[61] The estate thus formed passed into the hands of the Chalkhill family in the late 14th century.[62] In 1533 the property comprised three messuages, 40 a. of land, 16 a. of meadow, 100 a. of pasture, and 10 a. of wood in Kingsbury and Harrow-on-the-Hill, presumably at Tokyngton.[63] In 1597 Chalkhill Place and another messuage were sited in the corner between Forty Lane and Salmon Street.[64] The 1597 map shows the boundaries of land in the Harrow border, south of the demesne of Kingsbury manor, and the northern boundary of the main part of the estate, which may be presumed to occupy all the south-western corner of Kingsbury, with the exception of one field, giving a total area of approximately 152 a.

Jon Chalkhill, who succeeded his father, Jon or Eyan Chalkhill, in 1605,[65] was still in possession in 1609,[66] but the estate had passed to John Scudamore of London (d. 1647) before 1617.[67] Scudamore's widow, Elizabeth, sold Chalkhill,

[42] St. Paul's MS., Box A 58a.
[43] M.R.O., Acc. 262/27(1).
[44] Ibid.; Bodl. MS. D.D. All Souls c246/2; *Return of Agreements for commutation of tithe*, H.C. 555, p. 23 (1839), xli.
[45] Tithe-rent redemption certs. A9/20–60 *penes* Holy Innocents church, Kingsbury.
[46] Church Com., file 67417; M.R.O., Acc. 400/66. For Townsend, see p. 64.
[47] Church Com., S4 surveys, p. 537.
[48] Ibid. p. 530A.
[49] All Souls Coll., Hovenden maps, portfolio II, nos. 9, 15.   [50] M.R.O., Acc. 262/27(1).
[51] Church Com., file 51708.
[52] *Kelly's Dir. Wembley* (1937).
[53] Age of Bldgs. map *penes* Brent L.B., Dept. of Planning and Research.
[54] Harmer, *Anglo-Saxon Writs*, 344–5.

[55] *Reg. Regum Anglo-Norm.* i, no. 89; ii, p. 392.
[56] *V.C.H. Mdx.* i. 123.
[57] C.P. 25(1)/146/10/139.
[58] Harmer, *Anglo-Saxon Writs*, 497.
[59] B. T. Harvey, 'Abbot Gervase de Blois and the fee-farms of Westminster Abbey', *Bull. Inst. Hist. Res.* xl. 131.
[60] *Rot. Cur. Reg.* (Rec. Com.), ii. 95; Bodl. MS. D.D. All Souls c76/116–17; c75/8.
[61] Bodl. MS. D.D. All Souls c37/2.
[62] Ibid. /4, /7; c56/11–12a; c75/39.
[63] C.P. 25(2)/27/182/7.
[64] All Souls Coll., Hovenden map, portfolio II, no. 14.
[65] Bodl. MS. D.D. All Souls b1/19.
[66] Ibid. c78/187.
[67] M.R.O., Acc. 276/6, where Scudamore is called 'gentleman', although he is usually distinguished from his namesake in rentals as 'esquire'. And cf. C 6/105/136; C 8/126/197.

then described as a mansion house and 161 a., to Ralph Hartley, apothecary of London, in 1649.[68] John Scudamore had added Haw or Holcroft (3 a.) before 1631,[69] and 5 a. of Mosshatches, both north of Forty Lane, as well as Findens (12 a.), freehold land on either side of Blackbird Hill and a house north of Old Church Lane in the 1640s, which was held at a nominal rent from the heirs of Francis Roberts.[70] The rest of Mosshatches (10 a.) had become part of the Chalkhill estate by 1726.[71]

In 1684 Hartley mortgaged the property and shortly afterwards it passed by sale or mortgage in trust to Richard Bowater, mercer of London, who was related to Hartley by marriage.[72] Bowater was succeeded, on his death in 1726, by his nephew of the same name,[73] whose son, also called Richard Bowater, was still in possession in 1786.[74] George Worrall of Frenchay (Glos.) was the owner in 1819[75] and 1823.[76] He sold the estate to Capt. George Rooke of Bigsweir (Glos.) in 1830.[77] George Rooke was in possession in 1839 of 180 a.[78] and Hannah Rooke, probably his widow and possibly his daughter of George and Hannah Worrall, was the owner in 1842 and 1846. John W. Prout, who held the estate in 1859,[79] sold 20 a. on the Harrow border, north of Forty Lane, to All Souls College between 1868 and 1879.[80] H. D. Rawlings was the owner in 1882.[81] Chalkhill was referred to as 'the Nicoll estate' by 1901 and in that year Mrs. Nicoll sold 8 a. adjoining the river Brent and the Metropolitan railway to Kingsbury U.D.C. for use as sewage works.[82] Most of the estate had apparently been sold to the Metropolitan Railway Co. Estates Ltd. before 1919, when the company planned to develop it.[83] Building began there in 1920.[84]

Chalkhill Place or House was the home of the Chalkhill family and may have been used as a residence by the Bowaters and other owners, but most of the estate was leased out.[85] From the mid 18th century it was usually divided among two or more lessees,[86] although sometimes, as in 1819 and in the 20th century, it was administered as part of a much larger area of leased land.[87] A messuage was attached to 'Chalkhilland' in 1350.[88] As 'Eyan Chalkhill's tenement', it was depicted in 1597 as a typical Elizabethan house with a main block and projecting wings, situated south of Forty Lane.[89] The house was rebuilt and added to several times. Tudor pottery and bricks in the cellar floor were found when the site was excavated. The brick-built ground-floor and timbered attic were of 17th-century date. The northern wing was probably built in the late 18th century and a western extension was added in the early 19th century. Conservatories erected during the 19th century had been removed by 1963. The house was then a large stuccoed building of two storeys and attics. The front, which faced south, had two bays and there were three gables on the east. The building, which housed Kingsgate school from 1946 until 1961, was demolished in 1963.[90]

In addition to the freehold manors and estates, there were three mainly copyhold farms south of Kingsbury Road — Bush farm, Little Bush farm, and Townsend.[91] The southernmost was Little Bush farm, which lay mostly west of Salmon Street, intermingled with the demesne lands of Hill farm. The core of the estate was a medieval tenement, called Edwins after the family which held it in the late 13th and 14th centuries. In 1276–7 Thomas Edwin held $\frac{1}{2}$ virgate and 1 a. for 3s. $1\frac{3}{4}d.$ rent and $9\frac{1}{2}d.$ services from Edgware manor.[92] The Edwins disappear from the court rolls in the late 14th century[93] and in 1426 a tenement and $\frac{1}{2}$ virgate, described as once Richard Edwin's, were held by John Lynford for 3s. rent and $11\frac{1}{2}d.$ services.[94] When Lynford died in 1434, Edwins was inherited by his daughter, Agnes, and her husband, Richard Edward, whence it descended to their son, John Edward, and his wife Joan. In 1463 Joan and her second husband, John Burton of Fulham, conveyed Edwins to William and Agnes Shepherd.[95] In 1572 Thomas Shepherd surrendered it to Vincent Poynter, draper of London, who in 1574 conveyed $9\frac{1}{2}$ a. to Robert Norton and $13\frac{1}{2}$ a. to John Franklin. The property was united again in 1579 when Franklin conveyed his portion to Thomas Scudamore (Skidmore), who had already received the other portion from William Norton in 1575.[96]

Thomas Scudamore extended the estate. He acquired Warrens, 11 a. joining Edwins on the north, from his brother Richard in 1587, inherited 47 a. about Kingsbury Green after the death of his father, Erasmus, in 1580, and acquired another 26 a. there in 1578 and 1595.[97] In 1597 he had an estate of 107 a., consisting of Edwins in the south-west and several medieval tenements around Kingsbury Green — Jack Johns, Collins, Payces, and Brasiers; a strip of land, called Stonepits, Barefield, and Hay Hills, ran along Buck Lane from the green to Hay Lane.[98] In 1604 Thomas acquired another 4 a., Hog Hills, adjoining it.[99] Thomas

[68] C.P. 43/267 m. 17.
[69] Bodl. MS. D.D. All Souls c78/187b.
[70] Ibid. c57/17, /20; C.P. 43/269 m. 17; M.L.R. 1714/5/69.
[71] Bodl. MS. D.D. All Souls c40/51.
[72] C 78/1445 no. 1.
[73] Bodl. MS. D.D. All Souls c40/51, mm. 1–1d.
[74] Ibid. c245/34z; Abstract of Returns of Char. Dons. 1786–8, H.C. 511, pp. 752–3 (1816), xvi(1).
[75] M.R.O., Acc. 262/30.
[76] 9th Rep. Com. Char. H.C. 258, pp. 266–7 (1823), ix.
[77] M.L.R. 1830/4/742.
[78] M.R.O., TA/KIN.
[79] Bodl. MS. D.D. All Souls c245/34z; Char. Com. file 205797/A1.
[80] See p. 58.
[81] Char. Com. file 205797/A1.
[82] Kingsbury U.D.C., Wks. & Finance Cttee. Mins. (1900–2), 31, 47; O.S. Maps 1/2,500, Mdx. XI. 13 (1914 edn.).
[83] Kingsbury U.D.C., Min. Bk. (1915–22), 252.

[84] See p. 54.
[85] e.g. in 1649: C.P. 43/267 m. 17; in 1680: C 8/267/127.
[86] M.L.R. 1757/2/254; 1830/41/742; M.R.O., TA/KIN.
[87] M.R.O., Acc. 262/30; Kingsbury U.D.C., Wks. & Finance Cttee. Mins. (1900–2), 57.
[88] Bodl. MS. D.D. All Souls c37/2.
[89] All Souls Coll., Hovenden map, portfolio II, no. 14.
[90] Wemb. Hist. Soc., Acc. 412/4, Acc. 962; Wemb. Hist. Soc., Photo. Coll., Acc. 96/71, /9–10, /12, /14–17, /19–20, /23, /26, /28–29, /31–33; Wemb. Hist. Soc., Jnl. N.S. ii(4–6).
[91] O.S. Map 1/2,500, Mdx. XI. 9, 10 (1873 edn.).
[92] S.C. 11/439.
[93] S.C. 2/188/54; Bodl. MS. D.D. All Souls c37/1, /3–5.
[94] Bodl. MS. D.D. All Souls c56/2.
[95] Ibid. c37/8, /9. See p. 63.
[96] Bodl. MS. D.D. All Souls c39/18.
[97] Ibid. c38/16; c39/18; c52, ct. bk., ff. 5d.–6, 7d.–8, 9–11d.; c56/11; c243/27.
[98] All Souls Coll., Hovenden maps, portfolio II, nos. 12–14.
[99] Bodl. MS. D.D. All Souls b1/19.

Scudamore died in 1626, leaving his property to several of his six sons and five daughters.[1] His eldest son, Henry, inherited most of the land to the east of Buck Lane, which he conveyed to John Scudamore esquire of Chalkhill in 1627.[2] John, another of Thomas's sons, usually called 'gentleman' to distinguish him from the John Scudamore of Chalkhill, inherited 67 a., including Edwins. He also acquired 6 a. from his sister Ann in 1627 and 6 a. after his brother Francis's death in 1631.[3] After John's death c. 1653, his property was held by his widow, Mary,[4] until her death in 1669, when it was divided between their daughters, Katharine and Elizabeth.[5]

Edwins, which was held by Katharine, passed in 1691 to Samuel Twinn, whose daughter, Ann, surrendered it to William Thorpe of St. Clement Danes (City of Westminster) on the death of her father in 1731.[6] When William's son, Thomas Thorpe of St. Marylebone, died in 1782, the estate passed by will to trustees who conveyed it to Thomas Furnell in 1783.[7] Furnell died in 1802, leaving his property in trust for his wife's adopted daughter, Ursula Desting. In accordance with Ursula's will, proved 1814, the property was sold in 1820 to Francis Stubbs, coach-maker of Long Acre.[8]

John Scudamore's other daughter, Elizabeth, and her husband, John Owen, inherited the rest of his property, mostly concentrated around Kingsbury Green.[9] By 1698 it was in the hands of Thomas Crane[10] and in 1716 it passed to Mary Rawlings. Mary and Charlotte Rawlings were in possession in 1770 and in 1773 Mary and her husband, Bisby Lambert, surrendered their interest to Charlotte and her husband, John Carter.[11] In 1806 Carter conveyed 22 a. at Kingsbury Green and Buck Lane to Francis Stubbs and another 9 a., originally part of the Edwins estate, to William Evans. Evans surrendered it in 1817 to Stubbs,[12] who accumulated other property between 1809 and 1839[13] and in 1839 had an estate of 108 a., consisting of Edwins in the south-west and scattered fields in central and northern Kingsbury.[14] After Stubbs's death in 1843, his property was sold by trustees under his will. All Souls College bought Edwins (44 a.) in 1843 and another 5 a. in 1845;[15] 36 a. were sold in 1845 to William Field, who mortgaged them in 1882;[16] 25 a. in north-eastern Kingsbury were sold in 1844 to John H. Essex.[17]

Edwins or Little Bush farm was normally leased out. Although houses, probably fronting Salmon Street, were attached to both Edwins and Warrens in the Middle Ages, they had disappeared by 1597. A cottage was built on Newlands, a field bounded by Salmon Street in the east, Richards on the north, and Edwins on the south, between 1597 and 1631.[18] Little Bush farm-house was built by Stubbs on the site of the cottage between 1823, when he added it to the Edwins estate,[19] and 1835.[20] The farm-house was bombed during the Second World War and the site subsequently let on building leases.[21]

Bush or Big Bush farm lay west of the junction of Salmon Street with Slough Lane, its lands bounded on the south by those of Little Bush farm and on the north by those of Pipers farm. Bush farm originated in a copyhold tenement called Richards, after the family which held it in the late 13th and 14th centuries.[22] In 1426 it was a tenement and $\frac{1}{2}$ virgate held from Edgware manor for 5s. 11d. rent and 1s. $5\frac{1}{2}d$. services by Richard Edward and John Lynford.[23] After John Lynford's death in 1434 the property was divided between his daughters, Agnes, wife of Richard Edward, and Alice, wife of Richard Page.[24] Agnes's descendants held half Richards until 1466 when her grandson, John Edward, and his mother, Joan Burton, conveyed it to William Shepherd.[25] Both halves were united in the hands of Richard Shepherd by 1482.[26] In 1541 William Shepherd, draper of London, surrendered the reversion to Richard Shelley,[27] who had apparently entered the property by 1551 when he surrendered it to the use of himself and his wife Agnes for life with remainder to Agnes's son, John James of Hampstead.[28] James, who took possession after Shelley's death in 1559, conveyed the estate to John Franklin in 1565. In 1585 Franklin surrendered it to William Marsh of Willesden, who in 1592 conveyed it to Robert Golding, baker of Westminster.[29] In 1597 Golding had an estate of 37 a., consisting of Richards (32 a.), a farm-house and land stretching in a narrow band from Slough Lane to the border with Harrow, and of Seakins, at the junction of Hay Lane and Stag Lane.[30] After Robert Golding's death in 1630, Richards passed to his daughter, Elizabeth, wife of Charles Dethwick,[31] and in 1714 Charles Dethwick of Holborn sold it to Joseph Stent, also of Holborn.[32] Stent's son, Matthew, conveyed it to William Harrison in 1747.[33] On the death of Mary Harrison in 1834, the estate passed by will to her nephews, William Harrison Ashby and Edward Ashby.[34] In 1873 it passed to George H. R. Harrison.[35]

The estate was leased out in 1464,[36] and, except

[1] Bodl. MS. Rawl. B 389 b, ff. 85–86.
[2] Bodl. MS. D.D. All Souls c52, ct. bk. (1616–49). For the subsequent history of this land, see p. 65.
[3] Bodl. MS. D.D. All Souls c52, ct. bk. (1616–49).
[4] Prob. 11/231 (P.C.C. 332 Brent, will of John Scudamore).
[5] Bodl. MS. Rawl. B 389 b, ff. 85–86.
[6] Bodl. MS. D.D. All Souls c43, pp. 42–3; c57/20; c151/H/19.
[7] Ibid. c151/H/2–4, /19–21, /23, /26–28; c245/34z.
[8] Ibid. c151/H/5, /10, /43.   [9] Ibid. c57/20.
[10] Ibid. /25.   [11] Ibid. c151/H/25; c245/34z.
[12] Ibid. c53, ct. bk. (1805–30); c151/H/7, /35, /43.
[13] Ibid. c46, pp. 158–9, 373–4; c53, ct. bks. (1805–30), (1831–61); c151/H/10, /13; /F/3.
[14] M.R.O., TA/KIN.
[15] Bodl. MS. D.D. All Souls c151/F/4–5; /H/15–16, /28, /41–42. See p. 58.
[16] Ibid. b4/143; c51, pp. 39–43.
[17] Ibid. b4/142. See p. 69.

[18] Bodl. MS. D.D. All Souls c30/54; All Souls Coll., Hovenden maps, portfolio II, no. 12.
[19] Bodl. MS. D.D. All Souls c151/H/11–13, /36, /42.
[20] Ibid. /14.
[21] Ex inf. Daniel Smith, Briant and Done.
[22] S.C. 2/188/54; Bodl. MS. D.D. All Souls c37/1.
[23] Bodl. MS. D.D. All Souls c56/2.
[24] Ibid. c37/7.
[25] Ibid. /9.
[26] Ibid. c56/5.
[27] Ibid. c38/13.
[28] Ibid. /16.
[29] Ibid. c39/18; c52, ct. bk., ff. 341–35.
[30] All Souls Coll., Hovenden maps, portfolio II, nos. 12–13. See map on p. 52.
[31] Bodl. MS. D.D. All Souls c52, ct. bk. (1616–49).
[32] Ibid. c42, p. 180.   [33] M.R.O., Acc. 262/27 pt. 1.
[34] Bodl. MS. D.D. All Souls c53, ct. bk. (1831–61).
[35] Bodl. MS. D.D. All Souls c245/34z.
[36] Ibid. c37/9.

under Samuel Harrison in the early 19th century, was probably always leased out by its owners from the 17th century, if not earlier.[37] A house was part of Richards at least since 1426.[38] It was depicted in 1597 as a farm with buildings on three sides of a yard and bordering orchards, set well back from the road.[39] In 1928–34 it was a two-storeyed, plain plastered building with a slate roof, probably dating from the 18th century, flanked by large wooden barns.[40] The farm-house was demolished shortly before 1947.[41]

The lands of Townsend farm lay intermingled with those of Hyde farm, south of Kingsbury Road on the eastern border with Hendon. The farm originated in a copyhold estate built up by a branch of the Chalkhill family in the 15th century. The farm-house, in 1426 a cottage called Perrys (le Pyryes),[42] probably originated as the tenement belonging to the Perry family, which held land in Kingsbury in the late 13th and 14th centuries.[43] Although most of the Perry lands were lost to the family by the 1330s,[44] the cottage was held by Christine Perry (atte Pyrye), who was presented for leyrwite by the homage of Kingsbury in 1330 and who married Henry Page in 1333.[45] In 1426 Perry's cottage was held by Ralph Chalkhill from Edgware manor for 5s. rent. Chalkhill also held Withy lands, 10 a. east of Townsend Lane, in 1426 a quartron or quarter-virgate held from Edgware manor for 1s. 5d. rent, once part of Robert Leman's land.[46] Between 1444 and 1446 Chalkhill acquired Silverlands, part of ½ virgate once held by the Clark family, from John Mosshatch (Mussach).[47] In 1462 Ralph Chalkhill's son, Peter, conveyed all these lands to William Shepherd,[48] whose son, Robert, had by 1502 acquired Sales croft, once part of Robert Leman's estate but held by the Hamond family since 1426.[49] John Shepherd surrendered the reversion to the estate to John Lamb of Tokyngton in 1542.[50] In 1597 his son, John Lamb of Hatton (E. Bedfont) had an estate of 27 a. in scattered fields on either sides of Townsend Lane, with one field, Hog Hills, north of Kingsbury Road.[51]

In 1604 John Lamb conveyed the estate to Henry Townsend, who was already the lessee of part of it. Townsend surrendered Hog Hills to Thomas Scudamore and the rest of the estate to Jon Franklin.[52] Franklin split the estate still further, conveying

most of it in 1629 to Richard Collett and a small portion in 1638 to Laurence Davis, merchant tailor of London.[53] Collett's lands descended to his son, Matthew, who conveyed them in 1708 to John Oxton of St. Stephen (Herts.); Oxton surrendered them in 1711 to Alice Field of Paddington, upon whose death in 1719 the property descended to her sisters and heirs, Margaret Robinson and Ann Ingle, who conveyed them to William Harrison of Brent Bridge, Hendon.[54] Laurence Davis's portion passed to William Williams between 1672 and 1698, to Francis Newman in 1700 and, together with other property acquired by Newman, to William Harrison in 1752.[55] Harrison bought Clarks croft, 9 a. south of Wood Lane, from Henry, duke of Chandos, in 1753.[56] The combined estate thus formed, 44 a., remained in the hands of the Harrison family until 1856, when it passed to William Field, who secured its enfranchisement.[57] In 1858 Field exchanged two fields east of Townsend Lane with All Souls for two fields adjoining the farm-house west of the lane.[58] Between 1858 and 1866 a field at Salmon Street was exchanged with St. Paul's for 9 a. between Wood Lane and Townsend Lane.[59]

Richard Collett in the 1660s[60] and Samuel Harrison in 1819[61] occupied the farm but most owners leased it out. In 1604 and 1713 the lessees were Townsends,[62] and leases may even have become hereditary in the family which gave its name to the farm and lane.[63] There was probably a building on the site west of Townsend Lane from the 14th century. It was described as a cottage in 1426[64] but was depicted in 1597 as three buildings around a courtyard facing Townsend Lane.[65] It was, however, probably always a small house. In 1664 only 4 hearths were assessed[66] and in 1839 it was called a cottage.[67] The house was demolished and the estate developed for industry in the north and housing in the south during the 1920s.[68]

Most of the land north of Kingsbury Road belonged to farms which developed from copyhold tenements. Two 19th-century farms in the north-west, Gore farm and Valley farm,[69] originated in an estate built up by the Lyon family. Boyfords Heal or Hole, 7½ a. on the border with Harrow, was held by the family in 1395[70] and Small Withies, 16 a. south of it, was in the hands of William Lyon in 1426.[71] By 1441 John Lyon of Preston had acquired

[37] e.g. in 1664: M.R.O., MR/TH/5; in 1747: M.R.O., Acc. 262/27 pt. 1; in 1839: M.R.O., TA/KIN; in 1851: H.O. 107/1700/135/2 ff. 310–28; in 1870: M.R.O., Acc. 262/27 pt. 1.
[38] Bodl. MS. D.D. All Souls c56/2.
[39] All Souls Coll., Hovenden maps, portfolio II, no. 12.
[40] Wemb. Hist. Soc., Photo. Coll., Acc. 333/6A, /24, /25.
[41] Ex inf. Brent L.B., Planning and Research Dept. (1971).
[42] Bodl. MS. D.D. All Souls c56/2.
[43] Ibid. c37/1; S.C. 2/188/54 m. 2; S.C. 11/439.
[44] See p. 65.
[45] Bodl. MS. D.D. All Souls c37/1.
[46] Ibid. c56/2.
[47] Ibid. c37/8; c52, ct. bk., ff. 52–53.
[48] Ibid. c37/9.
[49] Ibid. /8, /10; c52, ct. bk., ff. 52–53; c56/2.
[50] Ibid. c38/13; c52, ct. bk., ff. 52–53.
[51] All Souls Coll., Hovenden maps, portfolio II, nos. 13, 15; Prob. 11/34 (P. C. C. 1 Bucke).
[52] Bodl. MS. D.D. All Souls b1/19; c52, ct. bk., ff. 52–53. For the descent of Thomas Scudamore's estate, see above.
[53] Bodl. MS. D.D. All Souls c52, ct. bk. (1616–49).
[54] Ibid. c42, pp. 135, 165, 219.
[55] Ibid. c44, pp. 31–2, 124; c57/20, /25; c245/34z.
[56] Ibid. c44, pp. 146–7.
[57] Ibid. b5/154; c245/34z; M.R.O., Acc. 262/30; TA/KIN.
[58] Bodl. MS. D.D. All Souls c77/149c. See p. 61.
[59] M.R.O., Acc. 400/66; Church Com., file 67417.
[60] M.R.O., MR/TH/5, 26, 53, 75.
[61] M.R.O., Acc. 262/30.
[62] Bodl. MS. D.D. All Souls b1/19; c42, p. 165. And see M.R.O., TA/KIN; M.R.O., Acc. 262/27 pt. 1; H.O. 107/1700/135/2 ff. 310–28.
[63] Cf. C 8/74/166.
[64] Bodl. MS. D.D. All Souls c56/2.
[65] All Souls Coll., Hovenden map, portfolio II, no. 15.
[66] M.R.O., MR/TH/5.
[67] M.R.O., TA/KIN.
[68] Kingsbury U.D.C., Min. Bk. (1922–6), 45, 138, 367; (1926–9), 43; O.S. Map 1/2,500, Mdx. XI. 10 (1935 edn.).
[69] O.S. Map 1/2,500, Mdx. XI. 5 (1896 edn.).
[70] E. J. L. Scott, Recs. of Grammar Sch. at Harrow on Hill, 4.
[71] Bodl. MS. D.D. All Souls c56/2.

TOTTENHAM: THE HIGH CROSS AND HIGH ROAD IN 1827, FROM THE SOUTH

HENDON: BRENT CROSS FLY-OVER AND THE NORTH CIRCULAR ROAD FROM THE NORTH-EAST
Brent station and the Northern line to Edgware are in the foreground

Tottenham: Broadwater Farm estate from the south-west

Hendon: the centre of Hampstead Garden Suburb from the south-west

an interest in Gore field, 37 a. north of Kingsbury Road,[72] which is identifiable with ½ virgate held by Richard Lorchon *alias* Page (fl. 1339) from Edgware manor for 3*s.* rent and 1*s.* 1*d.* services.[73] When John Lyon died in 1457 he was seised of two ½ virgates, Small Withies, and two crofts which were lost to the Shepherd family in 1492.[74]

In 1580 John and Joan Lyon acquired Half Yards and Hogsheads, 31 a. south of Kingsbury Road near the border with Harrow.[75] This land originated in ½ virgate held *c.* 1280 by Laurence Page[76] and in 1426 by Alice Savuy from Edgware manor for 3*s.* rent and 1*s.* 1*d.* works.[77] John Barnville of Tokyngton was in possession by 1441[78] and the property descended to his daughter Elizabeth (d. 1515) and her husband Sir Thomas Frowyk, and to their daughter Frideswide (d. 1528) and her husband, Sir Thomas Cheyney (d. 1558). Their son Thomas (d. 1544) was succeeded by his sisters, Anne, Katharine, and Frances.[79] The interest of Anne (d. 1562), wife of Sir John Parrott, passed to her son, Thomas, who sold it in 1574 to William Nicholas, who conveyed it in 1576 to Paul Pope, engraver. The other two sisters conceded their interest to Pope, who surrendered the property in 1579 to John Wickham, gentleman of Horsmonden (Kent). Wickham surrendered it to Robert Strensham, who in 1580 conveyed it to John and Joan Lyon.[80] In 1581 the Lyons acquired Great Framesland, 12 a. north of Kingsbury Road, from William Crosley.[81]

In 1597 Joan Lyon, widow, held 116 a. in west Kingsbury, mostly situated on either side of Kingsbury Road but including fields in the extreme north-west of the parish.[82] The estate, which bordered Harrow parish, was farmed as an extension of the Lyons' farm in Preston.[83] The land in Kingsbury was not included in John Lyon's endowment of Harrow School although wood for fuel was, according to the statutes of the school, to be taken from his estate there.[84] In 1594 Richard Millett of Hayes, John Lyon's nephew and heir, surrendered the reversion to the Kingsbury portion to three people, thus ensuring the break-up of the estate after Joan Lyon's death in 1608.[85]

The reversion to 33 a., consisting of Picked Acre in the north-west and the bulk of Gore field on the border with Harrow, was surrendered in 1594 to Robert Pollett, who conveyed it to John Workhouse in 1597. Workhouse surrendered it in 1598 to Cuthbert Lyne,[86] whose son, Humphrey, conveyed the property in 1610 to Henry Scudamore. Scudamore surrendered Picked Acre to William

Page of Harrow Weald in 1615 and Gore field to Clement Scudamore in 1620. Gore field was conveyed to Richard Nicholl of South Mimms in 1624,[87] to Richard Haley in 1652,[88] and to Robert Tanner in 1655.[89] Robert's son, Thomas, citizen of London, sold the estate in 1678 to Nathaniel Walter of Kenton,[90] who sold it in 1714 to James Brydges, later duke of Chandos,[91] in whose family it remained until 1800, when it was sold to Christopher Hill the younger of Stanmore.[92] Hill sold it to Benjamin Weall in 1805. Under the will, dated 1818, of John Weall, five coparceners, members of the Rice family, were admitted to the property in 1861, when they sold it to John Procter of Rickmansworth. The estate was enfranchised in 1874.[93] Dr. Arthur Calcutta White was the owner in 1906.[94]

For most of the 18th century Gore field formed one farm with Lower farm, the demesne lands of Kingsbury manor leased by the Brydges family. A barn fronting Kingsbury Road had been recently erected in 1714.[95] A farm-house, Gore Farm, was built on the site in the late 19th century.[96] It was probably demolished after 1928 when the farm-land was given over to building development.[97]

The reversion to 26 a., which joined Gore farm-lands on the east, was surrendered by Richard Millett in 1594 to Edward Pollett.[98] Pollett conveyed the land in sections to Thomas Marsh in 1638, 1639, and 1640.[99] Marsh conveyed it to Edward Nicholl and Susan Child in 1683 and Nicholl's widow, Susannah, surrendered it to Thomas Coleman, chandler of Westminster, in 1706.[1] The estate descended to Coleman's nephew, Thomas Norris, in 1756 and he apparently sold it in the same year to Isaac Mencelin of Cricklewood, who conveyed it to Thomas Heming in 1797.[2]

The reversion to the rest of Joan Lyon's estate was surrendered by Richard Millett in 1594 to Daniel Pate. His estate consisted of 57 a., made up of fields on the north-west border with Harrow and Half Yards and Hogsheads, south of Kingsbury Road.[3] The fields on the north-west border were lost to the estate during the earlier 17th century, but the rest was conveyed in 1639 by Daniel Pate to Daniel Brown, who conveyed it in 1647 to John Scudamore.[4] By 1672 it was in the hands of the heirs of Sir Francis Prujean M.D. (Privian).[5]

In 1672 the Prujean family had an estate of 95 a., which they had acquired from various sources in the mid 17th century. Adjoining Half Yards and Hogsheads on the east were Masons or Perry fields (20 a.). The name Masons was probably taken from John Lyon, mason, the holder in 1426,[6] and Perry

[72] Ibid. c37/8.
[73] Ibid. /3.
[74] Ibid. /8, /11.
[75] Ibid. c39/18.
[76] Ibid. c52, ct. bk. ff. 23–24; S.C. 2/188/54.
[77] Bodl. MS. D.D. All Souls c56/2.
[78] Ibid. c37/8.
[79] Ibid. c38/13; c39/18; c56/5; W. C. Davis, *Ancestry of Mary Isaac*, 196, 259. See *V.C.H. Mdx.* iv. 208.
[80] Bodl. MS. D.D. All Souls c39/18; c52, ct. bk., ff. 23–24; M.R.O., Acc. 182/1–2.
[81] Bodl. MS. D.D. All Souls c39/18.
[82] All Souls Coll., Hovenden maps, portfolio II, nos. 10, 12.
[83] *V.C.H. Mdx.* iv. 213.   [84] Elsley, *Wembley*, 98.
[85] Bodl. MS. D.D. All Souls b1/19; *V.C.H. Mdx.* i. 299.
[86] Bodl. MS. D.D. All Souls c39/18.
[87] Ibid. b1/19.   [88] Ibid. /21.
[89] M.R.O., Acc. 262/27 pt. 2/9.   [90] Ibid. /12, /14.

[91] Bodl. MS. D.D. All Souls c42, p. 187.
[92] M.R.O., Acc. 262/27 pt. 1.
[93] Bodl. MS. D.D. All Souls c53, ct. bk. (1861–1914); c245/34z.
[94] Rep. on Kingsbury U.D. 1906, p. 13, *Reps. of Local Inqs.* (1895–1907) *penes* M.R.O.
[95] Bodl. MS. D.D. All Souls c42, p. 187.
[96] O.S. Maps 1/2,500, Mdx. XI. 5 (1873, 1896 edns.).
[97] Kingsbury U.D.C., Min. Bk. (1926–9), 307.
[98] Bodl. MS. D.D. All Souls c39/18.
[99] Ibid. c52, ct. bk. (1616–49).
[1] Ibid. c42, p. 119.
[2] Ibid. c40/51, m. 5; c53, ct. bk. (1756–77); c245/34z; M.L.R. 1776/6/279.
[3] Bodl. MS. D.D. All Souls c30/54; c39/18.
[4] Ibid. c30/54; c52, ct. bk. (1616–49); c57/16.
[5] Ibid. c57/20, where the holder is given as Sir Francis although he had died by 1666: C 9/37/27.
[6] Bodl. MS. D.D. All Souls c56/2.

fields, while possibly derived from pear trees,[7] was probably named after the medieval Perry family.[8] William of Aldenham, gold-beater of London (fl. 1333),[9] held the property which in 1426 was described as a tenement and ½ virgate held from Edgware manor for 2s. 10¼d. rent and 1s. 1d. services.[10] The property was held by the Lyon family in 1426 and 1457[11] but it was granted by the lord of the manor in 1476 to Robert Mosshatch[12] and surrendered by his son, John, in 1488 to Thomas Page.[13] The Pages retained it until Richard Page died in 1649, leaving his daughters, Mary and Prudence, as coheirs.[14] In 1640 Richard Page had acquired Honey Sloughs, 6 a. on the border with Harrow, an under tenement which had been in the hands of the Hamond family at least since 1495.[15] Between 1649 and 1672 Page's estate passed to the Prujeans.[16]

The Prujean family acquired 37 a. lying between Kingsbury Green and Hay Lane between 1641 and 1672.[17] Randolfs tenement at Kingsbury Green, of which Richard Randolf died seised in 1331,[18] and which was held by the Shepherd family from 1512 until 1641,[19] was conveyed by William Peters to Francis Prujean in 1660.[20] Henry Scudamore's property — Brasiers, Stonepits, Dawes, Hay Hills, and Hog Hills (35 a.) — was surrendered in 1627 to John Scudamore of Chalkhill,[21] who conveyed it to Prujean in 1647.[22]

The estate thus formed remained in the hands of the Prujean family until 1789 when it was sold by trustees to George Heming, goldsmith of Bond Street (Westminster).[23]

In 1854 the combined estate was divided among five members of the Heming family as coparceners, who secured enfranchisement of the copyhold in 1869.[24] It was still referred to as the Hemings estate, owned by trustees under the will of Richard Heming, in 1906[25] and 1916.[26] In 1839 Richard Heming held 158 a., grouped in two blocks, one in western Kingsbury on either side of Kingsbury Road and the other stretching along Buck Lane from Kingsbury Green to Hay Lane.[27] The two blocks were usually leased out separately. There was a barn on the western block, north of Kingsbury Road, to the east of Gore farm, by 1729–38.[28] Vale or Valley Farm was built on the site in the late 19th century.[29] Most of the farm-land had been developed by 1935 but the house itself was not demolished until after the Second World War.[30] The other block of land was administered from Brasiers, a freehold messuage which existed by 1521.[31] In 1597 it was a large house north of Kingsbury Green.[32] The house was still there in 1729–38[33] but it had been pulled down by 1789.[34] The farm-land had been given over to housing by 1935.[35]

The Hamond family began to build up an estate next to Gorelands in the 15th century. In 1426 John Hamond held land which had once belonged to Geoffrey Roe (fl. 1330),[36] including a tenement and three quartrons held from Edgware manor for 4s. 6d. rent and 1s. 3¼d. services. Richard Hamond held, jointly with John Lyon of Preston, one virgate called Crabsland Gore field from Edgware manor for 6s. rent and 1s. 5½d. services;[37] it was part of an estate held by John John in the late 14th century.[38] Both holdings were united by 1482 in the hands of Simon Hamond,[39] who conveyed them to Richard Shepherd in 1498.[40] In 1597 John Shepherd had an estate of 64 a., farming an almost continuous strip of land from Crabsland, through Broad field to the southern side of Roe Green.[41]

John Shepherd conveyed the estate in 1599 to John Bull,[42] who in 1621 surrendered it to the use of his wife, Katharine, for life with remainder to be divided among his sons, Laurence, Dickens, John, and Francis, and his daughters, Katharine and Frances. Portions were surrendered by Laurence to Henry Haley the elder in 1623, by Frances to Thomas Marsh of Hendon in 1633 and to Henry Haley the younger in 1624, and by Katharine to John Edlin of Great and Thomas Ewer of Little Stanmore in 1624. There was a reorganization of field boundaries in 1624 and Edlin and Ewer surrendered their portion to Henry Haley the younger of Hendon.[43] By 1641 the whole of the Bull estate had been divided between Thomas Marsh and Henry Haley.[44]

Henry Haley's portion, consisting of Crabsland and Little Rowens in north-west Kingsbury, passed to John Haley's daughter, Mary, in 1675[45] and had been divided by 1698 among Lydia Brown, John Marsh, and Henry Haley.[46] Lydia Brown, who held about 12 a., died in 1729 and was succeeded by her daughter, Rebecca Savage;[47] when Rebecca died in 1757, her portion passed to her granddaughter, Lydia Wheeler,[48] whose descendant Thomas Wheeler obtained enfranchisement in 1856.[49]

[7] P.N. Mdx. (E.P.N.S.), 39.
[8] See p. 64.
[9] Bodl. MS. D.D. All Souls c37/1; Ft. of F. Lond & Mdx. i. 78.
[10] Bodl. MS. D.D. All Souls c56/2.   [11] Ibid.; c37/8.
[12] Ibid. /9.
[13] Ibid. /10.
[14] Ibid. c52, ct. bk., f. 60; M.R.O., Acc. 262/27 pt. 1.
[15] Bodl. MS. D.D. All Souls c30/54; c37/10; c52, ct. bk. (1616–49); c56/11; c57/17; c78/187.
[16] Ibid. c57/20.
[17] Ibid. /17, /20.
[18] Ibid. c37/1.
[19] Ibid. c30/54; c38/13; c52, ct. bk., ff. 44–45; c57/17.
[20] Ibid. b1/21, /22, m. 2.   [21] See p. 63.
[22] Bodl. MS. D.D. All Souls c52, ct. bk. (1616–49).
[23] Ibid. c45, pp. 175, 205; c245/34z; M.R.O., Acc. 583/14; M.L.R. 1774/4/148; 1788/7/391; 1799/3/215.
[24] Bodl. MS. D.D. All Souls c245/34z.
[25] Rep. on Kingsbury U.D. 1906, p. 35, Reps. of Local Inqs. (1895–1907) penes M.R.O.
[26] Kingsbury U.D.C., Min. Bk. (1915–22), 28.
[27] M.R.O., TA/KIN.
[28] M.R.O., Acc. 262/72/1–2.
[29] O.S. Maps 1/2,500, Mdx. XI. 5 (1873 and 1896 edns.); Kelly's Dir. Lond. (1880), 206.
[30] O.S. Maps 1/2,500, Mdx. XI. 5 (1935 and 1940 edns.); Age of Bldgs. map penes Brent L.B., Planning and Research Dept.
[31] Bodl. MS. D.D. All Souls c56/12.
[32] All Souls Coll., Hovenden map, portfolio II, no. 13.
[33] M.R.O., Acc. 262/72/1 & 2.
[34] M.R.O., Acc. 583/14.
[35] O.S. Map 1/2,500, Mdx. XI. 6 (1935 edn.).
[36] Bodl. MS. D.D. All Souls c37/1.
[37] Ibid. c56/2.
[38] Ibid. c37/3, /5.
[39] Ibid. c56/5.
[40] Ibid. c37/10.
[41] All Souls Coll., Hovenden maps, portfolio II, nos. 10, 13.
[42] Bodl. MS. D.D. All Souls c39/18.   [43] Ibid. b1/19.
[44] Ibid. c57/17.
[45] Ibid. G1/28.
[46] Ibid. c57/25.
[47] Ibid. c40/51, m. 9.
[48] Ibid. c44, p. 181.
[49] Ibid. c245/34z.

John Marsh conveyed his portion, about 10 a., to Daniel Weedon in 1744, in whose family it remained until the death of James Weedon in 1799, when it passed to his nephew, John Nicoll.[50] About 28 a. remained in the hands of the Haley family until 1809, when John Haley conveyed them to John Nicoll. Nicoll alienated Little Rowens to Francis Stubbs in 1809[51] and the rest of the estate to Philip Rundell of Ludgate Hill (City of London) in 1819. In 1829 it passed by will to Joseph Neeld,[52] who in 1839 had an estate of 46 a. in north-west Kingsbury;[53] Sir John Neeld was in possession in 1861.[54]

The estate held by Thomas Marsh in 1641 comprised most of the former Roe holding, centred upon Roe Green.[55] In 1695 it was conveyed by Thomas Marsh of Roe Green to Thomas Nicoll the younger of Totteridge (Herts.). In 1711 the Nicoll family conveyed the estate to John Cranmer of Eccleshall (Staffs.), from whom it passed in 1718 to John Beckett, goldsmith of Holborn, and his wife Mary. Beckett was dead by 1733 and Mary married Alexander Ward of Whitehall (Westminster) in 1736.[56] Trustees under the will of Thomas Ward (d. 1773) sold the estate to William Allsop.[57] In 1839 John Allsop had an estate of 62 a., mostly made up of the former Shepherd estate, but including some land between Bacon Lane and Stag Lane which had formed part of Grove farm in 1597.[58] John Thomas Allsop secured the estate's enfranchisement in 1878.[59] The estate, which was often leased out,[60] was centred on a house at Roe Green, approximately where Haydon Close now is. A house had probably stood there since the 14th century,[61] and, as Roe tenement, it was marked on the map of 1597.[62] It was assessed for 8 hearths in 1664.[63] By 1729–38 there were two houses on the site.[64] The northern one, which was probably the more important, was called Roes; that to the south seems to have been a farm-house.[65] In 1851 the southern one was still a farm-house, although for most of the later 19th century it was called Roe Green House.[66] In 1896 and 1914 its name was Fairfields.[67] The house, once again called Roegreen House, was still standing in 1970.[68] The house north of it, called Haydon House by 1887,[69] was demolished between the two World Wars.[70]

Grove farm in north-east Kingsbury originated in land held by the Grove family of Stanmore in the early 14th century.[71] It can probably be identified

with ½ virgate held in 1276–7 by Richard Grove from Edgware manor for 2s. 11½d. rent and 9½d. services.[72] Richard almost certainly held land in north-east Kingsbury at the end of the 13th century,[73] which may have come to him through his marriage with Clarice, one of the coheirs of William Paris (d. 1271),[74] who had held 227 a., mostly in Kingsbury.[75] By 1426 Groves consisted of a messuage and virgate held from Edgware manor for 6s. rent and 1s. 7½d. services. It was then held by John Grove, who also held one quartron, Mill Hill, east of Townsend Lane,[76] which was lost to the estate by 1441[77] and subsequently became part of Hyde farm.[78]

John Grove was in possession of Groves in 1461[79] and he was still alive in 1470 but in 1475 John Wise quitclaimed rights in John Grove's property to Richard Jordan, who in 1479 surrendered Groves, then described as 30 a. 'in divers parcels' to William Jordan and his wife Joan.[80] They extended the estate, acquiring Grove field, 12 a. abutting Groves on the east and south, between 1462 and 1482,[81] and Lemans or Bush fields, 12 a. adjoining Groves on the east, from John Hopcock (Hobcok), and Trigsbough, 2 a. west of Stag Lane, from John Wrench in 1485. William Jordan died in 1486 and in 1488 Joan and her second husband, Hugh Morland, received Long mead, 12 a. north of Groves, and in 1489 Short crofts (8 a.) from John Wrench.[82]

In 1496–7 Hugh and Joan Morland conveyed the estate to Richard Stone and John Edward and in 1528 Edward surrendered it to his own use for life, with reversion to Joan Pluckington and her heirs. When Joan, who married John Nicholl of Hendon and then one Harding, died seised of the property in 1578, it passed to her son, Alan Nicholl of Hendon Hall, usually called Alan Nicholl the elder.[83] Alan had already inherited land at Redhill after his grandfather's death in 1558,[84] and he was active in building up the estate. He acquired Little Dawes and Hay Hills, south of Hay Lane, in 1581 but sold them to Thomas Scudamore in 1589. In that year he extended his estate westward by exchanging land in Edgware for some of John Marsh's land in Kingsbury.[85] By 1597 Alan Nicholl the elder had an estate of 162 a. in north-east Kingsbury.[86]

On his death-bed in December 1599, Alan Nicholl surrendered 80 a., mostly comprising the northern part of the estate, but including Bush

---

[50] Ibid. c40/52, m. 8d.; c46, p. 109.
[51] Ibid. c46, pp. 373–4; c245/34z.
[52] Ibid. c53, ct. bk. (1805–30).
[53] M.R.O., TA/KIN.
[54] Bodl. MS. D.D. All Souls c45, pp. 176–7.
[55] Ibid. c57/17.
[56] Bodl. MS. D.D. All Souls c42, pp. 155–6, 212; c43, pp. 99–100, 105.
[57] Ibid. c45, pp. 134–5.
[58] M.R.O., TA/KIN. Cf. All Souls Coll., Hovenden maps, portfolio II, nos. 11, 13.
[59] Bodl. MS. D.D. All Souls c53, ct. bk. (1861–1914).
[60] e.g. in 1718: Bodl. MS. D.D. All Souls c42, p. 212; 1800: M.L.R. 1802/7/512; 1839: M.R.O., TA/KIN.
[61] Bodl. MS. D.D. All Souls c37/1.
[62] All Souls Coll., Hovenden map, portfolio II, no. 13.
[63] M.R.O., MR/TH/5.
[64] M.R.O., Acc. 262/72/1.
[65] M.L.R. 1801/4/295; 1802/7/512.
[66] H.O. 107/1700/135/2 ff. 310–28; Home Cnties. Dir. (1851), 546; Kelly's Dir. Lond. (1872), 142.
[67] O.S. Maps 1/2,500, Mdx. XI. 6 (1876 and 1916 edns.).

[68] Bartholomew's Ref. Atlas of Greater Lond. (1968 edn.).
[69] H. J. Foley, Our Lanes and Meadow Paths, 43.
[70] Age of Bldings. map penes Brent L.B., Planning and Research Dept.
[71] Bodl. MS. D.D. All Souls c76/137, /141.
[72] S.C. 11/439.
[73] D.L. 25/159; Bodl. MS. D.D. All Souls c76/133.
[74] Cat. Anc. D. ii, A 2296; iv, A 6256, A 6311; Davenport MSS.: Ct. of Husting, roll 4, nos. 124–5; Baylis, Edgware and the Stanmores, 6.
[75] S.C. 11/439.
[76] Bodl. MS. D.D. All Souls c56/2.
[77] Ibid. c37/8.
[78] See p. 57.
[79] Bodl. MS. D.D. All Souls c37/8.
[80] Ibid. /9.
[81] Ibid. /8; c56/5.
[82] Ibid. c37/10.
[83] Ibid. c39/18; c52, ct. bk., f. 51.
[84] Ibid. c38/16.
[85] Ibid. c39/18.
[86] All Souls Coll., Hovenden maps, portfolio II, nos. 9–11, 13.

fields, to his son Edward, and Hobcocks cottage in Hay Lane to his wife, Parnel, for life with remainder to Edward.[87] Alan's death was presented in 1600 and his heirs to the rest of the property were his grand-daughters, Agnes and Parnel, daughters of his deceased eldest son, Alan. But in 1597 and 1599 the elder Alan had mortgaged most of Groves to Cuthbert Lyne (d. 1608), grocer of Westminster, who entered the property after Alan's death. Although Alan's widow and granddaughters brought an action against Lyne, who, they alleged, foreclosed by fraud, they were unsuccessful[88] and by 1609 they were in possession of only 16 a. at High Tunworth, west of Stag Lane.[89]

Cuthbert Lyne's son, Humphrey, sold Groves in 1610 to Thomas Gawen of Hornchurch (Essex),[90] who had acquired Bush fields from Edward Nicholl by 1631.[91] Gawen conveyed the estate to William Bell of Westminster in 1637.[92] Bell was dead by 1658[93] and Robert Nicholl was in possession by 1672,[94] although by what title is unknown. In 1698 Groves was in the hands of William Nicholl, who also held 24 a. to the west of Roe Green and Bacon Lane, which had come to him from another branch of the Nicholl family.[95] When William died in 1729, the estate passed to his sisters and coheirs, Ellen Nicholl and Ann Coghill, a widow.[96] Ann Coghill's daughter, Sarah, wife of Robert Hucks of St. George's, Bloomsbury, inherited her mother's moiety in 1742[97] and her aunt's in 1759.[98] Groves, once again united, descended to her son, Robert Hucks, in 1771[99] and thence to Sarah and Ann Noyes, coparceners by descent from Robert Nicholl (d. 1690) and Robert Hucks (d. 1815) in 1815. Ann predeceased Sarah, who had an estate of 93 a. in 1839. Sarah died in 1844, leaving Groves as moieties to John Smith and Henry Hucks Gibbs, heirs respectively of Robert Nicholl and Robert Hucks.[1]

Smith's portion passed in 1862 to William Lovejoy and William Shelleys Wood. In 1871 Thomas John Bolton, who had been a lessee from 1855, acquired both moieties and in 1873 he secured the enfranchisement of the estate,[2] which in 1874 consisted of 94 a.[3] Mrs. Bolton lived at the Grove in 1880[4] but by c. 1890 it was occupied, and possibly owned, by Michael Walton.[5] From 1892 until 1904 it was described as William Walton's.[6] Most of the land was sold for industry after the First World War.[7]

The estate was leased out from the early 17th century,[8] although Humphrey Lyne in 1609[9] and

the Bolton family in the 19th century lived in the house.[10] A messuage, first mentioned in connexion with the estate in 1426,[11] was already called Groves Place in 1441.[12] It was depicted in 1597 as a typical farm-house — a yard enclosed on three sides by buildings, two other buildings, a pond and orchard and two barns on the edge of the home field.[13] In 1608 Alan Nicholl's granddaughters accused Cuthbert Lyne of 'putting down and altering the mansion house'.[14] A year later the house was broken into and goods worth £14 11s., mostly linen, clothing, curtains and carpets, were stolen from Humphrey Lyne.[15] Groves was assessed for 9 hearths in 1664.[16] Grove Park consisted of an Elizabethan or Jacobean core with 18th-century additions. It had a tower and a long, east-facing drawing-room. There were also hot-houses which were used for market-gardening in the 1920s. The house served as a private boys' school from c. 1923 until the Second World War. It then remained empty and became dilapidated; it was demolished shortly after the war.[17]

In the 15th century the Seakin family began to build up an estate in the north-east corner of Kingsbury, in the area known as Tunworth or Redhill and in Colmans Dean, which had probably formed part of the manor of Stanmore Chenduit in the 13th century.[18] In 1426 William Seakin held a messuage, quartron, croft, and parcel of land and, jointly with John Hamond, another messuage and virgate.[19] The property was scattered throughout the parish but it included land adjoining Edgware Road at Bakers Tunworth and Colmans Dean. Peter Seakin acquired 12 a. at Redhill from Thomas Molesley in 1465 and 16 a. in Colmans Dean from William and Cecily Edmond in 1466.[20] After the death of Peter's widow, Alice, in 1486, the property, then about 100 a., was divided. Part was sold to maintain an obit and charity in accordance with Peter's will and the rest descended to his heirs.[21]

About 30 a., including Warrens[22] and Seakins tenement at Hay Lane, were sold to John Shepherd, and about 26 a. at Redhill was sold before 1500–1 to Thomas Nicholl,[23] who had acquired Honeymans Tunworth next to it from Simon Hamond in 1493.[24] Thomas Nicholl's widow Joan held his property until her death in 1527, when it reverted to his daughters and heirs, Christine Norris, Agnes Greenhill, and Margaret Bellamy, all widows, and to his grandson Alan Nicholl (d. 1558), son of his presumably deceased daughter Joan Nicholl. Two years later the sisters surrendered all their rights

[87] Bodl. MS. D.D. All Souls c39/18.
[88] Ibid. C 2/Jas. I/B8/34; C 3/283/17.
[89] Bodl. MS. D.D. All Souls c78/187.
[90] Ibid. b1/19.
[91] Ibid. c30/54.
[92] M.R.O., Acc. 210/38.
[93] Prob. 11/282 (P.C.C. 561 Wootton).
[94] Bodl. MS. D.D. All Souls 57/20.
[95] Ibid. c57/20, /27.
[96] Ibid. c40/51, m. 9; c43, pp. 32–3.
[97] Ibid. c40/52, m. 1.
[98] Ibid. c44, pp. 198–9.
[99] Ibid. c245/34z; M.L.R. 1775/5/446.
[1] Bodl. MS. D.D. All Souls b4/142; M.R.O., TA/KIN.
[2] Bodl. MS. D.D. All Souls c41/160; c53; c245/34z; Kelly's Dir. Lond. (1860), 66; Par. reg., baptisms (1813–64), A1/3 penes Holy Innocents church, Kingsbury.
[3] Ret. of Owners of land [C. 1097], H.C., p. 2 (1874), lxxii(1).
[4] Kelly's Dir. Lond. (1880), 206.
[5] Wemb. Hist. Soc., Jnl. N.S. i(1), p. 7.

[6] Kelly's Dirs. Lond. (1894), 364; (1900), 304; Kingsbury U.D.C. Wks. & Finance Cttee. Mins. (1900–2), 33; Min. Bk. (1903–15), 30.
[7] Tithe rent-charge apportionments, A9/4–19 penes Holy Innocents church, Kingsbury.
[8] C 3/283/17; Bodl. MS. D.D. All Souls b1/19; c40/51, m. 9.
[9] Mdx. Cnty. Recs. ii. 53–4.   [10] See above.
[11] Bodl. MS. D.D. All Souls c56/2.   [12] Ibid. c37/8.
[13] All Souls Coll., Hovenden map, portfolio II, no. 13.
[14] C 2/Jas. I/B8/34.   [15] Mdx. Cnty. Recs. ii. 53–4.
[16] M.R.O., MR/TH/5.
[17] Hendon Libr., Print L. 2136; S. C. Holliday, 'Notes on hist. of Grove Park', Phoenix, Winter 1954.
[18] S.C. 11/439.
[19] Bodl. MS. D.D. All Souls c56/2.
[20] Ibid. c37/9.
[21] Ibid. /9, /10. Obit in St. Margaret's church, Edgware.
[22] Later part of Little Bush farm, see p. 62.
[23] Bodl. MS. D.D. All Souls c38/13; C 1/239/25.
[24] Bodl. MS. D.D. All Souls c37/10.

in the property to Alan Nicholl,[25] whose grandson, usually called Alan Nicholl the elder, succeeded him in 1558.[26] When this Alan Nicholl the elder inherited his mother's lands in 1578, Redhill became part of Groves until the division of his estates after his death in 1600.[27] Redhill, which was part of the land which passed to Alan's son, Edward, was surrendered by Edward to John Nicholl of Cookes, Hendon, in 1605.[28] Between 1641 and 1672 it passed to John Haley[29] and in 1700 it was conveyed by Richard Haley to John Page of Wembley.[30]

Peter Seakin's executor, Thomas Ederych, retained, in defiance of Seakin's will, 23 a. of Seakin's estate at Colmans Dean, which descended in 1538 to John Ederych's daughter, Elizabeth, wife of Robert Nicholl.[31] When she died in 1590, she was succeeded by her son, usually called Alan Nicholl the younger to distinguish him from the holder of Groves and Redhill.[32] Alan conveyed Colmans Dean to Randolph Marsh in 1598 and in 1700 Robert Marsh surrendered it to John Page of Wembley.[33] John Page thus had a compact estate of 59 a. in north-east Kingsbury. When Richard Page died in 1760, the estate passed to his sister Ann Salter, widow, of Wembley, and his niece, Susanna, wife of Richard Page of Harrow.[34] Susanna and her son, yet another Richard Page, conveyed the estate in 1780 to Isaac Mencelin,[35] whose widow, Harriet, and other trustees under his will, sold it on his death in 1787 to John Nicholl[36] of the Hyde in Hendon.[37]

The remainder of Peter Seakin's property left after the sale of Warrens, Redhill, and Colmans Dean in 1486, about 24 a. on the border with Little Stanmore, passed to his sister and heir, Rose, and her husband, George Collins.[38] In 1519 their son, George, conveyed it to Richard Tyler, who conveyed 6 a. to Henry Platt and 18 a. to Roger Shepherd in 1543.[39] Robert Shepherd surrendered the 18 a. in 1593 to John Franklin, whose son, Richard, acquired 9 a. adjoining it on the east in 1594 through his wife, Margaret, *née* Spurling.[40] Richard Franklin conveyed the combined estate to Nicholas Holland, minister of Little Stanmore, in 1653.[41] The property was split up among various holders during the late 17th and early 18th centuries, but, together with Piggsland, 17 a. joining it on the south-west, had

been reunited in the hands of the Pike family by 1732.[42] John and Ann Pike conveyed the combined estate in 1770 to William Hallet, whose grandson surrendered it to Thomas Day, oilman of Aldersgate Street, in 1788.[43] Day conveyed it to John Nicoll in 1802.[44]

By 1819 John Nicoll had an estate of 140 a. in north-east Kingsbury and 58 a. joining it in Little Stanmore.[45] Apart from the former Seakin lands, acquired in 1787 and 1802,[46] Nicoll had acquired Coghills in 1793,[47] Threshbeing Acre in 1799,[48] Bean croft (the 6 a. conveyed by Richard Tyler to Henry Platt in 1543),[49] in 1804,[50] and High Tunworth, part of Alan Nicholl's estate which had descended to his granddaughters,[51] in 1805.[52]

By the 1830s, however, John Nicoll (d. 1839) was in financial difficulties.[53] He sold 25 a. west of Stag Lane to Francis Stubbs in 1830 and 25 a. at Colmans Dean to Jason Smith in 1833, and mortgaged 50 a. on the Stanmore border in 1834.[54] His executors sold Threshbeing Acre (4 a.) to All Souls in 1842[55] and 115 a. on either side of the Stanmore border to John Hezekiah Essex in 1844.[56] Essex (d. 1848) also acquired Francis Stubbs's lands in north-east Kingsbury in 1844, giving him an estate of 140 a. in Kingsbury and Little Stanmore.[57] On the death of his widow, Margaret, in 1853 the land passed to her nephew, Thomas Cowper, who secured its enfranchisement in 1866.[58] The trustees of Cowper Essex were in possession in 1875.[59] In 1930 the owners of Burnt Oak farm on the Stanmore border were Henry Boot & Sons Ltd.[60]

Redhill farm (34 a.), which was encumbered with the marriage settlement of 1819, was sold by Samuel Nicoll, one of the trustees appointed by John Nicoll, to John Hetherington, the lessee, in 1875.[61] The lands at Redhill and Colmans Dean were leased out at least since the early 17th century, and, until the end of that century, were farmed with neighbouring land belonging to other estates.[62] A windmill was marked next to Edgware Road at Redhill c. 1677[63] and a windmill and cottage, mentioned in 1684,[64] were recorded in 1729–38.[65] John Page referred in 1716 to his farm called Colmans Dean at Redhill, where his lessee occupied a house and barns in 1728.[66] The farmstead was marked on the maps of 1819[67] and 1839.[68] By 1875 the original

[25] Ibid. c38/13.
[26] Ibid. /16.
[27] Ibid. c39/18. See p. 68.
[28] Bodl. MS. D.D. All Souls b1/19.
[29] Ibid. c57/17, /20.
[30] Ibid. c42, p. 66.
[31] Ibid. c38/13; C 1/239/25.
[32] Bodl. MS. D.D. All Souls c39/18.
[33] Ibid. c39/18; c42, p. 68.
[34] Ibid. c44, pp. 208–9.
[35] The wording suggests that Ann Salter's portion passed to her nephew: Bodl. MS. D.D. All Souls c45, pp. 173–4.
[36] By the late 18th cent. the Nicholl family was spelling its name 'Nicoll'.
[37] Bodl. MS. D.D. All Souls c45, pp. 235–7.
[38] Ibid. c37/9, /10.
[39] Ibid. c38/13.
[40] Ibid. c39/18.
[41] Ibid. b1/21.
[42] Ibid. c42, pp. 158, 234; c43, pp. 51–2, 54–5; c57/20, /25.
[43] Ibid. c45, pp. 92–3, 194–5, 241–2; B.M. Maps 188 b2(16).
[44] Bodl. MS. D.D. All Souls c46, p. 159.
[45] M.R.O., Acc. 262/30; Hendon Libr., MS. L. 1723.
[46] See above.
[47] Bodl. MS. D.D. All Souls c46, pp. 35–6.
[48] Ibid. p. 109.
[49] See above.
[50] Bodl. MS. D.D. All Souls c46, p. 179.
[51] See p. 68.
[52] Bodl. MS. D.D. All Souls c46, p. 179.
[53] Hendon Libr., MSS. L. 1707, L. 1710.
[54] Ibid. L. 1718, L. 5501; Bodl. MS. D.D. All Souls c53, ct. bks. (1805–30, 1831–61); c151/G/7; c245/34z.
[55] See p. 58.
[56] Bodl. MS. D.D. All Souls b4/142; Hendon Libr., MS. L. 5501.
[57] Hendon Libr., MS. L. 5501.
[58] Bodl. MS. D.D. All Souls b5/151; c245/34z.
[59] Hendon Libr., MS. L. 5503.
[60] Tithe-rent redemption certs. A9/20–60 *penes* Holy Innocents church, Kingsbury.
[61] Bodl. MS. D.D. All Souls c53, ct. bk. (1861–1914); Hendon Libr., MS. L. 1707.
[62] e.g. 1604 & 1605: Bodl. MS. D.D. All Souls b1/19; 1725: c42, p. 158; 1800: c46, pp. 139–40; 1870: c41/159.
[63] Ogilby, *Map of Mdx.* (c. 1677).
[64] Bodl. MS. D.D. All Souls b2/34.
[65] M.R.O., Acc. 262/72/1.
[66] Bodl. MS. D.D. All Souls c40/51, mm. 5d.–6, 8.
[67] M.R.O., Acc. 262/30.
[68] M.R.O., TA/KIN.

homestead was being used as a foreman's dwelling-house and a 'modern villa residence' had been built beside it.[69] Redhill Farm disappeared between 1926[70] and 1938.[71]

A barn had been erected at Burnt Oak in the extreme north-east corner of Kingsbury by 1844[72] and a farm had been built there by 1865.[73] There was still a cowkeeper there in 1922,[74] but the farm was probably demolished during the 1930s.

In a parish where most of the larger landowners were absent, leasehold estates were very important. In 1317 Kingsbury manor was leased for life to James Palmer, mercer of London,[75] and in 1434 to John Barnville, lord of the neighbouring manor of Tokyngton.[76] A local family, the Shepherds, were the lessees from 1450 until 1618.[77] The lessee in the mid 17th century was John Wingfield, also a native of Kingsbury,[78] who sold the lease in 1664 to Daniel Waldo, presumably a member of the London merchant family which had property in Harrow.[79] The lease of Kingsbury manor descended to Daniel's sons, Edward (d. 1707) and Peter, who sold it in 1712 to James Brydges, later duke of Chandos (d. 1744),[80] who was building up an estate centred on Canons in Little Stanmore (q.v.).[81] His descendants continued to lease the manor lands until 1867.[82]

From 1700 until the 1860s Kingsbury manor demesne lands were sub-leased. In 1712 there were four under-tenants holding by 16- or 17-year leases.[83] Their four farms or estates remained the basic division of the demesne until well into the 19th century. The most important of the four was Hill farm, the southernmost block of land, consisting of about 118 a. on either side of Salmon Street, centred on Hill farm-house, the former home farm of the manor.[84] In 1788 it was a 'good, square brick house', with three barns, a stable, cow-house and other outbuildings.[85] The farm-house, with 3 a. surrounding it, was let on a building lease in 1960 and pulled down shortly afterwards.[86]

The second farm, Pipers, which took its name from an adjacent tenement,[87] consisted of about 47 a.–66 a. north of Great Bush farm.[88] The farm-house, which was in existence by 1729–38, lay just outside the demesne lands.[89] Pipers ceased to be run

as a separate farm after 1867 and by 1894 the farm-house had been replaced by Fern Dene, which survived until after the Second World War.[90]

The third farm, called in the 19th century Lower or Hungry Down farm, consisted of 66 a.–96 a. in north-west Kingsbury which was leased separately as early as 1438–9.[91] It was leased together with Gore fields after they had been acquired by the Brydges family.[92]

Shoelands, the fourth farm, grew out of Stratford Long (37 a.) in north-east Kingsbury which was leased separately in 1438–9.[93] There was a barn on the estate next to Edgware Road by 1729–38[94] and a farm-house had been built there by 1864–5.[95] The farm still existed in 1917,[96] but a factory was already producing motor bodies there in 1914[97] and the whole area was converted to factory development after the First World War.[98]

Except for the period 1584–94[99] Hyde farm, 85 a. in 1597,[1] was always leased separately from the other All Souls estates. The Shepherd family leased Hyde farm in 1534–66[2] and 1584–94, when both Hill and Hyde farms were leased by Thomas Shepherd.[3] Michael Page, a relation by marriage of the Shepherds,[4] was the lessee in 1597[5] and 1620,[6] and Margaret Stockdale in the 1660s.[7] From 1779 until 1800 the lease was held by Maximilian Western of Cavendish Square (Westminster),[8] who probably sub-let it. Robert Selby, the lessee in 1807–39,[9] said that his father was the farmer there in 1771–4.[10] Other lessees included Harbut John Ward, builder of Blackfriars (City of London) in 1842,[11] John King, brewer of Southampton in 1849,[12] James Arbon in 1870,[13] and Henry Ward, horse-dealer of Edgware Road, 1880–1905.[14] A tenement was attached to the original Lorchons or Hamonds holding in the 14th century.[15] In 1597 the farm-house was a typical Elizabethan house with a main block and two projecting wings. There were three other buildings, possibly barns or labourers' cottages, about the yard.[16] Hyde Farm was assessed for 12 hearths in 1664.[17] The house was rebuilt in the late 18th or early 19th century and described in 1837 as a superior farm-house.[18] It was a plain, stuccoed building with two storeys and

[69] Hendon Libr., MSS. L. 5500, L. 5502.
[70] *Kelly's Dir. Hendon* (1926).
[71] O.S. Maps 1/2,500, Mdx. XI. 1 (1938 edn.).
[72] Hendon Libr., MS. L. 5501.
[73] O.S. Map 1/2,500, Mdx. XI. 1 (1873 edn.).
[74] Kingsbury U.D.C., Min. Bk. (1915–22), 450.
[75] Bodl. MS. D.D. All Souls c75/1.
[76] Ibid. c76/55.
[77] Ibid. c79/4, /34; Davenport MSS.: All Souls Coll., Bursars' Accts.; see p. 73.
[78] Bodl. MS. D.D. All Souls c30/56; c77/182.
[79] *V.C.H. Mdx.* iv. 216.
[80] M.R.O., Acc. 262/27(1), /29.
[81] He bought Gore fields in 1714 (see above) and leased the Freren estate in 1720 (see below).
[82] Bodl. MS. D.D. All Souls c80/4–7, /49; c82/71, /75; c83/84, /95, /99; c85/123, /138; M.R.O., Acc. 262/27(1), /28, /29; /61/21.
[83] M.R.O., Acc. 262/29.
[84] For the earlier history of the house, see s.v. manors, above.
[85] Bodl. MS. D.D. All Souls c245/341.
[86] Ex inf. Daniel Smith, Briant and Done.
[87] See p. 53.
[88] O.S. Map 1/2,500, Mdx. XI. 5 (1873 edn.).
[89] M.R.O., Acc. 262/72/1, /2.
[90] Bodl. MS. D.D. All Souls c85/138. See p. 53.
[91] Bodl. MS. D.D. All Souls c78/184.
[92] See p. 65.

[93] Bodl. MS. D.D. All Souls c78/184.
[94] M.R.O., Acc. 262/72/1, /2.
[95] O.S. Map 1/2,500, Mdx. XI. 6 (1873 edn.).
[96] Kingsbury U.D.C., Min. Bk. (1915–22), 85.
[97] Ibid. (1903–15), 419, 429.
[98] See p. 77.
[99] Bodl. MS. D.D. All Souls c79/25, /28.
[1] Of which 63 a. lay in Kingsbury: All Souls Coll., Hovenden maps, portfolio II, nos. 9, 13, 15.
[2] Bodl. MS. D.D. All Souls c79/11, /15, /18, /21.
[3] Ibid. /25, /28.
[4] Bodl. MS. D.D. All Souls c77/172.
[5] All Souls Coll., Hovenden maps, portfolio II, nos. 9, 13, 15.
[6] Bodl. MS. D.D. All Souls c79/36a.
[7] Ibid. c30/56; c80/39.
[8] Ibid. c80/40, /51; c81/62.
[9] Ibid. c82/69; c83/80, /89; c84/96, /105; M.R.O., TA/KIN.
[10] Prior, *Goldsmith*, ii. 332.
[11] Bodl. MS. D.D. All Souls c85/116.
[12] Ibid. /127.
[13] Ibid. /140.
[14] Ibid. /143–4a; Kingsbury U.D.C., Min. Bk. (1903–15), 80.
[15] Bodl. MS. D.D. All Souls c37/3, /5; c56/2.
[16] All Souls Coll., Hovenden maps, portfolio II, no. 13.
[17] M.R.O., MR/TH/5.
[18] Prior, *Goldsmith*, ii. 332.

a slate roof.[19] In 1929 the site was let on a building lease and the house was demolished in 1932.[20]

Freren manor, including the rectory, tithes,[21] and seigneurial rights, was leased out by 1505 to a chaplain.[22] In 1524 it was leased to a layman, Guthlac Overton, gentleman, for 60 years,[23] but by 1540 the lease had passed to Richard Bellamy[24] and it was subsequently held by his son, William.[25] Other lessees were Michael Page (1588),[26] his son Richard (1589, 1640),[27] Ralph Hartley (1668),[28] John (1680, 1699) and Richard Prince (1711) of Flaunden (Herts.).[29] From 1540, if not earlier, Freren was leased to absentee lessees who held it as part of larger neighbouring estates and sub-leased to local farmers. The Bellamys and Pages were primarily concerned with Tokyngton and Uxendon and Hartley with Chalkhill and Findens. In 1720 Richard Prince sold the lease to James Brydges, duke of Chandos, whose descendants leased Freren until 1886.[30]

Until the late 19th century all the land in southern Kingsbury and Hendon was farmed by the under-lessees as a single farm centred on Freren farm-house. In 1886 it was divided into two farms: Freren (105 a.), which was leased directly to Frederick Reynolds, and the Hendon lands (85 a.), leased directly to Henry Ward.[31]

From 1333 the Coffers estate was always leased out,[32] usually among several people.[33] Lessees during the 16th century included members of the Shepherd[34] and Grove families.[35]

ECONOMIC HISTORY. AGRICULTURE. In 1086 Kingsbury was divided between two holdings. The largest, held by Albold, consisted of $7\frac{1}{2}$ hides, made up of land for 7 ploughs, enough meadow for $\frac{1}{2}$ plough, and woodland for 1,000 pigs yielding £1. Of the arable land, 2 ploughs were on the demesne and 5 on the land held by peasants. The whole estate, worth £4 in 1086 and £6 T.R.E., was worth only £1 when Albold received it, suggesting considerable devastation after the Conquest. The second estate, at Chalkhill, consisted of $2\frac{1}{2}$ hides, composed of land for 2 ploughs and woodland for 200 pigs. Of the arable, 1 plough was in demesne and one divided among the 5 villeins, who each held a virgate, and one cottar. The estate, worth £1 10s. in 1086, had been valued at £3 T.R.E.[36]

Of the cultivated land in Kingsbury in 1086 6 ploughs were required on the peasant land, approximately 4 hides, and 3 ploughs on the freehold demesne land, probably about 3 hides. If there was more customary than freehold land in cultivation,

there was also a large area of uncultivated, probably wooded, land. Most had been granted out by the end of the 13th century, part forming freehold estates like those of the de la Hayes in northern and of the Brancasters in southern Kingsbury,[37] and part forming new villein holdings. In 1276–7 there were 16 virgates and 20 a. of copyhold land of Edgware manor in Kingsbury.[38] By c. 1350 most of the freehold land in northern Kingsbury had been absorbed into the demesne of Kingsbury manor, which then consisted of approximately 320 a.[39] Southern Kingsbury was predominantly freehold. By c. 1350 the Westminster estate at Chalkhill had been replaced by a freehold estate of 40 a., a few small freehold estates, and $3\frac{3}{4}$ virgates and 22 a. of copyhold land held from Kingsbury manor; south-eastern Kingsbury was occupied by the freehold Brancaster estate. Copyhold land, which was at its greatest extent during the early Middle Ages, contracted during the 15th and 16th centuries as it was absorbed into the larger freehold estates of Chalkhill and Kingsbury manor.[40] By 1597 750 a. out of a total of 1,580 a. (48 per cent) was freehold land.[41] This proportion remained until the copyhold contracted still further with new acquisitions by All Souls College and enfranchisements in the 19th century.

Accounts made by the bailiff of Geoffrey le Scrope for the period Feb. 1325–Michaelmas 1326 are the only evidence for the organization of the economy on the freehold demesnes.[42] The work was directed by the bailiff and carried out by *famuli*, permanent and hired workers, and villeins performing customary services. Permanent labourers, who included a dairyman, a swineherd, a herdsman, a drover, a carter, two ploughmen, a boy to watch the horses and a woman to make ale, were paid in money and grain. Hired workers performed all the mowing of hay, collecting, binding and stacking, winnowing, most of the threshing and part of the weeding and reaping of grain. *Famuli*[43] carried out half the weeding, a small part of the threshing, and part of the collecting of hay and building of hayricks. The rest of the reaping of grain and collecting of hay and building of hayricks was performed by boon-workers.

In 1304 Thomas of Brancaster alluded to service owed him by William Gospriest and Richard Simond.[44] Although Ralph Gospriest and Ralph Simond were among the six tenants who paid assized rents to Geoffrey le Scrope in 1325,[45] there is no evidence that customary services other than boon-works were ever exacted on the Coffers estate. Most people in Kingsbury owed customary

[19] Wemb. Hist. Soc., Acc. 445/1.
[20] Ex inf. Daniel Smith, Briant and Done; F. K. Malyon, *Kingsbury Par. Ch.* (pamphlet).
[21] Tithes were sometimes leased separately from the rest of the estate: Davenport MSS.: Com. Ct. Lond., Reg. 1585–92, f. 127; M.R.O., Acc. 262/28 pt. 2, /29.
[22] B.M. Cott. MS. Claud. E. vi, f. 14; see p. 83.
[23] Ibid. f. 241.   [24] S.C. 6/Hen. VIII/2402 m. 9d.
[25] M.R.O., Acc. 853/10.
[26] Davenport MSS.: Com. Ct. Lond., Reg. 1585–92, f. 127.
[27] Bodl. MS. D.D. All Souls c39/18; C 54/3556 no. 24, mm. 10 sqq.
[28] St. Paul's MS., Box A 58a.
[29] M.R.O., Acc. 262/27 pt. 2, /29; C 8/267/127.
[30] Bodl. MS. D.D. All Souls c85/42; M.R.O., Acc. 262/28; /50/9; /72/1; Church Com., file 51708; deeds 169053–62.

[31] Church Com., files 51708, 67417.
[32] B.M. Cott. MS. Nero E. vi(1), f. 75.
[33] e.g. in 1394 'tenants of the land formerly John Farnborough': Bodl. MS. D.D. All Souls c37/5. There were 5 lessees in 1716: M.L.R. 1716/6/138.
[34] Bodl. MS. D.D. All Souls c38/13.
[35] M.R.O., Acc. 727/2; Req. 2/25/157.
[36] *V.C.H. Mdx.* i. 123, 126. And see below, p. 76.
[37] See pp. 57–8.
[38] S.C. 11/439.
[39] See p. 57.
[40] See pp. 57, 61.
[41] All Souls Coll., Hovenden maps, portfolio II, nos. 9–15.
[42] W.A.M. 27844–5.
[43] They received food, porridge made from oats and salt.
[44] D.L. 25/162.
[45] W.A.M. 27844–5.

services to Edgware manor. The services appear to have been evenly divided between Kingsbury and Edgware, being respectively worth £1 6s. 10¾d. and £1 6s. 11¼d. in 1276–7[46] and £1 7s. ¼d. and £1 9s. 3d. in 1426. In 1426 23 tenements in Kingsbury, representing 13¾ virgates, owed a total of 289 works: 50 carrying works (*averagia*), 23 each of hedging, harrowing, hoeing, and binding corn, 92 reaping and 55 carrying corn works. Apart from one tenant who had to mow Rush Mead, there was no mention in 1426[47] of any works connected with hay, in contrast to 1276–7 when mowing, carrying, and building haystacks were demanded from all customary tenants.[48] In 1438–9 11 customary tenants of Kingsbury manor owed services of harrowing and hoeing, boon-works of mowing, lifting and carrying, and certain autumn works, valued in all at 7s. a year.[49] Although services were included in the appurtenances of Freren manor leased in the early 16th century,[50] there is no evidence that any were performed. The tenants of Freren were said in 1358 to be free[51] and of the 13 tenants mentioned in 1510–12, many held land in Hendon and Harrow.[52]

Most services had probably been commuted by 1276–7,[53] although there was some presentment of tenants of Edgware manor for failure to perform ploughing-services in 1280[54] and 1331[55] and mowing was expected from tenants in Kingsbury in 1433.[56] On Kingsbury manor tenants had to mow Honeyslough meadow in 1350[57] and 16 people were presented for default at 'the time of mowing' in 1379; at the same court Robert Wrench was presented for having 30 autumn works in arrears.[58]

None of the customary holdings in Kingsbury during the Middle Ages was very large. On the main manor in 1086 8 villeins held a virgate each, 3 villeins held a half-virgate each, and 5 bordars held 5 a. each; there was one cottar.[59] In 1276–7 holdings consisted of a virgate and a quartron or quarter-virgate, 6 virgates, 6 triple-quartrons, 7 half-virgates, 3 quartrons, and two 5-acre holdings. Except for Tollesland and Allechonland, two triple-quartrons which were probably held in common, each was held by one tenant, giving a total of 23 tenants.[60] By 1426 customary land in Kingsbury held from Edgware manor comprised 4 virgates, 3 triple-quartrons, 10 half-virgates, 10 quartrons, and 24 other holdings, mostly crofts. There were 32 tenants, ranging from John Hamond, who held part of a virgate, a triple-quartron, a quartron and 4 a., to John Lyon of Boys, who had 2 a.[61]

A comparison of the figures for 1086, 1276–7, and

1426 suggests that, as the population of Kingsbury grew, the larger holdings were divided and by 1426 many under-holdings had become separated from the main tenement. Since the total amount also expanded, however, there must have been continuous assarting. Colmans Dean, the valley of the charcoal man,[62] was presumably once densely wooded, but by 1276–7 it was a field of 70 a. belonging to the manor of Stanmore Chenduit.[63] The same process took place elsewhere in Kingsbury, although most areas, when cleared from the forest, formed small assarts surrounded by wood rather than large open fields. In eastern Kingsbury in the late 13th and early 14th century land was held in 1 r. strips or selions by about five or six people in Apsfurlong, Streetfurlong (identifiable with Stratford Long or Shoelands),[64] Oldham, Arneyshaw, Sneteleshale, and Hay Dean.[65] In 1350 customary land held from Kingsbury manor included 7 half-virgates, one quartron, one 7-acre and one 11-acre holding.[66] Unlike Edgware manor, where there were no free holdings apart from the large estates, there were four freehold estates held from Kingsbury manor: Chalkhill, consisting of 40 a. in 1350, and three one-acre holdings. The land held from Kingsbury manor consisted of scattered holdings like Brasiers at Kingsbury Green, Dawes on Edgware Road, strips in Tunworth and strips and closes in south-west Kingsbury.[67]

The process of consolidating and inclosing selions by exchange[68] and by accumulating under-sets[69] was furthered when the Black Death considerably reduced the numbers of landholders, especially on Kingsbury manor. Colmans Dean had probably been inclosed by 1426, when it was parcelled among six tenants,[70] and consolidation had been carried a stage further by 1482 when it was held by two tenants.[71] By 1597 strip-cultivation was confined to a small area of Broad field between Bacon Lane, Stag Lane, and Roe Green.[72] The inclosure of strips into closes took place in Tunworth in the 15th century,[73] on Freren manor at the beginning of the 16th century,[74] and to the west of Stag Lane in 1584.[75] It had begun in Broad field by 1479[76] and was completed by 1752.[77] Much of the land in the south-west became absorbed into Kingsbury demesne and Chalkhill, while much of the rest was incorporated into the estates built up by the Shepherd, Scudamore, and Nicholl families.

During the 13th, 14th, and 15th centuries most customary land was held by local peasant families, the Mosshatches, Randolfs, Lewgars, Roes, Lemans, Hamonds, Edwins, Richards, Simonds, Dibels, Wrenches, Warrens, Dawes, Pages, Lyons, and

[46] S.C. 11/439. The extent is discussed in full *sub* V.C.H. Mdx. iv. 158, where, however, the importance of Kingsbury is underestimated.
[47] Bodl. MS. D.D. All Souls c56/2.
[48] S.C. 11/439.
[49] Bodl. MS. D.D. All Souls c78/186a.
[50] B.M. Cott. MS. Claud. E. vi, ff. 14, 39v.; S.C. 6/Hen. VIII/2402 m. 9d.
[51] C 143/329/3.
[52] S.C. 2/191/45.
[53] S.C. 11/439.
[54] S.C. 2/188/54.
[55] Bodl. MS. D.D. All Souls c37/1.
[56] Ibid. /7(2).
[57] Ibid. /2.
[58] Ibid. /4.
[59] V.C.H. Mdx. i. 126.
[60] S.C. 11/439.

[61] Bodl. MS. D.D. All Souls c56/2.
[62] Cf. P.N. Mdx. 184.
[63] S.C. 11/439.
[64] See p. 58.
[65] Bodl. MS. D.D. All Souls c76/113–14, /136, /138, /140–2; D.L. 25/159–60.
[66] Bodl. MS. D.D. All Souls c37/2.
[67] e.g. ibid. c77/150–1.
[68] e.g. ibid. c37/1; c76/138.
[69] Ibid. c37/9.
[70] Ibid. c56/2.
[71] Ibid. /5.
[72] All Souls Coll., Hovenden maps, portfolio II, no. 13.
[73] Bodl. MS. D.D. All Souls c37/7(1), /9, /10.
[74] S.C. 2/191/45.
[75] Bodl. MS. D.D. All Souls c56/12a.
[76] Ibid. c37/9.
[77] Ibid. c245/34z.

Groves.[78] The Hamonds had the longest association with Kingsbury. Hamon Constantine, hanged in 1280,[79] was succeeded by his son John Hamond, whose descendants remained landholders in Kingsbury until 1641.[80] The Wrench family, which held a half-virgate in 1276-7,[81] was active in Kingsbury until 1530.[82] Most of the Wrench lands passed to the Shepherd family. A William Shepherd had an interest in land in Kingsbury in 1306[83] but the main connexion of the family with the parish dates from the mid 15th century. The Shepherds were lessees of Kingsbury manor demesne (1450-1618), of Hyde farm (1534-66 and 1584-94), and of Coffers (c. 1541).[84] Of the copyhold estates, they held Edwins (1463-1572), Richards (1466-1541), Townsend (1462-1542), land around Roe Green (1498-1599), and part of Colmans Dean (1543-93).[85] The family was at its height c. 1540 when it held 285 a. and leased 783 a., 46 per cent of Kingsbury parish. In 1597 Thomas Shepherd leased 233 a. of Kingsbury manor demesne and 5 other members of the family held a total of 118 a.[86] In 1631 9 members, mostly sons of Michael Shepherd, held 66 a.;[87] four houses, all small, were charged to the family in 1664.[88] In 1698 three Shepherds held 28 a.;[89] the remaining land was lost and the family died out in the early 18th century.[90]

The rise and decline of the Shepherds illustrates the part played by local families. During the Middle Ages only one large freehold estate, Chalkhill, was held by such a family but most customary lands were in the hands of local peasants. Towards the end of the medieval period control began to pass to three groups of outsiders: those whose main interests were in neighbouring parishes, those who received estates in Kingsbury as a reward for services elsewhere, and the Londoners. Among the first group were the Pages, who originally acquired Kingsbury manor as an extension of their estate in Stanmore. The Barnvilles, Bellamys, Pages, Lyons, and Walters extended their Harrow estates into Kingsbury. Colmans Dean and Redhill were closely linked with Little Stanmore and Coffers with Willesden, and the Franklin and Roberts families, who held land in southern Kingsbury, were primarily concerned with Willesden. The most important of this group was the Brydges family, centred on Canons in Little Stanmore.

The second group was especially important in the Middle Ages. The de la Hayes and Poleyns were vassals of the earls of Lincoln. Geoffrey le Scrope was a royal favourite who may have obtained his estate near Hendon through his brother, Henry. John Warner, Christopher Hovenden, and Robert Strensham, warden and fellows of All Souls College, and their relatives, had interests in Kingsbury in the 16th century,[91] which were maintained, in the latter's case, even against royal pressure.[92]

The third class of outsiders, the Londoners, was always influential. Kingsbury manor was leased to Londoners in the 14th century and owned by London merchants during the early 15th century. In the south a large area was held by Gilbert of Brancaster, the son of a London citizen, and by his daughter, who married another. Although most of these two estates passed into the hands of institutions, All Souls College and the Knights Hospitallers and later St. Paul's Cathedral, Chalkhill and Coffers and most of the copyhold land were acquired by Londoners. By 1597 only 35 per cent of Kingsbury was owned by people who lived in the parish.[93] The proportion continued to decline, to 26 per cent in 1672,[94] 17 per cent in 1839,[95] 12 per cent in 1887, and 0·2 per cent in 1917.[96]

Although more and more land passed to outsiders, the size of estates remained much the same. From the Domesday survey until the 19th century most estates were of between 5 and 50 a.[97] During the 19th century there were more large estates and new cottages were erected.

The most important tenure for most of Kingsbury's history, however, was not freehold or copyhold but leasehold. Few outsiders were prepared to farm the land themselves. Land was leased. sometimes to the local peasant families but increasingly to other outsiders, who in turn sub-let it to local farmers. The most important figures in 18th- and early-19th-century Kingsbury were not owners but the duke of Chandos and his heirs who from 1714 until 1800 held, mainly by lease, 38 per cent (640 a.) of the parish.[98] Thus, especially on the larger freehold estates, there was a chain of leasing and under-leasing which was a major cause of the backward character of rural Kingsbury. Middlesex was the most highly rented county in England in 1833[99] and the high rents for cottages were given in 1834 as the main cause of poverty.[1] The farmers were themselves lessees and, although their rents were lowered in the 1830s,[2] often insolvent.

High rents for short leases did not encourage long term investment and land became exhausted and farm-houses dilapidated. Another effect of leasing was the lack of authority in the parish. All Souls College and St. Paul's regarded the estates purely in terms of profit. Everything that could be leased

[78] S.C. 2/188/54; S.C. 11/439; Bodl. MS. D.D. All Souls c37/1, /2, /4.
[79] S.C. 2/188/54.
[80] Bodl. MS. D.D. All Souls c30/54; c56/2, /5, /11; c57/17.
[81] S.C. 11/439.
[82] S.C. 2/185/54; Bodl. MS. D.D. All Souls c38/13; c56/2, /5.
[83] Bodl. MS. D.D. All Souls c76/138.
[84] See p. 59.   [85] See pp. 62, 64, 66.
[86] All Souls Coll., Hovenden maps, portfolio II, nos. 9-15.
[87] Bodl. MS. D.D. All Souls c30/54.
[88] M.R.O., MR/TH/5.
[89] Bodl. MS. D.D. All Souls c57/25.
[90] Ibid. c245/34z; Eliz. Shepherd's will (1711), Davenport MSS.: Com. Ct. Lond. Reg. lv.
[91] Bodl. MS. D.D. All Souls c32/15-16; c38/13; c56/11; Alumni Oxon. 1500-1714.

[92] See V.C.H. Mdx. iv. 157.
[93] All Souls Coll., Hovenden maps, portfolio II, nos. 9-15. Landholders have been identified by means of wills, court rolls and deeds.
[94] Bodl. MS. D.D. All Souls c57/20; M.R.O., MR/TH/5, 26, 53, 75.
[95] M.R.O., TA/KIN.   [96] M.A.F. 68/1105, /2815.
[97] Inf. based upon V.C.H. Mdx. i. 123, 126 (1086); S.C. 11/439 (1276-7); Bodl. MS. D.D. All Souls c56/2 (1426); All Souls Coll., Hovenden maps, portfolio II, nos. 9-15 (1597); Bodl. MS. D.D. All Souls c30/54 (1631); ibid. c57/25 (1698); M.R.O., Acc. 262/27 pt. 1 and TA/KIN (1839); M.R.O., Acc. 262/27 pt. 1 (1870).
[98] M.R.O., Acc. 262/72/1-2. See pp. 56-60, 65.
[99] G. B. G. Bull, 'Changing Landscape of Rural Mdx. 1500-1850' (Lond. Univ. Ph.D. thesis, 1958), 150.
[1] Rep. of Poor Law Com. App. B(2), p. 105.
[2] e.g. on land leased from the duke of Buckingham: Eton Coll. Recs. 49/55.

out, including seigneurial and church rights and appurtenances,[3] was leased, usually to men who rarely visited Kingsbury. In the absence of the lord and his bailiff and with courts held at Edgware, it is not surprising that court orders were ignored and that neglect, quarrels and corruption became something of a tradition, from the cases of fraud and forgery in the 15th and 16th centuries[4] to the local government feuds of the 20th century.[5]

Leasing began on the freehold estates in the Middle Ages. Geoffrey le Scrope's estate was administered for him by a bailiff in 1325[6] but it was probably leased out from 1333.[7] Walter Saling may have farmed Kingsbury manor in the 1330s but most of the owners were absentees who leased it out. From 1458 the manorial demesne was let on 10-year leases at £8 a year.[8] It was held on 20-year leases at £8 13s. 4d. from 1508 until the end of the century[9] when a mixed money and corn rent was introduced which lasted, with little variation,[10] until 1867 when a more realistic rent of £420 a year was demanded.[11] Hyde farm was let on 20-year leases at £6 a year in 1534[12] and for a mixed money and grain rent from 1584[13] until 1870, when the 139-acre farm was let at £340 a year.[14] Freren manor was leased in the early 16th century for £8 and its woods were leased in 1524 for £1.[15] From the mid 16th century until 1886 the Freren estate was held by 21-year leases at £9 or £9 10s. a year rent with the addition, from the mid 17th century, of an annual payment to the curate (£40), and from the early 19th century, of an annual redeemed land-tax payment of £66.[16] In 1886, when the connexion with the dukes of Buckingham came to an end, the estate was divided into two farms, leased for £210 and £204 respectively.[17]

During the 16th century leasing became widespread on the copyhold estates. Sometimes a father or elder brother leased portions of the estate to other members of the family[18] but most leasing was by outsiders to local farmers. The farms were rarely conterminous with the estates but, from the 17th century, were usually small, of between 30 a. and 150 a. Large estates, notably those of All Souls College, were divided into several farms, while smaller estates were combined. In 1870, for example, William Field's farm of 236 a. was formed from land owned by 9 people, he himself owning only 7 a.[19] The acreage of farms remained much the same throughout the 19th century, although there was a tendency towards large farms, the largest in 1870 being of 282 a., compared with 212 a. in 1839.[20]

The size and shape of farms was intimately connected with agriculture. The quartron and

virgate strip-holdings of the early Middle Ages were part of a predominantly arable farming system. Wheat, oats, and beans were grown.[21] In 1350 there were at least 18 oxen on the demesne of Kingsbury manor[22] and in 1426 wheat was grown in Paradise, possibly identified with Cow Leas, west of Salmon Street.[23] During the 15th century oats were frequently sold by the lessee to the stables of All Souls College in Oxford.[24]

Oats were apparently the most important crop grown in 1325–6 at Geoffrey le Scrope's Kingsbury grange which produced nearly 43 qr. of oats and 18½ qr. of oats and wheat growing together compared with 10¼ qr. of wheat, 11¼ qr. of maslin, and 1 qr. 6 bu. of beans. About 28 per cent of the wheat and 50 per cent of the beans were sold and some wheat was sent to the lord's house in London, but all the other produce was consumed at Kingsbury, as seed, payment for manorial workers and officials, and food for servants, dogs, and stock. Compared with 106 a. producing grain crops, there were only 17½ a. of meadow and the only pasture was at Wakemans Hill, which was leased out. The cattle, of which at Michaelmas 1325 there were 20 cows, 16 calves, a bull and 4 bullocks, were also leased out. Other stock included 9 oxen, 4 plough-stots, 2 carthorses, 15 pigs, and poultry. There were no sheep although a sheephouse (domus bercar') was mentioned. There were also apples in a garden.[25]

The relative unimportance of meadow and pasture compared with arable land on the le Scrope estate seems to have been general throughout Kingsbury in the Middle Ages. In 1086 there was only enough meadow for ½ plough, presumably water-meadow along the Brent. There was extensive woodland, enough for 1,200 pigs,[26] and some of it may have been cleared by c. 1200 to give pasture for cattle.[27] Nevertheless, pannage was still demanded in 1333[28] and pigs and draught animals figured more frequently than cattle in suits of trespass during the 14th and early 15th centuries.[29] Meadow formed a very small proportion of estates during the 14th century and pasture is rarely recorded before 1430.[30] Meadow was apparently held in common in 1284.[31] The lord's meadow was mentioned in 1379[32] and hay was grown on the demesne of Kingsbury manor during the 15th century.[33]

The conversion of arable to grassland may intitially have been connected with the inclosure of arable strips and building up of estates. It was well-advanced in some areas by the late 15th century and by 1597 arable formed only 30 per cent of the 1,240 a. marked on the All Souls map.[34] Of the area in south Kingsbury not marked on the map, Coffers (366 a. in

[3] e.g. Bodl. MS. D.D. All Souls c32/8; c79/12; St. Paul's MS., Box A 58a.
[4] C 1/60/76; C 1/709/5; Req. 2/19/11; Req. 2/25/157.
[5] See p. 81.   [6] W.A.M. 27844–5.
[7] B.M. Cott. MS. Nero E. vi(1), f. 75.
[8] Bodl. MS. D.D. All Souls c79/4; Davenport MSS.: All Souls Coll., Bursars' Accts.
[9] Bodl. MS. D.D. All Souls c79/9.
[10] Ibid. /27; c82/75a; c83/84c.
[11] Ibid. c85/138.   [12] Ibid. c79/11, /15.
[13] Ibid. c83/80, /89; c85/127.
[14] Ibid. c85/140.
[15] B.M. Cott. MS. Claud. E. vi, ff. 39v., 241.
[16] B.M. Add. Ch. 2018; C 54/3556 no. 24; M.R.O., Acc. 262/27 pt. 1; Church Com. deeds 169053–62.
[17] Church Com. file 51708.
[18] e.g. Michael Page (1588), Davenport MSS.: Com. Ct. Lond., Reg. 1585–92, f. 127.

[19] M.R.O., Acc. 262/27 pt. 1.
[20] M.R.O., TA/KIN; Acc. 262/27 pt. 1 (1839); Acc. 262/27 pt. 1 (1870); M.A.F. 68/2815 (1917).
[21] S.C. 2/188/54; Bodl. MS. D.D. All Souls c37/7(1).
[22] Bodl. MS. D.D. All Souls c37/2.
[23] Ibid. /7(1).
[24] Davenport MSS.: All Souls Coll., Bursars' Accts.
[25] W.A.M. 27844–5.   [26] V.C.H. Mdx. i. 123, 126.
[27] Rot. Cur. Reg. (Rec. Com.), ii. 95.
[28] Bodl. MS. D.D. All Souls c37/1.
[29] Ibid. /4, /7(1).
[30] Ibid. c75/41; c76/144; C.P. 25(1)/150/64; C.P. 25(1)/152/88; C 47/68/8/170; Cal. Close, 1422–9, 316.
[31] S.C. 2/188/54.
[32] Bodl. MS. D.D. All Souls c37/4.
[33] Davenport MSS.: All Souls Coll., Bursars' Accts.
[34] All Souls Coll., Hovenden maps, portfolio II, nos. 9–15.

Kingsbury, Hendon, and Willesden) had 33 per cent arable in 1478–9,[35] Chalkhill (166 a.) had 24 per cent arable in 1533,[36] and Freren (184 a.) had 41 per cent arable in 1650.[37] Although Kingsbury was on the edge of the wheat-growing belt and grain was still grown, animal farming became increasingly important during the 16th century. Sheep and cattle, especially bullocks for the London meat market, were raised.[38] Kingsbury's position on Edgware Road was excellent for middlemen operating between London and the animal-raising regions of Hertfordshire. John Molesley, a drover from London, acquired a small estate at Redhill in 1445.[39] Between 1615 and 1617, 8 inhabitants of Kingsbury were licensed as drovers, badgers, and kidders.[40]

Pasture continued to increase throughout the 17th and 18th centuries, until by 1838 it covered 97 per cent of Kingsbury. Boundaries were rearranged and arable was converted to pasture at Gore fields during the early 17th century.[41] The process was completed in eastern Kingsbury, bordering Edgware Road, by the mid 18th century,[42] at Hungry Down by 1812,[43] at Pipers farm by 1832,[44] Freren farm by 1866,[45] and at Hill farm by 1867.[46] A three-field system involving fallowing and the use of leas was long practised on farms before the total conversion to grassland. Another feature was the conversion of woodland to arable before it was turned over to pasture.[47] By the mid 18th century most of the grassland in Kingsbury was given over to hay, which was taken to London by waggon along Edgware Road[48] and remained the chief crop until well into the 19th century.[49] The dependence on hay, while possibly helping the farmers during the agricultural depression of the 1830s, increased the poverty of the labourers. While Irishmen were hired during the harvest, local farm-workers became chargeable on the parish during the winter.[50] In 1851 30 labourers were employed on 7 of the 11 farms in Kingsbury; since 95 labourers, a shepherd, three farm servants, and a farmer's boy lived in the parish, many must have been unemployed for most of the year.[51] Hay-farming began to decline at the end of the 19th century when cheap foreign hay

could be imported and when motor traffic replaced horse traffic.[52]

Some diversification was introduced into farming during the 19th century. Crops were never important. In 1867 there were 9 a. of mangolds, 3 a. of turnips, and 180 a. of clover and artificial grass, all presumably grown as fodder crops.[53] Mushrooms were grown at Blackpot Hill farm in 1909[54] and fruit and vegetables together covered 11½ a. in 1917.[55]

There was a shepherd in Kingsbury in 1851[56] and Grove House was in the hands of a sheep salesman between 1868 and 1880.[57] There were 851 sheep in 1867 but only 332 in 1917. During the same period the number of pigs rose from 100 to 486.[58]

Gore farm, owned by Dr. Arthur Calcutta White, was a pig farm from 1901[59] and there were piggeries at Grange farm, Shoelands, and Fryent farms by 1915.[60] Horses were probably reared in consequence of the hay trade. There were two jobmasters in 1851[61] and from that date until 1900 Redhill farm was in the hands of horse-dealers.[62] In 1921 it was leased by Capt. Bertram Mills as a stud farm for hackney horses.[63] The lessees of Hyde farm in 1882[64] and of Freren farm from 1882 until 1915 were horse-dealers.[65] There were stud farms at Roe Green in 1904[66] and at Kingsbury House in 1913,[67] and in 1917 Shoelands farm was licensed as a slaughter-house of horses for human consumption.[68] The number of horses increased from 80 in 1887 to 146 in 1917.[69]

Like hay-farming horse-breeding declined with the growth of motor traffic and was mostly replaced by dairy farming. A cowkeeper was mentioned in 1823[70] but most farms did not transfer to dairy farming until the end of the century. It was practised at Blackbird farm by 1894,[71] at Grange farm by 1900,[72] and at Valley farm, Chalkhill farm, and the Hyde by 1901.[73] It was introduced at Hyde farm in 1911,[74] and Freren farm passed from a jobmaster to a dairy farmer from Willesden in 1915.[75] The number of cattle increased from 68 in 1867 to 225 in 1887 and 472 in 1917.[76] Nine dairy farmers were registered in 1922[77] but suburban building development began to encroach on farming land soon

[35] C.P. 25(1)/152/98.
[36] C.P. 25(2)/27/182/7.
[37] C 54/3556 no. 24, mm. 10 sqq.
[38] Prob. 11/28 (P.C.C. 3 Alenger, will of Alice Cowper); Bodl. MS. D.D. All Souls c38/13, /16; c39/18; c77/172; Davenport MSS.: Com. Ct. Lond., Reg. xv, f. 234; Reg. 1585–92, f. 127; there were sheep at Chalkhill in 1683: C 10/214/39.
[39] Bodl. MS. D.D. All Souls c37/8.
[40] Mdx. Sess. Recs. i. 82, 256, 449; ii. 120, 294; iii. 69, 237; iv. 159. At one session in 1613, 5 were licensed, more than in the much larger parishes of Hendon and Harrow.
[41] See p. 65.
[42] M.R.O., Acc. 262/72/1; J. Rocque, Map of Mdx. (1754).
[43] Bodl. MS. D.D. All Souls c245/34i, /34o.
[44] Ibid. /34r; M.R.O., Acc. 262/61/1.
[45] M.R.O., Acc. 400/66; Church Com., file 67417.
[46] M.R.O., Acc. 262/27 pt. 1; Bodl. MS. D.D. All Souls c85/138.
[47] Bodl. MS. D.D. All Souls c245/34i.
[48] M.R.O., Acc. 262/72/1.
[49] G. B. G. Bull, 'Changing Landscape of Rural Mdx. 1500–1850' (Lond. Univ. Ph.D. thesis, 1958), 55–76, 96.
[50] Rep. of Poor Law Com. App. B(2), p. 105; examinations for settlement (1822–6) penes Harrow Cent. Ref. Libr.
[51] H.O. 107/1700/135/2 ff. 310–28.
[52] Church Com., file 51708.   [53] M.A.F. 68/136.
[54] Kingsbury U.D.C., Min. Bk. (1903–15), 281.

[55] M.A.F. 68/2815.
[56] H.O. 107/1700/135/2, ff. 310–28.
[57] Kelly's Dirs. Lond. (1868), 108; (1880), 206.
[58] M.A.F. 68/136, /2815.
[59] Kingsbury U.D.C., Wks. & Finance Cttee. Mins. (1900–2), 45; Kingsbury U.D.C., Min. Bk. (1903–15), 6; Rep. on Kingsbury U.D. 1906, Reps. of Local Inqs. (1895–1907), 12–14; for White's activities, see pp. 81–2.
[60] Kingsbury U.D.C., Min. Bk. (1903–15), 287, 299; (1915–22), 3.
[61] Home Cnties. Dir. (1851), 546.
[62] Kelly's Dirs. Lond. (1868, and subseq. edns.).
[63] Kingsbury U.D.C., Min. Bk. (1915–22), 366; Phoenix (magazine of Phoenix Telephone & Electric Co.), xiii(6), p. 14.
[64] Bodl. MS. D.D. All Souls c51, p. 76.
[65] Ibid. pp. 39–43; Church Com., file 51708.
[66] Kingsbury U.D.C., Min. Bk. (1903–15), 22.
[67] M.R.O., Acc. 549/58.
[68] Kingsbury U.D.C., Min. Bk. (1915–22), 85.
[69] M.A.F. 68/1105, /2815.
[70] Bodl. MS. D.D. All Souls c151/H/12.
[71] Kelly's Dir. Lond. (1894), 364.   [72] Ibid. (1900), 304.
[73] Kingsbury U.D.C., Wks. & Finance Cttee. Mins. (1900–2), 55, 57.
[74] Kingsbury U.D.C., Min. Bk. (1903–15), 335.
[75] Church Com., file 51708.
[76] M.A.F. 68/136, /1105, /2815.
[77] Kingsbury U.D.C., M.O.H. Ann. Rep. (1922).

afterwards and by 1933 there were only three.[78] The last of the farms disappeared after the Second World War but cattle were still grazed in Kingsbury, on Fryent open space, in 1970.[79]

A pound-keeper had been granted Radletts cottage in 1489[80] but no pound was marked on the map of 1597. Hyde pound existed by 1698[81] and was dilapidated in 1857.[82] In 1844, when there was no hayward or pound-keeper for Kingsbury, one man was appointed to hold both offices.[83]

WOODS. In 1086 there was enough woodland, yielding £1, for 1,000 pigs on the main estate at Kingsbury and woodland for another 200 pigs on the Westminster abbey estate,[84] which had been described in Edward the Confessor's grant of 1044–50 as the 'wood, which belongs to Kingsbury, which is held in common as it was constituted in olden times'.[85] By c. 1200 the common wood had become common pasture,[86] considerable clearance presumably having taken place in the meantime.

There were four woods, Oldfield wood, Roberts grove, Faytes grove, and Honeyslough, on the demesne land of Kingsbury manor c. 1438.[87] Roberts grove was leased out as early as 1370[88] but usually All Souls reserved the wood grounds, calculated in 1597 as 113 a.,[89] when it leased out the rest of its lands. Mid-15th-century leases of Kingsbury manor allowed lessees ploughbote, firebote, and cartbote but reserved all other wood.[90] For about a century from 1470 the college found a lucrative source of income in selling the right to fell wood in certain fields for two-year periods, providing that sufficient storers were left and hedges maintained to protect the young trees.[91]

In 1580 Robert Hovenden, warden of All Souls, leased all the college's woods in Middlesex to Christopher Hovenden, presumably a relative, for 20 years. The college maintained the grant, even against royal pressure.[92] In spite of a decision in 1661 that leasing woods and hedgerows was contrary to the statutes of the college,[93] such leases continued to be made from 1667, usually to the lessee or under-lessee of the farm-lands.[94] On other estates the practice was probably the same. In 1524 the Knights Hospitallers reserved oaks and elms over 60 years of age but allowed the lessee to uproot 12 a. of woodland on payment of £10.[95] Great trees over 60 years old continued to be reserved.[96] The lessee of Freren paid £40 on his entry for underwood c. 1668.[97]

During the Middle Ages there were frequent presentments for illegally taking wood, sometimes large amounts, like the 26 oaks which Jon Chalkhill had cut down in 1479.[98] It was probably during the 16th century, however, that the reduction of woodland reached alarming proportions. Oaks were felled on Hyde farm in 1551[99] and wood on the borders of Harrow and Kingsbury was cut down by Joan Lyon in 1593.[1] Wood mentioned at Tunworth in 1558[2] had been cut down by 1597.[3] By that date woodland, mostly in bands around fields, comprised rather more than 11 per cent of the known area of Kingsbury. The largest areas were Roberts grove (7 a.), Dawes (7 a.), Oldfield grove (4½ a.), Crabsland (4¼ a.), Hogsheads (3½ a.), and Frowicks (3¼ a.).[4]

Woodland seems to have been preserved longer on the demesne lands of Kingsbury and Freren estates than on the copyhold estates. In 1662 All Souls owned 730 oaks, 213 elms, and 16 ashes worth a total of £652.[5] Trees were cut down on the Groves estate at the beginning of the 17th century[6] and copses were uprooted at Gore field and Framesland between 1706 and 1722.[7] By 1729–38 woodland occupied about 4 per cent of the parish and was mostly concentrated on the demesne lands of Hill and Pipers farms.[8] There were still 43 a. of woodland on All Souls estates[9] in 1788, 23 a. having recently been converted to farm-land. The land was thought to grow very fine timber but to be less productive than if it had been laid down to grass.[10]

The woodland on the old demesne lands was cleared during the next 50 years. Two acres of wood ground were grubbed up at Hyde farm in 1800,[11] some more on Pipers farm in 1803,[12] and Roberts wood disappeared between 1800[13] and 1819. The 24 a. of woodland which survived in 1819,[14] were reduced by 1839 to 4 a., mostly on the Chalkhill estate.[15] Many trees remained — in 1843, for example, there were 65 oaks, 174 elms, 3 ashes and 3 willows on Little Bush farm — but there was no separate acreage for woodland.[16]

MILLS. There was a mill rendering 3s. on the land of Ernulf of Hesdin in 1086.[17] 'Brentmill', which was farmed, was recorded from 1461 until 1499,[18] but it may have been in Kingsbury, Hendon, or Willesden. The site of a water-mill was included among appurtenances of Coffers manor in 1556[19] but it, too, might have lain in Kingsbury or Hendon. There was a Mill field approximately on the site of the present

[78] Kingsbury U.D.C., *M.O.H. Ann. Rep.* (1933).
[79] Ex inf. Mr. Paul Lory.
[80] Bodl. MS. D.D. All Souls c37/10.
[81] Ibid. c57/25.
[82] Ibid. c53, ct. bk. (1831–60).   [83] Ibid. b4/142.
[84] *V.C.H. Mdx.* i. 123, 126.
[85] *Anglo-Saxon Writs*, 344–5, 498–9.
[86] *Rot. Cur. Reg.* (Rec. Com.), ii. 95.
[87] Bodl. MS. D.D. All Souls c37/7(1); c78/186.
[88] Ibid. c75/20.
[89] Probably including woodland in Hendon belonging to Hyde farm: All Souls Coll., Hovenden map, portfolio II, no. 9d.
[90] Bodl. MS. D.D. All Souls c79/3.
[91] Ibid. c242/2–37.
[92] Ibid. c32/16; *V.C.H. Mdx.* iv. 157.
[93] Bodl. MS. D.D. All Souls c77/182.
[94] M.R.O., Acc. 262/27–29.
[95] B.M. Cott. MS. Claud. E.vi, f. 241.
[96] Church Com., deed 169397.
[97] St. Paul's MS., Box A 58a.

[98] Bodl. MS. D.D. All Souls c37/9.
[99] Ibid. c268/229b.
[1] Ibid. c39/18.
[2] Ibid. c38/16.
[3] All Souls Coll., Hovenden map, portfolio II, no. 11.
[4] Ibid. nos. 9–15.
[5] Bodl. MS. D.D. All Souls c30/56.
[6] C 2/Jas. I/B8/34.
[7] Bodl. MS. D.D. All Souls c40/51, m. 5; M.R.O., Acc. 262/28 pt. 2.
[8] M.R.O., Acc. 262/72/1.
[9] Excluding Hyde farm.
[10] Bodl. MS. D.D. All Souls c245/34i.
[11] Ibid. c81/62.
[12] Ibid. /65.
[13] Milne, *Plan of Lond. etc.* (1800).
[14] M.R.O., Acc. 262/30.   [15] M.R.O., TA/KIN.
[16] Bodl. MS. D.D. All Souls c151/H/44.
[17] *V.C.H. Mdx.* i. 126.
[18] Davenport MSS.: All Souls Coll., Bursars' Accts.
[19] C.P. 25(2)/74/630/10.

Willesden cemetery.[20] Shortly before 1596 Jon Chalkhill erected a mill over the Brent to the south-west of Blackbird Hill.[21] A windmill, which stood at Redhill from 1675 at least until 1729–38,[22] had been blown down by 1754.[23]

TRADE AND INDUSTRY. Agriculture, the main occupation throughout most of Kingsbury's history, was followed, in terms of numbers, by domestic service. In 1831 there were 30 servants, compared with 56 agricultural labourers. Twenty years later the figures were 63 and 100 respectively. Merchants and professional men numbered 10 in 1831 and included an architect, a solicitor, a civil engineer, a civil servant, three landed proprietors and two 'gentlemen' in 1851.[24]

Apart from charcoal-burners who may have flourished in Colmans Dean in the early Middle Ages[25] and a 'collier' who lived in Kingsbury in 1528–9,[26] the only crafts were those which sprang directly from an agricultural community. There was a tailor in 1615,[27] a tallow-melter in 1826, and a plumber in 1835,[28] and tradesmen included a milliner, a carriage-painter, a dressmaker, and a fruit-seller in 1851.[29] Most of the tradesmen lived at the Hyde, although there was probably a general store or grocer's shop at Kingsbury Green. In 1906 it was said that all the local shopping had to be done at Hendon.[30] Shops came to Kingsbury with the development between the World Wars. Kingsbury and Queensbury Chamber of Commerce was founded in 1938.[31] In 1967 there were shopping centres at Burnt Oak, the Hyde, and the western part of Kingsbury Road.[32]

Industry was attracted by government intervention during the First World War, when Kingsbury's proximity to Hendon Aerodrome made it a centre of aircraft and munitions production. Edgware Road provided good communications with the main market, London, and with the source of much of the raw material, the Midlands. Labour, mostly unskilled, was initially brought from more densely-populated areas in the south by cheap trams and electric railways and later housed in estates built on farm-land. After the First World War, new concerns, mainly motor and engineering factories, were officially encouraged to employ the many made idle by the collapse of the war industries.[33] By 1923 there were 23 factories employing thousands.[34] More recently, the high price of land and cramped conditions have forced many companies farther out into the country, leaving their sites to small, new

firms making goods such as plastics or electronic components. There are three industrial areas in Kingsbury: Edgware Road and its extensions, Kingsbury Road, and Honeypot Lane.

Messrs. Thrupp & Maberly were making motor bodies at Shoelands Farm in 1914[35] and Messrs. Handley Page were permitted to erect buildings at the back of Thrupp & Maberly's factory in 1915.[36] The Aircraft Manufacturing Co. (Airco), which had been founded in 1912 in Hendon, extended its premises to the Kingsbury side of Edgware Road in 1915 and by the end of the war had acquired all the area between Hay Lane and Carlisle Road, stretching westward across Grove Park, which was used as a take-off field. Airco failed to adapt itself to peace-time production and in 1920 it was sold to the Birmingham Small Arms Co.[37] The site was occupied by factories mostly concerned with motor engineering, including the Daimler Co., Beardmore Motors, Windover, and Desoutter Bros.[38] The American firm of General Motors opened a branch with 6 employees in Edgware Road in 1923, beginning the production of American and later of Vauxhall vehicles in 1928. Frigidaire, a division of General Motors, occupied part of the premises in 1931 and took over the whole site when Vauxhall moved to Luton (Beds.) in 1946. By 1969 Frigidaire occupied 25 a. and employed over 2,000 people in Kingsbury.[39]

One of the largest Edgware Road factories was that of the Phoenix Telephone & Electric Works, which started in 1912 in Cricklewood, became the War Department Signal Factory, and moved to Kingsbury in the early 1920s.[40] At its height it employed 1,600 workers but there were only 1,000 at the factory's closure in 1968–9.[41] In 1920 Thrupp & Maberly's premises were acquired by Lamson Paragon, which had been established in the City of London in 1886 as the Paragon Check Book Co. The factory was opened in 1922 as Papercraft Works, manufacturing bags and wrappings but became inadequate after the Second World War, when most production was moved to West Hartlepool (co. Dur.). A new factory and offices were being built in Carlisle Road in 1969,[42] when the old premises were occupied by Hupfield Bros. and Hedges Reinforced Plastics.[43] Carlisle Road was built as a westward extension from Edgware Road in the 1930s and was occupied mostly by small factories like Acorn Products Ltd., which was founded in 1928 and moved from Camden Town in 1936. It changed its name in 1965 to Acorn

[20] M.R.O., Acc. 262/72/1–2.
[21] Bodl. MS. D.D. All Souls c77/179a; All Souls Coll., Hovenden map, portfolio II, no. 14.
[22] Ogilby, *Map of Mdx.* (c. 1677); M.R.O., Acc. 262/72/1. See p. 69.
[23] Rocque, *Map of Mdx.* (1754); Bodl. MS. D.D. All Souls c245/34z.
[24] *Census,* 1831; H.O. 107/1700/135/2 ff. 310–28.
[25] See p. 49.
[26] Bodl. MS. D.D. All Souls c56/11.
[27] *Mdx. Cnty. Recs.* N.S. iii. 102.
[28] Par. reg., baptisms (1813–64), A1/3 *penes* Holy Innocents church, Kingsbury.
[29] H.O. 107/1700/135/2 ff. 310–28.
[30] Rep. on Kingsbury U.D. 1906, *Reps. of Local Inqs.* (1895–1907), 38, 42 *penes* M.R.O.
[31] Wemb. Hist. Soc., Acc. 283.
[32] *Background to Brent* (Rep. by Brent L.B., Planning and Research Dept., 1967), 49–50.

[33] D. H. Smith 'The Recent Industrialization of the Northern and Western sectors of Greater London' (Lond. Univ. Ph.D. thesis, 1932), 93–114; A. J. Garrett, 'Hist. Geog. of Upper Brent Valley' (Lond. Univ. M.A. thesis, 1935), 167; Kingsbury U.D.C., Min. Bk. (1915–22), 230, 438.
[34] Kingsbury U.D.C., *M.O.H. Ann. Rep.* (1923).
[35] Kingsbury U.D.C., Min. Bk. (1903–15), 419, 421, 429.
[36] Ibid. (1915–22), 3.
[37] Ibid. 21; C. M. Sharp, *D.H. An Outline of de Havilland History,* 43–69.
[38] Kingsbury U.D.C., Min. Bk. (1922–6), 201, 205, 329; *Kelly's Dir. Hendon* (1926); O.S. Map 1/2,500, Mdx. XI. 1 (1938 edn.).
[39] Ex inf. Frigidaire (Division of General Motors Ltd.), 1969. [40] *Phoenix,* 1954, 1956, 1958.
[41] *Wembley News,* 11 Oct. 1968.
[42] Kingsbury U.D.C., Min. Bk. (1915–22), 255; ex inf. Lamson Paragon Ltd. (1969).
[43] Ex inf. Hedges Reinforced Plastics Ltd. (1969).

Aluminium Products and was closed down in 1968.[44]

The farthest extension westward of the Edgware Road industrial complex was the de Havilland works in Stag Lane. The de Havilland Aircraft Co. Ltd. was founded in 1920 by a group from Airco which leased and in 1921 bought the 76-acre site from two flying instructors. Factory buildings for aircraft bodies and engines were erected west of Stag Lane, around the later De Havilland Road, while the rest of the site, to the north and west, was occupied by the airfield. The company opened the de Havilland Aeronautical Technical school in 1928, and by 1929 it employed 1,500 people. In 1932, however, owing to the depression and to increasing air congestion, all but 14 a. of the Stag Lane site were sold to builders and a new factory was opened at Hatfield (Herts.). Manufacture, notably of propellers, continued at Stag Lane, and during the Second World War other factories, including some in Carlisle Road and Honeypot Lane, were requisitioned.[45] The Stag Lane works were acquired in 1946 by the de Havilland Engine Division, itself taken over in 1960 by the Hawker Siddeley Group, which used it as a Rolls Royce works[46] until the sale of the site in 1969 to Brixton Estate.[47]

The second area of industry is at the Kingsbury Works, south of Kingsbury Road.[48] The works were built for the Kingsbury Aviation Co., which was formed in 1917 as a subsidiary to Barningham Ltd., machine tool engineers, to make aeroplanes and motor-cars. The company occupied 109 a., including an airfield stretching from Church Lane across Jubilee park, and in 1918 it employed 800 people building aero engines. As Kingsbury Engineering Co.,[49] it tried to transfer to motor-car manufacture after the war but went into liquidation in 1921. The works remained empty until 1924, when several firms were attracted by the improvements to Kingsbury Road which linked the site with Edgware Road. The main hangar was taken over by Vanden Plas (England) 1923 Ltd., which had been formed after the failure of Vanden Plas (England) 1917 Ltd., the firm at Colindale formed out of Airco. The new firm built up a reputation for high-quality motor-car bodies and gradually extended its site, purchasing Kingsbury House in 1926. It made aircraft during the Second World War and reverted to motor cars in 1946, when it became a subsidiary of the Austin (later British) Motor Co. In 1969 it was building Daimlers as part of British Leyland.

With the exception of the Albion Food Mills, most industry at Kingsbury Works has been concerned with engineering and most firms have been small and relatively short-lived.[50] Firms in the 1920s included the Power Co., Ajax Motor & Engineering Co., and Fry's Metal Foundry.[51] The Power Co., founded in Cricklewood in 1919,

moved to premises in Kingsbury Works in 1924 and to adjacent premises in 1937, the old factory being occupied by Linotype-Paul in 1969.[52] Linotype-Paul, formerly known as K. S. Paul & Associates, has made electronic equipment since it started at Kingsbury Works in 1961 and by 1969 had three factories employing over 250 people.[53] In 1962 Harry Neal, engineers, took over the premises occupied since 1947 by another engineering firm, Charles R. Price, and was in 1969 employing 135 people.[54] India Tyres occupied Semtex's premises from 1954 until it moved to Park Royal in 1968.[55] Purdy & McIntosh (Electronic Developments) moved into Scott's Wire Works in 1962, took over the adjoining factory of K. S. Paul & Associates in 1967, and moved to Wembley in 1969.[56]

The third industrial region at Honeypot Lane and its extensions, Cumberland and Westmoreland roads, grew up during the 1930s after the building of Honeypot Lane and of the Stanmore line and after the opening of Kingsbury and Queensbury stations in 1932 and 1934.[57] The largest firm in 1965 was Rotaprint, which built its first factory in 1936 and steadily expanded until in 1969 it had 8 factories in the area and one in east Kingsbury, employing a total of 1,200 people.[58] Injection Moulders opened its first factory in Westmoreland Road in 1935 with three employees. By 1939 there were 60 employees and a second factory was opened in Dalston Gardens, Great Stanmore. Three other factories followed, the last, opened in 1960, being in Honeypot Lane. By 1969 the firm, which was taken over in 1966 by G. K. N. Sankey, employed some 400 people in Kingsbury, although the main plant had been moved to the Midlands.[59] The Gee Tee Co., manufacturers of paper products, which was founded at King's Cross, London, in 1926, moved to Colindale Avenue, Hendon, in 1931 and thence to a new factory in Cumberland Road in 1936. During the Second World War the factory was requisitioned for work on torpedoes; although the company afterwards returned, there was no room for expansion and in 1966 it moved to Thetford (Norf.).[60]

In 1965, 21 firms in Edgware Road employed 5,511 people, 20 firms in Kingsbury Road employed 1,164 people, and 26 firms in Honeypot Lane employed 3,822 people.[61]

SOCIAL LIFE. Although Kingsbury was heavily wooded, little evidence remains of early hunting beyond the maintenance of dogs and horses by Geoffrey le Scrope in 1325.[62] Hunting and hawking rights formed part of the appurtenances of Kingsbury and Freren manors which were sometimes leased out with the rest of the estate.[63] In 1713 the

[44] Ex inf. Acorn Anodising Co., Ealing (1969); Brent L.B., *Official Guide* [1965].
[45] Sharp, *D. H. Outline of de Havilland Hist.* 71–72, 80–155, 199, 233, 343–4; Land Util. Survey Map 1″, sheet 106 (1935 edn.).
[46] Ex inf. Hawker Siddeley Aviation Ltd. (1969).
[47] Ex inf. Brixton Estate Ltd. (1969).
[48] Unless otherwise stated, the following two paras. are based on inf. supplied by British Leyland (Austin–Morris) Ltd., Vanden Plas Division (1969).
[49] *The Times*, 7 Jan. 1920, 17b.
[50] *Kelly's Dir. Hendon* (1926); *Kelly's Dir. Wembley* (1937); O.S. Map 1/2,500, Mdx. TQ 2088 (1956 edn.); Land Util. Survey Map 1/25,000, sheet 224 (1967 edn.).

[51] Kingsbury U.D.C., Min. Bk. (1922–6), 201; (1926–9), 22.
[52] Ex inf. Power Equipment Co. Ltd. (1969).
[53] Ex inf. Linotype-Paul Ltd. (1969).
[54] Ex inf. Harry Neal Ltd. (1969).
[55] Ex inf. India Tyres (1969).
[56] Ex inf. Purdy & McIntosh (1969).
[57] See p. 51.
[58] Ex inf. Rotaprint Ltd. (1969).
[59] Ex inf. G.K.N. Sankey Ltd. (1969).
[60] Ex inf. Gee Tee Co. (1969).
[61] *Background to Brent*, 34.
[62] W.A.M. 27844.
[63] C 54/3556 no. 24; Bodl. MS. D.D. All Souls c79/26.

lessee, James Brydges, later duke of Chandos, was given the formal title of gamekeeper by All Souls College.[64] Much later, a drag hunt met at Bacon Lane.[65] Free fishing in the Brent formed an appurtenance of Coffers manor[66] and apparently passed to the Regents Canal Co., which leased it out, together with rights of fowling and shooting, in 1844.[67]

Before the 19th century recreation was virtually confined to the inns. One in nine houses in 18th-century Kingsbury was an inn. The King's Arms in Edgware Road may have existed in the early 17th century[68] and the Old or Lower King's Arms at the Hyde, although not mentioned by name until 1698,[69] was probably even earlier. Other early inns were the Plough at Kingsbury Green (1748)[70] and the Black Horse (1711)[71] and two Chequers inns (1751),[72] whose sites are unknown. The Old King's Arms ceased to be an inn between 1803 and 1851.[73] The New King's Arms passed by 1785 into the hands of Thomas Clutterbuck,[74] whose family owned most of the local inns in the late 18th and early 19th centuries, and was rebuilt further north before 1914.[75] The old Plough, a weatherboarded building with a tiled roof, was demolished in 1932 and replaced by the present building.[76] The Black Horse and the two Chequers inns had disappeared by 1803[77] but the Red Lion on the corner between Edgware Road and Kingsbury Road had probably opened by 1839.[78] It was rebuilt in 1931.[79] Three more inns or beer-houses had been opened by 1851:[80] the Green Man at Pipers Green, rebuilt in 1931,[81] and the Two Poplars and the Boot, both at the Hyde and both still there in 1901.[82]

Kingsbury's proximity to London and its association with horsedealers[83] made it an ideal place for horse-racing. Kingsbury races, which flourished from 1870 until their suppression in 1878, were held near Bush Farm until 1873 and then on land leased by William Perkins Warner, who was also the proprietor of the Old Welsh Harp. The races, which were held five times a year, attracted 'thousands of the scum of London', were denounced as a carnival of vice, and were said to have caused several families to leave the district.[84] Greyhound racing, said to be taking place at Hill farm in 1928, was defended as private, for 'the training and convalescence of dogs'.[85] The connexion of the

district with horses may also account for the presence of three polo grounds, one on each side of Bacon Lane and one north of Forty Lane, in 1914.[86] At the same date there was a shooting ground in south-east Kingsbury,[87] probably identifiable with the practice-grounds on Blackbird farm which were used by the Metropolitan School of Shooting in 1907.[88]

The growth of the aircraft industry led to the opening of the London and Provincial Flying School at Stag Lane, where pilots were trained during the First World War. In 1923 the London Aeroplane Club, under the auspices of de Havilland, took over the airfield in Stag Lane, where Amy Johnson learnt to fly and where the National Aviation Display took place in 1932.[89] During the 19th and early 20th centuries Kingsbury, a picturesquely rural district a short distance from London, attracted many walkers[90] and cyclists, and the Plough inn was once the headquarters of 13 cycling clubs. It was at the Plough, too, that four Frenchmen and their three performing bears used to stay.[91]

Kingsbury cricket club was founded in 1828 and used a field in Townsend Lane,[92] possibly the field adjoining Kingsbury House which was called the Cricket Field in 1882,[93] or Silver Jubilee park. Townsend cricket club, probably a descendant of the earlier club, existed by 1928.[94] Sporting clubs multiplied with suburban building and the opening of factories. Phoenix Telephone & Electric Co. had a social and athletic club by 1918.[95] There was a winter tennis club by 1923[96] and a tennis club at Roe Green by 1925.[97] There were already four athletic grounds in south-west Kingsbury by 1914[98] and many more by 1938, when most of Fryent open space was divided into sports grounds.[99] A large open-air swimming bath was opened in Kingsbury Road in 1939.[1] By 1948 there were two cricket clubs, two football clubs, and a swimming club.[2] The Kingsbury Community Association provided other sporting and dancing facilities during the 1950s.[3]

There was a literary and social club at the Hyde in 1900[4] and a horticultural society by 1923.[5] Cinemas were built in the 1930s. There were two in Edgware Road: the Savoy, also called the Essoldo, which in 1970 was used for bingo and wrestling, and the Curzon, formerly the Odeon. The

[64] M.R.O., Acc. 262/27 pt. 1.
[65] Phoenix, 1960. The names Stag and Buck Lane, sometimes cited as evidence of hunting, were comparatively late and derived from the near-by Bald Faced Stag inn.
[66] C.P. 25(2)/74/630/10; M.L.R. 1716/6/138.
[67] M.R.O., Acc. 526/32.
[68] Mdx. Cnty. Recs. ii. 323; Bodl. MS. D.D. All Souls c57/16.
[69] Bodl. MS. D.D. All Souls c57/25.
[70] Ibid. c245/34z.
[71] M.R.O., Acc. 262/29.
[72] M.R.O., L.V. 7/1.
[73] M.R.O., L.V. 10/113; H.O. 107/1700/135/2, ff. 310–28.
[74] Bodl. MS. D.D. All Souls c245/34z.
[75] O.S. Map 1/2,500, Mdx. XI. 6 (1896 and 1914 edns.).
[76] Wemb. Hist. Soc., Acc. 907/107; Photo. Coll., Acc. 412/1; Acc. 906/51; Hendon Libr., Print L. 2490.
[77] M.R.O., L.V. 10/113.
[78] When the site was owned by Thos. Clutterbuck: M.R.O., TA/KIN.
[79] Wemb. Hist. Soc., Acc. 907/115.
[80] H.O. 107/1700/135/2, ff. 310–28; O.S. Map 1/2,500, Mdx. XI. 5, 6 (1873 edn.).
[81] Wemb. Hist. Soc., Photo. Coll., Acc. 380/18.

[82] Kingsbury U.D.C., Wks. and Finance Cttee. Mins. (1900–2), 57.   [83] See p. 75.
[84] The Times, 29 Jan. 1877, 11 Jan. 1878; Church Com., file 51708; Wemb. Hist. Soc., Acc. 700; Kelly's Dir. Lond. (1872), 142.
[85] Kingsbury U.D.C., Min. Bk. (1926–9), 303.
[86] O.S. Map 1/2,500, Mdx. XI. 5, 9 (1914 edn.).
[87] Ibid. 10.
[88] Kingsbury U.D.C., Min. Bk. (1903–15), 180.
[89] J. Hopkins, Hist. of Hendon, 85; C. M. Sharp, D. H. An Outline of de Havilland Hist. 72, 78, 80, 96.
[90] H. J. Foley, Our Lanes and Meadow Paths, 34–43.
[91] Wemb. Hist. Soc., Photo. Coll., Acc. 906/51.
[92] Wemb. Hist. Soc., Acc. 637/16.
[93] Bodl. MS. D.D. All Souls c51, pp. 37–38.
[94] Kingsbury U.D.C., Min. Bk. (1926–9), 290.
[95] Ibid. (1915–22), 151.
[96] Ibid. (1922–6), 17.   [97] Ibid. 330.
[98] O.S. Map 1/2,500, Mdx. XI. 9, 13 (1914 edn.).
[99] Ibid. XI. 5, 6, 9 (1932, 1935 and 1938 edns.).
[1] Wemb. Hist. Soc., Acc. 217.
[2] Wembley Dir. (1948 & 1949).
[3] Wemb. Hist. Soc., Acc. 336/1.
[4] Kelly's Dir. Lond. (1900), 276.
[5] Kingsbury U.D.C., Min. Bk. (1922–6), 6.

Essoldo at Queensbury was also, in 1970, used for bingo. The Odeon in Kingsbury Road, near Honeypot Lane, served western Kingsbury.[6]

The *Kingsbury and Kenton News* was founded as an edition of the *Wembley News* in 1930.[7]

LOCAL GOVERNMENT. Most land in Kingsbury was held from Edgware manor, and its holders owed suit at the court held at the George inn, Edgware.[8] Courts, view of frankpledge, assizes of bread and ale, infangthief, and outfangthief were part of the appurtenances of Kingsbury manor by 1325.[9] There are court rolls from 1339 to 1486, with gaps.[10]

Freeholders and copyholders owed suit at Kingsbury manor court twice a year.[11] A view of frankpledge and court leet were usually held at the beginning of May, often followed by a second court in November. More rarely other courts were held, as in 1349–50, when, presumably because of the Black Death, courts in December and March dealt with the exceptional number of presentments of deaths and the subsequent transfers of land.[12] After Kingsbury and Edgware manors were united in the possession of All Souls College, confusion between the two grew until separate courts for Kingsbury lapsed altogether. After the last recorded view of frankpledge in 1470,[13] annual courts were held in May until 1486.[14] Homagers were not recorded in the early court rolls but there was normally a jury of 13 in the 1420s,[15] although the number had dwindled to 3 by 1486.[16] There were probably about 20 suitors in the 15th century but they had been reduced by amalgamation and escheat to 15 in 1521.[17]

Richard, the reeve of Kingsbury mentioned *c.* 1274,[18] may have belonged to Edgware manor. The homage elected the reeve of Kingsbury manor at the May view and in 1350 the lord chose him from two people elected by the homage.[19] There was a reeve of the meadow in the 1420s and 1430s and a beadle from the 1460s.[20] Headboroughs and aletasters, first mentioned in 1339,[21] were usually elected at the view. There were four headboroughs in 1428.[22]

Throughout the period 1339–1486 Kingsbury manor court was mainly concerned with land transactions, and with trespass, strays, and obstruction, for which last offence the lord himself was fined in 1428 and 1434.[23] Breaking the assize of ale was common in the 14th century but only one instance, in 1468, was recorded during the 15th

century.[24] There are only two recorded cases of the hue having been raised, in 1350 and 1379,[25] and two involving fighting, in 1350 and 1435.[26] Failure to perform customary works was a feature of the 14th century[27] and in 1393 tenants of Edgware manor, including John Chalkhill, were refusing suit of court.[28]

There are two extant court rolls of Freren manor, for 1510–12,[29] dealing almost entirely with encroachments and the destruction of wood, although the second roll refers to a view of frankpledge. There was a jury of four at one court and of five at the other. A court was apparently still held by the lords of Freren in 1622 but it lapsed soon afterwards.[30] There may have been a court on Geoffrey le Scrope's estate in 1325[31] but there is no evidence of a court on Coffers manor.

Officials continued to be elected at the court of Edgware manor until 1914.[32] Two constables were elected for Kingsbury in 1543[33] but thereafter there was only one. The election of a headborough is not recorded from 1780 to 1831.[34] Women were elected as a beadle in 1466,[35] as a reeve in 1543,[36] and as a constable in 1726.[37]

In the absence of records very little is known of early parish government.[38] The vestry minutes date from 1802,[39] and there is a book of examinations of paupers for settlement certificates from 1822 until 1826.[40] Accounts were drawn up by the churchwardens and surveyors of the highway but the parish chest was kept in private houses and many records have been lost. The vestry met monthly in the church or at one of the inns, usually the Plough and sometimes the Upper King's Arms. Meetings were attended by between four and eleven people, presided over by the curate until 1820 when a chairman was elected. A salaried vestry clerk was appointed in 1802.

There were normally two churchwardens from the late 15th century,[41] although in 1802 there was only one. From 1802, and possibly from 1776,[42] there were two overseers of the poor, usually farmers who held office for several years; there was a surveyor of the highways by 1803. The parish constable and headborough were nominated by the vestry and presumably formally elected at the manor court. As a result of a lawsuit over the constable's expenses in 1804, it was decided that no money except poor-relief was to be paid by parish officers without the approval of five parishioners in vestry. The parish clerk, who received expenses in 1805,

[6] *Kelly's Dir. Wembley* (1937); *Wembley Dir.* (1948 & 1949); O.S. Map 1/2,500, Mdx. XI. 1 (1938 edn.); Mdx. Local Hist. Council, *Bulletin*, xviii. 8, 16.
[7] *Willing's Press Guide* (1973).
[8] Treated under Edgware: *V.C.H. Mdx.* iv. 161–2.
[9] Bodl. MS. D.D. All Souls c75/2.
[10] Ibid. c37/2, /4, /7(1), /9, /10.
[11] Ibid. c37/2, /7(1).
[12] Ibid. /2.
[13] Ibid. /9.
[14] Ibid. /10.
[15] Ibid. /7(1).
[16] Ibid. /10.
[17] Ibid. c56/12.
[18] J.I. 1/539 m. 16d.
[19] Bodl. MS. D.D. All Souls c37/7(1).
[20] Ibid. /9.
[21] Ibid. /2.
[22] Ibid. /7(1).
[23] Ibid.
[24] Ibid. /9.
[25] Ibid. /2, /4.
[26] Ibid. /2, /7(1).
[27] See p. 72.
[28] Ibid. /5.
[29] S.C. 2/191/45.
[30] Church Com. deed 169397; St. Paul's MSS., Box A 58.
[31] W.A.M. 27844. The evidence is ambiguous.
[32] Bodl. MS. D.D. All Souls c53, ct. bk. (1861–1914).
[33] Ibid. c38/13.
[34] Ibid. c53, ct. bks. (1780–1804, 1805–30).
[35] Ibid. c37/9.
[36] Ibid. c38/13.
[37] Ibid. c40/51 m. 1.
[38] Except where otherwise stated the foll. paras. are based upon Kingsbury Vestry Min. Bk. (1802–34) *penes* Brent Cent. Ref. Libr.; *Rep. Poor Law Com. App. B(2)*, p. 105.
[39] Kingsbury Vestry Min. Bks. (1802–60) *penes* Brent Cent. Ref. Libr.
[40] *Penes* Brent Cent. Ref. Libr.
[41] Bodl. MS. D.D. All Souls c37/10; c29/21.
[42] *Rep. Cttee. on Rets. by Overseers, 1776*, p. 396.

KINGSBURY: THE NEW CHURCH OF ST. ANDREW

ENFIELD WASH: ST. GEORGE'S CHURCH

HENDON: ST. MARY'S CHURCH IN 1798

ENFIELD: ST. ANDREW'S CHURCH IN 1793

KINGSBURY: THE OLD CHURCH OF ST. ANDREW IN 1796

GREAT STANMORE: ST. JOHN THE EVANGELIST'S CHURCH c. 1800

enjoyed a salary in 1808 after he had sued the churchwarden for not paying him. A salaried doctor for the poor was appointed in 1805, midwifery and venereal cases being excluded from his duties. In 1832, after the sexton had been dismissed for being drunk on duty, the posts of sexton and parish clerk were combined in one salaried official.

The parish was revalued for rating in 1802 and 1825. The church-rate, which varied between 1½d. and 6d. in the £, was levied for specific purposes, like repairs to the church. The poor-rate, always 6d. in the £, was usually levied once a year. Between 1776 and 1824 it raised between £12 and £174, the proceeds rising to £212 in 1831 and £339 in 1835. Expenditure on poor-relief averaged £171 a year from 1831 to 1834.[43] Relief in money and kind was given for specific purposes, such as funeral expenses, and the rents of paupers were paid until 1821, when the vestry forbade the practice. Weekly allowances of money and clothing were also made, usually to widows or bastards. Seven persons received regular relief in 1833. From 1822 until 1826 between two and four people were examined for settlement certificates each year, although in 1824 there were as many as 14.[44]

A poorhouse, inhabited by four widows in 1786,[45] may have originated in the charity of Robert Kitchingman.[46] The building, which was at the Hyde, was very dilapidated by 1802 but it was not until 1823 that it was replaced by two small cottages. They were occupied in 1834 by two large families and were sold in 1838 to help pay for the new union workhouse.[47]

The able-bodied poor could be employed on the roads or in digging gravel. In 1826 a single man was paid 5s., and a man with a wife and child 7s. 6d., with 1s. for each extra child up to 10s. In winter when there was no work the able-bodied received relief. A workhouse was proposed in 1802 but Kingsbury, being small, preferred to rely on workhouses in neighbouring parishes. In 1815 Kingsbury paid for a pauper at Stanmore and later it used the new workhouse which, although called Redhill, was situated in Hendon.

By the Poor Law Amendment Act of 1834, Kingsbury became part of Hendon union.[48] The parish became part of Edgware highway district under the Highway Act of 1863.[49] Thereafter roads as well as sanitation became the responsibility of Hendon rural sanitary authority,[50] of whose district Kingsbury became a part under the Public Health Act of 1872.[51]

From 1881 the population decreased, leading to a slight fall in the rateable value between 1889[52] and 1893.[53] Poor and backward, the parish was not welcomed by any of its neighbours when urban districts were formed in 1894, especially since sewerage had already caused friction with Hendon.[54] After Kingsbury became a ward of Wembley U.D., Wembley's 9 councillors resented paying for sewerage schemes for Kingsbury, while Kingsbury's 3 councillors were frustrated through being in a permanent minority. Personal jealousies exacerbated the situation, money was wasted in litigation, and in 1899 the inquirer from Middlesex C.C. considered Wembley U.D.C. 'an object lesson in misgovernment'.[55]

In 1900 Kingsbury became a separate urban district with 6 councillors,[56] a clerk who also acted as surveyor, inspector of nuisances and collector of rents, and a medical officer of health. After more turbulence, however, another inquiry was held in 1906,[57] when the district council was described as having furnished an example of maladministration. The trouble was partly inherent in Kingsbury's situation. As a sparsely populated district the rateable value was insufficient to provide essential services except by high rates, which discouraged people from settling there. More important, however, was the struggle among the councillors, the reds and blues, for control of the chair. The two most notorious members were Dr. Arthur Calcutta White of Kenton Grove Farm and José Diaz, a Spaniard who lived at Fern Dene until his death in 1915.[58] White, who had been largely responsible for the trouble with Wembley, owned Gore farm and caused offence with his piggeries and rubbish dumps in Honeypot Lane. Attempted improvements by the medical officer of health or the inspector of nuisances were blocked by White, who in 1904 responded to a summons by dismissing the clerk. Diaz, after his enforced resignation from the chair as an alien in 1904, continued to instruct his faction from the floor. Government collapsed altogether in 1906, when minutes were rescinded, a rate was cancelled, and bills were left unpaid. Ratepayers petitioned for an inquiry, as a result of which the number of councillors was increased to nine. A works and finance committee and an outdoor committee were formed and salaried officials, a medical officer of health, a sanitary inspector, a clerk, and one man to serve as surveyor, assistant clerk and rate-collector, were appointed.[59] Diaz, now naturalized, was elected chairman, however, and in 1909 White began to interrupt meetings, which became so stormy that the police were called.[60] Two opponents of both Diaz and White ceased to attend in 1910 and Diaz retained control until his death in 1915.

Diaz's death coincided with the building of

[43] Ibid.; *Abstract of Rets. by Overseers, 1787*, p. 628; *Reps. from Sel. Cttee. on Poor Rate Returns*, H.C. 748, p. 100 (1821), iv; H.C. 334, p. 132 (1825), iv; *Poor Law Com. 1st Rep.* 251.
[44] Examinations for settlement (1822–6) *penes* Brent Cent. Ref. Libr.
[45] *Abstract of Rets. of Char. Dons. 1786–8*, H.C. 511, pp. 752–3 (1816), xvi(1).
[46] See p. 88.
[47] *Poor Law Com. 4th Rep.* H.C. 147, p. 87 (1838), xviii, App. D; *Poor Law Com. 9th Rep.* H.C. 494, p. 278 (1843), xxi, App. C.
[48] *Poor Law Com. 1st Rep.* 251.
[49] 25 & 26 Vic. c. 61; *Lond. Gaz.* 13 Mar. 1863, p. 1480.
[50] M.R.O., LA. HW., Hendon Rural Sanitary Auth., gen. ledger (1882–91).
[51] 35 & 36 Vic. c. 79.

[52] M.R.O., LA. HW., Hendon Rural Sanitary Auth., gen. ledger (1888–90), f. 153.
[53] Ibid. bd. ledger (1892–3), f. 144.
[54] Hendon Rural Sanitary Dist., Inq. 1894, M.R.O., *Reps. of Local Inqs.* (1889–94), 11 sqq.; Wemb. Hist. Soc., *Jnl.* N.S. i(1), p. 7.
[55] Rep. on separation of Kingsbury from Wembley U.D. 1899, M.R.O., *Reps. of Local Inqs.* (1895–1907), 4.
[56] Ibid.; Wemb. Hist. Soc., *Jnl.* i(4), 20–2.
[57] Unless otherwise stated the para. is based upon Rep. on Kingsbury U.D. 1906, M.R.O., *Reps. of Local Inqs.* (1895–1907).
[58] Kingsbury U.D.C., Min. Bks. (1903–15), 74; (1915–22), 8.
[59] Ibid. (1903–15), 151–5.
[60] Ibid. 250, 255, 258.

factories and the beginning of Kingsbury's long-awaited development, which increased the rateable value eightfold between 1922 and 1933.[61] By 1926 the council had committees for allotments, highways and works, finance, housing, and special amalgamation.[62] It employed a clerk, a medical officer, a rate-collector and a joint engineer, surveyor and sanitary inspector.[63] The offices were at Kingsbury Green.[64]

BOROUGH OF WEMBLEY. *Vert, two seaxes crossed saltirewise passing through a Saxon crown or* [Granted 1938]

LONDON BOROUGH OF BRENT. *Per chevron gules and vert, a chevron wavy argent between in dexter chief an orb and in sinister chief two swords crossed saltirewise or points upwards and in base two seaxes crossed saltirewise passing through a Saxon crown or* [Granted 1965]

In 1934 Kingsbury was amalgamated with Wembley in a new Wembley U.D., which was incorporated in 1937. It was divided into wards, of which four, Roe Green, Fryent, Chalkhill, and Hyde, were formed out of old Kingsbury parish. In 1965, under the London Government Act, 1963, Wembley joined with Willesden in the London Borough of Brent. Three of Brent's 26 wards, Kingsbury, Queensbury, and Chalkhill, were formed from Kingsbury parish. In 1968, however, the new wards of Kingsbury, Queensbury, Roe Green, and Fryent were created, which completely ignored former parish boundaries.[65]

PUBLIC SERVICES. Some sewage was piped into the sewers of Hendon local board[66] but little was spent on the rest, the responsibility of Hendon rural sanitary authority, between 1883 and 1893.[67] After 1894 Hendon U.D.C. served the Hyde while Wembley U.D.C. dealt with the rest. There was a series of tanks for the Chalkhill area but elsewhere untreated sewage drained through open ditches to the Brent.[68] Pollution was already an issue in 1894,[69] and in 1901 a complaint by the Thames Conservancy forced the new Kingsbury U.D.C. to draw up a sewerage scheme. Although the project was very expensive, the council acquired 5 a. in the south-west, between the Metropolitan railway line and the river, for a sewage farm[70] which was opened in 1902 and connected to the whole of Kingsbury except the north-east corner.[71] In 1903 there was serious flooding and in 1906 there was a complete breakdown on the farm after Dr. White dismissed the clerk and surveyor, who himself had dismissed the workers for lack of money to pay them. White took charge personally, employing unskilled men, with the result that the farm crop was destroyed and untreated sewage contaminated the Brent.[72]

Under an agreement made with All Souls College in 1904, Kingsbury U.D.C. constructed filter beds on Stratford Long, east of Stag Lane, to serve the north-east corner of the parish.[73] A new sewage farm was built there in 1908.[74] The southern farm, which was called Neasden or Kingsbury Lane works, was reconstructed in 1924[75] and the Stag Lane works were sold in 1925.[76] Wembley U.D.C. took over the Kingsbury Lane works in 1934[77] and closed them in 1936, when the central works at Mogden were opened under the West Middlesex Sewerage and Sewage Disposal Scheme of 1933.[78]

The Colne Valley Water Co. was supplying piped water from Bushey by 1895.[79] In 1900 Edgware Road was lit by the Harrow and Stanmore Gas Co. and the rest of Kingsbury by the Gas Light and Coke Co.,[80] which the council failed to pay in 1906. An agreement with the North Metropolitan Electric Power Supply Co. in 1905 was rescinded by White's party[81] and it was not until 1910 that the company could introduce electricity. In 1910 the old post office at the Hyde, which had been in existence at least since 1851,[82] was made into a telephone exchange.[83] Although three policemen lived there in 1851,[84] Kingsbury relied on its neighbours for police and fire services, especially Hendon and Wembley.[85]

Kingsbury also made use of nearby hospital services and it was not until 1919,[86] having resisted since 1903,[87] that it joined the Middlesex Districts

61 Kingsbury U.D.C., *M.O.H. Ann. Reps.* (1922, 1924, 1933).
62 Kingsbury U.D.C., Min. Bk. (1926–9), 83.
63 *Kelly's Dir. Hendon* (1926).
64 Wemb. Hist. Soc., Acc. 411/37.
65 *Census,* 1951–61; Wemb. Hist. Soc., Acc. 701/1; Acc. 820/2; Boro. of Wembley, *Official Guide* [n.d.].
66 Hendon Rural Sanitary Dist., Inq. 1894, M.R.O., *Reps. of Local Inqs.* (1889–94), 11 sqq.; Rep. on separation of Kingsbury from Wembley U.D. 1899, ibid. (1895–1907), 4, 8.
67 M.R.O., LA. HW., Hendon Rural Sanitary Auth., gen. ledgers (1882–91, 1888–90); bd. ledger (1892–3).
68 Rep. on separation of Kingsbury from Wembley U.D. 1899, M.R.O., *Reps. of Local Inqs.* (1895–1907), 9–10.
69 Hendon Rural Sanitary Dist., Inq. 1894, M.R.O., *Reps. of Local Inqs.* (1889–94), 13–14.
70 Kingsbury U.D.C., *San. Reps.* (1901, 1902); O.S. Map 1/2,500, Mdx. XI. 13 (1914 edn.).
71 Kingsbury U.D.C., *San. Reps.* (1902, 1904).
72 Rep. on Kingsbury U.D. 1906, M.R.O., *Reps. on Local Inqs.* (1895–1907), 25–32; Kingsbury U.D.C., Min. Bk. (1903–15), 1, 92.
73 Kingsbury U.D.C., Min. Bk. (1926–9), 76.

74 Ibid. (1903–15), 224; Kingsbury U.D.C. *San. Rep.* (1908); O.S. Map 1/2,500, Mdx. XI. 6 (1914 edn.).
75 Kingsbury U.D.C., *M.O.H. Ann. Rep.* (1924).
76 Kingsbury U.D.C., Min. Bk. (1922–6), 329.
77 O.S. Map 1/2,500, Mdx. XI. 13 (1935 edn.).
78 Hendon R.D.C. *Rep. of Principal Activities, 1929–31, penes* Harrow Cent. Ref. Libr.; Wemb. Hist. Soc., Acc. 212.
79 M.O.H., *Rep. on San. Condition of Wembley U.D.* (1896).
80 Kingsbury U.D.C., Wks. and Finance Cttee. Mins. (1900–2), 15.
81 Rep. on Kingsbury U.D. 1906, M.R.O., *Reps. of Local Inqs.* (1895–1907), 6, 28; Kingsbury U.D.C., Min. Bk. (1903–15), 42, 65.
82 H.O. 107/1700/135/2 ff. 310–28; O.S. Map 1/2,500, Mdx. XI. 6 (1873 edn.).
83 Kingsbury U.D.C., Min. Bk. (1903–15), 308–9.
84 H.O. 107/1700/135/2 ff. 310–28.
85 Rep. on separation of Kingsbury from Wembley U.D. 1899, M.R.O., *Reps. of Local Inqs.* (1895–1907), 3–16; Rep. on Kingsbury U.D. 1906, ibid. 38; Kingsbury U.D.C., Min. Bks. (1903–15), 37; (1922–6), 89; *Kelly's Dir. Wembley* (1937); *Wembley Dir.* (1948–9).
86 Kingsbury U.D.C., *M.O.H. Ann. Rep.* (1919).
87 Kingsbury U.D.C., Min. Bk. (1903–15), 41.

Joint Smallpox Hospital Board. In 1901 Willesden U.D.C. rented, and in 1914 bought, 10 a. in north-west Kingsbury, bordering Honeypot Lane, for temporary buildings for a smallpox hospital. Some buildings were burnt down in 1912, the hospital was rebuilt in 1927, and in 1931 it was converted to a maternity hospital of 29 beds; it was expanded to its present complement of 56 beds in 1935. Under the National Health Act it became part of the Central Middlesex group and in 1949 changed its name from Willesden to Kingsbury maternity hospital. It was transferred to the Charing Cross Teaching Hospital group in 1952.[88]

In 1894 there was no burial board in Kingsbury and all interments took place in the churchyard.[89] Apart from extensions to the churchyard in 1900[90] the situation was still the same in 1970, although Willesden U.D.C. acquired a large area in south-east Kingsbury for use as a cemetery after 1928.[91]

In 1965 there were 262 a. of open space,[92] most of which had been acquired from All Souls College. The college sold Silver Jubilee park (36 a.) to Wembley U.D.C. in 1936 and Fryent open space (160 a.) to Middlesex C.C. in 1938.[93] Roe Green park (20 a.) had been acquired in 1934.[94]

CHURCHES. In 1086 a priest held a virgate in Kingsbury.[95] The church had been appropriated to the hospital of St. John of Jerusalem by c. 1244–8[96] and the benefice thereafter remained a donative or curacy in the gift of the hospital and, after 1544,[97] of the chapter of St. Paul's cathedral until 1834 when it became a perpetual curacy,[98] after 1868 styled a vicarage.[99] In 1884 a new parish church, Holy Innocents, was built and the old church of St. Andrew became its chapel of ease.[1]

The Knights Hospitallers were regarded as rectors and the rectorial glebe and parsonage house have been treated under Freren manor (q.v.). The curates were instituted by the hospital and chapter, except for a short period after 1650 when Sir William Roberts exercised the patronage.[2]

Roger, chaplain of Kingsbury, was apparently living there in 1291 when his 'houses' and the church were burgled.[3] Although it was never effected, the lease of Freren manor in 1505 was to John Nelson, a chaplain,[4] which suggests that early leases were made to clerks who were expected to serve the cure themselves. From 1506 the leases

were made to laymen who had to find a chaplain to serve the cure,[5] and the close connexion continued with Freren farm-house, described in 1650 as 'commonly called Kingsbury parsonage house'.[6] In 1588 the curate lived in a loft in the church-house which then belonged to Michael Page, the lessee of Freren;[7] but it is not clear whether the building was the small one near the church[8] or Freren farm-house. In 1650 the minister had 'two chambers'[9] and in 1661 the lessee had to allow him a room with a chimney, called the church loft, or pay him an extra £5 a year.[10] In 1699 a lease reserved a cottage and two pightles near the church for the accommodation of the curate.[11] Like all subsequent leases, it said that the property was then in the occupation of Thomas Gosling, who lived in the 1660s.[12] The cottage probably fell into disuse when curates were non-resident. When they began again to live in the parish in the 19th century, it was usually in a private house. Henry Atcheson lived at Hill House in 1851[13] and at the Hyde in 1872.[14] The two pightles, Little and Great Church field, were in 1839 described as glebe worth £3 10s., owned by the incumbent.[15]

The minister was paid an annual stipend of £20 by the lessee of Freren in 1650[16] and an additional £20 was approved in 1657 by the trustees for the maintenance of ministers.[17] The lessee of Freren had to pay the curate £30 a year in 1661,[18] £40 a year from 1720 to 1834,[19] when a grant of £200 was made by Queen Anne's Bounty,[20] and £80 a year thereafter.[21] In 1851 the perpetual curate's endowment was described as £4 10s. in land, £6 10s. from Queen Anne's Bounty and £80 from other endowment.[22]

In 1423 it was said that William Bury and his wife Margaret, William Page's daughter, had been granted Page's property in Hendon on condition that they found a suitable chaplain for the church of Kingsbury to pray for the souls of Page and his ancestors for 10 years after the death of Page, who was still alive in 1410.[23] In 1531 John Edward surrendered property worth 20s. a year rent to the use of his wife, on condition that she provided an obit with a dirge and mass in Kingsbury church for him and his parents.[24] Elizabeth Frowyk, by will proved 1516, provided for torches in several churches, including Kingsbury.[25] Michael Roberts left 3s. 4d. for Kingsbury altar by will proved 1544.[26] In 1547 it was said that John Edward had given a

[88] Ex inf. the sec.
[89] Hendon Rural Sanitary Dist., Inq. 1894, M.R.O., *Reps. of Local Inqs.* (1889–94), 11.
[90] See p. 85.
[91] Kingsbury U.D.C. Min. Bk. (1926–9), 295.
[92] *Background to Brent*, 8.
[93] Ex inf. Daniel Smith, Briant and Done; see p. 58.
[94] C. Radcliffe, *Mdx.* 163.
[95] *V.C.H. Mdx.* i. 126.
[96] St. Paul's MS., W.D. 9, f. 85v.
[97] *L. & P. Hen. VIII*, xix, p. 495.
[98] After the grant by Queen Anne's Bounty; see below.
[99] Under the District Church Tithes Act Amendment Act, 1868.
[1] See below.
[2] *Home Cnties. Mag.* i. 322; *Cal. S.P. Dom.* 1652–3, 398.
[3] J.I. 3/36/1 m. 3.
[4] B.M. Cott. MS. Claud. E. vi, f. 14.
[5] Ibid. ff. 39v., 241; S.C. 6/Hen. VIII/2402 m. 9d.; /2405.
[6] C 54/3556 mm. 10 sqq.

[7] Davenport MSS.: Com. Ct. Lond., Reg. 1585–92, f. 127.
[8] See below.
[9] *Home Cnties. Mag.* i. 322; C 54/3556 mm. 10 sqq.
[10] Church Com. deed 169397.
[11] M.R.O., Acc. 262/27(2).
[12] M.R.O., MR/TH/5, 75.
[13] *Home Cnties. Dir.* (1851), 546.
[14] *Kelly's Dir. Lond.* (1872), 132.
[15] M.R.O., TA/KIN; *Return of Agreements for commutation of tithe*, H.C. 555, p. 23 (1839), xli.
[16] *Home Cnties. Mag.* i. 322; C 54/3556 mm. 10 sqq.
[17] *Cal. S.P. Dom.* 1657–8, 198.
[18] Church Com. deed 169397.
[19] Ibid. 169053–62; M.R.O., Acc. 262/27(2).
[20] Hodgson, *Queen Anne's Bounty*, p. cccxiv.
[21] M.R.O., Acc. 400/66.
[22] H.O. 129/135/2/4/4.
[23] Bodl. MS. D.D. All Souls c75/31–2.
[24] Ibid. c38/13.
[25] Prob. 11/18 (P.C.C. 13 Holder).
[26] Prob. 11/30 (P.C.C. 14 Pynnyng).

close to maintain a church-house,[27] perhaps a small building which adjoined the churchyard in 1597.[28]

Little is known about the parish priests of Kingsbury. In 1435 John Ingram, chaplain, was amerced in the manor court of Kingsbury for striking Maud Chalkhill.[29] In 1503 Thomas Chalkhill was pardoned for killing John Fell, chaplain and curate of Kingsbury, in self-defence.[30] In 1525 William Cheshire, who may have been a former curate of Kingsbury, attacked John Bishop, curate of Kingsbury and later vicar of Willesden.[31] John West, curate in 1538, was a supporter of Henry VIII's religious innovations.[32] Robert Whiting, curate 1580–92, was 'simple'.[33] Thomas Fox, appointed curate in 1639, was ejected[34] and replaced in 1650 by Thomas Gardiner, a learned Presbyterian. When Gardiner moved to a more important post in 1654,[35] he was succeeded by Samuel Stancliffe, late rector of Great Stanmore.[36] The last of Kingsbury's 'Puritan' curates was James Prince, appointed in 1657 and ejected in 1662.[37]

Most early curates, often young men straight from university, were either poor or undistinguished, but from the late 17th century there were many pluralists, often incumbents of neighbouring parishes or canons of St. Paul's. Joseph Wilcocks, curate 1683–1702, was at the same time vicar of Harrow; William Hawkins, curate 1702–36, and Henry Fly, curate 1821–33, were also vicars of Willesden and canons of St. Paul's; Thomas Hilman, curate 1736–64, was another canon. William Clarke held Kingsbury in plurality with Willesden from 1795 and his successor, Thomas Woodman, held it with Twyford in 1820.[38] Moses Wight, curate 1764–95, vicar of Willesden and canon of St. Paul's, was a fashionable London preacher who appointed the learned Samuel Parr, then a master at Harrow School, as assistant curate with a salary of £25 a year.[39] Robert Dillon, assistant curate of Kingsbury and Willesden in 1824, was also a popular preacher, especially favoured by women.[40] In 1833 after complaints about non-residence[41] the chapter appointed Henry Atcheson, an extreme Evangelical, who was resident in the parish for over 40 years.[42]

In 1497 a Welsh boy of about five years of age was found bound in the cemetery of Kingsbury church. After adoption by a tenant of the manor, he was named David Welch and apprenticed.[43] In 1685 orders were given that the communion table was to be railed in.[44] During the 18th century there was one service on Sundays, usually in the afternoon, except three or four times a year when communion was administered.[45] A morning service was introduced in 1833 after complaints by the parishioners[46] and on census day 1851, the morning and afternoon services were attended by 55 and 36 people respectively,[47] presumably including the choir of red-hooded girls who occupied the gallery after it was built in 1840.[48] In 1883 a morning service at 11.0 a.m. was held at St. Andrew's while a service at 3 p.m. and a choral service at 6.30 p.m. were held at the chapel at the Hyde. Church activities included a guild of St. Andrew and Kingsbury clothing club.[49]

The old church of *ST. ANDREW*,[50] called in 1393 the church of St. Andrew and St. John the Baptist,[51] presumably because of its connexion with the Hospitallers, is situated in the southern extremity of the ancient parish of Kingsbury. The small church is built of flint rubble and Roman bricks and tiles and consists of undivided nave and chancel, west turret, and short spire. The modified long-and-short work of the western quoins may be a Saxon feature but other evidence, including the position of the 12th-century doorway, suggests a post-Conquest date. The chancel and nave contain 13th-century work with 14th- and 15th-century additions, including a trussed rafter roof. The parish was always too poor to enlarge the church and a relaxation of penance granted in 1393 to those who contributed to the conservation of St. Andrew's,[52] suggests that even the existing fabric was sometimes in danger. Pictures of 1796[53] and 1822[54] shows a dilapidated small country church. In 1840, however, it was drastically restored. The 14th-century timber south porch, the carved roof bosses and the rood screen were removed; the exterior was covered with roughcast and the roof with plaster; plain glass replaced quarries, a gallery was added, and a brick vestry was erected in front of the priest's door. In 1870 the wooden bell-turret and spire were rebuilt[55] and in 1888 the church was again restored; the mid-Victorian roof plaster and brick vestry were removed and a new vestry was built on the north side. The roof was re-tiled in 1906 and further restoration took place in 1955.[56]

The font, a circular bowl with octagonal rim, is probably 13th-century. It has no drainage hole and may have been a domestic mortar. According to local tradition, it was thrown into a pond in 1840,

27 E 301/34 m. 32; Bodl. MS. D.D. All Souls c52, ct. bk., ff. 11–11d., 57d.
28 All Souls Coll., Hovenden map, portfolio II, no. 14.
29 Bodl. MS. D.D. All Souls c37/7(1).
30 Cal. Pat. 1494–1509, 312.
31 Bodl. MS. D.D. All Souls c38/13; Req. 2/19/11. See p. 85.
32 L. & P. Hen. VIII, xiii(2), p. 142.
33 Guildhall MS. 9537/6, f. 173v.
34 Hennessy, Novum Repertorium, 262–3; Potter, Old Kingsbury Ch. 18–19.
35 Matthews, Calamy Revised, 217.
36 Ibid. 458; see p. 106.
37 Matthews, Calamy Revised, 399.
38 Hennessy, Novum Repertorium, 262–3; Le Neve, Fasti, 1541–1857, St. Paul's, 46, 65n.; Clerical Guide (1822), 92; Lysons, Environs, iii. 621, Suppl. 222.
39 Guildhall MS. 9557, f. 39; S. Holliday, Hist. of Kingsbury [pamphlet penes Hendon Libr.].
40 D.N.B.
41 Kingsbury Vestry Min. Bk. (1802–34) penes Brent Cent. Ref. Libr.
42 Hennessy, Novum Repertorium, 263; Potter, Old Kingsbury Ch. 26.
43 Bodl. MS. D.D. All Souls c37/10.
44 Guildhall MS. 9537/20, f. 107.
45 Guildhall MSS. 9550, 9557, f. 39.
46 Kingsbury Vestry Min. Bk. (1802–34) penes Brent Cent. Ref. Libr.
47 H.O. 129/135/2/4/4.
48 Potter, Old Kingsbury Ch. 26.
49 Hendon etc. Dir. (1883).
50 Except where otherwise stated, the foll. paras. are based upon Hist. Mon. Com. Mdx. 88–89; Pevsner, Mdx. 120; Potter, Old Kingsbury Ch.; Yates, 'Kingsbury Old Church', Jnl. of London Soc. ccx. 117–20; T.L.M.A.S. xviii(2), no. 209; G. H. Ayerst, Short Acct. of parish of Neasden-cum-Kingsbury [pamphlet c. 1907]; Wemb. Hist. Soc., Jnl. N.S. i(1), 15–19.
51 Cal. Papal L. iv. 450.
52 Ibid.
53 See plate facing p. 81.
54 Potter, Old Kingsbury Ch., plate facing p. 25.
55 For views of the church in 1815 and 1875, see Wemb. Hist. Soc., Photo. Coll., Acc. 412/3; 454/1.
56 Wemb. Hist. Soc., Jnl. N.S. i(1), 9.

whence it was rescued by the owner of Lewgars, who used it as a flower pot until he was persuaded, on his death-bed in 1905, to restore it to the church. The pedestal is modern. The church contains a late-17th-century oak lectern, which was taken from a City church in the 1880s and from which Gladstone read the lesson when he was staying in Willesden at the end of the 19th century. There are three original brasses, including one in the chancel to John Shepherd (d. 1520), his wives, and 18 children. There is a floor-slab to John Bull (d. 1621)[57] in the chancel and a table-tomb to Mary Scudamore (d. 1669) in the churchyard. There are three bells: (i) c. 1350, by Peter de Weston; (ii) 1604, by James Butler; (iii) 1708, by Samuel Newton.[58] The plate and registers have been transferred to Holy Innocents church.

When L. C. Edwards, a master at Harrow School, became curate of Kingsbury in 1883, St. Andrew's church was too small and the population was concentrated in the northern part of the parish and especially at the Hyde. There was a chapel at the Hyde where his predecessor conducted afternoon and evening services in 1883,[59] but it was on Edwards's initiative that a new church was built by subscription on a site given by All Souls College.[60] The church was consecrated in 1884 as the parish church of Kingsbury, all the endowments and rights of St. Andrew's being transferred to the new benefice, which was ordained a vicarage in the patronage of the chapter of St. Paul's.[61] It was attended on census day 1903 by 96 people in the morning and 92 in the evening.[62] The old church became a chapel of ease, against the wishes of many of the parishioners who, led by one of the churchwardens, sang psalms and hymns there while the vicar officiated at the first service in the new parish church.[63]

In 1887 the Ecclesiastical Commissioners granted a perpetual annuity of £205 and for the rest of the century the vicar's income was about £300 a year. The commissioners also granted £60 for a curate during the absence of the vicar.[64] The glebe, the two fields on either side of St. Andrew's church, which produced a rental of £7 a year, was sold in 1900 for use as an extension to the burial ground.[65] In 1887 the Ecclesiastical Commissioners made a grant of £1,500 for a parsonage, a large but insanitary building north of the church.[66] The London Diocesan Fund purchased a site at Roe Green in 1929 for a church, vicarage and hall. A hall was built there and used for public worship

in the 1930s. A site opposite was purchased for a new, smaller, vicarage, which was built in 1931, the old vicarage being used successively by the Children's Adoption Society, the Jewish Children Refugees, and Dr. Barnardo's Homes[67] until it was demolished between 1956 and 1963.[68]

The church of *HOLY INNOCENTS* stands at the highest point of Kingsbury Road, opposite its junction with Townsend Lane. The nave, chancel, Lady chapel and south porch were built in the Gothic style by William Butterfield in 1884 in yellow stock brick with varicoloured brick patterning. A small western turret was added in 1895 and a vestry in 1909; narthex, north aisle and choir vestry were added in 1957. There is one bell.[69] The plate, transferred from old St. Andrew's, includes a silver cup and paten cover, dated 1704, given by Richard Bowater.[70] Although an order was given to keep the registers in 1685,[71] the registers of births and deaths are complete only from 1732, and of marriages from 1735.

In 1885 old St. Andrew's became a consolidated chapelry under the name of Neasden-cum-Kingsbury, formed from parts of the parishes of Kingsbury and Willesden. It was a chapel of ease in the gift of the vicar of Kingsbury until he surrendered the right of presentation to the chapter of St. Paul's,[72] who retained it until the benefice became a vicarage in 1934 and the patronage passed to the Crown.[73] The Ecclesiastical Commissioners granted £1,500 in 1885[74] for a vicarage house, for which a site was found in 1887. An annuity of £95 was granted to the perpetual curate in 1887[75] and an annuity of £30 was added in 1907 to maintain an assistant curate. The benefice was worth £285 a year in 1903, by which date it had a chapel of ease, St. Catherine's Neasden-cum-Kingsbury.[76] With the development of southern Kingsbury after 1924 old St. Andrew's church could not accommodate the expanding population and a large church from Wells Street (St. Marylebone) was moved to an adjacent site to become the parish church.[77]

The new church of *ST. ANDREW* was originally built by S. W. Dawkes and Hamilton in 1847 and moved to Kingsbury by W. A. Forsyth in 1933. One of the earliest neo-Gothic churches, it is built of limestone rubble with freestone dressings in the Somerset Perpendicular style and consists of aisled and clerestoried nave incorporating the chancel, south porch, and north-west tower and spire.[78] As a centre of Anglo-Catholicism,[79] it acquired many

[57] See p. 49.
[58] *T.L.M.A.S.* xvi. 311–12; Wemb. Hist. Soc., *Jnl.* N.S. i(2), 12.
[59] See above.   [60] Church Com., file 67417.
[61] *Lond. Gaz.* 6 June 1884, p. 2494; *37th Rep. of Eccl. Com.* [C. 4323], pp. 66, 71, H.C. (1884–5), xxi.
[62] R. Mudie-Smith, *Religious Life of London*, 422.
[63] F. K. Malyon, *Holy Innocents Church, Kingsbury* (pamphlet), 3.
[64] *40th Rep. of Eccl. Com.* [C. 5330], p. 33, H.C. (1888), xxxiv; *Clergy List* (1892), 185; licence for curate, A6/1 and letters from Eccl. Com., A8/2–3 *penes* Holy Innocents church, Kingsbury.
[65] *Return of Glebe Lands*, H.C. 307, p. 88 (1887), lxiv; Ayerst, *Neasden-cum-Kingsbury*, 13.
[66] *40th Rep. of Eccl. Com.* [C. 5330], p. 33, H.C. (1888), xxxiv; *Lond. Gaz.* 8 July 1887, p. 3691; plans for vicarage, A8/7–9 *penes* Holy Innocents church, Kingsbury.
[67] F. K. Malyon, *Holy Innocents Church*, 4; correspond. on church hall, B3/1–2 *penes* Holy Innocents church, Kingsbury.

[68] Ex. inf. Brent L.B., Planning and Research Dept.
[69] *T.L.M.A.S.* xviii(2), no. 211; Malyon, *Holy Innocents Ch.*
[70] Freshfield, *Communion Plate*, 37.
[71] Guildhall MS. 9537/20, f. 107.
[72] *Lond. Gaz.* 21 July 1885, p. 3365; *Return of Parishes Divided*, H.C. 386, p. 8 (1890–1), lxi; transfer of right of presentation, A1/4 *penes* Holy Innocents church, Kingsbury.
[73] *Crockford* (1935).
[74] *38th Rep. of Eccl. Com.* [C. 4679], p. 36, H.C. (1886), xx.
[75] *40th Rep. of Eccl. Com.* [C. 5330], p. 72, H.C. (1888), xxxiv.
[76] *Kelly's Dir. Essex etc.* (1903), ii. 358.
[77] Malyon, *Holy Innocents Ch.*; F. G. Springford, *Hist. of St. Andrews* [pamphlet].
[78] See plate facing p. 80.
[79] 'Considered from a ritual point of view, it is the most satisfactory church yet built in London': *Ecclesiologist*, viii. 79.

interior embellishments. The metal chancel screen and pulpit are by Street, who also designed the reredos, which was sculptured by James Redfern. J. L. Pearson designed the font-cover and W. Butterfield the lectern. Most of the windows are by Clayton and Bell, except for the east window, a modern one designed by Goddard and Gibbs to replace a Pugin window, which was destroyed during the Second World War. Eight bells were presented to the church in 1880. A temporary church hall, built near the old church after 1907, was replaced by a permanent building in 1950.[80]

The parish of All Saints, Queensbury, which grew out of a Home Mission, was created in 1932 as a conventional district with a priest-in-charge. It was formed from the old parishes of Kingsbury and Little Stanmore, and includes all the area between Honeypot Lane and Edgware Road, between Camford Avenue in the north and Girton and Homstall avenues in the south. In 1941 it became a parochial district, the benefice becoming a vicarage in the patronage of the Crown. Worship was conducted in a hall in Dale Avenue, Little Stanmore, then in a marquee erected as part of a mission in Waltham Drive, and from 1938 in a wooden hut built on the site of the marquee. The church of ALL SAINTS, built next to the hall, was consecrated in 1954. Built by Romilly B. Craze, it is a brick building in a plain style and has a nave, chancel, north and south aisles, north-east chapel, and north tower.[81]

ROMAN CATHOLICISM. Only one recusant, Edward Robinson in 1624,[82] was associated with Kingsbury, where in 1676[83] and 1706 there were said to be no papists[84] There were some Irish Roman Catholics in 1851,[85] but there is no further evidence of Roman Catholicism before the period of suburban expansion.

In 1924 the diocese of Westminster purchased a cottage and field adjoining Haydon House in Hay Lane for use as a camping ground for the Westminster Cathedral boy scouts. A small church was built there in 1925 and registered for worship in 1926.[86] It was dedicated to St. Sebastian and St. Pancras, the patron saints of scout officers and cadets respectively. In 1930 a permanent parish priest was appointed and the church was enlarged. Further enlargements took place in 1938 and 1958.[87]

The church of the English Martyrs in Barnhill Road, Chalkhill, was licensed for worship in 1930[88] and opened, together with a presbytery, in 1931.[89]

A new circular church in a contemporary style by John E. Sterrett and B. D. Kaye was opened in 1970 on a site in Blackbird Hill, to replace the former temporary structure.[90]

PROTESTANT NONCONFORMITY. A single nonconformist was noted in 1676.[91] Dissenters, led by their minister, William Foxwell, obtained licences for worship in several private houses at the Hyde in 1803 and 1804.[92] They were probably Baptists and may have been connected with a short-lived chapel in the Hendon part of the Hyde, founded in 1843.[93]

It is more likely, however, that some of the dissenters of 1804[94] joined the Congregationalists who licensed one of Elizabeth King's houses on the Kingsbury side of the Hyde in 1818.[95] The meeting-place apparently moved to the Hendon part in 1836[96] but had returned to Kingsbury by 1851, when it was held in Henry Billing's house in Edgware Road, just north of the King's Arms. A minister had average congregations of 20 'mixed Christians' at the two Sunday services.[97] A Congregational chapel in Edgware Road, south of the King's Arms, was registered in 1860[98] and conveyed to church members as trustees in 1878. By 1912 the chapel was 'practically at an end' and in 1913 the trusteeship was vested in the London Congregational Union (Incorporated), in order that the building could be used as a mission hall by Cricklewood Congregational church. A new Congregational church was opened in 1933 on the Hendon side of Edgware Road and the old chapel was sold to the Salvation Army, which used it until 1935 when the licence to worship was cancelled.[99]

Kingsbury Free church was built in 1931 for Baptists[1] who had been meeting in a builder's hut. It is a brick building with timber and plaster decoration, at the junction of Slough Lane and Salmon Street. A church hall was erected next to the church in the 1930s.[2]

Methodists met on the new Queensbury estate in 1935 and in 1936 an empty shop near Queensbury station was opened for temporary use as a Sunday school and for worship. A brick church, designed by H. R. Houchin in a cinema-modernistic style, was opened in Beverley Drive in 1938. A new church hall was added in 1958.[3]

There was a gospel hall in Bacon Lane in 1936[4] and Roe Green hall in Princes Avenue was registered for undenominational worship in 1937 by members of Woodcroft Evangelical church.[5]

80 *T.L.M.A.S.* xviii(2), no. 208; Pevsner, *Mdx.* 120–1; Springford, *Hist. of St. Andrews*; Ayerst, *Neasden-cum-Kingsbury*, 18–19.
81 *T.L.M.A.S.* xviii(2), no. 210; Wemb. Hist. Soc., Acc. 907–21; *All Saints', Queensbury, Dedication* [souvenir pamphlet, 1954]. 82 *Mdx. Cnty. Recs.* ii. 238.
83 William Salt Libr., Stafford, Salt MS. 33, p. 40.
84 Guildhall MS. 9800.
85 H.O. 107/1700/135/2 ff. 310–28.
86 G.R.O. Worship Reg. no. 50553.
87 Ex inf. the par. priest, 1969.
88 G.R.O. Worshop Reg. no. 52463.
89 H. W. R. Elsley, *Wembley through the Ages*, 195.
90 *Wembley News*, 10 July 1970.
91 William Salt Libr., Stafford, Salt MS. 33, p. 40.
92 Guildhall MS. 9580/2; G.R.O. Worship Returns, Lond. dioc. nos. 584, 608. The application for Foxwell's house in 1803 gives it as in Hendon and the denomination as Baptists.
93 See p. 40.
94 e.g. James Reopath or Redpath appears in both certs.
95 Guildhall MS. 9580/2; G.R.O. Worship Returns, Lond. dioc. no. 1073. For Elizabeth King's houses, see M.R.O., Acc. 262/30.
96 See p. 39.
97 H.O. 107/1700/135/2 ff. 310–28; H.O. 129/135/2/4/6.
98 G.R.O. Worship Reg. no. 9385; O.S. Map 1/2,500, Mdx. XI. 6 (1873 edn.).
99 G.R.O. Worship Reg. no. 9385; Char. Com. file 89916; see p. 41.
1 G.R.O. Worship Reg. no. 53464.
2 Ex inf. the sec. (1969).
3 Material supplied by Queensbury Meth. ch.; G.R.O. Worship Reg. no. 58015.
4 Char. Com. file 119315.
5 G.R.O. Worship Reg. no. 57127; ex. inf. Mr. J. A. Gardiner (1969).

In 1937 meetings were held by the Protestant Apostolic Church in Oakleigh Avenue,[6] at a mission hall which was registered in 1939.[7]

JUDAISM

A congregation of Jews affiliated to the United Synagogue first appeared in Kingsbury in 1939.[8] In 1942 Eden Lodge at Kingsbury Green was registered for worship,[9] becoming Kingsbury district synagogue in 1954.[10] A new synagogue was built on the site by David Stern & Partners, architects, in 1967.[11] It is a dark grey brick building with rough-cast buttresses, full-length stained glass windows and a wooden roof.

EDUCATION

John Bishop, curate of Kingsbury, kept a school there c. 1530,[12] but there is no further evidence of schooling in the parish before the 19th century. In 1819 about 35 children were clothed and educated and a mistress was paid by annual subscriptions,[13] perhaps at the Sunday school to which George Worrall contributed £10.[14] A day-school, opened in 1822, had 30 children in 1833. It was supported by subscriptions, collections, and school pence at the rate of 1d. a week for each child:[15] from 1827 the National Society made an annual grant of £20.[16] The school, which was situated on waste land near the junction of Roe Green and Kingsbury Road, was owned by the vicar.[17] In 1846–7 there was one mistress and one schoolroom, accommodating 17 boys, 14 girls, and 13 infants.[18] The school was still in use in 1872 but had closed by 1876.[19] The school-house, converted into a private dwelling, still stood in 1937.[20]

In 1846–7 it was stated that nearly all the children in Kingsbury attended some school. Some boys went to Hendon and 6 boys and 20 girls attended a dame's school at the Hyde, supported by school pence.[21] In 1851, however, there were some Irish Catholic children at the Hyde and 'no school in the district'.[22] In 1865 a Roman Catholic school was established in a schoolroom attached to the stable of the Revd. George Ballard at the Hyde, where it was attended by about 36 children.[23]

The dame school at the Hyde was apparently short-lived and in 1861 an infants' school was built north of the Congregational chapel in Edgware Road.[24] The infants' school was replaced in 1870 by a British school at the Hyde end of Kingsbury Road, where about 40 boys, girls, and infants were taught by a mistress. The school was financed by voluntary contributions, school pence,[25] and, from 1870, regular parliamentary grants. The schools' inspector was dissatisfied, apparently because of the cramped premises, and Kingsbury school board, formed in 1875, replaced it with a board school with accommodation for 120 children in 1876.[26]

The board school, after 1903 called Kingsbury council school,[27] became a senior mixed school after infants had been transferred to a new school in Kenton Lane in 1922.[28] When Kenton Lane council school at Kingsbury Green was opened as a senior school in 1928, its juniors and infants were transferred to the old board school where they remained until it was bombed in the Second World War. In 1948 Kenton Lane council school, renamed Kingsbury Green school, opened for juniors and infants.[29]

Among primary schools built between the World Wars were Fryent, opened in Church Lane in 1931, Roe Green, opened in Princes Avenue in 1932, and Oliver Goldsmith, opened at the corner of Kingsbury Road and Coniston Gardens in 1938. Glenwood primary school in south-east Kingsbury existed from 1954 until 1959. Blessed Robert Southwell Roman Catholic primary school was opened in Slough Lane in 1967 and Chalkhill infants' school was opened to serve the new Chalkhill estate in 1970.[30]

A mixed secondary school, Kingsbury county, was housed in a building once belonging to the Aircraft Manufacturing Co. and adapted to take 380 pupils from 1925 until 1931, when a new school was built in Princes Road. Extensions were made in 1954.[31] Building started on a second mixed secondary school at a site in Bacon Lane in 1939 but it was not until 1952 that Tyler's Croft county secondary schools, redesigned as separate boys' and girls' secondary modern schools, were opened. Under the comprehensive scheme for education, which was adopted by Brent L.B. in 1967, Kingsbury county and Tyler's Croft schools were amalgamated as Kingsbury high school.[32]

There were several private schools in Kingsbury, mostly in large private houses. In 1851 49 girls, some drawn from Bombay, Australia, and the West Indies, and seven mistresses, in addition to the proprietor and his wife, were boarded at Kingsbury House, where subjects included French, English, and music.[33] The school had closed by 1861[34] but another ladies' seminary had been opened, at Redhill, by 1872.[35] At the turn of the century two members of the Wyand family ran

[6] Kelly's Dir. Wembley (1937).
[7] G.R.O. Worship Reg. no. 58778.
[8] Jewish Yr. Bk. (1939).
[9] G.R.O. Worship Reg. no. 60273.
[10] Ibid. 64546.
[11] Plaque at synagogue.
[12] Req. 2/19/11.
[13] Educ. of Poor Digest, 538.
[14] 9th Rep. Com. Char. 266–7.
[15] Educ. Enquiry Abstract, p. 567.
[16] Nat. Soc. 16th Annual Rep. (1827).
[17] M.R.O., Acc. 262/27 pt. 1; M.R.O., TA/KIN.
[18] Nat. Soc. Church Schs. Enquiry, 1846–7, Mdx. 8–9.
[19] Kelly's Dir. Lond. (1872, 1876).
[20] Kelly's Dir. Wembley (1937).
[21] Nat. Soc. Church Schs. Enquiry, 1846–7, Mdx. 8–9.
[22] H.O. 107/1700/135/2 ff. 310–28.
[23] Ed. 7/87/23.
[24] O.S. Map 1/2,500, Mdx. XI. 6 (1873 edn.).
[25] Ed. 7/86/48; Kelly's Dir. Lond. (1872), 132.

[26] Reps. of Educ. Cttee. of Council, 1870 [C. 406], H.C. p. 499 (1871), xxii; 1877–8 [C. 2048–I], H.C. p. 765 (1878), xxviii; 1878 [C. 2342–I], H.C. p. 745 (1878–9), xxiii; Lond. Gaz. 7 Dec. 1875, p. 6300; Kelly's Dir. Lond. (1900), 304; O.S. Map 1/2,500, Mdx. XI. 6 (1896 edn.).
[27] List of Schs. under admin. of Bd. 1903 [Cd. 2011], H.C. p. 169 (1904), lxxv.
[28] Ed. 7/86/48A; Kingsbury U.D.C., Min. Bk. (1922–6), 120.
[29] Mdx. Educ. Cttee. Schools Gaz. x(2), 23; ex inf. the headmistress.
[30] Brent L.B., Educ. Cttee., List of Schools (TS. 1969); O.S. Map 1/2,500, Mdx XI. 5 (1932 edn.); XI. 10 (1935 edn.); ex inf. chief educ. officer, Brent L.B.
[31] The Times, 18 Jan. 1926; Kingsbury County Sch. Mag. (1966); ex inf. history master at Kingsbury high sch.
[32] Ex inf. history master at Kingsbury high sch. (1969); Wemb. Hist. Soc., Acc. 336/7.
[33] H.O. 107/1700/135/2, ff. 310–28.
[34] Census, 1861.   [35] Kelly's Dir. Lond. (1872), 142.

schools, Halvergate preparatory school in Edgware Road and a boarding-school,[36] possibly the school in Kingsbury Lane mentioned by the medical officer of health in 1902.[37] There was a boys' preparatory school in Grove Park in the 1920s and 1930s and another preparatory school in Valley Drive in 1937.[38] Chalkhill House housed a girls' school in 1930[39] and a mixed preparatory school from 1946 until 1961. The latter had started as Kingsgate school in Salmon Street in 1932.[40]

There were two special schools in 1969. Woodfield school for educationally sub-normal children was opened in 1959 in premises formerly occupied by Glenwood primary school.[41] A school for physically handicapped children was transferred from Harlesden to Grove Park in 1968.[42]

An annexe for Kilburn Polytechnic was opened in 1950 in the building in Edgware Road formerly occupied by Kingsbury county school.[43]

CHARITIES FOR THE POOR. John Edward (d. c. 1532) devised land to the parson and church-wardens of Kingsbury, the rent from which was to be distributed annually to the poor in meat, drink, and money. By will proved 1540 Alice Cowyer bequeathed 8 kine to be used as an obit; in 1547 it took the form of annual payments of 10s. to the poor.[44] Robert Kitchingman, curate of Kingsbury from 1669 to 1683, bequeathed £400 to build an alms-house to house three people and to endow its maintenance.[45] The alms-house, unless it is the same as the later poorhouse,[46] does not seem to have been built.

By will dated 1719 Richard Bowater (d. 1726) of Chalkhill left 7 a. in Greenwich, then worth £4 or £5 a year, to the owner of his estate at Chalkhill to distribute the income therefrom annually to the poor of Kingsbury.[47] In 1786 the yield from the Greenwich estate was said to be £3 7s. a year but there had been no payments since 1773.[48] When George Worrall of Bristol became the owner of Chalkhill, he passed the responsibility for the charity to his tenant. Mrs. Ranking, tenant until 1820, distributed the charity in the form of clothes, flannel, sheets, and blankets, but from 1821 there was no tenant at Chalkhill and the money accumulated.[49] By 1843 the Greenwich land yielded £21 a year.[50] In 1846 it was conveyed to trustees, including Hannah Rooke, owner of Chalkhill, to let on building leases, thus increasing the annual income to £82 by 1880. By a Scheme of 1852 the income was to be paid in money or kind to those who 'from age, infirmity or poor circumstances had insufficient means of subsistence'. There were 47 recipients in 1880. By will proved 1842, Francis Perry Stubbs bequeathed £666 to trustees to invest in stock and to apply the income to purchasing coal and potatoes for the poor and needy at Christmas. In 1880 the income was £20 and 49 people received coal and potatoes.

The Charity Commissioners instituted an inquiry in 1882 at the request of the parishioners, who especially objected to absentee trustees, the choice of recipients, and the secrecy surrounding the charity accounts. As a result the two charities were amalgamated, as Bowater and Stubbs, and trustees were appointed from the parish.[51] A comprehensive Scheme was drawn up in 1902 by which trustees were to be appointed by Kingsbury U.D.C. and the income was to be spent on a wide variety of aid to the poor. Modifications were made by Schemes of 1938, 1953, and 1954, the main effect of which was to purchase from Wembley borough a site between Kingsbury Road and Buck Lane for 14 alms-houses for old people. The alms-houses, called Bowater Close, were opened in 1954 by Sir Noel Bowater, Lord Mayor of London. Income of the Bowater and Stubbs charity increased from £100 a year in 1902 to £16,404 in 1968.[52]

Kingsbury District Nursing, founded in 1925 and reconstituted in 1941, by a Scheme of 1956, purchased two alms-houses in Bowater Close and maintained them for almspeople suffering from chronic disease. The endowment, originally consisting of annual subscriptions, was later invested and yielded £542 a year in 1968.

GREAT STANMORE

GREAT STANMORE[1] was a parish of 1,441 a. in 1841.[2] It was roughly the shape of an elongated rectangle, running from north-north-west to south-south-east, and the village at its centre lay some 10 miles from London.[3] Stanmore was divided before the Conquest into estates foreshadowing the later parishes of Great and Little Stanmore,[4] although the name of Great Stanmore does not occur until 1354.[5] Throughout its history the main settlement, to which there was no equivalent in Little Stanmore, was often called merely Stanmore,[6] as were the old village and its surrounding district in 1971.

The parish was delimited by few natural features or roads.[7] Its northern boundary crossed Bushey

[36] Kelly's Dirs. Lond. (1894), 364; (1900), 276, 304.
[37] Kingsbury U.D.C., San. Rep. (1902).
[38] Kelly's Dir. Hendon (1926); Kelly's Dir. Wembley (1937).
[39] Truman and Knightley, Schools (1930).
[40] Wemb. Hist. Soc., Acc. 907/73; Acc. 952/4.
[41] Ex inf. chief educ. officer, Brent L.B.
[42] Ex inf. the headmaster.
[43] Ex inf. chief educ. officer, Brent L.B.
[44] E 301/34 m. 32; Prob. 11/28 (P.C.C. 3 Alenger, will of Alice Cowyer); S.C. 6/298/1 m. 57.
[45] Prob. 11/372 (P.C.C. 47 Drax, will of Robt. Kitchingman); Hennessy, Novum Repertorium, 262–3.
[46] See p. 81.
[47] 9th Rep. Com. Char. 266–7; Bodl. MS. D.D. All Souls c40/5, mm. 1, 1d.
[48] Abstract of Returns of Char. Dons. 1786–8, H.C. 511, pp. 752–3, xvi(1).   [49] 9th Rep. Com. Char. 266–7.

[50] Analytical Digest of Reps. of Char. Com. i [433], H.C. pp. 804–5 (1843), xvi.
[51] Except where otherwise stated, the remainder of the section is based on Char. Com. files.
[52] Hopkins, Hendon, 105.
[1] The article was written in 1971. Any references to later years are dated. The help of Mr. R. W. Thomson in making material available and commenting on the article is gratefully acknowledged.   [2] Census, 1841.
[3] Except where otherwise stated, the rest of the para. and the following para. are based on O.S. Maps 6", Mdx. V. SE.; X. NE.; XI. NW. (1865 and later edns.).
[4] V.C.H. Mdx. i. 125, 128.   [5] See below, p. 96.
[6] e.g. Rocque, Map of Mdx. (1754).
[7] The bounds were first recorded at a court of survey in 1680: Davenport MSS., Gt. Stan. ct. rolls. For the Davenport MSS. relating to Gt. Stanmore, see p. 102.

Heath, where the limits of the manors of Great Stanmore and Bushey were surveyed in 1595, and became that of the county.[8] The inclusion of Stanmore marsh was not finally determined, by agreement with Little Stanmore, until the 1820s.[9] After that time the eastern boundary, running from Hertfordshire along the west side of Cloisters wood to the bottom of Dennis Lane, continued south down Marsh Lane[10] and bulged outwards at Stanmore marsh before heading almost as far south as the site of Queensbury station. The southern boundary, with Harrow, ran for a short way along Honeypot Lane before turning west a little to the south of the modern Streatfield Road. The western boundary, also with Harrow, was later marked by a line slightly east of Uppingham Avenue, curving north-west towards Vernon Drive. Thence it crossed Belmont, a mound constructed by James Brydges, duke of Chandos (d. 1744),[11] Stanmore Park, the Uxbridge road, and the grounds of Bentley Priory, east of the mansion, to reach Hertfordshire where Magpie Hall Road meets Heathbourne Road. Great Stanmore civil parish was included in Hendon R.D. from 1894 until 1934. Thereafter most of both Great and Little Stanmore lay within the ward of Stanmore North, which formed part successively of the urban district, borough, and London Borough of Harrow.[12]

The soil is predominantly London Clay. A band of pebble gravel fringed by Claygate Beds crosses the parish along a high ridge in the north, stretching from Wood Lane over the southern part of Stanmore Common and into the grounds of Bentley Priory.[13] One of the ponds on the gravel, possibly Spring pond, may have been the 'stony mere' which gave its name to the locality.[14] A narrow strip of alluvium lies along the boundary north of Stanmore marsh.[15]

The main contours run from east to west. Apart from Belmont the southern half is almost flat, rising from less than 200 ft. very gradually to reach 300 ft. about 150 yards above the foot of Stanmore Hill. From that point the ground rises steeply to 475 ft. at the southern edge of the common and in the north-west, although it falls away to 350 ft. in the north-eastern corner, which is drained towards Aldenham reservoir (Herts.). The Stanburn stream flows from the lake of Bentley Priory in Harrow south-eastward, past Boot pond and through Temple pond, to the southern end of Stanmore marsh; there, as Edgware brook, it turns south to follow the boundary before a second turn leads it eastward across Little Stanmore.[16] Spring pond, on the southern edge of the common, was probably the 'great pond' from which water was taken down Stanmore Hill by 1640.[17]

John Warner (d. 1565), physician, and William Wigan Harvey (1810–83), divine, son of George Daniel Harvey of Montagues, were natives of the parish.[18] General Robert Burne died in retirement at Berkeley Cottage, Stanmore, in 1825. Charles Hart (d. 1683), Baptist Wriothesley Noel (1798–1873), divine, and Arthur Hamilton-Gordon (1829–1912), colonial governor, were also resident. In 1893 the last was created Lord Stanmore of Great Stanmore,[19] a title which became extinct in 1957.[20] Other prominent residents are mentioned elsewhere in this article, where their homes are described.

In the Middle Ages the busiest road was that running from Watling Street to Watford, mentioned c. 1170.[21] The section which entered from Little Stanmore, probably near the crest of the ridge at Spring pond was rendered useless in the early 18th century by the duke of Chandos's diversions around Canons[22] but the north-western stretch was left to follow the old route along the edge of Stanmore Common and into Harrow parish.[23] At the bottom of the ridge a lesser route cut south-westward through the parish, linking Watling Street with Harrow Weald and Uxbridge.[24] It followed the line of the modern Broadway and Church Road, continuing between the sites of the existing church and the rectory along Colliers Lane[25] before that stretch was foreshortened by the building of Stanmore Park; later Uxbridge Road, a 'new' road in 1800,[26] was laid out with its bulge to the north. Across it ran two ways from the high ground: Dennis Lane, which joined it at the boundary and continued south as Marsh Lane and Honeypot Lane, and Green Lane. The second continued south as Old Church Lane, before turning east to meet Marsh Lane, and as Watery Lane, which itself turned to join Honeypot Lane. Dennis Lane, so called by 1578,[27] and its southerly extensions may mark a north to south trackway older than Watling Street;[28] the route along Green and Old Church lanes, mentioned respectively in 1580 and 1633,[29] led to the main medieval settlement.

The road called Stanmore Hill, reaching the Uxbridge road between Dennis Lane and Green Lane, may have started as a branch from Green Lane, which it meets half-way up the slope; since the 18th century, however, Stanmore Hill has also been the name for the old stretch between that fork and the top of the ridge. Following the duke of Chandos's building around Canons, most travellers from Watford descended Stanmore Hill before meeting those coming from Uxbridge. East of the junction, at the bottom of Dennis Lane, they could reach Watling Street by taking the new London road straight across Little Stanmore or by going south down Marsh Lane before turning into Whitchurch Lane.[30] Marsh Lane became important only in the 1930s, when improvements there and along the

[8] E 178/1463.
[9] See p. 121.
[10] T.L.M.A.S. xiii. 222–3.
[11] W. W. Druett, Stanmore and Harrow Weald, 112.
[12] See below, p. 104.
[13] Geol. Surv. Map 1″, drift, sheet 256 (1951 edn.).
[14] P.N. Mdx. (E.P.N.S.), 65.
[15] Geol. Surv. Map 6″, Mdx. XI. NW. (1920 edn.).
[16] Except where otherwise stated, the para. is based on O.S. Maps 6″, Mdx. V. SE.; X. NE.; XI. NW. (1865 and later edns.).
[17] See p. 104.
[18] Except where otherwise stated, the para. is based on D.N.B.
[19] Complete Peerage, s.v. Stanmore.

[20] Who Was Who, 1951–60, 1036.
[21] Cat. Anct. D. ii, A 2097.   [22] See p. 111.
[23] C. F. Baylis, Short Hist. of Edgware and the Stanmores in the Middle Ages, map facing p. 1.
[24] Except where otherwise stated, the rest of the para. and the following para. are based on O.S. Maps 6″, Mdx. V. SE.; X. NE.; XI. NW. (1865 and later edns.).
[25] Druett, Stanmores and Harrow Weald, 79 and map facing p. 32.
[26] M.L.R. 1800/1/501.
[27] P.N. Mdx. (E.P.N.S.), 66.
[28] A. J. Garrett, 'Hist. Geog. of Upper Brent' (London Univ. M.A. thesis, 1935), 27–8.
[29] Davenport MSS., Gt. Stan. ct. rolls.
[30] See p. 111.

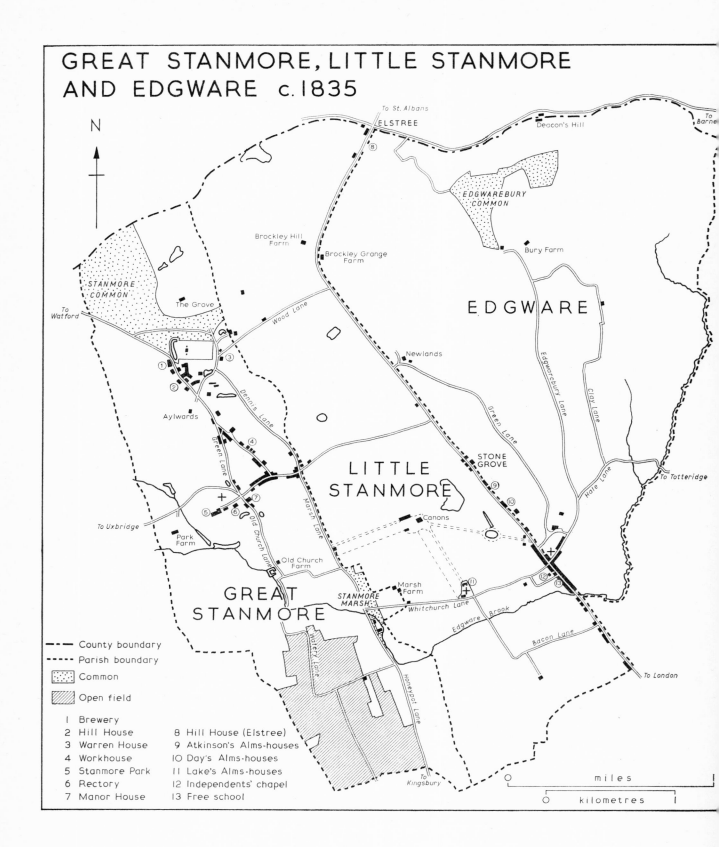

GREAT STANMORE, LITTLE STANMORE AND EDGWARE c.1835

N

To St. Albans
ELSTREE
To Barne
Deacon's Hill
8

EDGWAREBURY COMMON

Brockley Hill Farm
Brockley Grange Farm
Bury Farm

EDGWARE

STANMORE COMMON

The Grove

To Watford

Wood Lane

Newlands

Edgwarebury Lane

Clay Lane

1
3
2

Dennis Lane

Aylwards

Green Lane

STONE GROVE

To Totteridge

Hale Lane

4

LITTLE STANMORE

9
10

Green Lane

Marsh Lane

Canons

To Uxbridge

5 6 7

Park Farm

Old Church Lane

Old Church Farm

12
13

GREAT STANMORE

STANMORE MARSH

Marsh Farm

11

Whitchurch Lane

Edgware Brook

Bacon Lane

To London

Watery Lane

Honeypot Lane

To Kingsbury

County boundary
Parish boundary
Common
Open field

1 Brewery
2 Hill House
3 Warren House
4 Workhouse
5 Stanmore Park
6 Rectory
7 Manor House

8 Hill House (Elstree)
9 Atkinson's Alms-houses
10 Day's Alms-houses
11 Lake's Alms-houses
12 Independents' chapel
13 Free school

miles

kilometres

decayed Honeypot Lane[31] allowed traffic to head south along a course parallel to Watling Street. Gordon Avenue, running westward to link Old Church Lane with Kenton Lane in Harrow, was laid out after Frederick Gordon bought the Bentley Priory estate in 1882.[32] The network of residential roads covering the south part of the parish[33] was constructed between the World Wars.

The Stanburn flowed through a culvert under the Uxbridge road, west of the parish church, in 1826. There were also said to be two footbridges at Stanmore marsh,[34] although one was probably farther west, where Watery Lane crossed the stream in 1865.[35] It may have been the stone bridge mentioned in 1576 and the bridge leading from Stanmore town to the marsh which needed repair in 1639. A bridge at the marsh itself had disappeared by 1699, when the lord was asked to put up another.[36]

Coaches ran between Stanmore and Holborn as early as 1803[37] and a coach for Oxford Street left twice daily from the Abercorn Arms on Stanmore Hill by 1826.[38] Conveyances ran thrice daily from there to London in 1845, when there were also coaches to Chesham (Bucks.), Watford, Rickmansworth, and Hemel Hempstead (Herts.), and when the London coach from Bushey called twice a day at the Vine.[39] In 1905 it was planned to extend the tramway from Edgware through Great Stanmore as far as Watford but the route was taken only a little farther along Edgware Road.[40] The London General Omnibus Co. introduced a Sunday motor-bus service from Charing Cross to Harrow Weald through Stanmore village in 1912 and ran motor-buses from Kilburn to Watford through Stanmore from 1913.[41] By 1925 motor-buses linking Mill Hill and Edgware with Stanmore and Harrow crossed the parish from east to west. While services continued along the old routes, buses were using Marsh Lane and Whitchurch Lane[42] by 1934 and were afterwards introduced into the south part of the parish, along the new Wemborough Road and Honeypot Lane.[43]

The nearest railway stations were at Harrow (later Harrow and Wealdstone) and at Edgware until 1890,[44] when the Harrow and Stanmore Railway Co. opened a branch line from the L. & N.W.R. main line station at Harrow. The company, which had been incorporated in 1886, was controlled by Frederick Gordon of Bentley Priory. It tried to placate the parish council by building the red-brick Stanmore railway station, on the west side of Old Church Lane, in an ecclesiastical style and by promising that there should be no Sunday service for 40 years. Under an Act of 1899 the L. & N.W.R. took over the working of the new line, on which an intermediate station was opened at Belmont, on the

Harrow side of the boundary, in 1932. Thirty-six trains ran each way on weekdays along the entire length in 1952, when the section between Belmont and Stanmore was closed.[45] Since that date the nearest station to the old village has been the Stanmore terminus of the Bakerloo line, in Little Stanmore.[46]

Settlement in the Middle Ages presumably centred upon the manor-house, at the corner of the later Wolverton Road and Old Church Lane, and the church which stood a few yards north of it.[47] It is not certain whether, as in Kingsbury,[48] the Black Death played a part in the decay of the old village and the choice of a more northerly site.[49] Increasing traffic may have made the route to Uxbridge more attractive than a position $\frac{1}{4}$ mile down a branch road such as Old Church Lane. The sites of head tenements, though not recorded until the late 16th century,[50] suggest that many medieval holdings were scattered well to the north of the manor-house: Montagues lay on the south side of the road to Uxbridge, Fiddles nearly opposite at the west corner of Dennis Lane,[51] Pynnacles at the east corner of Green Lane, and Aylwards higher up, off the west of Stanmore Hill.[52]

A northward shift in the centre of population may explain why, by 1582, the three common fields were known as Hither, Middle, and Further fields.[53] Lying either side of Old Church Lane and stretching beyond, around Watery Lane, to the Kingsbury boundary, they surrounded the old village but were all south of the houses along the way to Uxbridge.[54] The fields adjoined those of Harrow Weald to the west and of Kenton farther south, from which holders had been ordered to separate them by hedges and ditches before 1579, when boundary stones were planned.[55] On the eve of inclosure in 1839, under an Act of 1813, the fields were confined to one corner of the parish, south of the Stanburn and west of Honeypot Lane; they straddled Watery Lane and, with the roadway, covered no more than 308 a.[56]

East of the common fields and astride the ill-defined parish boundary lay Stanmore marsh, where in 1582 the homage of Great Stanmore admitted that certain tenants of Little Stanmore also had pasture 'of right immemorial'. A cottage recently built there was ordered to be taken down, as an encroachment, in 1679, and in 1680 Sir Lancelot Lake of Canons was presented for having inclosed part of the marsh some twenty years previously.[57] By 1838 the marsh consisted of a narrow strip along the east side of Marsh Lane, stretching from a point opposite Old Church Lane to a few yards south of Whitchurch Lane.[58] A shortened strip of some 10 a.

[31] See p. 51.
[32] V.C.H. Mdx. iv. 206.
[33] See below.
[34] Rep. on Bridges in Mdx. 208.
[35] O.S. Map 6", Mdx. X. NE. (1865 edn.).
[36] Davenport MSS., Gt. Stan. ct. rolls.
[37] Ex inf. Mr. R. W. Thomson.
[38] Pigot, Com. Dir. (1826–7).
[39] P.O. Dir. Home Cnties. (1845).
[40] Garrett, op. cit. 132 and fig. 15.
[41] Harrow Gaz. 5, 12, 19 Apr. 1912; Harrow Observer, 27 Feb. 1964; A. W. McCall, Omnibus Soc. Hist. Notes, 1964, 13.
[42] Garrett, op. cit. 133, 135, 138, 141, and figs.
[43] Harrow L.B., Official Guide [1967].
[44] V.C.H. Mdx. iv. 152, 198.

[45] Railway Mag. lxxxviii, 203–4; xcix, 91–4.
[46] See p. 111.
[47] Druett, Stanmores and Harrow Weald, 78; see below, pp. 98, 106.
[48] See p. 53.
[49] Druett, op. cit. map facing p. 32.   [50] See p. 100.
[51] Enfranchised in 1865 and 1859 respectively: M.R.O., Acc. 658/6, ff. 275, 199.
[52] See below, p. 100.
[53] Druett, op. cit. 79; Davenport MSS., Gt. Stan. ct. rolls.
[54] Druett, op. cit. map facing p. 32.
[55] Davenport MSS., Gt. Stan. ct. rolls.
[56] M.R.O., TA/S'MORE Gt.
[57] Davenport MSS., Gt. Stan. ct. rolls.
[58] M.R.O., TA/S'MORE Gt.

by the corner of Whitchurch Lane constituted the open space called Stanmore marsh in 1972.[59]

Most of the waste lay in the north-west part of the parish. It was originally considered part of Bushey Heath[60] but was known by 1637 as Stanmore heath and later as Stanmore Common. Five cottages there were condemned as encroachments in 1679.[61] Stanmore Common in 1838 stretched half-way along the Hertfordshire boundary and south to the Watford road and the reservoir, with an arm reaching almost to the eastern boundary south of the Grove. Below the reservoir was Little Common, probably the site of the 17th-century encroachments and with many more cottages 150 years later.[62] Stanmore Common covered the same area, 120 a., in 1838 as in 1972,[63] when Hadley Common was the only comparable uninclosed space in what had been north-west Middlesex.[64]

By 1754, after the rerouting of traffic to Watford, settlement was concentrated along the Uxbridge road, along Stanmore Hill and, at the top, around Little Common.[65] The presumed medieval village was marked only by the moat of the manor-house and, on the opposite side of Old Church Lane, by Old Church Farm. Fields stretched around, with no other houses south of the Uxbridge road save a summerhouse at Belmont.[66] The new manor-house, the Rectory, the church, which had been moved to a new site in 1632, and other dwellings stood around the intersection of Old Church and Green lanes with the Uxbridge road; to the west Stanmore Park may already have been built on the site of an older residence. Houses were close together on both sides of Church Road near the foot of Stanmore Hill, with others on the lower part of the hill itself. A small group at the corner of Dennis Lane and the London road, although it lay within Little Stanmore, also formed part of the village. More buildings clustered at the top of the triangle formed by Green Lane, Church Road, and Stanmore Hill. Others, including the brewery,[67] were dotted along the road towards the crest of the ridge and at Little Common. There were buildings on or near the later sites of Warren House and Aylwards but none farther north than the bowling green,[68] which separated Little Common from the main expanse of heath and thereby may have given Little Common its name. Forty years earlier Bowling Green House had stood there but it was probably replaced by a banqueting house built for the duke of Chandos (d. 1744).[69]

An inn called the Queen's Head existed by 1714,[70] and the King's Head, formerly the Three Pigeons, stood in 1730 on Stanmore Hill.[71] The Queen's Head, the Red Lion on Stanmore Hill, and the Vine on Stanmore Common were licensed by 1751.[72] The first stood on the corner of the hill and Church Road

in 1888, when it was no longer an inn; the Red Lion was last mentioned in 1860.[73] The Abercorn Arms on the hill, the Crown in the later Church Road, and the Vine were licensed in 1803.[74] It was at the Abercorn Arms that the Prince Regent met Louis XVIII of France in 1814, after the king had ended his years of exile at Hartwell (Bucks.).[75] All three of the inns recorded in 1803 survived in 1971, although the Abercorn Arms, still so called in 1863, had been temporarily renamed the Royal hotel by 1865.[76] Two beer-sellers living on Stanmore Hill in 1851 presumably occupied the Black Horse, recorded between that date and 1879, by which time its name had changed, and the Load of Hay, which comprised three former cottages in 1868. A beer-seller at Stanmore marsh in 1851 perhaps ran the Green Man beershop, so named in 1865.[77]

Housing spread little in the late 18th and early 19th centuries,[78] although the village became a more important centre, with a workhouse on the east side of Stanmore Hill from 1788 and probably a separate school-house from c. 1826. By 1865, after the workhouse had been closed, an infants' school stood higher up the slope and a National school near the bottom of the hill. A post office adjoined a smithy slightly higher up than the infants' school, on the western side. Buildings were close together only where some had stood a hundred years earlier: towards the eastern end of the later Church Road, up Stanmore Hill, at the fork between the hill and Green Lane, and on island sites between the Watford road and Spring pond on Little Common. There were gaps along the hill between the National school and the old workhouse, between the infants' school and the Royal hotel, and opposite the infants' school. Buildings at the cross-roads formed by Dennis and Marsh lanes and the London road included a farm[79] in the south-west corner. Green Lane had no houses between Pynnacles, at its southern end, and a group of over a dozen small dwellings near its junction with Stanmore Hill.

East of the houses lining Stanmore Hill, Dennis Lane in 1865 sloped upwards between fields and, near the top, between the grounds of Stanmore Hall and Warren House. West of the village stretched part of the estate of Bentley Priory, with that of Stanmore Park, including Park farm, south of the Uxbridge road. The flat southern half of the parish was mainly grassland, purchased by St. Bartholomew's hospital. Labourers inhabited the decaying Old Church Farm, whose tenant lived at what had been Ward's Farm at the corner of Marsh Lane. Belmont Terrace, an isolated row of six cottages, had been built since 1827 west of the junction of Watery Lane with Honeypot Lane;[80] at Stanmore marsh, in addition to the Green Man, there was a group of

[59] Ex inf. Harrow L.B., legal and admin. dept.
[60] E 303/9/223.
[61] Davenport MSS., Gt. Stan. ct. rolls.
[62] M.R.O., TA/S'MORE Gt.
[63] Ex inf. Harrow L.B., legal and admin. dept.
[64] E. C. Willatts, *Mdx. and the London Region*, 298.
[65] Except where otherwise stated, the para. is based on Rocque, *Map of Mdx.* (1754).
[66] H. H. Bolitho and D. Peel, *Drummonds of Charing Cross*, 36–7, 207–8.
[67] See below, p. 101.
[68] See p. 102.
[69] Lysons and others connect the banqueting house with a bowling green laid out by Chandos but the green was much older: see p. 102.

[70] M.L.R. 1714/6/136.
[71] Davenport MSS., Gt. Stan. ct. rolls.
[72] M.R.O., L.V. 7/1.
[73] Harrow Cent. Ref. Libr., sales parts. (Stanmore Hall).
[74] M.R.O., L.V. 10/113.
[75] Druett, *Stanmores and Harrow Weald*, 159–60.
[76] O.S. Map 6″, Mdx. V. SE. (1865 edn.).
[77] H.O. 107/1700/135/2; O.S. Map 6″, Mdx. XI. NW. (1865 edn.).
[78] Except where otherwise stated, the foll. three paras. are based on O.S. Maps 6″, Mdx. V. SE.; X. NE.; XI. NW. (1865 edn.).
[79] See below.
[80] St. Barts. Hosp., Surveyors' Reps. EO 8/1, pp. 171–2; EO 8/6, pp. 32, 186.

cottages, numbering four in 1838,[81] and a recently erected gas-works. The northernmost part of the parish, too, was empty, being divided between Stanmore Common and the estate in the north-east belonging to the Grove. To the north-west some large houses along Heathbourne Road included one, Stanmore Villa, just within the parish boundary.

The most striking change between 1754 and 1865 was the building or enlargement of several gentlemen's residences. In addition to Stanmore Park and the manor-house, near the church, the village contained the head tenements of Montagues, Fiddles, Pynnacles, and Aylwards,[82] all of which were marked in 1827 by substantial houses. Oak Villa, Townsend Villa (later Belmont Lodge), Rose Cottage, and Vine Cottage formed an extension of the village, into Little Stanmore, at the corner of Dennis Lane and the London Road. Near the crest of the hill, on the west, Hill House and Broomfield stood between the drive leading to Aylwards and the residence next to the brewery. It was at Hill House, then called the Great House,[83] that Dr. Samuel Parr had briefly opened his school in 1771 and that the antiquary Charles Drury Edward Fortnum, who bequeathed most of his treasures to the Ashmolean Museum, Oxford, lived from 1852 until 1899.[84] Broomfield, later Broomfield House, was designed c. 1860 by James Knowles.[85] On the opposite side of the road, south of the corner with Wood Lane, a house erected by the duke of Chandos (d. 1744) had been enlarged in the late 18th century by James Forbes of the East India Company, who had adorned the grounds with the first pieces of Hindu sculpture to be seen in England.[86] The mansion itself had been rebuilt, as Stanmore Hall, in 1847.[87] Forbes had also owned Warren House, farther east along Wood Lane, which he sold in 1813.[88] By 1827 it had passed to the architect Robert Smirke, who held it with 23 a. in Great Stanmore and 108 a. in Little Stanmore in 1838.[89] Almost opposite Warren House a drive led northeast to the Limes, which had been built by 1851 on the Little Stanmore side of the border.[90] Beyond Little Common the banqueting house attributed to Chandos had been the seat of George Hemming in 1795 and of his widow in 1816;[91] it had recently been pulled down in 1820.[92] Farther north stood the Grove, where a Jew named Aaron Cappadoce had died in 1782; a grotto and other embellishments made by his successor, one Fierville, were to survive a remodelling of the mansion in the 1870s.[93] Spacious grounds in many places restricted the spread of humbler housing: in 1865 the gardens of the manor-house and Pynnacles stretched along the western end of Church Road, and those of Aylwards and Stanmore Hall separated the main village from the settlement around Little Common. The rich owners of such houses, led by Col. Hamilton Tovey-Tennent of Pynnacles[94] and encouraged by the Hamilton-Gordons and Queen Adelaide of Bentley Priory, had been responsible for abandoning the 17th-century church in favour of a larger one, consecrated in 1850.

The parish as a whole changed little between the mid-19th century and the First World War. Stanmore village, considered attractive because it was situated on a slope and bordered by much fine parkland, retained the genteel character for which it was noted in 1876.[95] William Morris in 1888 found it 'pretty after a fashion, very well wooded ... but much beset with "gentlemen's houses". Nothing but grass fields everywhere'.[96] The naturalist Mrs. Eliza Brightwen lived from 1872 to 1906 at the Grove, where she kept her collection of plants and animals which she described in a series of popular books. Warren House became the home of Charles Keyser, chairman of the Colne Valley Water Co., and his sister Agnes, a friend of the royal family, and from c. 1890 of the banker Henry Bischoffsheim (d. 1908), who was often visited there by Edward VII. Woodlands, on the west side of the lower part of Stanmore Hill, was until 1899 the country home of the Lord Chancellor, the earl of Halsbury (d. 1921).[97]

New houses were mostly large and set in extensive gardens. The Elms had been built by 1879 behind the buildings lining the north side of Church Road, with a drive east of the Crown.[98] In 1897 the west side of Green Lane was almost entirely taken up by four houses: Culverlands, in the north, Benhale, Woodside, built c. 1893 by Arnold Mitchell in the style of Norman Shaw, and Clodiagh. There was a house at the east end of Uxbridge Road and there were others along the west side of Old Church Lane, where growth had probably started with the opening of the railway station and of a cottage hospital in 1890 and the construction of Gordon Avenue. Orme Lodge occupied the northern corner of Gordon Avenue, with Herondale to the west, and more houses stretched south of the hospital.[99] In 1920 the Dearne stood on the north side of Uxbridge Road, and large houses lined the south side of Gordon Avenue as far as the boundary. By that date detached houses had also been built in Elm Park, a cul-de-sac leading south from Church Road, and extended into Little Stanmore at the corner of Marsh Lane and London Road.[1]

The southern half of the parish assumed its modern appearance in the 1930s, after St. Bartholomew's hospital sold its farm-land[2] and when private building was encouraged by improvements to Honeypot Lane, the opening of Belmont station, and the extension of the Bakerloo line into Little Stanmore. Purchasers from the hospital included London companies seeking convenient sports grounds, local builders, notably Henry J. Clare, and larger construction firms, among them John Laing & Co.[3] By 1935 building was in full spate to the west of Honeypot

[81] M.R.O., TA/S'MORE Gt.
[82] See p. 101.
[83] Davenport MSS., Gt. Stan. ct. rolls (1782).
[84] Druett, Stanmores and Harrow Weald, 199–200; Who Was Who, 1897–1916, 254.
[85] TS. notes penes Harrow Cent. Ref. Libr.
[86] Ambulator (1792, 1820).
[87] TS. notes penes Harrow Cent. Ref. Libr.
[88] M.L.R. 1813/9/271.
[89] M.R.O., Acc. 262(26); TA/S'MORE Gt; TA/S'MORE Lt.
[90] H.O. 107/1700/135/2.

[91] Lysons, Environs, iii. 395; Brewer, Beauties of Eng. and Wales, x(5), 629.
[92] Druett, op. cit. 185.
[93] Brewer, Beauties of Eng. and Wales, x(5), 630–1.
[94] D.N.B.
[95] Thorne, Environs, ii. 563.
[96] Letters of Wm. Morris, ed. P. Henderson, 306.
[97] Druett, op. cit. 182–5, 187–9, 201–2.
[98] Harrow Cent. Ref. Libr., sales parts.
[99] O.S. Map 6″, Mdx. V. SE. (1897 edn.).
[1] Ibid. (1920 edn.). [2] See p. 99.
[3] St. Barts. Hosp., Journals of Governors, Ha 1/30, /31.

Lane; Pearswood Gardens and Anmersh Grove were lined with houses, a start had been made along Portland Crescent, and Langland Crescent, Streatfield Road, and other avenues had been planned and named. By 1938 the network of residential roads was almost complete: Watery Lane had disappeared and the line of Old Church Lane had been extended southward by building along Abercorn Road, St. Andrew's Road, and the partly finished Culver Grove. The line was crossed by rows of houses stretching west from Honeypot Lane: Wemborough Road, Crowshott Avenue, and, at the southern boundary, Streatfield Road. Wetherall Drive, Bush Grove, and most of the other offshoots from those roads had also been built up.[4]

Many houses in Old Church Lane and its offshoot, the Ridgeway, were detached, in contrast to the smaller, semi-detached houses along Abercorn Road and covering the south of the parish.[5] Council building between the World Wars was confined to 32 houses on the Wolverton Road estate and 111 houses on the Glebe estate, south of the Broadway.[6] A few shops were built near the Green Man at Honeypot Lane's junction with Wemborough Road, and in the extreme south along Honeypot Lane and Streatfield Road. A site south of the Green Man, entered from the west but extending into Little Stanmore, had been bought by the Canons Park Estate Co. in 1904 on behalf of the London Playing Fields Society, which in 1931 sold it to the London Passenger Transport Board.[7] No farm-land was left, other open spaces being limited to a golf course in part of Stanmore Park, school playing fields, and a few public recreation grounds.[8]

Stanmore village was joined to the suburban building which spread over the south part of the parish. During the 1930s the main changes took place along the foot of the slope, where demolitions and road widening were followed by the appearance of new shops in Church Road and the Broadway.[9] The 10 a. surrounding Pynnacles were advertised in 1927 as ripe for development;[10] Pynnacles itself was burned down in 1930, after which a corner of its garden was cut off and detached houses, stretching up Green Lane, were built over the remainder. On the opposite side of Church Road the manor-house was pulled down in 1930 and at the far end of the village Fiddles had been demolished by 1938.[11] Aylwards was last recorded in 1934, although the lodge, with later additions, survived in 1974.[12] More detached houses were built away from the main shopping thoroughfare. By 1939 they stood in Bentley Avenue and Old Lodge Way, where the Bentley Priory estate had bordered Uxbridge Road, on the Aylwards estate, along the south-western side of the Watford road to Priory Close, and along part of Dennis Lane.[13] Between the World Wars prominent people continued to live in and around the

village. Sir John Rees, Bt., M.P. (d. 1922) and his son Sir Richard successively owned Aylwards, Maj.-Gen. Sir John Fitzgerald, Bt., Henry Bischoffsheim's grandson, lived at Warren House,[14] and Frederick (later Sir Frederick) Handley Page (d. 1962) at Limes House. The aircraft designer Captain Geoffrey (later Sir Geoffrey) de Havilland owned the White House, London Road, on the Little Stanmore boundary, before moving to Harrow Weald.[15] Heriots was built in grounds of 16 a., south-west of the Watford road, as late as 1926.[16]

The site of Stanmore Park was rapidly covered with buildings after its acquisition as a Royal Air Force station in 1938.[17] The original hangars and many offices were replaced from the 1950s, while married quarters were built in Cherry Tree Way and other roads off Old Church Lane, as well as in new roads immediately east of the Chase.[18] Growth elsewhere after the Second World War consisted mainly of filling gaps in existing lines of houses and of building closes in former gardens. A shopping parade replaced the early-18th-century Buckingham House and Buckingham Cottage[19] at the corner of Stanmore Hill and the Broadway. Stangate Gardens, Hill Close, and Spring Lake extended as cul-de-sacs from the east side of Stanmore Hill by 1963, when Old Forge Close, Heriots Close, and Fallowfield were among those higher up. Pynnacles Close, Ray Gardens, and Halsbury Close, on the site of Woodlands, occupied the triangle between the hill, Church Road, and Green Lane. Benhale had given way to a close off Green Lane and Rectory Close ran south of the church.[20] In 1971 private building was still in progress in the central triangle and farther up the slope, and ranged from detached dwellings to terraced houses, often in a neo-Georgian style, and flats. It was also in progress along Old Church Lane, on the site of the former railway station and beyond the hospital, where some houses built earlier in the century were giving way to more concentrated development. Little space was left for council building: 47 houses and flats were built along Dennis Lane, followed by 44 flats at Bernays Close, 30 old people's flats at Honeypot Lane, and 44 houses and flats on the Wemborough Road estate.[21] The site owned by the London Passenger Transport Board in Honeypot Lane, which had been requisitioned during the war and covered with single-storeyed buildings, was conveyed in 1951 by the British Transport Commission to the Ministry of Works and used in 1971 by the Department of the Environment and other government bodies.[22]

In 1971 there were striking contrasts between the monotonous suburban avenues covering the south of the parish, the old village in the centre, and the partly wooded common in the north. The road ascending Stanmore Hill retained many 18th- and 19th-century houses, while others were recalled by the mellow

[4] O.S. Maps 6″, Mdx. X. NE., XI. NW. (1935 and 1938 edns.).
[5] Except where otherwise stated, the para. is based on O.S. Maps 1/2,500, TQ 1790, 1791 (1963 edn.).
[6] Boro. of Harrow, *Facts & Figures* (1963–4).
[7] Ex inf. Dept. of the Environment.
[8] See p. 105.
[9] Druett, *Stanmores and Harrow Weald*, 259.
[10] M.R.O., Acc. 262/23(c).
[11] Druett, op. cit. 210, 260.
[12] *Kelly's Dir. Edgware* (1934); ex inf. Mr. R. W. Thomson.
[13] O.S. Map 1/25,000, TQ 19 (1950 edn.).

[14] Druett, op. cit. 189, 198; Burke, *Peerage, Baronetage and Knightage* (1931), 971, 1984.
[15] *Kelly's Dir. Edgware* (1933); *Who Was Who, 1961–70*, 864.
[16] M.R.O., Acc. 262/23(c).
[17] See p. 99.
[18] O.S. Map 1/25,000, TQ 19 (1950 edn.); *R.A.F. Stanmore Pk. Inf. Handbk.* 19, 24–5, 48.
[19] Min. of Town and Country Planning, List of Bldgs. (1950).
[20] O.S. Map 1/2,500, TQ 1792 (1963 edn.).
[21] Boro. of Harrow, *Facts & Figures* (1963–4).
[22] Ex inf. Dept. of the Environment.

red-brick garden-walls and established trees which sheltered later buildings.

Along the foot of the ridge the oldest survivals are scattered. Oak Lodge, Belmont Lodge, and Rose Cottage, built of yellowish-brown brick *c.* 1800, are on the corner of Dennis Lane and just within Little Stanmore. On the far side of a busy cross-roads is a timber-framed range of two-storeyed tenements, nos. 57–65 the Broadway, built in the early 17th century as one house, possibly as an inn, but with later doors and windows. The building is plastered outside and contains, in no. 59, an elaborate chimney-piece and panelling. Despite the loss of a ninth bay at the western end, the jettied upper storey facing the street for 98 feet is unequalled in Middlesex and one of the longest continuous jetties in the country.[23] Farther west the upper storeys of an early-18th-century house,[24] formerly no. 33, are scarcely distinguishable from those of a red-brick shopping parade into which the building has been incorporated.

Close to the neo-Georgian Crown inn in Church Road, which continues the line of shops, is the two-storeyed Regent House,[25] whose red-brick front contains an early-18th-century doorcase with a broken pediment. Bernays memorial gardens, at the west end of Church Road, look upon the back of Church House, a rambling building in the Tudor style, where old timbering is incorporated in a church hall.[26] Opposite its entrance, at the top of Old Church Lane, a tithe barn has been converted into cottages. The buildings, with trees in the memorial gardens and around the church, give what was once the western end of the village a rustic air belied by the heavy traffic.

Many houses dating from the time when Stanmore was a select village survive along Stanmore Hill between later buildings, entrances to closes, and sites awaiting development. Along the west are Elm House, early-18th-century with a later addition, Nunlands, with a 19th-century stucco refacing, Hilldene, the Old House, and the Coach House. Farther up no. 73 is an early-18th-century house of two storeys and attics, parapeted, with a pedimented doorcase and, in the south front, a venetian window. It was called Robin Hill in the 1930s and Loscombe Lodge in 1899, when it became for nearly two years the home of Edward Wilson (1872–1912), the naturalist and Antarctic explorer.[27] Close by a cluster of 19th-century brick cottages and shops, some whitewashed or part weatherboarded, fills the fork between Stanmore Hill and Green Lane.

The east side contains a stuccoed two-storeyed early-19th-century residence, formerly called Raven Dene, which has been divided; Doric columns flank the central porch, facing Stangate Gardens, and a balustrade surmounts the centre of the west front. Higher up are Ivy Cottage (no. 52) and the Abercorn Arms, a three-storeyed pedimented building of

c. 1800 in red brick, with a verandah along the end facing the road and an extension, built about 100 years later, to the north. Near the crest of the hill on Little Common are more 19th-century cottages, many with black diapering on their brickwork. Other cottages border the road next to the Vine, a two-storeyed yellow-brick building of *c.* 1800. Almost opposite is the 18th-century Hill House, built of red brick with stone dressings and comprising a para-peted main block of two storeys with pedimented one-storeyed wings; the house has been much altered and divided into flats.[28] To its north stand the Rookery, pink-brick and early-18th-century, with its stable range and the premises of the brewery.

On the north side of Wood Lane near the corner with Stanmore Hill, high walls, a lodge, and massive gate pillars guard the approach to Stanmore Hall.[29] After its conveyance by Thomas Teed to Matthew John Rhodes in 1842 the house was resited,[30] so as to command south-easterly views. It was bought by Teed's son-in-law Robert Hollond, M.P., in 1847 and became in turn the home of his widow Ellen Julia Hollond, authoress and founder of London's first crèche, who died there in 1884, and of William Knox D'Arcy, who made one fortune from Austra-lian gold and another from Iranian oil. D'Arcy bought the estate in 1889, greatly enlarged the house, decorated the interior, and landscaped and lavishly stocked the gardens. The house was used as assize courts after D'Arcy's death in 1917,[31] by United States troops in the Second World War, and as a nurses' home for the Royal National Orthopaedic hospital in 1947. It stood empty in 1972, having been vacated by the hospital in the previous year.[32]

Stanmore Hall is an impressive building in the Tudor style, with an intricate silhouette from its tower and many gables; its walls are of Kentish rag and freestone, like those of the lodge, and the roof is of greenish slate.[33] The mid-19th-century house was in the villa-gothic style, having a symmetrical plan with contrived asymmetry in the arrangement of the main elevations. In its enlargement D'Arcy employed Brightwen Binyon as his architect and, apparently simultaneously, William Morris & Co. and Howard & Co. to decorate the interior.[34] Binyon extended the south elevation in sympathy with the original house but added an east front in a Flemish Renaissance style which is continued in Howard's decorations. Most of the work by Morris, which includes a stair-case, ceilings, fireplaces, and mosaic floors, was within the earlier house but the most important feature, the Holy Grail tapestries by Burne-Jones, was for the dining room in the extension.[35]

Farther east along Wood Lane stretches the back of the former Warren House, sold in 1951 by Sir John Fitzgerald and used in 1972 as a hospital, called Springbok House.[36] It is an 18th-century building considerably extended in the Jacobean style.[37] Opposite stands a lodge which belongs to

[23] Ex inf. G.L.C. Hist. Bldgs. Div.; see plate facing p. 241.
[24] Min. of Town and Country Planning, List of Bldgs. (1950).
[25] Except where otherwise stated, the foll. three paras. are based on Pevsner, *Mdx.* 146; Robbins, *Mdx.* 331–2; and Min. of Town and Country Planning, List of Bldgs. (1950).
[26] See below, p. 95.   [27] *D.N.B.*
[28] *Kemp's Dir. Harrow* (1971).
[29] Except where otherwise stated, the foll. two paras. are based on TS. notes on Stanmore Hall *penes* Harrow Cent.

Ref. Libr.; Druett, op. cit. 192–6; and inf. supplied by G.L.C. Dept. of Architecture and Civic Design.
[30] *Handbk. to Harrow on the Hill (1850)*, ed. T. Smith, 16. The new ho. was by J. M. Derick: W. Keane, *Beauties of Mdx.* (1850).
[31] *Who Was Who, 1916–28,* 263.
[32] Ex inf. the sec., Royal Nat. Orthopaedic hosp.
[33] Pevsner, *Mdx.* 146; see below, plate facing p. 160.
[34] See plate facing p. 160.
[35] *Studio,* i. 214–26; iii. 99–101.   [36] See below, p. 105.
[37] Pevsner, *Mdx.* 146; Druett, op. cit. plate facing p. 160.

Limes House, whose drive is reached from a road leading north, across a wooded arm of the Common, towards the Grove. Limes House is a three-storeyed stone-faced mansion probably dating from the 1870s, when outbuildings to the north replaced older ones farther west, but later extended. It was bought with 22 a. from the executors of Sir Frederick Handley Page in 1969 by Limes Country Club.[38] The Grove was remodelled in 1877 by Brightwen Binyon in a half-timbered style similar to that employed by Norman Shaw at Grim's Dyke.[39] It was acquired in 1949 by the General Electric Co., which erected many smaller buildings in the grounds; the house and about 30 a. were occupied by Marconi Space and Defence Systems in 1971.[40]

There were 130 communicants in Great Stanmore in 1547[41] and 82 adult males who took the protestation oath in 1642.[42] The population rose slowly but steadily from 722 in 1801 to 1,318 in 1861. After scarcely changing for 20 years, it reached 1,473 in 1891 and 1,827 ten years later but was no more than 1,849 in 1921. The figure was 2,688 in 1931, giving a density of 1·2 person an acre on the eve of the rapid spread of suburban housing and the absorption of the civil parish into Harrow U.D. In 1951 Stanmore North ward, with an area some 85 per cent larger than that of the old parish, had a population of 17,395. Building in the grounds of old houses allowed numbers to continue to rise, in contrast to the trend in more populous suburbs; there were 19,603 persons in 1961, although the density remained low for Middlesex, at 7·5 an acre.[43]

MANOR AND OTHER ESTATES. Offa, king of Mercia, was said to have included 10 *mansiones* in Stanmore among the lands granted to St. Albans abbey on its foundation *c.* 793.[44] Although Offa's charter, recorded by Matthew Paris, was probably spurious,[45] the abbey's lands in 957 stretched southward across Stanmore as far as the later boundary with Kingsbury.[46] At least some of them were lost before the Conquest, in spite of Thomas Walsingham's story that William I deprived the monks of nearly all their property between Barnet and London.[47] Nine and a half hides at Stanmore were held by Edmer Atule, a thegn of Edward the Confessor, and in 1086 by William I's half-brother Robert, count of Mortain,[48] whose son William had restored them to St. Albans by 1106.[49]

The division of Stanmore, first recorded in Domesday Book, persisted, although it was not until 1274 that the abbey's property was said to lie in Great Stanmore[50] and not until 1354 that it was called the manor of *GREAT STANMORE.*[51] Abbot

Richard (d. 1119) granted the 'town' of Stanmore to Serle and his heirs, in fee farm for 60s. a year.[52] Serle's son Robert of Stanmore exchanged part of the estate in the north with the abbot, by whom it was incorporated into Aldenham (Herts.), and the rest passed to Robert's daughter Marsilia, whose husband, also called Robert, pledged it to a Jewish moneylender. In 1221, when the inheritance was disputed between William, Marsilia's grandson, and Richard de la Grave, descended from a younger son of Serle, St. Albans resumed possession.[53] The rights of William's sisters Maud and Felice were secured by a fine of 1244–5 and those of William's widow Alice and her second husband, John de Ros, in the following year.[54] Aloys of Stanmore, perhaps the son of the younger Robert of Stanmore by a different marriage, quitclaimed his interest at about the same time but regained possession by a writ of mort d'ancestor against Abbot Roger (1260–90), who had mislaid the title deeds.[55] In 1274, however, Aloys's son Robert surrendered all his rights in Great Stanmore to Edward the goldsmith and in 1279 it was agreed between Robert and the abbot that Edward and his heirs should hold the lands, paying 15 marks a year during the lifetime of John Clarel, to whom the abbot had leased the property, and 10 marks thereafter.[56] John de Shorne and his wife Isabel held the estate in 1307[57] and in 1349 Walter de Shorne conveyed his interest in Broadcroft, Hall mead, and other lands in Great Stanmore to Roger Wendout, who was probably acting for the Francis family of London. In 1354 Walter's son John de Shorne released to Ellis Francis and Thomas de Loughtborough all his claims in the manor, which they had acquired from Simon Francis.[58] Simon died in 1358, seised jointly with his wife Maud of the manor of Great Stanmore.[59] In 1362 the prior of St. Bartholomew's, Smithfield, was licensed to acquire the manor in mortmain from David of Wooler, Keeper of the Rolls of Chancery, who was to have had the reversion on Maud's death.[60]

St. Bartholomew's priory, which already held the manor of Little Stanmore, in 1359 had been licensed to acquire other lands in Great Stanmore:[61] a house and 168 a. from Hugh de la More of Carleton, chaplain, and 20 a. from John de Affebrigge.[62] In 1392 the abbot of St. Albans was permitted to receive 5 marks for the manor of Great Stanmore whenever the priory of St. Bartholomew's was vacant, since he had been paid a relief of twice the rent on the death of each tenant before the priory's acquisition in mortmain.[63] In 1535 St. Bartholomew's, which drew profits of £20 a year from all its property in Great Stanmore, was still paying the old rent of 10 marks (£6 13s. 4d.) to St. Albans.[64]

[38] Ex inf. Clarke & Hale (Pinner).
[39] Harrow Cent. Ref. Libr., sales parts.
[40] Ex inf. Marconi Space and Defence Systems Ltd.
[41] E 301/34/172.
[42] H.L., Mdx. Protestation Rets.
[43] Census, 1801–1961.
[44] Cart. Sax. ed. Birch, i, p. 373.
[45] P. H. Sawyer, Anglo-Saxon Charters, pp. 105–6.
[46] P.N.Mdx. (E.P.N.S.), 219.
[47] Thos. Walsingham, Gesta Abbatum (Rolls Ser.), ed. H. T. Riley, i. 50.
[48] V.C.H. Mdx. i. 103, 125.
[49] Regesta Regum Anglo-Normannorum, ii, ed. C. Johnson and H. A. Cronne, no. 741.
[50] Cal. Close, 1272–9, 224.

[51] Ft. of F. Lond. & Mdx. i. 134.
[52] Walsingham, Gesta Abbatum, i. 72.
[53] C. F. Baylis, Edgware and the Stanmores, 21–2; Cur. Reg. R. x. 252–3.
[54] Ft. of F. Lond. & Mdx. i. 29, 30.
[55] Walsingham, Gesta Abbatum, i. 466–7.
[56] Cal. Close, 1272–9, 224; Ft. of F. Lond. & Mdx. i. 55.
[57] Baylis, op. cit. 23.
[58] Cal. Close, 1346–9, 614; 1354–60, 96.
[59] Cal. Inq. p.m. x, p. 349.
[60] Cal. Pat. 1381–4, 141.
[61] Cal. Pat. 1358–61, 185.
[62] E. A. Webb, Recs. of St. Bartholomew's, Smithfield, i. 166.
[63] Ibid. 348.
[64] Ibid. 407.

Geoffrey Chamber, formerly chief steward for St. Bartholomew's in Great Stanmore[65] and from 1536 surveyor and receiver-general in the Court of Augmentations,[66] leased the manor for 15 years in 1538, acquitting the prior of payments to St. Albans.[67] Great Stanmore was among the manors granted for life to Robert Fuller, the last prior, in 1540,[68] the year after his surrender of the house, but it was granted to Chamber and his heirs in 1542.[69] Chamber sold some of his property there to Sir Pedro de Gamboa, a Spanish mercenary in the royal service, in the same year[70] and died in 1544, heavily in debt to the Crown.[71] The manor and its lands were forfeited and in 1547, when they covered 276½ a., they were granted to Gamboa in tail male, together with the land bought from Chamber in 1542.[72] Great Stanmore escheated on Gamboa's murder in 1550,[73] when it was leased to Sir George Blage at a rent which was slightly reduced after some lands had been granted to Hugh Losse, lord of Little Stanmore, in 1552.[74] Chamber's last surviving son Edward, an exiled Roman Catholic priest, vainly claimed the manor as late as 1593 and ascribed the Crown's refusal to sell it to the existence of a rightful heir.[75] Leases were made to Blage's widow Dorothy in 1563[76] and, in reversion, to Thomas Marshe in 1576.[77] Marshe had conveyed his interest by 1587–8 to John Kaye, clerk of the Green Cloth,[78] whose son John obtained a lease in reversion in 1594[79] but assigned it to John Burnell, a clothworker of London,[80] c. 1599.[81]

In 1604 the lordship of Great Stanmore was sold in reversion for £600 to Sir Thomas Lake, a secretary of state, who already held Little Stanmore. A fee farm rent was reserved to the Crown but granted in 1623 to the chapter of Westminster.[82] Lake's son, another Sir Thomas, secured possession in 1638 by buying in the Burnells' lease from Anne Rewse, widow of John Burnell's son and namesake. After the younger Sir Thomas's death in 1653[83] the children of his first marriage, Thomas, Dorothy, and Elizabeth, claimed that Great Stanmore had been among the estates settled by their grandfather for 60 years and therefore that the profits could not be withheld because of any conveyance to their uncle, the earl of Rutland, who was in league with their step-mother.[84] More prolonged discord arose when the two sisters, supported by their uncle Sir Lancelot Lake of Canons, alleged that Thomas, who married while still a minor, was under the influence of his brother-in-law William Bockenham, formerly their father's steward.[85] Thomas mortgaged the

manor to Thomas Mann, an associate of Bockenham, in 1661[86] and died in 1662, leaving Great Stanmore to his widow Mary and Bockenham. After further litigation[87] Bockenham in 1663 agreed to sell most of the demesne lands to Sir Lancelot and to pay £9,000 to Dorothy and Elizabeth Lake.[88] The remaining lands, with the manor-house, were left to Bockenham and his co-feoffees, in whose names courts were held in 1664 and 1666.[89] Attempts by Thomas Lake and Bockenham to raise money encumbered the estate with many conflicting claims throughout the 1660s and 1670s, although as a result of one of Bockenham's mortgages possession passed to Mary Lake shortly before her second marriage, to Richard (later Sir Richard) May, a baron of the Exchequer.[90] May held the manor by 1668[91] and mortgaged it in 1679 to Dame Barbara Wyndham. Both Bockenham and May evidently conveyed their interests to a London embroiderer, Matthew Smith, and other trustees, in whose names courts were held in 1679–80.[92]

Matthew Smith, hoping to entail the manor on his eldest grandson Thomas, empowered the trustees to sell some property to redeem the mortgage. Part was accordingly sold, with the consent of Smith's widow Margaret, to John and William Powell in 1681. The manor itself changed hands but unspecified lands were retained, to be disputed among Smith's heirs at least until 1713. John Powell, a London vintner, was the sole lord from 1685 to 1700, when he was followed by John Rogers.[93] Differences arose between Rogers and Warwick Lake of Canons over the payment of the fee farm rent to Westminster abbey: Rogers, maintaining that most of the charge should be borne by the Lakes, alleged that Sir Lancelot had bought as much as two-thirds of the demesne lands, leaving only 150 a. to the lords of Great Stanmore.[94]

In 1714 the manor was acquired from John Rogers by Humphrey Walcot,[95] presumably on behalf of his patron James Brydges, earl of Carnarvon and from 1719 duke of Chandos.[96] In 1715 Great and Little Stanmore were united under the Brydges family, as they had been under the Lakes. After the third duke's death in 1789[97] courts were held for his widow Anne Eliza, a lunatic whose estates were leased out under an Act of 1793,[98] and in 1795 for his daughter Lady Anna Elizabeth Brydges, *de jure* Baroness Kinloss. Anna Elizabeth in 1796 married Richard Nugent-Temple-Grenville, Earl Temple, who in 1813 succeeded as marquess of Buckingham and in 1822 was created duke of Buckingham and Chandos. His

[65] Webb, *Recs. of St. Barts.* i. 383.
[66] W. C. Richardson, *Hist. of Court of Augmentations*, 53, 493.
[67] E 303/9/223.
[68] *L. & P. Hen. VIII*, xvi, p. 716.
[69] *Ft. of F. Lond. & Mdx.* ii. 58.
[70] *L. & P. Hen. VIII*, xxi(2), p. 419.
[71] Richardson, op. cit. 116.
[72] *L. & P. Hen. VIII*, xxi(2), p. 419.
[73] John Stow, *Annales of England* (1631), 603.
[74] *Cal. Pat. 1560–3*, 608.
[75] *Cal. S.P. Dom. 1591–4*, 400; *1595–7*, 359.
[76] *Cal. Pat. 1560–3*, 608.
[77] M.R.O., Acc. 262/15 (documents unnumbered): copy of grant (1604).
[78] M.R.O., Acc. 262/15: survey (1587/8).
[79] Hist. MSS. Com. 9, *Hatfield*, iv, p. 341; M.R.O., Acc. 262/15: copy of grant (1604).
[80] P. Davenport, *Old Stanmore*, 101.
[81] C 2/Chas. I/B 36/62.

[82] M.R.O., Acc. 262/15; *Cal. S.P. Dom. 1623–5*, 135.
[83] Davenport, *Old Stanmore*, 16.   [84] C 7/426/73.
[85] Davenport, *Old Stanmore*, 16.
[86] C.P. 25(2)/689/13 Chas. II Hil. Mdx.
[87] C 6/159/89; C 6/159/91.
[88] M.R.O., Acc. 262/17: case of Mr. Rogers.
[89] Davenport MSS., Gt. Stan. ct. rolls 1664, 1666.
[90] C 5/61/10; M.R.O., Acc. 262/15: answer of Sir Lancelot Lake (1671); C 5/446/25.
[91] M.R.O., Acc. 262/16a, f. 9.
[92] C 6/261/73; Davenport MSS., Gt. Stan. ct. rolls.
[93] C 6/261/73; C 5/631/49; Davenport MSS., Gt. Stan. ct. rolls.
[94] M.R.O., Acc. 262/17: case of Mr. Rogers.
[95] Davenport MSS., Gt. Stan. ct. rolls; Lysons, *Environs*, iii. 394.
[96] C. H. C. and M. I. Baker, *Life and Circumstances of James Brydges, First Duke of Chandos*, 12–13.
[97] M.R.O., Acc. 943.
[98] M.R.O., Acc. 262/57/3 [33 Geo. III, c.79 (Priv. Act)].

son, Richard Plantagenet Temple-Nugent-Brydges-Chandos-Grenville, succeeded in 1839 and sold the manor in 1840 to James Hamilton, marquess (later duke) of Abercorn[99] and owner of Bentley Priory.[1] In 1863 the manor was bought by John Kelk (later Sir John Kelk, Bt.),[2] the railway engineer, who in 1882 sold it to Thomas Clutterbuck of Micklefield Hall, Rickmansworth (Herts.).[3]

The Clutterbucks had held property in the parish at least since 1749, when a messuage was granted to Thomas Clutterbuck, a brewer.[4] In 1762 he had acquired the Vine at the top of Stanmore Hill and in 1763, on behalf of his son Thomas, a brewery which stood a few yards farther north on the opposite, western, side of the road.[5] Although not large land-owners in Great Stanmore, the family had acquired many buildings, including the Crown in 1769, the Black Horse on a lease in 1851, and the Load of Hay in 1868, as well as many wastehold parcels.[6] The purchaser of the manor was described as of Great Stanmore in 1844, of Red Hall (Herts.) in 1847, and of Micklefield Hall in 1851.[7] The manor passed in 1895 to his son Thomas Meadows Clutterbuck (d. 1919) and to his grandson Captain Rupert Clutterbuck (d. 1933), both of Micklefield Hall.[8] Many manorial rights were sold in the 1920s, including those in the common and Stanmore marsh, for which Hendon R.D.C. paid £1,000 in 1929.[9] The last rights were extinguished by Captain Clutterbuck's widow and her co-executor, in whom the manor was vested, in 1935–6.[10]

According to Thomas Walsingham a manor-house was built by John, abbot of St. Albans 1235–60.[11] Presumably it occupied the moated site in the medieval village, south of the vanished St. Mary's church, between Old Church Lane on the east and the Stanburn on the west.[12] Four sides of the moat enclosed a rick-yard in 1838[13] but only two survived in 1865.[14] Traces were visible in private gardens on the northern corner of Old Church Lane and Wolverton Road in the 1930s.[15] The 'capital mansion-house' recorded in 1587–8[16] may have been a new building, ancestor of the later Manor House which stood at the northern end of Old Church Lane, opposite the Rectory. John Burnell (d. 1605) was said by his son to have spent over £800 in reconstructing and repairing his residence there.[17] It was assessed at 16 hearths in 1664,[18] again restored in 1682 and much altered in the 18th or early 19th century,[19] but was leased out after its acquisition by the owners of Canons:

Humphrey Walcot held the lease for two lives in 1734[20] and there was a yearly tenant in 1837, when the house and 14 a. were put up for sale.[21] Later occupants of the Manor House, which was demolished in 1930,[22] included Mrs. Sperling, Eugene Noel, and Charles Hartridge.[23] The so-called New Manor House, farther south in the same road and opposite the junction with Gordon Avenue, was merely a lavish Tudor-style remodelling, dating from 1930–3, of a late Victorian residence, the Croft. At the expense of Samuel Wallrock many ancient materials were incorporated in the new house[24] and in Church House, a range of former outbuildings to the north which included a banqueting room afterwards used as a church hall.[25] The New Manor House was bought with 5½ a. by the Ministry of Defence in 1940[26] and was used as a residence for senior officers in 1971.[27]

In 1838 the Drummond family held 408 a. in Great Stanmore, twice as much as the next largest landowner, the duke of Buckingham and Chandos,[28] and part of a 1,406-acre estate which stretched westward into Harrow Weald. The Drummonds' connexion with the parish was foreshadowed in 1725, when the duke of Chandos opened an account at the Charing Cross bank of Andrew Drummond, founder of the family's fortune.[29] In 1729 Andrew was admitted to a copyhold tenement called Hodgkins, which he had bought from John Shepherd, a London merchant.[30] Many subsequent purchases were made by Andrew, who died in 1769 seised of at least 56 a. of copyhold land,[31] including three of the manor's head tenements.[32] Small parcels of waste were added by Andrew's son John (d. 1774) and John's son George (d. 1789).[33]

By 1788 the estate included Belmont, a mound constructed by the first duke of Chandos and surmounted by a summer-house which terminated the vista along the western avenue from Canons. Andrew Drummond is said to have lived at Belmont but it is more likely that his early home was south-west of the church, on the site of a Palladian mansion begun in 1763 by John Vardy and completed by Sir William Chambers.[34] The mansion later was mistakenly known as Belmont[35] and was called Stanmore House in 1816, when it was occupied by the Countess of Aylesford. Lord Castlereagh is said to have lived there for a short time,[36] presumably, like Lady Aylesford, as the tenant of George Drummond's spendthrift son, George Harley Drummond (d. 1855). The mansion

[99] M.R.O., Acc. 943; Acc. 658/5; *Complete Peerage*, s.v. Buckingham, Abercorn.
[1] *V.C.H. Mdx.* iv. 206.
[2] M.R.O., Acc. 502/34.
[3] M.R.O., Acc. 658/2, f. 278.
[4] M.R.O., Acc. 943, ff. 42–3.
[5] Davenport MSS., Gt. Stan. ct. rolls.
[6] Ibid. 1769; M.R.O., Acc. 943, f. 154 and passim; Acc. 658/5, passim; /6, passim.
[7] M.R.O., Acc. 658/5, f. 325; /6, ff. 58, 107.
[8] Druett, *Stanmores and Harrow Weald*, 163.
[9] M.R.O., Acc. 658/7, ff. 257–9, passim.
[10] Ibid. ff. 261–5.
[11] *Gesta Abbatum*, i. 315.
[12] Druett, op. cit. 77–8 and map facing p. 32.
[13] M.R.O., TA/S'MORE Gt.
[14] O.S. Map 6", Mdx. V. SE. (1865 edn.).
[15] Druett, op. cit. 78.
[16] M.R.O., Acc. 262/15: survey (1587/8).
[17] C 2/Chas. I/B 36/62. [18] M.R.O., MR/TH/5.
[19] Davenport, *Old Stanmore*, plate VI.
[20] M.R.O., Acc. 262/17 (documents unnumbered): Earl Temple's abstract of title.

[21] M.R.O., Acc. 262/23(a).
[22] Druett, op. cit. 210; Davenport, op. cit. plate VI.
[23] *Kelly's Dirs. Mdx.* (1867, 1882, 1908).
[24] Davenport, op. cit. plate VII; Druett, op. cit. 210–11. For Wallrock, see newspaper cutting *penes* Harrow Cent. Ref. Libr.
[25] Harrow Cent. Ref. Libr., photographs and newspaper cutting.
[26] Ex inf. the Defence Land Agent.
[27] Ex inf. R.A.F. Stanmore Pk.
[28] M.R.O., TA/S'MORE Gt.
[29] Bolitho and Peel, *Drummonds of Charing Cross*, 112, 36.
[30] Davenport MSS., Gt. Stan. ct. roll.
[31] Ibid. 1769.
[32] See p. 100.
[33] M.R.O., Acc. 943, ff. 19–20, 136–7.
[34] *Drummonds of Charing Cross*, 36–7, 111, App. III. The successive façades by Vardy and Chambers are illus., ibid., plates 6 and 16. See also J. Harris, *Sir William Chambers*, 247 and plate 67.
[35] *Ambulator* (1792, 1820).
[36] Brewer, *Beauties of Eng. and Wales*, x(5), 630.

stood in extensive grounds, which form the setting for Zoffany's painting of Andrew Drummond's family;[37] in 1838 they included South park, 87 a. extending from Temple pond to Belmont, and North park, 66 a. including Boot pond, north of Uxbridge Road. Park or Home farm, west of the mansion, and Old Church farm also formed part of the Drummonds' property,[38] which was bought by the marquess of Abercorn, as the Stanmore Park estate, in 1839.[39] Abercorn, having his own seat at Bentley Priory, sold the Stanmore mansion in 1848 to George Carr Glyn, later Lord Wolverton (d. 1873), a partner in Glyn, Mills & Co. The house, after some 50 years as a boys' preparatory school, was sold with 56 a. and pulled down in 1938[40] to make way for no. 3 Balloon Centre of the Royal Auxiliary Air Force. The site was occupied in turn by Balloon Command H.Q., and by groups of Transport Command and Fighter Command. In 1971 Stanmore Park was a station in no. 11 (Fighter) Group of Strike Command, whose headquarters were at Bentley Priory,[41] although part of the old park survived as Stanmore golf course.

When the earl of Abercorn bought Bentley Priory in 1788,[42] its grounds already encroached from Harrow into Stanmore. In 1795 the marquess of Abercorn was licensed to inclose part of the turnpike road which led north-west across Stanmore Common, with some adjoining waste-land, on condition that he made a new road and did not build anything other than 'lodges, temples and other ornamental buildings' of an approved design.[43] His grandson and heir thus already held 97 a. in the north-west of the parish,[44] before he bought the Drummonds' property and other lands, with the lordship, from the duke of Buckingham and Chandos's estates. Aylwards,[45] east of the Bentley Priory grounds, was acquired in 1842.[46] All the lands were mortgaged,[47] however, and the sale of Stanmore Park was followed by that of extensive farm-land in the south, whose purchase by St. Bartholomew's hospital was completed after three years in 1856.[48] The parkland attached to Bentley Priory was conveyed in 1857 to John Kelk, whose purchase of Aylwards at the same time as that of the manor ended Great Stanmore's connexion with a family which, twenty years earlier, had owned nearly half the parish.[49]

The Stanmore lands bought by St. Bartholomew's hospital comprised Kenton Lane, Old Church, and Marsh farms. Apart from a farm-house at the corner of Marsh Lane they formed a compact block which amounted to 808 a. in 1857, when it was by far the largest of the hospital's estates in Middlesex. No more than 440 a., however, were in Great Stanmore, for part of Marsh farm lay in Little Stanmore and most of Kenton Lane farm in Harrow.[50] The homestead of Marsh farm was sold with 7 a. to Dr. Begg of Canons in 1863 and a small additional purchase was made in 1864[51] but much of the property, because of its value as building land, was retained after a general decision to dispose of the hospital's country estates in 1919.[52] The first sales took place in 1926 and the last, to John Laing & Co., the biggest purchasers, in 1934.[53]

ECONOMIC HISTORY. AGRICULTURE. In 1086 Great Stanmore was assessed at 9½ hides, which included land for 7 ploughs, pasture for the cattle of the vill, and woodland for 800 pigs. The value had fallen from £10 T.R.E. to 10s. when Robert of Mortain received it, but had risen to 60s. at the time of the Domesday survey. The lord had 2 ploughs and room for one more on his 6½-hide demesne, and his tenants had 1½ plough, with room for 2½ more. The tenants consisted of a priest, who had ½ hide, 4 villeins each on one virgate, 2 more on one virgate, 3 cottars on 10 a., and 3 others on 1 a.[54]

The lord occupied Great Stanmore manor-house and lands totalling 40 a. in 1587–8. The remaining 362 a. in demesne, including 45 a. in Harrow parish, were divided among 17 tenants, whose holdings ranged from 88 a. to a single acre, fourteen of them being less than 30 a. Four freeholders owed quit-rents totalling 9s. 8d. and copyholders paid a total of £1 13s. 8d. for 20 holdings,[55] which included 13 of the head tenements.[56] By 1714, after the manorial estate had been divided and the demesne reduced to 208 a., as many as 109 a. were in hand. The remainder was farmed by five tenants, four of them tenants at will and the largest enjoying a lease for 21 years.[57] Much of the duke of Chandos's land, covering 778 a. or slightly more than half of the parish, was let on 21-year leases from the 1730s,[58] when his chief farming tenants were Samuel Ward, who leased some 161 a., and William Street of Old Church farm, who leased 175 a.[59] Few enfranchisements took place before the mid 19th century.[60]

The parish contained 1,333 a. of farm-land in 1867,[61] by which time the tenant of Old Church farm lived in the former homestead of Ward's farm. From 1871 he also leased 199 a. of Marsh farm, stretching into Little Stanmore, after the sale of its farm-house and 7 a. by St. Bartholomew's hospital. Old Church and Marsh farms, at first together covering 376 a.,[62] continued to be leased to a single tenant until the break-up of the hospital's estates.[63] In 1897 Great Stanmore had 967 a. of farm-land, divided among 19 farmers or small-holders. In 1917 there were 20 returns for 847 a., sixteen of them for holdings of under 20 a.[64]

None of the head tenements bore a personal name

[37] Drummonds of Charing Cross, plate 4.
[38] M.R.O., TA/S'MORE Gt.
[39] Drummonds of Charing Cross, 111–12.
[40] Druett, Stanmores and Harrow Weald, 203, 206–7.
[41] R.A.F. Stanmore Pk. Inf. Handbk. 19, 47–8.
[42] V.C.H. Mdx. iv. 206.
[43] M.R.O., Acc. 943, ff. 132, 181–2.
[44] M.R.O., TA/S'MORE Gt.   [45] See p. 100.
[46] M.R.O., Acc. 658/5, f. 313.
[47] M.R.O., Acc. 502/24; /25.
[48] Ibid. /31; St. Barts. Hosp., Journals of Governors, Ha 1/20, pp. 415, 478; Ha 1/21, p. 229.
[49] M.R.O., Acc. 502/34.
[50] St. Barts. Hosp., map of Stanmore estate, Hc 1916A/49.

[51] St. Barts. Hosp., Ha 1/22, pp. 200, 296, 373, 380.
[52] St. Barts. Hosp., Ha 1/30, p. 354.
[53] Ibid. pp. 354, 369, 418; Ha 1/31, pp. 8, 19, 57, 109, 232–3.
[54] V.C.H. Mdx. i. 125.
[55] M.R.O., Acc. 262(15).   [56] See below.
[57] M.R.O., Acc. 262(17): survey.
[58] M.R.O., Acc. 262/72/1; Acc. 262(17): leases.
[59] M.R.O., Acc. 262/71/1.
[60] M.R.O., Acc. 658/6; /7.   [61] M.A.F. 68/136.
[62] St. Barts. Hosp., EO 8/6, pp. 32, 117.
[63] See above.
[64] M.A.F. 68/1675; M.A.F. 68/2815. In 1917 eight holdings were of 5 a. or less, which would not have been included in returns before 1892.

which persisted into the 16th century save Aylwards, named from the Aylward or Ayleworth family recorded from 1489 to 1586.[65] By 1679 some had already been divided and one, Pathsgate otherwise Brains,[66] had come to form two head tenements. In that year there were 15: Fiddles, Pathsgate, Montagues, Thrums, Pynnacles, Mackerels, Aylwards, Rooks, and Buggs were described as houses or tenements, while Barretts, Heriots Wood, Brooks, Simrookes, Brains, and Cock Allens were merely fields.[67]

Four men held the 13 head tenements recorded in 1587–8.[68] The families in whose hands the head tenements had become concentrated were also represented in neighbouring parishes and comprised both yeomen and gentry.[69] Richard Franklin, who held Fiddles, had a cousin and namesake who was a leading tenant in Little Stanmore.[70] Thomas Nicholl, who held five head tenements, came from a widespread family related to the Franklins.[71] Thomas Norwood of Pinner, holding land in Great Stanmore in the right of his wife Joan, had surrendered five head tenements and parcels of two others in 1582 and 1583 to his son Warner Norwood. The parcels were held in 1587–8 by Joan Norwood's son and Warner's half-brother Thomas Tailor, who also held yet another head tenement. Franklin's head tenement, and seven of those held by Nicholl, the Norwoods, and Tailor, were acquired in the 17th century by the Burnells.[72] By 1679 only two men held as many as two head tenements.[73] Edward Norwood the elder, Edward Norwood the younger, and John Norwood, a substantial landowner in Pinner,[74] each had one of the head tenements formerly held by Warner Norwood, Nathaniel Nicholl had two of those which had been held by Thomas Nicholl, and John Burnell had two which had been held by his uncle Thomas Burnell. The Burnells ceased to hold any head tenements after surrenders by John Burnell's daughter Elizabeth Webb in 1692 and 1700. A Thomas Nicholl of Watford held Nathaniel's former head tenements in 1730 and Ruth Norwood of Guildford (Surr.), widow of Richard Norwood, surrendered one of the Norwoods' holdings as late as 1736. Another had already been surrendered by the younger Edward's daughter Priscilla Norwood in 1711 and a third, Aylwards, had passed to Priscilla's cousin William Boys, whose family held the Norwoods' lands in Pinner[75] and retained Aylwards until 1822. Six head tenements were not recorded as such after the early 18th century. Four others were bought by Andrew Drummond and presumably passed with the Drummonds' estate to Lord Abercorn.[76]

The lord, Geoffrey Chamber, claimed in 1544 that any homage should be forfeit if it had fallen into decay.[77] In 1679 a homage of nine, including six head tenants, swore that a best beast was owed as heriot for a single head tenement and 3s. 6d. for any

others. Undersetters were to pay rent to the head tenant, as before, rather than to the lord's steward who had admitted them. Copyholders wishing to alienate property must surrender it to two head tenants, who were to present the surrender at the next court baron on pain of forfeiting their own holdings.[78] The homage also repeated a presentment of 1664 that, if an underset holding was to be sold, the head tenant should have time in which to buy it for the price offered by the third party. In 1725 several lawyers pointed out that the homage of 1679 had been unrepresentative; the lord had been denied his proper heriots and the claim to buy back undersets was attributed to one head tenant's desire to be paid a commission for agreeing to a sale. Chandos's own steward thought it wrong that sales should be held up without good security[79] but, despite the many doubts, no new custumal was drawn up. Sums of £7 and £15, in lieu of live beasts, were paid on entering head tenements as late as 1846 and 1858.[80]

Head tenements and undersets were heritable by females,[81] although in 1679 they could not be vested in widows, whose yearly income would be assessed on the lands by the homage. Guardians were to be appointed for heirs under the age of fourteen. The lord received a relief of a year's rent for copyhold land and one year's rent when it was alienated. Copyhold land could not be sublet for more than three years without licence: in 1664 Hester Burnell forfeited her head tenement, Fiddles, for making a long lease to her son John, who, however, was soon readmitted.[82] Leases for terms of 21 years or less were often licensed from the 17th to the 19th centuries.

Parishioners were forbidden to pasture any sheep other than their own in 1684 and were repeatedly fined for overburdening the common. In 1640 grazing rights for 20 sheep and 4 steers were allowed to a head tenant and for half that number to an under-tenant, as well as 5 sheep for every acre of leyland and 3 for every acre of fallow. A different custom was asserted in 1646, permitting all tenants to graze 2 sheep for an acre of arable, 5 for an acre of meadow, and 3 for an acre of leyland. Pigs were to be yoked from Christmas until harvest time and always to be kept ringed, according to an order often repeated from 1580.[83]

By 1714 grassland exceeded arable. Some 60 a. of the lands in hand were meadow and 36 a. were arable. The largest block of demesne lands leased out, 44 a. with Warren House, was arable, but the four other demesne holdings consisted entirely of grassland.[84] Meadow predominated on the holdings of the duke of Chandos's most substantial tenants, Samuel Ward and William Street.[85] By 1798 arable covered 300 a. out of the 1,400 a. in the parish, more than twice as much as in Little Stanmore.[86] Grass was reckoned to cover 850 a., the remaining 250 a. being waste. The rector probably underestimated the area

[65] Davenport MSS., Gt. Stan. wills (com. ct. of Lond.); Prob. 11/9 (P.C.C. 26 Dogett).
[66] M.R.O., Acc. 262(15).
[67] M.R.O., Acc. 262(16).
[68] M.R.O., Acc. 262(15).
[69] Except where otherwise stated, the para. is based on Davenport MSS., Gt. Stan. ct. rolls.
[70] See p. 118.
[71] See p. 68.
[72] See p. 97.
[73] M.R.O., Acc. 262(16).
[74] V.C.H. Mdx. iv. 213.
[75] Ibid.
[76] See p. 99.
[77] C 1/961/15.
[78] M.R.O., Acc. 262(16).
[79] Davenport MSS., Gt. Stan. ct. rolls.
[80] M.R.O., Acc. 658/6, ff. 19, 184.
[81] Davenport MSS., Gt. Stan. ct. rolls.
[82] Ibid.; M.R.O., Acc. 262(16).
[83] Davenport MSS., Gt. Stan. ct. rolls.
[84] M.R.O., Acc. 262(17).
[85] M.R.O., Acc. 262/72/1.
[86] Middleton, View, 560.

under crops, at 163 a., in 1801,[87] for in 1867 there were still 124 a., excluding fields of clover or temporary grasses, compared with 1,208 a. under grass.[88] The last arable on Old Church farm, 36 a., and on Marsh farm, 78 a., was laid down to grass between 1857 and 1871, when the tenant was forbidden to reconvert it.[89] Arable had dwindled to 28 a. by 1897 and 16 a. by 1917, while grassland slowly shrank from 939 a. to 831 a.[90]

Beans, covering 92 a., were the largest crop in 1801, when corn was grown on about 60 a.[91] By 1867 there were corn on 48 a., beans on 14 a., and potatoes on 24 a. Sheep were the main livestock in that year, when 1,044 were kept. By 1897 there were no more than 68,[92] presumably because of a wet season in 1879–80 which had caused the loss of the entire flock, upwards, of 1,000 sheep, on Old Church and Marsh farms.[93] London's demand for hay was still high, so that 634 a. or some two-thirds of the farm-land supported grass for mowing, whereas slightly under 300 a. were devoted to grazing. The number of cattle fell from 132 in 1867 to 95 in 1897 but hardly changed during the next 20 years. There were as many as 374 sheep in 1917, when 467 a. were devoted to hay and 355 a. to pasture.[94]

WOODS. St. Bartholomew's priory leased or sold woods separately, as in Little Stanmore, during the early 16th century.[95] Geoffrey Chamber claimed the forfeiture of Heriots wood in 1544, after over 100 large trees had been felled, but he was opposed by the homage and forced to sue his tenant.[96] In 1679 the homage claimed that a copyhold tenant by inheritance could fell the timber on his land without licence but that no one holding for life, for a term of years, or in the right of another could do so. Any tenant who had planted trees on the waste, to shelter his property, was free to lop them.[97]

In 1520 there was a dispute over Wapats or Wabbetts wood, which, with woods and hedgerows in Little Stanmore, had been sold by St. Bartholomew's at least 8 years previously.[98] Wabbetts wood, adjoining the common, covered 20 a. in the late 17th century, when it was the only woodland on the demesne.[99] By 1838 the parish had 83 a. of woodland. A quarter of it consisted of patches in Stanmore Park belonging to George Harley Drummond but the largest block, 19 a., lay along the Watford road north-west of the brewery in Lord Abercorn's Bentley Priory estate.[1]

MILLS. There was a mill at Stanmore, presumably Great Stanmore, in 1352.[2] Two horse-mills and a windmill, late of St. Bartholomew's priory, were granted with the manor to Pedro de Gamboa in 1547 but were not recorded at any later date.[3] A 'little house called a mill-house' was claimed by a customary tenant in 1665.[4]

TRADE AND INDUSTRY. A tailor, mentioned in 1613, a victualler, indicted in 1617,[5] and a butcher whose offal fouled the highway in 1637,[6] were the only tradesmen recorded until the 19th century. Commercial life was more restricted than in Little Stanmore, with its houses lining Edgware Road. In 1801 Great Stanmore contained 89 persons employed in trade or crafts, 100 on the land, and 533 in other occupations, most of them presumably in domestic service. Thirty years later, after the population had exactly doubled, there were 71 families in trade or crafts, no more than 36 in agriculture, and 99 in other callings.[7] Apart from the brewery,[8] the largest employer in 1851 was a builder called John Chapman, who had 18 workmen at his yard next to Montagues, on the south side of the high road.[9]

Mid-19th-century Stanmore offered many of the services of a small town. Householders following the commoner trades included 12 carpenters or sawyers, 6 grocers, 6 bakers, and 7 boot-makers, some of them employing one or two assistants. Several women, apart from 4 householders, practised dress-making to serve the neighbourhood's many rich residents and retired people. More specialized tradesmen included a 'historical engraver', whose customers presumably were drawn from a wide area, a fish-monger, a chimney-sweep, a hair-dresser, a book-seller, and a watch-maker.[10]

In 1851 James Wilshin employed 30 men at the Clutterbucks' Stanmore brewery, at the top of Stanmore Hill.[11] Since the buildings stood almost opposite the Vine, which Thomas Clutterbuck acquired in 1763, they probably included the brewhouse to which Clutterbuck had been admitted in 1749.[12] Brewing was discontinued in 1916,[13] whereupon the main building became a bottle-store until the premises were sold by Capt. T. R. Clutterbuck to Harold Pattisson Cole in 1926. Thereafter they were used by H. Pattisson & Co., who employed 60 persons in designing and manufacturing turf maintenance and golf course equipment in 1971.[14] The 18th-century buildings in that year comprised a private house, offices, and a factory in the former brewery. All were of red brick, the old brewery being surmounted by a weatherboarded clock-tower, with a cupola and a bell dated 1726.

After the Grove and its estate had been acquired by the General Electric Co. in 1949,[15] many buildings for research and development were erected on behalf of the Ministry of Supply. They were used in 1971 by Marconi Space and Defence Systems, a part of G.E.C.-Marconi Electronics, whose 1,100 employees made it the largest firm in Great Stanmore.[16]

Other industries have been confined to the south of the parish where Honeypot Lane, continuing into Kingsbury, was built in the early 1930s.[17] Eight firms occupied sites along the east side of Honeypot Lane in 1971, when lack of space had forced some

[87] H.O. 67/16.
[88] M.A.F. 68/136.
[89] St. Barts. Hosp., EO 8/6, pp. 59–60.
[90] M.A.F. 68/1675; M.A.F. 68/2815.   [91] H.O. 67/16.
[92] M.A.F. 68/136; M.A.F. 68/1675.
[93] St. Barts. Hosp., EO 8/6, p. 188.
[94] M.A.F. 68/136; M.A.F. 68/1675; M.A.F. 68/2815.
[95] See p. 119.   [96] C 1/961/15.
[97] Req. 2/3/184.   [98] M.R.O., TA/S'MORE Gt.
[99] Davenport MSS., Gt. Stan. ct. roll.
[1] M.R.O., TA/S'MORE Gt.
[2] K.B. 9/66/19.

[3] L. & P. Hen. VIII, xxi(2), p. 419.
[4] Davenport MSS., Gt. Stan. ct. rolls.
[5] Davenport MSS., Gt. Stan. ct. rolls.
[6] Mdx. Sess. Recs. i. 234; iv. 160.
[7] Census, 1801, 1831.   [8] See below.
[9] H.O. 107/1700/135/2.
[10] Ibid.   [11] Ibid.
[12] See p. 98.
[13] F. A. King, Story of the Cannon Brewery, 33.
[14] Ex inf. Mr. K. H. Hemingway, man. dir.
[15] Ex inf. Marconi Space and Defence Systems Ltd.
[16] See p. 96.   [17] See p. 51.

companies to move and others to open branches elsewhere. Computer Machinery Co., for example, took over a 12,500 square ft. factory in 1970 only to move to Hertfordshire after 18 months; the company, a subsidiary of a United States computer-controlled system manufacturer, employed 70 people at Stanmore.[18] G. H. Bloore, stockists and distributors of plastics, moved from Mill Hill to Honeypot Lane in 1961; ten years later it had some 50 employees there and twice that number at its provincial branches.[19] In Dalston Gardens, leading off Honeypot Lane, premises were acquired in 1969 by Elliott Bros. (London), later Marconi-Elliott Avionic Systems, which previously had been in Honeypot Lane itself.[20] Other sites were occupied by Price & Co., bakers, Sew-Tric, sewing machine manufacturers, and Service Electric Co., as well as by the laboratories of Parnosa of London and the main garage of Middlesex Motors.

SOCIAL LIFE. Fines were ordained by the manorial court in 1584 for any person found at 'tables or other unlawful games for money'. In 1637 the lord agreed to a request that about one acre of land on Stanmore Common should be inclosed as a bowling green.[21] The green itself, with Bowling Green House,[22] was leased out with a further 9 a. in 1714[23] and may still have existed in 1754.[24] Coursing for hares was punished by fines in 1638 and 1640, and four members of the Norwood family were twice fined for shooting with crossbows or guns within the manor.[25]

There was a coney warren on the common by 1667.[26] Nine years later 200 a. of warren ground, furze, and heath had been leased out with two messuages, the Round House, mentioned in 1579,[27] and the White House,[28] one of which was presumably the ancestor of Warren House. Hunting over the heavy soil by the Old Berkeley Hounds, which was not a local pack, drew protests in 1808 from many landowners, including Lord Abercorn, George Harley Drummond, and the rector. Legal actions led to the temporary dispersal of the hounds[29] but hunting was still carried on in the neighbourhood in 1840.[30]

A messuage called the assembly room passed from John Snoxall to his son Joseph Ironmonger Snoxall in 1764 and to Joseph's son Edward in 1810, by which time it had been divided into six dwellings. After Edward Snoxall's death in 1813 it was bought from his executors by the surgeon Richard Andrews, who leased it out for 21 years in 1847. The old assembly room stood on the east side of Stanmore

Hill, south of the workhouse.[31] The Ernest Bernays memorial institute, a red-brick building with stone dressings on the south side of Broadway, was built in 1870 to commemorate a son of L. J. Bernays,[32] rector from 1860 until 1883.

Stanmore cricket club was established in 1853 after the lord had granted some 7 a. in trust for a cricket ground or, if there should be no club, for the parishioners' general recreation. The lord's right passed to Hendon R.D. in 1929 but six years later, after an electors' meeting, the club persuaded Harrow U.D. to abandon a Bill which would have vested ownership of the land in the local authority.[33] Stanmore golf club was founded in 1893. The club-house stood south of Gordon Avenue in 1971, when the golf course comprised some 120 a., which covered part of the former grounds of Stanmore Park and extended into Harrow parish.[34]

LOCAL GOVERNMENT. No medieval court rolls survive for Great Stanmore. In 1294 a jury upheld the abbot of St. Albans in his claim to exercise view of frankpledge and the assizes of bread and ale.[35] The abbot retained some jurisdiction after the manor had passed to St. Bartholomew's priory: his cellarer, who acted as an itinerant justice at six-monthly halimotes on the abbey's estates from the early 13th century, was still visiting Stanmore in 1399.[36] Of the regular courts presumably held by the priors of St. Bartholomew's only one, that of 1508, is recorded, in a transcript.[37] A few late-16th- and early-17th-century proceedings are also recorded,[38] and surviving court books run from 1666 until 1936.[39] Until the mid 17th century a court baron normally met in the spring and a view of frankpledge, occasionally called a court leet, and further court baron were held in the autumn; sometimes the view was held in the spring, as became common in the late 17th century. For most of the 18th century there was a view with a court baron in the spring or early summer and occasionally also a special court baron. General courts baron were held annually in the early 19th century, when views and special courts might also be held. They met at the Abercorn Arms from 1794 until 1815, then at the Crown until 1836, and subsequently again at the Abercorn Arms,[40] where a general court baron was held as late as 1892.[41]

In 1576, and presumably earlier, the assizes of bread and ale were exercised and a constable, two headboroughs, and two aleconners were appointed for the year. Similar appointments were made at views of frankpledge until 1681, after which aletasters, as they had come to be called, were no longer

---

[18] Ex inf. Computer Machinery Co. Ltd.
[19] Ex inf. G. H. Bloore Ltd.
[20] Ex inf. Marconi-Elliott Avionic Systems Ltd.
[21] Davenport MSS., Gt. Stan. ct. rolls.   [22] See p. 92.
[23] M.R.O., Acc. 262 (17).
[24] Rocque, *Map of Mdx.* (1754).
[25] Davenport MSS., Gt. Stan. ct. rolls.
[26] M.R.O., Acc. 262 (15): John Smith v. Ric. Eades.
[27] Davenport MSS., Gt. Stan. ct. rolls.
[28] Davenport MSS., Chancery Procs., Eliz. Mann v. John Powell.
[29] *Mdx. & Herts. N. & Q.* iii. 76–7, 159–63.
[30] See p. 120.
[31] Davenport MSS., Gt. Stan. ct. rolls.
[32] Druett, *Stanmores and Harrow Weald*, 208.
[33] D. Pritchard, 'Aspects of Ancient Man of Gt. Stanmore', TS. *penes* M.R.O.
[34] Ex inf. the sec.

[35] *Plac. de Quo Warr.* (Rec. Com.), 478.
[36] *A. E. Levett, Studies in Manorial Hist.* ed. H. M. Cam and others, 136–7.
[37] Davenport MSS., Gt. Stan. ct. rolls.
[38] Ibid. transcripts for 1576, 1580, 1582–4, 1586, 1633, 1637–41, 1645–6, and 1664. They were made in 1930 and 1931 by Percy Davenport from a book in the possession of Fred. Wilson, steward of the manor; the book itself, ending in 1737 and probably compiled for the duke of Chandos, cannot be traced. Its later entries, also transcribed, are identical with those of the surviving ct. bks.; see below.
[39] M.R.O., Acc. 262(16); Acc. 658/5–8; Acc. 943. A ct. roll for 1737 is in M.R.O., Acc. 262(17).
[40] M.R.O., Acc. 262(16); Acc. 658/5–8; Acc. 943; Davenport MSS., Gt. Stan. ct. rolls.
[41] D. Pritchard, 'Aspects of Ancient Man. of Gt. Stanmore', TS. *penes* M.R.O.

recorded. Land transactions, which formed the bulk of the courts' business by the 17th century, led to several disputes and attempts to define the customs of the manor. In 1681 some discontented copyholders seized the court book and interrupted the steward, who fined the constable for refusing to intervene. Courts continued to name a constable and headborough, for the leet until 1719 and thereafter for the town or parish, until 1805. From 1580 attempts were made to prevent vagrants from becoming a burden by fining parishioners who harboured them.[42]

In 1508 Prior Bolton granted a close called Staples to a group of parishioners, for the support of a parish clerk.[43] The land comprised 8 a. of arable in 1547, when it was worth 20s. a year.[44] It was often regranted at subsequent courts[45] and became known as Clerks Staples, amounting to two fields totalling 14 a. in 1823. At that date the clerk, who still enjoyed it in lieu of salary, leased it out for £30 a year.[46] There were two churchwardens in 1580[47] and a subconstable in 1613[48] but the earliest records of a vestry, the order books, date only from 1730[49] and the churchwardens' accounts from 1832.[50] At first all the vestry meetings may not have been recorded: there seem to have been none in 1741 and nine in 1742, while attendance varied from 4 to 16.[51] The rector often took the chair, as did his successors, and both Andrew Drummond and the first Thomas Clutterbuck were present on occasion. The vestry usually met 3 or 4 times a year in the 1750s, almost monthly at the end of the century, and 3 or 4 times a year in the 1850s, while the average attendance rose from about 7 to 8 or 9 and eventually to 15. The first known meeting-place was the Queen's Head, in 1742, whither the vestry sometimes adjourned even after a special room for it had been furnished at the church in 1750. From 1789 until 1835 meetings were held in the workhouse, as well as at the church, the Crown, and the Abercorn Arms; from 1844 the new schoolroom was the usual meeting-place.

The churchwardens, one nominated by the rector, submitted their accounts to the vestry and were reimbursed from church-rates. For a long time they retained wide responsibilities: in 1801 the signature of a churchwarden, or of an overseer, was required for every admission to the workhouse. By 1730 there were two overseers of the poor and by 1750 two surveyors of the highways, all of them chosen at quarter sessions from nominees of the vestry. Overseers' accounts run from 1784 to 1804,[52] and surveyors' accounts from 1772 until 1826.[53] It was decided that a vestry clerk was no longer needed in 1743 but a new one was appointed by wage a few months later. The constable's expenses for 1779 were paid three years later, although it was not until the early 19th century that the vestry itself appointed either constable or headboroughs. An assistant overseer was to be appointed by wage in 1832 and a beadle in 1834, but the only paid officers recorded in 1837 were a vestry clerk, organist, sexton, and pew-opener.

Eighteenth-century poor-rates were 6d. in the £; at least two a year became necessary in the 1790s and from 1806 a shilling rate was common. In 1775-6 out of £214 raised, £194 was spent on the poor, more than three times the figure for Little Stanmore.[54] Expenditure varied considerably in the early 19th century, rising from £391 in 1818 to £813 in 1821, only to fall to £602 in the two succeeding years[55] and thereafter to rise to an average of £851 from 1831 to 1834.[56] Apart from an income from the parish charities, whose regulation occasioned several vestry meetings, money for the poor was often exacted at late-18th- and early-19th-century courts in return for licences to inclose parcels of waste; the overseers received as much as £70 for the inclosure of 3 a. of Stanmore Common in 1802.[57] An acre at Stanmore marsh, given to accommodate the poor by the lord of the manor in 1802, was sold to Sir Thomas Plumer in 1824 and 2 a. awarded at inclosure on the common were leased out.

Paupers were paid regular weekly allowances, totalling 13s. 6d. in May 1730, when there were 8 recipients, and £1 16s. 6d. in 1784; many casual expenses such as bills for clothing, nursing, medicine, or laundry, were also met. Attempts were made in 1734 and 1748 to enforce the badging of paupers, and out-parishioners often had to produce settlement certificates; when the magistrates refused to order a removal in 1781, legal advice was sought. Cheap food and coal were distributed several times between 1799 and 1801, when it was decided to give as much relief as possible in kind rather than in money.

Two parish houses were repaired in 1752, when four spinning wheels were bought for the inmates. The garden, adjoining the churchyard, was split up into allotments in 1783 and the site was ordered to be sold four years later. A workhouse was built on the east side of Stanmore Hill in 1788. In 1790 it was fenced in and special permission was required for inmates to go outside. The vestry supplied furnishings, carried out repairs, and always paid the medical officer, while other expenses, including those of the constable, were periodically assigned to a farmer or contractor. The poor were first farmed in 1791 for £147 a year, but the cost rose steadily, reaching £220 by 1795 and £410 by 1807. Sometimes no suitable tender could be secured and often an agreement had to be terminated, as in 1798 when the contractor was gaoled or in 1818 and 1825, when the vestry declined to pay extra despite the large numbers out of work. At such times the vestry itself assumed responsibility for the poor, appointing a master or superintendent of the workhouse and arranging for the supply of provisions. Although many felt that direct administration was cheaper, there were repeated reversions to a farmer, who received £570 in 1826 and £700 in 1833.

In 1752, after several robberies, the overseers were

[42] Davenport MSS., Gt. Stan. ct. rolls.
[43] M.R.O., Acc. 262(16)A, f. 97; ref. to original grant.
[44] E 301/34/172.
[45] e.g. M.R.O., Acc. 262(16)A, f. 40.
[46] 9th Rep. Com. Char. 271.
[47] Guildhall MS. 9537/4.
[48] Mdx. Sess. Recs. i. 251.
[49] M.R.O., D.R.O. 14/C1/1(1730-74), /2(1776-84), /3 (1804-27), /4(1827-76).
[50] Ibid. B1/1-4.

[51] Except where otherwise stated, the rest of the section is based on M.R.O., D.R.O. 14/C1/1-4 (unpaginated).
[52] M.R.O., D.R.O. 14/F1/1-2. Examinations of paupers are ibid. F2/1 and contracts for farming out the poor F3/1-5.   [53] Ibid. G1/1.
[54] Rep. Cttee. on Rets. by Overseers, 1776, 101.
[55] Rep. Sel. Cttee. on Poor Rate Returns, H.C. 748, p. 100 (1821), iv; ibid. H.C. 334, p. 132 (1825), iv.
[56] Poor Law Com. 1st Rep. 251.
[57] M.R.O., Acc. 943, ff. 232-3.

authorized to pay two men to keep watch at night, and in 1829 handbills were to be printed, cautioning gangs of boys who caused annoyance in the evenings. A cage for prisoners which was attached to the work-house in 1791 needed repair in 1805 and at that date was probably rebuilt in the workhouse yard, whither the parish stocks, first mentioned in 1639,[58] were similarly moved in 1819. In 1829 it was proposed that the fire-engines,[59] too, should be kept next to the workhouse.

Medicines were ordered for paupers as early as 1730 and a surgeon was paid to attend the poor in 1761. A successor received a fixed sum for all visits and prescriptions, except attendance at childbirth, from 1782 until 1797, when his salary was doubled, and a grateful vestry refused to replace him in 1822. Other measures for public health included the white-washing of all cottage interiors and provision of proper 'breeches' in 1801 and free vaccination against smallpox in 1819.

Hendon instigated discussions on poor-relief with representatives of the Stanmores, Edgware, and Kingsbury, in 1829. In 1835 all five parishes joined Harrow, Pinner, and Willesden to form Hendon poor law union.[60] The new board of guardians at once caused alarm by proposing extensive alterations to the workhouse and demanding the removal of the cage and engine-house, which remained the parish's responsibility. After two years of argument the guardians were permitted to sell the workhouse to William Rogers, a neighbouring surgeon, whose family lived there until its sale by trustees in 1893.[61] Great Stanmore paid more than most members of the union towards the new workhouse at Redhill, since the land awarded at inclosure was also sold.[62]

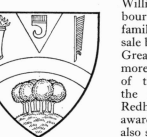

URBAN DISTRICT (LATER BOROUGH AND LATER LONDON BOROUGH) OF HARROW. *Or, a fess arched vert; in chief a pile gules charged with a clarion or, on the dexter side of the pile a torch sable with flames proper, and on the sinister side a quill pen sable; and in the base of the shield a hurst of trees growing out of a grassy mount*
[Granted 1938]

The parish steadily resisted the erosion of its authority in the 19th century. Great Stanmore, along with its neighbours, was included in the Metropolitan Police District in 1840[63] but in 1842 the vestry complained to the Home Secretary about the consequent expense and inadequate protection. A proposal to adopt the Lighting and Watching Act of 1834 was defeated at meetings of ratepayers in 1836 and 1859 but unanimously accepted in 1861, whereupon six inspectors were appointed, answerable to the vestry. In 1863 the parish vainly protested against its inclusion in the new Edgware highway district.[64]

Sums raised by the overseers and spent by Edgware highway board in Great Stanmore were much the same as those in Little Stanmore.[65] A nuisance removal committee was set up by the vestry under an inspector in 1857 but was superseded under the Public Health Act of 1872[66] by the new Hendon rural sanitary authority, which in 1879 also took over the functions of Edgware highway board.[67] Hendon rural sanitary authority in 1895 became Hendon R.D., which was dissolved in 1934 when the Stanmores joined Harrow U.D., itself created a municipal borough in 1954. Stanmore North and Stanmore South formed two of the new urban district's 12 wards (15 from 1948); some two-thirds of Great Stanmore was included in Stanmore North but the southern part lay mostly in Stanmore South and later in Belmont and Queensbury wards.[68] Since 1965 both Great and Little Stanmore have lain within Harrow L.B. The postal address for many of its offices is Stanmore, as it was for those of the old urban district, but all are located on the Harrow side of the parish boundary.

PUBLIC SERVICES. Two fire-engines, which in 1782 might be used by other parishes for a fee,[69] were ordered to be regularly tested from 1813. It was decided to ask neighbouring parishes to contribute towards the upkeep in 1837 and, after the sale of the workhouse, to commission a new engine-house on Stanmore Common[70] in 1842. A paid keeper was appointed but in 1866 it was resolved to support him from subscriptions rather than church-rates and the post was not filled. The vestry was still responsible for repairing a hand engine in 1875. A fire station was built by the county council on waste ground at the corner of Honeypot Lane and Wigton Gardens in 1961. It replaced fire stations at Weald-stone and Kingsbury.[71]

By 1640 water was brought to the manor-house from a 'great pond' on Stanmore Hill. The source was probably Spring pond, since John Norwood the younger was accused of diverting part of the supply through leaden pipes to a house on the common,[72] although by the 19th century water was also collected in a pond which had been dug at the foot of the hill.[73]

Repairs were ordered to a well on the common in 1783. A new well and pump were contemplated in 1802, for the use of subscribers and specified paupers, and more wells four years later. In 1824 there was a fund for laying on plentiful soft water and in 1846 4 a. near the engine-house were granted by the lord for a reservoir.[74] A pump near the churchyard had often to be kept locked in 1873, when a service was proposed by the Colne Valley Water Co., which has

[58] Davenport MSS., Gt. Stan. ct. rolls.
[59] See below.
[60] *Poor Law Com. 1st Rep.* 251.
[61] M.R.O., Acc. 658/5, ff. 222–4; /7, f. 87.
[62] *Poor Law Com. 9th Rep.* H.C. 494, App. C, pp. 278–9 (1843), xxi.
[63] *Lond. Gaz.* 13 Oct. 1840, p. 2250.
[64] Ibid. 3 Mar. 1863, p. 1480.
[65] M.R.O., LA. HW., Edgware highway bd. par. ledger (1863–79).   [66] 35 & 36 Vic. c. 79.
[67] For the remainder of the para. see *V.C.H. Mdx.* iv. 243, 245.

[68] For the ward boundaries see Harrow L.B., North Star, map of Harrow U.D., 1935, and Harrow Cent. Ref. Libr., Harrow ward boundaries map, 1963.
[69] Except where otherwise stated, the first two paras. of the section are based on M.R.O., D.R.O. 14/C1/2, /3, /4.
[70] M.R.O., Acc. 658/5, f. 262.
[71] Ex inf. chief officer, Lond. Fire Brigade.
[72] Davenport MSS., Gt. Stan. ct. rolls (1640, 1641).
[73] Druett, *Stanmores and Harrow Weald*, 250 and pl. facing p. 176.
[74] M.R.O., Acc. 658/6, ff. 21, 48.

since always supplied the parish.[75] Despite optimistic reports from the nuisance removal committee, the vestry was taken to task by the Hendon guardians in 1866 and admitted the danger to the lower part of the village from nine open drains running through the fields. The drains were subsequently closed in, leaking earthen pipes were replaced with iron ones, and by 1871 a sewer by Old Church Lane had been enlarged to become the main sewer. At the end of the century the parish was served by Edgware and Little Stanmore sewage farm, which lay in Kingsbury[76] and which was superseded by trunk sewers leading to a central works at Mogden under the West Middlesex Sewerage and Sewage Disposal Scheme of 1933.[77]

Half an acre at Stanmore marsh, where the parish boundary bulged east of Marsh Lane, was approved as the site for a gas-works in 1858.[78] Stanmore gas works were opened in 1859[79] and still stood there in 1969. Gas was first supplied from Harrow by a private contractor, John Chapman, whose concern was later called Stanmore Gas Co.[80] In 1894 it was joined with Harrow District Gas Co. to form Harrow and Stanmore Gas Co., which was taken over in turn by Brentford Gas Co. in 1924 and the Gas Light, and Coke Co. in 1926.[81] Under an Act of 1906 electricity was supplied by Northwood Electric Light and Power Co.[82]

Stanmore cottage hospital was built in 1890, near the railway station and on the west side of Old Church Lane, at the expense of Emily and Katharine Wickens of the Pynnacles. The hospital, which originally contained 7 beds and a cot, was endowed by the Misses Wickens and afterwards run by four trustees, who could decide on admissions and charges.[83] After nationalization in 1948 it was converted into a home for old people. In 1971, when it was administered by Hendon group hospital management committee as a geriatric sub-unit of Edgware general hospital, there was accommodation for 14 inmates.[84] An isolation hospital, with separate blocks for diphtheria and scarlet fever, was built in 1902 on the east side of Honeypot Lane. After epidemics in 1928 and 1929 Hendon R.D.C. decided to double the accommodation of 26 beds and cots. On nationalization the hospital was handed over to the county council and converted into Stanmore residential nursery, for children below five. It was transferred in 1965 from Harrow L.B., which placed few of the children there, to Brent L.B.[85] Warren House was acquired with 11 a. from Sir John Fitzgerald in 1951 by the National Corporation for the Care of Old People and, as Springbok House, was transferred in 1964 to the Hendon group.[86] Orme Lodge, a late Victorian building in Gordon Avenue, was sold by the Robinson family in the 1930s, used by the R.A.F.

during the Second World War, and afterwards acquired by the county council as an old people's home. In 1971 both Warren House, with 53 beds, and Orme Lodge, with 22, were geriatric sub-units of Edgware general hospital.[87]

In the 1960s by far the largest open space was Stanmore Common, 120 a. stretching from the Hertfordshire border south as far as the reservoir.[88] The adjoining cricket ground,[89] granted as such by the lord in 1853,[90] comprised nearly 7 a., as did Little Common on the far side of the reservoir. Much of the Grove estate, 63 a. bordering the common on the east, and most of the Warren House estate, 123 a. east of Little Common and stretching south along Dennis Lane, had been bought by Harrow U.D.C. to form part of the Green Belt in 1937. The Bentley Priory estate, purchased in 1936, lay mainly in Harrow parish, although its eastern strip was in Great Stanmore. Stanmore recreation ground, between Dennis Lane and Stanmore Hill, covered only 6½ a. Most of Stanmore golf course[91] also lay within the parish, forming the largest open space in the southern half, where Stanmore marsh covered a further 10 a. The Whitchurch schools playing field, administered in 1971 by Harrow L.B., lay north of Wemborough Road and the North Western Polytechnic sports ground lay west of Honeypot Lane. Farther south the 23 a. of Centenary park, bordering Culver Grove, had been acquired in 1934.[92]

CHURCH. In 1086 a priest held ½ hide at Great Stanmore.[93] A church, presumably the rectory and advowson, was among the possessions recovered by Richard, abbot of St. Albans (d. 1119)[94] and evidently was part of the property which William of Mortain had restored by 1106.[95] Although new sites were found for the building in the 17th and 19th centuries,[96] a single church has always served the whole parish.

The rights of St. Albans were confirmed by Pope Clement III in 1188, to provide vessels for the monks' refectory,[97] and by Honorius III in 1219.[98] Thereafter it seems that the abbots retained the advowson until the Dissolution, although by the mid 13th century they owned nothing else, save a portion which presumably was used on buying vessels.[99] The first recorded date of a presentation is 1322.[1] The Crown presented three times in 1349, when there was no abbot, and once in 1373, for reasons unknown.[2] In 1464 the next presentation to the rectory was granted to the Lord Chancellor George Neville, who, when archbishop of York, exercised his right six years later.[3] From 1539 it passed with the lordship of the manor to the Crown and afterwards,

[75] Druett, op. cit. 251.
[76] O.S. Map 6″, Mdx. XI. NW. (1897 edn.).
[77] V.C.H. Mdx. iv. 249.
[78] M.R.O., Acc. 658/6, f. 184.
[79] Harrow Gaz. and Gen. Advertiser, 1 Apr. 1859.
[80] Druett, op. cit. 249.　　　　[81] V.C.H. Mdx. iv. 249.
[82] 6 Edw. VII, c. 129.　　　[83] Druett, op. cit., 212.
[84] Ex inf. sec., Edgware gen. hosp. geriatric sub-group; Hosp. Yr. Bk. (1971).
[85] Ex inf. dir. of community services, Harrow L.B.
[86] Ex inf. asst. sec., Nat. Corp. for Care of Old People.
[87] Ex inf. sec., Edgware gen. hosp. geriatric sub-group; Hosp. Yr. Bk. (1971).
[88] Except where otherwise stated, the para. is based on Boro. of Harrow, Facts & Figures (1963–4).

[89] O.S. Map 6″, Mdx. V. SE. (1865 edn.).
[90] Pritchard, 'Aspects of Man. of Gt. Stanmore', penes M.R.O., 5–6.
[91] See p. 102.
[92] C. Radcliffe, Mdx. (rev. edn.), 161.
[93] V.C.H. Mdx. i. 125.
[94] Thos. Walsingham, Gesta Abbatum (Rolls Ser.), ed. H. T. Riley, i. 68.
[95] See p. 96.　　　　　　　　[96] See below, p. 106.
[97] Mat. Paris, Chron. Majora (Rolls Ser.), vi. 46.
[98] Cal. Papal Regs. i. 63.　　　　　　[99] See below.
[1] Hennessy, Novum Repertorium, 406.
[2] Cal. Pat. 1348–50, 276, 329, 421; 1370–4, 346.
[3] Registrum Abbatiae Johannis Whethamstede (Rolls Ser.), ed. H. T. Riley, ii. 91.

in turn, to Geoffrey Chamber, Sir Pedro de Gamboa,[4] successive lessees of the manor, and the families of Lake and Brydges.[5] James Brydges, duke of Chandos, by will dated 1742, left the advowson to trustees, who presumably sold it to Andrew Drummond, thereby separating it from the manor. William Hallett, the purchaser of Canons, claimed the advowson from Henry, duke of Chandos,[6] but Drummond presented in 1749 and his grandson in the 1780s. The marquess of Abercorn held both lordship and advowson, presenting in 1847 and 1848, but in 1857 presentation was by the Revd. Leopold John Bernays of Elstree (Herts.). The right has since remained with the Bernays family or its trustees, Mrs. N. Bernays being the patron in 1965.[7]

The church was said to be worth 6 marks in the mid 13th century, when the abbot of St. Albans took 2 marks from the profits,[8] and £2 in 1291, when the abbot received £1.[9] Great Stanmore was expressly excluded from the taxation on churches in 1428.[10] The rectory was valued at £13 6s. 8d. in 1535[11] and at £10 in 1547.[12] Early in the 18th century the benefice was estimated to be worth £100,[13] as it was at the close,[14] and by 1835 the net income was £566.[15] In 1838 the rector was awarded a rent-charge of £444 in lieu of all tithes, a sum which was still payable in 1887.[16]

The glebe in 1680 amounted to more than 32 a.; 9 a. adjoined the parsonage house, 7 a. lay south of the old churchyard, and the rest was scattered in the common fields.[17] Under an Act of 1784[18] some 12 a., worth £25 a year and including the old churchyard, were exchanged with George Drummond for nearly 20 a., worth £35.[19] There were 41 a. in 1838, some 6 a. lying next to the rectory house and the rest in two blocks to the south of Old Church Lane. The glebe was then worth £82 a year[20] but had shrunk to 23 a., worth £64 11s., by 1887, to 12 a. by 1926, and to 2 a. by 1940.[21]

It is not certain where the parsonage house stood before 1721, when George Hudson, rector 1715–49, built a new one to the south-east of the church, at the top of Old Church Lane. The duke of Chandos gave the timber and perhaps also paid the architect, Edward Shepherd, whom he often employed as a surveyor. The building was red-brick and three-storeyed, facing south across a pond.[22] A wing was added in 1850 but the house was divided in 1949 and pulled down in 1960, when the present Rectory was built a few yards to the north-west.[23]

Most early incumbents were probably pluralists or absentees, since Great Stanmore was not a rich living. John Nicholl exchanged it for West Angmering (Suss.) in 1423[24] and John Cortell was licensed to hold it with one other benefice in 1476.[25] Alfonso de Salignas, presumably a nominee and fellow countryman of Sir Pedro de Gamboa, paid a priest to serve the cure in 1547.[26] After the building of the 18th-century rectory house, incumbents seem normally to have been resident. Arthur Chauvel, rector 1788–1847, was also a canon of St. Paul's and vicar of Chigwell (Essex) in 1835.[27]

All the parishioners, it was said, could conveniently attend the church in 1650.[28] The Presbyterian Samuel Stancliffe, later one of the first managers of the Common Fund, was rector from 1658 until his ejection in 1662.[29] A Sunday school, started by 1790,[30] was attended by between 30 and 40 children in 1819.[31] Services took place twice every Sunday at the end of the 18th century, when between 50 and 70 people received the sacraments four times a year. By 1810 the sacraments were administered 'nearly monthly'.[32] Two Sunday services were still held in 1851, attended by some 450 people in the morning and 400 in the afternoon, as well as about 80 children from the Sunday school.[33] There has usually been an assistant curate, paid £50 in 1782 and 1797, since the late 18th century.[34]

From c. 1300 until 1632 the parish church, probably dedicated to St. Mary, stood north of the moat[35] on what became the corner of Old Church Lane and Wolverton Road.[36] Possibly there had been earlier churches here, of which nothing is known. Fragments uncovered by builders in 1892 showed the medieval church to have measured no more than 81 ft. by 22 ft., with small transepts and a 15th-century extension.[37] No trace survives, apart from the tomb of Baptist Willoughby, rector 1563–1610, later in the garden of Haslemere (no. 44 Old Church Lane), and the Burnell monument in the modern parish church.[38] In 1632 William Laud, as bishop of London, consecrated the church of St. John, whose ivy-clad ruins still stand at the western end of the churchyard. The building was paid for by Sir John Wolstenholme and so later denounced by the Puritans as a private chapel.[39] Its roofless walls and three-stage battlemented tower are of brick with stone dressings; the body forms a plain rectangle with no separate chancel, although one 18th-century annexe to the north remains and there are traces of another. The south doorway, attributed to Nicholas Stone,

[4] L. & P. Hen. VIII, xxi(2), p. 419.
[5] Hennessy, op. cit. 406.
[6] Baker, Chandos, 445, 466.
[7] Hennessy, op. cit. 406; Crockford (1896 and later edns.).
[8] Val. of Norw., ed. Lunt, 359.
[9] Tax. Eccl. (Rec. Com.), 17, 20.
[10] Feud. Aids, iii. 380.
[11] Valor Eccl. (Rec. Com.), i. 433.
[12] E 301/34/172.
[13] Bodl. MS. Rawl. B 389b, f. 96v.
[14] Guildhall MS. 9557, f. 24.
[15] Rep. Com. Eccl. Revenues, 672–3.
[16] Return of Tithes Commuted, H.C. 214, p. 123 (1887), lxiv.
[17] M.R.O., Acc. 262 (16).
[18] 24 Geo. III, c. 10 (Priv. Act).
[19] M.R.O., Acc. 398/11.
[20] M.R.O., TA/S'MORE Gt.; Return of Tithes Commuted, 123; Return of Glebe Lands, H.C. 307, p. 92 (1887), lxiv.

[21] Crockford (1926, 1940).
[22] Druett, Stanmores and Harrow Weald, 207–8 and pl. facing p. 96; Baker, Chandos, 280.
[23] Guide to ch. of St. John the Evangelist, Gt. Stanmore (1965), 19; photographs penes Harrow Cent. Ref. Libr.
[24] Cal. Pat. 1422–9, 141.
[25] Cal. Pap. Regs. xiii(2), 526.   [26] E 301/34/172.
[27] Rep. Com. Eccl. Revenues, 673.
[28] Home Cnties. Mag. i. 319.
[29] Calamy Revised, ed. Matthews, 458.
[30] See p. 108.
[31] Educ. of Poor Digest, 555.
[32] Guildhall MSS. 9557, 9558.
[33] H.O. 129/135/2/1/1.
[34] Guildhall MSS. 9557, 9558; Rep. Com. Eccl. Revenues, 673; Crockford (1896 and later edns.).
[35] See p. 92.
[36] O.S. Map 1/2,500, TQ 1691 (1963 edn.).
[37] T.L.M.A.S. xiii. 219; Home Cnties. Mag. iii. 170.
[38] See p. 107.
[39] Robbins, Mdx. 331.

and most of the windows are round-headed; the east window is venetian, an early occurrence of this feature.[40] The table-tomb of Sir John Wolstenholme, his father, and two grandsons, dated 1639, stands within the ruins, together with the ornate mausoleum of the Hollond family, dated 1866; there are several tablets of the late 17th and early 18th centuries, but most of the more elaborate monuments have been moved to the new church.[41]

After the Laudian church had been pronounced too small and unsafe, the foundation stone of *ST. JOHN THE EVANGELIST* was laid in 1849 by Queen Adelaide at her last public appearance.[42] The church, consecrated in 1850, was built on near-by land given by Col. Tovey-Tennent of the Pynnacles, at a cost of £7,855, of which £3,000 was raised by a church-rate and a similar sum given by the earl of Aberdeen and his son, the Hon. Douglas Gordon, who was rector from 1848 until 1857. Henry Clutton, the architect,[43] used Kentish rag and Bath stone in the Decorated style to build a church comprising a wide chancel with a chapel to the south, nave, north and south aisles, and north-west tower. The organ was later moved to the chapel from near the south door. Vestries on the north side of the chancel were converted into the chapel of St. George by E. B. Glanfield in 1955, and a new vestry was built further north. Alterations to lighten the chancel and emphasize the altar were completed in 1961; they included whitening the walls, removing the brass communion rails and much woodwork, including the choir-screen, and lowering and re-tiling the sanctuary floor. The central light of Thomas Willement's east window, erected in memory of Queen Adelaide, was redesigned in 1950. Despite such changes there are many fittings, among them a font given by Queen Adelaide and a stained glass window in the south aisle attributable to William Morris & Co.,[44] to recall the wealth of Victorian Stanmore.

The oldest fittings, which must have been in the two earlier churches, are a brass inscription to John Burnell (d. 1605) and, above it, a marble and alabaster wall monument erected by his widow Barbara, with kneeling figures of herself, her husband, and eight children; details of the Burnells' charities are inscribed, with the provisions, still observed, for the monument's maintenance by the Clothworkers' Company of London. Other pieces from the Laudian church include an octagonal font, bearing the Wolstenholmes' arms, of white marble on a grey marble baluster-stem, and a white marble recumbent effigy from the tomb of Sir John Wolstenholme (d. 1639), both of them by Nicholas Stone. A large stone monument, crammed beneath the tower and perhaps wrongly reassembled, depicts John Wolstenholme (d. 1669), his wife, and two children, lying in a heavily draped four-poster bed. A black marble and alabaster tablet commemorates the wife and

three daughters of John Collins, dated 1670,[45] some memorials to the Dalton family include one to John Dalton by John Bacon the younger, dated 1791,[46] and there is an effigy by J. E. Boehm of George Hamilton-Gordon, earl of Aberdeen (d. 1860), former Prime Minister and father of the rector Douglas Gordon. A mid-17th-century record of the parish's charities hangs in the north aisle. The churchyard contains the unmarked grave of William Hart (d. 1683), son of Shakespeare's sister Joan,[47] table-tombs of 1705 and 1714,[48] and a winged figure over the grave of Sir William Gilbert (d. 1911); Lord Halsbury (d. 1921), three times Lord Chancellor, is also buried there.[49]

The tower has eight bells, six of them from the Laudian church: (i) and (ii) 1684, James Bartlett; (iii) 1632, Brian Eldridge; (iv) 1756, Lester and Pack; (v) 1632, Brian Eldridge (recast 1888); (vi) 1632, Brian Eldridge.[50] The plate includes a flagon of 1616, given by Barbara Burnell, paten covers of 1632 and 1637, and a stand-paten of 1709, all silver-gilt.[51] Registers record baptisms, marriages, and deaths from 1599.[52]

ROMAN CATHOLICISM. Edward Chamber, whose father Geoffrey had been forced to surrender Great Stanmore in 1546, became a Roman Catholic priest. In 1597, as the only surviving son, the exiled Edward offered to sell his interest in the manor, but he may not have lived in Stanmore after his youth.[53] Recusants indicted in 1581 and 1582 included Thomas Norwood of Great Stanmore, gentleman, one of the Norwoods of Astwood (Bucks.) and Ashwell (Herts.), whose family also held property in Harrow.[54] Agnes Mills of Stanmore was among those indicted in 1598.[55] No further Roman Catholic activity was recorded until the 20th century. Worshippers used the new chapel of St. Thomas's convent, on the Little Stanmore side of Marsh Lane, in the 1930s and were served by the near-by church of St. William of York from 1960.[56]

PROTESTANT NONCONFORMITY. Stanmore was included in a list of parishes where a meeting-house is said to have been licensed between 1689 and 1719.[57] A house was certified as a meeting-place by Samuel Gadsden in 1826, but no denomination was recorded, and William Coughtrey certified a building for Independents in 1833. Neither place was used for long by worshippers, nor was a room in a house on Stanmore Hill, certified by James John Foster of Edgware, a dissenting teacher, in 1850.[58] Primitive Methodists registered a preaching room in 1882 but the registration was cancelled in 1896.[59] The registration by Baptists of a meeting room in Church Road in 1889 was cancelled in 1954.[60]

[40] See plate facing p. 81.
[41] Hist. Mon. Com. *Mdx.* 114; Pevsner, *Mdx.* 145.
[42] Except where otherwise stated, the para. is based on *Guide to ch. of St. John*, 4–10 and plan facing p. 1.
[43] Two Hen. Cluttons practised *c.* 1848. The architect of Gt. Stanmore church was of no. 8 Whitehall Place, Westminster: M.R.O., D.R.O. 14/B2/23.
[44] Damaged *c.* 1974.
[45] Hist. Mon. Com. *Mdx.* 114 and plates 12, 163, and 173.
[46] Pevsner, *Mdx.* 146.
[47] Ibid.; *Guide to ch. of St. John*, 6–7, 18.
[48] Hist. Mon. Com. *Mdx.* 114.

[49] *Guide to ch. of St. John*, 19.
[50] *T.L.M.A.S.* xvii. 239.
[51] Freshfield, *Communion Plate*, 41.
[52] *Guide to ch.* 17. The registers from 1599 to 1934 are in M.R.O., D.R.O. 14/A1–16.
[53] *Cal. S.P. Dom. 1591–4*, 400; *1595–7*, 359.
[54] *Mdx. Cnty. Recs.* i. 122, 127, 129; *Vis. Bucks.* 1566, ed. W. C. Metcalfe, 26.   [55] *Mdx. Cnty. Recs.* i. 242.
[56] See p. 124.   [57] Guildhall MS. 9579.
[58] G.R.O. Worship Returns, Lond. dioc. nos. 1511, 1786, 2365.
[59] G.R.O. Worship Reg. no. 26119.   [60] Ibid. 31454.

In the early 1930s weekly lunch-time meetings were held for workmen employed by Henry J. Clare, who was building houses in Abercorn Road, Belmont Lane, and Old Church Lane. The meetings, although Baptist in character, were undenominational and took place in the Old Barn, a brick building once part of Old Church Farm and later converted to residential use as part of Stanburn House, no. 69 Old Church Lane. When the new houses were occupied, Sunday services were started in the Old Barn.[61] Stanmore Baptist church was registered in 1934 and the foundation-stone of the existing church, on the corner of Abercorn Road and Old Church Lane, was laid in 1935. The new building, of pale brown brick and including a small hall, classrooms, and vestry, was registered in 1936. The church was enlarged to seat 270 people in 1963, when a bigger hall, with classrooms overhead, and new rooms along the Abercorn Road frontage were also added.[62]

Stanmore chapel, which is affiliated with the Fellowship of Independent Evangelical Churches, was founded in 1932 as an independent Baptist church. Services were held in the Old Barn until 1935 and at no. 1 Abercorn Road for a further two years. The title of Stanmore Baptist church was adopted in 1934 but the original name had been revived by 1937, to avoid confusion with the church in Old Church Lane, which is a member of the Baptist Union. The existing chapel, on the corner of Marsh Lane at the junction with Nelson Road, was opened in 1937 and registered in 1938 and again in 1941. The building, of red brick, has seating for 150 and adjoins a hall, built later with seating for 200.[63]

Stanmore free church was registered in 1936, although evangelical services had been held for several years in private houses.[64] It is a brown rough-cast building, set back from the north side of Church Road and east of the post office. After meeting in private houses Brethren registered Culver Grove gospel hall, on the corner of Crowshott Avenue and Culver Grove, in 1938.[65] The building, which has about 200 seats, is of red brick and is attached to a second hall.

JUDAISM. The Belmont and District affiliated synagogue, which is attached to the United Synagogue, was established in 1966. The synagogue had no premises of its own in 1969, when services were held in local church halls.[66]

EDUCATION. In 1790 the master of the workhouse was made responsible for teaching paupers' children; £80 was borrowed from the funds of the Sunday school and, by 1798, a schoolroom was built in the workhouse.[67] In 1819 the rector stated that the poor were not without the means of educating their children.[68] By 1833 19 boys and 33 girls attended an infant school, supported by school pence and by subscription.[69]

Great Stanmore infants' school, next to no. 56 Stanmore Hill, was erected in 1845 at the expense of Miss Catherine Elizabeth Martin of Woodlands, who endowed it with £1,000. The building, in an ornamental half-timbered style, consisted of a schoolroom with seating for 100 and an adjoining mistress's house. The average attendance of 70–80 pupils, first recorded in 1871,[70] varied little in the late 19th century, although the school was enlarged to accommodate 175.[71] Control was vested in the rector until 1899, when the infants' school was placed under the same management as the National school.[72] Conditions in the schoolroom and classroom were criticized by the county council's surveyor in 1904 but after repairs[73] the structure remained in use until 1960, when the pupils moved to the near-by National school building.[74] They were moved to St. John's school in Green Lane in 1964, soon after the former infants' school had been demolished.[75]

Great Stanmore National school was founded by 1826, the year of its union with the National Society.[76] The school, which was supported by voluntary contributions, was attended by 20 boys and 40 girls in 1833, but its site was not recorded.[77] Land on Stanmore Hill, south of the infants' school, was acquired in 1859 and a new building was opened in 1861. Accommodation comprised a boys' schoolroom, girls' schoolroom, and classroom, with an adjoining house for the teacher. The income came mainly from voluntary contributions, supplemented by school pence, a sermon, and a rent of £30 from a piece of land. Part of the land, which presumably had formed the endowment of the earlier National school, was soon sold to meet building costs,[78] although an annual grant was paid from 1863.[79] A new schoolroom was proposed in 1880, when the rector feared the establishment of a school board,[80] and in 1885–6 the school, which had accommodated 151 pupils, was enlarged to take 287.[81] Average attendance, however, after rising from 75 in 1861 to 158 by 1882–3, was little affected.[82] The girls' classroom was pronounced totally unsuitable in 1904, whereupon the trustees agreed to carry out extensive improvements.[83] In 1906 Great Stanmore National school could accommodate 317 juniors and 171 infants, although the average attendance figures

[61] Druett, *Stanmores and Harrow Weald*, 258; ex inf. the sec.

[62] G.R.O. Worship Reg. nos. 55642, 57611; *Baptist Handbk.* (1969); ex inf. the sec.

[63] Ex inf. the sec.; Gen. Reg. Off., Wship. Reg. 58002, 59722.

[64] G.R.O. Worship Reg. no. 57100; ex inf. the sec.

[65] Ex inf. Mr. S. R. Fowler; G.R.O. Worship Reg. no. 57823.

[66] *Jewish Yr. Bk.* (1969); ex inf. the sec.

[67] M.R.O., D.R.O. 14/C1/2.

[68] *Educ. of Poor Digest*, 555.

[69] *Educ. Enquiry Abstract*, 580.

[70] Ed. 7/86/20; plan and description *penes* Harrow Cent. Ref. Libr.

[71] *Rep. of Educ. Cttee. of Council, 1878* [C. 2342–1], p. 948, H.C. (1878–9), xxiii.

[72] *Schs. in receipt of Parl. grants, 1899* [Cd. 332], p. 168, H.C. (1900), lxiv.

[73] Nat. Soc. file.

[74] Ex inf. the headmaster, St. John's school.

[75] *Hendon & Finchley Times*, 19 June 1964; ex inf. the headmaster. See below.

[76] National Society, *17th Annual Report* (1828), 80.

[77] *Educ. Enquiry Abstract*, 580.   [78] Ed. 7/86/20.

[79] *Rep. of Educ. Cttee. of Council, 1862–3*, p. 445, H.C. (1863), xlvii.

[80] Nat. Soc. file.

[81] *Rep. of Educ. Cttee. of Council, 1884–5* [C. 4483–1], p. 593, H.C. (1884–5), xxiii; ibid. *1885–6* [C. 4849–1], p. 556, H.C. (1886), xxiv.

[82] Ed. 7/86/20; *Rep. of Educ. Cttee. of Council, 1882–3* [C. 3706–1], p. 696, H.C. (1883), xxv.

[83] Nat. Soc. file.

were only 153 and 68;[84] there was accommodation for 253 juniors and 156 infants between 1919 and 1932 and, after reorganizations, for a total of 261 children in 1936 and 169 in 1938.[85] In 1960, after protracted negotiations, the juniors were moved to St. John's school, which had been built by the county council but which was to be managed by the London Diocesan Board of Education. When the infants followed in 1964 the new school, north of the junction of Stanmore Hill and Green Lane, became known as St. John's Church of England junior and infants' school.[86] In 1970 it was full, with 320 pupils, although there were plans to double the accommodation. The old school building and master's house, of red brick with stone dressings, stood empty, awaiting demolition.[87]

Stanburn school, for juniors and infants, opened in temporary premises in 1936.[88] A new building in Abercorn Road was opened in 1938,[89] when it accommodated 250 children.[90] Four huts, added in 1947, were still used as classrooms in 1970 and children were also taught for a time in a clinic in Honeypot Lane and, from 1949 until 1960, in the Baptist church halls. A block of four more classrooms was built in 1969, for both juniors and infants. In 1970, with 480 juniors and 335 infants on the roll, there were further plans for building.[91]

Chandos secondary school for boys and Chandos secondary school for girls opened in Thistlecroft Gardens in 1939. Hutted classrooms were added to the girls' school after the Second World War and later a new brick building was shared by both schools. In 1970 there was accommodation for 650 girls and 453 boys.[92]

Dr. Samuel Parr, after being refused the headmastership of Harrow, opened a rival school in Stanmore Hill in 1771.[93] Although he began with 60 boys, the venture failed. In 1776 he moved to Colchester[94] and in 1780 his property at Stanmore, a copyhold known as the Great House, was sold.[95] In 1794 four pews in the church were temporarily taken away from a Mr. Dwyer, who had used them for many years for his school.[96] By 1833 there were 6 private schools in the parish, all of them established during the previous 15 years and together containing 86 boys and 27 girls.[97] In the late 1880s a boys' preparatory school moved from Brighton to Stanmore Park, which had been sold by Lord Wolverton.[98] A well-known cricketer, the Revd. Vernon Royle, was headmaster from 1901 until his death in 1929. After the school's move to Hertford in 1937 the mansion was demolished.[99] Alcuin House, a boys' preparatory school, opened in Old Church Lane in 1927 and closed in 1962.[1] Other private schools between the first and second World Wars

included St. Nicholas's preparatory school for girls, in Gordon Avenue in 1926 and at Pynnacles Corner in 1929, and St. Brendan's girls' school, in Marsh Lane from c. 1933 until c. 1958.[2]

CHARITIES FOR THE POOR. Robert Hillson, mercer of London, by will proved 1585, left a house in Edgware to his widow. After her death the rent was to be spent on the poor of Great Stanmore.[3] John Burnell, by will proved 1605, left £100 to the Clothworkers' Company of London, which was to pay part of the annual interest, 26s., for 6 pennyworth of bread a week for the poor. His son John, also a clothworker, by will proved 1623, left a rentcharge of 40s. a year to the poor.[4] The testator's daughter, Anne Coo, was accused of withholding payment in 1668[5] and the vestry was persistent in claiming arrears from the marquess of Buckingham, as owner of Ward's farm, from 1815.[6] By 1823 stock worth £50 had been bought, mainly out of 19 years' arrears, and half a year's interest, with the rentcharge, had been spent on 3s. worth of coal for 20 poor people.[7] In 1964 each of the three charities had an income of less than £5 a year.[8]

Barbara, widow of John Burnell the elder, by will dated 1630, left £300 to the Clothworkers' Company, which was to spend £7 a year on bread for 12 of the poor and for the parish clerk, on a payment of 2s. to the parish clerk, and on gowns for 6 poor women; all six women were to come from Stanmore one year and two were to come from Bushey (Herts.), two from Harrow Weald, and two from Edgware, in the following year. Thomas Burnell, by deed of 1655, augmented Barbara Burnell's gift by 30s. a year for clothing and 18d. a week for cheese. In 1823 the Clothworkers' Company paid £15 0s. 8d. for the gifts of Barbara and Thomas Burnell; although the clerk no longer received 2s. the total amount spent was £15 2s., the difference being paid out of the church-rate.[9] In 1963 £7 4s. 10d. from the Barbara Burnell trust was spent on bread and £5 3s. 4d. on an exhibition at Oxford University, which the Clothworkers' Company increased from its own resources. The income from the charity of Thomas Burnell, also paid by the company, was between £5 and £10 in 1966.[10]

Sir John Wolstenholme, by will dated 1639, gave the income on £200 to the poor of Great Stanmore, as well as whatever should be left from the income on another £200 which was intended for repairs to the church. His son John, by deed of 1655, accordingly settled land in Billiter Lane (London) on trustees.[11] In the 1720s two tenants there each paid £10 a year, although in 1740 the vestry, which often

[84] Public Elem. Schs. 1906 [Cd. 3510], p. 447, H.C. (1907), lxiii.
[85] Bd. of Educ., List 21 (H.M.S.O. 1919, 1922, 1927, 1932, 1936, 1938).
[86] Hendon & Finchley Times, 25 Mar. 1960, 19 June 1964.
[87] Ex inf. the headmaster, St John's sch.
[88] Ex inf. the headmaster.
[89] Bd. of Educ., List 21 (H.M.S.O. 1936).
[90] Ibid. (1938).
[91] Ex inf. the headmaster.
[92] Ex inf. the headmistress and the headmaster.
[93] Brewer, Beauties of Eng. & Wales, x(5), 629.
[94] V.C.H. Mdx. i. 244–5.
[95] Davenport MSS., Gt. Stan. ct. roll, Nov. 1780.
[96] M.R.O., D.R.O. 14/C1/2.

[97] Educ. Enquiry Abstract, 580.
[98] See p. 99.
[99] Druett, Stanmores and Harrow Weald, 203, 206–7; Who Was Who, 1929–40, 1178.
[1] Harrow Gaz. 26 July 1962.
[2] Kelly's Dir. Mdx. (1926, 1929); Kelly's Dir. Edgware (1933); Kemp's Dir. Harrow (1958).
[3] Prob. 11/66 (P.C.C. 20 Butts).
[4] P. Davenport, Old Stanmore, 98, 108.
[5] C 93/30/7.
[6] M.R.O., D.R.O. 14/C1/3.
[7] 9th Rep. Com. Char. 267–8.
[8] Char. Com. files.
[9] 9th Rep. Com. Char. 267.
[10] Char. Com. files.
[11] 9th Rep. Com. Char. 268.

discussed the affairs of the charity, had to be content with rents of £8.[12] The annual rent amounted to £13 in 1823, when half was spent on the church and half, supplemented by the parish, on beef for 60 poor people at Christmas. In 1964 the income was between £25 and £50.

Rose Archer (d. 1686) is said to have left the income on £20 to six poor women.[13] In 1823 it was reported that the capital had been spent nearly forty years previously, on legal costs over the houses in Billiter Lane, and the vestry agreed to reinstate the charity with £20 from the church-rates.[14] By 1899 there was stock worth £77 6s. and in 1964 the income amounted to less than £5 a year.[15]

John Pardoe, by deed of 1757, left his great tithes on some 230 a. in Hendon to ten poor widows aged 40 or over on Stanmore.[16] A rent-charge payable in lieu of great tithes was gradually redeemed for stock between 1909 and 1943. Henry Hooper, by deed of

1850, left four cottages on Stanmore Hill to be used as alms-houses for poor widows. The cottages were not endowed and the rector reported that they were very dilapidated in 1883, when the tenants were paying 6d. a week. The buildings, condemned by 1903, had been pulled down by 1915, when a Scheme directed that their site should be let as a garden and that the income should be used, after helping former inmates to pay rent elsewhere, to augment Pardoe's charity. The land, let for £10 in 1947, was sold for £1,250 in 1967. Frances Wilson of Belmont Lodge began to build four alms-houses for widows in Elm Terrace, Old Church Lane, in 1922, and, by will proved in the following year, left the income on £500 towards repairs. In 1963, when the annual income was £26 6s. 2d., a Scheme empowered the trustees to charge weekly contributions of 10s. or less towards the cost of upkeep. The alms-houses, forming a single-storeyed red-brick building, survived in 1971.[17]

LITTLE STANMORE

LITTLE STANMORE[1] parish was similar to Great Stanmore in alignment, although longer and thinner in shape. Its area was slightly larger, 1,552 a. in 1841,[2] and its centre of population lay closer to London, which was less than 9 miles from Edgware High Street.[3] By 1538 the parish was also known as Whitchurch, presumably because of the colouring of the church walls.[4] During the 17th and 18th centuries that name was sometimes used to distinguish the church and its very few near-by buildings from the houses along Watling Street.[5]

The northern boundary, across Bushey Heath, followed that of the county.[6] The eastern boundary was formed by Watling Street, which ran south-west from Elstree to Brockley Hill, where it resumed its south-easterly course to London, separating Little Stanmore from Edgware as far as Edgware brook and from Hendon between the brook and Burnt Oak. The parish was bordered by Kingsbury on the south and Great Stanmore on the west.

Little Stanmore, where James Brydges, duke of Chandos (d. 1744), built his mansion of Canons, has always shared its main areas of settlement with Edgware. In the extreme north both parishes included part of the village of Elstree. Most of their inhabitants lived farther south along Watling Street, where houses along the Little Stanmore side were normally thought to belong to the high street of the village or town of Edgware.[7] Since the 17th century, however, the administrative history of Little Stanmore has been more closely bound up with that of Great Stanmore. The civil parish lay within Hendon R.D. from 1894 until 1934 before it was divided to form part of the wards of Stanmore North and

Stanmore South in the urban district (later borough and later London Borough) of Harrow.[8]

The soil is mainly London Clay, as in the parishes to east and west. Pebble gravel, edged with Claygate Beds, covers the highest ground, from Brockley Hill along Wood Lane to Great Stanmore; in the south alluvium lies along the border at Marsh Lane.[9] From less than 200 ft. in the south the ground slopes slowly up to 300 ft. at the bottom of Brockley Hill and from there rises rapidly to 400 ft. at Wood Lane, which itself reaches 475 ft. near the western boundary. Northward from its crest the level dips to 350 ft., only to rise to 425 ft. at Elstree, in the extreme north-east. West of Elstree a small part of Aldenham reservoir, one of five reservoirs built by 1819 for the Grand Junction Canal Co., lies within the parish.[10] A small stream, arising from springs in Cloisters wood, flows southward to form part of the western boundary; below Stanmore marsh Edgware brook crosses the parish to join Dean's brook in Edgware.

Oliver Goldsmith (1728–74), who spent three years in Kingsbury, is said also to have lived in an unidentified house 'at the back of Canons', where he laid out a small but elaborately ornamented garden. Albert Chevalier (d. 1923), the singer, lived at Brockley Hill.[11] All other well-known residents were owners of Canons, or persons connected with them, or incumbents.

The busiest road has always been Watling Street, the Roman road from London to St. Albans (Herts.) and Chester.[12] Since the mid 19th century the northernmost stretch has been known as Elstree Hill

[12] M.R.O., D.R.O. 14/C1/1.
[13] 9th Rep. Com. Char. 268–70; Char. Com. files.
[14] M.R.O., D.R.O. 14/C1/3.
[15] Char. Com. files.
[16] 9th Rep. Com. Char. 271.
[17] Char. Com. files.
[1] The article was written in 1971. Any references to later years are dated. The help of Mr. R. W. Thomson in making material available and commenting on the article is gratefully acknowledged.
[2] Census, 1841.
[3] Except where otherwise stated, the rest of the para.

and the following para. are based on O.S. Maps 6″, Mdx. V. SE.; VI. SW.; XI. NW. (1865 and later edns.).
[4] P.N. Mdx. (E.P.N.S.), 66.
[5] e.g. J. Ogilby, Map of Mdx. (c. 1677); J. Rocque, Map of Mdx. (1754).
[6] See p. 114.
[7] V.C.H. Mdx. iv. 151.   [8] See p. 121.
[9] Geol. Surv. Map 1″, drift, sheet 256 (1951 edn.); ibid. 6″, Mdx. XI. NW. (1920 edn.).
[10] A. Rees, Cyclopaedia (1819 edn.), vi, s.v. 'Canal'.
[11] Druett, Stanmores and Harrow Weald, 190–1.
[12] V.C.H. Mdx. iv. 151–2.

and the slope from the ridge farther south as Brockley Hill.[13] The name Edgware Road, applied to much of Watling Street in the south part of the parish and beyond, first appeared as Edgware highway in 1574. In 1971 shorter sections of the road were known as Stone Grove, High Street, and Burnt Oak Broadway.

From the Middle Ages until the early 18th century a main road, leaving Watling Street at Stone Grove, led north-west across both Little Stanmore and Great Stanmore to Watford.[14] In 1718 James Brydges, then earl of Carnarvon, was licensed to inclose the Little Stanmore section of the Watford road in the grounds of Canons.[15] Brydges in compensation improved the modern London Road from Canons Corner, farther north than Stone Grove, south-westward across the parish to Great Stanmore village, along the line of an older way connecting Watling Street with Harrow and Uxbridge.[16] Parallel routes across the parish were Wood Lane, following the crest of the ridge from Brockley Hill by 1754, and Whitchurch Lane, running west from the high street past the isolated parish church to meet the western boundary at Stanmore marsh. Bacon Lane, running south from the parish church to Roe Green in Kingsbury, had largely fallen into disuse by 1754, when it also had an easterly branch leading to Watling Street below Edgware bridge.[17] A track still led south in 1827[18] but by 1865 the branch from Watling Street, marked by the present Bacon Lane, alone remained, to peter out among the fields.[19] Apart from the drives running through the park of Canons, there were no other roads until the first suburban avenues were laid out shortly before the First World War.[20] In 1971 the north-eastern corner of the parish, including new roads in the Little Stanmore quarter of Elstree village, was cut off by two major roads: the Watford by-pass, finished in 1927, there ran parallel with the M1 motorway, opened in 1967 and intersecting with the by-pass east of Brockley Hill, in Edgware.[21]

In 1826 Edgware brook flowed through a culvert near the church,[22] perhaps under Bacon Lane, and under a bridge which had existed in some form since 1597[23] at the south end of Edgware village.[24]

Watling Street, although often in need of repair, brought comparatively good communications with London before the railway age: in 1832 the Royal Mail called every day and other coaches left almost hourly from inns along the village high street.[25] Apart from coaches to Great Stanmore,[26] however, public transport was restricted to Watling Street until the 20th century. Horse-drawn omnibuses, opposed by Edgware vestry,[27] had reached Cricklewood by 1896 and Edgware a few years later.[28] In 1904 the Metropolitan Electric Tramways Co.

opened a service along the route but a proposed extension went no farther north than the corner of London Road, where Canons Park became the terminus from 1907.[29] By that date the London General Omnibus Co. was running motor-buses to Great Stanmore and Watford along London Road itself. In 1934 motor-buses ran the entire length of the parish, up Brockley Hill to Elstree, and also reached Great Stanmore via Whitchurch Lane and Marsh Lane.[30] All the routes were used in 1971, when the southern area which had been densely built up in the 1930s enjoyed services linking Edgware and Queensbury stations along Camrose Avenue.[31]

Although no railway reached the parish until the 1930s, most inhabitants could conveniently use the Great Northern branch line from Edgware station, opened in 1867, or the Underground which ran from there after 1924.[32] A branch of the Metropolitan line, driven north from Wembley Park through Kingsbury to Little Stanmore, was opened in 1932. It became part of the Bakerloo line in 1939.[33] Stanmore station, its terminus at London Road, and Canons Park station, near the western end of Whitchurch Lane, also served much of Great Stanmore after the closure of the old Stanmore railway station in 1952.[34]

Settlement probably was always densest along Watling Street. A 15th- or 16th-century house survived, as no. 47 High Street, until after 1950[35] and was one of a line of buildings which stretched from Whitchurch Lane to Edgware brook by 1597.[36] Together with those forming part of Elstree in the north and others encroaching from Great Stanmore, they left no need for a central village in such a long, narrow parish. From the Middle Ages until the 20th century there were very few buildings between the eastern and western boundaries apart from the church, first mentioned c. 1130,[37] and the manor-house of the priors of St. Bartholomew, Smithfield, to the north. No traces survive of a medieval village around the church nor of any open fields.[38] The most distinctive feature of the parish became the manor-house, known by the early 16th century as Canons,[39] which was completely rebuilt at least three times. The duke of Chandos's famous mansion had the shortest life but its extensive grounds, stretching from Watling Street to the western border, helped to limit the spread of modern building.

In the early 18th century,[40] after improvements carried out by the duke of Chandos, Canons stood at the centre of a square formed by Watling Street, London Road, Marsh Lane, and Whitchurch Lane. The principal drive led south-east to two lodges at the north end of the houses along Watling Street and

[13] O.S. Map 6″, Mdx. V. SE. (1865 edn.).
[14] C. F. Baylis, *Edgware and the Stanmores*, 5 and map facing p. 1.
[15] M.R.O., MJ/SBB. 766/33.
[16] Baylis, op. cit. map facing p. 1.
[17] Rocque, *Map of Mdx.* (1754).
[18] M.R.O., Acc. 262/71/2.
[19] O.S. Map 6″, Mdx. XI. NW. (1865 edn.).
[20] See p. 112.
[21] *V.C.H. Mdx.* iv. 152.
[22] *Rep. on Bridges in Mdx.* 207.
[23] *V.C.H. Mdx.* iv. 151.
[24] *Rep. on Bridges in Mdx.* 207.
[25] *Pigot's Com. Dir.* (1832–4).
[26] See p. 91.
[27] *V.C.H. Mdx.* iv. 152.

[28] A. J. Garrett, 'Hist. Geog. of Upper Brent' (London Univ. M.A. thesis, 1935), 130–2 and maps; ex inf. Mr. H. V. Borley.
[29] *V.C.H. Mdx.* iv. 153.
[30] Garrett, op. cit. 133 and maps.
[31] Harrow L.B., *Official Guide* [c. 1967].
[32] *V.C.H. Mdx.* iv. 152–3.
[33] C. E. Lee, *Sixty Years of the Bakerloo*, 22–3.
[34] See p. 91.
[35] Min. of Town and Country Planning, List of Bldgs. (1950).
[36] All Souls Coll., Oxford, map of Edgware man. 1597; *V.C.H. Mdx.* iv, plate facing p. 127.
[37] See p. 122.
[38] Garrett, op. cit. 58.   [39] See p. 114.
[40] The para. is based on Rocque, *Map of Mdx.* (1754).

was balanced by a tree-lined ride leading north-east. Avenues, terminated by lodges, also radiated north, west, and south. Parkland covered most of the eastern part of the square but there were inclosed fields along Marsh Lane surrounding Marsh Farm in the south-western corner. The church, with 17th-century alms-houses to the north[41] and, probably, a minister's house,[42] stood at the end of the southern avenue in Whitchurch Lane. There were no other buildings of any importance away from the main road save at Brockley Hill.[43] Houses stood close together along the high street of Edgware village from a point south of Edgware brook to the gates of Canons. There were a few others at the south corner of Bacon Lane and one or two at Elstree.

Tenements within the manor of Little Stanmore called the Lion, the Falcon, and the Crown, whose holders had pasture rights in Stanmore marsh in 1582,[44] were presumably inns in the high street. Part of the inn later called the Crane or the Chandos Arms stood there by 1600 and the later White Hart was rebuilt in the 17th century.[45] The sole inn recorded away from Watling Street was the King's Head, recently erected on the old Watford road near Pear wood in 1720 and still existing in 1729.[46] A divided tenement called the Greyhound in 1719, which had been rebuilt as the Green Man inn by 1724,[47] was licensed in 1751, together with the White Horse, the Coach and Horses, the White Lion, the White Hart, the Crane, latterly also known as the Chandos Arms, and the Mason's Arms. The last four, whose sites ranged from the modern Burnt Oak Broadway northward to the corner of Whitchurch Lane, were the only inns licensed in 1803.[48] Apart from the Chandos Arms, awaiting demolition in 1937, they survived in 1971, although the White Lion and the Mason's Arms had been rebuilt. An inn called the Load of Hay stood south of Bacon Lane in 1865.[49]

There was very little new building away from Watling Street in the late 18th and early 19th centuries. Oak Villa and other residences at the corner of London Road and Dennis Lane formed part of Great Stanmore village, although they were in Little Stanmore parish, and the Limes (later Limes House), a mansion at the west end of Wood Lane, was approached from across the boundary.[50] The Little Stanmore side of Watling Street boasted 18th-century gentlemen's residences in Albany House and its neighbour, as well as a chapel from 1834[51] and a police station in Whitchurch Lane from 1853,[52] but in 1865 there were more houses on the Edgware side, both along the high street and in adjoining roads.[53] In 1887 the park of Canons stretched along the main road, with the result that north of the lodges there were still no buildings to face those on the Edgware side, except where the 18th-century Stone Grove House stood immediately

south of Stone Grove Lodge and Stone Grove Cottage.[54] At Elstree the post office was in Little Stanmore, south-west of the cross-roads.[55]

Growth along the Little Stanmore side of Edgware Road was made possible by sales of Canons and the gradual reduction of its surrounding estate.[56] A small plot on the north side of Whitchurch Lane, near the high street, and 10 a. on the south side, beyond the church, were advertised for building in 1887. The Canons Park Estate Co. in 1898 announced plans for building on the remaining 479 a.[57] and in 1905 land was sold for Whitchurch gardens, where semi-detached houses were under construction in 1911.[58] By 1919 several houses had been built between the lodges and Stone Grove, and along Whitchurch Lane from the high street towards the church. Meads Road and Montgomery Road with its offshoots were also built up.[59]

The southern part of Little Stanmore, like that of Great Stanmore, was built up in the period between the World Wars. The park of Canons, although much reduced,[60] still extended north-east of a lake along the north side of the main avenue in 1920.[61] Much of it was bought in 1926 by George Cross[62] and soon afterwards large detached houses were built along the main avenue, which was renamed Canons Drive, and along adjoining roads. Farther south houses lined both sides of Whitchurch Lane, from Edgware to the new Canons Park tube station, by 1935. By that date the fields beyond, in the extreme south part of the parish, had been covered with rows of semi-detached houses. Camrose Avenue stretched almost across the parish to Turner Road, which was under construction, and was linked by Dale Avenue and other offshoots to Mollison Way.[63] The council built the Chandos estate around Buckingham Road and the Berridge estate around Bacon Lane, which together contained 304 houses.[64] Most of the shops were in Edgware High Street or its southern continuation Burnt Oak Broadway, where new building and alterations took place. The new suburb was also served by a small shopping parade in Whitchurch Lane, west of the tube station, and in the south by shops over the parish boundary, around Honeypot Lane and Queensbury station.[65]

North of Canons Park building was in progress along both sides of London Road before the Second World War.[66] New roads included Merrion Avenue west of Stanmore tube station, Court Drive and its offshoots, and Pangbourne Drive near Edgware Road, although in 1950 there was empty ground immediately east of the railway. Parts of Valencia and Glanleam roads, north of London Road, were also built up along the foot of Brockley Hill. Contrasting conditions prevailed in the extreme north part of the parish. The acquisition of a nursing home by the Royal National Orthopaedic hospital in 1920 and the subsequent extension of its grounds

[41] See p. 127.
[42] See p. 123.
[43] See p. 113.
[44] Davenport MSS., Gt. Stan. ct. rolls.
[45] Hist. Mon. Com. *Mdx.* 115; see below, p. 113.
[46] M.L.R. 1720/2/201; 1729/3/388.
[47] M.L.R. 1719/3/18; 1724/6/453.
[48] M.R.O., L.V. 7/1; L.V. 10/113.
[49] O.S. Map 6″, Mdx. XI. NW. (1865 edn.).
[50] See p. 96.
[51] See p. 124.
[52] See p. 122.
[53] O.S. Map 6″, Mdx. VI. SW. (1865 edn.).
[54] Harrow Cent. Ref. Libr., sales parts.

[55] O.S. Map 6″, Mdx. VI. NW. (1865 edn.).
[56] See p. 116.
[57] Harrow Cent. Ref. Libr., sales parts.
[58] A. A. Jackson, *Semi-detached Lond.* 249.
[59] O.S. Map 6″, Mdx. VI. SW. (1919 edn.).
[60] See p. 116.
[61] Harrow Cent. Ref. Libr., sales parts.
[62] See p. 116.
[63] O.S. Map 6″, Mdx. VI. SW. (1935 edn.).
[64] Boro. of Harrow, *Facts & Figures* (1963–4).
[65] See pp. 55, 111.
[66] The para. is based on O.S. Maps 6″, Mdx. V. SE. (1938 edn.); 1/25,000, TQ 19 (1950 edn.).

ensured that a large area stretching north and west to the Hertfordshire boundary should remain free of housing, although additions were made to the hospital buildings near Wood Lane.[67] From 1927 the north-eastern corner of the parish was cut off by the Watford by-pass. A depot was built along the by-pass by the London Passenger Transport Board[68] and building started in Sullivan Way and its off-shoots at the Little Stanmore corner of the Elstree cross-roads.

Small council estates, comprising 56 flats and houses in Camrose Avenue and 24 at the junction of the avenue with Edgware Road, helped to cover what little building land was left in the south after the Second World War. Between the Kingsbury boundary and Whitchurch Lane there were no open spaces, apart from playing fields and the 27 a. of Chandos recreation ground immediately south of Edgware brook.[69] Farther north many houses were more expensive because of their proximity to Canons and its grounds. Land stretching east to Seven Acre lake was saved by the North London Collegiate school, which bought the mansion in 1929, while nearly 50 a. became a public park incorporating a garden.[70] In 1971 an avenue of trees, cut by the Bakerloo line which had become the western boundary of the park itself, still stretched to the former gateway in Marsh Lane, and a second avenue led south alongside the main park to the churchyard. The entrance in Whitchurch Lane afforded a vista across nearly half a mile of finely timbered land to the south front of Canons, whose modern extensions were largely masked by trees.

North of the park many gaps were filled on either side of London Road between 1950 and 1963.[71] Westbere Drive and Aylward school were built east of the railway and more detached houses appeared in and around Glanleam Road. Land at the corner of London Road and Brockley Hill was acquired by the Ministry of Works in 1946 and an additional plot to the north was bought in 1957.[72] Government offices, most of them single-storeyed buildings, stretched for more than half a mile up Brockley Hill in 1971, when they were used by the Department of the Environment, the Ministry of Defence, and several other bodies. Farther north the sports ground and club-house of George Wimpey & Co. adjoined a slope of open country, crowned with woods. Beyond Wood Lane more additions were made to the Royal National Orthopaedic hospital and from 1967 Watling Street was carried on a bridge over the M1 motorway. At Elstree building continued along Schubert Road and other offshoots of Sullivan Way; a few modern houses were all that stood on the Little Stanmore side at the top of Elstree Hill in 1971, although some 19th-century cottages survived along the Bushey–Barnet road.

Apart from St. Lawrence's church and Canons, there are no notable pre-20th-century buildings away from Watling Street.[73] Near the corner of Camrose Avenue a late-18th-century red-brick residence, with adjoining stables, awaited demolition in 1971.[74] Albany House, a similar building of c. 1750, stands to the north. Beyond Edgware brook is the stuccoed, three-storeyed White Hart, 17th-century but with timbering of c. 1500;[75] Victorian alterations have been made to its ground floor. Farther north an 18th-century red-brick house has been divided into two shops, nos. 59 and 61 High Street, as has the 17th-century timber-framed building which contains nos. 65 and 67. On the far side of the junction with Whitchurch Lane most of a 17th-century timbered row survives in nos. 81 to 101; the ground floors are used as shops or as part of the Dick Turpin, nos. 99 and 101 having comprised the Sawyers' Arms, dated 1650. Farther north Stone Grove Court, stuccoed and early-19th-century, stands about mid-way between Canons Drive and London Road. Over a mile beyond are Brockley Hill House, a stuccoed mid-19th-century residence in the grounds of the Royal National Orthopaedic hospital, and the 17th-century brick and weatherboarded Brockley Hill Farm, with weatherboarded barns. An older Brockley Hill House, first mentioned in 1725[76] and later the seat of William Sharpe,[77] probably stood farther west. Close to the Great Stanmore boundary, in the grounds of the hospital, is an obelisk erected by Sharpe in the mid 18th century; its inscription, renewed at the expense of the governors, claims that Cassivellaunus made a successful stand there against the Romans.[78]

There were 127 communicants in Little Stanmore in 1547[79] and 91 adult males, including the minister, who took the protestation oath in 1642.[80] The population rose from 424 in 1801 to 891 in 1861 but was no more than 862 in 1881 and 1,069 in 1891. It rose more sharply in the early 20th century, reaching 1,761 in 1911, 2,015 in 1921, when numbers overtook those in Great Stanmore, and 6,918 in 1931. The density increased from 1·3 persons per acre in 1921 to 4·35 ten years later. Stanmore South ward, covering much of the south of the parish, had 13,363 inhabitants in 1951 and the high density of 30·5 to an acre in 1951. By 1961 numbers had fallen to 11,365, reducing the density to 25·9.[81]

MANORS. In the reign of Edward the Confessor 9½ hides in Stanmore, presumably part of the lands which had been granted by Offa to St. Albans,[82] were held by Algar, the man of Earl Harold. In 1086 they formed part of the fief of Roger de Rames, who was also lord of Charlton but whose main property lay in Essex.[83] The lands, which probably included the later manors of both *LITTLE STANMORE*,

[67] See p. 122.
[68] See p. 120.
[69] Boro. of Harrow, *Facts & Figures* (1963–4).
[70] See p. 122.
[71] Except where otherwise stated, the para. is based on O.S. Maps 1/25,000, TQ 19 (1950 edn.); 1/2,500, TQ 1792 (1963 edn.); 1/2,500, TQ 1793 (1964 edn.).
[72] Ex inf. Dept. of the Environment.
[73] Except where otherwise stated, the para. is based on Hist. Mon. Com. *Mdx.* 115 and Min. of Town and Country Planning, List of Bldgs. (1950).
[74] It was called Edgware Ho. in 1897, when another

Edgware Ho. (later Edgware Place) stood farther north on the east side of Watling Street: O.S. Map 6″, Mdx. XI. NW. (1897 edn.); *V.C.H. Mdx.* iv. 154.
[75] *Harrow Observer*, 10 Oct. 1972.
[76] M.L.R. 1725/4/368.
[77] *Ambulator* (1807).
[78] Druett, *Stanmores and Harrow Weald*, 12–13 and plate facing p. 16.
[79] E 301/34/127.
[80] H.L., Mdx. Protestation Rets.
[81] *Census*, 1801–1961.
[82] See p. 96.
[83] *V.C.H. Mdx.* i. 116, 128.

sometimes called *CANONS*, and Edgware, passed to Roger's son William but were divided, with the rest of the Rames barony, between his sons Roger (II) and Robert by *c.* 1130. Their holdings were separated by the road running north-westward from Stone Grove in Watling Street towards Watford. Part of the Domesday manor east of Watling Street, i.e. most of Edgware, may have passed from the Rames family on the marriage of Adelize, probably Roger's daughter, to Edward of Salisbury. After the rest had been divided between the two brothers, the property north of the old Watford road was treated as part of the vill of Edgware, while that to the south was considered to belong to Stanmore and eventually, since it was smaller than the St. Albans estate, to form Little Stanmore. The reunion of the two Rames estates under Roger's son, Roger (III), made the name Little Stanmore less appropriate, although the northern part was for long described as in Edgware.[84]

Alienations of the Domesday manor began with gifts to the priory of St. Bartholomew the Great, West Smithfield, by Roger (II) and Robert de Rames. In the south Roger (II) gave St. Lawrence's church, with land stretching east to Watling Street and north as far as the Watford road, while in the north-western corner of Edgware Robert gave the church of St. Bartholomew, 'Elstree'. Roger (III) granted half his lands in Edgware and Stanmore, except his dwelling-house, the church and an adjoining meadow, to Adam, son of Ranulph Bucointe, to be held as ½ knight's fee, and pledged 30 a. which the family had retained in Edgware to Humphrey Bucointe. Roger's son William (II), to recover the 30 a., surrendered to Humphrey 120 a. in the northern angle between Watling Street and the old Watford road. William also gave land in the north to St. Bartholomew's and, by 1191, lands to the south along Watling Street to Waleran, the husband or future husband of Lucy, Humphrey Bucointe's daughter. William was succeeded *c.* 1196 by his son and namesake and in *c.* 1203 by his grandson, also called William, a minor, who rebelled against King John but was restored in 1217. William de Rames (IV), for £42 and land in Essex, in 1238 released to St. Bartholomew's all his reversionary interest in Little Stanmore which was enjoyed by his mother Gille, although in 1241 the prior sued Gille and her husband, William Hanselin, for despoiling her dower lands. Meanwhile the lands of Adam Bucointe had passed to his son Henry and those of Humphrey Bucointe and of Waleran to the latter's daughter Lucy Waleran.[85] In 1242–3 the former Rames holding in Little Stanmore, which had constituted one knight's fee in 1210–12, was divided into ½ knight's fee held by Henry Bucointe and two ¼ knight's fees, held by Lucy Waleran and William Hanselin, all held of St. Bartholomew's.[86]

Within a century of acquiring the remaining interest of William de Rames, St. Bartholomew's had secured most of the lands which his ancestors had granted to the Bucointes. Land in the north-west, extending into Great Stanmore, had been conveyed by Adam Bucointe to the abbot of St. Albans, who incorporated it into Aldenham and so shifted the boundary of the Stanmores and of Middlesex to the south-east,[87] and Adam's son Henry had granted a house and a croft, with land in Stanmore marsh, to the Knights of St. John of Jerusalem.[88] The rest of Henry's property passed in turn to his sons, Henry and Ranulph, the second of whom retained part for his mother Joan and his two daughters but sold the rest to Thomas Esperun, who sold it to Nicholas Longespée. Nicholas gave his lands in Little Stanmore to his daughter Alice on her marriage to Geoffrey de Jarpenville, but by 1277 Jarpenville's lands and those of Ranulph Bucointe's mother and daughters were fraudulently acquired by the moneylender Adam de Stratton. In the meantime the estate of Lucy Waleran, wife of Robert de Paris and later of Andrew Blund and Sir John Garland, passed to her son William de Paris (d. 1271). William's widow Sibyl and her daughters Lucy, wife of John Pypard, and Clarice, wife of Richard de la Grave, all surrendered their rights to Adam de Stratton but regained them on his disgrace in 1290.[89] Their lands, ⅕ knight's fee held by William Pypard and William de la Grave in 1306,[90] were acquired by St. Bartholomew's in 1314, when William Pypard was licensed to alienate 182 a. John de Barnville, who presumably had acquired part of Henry Bucointe's former estate, alienated land to the priory in 1316.[91] More land, which probably formed at least part of that given to the Knights Hospitallers by Henry Bucointe, was acquired by exchange in 1330. John le Blount of Biggleswade (Beds.) conveyed land in 1331 and Henry le Hayward and Roger de Creton, to support a chantry in the priory church, in 1335.[92] The priory's total acreage in Little Stanmore, 379½ a. in 1306, was thus raised to 957½ a.[93] Held as one knight's fee in 1353,[94] it remained the largest single estate of St. Bartholomew's until the Dissolution.[95]

In the 16th century, if not earlier, the priors leased out many portions of their property in Little Stanmore, normally for at least 30 years. A lease in 1501 of the manor of 'Little Stanmore called Canons' provides the earliest instance of an alternative name being given to the manor,[96] Canons originally having been the land granted to the priory in 1330.[97] Thereafter the second name became increasingly common, until it was often used on its own, although a few documents, including a will dated 1693, continued more accurately to refer to the manor of Little Stanmore and the capital message called Canons.[98] It was as the manor of Canons that the great manor-house and gardens were leased, separately from most of the estate, to William Daunce of Whitchurch in 1535.[99]

St. Bartholomew's was surrendered in 1539 and Little Stanmore, like Great Stanmore, was granted for life to the last prior, Robert Fuller, in 1540.[1] It

84 Baylis, *Edgware and the Stanmores*, 2, 4–5.
85 Ibid. 4, 6, 8–9, 14–15.
86 *Book of Fees*, ii. 898.
87 Baylis, op. cit. 6, 8.
88 *Cat. Anct. D.* ii, A 2396; iv, A 7268.
89 Baylis, op. cit. 15–16.
90 E. A. Webb, *Recs. of St. Bartholomew's, Smithfield*, i. 450.
91 *Cal. Pat.* 1313–17, 114, 558.

92 Ibid. 1330–4, 13, 195; 1334–8, 97.
93 Webb, *Recs. of St. Barts.* i. 350–1.
94 *Feud. Aids*, iii. 376.
95 Webb, *Recs. of St. Barts.* i. 351.
96 C 1/572/35.
97 *P.N. Mdx.* (E.P.N.S.), 67.
98 Prob. 11/418 (P.C.C. 35 Box).
99 E 303/9/281.
1 *L. & P. Hen. VIII*, xvi, p. 716.

reverted to the Crown on Fuller's death later in that year and in 1543 the manor-house of Canons, as leased to William Daunce, was granted to the sitting tenant Hugh Losse and his heirs.[2] Losse, a merchant who accumulated much monastic property, obtained more lands formerly of St. Bartholomew's in Little Stanmore in 1544 and 1546,[3] and bought the rectory and most of the other property once leased out by the priory there in 1552.[4] He was succeeded in 1556 by his son Robert[5] and afterwards by Robert's son Hugh, knighted in 1603, who in 1604 sold the manor of Canons otherwise Stanmore the Less to James I's secretary of state, Sir Thomas Lake, and his wife Mary.[6] In 1630 it passed to Lake's son, Sir Thomas, who in 1641 conveyed it in reversion, on the death of his mother, to Dame Frances Weld,[7] who in turn transferred it to Sir Thomas's younger brother Lancelot in 1654.[8] Sir Lancelot, knighted in 1660, was followed in 1680 by his second son, Lancelot, who in 1689 left the manor to Lancelot (III), son of his late elder brother, another Sir Thomas (d. 1673). Lancelot (III) died in 1693, leaving Canons to his father's younger brother Warwick Lake, who in 1709 sold it to James Brydges, husband of Lancelot (III)'s sister Mary. Warwick's death in 1713 gave possession of Canons to Brydges, its most famous resident, soon to succeed as Lord Chandos of Sudeley and to rise through the peerage to become, in 1719, duke of Chandos.[9]

In the 18th and 19th centuries the manor was normally described as Little Stanmore, to distinguish it from the mansion of Canons. James, duke of Chandos (d. 1744), having made a fortune as paymaster of the duke of Marlborough's armies, had land in several counties. The debts left at his death were not serious but by that time his surviving son Henry had incurred much heavier liabilities. An Act of 1746 accordingly authorized Henry to sell the two Stanmore manors, with Canons and much other property in Middlesex and Hertfordshire.[10] Despite the break-up of the Canons estate,[11] the lordship of Little Stanmore, like that of Great Stanmore, remained in the Brydges family and so passed to the duke of Buckingham and Chandos.[12] In 1838 the duke still owned fields along Marsh Lane and farther north, on the other side of London Road, bordered on the east by the much larger estate of the Plumers, who had acquired Canons. The duke's land, 103 a. in 1838,[13] had been reunited with Canons by 1887,[14] although the manor continued to pass through the same hands as Great Stanmore.[15]

The manor-house in 1535 was to be kept in repair by the tenant, William Daunce, who had to reserve four chambers for the use of the prior.[16] The

building which passed to Brydges in 1713, traditionally ascribed to John Thorpe (fl. 1570–1610), presumably had been designed for the first Sir Thomas Lake.[17] Something is known of it from two plans of c. 1606, one of them inscribed 'Canons, my Lady Lake's house',[18] and it was evidently of brick, since Brydges before deciding to rebuild merely contemplated alterations, including a new brick façade. Work began on outlying offices as early as 1713, under William Talman, but Brydges, increasingly ambitious yet often indecisive and cheese-paring, turned to a series of architects whose individual contributions cannot now be distinguished. John James, from 1714 to 1715, and James Gibbs, from 1716 to 1719, received the largest sums, but advice was also sought from Sir John Vanbrugh and Robert Benson, Lord Bingley. Gibbs, who claimed to have been the architect, at least modified the external design, whereas it is unlikely that more than the final touches were put by John Price, named as architect on engravings of the south and east elevations. The engravings, the only depictions of that time to survive, are dated 1720.[19] By that year the outside was probably finished, although work on some of the rooms continued until 1723.

Chandos's mansion was almost square, with a central courtyard, built on an axis north-north-west to south-south-east. A chapel, at a right angle to a projecting wing of offices, probably jutted out from the north-east corner[20] and a second wing may have projected north from the north-west corner. The great entrance hall was in the centre of what may be called the south range, with the saloon overhead; the second or main floor also boasted the largest room, the library, which filled the centre of the north range.[21] The entire building, stone-faced and contained in an Ionic order, may have appeared monotonous, for it lacked the stamp of one man's genius. Measuring 146 ft. × 124 ft., it was not enormous by the standards of its age. The interior, thanks to Chandos's obsession with opulent detail, was more remarkable: rare woods and marbles vied with ceilings painted by Thornhill, Kent, Belucci, and Laguerre, with Gobelins tapestries, and with art treasures which included cartoons by Raphael. The grounds too were outstanding, with their sculpture and wrought iron, their canals and parterres, their 87 a. of pleasure garden, the hothouses, the aviary, and the lines and clumps of elms. After the closure of the road from Edgware to Watford, avenues radiated from the house northward to London Road, westward to Marsh Lane in Great Stanmore, south to St. Lawrence's church, and south-east to Edgware. Most visitors presumably used the third

[2] Ibid. xviii(1), p. 364.

[3] Ibid. xix(1), p. 644; xxi(2), p. 162.

[4] Cal. Pat. 1550–3, 457.

[5] Ibid. 1555–7, 67.

[6] C.P. 25(2)/323/2 Jas. I. Trin. Mdx.

[7] C.P. 25(2)/458/17 Chas. I Hil. Mdx.

[8] C.P. 25(2)/575/1654 Hil. Mdx.

[9] C.H.C. and M. I. Baker, Life . . . of James Brydges, First Duke of Chandos, 13–17. The authors cite family records, ibid. xii–xiii, which were moved to Stowe on the marriage of Lady Anna Eliz. Brydges (see above, p. 97) and which in 1925 were bought for the Huntington Libr., California.

[10] Listed in Baker, Chandos, 452–65.

[11] See below.

[12] See above, p. 97.

[13] M.R.O., TA/S'MORE Lt. and map (1838).

[14] Harrow Cent. Ref. Libr., sales parts. (1887).

[15] See above, p. 98.

[16] E 303/9/281.

[17] Except where otherwise stated, the foll. five paras. are based on Baker, Chandos; chapters VI, VII, VIII, and XX, deal respectively with the building of Canons, the grounds and an inventory of the contents, the household economy, and the estate after Chandos's death.

[18] Bk. of Architecture of John Thorpe (Walpole Soc. xl), 5, 7, 56, and plate 20; the original is in Sir John Soane's Mus.

[19] See plate facing p. 161; a conjectural sketch of the south front is in Robbins, Mdx. pl. 13.

[20] Baker, Chandos, 144. The chapel is shown projecting north from the north-west corner in a conjectural sketch and ground-plan by I. Dunlop, Country Life, cvi (1949), 1950, 1952.

[21] Contemporary plans, in the Huntington Libr., are reproduced in Baker, Chandos, facing pp. 125, 129, 144.

avenue, 1,300 yards long, and so, by approaching at an angle, glimpsed two fronts totalling 270 ft., as did the enraptured Defoe.[22] Pope, who, despite his denials, was widely believed to have pilloried Canons as Timon's Villa, scorned such a setting, where

> The suffring eye inverted Nature sees,
> Trees cut to statues, statues thick as trees.[23]

His invective, and the easy journey for gaping tourists from London, helped to make Canons a byword for ostentation. So too did the style of living of 'princely Chandos', who maintained a corps of Chelsea pensioners, lodged in pairs of houses at the three main gates, as well as his famous private orchestra,[24] and whose collecting mania led agents to scour the known world for exotic birds, animals, and plants. Popular interest, attracted on so many counts, was afterwards gratified by reflections on the transience of Canons's glory.

As late as 1731 it was hoped to extend the southern avenue for 2½ miles beyond St. Lawrence's church. Other expenses, however, were being pruned and Henry, duke of Chandos, could reside only briefly at Canons after his father's death there. The first sale, of books and pictures, took place early in 1747, followed by auctions of furniture in the following year. The mansion itself, denuded, had been pulled down by 1753, when the site and everything left on it were bought by William Hallett, a cabinet-maker of Long Acre who himself had worked for Chandos. Much of the land also went to Hallett or to a Col. Fitzroy, the purchases not being completed until at least 1754. Relics of Canons which perished later included the marble staircase, taken to Lord Chesterfield's London house,[25] and a figure of George I in Leicester Square. Surviving treasures include an equestrian statue of George II in Golden Square (Westminster), two wrought iron side-gates and some railings bought for St. John's churchyard, Hampstead, another gate at the Durdans, near Epsom (Surr.), and a panel by Grinling Gibbons from the library, the Stoning of St. Stephen, which eventually reached the Victoria and Albert Museum. Much has been rescued from the chapel, which was dedicated in 1720 and demolished in 1748: its windows and the centre of Belucci's ceiling, with papier-mâché mouldings of Bagutti's stucco-work, are now at St. Michael's church, Great Witley (Worcs.),[26] the organ is at Holy Trinity, Gosport (Hants), and the pulpit, altar, and some panelling are at Fawley (Berks.). It is no longer thought likely that Canons supplied railings for New College, Oxford, or the outsize portico at Hendon Hall.[27]

William Hallett (d. 1781)[28] built a villa on the same site. The bulk of his estate had been en-

franchised and evidently followed the same succession as some copyhold property which included the coach-house of North Lodge.[29] Hallett's grandson William, the young man in Gainsborough's 'The Morning Walk',[30] sold the copyhold in 1786 or 1787[31] to Col. Dennis O'Kelly (d. 1787),[32] a race-horse owner enriched by his stallion Eclipse.[33] Philip O'Kelly was admitted as the colonel's brother and heir in 1790 and was succeeded in 1811 by his son Andrew. In the following years Andrew O'Kelly conveyed his copyhold property[34] to Sir Thomas Plumer (d. 1824), later vice-chancellor of England and Master of the Rolls.[35] His son, Thomas Hall Plumer (d. 1852),[36] owned more than 450 a. of farmland in 1838, when he was the largest landowner.[37] Soon after Lady Plumer's death there in 1857 Canons was offered by her grandson Hall Plumer to a German speculator, one Strousberg, and finally sold in 1860 to Dr. David Begg. Begg died at Canons in 1868 and his widow in 1887, whereupon the estate was offered for sale in nine lots by trustees.[38] At that date the land stretched from Whitchurch Lane north beyond London Road, and from Edgware Road westward to Marsh Lane. Apart from the mansion it contained the farm-house which had belonged to Marsh farm, North and South lodges, at the Edgware gates, and Stone Grove House, Lodge, and Cottage, along Edgware Road; there were also four 'superior' houses at the corner of Dennis Lane and London Road[39] and fields at the corner of Marsh Lane and London Road which in 1838 had belonged to the duke of Buckingham and Chandos.[40] Morris Jenks bought the entire estate, amounting to some 479 a., and sold it in 1896 to the Canons Park Estate Co.,[41] which in 1898 issued a prospectus of its plans for development.[42] Arthur du Cros, founder of the Dunlop Rubber Co. and later a baronet, bought the mansion but in 1905 sold part of the estate. In 1919 he formed a trust, the Pards Estate, and in 1920 Canons itself was offered for sale, with lands that had been greatly reduced in the north, west, and south-east. Canons Park, formerly Marsh, farm-house and the other houses had been sold and 150 a. remained, almost corresponding to the present open space but still stretching eastward, along the north of the avenue, to reach as far as Edgware Road. In 1926 George Cross bought 85 a. and in 1928 the remainder was bought by Canons Ltd. and, on the west, by Harrow U.D.C. as a park. The mansion and 10 a. were sold in 1929 to the North London Collegiate school. More land was acquired by the school in 1936 and by the county council for playing fields, which were lent to the school.[43]

Some of Chandos's materials were used for the

[22] Daniel Defoe, *Tour through Eng. and Wales* (Everyman edn.), ii. 5–8.
[23] *Epistle to Ric. Boyle, Ld. Burlington*, l. 119–20. Timon's Villa was not modelled on Canons alone: *Alex. Pope, Epistles to Several Persons*, ed. F. W. Bateson, 146–52, 170–4.   [24] See below, p. 120.
[25] Pevsner, *Mdx.* 147. An account of the relics in *Country Life*, xxxv (1914), is corrected by Baker, *Chandos*, 436–49. Many relics are illus. by Baker and *Country Life*, cvi.
[26] Pevsner, *Worcs.* 172–3.   [27] See p. 9.
[28] *Gent. Mag.* lii. 45–6, *pace* Baker, *Chandos*, 438.
[29] M.R.O., Acc. 658/1, f. 40.
[30] W. Myers, 'Canons', in *North London Collegiate Sch. 1850–1950*, 181. A painting by Francis Hayman of the first Wm. Hallett and his family at Canons is in ibid. facing p. 161.

[31] M.R.O., Acc. 658/1, ff. 59–61, 74.
[32] *Gent. Mag.* lvii(2), 1197.
[33] The mistaken story that Eclipse was buried in the park at Canons apparently originated in Lysons, *Environs*, iii. 408.
[34] M.R.O., Acc. 658/1, ff. 77, 181, 206–7.
[35] *D.N.B.*   [36] Tablet in ch. porch.
[37] M.R.O., TA/S'MORE Lt.   [38] M.R.O., Acc. 784/1.
[39] Oak Villa and its neighbours; see p. 93.
[40] Harrow Cent. Ref. Libr., sales parts.; M.R.O., TA/S'MORE Lt.
[41] M.R.O., Acc. 784/1.
[42] *Mdx. and Herts. N. & Q.* iii. 16; Harrow Cent. Ref. Libr., debenture prospectus.
[43] Jackson, *Semi-det. Lond.* 249, 253–4. Harrow Cent. Ref. Libr., sales parts.

new Canons. The third duke, on a visit in the 1780s, thought the result elegant but rather modest for the grounds, whose richness defied description.[44] Humphry Repton landscaped the gardens for Sir Thomas Plumer[45] and by 1887 evergreens had been planted along the south-eastern avenue to replace trees which had been felled by Dr. Begg.[46] Sir Arthur du Cros heightened and brought forward the third, attic, storey, and added a new entrance forecourt to the east, with a kitchen wing to the north balanced by a screen to the south; beyond the screen, and also on the northern side, paved gardens were laid out.[47] Hallett's stone house, so extended, remains the core of the school buildings, although large brick additions, of the same height, have been made to the north.[48]

The manor of *STANMORE CHENDUIT*, so described in 1276-7,[49] originated in the land settled by Nicholas Longespée on his daughter Alice and her prospective husband, Geoffrey de Jarpenville,[50] in 1260-1. The property comprised a house and one carucate in the south-east of Little Stanmore and lands in Colmans Dean, which lay in Kingsbury.[51] In 1272-3 Geoffrey and his wife gave a messuage, land, and rents in Little Stanmore, with land in Edgware, to Stephen Chenduit, in exchange for an estate at Langley Chenduit or Shendish,[52] his manor in Kings Langley (Herts.).[53] All that Stephen Chenduit had received from the Jarpenvilles was conveyed in 1274-5 to Adam de Stratton.[54] In 1276-7 Stanmore Chenduit contained a 'court' and 396 a., of which a field called Wimborough comprised 120 a., marshland 94 a., and Colmans Dean 70 a.[55] The manor is not recorded again and in the 14th century was presumably merged in the other lands of St. Bartholomew's.

The reputed manor of *WIMBOROUGH* was so called in 1540, when it was granted for life to Robert Fuller.[56] Wimborough, possibly Wina's hill, a field-name in 1276-7,[57] had become a separate estate by 1528, when the tenant was Geoffrey Chamber's father-in-law Nicholas Burgh.[58] In 1534 it was again leased out by St. Bartholomew's, to Richard Warde. Warde's sons Christopher and John sold their respective interests to John Franklin and William Hawtrey, who in turn sold them to Robert Losse.[59] Although the lands granted to Fuller were said to include the manors of Little Stanmore, Canons, and Wimborough, in the late 16th and 17th centuries the last two names were often used to denote the manor of Little Stanmore. It is not clear, when both names occur, which parcels belonged to Canons and which to Wimborough: in the 17th century Wimborough was apparently the larger, whereas its profits had accounted for only £6 out of the priory's income of £19 19s. 4½d. from Little Stanmore at the Dis-

solution.[60] Sometimes only Canons was named, as in 1641 when it was said to include two parcels called Lower Wimborough, two called Wimborough hill, and Wimborough house field (perhaps the Wimborough Wicks of 40 years later).[61] Wimborough was reputed a manor between 1691 and 1753, after which the name died out,[62] until its revival for the modern Wemborough Road.

ECONOMIC HISTORY. AGRICULTURE. In 1086 Little Stanmore, like Great Stanmore, was assessed at 9½ hides and included land for 7 ploughs, pasture for the cattle of the vill, and woodland for 800 pigs. It was worth £10 T.R.E., a mere 20s. when received by Roger de Rames, and 60s. at the time of Domesday Book. There was one plough, with room for two more, on the 4-hide demesne, and the tenants had 3 ploughs, with room for one more. One villein had a virgate, 8 villeins each had ½ virgate, and 3 bordars each had 5 a.; there were 2 serfs.[63]

On some 379 a. held by St. Bartholomew's priory in 1306, 6 houses and 3 carucates were held by free tenants in demesne, and 13 houses and about 100 a. were held by freemen or serfs in villeinage. There were 18 demesne holdings, with 13 individual tenants, and 34 holdings in villeinage, with 17 tenants, three of whom also held in demesne. Most of the villein holdings comprised less than 5 a. and no more than three exceeded 10 a. Villeins enjoyed all the customs of the prior's manor of Langley (Essex), save that a widow might not hold more than one third of any tenement of which her husband had been seised.[64] The customs of Langley were themselves based on those of Shortgrove (Essex), with the difference that at Shortgrove no heriots were owed.[65]

In 1276-7 services for mowing, haymaking, and weeding were owed by three tenants of Stanmore Chenduit manor. The total value was only 2s. 2d. a year, whereas services had been commuted by one of the tenants for part of his holding and by five others for 27s. 7d. A cock and two hens, worth 3d., were also owed.[66] More than half of the tenants on the St. Bartholomew's estate in 1306 owed customary services: 22 performed weeding works, 22 haymaking, 11 harrowing, and 26 reaping. The total value of the works and of two hens and a cock was 4s. 9½d. Twenty-eight tenants also attended the lord's great reaping days, when more was taken than the value of the works. One man performed all the usual services, although the previous holder had been allowed to commute them. At Langley, and therefore presumably at Little Stanmore, commutation was not the custom.[67] A tenant of Little Stanmore still owed autumn works in 1541.[68]

Arable accounted for 156 a. or slightly over 40 per

[44] A drawing of the house from the south by J. A. Gresse, first published in Watts's *Seats of the Nobility and Gentry* (1782), is in Baker, *Chandos*, plate facing p. 436.
[45] Brewer, *Beauties of Eng. and Wales*, x(5), plate facing p. 643.
[46] Harrow Cent. Ref. Libr., sales parts.
[47] *Building News*, ci. 476.
[48] Baker, *Chandos*, plate facing p. 448; N. *Lond. Coll. Sch. 1850-1950*, plate facing p. 97.
[49] S.C. 11/439.
[50] Baylis, *Edgware and the Stanmores*, 15.
[51] C.P. 25(1)/147/21/416.
[52] C.P. 25(1)/284/20/8.
[53] *V.C.H. Herts.* ii. 240.
[54] C.P. 25(1)/148/25/24; E 42/25.

[55] S.C. 11/439.
[56] *L. & P. Hen. VIII*, xvi, p. 716.
[57] *P.N. Mdx.* (E.P.N.S.), 66.
[58] Prob. 11/22 (P.C.C. 31 Porch).
[59] C 2/Eliz. I/L11/60.
[60] Webb, *Recs. of St. Barts.* i. 352.
[61] Davenport MSS.: copy of indenture.
[62] Ibid.; M.L.R. 1753/3/36.
[63] *V.C.H. Mdx.* i. 128.
[64] The figures are based on Webb, *Recs. of St. Barts.* i. 449-55, containing the Mdx. entries on a rental (Bodl. Middlesex Roll I) transcribed in ibid. i. 428-77.
[65] Ibid. i. 436, 440.   [66] S.C. 11/439.
[67] Webb, op. cit. i. 450-5, 440.
[68] S. C. 6/Hen. VIII/2396 m. 123d.

cent of the priory's estate in 1306, pasture for 167 a. or nearly 45 per cent, and woodland for the remainder. Villein holdings contained little more than 8 a. of grassland.[69] Of the 578 a. subsequently acquired by St. Bartholomew's, 465 a. were arable, a mere 38 a. were meadow or pasture, and 75 a. were woodland. By 1335 the priory thus held 957½ a., of which 621 a. or nearly 65 per cent was arable and slightly over 20 per cent grass.[70] In the early 16th century the priory's tenants were normally forbidden to plough up meadow land and had to leave arable fallow for ten years after it had borne three years' crops.[71]

One third of the pasture on the priory's estate in 1306, at Lurspit and 'Pyrifeld', was for cows and cart-horses. The remaining 113 a., at Grimsditch, were for heifers.[72] Lurspit lay in the centre of the parish, north of Whitchurch Lane,[73] and Grimsditch entered from Edgware in the north-east, near the crest of Brockley Hill.[74] There were also separate fields and commons for 140 sheep. The villeins enjoyed pannage but were liable to fines of ½d. or 1d. if their pigs trespassed on the demesne.[75] By 1501 there was a dove-house at Canons, where in 1535 the moat was stocked with fish.[76] There was a pound in 1736, probably farther east than one which stood in 1865 at the north end of Marsh Lane; the second pound had gone by 1897.[77]

St. Bartholomew's let blocks of its estate on long leases many years before it was threatened by the Dissolution. Canons was leased out for 40 years in 1501,[78] as well as for a further 50 years in 1535.[79] The Great Marsh and other fields, previously let for 30 years in 1520, were let again at an unchanged rent for 41 years from 1535. An adjoining meadow was let for 30 years from 1526 and a block in the north of the parish was likewise let from 1530. Tenants normally could not sub-let any parcel of land for more than one year without the lord's consent.[80]

In 1541 the annual rents of St. Bartholomew's former lands in Little Stanmore totalled some £98, of which over £75 was paid by 5 tenants. The most substantial was Peter Franklin, who held lands worth £20, extending into Great Stanmore, under a lease of 1527. The others were Henry Hyde, Simon Hoddesdon, a local yeoman, John Goodwin, a London tallow-chandler, and William Daunce, who paid £13 6s. 8d. a year for Canons.[81] The Franklins were widespread, related to the Nicholls and with members in both Stanmores, Edgware, Kingsbury, and Willesden, embracing servants, yeomen, and gentry. John Franklin (d. by 1596)[82] and his son Richard (d. by 1615)[83] were described as of Canons,[84] although they never lived in the manor-house; the

house owned by John was probably the farm-house adjoining Canons which Richard held in 1604.[85] Theirs was the most prosperous branch of the family, for John held manors in Bedfordshire and Oxfordshire which passed to his son and then to his grandson Sir John Franklin,[86] lord of Cowley Peachey and of Hayes.[87] Neither Richard nor Sir John, who were residents of Willesden, died holding property in Little Stanmore.[88]

In c. 1729, when the duke of Chandos owned 1,492 a. of Little Stanmore, almost one third, 481 a. formed the demesne of Canons. The remainder was leased out, usually for 21 years although a few holdings were leased for 14 years and others during pleasure; the length of some terms was not recorded. John Phillpot, the duke's leading tenant, held 207 a., including the 54 a. of Grub's farm; Old farm contained 65 a. and New farm 90 a.[89] In 1867 ten farmers or smallholders submitted returns, when there were still 1,363 a. of agricultural land.[90] By 1897 many estates were smaller, for 21 returns were made for 1,220 a. In 1917 there were 18 returns for 1,183 a., ten being for holdings of under 20 a. and only three for holdings of over 150 a.[91]

The lands attached to Canons, being largely ornamental, distorted any picture of the economy of the parish in the early 18th century. They included 27 a. 'within the iron palisadoes', 63 a. making up the rest of the pleasure gardens and the physic garden, and 172 a. of woodland. On most holdings meadow predominated, although John Phillpot held as many as 136 a. of arable, including the whole of Grub's farm. Arable accounted for a quarter, 16 a., of the land on Old farm and for less than a quarter, 17 a. on New farm.[92] By 1798 arable covered less than one tenth of the parish, about 130 a.,[93] and by 1867 it had shrunk to 100 a., although there were still 1,363 a. of farm-land. Thereafter it virtually disappeared, amounting to 2 a. out of 1,220 a. in 1897 and 12½ a. out of 1,183 a. in 1917.[94]

Corn, chiefly wheat, was grown on about 60 per cent of the arable in 1801 and 1867. Beans were the next largest green crop in 1801, when they covered 25 a., but had become less important than root crops by 1867. Potatoes, turnips, and mangolds alone were grown 50 years later. Sheep were the main livestock in 1867, when 1,775 were kept. By 1897 there were no more than 120, although the number of cattle had roughly trebled, to 161, and that of pigs had fallen very little, to 55. Well over two-thirds of the farm-land, 875 a., supported permanent grass for mowing at that date, when London's demand for hay was at its height. Twenty years later livestock had again increased, to 844 sheep, 320 cattle and 183 pigs;

[69] Webb, op. cit. i. 450–5.
[70] Cal. Pat. 1313–17, 114, 558; 1330–4, 13, 195; 1334–8, 96–7; Webb, op. cit. i. 351.
[71] E 303/9/218; E 303/9/237; E 303/9/290.
[72] Webb, op. cit. i. 450.
[73] P.N. Mdx. (E.P.N.S.), 212; M.R.O., TA/S'MORE Lt.
[74] T.L.M.A.S. xiii. 383.
[75] Webb, op. cit. i. 450, 455.
[76] C 1/572/35; E 303/9/281.
[77] M.L.R. 1736/4/38; O.S. Maps 6″, Mdx. V. SE. (1865 and 1897 edns.).
[78] C 1/572/35.   [79] See above, p. 114.
[80] E 303/9/218; E 303/9/237; E 303/9/264; E 303/9/290.
[81] S.C. 6/Hen. VIII/2396 mm. 122–3.
[82] Prob. 11/87 (P.C.C. 19 Drake).
[83] Prob. 11/126 (P.C.C. 70 Rudd).

[84] Prob. 11/100 (P.C.C. 81 Montague, will of Agnes Franklin); Davenport MSS., Gt. Stan., will of Ric. Franklin (1599).
[85] Davenport MSS., Lt. Stan., sale of man. by Sir Hugh Losse.
[86] Prob. 11/87 (P.C.C. 19 Drake); Prob. 11/126 (P.C.C. 70 Rudd); Prob. 11/200 (P.C.C. 85 Fines).
[87] V.C.H. Mdx. iii. 173; iv. 26.
[88] Prob. 11/126; Prob. 11/200.
[89] M.R.O., Acc. 262/72/1.   [90] M.A.F. 68/136.
[91] M.A.F. 68/1675; M.A.F. 68/2815. Until 1895 holdings of 5 a. or less were not included but there were only two of them in 1917.
[92] M.R.O., Acc. 262/72/1.
[93] Middleton, View, 560. Arable was some 125 a. in 1801: H.O. 67/16.
[94] M.A.F. 68/136; M.A.F. 68/1675; M.A.F. 68/2815.

fields used for grazing had expanded to cover 609 a., whereas grass for mowing had shrunk to 559 a.[95] Stanmore Dairies operated in the 1960s at Wood farm, south of Wood Lane, but the farm was used mainly for pig-breeding, with a stock of 300–350 sows, in 1972.[96] At that date agriculture was still carried on in the north, at Brockley Hill farm.

WOODS. There were 56 a. of woodland on the priory's 379 a. in 1306 and a further 75 a. among the 578 a. of land which were soon afterwards acquired. In 1335, therefore, some 15 per cent of the 957-a. estate was wooded.[97] Woods and underwoods were often reserved in early-16th-century leases, although tenants were granted hedgebote. Tenants could keep the wood from any hedgerows grubbed up to make arable or pasture but must care for the remaining hedges and for the young trees. Woods might be sold separately and inclosed by the buyer.[98] A number of hedgerows and groves were leased out in 1534, some of them for one year and some for 18 years; future supplies were to be assured by preserving as many standards as was customary.[99] When William Daunce leased Canons in 1535, he was permitted to lop or grub up any trees within the grounds.[1]

The former monastic property granted to Hugh Losse in 1552 included Pear or Pares wood, recorded in 1538,[2] Bromfield grove, mentioned in 1512,[3] Anmers grove, and Giles park.[4] The first three covered 200 a., 80 a., and 30 a. respectively when mortgaged by Robert Losse in 1589.[5] They had been much reduced by 1640, when Pear wood and Bromfield heath together contained 180 a. and Anmers grove a mere 10 a.; Giles park then contained 22 a. and a further 34 a. were divided equally between springs near the manor-house and others in Wimborough.[6] At that date Cloisters wood, also recorded in 1541, and Crabtree orchard belonged to the rectory but by 1691 they too formed part of the Canons estate, which contained 320 a. of woodland.[7] By 1838 woods, plantations, and nurseries together made up no more than 58 a. of the parish. They comprised chiefly the 31 a. of Pear wood and 12 a. of Cloisters wood, belonging to Sir Robert Smirke, whose seat, Warren House, lay in Great Stanmore.[8] Both woods covered the same areas in 1971.[9]

MILL. The cellarer of St. Bartholomew's received 46s. 8d. a year from a windmill at Grimsditch in 1306.[10] Its profits were not recorded again, although a mill-house was among the appurtenances of Canons leased to Hugh Losse in 1543[11] and a mill among those surrendered to Sir Thomas Lake in 1604.[12] The former windmill was said in 1680 to have stood near the boundary with Great Stanmore, on the crest of Brockley Hill.[13]

MARKETS AND FAIRS. Sir Thomas Lake was granted the right to hold a weekly market and two annual fairs at Little Stanmore in 1604.[14] Fairs were not recorded again but a market was said to belong to the manor of Canons in 1640.[15] Presumably it had been discontinued by 1749, when the master of the free school was authorized to convert for his own use part of the market-house under the schoolroom.[16] Markets at Edgware probably served Little Stanmore until they, too, ceased to function at the end of the 18th century.[17]

TRADE AND INDUSTRY. The earliest known tradesman was a maltman, first recorded in 1571.[18] Others included a baker in 1572, a chandler in 1597,[19] a brewer and a cordwainer in 1613, a collier in the following year,[20] a mealman in 1635,[21] and a collar-maker in 1696.[22] The first shop-keeper was mentioned in 1726.[23] Such references do not give an accurate picture, however, since anyone living on the east side of the village high street was described as of Edgware.

Gravel had recently been dug near Pear wood in 1538.[24] There were bricklayers in 1659 and 1715.[25] A local brick-maker worked under John James at Canons early in 1714 but soon an outsider was brought in and bricks were ordered from Brentford.[26] At Brockley Hill bricks had been dug on what had become arable land by 1725,[27] presumably where Brick field lay south-west of Brockley Hill farm in 1838.[28] A brick-kiln was among the duke of Chandos's possessions in the parish in 1744.[29]

In 1801 there were 42 farmworkers and as many as 73 tradesmen or craftsmen, most of whom presumably worked in businesses along Edgware Road. Three-quarters of the population fell within neither category. By 1831, when numbers had almost doubled, 45 families were employed in agriculture, 68 in trade or manufacturing, and 77 in other occupations.[30] None of the tradesmen or craftsmen who lived along the west side of Edgware Road in 1851 employed more than two assistants; the shops, although less varied than in Great Stanmore, included a confectioner's and an umbrella-maker's.[31]

Growth in the 20th century was overwhelmingly residential. In 1915 The Leto Photo Materials Co. had a works in Meads Road, which was occupied by

[95] Middleton, *View*, 560; M.A.F. 68/136; M.A.F. 68/1675; M.A.F. 68/2815.
[96] Ex inf. the lessee.
[97] Webb, *Recs. of St. Barts.* i. 350–1.
[98] C 1/572/35; E 303/9/218; E 303/9/237; E 303/9/290.
[99] E 303/9/250; E 303/9/281.
[1] E 303/9/281.
[2] E 303/9/223.   [3] Req. 2/3/184.
[4] *Cal. Pat.* 1550–3, 457.
[5] Davenport MSS., Anc. Deeds A 5762.
[6] Davenport MSS., indenture betw. Sir Thos. and Dame Dorothy Lake and Dame Frances Weld.
[7] Ibid., indenture betw. Warwick Lake and Jas. Brydges and others.
[8] M.R.O., TA/S'MORE Lt.
[9] O.S. Map 6", Mdx. V. SE. (1865 edn.); Bartholomew, *Ref. Atlas Greater Lond.* (1968 edn.).
[10] Webb, *Recs. of St. Barts.* i. 450–1.
[11] S.C. 6/298/1.
[12] C. P. 25(2)/323/2 Jas. I Trin. Mdx.

[13] Davenport MSS., Gt. Stan. ct. rolls.
[14] *Cal. S.P. Dom.* 1603–10, 171.
[15] Davenport MSS., parts. of man. of Canons.
[16] Vestry order bk.
[17] *V.C.H. Mdx.* iv. 161.
[18] Prob. 11/53 (P.C.C. 29 Holney, will of Thos. Oxton).
[19] Davenport MSS., Com. Ct. Lond., ff. 116, 410.
[20] *Mdx. Sess. Recs.* i. 49, 102; iii. 172.
[21] Davenport MSS., Com. Ct. Lond., f. 127.
[22] Prob. 11/431 (P.C.C. 70 Bond, will of John Holmes).
[23] Davenport MSS., Com. Ct. Lond. reg. no. 64.
[24] E 303/9/223.
[25] Prob. 11/297 (P.C.C. 6 Nabbs, will of Isaac Doughty); Davenport MSS., Com. Ct. Lond. reg. no. 57.
[26] Baker, *Chandos*, 116–17.
[27] M.L.R. 1725/4/368.
[28] M.R.O., TA/S'MORE Lt.
[29] M.L.R. 1744/1/305.
[30] *Census*, 1801, 1831.
[31] H.O. 107/1700/135/2.

Wellington & Ward in 1923 and later by Harper & Tunstall, makers of drawing office equipment.[32] Land in the north-east, between the Watford by-pass and Elstree village, was acquired by the London Passenger Transport Board under its New Works Programme of 1935–40, as a depot to serve the proposed extension of the tube line from Edgware to Aldenham (Herts.). During the Second World War an aircraft factory occupied the site, where in 1956, after plans for the tube had been abandoned, London Transport opened a depot for overhauling buses. In 1971 nearly 1,000 people were employed at Aldenham Bus Works, which covered 17 a.[33] The only other large factory at that date was Terminal House, on the corner of London Road and Merrion Avenue, which had been occupied on its completion in 1964 by Aircraft-Marine Products (G.B.), later AMP of Great Britain. The firm's United States parent-company pioneered the system of crimping terminals to electric wire, serving the marine and aircraft industries and later a wide range of mass-produced articles. In 1971 AMP employed 320 persons at its Stanmore factory.[34] The other industrial sites, off Burnt Oak Broadway and Edgware High Street, were largely occupied by garages and by new and second-hand car dealers. Among the firms was a branch of W. Harold Perry, the largest Ford main dealers, which acquired nos. 51 to 55 High Street in 1958 and by 1972 employed about 130 people.[35] Movitex Signs, makers of information boards, lettering sets and similar products, acquired a site off the main street north of Whitchurch Lane in 1968; about 100 people worked there in 1972.[36] Close by was the entrance to Ballards Yard, which was used by several small firms concerned with manufactures in metal.

SOCIAL LIFE. In the 1720s Canons held a place in the world of fashion unrivalled by any neighbouring seat. A household staff which numbered 93 by 1722 enabled the duke of Chandos to give banquets for his fellow peers, as well as chieftains from Africa and America; European royalty, too, may have dined there, since servants of the kings of Denmark and Prussia were entertained below stairs. Parties from London were eager to be shown over the mansion and to stroll in its grounds. Although high fees were paid, causing jealousy between the housekeeper and the groom of the chambers, the duke eventually was forced to exclude sightseers on Sundays and to keep the library closed.[37] Long after the estate had been sold, Chandos's love of music ensured that Little Stanmore was remembered for its connexion with Handel, who composed the Chandos anthems for his patron from 1717 and periodically played the organ in the rebuilt parish church before the dedication of the chapel at Canons in 1720. The orchestra or 'concert', numbering 24 performers in 1719, had its own table in the duke's dining room. From 1719 until 1731 or 1732 the director was the composer and teacher John Christopher Pepusch (1667–1752),[38] later organist to the Charterhouse.[39]

Despite earlier local protests against hunting,[40] in 1840 the parish's future incumbent Benjamin Armstrong recorded a good outing with the Queen's stag hounds before the deer was taken at Stanmore.[41] The parish proved too small to support many of the clubs which were a feature of the late 19th century, when people presumably attended the fairs and other amusements in Edgware.[42] Under a Scheme of 1899 the old National school building on the south side of Whitchurch Lane was to be used as a Sunday school and for the general benefit of the parishioners. The building was known as the institute and used as a hall and working men's club[43] until its demolition for road widening in 1930. The Whitchurch institute was built on the corner of Buckingham Road and Chandos Crescent in 1932.[44]

LOCAL GOVERNMENT. In 1294 the prior of St. Bartholomew's claimed view of frankpledge, the assizes of bread and ale, infangthief, outfangthief, and the right to erect a gallows in Little Stanmore, by virtue of a grant from William de Rames (IV). A jury upheld the first two claims but found that the three remaining rights had always belonged to the king.[45] View of frankpledge was duly ascribed to the prior in 1306.[46]

The earliest court recorded, in a modern transcript, is that held for Prior William Bolton in 1508.[47] Transcripts also record some 17th- and 18th-century proceedings,[48] and surviving court books run from 1775 to 1924.[49] A view of frankpledge was usually held with a court baron every spring until 1736; from 1775 a general court baron was held alone, sometimes with an additional one or a special court at some other season. They met at the Crane, from 1731 the Duke of Chandos's Arms and Crane, where the last court was held in 1890.[50]

A vestry minute book, beginning with some accounts of surveyors of the highways from 1654, records the annual elections of parish officers from 1661 until the present day. Churchwardens' accounts run from 1729 to 1831 and vestry order books from 1739 to 1815.[51] Eighteenth- and early-nineteenth-century vestries normally met every month, with an average attendance of 7 or 8; the incumbent or his curate often presided and others who were occasionally present included the elder William Hallett and two of his successors at Canons, Philip and Andrew O'Kelly. Meetings took place in the vestry room at the church from 1795, although they might be adjourned to one of four near-by inns.[52]

From 1668 the vestry nominated a constable and

[32] *Kelly's Dir. Watford* (1915–16); *Kelly's Dirs. Edgware* (1923, 1938); *Kemp's Harrow and Dist. Dir.* (1973).
[33] Ex inf. London Transport.
[34] Ex inf. W. Harold Perry Ltd.
[35] Ex inf. AMP of Great Britain Ltd.
[36] Ex inf. Movitex Signs Ltd.
[37] Baker, *Chandos*, 126, 181–2, 194–5.
[38] Ibid. 129–30.
[39] *D.N.B.*
[40] See p. 102.
[41] *T.L.M.A.S.* xvii. 177.
[42] *V.C.H. Mdx.* iv. 161.
[43] *Kelly's Dir. Edgware* (1915–16).
[44] Char. Com. files.
[45] *Plac. de Quo Warr.* (Rec. Com.), 478.
[46] Webb, *Recs. of St. Barts.* i. 350.
[47] Davenport MSS., Lt. Stan. ct. rolls.
[48] Ibid. ct. rolls for 1642–3, 1717–19, 1733–5, and 1775–92.
[49] M.R.O., Acc. 658/1–3.
[50] Davenport MSS., Lt. Stan. ct. rolls; M.R.O., Acc. 658/1–3.
[51] In 1971 they were kept at the church; there are transcripts in Davenport MSS.
[52] Vestry min. and order bks.

headborough, although their formal elections took place at the manorial court at least until 1736; both officers later had their expenses paid by the vestry and continued to be nominated until 1864.[53] There were two churchwardens in 1580[54] and a sub-constable in 1613.[55] One churchwarden was chosen by the incumbent and one by the parishioners in 1661. From that date the vestry also named two surveyors of the highways and two overseers of the poor, although surveyors are not recorded between 1691 and 1796. Overseers' accounts survive for 1782 to 1801.[56] An assistant overseer was appointed by wage in 1830. Other officers included a parish clerk in 1780, an organist who in 1799 had to teach children to sing before Sunday services, a beadle, recorded once in 1814, and a sexton, by 1837. The salaries of the clerk and organist came from rents from the free school lands.

Poor-rates and church-rates were levied from the mid 18th century. In 1776 £85 were raised and £60 spent on the poor.[57] Expenditure rose from £352 in 1816 to £468 in 1820, thereafter declining[58] and then rising again to average £544 from 1831 to 1834.[59] Weekly allowances were authorized by the vestry, which in 1810 paid for 16 weeks in advance to enable one recipient to undertake a sea-bathing cure; the usual range of casual expenses, notably for clothing, was also paid. Part of the surplus from the free school lands was used for apprenticing boys or placing girls in service. In 1799, as an apparently short-lived experiment, two adults and six children were farmed out; the overseers were to clothe them and two visitors were to carry out monthly inspections at the contractor's house. In 1807 paupers were to dig gravel from a new pit at Stanmore marsh. The parish was as keen as Great Stanmore to reduce the burden of relief: illegal settlers were repeatedly removed and in 1749 the constable, himself accused of conducting vagrants into Hendon without leave, refused to accept others from Great Stanmore, on the grounds that their pass referred to Little Stanmore as Whitchurch.

No workhouse was built, presumably because the parish was small and had other accommodation. Apart from filling vacancies at the alms-houses, which were separately endowed,[60] the vestry kept up various parish houses, the first of which was recorded in 1713.[61] Repairs were ordered to the thatched roof of one in 1758, since inmates were soaked in their beds; it was probably the thatched poor house 'up town', which was burned down in 1785. Another parish house, 'below the turnpike', was recorded in 1778. Part of a third parish building by the Ninepin and Bowl, previously used for storing wood, was converted to hold extra paupers in 1773; it still stood 20 years later but was pulled down before the overseers sold the site in 1837.[62]

The vestry often acted in concert with its neighbours. In 1767 a cage was to be built and used jointly with Edgware. The constable of Little Stanmore had a key to the cage by 1772 but Edgware did not pay its half of the cost until 1780. The appointment of an assistant overseer was also discussed with Edgware in 1824, six years before Little Stanmore named one of its own. As in Great Stanmore medicines for the poor were provided by 1741, a family was given vaccination in 1768, and regular medical attendance was paid for by 1754. Both parishes retained the same 'surgeon and apothecary' in 1761, at identical salaries, and 1782, although soon afterwards Little Stanmore again had its own officer. Committees were set up by the two vestries in 1803, to avoid litigation over a disputed boundary at Stanmore marsh; more committees were formed in 1825 and lawyers' arbitration was eventually accepted.[63]

Little Stanmore became part of Hendon poor law union in 1835, whereupon a mere £37 was raised by selling parish property and contributed towards the new union workhouse at Redhill.[64] A nuisance removal committee was set up, under an inspector, in 1857 or 1858.[65] The parish was included in Edgware highway district in 1863, thereafter being governed by the same authority as Great Stanmore.[66] In 1934 much of Little Stanmore was assigned to the new Stanmore North ward and the area south of Edgware brook to Stanmore South; the boundary of Stanmore South was later moved to Whitchurch Lane and a portion in the south-west included in Belmont.[67]

PUBLIC SERVICES. The fire engines at Great Stanmore were presumably used in Little Stanmore, where the vestry did not decide to buy an engine and other equipment until 1883. Nothing had been done by 1887 but thereafter sums were regularly voted for a fire brigade.[68] An engine house stood behind the Chandos Arms in 1896.[69] Subscriptions for a new pump, which would be used jointly with Edgware, were suggested in 1843;[70] perhaps it was the hand pump near Edgware churchyard, where people from both parishes queued for their sole supply thirty years later, when a service was proposed by the Colne Valley Water Co.[71] In 1858 much 'low fever' was reported near the bridge over Dean's brook, at the southern end of the village; presumably the cause was bad drainage, although the newly formed nuisance removal committee declared itself mystified.[72] By 1896 the parish was served by the Edgware and Little Stanmore sewage farm, in north-east Kingsbury, which was superseded under the sewerage scheme of 1933. As at Great Stanmore, gas was first supplied by John Chapman of Harrow c. 1860 and electricity under an Act of 1906.[73]

By 1853 the police commissioners had acquired

[53] Except where otherwise stated, the foll. four paras. are based on the vestry min. and order bks.
[54] Guildhall MS. 9537/4.
[55] *Mdx. Sess. Recs.* i. 251.
[56] M.R.O., LA. HW. 779–80.
[57] *Rep. Cttee. on Rets. by Overseers, 1776*, 101.
[58] *Rep. Sel. Cttee. on Poor Rate Returns*, H.C. 748, p. 108 (1821), iv; ibid. H.C. 334, p. 132 (1825), iv.
[59] *Poor Law Com. 1st Rep.* 251.
[60] See p. 126.
[61] M.R.O., Acc. 658/1, ff. 64–5.
[62] M.L.R. 1837/6/43.

[63] See p. 89.
[64] *Poor Law Com. 9th Rep.* H.C. 494, App. C, pp. 278–9 (1843), xxi.
[65] Vestry min. bk.   [66] See p. 104.
[67] For the ward boundaries in 1935 and 1963, see above, p. 104, n. 68.
[68] Vestry min. bk.
[69] O.S. Map 1/2,500, Mdx. VI. 13 (1897 edn.).
[70] Vestry min. bk.
[71] Druett, *Stanmores and Harrow Weald*, 251.
[72] Vestry min. bk.
[73] See p. 105.

the site of the present police station, on the south side of Whitchurch Lane near its junction with Edgware Road.[74] The station, immediately east of the National school, had been built by 1865.[75]

A hospital for children recovering from infectious diseases was founded in 1882 by Miss Mary Wardell, who converted her house, Sulloniacae, near the junction of Wood Lane with Brockley Hill. The building became a military convalescent home in 1915 and was bought by the Shaftesbury Society at the end of the First World War on the death of Miss Wardell, who had retained a smaller house to the west. The Royal National Orthopaedic hospital bought the property in 1920 as a country branch, together with 4 a. of garden, after undertaking to provide convalescent treatment in accordance with a trust set up by Miss Wardell. Rapid expansion followed the admission of the first patient in 1922, the number of beds being doubled to 100 in 1923. Purchases added 30 a. running westward along Wood Lane as far as Moor House in 1923, a further 70 a. in 1927, and Brockley Hill House with its grounds in 1935. Wings were added to the 19th-century hospital and new wards were built, raising the accommodation to 275 beds in 1929. A block, later called the Zachary Merton wards, was opened in 1936 to the north-west, near the obelisk, and a training college and workshops (replacing the Wrights Lane Home for Crippled Boys, in Kensington) were opened near by in 1937; after the final disbanding of the college in 1948 its buildings were enlarged for the nursing staff and part of the workshops was leased to the Institute of Orthopaedics. In 1972 the hospital's grounds covered some 115 a., including land leased to the institute. There were 305 beds and a total staff of 800, of whom about 100 were the institute's employees. At that date the Wardell hospital building, of yellow-brown brick, was still in use, while Brockley Hill House, previously a home for student nurses, was being converted into flats for married staff.[76]

In 1970 much of the north of the parish was open space, since the Warren House estate stretched over the border from Great Stanmore, to adjoin the grounds of the Royal National Orthopaedic hospital. Near the centre of the parish Harrow U.D.C. limited building by buying the 49 a. of Canons Park extension, south of the mansion occupied by the North London Collegiate school, early in 1936 and the 7 a. of Lake Grove recreation ground, north of the park's lake, a few months later; part of the extension was opened as the King George V memorial garden in 1937. Farther south the Chandos recreation ground, between Edgware brook and Camrose Avenue, covered 27 a.[77]

CHURCH. The church of St. Lawrence at Little Stanmore was given by Roger de Rames (fl. 1130) to St. Bartholomew's priory,[78] recorded as the appropriator c. 1244. There was a vicarage by that date[79] and 16th-century incumbents were described as vicars.[80] The living, however, first listed as a donative in 1708,[81] was considered from the 17th to early 19th centuries to be a perpetual curacy.[82] Incumbents during that period normally called themselves ministers, presumably in order to be distinguished from their salaried curates. Henry Poole styled himself rector from 1785,[83] although it was not until after the District Church Tithes Act of 1865 that Little Stanmore was raised to become a rectory, in 1868.[84] St. Lawrence's church served the whole parish, save during a brief period when the duke of Chandos maintained his chapel at Canons,[85] until 1932. The conventional district of All Saints, Queensbury, was then constituted out of the southern part of Little Stanmore and northern Kingsbury, becoming a separate parish in 1941.[86]

After the Reformation the church was impropriated by the lay lords of the manor, being acquired by Hugh Losse in 1552[87] and passing from his grandson to the Lake family.[88] Although the profits were vested in trustees under the will of Sir Lancelot Lake,[89] the right of presentation was retained by his heirs and afterwards, at least until 1786, by the dukes of Chandos.[90] In 1810 the trust had been 'inefficient for some time'[91] and in 1811 the advowson was the subject of a Chancery suit, which perhaps stemmed from a claim that William Hallett had bought it after the first duke's death.[92] From 1811 until 1829 the rector of Great Stanmore acted as minister.[93] In 1832 trustees presented George Mutter,[94] who himself soon acquired the advowson[95] and all tithes on most of the parish, although those on some 127 a. became payable to Sarah Noyes and the Grand Junction Canal Co.[96] The right of presentation was exercised by Maria Mutter in 1844, by Thomas Murray Mackie in 1850, by Dorothy Norman in 1868, and by the retiring rector, John Burton Norman, in 1897.[97] It passed between 1907 and 1915 to Muriel, Countess De La Warr,[98] and was transferred in 1929 to the bishop of London.[99]

The church was valued at 30s. c. 1244-8[1] and £2 in 1291.[2] The vicarage was said to be worth 3 marks c. 1244[3] and the vicar was paid 46s. 8d. by St. Bartholomew's in 1535.[4] It was alleged in 1638 that the 'curate', apparently the incumbent, had for long received one penny out of every shilling for the yearly value of all unploughed and pasture lands but that Lady Lake would pay nothing for her many hundreds of acres, had forbidden other parishioners to pay, and had laid claim to his dwelling house. The

[74] Nat. Soc. files (plan of sch.).
[75] O.S. Maps 6", Mdx. VI. SW. (1865 edn.).
[76] Ex inf. the sec.
[77] Boro. of Harrow, Facts & Figures (1963-4).
[78] Webb, Recs. of St. Barts. i. 349, 479-80.
[79] St. Paul's MS. W.D. 9, f. 85v.
[80] Valor Eccl. (Rec. Com.), i. 407; Hennessy, Novum Repertorium, 406.
[81] Newcourt, Repertorium, i. 731.
[82] Ibid.; Rep. Cttee. Eccl. Revs. H.C. 67, p. 673 (1835), xxii.
[83] Vestry min. bk.
[84] 21st Rep. Eccl. Com. [4118], p. 122, H.C. (1868-9), xix(1).
[85] See pp. 115-16.   [86] See p. 86.
[87] Cal. Pat. 1550-3, 457.

[88] Home Cnties. Mag. i. 320.
[89] 9th Rep. Com. Char. H.C. 258, pp. 272-3 (1823), ix.
[90] John Ecton, Liber Regis (1786), 582.
[91] Guildhall MS. 9558, f. 478v.
[92] Lysons, Environs, iii. 411, suppl. 287.
[93] Vestry min. bk.
[94] Hennessy, Novum Repertorium, 406.
[95] Rep. Cttee. Eccl. Revs. 673.
[96] M.R.O., TA/S'MORE Lt.
[97] Hennessy, Novum Repertorium, 406-7.
[98] Crockford (1907 and later edns.).
[99] Par. recs. penes the Rectory, AS/1.
[1] St. Paul's MS. W.D. 9, f. 85v.
[2] Tax. Eccl. (Rec. Com.), 17b.
[3] St. Paul's MS. W.D. 9, f. 85v.
[4] Valor Eccl. (Rec. Com.), 407.

council referred the complaint to the Attorney-General for prosecution and ordered that meanwhile the curate should enjoy his customary rights.[5] Lancelot Lake, as impropriator, received tithes worth about £50 a year and paid £40 to the minister in 1650;[6] in his will, proved in 1680, however, the profits were reckoned at £100.[7] After tithes had been demanded from the tenants of the free school lands, the vestry in 1792 forbade payment and resolved to meet the costs of any action which the incumbent might bring.[8] In 1835 the net income of the incumbent and chief tithe-owner, George Mutter, was £267.[9] A rent-charge of £415 10s. was awarded in 1838 to Mutter and a further £36 10s. to Sarah Noyes and the Grand Junction Canal Co., in lieu of all tithes.[10] Similar sums were payable in 1887, when there was no glebe.[11]

In 1638 it was stated that for about 40 years the curates had enjoyed a dwelling house near the church, where Lady Lake was ordered to leave the incumbent undisturbed.[12] A vicarage house, with its yard and great orchard and an orchard adjoining the churchyard on the north, was mentioned in 1666.[13] It may have been the house, 'fit for residence' in 1835,[14] which stood west of the church, with a garden on the south side of Whitchurch Lane.[15] The building was replaced in 1852 by one designed by Anthony Salvin, east of the church and on what is now the north-west side of St. Lawrence Close.[16] Salvin's rectory was pulled down in 1967 and a smaller house built in St. Lawrence Close in 1970.[17]

William Paris, by will dated 1271–2, left 5s. for the fabric of Little Stanmore church and 24 sheep to support a light there.[18] In 1547 there was a church house for which the tenant William Stile, perhaps a relative of the vicar John Stile, paid 5s. a year.[19] A church hall had been built in Whitchurch Lane, between Meads and Montgomery roads, by 1911. After fires in 1966 and 1970, a new one was opened in 1972.[20]

The curate Richard Davy, a former Carthusian, was denounced to Cromwell in 1538 by the curates of Kingsbury and Hendon for objecting to the suppression of images.[21] Davy presumably was a salaried curate, like the one paid by the vicar in 1547.[22] Lady Lake's hostility was said in 1638 to have endangered the service of God by threatening the incumbent with destitution[23] but his successor, Nicholas Holland, was a 'constant preaching minister' in 1650, when all the parishioners could conveniently attend the church.[24] The most distinguished incumbent was the Huguenot refugee

John Theophilus Desaguliers, natural philosopher and inventor of the planetarium, who was nominated in 1714.[25] Offence was caused by his many distractions, which included superintending the water engineering for Canons, and Chandos himself pointed out that a corpse had lain three days in the church, since neither the incumbent nor his curate could be bothered to bury it. Desaguliers quarrelled with his patron in 1741 but retained the living until his death in a London coffee-house in 1744.[26]

Services were held once on Sundays in 1810, when the sacraments were administered four times a year to only ten communicants,[27] perhaps because most parishioners, who lived along the west side of Edgware Road, found it easier to reach Edgware parish church. Benjamin John Armstrong, incumbent from 1844 to 1850, prided himself on having sometimes doubled his congregation to 300, in spite of the church's isolation, and recalled hearing that c. 1835 a bell-ringer had locked up the building for want of any worshippers.[28] Two Sunday services were held in 1851, attended by some 170 people in the morning and 130 in the afternoon, as well as by about 30 children from Sunday school, when bad weather was blamed for keeping the numbers unusually low.[29] In 1835 the incumbent, George Mutter, was also rector of Chillenden (Kent) and perpetual curate of Broadway Chapel, St. Margaret's, Westminster; he often attended vestry meetings[30] but paid £80 a year to a curate.[31] Mutter's successor, Armstrong, described his own parish work in a diary[32] and wrote a popular book on the church.[33] Since 1961 the rector has normally been assisted by a curate.[34]

The church of *ST. LAWRENCE* stands on the north side of Whitchurch Lane, its churchyard and the south entrance to Canons Park forming a gap in a line of semi-detached houses of the 1930s. Nothing survives of the building recorded in 1272. The oldest part of the present fabric is the early-16th-century west tower, of red brick and flint rubble rendered with cement; it is battlemented and three-storeyed, with a north-east stair turret.[35] The remainder was rebuilt for the duke of Chandos (d. 1744), as an unaisled nave and retrochoir with, slightly later, a pantheon to the north. The work was largely carried out by John James in 1714,[36] although the rain-water heads are dated 1715, and is now the only architectural memorial to the duke's taste. The walls outside are simple, of purplish brick with plain stone-arched windows and broad Tuscan corner pilasters.[37] Inside the nave walls are panelled and painted in *grisaille*,

[5] *Cal. S.P. Dom.* 1638–9, 62, 396.
[6] *Home Cnties. Mag.* i. 320.
[7] *9th Rep. Com. Char.* 273.   [8] Vestry order bk.
[9] *Rep. Com. Eccl. Revenues*, 673.
[10] M.R.O., TA/S'MORE Lt.
[11] *Return of Tithes Commuted*, H.C. 214, p. 123 (1887), lxiv; *Return of Glebe Lands*, H.C. 307, p. 92 (1887), lxiv.
[12] *Cal. S.P. Dom.* 1638–9, 62.
[13] Davenport MSS., marriage settlement for Thos., s. of Sir Lancelot Lake, and Rebecca Langham.
[14] *Rep. Cttee. Eccl. Revs.* 673.
[15] Ex inf. Mr. C. L. Holness (1970).
[16] Robbins, *Mdx.* 335; O.S. Map 6″, Mdx. XI. NW. (1865 edn.).
[17] *Harrow Observer*, 14 Aug. 1970.
[18] *Cat. Anct. D.* ii, A 2296.
[19] Hennessy, *Novum Repertorium*, 406.
[20] O.S. Map 1/2,500, Mdx. VI. 13 (1914 edn.); *Harrow Observer*, 29 Dec. 1966, 7 Apr. 1970, 19 Apr. 1974.
[21] *L. & P. Hen. VIII*, xii(2), p. 142.

[22] Hennessy, *Novum Repertorium*, 406.
[23] *Cal. S.P. Dom.* 1638–9, 62.
[24] *Home Cnties. Mag.* i. 320.
[25] *D.N.B.*
[26] Baker, *Chandos*, 152, 429.
[27] Guildhall MS. 9558, f. 478v.
[28] *T.L.M.A.S.* xvii. 112.
[29] H.O. 129/135/2/2/2.   [30] Vestry min. bk.
[31] *Rep. Cttee. Eccl. Revs.* 673.
[32] Extracts relating to Armstrong's later years have been published as *A Norfolk Diary*, ed. H. B. J. Armstrong (1949).
[33] *T.L.M.A.S.* xvii. 105–12. The book was first pub. in 1849.
[34] *Crockford* (1961 and later edns.).
[35] Hist. Mon. Com. *Mdx.* 114. Except where otherwise stated, the rest of the para. and the foll. para. are based on Pevsner, *Mdx.* 148–9, and Robbins, *Mdx.* 334–5.
[36] Baker, *Chandos*, 117, 119, 126.
[37] Robbins, *Mdx.* plate 23.

probably by Francesco Sleter assisted by Gaetano Brunetti.[38] Together with the vaulted ceiling, painted by Louis Laguerre, they form a baroque monument unique in England. At the west end is a wooden gallery with the duke's box beneath a canopy painted by Belucci. At the east end there are wooden Corinthian columns on each side of the altar, making the organ, beyond, appear as if on a stage; both altar and organ are flanked by paintings attributed to Belucci (the Nativity and Pietà) and Laguerre. On the north the pantheon, designed for the Brydgeses' monuments[39] and later converted into a vestry, leads to a farther painted room, the Chandos mausoleum, completed by James Gibbs in 1735. Restorations were carried out to the whole fabric in 1854, to the mausoleum in 1936, to the tower by Sir Albert Richardson in 1951, and to the interior by a local artist, W. P. Starmer, in 1953.[40] In 1971, when the painted plaster along the north wall of the nave had been shored up for several years and after extensive damage to the mausoleum, a national appeal was launched to save the church.

Apart from Victorian glass in the south windows and a wooden altar-screen erected in 1900,[41] when the old one was moved to the entrance to the mausoleum, the interior has been little changed. The oak box-pews are original, as are the iron rings to which service books were chained, the wrought iron altar-rails, and the font. The pulpit, also 18th-century, was altered in 1854. Several of the books are kept by the organ, together with a copy of the 'vinegar Bible' of 1716, presented by Chandos. The organ, built by Abraham Jordan and in a case perhaps by Grinling Gibbons, has been enlarged and much renovated.[42] It was played by Handel when the duke's household attended church, before the completion of the chapel at Canons; Handel, however, was not the regular organist nor need he have composed the Chandos anthems here, as stated on a brass plate.[43] An impressive white marble monument to James, duke of Chandos (d. 1744), stands against the east wall of the mausoleum; it is probably by Andrew Carpentier and depicts the duke, in Roman costume, between kneeling figures of his first two wives.[44] Against the south wall are the sarcophagi of his daughter-in-law Mary, marchioness of Carnarvon (d. 1738), by Sir Henry Cheere, and of Margaret, marchioness of Carnarvon (d. 1760). In the church-yard to the south is the table-tomb of John Franklin, with a recut inscription bearing the old-style date 1596. Another stone, erected in 1868, alleges that William Powell was the 'harmonious blacksmith' once thought to have inspired Handel; in reality Powell was the parish clerk and the blacksmith no more than an apprentice, William Lintern, who took

up music and gave his own nickname to one of Handel's compositions.[45] In 1863 it was ordered that coffins beneath the monument rooms be reinterred and the vaults closed up and in 1864 that no new burials should normally be made in the eastern part of the churchyard.[46]

The church has one bell, cast in 1774 by Thomas Janaway.[47] A set of silver-gilt plate, dated 1715, was given by Chandos when he was earl of Carnarvon in 1716; it comprises a flagon, two large cups, two patens, and an alms-dish.[48] Registers record baptisms from 1559, marriages from 1552, and burials from 1556.[49]

When All Saints, Queensbury, was created a conventional district in 1932, worshippers first attended a hall in Dale Avenue, Little Stanmore. By 1938, however, services were held in Waltham Drive, close to the site of the existing church, which is in the old parish of Kingsbury.[50]

ROMAN CATHOLICISM. Richard Gill, late of Little Stanmore, was indicted for recusancy in 1611 and two widows, Joan Brickhill and Alice Rumball, were repeatedly indicted between 1624 and 1635.[51] Thereafter no Roman Catholic activity is recorded until the building of the Dominican convent of St. Thomas Aquinas in the 1930s, on the east side of Marsh Lane.[52] After the parish of St. William of York had been founded in 1938, mass was said on weekdays in the chapel of the near-by convent and on Sundays in the hall of the adjoining St. Thomas's school.[53] The existing church, on the north side of Du Cros Drive, was opened in 1960 and registered for worship in 1961.[54] It is of pale brown brick, with a porch of three round-headed stone arches and a tower. There is seating for 500 and there is a small wooden hall at the rear.[55]

PROTESTANT NONCONFORMITY. In 1801 the house of Daniel Gardner was registered as a meeting-place for Independents.[56] In 1829 they worshipped in an upper room in Watling Street and in 1834 they built and registered the building known as Edgware chapel,[57] which was set back from the Little Stanmore side of the street, south of the Mason's Arms.[58] In 1851, when a Sunday school was also held there, the chapel could seat 120 worshippers; on Sundays about 40 people attended service in the morning and about 60 in the evening.[59] The chapel, which was closed after 1881 but re-opened in 1893, was replaced by a building in Grove Road, Edgware, in 1937.[60]

In 1934 Baptist services were held in a tent and

[38] Letter from Edw. Croft-Murray (1967) *penes* the rector. See frontispiece.
[39] Baker, *Chandos*, 416.
[40] *T.L.M.A.S.* xviii(2), no. 94.
[41] *Architect*, lxiii (1900), 64.
[42] C. L. Holness, *Short Guide to par. ch. of Lt. Stanmore* (1942 edn.), 8.
[43] R. A. Streatfield, *Handel, Canons and the Duke of Chandos*, 16–17, 19.
[44] Pevsner, *Mdx.* plate 28(b). The lengthy inscriptions are in Baker, *Chandos*, 420–2.
[45] W. H. Cummings, *Handel, the Duke of Chandos, the Harmoniuous Blacksmith*, 21.
[46] *Lond. Gaz.* 15 Sept. 1863, p. 4517; 4 Aug. 1864, p. 3872.
[47] *T.L.M.A.S.* xvii. 240.

[48] Freshfield, *Communion Plate*, 54.
[49] *T.L.M.A.S.* xviii(2), no. 94. In 1971 the registers were at the church.
[50] See p. 86.
[51] *Mdx. Cnty. Recs.* ii. 72, 238; iii. 23, 32, 59, 136–7.
[52] Druett, *Stanmores and Harrow Weald*, 257.
[53] Ex inf. the Revd. L. F. Allan.
[54] *Westminster Dioc. Yr. Bk.* (1969); G.R.O. Worship Reg. No. 68151.
[55] Ex inf. the Revd. L. F. Allan.
[56] Guildhall MSS. 9580/2.
[57] Letter from C. L. Holness *penes* Harrow Cent. Ref. Libr.; G.R.O. Worship Returns, Lond. dioc. no. 1840.
[58] O.S. Map 1/2,500, Mdx.
[59] H.O. 129/135/2/2/5.
[60] *V.C.H. Mdx.* iv. 167.

subsequently in a timber hall in Camrose Avenue. The hall, seating about 60 people, was registered as Camrose Baptist church in 1935 and was still standing in 1969.[61] A permanent church, on the corner of Camrose Avenue and Haverford Way, was founded later in 1935 and registered in 1936.[62] The church, of brick with stone dressings, has seats for 250 and stands next to a brick hall, built *c.* 1948 to seat some 60 people.[63] The Christian Science Society registered a hall on the north side of Valencia Road in 1949.[64] The Assemblies of God registered a brick hall on the north side of Bacon Lane in 1963.[65]

JUDAISM. After the Second World War Jews worshipped in private houses, in the Bernays institute, and in huts which served as a community centre in Merrion Avenue. In 1970 the Bernays institute was still used on high holydays but the huts had been replaced by Terminal House.[66] Stanmore and Canons Park District synagogue, whose members belong to the United Synagogue,[67] was consecrated in 1951.[68] The building, in London Road, is of yellow-brown brick and has a flat roof. It adjoins the Stanmore Jewish community centre, built of similar materials and comprising a hall and classrooms, which was opened in 1963. The synagogue itself was reconsecrated, after internal alterations, in 1969.[69]

EDUCATION. In 1656 Sir Lancelot Lake settled 20 a. at Stanmore marsh on trustees, who were to pay £15 p.a. to a schoolmaster. In his will, proved in 1680, Lake instructed that a school-house which he had built should also be settled on trustees.[70] When the school lands were let in 1740 for 21 years, the rent was to rise from £15 to £20 after 11 years. Further increases enabled the vestry to raise the schoolmaster's salary in 1777 and 1796.[71] By 1823 the income was £60 p.a., out of which the master received £30 and the parish organist £10.[72] In 1749 the master was allowed to convert part of the 'market house' beneath the schoolroom for his own use.[73] Between 1817 and 1823 nearly £300 was spent on repairs to the school and the adjoining master's house, although it was not known whether either building was the one which had been left by Lake.[74]

Two masters had their salaries stopped in the 1750s, for refusal to teach a parishioner's child. In 1789 the overseers were ordered to provide books for all pupils at the free school.[75] Although any parishioner might send his children there in 1823, the master's wife had to be paid for needlework. Numbers were then reported to have declined to about 30 following the establishment of a National school,[76] although four years previously Lake's free school was said to have only 21 boys and two girls.[77] Some 30 pupils still attended the free school in 1843.[78]

A charity school for 12 girls was opened in 1710, after a visitor from Westminster had appealed to the S.P.C.K. and persuaded his friends to subscribe to it. Further subscriptions at London, followed by collections at the churches of Great and Little Stanmore and Edgware, enabled the number of girls to be raised to 18 in 1711 and 24 in 1712. The pupils were given clothing in 1713, when 6 boys were added, and by 1724 the school had 'come to a considerable bigness', but thereafter nothing is known of it.[79]

The origin of Little Stanmore National school, which existed by 1823,[80] is obscure: in 1819 the free school was said to be the only one in the parish,[81] whereas 7 daily schools were recorded in 1833, only three of them having started since 1818.[82] In 1853 Thomas Clutterbuck conveyed a plot in Whitchurch Lane, west of the police station, for a school which was to be affiliated to the National Society,[83] and in 1855 the new building, a single room next to the mistress's house, was opened. The new school apparently came to replace Sir Lancelot Lake's free school. In 1863 there was one mistress, receiving £60, and an annual income of £78, from an endowment fund (perhaps created from the sale of Lake's land) and school pence paid by the 35 pupils.[84] A parliamentary grant was paid from 1870, when the average attendance had risen to 64.[85] In 1884–5 the school, which had accommodated 80 pupils, was enlarged to take 143.[86] Attendance had risen to 110 by 1896, when Little Stanmore National school was amalgamated with Edgware board school.[87] Under a Scheme of 1899 Lake's endowment and the buildings in Whitchurch Lane were consolidated as the charity of Sir Lancelot Lake with the school of 1853; the premises were to be used as a Sunday school and otherwise for the benefit of the parishioners, £15 a year was to be distributed to local schoolchildren or those at institutes of higher education, and the remaining income was to be divided between the buildings or other charitable causes and the church. By an order of 1905 the £15 was to be provided from £600, which was to be set aside from the total endowment of £2,337 as Sir Lancelot Lake's Educational Foundation. The old school buildings were demolished in 1930 and the Whitchurch institute was built in Buckingham Road two years later.[88]

Camrose school, for juniors and infants, opened in 1931. Of 441 children admitted, 82 were accommodated in St. Lawrence's church hall and the remainder in a temporary wooden building in

[61] Ex inf. Mr. E. J. T. Neal; G.R.O. Worship Reg. No. 55778.
[62] Date on building; G.R.O. Worship Reg. no. 56730.
[63] *Baptist Handbk.* (1969); ex inf. Mr. E. J. T. Neal.
[64] G.R.O. Worship Reg. no. 62209.
[65] Ibid. 69142.
[66] Ex inf. the minister.
[67] *Jewish Yr. Bk.* (1969).
[68] G.R.O.Worship Reg. no. 62892; ex inf. the minister.
[69] Ex inf. the minister.
[70] *9th Rep. Com. Char.* 275.   [71] Vestry order bk.
[72] *9th Rep. Com. Char.* 276.
[73] Vestry order bk.
[74] *9th Rep. Com. Char.* 276.
[75] Vestry order bk.
[76] *9th Rep. Com. Char.* 276.

[77] *Educ. of Poor Digest*, 555.
[78] *Digest of Schs. & Chars. for Educ.*, H.C. 435, p. 182 (1843) [1–182], xviii.
[79] *V.C.H. Mdx.* i. 223.
[80] See above.
[81] *Educ. of Poor Digest*, 555.
[82] *Educ. Enquiry Abstract*, 580.
[83] Nat. Soc. file.
[84] Ed. 7/87.
[85] *Rep. of Educ. Cttee. of Council 1870–1* [C. 406], p. 562, H.C. (1871), xxii.
[86] Ibid. *1883–4* [C. 4091–1], p. 677, H.C. (1884), xxiv; *1884–5* [C. 4483–1], p. 593, H.C. (1884–5), xxiii.
[87] *Schs. in Receipt of Parl. Grants, 1896–7* [C. 8546], p. 167, H.C. (1897), lxix.
[88] Char. Com. files.

St. David's Drive.[89] A senior department was opened as a separate school, Camrose secondary school, in 1932, with accommodation for 560. The number of juniors and infants rose to 666 in 1935–6[90] but was later reduced on the opening of Stag Lane and Stanburn schools. A new hall and canteen for Camrose junior and infants' school were opened in 1964 and there were plans for a new school building in 1970, when the number of pupils was 214.[91]

Stag Lane school opened in 1935, in temporary huts for 450 children, on part of its later site in Collier Drive. In 1937 the junior and infants' departments were separated and moved into a permanent building, holding 484, although the huts remained in use until four new classrooms were ready in 1964. In 1970 the land where the huts had stood was intended for a public library.[92]

Downer grammar school, named after Thomas Downer (d. 1502) of Harrow, was opened at the south end of Shaldon Road in 1952. In 1970 there were 643 boys and girls on the roll.[93]

Both the junior and infants' departments of Aylward school opened in 1952 in Pangbourne Drive. No additions had been made to the original buildings by 1970, when there were 220 infants and 330 juniors on the roll.[94]

In 1942 a prefabricated bungalow accommodating 40 children was built as a day nursery on a bombed site in Buckingham Road. Since 1946, when it was taken over as Buckingham nursery school, it has been the only nursery school provided by the local authority in Great or Little Stanmore.[95]

Teaching at the Royal National Orthopaedic hospital school began in 1923, one year after the hospital opened its country branch at Brockley Hill. Responsibility passed in 1948 from the hospital to the county council and in 1965 to Harrow L.B. which, with the hospital's board of governors, appoints the governing body. The school, comprising six wards accommodating 100–110 children, provides full-time general education until the age of 16 or to advanced level. Adult education has been provided since 1952.[96]

In 1851 Edgware House commercial school, near the White Lion, held more persons than any other building along the Little Stanmore side of Edgware Road. The principal was James Earle, who, with an assistant teacher and a French teacher, had charge of 40 boys aged between 7 and 15.[97] Miss Euphemia Miles ran a school at Edgware House from 1910 to 1922.[98]

The North London Collegiate school acquired Canons in 1929. Ten years later work began on a new building adjoining the Georgian house and in 1940 the entire school moved to Canons, where it has greatly expanded.[99] Other private schools have included Mornington school of commerce, a business training college which occupied a Victorian mansion

south of Stone Grove House at least from 1926 until 1938, and Whitchurch school, in Buckingham Road in 1937.[1]

CHARITIES FOR THE POOR. John Franklin, by will proved 1596,[2] left 20s. a year charged on lands in East Barnet to the poor of Little Stanmore but in 1823 there was no record that the money had ever been paid.[3] A churchwardens' account of the disbursement of £5, 'the annual gift of Sir John Franklin', in 1693[4] presumably refers to a deed of Richard Franklin, confirmed in his will (proved 1615),[5] whereby a rent of £5 a year was left to the poor. Richard's grandson and namesake accordingly settled a rent-charge of £5 on Litten's Mead in Hendon in trust in 1652. The money was to be distributed by the churchwardens on All Saints' Day but in 1823 payments, of 1s. to 4s., were made on St. Thomas's Day (21 December).[6] Sir Thomas Plumer supplemented the payments by 30s. a year, representing five per cent interest on £30; in 1811 the sum had been owed as a fine to the duke of Buckingham in return for inclosing a piece of wasteland, but the duke had given the money to the poor. In 1963 the income of Richard Franklin's charity, £4 3s. 4d. from 2½ per cent consols, was distributed among at least 20 old people.[7]

Alms-houses were built in Church field by Dame Mary Lake, who, by will proved 1646, instructed her son Sir Lancelot to settle a rent-charge of £33 a year to support the inmates, four old men and three old women, all of them unmarried churchgoers. The almspeople were to receive 1s. a week, 20s. worth of coal every summer, and a black gown, worth 20s., at Christmas; vacancies were to be filled by the churchwardens and parishioners, with the approval of the owner of Canons so long as he should be of the blood of Sir Thomas Lake. Sir Lancelot, by will proved 1680, therefore left all the tithes of Little Stanmore, worth about £100 a year, to his executors, who were to maintain the almspeople and assign the remaining profit to the incumbent. Since the incumbent had been granted most of the profits for life, Sir Lancelot's heir Warwick Lake in 1694 agreed to pay £33 a year to the trustees until the expiry of the lease. Warwick also supplemented the income by £11 13s. 4d. a year, charged on 13 a. called Crowshots which had been bought with £300 bequeathed to the poor by Sir Lancelot's grandson, Lancelot Lake, in 1693.[8] Under a Scheme of 1870 the rector himself was to pay the £33 to the trustees. A further Scheme in 1880 regulated the charities of Dame Mary, Sir Lancelot, and Lancelot Lake, i.e. the alms-house buildings, the payment from the rector, and the rent from Crowshots, to which had been added the income on £1,000 given by the executors of Miss Harriett Hurst,[9] whose will had

[89] Ex inf. the headmaster, Camrose jnr. and inft. sch.
[90] Bd. of Educ., List 21 (H.M.S.O., 1932, 1936, 1938).
[91] Ex inf. the headmaster.
[92] Bd. of Educ. List 21 (H.M.S.O. 1936, 1938); ex inf. the headmistress, Stag Lane jnr. sch.
[93] Ex inf. the headmaster.
[94] Ex inf. the headmistress, Aylward jnr. sch.
[95] Ex inf. the headmistress.
[96] Ex inf. the headmistress.
[97] H.O. 107/1700/135/2.
[98] Kelly's Dirs. Watford (1910–11, 1922).

[99] For the North Lond. Collegiate sch., see V.C.H. Mdx i. 310.
[1] Kelly's Dirs. Mdx. (1926, 1929, 1937); Kelly's Dir. Edgware (1938).
[2] Prob. 11/87 (P.C.C. 19 Drake).
[3] 9th Rep. Com. Char. 277.
[4] Vestry min. bk.
[5] Prob. 11/126 (P.C.C. 70 Rudd).
[6] 9th Rep. Com. Char. 277.
[7] Char. Com. files.
[8] 9th Rep. Com. Char. 271–5.
[9] Char. Com. files.

been proved in 1878;[10] the number of almspeople was reduced to 2 men and 2 women, who were to receive at least 7s. a week each. In 1903 the number was fixed at two men and one woman, who were 'diligently' to attend church (a provision omitted in 1880); part of the building was to be let and £100 from Harriett Hurst's stock was to be spent on repairs. The charities were consolidated as the alms-house charity of Dame Mary Lake and others in 1920, by which time the land forming Lancelot Lake's endowment had been converted to stock worth £466 13s. 4d.[11] The alms-houses, originally eight tenements, formed a half **H**-shaped block of one storey, north of the church. They were said to be in good repair in 1937, when the brick walls had been cement-rendered,[12] but in 1938 the urban district council's surveyor found them damp; the last inmate left in 1953 and the site was added to the churchyard four years later. After stock had been bought with the proceeds of the sale, the charity in 1962 had a total income of c. £80, which was distributed in food, fuel, clothing, and weekly allowances. The income, from stock and the surplus of the account of the Whitchurch institute, was more than £250 in 1970.[13]

[10] Principal Probate Reg. 1878, vol. 8, f. 318.
[11] Char. Com. files.

[12] Hist. Mon. Com. *Mdx.* 115.
[13] Char. Com. files; see pp. 120, 125.

EDMONTON HUNDRED

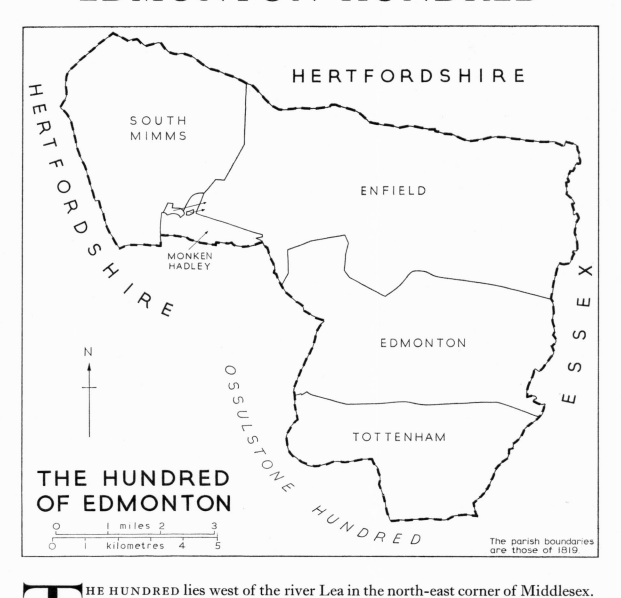

HERTFORDSHIRE

SOUTH MIMMS

HERTFORDSHIRE

ENFIELD

MONKEN HADLEY

N

OSSULSTONE HUNDRED

EDMONTON

ESSEX

THE HUNDRED OF EDMONTON

TOTTENHAM

0   1 miles 2   3
0   1 kilometres 4   5

The parish boundaries are those of 1819.

THE HUNDRED lies west of the river Lea in the north-east corner of Middlesex. Crossed by the Great North Road and Ermine Street, it is bounded by Hertfordshire in the north, north-east, and north-west, and by Ossulstone in the south and south-west. In 1881 it covered 31,805 a.[1] South Mimms, Monken Hadley, and part of Enfield project westward into Hertfordshire and from the later 19th century have been transferred piecemeal to that county.

In 1086 the hundred comprised the manors of Enfield, Tottenham, and Edmonton with the berewick of South Mimms, which presumably included Monken Hadley. It was then assessed at only 70 hides, less than any other Middlesex hundred.[2] From 1130 it was frequently described as a half hundred.[3] The early-12th-century Middlesex

[1] Census, 1881.
[2] V.C.H. Mdx. i. 83–4.
[3] Pipe R. 1130 (H.M.S.O. facsimile), 151; Chanc. R. 1196 (P.R.S. n.s. vii), 295; J.I. 1/544 rott. 61, 63d.

Hidagium calls it the 'half hundred of Mimms' but some of the details for the area are missing.[4]

The components of the hundred hardly varied after 1086. By 1316 they consisted of the vills of Edmonton, Enfield, South Mimms, and Tottenham.[5] Monken Hadley was expressly mentioned as a constituent in 1524.[6] By the late 15th century the number of manors in the hundred had increased to *c.* 16, excluding those of East and Chipping Barnet and Brookmans, part of whose lands lay in South Mimms.[7]

The hundred apparently was never alienated by the Crown.[8] In 1273–4 Tottenham and Edmonton were presented for not attending the hundred court,[9] to which they owed suit. Only Roger Lewknor at South Mimms and the abbot of Walden and Humphrey de Bohun sustained their claims to view of frankpledge in 1294.[10]

A bailiff was mentioned in 1273–4 and from 1294 there was a chief bailiff.[11] In the early 17th century the term of office was apparently indefinite. The chief bailiff, four electors of jurors, and eight other jurors represented Edmonton at the eyre of 1294.[12] In 1305 actions were heard before a constable of the peace for the hundred.[13] There was a chief constable in 1486, who was a maltman from Enfield,[14] and by 1613 there were three chief constables, all gentlemen, responsible respectively for Edmonton, Enfield, and Mimms and Hadley.[15] Later known as high constables, until at least 1747[16] they were elected and sworn at quarter sessions, initially for a three-year term,[17] although some served for as long as five years.[18] In the early 17th century about 16 petty constables were responsible to them.[19] From 1559[20] to 1729[21] Edmonton was normally associated with Gore and Ossulstone hundreds for musters to arms and administering the county funds.

The meeting-place of the hundred may have been near Potters Bar.[22] In 1658 a track led from Mutton Lane (the lane near which the moots were held)[23] to an area of 109 a. in Enfield Chase marked as 'mote plane'.[24] After the Middlesex county court had been reorganized under the Small Debts, Middlesex, Act of 1750,[25] the court for Edmonton hundred suitors was held from at least 1808 at the George, Enfield.[26] The court ceased to function in that form after the passage of the County Courts Act, 1846.[27]

The bronze matrix of the hundred seal, round, 2.7 cm., made in 1390–1 to seal the passes required by the Statute of Cambridge (1388), survives.[28] Legends, black letter, EDELME/TONE and SIGILLUM/COMITATUS MIDD' and on the reverse ED.

[4] *V.C.H. Mdx.* i. 136, 138.

[5] *Feud. Aids*, iii. 373.

[6] E 179/141/111.

[7] These figures are from the par. histories below.

[8] South Mimms and Enfield were included in the honor of Mandeville, later the honor of Clare, and thereby formed part of the duchy of Lancaster.

[9] J.I. 1/538 rot. 18.

[10] *Plac. de Quo Warr.* (Rec. Com.), 476, 478–9.

[11] J.I. 1/538 rot. 24; J.I. 1/544 rot. 67.

[12] J.I. 1/544 rot. 67.　　　[13] J.I. 3/39/1 rot. 4.

[14] K.B. 9/371/36; K.B. 29/116 rot. 15.

[15] *Mdx. Sess. Recs.* i. 250; ii. 96.

[16] M.R.O., Cal. Mdx. Sess. Bks. 1743–5, 125.

[17] *Mdx. Sess. Recs.* ii. 117; iv. 207.

[18] M.R.O., Cal. Mdx. Sess. Bks. 1732–5, 105.

[19] *Mdx. Sess. Recs.* i. 250–1; ii. 96.

[20] *Cal. S.P. Dom.* 1547–80, 122.

[21] M.R.O., Cal. Mdx. Sess. Bks. 1727–9, 126.

[22] *T.L.M.A.S.* xvi. 149–50.

[23] Ibid. citing Ekwall, *Dict. of Eng. Place-Names* (1960), 334, for Mutford and Mutlow (ford and mound where moots were held).

[24] M.R.O., F. 57.

[25] 23 Geo. II, c. 33.

[26] *Holden's Triennial Dir.* i. 115; *P.O. Dir. Lond.* (1847), p. 1464.

[27] 9 & 10 Vic. c. 95.

[28] E 364/25 B; A. B. Tonnochy, *Cat. of Brit. Seal-Dies in B.M.* (1952), no. 174. A wax impression, probably made in 1854, is among the coll. of the Soc. of Antiquaries of London, D. 28: *Arch. Jnl.* xi. 379.

EDMONTON,[1] noted for its witch and devil, for John Gilpin and its 18th-century fairs, lay about 7 miles from London on the main road to Ware and the north. Southgate, known for its elegant mansions and the cricketing Walker brothers, lay some $2\frac{1}{4}$ miles west of Edmonton village. Edmonton parish was a compact rectangle in shape, approximately 5 miles long and $2\frac{1}{4}$ miles from north to south until the Act for inclosing Enfield Chase in 1777[2] added 1,231 a. jutting into Enfield from the north-west corner. About 1860 part of the Chase allotment, which was owned by the lord of the manor and the tithe owners of Enfield, was assigned to Enfield parish, leaving Edmonton with a very irregular boundary and a small isolated piece of land at World's End, which was transferred to Enfield in 1926. Southgate, a separate local government unit from 1881, received a strip of land from Enfield in the north-west between 1931 and 1951 and there were minor boundary changes with Wood Green in 1892 and with Friern Barnet by 1951. The total acreage varied little, rising from 7,480 a. in 1831 to 7,491 a. in 1901 and 7,660 a. in 1951.[3] Edmonton and Southgate united with Enfield to form the London Borough of Enfield in 1965.[4]

The eastern boundary followed the river Lea, whose tributaries formed part of the boundary with Enfield.[5] Tottenham mark, mentioned many times in the 13th century,[6] was a ditch or hedge between Tottenham and Edmonton.[7] Bounds Green and Waterfall Road formed part of the boundaries in the south-west with Tottenham and Friern Barnet but the rest of the western boundary with East Barnet (Herts.) and the northern one with Enfield ran through woodland containing only estate boundaries and the gates of the Chase.[8] The portion of Enfield Chase allotted to Edmonton after 1777 was marked by straight lines bearing no relation to natural features.

Apart from the alluvium forming Edmonton marsh along the eastern border the eastern half of the parish is mainly valley brickearth. Flood plain gravel covers the north-east and pushes tongues southward along Fore Street and westward along the river valleys. In the west London Clay is predominant with large outcrops of plateau gravel in the west and north.[9] Most of Edmonton is flat with a gentle rise from 36 ft. in the marshy Lea valley to 304 ft. in the north-west. Streams drain from the west to the river Lea.[10]

In 894 the Danes sailed 20 miles up the Lea[11] but during the Middle Ages the marshy river banks restricted navigation. Edmonton marsh formed a band about $\frac{1}{2}$ mile wide, bordered and crossed by innumerable watercourses.[12] An Act of 1571[13] authorized the City of London to make the Lea navigable as far as Ware (Herts.). The New Cut, as it was called, was used for barges, mostly transporting grain from Hertfordshire to London[14] and there is little evidence that it benefited Edmonton until the late 18th century and the nineteenth. A new straight canal was begun a little to the west of the meandering river in 1770.[15] The Lee Conservancy Board,[16] which was established in 1868, was taken over by the Metropolitan Water Board in 1904. The course of the river was obliterated by the construction of Banbury reservoir in southern Edmonton and Tottenham in 1903[17] and by the much larger William Girling reservoir in Edmonton and Enfield in 1951.[18]

The two main tributaries of the Lea which run eastward through Edmonton are Pymme's and Salmon's brooks. Pymme's brook, which throughout the Middle Ages was called the Medesenge[19] and afterwards sometimes Millicents brook (1675)[20] and Bell brook (1765)[21] enters Southgate at Arnos Park, where in 1567 it was known as Hawland brook,[22] and flows to meet the network of watercourses along Edmonton marshes. Bounds (1659)[23] or Bounds Green brook, which enters New Southgate with the North Circular Road, joins Pymme's brook at the eastern end of Arnos Park. Salmon's brook,[24] in the 13th century called Stebbing,[25] enters Edmonton at Bush Hill[26] and flows to Edmonton Green, where it turns south and then east at approximately the site of the former town hall. In the 16th century it was joined by a tributary near the later junction of Brettenham and Brookfield roads and thence flowed southward along John a Marsh Green to join Pymme's brook at Watery Lane (later Angel Road).[27] The tributary (which is treated below) had largely disappeared by 1801 and most of the

[1] The article was written in 1972–3. Any references to later years are dated. The help of Mr. D. O. Pam in making material available and commenting on the article is gratefully acknowledged. [2] See p. 207.

[3] Census, 1801–1961; O.S. Maps 6″, Mdx. VII, XII (1865 and later edns.). See below, p. 207.

[4] See p. 179.

[5] Hatfield C.P.M. Suppl. 27 (late-16th-cent. map of Edmonton); inclosure map in W. Robinson, Hist. and Antiquities of Edmonton (1819).

[6] e.g. E 40/2040; E 40/2190; E 40/2294; E 42/99.

[7] Probably a hedge, hence Langhedge field.

[8] Hatfield C.P.M. Suppl. 27; inclosure map in Robinson, Edmonton. See description of boundaries in 1605: M.R.O., Acc. 695/42, f. 72.

[9] Geol. Surv. Map 1″, drift, sheet 256 (1951 edn.).

[10] O.S. Map 6″, Mdx. VII (1865 edn.).

[11] Anglo-Saxon Chron. ed. Dorothy Whitelock (1961), 56. The story, quoted by Robinson (Edmonton, 10 n. 20) that Alfred drained the Lea to strand the Danish boats is based upon a probably mistaken interpretation of the chronicle and other sources.

[12] Hatfield C.P.M. Suppl. 27; inclosure map in Robinson, Edmonton.

[13] 13 Eliz. I, c. 18.

[14] Robinson, Edmonton, 12–14. [15] See p. 208.

[16] The spelling 'Lee', used in Acts of Parliament, was adopted by the Board. 'Lea', however, was used by topographical writers and map-makers: ex inf. Metropolitan Water Bd. (1973).

[17] Robbins, Mdx. 68; Mdx. Quarterly, N.S. xix. 11.

[18] Ex inf. Metropolitan Water Bd.

[19] e.g. 1204: C.P. 25(1)/146/3/36; 1372: BM. Add. Ch. 40526.

[20] C 10/201/50.

[21] D. O. Pam, Stamford Hill, Green Lanes Turnpike Trust, i (Edmonton Hund. Hist. Soc. 1963), 16.

[22] B.M. Add. Ch. 40589.

[23] Prob. 11/295 (P.C.C. 496 Pell, will of Thos. Cranaway).

[24] So called by 1605: M.R.O., Acc. 695/42, f. 22. There was a medieval family called Salmon in Edmonton: W.A.M. 50, 232; C.P. 25(1)/149/42/84; C.P. 25(1)/148/37/321.

[25] Hatfield C.P. 291.1, nos. 88, 105 (cartulary of Adam Francis).

[26] O.S. Map 6″, Mdx. I. SE.; II. SW.; VII. NE., SE. (1865 edn.). [27] Hatfield C.P.M. Suppl. 27.

portion between Edmonton Green and Pymme's brook was culverted between 1897 and 1920. Thereafter Salmon's brook ran due eastward from Edmonton Green to the edge of the marsh, whence it flowed south to join Pymme's brook by a drainage channel near the border with Tottenham.[28]

Merryhills brook in the north and Hounsden gutter at the south of Edmonton's portion of Enfield Chase both ran eastward across Southgate and Winchmore Hill to join Salmon's brook in Enfield. In the 16th century a stream, probably Bridgewater, which was described in 1322 as south of the Hyde,[29] flowed south-eastward from a point near Fords Green to Fore Street, where it turned northward for a short distance before striking east to join Salmon's brook near the later Brettenham Road.[30] By 1801 most of it apparently had disappeared in the lakes and streams of Pymmes Park[31] and by 1895 it terminated at Morees pond west of Fore Street.[32] In the 16th century a stream, possibly the medieval Hakebrook[33] and called in 1605 Hobb Hale[34] and in 1826 Bury Street stream,[35] formed the boundary with Enfield from Bush Hill to a point almost due north of Bury Farm. Thence it ran southward to cross Bury Street, form the mill stream of Sadlers mill, and flow eastward close to the later Nightingale Hall farm, whence it followed the road south to John a Marsh Green before turning east again towards Edmonton marsh.[36] In the 19th century it became a tributary of Salmon's brook after the changes to the latter's southern section.[37] Unidentified watercourses include Melflet in the 13th century,[38] Church brook in the 14th century,[39] and Rowes brook in 1616.[40]

Almost all the streams have been straightened and often diverted into underground sewers. Pymme's and Salmon's brooks were widened and deepened in 1766 and 1772.[41] After severe flooding in 1881 Salmon's brook, which had formed a pond at Edmonton Green, and Pymme's brook at Montagu Road were confined between concrete walls. In 1921 Pymme's brook was culverted and its western course straightened.[42]

The New River, which was constructed in 1608–13 to bring drinking water from Chadwell and Amwell (Herts.) to Islington, crossed Edmonton parish from Bush Hill to Bowes. At Bush Hill a wooden aqueduct carried the river across a stream, presumably Salmon's brook. The Gordon rioters threatened to destroy the aqueduct in 1780[43] and in 1784 it was removed and the landscape remodelled.[44]

The New River was dependent on the contours and in the southern portion of Southgate and Bowes Park it followed a very meandering course until 1857–8, when an embankment was constructed to carry it across the valley of Pymme's brook.[45]

Edmonton was noted in Jacobean literature. Elizabeth Sawyer, married to a local labourer, was suspected of felony in 1615[46] and apparently hanged for killing by witchcraft. Her story, told to a minister who visited her in prison, was published in a tract in 1621, which immediately became the basis for the play, the *Witch of Edmonton*, by Ford, Dekker, and William Rowley. Another popular play, the *Merry Devil of Edmonton*, was probably written by Michael Drayton and first performed c. 1606. According to the play's preface the protagonist Peter Fabell was commemorated on a monument in Edmonton church.[47] Presumably he was Peter Favelore (d. 1360).[48]

During its heyday, in the 18th and early 19th centuries, several literary and artistic people lived in Edmonton, where there were good communications and wealthy patrons. Charles Lamb (d. 1834), who moved there from Enfield in 1833, remarked on the frequency and cheapness of coaches to London.[49] Alexander Cruden (1701–70), author of the biblical concordance, was in his youth the tutor of a gentleman at Elm Hall, Southgate.[50] John T. Smith, the artist and author, came to live in Edmonton in 1788 at the invitation of Sir James Winter Lake of the Firs.[51] The duke of Chandos was the patron of Isaac Hunt, whose son James Henry Leigh Hunt (d. 1859) was born in Southgate in 1784. John Keats (d. 1821) lived in Church Street from 1805 and from 1810 until 1815 was apprenticed to the local doctor, Thomas Hammond.[52] Henry Crabb Robinson (d. 1867), diarist, lived at Southgate in 1812[53] and Thomas Hood (d. 1845), poet, at Winchmore Hill from 1829 to 1832. Among painters John Clayton (1728–1800) came from a Bush Hill family and Abraham Cooper (1787–1868) was a child at Edmonton, where his father was an innkeeper.[54]

Sir John Moore (d. 1702), Lord Mayor of London in 1681, lived in Southgate c. 1674[55] and Reuben Bourne (d. 1695), author of a play set in Edmonton, had property there and probably came of an Edmonton family.[56] Natives[57] included Brook Taylor (1685–1731), mathematician; Robert Taylor (1784–1844), deistical writer; J. D. G. Pike (1784–1854), Baptist author; Sir William Maule (1788–1858), the

[28] Inclosure map in Robinson, *Edmonton*; O.S. Maps 6″, Mdx. VII. SE. (1865 and later edns.).
[29] St. Paul's MS., Box A 31, no. 533.
[30] Hatfield C.P.M. Suppl. 27.
[31] Inclosure map in Robinson, *Edmonton*; and see O.S. Map 6″, Mdx. VII. SE. (1865 edn.).
[32] O.S. Map 6″, Mdx. VII. SE. (1897 edn.).
[33] Near Heyegate and South field. St. Paul's MS., Box A 26, no. 99; Hatfield C.P. 291.1, no. 887.
[34] M.R.O., Acc. 695/42, f. 22.
[35] *Rep. on Bridges in Mdx.* 107.
[36] Hatfield C.P.M. Suppl. 27; inclosure map in Robinson, *Edmonton*.   [37] See above.
[38] E 40/2376; E 40/2378. It was south of Medesenge and therefore possibly a branch of Pymme's brook.
[39] Hatfield C.P. 291.1, nos. 655, 969. Possibly Salmon's brook at John a Marsh Green.
[40] M.R.O., Acc. 349/58.
[41] Pam, *Stamford Hill, Green Lanes Turnpike Trust*, i. 18.
[42] G. W. Sturges, *Edmonton Past and Present*, 63, 65; M. S. Briggs, *Mdx. Old and New*, 81.

[43] Robinson, *Edmonton*, 14–19.
[44] *Gent. Mag.* liv. 643, 723; lviii. 460.
[45] Inclos. map in Robinson, *Edmonton*; T. Mason, *Southgate Scrapbook*, 54.
[46] *Mdx. Sess. Recs.* iii. 1.
[47] G. W. Sturges, *Edmonton Heritage*, 2–35; *Mdx. Quarterly*, N.S. xiv. 13; xv. 15.
[48] See p. 182.
[49] Sturges, *Edmonton Heritage*, 102.
[50] *D.N.B.*
[51] Extracts from *Bk. for a Rainy Day*, a journal of his life in Edmonton, are in Sturges, *Edmonton Heritage*, 59–68.
[52] Burnby, *Hammonds of Edmonton* (Edmonton Hund. Hist. Soc. 1973).
[53] *D.N.B.*; Robbins, *Mdx.* 158.
[54] *D.N.B.*
[55] C 7/63/30.
[56] C 7/358/10; M.R.O., Acc. 689/5; Prob. 11/250 (P.C.C. 408 Aylett, will of Reuben Bourne).
[57] Except where otherwise stated, the foll. two paras. are based on *D.N.B.*

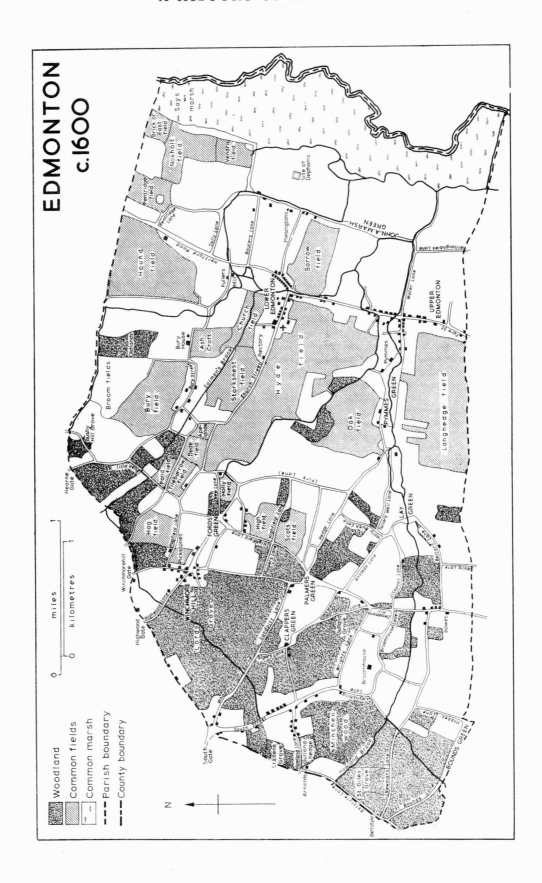

judge; H. W. Woolrych (1795–1871), biographer and legal writer; J. A. Dorin (1802–72), Indian administrator; and Frances Broderip (1830–78), daughter of Thomas Hood and herself an author. The father (d. 1760) of Nathaniel Bentley (1735?–1809), the beau known as 'Dirty Dick', had a country house at Edmonton. Charles Molloy (d. 1767), journalist and dramatist, may have spent his last years at Edmonton, where he was buried,[58] and Isaac Taylor (1730–1807), the engraver, retired there in 1780.

Most of the prominent people associated with the parish since the mid 19th century are treated below. The painter George Patten died in 1865 at his house at Winchmore Hill.[59] The Hebraist C. D. Ginsburg (1831–1914), the authority on Old English language and literature, Professor R. W. Chambers (1874–1942), and Benjamin Waugh (1839–1908), the philanthropist and a founder of the National Society for the Prevention of Cruelty to Children, lived in the area.[60]

COMMUNICATIONS. There were probably two Roman roads through Edmonton: Ermine Street, from Bishopsgate, and a route from Cripplegate to Hatfield through Southgate and Chase Side, whose course is uncertain.[61] Ermine Street passed through Edmonton approximately along the line of Fore Street and Hertford Road or to the west of it.[62] Fore Street was parallel to the Lea and far enough west to run on gravel rather than the brickearth and alluvium of the river valley but was crossed by four streams which caused great damage to the road surface. In the 18th century the portion between the junction with Silver Street and Edmonton Green was called Duck Lane.[63] The stretch between the Tottenham border and Edmonton Green was the most important road in Edmonton, called the high street (1341),[64] Edmonton Street (1593),[65] or Fore Street (1535–6).[66] Only later was the northern portion named Hertford Road. By an Act of 1713[67] the Stamford Hill turnpike trust was set up to administer the road between Enfield and Shoreditch, and by an Act of 1826 the trust was succeeded by the commissioners for the metropolitan turnpike roads.[68] Fore Street was widened to accommodate trams in 1906.[69]

By the late 16th century Green Lanes formed a second route to the north, entering Edmonton at Bowes and passing through Palmers and Fords greens and Bush Hill, while another route ran from Palmers Green through Winchmore Hill to the north-west.[70] Green Street, mentioned in 1330,[71] may be identifiable with Green Lanes but c. 1600 Green Street or Green Lanes consisted of a series of linking lanes, each with a different name. From south to north they were Deadman's Hill, Palmers Green,[72] Highfields Lane, and Fords Green Lane.[73] The 13th-century Rod Way or Rod Street may have been part of Green Lanes between Palmers Green and Fords Green.[74] Under an Act of 1789[75] the portion of Green Lanes within Edmonton parish passed under the control of the turnpike trust which was already responsible for Fore Street. Thereafter extensive improvements were made to Green Lanes, which led to a great increase in traffic[76] and contributed to the growth of Southgate. In 1826 responsibility for Green Lanes passed to the commissioners for the metropolitan turnpike roads.[77] Some straightening of Green Lanes took place in 1905 and 1907[78] but its course remained essentially the same in 1973 as it had been c. 1600.

By an Act of 1728 the Stamford Hill turnpike trust, hitherto responsible only for the north road, extended its control to the road from the watch house in Edmonton to the market-place in Enfield.[79] The road included Church Street, which, although not mentioned by name until c. 1530,[80] must have been one of the oldest streets in Edmonton. By c. 1600 it ran north-west from Edmonton Green and joined Bush Hill Road and Bush Hill.[81] Green Lanes joined it at Bush Hill. It was much altered at Bush Hill in 1805[82] and in 1807 extensive improvements were made to Church Street.[83]

All other roads remained the responsibility of the parish. The road pattern was established by c. 1600 and changed little until the mid 19th century.[84] No through route ran from west to east until the Lea was bridged in the 19th century. Angel Road, called Watery Lane in 1557[85] and Marsh Lane in the late 16th century,[86] followed Pymme's brook from Fore Street to Edmonton marsh. The route ran westward from Fore Street as Fords Street (1312),[87] Pymme's Green, Silver Street,[88] or Weir Hall Road.[89] At Tanners End, Hedge Lane ran north-westward to Palmers Green and c. 1600 Tailors Well Lane[90] and

[58] His wife was buried there in 1758: Robinson, *Edmonton*, 105.

[59] *D.N.B.*

[60] In Oakthorpe Road, Selborne Road, and Southgate Green respectively: Mason, *Southgate Scrapbook*, 27–8; *D.N.B.*

[61] I. D. Margary, *Roman Roads in Britain*, 201.

[62] The Roman road may have run west of Fore Street because the alignment is not due north from Tottenham High Road: Margary op. cit. 195. The only portion of the Roman road to be excavated is at Snells Park near the Tottenham border: G. R. Gillan, 'Prehist. and Rom. Enfield', Enfield Arch. Soc., *Research Rep.* iii (1973).

[63] Pam, op. cit. i. 5 and map.

[64] C.P. 25(1)/150/59/152.

[65] Norden, *Spec. Brit.* 19.

[66] S.C. 6/Hen. VIII/2102 m. 2.

[67] 12 Anne, c. 19.

[68] 7 Geo. IV, c. 142.

[69] *The Times*, 6 Apr. 1906.

[70] Hatfield C.P.M. Suppl. 27.

[71] Hatfield C.P. 291.1, no. 978; and see M.R.O., Acc. 695/42, f. 26.

[72] The 'highway called Palmers Green' was mentioned in 1324: W.A.M. 318.

[73] Hatfield C.P.M. Suppl. 27; Hatfield C.P. 291.1, ff. 119 sqq.

[74] E 40/1693; E 40/2147.

[75] 29 Geo. III, c. 96.

[76] Pam, op. cit. ii. 20, 22, 24–5.

[77] 7 Geo. IV, c. 142; Pam, op. cit. ii. 29.

[78] M.R.O., S.B. 2506/82; 2508/68.

[79] 2 Geo. II, c. 14; Pam, op. cit. i. 3.

[80] C 1/647/17–18.

[81] Hatfield C.P.M. Suppl. 27.

[82] M.R.O., S.R. 3727/85.

[83] Pam, op. cit. ii. 28.

[84] Cf. maps of c. 1600 (Hatfield C.P.M. Suppl. 27) and 1801 (inclosure map in Robinson, *Edmonton*).

[85] Prob. 11/39 (P.C.C. 46 Wrastley, will of Wm. Gilbarne).

[86] Hatfield C.P. 143/111, f. 151.

[87] W.A.M. 257. Cf. position of Fords field: Hatfield C.P. 291.1, ff. 119 sqq.

[88] Mentioned 1546: Hatfield C.F.E.P. (Deeds) 89/13; but Silver St. was also an *alias* for Church St. in 1568: C 142/152/91.

[89] e.g. in 1887: M.R.O., Acc. 815/37.

[90] The old lane next Tailors field was mentioned in 1337: W.A.M. 185.

Belsers Lane (otherwise Tile Kiln Lane or Tottenhall Road), which was diverted in 1905,[91] twisted about the Pymme's valley to Green Lanes at Bowes. From Green Lanes Bowes Road, called Bowes Street[92] and Newmans Lane (1574)[93] and later Betstile Road,[94] *c.* 1600 ran westward to Betstile, the south-western corner of the parish. There was a network of roads to the east of the north road, mainly to serve isolated farms. John a Marsh[95] or Jeremy's Green and Lane (later Montagu Road) ran parallel with Fore Street from Watery Lane to Claverings. From north to south it was linked to Fore Street by Pentridge (1598)[96] or Dyer's *alias* Cuckoohall Lane,[97] Colly Lane (Colles Lane 1328),[98] which disappeared between 1801 and 1865,[99] Boursers (1333)[1] or Bounces Lane, and Wrights[2] or Town Lane (1765).[3] A short section of Brettenham Road, which was called Board's Lane after a local farmer in 1851,[4] existed *c.* 1600, as did Cow Lane (1818)[5] or Claremont Street. Dyson's Road, which joined Angel Road and Tottenham, may be identifiable with Willoughby Lane.[6]

Three important roads ran westward from Fore Street: Silver Street, Church Street and, in the north, Bury Street, which was mentioned in 1269.[7] It was linked to Church Street by several side-roads one of which was stopped up in 1903.[8]

About 1600 Green Lanes formed the backbone of a group of lanes linking hamlets at Palmers, Clappers, and Fords greens and Winchmore Hill.[9] From Palmers Green Ansteds or Hazelwood Lane, Hedge Lane, and an unnamed lane, perhaps the 13th-century Scottes Lane,[10] ran eastward to Tanners End; Hoppers Road[11] went northward to Winchmore Hill, and Sandpitt or Dog and Duck Lane[12] and Wapull Borne[13] (later Bourne Hill and the Bourne) ran westward to Southgate. From Winchmore Hill Highwood Lane or Church Hill and the later Wade's Hill[14] led to gates at the edge of Enfield Chase. Hagfield Lane (1349)[15] or Vicar's Moor Lane,[16] Middle Lane (1865)[17] or Station Road, and the later Compton Road led eastward to Fords

Green. At Fords Green New Lane or Fords Grove, Holly Field Lane or Farm Road, and Highfield Row (1851)[18] or Road ran eastward to join the north-south route, Firs Lane, which may have been the medieval Garsonsway.[19] Farther south Highfield Lane or Barrowell Green joined Green Lanes and Firs Lane. From Clappers Green, Sigors Lane (*c.* 1530)[20] ran north to Wapull Borne and an unnamed lane, possibly Rosewell Lane (1685),[21] ran south-eastward to Green Lanes. The whole of the route was later called Fox Lane and at least part of it may be identifiable with Fox Street, mentioned in 1334.[22] Pricketts Want and Barnfield Lane, branching southward from Fox Lane to join Green Lanes farther south, disappeared between 1801 and 1865.[23] An unnamed lane ran westward to South Street.

High Street, Southgate, was called South Street (1339)[24] or the road to Southgate (1370).[25] Its continuation southward from Southgate Green (later called Cannon Hill and Powys Lane) was called Mynching Lane *c.* 1600.[26] Armolt Street (1322)[27] or Hawland Lane ran westward from Southgate Green to the border, which it followed as the road to Betstile (13th cent.)[28] or Betstile Lane (1567).[29] The whole of the road became Waterfall Road. In the south-west corner of the parish it joined Bowes Road and Bounds Lane and Green. Hobbes (1574)[30] or Jones's Lane[31] (later Warwick Road) joined Bounds Green to Bowes Road. Wrights Lane or Alderman's Hill and Broomhouse Lane (later Powys Lane and Broomhouse Lane) linked Mynching Lane with Green Lanes. Wolves Lane (1336)[32] ran southward to Tottenham from Tottenhall Road and Jickocks Lane (later Oakthorpe Road) joined Green Lanes to Lay Green. Lay Green and Holly Bush Lane by 1702 formed Blind Lane,[33] probably a cul-de-sac caused by difficulty in crossing Pymme's brook.

Other early roads in Edmonton cannot be identified. Colwell Street (13th cent.)[34] or Lane (1576)[35] may have been Colly Lane but the positions of Hog Lane (*c.* 1530),[36] Rowe Lane (1312),[37] Stony Street (13th cent.),[38] Wodenes

[91] M.R.O., S.B. 2506/77.
[92] M.R.O., Acc. 695/42, f. 19.
[93] B.M. Add. Ch. 40591.
[94] O.S. Map 6″, Mdx. VII. SW. (1865 edn.).
[95] See p. 167.
[96] M.R.O., Acc. 727/72.
[97] Rocque, *Map of Mdx.* (1754); O.S. Map 6″, Mdx. VII. SE. (1938 edn.).
[98] E 164/18 ff. 12 sqq.
[99] Approximately on the site of Grosvenor Rd.: O.S. Map 6″, Mdx. VII. SE. (1865 edn.).
[1] Hatfield C.P. 291.1, no. 1045.
[2] e.g. 1860: C 54/15556 no. 10.
[3] Edmonton Publ. Libr., Fore Street, D 11.
[4] H.O. 107/1703 p. 43.
[5] C 54/9751 no. 9.
[6] It ran beside Willoughby manor: E 310/19/93 f. 2; M.R.O., Acc. 695/42, f. 38. See below, p. 333.
[7] Hatfield C.P. 291.1, no. 340.
[8] M.R.O., S.B. 2504/43.
[9] Hatfield C.P.M. Suppl. 27; Hatfield C.P. 291.1, ff. 119 sqq.
[10] W.A.M. 5, 60; see proximity to Scots field.
[11] Though unnamed *c.* 1600, the road probably took its name from a medieval family: *Cur. Reg. R.* xi. 149; Hatfield C.P. 291.1, nos. 41, 1058.
[12] Sales parts. (1908) *penes* Broomfield Mus., Southgate.
[13] 'Wopoleshull' was mentioned in 1335: Hatfield C.P. 291.1, no. 285. 'Wapull Borne' was probably the name of Salmon's brook and became transferred to the broad track which crossed it.

[14] Called Manns Lane in 1851: H.O. 107/1703 pp. 249 sqq.
[15] W.A.M. 273. Land there was held by Wm. Viker.
[16] Vickers More pasture was mentioned in 1605: M.R.O., Acc. 695/42, f. 8.
[17] O.S. Map 6″, Mdx. VII. SW. (1865 edn.).
[18] H.O. 107/1703 p. 275.
[19] Described as east of the Hyde in 1294: St. Paul's MS., Box A 27, no. 103; in 1500: M.R.O., Acc. 349/28.
[20] C 1/647/17–18. Named after the medieval Sigor or Sigar family: E 40/1478; E 40/2304; E 40/11138.
[21] C 8/441/27.
[22] E 326/9820.
[23] Cf. inclosure map in Robinson, *Edmonton*, and O.S. Map 6″, Mdx. VII. SW. (1865 edn.).
[24] Hatfield C.P. 291.1, no. 199.
[25] E 326/1478.
[26] Hatfield C.P.M. Suppl. 27.
[27] Hatfield C.F.E.P. (Deeds) 102/10.
[28] E 40/2278; W.A.M. 339.
[29] B.M. Add. Ch. 40589.
[30] Ibid. 40591.
[31] O.S. Map 6″, Mdx. VII. SW. (1865 edn.).
[32] St. Paul's MS., Box A 31, no. 527.
[33] M.R.O., Acc. 276/182.
[34] Hatfield C.P. 291.1, no. 496.
[35] M.R.O., Acc. 241/3a.
[36] C 1/647/17–18.
[37] Hatfield C.P. 291.1, no. 522.
[38] E 40/2198.

Street (13th cent.),[39] Worde Street (13th cent.),[40] and Wyke Lane (1323)[41] are unknown.

The Edmonton maps of *c.* 1600 do not include Enfield Chase but routes through the Chase were marked, though not named, in 1658.[42] They included Chase Side, Chase Road, and a road from Winchmore gate, which all ran north-westward to Cockfosters, the east-west route later called Bramley Road, and a group of roads leading northward to Enfield and Theobalds. Cock Hill or Eversley Park Road, which ran north from Winchmore or Highmore gate, may be identifiable with Highgate Street (*c.* 1255)[43] and Highgate Lane near Green Street (1330).[44] At Old Park Corner it was joined by Green Dragon Lane, which may have been the earlier Park Street (13th cent.)[45] and Park Lane (1321).[46]

'Chase Side', mentioned in 1668,[47] was probably Winchmore Hill Road which ran along the border of Southgate and the Chase. A road west from Upper Fore Street, called Meeting House Lane, Church Road, Union Road, or Bridport Road,[48] existed in part by 1754[49] and Bull Lane joined it to Silver Street by 1801.[50] A new major road, Great Cambridge Road, was driven through the centre of Edmonton parish in 1923–4[51] and in 1924–7 Bowes Road, Silver Street, and Angel Road were transformed into the North Circular Road.[52] In 1974 a new section of the North Circular was being constructed south of the narrow and congested Silver Street.

The roads, bearing heavy traffic over ill drained clay, were hard to maintain. In 1365 the main road between Hackney and Edmonton was almost impassable and tolls were levied to repair it.[53] Bequests were made by Richard Askew (1551),[54] Ralph Davenant (1552),[55] William Gilbarne (1557),[56] John Sadler (1560),[57] and John Wilde (1665),[58] chiefly for repairs to Watery Lane and Church Street, and Wilde set up a charity to drain the highways into ditches during the winter.[59] In 1695 the road through Edmonton to London after a spring shower was so full of water that meeting loaded waggons was dangerous,[60] in 1713 it was estimated that 10,000 loads of gravel were needed for Duck Lane,[61] and in 1762 the Stamford Fly overturned in floods near the 7-mile stone at Edmonton.[62] A concerted effort to improve the

road to London began in 1764, before bridges were built over Pymme's and Salmon's brooks.[63]

Bridges in the 13th century included the long bridge near Langhedge,[64] a stockbridge near the mill,[65] and a bridge over the Medesenge.[66] Highgatesbridge, probably over Salmon's brook or Hobb Hale,[67] Alnenebridge, east of a road to Winchmore Hill,[68] and Pipplebridge in Northmarsh[69] existed in the 14th century, and Stonebridge in north-east Edmonton[70] and Cowbridge at Edmonton marsh (1564)[71] in the 16th.

In 1605 the lord of the manor was responsible for seven bridges.[72] A timber footbridge crossed Pymme's brook in Fore Street just north of its junction with Silver Street in the early 19th century,[73] when another footbridge crossed it in Love Lane, which led to the Hyde.[74] There were three bridges over Salmon's brook. In the north a cart bridge at Bush Hill marked the boundary between Edmonton and Enfield. It was called Balstepgrove bridge in 1623, when the inhabitants of the two parishes were indicted for neglecting it,[75] and Red bridge by *c.* 1801.[76] There was another bridge in Church Street, near its junction with Hertford Road, where the brook formed a wash, later the pond at Edmonton Green.[77] The third bridge was presumably between those two, over a side road leading to Bury Street.[78] There were two cart bridges over Hobb Hale, one in Hertford Road at Sadlers mill[79] and another leading to the common marsh near Claverings.[80] The latter may have been removed as part of the improvements initiated by the turnpike trust in 1772.[81]

By 1826[82] there was still no bridge over the river Lea, which was crossed at Cook's ferry. Pymme's brook was still bridged at Fore Street by Angel bridge, a three-arched brick and stone structure built in 1766 by the road trustees[83] and maintained by the county. The bridge in Love Lane had probably disappeared by 1826 but there were several other brick bridges over Pymme's brook. One of two arches had been built in 1772 at Tanners End with money raised from subscriptions and was maintained by the parish. Bowes Farm bridge, presumably Deadman's bridge in Green Lanes, a single arch, was built in 1789 by the road trustees and repaired in 1822 by the county. Another single arch, Woodlands bridge, was built, presumably

[39] Hatfield C.P. 291.1, no. 138.
[40] Ibid. nos. 201, 391.
[41] Ibid. no. 488.
[42] M.P.C. 50A.
[43] Hatfield C.P. 291.1, no. 18.
[44] Ibid. no. 978.
[45] Ibid. nos. 137, 404.
[46] Ibid. no. 584.
[47] Prob. 11/338 (P.C.C. 54 Eure, will of John Wynne).
[48] Named after Alexander Hood, Viscount Bridport (d. 1814) who married an Edmonton woman and had land in the area: D.N.B.; Robinson, *Edmonton*, 248.
[49] Rocque, *Map of Mdx.* (1754).
[50] Inclosure map in Robinson, *Edmonton*.
[51] Robbins, *Mdx.* 243.
[52] 'St. Paul's, New Southgate', (TS. *penes* the vicar, 1972); plate on Lea Valley viaduct.
[53] *Cal. Pat.* 1364–7, 183.
[54] Prob. 11/34 (P.C.C. 31 Bucke, will of Ric. Askew).
[55] Prob. 11/36 (P.C.C. 2 Taske, will of Ralph Davenant).
[56] Prob. 11/39 (P.C.C. 46 Wrastley, will of Wm. Gilbarne).
[57] Prob. 11/43 (P.C.C. 49 Mellershe, will of John Sadler).
[58] Prob. 11/316 (P.C.C. 9 Hyde, will of John Wilde).
[59] See p. 204.
[60] Ralph Thoresby's diary quoted in Pam, op. cit. i. 1.
[61] Pam, op. cit. i. 3.
[62] Ibid. 4–6.
[63] Ibid. 15–17.
[64] E 40/2140.
[65] Hatfield C.P. 291.1, no. 85.
[66] J.I. 1/540 m. 19.
[67] W.A.M. 73.
[68] Hatfield C.P. 291.1, no. 648.
[69] *Publ. Works in Medieval Law*, ii (Selden Soc. xl), 36–7.
[70] D.L. 1/19 no. E 1.
[71] E 310/19/90 f. 7.
[72] M.R.O., Acc. 695/42, f. 22.
[73] i.e. the Angel: M.R.O., Acc. 695/38. See below, p. 173. Cf. Hatfield C.P.M. Suppl. 27 and O.S. Map 6", Mdx. VII. SE. (1865 edn.).
[74] M.R.O., Acc. 695/38; Hatfield C.P.M. Suppl. 27; O.S. Maps 6", Mdx. VII. SE. (1865 and 1920 edns.).
[75] *Mdx. Cnty. Recs.* ii. 238.
[76] M.R.O., Acc. 695/38.
[77] Hatfield C.P. 291.1, ff. 119 sqq. (1606 survey of Cecil estates).
[78] Hatfield C.P.M. Suppl. 27.
[79] Hatfield C.P. 291.1, ff. 119 sqq.
[80] See Hatfield C.F.E.P. (Accts.) 5/22.
[81] Pam, *Stamford Hill, Green Lanes Turnpike Trust,* i 18–19.
[82] *Rep. on Bridges in Mdx.* 106–111.
[83] Pam, op. cit. i. 17.

in Bull Lane, c. 1792 by a Mr. Whitehead and maintained by the county. Betstile bridge, with three arches, was erected at Waterfall Road by Sir William Curtis or John Schneider, probably c. 1800.[84] There was also a ford and footbridge over Pymme's brook in Tile Kiln Lane.

In 1605 and 1826 Salmon's brook was bridged in three places. Red bridge had probably become Salmon's brook bridge, described as east of Bush Hill and on the road from Lower Edmonton to Enfield, which was the responsibility of the lords of Enfield and Edmonton manors although it had been repaired in 1821 by the county. A three-arched brick bridge had been built there c. 1779 by the road trustees. Lower Edmonton bridge marked the site of the older bridge in Church Street. Only a footbridge in 1675, it had been replaced by a bridge of two arches of brick and stone by the road trustees in 1766[85] and repaired in 1819 by the county, which maintained it. The third bridge was Bush Hill bridge, where Bush Hill and the New River crossed Salmon's brook. It had been built in brick with one arch by the New River Co. in 1682 and subsequently maintained by them. By 1826 Bury Street stream had been culverted in Bury Street and Hertford Road and the two bridges of 1605 had disappeared. There were, however, eleven bridges over the New River, all maintained by the company: one west of Bush Hill Park, one at Bush Hill, one at Butt's Farm, two at Boston Lodge, two at Huxley Farm, and four near Broomfield House. They included a bridge at Deadman's Hill which needed rebuilding in 1810 and an iron bridge of 1814 at Tile Kilns.[86]

By 1865 the Lea had been bridged.[87] Although the inhabitants asked the lord for a footbridge over Pymme's brook at the junction of Jeremy's Green Lane (later Montagu Road) with Watery Lane (later Angel Road) in 1799,[88] there was still only a ford there in 1865.[89] A wooden bridge had been erected by 1881 when it was washed away by floods and replaced by an iron one. Angel bridge in Fore Street was widened when the tramway (see below) was electrified.[90]

In spite of the bad roads Edmonton was considered to be easily accessible from London and by 1722 there was a daily coach service to Bishopsgate.[91] In 1807 hourly coaches ran to Edmonton from Bishopsgate and four coaches a day from Snow Hill.[92] In 1825 17 coaches made 39 return journeys a day from Edmonton and one coach made a daily return journey from Southgate.[93] By 1839 there were eight omnibuses and five short-stage coaches running between Edmonton and Bishopsgate, two omnibuses and three short-stage coaches to Snow Hill, and one omnibus and one short-stage coach

to the Bank. There were two short-stage coaches between Southgate and Snow Hill. Most services were in the hands of the Matthews and Isaac families.[94]

In 1851 there were two coach and nine omnibus proprietors concentrated in Church Street and Chase Side.[95] By then, however, omnibuses were becoming restricted to local journeys to railway stations. In the 1860s an omnibus ran from the King's Head in Winchmore Hill to Bishopsgate via Fore Street and another from the Green Dragon in Winchmore Hill to London Bridge via Green Lanes. Both services were discontinued in 1869.[96] An omnibus ran ten times a day between Avenue Road, Southgate, and Palmers Green station in 1890 and 1908.[97]

In 1840 the Northern and Eastern Railway[98] (from 1844 the Eastern Counties and from 1862 the Great Eastern Railway) opened a line along the Lea valley from London to Broxbourne (Herts.)[99] with a station at Edmonton (Water Lane, later Angel Road). A branch line was opened in 1849 between Angel Road and Enfield Town, with a station at Church Street (later Lower Edmonton) and from 1880 another at Bush Hill Park.[1] In 1872 a second branch line, from Bethnal Green to Edmonton, joined the first just north of Edmonton Green and another Lower Edmonton station was built just south of Church Street;[2] a station was also opened at Silver Street. In 1891 a line to Cheshunt was opened from the one from Angel Road to Enfield Town at a point just north of Bury Street. Suburban growth was not so rapid as expected and in 1909 the line was closed, though reopened for munitions workers between 1915 and 1919 and for electric trains from Liverpool Street to Hertford and Bishop's Stortford (Herts.) in 1960. The section of the line between Angel Road and Lower Edmonton, together with Lower Edmonton (Low Level) station, was closed in 1939.[3]

The main line of the Great Northern Railway,[4] which crossed the south-western corner of Edmonton parish in 1850, had a station at Colney Hatch or New Southgate.[5] Boundary adjustments later placed this line outside the parish. In 1871 the G.N.R. opened a branch line between Wood Green and Enfield with stations at Bowes Park (in Tottenham), Palmers Green, and Winchmore Hill. In spite of schemes in 1902 and 1919 to bring the railway to Southgate it was not until 1932 that the London Electric Co. extended the Piccadilly line to Arnos Grove, where Charles Holden designed a striking circular station.[6] In 1933 the line reached Cockfosters with intermediate stations, also designed by Holden, at Southgate and Enfield West (later Oakwood).[7]

---

[84] See inclosure map in Robinson, *Edmonton*.
[85] Pam, op. cit. i. 17.
[86] Ibid. 11, 26.
[87] O.S. Map 6", Mdx. VII. SE. (1865 edn.).
[88] M.R.O., Acc. 695/41.
[89] O.S. Map 6", Mdx. VII. SE. (1865 edn.).
[90] F. Fisk, *Hist. Edmonton*, 136–7.
[91] Sturges, *Edmonton Past and Present*, i. 116.
[92] *Ambulator* (10th edn.), unpag.
[93] T. C. Barker and M. Robbins, *Hist. Lond. Transport*, i. 391.
[94] Ibid. 396, 402.
[95] H.O. 107/1703 pp. 100, 112, 182, 195, 199, 212, 215 sqq.
[96] Helen Cresswell, *Winchmore Hill*, 93.
[97] *Kelly's Dirs. Mdx.* (1890, 1908).
[98] Except where otherwise stated, inf. about this rly. is taken from C. J. Allen, *Gt. Eastern Rly.*

[99] The line reached Cambridge in 1845.
[1] Ex inf. Mr. H. V. Borley.
[2] The first station was called Low Level, the Green, and second High Level, Church Street: *Kelly's Dir. Mdx.* (1890).
[3] J. E. Connor and B. L. Halford, *Forgotten Stations of Greater Lond.* 34.
[4] Except where otherwise stated, the hist. of this rly. is based upon C. H. Grinling, *Hist. of Gt. Northern Rly.*
[5] Ex inf. Mr. H. V. Borley.
[6] See plate 18 in Jackson, *Semi-Det. Lond.*
[7] C. E. Lee, *Sixty Yrs. of the Piccadilly* (London Transport pamphlet), 11, 20, 22; A. E. Bennett and H. V. Borley, *London Transport Rlys.* 11, 13. The London Passenger Transport Bd. built the section between Oakwood and Cockfosters.

In 1881 the North London Tramways Co. opened a service from Stamford Hill along Fore Street to Lower Edmonton, where a tram station was erected at Tramway Avenue, and in 1882 it extended the line along Hertford Road to Ponders End. The company was taken over by the North Metropolitan Tramways Co. in 1891.[8] Steam and horse trams ran until 1905, when the Metropolitan Electric Tramways Co. introduced a service from Stamford Hill to Silver Street. Later in 1905 electric trams were extended to Lower Edmonton and in 1907 to the Hertfordshire boundary. In 1907 the company began services from Bounds Green to New Southgate (extended to North Finchley in 1909) and from Wood Green along Green Lanes to Palmers Green and later to Winchmore Hill (1908) and Enfield (1909).[9] In 1933 control passed to the London Passenger Transport Board and in 1938 trams were replaced by trolley-buses, of which there were five services in Edmonton in 1939. They were withdrawn in 1961.[10] The London General Omnibus Co. introduced motor-buses between Victoria station and the Angel, Fore Street, and by 1914 there were also services from Victoria to Palmers Green and Southgate.[11] There were nine services within Edmonton borough in 1939[12] and 26 London Transport suburban services and two Green Line routes within Edmonton and Southgate c. 1970.[13]

GROWTH BEFORE 1851. A mesolithic tool has been found at Winchmore Hill,[14] people lived near Ermine Street from c. 100–350 A.D.,[15] and a few fragments of Roman pottery were discovered at the Ridgeway, near the Bourne in Southgate.[16] Nevertheless continuous settlement probably dates from the Anglo-Saxon period, as the name Edmonton (Adelmetone) indicates.[17]

Early habitations were probably along Fore Street, particularly on the gravel west of the road, watered by wells[18] and by the east-flowing streams that served as public sewers. Upper Edmonton, at the junction with Silver Street, and Lower Edmonton, at the junction with Church Street, represent the earliest concentrations of dwellings. Few named medieval houses can be located[19] but they were usually near a church;[20] Gisors Place or Polehouse, Pymmes, and Caustons were probably

near Silver Street by the mid 14th century. Thurstones stood on the east side of Fore Street, next to Salmon's brook, by 1423[21] and Trumpton Hall between Fore Street and Langhedge field by 1500.[22] Cookes existed on the south side of Silver Street by 1461[23] and the Lyon stood in 1523 on the east side of Silver Street from Fore Street.[24] Goodhouse was in Fore Street by 1548[25] and Paycock or Peacock Farm in Church Street by 1559.[26]

Upper and Lower Edmonton were served by open-field systems mostly west of Fore Street. More open fields probably lay to the north, primarily serving the manorial demesne farm north of Bury Street. At least one other house existed in Bury Street in 1269[27] and Fullers was there by 1467.[28]

Winchmore Hill, Wynsemerhull in 1319, probably originated as a hamlet served by assarted fields which existed by the 13th century.[29] The Vikers family had a house there in 1349[30] and Dacres tenement existed there in 1546.[31] The house by Highgate, mentioned in the 13th century, was probably near by.[32]

Southgate, the south gate of Enfield Chase, was first mentioned 1166 × 1189[33] and South Street, the road leading to the gate, in 1321.[34] Houses seem to have been erected there by 1321 and one of them, Ryneshamstall, was so named in 1338.[35] Pottery probably dating from the 13th century has been found south of the Bourne.[36] No medieval field system was associated with Southgate, whose inhabitants were woodmen rather than farmers. There was probably a small agricultural settlement at Clappers Green by the early 14th century, where the Clapper and Sigar families held land and Holy Trinity priory a grange.[37]

Palmers Green was mentioned as a highway in 1324.[38] There are allusions to Palmers field (1204),[39] Palmersland (1322),[40] and Palmers Grove (1340),[41] but there is no evidence of settlement there before the late 16th century.[42]

In the Middle Ages there were several moated farm-houses, mainly east of Fore Street, although one was at Fords Grove and another at Bowes in the west of the parish. Dephams probably dated from the 12th century and Fords Grove from the 13th century[43] but most were created when land holdings were consolidated during the 14th century.[44]

[8] Barker and Robbins, Hist. Lond. Transport, i. 241, 267.
[9] Jackson, Semi-Det. Lond. 329–31.
[10] Edmonton, Official Guide [1939]. See p. 312.
[11] Jackson, Semi-Det. Lond. 334.
[12] Edmonton, Official Guide [1939].
[13] Enfield L.B. Inf. Handbk. [1970]; London Transport, Map & List of Routes.
[14] V.C.H. Mdx. i. 28.
[15] Ibid. 66, 69.
[16] Enfield Arch. Soc. Bulletin, xxxiii (1969).
[17] P.N. Mdx. (E.P.N.S.), 67.
[18] e.g. well in Church St. mentioned in 1559: Prob. 11/43 (P.C.C. 49 Mellershe, will of John Sadler).
[19] e.g. William son of Fubert's capital messuage next Stonifeld before 1224: Clerkenwell Cart. (Camd. 3rd ser. lxxi), 107–8; Kingent in 13th cent.: E 40/2283; Sopereshawe in 1317: Hatfield C.P. 291.1, no. 563; Picots tenement in 1349: W.A.M. 17; Silveynes in 1340: St. Paul's MS., Box A 35, no. 911; Ansties, Hamonds and Heghammes in 1359: W.A.M. 11, 55; le Lecheslonde in 1368: E 326/1227; Littlecooks and Mayhouse c. 1530: C 1/647/17–18.
[20] The 13th-cent. rectory and vicarage houses were probably in Church Street.
[21] Hatfield C.F.E.P. (Deeds) 109/20.

[22] M.R.O., Acc. 349/28.
[23] Ibid.; C 10/201/50.
[24] M.R.O., Acc. 349/10.
[25] Prob. 11/32 (P.C.C. 10 Populwell, will of John Hilmer).
[26] Prob. 11/34 (P.C.C. 49 Mellershe, will of John Sadler).
[27] Hatfield C.P. 291.1, no. 340.
[28] Hatfield C.F.E.P. (Deeds) 236/25.
[29] See p. 166.
[30] W.A.M. 273. For Vicars Moor Lane, see above.
[31] Hatfield C.F.E.P. (Deeds) 89/13.
[32] W.A.M. 254.
[33] Hatfield C.P. 291.1, no. 826.
[34] St. Paul's MS., Box A 27, no. 107.
[35] W.A.M. 173.
[36] E 40/2304; E 40/2670; E 40/11138.
[37] Enfield Arch. Soc. Bull. xxxiii.
[38] W.A.M. 318.
[39] C.P. 25(1)/146/3/36.
[40] Hatfield C.P. 291.1, no. 593.
[41] Ibid. no. 1058.
[42] See map on p. 132.
[43] Robert Ford's house was mentioned c. 1274: J.I. 1/540 m. 18d.
[44] V.C.H. Mdx. ii. 4, 9; Hist. Mon. Com. Mdx. 112. The moats were probably for drainage rather than defence.

Much building was the work of individuals, particularly London merchants, who divided up the common fields.[45] Plesingtons, Claverings, and Willoughbies in the east, Bowes in the south-west, and Weir Hall at Tanners End were probably all established during the 14th century. Pentridge Farm in the north-east existed by 1483.[46]

In the 16th century the main centres of population were still Lower Edmonton, near the church, and Upper Edmonton, along Fore Street. About 1535 the tenants of Edmonton manor were divided into six groups, which, although not yet called wards, were the precursors of wards which served from the 17th century as parish government divisions.[47] Customary rents suggest that Church Street ward, which paid 57 per cent of the total, was by far the most populous and Fore Street, paying 21 per cent, the next. To the north Bury Street ward paid 7 per cent and in the west Winchmore Hill paid 11 per cent and South Street and Bowes 2 per cent each.[48] Apart from the church no medieval or early Tudor building suvives in the parish. About 182 houses are marked on late-16th-century maps,[49] probably too few but some indication of the pattern of settlement. Buildings were concentrated at Lower and Upper Edmonton, with smaller hamlets at Winchmore Hill and Southgate. There were a few houses at Bowes, Bury Street, Tanners End, Marsh Lane, and Clappers Green, four at Palmers Green, and one at Bush Hill. The most notable change in the 16th century took place at Fords Green, where fields were assarted and houses probably erected at the same time. Butts Farm stood a little to the north by 1591.[50]

From the 16th century growth was continuous. As communications improved more Londoners acquired houses in Edmonton, some, like one Avery of Basinghall in 1665, as summer residences for their families,[51] others as permanent homes. Brick was not the only building material, for weatherboarding was particularly common in Southgate and Winchmore Hill, while dilapidated hovels with thatch and even turf roofs survived into the late 18th century, when they were depicted in a romantic manner by the local painter John T. Smith.[52] New houses were normally erected on old sites, bordering the roads and greens, and frequently several dwellings were built where there had once been only one. In place of houses set in spacious gardens, buildings presented an uninterrupted front to the street, especially along Fore Street and Edmonton Green. In Silver Street, for example, there were in 1675 several houses where Cookes had stood.[53] In Southgate a site which in 1743 contained only the Woolpack inn was covered by two houses in 1750, three in 1782, and five in 1824.[54] West of South Street a large house was pulled down by 1769 and replaced by three houses in 1778, to which two more had been added by 1798.[55] The number of houses in the parish increased to 423 in 1664,[56] about 800 in the late 18th century,[57] 901 in 1801, and 1,726 in 1851.[58] Growth therefore appears to have gathered pace. Although there were no new centres of population, the older ones expanded at varying rates.

Of the four wards which existed from the mid 17th century, Fore Street eventually became the most populous. There were 88 houses in 1664,[59] 229 1801,[60] 368 in 1811, 506 in 1841,[61] and 611 in 1851.[62] Polehouse and Trumpton Hall[63] survived on their medieval sites and Neales, the home of the Rogers family, was in Fore Street in 1659.[64] The largest houses in the ward in 1664 were Weir Hall, with 20 hearths, and another with 18 hearths.[65]

Fashionable residents increasingly settled in Fore Street during the 18th century, many of them attracted by the regular coach services. John T. Smith remarked in 1789 on the inhabitants 'within their King William iron gates and red brick, crested piers', who excluded the villa-building tradesmen from their neighbourhood.[66] At the same time crowds of visitors attended the famous Edmonton fair.[67] The story of John Gilpin, written by William Cowper in 1782, shows Edmonton's popularity as a place of relaxation for Londoners.[68]

Large houses of the early 18th century in Fore Street included Eagle House, built in 1713 on the west side just north of Pymme's brook, and Elm House, with a mansard roof, on the east; the first was demolished in 1713, the second in 1952.[69] Edmonton House stood opposite Elm House by 1801.[70] There were two mid-18th-century houses, nos. 258 and 260, on the eastern side of Fore Street north of Elm House[71] and a large old house opposite,[72] which may have been Strawberry House.[73] Angel Place or Row, four pairs of adjoining two-storeyed houses with attics, was built in the 18th century on the west side of Fore Street between the Angel inn and Pymme's brook.[74]

[45] See p. 167.
[46] Hatfield C.F.E.P. (Deeds) 10/8.
[47] See p. 176.
[48] S.C. 6/Hen. VIII/2102 m. 2.
[49] Hatfield C.P. 291.1, ff. 119 sqq.; C.P.M. Suppl. 27.
[50] M.R.O., Acc. 241/8.
[51] M.R.O., Cal. Mdx. Sess. Bks. 1664–73, 9–10.
[52] John T. Smith, *Remarks on Rural Scenery* (1797), unpag. Cf. engravings of cottages in Church St., Bury St., and Palmers Green.
[53] C 10/201/50.
[54] M.R.O., Acc. 98/83–8.
[55] M.R.O., Acc. 718/1.
[56] M.R.O., MR/TH/5, mm. 1–4d.
[57] Lysons, *Environs* (1795), ii. 269 gives 810. Claims at inclosure based on ct. rolls give 792 but the actual number at the award c. 1804 was 905: M.R.O., Acc. 695/42.
[58] *Census*, 1801, 1851.
[59] M.R.O., MR/TH/5, m. 4–4d.
[60] The 1801 census returns are not broken down into wards. Figures are based upon the inclosure claims and award, identifying Fore St. up to the green, Brettenham Rd., Angel Rd., and Silver St. as Fore St. ward: M.R.O., Acc. 695/62; Robinson, *Edmonton*, App. II.

[61] *Census*, 1811, 1841.
[62] H.O. 107/1703 pp. 1–100.
[63] Held by a London merchant, it was assessed for 13 hearths in 1664: M.R.O., MR/TH/5, m. 4.
[64] Prob. 11/292 (P.C.C. 330 Pell, will of Edw. Rogers). It was assessed for 15 hearths in 1664: M.R.O., MR/TH/5, m. 4.
[65] M.R.O., MR/TH/5, m. 4.
[66] John T. Smith, *Book for a Rainy Day*, ed. W. Whitten, 134–5. [67] See p. 169.
[68] There is no evidence that Cowper himself visited Edmonton.
[69] Fisk, *Edmonton*, 73; O.S. Map 6", Mdx. VII. SE. (1865 edn.); Briggs, *Mdx. Old and New*, 76; Min. of Housing and Local Govt., List of Bldgs. (1952); photographs *penes* Edmonton Publ. Libr.
[70] No. 703 on inclosure map.
[71] Min. of Housing and Local Govt., List of Bldgs. (1952).
[72] Briggs, *Mdx. Old and New*, 79.
[73] i.e. in Duck Lane near the Horse and Groom: H.O. 107/1703 p. 182.
[74] Nos. 183 and 185 Fore St.: Min. of Housing and Local Govt., List of Bldgs. (1952); see below.

South of Elm House was Addison House, nos. 224 and 226 Fore Street.[75] Other houses which had been built in Fore Street before 1851 included on the east side Almond House, which was probably opposite St. James's church, Sycamore House between Angel Road and Claremont Street, and Bridge House by Pymme's brook and, on the west side, Hatford House and Old House near the junction with Church Road and College House just north of the Bell.[76] Many large houses with gardens and orchards, particularly in the Duck Lane portion of the street, survived well into the 19th century.[77]

Silver Street was in many ways an extension of Fore Street. It contained Pymmes, Weir Hall, Russell House, a small early-18th-century building,[78] and, by 1819, Woodlands.[79] Millfield House was built in the late 18th century and occupied in 1796 by the Russian ambassador.[80] Other houses of the same period included Bridport Hall and two large houses opposite Pymmes, which were destroyed during the Second World War.[81] There were also many cottages and shops, including the Parade, built by 1801.[82]

Fore Street was never wholly occupied by the rich. Increasingly, particularly south of Angel Road and Silver Street, the area came to be covered with small, overcrowded tenements and lodging houses. Typhus was prevalent in 1838 at Eaton Place,[83] where 9 tenements were built in 1795 and 15 existed in 1801,[84] and at Orchard Street 30 lodgers were found in one room in 1844.[85] Industry, particularly coach-building, concentrated in the area. Probably the first example of building beyond the ancient street front was on the estate of Snells Park, a three-storeyed house 'of ancient date'[86] with park-land stretching on the west side of Fore Street from the Tottenham border to Church Road, which was sold in 1848 and covered with small houses.[87] Opposite, Claremont Street, where non-conformist chapels were erected in 1818 and 1845, was built up before 1851.[88]

Much of Edmonton thus lost its exclusiveness[89] and as prosperous traders moved in the gentry moved out. By 1800 it was inhabited by 'retired embroidered weavers, their crummy wives and tightly laced daughters',[90] and a working-class character was later widely apparent.[91] While some houses in Fore Street still had occupiers of in-dependent means in 1851, others had been converted into boarding schools.[92] Silver Street, too, declined socially: Weir Hall was demolished in 1818 and Millfield House had by 1851 been taken over by the West London union school.[93]

The spread of building in Church Street ward was at first much slower, although statistics for the ward as a whole probably conceal rapid growth in parts, especially at Edmonton Green. The number of houses rose from 72 in 1664[94] to 191 c. 1801,[95] 210 in 1811, 346 in 1841,[96] and 374 in 1851.[97] Church Street itself contained Wilde's alms-houses (by 1662) and Style's (by 1679), Latymer school (c. 1623) and the girls' charity school (1778), the workhouse (1732), and the watch-house (c. 1714), as well as the Rectory and Vicarage which were rebuilt c. 1600 and c. 1700 respectively. A house in the ward which was assessed for 18 hearths in 1664[98] may have been Hyde House, a large house near the Rectory in 1750.[99] Among several smaller houses[1] were Bay Cottage, later Lamb's Cottage, dating from c. 1700, and no. 2A Church Street, next to the girls' charity school, built in the 18th century.[2] The house where Keats was apprenticed to a surgeon in 1810 was pulled down in 1931[3] but some 37 17th- and 18th-century buildings survived about Edmonton Green until after 1937. Numbers 5–9, 17–17A, 33, and 35 on the north side of the green and nos. 30–4 and 36 on the south side, though much altered in the 18th century, were essentially of the 17th century.[4] By 1806 buildings presented a continuous front on both sides of the green.[5] There were 101 dwellings at Lower Edmonton and 51 in Church Street in 1801. Of these about eight at Lower Edmonton and two in Church Street were comparatively recent.[6]

Marsh Side, at the junction of Bounces and Town roads, and a few scattered farms in the north-east also lay in Church Street ward. Plesingtons (Pleasantine Hall) and Claverings, though rebuilt, survived on their medieval sites and Dephams was rebuilt near its old site c. 1679. Two, possibly three, farms were created during the 17th century. Cuckoo Hall in the north-east and Causeyware Hall near Hertford Road in the north probably existed by 1650;[7] Nightingale Hall, opposite Claverings, may have derived its name from John Nightingale (fl. 1617)[8] and certainly existed by the mid 18th

[75] Briggs, *Mdx. Old and New*, 76.
[76] H.O. 107/1703 pp. 10, 17, 43, 84, 70.
[77] O.S. Map 6", Mdx. VII. SE. (1865 edn.).
[78] Briggs, *Mdx. Old and New*, 76.
[79] Greenwood, *Map of Mdx.* (1819).
[80] Enfield Arch. Soc. *Bull.* lii (Mar. 1974).
[81] Photographs *penes* Edmonton Publ. Libr.
[82] Robinson, *Edmonton*, 306.
[83] S. I. Richardson, *Edmonton Poor Law Union, 1837–54* (Edmonton Hund. Hist. Soc., n.d.), 64.
[84] Sale cat. (1800) *penes* Enfield Libr.
[85] Richardson, op. cit. 64.
[86] Sales parts. of Snell estate (1848) *penes* St. James's ch.
[87] Cf. inclosure map and O.S. Map 6", Mdx. VII. SE. (1865 edn.).
[88] H.O. 107/1703 pp. 1, 10.
[89] For examples of the aristocracy and gentry, see extracts from ch. regs. in Robinson, *Edmonton*, 69 sqq.
[90] Smith, *Bk. for a Rainy Day*, 136.
[91] H.O. 107/1703.
[92] See p. 202.
[93] *Census*, 1841. It was later Strand union training sch. and St. David's hosp.
[94] M.R.O., MR/TH/5, mm. 1–4d.
[95] M.R.O., Acc. 695/62; Robinson, *Edmonton*, App. II.

[96] *Census*, 1811, 1841.
[97] H.O. 107/1703 pp. 179–234. The ward includes Hertford Road and Marsh Side.
[98] M.R.O., MR/TH/5, mm. 1–4d.
[99] Robinson, *Edmonton*, map facing p. 5.
[1] Cf. photograph of weatherboarded thatched cottages in Church St.: Sturges, *Edmonton Past and Present*, i. 15.
[2] Min. of Housing and Local Govt., List of Bldgs. (1952).
[3] Illus. in Burnby, *Hammonds of Edmonton* (Edmonton Hund. Hist. Soc. 1973), unpag.
[4] Hist. Mon. Com. *Mdx.* 19 (publ. 1937). The buildings apparently had been demolished by 1952: ex inf. Mr. M. Saunders.
[5] Engraving *penes* Edmonton Publ. Libr.
[6] Robinson, *Edmonton*, App. II; M.R.O., Acc. 695/62.
[7] When they gave their names to common fields: M.R.O., Acc. 695/15. Cuckoo Hall was named in 1697: M.R.O., Acc. 349/105; the house on Causeyware field was mentioned in 1654: Prob. 11/233 (P.C.C. 9 Alchin, will of Robt. Halsey). Photograph of Cuckoo Hall *penes* Edmonton Publ. Libr.
[8] *Mdx. Sess. Recs.* iv. 258. There was also a Nightingale Hall at Wood Green: see below, p. 319.

century.[9] There were a few cottages and an inn at Marsh Side, as there had been c. 1600, but the total number of buildings, including the farms, was still only 31 in 1801.[10]

In the early 19th century Marsh Side continued to stagnate while building in the rest of Church Street ward outstripped that in any other district, including Fore Street. Housing spread westward along Church Street and in 1849 New Road was built along the east side of the green, which was soon lined with houses, by the G.E.R. to take traffic interrupted by the low level railway.[11] Building also spread eastward along Town Road and northward along Hertford Road. The most striking feature was the Crescent, 25 adjoining houses with lodges, erected between 1826 and 1851 as an unsuccessful speculation by a London solicitor.[12]

Bury Street ward, in the north of the parish away from the turnpike roads, had as many as 169 houses in 1664 but later remained much the most rural area. It had only 187 houses c. 1801, 239 in 1811, 269 in 1841, and 301 in 1851.[13] There was an unusually large number of one-hearth cottages in 1664,[14] many of them probably squatters' homes, later removed from the edge of Enfield Chase. Two large houses were Bush Hill (31 hearths) and a house with 17 hearths which was probably Bury Hall.

Bury Street itself changed little in the 250 years after 1600.[15] Bury farm-house stood on the site of the demesne farm and next to Warren Lodge, so named in 1607.[16] Salisbury House, although not named until much later, was described in 1605 as a two-storeyed mansion house.[17] Brook House stood near the site of Sadlers mill and the Stag and Hounds and a few near-by cottages stood where there had been buildings c. 1600. Bury Hall was built by 1627 and Bury House by 1754.[18] In 1801 there were 52 houses and cottages in Bury Street, of which 7 were new.[19] Montefiore's Place in Little Bury Street, which joined Bury Street and Church Street, contained brick cottages built in 1789.[20]

Winchmore Hill, the main settlement in Bury Street ward, was already one of the biggest hamlets in the parish c. 1600. The King's Head, a stopping place of omnibuses from London, encouraged its growth and there was an active community of early Quakers. In the early 19th century the discovery of a well with Epsom Salts brought Winchmore Hill a reputation as a spa.[21] The village consisted mostly of weatherboarded cottages but a few larger houses were built in the 18th and early 19th centuries. At the green were Rowantree House and Woodside House, mid-18th-century and of painted brick, Roseville, late-18th-century and stuccoed with a fluted Doric porch,[22] and Uplands, a brown brick Georgian house.[23] Devon House in Church Hill also dates from the 18th century.[24] In Vicars Moor Lane were Rose Cottage, with bay windows and a pedimented doorway, where Thomas Hood the poet lived from 1829 to 1832,[25] and Percy Lodge, the home of Sharon Turner (d. 1847), historian and friend of Isaac D'Israeli.[26] Prospect House on the north side of the road was built after 1801 but Moor Park, rebuilt in the 1890s by the brewer Sir Edward Mann,[27] and Roseneath, on the south side, probably both existed before inclosure.[28] Beaumont Lodge, at the junction of Vicars Moor Lane and Wade's Hill, which also probably existed in 1801, was c. 1840 the largest house in the area and the home of John Wade, a merchant tailor.[29] Glenwood House was built on the west side of Wade's Hill in the early 19th century and Belmont in Hoppers Road in the 18th century.[30]

South-east of Winchmore Hill there were about nine buildings at Fords Green, eleven in Highfields Road, and four at Barrowell Green in 1801. A mansion at Fords Green in 1605[31] was possibly the house where George Fox visited the London haberdasher Edward Mann in the 1680s.[32] As Ford Grove, it was the home of the Goulds and Tesh-makers in the 18th century[33] and of the Busks in the 19th.[34] There was an alehouse, possibly the precursor of the Orange Tree, at Highfield in 1611[35] and there was a Highfield House in 1677 and 1703,[36] probably in Highfield Road rather than on the site of the 19th-century Highfield House.[37] The most important house in the area was the Firs west of Firs Lane,[38] the 18th-century residence of the Lake family, which was pulled down in 1810 but replaced by another house of the same name north of Barrowell Green.[39] In the northern part of Firs Lane was Beaulieu, set in grounds adorned with an 18th-century ruin and grotto and in 1801 the residence of John Gray.[40] On the edges of Winchmore Hill, bounded on the north by the western portion of Church Street, was an estate belonging to John Wilde's charity. Apse farm-house probably stood there by 1662 and in 1805 a new house and cottage

[9] Robinson, *Edmonton*, 99; Rocque, *Map of Mdx.* (1754); photograph *penes* Edmonton Publ. Libr.
[10] Robinson, *Edmonton*, App. II; M.R.O., Acc. 695/62.
[11] *Illustrated Lond. News*, 3 Mar. 1849.
[12] M.R.O., Hist. Notes 7.6.72A (A. F. Kelsall): Min. of Housing and Local Govt., List of Bldgs. (1952).
[13] M.R.O., MR/TH/5, mm. 1–4d.; Robinson, *Edmonton*, App. II; M.R.O., Acc. 695/62; *Census*, 1811, 1841; H.O. 107/1703 pp. 235–80.
[14] Twenty-one occupiers were listed separately as cottagers: M.R.O., MR/TH/5, mm. 1–4d.
[15] Cf. Hatfield C.P.M. Suppl. 27 and O.S. Map 1/2,500, Mdx. VII. 11 (1865 edn.).
[16] i.e. Waringe Lodge: Sta. Cha. 8/11/17; Sta. Cha. 8/196/7.
[17] M.R.O., Acc. 695/42, f. 48; Hatfield C.P.M. Suppl. 27.
[18] Rocque, *Map of Mdx.* (1754). Photograph of simple Georgian house *penes* Edmonton Publ. Libr.
[19] M.R.O., Acc. 695/42; Robinson, *Edmonton*, App. II.
[20] Photograph *penes* Edmonton Publ. Libr.
[21] Cresswell, *Winchmore Hill*, 85.
[22] Min. of Town and Country Planning, List of Bldgs. (1949).
[23] H. G. Regnart, *Memories of Winchmore Hill*, 25.

[24] Min. of Town and Country Planning, List of Bldgs. (1949).
[25] Regnart, *Winchmore Hill*, 72, illus. p. 73.
[26] Ibid. 43.
[27] Ibid. 71.
[28] Cf. inclosure map in Robinson, *Edmonton*, and O.S. Map 1/2,500, Mdx. VII. 6 (1867 edn.).
[29] Regnart, *Winchmore Hill*, 8–9; H.O. 107/1703 pp. 249 sqq.
[30] Briggs, *Mdx. Old and New*, 88.
[31] M.R.O., Acc. 695/42, f. 15.   [32] See p. 188.
[33] Robinson, *Edmonton*, 109.
[34] H.O. 107/1703 p. 274.
[35] M.R.O., Cal. Mdx. Sess. Recs. 1610–11, 161.
[36] C 5/260/9; C 5/494/47.
[37] Cf. inclosure map in Robinson, *Edmonton*, and O.S. Map 1/2,500 Mdx. VII. 6 (1867 edn.).
[38] No. 367 on inclosure map. Cf. O.S. Map 6″, Mdx. VII. SW. (1865 edn.).
[39] Robinson, *Edmonton*, 72–3; Sturges, *Edmonton Past and Present*, ii. 102. See illus. in Burnby, *Hammonds of Edmonton*.
[40] Robinson, *Edmonton*, 272; Cresswell, *Winchmore Hill*, 59.

occupied the site of the old farm, perhaps Rowan-tree House.[41]

Bush Hill, also part of Bury Street ward, had 11 houses in 1801, including Quakers Row[42] and the mansions of John Blackburn and William Mellish, which were established in the early 17th and early 18th centuries respectively.[43]

South Street ward, which included Palmers Green and Bowes, was second only to Fore Street in its rate of growth. From 94 houses in 1664,[44] it increased to 'about 180' c. 1795,[45] 265 in 1801, 340 in 1811, 424 in 1841,[46] and 441 in 1851.[47] In 1664 the largest house in the ward was Broomfield, assessed for 14 hearths; three others had 12 hearths each.[48]

Southgate was settled late because it was so densely wooded and because wells could not be sunk in the clay soil, although the New River made piped water available to the richer landowners. Attracted by the scenery the wealthy began to settle, stimulating trade and clearing the woods for farm- and park-land. In 1746 Southgate was described as one of the pleasantest villages in England[49] and Leigh Hunt, who was born there in 1784, wrote that 'Middlesex in general is a scene of trees and meadows, of "greenery" and nestling cottages, and Southgate is a prime specimen of Middlesex'.[50] In the early 19th century, when the gentry were moving out of Edmonton, attention was often drawn to Southgate's 'superior residences'.[51]

Early buildings included Russells in South Street by 1654,[52] Minchenden, assessed for 35 hearths in 1672,[53] and the Cherry Tree inn at Southgate Green in 1695.[54] The transformation of Southgate, however, took place in the 18th century. Among the mansions Minchenden was rebuilt in 1738; Cullands Grove was built by the mid 18th century, Grove-lands in 1798, and Southgate House c. 1800. At Southgate Green Arnoside and Essex House (nos. 3–4) date from the early 18th century,[55] (nos. 23–32 from 1777,[56] and Norbury House and Sandford House (nos. 38–9) from the late 18th century.[57] Three houses were built on the site of a former mansion in High Street between 1769 and 1778 and two others added near by before 1798.[58] Eagle Hall, on the west side of High Street, existed by c. 1783 when Leigh Hunt's father moved there.[59] Among late-18th- and early-19th-century brick and

weatherboarded buildings in High Street were Croft Cottage, Holcombe House, Avington House, and Brackley House, a three-storeyed stuccoed house with a pedimented Doric doorcase. In Blagden's Lane was the Wilderness, a late-18th-century house of yellow brick with a Doric porch.[60] Cannon House in Cannon Hill dates from the early 19th century. Bone Grove, which, like Cullands Grove, was demolished by J. D. Taylor c. 1840, stood near Grovelands and was described as ancient in 1834.[61] Waterfall Road contained Ivy Cottage, probably 18th-century like Beaver Hall, which in the early 19th century housed the Schneiders, steel manufacturers, and Joseph Thornton, a wealthy railway contractor.[62] By c. 1801 there were about 91 houses in High Street, Cannon Hill, Southgate Green, and Waterfall Road.

The Bourne consisted of a hamlet of cottages c. 1801. At Clappers Green[63] 6 cottages had been pulled down in the 1790s and only four were left c. 1801.[64]

The former Enfield Chase portion of Southgate experienced the fastest growth in the late 18th and early 19th centuries. About 1600 there were two buildings on the edge of the Chase, one of which made way for Hope House, a long two-storeyed building used as a dower-house by the Walkers and Taylors.[65] There were houses at Chase Side in the late 17th century[66] but little settlement took place until after the Chase had been divided and then only along the roads at its edges — the modern Chase Side and Winchmore Hill Road. By c. 1804 there were about 24 buildings at Chase Side and 43 in Winchmore Hill Road, of which about half were new. In Winchmore Hill Road building was on the northern side of the road, mostly near Winch-more Hill village.[67] By 1819, when Eastpole (called Chase Farm) and Westpole (unnamed) farms existed in Bramley Road and Oak Lodge off Chase Road, building was spreading on all sides of Southgate circus.[68] College House stood on the north side of Chase Side by 1851.[69] The district later known as New Southgate remained uninhabited except for Betstile Lodge, which had appeared by 1851.[70]

Palmers Green grew from a few isolated houses c. 1600 to a village of about 54 buildings, including two inns, c. 1801.[71] There were two farms, Hazel-wood and Huxley,[72] and houses on the site

[41] Robinson, Edmonton, 160, 270. O.S. Map 6", Mdx. VII. SE. (1865 edn.).

[42] For position, see M.R.O., Acc. 1076/17a/c.

[43] Robinson, Edmonton, App. II; M.R.O., Acc. 695/62.

[44] M.R.O., MR/TH/5, mm. 1–4d.

[45] Lysons, Environs, ii. 269.

[46] Census, 1801, 1811, 1841.

[47] H.O. 107/1703 pp. 100–78.

[48] M.R.O., MR/TH/5, mm. 1–4d.

[49] S. Simpson, Agreeable Historian, ii. 615.

[50] From his autobiography, quoted in Sturges, Edmonton Heritage, 146–7.

[51] Brewer, Beauties of Eng. and Wales, x(5), 709; Ambulator (12th edn., 1820), 291.

[52] Prob. 11/233 (P.C.C. 11 Alchin, will of Edw. Sanderson).

[53] M.R.O., MR/TH/22.

[54] C 7/644/29. Parts of the bldg. are probably earlier.

[55] Min. of Town and Country Planning, List of Bldgs. (1949).

[56] M.R.O., Hist. Notes 7.6.72B (A. F. Kelsall).

[57] Min. of Town and Country Planning, List of Bldgs. (1949).

[58] M.R.O., Acc. 718/1.

[59] W. Round, Southgate and Winchmore Hill, 32, 34; sales parts. (1885) penes Broomfield Mus.

[60] Min. of Town and Country Planning, List of Bldgs. (1949).

[61] H. W. Newby, Old Southgate, 13; sales parts. (1834) penes Broomfield Mus.

[62] Robinson, Edmonton, 258 (no. 247), 308 (no. 405); Round, Southgate and Winchmore Hill, 34.

[63] Rocque, Map of Mdx. (1754).

[64] Robinson, Edmonton, App. II; M.R.O., Acc. 695/62.

[65] Robinson, Edmonton, 322 (no. 37); Regnart, Winchmore Hill, 67.

[66] C 8/344/142; Prob. 11/338 (P.C.C. 54 Eure, will of John Wynne). Chase Side here probably refers to Winchmore Hill Road. See Mr. Cornish's house marked there on map of the Chase of 1658: M.P.C. 50A.

[67] Robinson, Edmonton, App. II; M.R.O., Acc. 695/62. The hos. in Winchmore Hill Road came after the inclosure map (1801) but before the award (1804).

[68] Greenwood, Map of Mdx. (1819).

[69] H.O. 107/1703 pp. 100 sqq.

[70] Ibid. pp. 154 sqq.

[71] Robinson, Edmonton, App. II; M.R.O., Acc. 695/62.

[72] Robinson, Edmonton, 242 (no. 363), 280 (no. 381); O.S. Map 6", Mdx. VII. SW. (1865 edn.).

of Eaton Villa,[73] Hazelwood House[74] and Hill House.[75]

Bowes, a hamlet around the manor-house and Cock inn, changed little from *c.* 1600 until the mid 19th century. There were houses near Deadman's Hill by 1623[76] and Truro House was built at the junction of Green Lanes and Oakthorpe Road in the 1820s. Another small hamlet at Tile Kilns and Chequers Green grew from 11 buildings *c.* 1801[77] to 28 in 1851, when it consisted of a farm and farmworkers' cottages.[78]

There were 600 communicants in the parish in 1547[79] but numbers may have declined later because of the plague, which claimed 85 out of a total of 145 buried in 1603 and 53 out of 157 buried in 1625.[80] In 1642 537 adult males took the protestation oath[81] and in 1676 there were 483 conformists, 2 papists, and 15 other nonconformists.[82] The population, estimated *c.* 1716 as 'about 600',[83] had risen to 5,093 by 1801 and grew steadily during the early 19th century to reach 9,708 in 1851.[84]

GROWTH AFTER 1851. Inclosure of the common fields in 1804 greatly altered the appearance of the countryside, particularly in the eastern half of the parish, but had little effect upon the pattern of settlement, except in the Chase portion of Southgate. The spread of housing in the late 19th century was caused chiefly by the railway. After a station was opened at Colney Hatch in 1850 to serve the county lunatic asylum, in Friern Barnet, a settlement grew up at New Southgate in the 1850s and 1860s.[85] Building took place at Edmonton Green after the opening of a station there in 1849[86] but not in Angel Road, where a station had existed from 1840. In 1872, however, when the line through Silver Street and Lower Edmonton was opened, the G.E.R., in accordance with the Great Eastern Railway (Metropolitan Station and Railways) Act[87] of 1864, introduced cheap workmen's tickets and when Liverpool Street station was built in 1874, the displaced population moved out to places like Edmonton. Consequently the areas bordering the railway grew rapidly.[88] Between 1861 and 1871 the number of houses in Edmonton rose from 2,079 to 2,539; in the next decade it increased to 3,887. The introduction of trams along Fore Street and Hertford Road in 1881–2 was an additional stimulus and the number of new houses doubled each decade, reaching 6,232 in 1891 and 10,613 in 1901.[89]

Most of the new housing was in the former Fore Street and Church Street wards. Around Lower Edmonton houses were being built in Hertford Road in 1878,[90] westward along Bury Street in 1881 and 1886,[91] and on the Millbrook estate to the south-west in 1882.[92] Chiswick and Kingston roads near by, the property of the British Land Co., were being built up in 1898.[93] On the eastern side of Hertford Road houses were spreading towards the marshes along Town Road in the late 1870s[94] and St. Mary's Road in 1882.[95] The United Counties Land Building and Investment Society was laying out the Orchard estate between New Road and the railway in 1899.[96] There was further extension west and north from Church Street, where Hyde House estate was built up in the 1880s.[97] By 1897 new streets branched off the main ancient roads, Hertford Road, Church Street, the eastern end of Bury Street, Town Road, and Bounces Road.

It was in Fore Street ward, round Upper Edmonton, that growth was most striking during the later 19th century. The area south of Silver Street had already been built up by 1851 and there were few changes except where the Bell inn was rebuilt in 1878 and Gilpin Grove was built on its gardens.[98] North of Silver Street and westward and eastward along Silver Street and Angel Road large-scale building, mostly of terraced houses, took place in the 1880s and 1890s. In 1889 Fore Street ward was divided into three, Fore Street itself with 715 houses, Silver Street with 702, and Angel Road with 880.[99] By 1893 there were 876, 984, and 999 houses respectively.[1] The growth in Angel Road, hitherto uninhabited because of its liability to flooding, became possible after the road was made up and the stream confined by concrete in 1883.[2] Workers moved there because Angel Road station provided convenient transport and the gasworks and Whitley's offered local employment. New roads began to appear on both sides of Silver Street; Ashwell Grove off Bull Lane existed by 1889[3] but the two union workhouses to the south and the purchase by the council in 1899 of Pymmes Park to the north prevented further building. At the western end of Silver Street 57 a. of the Huxley estate were sold in 1887. Nineteen acres were sold between 1888 and 1894, and another 23 a. in 1898–1900 to Frederick G. Lacey, a local builder, on condition that no building selling intoxicating liquors was erected there.[4] North of Angel Road houses spread from Fore Street eastward towards the railway line and along Fore Street itself there

[73] Wm. Eaton's house: Robinson, *Edmonton*, 270 (no. 337); Edmonton Publ. Libr., D. 23. For the modern Eaton Villa, see below.
[74] Robinson, *Edmonton*, 244 (no. 352); O.S. Map 6", Mdx. VII. SW. (1865 edn.).
[75] Robinson, *Edmonton*, 288 (no. 523); O.S. Map 6", Mdx. VII. SW. (1865 edn.). Hill House was large and probably early-19th-century: M.R.O., Acc. 815/8.
[76] C 2/Jas. I/F 8/14.
[77] Robinson, *Edmonton*, App. II; M.R.O., Acc. 695/62.
[78] H.O. 107/1703 pp. 175–8.
[79] E 301/34 mm. 31d.–32.
[80] Lysons, *Environs*, ii. 269.
[81] H.L., Mdx. Protestation Rets.
[82] Wm. Salt Libr., Stafford, Salt MS. 33, p. 40.
[83] Bodl. MS. Rawl. B. 389b, f. 15.
[84] *Census*, 1801–51.
[85] H.O. 107/1703 p. 131; O.S. Map 1/2,500, Mdx. VII. 13 (1867 edn.).
[86] *Illustrated Lond. News*, 3 Mar. 1849.

[87] 27 & 28 Vic. c. 313 (Local Act).
[88] Barker and Robbins, *Hist. Lond. Transport*, i. 216–17; Allen, *Gt. Eastern Rly.* 63.
[89] *Census*, 1861–1901. The number of hos. is not recorded after 1901.
[90] Rose Villas, datestone.
[91] Alfred and Matlock villas, datestones.
[92] M.R.O., Acc. 704/8.
[93] Ibid. /13.
[94] *Building News*, xxxix. 31.
[95] M.R.O., Acc. 1076 (Bldg. lease, 1882).
[96] M.R.O., Acc. 704/13.
[97] Datestones (1881, 1885); M.R.O., Acc. 894/11–15.
[98] Fisk, *Edmonton*, 109.
[99] M.R.O., *Reps. of Local Inqs.* (1889–97), 119–34, *Edmonton*, division into wards (1889).
[1] Ibid. (1889–94), unpag., Edmonton, division into wards (1894).
[2] Sturges, *Edmonton Past and Present*, i. 65.
[3] M.R.O., Acc. 290/12.
[4] M.R.O., Acc. 815/6/6, /10, /13, /37.

was infilling and rebuilding.[5] The Golden Fleece, for example, was rebuilt in 1892 and a parade of shops near by was erected in 1898.[6] The centre of civic activity then shifted from Church Street to Fore Street, where several public buildings were erected, the town hall in 1884, the public library in 1897, and the public baths in 1899.[7]

Social decline continued, as the surviving large 18th-century houses lost their spacious gardens and were surrounded by building. Edmonton was considered a suburban village as early as 1876[8] and in 1884 its transformation, with that of Tottenham, was thus described by the general manager of the G.E.R., who well appreciated the effect of the workmen's tickets: 'each good house was one after another pulled down and the district given up entirely . . . to the working man'.[9] Speculators quickly erected small houses, close together and with shoddy materials. In 1880 some 'jerry builders' were prosecuted by the council and forced to pull down their constructions.[10]

At Bowes, Palmers Green, and Winchmore Hill the advent of the railway in 1871 did not immediately lead to building, mainly because big landowners resisted the sort of change which they had seen farther east. Building, therefore, usually followed the sale of an estate after a death. The church of St. Michael-at-Bowes (1874) and a few large houses, including Avondale College, had been built in Palmerston Road by the 1880s. In 1889 and 1890 Bowes Manor was put up for sale and by 1897 there was building on either side of the railway line, although Bowes Manor and its grounds were still untouched.[11] In 1879 the Eaton Park estate at Palmers Green, which included Eaton Villa and Highfield, a large red-brick house built after 1865, was offered in plots. Apart from a few houses, however, including one erected in Stonard Road in 1881,[12] building had not taken place by 1897. Hazelwood House and the Skinners' alms-houses (1895) were the only other buildings erected at Palmers Green before 1897.[13] Although Winchmore Hill long retained its wooded 'idyllic' character,[14] it contained 400–500 houses by 1882.[15] There was some building near the station and along Hoppers Road, Compton Road, Middle Lane (Station Road) and Wade's Hill. Large new houses included Stone Hall in Church Hill, built c. 1872,[16] and Broadfields in Wade's Hill. There were also several nurseries, mostly east of Winchmore Hill.[17] Apart from the portion next to Hertford Road, and a few houses built near the Stag and Hounds in 1899,[18] Bury Street remained unchanged throughout the later

19th century. At Bush Hill the two most important estates passed to builders, Bush Hill Park to the Bush Hill Park Co. in 1872 and Bush Hill after the death of Horace Harry, the owner, between 1890 and 1908.[19]

The rural character of Old Southgate, far from the railway and dominated by a few landowners, persisted throughout the later 19th century. It was the contrast with the rapidly changing eastern part of the parish that led to the separation of Southgate from Edmonton in 1881. Social changes nonetheless took place. Large crowds attended the cricket matches of the Walker brothers[20] and by 1876 it was said that Southgate had once 'boasted its patrician residents, but its aristocracy now consists of opulent citizens, with an occasional nabob'.[21] Brewers were particularly associated with Southgate and Winchmore Hill, where the Walkers, Taylors, Paulins, Booths, and Sir Edward Mann lived during the 19th century.[22] Minchenden was demolished in 1853 and Beaver Hall c. 1870[23] and Mayfield and Laverock Cottage were built, probably between 1851 and 1865.[24] Apart from the erection of the village hall in 1882, however, there was virtually no change in Southgate High Street.

Meanwhile the countryside around Old Southgate gave way to suburbs, although inns and tea-rooms continued until 1914 to cater for walkers and cyclists from London.[25] To the north c. 1853 the Lambeth and Provincial Street Borough, a development society, planned a 241-acre estate stretching from Chase Side to Chase Road and Bramley Road. The plan included shops, 3 taverns, and 347 plots. The first house was erected in Avenue Road but the area was still too remote and building slowed down[26] until the construction of a reservoir allowed water mains to be laid and stimulated progress from the 1870s.[27] Cottages were built in Bramley Road in the 1860s,[28] and in Chase, Farm, Ivy, Chelmsford, and Nursery roads during the 1870s and 1880s.[29] Farther east Eversley Park in Green Dragon Lane was erected in 1865[30] and a hospital was built on a 36-acre site next to World's End Road in 1886.[31] To the south growth continued during the 1880s and 1890s at New Southgate until by 1897 almost all available land in the triangle formed by Bowes Road, Palmers Road, and the Wood Green border was built up.[32] In 1905 New Southgate ward (175 a.) contained 698 houses;[33] most were for the middle-class, although a resident in 1912 complained of the smell from the near-by gas-works and the poverty of children in High Road.[34]

The district along the railway through Bowes Park,

[5] O.S. Map 6″, Mdx. VII. SE. (1897 edn.).
[6] Datestones. [7] Fisk, *Edmonton*, 133, 134, 193.
[8] Thorne, *Environs*, i. 164.
[9] Barker and Robbins, *Hist. Lond. Transport*, i. 217.
[10] *Building News*, xxxix, 31, 114; Fisk, *Edmonton*, 19.
[11] Sales parts. (1889 and 1890) *penes* Broomfield Mus.; O.S. Map 6″, Mdx. VII. SW. (1897 edn.).
[12] Edmonton Publ. Libr. D 23; datestone.
[13] O.S. Map 6″, Mdx. VII. SW. (1897 edn.).
[14] Cf. Cresswell, *Winchmore Hill*. Written in 1912 about the village in her girlhood, the book has much of the flavour of Flora Thompson's *Lark Rise to Candleford*.
[15] E. Walford, *Greater Lond.* i. 346.
[16] Regnart, *Winchmore Hill*, 52. The stone came from Blackfriars bridge and Beaver Hall.
[17] O.S. Map 6″, Mdx. VII. SE. (1897 edn.).
[18] M.R.O., Acc. 687/6–7.
[19] *Kelly's Dirs. Mdx.* (1890, 1908); Fisk, *Edmonton*, 184–6.

[20] See p. 175.
[21] Thorne, *Environs*, ii. 560.
[22] T. Mason, *Story of Southgate*, 7; Regnart, *Winchmore Hill*, 71, 76.
[23] Round, *Southgate and Winchmore Hill*, 40.
[24] Cf. H.O. 107/1703 pp. 131 sqq.; O.S. Map 6″, Mdx. VII. SW. (1865 edn.).
[25] Fisk, *Edmonton*, 196; Mason, *Story of Southgate*, 41.
[26] Newby, *Old Southgate*, 47–9. [27] See p. 179.
[28] Datestones on Oak cottages (1866) and Ashwood House (1869).
[29] Datestones, e.g. Brook Terrace (1872), Chase Terrace (1881); Newby, *Old Southgate*, 55.
[30] Regnart, *Winchmore Hill*, 46.
[31] Fisk, *Edmonton*, 182.
[32] O.S. Map 6″, Mdx. VII. SW. (1897 edn.).
[33] M.R.O., *Reps. of Local Inqs.* (1895–1907), Southgate, division into wards (1906).
[34] Jackson, *Semi-Det. Lond.* 43.

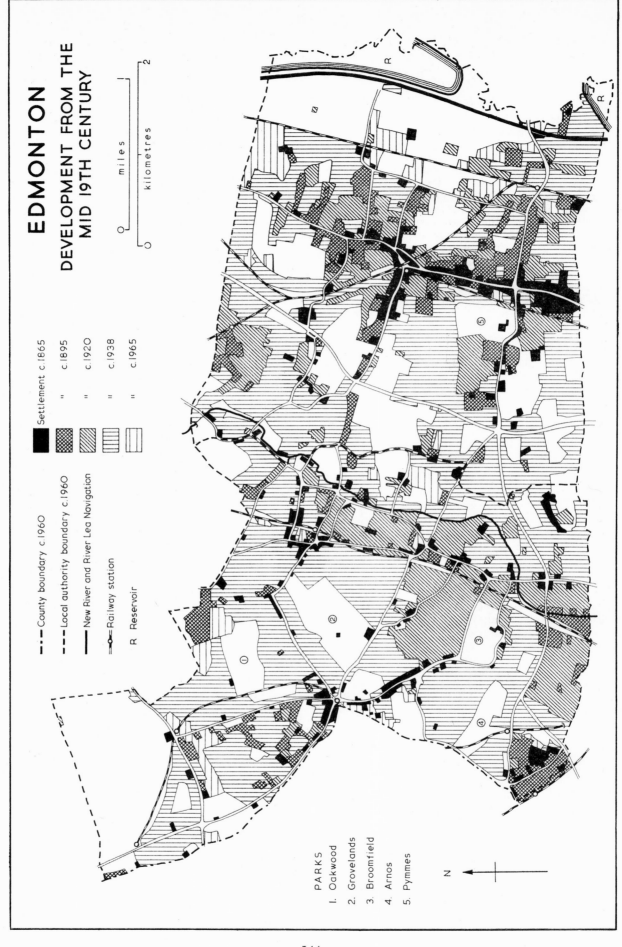

EDMONTON

DEVELOPMENT FROM THE MID 19TH CENTURY

Settlement c.1865
" c.1895
" c.1920
" c.1938
" c.1965

--- County boundary c.1960
--- Local authority boundary c.1960
— New River and River Lea Navigation
— Railway station
R Reservoir

miles
kilometres

PARKS
1. Oakwood
2. Grovelands
3. Broomfield
4. Arnos
5. Pymmes

N

Palmers Green, eastern Southgate, and Winchmore Hill, became a middle-class suburb between 1900 and 1918. Housing was in demand by those able to afford the higher fares on the G.N.R. and on the trams, which were introduced along Green Lanes in 1907,[35] and at the same time land became available as estate owners died. In 1900 a Mr. Hill proposed to build 2,000 houses and shops on 120 a. at Bowes Park.[36] By 1905 Bowes Park ward, which included the area next to the railway, contained 1,578 completed houses on 240 a.[37] In 1900 there were plans for 400–500 houses on the 60-acre Hazelwood Park estate between Green Lanes and Hazelwood Lane and for 30 on the Highfield estate.[38]

The largest estate to be broken up was Grovelands (600 a.). It was offered for sale in lots in 1902 by the executors of Major R. K. Taylor, whose father (d. 1885) had resisted the introduction of the railway and refused to sell land for building.[39] Grovelands itself, consisting of 314 a. between the Bourne, Winchmore Hill Road, Church Hill, and the railway, and the Lodge estate, 27 a. between Green Lanes and Hazelwood Lane, were withdrawn unsold. Home farm, 62 a. north of Winchmore Hill Road, was sold as farm-land and the Waterfall estate (24 a.) lay outside Southgate but the rest of the land was acquired by builders. Old Park estate (130 a.), bounded by Alderman's Hill, Fox Lane, and the railway, was bought by the British Land Co., 2½ a. fronting Hoppers Road were bought by the Town and Country Land Co., and 9 a. fronting Green Lanes were sold for shops.[40] The unsold land was again on the market in 1909.[41] In 1910 Southgate U.D.C. bought 63 a. of Grovelands for a park and the rest was laid out for middle-class housing which, however, had not appeared by 1920.[42] The Lodge estate was being laid out in 1911,[43] although this, too, had apparently not been built up by 1920.[44]

Palmers Green ward contained 765 completed houses by 1905.[45] In contrast to Edmonton with its terraces of stock brick, heavy bay windows, and slate roofs, Palmers Green became a middle-class Edwardian suburb of lighter, red-brick houses with gables and timbering, derived from Norman Shaw and C. F. A. Voysey,[46] and parades of shops along Green Lanes in the 'Metropolitan Electric' style of c. 1880.[47] The Old Park estate had been built up by 1908 when the adjoining Clappers Green farm, 46 a. between Fox Lane and Bourne Hill, was sold for building.[48] Broomfield Park

estate, 200–300 a. south-west of Palmers Green, became available in 1901. Southgate U.D.C. bought the house with 54 a. in 1903 and the rest, to the south and east, was covered by housing.[49]

Building spread northward from Palmers Green to Winchmore Hill, where 70 shops and 200–300 houses were planned in 1900[50] and where there were 1,052 completed houses by 1906.[51] Their styles, with half-timbering, gables, towers, and finials, were intended to avoid the monotony of other neighbourhoods and to preserve a rural air,[52] although contemporaries considered that the charm of the district was being destroyed.[53]

At Bush Hill Park building continued and spread southward toward Bury Street. Some large detached houses, similar to those of Hampstead Garden Suburb, were built during the late 19th and early 20th centuries along Chase Side.[54] Southgate U.D.C. erected 82 houses before 1914, in Chase and Chelmsford roads in the former Chase area and in Tottenhall Road.[55]

Edmonton's working-class character became increasingly apparent c. 1900. After battles with the 'jerry builders' the U.D.C. decided in 1899 to provide council housing but negotiations to buy Brookfield estate were unsuccessful and no houses were built until after the First World War.[56] The introduction of the electric tram (1905) and the motor-bus (1913) to Fore Street attracted still more people. More large houses were demolished[57] and building spread eastward from Fore Street and Hertford Road, the Fairfield estate being built during that period.[58] Industry, attracted by the large population, grew steadily in Angel Road and spread northward along the canal.[59]

The remaining landed estates were sold for building in the period between the World Wars, when all parts of the area became accessible after the construction of Great Cambridge Road (1923–4), the North Circular Road (1931), and the Piccadilly line (1932–3). Huxley estate, which originally stretched from Silver Street to Palmers Green, had been reduced from 221 a. in 1888 to 179 a. in 1920. Hill House at Palmers Green was sold in 1922[60] and a large area south of Hedge Lane, near the North Circular and Great Cambridge roads, was bought by Frank J. Lawes, a builder from Crouch Hill, in 1929.[61] The rest of the Huxley estate, including the farm and fields north of Hedge Lane and east of Great Cambridge Road, was sold in lots in 1930–32[62] and built up shortly afterwards.

[35] See above. The cheapest fares were on the G.E.R. and the next cheapest on the trams: Jackson, *Semi-Det. Lond.* 41.
[36] M.R.O., *Reps. of Local Inqs.* (1895–1907), Southgate, increase in U.D.C. members (1900).
[37] Ibid., Southgate, division into wards (1906).
[38] Ibid., Southgate, increase in U.D.C. members (1900).
[39] Regnart, *Winchmore Hill*, 29.
[40] Sales parts. *penes* Broomfield Mus.; Mason, *Story of Southgate*, 31–4.
[41] *Recorder*, Nov. 1908, ii(1) *penes* Broomfield Mus.
[42] *The Times*, 29 June, 5 Oct. 1910, 6 Nov. 1911; O.S. Map 6″, Mdx. VII. SW. (1920 edn.); Jackson, *Semi-Det. Lond.* 37.
[43] M.R.O., Acc. 815/7/2.
[44] O.S. Map 6″, Mdx. VII. SW. (1920 edn.).
[45] M.R.O., *Reps. of Local Inqs.* (1895–1907), Southgate, division into wards, 1906.
[46] Jackson, *Semi-Det. Lond.* 44–5, pl. 5.
[47] A style spreading from London along the tram route: Robbins, *Mdx.* 82; e.g. parade at Queen's Ave., 1911.

[48] Sales parts. (1908) *penes* Broomfield Mus.
[49] M.R.O., *Reps. of Local Inqs.* (1895–1907), Southgate, increase in U.D.C. members, 1900; *Opening of Broomfield Park, 1928* [programme *penes* Broomfield Mus.].
[50] M.R.O., *Reps. of Local Inqs.* (1895–1907), Southgate, increase in U.D.C. members, 1900.
[51] Ibid., Southgate, division into wards, 1906.
[52] *Builder*, lxxviii. 321; *Architect*, lxx. 328. Cf., e.g., hos. in Compton Rd.
[53] *Home Cnties. Mag.* viii. 303.
[54] Robbins, *Mdx.* 182.
[55] Southgate, *Official Guide* [1963].
[56] Fisk, *Edmonton*, 166; ex inf. Enfield L.B. planning officer.
[57] e.g. Woodlands (1903): photograph *penes* Edmonton Publ. Libr.; Fleecefield (1911): M.R.O., Acc. 704/16; Eagle House (1913): Fisk, *Edmonton*, 73.
[58] Fisk, *Edmonton*, 48.
[59] O.S. Map 6″, Mdx. VII. SE. (1920 edn.).
[60] M.R.O., Acc. 815/6/9.   [61] M.R.O., Acc. 525/5.
[62] M.R.O., Acc. 815/27.

Much new housing was on land made available by the Church Commissioners, who granted building leases on 30 a. at Bowes Park in 1913. By 1923 there were 72 houses east of Green Lanes and south of Tottenhall Road and another 100 were planned. Nine acres east of Wolves Lane were leased in 1928 and 19 a. of the Tottenham rectory estate east of Tottenhall Road in 1933, with an agreement to build 30 houses a year until there should be 270.[63] In 1920 the Church Commissioners sold their largest estate, 170 a. of the former Hyde field south of Church Street, between Firs Lane and Victoria Road, to Edmonton U.D.C.[64] and by 1926 it was laid out as a garden suburb.[65] The Commissioners also sold 10 a. west of Green Lanes at Palmers Green to the Church Army Housing Co. in 1926 and 34 a. on the Enfield border, west of Hertford Road, to Edmonton Estates in 1932–4.[66]

Growth continued unevenly. Fords Grove estate, 75 a. east of Green Lanes, was offered for sale in 1920 for 'moderate sized residencies and cottages', which were said to be in great demand.[67] It sold but Oak Lodge estate, 239 a. east of Chase Road, failed to find a buyer because of its remoteness.[68] The Southgate House estate, 64 a. between Southgate High Street and the Bourne, became available after the death of the last Walker brother in 1922. The house and grounds were bought by the council for a school and the rest of the land by Edmondson's, a Muswell Hill firm which had already built up much of Winchmore Hill.[69] Houses in Southgate U.D. increased from 1,694 in 1881 to 5,051 in 1905 and 14,750 in 1931,[70] but building was mostly on the borders of the district, at New Southgate, Bowes Park, Palmers Green, and Winchmore Hill. The opening of the Piccadilly line transformed Southgate itself, where by 1934 750 houses round the station were planned for completion. Although growth was slower near the more northerly stations of Oakwood and Cockfosters, by 1937 continuous building stretched southward from the railway line to New Southgate.[71] Meanwhile in Edmonton U.D. a new industrial area arose at Bridport Road south of Silver Street and housing spread to the farm-land, nurseries, and brick-fields of the north and north-east.[72]

As farm- and park-land disappeared, speculators turned to the large houses. In Edmonton Bury Hall was demolished in 1920, Bury House c. 1933, Bury Lodge in 1936, and Weir Hall in 1934.[73] Mayfield in Southgate High Street was demolished,[74] Roseneath (11 a.) and Broadfields (14 a.) in Winchmore Hill were sold in 1931,[75] and Beaulieu

(1¼ a.) in Firs Lane was sold in 1936.[76] Southgate U.D.C., faced with the spread of housing, bought part of each large estate that was offered for sale to provide public parks. In 1927 it purchased Oakwood Park (50 a.) from Sugden's executors[77] and in 1928 Arnos Park (44 a.) from Lord Inverforth.[78] In 1937, following the sale in 1933 of 100 a. of Chase land near the new railway[79] and in 1935 of Westpole farm (75 a.),[80] the council made an agreement with Sir Philip Sassoon to preserve the area south of the Enfield border as an open space.[81]

Most housing estates were private, the work of firms like Comfy Housing Estates which in 1936 erected houses in Cavendish Road to M. M. Lyons's design.[82] The first council estate in Edmonton was also the largest: under the Act of 1919 1,760 houses were planned on the Hyde estate, where contractors had built 232 by 1925 when the council changed to direct labour. By 1940 1,124 houses had been built on the Hyde estate, 208 on the Brookfield and 147 on the Montagu estates, both lying east of Fore Street and south of the railway line, 164 on Woolmer estate south of Angel Road, 153 on Galliard estate in the north between the railway and Galliard Road, and 114 at Wilbury Way south of Silver Street and east of Great Cambridge Road. There were also 86 on either side of Great Cambridge Road and 25 on the Houndsfield estate west of Hertford Road.[83] Meanwhile Southgate council had built 639 houses, mostly on two estates: in the Chase between Trent Gardens, Green Road, and Reservoir Road, and east of Green Lanes near Highfield Road, where land had been purchased before the war but where houses, of concrete made from clinker, were built only in the early 1920s.[84]

During the Second World War 433 houses were totally destroyed and 971 badly damaged in Edmonton borough alone.[85] The demand for housing was greater than ever in 1945 when, except in the north-east, there was little land left. Most of Nightingale farm had been laid out for housing in 1938 and the farm-house was replaced by factories after the war.[86] In 1949 Edmonton B.C. decided to locate industry at Claverings farm, where factories were built in the 1950s and early 1960s, and in the north it acquired Cuckoo Hall farm, where houses were built during the 1950s.[87] In Southgate building was resumed on the Chase and still proceeded in the early 1970s.[88] Most post-war construction has been either small-scale, on a nursery or large garden, or has taken the form of re-building. Examples of the former are the council housing in the old grounds of Halliwick at Bush Hill,

[63] Church Com. files 85682, 89842 pt. 1, 91286 pt. 1, 93058 pt. 1.
[64] Ibid. file 88068.
[65] [H. J. Griffin], *Hist. Articles on Old Tottenham and Edmonton*, 105.
[66] Church Com. S4 surveys, pp. 368–70; map 15495a.
[67] Sales parts. (1920) *penes* Broomfield Mus.
[68] Ibid.
[69] M.R.O., Acc. 848/1–2; see above.
[70] M.R.O., *Reps. of Local Inqs.* (1895–1907), Southgate, division into wards, 1906; *Southgate, Fifty Yrs. of Progress* [pamphlet, 1931] *penes* Broomfield Mus.
[71] Jackson, *Semi-Det. Lond.* 238.
[72] O.S. Map 6″, Mdx. VII. SE., NE. (1938 edn.).
[73] Sturges, *Edmonton Past and Present*, ii. 64; photographs *penes* Edmonton Publ. Libr.
[74] O.S. Maps 6″, Mdx. VII. SW. (1920 and 1938 edns.).
[75] Sales parts. (1931) *penes* Broomfield Mus.
[76] Sales parts. (1936) *penes* Broomfield Mus.

[77] Mason, *Story of Southgate*, 54–7; O.S. Map 6″, Mdx. VII. NW. (1938 edn.).
[78] Mason, *Story of Southgate*, 63; *The Times*, 18 July 1928.
[79] *The Times*, 27 Jan. 1933.
[80] Jackson, *Semi-Det. Lond.* 238–9.
[81] *The Times*, 29 Dec. 1937.
[82] Plaque on bldg.
[83] There were also 194 houses at Hoe Lane in Enfield: Edmonton, *Official Guide* [1939]; Boro. of Edmonton, *Official Guide* [1963]; ex inf. Enfield L.B. planning officer.
[84] Boro. of Southgate, *Official Guide* [1963]; *The Times*, 26 Apr. 1920.
[85] Boro. of Edmonton, *Official Guide* [1963].
[86] O.S. Maps 6″, Mdx. VII. SE. (1938 and 1965 edns.).
[87] Ex inf. Enfield L.B. planning officer.
[88] e.g. Priory Close off Green Road and Eversley Park Rd.

the houses at Hydefield Close and Myrtle Road on former nurseries, the building in Blagden Lane, where the Wilderness had been, and Skinners Court, the flats at Palmers Green which replaced the Skinners' alms-houses. Edmonton B.C. rehoused substantially, replacing 19th-century terraces by tower-block flats, particularly in the 'jerry-built' areas of the 1870s and 1880s.

Between 1945 and 1963 Edmonton completed 3,911 houses and flats, of which 1,248 were at Potters Bar and Cheshunt (Herts.).[89] In the 1950s council housing, mostly blocks of flats,[90] was erected on Cuckoo Hall farm, on nursery ground east of Fox Lane, and on older sites south of Lower Edmonton and east of Fore Street, between Fore Street and the Enfield Town railway, at Snells Park, Jeremy's Green, and Barrowfield Close. The Galliard Road estate was continued and there were smaller sites in Church Street, Great Cambridge Road, and off Little Bury Street. In 1953 18 a. were acquired at Montagu South for industry. Since 1960 council housing has been built in the grounds of Halliwick, Barbot Street at Victoria Road, St. Mary's Road, Goodwin Road north of Bounces Road, Brettenham Road East, Angel Road North and South, College Gardens and Snells Park west of Upper Fore Street, Bolton Road at Silver Street, two sites in Church Street, and Walmer House in Bury Street.

In 1965 Enfield L.B. approved a comprehensive rebuilding scheme for 61 a. at Edmonton Green. The first stage was completed in 1970 when a shopping precinct, swimming pool, entertainment centre, and blocks containing 376 flats were opened on the east side of the old green. The second stage, comprising shops north of the new area, was nearing completion in 1974.[91]

Southgate erected about 500 houses and flats between 1945 and 1963. Shortly after the war about 250, mostly semi-detached, houses were built south of Barrowell Green and a few more at Barber Close, east of Wade's Hill. Later council housing consisted chiefly of three-storyed blocks in numerous small areas, usually surrounded by private dwellings. In the 1950s most building was in the Chase although there was also a little north of the North Circular and at New Southgate. Work continued during the 1960s and early 1970s on several relatively small sites, mainly in the Chase but also in Old Southgate, Winchmore Hill, and Tottenhall Road. The most important municipal project was the redevelopment of almost the whole of New Southgate, begun in the 1950s and still in progress in 1974.[92] Private firms then were replacing some large houses, as in Alderman's Hill and parts of Victorian Bowes Park, by blocks of flats.

After the building of Great Cambridge Road in 1923–4 Fore Street ceased to be the main north-south route through Edmonton but in 1974 it was still the main shopping centre and focus of social life. Examples of many styles, from classical 18th-century houses to extravagantly Gothic late-19th-

century public buildings and chequer-board tower blocks of the 1960s, lined the street, usually behind shop fronts of the 1930s. On the east side of Fore Street no. 238 is an early-18th-century three-storeyed building with Doric pilasters, entablature, and architrave, and nos. 258 and 260 are three-storeyed houses with Ionic pilasters and entablatures dating from the 18th century.[93] Angel Place, four pairs of adjoining brown brick houses with open pedimented Roman Doric doorways, is also 18th-century but in bad repair.[94] There are a few mid-Victorian houses north of the junction with Angel Road and one house of c. 1830 almost opposite St. James's church, which, with its mid-Victorian vicarage, stands surrounded by buildings of the 1960s and 1970s. To the north Fore Street enters the area where Edmonton Green was being transformed in 1974. The concrete masses of the new shopping precinct then looked across roadworks on the green to buildings awaiting demolition on the west, relieved only by the high tower and striking architecture of the National Coal Board heating station erected c. 1971 next to Salmon's brook. The air of decay persisted in Hertford Road, leading northward from the green, where villas and terraces of the late 19th and early 20th centuries were interspersed with modern flats and garages. In 1974 its one striking group of buildings, badly preserved, was the Crescent, segmental and of three storeys and basement, built of brown brick and stucco with Corinthian pilasters and a central pediment.[95]

The main east-west route through Edmonton remains Angel Road and Silver Street, transformed into the North Circular Road. Heavy traffic travels eastward along the wide Angel Road towards the factories and canals, and much of it turns north along Montagu Road with its industrial estates. To the east lies the railway and beyond it are the sewage works, allotments, waste-land, and reservoirs that mark the former Edmonton marsh, in 1974 being transformed into the Lee Valley regional park. Almost all the rest of the area between the railway and Fore Street and much to the west of Fore Street consists of small shopping parades and varied working-class housing, from the terraced and semi-detached houses of the 1920s and 1930s in the north to the mixture of mid-20th-century blocks of flats and 19th-century terraces in the south, the latter often brightly painted by the West Indian immigrants who form much of the population.

West of Fore Street the three ancient roads, Silver, Church, and Bury streets, have retained their identity amidst the building. Silver Street, predominantly 19th century, contains Pymmes Park, although not the house, and Millfield House, in 1974 awaiting conversion into an arts centre.[96] The latter, a late-18th-century mansion of brown brick, has a slate roof, Doric columns, and frieze. Inside it has an oval hall and original doorways and chimney pieces.[97] In Church Street styles are mixed. On the south side near Fore Street the girls' charity school of 1784 adjoins the former schoolmistress's house, an

[89] Boro. of Edmonton, *Official Guide* [1963]. There are photographs of the Cheshunt estate (c. 1950) *penes* Edmonton Publ. Libr.

[90] e.g. two 23-storey tower blocks opened in 1968: *The Times*, 11 Apr. 1968.

[91] Ex inf. Enfield L.B. planning offr. See pl. facing p. 177.

[92] Boro. of Southgate, *Official Guide* [1963]; ex inf. Enfield L.B. planning officer.

[93] Min. of Housing and Local Govt., List of Bldgs. (1952).

[94] Odd nos. 183–5 Fore St.: Min. of Housing and Local Govt., List of Bldgs. (1952).

[95] Min. of Housing and Local Govt., List of Bldgs. (1952).

[96] Enfield Arch. Soc. *Bull.* lii (Mar. 1974).

[97] Min. of Housing and Local Govt., List of Bldgs. (1952); photographs *penes* Edmonton Publ. Libr.

18th-century red-brick cottage with a pantile roof. To the west on the opposite side of the road is Lamb's Cottage, a two-storeyed building of *c.* 1700 with a mansard roof and 18th- and 19th-century door and fittings.[98] The medieval church stands away from the road in its churchyard, surrounded on three sides by mostly modern houses. Apart from the alms-houses (1903) and the Lamb institute (1907)[99] Church Street consists mainly of Victorian detached and semi-detached houses, although there are council houses at the western end. Only one of the early houses of Bury Street survives. At the western end of the street amidst houses of the 1920s and 1930s stands Salisbury House, the oldest secular building in Edmonton, a gabled structure of *c.* 1600 with a brick ground floor and timber-framed upper storeys. There are modern additions on the western side. The interior contains 17th-century doors, panelling, and other fittings.[1]

Bush Hill, to the north-west beyond Great Cambridge Road, is a district of terraced and semi-detached houses of the late 19th and early 20th centuries, relieved only by a wooded golf course on the Enfield border. Of the two large houses near by only Halliwick, formerly Bush Hill House, survives.[2]

Winchmore Hill in parts retains the air of a large village or superior suburb. The King's Head, rebuilt in 1896[3] and with an art nouveau interior, faces the green, where five roads meet. The northern side of the green is lined mostly with antique shops in a parade dated 1895. Despite much rebuilding Rowantree House and Woodside House on the south-west, of painted brick with slate roofs, attic windows, and eaves cornices, survive from the mid 18th century with 19th-century extensions.[4] Church Hill, which runs north-east from the green, contains the late-18th-century Quaker meeting-house, the early Victorian Gothic St. Paul's church, the 18th-century Devon House, of brown brick with dormers,[5] and a few 19th-century weather-boarded cottages and large semi-detached houses, besides later dwellings. Some early-19th-century weatherboarded and brick cottages and Glenwood House, of the same date, are in Wade's Hill, which also runs north from the green. Early-19th-century houses with Doric porches stand in Vicars Moor Lane,[6] leading east from Wade's Hill.

Green Lanes and most of Palmers Green are characterized by late-19th- and early-20th-century shops and housing, stretching eastward from Winchmore Hill along Station and Compton roads. Other old buildings survive south of Winchmore Hill. Eaton Villa, a square detached house at the Palmers Green end of Bourne Hill, is mid-19th-century and Truro House, named after the Lord Chancellor Thomas Wilde, created Lord Truro of Bowes in 1850, is a buff-coloured brick house of the 1820s[7] with a timber-framed addition of 1917 and a late-18th-century doorcase with Corinthian capitals. Edwardian Palmers Green is surrounded by housing estates of the 1920s and early 1930s.

Green Lanes leads south to Bowes Park, where a

Greek Cypriot community gives variety to the otherwise uniform terraced houses and shops of *c.* 1900. A few earlier large Victorian houses survive in Palmerston Road. Both Bowes Park and its westerly neighbour, New Southgate, once full of 19th-century villas but later a working-class semi-industrial district, have much decayed housing which in 1974 was being replaced by flats.

Southgate, on higher ground farther north, is separated from New Southgate and Bowes Park by the wooded Arnos and Broomfield parks. Although predominantly a middle-class suburb of the 1930s, its centre is the much older green and High Street, formerly South Street. The street leads to Southgate Circus, created in 1933 around Southgate station which is on or near the site of the south gate of the Chase. In High Street older buildings are interspersed among houses and flats built before and after the Second World War. Croft Cottage, Holcombe House, and Avington (nos. 111–5) were built in the late 18th century as a unit, with a central three-storeyed house flanked by two-storeyed houses, each with reeded flat-topped doorcases.[8] Numbers 107–109 date from the early 19th century. On the eastern side amid playing fields is Minchenden school, which incorporates Southgate House, the home of John Lawrence (d. 1879), 1st Lord Lawrence of the Punjab, a late-18th-century yellow-brick building, much altered. Minchenden Lodge in Blagden's Lane is a large square mid-19th-century house with a later conservatory and there are terraced 19th-century brick and weatherboarded cottages on the east side of High Street. Ash Lodge (no. 40), a small early-19th-century grey-brick house with a round-headed arched doorway, and Norbury and Sandford Houses (nos. 38–9), a late-18th-century brown-brick pair with pedimented door and 19th-century bay windows, form a group on the east where High Street runs into the green. A little to the south the Cherry Tree inn, 17th-century but much altered, is set in a terrace designed by Michael Searles (d. 1813).[9] On the north side of the green next to some modern flats are Old House (no. 2), late-18th-century, and Arnoside and Essex House, an early-18th-century brown-brick pair with a parapet, wrought iron gates, and stone urns. On the south of the green there are large detached houses and flats of the 1930s and to the west the road leads to Christ Church and the cricket fields. Cannon Hill, which runs south to Broomfield Park, is lined mainly by detached houses of *c.* 1910 and *c.* 1930 but also contains Northmet House, formerly Arnos Grove, Cannon House, an early-19th-century brick villa, and the Hermitage, a mid-19th-century *cottage orné*.

Several roads radiate from Southgate Circus. The Bourne, running south-eastward to Palmers Green, has a mixture of houses built between 1910 and 1939 and forms the southern boundary of Grovelands Park, wooded grounds which contain a lake and surround the house, later a hospital, designed by John Nash. Running north-eastward from South-

[98] Min. of Housing and Local Govt., List of Bldgs. (1952).
[99] Datestones.
[1] Hist. Mon. Com. *Mdx.* 19 and plates 55–6.
[2] See p. 161.
[3] Regnart, *Winchmore Hill*, 25.
[4] See Mason, *Southgate Scrapbook*, 91–4.

[5] Min. of Town and Country Planning, List of Bldgs. (1949).
[6] Nos. 68–76 probably date from the 1830s; nos. 78–106 are probably earlier.
[7] Ex inf. Mr. M. Saunders.
[8] Min. of Town and Country Planning, List of Bldgs. (1949).
[9] R.I.B.A. drawings coll.

gate Circus is Winchmore Hill Road, where among mostly modern houses, flats, and shops are Rose Cottage and Linden Lodge (nos. 229–31), 19th-century brick cottages near the junction with Church Hill. Chase Road and Chase Side, leading north and north-westward respectively, are characteristic of the southern part of the Chase, with houses of many dates and styles from the mid 19th century. Farm-land survives north of Bramley Road, forming part of the Trent Park estate in Enfield rather than the built-up district of Southgate.

The population of Edmonton rose from 9,708 in 1851 to 10,930 in 1861 but the steepest rise, reflecting the introduction of workmen's tickets on the railway, was from 13,860 in 1871 to 23,463 in 1881. The population thereafter increased at an ever faster rate, to 61,892 in 1901, 98,409 in 1911, and 133,215 in 1931. It reached 177,647 in 1951 and then declined to 164,315 in 1961.[10]

MANORS. The manor of *EDMONTON* was held by Ansgar the staller in 1066 and Geoffrey de Mandeville in 1086[11] and descended with Enfield until the death of William de Mandeville in 1189.[12] William's heir was his aunt Beatrice, sister of Geoffrey de Mandeville (d. 1144) and widow of William de Say (d. ?1144). Beatrice's eldest son William had died in 1177 and most of the Mandeville property, including Enfield, passed to his eldest daughter Beatrice and her husband Geoffrey fitz Piers. Beatrice's second son Geoffrey de Say claimed the Mandeville inheritance[13] and presumably obtained Edmonton, since he and his heirs held the manor in fee throughout the 13th century.[14] It was not until 1284, however, that the family agreed to the *de facto* division of the Mandeville lands, leaving the descendants of Beatrice and Geoffrey fitz Piers with Enfield and those of Geoffrey de Say with Edmonton, which was held of the Crown as a knight's fee.[15]

The manor descended in a direct line from Geoffrey de Say (d. 1214) to Geoffrey (d. 1230), William (d. 1272), William (d. 1295), Geoffrey (d. 1322), Geoffrey (d. 1359), and William (d. 1375).[16] Probably originally as part of a mortgage made *c.* 1361, William de Say granted the manor to Adam Francis (Fraunceys), mercer of London,[17] who had already built up an estate in Edmonton.[18] In 1369 Francis granted it to feoffees,[19] who in 1371 settled it

on him for life with remainder to his son Adam in fee.[20] Adam died in 1375 and was succeeded by his son,[21] later Sir Adam (d. 1417),[22] who left all his lands to be divided between his widow and his two daughters. Margaret, Sir Adam's widow, who married Edward Aske, died in 1445;[23] Elizabeth, Sir Adam's younger daughter, wife of Sir Thomas Charlton, died *c.* 1450[24] and Agnes, the elder daughter and wife of Sir William Porter, died in 1461. In 1461, therefore, the whole manor was reunited in the hands of Sir Thomas Charlton (d. 1465), Elizabeth's son.[25] Sir Thomas was succeeded by his son Sir Richard,[26] who supported Richard III and was killed at Bosworth in 1485, whereupon his estates were forfeit to the Crown.[27]

The manor and other estates in Edmonton were granted in tail male to Sir Thomas Bourchier in 1485[28] and the reversion was granted to Sir John Pecche and John Sharpe, the king's servants, in 1510.[29] By 1521 both Bourchier and Sharpe were dead and the king granted the reversion after the death of Sir John Pecche, who had no male heirs, to Henry Courtenay, earl of Devon and later marquess of Exeter.[30] Courtenay was in possession by 1523,[31] although the grant in fee was not made until 1530.[32] In 1532 he sold the manor and other property to William Sulyard and others[33] who were licensed in the same year to alienate a moiety of it.[34] The donation did not take effect and by 1535 the manor was in the hands of the Crown, administered by Thomas Cromwell as the king's bailiff.[35]

The manor remained with the Crown thereafter, except during the Interregnum when it was bought on behalf of John Reyner of St. Martin's-in-the-Fields.[36] For most of the 17th century it formed part of the queen's jointure; from 1629 until 1650[37] and from 1660 until her death in 1669 it belonged to Henrietta Maria and from 1672 until her death in 1705 it was assigned to Catherine of Braganza.[38]

Although the demesne lands, called Sayesbury or Bury manor or farm, had been leased out since the 15th century[39] and had been detached in 1571,[40] the manor with its perquisites was not leased until 1665.[41] It was then let on short leases, constantly extended and assigned by the lessees to others until in 1716 William Gould, merchant of London, purchased it in fee farm.[42] The connexion with the Crown, however, by then consisted of a nominal rent[43] and the lessee was thereafter regarded as lord of the manor.[44] William Gould (d. 1733) was

[10] *Census*, 1851–1961. The 1971 census returns do not distinguish between Edmonton and Southgate and the rest of Enfield L.B.

[11] *V.C.H. Mdx.* i. 126.

[12] See p. 224.

[13] *Complete Peerage* s.v. de Say; *Cur. Reg. R.* vii. 110–11.

[14] *Bk. of Fees*, i. 474; *Rot. Litt. Claus.* (Rec. Com.), i. 207; *Cal. Inq. p.m.* i, pp. 178, 281–2.

[15] D.L. 36/1/159; C 132/42/6.

[16] *Complete Peerage* s.v. de Say.

[17] Hatfield C.P. 291.1, nos. 1099, 1101, 1102; *Cal. Close, 1360–4, 290.*

[18] e.g. Dephams, see p. 150.

[19] *Cal. Pat. 1367–70*, 312–13; C 143/367/17.

[20] *Cal. Close, 1369–74*, 309.

[21] Although the inquisition post mortem stated that his daughter Maud was his heir, seisin was delivered to Adam's son, Adam. *Cal. of Wills in Court of Husting, London, 1258–1688*, ii, ed. R. R. Sharpe, p. 171; *Cal. Inq. p.m.* xiv, pp. 124–5; *Cal. Close, 1374–7, 133.*

[22] Prob. 11/2B (P.C.C. 38 Marche); *Cal. Inq. p.m.* (Rec. Com.), iv. 32.

[23] C 139/118/21; D. O. Pam, *The Fight for Common Rights*

in *Edmonton and Enfield, 1400–1600* (Edmonton Hund. Hist. Soc., Occas. Paper, 1974), 3.

[24] *Cal. Inq. p.m.* (Rec. Com.), iv. 249.

[25] C 140/179/39; E 41/297.

[26] C 140/17/31.

[27] *Rot. Parl.* vi. 276.

[28] *Cal. Pat. 1485–94*, 63.

[29] *L. & P. Hen. VIII*, i(1), p. 289.

[30] Ibid. iii(2), p. 750.

[31] E 326/6076.

[32] *L. & P. Hen. VIII*, iv(3), p. 2858.

[33] Ibid. v, p. 485; C.P. 25(2)/27/181/44.

[34] *L. & P. Hen. VIII*, v, p. 668.

[35] Ibid. ix, pp. 156–7; x, p. 513; S.C. 6/Hen. VIII/2102.

[36] E 320/L 36.

[37] *Cal. S.P.Dom. 1629–31*, 37; C 66/2511 m. 9.

[38] C 66/3172 m. 18; *Cal. Treas. Bks.* 1700–1, p. 416.

[39] D.L. 3/21/E 1ee.

[40] See p. 157.

[41] M.R.O., Acc. 695/42, f. 84v.

[42] Ibid. 84v., 87–87v., 90, 93–5.

[43] E 367/5270.

[44] Bodl. MS. Rawl. B 389b, f. 15.

succeeded by his son James (d. 1767). The manor passed to James's nephew Thomas Teshmaker (d. 1771), whose widow Sarah held it[45] until 1800, when it was conveyed in fee to Sir William Curtis, Bt. Curtis, who died in 1829, devised the manor in tail male to his son Sir William (d. 1847), who was succeeded by his son Sir William (d. 1870), whose successor was his grandson, Sir William Michael Curtis.[46] In 1916 it passed to a cousin, Sir Edgar Francis Egerton Curtis, and in 1943 to Sir Edgar's second cousin once removed, Sir Peter Curtis of Romsey and afterwards of Bishop's Waltham (Hants).[47]

The manor of *DEPHAMS* or Deephams took its name from a London citizen, Roger de Depham. Between 1314 and 1355 Depham acquired property in north-east Edmonton from 17 people, mostly by purchase or exchange,[48] but the largest estate came to him in 1347 as chief creditor after John le Venour had forfeited his estates for debt.[49] John le Venour had inherited most of his 196-acre estate from his mother, Sibyl, daughter and heir of Robert Blund (d. 1290).[50] The Blund inheritance had originated in a grant of ¼ knight's fee by Geoffrey de Mandeville to Robert Blund of London c. 1154–66.[51] In 1263 the Blund fee had been described as the 'manor of Edmonton'[52] and in 1281 the estate, although small in demesne, had included pleas of court, customary works, and other manorial appurtenances.[53] In 1353 the Blund ¼ fee, with ⅕ knight's fee held in 1242 by Geoffrey de Querendon,[54] was held by Roger de Depham, Robert de Plesington, and William Causton, all of whom had some interest in John le Venour's lands.[55]

In 1358 Roger de Depham conveyed all his property in Edmonton, Tottenham, and Enfield to feoffees who conveyed it to Adam Francis (d. 1375) in 1359.[56] Francis died seised of some of Depham's property[57] but he may have sold the manor, as its descent did not follow that of the capital manor and Francis's other lands. It was held by John Innocent, under-treasurer of England (d. c. 1401),[58] and may be identifiable with the house, land, and rent which Innocent bought in 1392 from John Hende, who had bought it in 1389 from Elisha Bocking, skinner of London, and his wife Isabel.[59] John Innocent gave Dephams to Isabel Rampton, who married Nicholas Brenchley of London. Brenchley sold it to the bishop of Winchester[60] who conveyed it to Jane de Bohun, countess of Hereford (d. 1419),

from whom it passed to the Crown, which exchanged it with Henry Somer for the manor of Graunt Courts (Felsted, Essex).[61] Somer, Chancellor of the Exchequer,[62] who had acquired other property in Edmonton, was confirmed in Dephams in 1422.[63] According to a later account by his bailiff Somer granted the estate to his daughter Anne, who married, probably as a child, Thomas Charlton the younger, heir to Edmonton manor, and when Somer died there was a violent dispute between his widow Catherine and Charlton's father, Thomas Charlton the elder. Anne was said then to have married Sir Richard Vere and Catherine to have given Dephams to Ralph de Cromwell, Lord Cromwell, Treasurer 1433–43, c. 1438.[64] In reality Somer did not die until 1450, when he still received issues from Edmonton, his daughter's name was Agnes, and his heir was his grandson James Vere.[65] Cromwell, however, as a fellow treasury official, may have had some interest in Dephams during Somer's lifetime. On Cromwell's death in 1455 Dephams passed to Sir Thomas Charlton the younger, then owner of a moiety of the capital manor,[66] and thereafter the manors descended together until 1531, when Henry Courtenay, marquess of Exeter, sold Dephams to Richard Hawkes.[67] In 1539 Robert Hawkes sold it to William Stanford of London[68] who conveyed it in the same year to John Grimston,[69] lessee of Dephams since 1535.[70] Grimston's grandson Gabriel Grimston was much in debt in the 1570s and in 1582 he mortgaged two-thirds of Dephams to William Curle and the reversion to a third, which was held by Gabriel's mother in dower, to Thomas Wroth.[71] The property was the subject of a dispute between Curle, who claimed to have purchased it, and Grimston's other creditors.[72] By 1588, however, all interest was surrendered to William Cecil, Lord Burghley, when he bought Curle's title,[73] having in 1585 acquired that of William Dowgill, a London haberdasher, who had acquired the interests of the other creditors.[74] Burghley's lands passed to Robert Cecil, earl of Salisbury, and in 1628 Robert's son William, earl of Salisbury, sold Dephams to Thomas Style, who had been the lessee since 1608.[75] Thomas Style was succeeded by his sons Maurice (d. 1659) and Thomas (d. 1679).[76] By will dated 1717 George Style of Peckham (Surr.) devised Dephams to his sister Sarah, who married into the Ravenscroft family, which retained the estate for most of the

[45] E 367/5270; Robinson, *Edmonton*, 45, 109.
[46] M.R.O., Acc. 727/128; M.A.F. 20/69/1011; M.A.F. 9/168/22118.
[47] Burke, *Peerage* (1959), 601–4; ex inf. Sir Peter Curtis Bt. (1973).
[48] W.A.M. 4, 9, 13, 15–16, 21, 23, 53, 63, 66, 71, 76, 85, 88, 91, 114–5, 120, 134, 143, 145, 153–4, 334; C.P. 25(1)/149/46/179; /150/61/215; Hatfield C.P. 291.1, no. 963; Hatfield C.F.E.P. (Deeds) 76/11.
[49] W.A.M. 3, 103, 303, 305; C.P. 25(1)/150/59/159; /64/287; Hatfield C.P. 291.1, nos. 948, 952–7.
[50] C.P. 25(1)/149/45/165; *Cal. Inq. p.m.* ii, p. 506; *Cal. Fine R.* 1272–1307, 437.
[51] Hatfield C.P. 291.1, nos. 6–8.   [52] C 132/30/6.
[53] *Cal. Inq. p.m.* ii, p. 509.
[54] *Bk. of Fees*, ii. 898.   [55] *Feudal Aids*, iii. 376.
[56] W.A.M. 52, 65; C.P. 25(1)/150/67/365.
[57] *Cal. Inq. p.m.* xiv, pp. 124–5.
[58] Prob. 11/2A (P.C.C. 1 Marche); Robinson, *Edmonton*, 100–1.
[59] C.P. 25(1)/151/79/104, /124.
[60] In possession in 1412: *Feudal Aids*, vi. 486–7.

[61] Pam, *Fight for Common Rights*, 12. For confirmation of Somer's connexion with Graunt Courts, see S.C. 2/172/6.
[62] *Feudal Aids*, iii. 382–3; *D.N.B.*
[63] *Cal. Pat.* 1416–22, 435.
[64] Pam, *Fight for Common Rights*, 12.
[65] For Somer, see *V.C.H. Cambs.* v. 163, 203; Lambeth Pal., Reg. Stafford, f. 183v.
[66] Pam, *Fight for Common Rights*, 12. Charlton had acquired other property of Somer's by 1462: *V.C.H. Cambs.* v. 163.
[67] *L. & P. Hen. VIII*, v, p. 237; C.P. 25(2)/27/181/32.
[68] C.P. 25(2)/27/183/43.
[69] Ibid. /41; *L. & P. Hen. VIII*, xiv(2), p. 158.
[70] Hatfield C.F.E.P. (Deeds) 178/6.
[71] Ibid. 89/9, 104/9.
[72] C 2/Eliz. I/G 8/51; Req. 2/79/17.
[73] Hatfield C.F.E.P. (Deeds) 104/5.   [74] Ibid. /8; 52/2.
[75] Hatfield C.P. 291.1, ff. 119 sqq.; C.F.E.P. (Deeds) 102/31.
[76] Prob. 11/292 (P.C.C. 346 Pell, will of Thos. Style); C 93/53/16. See p. 204.

18th century.[77] Thomas Hylord Ravenscroft alienated it to Thomas Cock of Tottenham and Thomas's son John was the owner in 1819.[78] John Cock sold Dephams in 1822 to Andrew John Nash and George Augustus Nash,[79] whose family still held land in the area in 1893,[80] although Dephams had become a sewage farm in the 1870s.[81]

A manor-house, probably dating from the Blunds' tenure in the 12th and 13th centuries,[82] was situated in the centre of Depham's estate, east of Jeremy's Green Lane and approximately on a line with Plesingtons. By 1585, however, the house had disappeared, leaving only a large barn and the moated site.[83] Sir Edmund Berry Godfrey (d. 1678), the murdered J.P. of the Popish Plot, was said to have lived at Dephams[84] and a 'new brick-built messuage' was referred to in 1679.[85] The 19th-century Dephams Farm, east of the earlier manor-house,[86] was pulled down between 1897 and 1920.[87]

The manor or manors of *BOWES* and *DERN-FORD*,[88] with the tenements of Polehouse and Fords sometimes called the manor of *POLE-HOUSE*,[89] derived from families of the 13th and 14th centuries. Land in south-west Edmonton and in Tottenham which had belonged to John Bowes (*de arcubus*), a mid-13th-century London citizen,[90] and land in north-west Tottenham which belonged to the late 13th- and 14th-century Dernford family of Tottenham,[91] had by 1370 become part of the estates of the Wykwane family of London and Edmonton.[92] In 1370 Thomas Wykwane sold a house, some 380 a. and rent in Edmonton, Tottenham, and Enfield to John Bernes, mercer of London,[93] and Henry Wykwane conveyed land in south-west Edmonton to Thomas Langham, vicar of Edmonton, from whom Bernes acquired them in 1372.[94] Polehouse took its name from John atte Pole (d. 1361), a London rope-maker, who conveyed his estate, which included land formerly held by the Ford family and $\frac{1}{12}$ knight's fee which had belonged in 1235–6 to William son of Geoffrey,[95] to Gilbert Nusom and William Gosselyn.[96] In 1362 the last two sold the estate, consisting of 5

houses, nearly 400 a. and rent in Edmonton and six other Middlesex parishes, to John Bernes (d. *c.* 1373).[97] Bernes's lands passed to his cousin Thomas King of Tottenham, who in 1383 conveyed them to John of Northampton, the former mayor of London.[98]

In 1395 Northampton conveyed the estate, for the first time called the manor of Bowes and Dernford, and the tenements of Polehouse and Fords, to feoffees, citizens of London,[99] who in 1402 conveyed it to other feoffees to the use of Henry Somer[1] and a subsidiary interest was quitclaimed at the same time by heirs of John Innocent.[2] The feoffees conveyed the manor in 1406 to Sir John Daubridgecourt and others[3] who sold it in 1410 to Thomas Langley, bishop of Durham, and others,[4] to whom Henry Somer quitclaimed in 1411.[5] The property was purchased with John of Gaunt's money and conveyed in 1411 to the king,[6] who granted it to the chapter of St. Paul's in 1412.[7] Bowes and Polehouse manor was a sub-manor of the capital manor[8] until 1572, when the Crown released it from suit of court, an annual rent, and the provision of a hunting dog.[9]

Except during the Interregnum, when Polehouse was sold to the lessee,[10] the chapter remained in possession until its property passed to the Ecclesiastical Commissioners in 1872.[11] Copyholds were progressively enfranchised between 1853 and 1936, after which the lordship of Bowes and Polehouse manor lapsed.[12] During the 15th century the manor was leased in its entirety to individual canons of St. Paul's[13] but the demesne was sub-let as two farms, centred on Bowes and Polehouse respectively, by 1438.[14] The two demesne farms were leased separately from the 16th century[15] and in 1804 the Bowes and Dernford estate was divided into six lots.[16] Part of Bowes, including the site of the manor-house, was sold to the lessee, Thomas Sidney *c.* 1866[17] and on his death in 1889 it was put up for auction as building land.[18] It was not sold, however, and was leased to the guardians of St. Mary's, Islington. In 1899 it was sold for building.[19] The

[77] M.L.R. 1747/3/37–8; 1754/2/198.
[78] Robinson, *Edmonton*, 56.
[79] M.R.O., Acc. 695/26, pp. 285–6, 293.
[80] *Kelly's Dir. Tottenham* (1893–4).
[81] See p. 180.
[82] e.g. messuage and gardens listed among John Blund's property in 1281: *Cal. Inq. p.m.* ii, p. 509.
[83] Hatfield C.P. 143.104, f. 141; C.P.M. Suppl. 27.
[84] Robinson, *Edmonton*, 56.
[85] C 93/53/16.
[86] Inclosure map in Robinson, *Edmonton*; O.S. Map 6", Mdx. VII. SE. (1865 edn.). A watercolour *penes* Edmonton Publ. Libr. shows a small, two-storeyed tiled building with attics and gables possibly dating from the 17th century.
[87] O.S. Maps 6", Mdx. VII. SE. (1897 and 1920 edns.).
[88] Although documents often refer to 'manors' in the plural there is no evidence for more than one manor.
[89] After St. Paul's acquired the property Polehouse was corrupted into 'Paul house'.
[90] E 40/1724, /2034, /2278; C.P. 25(1)/147/20/394.
[91] E 40/2209, /7076; E 326/6593, /8811; Guildhall, Church Com. MS. 168917.
[92] Cf. field names: St. Paul's MS., Box A 34, no. 895; B.M. Add. Ch. 40526 (1372) and Robinson, *Edmonton*, 266 (1801).
[93] C.P. 25(1)/151/72/486.
[94] St. Paul's MS., Box A 34, no. 895; B.M. Add. Ch. 40526.
[95] *Bk. of Fees*, i. 474; *Feudal Aids*, iii. 376.
[96] *Cal. of Wills in Ct. of Husting, London*, ii. 47; B.M. Add. Ch. 40515.

[97] C.P. 25(1)/150/68/396; B.M. Add. Ch. 40526; *Cal. Close, 1374–7*, 259.
[98] *Cal. Close, 1381–5*, 389.
[99] St. Paul's MS., Box A 27, no. 174.
[1] Ibid., nos. 175–7; Box A 34, no. 900; Box A 35, nos. 901, 906; *Cal. Close, 1399–1402*, 512.
[2] St. Paul's MSS., Box A 34, nos. 867, 871. According to Henry Somer's bailiff, speaking many years later, John Innocent was owner of Bowes which he gave to Lord Grey but there is no evidence to corroborate his claim: D.L. 3/21 f. 51.
[3] St. Paul's MS., Box A 27, no. 178.
[4] Ibid., no. 180.   [5] C.P. 25(1)/152/85/78.
[6] St. Paul's MS., Box A 27, no. 181; *Cal. Pat. 1408–13*, 372.
[7] *Cal. Pat. 1408–13*, 385.
[8] *Valor Eccl.* (Rec. Com.), i. 360–1.
[9] *Cal. Pat. 1569–72*, 335–6.   [10] C 54/3474 no. 7.
[11] *Lond. Gaz.* 13 Aug. 1872, pp. 3587–9.
[12] M.A.F. 9/169/514, /699, /734, /1906, /9960, /9980, /10148, /10242, /12097, /19266; Church Com., S 4 Survey, p. 5.
[13] St. Paul's MSS., Box A 27, no. 112; Box A 35, nos. 907–10.
[14] D.L. 3/21 f. 51.
[15] C 1/974/88–9; C 54/3474 no. 7; M.R.O., Acc. 695/42, f. 17; Robinson, *Edmonton*, 58–59.
[16] Guildhall, Church Com. MS. 168894.
[17] Ibid., MS. 169045; *The Times*, 22 Sept. 1869.
[18] Sales parts. *penes* Broomfield Mus.
[19] Mason, *Southgate Scrapbook*, 30.

rest of Bowes, except 25 a. which was sold to P. L. Powys Lybbe in 1895 and 40 a., mostly in Tottenham, which was sold to Wood Green U.D.C. in 1927,[20] was let on building leases in 1913 and 1923.[21] In 1958 the Church Commissioners sold their freehold interest in Bowes and the near-by Tottenham rectory estate. The purchasers were mostly tenants of the individual houses although the remaining houses were sold in 1960 to Mountsfield Properties Ltd.[22]

The Polehouse demesne farm was disposed of earlier. At inclosure in 1801 St. Paul's sold 25 a. to Joseph Dorin and 26 a. at Palmers Green to William Eaton.[23] Pauls grove (16 a.) at Winchmore Hill, originally part of the Polehouse estate but long leased separately, was sold in 1881 to J. Donnithorne Taylor.[24] In 1883 the commissioners conveyed 30 a. to Edmonton local board for a cemetery.[25] In 1920 the rest of the Polehouse estate was included in the sale of 170 a. of mostly rectorial land to Edmonton U.D.C. for building.[26]

Bowes manor-house was mentioned as 'the place of Bowes' in 1384[27] and the moated site survived in 1889.[28] The farm-house c. 1580 stood west of Green Lanes, just south of its junction with Tottenhall Road,[29] and was a plain, probably plastered building of two storeys and attics.[30] It was much altered in the mid 19th century by the lessees Thomas Wilde, Lord Truro, and Thomas Sidney, a former mayor of London,[31] but disappeared in the building development of 1900.[32]

Polehouse may be identifiable with Gisors Place, the house originally belonging to the powerful London family of that name, which had passed to John atte Pole by 1332.[33] It stood west of Fore Street, north of its junction with Silver Street,[34] included a hall and five chambers in 1649,[35] and in 1672 was assessed for 14 hearths.[36] By 1860 it was a brick-built and tiled house which had long been divided, half being occupied as a private house and half as Priory school.[37] It was demolished when the Great Eastern Railway line from Bethnal Green was built through the site in 1872.[38]

The manor of Willoughbies can be traced from 1305 when Philip Willoughby, dean of Lincoln,[39] died seised of a house, 189 a. of land and rent in Edmonton held of Geoffrey de Say for rent and suit of court and of Holy Trinity priory, the hospital of St. John of Jerusalem, and Richard le Keu for rent. Philip was succeeded by his brother

Sir William Willoughby, then aged over 80,[40] but the estate, by 1342 described as a manor,[41] was apparently held by the Beaumont family in 1328.[42] On John, Lord Beaumont's death (1396) the manor of *WILLOUGHBIES* passed to his son Henry, a minor.[43]

The manor was enlarged by the acquisition by marriage of an estate originally belonging to the Aguillons. In the early 13th century Sir William Aguillon had land and tenants in Edmonton,[44] as had Sir Robert Aguillon c. 1255.[45] In 1286 Robert had died seised of demesne meadow land and rents, held of William de Say,[46] and his widow Margaret Rivers had held the property as dower until her death in 1292, when it had passed to Robert's daughter Isabel, wife of Hugh Bardolf, Lord Bardolf.[47] Their grandson John, Lord Bardolf, had granted his demesne meadow land to William Causton in 1337[48] but the rest of his property in Edmonton seems to have descended to Thomas, Lord Bardolf (d. 1408), and through Thomas's daughter Joan and her husband William Phelip, Lord Bardolf, to their daughter Elizabeth who married John Beaumont, Viscount Beaumont (d. 1460), between 1425, and 1436.[49]

William, Viscount Beaumont, John's son, was attainted as a Lancastrian in 1461. The Yorkist William Hastings, Lord Hastings (d. 1483), was already drawing the profits of the manor, possibly as mortgagee, and in 1464 he was granted Willoughbies during the lifetime of Catherine, second wife of John, Viscount Beaumont (d. 1460).[50] In 1467 Hastings was granted, without any encumbrances, all Beaumont's estate in Edmonton and Tottenham,[51] and in 1475 he granted the manor to feoffees,[52] who in 1484 granted it to Hastings's widow Catherine.[53]

In 1485 Henry VII restored Willoughbies manor to William, Viscount Beaumont, who leased it in 1486 for life to Catherine Hastings and her son Edward.[54] The king, acting on behalf of Beaumont, who had lost his reason in 1487, confirmed the lease in 1505.[55] Beaumont died in 1507 leaving the children of his sister Joan (d. 1466) and her husband John, Lord Lovell, as his heirs. Since Joan's son Francis, Viscount Lovell, had died attainted in 1487, the Crown claimed Willoughbies after Beaumont's death.[56] In 1509 the king granted the manor as dower to William Beaumont's widow Elizabeth and her second husband John de Vere,

[20] Church Com. S 4 Surveys, pp. 351, 446.
[21] Church Com. files 85682, 89842 pt. 1.
[22] Ibid. files 89842 pts. 7 & 9, 571735.
[23] Guildhall, Church Com. MSS. 169027, 169029.
[24] Church Com. file 61439.
[25] Ibid. 23019.　　[26] Ibid. 88068.
[27] *Cal. Inq. Misc.* iv. 153–4.
[28] Sales parts. (1889) *penes* Broomfield Mus.
[29] Hatfield C.P.M. Suppl. 27.
[30] Broomfield Mus., print in Misc. Etchings file.
[31] Guildhall, Church Com. MS. 168902; *The Times*, 22 Sept. 1869; Sales parts. (1889) *penes* Broomfield Mus.
[32] Mason, *Southgate Scrapbook*, 30; O.S. Maps 6", Mdx. VII. SW. (1897 and 1920 edns.).
[33] W.A.M. 302; Robinson, *Edmonton*, 57.
[34] Hatfield C.P.M. Suppl. 27; Robinson, *Edmonton*, 268 (no. 698 on inclos. map).
[35] C 54/3474 no. 7.　　[36] M.R.O., MR/TH/22.
[37] Guildhall, Church Com. MS. 168957; H.O. 107/1703 pp. 43 sqq. See p. 202.
[38] O.S. Maps 6", Mdx. VII. SE. (1865 and 1897 edns.). See p. 136.

[39] Le Neve, *Fasti, 1300–1541, Lincoln*, 3; E 40/2193.
[40] *Cal. Inq. p.m.* iv, p. 182–3; C 143/59/2.
[41] *Cal. Close*, 1341–3, 389.
[42] [Henry], Lord Beaumont paid rent to Holy Trinity on behalf of his sister [Isabel] Lady de Vescy: E 164/18 ff. 12 sqq.
[43] C 136/91/8; *Cal. Pat.* 1399–1401, 172–3.
[44] E 40/1721.
[45] Ibid. /1705.
[46] *Cal. Inq. p.m.* ii, p. 360.
[47] Ibid. iii, p. 11; *Cal. Close*, 1288–96, 239.
[48] W.A.M. 164.
[49] G.E.C. *Complete Peerage*, s.v. Bardolf and Beaumont.
[50] *Cal. Pat.* 1461–7, 352; C 145/318/30; G.E.C. *Complete Peerage*, s.v. Beaumont.
[51] *Cal. Pat.* 1467–77, 26.
[52] Ibid. 516–17.
[53] B.M. Harl. MS. 3881, f. 22.
[54] *Cal. Close*, 1485–1500, 16–17.
[55] Ibid. 1500–9, 187–8.
[56] *L. & P. Hen. VIII*, iii(1), p. 553; G.E.C. *Complete Peerage* s.v. Beaumont.

earl of Oxford,[57] and in 1521 he granted the reversion in tail male to Sir Wistan Brown, knight of the body.[58] Brown was dead by 1543–4[59] and the manor was held by his son John in 1546, when the king conveyed a reserved rent and the reversion on Willoughbies to Sir Philip Hobby, gentleman of the privy chamber, in an exchange. Hobby granted it for life to Queen Catherine, who died in 1548.[60]

By 1551 the manor of Willoughbies, consisting of a toft, 130 a., and 40s. rent in Edmonton and Tottenham, was in the hands of Jasper Phesaunt, who conveyed it in that year to John Machell.[61] Machell's son, John, conveyed it in 1597 to Peter Collet (d. 1607), merchant tailor of London, whose daughters and coheirs were Hester, wife of Sir Anthony Aucher, and Sarah, wife of Peter Hayman.[62] The Auchers' portion was alienated to Sir Ferdinando Heybourne, from whom it passed to Ferdinando Pulford and his mother Anne, who sold it in 1638 to George Pryor. In 1638 Pryor also bought the Haymans' portion from Sir John Melton, who had purchased it from Sir Peter and Henry Hayman in 1631.[63] On the death of George Pryor in 1675 the whole manor descended to his son Charles, who died without issue in 1700 after conveying the Edmonton portion of Willoughbies to his step-daughter Lucy, wife of William Beteress, dyer of London. Charles's sisters in 1701 vainly contested the title of Lucy's son William Beteress,[64] who in 1708 mortgaged the Edmonton portion, which by this date had become detached from that in Tottenham, to Dr. Arthur Wolley of London.[65] William's sister and heir, Lucy, sold the Edmonton estate in 1717 to William Buckle and William Smith of London,[66] whose son William conveyed it in 1764 to William Snell of London.[67] Snell conveyed it in 1767 to Nathaniel Chauncey,[68] whose heirs were still in possession in 1800. Charles Snell Chauncey was the owner in 1819.[69]

Willoughby Moat, which probably surrounded the medieval manor-house, was in 1801 and c. 1865 in south-east Edmonton near the border with Tottenham, east of Dyson's Road.[70] By 1619, however, the main house had been built just inside Tottenham parish.[71]

The manor of *HOLY TRINITY* priory, Aldgate, in Edmonton[72] derived from the $\frac{1}{5}$ knight's fee held in the 12th century by Hugh Peverel.[73] Between 1235 and 1364 his grandson, also called Hugh Peverel,[74] conveyed the $\frac{1}{5}$ fee,[75] which included the

homage and customary services of tenants, a capital messuage (*managium*), at least 60 a. and rent to the canons in return for a corrody.[76] Between the 12th and 14th centuries, especially during the priorate of Richard de Temple (1222–48), Holy Trinity priory accumulated land and quit-rents in Edmonton from over 60 people.[77] There were some grants in free alms but most of the property was purchased in small amounts. Apart from Hugh Peverel, the most important grantors were the Heyruns and John Fitz John. Ralph Heyrun and his two sons, Ralph and Robert, conveyed property in the early 13th century[78] and John Bucointe, who also held from the Heyrun fee, made further grants in 1203[79] and 1217.[80] Many of the other grants were of land and rent held of the Heyrun fee and by 1242–3 Holy Trinity was being assessed for the $\frac{1}{4}$ knight's fee that had once been Ralph Heyrun's.[81] From John FitzJohn of Edmonton the priory obtained about 70 a. and rent between 1250 and 1265.[82] In 1253 the king granted the canons free warren in their demesne lands in Middlesex.[83]

Holy Trinity had a grange at Clapper's Green but it was leased out by 1303–14[84] and the priory preferred to draw quit-rents rather than farm its estates directly.[85] Most of the estate was granted out for quit-rents[86] and the rest, mostly in northern Edmonton or the woodland in the south and west, was entirely leased out in 1328, when the priory derived some two-thirds of its income in Edmonton from quit-rents.[87] By c. 1380 some of the property had become merged in Adam Francis's estate[88] and when the priory was suppressed in 1532, the quit-rents were cancelled because the property from which they issued was already in the hands of the Crown.[89] Some of the priory's demesne land in Edmonton was granted to St. Paul's in 1544 and was thereafter treated as part of Tottenham rectory.[90] After inclosure in 1801 the Edmonton portion of the estate totalled 67 a. in the south of the parish, east of the Bowes estate. Most was sold in 1930 and 1958–60.[91]

The rest of Holy Trinity's demesne, 150 a. of woodland in the west of the parish, was granted in 1543 to John Tawe and Edward Taylor,[92] who alienated it in 1545 to John Grimston of Edmonton.[93] Grimston granted the woods to his daughter Alice and her husband Nicholas Askew in 1546.[94] Alice's second husband Thomas Trussell sold the woods in 1564 to Geoffrey Walkeden, skinner of London, and

[57] *L. & P. Hen. VIII*, i(1), p. 134.
[58] Ibid. iii(1), p. 553.
[59] E 318/Box 13/576; S.C. 6/Hen. VIII/2105 m. 1.
[60] *L. & P. Hen. VIII*, xxi(1), p. 766; *Magna Britannia* (1724), iii. 33 [printed by E. & R. Nutt].
[61] C.P. 25(2)/61/474/58.
[62] C 142/329/181; Robinson, *Edmonton*, 54.
[63] Robinson, *Edmonton*, 54.
[64] C 78/1140 no. 3; /1194 no. 3. Beteress had doubtless tricked Pryor, who was a spendthrift and drunkard.
[65] C 7/377/99.
[66] M.L.R. 1717/5/41–3.   [67] M.L.R. 1764/5/382–4.
[68] M.L.R. 1774/2/416.
[69] Robinson, *Edmonton*, 54, 254.
[70] Inclosure map (no. 955) in Robinson, *Edmonton*; O.S. Map 6″, Mdx. VII. SE. (1865 edn.).
[71] Robinson, *Tottenham*, map of 1619. See below, p. 333.
[72] Although never called a manor, the estate possessed manorial courts: see p. 176.
[73] *Rot. Cur. Reg.* (Rec. Com.), ii. 243.
[74] i.e. son of Wm. son of Hugh: *Cur. Reg. R.* x. 214; E 40/1727.   [75] *Feudal Aids*, iii. 376.

[76] E 40/1727–9, /2192, /2257, /2292–4, /2638.
[77] Based on an analysis of many deeds, E 40. See also *Cal. Pat. 1317–21*, 145–6.
[78] E 40/1483, /2131, /2191.
[79] C.P. 25(1)/146/3/28.   [80] E 40/12344.
[81] *Bk. of Fees*, ii. 898.
[82] E 40/2147, /2151–3, /2268, /2270, /2276–7; C.P. 25(1)/147/22/434.
[83] *Cal. Chart. R.* i. 427.   [84] E 40/2670, /2671.
[85] *Cartulary of Holy Trinity, Aldgate*, ed. G. A. J. Hodgett (London Rec. Soc. vii), p. xvi.
[86] e.g. E 40/1693–4, /1738, /1798.
[87] E 164/18 ff. 12 sqq.
[88] E 40/1738, /1740, /7362, /11085.
[89] S.C. 6/Ed. VI/299 m. 16.
[90] *L. & P. Hen. VIII*, xix(1), p. 495.
[91] Church Com. S 4 survey, pp. 314, 325, 330, 333, 380–1; ibid. map 15495A.
[92] *L. & P. Hen. VIII*, xviii(2), p. 142; S.C. 6/Hen. VIII/2357 mm. 1d.–2.
[93] *L. & P. Hen. VIII*, xx(1), p. 59.
[94] Ibid. xxi(1), p. 582; Hatfield C.F.E.P. (Deeds) 89/13.

his son Thomas,[95] who sold them in 1574 to William Cecil, Lord Burghley.[96] The Cecils retained the woodland longer than their other lands but the former Holy Trinity estate was split up during the early 17th century. Some was sold to John Clapham in 1614,[97] some to George Huxley of Weir Hall before 1627[98] and some had become part of Sir William Curtis's estate by inclosure.[99]

OTHER ESTATES. When Geoffrey de Mandeville, earl of Essex (d. 1144) founded Walden abbey (Essex) in 1136–43, he endowed it, *inter alia*, with the church of Edmonton and lands there.[1] Shortly afterwards, during the disorders of Stephen's reign, Westminster abbey briefly took possession of Walden's revenues and granted 3 marks from Edmonton church to William de Costentin.[2] The first earl's son, Geoffrey de Mandeville (d. 1166) seized part of the glebe, leaving Walden abbey with 14 a. of his father's endowment.[3] The rectory, in practice mainly consisting of tithes, was worth £33 6s. 8d. during the 13th century.[4] In 1340–1 the 14 a. of glebeland consisted of meadow worth £2 2s.[5] During the Middle Ages and especially in the mid 13th century Walden received small grants in free alms from inhabitants of Edmonton.[6] Rents from these lands totalled £2 4s. 2d. in 1291[7] and £2 0s. 8d. in 1340–1.[8] By 1535 they had become indistinguishable from the glebe and the total value of the rectory was then £20 3s.[9]

In 1538 Walden abbey surrendered all its property, including Edmonton rectory, to the king, who granted it in the same year to Sir Thomas Audley.[10] He exchanged it with the king for other property in 1542[11] and it was granted to the chapter of St. Paul's in 1544.[12] The rectory was sold to William Wakefield, merchant of London, during the Interregnum[13] and in 1650 consisted of a house and cottage, 28 a. mostly scattered in the open fields and common marsh, and tithes, the whole valued at £220 a year.[14]

The estate, which reverted to St. Paul's at the Restoration, was sold at inclosure in 1801 to Joseph Dorin.[15] Under the terms of the inclosure settlement, St. Paul's as rector received 276 a. in lieu of tithes from common-field and marsh-land,[16] as well as corn-rents in lieu of tithes from old inclosures, which then amounted to £434.[17] An allotment of 56 a. was made to Trinity College, Cambridge, as owners of the rectorial tithes due from the Edmonton portion of Enfield Chase.[18] St. Paul's sold 83 a. to Edmonton local board in 1890, another 40 a. to local authorities by 1925, and 34 a. to Edmonton Estates Ltd. between 1931 and 1934.[19] The corn-rents were redeemed between 1886 and 1940.[20]

Walden abbey's house and court (*curia*), mentioned in the 13th century,[21] were probably on the site of the later Rectory House, in 1606 a large moated house on the north side of Church Street, west of the church.[22] An engraving of 1798 shows a large brick house of c. 1600, with gabled roofs. Dr. John Tillotson (d. 1694) lived there while he was dean of St. Paul's. The house disappeared between 1816 and 1865.[23]

There were conflicts between Walden and other religious houses with interests in Edmonton. When Geoffrey de Mandeville (fl. 1086) founded Hurley priory (Berks.), a cell of Westminster abbey, he granted it tithes and pannage from all his manors.[24] The second Geoffrey (d. 1144) substituted a payment of £5 yearly in lieu of all tithes except tithes of pannage.[25] About 1156–7 Hurley's pannage rights were augmented by a grant by Westminster abbey, which claimed to have enjoyed pigs and pence in Edmonton since the days of the first Geoffrey.[26] Although not expressly mentioned, Edmonton was probably included in the agreement between Hurley and Walden in 1255, whereby Hurley relinquished its tithes in many parishes.[27] In 1233, Walden, in return for a 3s. yearly payment, conceded a claim by the knights of St. John of Jerusalem that the tithes of hay from their meadows in Edmonton belonged to them by papal indulgence.[28]

William de Mandeville gave land worth £5 in Edmonton in free alms to the Augustinian canonesses of St. Mary, Clerkenwell, c. 1179–89.[29] John Blund made grants in free alms after 1190[30] and c. 1197[31] and Gillian, daughter of William Renger and wife of John Bucointe, made a grant from the Heyrun fee to the priory c. 1220–24.[32] Gundred de Warenne granted in free alms c. 1223–4 the house and extensive property which she had received from John Bucointe.[33] Only rents were thereafter granted to Clerkenwell, by William Blund c. 1222–50[34] and by John FitzJohn c. 1236–7.[35]

95 C 3/181/24; Hatfield C.F.E.P. (Deeds) 85/18.
96 Hatfield C.F.E.P. (Deeds) 146/10.
97 Hatfield C.P. 291.1, ff. 119 sqq.
98 Ibid.; C 142/435/130.
99 Robinson, *Edmonton*, 258.
1 *Reg. Regum Anglo-Norm.* iii, no. 913.
2 H. Collar, 'The Book of the Foundation of Walden Abbey', *Essex Rev.* xlv. 84.
3 Robinson, *Edmonton*, 80; B.M. Harl. MS. 3697, ff. 183–183d.
4 St. Paul's MS., W.D. 9, f. 85; *Val. of Norw.* ed. Lunt, 359; *Tax. Eccl.* (Rec. Com.), 17.
5 *Inq. Non.* (Rec. Com.), 197.
6 B.M. Harl. MS. 3697, ff. 182–3.
7 *Tax. Eccl.* (Rec. Com.), 13.
8 *Inq. Non.* (Rec. Com.), 197.
9 *Valor Eccl.* (Rec. Com.), vi, p. xii.
10 *L. & P. Hen. VIII*, xiii(1), pp. 212–13, 410.
11 E 305/C 58.
12 *L. & P. Hen. VIII*, xix(1), p. 495.
13 C 54/3552 no. 4.
14 Ibid.; *Home Cnties. Mag.* i. 316.
15 Guildhall Libr., Church Com. MS. 169029.
16 Robinson, *Edmonton*, 212, 268.
17 Ibid. 213–22, 236–8.
18 Ibid. 211, 322.
19 Church Com. S 4 survey, pp. 368–371.
20 Ibid. p. 338.
21 B.M. Harl. MS. 3697, f. 182v.; W.A.M. 12.
22 Hatfield C.P. 291.1, ff. 119 sqq. Cf. map & illustration (1750) in Robinson, *Edmonton*, 5.
23 Engraving (1798) *penes* Edmonton Publ. Libr.; Brewer, *Beauties of Eng. & Wales*, x(5), p. 707. Cf. remains of moat in grounds of Hydeside House: O.S. Map 6", Mdx. VII. SE. (1865 edn.).
24 W.A.M. 2001.
25 Ibid. 2182.
26 *A Medieval Miscellany for D. M. Stenton* (Pipe R. Soc. N.S. xxxvi), 104.
27 F. T. Wethered, *Lands and Tythes of Hurley Priory*, 24.
28 B.M. Harl. MS. 3697, f. 183v.; Cott. MS. Nero E. vi, f. 68.
29 *Clerkenwell Cart.* (Camd. 3rd ser. lxxi), p. 24.
30 Ibid. pp. 18–19.
31 Ibid. p. 18.
32 Ibid. pp. 115, 180.
33 i.e. a carucate and 10s. 10d. rent: *Clerkenwell Cart.*, pp. 107–8, 115–16; *Cur. Reg. R.* xii. 298. And see C.P. 25(1)/148/26/31.
34 E 40/1702; E 164/18 ff. 12 sqq.
35 *Clerkenwell Cart.*, p. 131.

In 1535 the priory had property in Edmonton worth £3 14s. 8d. in rent and 8 a. of woodland.[36]

When the priory was dissolved in 1539, the demesne lands in Edmonton were leased out[37] until 1547, when they were granted to Thomas Seymour, Lord Seymour of Sudeley (d. 1549).[38] After Seymour's attainder they were granted in 1550 to William Herbert, earl of Pembroke.[39] Herbert sold them to John Cock, whose son Sir Henry sold them in 1561 to Geoffrey Walkeden.[40] In 1574 Walkeden sold the estate to John Hudson, grocer of London, who conveyed it in the same year to William Cecil, Lord Burghley.[41]

In 1202 Ralph de Querendon granted a house and land to the leper hospital of St. Giles, Holborn,[42] which was granted a rent by John Bucointe at about the same time.[43] The most important part of St. Giles's holding in Edmonton, a wood of 35 a. in the south-west, had been acquired by the late 13th century and may have originated as part of the Querendon fee.[44] In 1412 the property of the hospital in Edmonton was worth £1[45] and in 1535 rents there totalled 13s. 4d. a year.[46] The hospital was dissolved in 1539 and its possessions in Edmonton were granted to John Dudley, Viscount Lisle, in 1544.[47] By 1566 they had passed to John Isham, mercer of London, who conveyed them in that year to Geoffrey and Thomas Walkeden.[48] St. Giles wood was conveyed with other woods to Lord Burghley in 1574[49] and was subsequently part of the Arnolds estate.[50]

Although the Benedictine nunnery of St. Helen, Bishopsgate, owned land in Edmonton c. 1274,[51] most of its later estate was probably granted out of Edmonton manor by Adam Francis, the priory's London benefactor.[52] In 1535 the nunnery owned woods in Southgate which were leased out at £1 8s. a year and quit-rents of 7s. 6d.[53] St. Helen's was dissolved in 1538, the quit-rents were cancelled, and the Crown continued to lease out the woods until 1547 when they were granted to Lord Seymour of Sudeley. Thereafter they descended with the former Clerkenwell estate.[54]

Ralph Heyrun granted to St. Bartholomew's priory a small parcel of meadow in free alms, worth 3s. a year by 1306.[55] Land in Edmonton and Tottenham was leased out by the priory in 1511[56] but there is no later reference to it.

Christine Marsh and her husband William Carter made small grants of meadow in Edmonton marsh to the hospital of St. Bartholomew, Smithfield, c. 1210.[57] Although the estate was granted to the City of London in 1547,[58] it was returned to the hospital, which in 1804 was allotted 1 a. in the marsh at inclosure.[59]

The Knights Hospitallers of St. John of Jerusalem acquired meadow land in Edmonton before 1233[60] and a rent from Hugh Peverel c. 1260.[61] By 1536 they had 24 a. in Edmonton marsh, which was leased out with meadow in adjoining parishes (3 a. in Tottenham and 7 a. in Enfield) and a 6d. quit-rent.[62] The priory was suppressed in 1540, re-endowed with its former lands by Mary in 1558,[63] and suppressed again by Elizabeth I, who granted the estate in 1560 to William Dodington.[64]

Part of the Pulteney estate in Edmonton marsh was granted by the bishop of Winchester and others to the Cistercian abbey of St. Mary Graces in 1396.[65] It was worth £1 in 1412.[66]

The Augustinian canonesses of Haliwell had land in Edmonton marsh, which was leased out in 1535 for £1 4s. a year.[67] In 1553 their meadow was sold by the Crown to Thomas and George Golding.[68] The hospital of St. Katharine by the Tower had meadow and quit-rents in Edmonton which it granted to Holy Trinity priory in 1222–48.[69] Sir John Elrington, who owned land in Edmonton,[70] probably granted it to the chantry which he founded in 1482 in the church of St. Leonard, Shoreditch.[71] At the suppression of the chantries St. Leonard's had 10 a. of woodland at Bush Hill and 2 a. in Enfield.[72] A small amount of woodland in Edmonton formed part of the Tottenham estate of the London Charterhouse.[73]

The largest secular estate in medieval Edmonton was built up between 1308 and 1349 by William Causton, mercer of London, who acquired more than 15 houses, 640 a. and £4 18s. 8d. quit rents from 54 people.[74] Most purchases were of small amounts, although those made from John atte Noke in 1338[75] and from John le Venour in 1342 were more substantial.[76] The largest acquisitions, however, were from John and Maud de Chilterne in 1339[77] and 1343.[78] John inherited from his uncle Adam de Chilterne[79] and Maud from her grandfather William Ford the elder.[80] The Ford estate had been

[36] *Valor Eccl.* (Rec. Com.), i. 395.
[37] *V.C.H. Mdx.* i. 171; S.C. 6/Hen. VIII/2396 m. 100d.; *L. & P. Hen. VIII,* xvi, p. 725; xviii(1), p. 556; xx(1), p. 681.
[38] *Cal. Pat.* 1547–8, 27–8.
[39] Ibid. 1550–3, 32.
[40] B.M. Add. Ch. 40597.   [41] Ibid. 40591–2.
[42] C.P. 25(1)/146/2/17.
[43] E 42/99.
[44] B.M. Harl. MS. 4015, f. 158v. Pace J. Parton (*Some Account of the Hosp. . . . of St. Giles-in-the-Fields,* 59), 'gravam' i.e. grove, not 'granam' i.e. granary.
[45] *Feudal Aids,* vi. 486–7.
[46] *Valor Eccl.* (Rec. Com.), iv. 153.
[47] *L. & P. Hen. VIII,* xix(i), p. 371.
[48] *Cal. Pat.* 1566–9, 97.
[49] Hatfield C.F.E.P. (Deeds) 146/10.
[50] M.L.R. 1747/1/277. For Arnolds, see below.
[51] J.I. 1/538 m. 2d.
[52] *V.C.H. London,* 457 sqq.
[53] *Valor Eccl.* (Rec. Com.), i. 392–3; S.C. 6/Hen. VIII/2396 m. 23d.
[54] S.C. 6/Ed. VI/299 m. 16; *Cal. Pat.* 1547–8, 27–8. See above.
[55] E. A. Webb, *Records of St. Bartholomew's Priory,* i. 446.

[56] E 303/9/268.
[57] *Cartulary of St. Barts. Hosp.* ed. N. J. M. Kerling, nos. 1181–6.
[58] *L. & P. Hen. VIII,* xxi(2), p. 414.
[59] Robinson, *Edmonton,* 248.
[60] B.M. Cott. MS. Nero E. vi, f. 68.
[61] Hatfield C.P. 291.1, no. 65.
[62] L.R. 2/62 f. 134; S.C. 6/Hen. VIII/2402 m. 7d.
[63] *Cal. Pat.* 1557–8, 313–14.
[64] Ibid. 1558–60, 387.
[65] *Cal. Close,* 1413–19, 509; Lysons, *Environs,* iii. 424; E 321/1/14.
[66] *Feudal Aids,* vi. 486–7.
[67] *Valor Eccl.* (Rec. Com.), i. 394; M.R.O., F 84/8c.
[68] *Cal. Pat.* 1553, 251.
[69] *Cart. of Holy Trinity,* Aldgate, ed. Hodgett, 195–6.
[70] C.P. 25(1)/152/98/58.
[71] L.C.C., *Survey of London,* viii. 93.
[72] E 315/67 p. 2; E 318/Box 28/1557.   [73] See p. 331.
[74] Based upon analysis of deeds *penes* W.A.M. and Hatfield Ho.
[75] C.P. 25(1)/150/57/115.
[76] Ibid. /59/164.   [77] Ibid. /57/119.
[78] Ibid. /61/213.   [79] W.A.M. 243.
[80] Ibid. 197.

held for $\frac{1}{12}$ knight's fee in 1235–6 by Laurence Ford,[81] by John Bucointe *c*. 1220,[82] and by Fubert in the 12th century.[83] Most of the land from the fee was granted to Clerkenwell and Maud's inheritance may have consisted mainly of rents.

In 1354 William Causton granted all his property in Edmonton, Enfield, and Tottenham to feoffees[84] who in 1355 conveyed it to Adam Francis and Peter Favelore.[85] Caustons, though considerably reduced in area, descended with Edmonton manor until 1571 when it was granted to Lord Burghley.[86] In the 16th century the house and a small amount of land were separated from most of the estate, which was attached to Pymmes.[87] William Cecil, earl of Salisbury, sold the house to Arthur Morgan, barber surgeon of London, in 1613.[88] Thereafter the descent is obscure. William Causton apparently had a house in Edmonton,[89] which by the 16th century was a farm-house north of Pymmes green and west of Pymmes house.[90]

Pymmes took its name from the family of William Pymme, who in 1371 granted all the land that he and John Clavering had received from William Viker to Adam Francis.[91] By 1502 Pymmes was held by Reynold Manser, whose father Robert had probably acquired it, together with Fullers messuage, in 1482 from Sir Richard Charlton, who had inherited Adam Francis's estate.[92] In 1502 Manser conveyed Pymmes to feoffees to the use of Robert Couch, after whose death it passed to Couch's widow Joan and then, in spite of a dispute over title, to Joan's nephew William Fox.[93] Fox conveyed it in 1525 to Sir Christopher Askew, alderman of London,[94] whose family held it[95] until it was sold in 1560 by Francis Askew to Elizabeth Gilburn.[96] In 1561 Elizabeth and her second husband Oliver Dawbeney, tallow chandler of London, conveyed Pymmes to Bartholomew Brokesby, gentleman of London,[97] who in 1562 enfeoffed Anthony Hickman, mercer of London.[98] In 1568 Pymmes passed to William Jephson[99] and from him to William Calton, an Edmonton tanner,[1] and in 1570 to Anthony Calton of Saffron Walden (Essex).[2] Calton conveyed it in 1574 to Nicholas Roldsby,[3] who sold it in 1579 to Thomas Wilson (d. 1581), secretary of

state.[4] Feoffees under Wilson's will sold it to Lord Burghley[5] in 1582, at about which date most of the lands belonging to Caustons was added.[6] The estate was still with the Cecil family in 1704[7] but by 1804 it was held by Henry Barker.[8] On Barker's death in 1808 it passed to his niece Ann and her husband Robert Ray and thence in 1824 to Henry Belward Ray[9] and in 1856 to Herbert Reginald Ray, who was of unsound mind by 1897 when Edmonton U.D.C. purchased it from the receiver of his estates.[10]

Pymmes house, north of Pymmes green,[11] was in 1562 a 'great messuage'.[12] Plans which were made for Thomas Wilson in 1579 show a hall of 33 × 20 ft. with a buttery and kitchen to the west, a large parlour to the east, and a long wing containing six lodgings to the north.[13] Pymmes was altered or rebuilt *c*. 1593[14] and it is not clear which building was the one described by Norden as 'a proper little house'.[15] It was again rebuilt in the early 18th century and a new south front, with a pediment and Ionic portico, was added later in the century. The building was of brick and timber-framing, with two storeys and attics, and the north front, which was plastered, had two projecting wings. The interior retained earlier panelling, staircases, and other features, possibly from Burghley's house.[16] Pymmes was burnt down in 1940.[17]

Robert de Plesington bought a house and lands from William Furneys, pepperer of London, in 1340,[18] and further houses and lands from Thomas Anesty in 1344,[19] and from Robert Anesty[20] and from John le Venour in 1346.[21] Robert de Plesington was dead by 1350 when his son Adam conveyed to Henry Walton, archdeacon of Richmond, property in Edmonton, Enfield, and East Barnet and the reversion of other property after the death of Adam's mother, Ellen.[22] Ellen and her second husband Gilbert Haydok conveyed their property in 1351 to Henry Walton,[23] who thereupon conveyed his lands to Roger de Depham, expressly including John le Venour's estate in which Depham already had an interest as creditor.[24]

In 1358 Roger de Depham granted all his property in Edmonton, Enfield, and Tottenham to

[81] *Bk. of Fees*, i. 474.
[82] *Clerkenwell Cart.*, pp. 107–8.
[83] *Cur. Reg. R.* vii. 341.
[84] W.A.M. 8.
[85] Ibid. 126.
[86] *Cal. Pat.* 1569–72, 270.
[87] Hatfield C.F.E.P. (Gen.) 55/23.
[88] Ibid. (Deeds) 225/30.
[89] e.g. deeds dated at Edmonton: W.A.M. 8, 175.
[90] Hatfield C.F.E.P. (Deeds) 146/13; Hatfield C.P. 143. 111, f. 151.
[91] *Cal. Close*, 1369–74, 262.
[92] Hatfield C.F.E.P. (Deeds) 119/7; 236/25.
[93] C 1/467/67–70.
[94] Hatfield C.F.E.P. (Deeds) 244/18.
[95] Ibid. (Legal) 33/4.
[96] Ibid. (Deeds) 147/3.
[97] Ibid. 152/8.
[98] Ibid. /10.
[99] Ibid. 246/10.
[1] Ibid. 247/3.
[2] Ibid. 68/10.
[3] Ibid. 190/19.
[4] Ibid. 88/23.
[5] Ibid. 129/20.
[6] Ibid. (Gen.) 55/23.
[7] T. Lewis and D. O. Pam, *Wm. and Robt. Cecil as Landowners in Edmonton and Southgate, 1561–1600* (Edmonton Hund. Hist. Soc., *c*. 1971), 6.

[8] Robinson, *Edmonton*, 246.
[9] M.R.O., Acc. 695/25, ff. 113, 162; /26, f. 351.
[10] Pamphlet on Pymmes Park *penes* Broomfield Mus.; Edmonton U.D.C. Act, 61–2 Vic. c. 63 (Priv. Act).
[11] Hatfield C.P. 143.111, f. 151.
[12] Hatfield C.F.E.P. (Deeds) 152/10.
[13] Ibid. 174/7; 219/21; ibid. C.P. 143.25; ibid. C.P.M. Suppl. 31; *pace* R. A. Skelton and J. Summerson, *Description of Maps and Architectural drawings in . . . Hatfield House* (Roxburghe Club, ccxxxv), 78, Burghley could not have rebuilt the house in 1579.
[14] The building of Pymmes was referred to in 1597 as '4 years past or thereabouts'. Hatfield C.F.E.P. (Accts.) 5/22.
[15] Norden, *Spec. Brit.* 38.
[16] Hist. Mon. Com. *Mdx.* 19; Sturges, *Edmonton Past and Present*, ii. 59–61; photographs *penes* Edmonton Publ. Libr.
[17] Pevsner, *Mdx.* 48.
[18] i.e. a house, grange and 32 a.: Hatfield C.P. 291.1, nos. 926–7.
[19] i.e. 2 houses and 114 a.: Hatfield C.P. 291.1, no. 924.
[20] i.e. 2 houses, 142 a., 34*s*. rent and the services of 27 tenants: C.P. 25(1)/150/64/294.
[21] i.e. a house and 162 a.: Hatfield C.P. 291.1, no. 948.
[22] Hatfield C.P. 291.1, no. 949.
[23] Ibid. no. 950.
[24] Ibid. nos. 955–7; W.A.M. 311; C.P. 25(1)/150/64/287. See p. 150.

feoffees,[25] who conveyed part of it to Adam Francis,[26] and in 1362 Richard, son of Adam de Plesington, granted all remaining interest in le Venour's estate to Francis.[27] Plesingtons descended with the capital manor until 1531 when Henry Courtenay, marquess of Exeter, sold it to John Grimston.[28] Thereafter it followed the same descent as Dephams manor.[29]

The main house on the Plesington estate, which, by the 18th century, was called Pleasantine Hall,[30] stood in a moated site west of Jeremy's Green Lane, at its junction with Town Road.[31] It may have originated in the enclosure containing a house, grange, other buildings and two gardens which William Furneys conveyed to Robert de Plesington in 1340.[32] About 1585 the mansion possessed a hall, parlour, and four chambers, as well as farm-buildings.[33] It was pulled down in 1906.[34]

Sayesbury or Bury farm was the demesne farm of Edmonton manor. In 1571 it was detached from the manor and granted by the Crown to Lord Burghley[35] whose grandson William, earl of Salisbury, sold it in 1614 to Roger Haughton of St. Martin-in-the-Fields.[36] In 1637 Eusebius Andrews sold it to Joshua Galliard, leather seller of London,[37] with whose descendants it remained until Pierce Galliard gave it to his daughter Mary and her husband Charles Bowles in 1787.[38] The Bowles family retained the estate until Arthur Humphrey Bowles sold it in 1893.[39] The house was purchased by W. C. Bowater.[40]

In 1272 the medieval manor-house possessed a garden, courtyard, and two dovecots.[41] By 1478, when it was leased out, it was a simple farmstead consisting of a dwelling, barns for corn and hay, two stables, and a long sheep-house.[42] A new house, probably Bury Hall, was built before c. 1627 on the south side of Bury Street, opposite the ancient farm-house.[43] Bury Hall was refronted c. 1750 and was the most important building in Bury Street until its demolition in 1920.[44] The presence of the Bradshaw arms over a fireplace gave rise to a story that the regicide John Bradshaw lived there. The only connexion was the marriage of a Galliard to a Bradshaw in the mid 18th century.[45] Bury Farm was pulled down about the same time as Bury Hall.[46]

Claverings, a freehold and copyhold estate first mentioned in 1486,[47] took its name from a 14th-century Edmonton family and was probably included in the estate conveyed by William Pymme to Adam Francis in 1371.[48] Claverings descended with the capital manor at least until 1532[49] and probably passed with it to the Crown before 1535.[50] It was granted to Edward Nowell the elder in 1563[51] and passed to his son Edward the younger (d. 1650).[52] John Highlord of Mitcham (Surr.) sold it in 1671 to Joseph Dawson, draper of London,[53] who died in 1693[54] and whose son Joseph, one of Edmonton's wealthiest men in 1694,[55] was dead by 1703.[56] Claverings passed to Peter Sykes and his wife Judith[57] and then to John Rowley (d. 1729), whose children in 1732 contested efforts by his executors to sell it.[58] By 1778 Claverings was held by Pierce Galliard, who sold it in that year to Thomas Woodham of Enfield.[59] Thomas's brother John Woodham succeeded him in 1783[60] and sold Claverings in 1784 to Charles Bowles of Stepney, who had other estates in Edmonton.[61] By will proved 1795 Charles Bowles devised his estates to his widow Mary, the owner in 1804.[62] The Bowles family were still in possession in 1888, when the copyhold of 79 a. was enfranchised. Arthur Humphrey Bowles was the owner in 1893.[63]

The Claverings estate lay north of Dephams and stretched from the farm-house at the northern part of Jeremy's Green (later Montagu Road) eastward to the river Lea.[64] Together with Dephams it became part of Edmonton U.D.C. sewage works and after 1949 the farm-house was demolished and the site developed as Claverings industrial estate.[65]

Weir Hall, an estate centred upon a house at the western end of Silver Street, probably took its name from the Wylehale or Wyrhale family, whose holding in Edmonton included land held in 1235-6 for $\frac{1}{40}$ knight's fee by Gilbert Prudhomme.[66] In 1349, when John Wyrhale and his son Richard both died, the estate consisted of a house and 100 a. John's widow Joan married Simon Bonde and, although she had as son another John Wyrhale, the Bondes granted the estate to John Golding, who was still in possession in 1371.[67] By 1397 the estate was in the hands of Richard Godestre.[68]

The Leake family, described as of Weir Hall in

[25] W.A.M. 52, 65.
[26] i.e. 2 houses, 320 a. and 50s. rent in Edmonton: C.P. 25(1)/150/67/365.
[27] Cal. Close, 1360-4, 411.
[28] Hatfield C.F.E.P. (Deeds) 190/9.
[29] See p. 150.
[30] Edmonton Publ. Libr., D 11.
[31] Hatfield C.P.M. Suppl. 27.
[32] Hatfield C.P. 291.1, no. 927.
[33] Hatfield C.P. 143.105, f. 142.
[34] Then called Moat House: V.C.H. Mdx. ii. 4.
[35] Cal. Pat. 1569-72, 270.
[36] Hatfield C.F.E.P. (Deeds) 197/20.
[37] C 142/588/76; Edmonton U.D.C., Official Guide [1923].
[38] Fisk, Edmonton, 147; C 5/576/12; Edmonton Publ. Libr., D 110.
[39] M.R.O., Acc. 727/246; Fisk, Edmonton, 147.
[40] Edmonton U.D.C., Official Guide [1923].
[41] C 132/42/6. And cf. 'manor of Say' 1328: E 164/18 ff. 12 sqq.
[42] Hatfield C.F.E.P. (Deeds) 40/3.
[43] Hatfield C.P.M. Suppl. 27; C 142/434/105.
[44] Fisk, Edmonton, 145; Sturges, Edmonton Past and Present, ii. 64; Edmonton U.D.C., Official Guide [1923]. There are many photographs of the interior and exterior of Bury Hall penes Edmonton Libr.
[45] Robinson, Edmonton, 28; N. & Q. 5th ser., vii. 25.

[46] O.S. Map 6″, Mdx. VII. SE. (1920 and 1938 edns.).
[47] Cal. Pat. 1485-94, 63.
[48] Cal. Close, 1369-74, 262. See above.
[49] L. & P. Hen. VIII, v, p. 485.
[50] See above.
[51] M.R.O., Acc. 695/42, f. 39.
[52] C 2/Jas. I/N7/60; Robinson, Edmonton, 93-4.
[53] M.R.O., Acc. 695/15, ff. 101v.-102.
[54] Ibid. /16, ff. 122v.-3.
[55] M.R.O., F 34/61-7.
[56] C 5/260/9.
[57] M.R.O., Acc. 695/18, ff. 237-8v.
[58] C 78/1750 no. 4. The eldest son claimed the freehold and the youngest the copyhold by Borough English.
[59] M.R.O., Acc. 695/22, f. 157.
[60] Ibid., Acc. 276/186.
[61] Ibid., Acc. 695/23, f. 69; Acc. 829.
[62] Ibid., Acc. 727/218; Robinson, Edmonton, 250.
[63] M.R.O., Acc. 727/238-241,/246; Acc. 1016/1/27.
[64] Hatfield C.P.M. Suppl. 27; inclos. map in Robinson, Edmonton.
[65] Edmonton U.D.C., Official Guide [1923]; ex inf. Enfield L.B. planning officer (1974).
[66] Bk. of Fees, i. 474; Feudal Aids, iii. 376.
[67] Cal. Inq. p.m. xiii, pp. 106-7; C.P. 25(1)/151/71/456.
[68] Cal. Close, 1396-9, 87-8. Cf. field names in 1397 with the description of Weir Hall alias Goldsters in 1605: M.R.O., Acc. 695/42, f. 3.

the early 16th century,[69] may have acquired the estate in 1491, when Thomas Fulnetby granted two houses and 122 a. to John Leake and others.[70] In 1605 Weir Hall formed part of 650 a. held by Jasper Leake.[71] In 1609 Sir John Leake sold Weir Hall to George Huxley, haberdasher of London,[72] and the estate thereafter descended in the direct male line until Thomas Huxley died in 1743. His estates were divided between his daughters Meliora Shaw (d. 1788) and Sarah Huxley (d. 1801), Sarah receiving the Weir Hall portion. In 1801 Sarah's estate was divided among five cousins but in 1814 four-fifths, including Weir Hall, were reunited by James George Tatem (d. 1854).[73] Tatem's son and namesake died in 1895, devising the estate by will to his nieces Ellen Anna and Elizabeth Margaret Harman,[74] who still possessed part of it in 1926.[75] The other fifth descended to the Parrotts, who sold it in 1852 to Richard Booth Smith.[76] On the death of his son John Smith in 1894 it passed to Edward C. Roberts, who was still in possession in 1900.[77]

In 1887 the estate, then referred to as the Huxley estate and consisting of 306 a., was put up for sale, but only about 57 a. were sold.[78] The Misses Harman for many years resisted the pressure of John Smith and later of Edward Roberts to sell but from 1898 they relinquished portions to builders, until the remnants were disposed of in 1930.[79]

The site of the house of 1349[80] is not known, since no medieval material was found where the later house stood at the western end of Silver Street, north of its junction with Hedge Lane. The Leake family had a mansion house by c. 1600,[81] and may have built it in the early 16th century at the time of the marriage of Henry VIII and Catherine of Aragon since a rose and pomegranate (the device of Aragon) adorned it. In 1611 George Huxley made substantial alterations, probably amounting to a virtual rebuilding,[82] and in 1664 the hall was one of the largest houses in Edmonton, assessed for 20 hearths.[83] It was built of brick and described in 1816 as lofty and spacious. A central projecting turret formed the entrance and the large windows and Dutch gables suggest a 17th-century date. The Leakes and Huxleys were resident but under James George Tatem the building was dilapidated and used as a boarding house before its demolition in 1818. Musket shot found in the walls gave rise to a conjecture that the house was besieged during the Civil War.[84] Its site afterwards served as a market-garden, where an old wall and outbuildings survived

into the 20th century.[85] A new house in a French château style,[86] called Weir Hall, was erected on the south side of Silver Street.[87] It was leased out as 'a high class inebriates' home' and a boys' school and was demolished in 1934.[88]

The estate centred on Broomfield House may have derived its name from John Broomfield, currier of London, who sold land in Southgate to Geoffrey Walkeden in 1566.[89] Walkeden was apparently the owner of Broomfield in the late 16th century,[90] and Richard Skevington, who lived there in 1593, may have been only the lessee.[91] 'Bromehowse' was in the possession of Sir John Spencer, alderman of London, in 1599 and 1606[92] and probably was acquired by the Jackson family[93] before 1624, when Joseph Jackson, merchant of London, was one of the principal inhabitants of South Street ward.[94] Broomfield House, a copyhold estate, remained with the Jacksons until 1773, when it passed to Mary Jackson and her husband William Tash. At inclosure in 1804 Tash had 582 a. mostly around Broomfield House and on the borders of Southgate and Tottenham, the second largest estate in Edmonton.[95] In 1816, when Tash died,[96] the estate was sold to Henry Philip Powys. Philip Lybbe Powys, who added the surname Lybbe to his name, sold the house and its 54-acre park to Southgate U.D.C. and the rest of the estate to builders in 1903.[97]

Although there was a house on the site in the 16th century, the structure of the southern part of the existing building is probably mid- to late-17th-century. Alterations were made c. 1725, when the staircase hall was probably added and one of the older rooms was repanelled. The house may then have extended farther north but the existing wing in that direction is probably c. 1800. During the 19th century there were further additions to the east, which squared off the plan of the house. The external appearance was altered c. 1930 by the application of false half-timbering.[98] The main feature of the interior is a group of classical paintings of 1723 by Gerrard Lanscroon, which cover the walls and ceiling of the staircase.[99] There was a park with formal avenues and a line of ponds in front of the house in 1754,[1] much of which survives.

Arnos Grove, formerly Arnolds and Arno's Grove, originated in Armholt, a 14th-century wood on the western borders of Southgate which became part of the Charterhouse estate.[2] In 1551 the Charterhouse wood was granted to Sir Thomas and George

69 *Mdx. Pedigrees* (Harl. Soc. lxv), 12–13.
70 C.P. 25(1)/152/100/31.
71 M.R.O., Acc. 695/42, ff. 2–5, 24–26.
72 C 2/Jas. I/H 23/27.
73 Robinson, *Edmonton*, 24, 96–7; M.R.O., Acc. 815/13.
74 M.R.O., Acc. 695/29, pp. 154–64, 445–54.
75 Ibid., Acc. 815/30.
76 Ibid. /20–21.
77 Ibid. /6/11–13.
78 Ibid., Acc. 815/37.
79 Ibid. /6/10–13; /9, /27, /37.
80 *Cal. Inq. p.m.* xiii, pp. 106–7.
81 Hatfield C.P.M. Suppl. 27; M.R.O., Acc. 695/42, f. 3.
82 Robinson, *Edmonton*, 24–6.
83 M.R.O., MR/TH/5, m. 4d.
84 Robinson, *Edmonton*, 24–6. See illus. in Brewer, *Beauties of Eng. & Wales*, x(5), p. 707.
85 Fisk, *Edmonton*, 196.
86 Briggs, *Mdx. Old & New*, 76; photographs *penes* Edmonton Publ. Libr.
87 O.S. Map 6", Mdx. VII. SE. (1865 edn.).
88 Fisk, *Edmonton*, 141, 196; Sturges, *Edmonton Past and Present*, ii. 64.
89 B.M. Add. Ch. 40591.
90 Hatfield C.P.M. Suppl. 27.
91 Norden, *Spec. Brit.* 17; E 179/253/3.
92 Hatfield C.P. 291.1, ff. 119 sqq.; Lewis and Pam, *Wm. and Robt. Cecil as landowners in Edmonton and Southgate, 1561–1600*, 8.
93 *Visitation of Mdx. 1663*, ed. Foster (priv. print 1887), 51.
94 C 93/50/33.
95 Robinson, *Edmonton*, 34, 318–22; *Mdx. Quarterly*, ii. 12–13.
96 C 54/14336 m. 42 no. 3.
97 Round, *Southgate and Winchmore Hill*, 24–5.
98 Briggs, *Mdx. Old and New*, 86.
99 Pevsner, *Mdx.* 140; guide and pamphlet *penes* Broomfield Mus.
1 Rocque, *Map of Mdx.* (1754).
2 E 164/18 ff. 12 sqq.; L.R. 2/61 ff. 145v.–6v.

Tresham.[3] Thomas Colte of Waltham Holy Cross (Essex) later held it and in 1584, after his death, his daughters and coheirs Catherine and Jane and their husbands, Thomas Cave of Baggrave (Leics.) and Nicholas Brookes of London, covenanted to convey Arnolds, then consisting of a house and 24 a., to Humphrey Weld, grocer of London.[4] Weld (d. 1611), who was later knighted, acquired 13 a. from Robert Cecil in 1610[5] and his son, Sir John Weld (d. 1623), the founder of Weld chapel, bought 150 a. near by from William Cecil, earl of Salisbury, in 1614.[6] Sir John's widow Frances sold the property in 1645 to Sir William Acton, Bt. (d. 1651). Acton's daughter and heir married Sir Thomas Whitmore, Bt., whose son, Sir William Whitmore, Bt. (d.s.p.) devised his estates to William Whitmore, who was succeeded by his son, Thomas Whitmore, later knighted.[7] In 1747 Sir Thomas sold Arnolds to James Colebrook,[8] a London mercer who had been acquiring property in Southgate since 1716.[9] His son Sir George Colebrook, Bt., sold it in 1762 to Abraham Hume[10] who in 1763 exchanged some land with the Minchenden estate[11] and in 1766 sold Arnolds to Sir William Mayne, Bt.,[12] later Lord Newhaven. Mayne conveyed the estate in 1775 to James Brown of Lombard Street (London)[13] whence it passed in 1777 to Isaac Walker of Cornhill (London).[14] In 1804 Walker was the owner and part occupier of 264 a.[15]

The Walkers retained the estate, which they increased to over 300 a. by buying Minchenden in 1853 and Beaver Hall in 1870, until Russell Donnithorne Walker, the last of the Walker brothers, sold it in 1918 to Andrew Weir, later Lord Inverforth, a shipowner. In 1928 Lord Inverforth sold the house to Northmet Electricity Co. (later the Eastern Electricity Board), 44 a. to Southgate U.D.C. as open space, and the rest to builders.[16]

Arnolds house, which existed by 1584[17] and which was described by Sir John Weld in 1623 as very small,[18] was situated next to Waterfall Road where it turns south to form the Southgate boundary.[19] During the late 17th and early 18th centuries the house was occupied by lessees,[20] one of whom in 1719 replaced the old house with a red-brick house to the east,[21] seven bays wide across the main fronts and three storeys high. The entrance hall and staircase in the centre of the east front have wall and ceiling paitings by Gerrard Lanscroon, dated 1723 and depicting the apotheosis of Julius Caesar.

Alterations from designs by Sir Robert Taylor were made to the principal rooms on the west front in 1788 and include a long drawing room with Adam-style plasterwork. During the early 19th century low wings were added to both the north and south. Towards the end of the century the east front was largely rebuilt, a new staircase was installed, and there was some modernization of the interior. The Northmet Co. added large wings for offices in 1929 and 1935.[22] There was a large park to the south and west.

Minchenden in Southgate, adjoining Arnos Grove, derived its name from the nuns (*myncen*) of Clerkenwell who had land there.[23] It was subsequently part of the Cecil estates and was sold as a wood of 50 a. by the earl of Salisbury in 1614 to John Weld of Arnolds.[24] It subsequently passed to Sir Thomas Stringer[25] who sold it before 1672 to Sir Thomas Wolstenholme.[26] Sir David Hechstetter, who occupied the house as lessee in 1714,[27] bought the land from Sir Nicholas Wolstenholme in 1716.[28] By 1738 it was in the possession of John Nicholl, a rich London merchant, probably conveyed to him by Heckstetter's widow in 1736.[29] In 1753 Nicholl's daughter and heir, Margaret, married James Brydges, marquess of Carnarvon and later duke of Chandos,[30] whereupon Minchenden became part of the extensive Brydges estates in Middlesex, which included the manors of Great and Little Stanmore. At its greatest extent the Brydges estate in Southgate consisted of a mansion, 18 other houses, and 500 a. of freehold land.[31] When James Brydges, duke of Chandos died in 1789, his widow Anne Eliza (d. 1813) received Minchenden House and about 105 a., mostly consisting of the former Minchenden wood,[32] for life but the rest of the estate passed to the duke's daughter and heir.[33] In 1853 the estate was sold to Isaac Walker, who merged it with Arnos Grove.[34]

Minchenden House, a large building on the south side of Waterfall Road, was built after 1664 by Sir Thomas Wolstenholme, who in 1672 was assessed for 35 hearths, the largest amount in the parish.[35] In 1738 John Nicholl carried out considerable alterations, mostly to the front of the house and including the coping of a parapet, a smoking-room, library, and staircase.[36] In 1747 there were repairs to a portico.[37] George II visited Minchenden,[38] which, after the demolition of Canons (Little Stanmore), became the main seat of the Brydges

---

[3] *Cal. Pat.* 1550–3, 202.
[4] M.R.O., Acc. 593/2–5.
[5] Ibid. /6; C 142/322/173.
[6] M.R.O., Acc. 593/7, /9.
[7] Robinson, *Edmonton*, 125 sqq.
[8] M.L.R. 1747/1/277.
[9] e.g. M.L.R. 1716/4/114–15.
[10] M.L.R. 1762/3/134–5.   [11] M.L.R. 1763/4/48.
[12] M.L.R. 1766/7/145–7.
[13] M.L.R. 1775/1/188.
[14] M.L.R. 1777/1/135–6.
[15] M.R.O., Acc. 695/62; Robinson, *Edmonton*, 322–3.
[16] Mason, *Story of Southgate*, 62–3.
[17] M.R.O., Acc. 593/2.
[18] Prob. 11/141 (P.C.C. 20 Swann).
[19] For its position on a map of 1599, see Lewis and Pam, *Wm. and Robt. Cecil as Landowners*, 10.
[20] M.L.R. 1735/1/383; 1747/2/1.
[21] Datestone in hall.
[22] Pevsner, *Mdx.* 140–1; Robbins, *Mdx.* 328; Colvin, *Dict. of Architects*, 604; Watts, *Views of Seats* (1784), pl. 63; 'Northmet Ho.' (TS. *penes* Northmet Ho.); Lysons,

Environs, suppl. 432. See illus. in Brewer, *Beauties of Eng. and Wales*, x(5), 709.
[23] *P.N. Mdx.* (E.P.N.S.), 69. See above.
[24] M.R.O., Acc. 593/7.
[25] M.L.R. 1714/1/164–5.
[26] M.R.O., MR/TH/22.
[27] M.L.R. 1714/1/164–5.   [28] M.L.R. 1716/3/86–9.
[29] M.L.R. 1731/1/108; 1744/2/48.
[30] M.R.O., Acc. 262/2/17; /51/3; C. H. C. and M. I. Baker, *Life . . . of James Brydges, First Duke of Chandos*, 262.
[31] M.R.O., Acc. 695/62.
[32] Robinson, *Edmonton*, 260.
[33] *Complete Peerage* and see p. 97.
[34] *Home Cnties. Mag.* xi. 178.
[35] M.R.O., MR/TH/5, m. 1–1d.; /TH/22. Cf. Ogilby, *Map of Mdx.* [c. 1677]. The map is dedicated to Sir Thos. Wolstenholme of 'Minsenden' and Minchenden is clearly marked as a very large house.
[36] M.R.O., Acc. 262/67/299, /314, /316.
[37] Ibid. /331.
[38] Mason, *Story of Southgate*, 177.

family and in 1816 was described as a capacious brick mansion.[39] Eighteenth-century prints depict a large plain house with a main front of nine bays probably dating from the early 18th century.[40] It was pulled down by Isaac Walker in 1853.[41]

Grovelands or Southgate Grove, an estate between Southgate and Winchmore Hill, was first mentioned in the 15th century as Lord's Grove, woodland treated as demesne of Edmonton manor.[42] It descended with the manor until 1571 when the queen granted it to Lord Burghley,[43] whose grandson the earl of Salisbury sold it, as 230 a. of woodland, to John Clapham, one of the six clerks of Chancery, in 1615.[44] Clapham was succeeded in 1619 by his cousin of the same name,[45] who died c. 1631 leaving the property to his widow Mary for life, with remainder to his son Luke.[46] Robert Marsh, merchant tailor of London, had possession in 1665[47] and sold it to Sir Thomas Wolstenholme (d. 1691), whereupon it became part of the Minchenden estate.[48]

Lord's Grove followed the descent of Minchenden until it was inherited by Anna Elizabeth, daughter and heir of the duke of Chandos (d. 1789) and after 1796 wife of Richard Nugent-Temple-Grenville, Earl Temple, later duke of Buckingham and Chandos.[49] In 1799 Temple sold it to Walker Gray, brandy merchant of London[50] and nephew of Isaac Walker of Arnos Grove. At inclosure Gray owned 231 a., almost precisely the area of the 17th-century Lord's Grove, although by c. 1804 the estate was entitled Southgate Grove and Winchmore Hill woods.[51] It descended in 1839 to Walker Gray's nephew John Donnithorne Taylor, a member of the brewing firm of Taylor Walker, who acquired other lands near by and died in 1885 possessed of over 600 a. in Southgate and Winchmore Hill.[52] The whole estate had been unsuccessfully put up for sale in 1834[53] and was offered again in 1902 after the death of Major Robert Kirkpatrick Taylor, J. D. Taylor's son and heir.[54] All the property was sold except Grovelands, which failed to reach the reserve price and so remained with Robert Taylor's son Captain John Vickris Taylor, who sold 64 a. to Southgate U.D.C. as a public park in 1910 and the house and the rest of the land to the Middlesex Voluntary Aid Detachment in 1921.[55]

In 1799 Walker Gray built a house, which he called Southgate Grove. It stands on a small spur, originally dotted with trees, overlooking a lake and park which were landscaped by Humphry Repton,

who is said to have chosen the site for the house.[56] John Nash, who was then just beginning a partnership with Repton, was the architect and designed an almost square block with three main elevations, each with a central feature of the Ionic order.[57] Inside the principal rooms are arranged round the central staircase and the decoration includes much scagliola in the hall, paintings in grisaille in the vestibule, and an octagonal breakfast room with walls and ceiling painted to represent the interior of a birdcage with, through the bars, the scenery of the park.[58] A feature of the basement is an ice-house between the two wine cellars. The house has suffered few structural alterations since it has been used as a hospital.[59] The dome lighting the staircase has been altered, there has been some subdivision of rooms, and the conservatory, which projected from the library at a corner of the main block, has been replaced by a link to a new ward. From 1840 until 1910 the park was stocked with fallow deer.[60]

Cullands or Cannons Grove was in the 16th century Gullands Grove, a triangular piece of woodland between Wrights Lane (later Alderman's Hill) and Barnfield Lane, which joined it from Clappers Green.[61] It belonged to the Cecils until the late 17th century[62] and was sold in the mid 18th century by Walter Henshaw and Henry Hadley to Stephen Peter Godin. Godin's estate, which included a house, was sold in 1787 by his daughters and devisees to William Curtis (d. 1829),[63] who, when granted a baronetcy in 1802, described himself as of Cullands Grove.[64] At inclosure c. 1804 Curtis owned 149 a. at Cullands Grove and in the south-west corner of Southgate.[65] The estate was put up for auction in 1832 and bought by John Donnithorne Taylor c. 1840 and added to his already extensive estates.[66] The 18th-century house, 'much improved' by Curtis, was a square, brick building with a pediment and pillared entrance. The interior, noted by J. N. Brewer for its 'unostentatious elegance', had been decorated by a painter called Kirke. George IV was a frequent visitor at Cullands Grove, where Curtis may have entertained the kings of France and Prussia and the Czar during their visit to England in 1814.[67] The house, which was set in gardens with a lake, was pulled down c. 1840.[68]

Bush Hill or Halliwick, the small estate centred on the house between the New River, Bush Hill, and Bush Hill Road, consisted c. 1600 of copyhold woodland which had been held by Robert Waleys

[39] Brewer, *Beauties of Eng. and Wales*, x(5), pp. 712–13.
[40] Print *penes* Broomfield Mus. (on display); *A New Display of the Beauties of Eng.* i (1776), illus.; Guildhall, Pr. V/SOU; illus. reproduced in Newby, *Old Southgate*, 8.
[41] Robbins, *Mdx.* 327.
[42] Hatfield C.F.E.P. (Deeds) 102/10.
[43] E 210/1410; *Cal. Pat. 1569–72*, 270.
[44] Hatfield C.F.E.P. (Deeds) 102/26.
[45] C 142/376/105.   [46] C 142/473/48.
[47] Prob. 11/324 (P.C.C. 75 Carr, will of Robt. Marsh); C 10/490/136.
[48] M.L.R. 1714/1/164–5.   [49] *Complete Peerage*.
[50] M.R.O., Acc. 695/24, f. 219; M.L.R. 1800/1/145.
[51] Robinson, *Edmonton*, 274–6.
[52] Newby, *Old Southgate*, 31; Mason, *Story of Southgate*, 49–50.
[53] Sales parts. (1834) *penes* Broomfield Mus.
[54] Ibid. (1902).
[55] Mason, *Story of Southgate*, 50–3. See p. 180.
[56] Dorothy Stroud, *Humphry Repton*, 98; engraving in *Peacock's Polite Repository* (1798).

[57] G. Richardson, *New Vitruvius Britannicus* (1802), 9, plates xxix–xxxi; T. Davis, *John Nash*, 35. See below, plate facing p. 161.
[58] T. Davis, *Architecture of John Nash*, plates 29–36; E. Croft-Murray, *Decorative Painting in England*, ii. 65, plate 124.
[59] For Grovelands hospital, see p. 180.
[60] *V.C.H. Mdx.* ii. 247.
[61] Hatfield C.P.M. Suppl. 27; ibid. C.P. 291.1, ff. 119 sqq.
[62] Hatfield C.F.E.P. (Deeds) 135/1; C 5/460/2.
[63] M.L.R. 1787/7/392.
[64] *Home Cnties. Mag.* xi. 176.
[65] Robinson, *Edmonton*, 258.
[66] Newby, *Old Southgate*, 17.
[67] Mason, *Story of Southgate*, 77, quotes the *Annual Register* (1815) but no reference to Culland's Grove has been found for 1814 or 1815.
[68] Brewer, *Beauties of Eng. and Wales*, x(5), p. 711; *Ambulator*, 12th edn. (1820), 80. For illustration see Newby, *Old Southgate*, 16–17 and print of 1797: Guildhall, Pr. V/SOU.

The South Front

The Entrance Hall

GREAT STANMORE: STANMORE HALL IN 1891

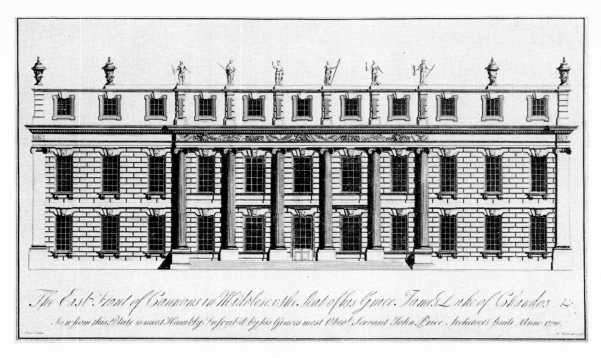

The East Front of Canons in Middlesex the Seat of his Grace James Duke of Chandos &

To whom this Plate is most Humbly Inscribed by his Graces most Obed.t Servant John Price Architect built Anno 1720

LITTLE STANMORE: CANONS IN 1720

SOUTHGATE: GROVELANDS *c.* 1800

(fl. 1523–60),[69] then by John Estry, and from 1588 by John's son Robert, who was still in possession in 1605.[70] Shortly afterwards Sir Hugh Myddelton, who is traditionally supposed to have built the house while he was constructing the New River, must have acquired the property.[71] By will proved 1631 he left the Bush Hill estate to his widow Elizabeth (d. 1643) for life, with remainder to his youngest son Simon.[72] Although Simon and his son Hezekiah (d. 1688) were buried in Edmonton, the Myddeltons seem to have sold the estate before 1650.[73]

John Bathurst, a London alderman, was in possession by 1664[74] and by will proved 1695 disinherited his son Sir Henry.[75] In 1696 the property was sold by Bathurst's daughter Catherine and her husband Josias Ent to John Clarke (d. 1701), merchant of London. The estate passed to John's brother Samuel (d. 1742) and from him to William Clarke (d. 1783), who left two daughters Anna Clarke and Mary Forbes. It was auctioned in lots in 1784, when the house and 39 a. were purchased by John Blackburn (d. 1798) of London, who was building up an estate in the area. Blackburn's son John sold Bush Hill in 1812 to Isaac Currie, banker of Cornhill.[76] The Curries retained the estate, which was leased in the 1850s to Sir Samuel Cunard, the shipowner, until 1878 when it was sold to Horace Barry. Barry was dead by 1908 when the house and 90-acre park, by then called Halliwick, was occupied by the Misses Fenton.[77] In 1911 the house and some grounds were bought by the trustees of the Girls Cripples' Home. The southern part of the estate was sold to builders.[78]

Sir Hugh Myddelton probably erected the first house at Bush Hill c. 1613.[79] By 1664 it was the largest in the parish, assessed for 31 hearths.[80] Nothing remains which can with certainty be identified as part of Myddelton's house. The late-18th-century house consisted of a main block three storeys high and nine bays long with two flanking wings each of three bays. A seven-bay portion remains of this building.[81] The main front on the south was modernized in the mid 19th century and additions were made to the east and west. After 1927 further additions were made to the north and west and the main front was largely rebuilt. More recently new classrooms have been added.[82] The house was set upon high wooded ground with commanding vistas over the winding New River, where John Blackburn laid out an elegant park.[83]

Bush Hill Park in north Edmonton originated in a small estate conveyed in 1671 by John Harvey to John Shale of London and in 1682 by Shale to Sir Jeremiah Sambrook (d. 1705).[84] It descended to Sir Samuel Vanacher Sambrook, Bt. (d. 1715), and then to Sir Jeremy Vanacher Sambrook, Bt. (d. 1740). Jeremy's sisters and coheirs, Judith, Elizabeth, and Susanna and the husbands of the last two, Sir Humphrey Monoux and John Crawley, sold the estate in 1745 to John Gore, who purchased about 37 a. near by from George Huxley in 1748. When Gore died in 1765, his trustees sold his lands to Joseph Mellish of Bishopsgate, London.[85] The estate reached its greatest extent under Mellish's great-grandson William Mellish (d. 1839), a merchant and M.P. for Middlesex.[86] At inclosure c. 1804 Mellish's estate was the third largest in the parish, consisting of 438 a., mostly at Bush Hill and Nightingale Hall farm in the north-east.[87] He also leased the Polehouse estate from St. Paul's from 1801 until 1822.[88] Nightingale Hall farm was conveyed to Robert Musket before 1828[89] and Bush Hill Park was sold by Mellish's executors, some of it to the New River Co. The house and part of the estate was bought by Lewis Raphael of Hendon (d. 1851) and passed to his nephew John Samuel Moorat (d. 1869) and then to Moorat's sons Samuel and Edward.[90] In 1872 the Bush Hill Park Co. acquired the land for building.[91]

The 'commodious brick mansion' of Bush Hill Park, in existence by 1724,[92] was set in grounds laid out by Le Nôtre. The house contained a wooden panel by Grinling Gibbons representing the stoning of St. Stephen,[93] which had come from Canons (Little Stanmore), and a clock tower which was pulled down in 1875.[94] The house, though set in a much smaller estate, was still a residence in 1914.[95] It was pulled down in 1929.[96]

ECONOMIC HISTORY. AGRICULTURE.

In 1086 Edmonton manor, which included the berewick of South Mimms and probably Monken Hadley, was assessed at 35 hides worth £40, the value T.R.E. and twice that when Geoffrey de Mandeville had received it. There was land for 26 ploughs, 22 of which belonged to the peasantry and only 4 to the demesne, although the demesne comprised 16 hides.[97]

In 1272 the demesne consisted of 593 a. of arable, 59 a. of meadow, 60 a. of several pasture, a

[69] S.C. 6/Hen. VIII/2102 m. 2; S.C. 6/Eliz./1415 m. 9d.; C 1/647/17–18.
[70] M.R.O., Acc. 695/42, ff. 33–4; Hatfield C.P.M. Suppl. 27.
[71] Lysons, *Environs*, ii. 261; *D.N.B.*
[72] *Wills from Doctors' Commons* (Camd. Soc. lxxxiii), 92–8.
[73] E 317/Mdx. 16 m. 3.
[74] M.R.O., MR/TH/5, m. 1d.
[75] The 'disobedient son', Sir Henry, received only books of history and divinity: Prob. 11/425 (P.C.C. 68 Irby, will of John Bathurst).
[76] M.R.O., Acc. 1076 (Bush House papers).
[77] Fisk, *Edmonton*, 184; *Kelly's Dirs. Mdx.* (1890, 1908).
[78] O.S. Maps 6", Mdx. VII. SE. (1897 and 1920 edns.). See p. 202.
[79] The only house c. 1600 lay to the north: Hatfield C.P.M. Suppl. 27.
[80] M.R.O., MR/TH/5, m. 1d.
[81] Guildhall Libr., illus. edn. of Lysons, *Environs*, ii, pt. ii, facing p. 260.
[82] Ex inf. Halliwick sch. (1974).

[83] *Ambulator*, 4th edn. (1792), 47; M.R.O., Acc. 1076/17a/c.
[84] M.R.O., Acc. 695/15, ff. 104v.–5; /16, f. 31.
[85] Ibid., Acc. 1076; Robinson, *Edmonton*, 292–5.
[86] *V.C.H. Mdx.* ii. 58.
[87] Robinson, *Edmonton*, 292–5; M.R.O., Acc. 695/43.
[88] Guildhall Libr., Church Com. MSS. 168992–4.
[89] Edmonton Publ. Libr., D 1.
[90] M.R.O., Acc. 695/27, pp. 243–5, 334–7; /28, p. 115; /29, p. 56.
[91] Fisk, *Edmonton*, 186–7.
[92] H. Moll, *New Description of Eng. and Wales* (1724), 134. A house was presumably in existence by 1705 when Sir Jeremiah Sambrook died in the garden: J. Walker Ford, *A sketch of Bush Hill Park*, 6.
[93] Brewer, *Beauties of Eng. and Wales*, x(5), p. 708.
[94] See illustration in J. Hassell, *Seats near London* (1804).
[95] Fisk, *Edmonton*, 187.
[96] Sturges, *Edmonton Past and Present*, ii. 64.
[97] *V.C.H. Mdx.* i. 126. South Mimms and Monken Hadley were probably mainly uninhabited woodland.

grove, and easement of vines.[98] The arable had been reduced by 1359[99] to 400 a., of which only 160 a. could be sown if it was well-tilled, in which case it was worth 4d. an acre. The rest, worth only ½d. an acre, was gravelly and sterile. Every third year it was laid open for common of pasture, when it was worth 2d. an acre. There was less reduction in the several pasture (40 a.)[1] and meadow (60 a.)[2] and the wood was specified as 40 a. The demesne was badly managed in 1359: the capital messuage had no net worth, the windmill was useless,[3] most of the soil was infertile, and the demesne had been reduced without any corresponding rise in rents.[4]

In 1478 the demesne, then 477 a. of open-field land, 56 a. of several pasture, and 45 a. of meadow in the common marsh, was leased out to the manorial bailiff for £14 a year.[5] From 1486 until his death in 1523 the bailiff was the powerful Nicholas Bone, a local man feared by his neighbours as a 'man of great possessions',[6] who was probably responsible for the separate leasing of part of the demesne which became Sadler's farm.[7] By 1523 Sayesbury demesne farm consisted of only 178 a. of open-field arable; 70 a. had been inclosed from Pury field for several arable and 30 a. for pasture. The several pasture and meadow remained unchanged.[8] The demesne was reunited by the Cecils after 1571[9] and in 1606[10] it consisted of 257 a. of arable: 171 a. in the open fields[11] and 86 a. of inclosed arable (Broom fields), 114 a. of inclosed pasture,[12] and 49 a. of meadow.

In 1086 most of the cultivated land, for 22 ploughs and consisting of 12½ hides and 40 a., was divided among 52 villeins, 17 bordars, and 14 cottars. There were also 4 serfs. Only one villein had one hide, three had ½ hide each, 20 had one virgate each, and 24 had ½ virgate each. There were 9 bordars on 3 virgates, 4 had 5 a. each, and 4 had 4 a. each. There were 4 cottars on 4 a. and 4 villeins and 10 cottars on one hide and one virgate.[13]

By 1272 there were 7 tenants by knight service,[14] tenants in socage whose rents (£12 13s. 1d.) provided threequarters of the total rental,[15] villeins holding 4⅘ virgates[16] and small molmen owing £2 17s. 11d. rent. Customary tenants owed 1,247 works a year. All customary tenants, presumably including the molmen, owed services of ploughing and harrowing in winter and Lent on 37 a., carting in summer on 18½ a., mowing 23 a. of meadow, threshing 6 qr. 1½ bu. of corn for winter fodder, and 171 carrying works from Michaelmas until Lammas. Forty customary tenants owed one day's corn-hoeing, one day's hay-lifting, and two boondays' reaping. Three of them, who held cottar land, owed 154½ works between Michaelmas and Midsummer and 72 works between Midsummer and Michaelmas. Twenty-four customary tenants owed one day's corn-binding and one day's hay-stacking.[17]

In 1359 the total rental from tenants was £16 a year, a little less than in 1272. All were free tenants except six bondmen (nativi), from whom the only customary works, reduced to hoeing and autumn and winter works, were demanded.[18]

Thereafter the proportion of freehold land seems to have remained much the same until the mid 16th century, when £12 9s. 1½d., 1 lb. pepper, and a hunting dog were the fixed annual rents of free tenants.[19] In the late 16th century, however, freehold rents dwindled to £5 3s. 2d. as estates were released from obligations to the central manor.[20] Rents from customary tenements increased greatly between 1359 (about £3 6s. 9d.) and c. 1525 (£82 7s. 7½d.).[21] In the mid 16th century they reached £87 7s. 3½d.[22] but by 1606 they had fallen to £73 10s. 10d.[23] James I tried to increase the profits of Edmonton manor but in return for increased admission fines he had to agree that customary rents should remain the same.[24] By 1650 freehold rents amounted to £7 13s. and copyhold to £77 1s. 6d.[25] About 1716 quit-rents totalled £96 a year.[26] On the eve of parliamentary inclosure, when only 22 per cent of the parish was unenfranchised, copyhold rents totalled £77 9s. 10d.[27]

Tenure by Borough English on copyhold land, which characterized Edmonton,[28] hindered the growth of estates, since the elder son would inherit his father's freehold and the younger his copyhold estate. Another factor was the fragmentation of free holdings among several children. John Marsh (d. by 1312) divided his lands among four sons and two daughters.[29] His family was long established, since William de Mandeville (d. 1189) had granted land to

---

[98] C 132/42/6.

[99] C 135/144/7.

[1] Worth £2 compared with £3 for 60 a. in 1272.

[2] Worth £9 (3s. an acre) compared with £7 6s. 10d. (2s. 6d. an acre) in 1272.

[3] See p. 169.

[4] See below.

[5] Hatfield C.F.E.P. (Deeds) 40/3. The arable consisted of 236 a. in Hounds field, 210 a. in Pury field, 29 a. in Ashcrofts, and 2 a. in Storksnest field.

[6] D.L. 3/21/E 1.

[7] Hatfield C.F.E.P. (Court Rolls) 15/25; Hatfield C.P. 143.103, f. 139.

[8] E 326/6076. The open-field land consisted of 110 a. in Hounds field, 36 a. in Pury field, 30 a. in Ashcrofts, and 2 a. in Storksnest field; Broom closes i.e. later Broom fields (64 a. of arable) and Broad leas and Hogs leas (30 a. of pasture) had been created from Pury field.

[9] See p. 157.

[10] Hatfield C.P. 291.1, ff. 119 sqq.

[11] i.e. 108 a. in Hounds field, 37 a. in Bury field, and 26 a. in Ashcrofts.

[12] Mostly consisting of closes between Hounds field and Pury field and including Oldland grove, which was probably the demesne grove mentioned in the 13th and 14th cents.: Hatfield C.P.M. Suppl. 27.

[13] V.C.H. Mdx. i. 126. These figures include the

berewick of South Mimms and probably the later parish of Monken Hadley.

[14] Paying 3s. a year rent; cf. Bk. of Fees, ii. 898.

[15] Total £16 3s. 9¾d. There were also rents in kind worth 1s., which probably represented ancient freehold estates.

[16] Paying 8s. 9¾d. rent.

[17] C 132/42/6.

[18] Worth 13s. 8d. compared with £4 8s. ¾d. in 1272: C 135/144/7.

[19] S.C. 6/Hen. VIII/2102 m. 2; S.C. 6/Hen. VIII/6159 p. 136; S.C. 6/Ed. VI/299 m. 15.

[20] e.g. Bowes (£1 2s. rent) was released in 1572: see p. 151. Willoughbies (16s. 9d.) had disappeared by 1605: M.R.O., Acc. 695/42, f. 73. Most of the woodlands granted to Burghley, which originated in monastic estates, owed no rent to Edmonton manor.

[21] C 135/144/7; S.C. 6/Hen. VIII/6159 p. 136.

[22] S.C. 6/Hen. VIII/2102 m. 2; S.C. 6/Ed. VI/299 m. 15.

[23] M.R.O., Acc. 695/42, f. 73.

[24] D. Avery, Manorial Systems in Edmonton Hund. in late Medieval and Tudor Periods (Edmonton Hund. Hist. Soc., n.d.), 10–11.

[25] E 317/Mdx. 16.

[26] Bodl. MS. Rawl. B. 389b, f. 15.

[27] M.R.O., Acc. 695/43, /62.

[28] Robinson, Edmonton, 45.

[29] Hatfield C.F.E.P. (Deeds) 102/10; W.A.M. 184.

Thurstan,[30] whose son Picot had taken the surname Marsh from the near-by Edmonton marsh.[31] The Marshes were active in local affairs during the 13th and 14th centuries but their land became part of the Causton and Depham estates and their connexion with Edmonton seems to have ended c. 1350.[32] The Fords also apparently lost their lands to Caustons in the mid 14th century.[33] The family had held land in Edmonton at least since 1202,[34] William Ford had married a sister of the lord of the manor in 1264,[35] and two Fords were knights.[36] Wolwyn le Sune received a small estate from William de Mandeville (d. 1189)[37] which his descendants retained until Agnes, daughter of Roger Sune, conveyed it to Roger de Depham in 1316.[38] Other local 13th- and early-14th-century families which in almost all cases lost their lands to William Causton and Roger de Depham were the Anesties, Berghs, Bursers, FitzJohns, Newmans, Salmons, le Venours, and Vikers.

There were precedents for the accumulation of land by Depham, Causton, and Francis. Londoners had been acquiring property in Edmonton, for residences or as investments,[39] since the 12th century and probably earlier. The Mandevilles themselves were powerful in London. Witnesses to one of Geoffrey de Mandeville's charters of c. 1086 included Roger Blund and Ralph Heyrun (de Hairun),[40] probably ancestors of the patrician London families which had been granted knights' fees in Edmonton in the 12th century.[41] Other such families[42] with land in Edmonton were the FitzAlufs (c. 1160),[43] the Bucointes (c. 1198–c. 1223),[44] who were related by marriage to the Renger or FitzReiner family (1191–1314),[45] the FitzAilwins (1203),[46] FitzAlans (1204),[47] Bukerels (1217–71),[48] Gisorses (c. 1230–1351),[49] which included John Gisors who assumed the debt of the town of Edmonton c. 1250,[50] Poles (1291–1362),[51] Wyrhales (1303–48),[52] and le Mires (1312–30).[53] The main landowners in the 14th century were William Causton the mercer (1308–54),[54] Roger de Depham, alderman (1314–58),[55] Adam Francis the

mercer and his son, Sir Adam (c. 1328–1417),[56] Causton's apprentice, the mercer John Bernes (c. 1333–75),[57] and John Northampton the draper (1383–95).[58] By 1400 at least nine mayors of London had been involved in dealings in land in Edmonton.[59] Another feature of land tenure in medieval Edmonton, and itself a corollary of the connexion with London merchants, was the large number of estates owned by religious houses, most of them in London.[60]

Land in Edmonton continued to be held by Londoners throughout its history.[61] In the 15th and 16th centuries several royal officials acquired an interest in the parish, among them John Innocent, Henry Somer, Sir John Pecche and John Sharpe, Sir Wistan Brown, Phillip Hobby, and Thomas Wilson. The most important was William Cecil, Lord Burghley, who between 1571 and 1588 acquired nearly 2,000 a. in Edmonton as part of his estates centred on Theobalds (Cheshunt, Herts.).[62] In 1606 the largest landholder after Robert Cecil, earl of Salisbury, and the chapter of St. Paul's was Sir Jasper Leake, with 650 a. There were no other very big landowners. Estates of 100–200 a. were owned by Richard Rogers, comptroller of the mint, Sir Henry Roe, alderman of London, Edward Nowell, father and son, Robert Estry, and Sir John Brett.[63]

At inclosure in 1804 half the land was owned by 11 proprietors and half by 287 people, mostly in parcels of less than 5 a. The largest estate (670 a.) belonged to St. Paul's. William Tash had 582 a., William Mellish had 438 a., Mary Bowles 403 a., and Sarah Huxley's devisees 383 a.[64]

Most owners regarded property in Edmonton as a source of income rather than as a country seat. The earliest deeds, of the 12th and 13th centuries, portray a very complicated tenurial structure in which rents played an important part. During the 18th century, as the woodland was cleared, gentlemen's residential estates appeared at Southgate but in 1800 and 1852 the amount of land occupied by the owners was very small.[65]

[30] Hatfield C.F.E.P. (Deeds) 109/29.
[31] Hatfield C.P. 291.1, nos. 16–17. For John a Marsh fields, see below.
[32] W.A.M. 63, 84.   [33] W.A.M. 197.
[34] C.P. 25(1)/146/2/14.
[35] Hatfield C.P. 291.1, no. 415.
[36] St. Paul's MS., Box A 27, no. 102.
[37] Hatfield C.P. 291.1, no. 826.
[38] W.A.M. 118, 134.
[39] A special feature of Edmonton's connexion with Londoners was mortgaging lands to Jews: G. A. Williams, *Medieval London from Commune to Capital*, 56; E 40/1478, /13420; *Hebrew Deeds of English Jews before 1290*, ed. M. D. Davis (Publs. of Anglo-Jewish Hist. Exhib. ii), p. 357.
[40] W.A.M. 2001.
[41] C.P. 25(1)/146/1/17; Hatfield C.P. 291.1, nos. 6–8; Williams, *Med. London*, 75, 123, 230, 264.
[42] The dates in brackets refer to the earliest and latest dated connexions with Edmonton.
[43] *St. Barts. Cart.* ed. N. J. M. Kerling, no. 1187; Williams, *Med. London*, 55.
[44] *Cur. Reg. R.* vii. 341; E 42/69; Williams, *Med. London*, 53, 73.
[45] *Clerkenwell Cart.* (Camd. 3rd ser. lxxi), p. 115; C.P. 25(1)/149/44/141; Williams, *Med. London*, 50–1, 329–30.
[46] C.P. 25(1)/146/3/31; Williams, *Med. London*, 74–5.
[47] C.P. 25(1)/146/3/36; Williams, *Med. London*, 5, 59.
[48] *Abbrev. Plac.* (Rec. Com.), 175; C.P. 25(1)/147/24/488; Williams, *Med. London*, 75, 324–5.

[49] E 40/2127; E 40/2380; *Cal. Close*, 1349–54, 363; Williams, *Med. London*, 68 sqq.
[50] E 368/25 m. 15d.
[51] St. Paul's MS., Box A 27, no. 118; B.M. Add. Ch. 40518–19.
[52] C.P. 25(1)/148/37/300; *Cal. of Wills in Ct. of Husting, London*, i. 561–2.
[53] C.P. 25(1)/149/43/101b; C.P. 25(1)/150/54/32; Williams, *Med. London*, 59.
[54] See p. 155.
[55] See p. 150.
[56] E 164/18 ff. 12 sqq.; *Cal. Inq. p.m.* (Rec. Com.), iv. 32.
[57] Hist. MSS. Com. 8, *9th Rep.*, St. Paul's, i, p. 31; *Cal. Close*, 1374–7, 259.
[58] *Cal. Close*, 1381–5, 389; St. Paul's MS., Box A 27, no. 174.
[59] Hen. FitzAilwin (1189–1212), Roger FitzAlan (1212), And. Bukerel (1231–7), John Gisors (1245–6, 1250, 1259), John Gisors (1311, 1314), Adam Francis (1352–3), John Bernes (1370–1), Wm. Walworth (1374), Nich. Brembre (1377, 1383–5).
[60] See pp. 154–5.
[61] See section on manors and other estates, *passim*.
[62] Hatfield C.P.M. Suppl. 27; Hatfield C.P. 291.1, ff. 119 sqq.; M.R.O., Acc. 695/42. For details see estates section.
[63] M.R.O., Acc. 695/42.
[64] Robinson, *Edmonton*, map and Apps. I & II.
[65] M.R.O., Acc. 695/62; Val. for poor rates (1852) *penes* Edmonton Publ. Libr.

For most of its history farming in Edmonton was mixed. Alluvium along the river Lea produced meadow land which was often waterlogged and supplied only hay or pasture. The London Clay in the west was wooded until the 17th and 18th centuries, providing mast for pigs and some pasture for cattle. Most of the valley brickearth and gravel in the centre supported arable farming.

Wheat, oats, rye, barley, maslin, peas, and beans were grown. In 1345, for example, John le Venour had 10 qr. of wheat, 10 qr. of rye, 20 a. sown with maslin, and 26 a. sown with oats.[66] In 1699 the court leet made regulations that gates or fences around common fields were to be made up by Michaelmas where wheat or rye were to be sown or by Lady Day where oats, peas, or barley were to be sown.[67] In the Middle Ages a three-course rotation was probably followed[68] but by the late 18th century the course was more complicated and fallowing was giving way to vegetable crops. The rotation in 1794 was potatoes, wheat, turnips on the wheat stubble, oats, tares, peas or beans, and wheat.[69]

In 1086 there was as much meadow as arable land, as well as pasture for cattle and woodland for 2,000 pigs.[70] Both oxen and horses were used for haulage until the 17th century.[71] John le Venour in 1345 had only 4 oxen, 2 draught animals (*affr'*), and a cow[72] but at Dephams in 1552 there were at least 25 bullocks, oxen, horses, pigs, geese, and chickens.[73] John Rockhill, in addition to a mixture of grain, had horses, cattle, and sheep in 1585.[74]

During the Middle Ages sheep were kept only by the wealthier farmers. There were sheep-houses on the estate of William Ford *c.* 1300[75] and at Sayesbury farm in 1478[76] and in 1340 the ninth was paid on wool and lambs by John Marsh, John le Venour, John Castle, William Viker, Edmund Pymme, and Thomas Anesty, all local men of substance.[77] Such men in the 14th and 15th centuries were responsible for inclosing and taking into severalty common-field land and converting much of it into pasture.[78] Cattle and sheep, presumably raised for the London market, were important in the 16th and early 17th centuries, when there were several cases of sheep-stealing.[79] Much livestock was driven through Edmonton to London. Between 1607 and 1617 11 drovers, 6 kidders, and a badger who dealt in wool, were licensed in Edmonton[80] and most of the 31 people granted licences in 1658 came from there.[81]

In 1368 John Manning, a fisherman from Chingford, granted John Berners of London a fishing weir at Neylond on the river Lea and all its attendant fishing rights.[82] In 1605 a meadow called le Neys belonged to Sir Robert Lee but free fishing in the river over the 1½ mile northward from the Tottenham boundary then belonged to the chapter of St. Paul's. The next ¼ mile was claimed by one Brothby.[83] In 1650 all fishing and fowling in the parish was said to belong jointly to the lord and tenants.[84] Fines were, however, imposed *c.* 1641 for fishing in the common sewer.[85]

Woodland in western Edmonton gave way to meadow land or pasture and livestock was kept on many estates in Southgate, partly perhaps for aesthetic reasons.[86] Welsh sheep and dairy cows, for example, grazed on the Minchenden estate in the 18th century.[87] In 1804, out of a total of 6,638 a., 4,571 a. (69 per cent) were under grass, compared with 1,903 a. (28 per cent) of arable land; there were 164 a. of woodland.[88]

Bad farming, recorded at Sayesbury in 1359[89] and on Bowes manor *c.* 1667,[90] was more general by the end of the 18th century. Agricultural writers were particularly scathing about the failure to grub up bushes and drain Edmonton's portion of Enfield Chase, which had been allotted in 1777[91] and where cattle lacked both shade and pasture. The common meadows of Edmonton marsh, too, were neglected. Divided into small strips of 5 a. or less,[92] their soil was chilled and their hay yield low. In both cases the recommended remedy was inclosure.[93]

Edmonton Inclosure Act was passed in 1800[94] and the award published in 1804.[95] Approximately 1,097 a. of open-field land, 413 a. of common marsh, 1,200 a. of Enfield Chase, and 29 a. of common waste in the form of small greens were inclosed. Old inclosures included 806 a. of arable, mostly in the central area near the common fields, 2,193 a. of meadow, and 765 a. of pasture which was scattered throughout the parish but mainly in the west and south-east.

There were 27 farms by the mid 19th century. In 1851 the largest were Huxley (350 a.), Broomfield (340 a.), Bury (300 a.), Nightingale (300 a.), and Cuckoo Hall (220 a.), all long-established farms. The greatest change since inclosure had been in the north-west, where six farms had been created on former Chase land: Model or Camelot, Eastpole, Westpole, Bohun, Oakhill, and Chase. Bush Hill Park Farm was built on former open-field land. Eaton Farm near Palmers Green, Dysons near the

[66] W.A.M. 305; cf. crops listed in will of John Rockhill in 1585: Prob. 11/69 (P.C.C. 3 Windsor).
[67] M.R.O., Acc. 695/42.
[68] e.g. C 135/144/7.
[69] Foot, *Agric. of Mdx.* 21–2; Middleton, *View*, 149.
[70] *V.C.H. Mdx.* i. 126.
[71] e.g. oxen at Claverings in 1620: C 2/Jas. I/N 7/60.
[72] W.A.M. 305.
[73] Prob. 11/35 (P.C.C. F 34 Powell, will of John Richardson *alias* Rowe).
[74] Prob. 11/69 (P.C.C. 3 Windsor).
[75] E 164/18 ff. 12 sqq.
[76] Hatfield C.F.E.P. (Deeds) 40/3.
[77] *Inq. Non.* (Rec. Com.), 197.
[78] See p. 167.
[79] *Mdx. Cnty. Recs.* i. 24–5; M.R.O., Cal. Mdx. Sess. Recs. 1608–9, 160; 1609–10, 18, 62; 1612 (2) 56; *Mdx. Sess. Recs.* N.S. iv. 74.
[80] M.R.O., Cal. Mdx. Sess. Recs. 1607–8, 83, 239; 1608–9, 132; 1609–10, 75–6; 1610 (1) 54; 1611 (2) 125; 1612 (1) 105, 221; 1612 (2) 172; *Mdx. Sess. Recs.* N.S. iv. 98.

[81] M.R.O., Cal. Mdx. Sess. Bks. 1657–64, 72.
[82] St. Paul's MS., Box A 34, no. 880.
[83] M.R.O., Acc. 695/42, f. 72.
[84] M.R.O., Acc. 695/15.
[85] S.C. 6/Chas. I/627 m. 4.
[86] See illus. of Weir Hall and Arnos Grove in Brewer, *Beauties of Eng. and Wales*, x(5), facing pp. 707, 709.
[87] M.R.O., Acc. 262/67/97; /56/2.
[88] Based upon an analysis of the inclosure map and award: Robinson, *Edmonton*, Apps. I & II.
[89] C 135/144/7. See above.
[90] St. Paul's MS., Box A 57, no. 5.
[91] See p. 168.
[92] Cf. John T. Smith's description of the floods in the late 18th century: *A Book for a Rainy Day*, ed. W. Whitten, 138.
[93] Foot, *Agric. of Mdx.* 38–55, 69–70; Middleton, *View*, 123, 219–20, 523.
[94] 39 & 40 Geo. III, c. 79 (Local and Personal).
[95] Both Act, award, and map (1801) are printed in Robinson, *Edmonton*, 207–331.

Tottenham border, and Betstyle in New Southgate, were all erected on old inclosed land. Despite the many farms, there was considerable unemployment. Twenty-one farmers employed 188 men, although there were as many as 541 farm-workers.[96]

In 1867[97] out of 5,885 a. of farm-land, 3,881 a. (66 per cent) were under grass, cereals were grown on 1,039 a. (18 per cent), fodder crops in 518 a. (8 per cent), vegetables on 392 a. (6 per cent), and the rest was fallow. There were 415 dairy cows, 196 other cattle, 882 sheep, and 959 pigs. Although farm-land contracted[98] with the spread of building, the percentage of it covered by grass and the proportionate number of animals remained much the same until well into the 20th century. In 1957 only 42 per cent of farm-land was under grass, by which time only pigs and fowls, which required little acreage, were reared in any number. Dairy cattle remained important, especially in Southgate, and dairy farms were a feature of Bush Hill Park and Winchmore Hill until the 1920s and 1930s.[99] In 1897 and 1917 there were roughly as many horses, 463 and 383, as there were cattle. Sheep dwindled to 188 by 1897, increased to 317 by 1917, and had disappeared by 1957.

Cereal crops continued to decline, covering only 261 a. (6 per cent of the farmland) by 1897. Fodder crops and vegetables became correspondingly more important, covering 518 a. (12 per cent) and 847 a. (20 per cent) respectively in 1897.

The acreage under vegetables was nonetheless important because it represented market-gardening and nurseries. About 1898 an acre of nursery land was let at £10 a year compared with £3 for farm-land.[1] According to a local tradition Edmonton had supplied London with vegetables during the Great Plague and in consequence had been given free standing in Covent Garden Market.[2] Fruit and vegetables were grown in the mid 18th century, although mainly in the gardens and conservatories of the wealthy in Southgate. A wide variety, including melons, was grown at Minchenden in 1740,[3] there was a melon ground at Bury Farm House in 1786,[4] and Culland's Grove had a 'grapery' at the end of the 18th century[5] and 24 orange and lemon trees in 1832.[6] Tobacco and sulphur were purchased in 1792 at Minchenden for the 'hot walls', probably the forerunners of the hot houses mentioned in 1811.[7] In 1816 there were hot houses at Arnos Grove and Culland's Grove and a conservatory at Southgate Grove.[8] Potatoes and

turnips were replacing fallowing in the rotation of crops and c. 1841 potatoes and vegetables were a feature of Edmonton.[9]

Market-gardening and particularly nurseries under glass began when head gardeners from the big houses exploited the London market. The soil, especially the brickearth, was good and the Lea provided easy transport for manure and for the coal to heat the glass houses.[10] As the traditional market-gardening areas of East London were built up, growers moved northward along the Lea valley,[11] until by c. 1800 nurseries were a feature of Tottenham.[12] In 1851 there were at least five nurseries in Edmonton, mostly in the southern part. Market-gardening was carried on at Cuckoo Hall farm in north-east Edmonton, where 23 persons were employed, at Marsh Side in eastern Edmonton and at Winchmore Hill.[13]

Seven of the horticultural firms of 1851 still existed in 1878. Cuckoo Hall farm had been taken over by Enfield as a sewage farm in 1877[14] and some of the nurseries in old Edmonton moved to the north and west. A new feature was the concentration of florists in Dyson's Road.[15] Most nurserymen specialized in cheap plants, tomatoes, and cucumbers for the new working-class suburbs. In 1894 Edmonton was among the 10 leading horticultural parishes in Middlesex,[16] there were 100 a. under glass in 1898 compared with 10 a. in 1870,[17] and the numbers of florists, nurserymen, and market-gardeners reached 66 in 1890 and 73 in 1908.[18] Long established firms included those of the Adams and Jifkins families from before 1851 until 1937, the Cuthberts of Southgate High Street from 1851 until 1926, the Hayes family from 1851 until 1908, and the Hills and Kings from 1890 until 1937.[19] The most important was that of Henry May, who arrived as a florist in 1870 and who by 1898 owned three nurseries employing 200 people. May grew a great variety of forced plants for Covent Garden, provincial markets, and export.[20] Still in Edmonton in 1908, he had left by 1926.[21]

As horticulture reached its height, it was menaced by encroaching building and by fogs.[22] The numbers of those employed dropped to 38 by 1926[23] and 25 by 1947,[24] as both nurseries and farms gave way to housing. The last farms were those in the north-west and after Oak Hill College farm, where dairy cattle and chickens had been kept, closed in 1973[25] only stables on the site of Eastpole farm were left.

[96] H.O. 107/1703; O.S. Map 6″, Mdx. VII (1865 edn.).

[97] Unless otherwise stated, the following two paras. are based upon M.A.F. 68/136; M.A.F. 68/1675; M.A.F. 68/2815; M.A.F. 68/4576.

[98] To 4,226 a. in 1897, 3,277 a. in 1917, and 182 a. in 1957.

[99] Regnart, Winchmore Hill, 8, 46, 53, 84; Sturges, Edmonton Past and Present, ii. 15.

[1] W. E. Bear, 'Flower and Fruit Farming in Eng.' Jnl. Royal Agric. Soc. ser. 3, ix. 525.

[2] Cresswell, Winchmore Hill, 40.

[3] M.R.O., Acc. 262/67/120–3.   [4] M.R.O., Acc. 829.

[5] John T. Smith, A Book for a Rainy Day, ed. W. Whitten, 139.

[6] Newby, Old Southgate, 20.

[7] M.R.O., Acc. 262/56/2, /16.

[8] Brewer, Beauties of Eng. and Wales, x(5), 711–12.

[9] S. Tymms, Compendium of Mdx. 16.

[10] E. C. Williatts, Mdx. and London Region, 222; M.R.O., Acc. 815/20; sales parts. of Snell estate (1848) penes St. James's church.

[11] L. G. Bennett, Horticultural Ind. of Mdx. 11.

[12] T. Milne, Plan of . . . London and Westminster, circumjacent towns and pars. (1800) [B.M. King's Topog. Coll. vi. 95].

[13] In 1851 14 people were described as market-gardeners and 8 as nurserymen but there may have been others among the 176 described as gardeners: H.O. 107/1703.

[14] See p. 243.

[15] Kelly's Dir. Mdx. (1878).

[16] Bennett, Horticultural Ind. of Mdx. 11, 20.

[17] Jnl. Royal Agric. Soc. ser. 3, ix. 525.

[18] Kelly's Dirs. Mdx. (1890, 1908).

[19] Ibid. (1878, 1890, 1908, 1926, 1937); H.O. 107/1703.

[20] Jnl. Royal Agric. Soc. ser. 3, ix. 523.

[21] Kelly's Dirs. Mdx. (1908, 1926).

[22] Jnl. Royal Agric. Soc. ser. 3, ix. 525–6; Williatts, Mdx. and London Region, 221–2.

[23] Kelly's Dir. Mdx. (1926).

[24] Bennett, Horticultural Ind. of Mdx. 38.

[25] Ex inf. Oak Hill College (1973).

COMMON FIELDS AND PASTURE. In reply to the parliamentary enquiry of 1650 the jurors of Edmonton listed 17 common fields;[26] 23 were recorded in the late 16th century[27] and 14 in 1801.[28] It has therefore generally been concluded[29] that Edmonton never had a classic two- or three-field system but was characterized by irregular fields. This view, based upon late evidence, takes no account of early modifications to Edmonton's economy, particularly by London merchants.

The largest common fields were also among the earliest[30] and imply a two- or three-field system. West of Fore Street lay Langhedge (c. 1166 × 1189),[31] which had 149 a. in 1804,[32] and the Hyde or Hyde field (c. 1166 × 1189),[33] a large field of 290 a. in 1750[34] and 272 a. in 1804. Its southern boundary was a stream, probably Bridgewater,[35] which divided it from Oak field (the 13th-century Hok field),[36] which had 79 a. in 1804. Oak field may be identifiable with Legha (1222 × 1250),[37] a field last mentioned in 1328.[38] The Hyde and Langhedge and probably Oak field seem to have formed a two- or three-field system for the community in Upper Edmonton, along Fore Street and Silver Street.

Another system in the north was used mainly and perhaps at first exclusively by the manorial demesne. It consisted of Bury field (1154 × 1166),[39] 112 a. in 1804, and Hounds or Ounce field (1478),[40] 236 a. in 1478[41] and 179 a. in 1804. Pury or Pery field (1252 × 1257),[42] where the Sayesbury demesne had 210 a. in 1478,[43] was another name for Bury field.[44] A third large field which probably formed part of this system lay south of Bury Street. It was later divided into three:[45] Storksnest field (c. 1260),[46] 23 a. in 1804, Church field (1280),[47] 50 a. in 1804, and Ashcroft (1478), which contained 29 a. in 1478[48] and was included in Church field and Storksnest field in 1804. Peacocks field (1495),[49] south of Church field, may have been an assart but was probably a division of Church field.

Common arable land appears to have covered most of the area east of Fore Street and Hertford Road and west of Edmonton marsh. East field (13th century)[50] originally covered much of north-east Edmonton although by 1605 it had shrunk to a close of 23 a., East or Brick field between Enfield and Sayes marsh.[51] There was also a West field (13th century)[52] but it was pasture by 1329[53] and its position is unknown. North and South fields (early 13th century)[54] seem to have lain south of East field adjoining the marsh and Amberlands.[55] These early common fields may have served the hamlet at Lower Edmonton.

Continuous assarting modified the simple two- or three-field system from an early date. Philip Godard had assarts in 1166 × 1189[56] and a piece of land assarted next to Enfield park was mentioned c. 1222 × 1250.[57] Land had been 'newly assarted' in High field in western Edmonton in 1566.[58] All the common fields in the west, serving Winchmore Hill and Fords Green, were small and apparently assarts. Hag field (in 1227 Heg field),[59] on the edge of Enfield Chase at Winchmore Hill, had 25 a. in 1804; Pickestones or Picketstones (1592)[60] to the south had 9 a. in 1605[61] but was completely inclosed by 1804.

A group of fields suggests the extension of cultivated land from Hyde field into the wooded land to the west. Dead field (13th century)[62] had 29 a. in 1804 which included Apslands (late 16th century),[63] called Dedesapelton in 1338.[64] Tile-barrow or Tilberyowe field, probably Tingelborh (late 12th century)[65] and Tithelberch (1252-7),[66] contained at least 10 a. in 1605.[67] Pond field (1321)[68] had at least 7½ a. in 1605.[69]

There were other fields east of Green Lanes, between Fords and Palmers greens: Holly or Hollis field (1605),[70] with at least 6 a. in 1605,[71] High field (1566),[72] 23 a. in 1804, and Scots field (1576),[73] 22 a. in 1804. Party or Partens field (1597)[74] at Winchmore Hill may have been another assart. Assarted fields farther south included Crabtree field (1605)[75] near Broomfield House and probably many at Bowes.

[26] M.R.O., Acc. 695/15.
[27] Hatfield C.P.M. Suppl. 27; Hatfield C.P. 291.1, ff. 119 sqq.
[28] Robinson, *Edmonton*, App. II.
[29] D. Avery, *Irregular Common Fields of Edmonton* (Edmonton Hund. Hist. Soc., c. 1965); H. L. Gray, *Eng. Field Systems* (1959 edn.), 381-2.
[30] The first recorded date is given in brackets. The location of the fields is based upon the late-16th-cent. Cecil map: Hatfield C.P.M. Suppl. 27.
[31] Hatfield C.P. 291.1, no. 826.
[32] All the acreages for 1804 are based upon the inclosure map and award: Robinson, *Edmonton*, App. II.
[33] Hatfield C.P. 291.1, no. 826.
[34] Robinson, *Edmonton*, map facing p. 5.
[35] See p. 131.
[36] Hatfield C.P. 291.1, no. 211.   [37] E 40/2127.
[38] E 164/18 ff. 12 sqq.
[39] As Berfeldie: Hatfield C.P. 291.1, no. 6.
[40] Hatfield C.F.E.P. (Deeds) 40/3. But Colwell, a parcel of Hounds field, was in existence in the early 13th cent. and Hounds field probably existed earlier under another name: W.A.M. 292; D.L. 1/19/E 1.
[41] Hatfield C.F.E.P. (Deeds) 40/3.
[42] E 40/1705.
[43] Hatfield C.F.E.P. (Deeds) 40/3.
[44] Hatfield C.P.M. Suppl. 27.
[45] The three fields were constantly confused even in their later history, e.g. M.R.O., Acc. 727/218.
[46] B.M. Harl. MS. 3697, f. 182.
[47] W.A.M. 37. Church field originally stretched to Hertford Rd. and Bury St.
[48] Hatfield C.F.E.P. (Deeds) 40/3.

[49] Prob. 11/10 (P.C.C. 30 Vox, will of Thos. Williams).
[50] E 40/2038; Hatfield C.P. 291.1, no. 73.
[51] M.R.O., Acc. 695/42, f. 41; Acc. 695/62.
[52] Hatfield C.P. 291.1, no. 123.
[53] Ibid. no. 1019.
[54] St. Paul's MSS., Box A 26, nos. 93-7.
[55] For Amberlands see Hatfield C.P.M. Suppl. 27.
[56] E 40/2199.
[57] E 40/2317.
[58] E 309/Box 2/8 Eliz./15 no. 1.
[59] E 40/2114.
[60] M.R.O., Acc. 689/1.
[61] M.R.O., Acc. 695/42, ff. 47, 52.
[62] Hatfield C.P. 291.1, no. 50.
[63] Hatfield C.P.M. Suppl. 27 where it is marked as a separate field.
[64] Hatfield C.P. 291.1, no. 698.
[65] E 40/1969.
[66] E 40/1705.
[67] M.R.O., Acc. 695/42, ff. 12, 39; Hatfield C.P. 291.1, ff. 119 sqq.
[68] Hatfield C.P. 291.1, no. 584.
[69] Avery, *Edmonton Common Fields*, 15. The 1605 survey upon which Avery's figures are based, is not, however, comprehensive. It omits all demesne land and all land not held from Edmonton manor.
[70] M.R.O., Acc. 695/42, f. 65.
[71] Avery, *Edmonton Common Fields*, 15.
[72] E 309/Box 2/8 Eliz./15 no. 1.
[73] Hatfield C.F.E.P. (Deeds) 146/13. There was a Scots-grove or croft in the 13th cent. (W.A.M. 5; E 40/2038).
[74] Prob. 11/104 (P.C.C. 66 Harte, will of Hen. Cade).
[75] M.R.O., Acc. 695/42, f. 52.

Broom field by Bury Street was listed in 1650[76] as a common field. While it may have originated as an assart or as an inclosure from Bury field, when first mentioned in 1523 it was as Broom closes (64 a.), wholly inclosed demesne land,[77] and it did not figure in the controversy over common-field rights in the late 15th and early 16th centuries.

There was probably assarting in the east, where it is difficult to distinguish between assarts and the divisions of an older common field. Nokholt or Nuccolds (13th cent.)[78] and Strode (1154 × 1166)[79] or Shrove field (c. 1515 × 1530)[80] alias Cuckoo Hall field (1605)[81] in the north are examples. Many fields were named after landowners of the 13th and 14th centuries, who probably accumulated strips by purchase and exchange[82] and then took their blocks into severalty, obliterating all the original common fields by the late 16th century.[83] The process probably started in the early 13th century when Geoffrey de Querenden[84] made grants in North field, South field, and Querenden Colwell to Ralph Bergh (Berewe or Burgh).[85] Bergh's re-arrangements may have given rise to Barrow field (1222 × 1263 Bergh field),[86] which contained 22 a. in 1804. The 13th-century le Sune family created Sounes field,[87] and John le Venour's Home field (1347)[88] had by c. 1493 become Venaris field.[89] Pentridges in 1483 was a farm and close[90] but was recorded as a common field in the late 16th century.[91] It was probably Causiware or Castleware field (1650),[92] 53 a. in 1804, and perhaps named after the Castle family of the 13th and 14th centuries.[93] Similarly Mays field, although not recorded before 1773,[94] may have taken its name from the 13th-century May family;[95] it contained 50 a. in 1804. Other names were derived from the Dephams, Gisorses, and Claverings, who were all active in the 14th century.[96]

Similar activity farther south, probably east of Montagu Road, created the early-14th-century John a Marsh field, which, with the adjoining Down field, covered about 50 a. in 1605.[97] In 1204[98] there were Dores, Chanterele, Palmers, Wulves, and Wenmares fields, and Great Rudings, none of them identifiable but all probably assarts. Two more, Stony field and the 'great field from William son of Fubert's house to the highway', which became Fuberts field (early 13th century),[99] lay between Fore Street and Montagu Road. They were conveyed in 1319 by the sons of John Marsh to William Causton.[1] Other probable assarts near by

were Squattokes field (1332)[2] and Rush field (1154 × 1166)[3] and Pratts or Spratts field alias Hungerdown (c. 1493),[4] whose name suggests its origin in poor, presumably marshy land.[5] It was during the 14th century, with the creation of Dephams, Plesingtons, Caustons, and Claverings, that eastern Edmonton was transformed.

Many fields were probably never fully common in the sense that several owners held strips in them. Common of pasture, the unstinted right to graze animals on the stubble after harvest, was claimed in many fields, which may have originated as assarts always held in severalty by one individual. Inclosure of both types of fields,[6] however, provoked opposition, from those dispossessed of arable or of herbage. Between 1413 and 1417 about 120 armed people broke down the 'pastures, closes, and severalties' on Willoughby manor to turn them into common.[7] The countess of Hereford (d. 1419) intervened against Henry Somer, who had inclosed Polehouse croft out of Hyde field, and the inclosure of John a Marsh fields by Lord Cromwell, lord of Dephams, led to a meeting in 1438 of the owners and lessees of all the important estates, who forced him to restore common rights. A second attempt to inclose John a Marsh field was made in 1475 by Richard Charlton, then lord of Dephams. Like all the fields in north and east Edmonton, John a Marsh field was intercommonable with Enfield. Tenants from Enfield led the opposition and after obtaining the advice of royal and duchy officials, between 200 and 300 commoners from Enfield, Edmonton, Hadley, and South Mimms broke up the hedges and ditches. Sir Richard later inclosed the field again and in 1486 the combined estates of Edmonton manor, Dephams, Plesingtons, Caustons, and Claverings passed to Sir Thomas Bourchier, who appointed as bailiff Nicholas Bone (d. 1523), the chief figure in the early inclosure movement.[8] Between 1486 and 1515 200 a. were inclosed by Bone and 100 a. by others, including St. Paul's, Holy Trinity, Haliwell, and Sir John Risley, lord of Tottenham. In Church field, Bone inclosed about 30 a. from the eastern and southern parts c. 1493[9] and 15 a. from the north c. 1495[10] and Robert Manser of Pymmes and James Bake created closes. Bone also inclosed 4 a. from Barrow field and leased other land on condition that the lessee kept the fields several and hedged them. Thus John a Marsh field and Downfield (30 a.), 24 a. in Hounds field, and 47 a. in East field were

[76] The suffix 'by Bury St.' makes it unlikely that they were alluding to the fields marked 'Bromfeld' next to Pickestones at Winchmore Hill, marked on the 16th-cent. map (Hatfield C.P.M. Suppl. 27). These were probably inclosed fields owned by John Broomfield.

[77] E 326/6076.

[78] St. Paul's MS., Box A 31, no. 532.

[79] Hatfield C.P. 291.1, no. 6.   [80] D.L. 1/1/E 5.

[81] M.R.O., Acc. 695/42, f. 24; Acc. 727/83.

[82] e.g. of exchanges, though not in this area: E 40/2209; E 40/2299.

[83] Hatfield C.P.M. Suppl. 27.

[84] See Hounds field, above.

[85] St. Paul's MS., Box A 26, nos. 93–101.

[86] Hatfield C.P. 291.1, no. 22.

[87] W.A.M. 292.

[88] W.A.M. 303.

[89] D.L. 1/1/E 5; cf. 'the field of Wm. le Venour' in 1308: W.A.M. 73.

[90] Hatfield C.F.E.P. (Deeds) 10/8.

[91] Hatfield C.P.M. Suppl. 27.

[92] M.R.O., Acc. 695/42.   [93] W.A.M. 73.

[94] B.M. Add. MS. 38477, ff. 48–56.

[95] e.g. 1235: E 40/1729; 1255: E 40/2293; 1274: J.I. 1/539 m. 7.

[96] Pam, Fight for Common Rights, 11. See above, pp. 150–1, 157.

[97] Though then inclosed and pasture: M.R.O., Acc. 695/42, f. 27.

[98] C.P. 25(1)/146/3/36.

[99] Hatfield C.P. 291.1, nos. 16, 30.

[1] Hatfield C.F.E.P. (Deeds) 57/18.

[2] W.A.M. 286. Between Montagu Rd. and Angel Rd.: Robinson, Edmonton, 314.

[3] Hatfield C.P. 291.1, no. 6.

[4] D.L. 1/1/E 5.

[5] West of Montagu Rd., probably between two streams.

[6] Unless otherwise stated, this section is based upon Pam, Fight for Common Rights.

[7] Sel. Cases in Chancery (Selden Soc. x), 112–13.

[8] For Bone, see above.

[9] i.e. Drabbs croft, Pypers, Peacocks field, and Fullers croft: Hatfield C.P.M. Suppl. 27.

[10] i.e. Calcotts.

inclosed. Between 1515 and 1530 Bone and his successor John Grimston inclosed another 100 a., mainly in the north and including Strode, Nokholt, Venaris, Dephams, Gisors, Pond, and part of Pury fields. By 1517 other inclosures included 54 a. by John Leake, of which 14 a. was in Langhedge, the whole of Pratt field, and Bows field.[11]

Since Bone intimidated the inhabitants of Edmonton, it was the Enfield tenants who appealed to Sir Reynold Bray, Chancellor of the duchy of Lancaster, in 1493 and won a case in the duchy court after 1523, when Grimston had impounded Enfield animals grazing in Pury field. The rights of Edmonton tenants to common of pasture in Enfield fields were upheld by the same decision but the people of Enfield were probably more dependent on cattle or had less pasture of their own and were therefore resented in Edmonton. The process was not halted but most of the inclosures of Bone and his associates remained in severalty, many were converted to pasture, and the cattle of both Enfield and Edmonton inhabitants were successfully excluded from pasture on the stubble. On the fields which remained fully common, pasture rights were restricted in 1699 to householders or those paying the poor rate in Edmonton.[12]

Possibly because the manor passed to the Crown in the 1530s, there was little further inclosure. Party field was apparently inclosed by 1597[13] and Tilebarrow, Holly field, Pickestones, and Crabtree field before 1804. In 1804 1,097 a. of open fields were inclosed, mostly west of Fore Street and Hertford Road. The Hyde (280 a.), Hounds field (179 a.), Langhedge (153 a.), and Bury field (112 a.) were the largest.[14]

The marshes on the alluvium by the Lea consisted of about 400 a.[15] which, like the common fields, were divided into many small strips and open for common pasture from Lammas to Lady Day.[16] The neighbouring parishes in Middlesex and Essex had a similar system and in the Middle Ages they shared rights of common in the marshes as they did in some of the common fields. Sir Adam Francis inclosed North or Sayes marsh at the beginning of the 15th century, denying common pasture rights to the inhabitants of Enfield. Although the countess of Hereford supported the Enfield tenants, they were still trying, presumably unsuccessfully, to regain their rights against the opposition of the inhabitants of Edmonton in 1561–2.[17] Thereafter Edmonton marshes were common only to parishioners. There was no stint but all animals had to be marked with the parish brand.[18] Numerous regulations about the opening and closing of the marshes, driving animals or carts, cutting grass, clearing ditches, or keeping mangy animals were enforced by haywards, chosen from eight heriot-paying holdings called hemstalls or haywards.[19]

The inhabitants of Edmonton, as of neighbouring parishes, had unstinted rights of common in Enfield Chase.[20] In 1272 the lord of Edmonton had timber and herbage rights in Enfield park worth £1 a year[21] but William de Say surrendered them in 1284[22] in return for 20 cartloads of brushwood a year from the foreign park of Enfield, presumably the Chase.[23] During the 16th and 17th centuries Edmonton joined its neighbours in defending common rights against officials of the Chase.[24] The struggle was largely between the humbler tenants and wealthy landowners who wanted pasture for their large flocks and herds uncontaminated by the inferior beasts of the poor. Under pressure from the larger landowners, an Act was passed in 1777 to inclose the Chase and Edmonton was allotted 1,231 a. to the north-west of Southgate, which was administered by salaried surveyors responsible to the vestry. Their main task was to cut down the remaining trees and from 1782 until 1785 the parish obtained an average of £1,865 a year, chiefly from the sale of wood.[25] A stint was introduced whereby each householder of less than £10 a year could pasture one horned neat beast, while two horned beasts or one horse were allowed for every subsequent £10. The Chase allotment was open for pasture from 12 May until Candlemas.[26] In 1800, however, it was included with Edmonton marsh and common fields in the Edmonton Inclosure Act.[27]

Edmonton manor court appointed a driver of cattle, a hayward, a parker and, after 1733, a pound-keeper.[28] Repair of the common pound was the responsibility of the lord.[29] Courts of Bowes and Polehouse appointed a hayward from 1674 to 1693, a common driver in 1694, and a pound-keeper in 1740.[30] In 1973 a pound survived at the junction of Fox Lane and the Bourne.

MILLS. A mill rendered 10s. in 1086.[31] In the late 12th century a mill was held by William son of Fubert. In 1204 it was granted by Roger FitzAlan to John Bucointe,[32] who leased it to Gundred de Warenne before 1224,[33] and in 1275 it formed part of the Ford fee confirmed by Laurence de la Ford to Clerkenwell priory.[34] It may be identifiable with Scerewesmill, which in 1256 was near the Medesenge or Pymme's brook[35] and with the water-mill and mill-house in Nuns field which was leased by

[11] C 47/7/2/2 m. 14.
[12] M.R.O., Acc. 695/41.
[13] Prob. 11/104 (P.C.C. 66 Harte, will of Hen. Cade).
[14] Robinson, *Edmonton*, App. II and inclosure map.
[15] 395 a., of which 193 a. were held by the lord and his lessees in 16th cent.: M.R.O., F 84/8a–d. There were 413 a. at inclosure (1804): Robinson, *Edmonton*, Apps. I & II.
[16] M.R.O., Acc. 695/15, /41; B.M. Cott. MS. Nero E. vi, ff. 68–9. The dates were St. Bartholomew to Candlemas in 15th cent.: D.L. 1/1/E 5.
[17] Pam, *Fight for Common Rights*, 4; D.L. 1/1/E 5; D.L. 1/46/M 7.
[18] Foot, *Agric. of Mdx.* 69–70.
[19] M.R.O., Acc. 695/41; E 317/Mdx./16 m. 8.
[20] e.g. 13th cent. rights of Holy Trinity, Aldgate: E 40/1740, E 40/2102.
[21] C 132/42/6.

[22] See p. 149.
[23] D.L. 36/1/159.
[24] e.g. D.L. 1/121/E 5; D.L. 1/200/A 44; E 317/Mdx. 17; see p. 235.
[25] E. Hoare, *Work of Edmonton Vestry, 1739–48 and 1782–98* (Edmonton Hund. Hist. Soc., 1968), 14–15, 28–35.
[26] Sturges, *Edmonton Past and Present*, ii. 11–12.
[27] See p. 164.
[28] Edmonton ct. bks.: see below, p. 176.
[29] E 317/Mdx./16 m. 8.
[30] Bowes ct. bks.: see below, p. 176.
[31] *V.C.H. Mdx.* i. 126.
[32] C.P. 25(1)/146/3/36.
[33] *Clerkenwell Cart.* (Camd. 3rd ser. lxxi), pp. 107–8.
[34] C.P. 25(1)/148/26/31.
[35] E 40/2378.

Nicholas Roldsby to William Calton, tanner of Edmonton, in 1577.[36]

Sadler's mill, named after its late-16th-century tenant Roger Sadler, was a copyhold water-mill south of Bury Street held by Lord Burghley in 1591.[37] It was sold to Edward Nowell in 1613[38] and survived as a place-name long after the mill had fallen into disuse.[39]

In 1605 a second water-mill, possibly the medieval one, belonged to Jasper Leake's freehold estate of Weir Hall. It was set among ponds and osiers near the mansion[40] and remained part of Weir Hall until the early 19th century[41] but had disappeared by 1851.[42]

A windmill belonged to Edmonton manor in 1272[43] and 1295[44] and in 1359 was worth nothing as it lacked a grinding stone.[45] A windmill erected on the Weir Hall estate between 1605 and 1627[46] stood in 1801 near the water-mill.[47] A new windmill was erected north of Silver Street, on the site of the later Windmill Road, before 1819[48] and was sometimes called Parfrey's mill after the miller in 1851.[49] It was a wooden post-mill with a round house used for grinding corn, to which a brick tower was later added for steam power. The mill was auctioned with the rest of the Huxley estate in 1887[50] and was derelict in the early 20th century; the last remnants were demolished in 1965.[51]

MARKETS AND FAIRS. About 1680, in response to a request by the local inhabitants, the high constable of Edmonton hundred proclaimed the first Edmonton statute fair on 14 September at the gateway of the George and Vulture near the corner of Marsh Lane. The fair was held for three days each year, at various public houses until c. 1730 and thereafter at the Bell.[52] By 1805 there were three sites: the Statute field (commemorated in Fairfield Road), the Bell, and the Angel, where a pie-powder court was held. It was originally a fair for the hiring of servants and was stated in 1813 to be the only one near London[53] but by 1819 it was 'only a holiday fair'.[54] Its heyday was in the late 18th and early 19th centuries, when it attracted crowds from London, many of whom were already excited after St. Bartholomew's fair, which immediately preceded it. Hackney carriages brought people from Shoreditch and in 1788, when John Nixon depicted the fair,[55] there were 25,000 people and 150 hackney coaches.[56] By 1816 it drew 30,000 people 'chiefly of the lower ranks',[57] causing offence to the middle class,[58] and it was suppressed in 1823.[59]

Two Beggar's Bush fairs, to be held on Ascension Day and the feast of St. Giles, were founded at Southgate in 1614, when the site formed part of Enfield Chase.[60] They were very thinly attended in 1816[61] but continued to be held until 1912 in a field near the Crown off Chase Side.[62] An open market was established at four sites in Southgate in 1919.[63]

TRADE AND INDUSTRY. Although agriculture long remained important, Edmonton was never wholly dependent upon it. Of a total population in 1801 of 5,093, 557 people were employed in trade, manufacture, and handicraft, compared with 412 in agriculture. In 1811, however, about 37 per cent of the population were in the former category, while 39 per cent depended on agriculture. South Street ward was the most rural with 46 per cent dependent on agriculture and Church Street and Fore Street wards were the most urban, with 50 per cent and 46 per cent respectively dependent upon trade and industry.[64] In 1851, of 9,708 persons, 642 worked in agriculture, 416 in trade and commerce, and 672 in craft and industry. As many as 691 were household servants.[65]

Brickearth and timber, together with Edmonton's proximity to London and a navigable waterway gave rise to early industry. The Romans had a brick- and tile-making works in Church fields.[66] Houses were built of brick, probably made locally, by the 16th century[67] and Tile Kiln Lane, recorded in 1597,[68] probably preserves the memory of an early works. A bricklayer was mentioned in 1613[69] and a brickmaker in 1704.[70] The churchwarden who encased the church in brick in 1772 was a bricklayer[71] and in 1851 there were two brick-makers, 46 bricklayers, and 5 builders.[72] In the late 19th century there were brick-fields at Bull Lane, Hedge Lane, Bury Street, Hertford Road, and Bush Hill Park. The Acton Brick Co. and Plowman's Brick Co. had works in Bridport Road and Houndsfield Road, Samuel South was in Bury Street and Snells Park, and W. D. Cornish, the most important brick-making firm, had its main works at Bush Hill Park. As the price of land rose the industry declined until Cornish, the last firm, closed in 1936.[73] Gravel deposits were worked at the end of the 19th century in Hedge Lane, Church fields, Montagu Road, and Pickett's Lock. The last were still exploited in 1951.[74]

[36] Hatfield C.F.E.P. (Deeds) 61/14.
[37] Hatfield C.F.E.P. (Accts.) 5/21; Hatfield C.P. 291.1, ff. 119 sqq.; M.R.O., Acc. 695/42, f. 23.
[38] Sturges, Edmonton Past and Present, ii. 3.
[39] e.g. H.O. 107/1703 pp. 21 sqq.
[40] M.R.O., Acc. 695/42, f. 3.
[41] Robinson, Edmonton, 282.
[42] H.O. 107/1703 pp. 56 sqq.
[43] C 132/42/6.
[44] C 133/71/19.
[45] C 135/144/7.
[46] M.R.O., Acc. 695/42, f. 3; C 142/435/130.
[47] Robinson, Edmonton, 282. On the inclosure map the water-mill was numbered 615, the windmill 617a, both south of Silver Street.
[48] Greenwood, Map of Mdx. (1819); poor rate valuation (1852) penes Edmonton Publ. Libr., no. 1335 on the inclosure map.
[49] H.O. 107/1703 pp. 56 sqq.
[50] M.R.O., Acc. 815/37.
[51] Mdx. Quarterly, N.S. ii. 4–6; Mdx. Pictorial and Greater London Rev. iv. 12, 24.
[52] Robinson, Edmonton, 8.
[53] Sturges, Edmonton Heritage, 72–4.
[54] Robinson, Edmonton, 8.
[55] Reproduced in Robbins, Mdx. plate 18.
[56] Gent. Mag. lviii. 832.
[57] Brewer, Beauties of Eng. and Wales, x(5), 716–17.
[58] e.g. M.R.O., Acc. 1017/1371; Robinson, Edmonton, 9.
[59] Edmonton Hund. Hist. Soc. N. & Q. ii (1970).
[60] C 66/2030/13; see map in Middleton, View, 532.
[61] Brewer, Beauties of Eng. and Wales, x(5), 716.
[62] Round, Southgate and Winchmore Hill, 37; Newby, Old Southgate, 65.
[63] The Times, 21 Aug. 1919.
[64] Census, 1801–11.
[65] H.O. 107/1703.
[66] Sturges, Edmonton Past and Present, ii. 15.
[67] e.g. see brick wall in garden at Pymmes.
[68] Hatfield C.F.E.P. (Accts.) 5/22.
[69] Mdx. Sess. Recs. i. 172.
[70] C 8/500/19.
[71] Robinson, Edmonton, 63.
[72] H.O. 107/1703.
[73] Sturges, Edmonton Past and Present, ii. 15–16; M.R.O., Acc. 815/29; Acc. 290/10–11; Kelly's Dirs. Mdx. (1890, 1908); O.S. Map 6", Mdx. VII (1897 and 1920 edns.).
[74] Sturges, Edmonton Past and Present, ii. 16; O.S. Map 1/25,000, TQ 39 (1951 edn.).

Woodland, concentrated in the west of the parish, supported hewers, cutters, peelers, sawyers, broom-makers,[75] colliers, and tanners,[76] probably from the Middle Ages. The first recorded collier died in 1547 but the heyday of charcoal-burning was the late 16th and early 17th centuries, when Lord Burghley and his son bought up and exploited large stretches of woodland, particularly in Southgate where about 40 a. of woodland every year were set aside for charcoal. At Michaelmas the hewers felled it and took it to the coal hearths,[77] where they hewed it and the colliers 'coaled' it. Edmonton was probably the nearest source to London, whither the fragile charcoal was sent in sacks.[78] Most colliers were small farmers or labourers for whom charcoal-burning was a seasonal and subsidiary occupation. After the Act of 1777 the Edmonton portion of Enfield Chase replaced the Southgate coppices for a while as a source of timber and in 1780 the vestry permitted two hearths to be erected there for charcoal-burning.[79]

William the tanner lived in Edmonton in the 13th century.[80] Tanning, a full-time occupation, flourished in the 16th and 17th centuries, when the Southgate woods provided the necessary bark. The tanners were interrelated by marriage, and sons tended to follow fathers. Tanners End near Silver Street may commemorate John Walker (d. 1590), one of the most prosperous of them. Local tanners may have had some organization, since in 1597 carriers were to take bark to 'the tanners' house'[81] and Jasper Leake's property in 1605 included 'the tanners' court'.[82] Twenty-two Edmonton tanners were recorded between c. 1562 and 1689,[83] by the end of which period the industry was in decline, probably because of the reduction in woodland. There was a tannery in Bury Street from the 17th century until 1802[84] but it had been replaced by 6 houses by 1861.[85] There was another tannery in Fore Street in 1787.[86] Tanning and charcoal-burning had died out by 1851, although there were still 12 sawyers, 3 leather-sellers, 19 cordwainers, and 49 shoemakers.[87]

Almost all Edmonton's other industries owe their existence to the London market and to the ease of transport of raw materials and finished goods. As a large village Edmonton in the early 17th century supported several brewers, tailors, and butchers, and, among more specialized craftsmen, a picture-maker and a clock-maker.[88] A weaver was mentioned in 1609[89] and a silk-weaver in 1610.[90] There was a weaver in 1772[91] and weaving probably long flourished as a cottage industry. There were 4 handloom weavers in 1851.[92] Silk-weaving, probably of stockings,[93] was carried on in mills or factories, whither workhouse children were sent in 1834.[94] William Kelsey lived and probably had his silk factory at Winchmore Hill in 1851, when at least six other people were involved in silk manufacture.[95]

The earliest factory was Aldersey's glass mill near the junction of Bury Street and Hertford Road in 1773. There was a hard soap factory at Edmonton in 1789.[96] A soap-boiler at Southgate in 1703[97] probably worked on his own. There was an un-identified factory on the eastern side of Fore Street near its junction with Angel Road in 1804.[98]

Wood and coal were cheaply transported by barge along the Lea. There was a wharf and warehouse on the Lea near Angel Road in 1804,[99] Corkers, the timber merchants, were established by 1839,[1] and there were 11 coal merchants and 10 warehousemen in 1851.[2] L. Hall (Edmonton) Ltd., timber importers and saw-millers, opened at Dorford Wharf near Angel Road in 1928 and employed some 100 people in 1973.[3]

Imported timber helped to establish both coach-building and furniture-making. Coach-building was among the features of Edmonton c. 1841[4] and involved 44 people in its various operations in 1851.[5] Eleazer Booker, whose firm existed at least from c. 1840 to 1878,[6] employed 41 men in Upper Fore Street in 1851.[7] There were coach-builders in Southgate in 1868,[8] in Southgate High Street in 1878[9] and 1908,[10] in Upper Fore Street, possibly Booker's successor, by 1893, and at New Southgate in 1908 and 1926.[11] There were 10 cabinet-makers in 1851, including one at Bury Hall who was also a plateglass-maker with 50 men.[12] A

---

[75] e.g. the witch, Eliz. Sawyer.
[76] Except where otherwise stated, information on char-coal burning and tanning is taken from T. Lewis and D. O. Pam, *Wm. and Robt. Cecil as Landowners in Edmonton and Southgate, 1561–1600* (Edmonton Hund. Hist. Soc., Occas. Paper, c. 1971), 17–23.
[77] e.g. 12 hearths for 37 a. (1593).
[78] Hatfield C.F.E.P. (Accts.) 5/22.
[79] Sturges, *Edmonton Past and Present*, ii. 12.
[80] Hatfield C.P. 291.1, no. 30.
[81] Hatfield C.F.E.P. (Accts.) 5/22.
[82] Leake's property, which centred on Weir Hall, in-cluded much in the vicinity of Tanners End: M.R.O., Acc. 695/42. f. 25.
[83] Hatfield C.F.E.P. (Deeds) 61/14; M.R.O., Cal. Mdx. Sess. Recs. 1607–8, 140; 1608–9, 210; 1610 (1), 67, 86; 1612 (2), 56; Cal. Mdx. Sess. Bks. 1644–52, 6; *Mdx. Sess. Recs.* i. 352; iii. 272; M.R.O., Acc. 276/176; Prob. 11/233 (P.C.C. 9 Alchin, will of Robt. Halsey); Prob. 11/247 (P.C.C. 260 Aylett, will of Robt. Webb); Prob. 11/266 (P.C.C. 274 Ruthen, will of John Harvey); Prob. 11/427 (P.C.C. 148 Irby, will of Jos. Guppy).
[84] Prob. 11/233 (P.C.C. 9 Alchin, will of Robt. Halsey); M.R.O., Acc. 276/176; Acc. 695/43; Acc. 727/218.
[85] M.R.O., Acc. 1016/2/65.
[86] Edmonton Publ. Libr., D 110.   [87] H.O. 107/1703.
[88] M.R.O., Cal. Mdx. Sess. Recs. 1608–9, 210; 1609–10, 45, 197; 1610 (1), 67, 86; 1610–11, 158; 1612 (1), 76; *Mdx. Sess. Recs.* i. 172, 217, 268, 352; ii. 272; iii. 111, 142, 272, 293; iv. 123, 133.

[89] M.R.O., Cal. Mdx. Sess. Recs. 1609–10, 27.
[90] Ibid. 1610 (1), 41.
[91] M.R.O., Acc. 276/184.
[92] H.O. 107/1703.
[93] W. J. Roe, *Tottenham, Edmonton and Enfield Historical Note-Book*, 89.
[94] *Rep. Poor Law Com.* H.C. 44, p. 92 (1834), xxxv, App. B 2.
[95] Probably 3 'weavers' should also be added: H.O. 107/1703. For a factory at Winchmore Hill in 1865, see C 54/16416 no. 5.
[96] Sturges, *Edmonton Past and Present*, ii. 17; map in Pam, *Stamford Hill, Green Lanes Turnpike Trust*, pt. 1 (Edmonton Hund. Hist. Soc., 1963).
[97] M.R.O., Acc. 698/6.
[98] No. 986 on inclosure map: Robinson, *Edmonton*, 314.
[99] No. 964 on inclosure map: Robinson, *Edmonton*, 286.
[1] Sturges, *Edmonton Heritage*, 82–6.
[2] H.O. 107/1703.
[3] Ex inf. L. Hall (Edmonton) Ltd. (1973).
[4] S. Tymms, *Compendium of Mdx.* (1841), 17.
[5] H.O. 107/1703.
[6] Sturges, *Edmonton Past and Present*, ii. 26; *Kelly's Dir. Mdx.* (1878).
[7] H.O. 107/1703 pp. 1 sqq.
[8] M.R.O., Acc. 1016/1/35.
[9] *Kelly's Dir. Mdx.* (1878).
[10] Ibid. (1908).
[11] Ibid. (1908, 1926); *Kelly's Dir. Tottenham* (1926).
[12] H.O. 107/1703 p. 239.

firm at Winchmore Hill in 1878 was manufacturing telescopic ladders by 1893.[13] In 1890 there were three cabinet-makers in Edmonton and one in Southgate High Street.[14] Some of the 20th-century furniture firms, like B. & I. Nathan, began as cabinet-makers.[15]

Other early factories included the gasworks of Tottenham and District Gas Co., opened in 1847 next to the railway line near the Tottenham border,[16] a horse-hair factory in Hertford Road in the 1840s[17] and an 'Oriental printer' in Bury Street who employed 70 people in 1851.[18] Fore Street, a densely populated area, became a centre of small-scale industry. There was a hair roller manufacturer in Lower Fore Street in 1866[19] and there were glass and oil factories in Upper Fore Street in 1890 and five firms, mostly cycle manufacturers, in 1908.[20] In 1970 there were only four firms in Fore Street[21] after the Snells Park area had been developed for housing and the small factories moved to Claverings industrial estate.[22]

Industry also spread around Lower Edmonton, especially northward along the railway line. There were mills, possibly saw-mills, at the Green in 1866[23] but growth took place mostly during the 1920s and 1930s, with seven firms in 1926.[24] There was a slipper factory in a new road, Chichester Road, by 1937[25] and in 1933 another slipper factory was erected in Rosebery Road, previously reserved for housing.[26] By 1970, however, there were only eight firms in the area.[27] Farther south factories were built in the 1920s and 1930s in Brettenham Road, east of Fore Street. There were three in 1926, eight in 1937, and eleven in 1970.[28]

Eley Bros. had a cartridge factory at Tile Kiln Lane near Weir Hall by 1865[29] and moved to Angel Road in 1903. The old works were sold in 1919 to a motor firm but apparently had disappeared by 1926.[30] A little farther east in Silver Street the former workhouse of the Strand union was occupied in 1926 by the Klinger Manufacturing Co., a stocking-making firm from Tottenham,[31] which employed 1,850 people in 1941[32] and sold its site in 1967 to the G.L.C.[33]

At Southgate, in addition to a coach-builder, there was one factory belonging to Hadfield Bros., varnish manufacturers, in 1878.[34] By c. 1889 the factory, in Chase Side, was occupied by the French Cleaning and Dyeing Co. There was a photographic plate factory in Chase Road by c. 1883[35] and Watkin and Son, manufacturers of 'the Chase bicycle', were in existence by 1895.[36] In 1970 there were twelve firms in Chase Road, including Newby Bros., old-established builders who employed about 100 men.[37]

There was little industry in New Southgate, apart from Colney Hatch gas-works in the extreme south-west. By 1890 Southgate Engineering Co. was in South Road, where there was a piano manufacturer's by 1908.[38] Knight and Co., engineers, were in Springfield Road from 1917 before moving to Chase Road in 1931[39] and there was one factory in Station Road by 1926.[40] There were a few factories in High Road in 1970, when eight were concentrated in Station Road.[41]

Enamel sign-making works were built in Hedge Lane near the home of the founder James Bruton c. 1883 and survived in 1937.[42] Most factories in Palmers Green, however, were built along the North Circular Road and Green Lanes during the 1920s and 1930s. One of the largest was that of the Metal Box Co., which in 1929 acquired a perfume factory established in 1914 in Blind Lane (Chequers Way). Metal Box started rebuilding in 1934, when Blind Lane disappeared in the North Circular, and had some 900 employees there in 1973.[43] Green Lanes had one factory in 1908 and 13 in 1970.[44] Firms included Die Casting Machine Tools, which opened in 1940 and employed about 100 people in 1973.[45] There has been very little industry in other parts of Edmonton, at Winchmore Hill, Bowes Park,[46] and Bush Hill Park.

Most industry is in the east of Edmonton, along Angel and Montagu roads. In Angel Road, conveniently situated between the Lea and the G.E.R., factories were built from the mid 19th century. The largest was that of Messrs. Ridley, Whitley and Co., established by 1865 at Angel Road works between the river and the New Cut.[47] The factory, which manufactured floor-cloths, employed 900 workers in its heyday but had only 100 by 1914, shortly before its closure.[48] In 1897 the Gothic works were erected south of Angel Road, east of the railway line but near the gas-works, by T. Glover & Co., who made gas meters, and by R. & A. Main, makers of gas stoves.[49] The two firms later amalgamated and were taken over in 1965 by Thorn Electrical Industries. A subsidiary

[13] *Kelly's Dir. Mdx.* (1878); *Kelly's Dir. Tottenham* (1893–4).
[14] *Kelly's Dir. Mdx.* (1890).   [15] Ibid. (1937).
[16] See p. 181.
[17] *Home Cnties. Dir.* (1845); M.R.O., Acc. 695/28, f. 29.
[18] H.O. 107/1703 pp. 215 sqq.
[19] *Stoke Newington Dir.* (1866).
[20] *Kelly's Dirs. Mdx.* (1890, 1908).
[21] *Kelly's Dir. London* (1970).
[22] Boro. of Edmonton, *Official Guide* [1963].
[23] *Stoke Newington Dir.* (1866); *Kelly's Dir. Mdx.* (1878).
[24] i.e. the Green, New Rd., Bridge Rd., Balham Rd., Winchester Rd.: *Kelly's Dir. Mdx.* (1926).
[25] *Kelly's Dir. Mdx.* (1937).
[26] *The Times*, 7 Jan. 1933.
[27] *Kelly's Dir. London* (1970).
[28] Ibid.; *Kelly's Dirs. Mdx.* (1926, 1937).
[29] O.S. Map 6", Mdx. VII. SE. (1865 edn.).
[30] Sturges, *Edmonton Past and Present*, ii. 27; *The Times*, 7 Feb. 1919; 4 Nov. 1925; H. P. Clunn, *Face of London*, 461.
[31] *New Mdx. Cnty. Pictorial*, N.S. v. 19–21.
[32] Sturges, *Edmonton Past and Present*, ii. 34.
[33] *The Times*, 15 Dec. 1967.

[34] *Kelly's Dir. Mdx.* (1878).
[35] Newby, *Old Southgate*, 55, 107.
[36] Trade Cat. (1898) *penes* Broomfield Mus.
[37] *Kelly's Dir. London* (1970); Enfield L.B., *Official Guide* [1970].
[38] *Kelly's Dirs. Mdx.* (1890, 1908).
[39] Ex inf. Knight & Co. (Engineers) Ltd. (1973).
[40] *Kelly's Dir. Mdx.* (1926).
[41] *Kelly's Dir. London* (1970).
[42] D. H. Smith, 'Industrialization of the Northern and Western sectors of Greater London' (Lond. Univ. Ph.D. thesis, 1932), 72; *Kelly's Dir. Mdx.* (1937).
[43] O.S. Map 6", Mdx. VII. SW. (1920 edn.); ex inf. Metal Box Co. Ltd. (1973).
[44] *Kelly's Dirs. Mdx.* (1908, 1926, 1937); *Kelly's Dir. London* (1970).
[45] Ex inf. Die Casting Machine Tools Ltd. (1973).
[46] Industry is concentrated in the Tottenham portion of Bowes Park, around Bounds Green: see p. 339.
[47] O.S. Map 6", Mdx. VII. SE. (1865 edn.); M.R.O., Acc. 815/37; *Kelly's Dir. Mdx.* (1878).
[48] Fisk, *Edmonton*, 137–8; *The Times*, 24 July 1914.
[49] Sturges, *Edmonton Past and Present*, ii. 26; *Kelly's Dir. Tottenham* (1913–14).

company, Main Enamel Manufacturing Co., was formed in 1946 and built a new factory on part of the Gothic works site in 1951.[50]

In 1901 Aerators Ltd., which was formed in Crayford (Kent) to make sparklet syphons in 1897, purchased a 3-acre site south of Angel Road, where a new factory was built. The firm, which changed its name to Sparklets, began to manufacture munitions during the First World War and extended its premises. After the war it contracted again and sold most of its site to the British Oxygen Co. Sparklets moved to Tottenham c. 1953 and British Oxygen gradually extended its premises to 23 a., where some 1,300 people were employed in 1973.[51]

When Eley Bros. (see above) moved from Tile Kiln Lane in 1903, they built extensive works north of Angel Road between the railway and Salmon's brook. In 1921 the firm moved to Waltham Cross (Herts.) and the site was divided among several firms of which the largest were the Great Eastern Cabinet Co., with 230 workers in 1941,[52] and the Ever Ready Co. (Great Britain), which moved there from London in 1935 and employed 450–500 people in 1973.[53]

After Angel Road became part of the North Circular Road (1924–7),[54] factories multiplied on either side. There were eight firms in 1926, 38 in 1937, and 80 in 1970, including 26 at Eley's estate to the north and 36 at the Lea Valley trading estate to the south.[55] Most factories were small and changed hands frequently. Only 37 per cent of the firms of 1937 were still there in 1970. Among the largest in 1941 were Rego Clothiers, which moved from east London in 1928 and employed 1,700 people, B. & I. Nathan, furniture manufacturers who moved from Hackney in 1930 and employed 300 people, and Atlas Lamp Works, which opened in 1931 and employed 200 people. In 1973 Nathan's had some 250 employees[56] but the largest firms were the British Oxygen Co. with about 1,300[57] and M. K. Electric Ltd. with about 3,000. M. K. Electric had been founded in 1919 as the Heavy Current Electric Accessories Co. in rented premises off Fore Street and in 1923 had changed its name and acquired its first factory in Wakefield Street. It opened other factories south of Angel Road and north of the gas-works in 1937 and 1969 and on the Eley estate in 1958, 1965, and 1974. By 1974 M. K. Electric had 12 factories and offices in Edmonton.[58]

The low price of land in the former marsh was instrumental in attracting industry to Angel Road. A second industrial area developed at Bridport Road, because the price of land depreciated after the top layer of soil had been removed during brick-making.[59] Eight factories were built in 1931–2[60] in the area between Bridport Road and the Tottenham border, bounded on the west by Bull Lane and on the east by the railway. There were 13 factories by 1937,[61] 16 by 1941,[62] and 23 by 1970.[63] The Dunlop Rubber Co. and the Enfield Clock Co. (London), which both started in 1932, had 1,500 and 300 employees respectively by 1941. Most firms, which included several furniture and clothing manufacturers, employed fewer than 100 people,[64] although in 1973 Fanfold Ltd., makers of business forms, who had moved from Cricklewood in 1957, employed about 320[65] and A. H. Meltzer, shoe manufacturers who had moved from east London in 1932, employed about 150.[66]

The most recent industrial concentrations, the Montagu South and Claverings industrial estates, are situated east of Montagu Road and west of the railway, adjoining the factories around Angel Road. There were two varnish manufacturers, James Price and Co. and Rolls and Co., at Marsh Side (later the northern part of Montagu Road) in 1890.[67] Rolls and Co. still existed on the Claverings estate in 1973.[68] The Pegamoid works, where leather cloths were made, had been erected by 1913 east of Montagu Road and the railway.[69] By 1941 there were about five factories[70] in the area but after the war the council planned industrial estates at either end of Montagu Road to house the many firms which would be displaced by rebuilding elsewhere. The 6½-acre site of Claverings farm was acquired in 1949 for small-scale industry, including clothing, furniture-making, and precision engineering. Montagu South, 18 a., was acquired in 1953 for depots, sand and ballast storage and the production of concrete.[71] By 1970 there were 25 firms in Montagu South industrial estate and 26 in Claverings industrial estate.[72] Charlton Road, which joined Montagu Road north of Claverings, contained Qualcast (Fleetway), which had moved from Tottenham in 1937 and employed about 290 people in 1973,[73] and Edward Doherty & Sons, which had moved from Tottenham in 1938 and employed about 250 in 1973.[74]

SOCIAL LIFE. Grants of free warren in their demesne lands were made to William de Say in 1245 and Holy Trinity priory in 1253.[75] There were frequent disputes in the 16th century between Edmonton inhabitants and the keepers of Enfield Chase[76] and in 1578 illegal hunters were pursued to Bush Hill.[77] Some of Henry VIII's servants

[50] Ex inf. Main Enamel Manufacturing Co. Ltd. (1973).
[51] Ex inf. British Oxygen Co. Ltd. (1973).
[52] Sturges, *Edmonton Past and Present*, ii. 27.
[53] Ex inf. Ever Ready Co. (Gt. Britain) Ltd. (1973).
[54] See p. 135.
[55] *Kelly's Dirs. Mdx.* (1926, 1937); *Kelly's Dir. London* (1970).
[56] Sturges, *Edmonton Past and Present*, ii. 27–31; ex inf. B. & I. Nathan Ltd. (1973).
[57] Ex inf. British Oxygen Co. Ltd. (1973).
[58] Ex inf. M.K. Electric Ltd. (1974).
[59] Sturges, *Edmonton Past and Present*, ii. 22.
[60] Smith, 'Industrialization of Greater London', 48–9.
[61] *Kelly's Dir. Mdx.* (1937).
[62] Sturges, *Edmonton Past and Present*, ii. 31–2.
[63] *Kelly's Dir. London* (1970).
[64] Sturges, *Edmonton Past and Present*, ii. 31–2; ex inf.

Hall's Carpets Ltd. and Dereta (Manufacturing) Ltd. (1973).
[65] Ex inf. Fanfold Ltd. (1973).
[66] Ex inf. A. & H. Meltzer Ltd. (1973).
[67] *Kelly's Dir. Mdx.* (1890).
[68] Enfield Dist. Manufacturers' Assoc. Ltd. list (1973–4).
[69] *Kelly's Dir. Tottenham* (1913–14); O.S. Map 6″, Mdx. VII. SE. (1920 edn.).
[70] Sturges, *Edmonton Past and Present*, ii. 36.
[71] Ex inf. Enfield L.B. Planning Officer (1974).
[72] *Kelly's Dir. London* (1970).
[73] Ex inf. Qualcast (Fleetway) Ltd. (1973).
[74] Ex inf. Edward Doherty & Sons Ltd. (1973).
[75] *Cal. Chart. R.* 1227–57, 282, 427.
[76] D.L. 1/121/E 5, /131/W 15, /170/54.
[77] Hist. MSS. Com. 9, *Hatfield House*, ii, pp. 174, 179, 189, 191–2; xiii, p. 155; Sturges, *Edmonton Heritage*, 36–9, 150–2.

'dwelling about Edmonton' were imprisoned for hunting in inclosed woods but later the Leakes seem to have hunted at will and in 1597 they were accused of causing scarcity of game in the Chase.[78] In 1820 Southgate offered 'excellent game' for the sportsman[79] and the Stag and Hounds in Bury Street was a meeting-place of stag hunts until the end of the 19th century.[80] About 1800 anglers paid a guinea a year to fish in weirs on the Lea at the Ferry House or Bleak Hall inn at Cook's ferry.[81]

London merchants, despite their property in Edmonton, played little part in social life before the 18th century. By 1776 the gentry had public assembly rooms,[82] which adjoined the Angel inn at the corner of Fore and Silver streets and still existed in 1880.[83] A theatre was built on the south side of Angel Road in the late 18th century. In 1805 it was opened with a company of comedians and was patronized by the ladies of the assembly rooms.[84]

The Bell at Edmonton, where John Gilpin attempted his rendezvous with his family, was well known. John Savile mentioned it in his account of James I's progress to London in 1603[85] and the petty sessions were held there in 1679.[86] Mention of the New Bell in 1688[87] suggests that there must then have been two inns of that name and in 1752 licences were granted to the Old Bell, the Oldest Bell, and the Six Bells.[88] Probably the Old Bell or Blue Bell, first mentioned in 1700[89] and by 1793 called the Angel,[90] was the original Bell and the New Bell, which then became the Bell, a lesser inn near it. The Angel, on land belonging to Latymer's charity at the crossing point of the London–Ware road with the route from Edmonton marsh to Palmers Green and Southgate, was rebuilt in the 1930s. The Bell, which was replaced by another building in 1878, lay south of the Angel, on the west side of Fore Street.[91]

There was a tavern in Edmonton in 1285,[92] an alehouse at Winchmore Hill in 1578,[93] and an inn at Southgate in the late 16th century in Waterfall Road, on a site approximately opposite Christ Church.[94] The George, mentioned in the *Merry Devil of Edmonton*,[95] may have been an inn of that name mentioned in 1675.[96] Other early inns were the Hart's Horn in Silver Street (1635),[97] the Fishmongers' Arms in Winchmore Hill (1668),[98] the Ship tavern (1671),[99] the King's Arms (1678),[1] the George and Vulture near Marsh Lane (1680),[2] the Swan (1682),[3] and the White Hart (1694).[4] The earliest inns that survive, in most cases as new or much altered buildings, are the Rose and Crown in Church Street (1667),[5] the Cross Keys at Edmonton Green (c. 1680s),[6] the Cherry Tree at Southgate Green (c. 1695),[7] the Golden Fleece in Fore Street (1715),[8] the Cock in Bowes Road (c. 1730),[9] the Woolpack in Southgate High Street (1743),[10] and the Green Dragon in Winchmore Hill (1750).[11] By 1752 there were 26 inns, including the Orange Tree in Highfield Road, Winchmore Hill, the Horse and Groom in Fore Street, the Fox at Palmers Green, the Cart Overthrown in Montagu Road, the Cock in Hertford Road, the Two Brewers and the Bull in Silver Street, the King's Head at Winchmore Hill, and the Golden Lion in Lower Edmonton.[12] There were 25 inns in 1803[13] and 32 inns and beerhouses in 1851.[14] The proportion of people to each public house, 204 in 1803 and 303 in 1851,[15] was relatively low and there does not appear to have been a strong temperance movement although some of the churches and chapels had their own temperance societies.[16]

Edmonton fair centred on the Angel and Bell inns. The Angel served as a meeting-place for 17th-century petty sessions, for 18th-century manorial courts[17] and turnpike trustees,[18] and for the board of guardians from 1837 until 1841.[19] The Cherry Tree in Southgate was noted for its skittles alley[20] and was used by several friendly societies, the first being the Loyal Britain society, which met there from 1800 to 1833.[21] At Winchmore Hill the Green Dragon was a centre for cock-fighting and prize-fights[22] and in 1794 was the meeting-place of a benefit society.[23] The Friendly and Constitutional society (1799–1841)[24] and the Prudent Sisters friendly society (1805–21)[25] met at the Golden Fleece; the Society of Tradesmen and Labourers

[78] Hist. MSS. Com. 9, *Hatfield House*, vii, p. 321.
[79] *Ambulator*, 12th edn. (1820), 291.
[80] Sturges, *Edmonton Past and Present*, i. 99.
[81] Sometimes wrongly identified as the inn visited by Izaak Walton: J. Dugdale, *New British Traveller*, iii. 458; Fisk, *Edmonton*, 65–9; Edmonton Publ. Libr., D 119.
[82] Quoted in Sturges, *Edmonton Past and Present*, i. 31.
[83] Illust. in ibid. i. 27; M.R.O., MCC/A/Pl. 1.
[84] *Mdx. Monthly*, iii. 30–2; Sturges, *Edmonton Heritage*, 72–5. For an engraving of 1805, see J. Winston, *Theatric Tourist*, pl. facing p. 46.
[85] Fisk, *Edmonton*, 106.
[86] M.R.O., Cal. Mdx. Sess. Bks., 1679–82, 21.
[87] Prob. 11/399 (P.C.C. 86 Dyke, will of Peter Beilby).
[88] M.R.O., L.V. 7/29.
[89] *Mdx. Cnty. Sess. Bks. 1689–1709*, 222.
[90] Edmonton Publ. Libr., D 119; Robinson, *Edmonton*, 146.
[91] O.S. Map 6″, Mdx. VII. SE. (1865 edn.); Fisk, *Edmonton*, 109; Briggs, *Mdx. Old and New*, 74; ex inf. Mr. D. O. Pam (1974).
[92] C 260/4 no. 5.
[93] Hist. MSS. Com. 9, *Hatfield House*, xiii, p. 155.
[94] Hatfield C.P.M. Suppl. 27.
[95] Robinson, *Edmonton*, 111; see above, p. 131.
[96] C 10/201/50.
[97] C 3/418/99.
[98] Mason, *Southgate Scrapbook*, 61.
[99] C 7/14/30.
[1] C 5/496/89.

[2] Robinson, *Edmonton*, 9.
[3] M.R.O., Acc. 349/92.
[4] Prob. 11/444 (P.C.C. 55 Lort, will of Geo. Waller).
[5] C 5/182/12.
[6] Robinson, *Edmonton*, 9.
[7] C 7/644/29.
[8] M.R.O., MR/RR 22/5.
[9] Robinson, *Edmonton*, 9. The Cock in South Street was mentioned in 1691 but may not have been an inn: M.R.O., Acc. 698/5–6.
[10] M.R.O., Acc. 98/83–8.
[11] M.R.O., Cal. Mdx. Sess. Bks., 1719–22, 100.
[12] M.R.O., L.V. 7/29. The Golden Lion was recently demolished.
[13] M.R.O., L.V. 10/111.
[14] H.O. 107/1703.
[15] *Census*, 1801, 1851.
[16] Recs. *penes* Greater Lond. Rec. Off. (County Hall) N/C/64; M.R.O., MA/CL 1888, 27e.
[17] See pp. 169, 176.
[18] Pam, *Stamford Hill, Green Lanes Turnpike Trust*, i. 6.
[19] Richardson, *Edmonton Poor Law Union, 1837–54*, 11.
[20] Mason, *Story of Southgate*, 39.
[21] F.S. 1/428/1118; F.S. 1/430/1272; F.S. 1/445/1827; F.S. 1/479/2993. Mason, *Story of Southgate*, 40.
[22] Cresswell, *Winchmore Hill*, 38.
[23] Indexed in F.S. 2/7.
[24] F.S. 1/428/1102.
[25] F.S. 1/425/1049; F.S. 1/439/1719.

(1794–1825) met at the Fox;[26] the Three Tuns was frequented by the Amicable Society of Tradesmen in 1794[27] and by the United society in 1811.[28] The Sons of Peace (1804–30) met at the Bell[29] and the Society of Good Fellowship (1808–13) at the King's Head, Lower Edmonton.[30] Later societies also met at the Rose and Crown, the Orange Tree, the Crown, Southgate, and, until 1869, at the Jolly Farmers and the Rising Sun, Southgate.[31] They also met at both Edmonton and Southgate National schools.[32]

The Edmonton mechanics' institution, which was active c. 1835, probably always met in Tottenham.[33] In Southgate there were assembly rooms next to the Cherry Tree[34] and at Winchmore Hill lectures were held at the Congregational church in 1860[35] and in St. Paul's school.[36] Festivities were held on Edmonton Green and menageries were exhibited there, leading in 1880 to a protest against the noise.[37]

Although most public houses in the late 19th and early 20th centuries were licensed for music and dancing,[38] they were superseded as meeting-places by public halls. Edmonton town hall, built in 1884 with accommodation for 675, was licensed for entertainments and in 1897 a free public library was built in Fore Street.[39] The Charles Lamb memorial hall and institute, designed by J. S. Alder, was opened in Church Street in 1908.[40] At Southgate a village hall, designed by A. R. Barker with accommodation for 400, was opened in High Street in 1883 under the auspices of the vicar. A library was erected by subscribers in Chase Side in 1889 and also served as a recreation centre.[41] In Winchmore Hill a village hall was opened near the green in 1887 and replaced in 1905 by St. Paul's parish hall and institute, which included a gymnasium, billiard room, and reading room.[42] By 1914 there were halls in Bowes Park, Palmers Green, New Southgate, and Bush Hill Park, as well as in the older areas of Edmonton and Southgate.[43] Most belonged to churches and chapels[44] but many were also used for lectures and entertainment.[45] Broomfield House was taken over by the local authorities and opened as a museum in 1925.[46]

The 18th-century theatre in Angel Road continued as the Theatre Royal until it was converted into the Hippodrome cinema c. 1920.[47] It was no longer used by 1952 and was demolished c. 1961.[48] The Empire theatre or music hall, where Marie Lloyd collapsed at her last performance in 1922, opened in New Road, Lower Edmonton, in 1908.[49] It was re-opened as a cinema designed by Cecil Masey in 1933, renamed the Granada in 1951 and pulled down in 1970.[50] The Intimate theatre, in Green Lanes, Palmers Green, was opened as a church hall in 1931 and taken over as a repertory theatre by John Clements, the actor, in 1937; apart from a brief period in 1969 when it served as St. Monica's church hall, it has remained a theatre.[51]

Cinema shows were held in the Grove and at the central hall in Southgate in 1909,[52] and in King's hall, Lower Edmonton, in 1913 and 1916.[53] The Edmonton cinematograph theatre opened in Fore Street, Lower Edmonton, in 1911 and closed between 1926 and 1937.[54] The first large cinema built in Middlesex was the Alcazar, which opened in Fore Street in 1913; it was modernized in 1934, damaged in 1942, and pulled down by 1952.[55] Other permanent cinemas in existence by 1913 were Queen's hall in Green Lanes, Palmers Green, which closed in 1967[56] and the New Southgate, later the Coronation, cinema in High Road, New Southgate, which had closed by 1958.[57] In addition to the two converted theatres,[58] there were the Palmadium in Green Lanes, Palmers Green, open by 1922 and demolished between 1948 and 1963,[59] the Capitol in Green Lanes, Winchmore Hill, in the 1930s, and the Odeon at the Bourne, Southgate, open by 1935 and closed by 1973.[60] The Regal in Silver Street[61] and the ABC, formerly the Ritz, in Bowes Road,[62] opened in 1934 and were still in existence in 1974.

Apart from hunting, there is no record of sport before the 18th century. There was an affray at a bull-baiting in 1746[63] and a bowling green in Southgate High Street had been in existence for some time before 1753.[64] Huxley cricket club was mentioned in 1858[65] but it was Southgate which became famous for cricket in the 19th century. Isaac Walker (d. 1853) of Arnos Grove had seven sons,

[26] F.S. 1/420/656.
[27] F.S. 2/7.
[28] F.S. 1/432/1383.
[29] F.S. 1/439/1717.
[30] F.S. 1/429/1180.
[31] F.S. 1/429/1238; F.S. 1/437/1584; F.S. 1/471B/2694; F.S. 1/481B/3351; F.S. 1/491/4298.
[32] F.S. 1/450/1908; F.S. 1/495/4712.
[33] T. Kelly, George Birkbeck, 314. See below, p. 340.
[34] Round, Southgate and Winchmore Hill, 39–40; Newby, Old Southgate, 52–3.
[35] North Mdx. and Southgate Messenger, Mar. 1860 (no. 43), penes Broomfield Mus.
[36] Regnart, Winchmore Hill, 27.
[37] Fisk, Edmonton, 104–5.
[38] M.R.O., MR/LMD; MCC/C/ENT passim.
[39] Kelly's Dir. Mdx. (1908); Boro. of Edmonton, Official Guide [1963], 25.
[40] The Times, 13 Nov. 1908; datestone (1907).
[41] Kelly's Dirs. Mdx. (1890, 1908).
[42] Regnart, Winchmore Hill, 27; Kelly's Dir. Mdx. (1908).
[43] O.S. Map 1/2,500, Mdx. VII. SE., SW. (1913–14 edn.).
[44] See sections on churches and protestant nonconformity.
[45] e.g. M.R.O., MCC/C/ENT 8/43, 57, 105.
[46] Boro. of Southgate, Official Guide [1963].
[47] M.R.O., MCC/S. EL 7; MCC/C/ENT 11/9; O.S. Maps, 1/2,500, Mdx. VII. 15 (1914 and 1936 edns.).
[48] Edmonton U.D.C., Official Guide [1939]; Kelly's Dir. Edmonton (1952); ex inf. Mr. D. O. Pam (1974).
[49] Kelly's Dir. Mdx. (1908); M.R.O., MCC/C/ENT 8/34; illust. penes Edmonton Hund. Hist. Soc.; Evening Standard, 29 Jan. 1974.
[50] Edmonton U.D.C., Official Guide [1939]; Boro. of Edmonton, Official Guide [1963]; ex inf. Mr. D. O. Pam (1974).
[51] Ex inf. the manageress (1973).
[52] Recorder for Palmers Green, Winchmore Hill and Southgate, Sept. 1909, penes Broomfield Mus.
[53] M.R.O., MCC/C/ENT 8/40.
[54] M.R.O., MCC/C/ENT 8/168; Kelly's Dirs. Mdx. (1926, 1937); ex inf. Mr. D. O. Pam (1974).
[55] M.R.O., MCC/C/ENT 8/41; MCC/S. EL 8; Kelly's Dir. Edmonton (1952); Edmonton U.D.C., Official Guide [1939].
[56] M.R.O., MCC/C/ENT 8/58; ex inf. Mr. D. O. Pam (1974).
[57] M.R.O., MCC/C/ENT 8/104; Mdx. Quarterly, N.S. XV. 14.
[58] i.e. the Hippodrome and Granada: see above.
[59] M.R.O., MCC/C/ENT 20/1–16; Mason, Story of Southgate, 34; Boro. of Southgate, Official Guide [1963].
[60] O.S. Map 1/2,500, Mdx. VII. 10 (1935 edn.); Kelly's Dir. Mdx. (1937).
[61] Ex inf. Mr. D. O. Pam (1974).
[62] Boro. of Edmonton, Official Guide [1963].
[63] M.R.O., Cal. Mdx. Sess. Bks., 1745–7, 81.
[64] M.R.O., Acc. 262/2/6.
[65] North Mdx. and Southgate Messenger, Oct. 1858 (no. 26), penes Broomfield Mus.

all good cricketers and including Vyell E. Walker, described in 1859 as the best all-round cricketer in the world. There had been a village cricket club, the Southgate Albert, which played on a field of John Walker, the eldest of the brothers, who c. 1850 made a proper pitch and established Southgate cricket club. The club played against local clubs, the universities and, from 1858 to 1863, against an all-England team before thousands who had been brought by special train to Colney Hatch station. From the Southgate club developed the county club, which played its first match at Southgate in 1859. The connexion of the Walker brothers with local cricket lasted until 1877, when Southgate ceased to be a private club.[66]

Annual cricket matches took place between the police and local tradesmen in Chapel fields until the 1880s, revived in 1899, and expanded into Southgate village sports in 1901. Enlivened by fireworks and a band, they lasted until c. 1913.[67] By 1963 there were 13 cricket clubs in Southgate and three in Edmonton, including Edmonton cricket club which was over 100 years old and had played at Starksnest field since c. 1913.[68]

Southgate football club was founded c. 1883 and played on the field behind the Cherry Tree.[69] Edmonton's Norsemen football club was founded in 1895 and by 1963 there were seven football clubs in Edmonton and six in Southgate.[70] Southgate Nondescript bicycle club was formed in 1882, changed its name to the Southgate cycling club in 1886,[71] and still existed in 1970.[72] There were five cycling clubs in Edmonton in 1963.[73]

Public swimming baths were built in 1900 to a design by W. Gilbee Scott as part of the town hall complex in Knights Lane.[74] They were replaced in 1970 by Edmonton Green swimming pool.[75] In Southgate swimming baths were erected at Barrowell Green in 1913[76] and at Winchmore Hill Road in 1966. In 1974 there was also a Lido in Edmonton, near Jubilee Park.[77]

Other popular sports in 1963 were tennis, with three clubs in Edmonton and 12 in Southgate, and bowls, with seven clubs in Edmonton and five in Southgate.[78]

Southgate reading society existed by 1849[79] and met in a cottage near Chase Corner until the library was built in 1889.[80] In 1861 the Edmonton Mutual Improvement and Recreation society replaced the Edmonton literary institute, which had recently dissolved.[81] There were literary societies at Winchmore Hill and Palmers Green by 1909.[82]

Palmers Green orchestral society and Palmers Green and Southgate choral society were founded in 1908,[83] Edmonton central hall choir existed by 1911, and by 1963 there were 20 music societies in Edmonton and 4 in Southgate. Of the 13 dramatic societies in 1963, the Thespians had been founded in 1924 and the Latymer Players in 1927. Edmonton Hundred Historical Society, usually meeting at Edmonton, was founded in 1938. The 15 horticultural societies in 1963 included Edmonton and Tottenham police society's horticultural section, founded in 1904, and the Edmonton allotment and horticultural association, founded in 1910.

Edmonton arts council, sponsored by the borough council, was in 1963 a federation of 46 societies. In 1957 Salisbury House was established as the first arts centre in London to be provided by a local authority.[84]

A newspaper called *Paul Pry* was published in Edmonton c. 1839[85] but indulged in personal attacks which led to its early closure.[86] The *Southgate Messenger*, which existed by 1857[87] had apparently become the *North Middlesex and Southgate Messenger* by 1858.[88] The *Southgate Chronicle*, one of the Barnet Press newspapers, was founded in 1859 and the *Southgate and Friern Barnet Sentinel* in 1895. The *Recorder for Palmers Green, Winchmore Hill and Southgate* circulated in 1909 and the *Palmers Green and Southgate Gazette* was founded in 1910. The *Palmers Green Weekly Herald*, one of the North London Weekly series, was founded in 1971. The latter survived in 1973, as did the *Palmers Green and Southgate Gazette*[89] and the *Tottenham and Edmonton Weekly Herald*, a successor to the *Tottenham and Edmonton Advertiser*.[90]

LOCAL GOVERNMENT. MANORIAL GOVERNMENT.

Manorial jurisdiction over the whole of Edmonton, of which South Mimms formed a berewick, seems to have originated before the Conquest.[91] Although there are no records for the capital manor before the 17th century, there are references to 13th-century courts held at Easter[92] and to an annual view of frankpledge in 1322.[93] A court leet or view of frankpledge was held annually on the Thursday in Whitsun week by 1359[94] and views, together with a general court baron, continued to be held at Whitsun until the last court in 1861.[95]

In 1372 Adam Francis, in theory at least, held a court every three weeks.[96] By the 16th century, however, there was only one court other than the

[66] W. A. Bettesworth, *The Walkers of Southgate*.
[67] Newby, *Old Southgate*, 99.
[68] Boro. of Edmonton, *Official Guide* [1963]; Boro. of Southgate, *Official Guide* [1963].
[69] Mason, *Story of Southgate*, 41.
[70] Boro. of Edmonton, *Official Guide* [1963]; Boro. of Southgate, *Official Guide* [1963].
[71] Newby, *Old Southgate*, 40–1, 43.
[72] Enfield L.B., *Official Handbook* [1970].
[73] Boro. of Edmonton, *Official Guide* [1963].
[74] *Building News*, lxxviii. 755; Fisk, *Edmonton*, 134.
[75] Boro. of Enfield, *Official Guide* [1970].
[76] *Incorp. of Southgate Boro.* (1933) [programme *penes* Broomfield Mus.].
[77] Boro. of Enfield, *Official Guide* [1970].
[78] Boro. of Edmonton, *Official Guide* [1963]; Boro. of Southgate, *Official Guide* [1963].
[79] Catalogue of bks. (1849) *penes* Broomfield Mus.
[80] Round, *Southgate and Winchmore Hill*, 39–40.
[81] *North Middlesex and Southgate Messenger*, Mar. 1861, *penes* Broomfield Mus.
[82] *Recorder for Palmers Green, Winchmore Hill and Southgate*, Sept. 1909, *penes* Broomfield Mus.
[83] *Southgate, Fifty Years of Progress* (1931) [pamphlet *penes* Broomfield Mus.]; *Mdx. Quarterly*, i (1953), 2.
[84] Boro. of Edmonton, *Official Guide* [1963]; Boro. of Southgate, *Official Guide* [1963].
[85] Sturges, *Edmonton Heritage*, 82–6.
[86] Couchman, *Reminiscences of Tottenham*, 73.
[87] Mason, *Story of Southgate*, 40.
[88] *North Mdx. and Southgate Messenger*, 1858–61, *penes* Broomfield Mus.
[89] *Willing's Press Guide* (1896 and later edns.); newspapers *penes* Broomfield Mus. [90] See p. 342.
[91] *V.C.H. Mdx.* i. 126. [92] E 40/1721; C 132/42/6.
[93] C 134/70/4. [94] C 135/144/7.
[95] M.R.O., Acc. 695/28, f. 366.
[96] *Cal. Inq. p.m.* xiii. 164.

general court, usually in December.[97] The frequency of other courts, known as special courts baron, was from the 17th century completely erratic. Only a few met in the 17th century; there were many more in the mid 18th century but by the 19th century the Whitsun court alone was held, most tenurial transactions being settled out of court.[98]

The court of Edmonton was probably originally held at the demesne farm of Sayesbury, the 'court' being described in 1280 as lying near Church field,[99] before the farm was divided from the lordship in 1571.[1] During the 18th century courts were held at public houses, usually at the Bell or Cross Keys, later at the Angel.[2] The only extant court rolls for the capital manor are for 1693–5 and 1700[3] but there is a complete series of court books from 1661 until 1933[4] and minute books from 1742 until 1844[5] and a court leet book covering the periods 1735–6 and 1745–1855.[6]

From 1661[7] the special courts baron were concerned wholly with tenurial business and the courts leet chiefly with electing officials whose presentments rarely appeared in the books. Administration was based upon the division of the manor and parish into wards, which may have originated as tithings. In the mid 16th century there were six wards: Fore Street, Bury Street, Church Street, South Street, Bowes, and Winchmore Hill.[8] The last two had disappeared by 1650[9] and four wards[10] remained until well into the 19th century. Each ward had its own constable and headborough, both first mentioned in 1607,[11] and its own aleconner. There was one parish constable from 1785. The election of officials was last recorded in 1855.

Most courts leet were concerned with scouring ditches especially in Edmonton marsh, impounding stray cattle, and preventing encroachments on the waste.[12] Stocks were mentioned c. 1548[13] and 1609[14] and there were whipping posts in Angel Road.[15] In 1714 a presentment was made at the leet court on the subject of two watch-houses[16] but by then criminal jurisdiction was generally left to the parish or magistrates. Even scouring ditches seems to have been the concern of the vestry rather than the manor by 1748.[17]

There is no evidence for courts on the manor of Bowes and Polehouse before the 16th century. In 1668 court rolls were extant from 1523–4[18] and there are still draft court rolls for 1536–42[19] and court books for 1669–1863.[20] Courts,[21] always a joint view of frankpledge and court baron, were held once a year, usually in May or June.[22] Manorial officials were appointed: a constable, a taster of bread and ale, and a headborough in the 1740s. There were stocks on Southgate Green, which survived in 1973. Occasional orders were made for scouring ditches but most of the business was tenurial and after the last court was held in 1863 settlements were made out of court until the last copyhold tenement was enfranchised in 1936.[23] In 1792 the chapter of St. Paul's emphasized that they could hold courts wherever they wished[24] and courts were apparently held alternately at Bowes and Polehouse during the 17th century.

John Blund held courts in 1281,[25] but there is no evidence that his successors, the lords of Dephams manor, or the holders of Willoughbies ever did so.

In 1328, in addition to 55 rent-paying tenants, the canons of the Holy Trinity had ten tenants of the fee of Peverel who owed suit of court, relief, and heriot as well as rent.[26] The courts were held at Edmonton twice yearly.[27]

In 1294 the abbot of Walden claimed view of frankpledge and the assizes of bread and ale from his men in several Middlesex parishes, including Edmonton but, when challenged, he acknowledged that his only liberties were in Enfield.[28] However, there was a court (*curia*) of Walden in Edmonton in the 13th century.[29]

PARISH GOVERNMENT TO 1837.[30] A churchwarden was mentioned in 1389,[31] a parish clerk in 1417 and 1529,[32] and two churchwardens and two *oeconomi* in 1580.[33] In the 18th century the churchwardens often served for two years. Overseers of the poor, first mentioned in 1639,[34] were appointed at the Easter vestry, one for each of the four wards.[35] By 1834 there were two salaried assistant overseers.[36] Paid officials appointed in the 18th century included the vestry clerk, who was usually the schoolmaster, the sexton, and the steward and

[97] S.C. 6/Hen. VIII/2102 m. 2d.; /2105 m. 1d.
[98] M.R.O., Acc. 695/15–28.
[99] W.A.M. 37. [1] See p. 157.
[2] M.R.O., Acc. 695/41 *passim*.
[3] Material *penes* Edmonton vestry office, docs. 5, 10–13. See M.R.O., D.R.O. 4.
[4] M.R.O., Acc. 695/15–30. Indices to court bks.: ibid. /31–33.
[5] M.R.O., Acc. 695/34–40.
[6] Ibid. /41.
[7] This para. is based upon the manorial records. See above.
[8] S.C. 6/Hen. VIII/2102 m. 2; Ed. VI/299 m. 15.
[9] E 317/Mdx./16.
[10] Hadley formed another division of Edmonton manor.
[11] Sta. Cha. 8/41/1.
[12] E 317/Mdx./16 m. 8.
[13] S.C. 6/Ed. VI/299 m. 16.
[14] M.R.O., Cal. Mdx. Sess. Recs. 1609–10, 120.
[15] Fisk, *Edmonton*, 192.
[16] See p. 179.
[17] E. Hoare, *Work of Edmonton Vestry, 1739–48 and 1782–98* (Edmonton Hund. Hist. Soc., Occas. Paper, N.S. xvi), 13.
[18] St. Paul's MS., Box A 57 no. 9.
[19] Ibid. B 59–60.
[20] 1669–93: St. Paul's MS., Box W.C. 7, ff. 89–116v.; 1694–1863: Bruce Castle Mus., D/MR/A/1–5. There are

also extracts from the court rolls 1661–1862 in the account bks. of the receiver general of St. Paul's: Guildhall MSS. 14213–5.
[21] Unless otherwise stated, this para. is based upon the court books: see above.
[22] The 16th-century courts were held from July to October.
[23] Church Com., S 4 survey, p. 51.
[24] Guildhall Libr., Church Com. MS. 168893.
[25] *Cal. Inq. p.m.* ii, p. 509.
[26] E 164/18 ff. 12 sqq.
[27] E 40/2670, /7838, /11131.
[28] *Plac. de Quo Warr.* (Rec. Com.), 479.
[29] B.M. Harl. MS. 3697, f. 182v. The context suggests that 'curia' was a court rather than a courtyard.
[30] Unless otherwise stated, this section is based upon D. Avery, *Edmonton Workhouse Cttee. 1732–7* and C. Hoare, *Work of Edmonton Vestry, 1739–48 and 1782–98* (Edmonton Hund. Hist. Soc., c. 1966 and 1968).
[31] *Cal. Close*, 1385–9, 571.
[32] Prob. 11/2B (P.C.C. 38 Marche, will of Sir Adam Francis); /23 (P.C.C. 15 Jankyn, will of John Kirton).
[33] Guildhall MS. 9537/4.
[34] S.C. 6/Chas. I/627 m. 3d.
[35] For the wards, originally a manorial division which was also applied to the parish, see above.
[36] *Rep. from Commrs. on Poor Laws*, H.C. 44, pp. 92 f–k (1834), xxxv–xxxvi.

COLLEGE HOUSE
Boarding School.
Upper Edmonton Middlesex
Conducted by
Mr D. J. WHITE.

VIEW FROM THE GYMNASIUM.

EDMONTON: COLLEGE HOUSE SCHOOL *c.* 1840

Edmonton Green: Tower Blocks around the Shopping Centre

Enfield: Brimsdown Power Station and Factories beside the Lea Navigation

beadle of the workhouse. The vestry instructed the surveyors of the highways, of whom there were two in 1683;[37] by 1835 there were four, one for each ward.[38] During the 18th century the post was often occupied by gentry who employed deputies.[39] After the inclosure of Enfield Chase in 1777 two salaried surveyors were appointed for the Edmonton portion. From 1785 there was only one surveyor but his salary was considerably higher.

The accounts of the churchwardens and overseers, which were submitted monthly to the vestry, have not survived and there is no evidence that the surveyors of the highways kept records. The surveyors of the Chase had to present their accounts in November and those for 1782–5 survived in the vestry minute book. Vestry minutes for 1739–48, 1782–98, and 1863–85 are extant;[40] those for 1798–1862 were given as salvage during the Second World War.[41] The vestry minute book for 1739–48 contains minutes of the workhouse committee for 1732–7. There are also minute books of the later workhouse committee for 1796–1801[42] and 1827–30[43] and for the select vestry for 1831–5.[44]

The vestry probably existed before 1739 when the minutes begin. In 1720 the poor-rate was made by 'the vicar, churchwardens, overseers and other inhabitants'.[45] The workhouse committee or board (1732–7), which derived its name from its meeting-place, seems to have been an early form of select vestry. It consisted of the trustees of the workhouse, the vicar, churchwardens, overseers, and parishioners probably elected at Easter. The committee had wide powers over the parish officers, charities, and church repairs, as well as poor-relief. By 1739 the vestry was the main authority and the workhouse committee which existed from 1741 was concerned solely with the administration of the workhouse. It consisted of a committee of three, chosen monthly and enlarged in 1782 to consist of the churchwardens, overseers, master of the workhouse, and two members[46] of each ward.

The vestry and the workhouse committees, especially during the early 18th century, were dominated by a few prominent inhabitants, like Merry Teshmaker who was also active in the manorial courts.[47] Teshmaker, Samuel Clarke of Bush Hill, Samuel Tatem, who married the daughter of John Huxley of Weir Hall, and Pierce Galliard of Bury Hall were J.P.s and the committees sometimes committed people to the parish watch-house or to Bridewell. Dawson Warren (vicar 1795–1839) was very conscious of his rights[48] and started legal proceedings in pursuit of his claim to the chairmanship of the vestry. Although the outcome is unknown, he was the dominant personality in parish government in 1834.[49]

Poor-relief was administered by the workhouse committee and the vestry with more humanity than in neighbouring parishes. Considerable efforts were made to give outdoor relief, in money or goods, and paupers were committed to the workhouse only as a last resort, although it was cheaper to keep them in the workhouse than outside it. Pauper children were apprenticed to tradesmen, mostly in Edmonton and London but also to factories in Lancashire and to the Hudson's Bay Co. in Canada. The latter connexion was probably established through the Lake family of the Firs; Sir Atwell Lake was a governor of the company and it was in his honour that Edmonton, Alberta, was named.[50]

A select vestry was formed in 1829 and, probably under Warren's influence, the treatment of paupers became harsher. Out-relief was refused to the able-bodied and emphasis was laid on economy.[51]

A poorhouse was erected on the waste in 1639.[52] A workhouse was built in 1731–2 in Church Street, west of Edmonton church and Latymer's school,[53] and a new building was added in 1782. Numbers in the workhouse at any one time ranged from 34 in September 1791 to 142 in December 1800 but in most years were 50–70; 1800 was exceptional in averaging 110 inmates.[54] There was an average of 87 people in 1829, but there were complaints by the managing committee of over-crowding, with 6 children to a bed.[55] The workhouse was run by a salaried master or steward until 1737, when a new master was paid a fixed amount for each inmate; in return he was to have the profits of the workhouse labour, the sale of mops made by the women, and the wages of men employed by local farmers and tradesmen. The committee and vestry supervised the master, ordering the cleansing of the house, the supply of new clothes, and the weekly diet. A paid beadle, usually himself an inmate, assisted the master and lived in the workhouse. A salaried parish physician and apothecary was also appointed to look after the workhouse and out-poor and to carry out vaccinations.

The alms-houses and pension and apprenticing charities eased the burden on the ratepayers of Edmonton.[56] There was also some private relief, such as the money given to 52 people in Southgate ward by the owners of Minchenden in 1778.[57] Nevertheless there were complaints in 1671,[58] 1720,[59] and 1749[60] of unfair or excessive rating and the poor-rate of 1733 was quashed.[61] The annual poor-rate rose from 1s. in the £ in 1764–5 to 4s. in 1800 and 6s. 6d. in 1818–19.[62] In 1740 the vestry paid out £433, of which £244 was spent on the workhouse, and in 1775–6 £460 was spent on the poor, out of a total raised of £847.[63] In 1797 £624 was spent on the workhouse. The amount spent on

[37] M.R.O., Cal. Mdx. Sess. Bks., 1683–6, 73.
[38] Edmonton Highway Rate (1835) penes Broomfield Mus.
[39] Pam, Stamford Hill, Green Lanes Turnpike Trust, i. 8.
[40] Penes Edmonton Publ. Libr.
[41] Mason, Southgate Scrapbook, 99.
[42] Penes Edmonton Publ. Libr.
[43] M.R.O., D.R.O. 4/Box 26/3.
[44] Penes Edmonton Publ. Libr.
[45] M.R.O., Cal. Mdx. Sess. Bks., 1719–22, 77–8.
[46] Increased in 1792 to 4.
[47] M.R.O., Acc. 695/18, /19.
[48] See p. 184.
[49] Rep. of Commrs. on Poor Laws, H.C. 44, pp. 92 f–k (1834), xxxv–xxxvi.
[50] Sturges, Edmonton Past and Present, ii. 101

[51] Rep. of Commrs. on Poor Laws, H.C. 44, pp. 92 f–k (1834), xxxv–xxxvi.
[52] S.C. 6/Chas. I/627 m. 3d.
[53] See map and illustration in Robinson, Edmonton, facing p. 5.
[54] Figures only for 1733–6 and 1782–1800.
[55] M.R.O., D.R.O. 4/Box 26/3. [56] See pp. 203–6.
[57] M.R.O., Acc. 262/2/34.
[58] M.R.O., Cal. Mdx. Sess. Bks., 1664–73, 143.
[59] Ibid. 1719–22, 77–8.
[60] Ibid. 1748–57, 33–4.
[61] Ibid. 1732–5, 62.
[62] Poor-rates penes Edmonton Publ. Libr.; Robinson, Edmonton, 76–7.
[63] Rep. Cttee. on Rets. by Overseers, 1776, 396.

the poor varied from £2,499 in 1803 to £4,561 in 1818; in 1836 it was £3,021.[64]

The church-rate, which was 6d. in the £ in 1818–19 and the highway-rate, variously 1s. or 9d. in the £,[65] were not regular exactions but were raised as circumstances required. In 1644 highways were being repaired with the labour of parishioners[66] but in 1698 by paid labour. The cost was met by a rate levied in 1705.[67] There are highway-rate books for 1830–1 and 1835.[68]

LOCAL GOVERNMENT AFTER 1837. Edmonton was the geographical centre of Edmonton union, created in 1837, and the board of guardians met there. Edmonton workhouse was used for all the able-bodied poor of the union until 1842 when a new workhouse to house all adult paupers was built in south Edmonton, on a site later occupied by the North Middlesex hospital.[69]

For most of the 19th century local government was divided among several bodies, although membership often overlapped. At the time of the cholera outbreak in 1853, the vestry appointed a committee to consider the sanitary state of the parish.[70] There was a watching and lighting committee, presumably set up after the Act of 1833,[71] and the overseers collected a lighting rate.[72] A board of the surveyors of the highway was responsible for the roads in the parish by 1841.[73] In 1837 Edmonton parish became a medical district within the poor law union and in 1842 it was divided into three, each with its own medical officer.[74]

Edmonton local board of health[75] was set up in 1850 under the Public Health Act of 1848. It immediately replaced the highway board and took over responsibility for street lighting under the Local Government Act of 1858. It consisted of 12 members who met twice a month at the watch-house in Church Street. Its salaried officials were a clerk, a combined inspector of nuisances and surveyor, and a collector of rates, who later received a percentage of the collected rates in place of a salary. The board was financed by a general district rate, although sometimes there was a separate highway-rate. Expenditure on highways was nearly always considerably greater than on sanitary improvements.

There were many complaints about sewerage, especially from Southgate, where in 1879 a petition for separation from Edmonton was drawn up by the leading landholders and signed by more than 500

people.[76] In 1881 Southgate was granted its own local board and Edmonton local board was reduced to 9 members.[77] Although the loss of the large houses in Southgate deprived it of valuable rates, the Edmonton board seems to have been more active after the separation. Jerry-builders were vigorously prosecuted during the 1880s.[78] During the 1880s and 1890s there were committees for the town hall, cemetery, works, finance, farms, engines, sanitation, and the library.[79] A town hall 'in municipal Perpendicular' was built facing Fore Street in 1884 and enlarged in 1903.[80]

Southgate local board had 9 members, whose first chairman was John Walker of Arnos Grove. The board met twice a month in Ash Lodge and in the village hall until 1893, when council offices were erected to a design by A. Rowland Barker, a Southgate resident;[81] they were enlarged in 1914.[82] Salaried officials were a clerk, treasurer, rate-collector, sanitary inspector, medical officer of health, and a combined surveyor and engineer.[83]

Under the Act of 1894 the two local boards became urban districts. Edmonton local board of health had used the traditional wards of Bury Street, Church Street, and Fore Street.[84] There had been proposals to add two new wards, Angel Road and Silver Street,[85] and the new U.D. was organized accordingly, with three councillors for each of the five wards. After an inquiry in 1903 the district again consisted of three wards, with nine councillors each.[86] In 1933 the area was divided into Bury Street, Church Street, Angel Road, and Silver Street wards, with seven councillors for each.[87]

BOROUGH OF EDMONTON. *Per pale wavy sable and azure, on a saltire or between two cogwheels in fess argent an open book proper bound gules edged gold*

[Granted 1937]

Southgate U.D.[88] had nine councillors in 1894 and twelve from 1900. In 1906 it was divided into four wards: Middle, South, North-east, and North-west.[89] Swimming baths and a refuse destructor were erected[90] but the most important achievement was control over the development of the area.

[64] *Rep. from Sel. Cttee. on Poor Rate Rets.* H.C. 748, p. 99 (1821), iv; ibid. H.C. 334, p. 132 (1825); *Rep. of Commrs. on Poor Laws,* H.C. 44, p. 92 f (1834), xxxv; *2nd Ann. Rep. of Poor Law Commrs.* H.C. 595–II, pp. 212–3 (1836), xxix.
[65] Robinson, *Edmonton,* 76.
[66] M.R.O., Cal. Mdx. Sess. Bks., 1644–52, 6.
[67] *Cal. Mdx. Cnty. Sess. Bks.* ed. W. J. Hardy, 281.
[68] M.R.O., D.R.O. 4/Box 27; Edmonton highway-rate (1835) *penes* Broomfield Mus.
[69] S. I. Richardson, *Edmonton Poor Law Union, 1837–54* (Edmonton Hund. Hist. Soc. n.d.).
[70] R. McIlven, *Edmonton Local Board of Health, 1850–60* (Edmonton Hund. Hist. Soc. n.d.), 18.
[71] Watching and Lighting Act, 3 & 4 Wm. IV, c. 90.
[72] McIlven, *Edmonton Local Board,* 26, 29.
[73] Richardson, *Edmonton Poor Law Union,* 34.
[74] Ibid. 70–1.
[75] Unless otherwise stated, this account is based upon McIlven, *Edmonton Local Board.*
[76] *The Times,* 18 Dec. 1879.
[77] Act to Divide District of Local Board of Health of Edmonton, 44 & 45 Vic. c. clv.
[78] Fisk, *Edmonton,* 19; *Building News,* xxxix. 31, 114.
[79] Minutes for cttees. *penes* Edmonton Publ. Libr.
[80] Robbins, *Mdx.* 244.
[81] *Southgate, Fifty Years of Progress* (1931) (pamphlet *penes* Broomfield Mus.); Newby, *Old Southgate,* 69.
[82] Broomfield Mus.; R. Phillip's Coll. of Photos., no. 12.
[83] *Kelly's Dir. Mdx.* (1890).
[84] The fourth ward, South Street, formed Southgate local board district. All Edmonton U.D.C. and boro. recs. are at Edmonton Publ. Libr., Fore St.
[85] M.R.O., *Reps. of Local Inqs.* (1889–94), 119–34; (1889–97), 113–35.
[86] Ibid. (1895–1907), unpag., Edmonton, alteration of wards (1903); *Census,* 1901, 1911.
[87] *Census,* 1951; Sturges, *Edmonton Past and Present,* ii. 179.
[88] All Southgate U.D.C. and boro. recs. after 1899 are kept at the Civic Centre, Silver St., Enfield.
[89] M.R.O., *Rep. of Local Inqs.* (1895–1907), unpag., Southgate, division into wards (1906).
[90] *Incorp. of Southgate Boro.* (1933).

Although the number of houses increased eightfold between 1881 and 1931, Southgate remained one of the 'most agreeable of the northern suburbs',[91] largely because of the council's regulations and its acquisition of 287 a. of park-land.[92]

Southgate was incorporated in 1933, retaining its four wards. The council, consisting of a mayor, 7 aldermen, and 21 councillors, was enlarged.[93] Edmonton was incorporated in 1937, after which it had four wards, a mayor, 8 aldermen and 24 councillors.[94] Southgate B.C. was consistently dominated by opponents of the Labour party, while Edmonton, at least after the Second World War, was controlled by Labour councillors.[95]

BOROUGH OF SOUTHGATE. *Azure, a sun rising or; on a chief or a four-barred gate azure*
[Granted 1933]

In 1965 Edmonton and Southgate were united in Enfield L.B., created under the London Government Act of 1963.[96] The names of three Edmonton wards, Angel Road, Church Street, and Silver Street, survived among the 30 wards of the new authority. Edmonton and Southgate town halls were retained to house the borough treasurer, architect, engineer and surveyor, area housing and town planning offices. The education department was housed in Church Street, Edmonton.[97]

PUBLIC SERVICES. By wills proved 1560 and 1612 John Sadler and Robert Brett left money for buckets, ladders, and hooks to be kept in the parish church.[98] A fire-engine was first provided in 1772, when a paid engine-keeper was appointed.[99] A proper carriage and harness were ordered in 1786 and sold in 1793, although the engine was still in use in 1796.[1] A volunteer fire brigade was formed in 1877, with a small contribution by the local board. There were complaints about its performance in 1882 and the local board set up an engine committee in 1887, and formed a brigade under the direction of the surveyor.[2] A fire station existed by 1893.[3] The modern station in Church Street was erected in 1940.[4] Southgate, which had its own fire brigade by 1933,[5] had a new station in the High Street by 1972.

Although an order was made in 1714 for two watch-houses or cages in Church Street and Fore Street wards respectively,[6] only one apparently was erected. In the 1730s it was the 'new prison' and seems to have been a cell next to the parish church.[7] The Stamford Hill turnpike trust provided watchmen over its roads from 1774.[8] During the 1780s and 1790s there were several requests for a cage at Southgate because the constable was finding it difficult to transport felons to Edmonton.[9] A new watch-house was built on the north side of Church Street in 1833[10] and after Edmonton became part of the Metropolitan Police district in 1840[11] it became the police station.[12] A new station was built in Fore Street c. 1870s[13] and rebuilt in 1916. Other police stations were erected in Chase Side by 1878,[14] in High Road, New Southgate, in 1888, and in Green Lanes in 1915.[15] The Chase Side station was rebuilt in 1970.[16]

The abundance of gravel facilitated the construction of wells in Edmonton and there were a few deep wells in the chalk at Winchmore Hill,[17] notably Vicarsmoor well, which was very pure.[18] In the western part of the parish, however, many cottages were still relying on rain-water butts in the late 19th century.[19] The New River was an additional source of supply from 1613, although initially only for the larger houses.[20] The New River Co. carried out improvements during the 19th century, drawing on the river Lea[21] and constructing a reservoir in the Chase in the 1870s, from which water mains were laid along some roads.[22] It was many years, however, before the company provided piped water to the whole area. In 1877, when the Bush Hill Park Co. built a housing estate near the New River at Bush Hill, its water was obtained from a specially sunk artesian bore.[23] In 1904 the Metropolitan Water Board took over the local water companies, including the New River Co., and the new Banbury reservoir on the borders of Tottenham.[24] In 1935 work started on the very large William Girling reservoir, which was not completed until 1951.[25]

Well-water was easily polluted, especially in

[91] Robbins, *Mdx.* 327.
[92] *Southgate, Fifty Years of Progress* (1931) (pamphlet *penes* Broomfield Mus.); *The Times*, 5 Oct. 1910; 6 Nov. 1911. See above.
[93] *Incorp. of Southgate Boro.* (1933) (programme *penes* Broomfield Mus.).
[94] Sturges, *Edmonton Past and Present*, ii. 180–2; *Census*, 1951.
[95] Election results in *The Times*, e.g. 2 Nov. 1933; 2 Nov. 1938; 14 May 1949; 11 May 1962.
[96] *Census*, 1971.
[97] Enfield L.B., *Information Handbook* [1971].
[98] Prob. 11/43 (P.C.C. 49 Mellershe); /119 (P.C.C. 15 Fenner).
[99] Fisk, *Edmonton*, 92.
[1] Hoare, *Work of the Edmonton Vestry*, 13.
[2] Fisk, *Edmonton*, 92; engine cttee. mins. 1887 *penes* Edmonton Publ. Libr.
[3] *Kelly's Dir. Tottenham etc.* (1893–4).
[4] Boro. of Edmonton, *Official Guide* [1963].
[5] *Incorp. of Southgate Boro.* (1933) [programme *penes* Broomfield Mus.].
[6] See above, p. 176.
[7] Avery, *Edmonton Workhouse Cttee.*, 12.
[8] Pam, *Stamford Hill, Green Lanes Turnpike Trust*, ii. 1, 5.

[9] Hoare, op. cit. 13; Sturges, *Edmonton Past and Present*, ii. 170–1.
[10] Sturges, *Edmonton Past and Present*, ii. 171.
[11] *Lond. Gaz.* 13 Oct. 1840, p. 2250.
[12] Poor Rate Valuation (1852), no. 899, *penes* Edmonton Publ. Libr.
[13] *Kelly's Dir. Tottenham* (1893–4); photographs *penes* Edmonton Publ. Libr.
[14] *Kelly's Dir. Mdx.* (1878).
[15] Datestones on bldgs.
[16] Ex inf. Southgate police station.
[17] Sturges, *Edmonton Past and Present*, i. 76; Cresswell, *Winchmore Hill*, 97.
[18] Robinson, *Edmonton*, 33. Name said to derive from a vicar who sunk the well, according to Cresswell (*Winchmore Hill*, 93) in the 17th cent. but it is more likely to have been derived from the medieval Viker family: see p. 134.
[19] Cresswell, *Winchmore Hill*, 93.
[20] Robinson, *Edmonton*, 14–19.
[21] M.R.O., 144; *Mdx. Quarterly*, N.S. i. 24–5.
[22] Newby, *Old Southgate*, 89.
[23] Sturges, *Edmonton Past and Present*, i. 77. The bore was filled in in 1925, leaving the tower of the water-works, the Wells: Robbins, *Mdx.* 361.
[24] See p. 346.
[25] Ex inf. Metropolitan Water Board (1973).

densely populated Upper Edmonton, where sewerage was totally inadequate in the mid 19th century.[26] The streams had always formed open sewers and in 1622 a presentment was made for fishing in the common sewer.[27] Maintaining the common sewers was in 1650 stated to be the lord's responsibility,[28] but in practice it was the tenants whose lands bordered the streams who were charged with maintaining them.[29] The growth of population and especially its concentration during the 19th century made the open sewers dangerous. Edmonton local board of health made only slow progress, laying sewers in the most populous areas during the 1850s,[30] and it was not until the 1870s that sewage works were constructed at Deephams Farm.[31] Southgate's case for separation in 1881 was largely based on complaints about sewage[32] but by 1893 both Edmonton and Southgate were said to be well-sewered. Sewage was treated at the 200-acre Deephams Farm,[33] which was extended in 1927.[34]

From the 18th century there was a parish physician and apothecary and after 1837 a medical officer.[35] About 1836 Winchmore Hill Independent Medical Club was set up to provide medicine and surgical attendance outside the parish system. It was financed by subscription.[36] An infirmary which formed part of the union workhouse buildings was too small and in 1844 sheds had to be converted into fever wards.[37] In 1910 a new union infirmary, with accommodation for 400 and an adjoining nurses' home, was opened east of the workhouse.[38] It was used as a military hospital during the First World War and in 1930, when the poor law union was dissolved, became a county hospital. In 1948, as the North Middlesex hospital, it came under the control of Edmonton group hospital management committee and catered mainly for acute cases.[39] By 1973 it had 667 beds and, like all the hospitals in Edmonton and Southgate except Grovelands and Highlands, it was administered by Enfield group management committee.[40]

In 1886 the Metropolitan Asylums Board purchased a 36-acre site from the Chaseville Park estate on former Chase land, where it opened a convalescent fever hospital. Control passed to the L.C.C. in 1930 and to the Northern group hospital management committee in 1948. The Northern hospital, after 1948 called Highlands hospital, consisted of 16 separate blocks with accommodation for 480 patients.[41] In 1973 it was a hospital for acute cases with 550 beds.[42]

In 1902, following a severe outbreak of smallpox, a temporary wooden building was erected by Edmonton U.D.C. in Picketts Lock Lane as an isolation hospital. It was pulled down after 1927.[43] In 1905 Edmonton and Enfield agreed to maintain a joint hospital for infectious diseases other than smallpox at South Lodge, inside Enfield but adjoining Highlands hospital.[44] About the same time Southgate U.D.C. opened an isolation hospital in Tottenhall Road. After the Second World War it became Southgate maternity annexe, then successively a children's hospital specializing in ear, nose, and throat cases, a hospital for the chronically sick, and a geriatric unit linked to the North Middlesex hospital.[45] In 1973, as Greentrees hospital, it had 73 beds for geriatrics.[46]

For most of the 19th century Millfield House in Silver Street housed children of the Strand poor law union. An infirmary was added in 1874. In 1917 the whole building was taken over by the Metropolitan Asylums Board as an epileptic hospital, which passed to the L.C.C. in 1930.[47] The hospital, then called St. David's hospital, had 328 beds in 1949 and was closed in 1971.[48]

Grovelands House was lent to the Middlesex Voluntary Aid Detachment in 1916 as a military hospital. In 1921 the detachment bought the house and 6 a. which it gave to the Royal Northern hospital as a convalescent home. Another 20 a. was purchased and the hospital was officially opened in 1926.[49] In 1973 Grovelands was a pre-convalescent unit of 56 beds run by the North London group hospital management committee.[50]

Edmonton churchyard was extended in 1772[51] and 1862[52] but burials were forbidden at Weld chapel in 1854[53] and at Edmonton church in 1882.[54] In 1880 a cemetery was opened in Waterfall Road, Southgate, and administered by a burial board of 6 members.[55] In 1882 Edmonton local board purchased 30 a. in Church Street from the Ecclesiastical Commissioners[56] which they opened in 1884 as Hyde Side cemetery.[57] In 1884 a Federation cemetery belonging to the Western Synagogue in St. Alban's Place (Islington) was opened west of Montagu Road.[58]

In 1815 the Stamford Hill turnpike trust introduced street lighting along Fore Street as far as the 7-mile stone and along Church Street to the parish church.[59] Edmonton vestry set up a watching and lighting committee soon after the 1833 Act[60] and by 1840 Edmonton village was said to be

---

[26] McIlven, *Edmonton Local Board of Health*, 19.

[27] M.R.O., Acc. 695/43 (end); S.C. 6/Chas. I/627 m. 3d. The fact that fish could be found in it suggests that the stream was not too polluted.

[28] M.R.O., Acc. 695/15 (end).

[29] e.g. 1799: M.R.O., Acc. 695/41.

[30] McIlven, op. cit. 12–13.

[31] Sturges, *The Silver Link*, 1.

[32] Sturges, *Edmonton Past and Present*, ii. 177.

[33] *Kelly's Dir. Tottenham* (1893–4).

[34] *The Times*, 5 Jan. 1925; 19 July 1927.

[35] See pp. 177–8.

[36] Prospectus *penes* Broomfield Mus.

[37] Richardson, *Edmonton Poor Law Union*, 39, 62.

[38] *The Times*, 26 July 1910; *Building News*, xciii. 37.

[39] Boro. of Edmonton, *Official Guide* [1963]; Sturges, *Edmonton Past and Present*, ii. 176.

[40] *Hosp. Yr. Bk.* (1973), 143.

[41] *Kelly's Dir. Tottenham* (1893–4); *Hosp. Yr. Bks.* (1947–9).

[42] *Hosp. Yr. Bk.* (1973).

[43] Fisk, *Edmonton*, 192; *The Times*, 3 Sept. 1927.

[44] Local Govt. Bd.'s Provis. Orders Confirmation (no. 17) Act, 5 Ed. VII, cxi. See p. 244.

[45] Ex inf. acting hosp. sec. (1973).

[46] *Hosp. Yr. Bk.* (1973).

[47] 'Rep. of Superintendent of Management Cttee., 1948' (TS. supplied by acting hosp. sec., N. Mdx. hosp., 1973).

[48] Ex inf. acting hosp. sec., N. Mdx. hosp. (1973); *Hosp. Yr. Bks.* (1947–9).

[49] Ex inf. the matron, Grovelands hosp. (1973).

[50] *Hosp. Yr. Bk.* (1973).

[51] Edmonton Publ. Libr., D 15, 18, 20.

[52] Fisk, *Edmonton*, 31.

[53] Edmonton Publ. Libr., D 17.   [54] Ibid. D 14.

[55] Ibid. D 13, 21; *Kelly's Dir. Mdx.* (1890).

[56] Church Com., file 23019.

[57] *Kelly's Dir. Tottenham* (1893–4).

[58] Plaque at cemetery.

[59] Pam, *Stamford Hill, Green Lanes Turnpike Trust*, ii. 1, 5.

[60] See above.

efficiently lighted with gas.[61] The Tottenham and
Edmonton Gas Light and Coke Co. was founded in
1847 and built gas-works in Dyson's Road, from
which the eastern part of Edmonton was supplied.
The company expanded, absorbing other companies
in 1914, 1928, 1930, and 1938 before itself being
taken over by the Eastern Gas Board.[62] In 1938 it
took over Southgate and District Gas Co., which
had been formed in 1858 as the Southgate and
Colney Hatch Gas Light and Coke Co., whose gas-
works in south-west Southgate supplied the western
side of Edmonton parish.[63]

The first house in Southgate to receive electric
light was Arnos Grove, in 1896.[64] In 1898 the
Tottenham and Edmonton Gas Act[65] empowered
the Tottenham and Edmonton Gas Light and Coke
Co. to produce and supply electricity. Edmonton
U.D.C. was made responsible for electric lighting
in 1902[66] and Southgate U.D.C. in 1904. After 1922
electricity for both districts was supplied by the
North Metropolitan Electric Power Supply Co.
(later the Eastern Electricity Board).[67]

By 1845 there were post offices in Fore Street,
Southgate and Winchmore Hill.[68] There was
another in Church Street by 1851[69] and two in
Southgate by 1865, one at Southgate Circus and the
other in High Street.[70] The High Street post office
moved to Southgate Green by 1890, by which date
there were also post offices at Palmers Green, Angel
Road, Hertford Road, and Lower Fore Street.[71]
The first telephone exchange was opened in 1905[72]
and a new one was built in Green Lanes in 1936.[73]

The Passmore Edwards library, designed by
Maurice Adams, was opened in Fore Street in
1897 and extended in 1931. A library had opened at
Bush Hill Park by 1923 and branches opened in
Houndsfield Road in 1937 and in Silver Street in
1938.[74] A new library opened in Ridge Avenue,
Bush Hill, in 1963.[75] There were four public
libraries in Southgate borough by 1963[76] and a new
branch was opened there in 1966.[77]

Edmonton U.D.C. bought the 53-acre Pymmes
estate in 1898 and opened it as the first public park
in the area.[78] The Church Commissioners sold 20 a.
at Church Street to the U.D.C. in 1902 for a
recreation ground.[79] Thirty-seven acres west of
Hertford Road was acquired by the council in
commemoration of George V's Silver Jubilee

(1935) and were being laid out as a park and
recreation ground in 1939.[80] Edmonton acquired
another 50 a. of open space at Firs farm after the
war.[81]

Southgate U.D.C. purchased most of the
Broomfield estate in 1903. The 54-acre grounds
became a park and the house was converted into a
local museum in 1925.[82] In 1911 the council
bought 64 a. of Grovelands, later increased to 91 a.
and forming the largest park in the area. Oakwood
Park (64 a.) and Arnos Grove (44 a.) were purchased
in 1927 and 1928 respectively.[83] Chapel Fields
cricket ground was a gift of the Walker brothers.
Among other sports grounds Bramley (20 a.) and
Hazelwood (12 a.) were the largest in 1963.[84]

Edmonton was one of the districts most affected
by the scheme to transform the derelict Lea riverside
into a recreational area. The Lee Valley regional
park authority, representing the local authorities,
was constituted in 1967 and Pickett's Lock centre,
containing many recreational facilities and set in
woods and park-land alongside the William
Girling reservoir, was opened in 1973.[85]

CHURCHES. Edmonton church is first mentioned
between 1136 and 1143,[86] a date consistent with the
earliest surviving portions of the fabric.[87] It was
appropriated to Walden abbey from 1136–43 until
1538 and granted to St. Paul's cathedral after 1544.[88]
A vicarage had been ordained by 1189–90 when the
prior of Walden granted it to master Peter de
Walde, to hold as William the chaplain had held it.[89]
The advowson descended with the rectory.

The vicarage was endowed with a small plot of
land and the small tithes c. 1189–90.[90] It was
valued at £6 13s. 4d. in the mid 13th century[91] and
at £5 in 1291,[92] but was subject to a yearly pension
of £2 to the abbot of Walden.[93] In 1535 the vicarage
was worth £18 a year[94] but in 1649 it was only £6.[95]
The valuation rose from £150 in 1723 to £300 in
1812,[96] until by 1835 the vicar's net income was
£1,550.[97] Small tithes were worth £1 16s. in 1535.[98]
In the 16th century the glebe consisted of 1 a. of
arable in the Hyde, a close of pasture (3 a.), and 1 a.
in the common marsh.[99] At inclosure in 1804 the
vicar was allotted 20 a. in the Hyde in lieu of small
tithes from common land, and corn-rents, then

[61] Pigot's Dir. Mdx. (1840).
[62] M.R.O., Acc. 1153/I; see pp. 346–7.
[63] M.R.O., Acc. 1153/II; O.S. Map 1/2,500, Mdx. VII.
13 (1867 edn.).   [64] Newby, Old Southgate, 75.
[65] 61 & 62 Vic. c. 161 (Local Act).
[66] Electric Lighting Orders Confirmation (No. 1) Act,
2 Ed. VII, c. xci.
[67] North Metropolitan Electric Power Supply Act, 12 &
13 Geo. V, c. lxxvii.   [68] Home Cnties. Dir. (1845).
[69] H.O. 107/1703 p. 212d.
[70] O.S. Map 6", Mdx. VII. SW. (1865 edn.).
[71] Kelly's Dir. Mdx. (1890).
[72] Sturges, Edmonton Past and Present, i. 131.
[73] Datestone on bldg.
[74] Edmonton U.D.C., Official Guide [1939].
[75] Boro. of Edmonton, Official Guide [1963].
[76] Boro. of Southgate, Official Guide [1963].
[77] Photographs penes Edmonton Publ. Libr.
[78] Acquis. of Pymmes Pk. Act, 61–2 Vic., c. lxiii.
[79] Church Com., S 4 Survey, p. 368.
[80] Edmonton U.D.C., Official Guide [1939].
[81] Boro. of Edmonton, Official Guide [1963].
[82] Pamphlet penes Broomfield Mus.
[83] Boro. of Southgate, Official Guide [1963]; Mason,
Story of Southgate, 5, 54, 64.

[84] Boro. of Southgate, Official Guide [1963].
[85] Evening Standard, 25 June 1974.
[86] Reg. Regum Anglo-Norm. iii, no. 913.
[87] See below.
[88] See p. 154.
[89] B.M. Harl. MS. 3697, f. 49, i.e. inspeximus of Richard
[FitzNeal], bishop of London (1189–98), of charter of
Reynold, prior of Walden (1164–90), and charter of Gilbert
Foliot, archdeacon of Middlesex (1181–96), who described
Peter de Walde as 'our clerk', possibly identifiable with
Peter de Waltham, archdeacon of London 1191–5.
William the chaplain flourished c. 1165–89: E 42/385.
[90] B.M. Harl. MS. 3697, f. 49.
[91] St. Paul's MS., W.D. 9, f. 85; Val. of Norw. ed. Lunt,
359.
[92] Tax. Eccl. (Rec. Com.), 17.
[93] B.M. Harl. MS. 3697, f. 49.
[94] Valor Eccl. (Rec. Com.), i. 433.
[95] Probably because of the decay of the house: Home
Cnties. Mag. i. 316.
[96] Guildhall MS. 9557, f. 30.
[97] Rep. Com. Eccl. Revs. [67], pp. 644–5, H.C. (1835),
xxii.
[98] Valor Eccl. (Rec. Com.), i. 433.
[99] Robinson, Edmonton, 83.

totalling £829, in lieu of small tithes from old inclosures.[1] In 1851 from a total income of £1,174, tithes accounted for £928 and glebe for £129.[2]

The vicar's house, on the site of the later vicarage, was mentioned in the mid 13th century.[3] It stood in an orchard south-east of the church[4] and was ruinous and uninhabited in 1649[5] and still so in 1673.[6] The vicar was apparently living elsewhere in 1664 and 1672.[7] The vicarage was rebuilt c. 1700 as a narrow, two-storeyed building with dormer-windowed attics and a steep roof. In 1819 it was described as 'a comfortable dwelling and in good repair'.[8] It was replaced by a large, Victorian brick house which was demolished in 1967[9] and in turn replaced by a smaller, modern vicarage.

Berenger le Romeyn founded a chapel in Edmonton church which his son-in-law, Sir Richard de Plessis (de Placetis) or Wrotham, by will dated 1292, endowed to maintain a chaplain.[10] It may be identifiable with the chantry of St. Thomas of Canterbury in the crypt, which was mentioned in 1461.[11] Before his death in 1360[12] Peter Favelore built a chapel within Edmonton church, which his colleague Adam Francis, by will proved 1375, endowed to maintain two chantry chaplains, vesting the patronage in the vicar of Edmonton.[13] In 1417 the chantries received an endowment of £13 6s. 8d. from property in London from John Church, a London grocer,[14] and in 1471 a house and garden were devised by William Age.[15] In 1535 the chantries were worth £7 8s. 4d. and £7 3s. 4d. a year respectively.[16] When they were suppressed in 1547, the two priests were receiving the £13 6s. 8d. of John Church's endowment from the chamber of London and £3 from their chantry house, two other houses, and c. 10½ a. in Edmonton.[17] In 1548 the property was granted to Thomas Wilkes and Thomas Atkins, both of London.[18]

In 1417 John Church also settled upon the chantry priests 13s. 4d. yearly for a lamp and 13s. 4d. for an obit.[19] By wills proved 1471, 1529, and 1540 respectively, William Age, John Kirton, and Jasper Leake founded obits[20] but only John Church's still survived in 1547.[21] There was a brotherhood of Our Lady in 1529.[22]

Richard Rogers the elder, by will proved 1579, left

his property in trust for, *inter alia*, 6s. 8d. for a sermon on the anniversary of his death.[23] Richard Rogers the younger left a rent-charge of £2 by will dated 1636, from which 3s. 4d. was to be paid for a sermon on the first Sunday in August. A further 3s. 4d. out of a rent-charge of £1 9s. 4d. was given towards a sermon on that day by Edward Rogers, by will proved 1659.[24] In 1867 13s. 4d. from the Rogers' charities was paid to the minister for a sermon on the first Sunday in August out of rent-charges totalling £7 1s. 4d.[25]

Although there is no evidence that vicars were non-resident, assistant curates were usual from the 13th century.[26] In 1641–2 there were two assistant curates, one of whom served Weld chapel,[27] and there was an assistant curate in 1706.[28] James Scott, the author of political and religious works, held the position as a young man from 1760–1.[29] There was one curate, paid £40 a year, in 1776[30] and two in 1835 had stipends totalling £250.[31] In 1883 the Ecclesiastical Commissioners granted the vicar £450 a year to employ three curates.[32]

In 1609 armed parishioners seized the crops of the vicar, William Hicks, who had been accused by the churchwarden, Walter Agard, of constantly breaking the canons.[33] William Muffet, who succeeded his father-in-law as vicar in 1631, was ordered in 1637 to remove a monument from the upper end of the chancel and replace it with a communion table and rail.[34] By 1643, however, he had been ejected as a royalist and execrated in a pamphlet as a drunkard, blasphemer, and man of violence.[35] He was restored in 1660.

The church was still suffering in the 1670s and 1680s from the neglect and ill-treatment of the Interregnum.[36] By will proved 1665, John Wilde of Edmonton devised property in trust for various charitable purposes, including an annual payment of £4 for bread and wine for the sacrament each Easter and the residue for the repair of the church.[37] By 1867 £90 from Wilde's charity was spent on church purposes[38] and when the Ecclesiastical Charities were instituted in 1899, £107 was allotted to them from this source.[39]

During the 18th century services were held twice on Sundays, communion was administered once a

[1] Ibid. 212–15, 326.
[2] H.O. 129/137/3/1/3.
[3] B.M. Harl. MS. 3697, f. 182. It was burgled in 1367: Cal. Pat. 1364–7, 387.
[4] Hatfield C.P. 291.1, ff. 119 sqq.; C.P.M. Suppl. 27.
[5] Home Cnties. Mag. i. 316.
[6] Guildhall MS. 9537/20, f. 19.
[7] He was assessed under Fore Street, not Church Street, ward for hearth tax: M.R.O., MR/TH/5 m. 4; E 179/143/370 m. 13.
[8] Robbins, Mdx. 244; Robinson, Edmonton, illust. facing pp. 5, 82.
[9] Photographs penes Edmonton Publ. Libr.
[10] J. Collinson, Hist. of Somerset, iii. 65.
[11] D. O. Pam, Late Medieval Religion in Enfield, Edmonton and Tottenham (Edmonton Hund. Hist. Soc., 1968), 6. Sir Richard's mother was a member of the Wrotham family, whose Kent connexions possibly account for the dedication to St. Thomas.
[12] Cal. Inq. p.m. x, p. 470.
[13] The Annals of St. Helen's, Bishopsgate, ed. J. E. Cox, pp. 372–3.
[14] St. Paul's MS., Box A 67, no. 63.
[15] Pam, op. cit. 6.
[16] Valor Eccl. (Rec. Com.), i. 433.
[17] E 301/34 mm. 31d.–32, no. 173.
[18] Cal. Pat. 1547–8, 385.

[19] St. Paul's MS., Box A 67, no. 63.
[20] Pam, op. cit. 6; Prob. 11/23 (P.C.C. 15 Jankyn); /28 (P.C.C. 22 Alenger).
[21] E 301/34 mm. 31d.–32, no. 173.
[22] Pam, op. cit. 9, 10.
[23] Prob. 11/61 (P.C.C. 22 Baker).
[24] Prob. 11/292 (P.C.C. 330 Pell).
[25] Gen. Digest of Endowed Chars. H.C. 433, pp. 14–15 (1867–8), lii, pt. 1.
[26] e.g. Roger and Simon (13th cent.): E 40/1690, /2140.
[27] Hse. of Lords, Mdx. Protestation Rets. f. 2.
[28] Guildhall MSS. 9550, 9800A.
[29] D.N.B.
[30] Guildhall MS. 9557, f. 30.
[31] Rep. Com. Eccl. Revs. [67], pp. 644–5, H.C. (1835), xxii.
[32] Lond. Gaz. 26 Jan. 1883, p. 473; 23 Nov. 1883, p. 5631.
[33] Sta. Cha. 8/38/12; M.R.O., Cal. Mdx. Sess. Recs. 1608–9, 214–15.
[34] Hennessy, Novum Rep. 145; Cal. S.P. Dom. 1636–7, 545.
[35] Walker Revised, ed. Matthews, 261; Robinson, Edmonton, 85 n. 186.
[36] Guildhall MS. 9537/20, ff. 19, 71.
[37] Prob. 11/316 (P.C.C. 9 Hyde).
[38] Gen. Digest of Endowed Chars. H.C. 433, pp. 14–15 (1867–8), lii, pt. 1.
[39] Endowed Chars. (Mdx.), H.C. 306, pp. 6–9 (1899), lxx.

month and children were examined in Lent. By 1778 prayers were also said on Wednesdays, Fridays and holy days. There were 70 communicants in 1770.[40] Several of the 18th-century vicars were canons of St. Paul's.[41] An exception was Henry Owen (vicar 1776–95), author of several theological works.[42] In 1825 Dawson Warren (vicar 1795–1839), author of a Paris journal and active in local affairs, proposed to present a petition to Parliament against concessions to Roman Catholics.[43] Henry W. Burrows (vicar 1878–82), canon of St. Paul's, was described as a 'High Churchman but not a ritualist'.[44]

Warren in 1810 blamed the increase in the numbers of dissenters on the lack of accommodation in the church.[45] Although this was mainly an excuse, the increasing population in the 19th century, especially in distant parts of the parish, did lead to the foundation of daughter churches. In 1828 a chapel of ease was erected at Winchmore Hill and St. John's in Upper Edmonton existed by 1839. In 1851, when Edmonton church was attended on census Sunday by 763 people in the morning, 590 in the afternoon, and 338 in the evening,[46] two daughter churches, St. Paul's Winchmore Hill and St. James's Upper Edmonton, were assigned separate parishes. Most missionary activity took place after 1880, with the creation of mission churches to serve the new suburbs. Most of these became separate parish churches,[47] St. Mary's in 1883, St. Peter's in 1898, St. Michael's in 1901, St. Aldhelm's in 1903, St. Stephen's in 1907, St. Martin's in 1911, and St. Alphege's in 1954. Among those which never developed into separate parishes was St. Barnabas's mission room, erected at the corner of Bury Street and Hertford Road in 1882 and superseded in 1902 by St. Michael's, Hertford Road.[48] A mission room, sometimes called St. Martin's, opened on the north side of Bury Street, between Bush Hill Road and the Stag and Hounds between 1882 and 1886 and was replaced by another mission room in 1902. This was St. Saviour's, opposite the Stag and Hounds,[49] which was attended by 26 people on the evening of census Sunday 1903,[50] and which closed between 1933 and 1937.[51] St. George's hall in St. George's Road was being used as a parish room by All Saints by 1893.[52] It was demolished in 1971.[53] St. Alban's or St. Peter's mission room opened in Goodwin Road in north-east Edmonton in 1888 and closed between 1933 and 1937.[54] In 1904 an iron room on the northern side of Malden Road

replaced an earlier mission in Walton Road. It was still there in 1938.[55] In 1905 All Saints took over Hyde mission hall in Victoria Road, which it used as St. Matthias's mission church until it was taken over by Brethren between 1917 and 1922.[56]

The church of *ALL SAINTS*,[57] so called in 1396,[58] is built of Kentish ragstone rubble and is faced, except for the tower, with brick. It consists of the chancel with chapels and north vestry, aisled nave, and west tower. The remains of a 12th-century arch and doorway were discovered in the south wall in 1889 and then incorporated into the west wall of a new aisle. The chancel, vestry (including the metal-plated door which survives), nave, north aisle, and west tower were rebuilt in the 15th century and the north chapel was added in the early 16th century. The roof of the north aisle probably dates from 1626 although it was ordered to be repaired in 1685.[59] In 1772 the churchwardens, a bricklayer and a carpenter, encased the outside, except for the tower, in brick and substituted wooden frames for the stone mullions of the windows.[60] The chancel was restored in 1858, the wood frames were replaced with stone mullions in 1868, and the south aisle and chapel added in 1889.[61]

There are many brasses dating from *c.* 1500 (Elizabeth and her husbands John Asplyn and Geoffrey Askew) to 1616 (Edward Nowell). There is a stone monument to John Kirton (d. 1529)[62] which has lost its brasses, but most monuments are of marble and date from the 17th and 18th centuries; several commemorate the Huxley family. The churchyard contains the tombs of Charles Lamb (d. 1834) and his sister.

In 1552 the church plate consisted[63] of a silver pax and two cruets bequeathed by John Kirton in 1529,[64] a silver pyx, and two chalices. Five salvers had been added by 1818, when all the plate was stolen.[65] The plate was replaced by a silver-gilt cup, bought in 1854, and a set made in 1880.[66] There are eight bells: (iii–vii) by Samuel Knight of Stepney, 1734; (i) and (ii) by Mears, 1788; (viii) by Mears, 1866. There is a sanctus bell by Mears, 1812.[67] The registers of burials are complete from 1557, those of baptisms and marriages from 1558.[68]

In 1615 Sir John Weld of Arnolds in Southgate erected a small chapel on his own land near his house for the use of his family and the inhabitants of South Street and Bowes.[69] It was consecrated in 1615 on condition that all the inhabitants should take Easter communion at the parish church and that the

[40] Guildhall MSS. 9550, 9557, f. 30; 9558, f. 431.
[41] Hennessy, *Novum Rep.* 145.
[42] Robinson, *Edmonton*, 87.
[43] *The Times*, 16 Apr. 1825.
[44] Hennessy, *Novum Rep.* 145; *The Times*, 12 Feb. 1878.
[45] Guildhall MS. 9558, f. 431.
[46] H.O. 129/137/3/1/3.
[47] See section on modern churches, below.
[48] *Kelly's Dir. Mdx.* (1882); *Kelly's Dir. Tottenham* (1893–4); *Kelly's Dirs. Enfield* (1901–2, 1902–3).
[49] *Kelly's Dirs. Mdx.* (1882, 1886); *Kelly's Dirs. Enfield* (1899–1900, 1902–3).
[50] R. Mudie-Smith, *Religious Life of London*, 400.
[51] *Kelly's Dirs. Mdx.* (1933, 1937).
[52] *Kelly's Dir. Tottenham* (1893–4).
[53] Ex inf. Mr. D. O. Pam (1974).
[54] *Kelly's Dirs. Mdx.* (1886, 1933, 1937); ex inf. Mr. D. O. Pam (1974).
[55] *Kelly's Dir. Enfield* (1904–5); O.S. Map 1/2,500, Mdx. VII. 15 (1938 edn.).
[56] *Kelly's Dirs. Enfield* (1904–5, 1905–6); *Kelly's Dir.*

Mdx. (1917); *Kelly's Dir. Tottenham* (1922). See section on Protestant nonconformity.
[57] Unless otherwise stated, the account of the church fabric is based upon Hist. Mon. Com. *Mdx.* 17–19; Pevsner, *Mdx.* 47.
[58] M.R.O., Acc. 349/28. It was called All Hallows in 1374 (*Cal. of Wills in Ct. of Hustings, London*, ii. 171) and 1519 (Prob. 11/21 (P.C.C. 7 Bodfelde, will of Nich. Bone)).
[59] Guildhall MS. 9537/20, f. 71.
[60] Robinson, *Edmonton*, 63.
[61] Fisk, *Edmonton*, 24–5.
[62] Prob. 11/23 (P.C.C. 15 Jankyn).   [63] E 315/498 f. 22.
[64] Prob. 11/23 (P.C.C. 15 Jankyn).
[65] Robinson, *Edmonton*, 65.
[66] Freshfield, *Communion Plate of Mdx.* 15.
[67] H. B. Walters, 'The Bells of Mdx.', *T.L.M.A.S.* xvii. 137; Edmonton Publ. Libr., D 48.
[68] Registers *penes* Edmonton church. See M.R.O., D.R.O. 4 for details.
[69] Unless otherwise stated, the account of Southgate chapel is based upon Robinson, *Edmonton*, 122–42.

vicar of Edmonton should consent to baptisms and marriages there.[70] The chapel was assigned a district chapelry in Southgate in 1851.[71]

The patronage of the chapel, which had been exercised by Sir John Weld, descended with Arnolds until 1762[72] when Sir George Colebrook, Bt., expressly reserved it when he sold the estate. His trustees sold the patronage and the chapel itself in 1774 to the Revd. Henry Shepherd, from whom it passed in 1784 to the Revd. William Barclay and in 1786 to Robert Winbolt of Enfield.

In 1813 Warren the vicar challenged the right of Robert Winbolt's widow to the patronage. Mrs. Winbolt appointed George William Curtis, nephew of the lord of the manor Sir William Curtis, as minister and she may have sold the patronage to Sir William at about that time. Warren took possession of the chapel as an appurtenance of Edmonton church and in 1814 Mrs. Winbolt sued him in King's Bench. In 1815, however, she renounced all her claims and the patronage passed to the vicar of Edmonton.

Sir John Weld made provision in 1615 for a minister or curate of at least £13 6s. 8d. a year[73] and, by will proved 1623, directed his trustees to purchase land to the value of £30 a year, out of which they were to pay £15 18s. 8d. to the poor and the remainder for the maintenance of the curate.[74] In 1625 Weld's widow and executrix, Frances, purchased an estate at Orsett (Essex) which she settled in trust. The profits of £40 a year, through negligence, had dwindled to £26 by 1709. By 1867 the annual rent was £170, of which £138 was spent on the church, mostly as an endowment for the curate.[75] The Orsett estate was subsequently sold and the proceeds, invested by the Charity Commission, were in 1974 applied in yearly grants to the incumbent.[76] The curate's income was supplemented in 1665 by £2 a year from the charity of Sir John Wilde[77] and members of the Weld family paid £18 a year, which was reduced to £12 until 1707 when it lapsed. By 1851 the total income of Weld chapel was £354, of which £160 came from the Weld chapel estate.[78]

Sir John Weld bequeathed £20 towards the building of a dwelling-house for the curate, which was pulled down in 1732 when the chapel was enlarged. The Ecclesiastical Commissioners made a grant in 1882 for a vicarage house,[79] but it was not built until 1900.[80] Southgate Church House was erected in 1934[81] and the foundation stone of a parish hall and new vicarage was laid in 1970.

WELD CHAPEL was a small brick building with narrow buttresses, windows in a College Gothic style, and a wooden turret.[82] Aisles were added to the original nave and chancel in 1715 and 1732 and there were alterations and enlargements in 1830.[83] On census Sunday 1851 the chapel was attended by 560 people in the morning, 430 in the afternoon, and 200 in the evening.[84]

The chapel was demolished in 1862 and replaced in 1863 by *CHRIST CHURCH*, Southgate, which was erected farther east on a site given by Isaac Walker. Built of stone in the Decorated style by Sir George Gilbert Scott, Christ Church consists of chancel with north chapel and south organ chamber, aisled nave, and spire. The stained glass windows in the south aisle, by D. G. Rossetti, date from 1865; those in the north aisle, by Burne-Jones, date from 1865, 1866, 1885, and 1898. The church contains 17th-century monuments from the original chapel, including one to the founder.[85]

The sanctus bell, the gift of Dame Joan Brooke, dates from 1616. The other bells, of which there are ten, date from 1872 to 1920 and are by Mears and Stainbank of London.[86] The plate includes a silver cup given by Dame Frances Weld in 1639, which was remodelled in 1894. There are also two plates of c. 1700, a tankard of 1738, a late-18th-century tumbler, and a set of modern plate, all in silver.[87] The registers of baptisms and burials date from 1695, those of marriages (incomplete) from 1702.[88]

The church of *ST. PAUL*, Winchmore Hill, was built in 1828 as a chapel of ease to Edmonton church. The bishop of London authorized marriages to be performed there in 1838 but was prevented from creating it a parish by the chapter of St. Paul's.[89] In 1851, however, Winchmore Hill became a district chapelry.[90] The benefice, a vicarage from 1874, is in the gift of the vicar of Edmonton.[91] On census Sunday 1851 the church was attended by 176 people in the morning and 176 in the afternoon.[92] By 1903 numbers had risen to 576 in the morning and 753 in the evening, making St. Paul's the best attended church in Edmonton.[93] The church, designed by John Davies and erected in 1828, is an early example of the neo-Gothic style. It was repaired in 1844 after thieves had stolen the communion plate and set fire to the building. The nave and chancel side windows date from 1846 and the chancel was enlarged in 1888 and 1928. Built of white brick in the Perpendicular style, it consists of an apsidal chancel with south chapel, a nave with north porch, and a bell turret.[94] St. Paul's parish hall and institute was built in 1905[95] and a corrugated iron mission room was erected in Highfield Row (later Road) in the early 1890s.[96]

[70] B.M. Harl. MS. 2176, ff. 23–5.
[71] *Lond. Gaz.* 29 Aug. 1851, p. 2205.
[72] See p. 159.
[73] B.M. Harl. MS. 2176, ff. 23–5.
[74] Prob. 11/141 (P.C.C. 20 Swann).
[75] *Gen. Digest of Endowed Chars.* H.C. 433, pp. 14–15 (1867–8), lii, pt. 1.
[76] Ex inf. Weld chapel trust (1974).   [77] See p. 204.
[78] H.O. 129/137/3/1/2.
[79] *Lond. Gaz.* 11 Aug. 1882, p. 3753.
[80] Mason, *Story of Southgate*, 65.
[81] *The Times*, 22 Oct. 1934.
[82] *Gent. Mag.* lxxii. 1097; Newby, *Old Southgate*, 8.
[83] Round, *Southgate and Winchmore Hill*, 18.
[84] H.O. 129/137/3/1/2.
[85] Hist. Mon. Com. *Mdx.* 112; Pevsner, *Mdx.* 139; Robbins, *Mdx.* plate 60; *T.L.M.A.S.* xviii(2), no. 149.

[86] H. B. Walters, 'The Bells of Mdx.', *T.L.M.A.S.* xvii. 141–3.
[87] Freshfield, *Communion Plate of Mdx.* 45.
[88] Registers of baptisms and burials 1695–1812 and of marriages 1702–54 *penes* Edmonton church: see M.R.O., D.R.O. 4; registers of baptisms and burials from 1813 and of marriages from 1838: *T.L.M.A.S.* xviii(2), no. 149.
[89] Fisk, *Edmonton*, 40, 182; Hennessy, *Novum Rep.* 147.
[90] *Lond. Gaz.* 29 Aug. 1851, p. 2205.
[91] Hennessy, *Novum Rep.* 147.   [92] H.O. 129/137/3/1/4.
[93] Mudie-Smith, *Religious Life of London*, 398–9.
[94] *T.L.M.A.S.* xviii(2), no. 156; Colvin, *Dict. of Architects*, 169; Cresswell, *Winchmore Hill*, 97.
[95] *Kelly's Dir. Mdx.* (1908). Since replaced by a new building.
[96] O.S. Map 1/2,500, Mdx. VII. 10 (1896 edn.); Regnart, *Winchmore Hill*, 188.

The church of *ST. JAMES*, Upper Edmonton, originated in mission work by the curate of All Saints, who held services in Northumberland House and who leased the meeting-place in Meeting House Lane for Anglican services.[97] As St. John's chapel it was licensed for marriages in 1839.[98] When John Snell died in 1847 he left 1½ a. of his park as a site for a church and school. The church, originally dedicated to St. Pancras, was erected in 1850 and a parish was assigned to it in 1851. The benefice, a vicarage, was in the gift of the vicars of Edmonton until 1901, when the patronage was transferred to the chapter of St. Paul's.[99] In 1877 the Ecclesiastical Commissioners granted the vicar an additional stipend to employ an assistant curate.[1] On census Sunday 1851 the church was attended by 500 people in the morning and 500 in the evening[2] and in 1903 by 141 in the morning and 258 in the evening.[3] The decline in attendance was attributable to the active mission work of St. James's. Mission halls were opened under its auspices in Upper Fore Street, on the east side just south of the junction with Claremont Street, c. 1880,[4] at Raynham Road (later St. John's, Dyson's Road) c. 1884, and on the north side of Gilpin Grove c. 1900.[5] The last was attended in 1903 by 74 people in the morning and 205 in the evening.[6] The Upper Fore Street mission room closed c. 1920[7] but that in Gilpin Grove remained as a church hall until it was burnt down and replaced by a new church hall in 1967.[8] St. James's church, built in 1850 in an early Gothic style by Edward Ellis of Angel Place, is a stone building accommodating 600 people and consists of apsidal chancel, nave with aisles and transepts, a west organ gallery, and western bellcot; it was restored in 1882 and 1896.[9] A large stone vicarage was built to the north of the church in 1868.[10]

The church of *ST. PAUL*,[11] New Southgate, originated in 1870 in a mission to the new district of Colney Hatch by the assistant curate of Christ Church, Southgate. In 1873 it became a consolidated chapelry, formed from Southgate and Friern Barnet parishes,[12] with the vicar of Southgate as patron. Attendance on census Sunday 1903 was 206 in the morning and 265 in the evening.[13] The High Church character of St. Paul's began with the introduction of high mass in 1914. Services were held in a temporary building in Ely Place until a church was built on land between Betstyle Road (later High Road) and Woodland Road probably given by G. Knights Smith, one of the largest subscribers. The foundation stone was laid in 1872 and the church, built of stone in the Early English style under the direction of George Gilbert Scott, was consecrated in 1873. It consists of chancel with north and south chapels and south bell turret and aisled nave.[14] The fabric, which was severely damaged by bombing in 1944, was restored by R. S. Morris by 1957. A stone vicarage, built in Woodland Road opposite the church in 1878–80, was demolished in 1964. A parish hall was built to the north of the church in 1908.

The parish of *ST. MICHAEL-AT-BOWES* was formed in 1874 as a consolidated chapelry out of the parishes of Southgate and St. Michael, Wood Green.[15] The church was built and endowed by Alderman Thomas Sidney of Bowes Manor, who presented the first vicar. After Sidney's death the patronage was exercised by his trustees until 1897, when it was transferred to the bishop of London.[16] St. Michael's was attended in 1903 by 370 people in the morning and 493 in the evening.[17] The church ran missions at Tile Kiln Lane in 1890,[18] at Wolves Lane from c. 1900 until after 1910,[19] and at St. Mary's, Tottenhall, from 1902 until after the Second World War, when it passed to St. Cuthbert's, Chitts Hill (Wood Green).[20] The Wolves Lane mission was attended by 134 people on the evening of census Sunday 1903.[21] The church, which was erected at the junction of Palmerston and Whittington roads in 1874, was built to an early Gothic design by Sir Gilbert Scott in rusticated Kentish ragstone and consists of chancel with north chapel, south tower, and south organ chamber, and aisled nave.[22] The vicarage and a small hall were built in 1892[23] and a new parish hall was opened in 1910.[24] In 1974 the vicarage was used for children in need.[25]

The church of *ST. JOHN*,[26] Dyson's Road, originated in mission work begun between 1882 and 1886 by St. James's, Upper Edmonton, in the Edmonton settlement, a hall on the north side of Raynham Road.[27] The district chapelry of St. John was formed from St. James's parish in 1906. The benefice was a vicarage in the patronage of the bishop of London.[28] In 1954 it was united with that of St. Mary as the parish of St. Mary with St. John

[97] Article on the history of the church in *St. James, Upper Edmonton Monthly Paper*, Aug. 1888 *penes* St. James's ch.

[98] *Lond. Gaz.* 19 July 1839, p. 1437.

[99] H.O. 129/137/3/1/1; *Lond. Gaz.* 29 Aug. 1851, p. 2205; *54th Rep. Eccl. Commrs.* [Cd. 1001], p. 60, H.C. (1902), xxii.

[1] *Lond. Gaz.* 27 July 1877, p. 4423.

[2] H.O. 129/137/3/1/1.

[3] Mudie-Smith, *Religious Life of London*, 400.

[4] *Kelly's Dirs. Mdx.* (1878, 1882); *Kelly's Dir. Tottenham* (1893–4).

[5] *Kelly's Dir. Enfield* (1899); *Kelly's Dir. Tottenham* (1901–2); lease *penes* St. James's church.

[6] Mudie-Smith, *Religious Life of London*, 400.

[7] *Kelly's Dir. Mdx.* (1917); *Kelly's Dir. Tottenham* (1922–3).

[8] O.S. Map 1/2,500, Mdx. VII. 15 (1938 edn.); ex inf. the vicar.

[9] Fisk, *Edmonton*, 103; *T.L.M.A.S.* xviii(2), no. 43.

[10] Datestone on bldg.

[11] Except where otherwise stated, this paragraph is based upon 'The Church of St. Paul, New Southgate' (TS. *penes* vicar, 1972).

[12] *Lond. Gaz.* 21 Nov. 1873, p. 5135.

[13] Mudie-Smith, *Religious Life of London*, 399.

[14] *T.L.M.A.S.* xviii(2), no. 155.

[15] *Lond. Gaz.* 30 Oct. 1874, p. 4770.

[16] *50th Rep. Eccl. Commrs.* [C. 8766], p. 52, H.C. (1898), xxi; Hennessy, *Novum Rep.* 146; *Building News*, xxxvii. 278.

[17] Mudie-Smith, *Religious Life of London*, 398.

[18] *Kelly's Dir. Mdx.* (1890).

[19] *Kelly's Dir. Barnet* (1900–1, 1910–11).

[20] St. Mary's, later called St. Cuthbert's Institute, was demolished in 1969: Church Com. file 81274.

[21] Mudie-Smith, *Religious Life of London*, 399.

[22] *T.L.M.A.S.* xviii(2), no. 154.

[23] *Kelly's Dir. Mdx.* (1908).

[24] *The Times*, 6 Oct. 1910.   [25] Ex inf. the vicar (1974).

[26] Unless otherwise stated, this account is based upon *The Parish Church of St. John, Upper Edmonton, 1906–1966* (pamphlet) and information supplied by the vicar (1972).

[27] *Kelly's Dirs. Mdx.* (1882, 1886); *Kelly's Dir. Tottenham* (1893–4).

[28] *59th Rep. Eccl. Commrs.* [Cd. 3377], p. 59, H.C. (1907), xx; *Crockford* (1935).

and the patronage was to be exercised alternately by the bishop of London and the chapter of St. Paul's.[29] The mission hall, by then called St. John's, was attended in 1903 by 74 people in the morning and 138 in the evening.[30] The hall continued to be used for social purposes until the late 1920s, when it became a motor-repairing shop. The church, which was erected in 1906 to a design by C. H. B. Quennell, is of buff brick in a Gothic style and has a chancel with side chapels, aisled nave with transepts and western bellcot.[31] Inside there is some 17th-century woodwork reset in a seat. The vicarage and parish hall were built north of the church in 1911.

The church of *ST. MARY*,[32] Fore Street, dates from the formation of a parish out of Edmonton in 1883. The benefice was a vicarage, originally in the gift of Robert S. Gregory, vicar of Edmonton, who gave £3,000 towards the cost of the church, and afterwards of the chapter of St. Paul's.[33] The church, which was built in 1884, was attended on census Sunday 1903 by 157 people in the morning and 131 in the evening.[34] The House of the Comforter, later called St. Mary's mission room, was erected next to the church in 1894 and was still in existence in 1922.[35] In 1954 the benefice was united with that of St. John, Dyson's Road. St. Mary's church, which was consecrated in 1884, was built to a characteristic design by W. Butterfield in red brick with stone dressings and consisted of nave, north and south aisles, and chancel. It contained candelabra and a carved seat dating from the 18th century.[36] A vicarage was erected in 1893.[37] The church was demolished in 1957 and in 1958 a small chapel was opened on the ground floor of the vicarage. The vicarage, however, was subjected to a compulsory purchase order and a new building, St. Mary's church centre, in Lawrence Road, replaced it in 1970. It contains a small church, a hall for meetings, and accommodation for a deacon and Sisters of the Community of St. Mary the Virgin.

The church of *ST. ALDHELM*, Silver Street, originated in mission services held by the London Diocesan Home Mission in a schoolroom in Windmill Lane *c.* 1885. An iron church in Silver Street was consecrated in 1895[38] and was superseded by a permanent church erected next to it on the corner of Windmill Road. It was consecrated in 1903 when a consolidated chapelry in the patronage of the vicar of Edmonton was formed from All Saints and Saint James's parishes.[39] St. Aldhelm's was attended by 407 people in the morning and 261 in

the evening on census Sunday 1903.[40] The church built in red brick with stone dressings to a design by W. D. Caroë,[41] and consisting of chancel, north organ chamber, vestry and south chapel, aisled nave with west gallery, and bell turret, was paid for out of the proceeds of the sale of St. Michael Bassishaw (London). A vicarage was built north of the church in 1907 and a mission hall was added in 1908.[42]

A corrugated iron chapel was erected in 1893 in Farm Road as a mission church of Christ Church, Southgate.[43] It was superseded by the church of *ST. ANDREW*,[44] Chase Side, to which in 1928 a vicarage in the patronage of the bishop of London was assigned.[45] St. Andrew's was attended on census Sunday 1903 by 129 people in the morning and 198 in the evening.[46] The foundation stone of the church was laid in 1903 although the completed building was not consecrated until 1916. Built in red brick with stone dressings to a design by A. R. Barker, with extensions by Barker and Kirk, it consists of nave, passage aisles, chancel, and chapel.[47] The Wesleyan chapel in Chase Side was bought for conversion into a church hall in 1929 and replaced by a new hall in 1957.[48]

Building began in 1896 of the church of *ST. PETER*, Lower Edmonton, to which a district chapelry taken from All Saints parish was assigned in 1898.[49] The living is a vicarage in the patronage of the bishop of London.[50] In 1903 St. Peter's was attended by 156 people in the morning and 291 in the evening.[51] A church with accommodation for 800, at the junction of Bounces Road with St. Peter's Road, was built in 1896–1900 to designs by Messrs. Newman & Newman. In 1902 J. S. Alder added the chancel, narthex, and porches. Built in red and yellow brick with stone dressings in the Perpendicular style, it consists of chancel with chapel and vestries, an aisled nave with transepts, and a west narthex. The vicarage was built to the north in a William and Mary style in 1901,[52] and a parish hall to the east of the church in 1908.[53]

The church of *ST. ALPHEGE*, Hertford Road, originated in 1897 as a mission church of All Saints. From 1905 it was run by a curate-in-charge under the auspices of the London Diocesan Home Mission[54] until the benefice became a vicarage in the patronage of the bishop of London in 1954.[55] A temporary iron chapel, attended in 1903 by 105 people in the morning and 110 in the evening,[56] was erected in 1897 on the east side of Hertford Road, just south of its junction with Tramway Avenue.[57] A permanent brick church with vestries, a campanile,

[29] *Crockford* (1965–6).
[30] Mudie-Smith, *Religious Life of London*, 400.
[31] *T.L.M.A.S.* xviii(2), no. 44; Nicholson & Spooner, *Recent English Ecclesiastical Architecture*.
[32] Unless otherwise stated, ex inf. the vicar (1972).
[33] *Lond. Gaz.* 31 Aug. 1883, p. 4270; *36th Rep. Eccl. Commrs.* [C. 3922], p. 415 sqq., H.C. (1884), xxii.
[34] Mudie-Smith, *Religious Life of London*, 400.
[35] *Kelly's Dirs. Tottenham* (1893–4, 1894–5, 1922–3).
[36] *T.L.M.A.S.* xviii(2), no. 46; photograph *penes* Edmonton Publ. Libr.
[37] *Kelly's Dir. Mdx.* (1933).
[38] Fisk, *Edmonton*, 175; *Crockford* (1896), 1641; ex inf. the vicar (1972).
[39] *56th Rep. Eccl. Commrs.* [Cd. 1966], p. 65, H.C. (1904), xviii; *Crockford* (1907).
[40] Mudie-Smith, *Religious Life of London*, 400.
[41] *T.L.M.A.S.* xviii(2), no. 42.
[42] Datestone; ex inf. the vicar (1972).

[43] Newby, *Old Southgate*, 55; O.S. Map 1/2,500, Mdx. VII. 9 (1896 edn.).
[44] Except where otherwise stated, this paragraph is based upon information supplied by Miss G. E. Morris (1972).
[45] *Crockford* (1935).
[46] Mudie-Smith, *Religious Life of London*, 398–9.
[47] *T.L.M.A.S.* xviii(2), no. 152.
[48] Datestone on bldg.
[49] *51st Rep. Eccl. Commrs.* [C. 9195], p. 54, H.C. (1899), xix.
[50] *Crockford* (1935).
[51] Mudie-Smith, *Religious Life of London*, 400.
[52] *T.L.M.A.S.* xviii(2), no. 48; *Architect*, lxxii. 72; pamphlet *penes* vicar (1974).
[53] Datestone on hall.
[54] Borough of Edmonton, *Official Guide* [1963]; *Kelly's Dir. Mdx.* (1908).
[55] *Crockford* (1951–2, 1955–6).
[56] Mudie-Smith, *Religious Life of London*, 400.
[57] *Kelly's Dir. Mdx.* (1908); *Kelly's Dir. Tottenham* (1912–13).

and statues of Christ and angels and of St. Alphege, was erected on the western side of Hertford Road, near the Enfield boundary in 1958.[58]

The church of *ST. MARTIN* began as a mission in 1900 in an iron church in Town Road.[59] A consolidated chapelry, in the patronage of the bishop of London, was formed from the parishes of All Saints and St. Mary in 1911.[60] The iron church was attended in 1903 by 109 people in the morning and 163 in the evening.[61] Money bequeathed by Miss Elizabeth Mason (d. 1909) for the erection of a new church, hall, and vicarage in the north-eastern London area, was allotted to St. Martin's, then described as a poor district. The church was consecrated in 1911, when the hall and vicarage were also completed.[62] The church, built in a mixed Gothic style of red brick with stone dressings to a design by E. L. Warre,[63] consists of chancel with south chapel, nave with aisles and transepts, and an organ gallery. The interior, which was restored in 1970 by John Phillips,[64] is plastered with exposed stone dressings, with a roof of exposed timber and gilded angels.

The church of *ST. MICHAEL*, Bury Street, was the second of two churches in Edmonton built with the proceeds from the sale of St. Michael Bassishaw (London).[65] A parish was assigned to it in 1901 and the living, a vicarage, was in the patronage of the chapter of St. Paul's.[66] In 1903 the church was attended by 163 people in the morning and 300 in the afternoon.[67] From 1973 the building was shared between Anglicans and the Greek Orthodox Church and is known to its worshippers as St. Demetrios. A red brick church was erected in 1901 to a debased Tudor design by W. D. Caroë. It consists of chancel, aisled nave, north chapel, and western narthex. A vicarage and church hall were erected at the same time.[68]

The church of *ST. STEPHEN*, Bush Hill Park, began in 1901 as a mission held in an iron church by an assistant curate of Edmonton. It was a chapelry with a conventional district from 1907 until 1909 when it became a vicarage in the patronage of the vicar of Edmonton.[69] Services on census day 1903 were attended by 94 people in the morning and 104 in the evening.[70] A church, at the corner of Park Avenue and Village Road, was begun in 1906 and a western end, designed by J. S. Alder, was added in 1916. Built in stone in a Decorated style with wooden barrel-vaulting,[71] it consists of chancel with north and south chapels, aisled nave with north and south porches, and a west baptistery. The south porch is built at the lowest stage of an intended tower.

The church of *HOLY TRINITY*, Winchmore Hill, originated as a mission of St. Paul's, Winchmore Hill, in 1903. The assistant curate who conducted it became the first vicar when Holy Trinity became a district chapelry in the patronage of the vicar of St. Paul's in 1913.[72] It was High Church in character in 1974. In 1907 the foundation stone was laid of a church in the corner between Green Lanes and Queens Avenue.[73] Built of red brick with stone dressings to a design in the Gothic style by J. S. Alder,[74] it consists of an apsidal sanctuary and an undivided and aisled chancel and nave with a tower rising from the western end of the north aisle.

The church of *ST. JOHN*,[75] Palmers Green, owed its foundation to the initiative of the vicar of Southgate, to V. E. Walker of Arnos Grove, who gave land, and to Mrs. Baird who gave money. The foundation stone of a church was laid in 1903 on a site at the corner of Green Lanes and Hoppers Road and in 1906 a consolidated chapelry in the patronage of the vicar of Southgate was formed from Southgate and Winchmore Hill parishes.[76] High Church practices have obtained since 1909. The church was consecrated in 1904 although not completed until 1909. Built in the Late Gothic style to a design by John Oldrid Scott,[77] it consists of chancel with south vestry, central tower, north chapel and south transept, aisled nave and north porch, and is of mixed flint, brick, and ashlar construction. The vicarage and parish hall, designed by J. S. Alder, were built in Bourne Hill, north-west of the church, in 1908.

The church of *ST. THOMAS*, Oakwood, dates from 1938 but there was an earlier, iron chapel of St. Thomas in Winchmore Hill Road which had been built between 1904 and 1908 by one of the daughters of Samuel Sugden (d. 1905) of Oak Lodge and which served as a chapel of ease to St. Paul's, Winchmore Hill.[78] A vicarage in the patronage of the bishop of London was created in 1938[79] and the foundation stone of a church at the junction of Prince George and Sheringham avenues was laid in 1939.[80] The church was built in stone-faced brick to a design by R. B. Craze and consists of nave, north and south aisles, and apsidal chancel, completed in 1941.[81] The west end, including a south-west tower with a copper spire, was built in 1965 to designs by William Mulvey. The spire was blown down in 1974.[82]

ROMAN CATHOLICISM. By will dated 1563 John Leake (d. 1572) left his biggest silver spoon to the church, 'if mass be ministered again'.[83] His widow and children were indicted for recusancy in

[58] Borough of Edmonton, *Official Guide* [1963].
[59] Fisk, *Edmonton*, 175; *Kelly's Dir. Mdx.* (1908).
[60] *66th Rep. Eccl. Commrs.* [Cd. 6111], p. 55, H.C. (1912–13), xxi; *Crockford* (1965–6).
[61] Mudie-Smith, *Religious Life of London*, 400.
[62] *The Times*, 26 Apr. 1909; 27 Feb. 1911.
[63] *T.L.M.A.S.* xviii(2), no. 45.
[64] Ex inf. the vicar's daughter (1972).
[65] See St. Aldhelm, above.
[66] *55th Rep. Eccl. Commrs.* [Cd. 1482], p. 63, H.C. (1903), xix; *Lond. Dioc. Bk.* (1972).
[67] Mudie-Smith, *Religious Life of London*, 398–9.
[68] Datestone on bldg.; *Building News*, lxxxii. 773.
[69] *62nd Rep. Eccl. Commrs.* [Cd. 5081], p. 64, H.C. (1910), xxii; *Crockford* (1935); *Kelly's Dir. Mdx.* (1908).
[70] Mudie-Smith, *Religious Life of London*, 400.

[71] *T.L.M.A.S.* xviii(2), no. 49; O.S. Map 1/2,500, Mdx. VII. 7 (1914 edn.).
[72] *66th Rep. Eccl. Commrs.* [Cd. 7301], p. 58, H.C. (1914), xxv; *Lond. Dioc. Bk.* (1970).
[73] Datestone; O.S. Map 1/2,500, Mdx. VII. 10 (1914 edn.).
[74] *T.L.M.A.S.* xviii(2), no. 151.
[75] Except where otherwise stated, ex inf. the vicar, 1972.
[76] *59th Rep. Eccl. Commrs.* [Cd. 3377], p. 60, H.C. (1907), xx. [77] *T.L.M.A.S.* xviii(2), no. 153.
[78] Mason, *Story of Southgate*, 56; *Kelly's Dir. Mdx.* (1908); O.S. Map 1/2,500, Mdx. VII. 10 (1935 edn.).
[79] *Lond. Dioc. Bk.* (1970), 116.
[80] Dated foundation stone.
[81] *T.L.M.A.S.* xviii(2), no. 157.
[82] Ex inf. Mr. D. O. Pam (1974).
[83] Prob. 11/54 (P.C.C. 32 Daper).

1587,[84] 1606, and 1608,[85] and in 1586 his widow's second husband John Cornwell was suspected of harbouring a priest and Leake's two sons, Joseph and Jasper,[86] were accused of using their position as justices of the peace to shelter him and of mocking the Anglican communion service.[87] There was suspicion in 1606 that Jesuits were being hidden in Edmonton.[88] Other recusants were Richard Palmer (1588),[89] Joan Ashley (1592–3),[90] Edmund Tayler (1599),[91] and John Gillett and his wife (1613),[92] who were mostly from yeoman families, and Thomas Gillett or Jellect and his wife (1615–1619)[93] and Philip Fursden and his family (1635),[94] who were gentry. A 'college' of Jesuits was resident in Edmonton for a time between 1624 and 1627[95] but there were said to be no recusants there c. 1640.[96]

There were two papists in 1676[97] and John Mulberry, yeoman, was indicted for recusancy in 1684.[98] In 1706 there were said to be no papists in Edmonton[99] but it must have been soon afterwards that William Le Hunt set up a large Roman Catholic seminary for young men who were then sent to foreign seminaries.[1]

No papists were recorded in the late 18th and early 19th centuries.[2] The first Roman Catholic church was that of the Precious Blood and St. Edmund King and Martyr, consecrated in 1907. Situated on the west side of Hertford Road, opposite Bounces Road, it is a neo-Gothic building of rusticated stone with a squat tower. It is served by Redemptorists[3] and was attended on census Sunday 1903 by 199 in the morning and 180 in the evening.[4] St. Monica's church in Palmers Green originated as a mission in 1910. The church, a stone building in the Gothic style, was built by Edward Goldie in 1914 at the corner of Green Lanes and Stonard Road.[5] There is a brick presbytery adjoining it and St. Monica's hall was built west of the church in 1931.[6]

In 1923 the first parish priest in New Southgate acquired a presbytery in Bowes Road and added a small extension which was used for services until

1935, when the church of Our Lady of Lourdes, a simple brick building, was erected next to it.[7] Benedictines of the priory of Christ the King were running a preparatory school at Cockfosters in 1936 and in 1937 they registered the priory chapel in Bramley Road, Southgate, for worship. The church hall was registered in 1940.[8] The priory is an austere building in white brick. A similar building, the priory of Our Lady, Queen of Heaven, originally known as Regina Pacis convent, was built for Olivetan Benedictine nuns in Priory Close, Southgate, in 1941.[9] The chapel was registered for worship in 1968.[10]

There is a chapel belonging to St. Joseph's nursing home in Church Street, an institution run by the Sisters of Charity of St. Vincent de Paul since 1910.[11]

PROTESTANT NONCONFORMITY.[12] Unlawful religious assemblies were being held at Edmonton in 1662[13] and it was said in 1666 that 'the head of the serpent', a reference to religious rebellion, dwelt in Edmonton and Enfield.[14] In the same year Arthur Jackson, an ejected London minister who had held conventicles, died at Edmonton.[15] There were 15 nonconformists at Edmonton in 1676.[16]

Most of the early nonconformists were probably Quakers. Gerard Roberts, a Quaker preacher, held a meeting there in 1669[17] and was among those indicted for attending conventicles in Edmonton in 1686.[18] Others indicted at the same time included Edward Mann, a London haberdasher who had a country house at Ford Green near Winchmore Hill,[19] and Robert Chair, a Winchmore Hill smith.[20] George Fox was a frequent visitor and conventicles were held at both Mann's and Chair's houses during the 1680s.[21] Fox also visited several people in Southgate, including James Lowrey (d. 1726), merchant and coachman,[22] and Bridget Austell, who kept a school there and at whose house a meeting was held in 1688.[23] Other Quakers of the 1680s included George Barr, a Londoner who had a house near Bury

---

[84] i.e. his widow Catherine and daughters Helen and Jane: *Mdx. Cnty. Recs.* i. 173.

[85] i.e. his son Edward: *Mdx. Cnty Recs.* ii. 19; M.R.O., Cal. Mdx. Sess. Recs. i. 236.

[86] For details of the Leakes, especially Jasper and Joseph, see D. Avery, *Popish Recusancy in the Elizabethan Hundred of Edmonton* (Edmonton Hund. Hist. Soc., c. 1967).

[87] When a poor couple were married at Winchmore Hill, Joseph Leake performed a mock communion service, singing 'a vile Profane song called "the Dogs of Tottenham"' instead of a psalm': *Cal. S.P. Dom.* 1581–90, 349.

[88] Hist. MSS. Com. 9, *Hatfield House*, xviii, p. 242.

[89] *Mdx. Cnty. Recs.* i. 176.

[90] *Cath. Rec. Soc.* xviii. 145.

[91] *Mdx. Cnty. Recs.* i. 254.

[92] Ibid. ii. 235.

[93] Ibid. 115, 131, 236; *Mdx. Sess. Recs.* iv. 289.

[94] *Mdx. Cnty. Recs.* iii. 58–9.

[95] *Cal. S.P. Dom.* 1628–9, 53.

[96] B M. Add. MS. 38856, f. 40.

[97] Wm. Salt Libr., Stafford, Salt MS. 33, p. 40 (Compton census).

[98] *Mdx. Cnty. Recs.* iv. 243.

[99] Guildhall MS. 9800A.

[1] M.R.O., MR/RR 22/5; RR 23/4; RR 25/7; RR 26/7; E. S. Worrall, *The Confessor Wm. Le Hunt, Priest and Schoolmaster of Enfield and Edmonton* (Edmonton Hund. Hist. Soc., n.d.).

[2] Guildhall MS. 9557, f. 30.

[3] *Westminster Yr. Bk.* (1966); G.R.O. Worship Reg. nos. 40379, 42463, 58040; O.S. Map 1/2,500, Mdx. VII. 11–12 (1914 and subseq. edns.).

[4] Mudie-Smith, *Religious Life of London*, 401.

[5] *Westminster Yr. Bk.* (1966); G.R.O. Worship Reg. no. 46077; O.S. Map 1/2,500, Mdx. VII. 10 (1935 edn.).

[6] Datestone on bldg.

[7] G.R.O. Worship Reg. nos. 48788, 55894; O.S. Map 1/2,500, Mdx. VII. 13 (1936 edn.); ex inf. priest-in-charge (1972).

[8] G.R.O. Worship Reg. nos. 57402, 59353; *Westminster Yr. Bk.* (1966); *Cath. Dir.* (1937).

[9] *Cath. Dirs.* (1940–1).

[10] G.R.O. Worship Reg. no. 71268.

[11] O.S. Map 1/2,500, Mdx. VII. 11 (1935 and subseq. edns.); *Westminster Yr. Bk.* (1969); *Kelly's Dir. Tottenham* (1912–3); *Cath. Dir.* (1910).

[12] Unless otherwise stated, locations are based upon O.S. Maps 1/2,500, Mdx. VII, XII (1867 and later edns.), attendance figures for 1851 upon H.O. 129/137/3/1 and for 1903 upon R. Mudie-Smith, *Religious Life of London*.

[13] *Mdx. Cnty. Recs.* iii. 325.

[14] *Trans. Baptist Hist. Soc.* iv. 58–63.

[15] *Calamy Revised*, ed. Matthews, 290.

[16] Wm Salt Libr., Stafford, Salt MS. 33, p. 40.

[17] G. L. Turner, *Original Recs. of Early Nonconformity*, 92.

[18] M.R.O., Cal. Mdx. Sess. Bks. 1683–6, 148, 149.

[19] *Jnl. of George Fox*, ed. N. Penney, ii. 422.

[20] *Short Jnl. & Itin. Jnls. of George Fox*, ed. N. Penney, 91.

[21] Ibid. 162; *Mdx. Cnty. Recs.* iv. 174, 302–4; M.R.O., Cal. Mdx. Sess. Bks. 1683–6, 148.

[22] *Short Jnl. & Itin. Jnls. of Geo. Fox*, 148.

[23] Ibid. 91, 111, 148, 187, 324.

Street,[24] and George Keith[25] and Christopher Taylor, who kept schools in Edmonton.[26] William Shacker, who had a house in Bury Street ward in 1672,[27] may have been the Shackler in whose yard a conventicle was held in 1686.[28] John Butcher (d. 1721), another Quaker, spent his last years at Palmers Green.[29] Quakerism came to be concentrated at Winchmore Hill, where John Oakley, a merchant tailor, offered his barn for meetings in 1682. A meeting-house was erected there in 1687, when John Freame and Thomas Gould, founders of Barclays Bank, were among those who gave assistance. Wealthy London merchants, especially bankers like the Barclay, Hoare, and Hodgkin families, maintained their connexion with the Winchmore Hill meeting-house, which they helped to rebuild in 1790.[30]

Isaac Walker was one of the Quaker trustees of 1790 and other brewers, like Jacob Yallowley of Whitbread's (d. 1801), who supported the Winchmore Hill Independent chapel,[31] were prominent nonconformists in the 18th and early 19th centuries. Three silkbrokers were the trustees of Lower Edmonton Wesleyan chapel in 1853[32] but humbler tradesmen formed the bulk of nonconformist congregations and increasingly took control,[33] as the rich moved out of Edmonton during the 19th century.

Apart from Quakers there were two ejected London ministers, John Jackson, son of Arthur, in Edmonton and one Chantrey, in Southgate, in 1690.[34] A dissenters' meeting-house had been erected by 1709[35] and by 1778 several denominations had their own meeting-houses.[36] At the end of the 18th century Quakers and Presbyterians each had their meeting-house and the Methodists, who had recently increased, had three.[37] Two of the Methodist meeting-houses were 'lately erected' in 1790[38] but the Methodists' success was not lasting, none of their early meeting-houses surviving until 1851 and one having already disappeared by 1819.[39]

A statement that Presbyterians had possessed a meeting-house in Edmonton since about the time of the Revolution, may refer to the meeting-house of 1709. It was here that Dr. Richard Price (d. 1791), the radical and moralist, began his ministry in 1744. The meeting-house was probably the chapel on the south-east side of Meeting House Lane (later Church and Bridport roads). A second Presbyterian meeting-house existed by 1803 but the old one had

been taken over by the Independents by 1819[40] and the second did not survive until 1851.

From the late 18th century Independents (later called Congregationalists) outstripped all the other denominations. They founded a permanent chapel at Winchmore Hill before 1785 and another in Upper Edmonton in 1788 which was enlarged in 1803. A house in Meeting House Lane was used for worship from 1803 until the Presbyterian meeting-house in the same road was taken over and a house in Chase Side, Southgate, was registered for worship in 1805[41] and superseded by a meeting-house erected there in 1806. Other houses were registered in Edmonton in 1807 and 1808,[42] in Silver Street in 1814, and at Winchmore Hill in 1815.[43] John Radford, a member of the Winchmore Hill chapel, registered a cottage and a building at Palmers Green in 1839 and 1840 respectively[44] and when the lease of the chapel expired in 1841 he supplied the site for a new one.

Wesleyan Methodists registered a house in Board Lane in 1814[45] and a room in Bury Street in 1826. The latter was superseded by a chapel built in Lower Edmonton in 1829. A group of Wesleyans registered a house at Winchmore Hill in 1843[46] and erected a chapel there in 1847. The meeting-house in Meeting House Lane, Upper Edmonton, which had been used by Presbyterians and Independents, was taken over by the Countess of Huntingdon's Connexion between c. 1819 and c. 1839.[47]

Two later Baptist chapels were established during the early 19th century, although Baptists themselves registered only one house, in 1830.[48] Ebenezer chapel in Claremont, registered as a Calvinistic Independent chapel in 1818, was serving Strict Baptists by the end of the century. Providence chapel in Vicars Moor Lane, Winchmore Hill, registered as Independent in 1825, belonged to the local Udallite sect. It was always based on Calvinist principles and was described as Strict Baptist by 1867.

Several meeting-places were registered by unspecified Protestant dissenters in the early 19th century: a house in Southgate in 1825,[49] houses at Palmers Green and Bourne Grove, Southgate, in 1826,[50] at Bowes Farm in 1828[51] and at Palmers Green in 1829,[52] a barn in 1829,[53] a schoolroom in Southgate in 1850,[54] and a room at Bowes Farm for those holding evangelical or Calvinist doctrines in 1841.[55]

[24] Ibid. 162, 307.
[25] D.N.B.
[26] Short Jnl. & Itin. Jnls. of Geo. Fox, 338. See below, p. 196.
[27] E 179/143/370 m. 13d.
[28] M.R.O., Cal. Mdx. Sess. Bks. 1683–6, 149.
[29] Jnl. of Geo. Fox, ii. 497.
[30] Regnart, Winchmore Hill, 58–9; W. Beck and T. F. Ball, London Friends' Meetings, 299–301; C 54/7344 no. 20.
[31] W. A. Oyler-Waterhouse, Revised Hist. of Our Church [Winchmore Hill Congreg. Church].
[32] C 54/14580 no. 6.
[33] e.g. the millers, gardeners, and shoemakers, trustees of Ebenezer chapel in 1818: C 54/9751 no. 9; local grocer, baker, and draper, trustees of Providence chapel 1835: C 54/15850 no. 4; baker and gas fitter, trustees of Congregational chapel in Queen's Rd. in 1860: C 54/15556 no. 10.
[34] A. Gordon, Freedom after Ejection, 2, 72; Calamy Revised, ed. Matthews, 291.
[35] Mdx. Cnty. Recs. Sess. Bks. 1689–1709, 351.

[36] Guildhall MS. 9558, f. 431.
[37] Lysons, Environs, ii. 268; Guildhall MS. 9557, f. 30.
[38] Guildhall MS. 9558, f. 431.
[39] Robinson, Edmonton, 186.
[40] Ibid. 185–6, 290 and map; C 54/12684 no. 8.
[41] Guildhall MS. 9580/2.
[42] Ibid. /3.
[43] Ibid. /4.
[44] Ibid. /8, ff. 50, 85.
[45] Ibid. /4.
[46] Ibid. /8, f. 163.
[47] Article on history of St. James's church in St. James, Upper Edmonton Monthly Paper, Aug. 1888 penes St. James's church.
[48] Guildhall MS. 9580/6, f. 293.
[49] Ibid. f. 4v.
[50] Ibid. ff. 103, 105.
[51] Ibid. f. 221.
[52] Ibid. f. 226.
[53] Ibid. f. 242.
[54] Ibid. /8, f. 58.
[55] Ibid. f. 108.

In 1851, out of a population of 9,708, the non-conformist chapels of Edmonton had a total attendance on census Sunday of 2,012. The Independents, with 1,613 attendances, formed 80 per cent of that total and were by far the largest denomination. The Wesleyans had 180 attendances (9 per cent), the Independent Calvinists 161 (8 per cent), and the Quakers 58 (3 per cent). The chapels were concentrated in and around Fore Street, particularly Upper Edmonton, and at Winchmore Hill.[56]

There was little change during the next three decades, when Independent chapels at Lower Edmonton Green and eastern Edmonton, a chapel for Evangelical dissenters at Lower Edmonton, and a room for Primitive Methodists near the Tottenham border were opened and closed. 'Episcopalian' dissenters registered Christ Church in Coach and Horses Lane in 1853[57] and Baptists opened a chapel in Lower Edmonton, extending their activities to Palmers Green and the middle-class suburb of New Southgate. In 1880 the chapels were still concentrated as they had been in 1851.

The greatest activity by all denominations was between 1880 and 1914, a period of rapid growth, especially in working-class housing. Quakers opened a meeting in Southgate in 1904 and a mission at Winchmore Hill in 1907. The Independents, by now called Congregationalists, extended their Winchmore Hill chapel in 1883 and 1913 and began missions in Bury Street in 1881 and in Church Street in 1899 although they lost their Chase Side chapel in 1890. Their Claremont Street chapel was closed but mission services were held in at least three places in Lower Edmonton during the 1880s and 1890s and a new chapel was built in Knights Lane between 1883 and 1914. Congregationalists started to meet at Palmers Green in 1907 and erected a chapel there in 1914.

Baptists enlarged the Lower Edmonton chapel in 1885 and rebuilt the Udallite chapel in Winchmore Hill in 1888. They replaced the New Southgate chapel by another twice its size in 1901 and expanded to Southgate in 1884, taking over the abandoned Congregational chapel at Chase Side in 1894. A Baptist mission was started in Palmers Green in 1878, where a chapel was built in 1905, and a chapel opened in Winchmore Hill in 1907. For a short time in the 1880s and early 1890s the Baptists ran a mission hall in Marsh Side in eastern Edmonton and in 1896 they opened a chapel in Bowes Park, although it soon passed to the Methodists.

The Methodists too made progress. Wesleyans built a chapel in Eaton Park, between Winchmore Hill and Palmers Green, in 1880 and replaced it in 1912. They built Central Hall in Lower Fore Street in 1911 and reached Southgate in 1891 and New Southgate in 1886. By 1904 they had taken over the Baptist chapel in Bowes Park, replacing it by a new chapel near by in 1907. Primitive Methodists began a mission in 1900 which resulted in a chapel in Hertford Road in 1902. They also built a chapel in New Southgate in the 1890s and began to meet in a new area, Bush Hill Park, in 1903. A Presbyterian church was built in Palmers Green in 1914.

Evangelical missions flourished in the late 19th century. The Salvation Army concentrated its work in New Southgate from 1886, and in old Edmonton where a mission was started in 1889. In the 1880s mission halls were opened by the Brethren in Bounces Road, eastern Edmonton, by the Gospel Union in Upper Edmonton, and by the London City Mission in Victoria Road. Halls were founded for general evangelical purposes at Tanners End c. 1890 and in 1913. Spiritualists began to meet in Lower Edmonton at the end of the 19th century.

The percentage of people attending nonconformist chapels nonetheless declined between 1851 and 1901, when the population multiplied six times, to 61,892, but attendances at chapels rose only three times, to 7,277. Edmonton had become a dormitory for predominantly working-class Londoners who were not church- or chapel-goers. In the better-off suburbs, like New Southgate, most people were churchmen or women.

Among Protestant nonconformists the Congregationalists, with 3,203 attendances, still maintained their lead in 1903, although it had dropped from 80 to 45 per cent of the total. The Baptists, with 1,625 attendances, accounted for 22 per cent and the Methodists, with 1,291 attendances, for 18 per cent. The Salvation Army had 719 attendances (10 per cent), general evangelical missions had 307, and the Brethren had 77. The Quakers had 55 attendances, almost the same as in 1851, but they formed less than 1 per cent of the total.[58]

Had a religious census been taken since 1903, it would almost certainly have shown a further decline. In the period between the World Wars chapels moved from the old centres of population to the new suburban estates. The Methodists closed a chapel in New Southgate in 1936, replaced their chapel in Chase Side by one in the Bourne in 1929, and opened new chapels at Grange Park in 1921 and at Oakwood in 1939. The Baptists opened a new chapel in New Southgate in 1926 and replaced their chapel in Chase Side by one in Oakwood Park in 1935. There were no important developments among the Congregationalists but the Brethren expanded, registering halls in Victoria Road c. 1920 and Croyland Road in 1926, a chapel in Bowes Park in 1934, and a room in Bury Street in 1938. New sects appeared during the 1920s and 1930s. Spiritualists opened a church in Linnell Road in 1929 and a house in Green Lanes in 1941. Christian Scientists registered a house in Palmerston Road in 1937, the Seventh Day Adventists registered a hall in Bounces Road in 1937, and Pentecostalists opened a mission room in Cowper Road c. 1930. In 1929 another mission hall, in Hertford Road, was registered for undesignated Christians.

Since 1945 there has been a steady contraction. In New Southgate the Baptist chapel in South Road closed in 1954 and the Quaker meeting-house in 1969. The Methodists closed Ripon Road chapel in 1964 and Central Hall in Fore Street in 1971, and in 1972 they amalgamated Bowes Park with Trinity chapel, Wood Green. The Congregationalists amalgamated their Upper and Lower Edmonton chapels in 1959 and although the Brethren opened a permanent chapel in Bury Street in 1951, their

[56] H.O. 129/137/3/1; *Census* (1851).
[57] G.R.O. Worship Reg. no. 721.
[58] *Census*, 1901; Mudie-Smith, *Rel. Life*, 337, 340, 342-3, 399, 401. There were 8,480 attendances for the Church of England and 379 for the Roman Catholics.

chapel at Bowes Park was taken over by Elim Pentecostalists in 1955. The Jehovah's Witnesses opened a Kingdom Hall in 1952 but despite a large immigrant population few new chapels opened, perhaps because many newcomers worshipped in Tottenham.

SOCIETY OF FRIENDS. A meeting-house was built at Winchmore Hill in 1687 to replace the barn used since 1682. It was ruinous in 1787 and in 1790 a new meeting-house was built on the same site, in what was later known as Church Hill.[59] It is a plain building of buff-coloured brick, described in 1819 as neat and substantial, and stands in a burial-ground which contains the remains of Dr. John Fothergill (d. 1780), the physician and botanist.[60] In 1819 the meeting-house accommodated 250 people although the congregation then consisted of fewer than 15 families.[61] On census Sunday 1851 the accommodation had contracted to 160, probably because a gallery had been removed. The attendance was then 42 in the morning and 16 in the afternoon. On census Sunday 1903 the attendance was 32 in the morning and 23 in the evening. From 1907 until 1954 the Quakers ran an adult school mission hall in Church Hill, Winchmore Hill.[62]

A Quaker meeting opened in 1904 at the institute in High Road, New Southgate, and closed in 1969.[63]

CONGREGATIONALISTS. The Congregationalist chapel in Compton Road descends from two previous chapels in Winchmore Hill.[64] The earliest, known as the Independent Old Meeting, existed by 1785 and was a wooden building with round-headed windows at one end and shuttered windows along the side, probably near the modern Branscombe Gardens. When the lease expired in 1841 John Radford gave the Independents a new site in Hoppers Road,[65] where the second chapel was opened in 1844.[66] The old chapel was pulled down in 1848. The Hoppers Road chapel, built in white brick in a Gothic style, accommodated 300 people and was attended on census Sunday 1851 by 80 people in the morning and 125 in the afternoon. The 1850s, however, brought financial difficulties and attendances reduced to five or six. The Great Northern Railway Co. planned to build a railway through the Hoppers Lane site and in 1869 it purchased the chapel. A temporary chapel was leased in 1871 and the third chapel, apparently an adaptation of the temporary building, opened in Compton Road in 1874.[67] A schoolroom was added in 1878 and extended in 1881 and there was accommodation for 320 in 1908.[68] Church membership rose until attendance on census Sunday 1903 was 186 in the morning and 136 in the evening, although by 1938 attendances had dropped to 19.

Winchmore Hill chapel bought Bury Street iron

mission room in 1881 and ran it as Belmont mission room until 1904, when it was replaced by a mission hall which had been erected on the Red Ridge estate in Church Street in 1899. Attendance on census Sunday 1903 was 32 in the morning and 43 in the evening. It was still standing in 1937.[69]

Edmonton and Tottenham or Snells Park Congregational chapel[70] derived from an Independent chapel which was opened on the east side of Fore Street, near the Tottenham boundary, in 1788. The building was enlarged in 1803 and in 1820 consisted of a chapel and vestry within a burial-ground.[71] A schoolroom was added in 1838. When John Snell's estate was sold in 1848, the Independents purchased a plot on the site of his mansion, between Langhedge Lane and Park Road (later Snells Park), for a larger chapel. The new chapel, built of yellow brick faced with stone and terracotta in a Gothic style to a design by Francis Pouget, was opened in 1850.[72] With accommodation for 850 people, it was twice the size of the old chapel. On census Sunday 1851 590 people attended in the morning and 498 in the evening, the highest figures for any nonconformist chapel, and in 1903 305 people attended in the morning and 432 in the evening. The old chapel continued in use as a schoolroom until the late 1960s[73] and in 1903 it was attended by 88 people in the morning and 220 in the evening. Lectures were given there in the 1870s, leading to a secession and the foundation of Lower Edmonton Congregational church in Knight's Lane. The two congregations reunited to form Edmonton Congregational church on a new site in 1959, although the Edmonton and Tottenham chapel continued to be used for worship until it was sold to the council and demolished c. 1965.[74]

There were several charities belonging to Edmonton and Tottenham Congregational chapel. By will proved 1866 Ann Smith left £200 and by will proved 1886 Jemima Stewart Barclay left £1,000, the income to be used for poor members of the congregation. Edward Chapman by will proved 1902 bequeathed £250 stock and Clarissa Cecilia Child by will proved 1923 left £500 to provide coal and Arthur James Howard bequeathed £200 stock, the interest to be distributed by the minister to 12 deserving poor at Christmas. In 1967 all the charities were transferred to the Edmonton Congregational chapel and in 1968 their total income amounted to £104.[75]

Edmonton and Tottenham Congregational chapel ran Olive Branch, Queen's Road, and Lower Edmonton chapels. Other missions were held at St. George's hall, New Road, from 1879 until 1896,[76] at the Angel assembly room[77] and at New hall in Knight's Lane from 1883 until 1896,[78] and in a room on the south side of Angel Road, just west of its junction with Dyson's Road, from c. 1884

[59] Beck and Ball, *Lond. Friends' Meetings*, 299–301.
[60] *D.N.B.*
[61] Robinson, *Edmonton*, 184–5; Robbins, *Mdx.* plate 45.
[62] G.R.O. Worship Reg. no. 42524.
[63] Soc. of Friends, Index of Meeting Recs. (Kent-Mdx.) *penes* Friends Ho. Libr.; *Kelly's Dir. Mdx.* (1908).
[64] Unless otherwise stated, this account is based upon W. A. Oyler-Waterhouse, *Revised History of Our Church* (pamphlet hist. of Winchmore Hill Congreg. Church).
[65] C 54/13273 no. 9.
[66] Guildhall MS. 9580/8, f. 209; M.R.O., Acc. 588/23.
[67] Registered in 1876: G.R.O. Worship Reg. no. 23098.

[68] *Kelly's Dir. Mdx.* (1908).
[69] *Kelly's Dirs. Mdx.* (1890, 1908, 1937); *Kelly's Dir. Tottenham* (1897–8); *Kelly's Dir. Enfield* (1899–1900).
[70] Unless otherwise stated, this account is based upon Fisk, *Edmonton*, 84–90.
[71] C 54/9904 no. 14; Guildhall MS. 9580/3.
[72] Pevsner, *Mdx.* 48.
[73] Photograph *penes* Edmonton Publ. Libr.
[74] Ex inf. Mr. L. J. Brockett (1972).
[75] Char. Com. files.
[76] G.R.O. Worship Reg. no. 24746.
[77] Ibid. no. 26808.
[78] Ibid. no. 26994.

until after 1937.[79] On census Sunday 1903 the Angel Road mission was attended by 149 people in the morning and 127 in the afternoon. The Gospel Union mission at Snells Park, usually regarded as undenominational, was listed as Congregational in 1903, when it was attended by 249 people in the morning and 432 in the evening.

A meeting-house in Chase Side, Southgate, opposite the Crown inn, was registered by Independents in 1806.[80] In 1851 112 people attended in the morning and 170 in the evening. As there were then only 120 sittings the congregation decided to raise a mortgage but numbers declined and in 1890 the chapel and its contents were sold by the mortgagee's order. The chapel was taken over by the Baptists.[81]

Independents who had used a room in Meeting House Lane since 1803,[82] had by 1819 moved into the Presbyterian meeting-house from which the road (later Church Road) took its name. The chapel, on the south-east side of the road, just north of Snells Park,[83] may have been St. John's chapel in Meeting House Lane, which served various sects before it was taken over by the Church of England before 1839.[84]

Olive Branch chapel, on the north side of Claremont Street, was erected in 1845 as a branch of Edmonton and Tottenham chapel and had 60 free sittings and an afternoon attendance of 38 in 1851. It was still run as a mission of Edmonton and Tottenham chapel in the late 19th century but had closed by 1893.[85]

Edmonton Congregational church in Fore Street, the third Congregational chapel in Lower Edmonton, originated in an Independent chapel registered at Edmonton Green from 1853 until 1866.[86] A breakaway group from Edmonton and Tottenham chapel, which had met in the old schoolroom, founded Lower Edmonton Congregational chapel in Knight's Lane in 1883. The building, which was still incomplete in 1914, was in the early Gothic style with accommodation for 750 people.[87] In 1903, with 241 people in the morning and 563 in the evening, it had the largest nonconformist congregation in Edmonton. Soon after 1959 the chapel was replaced by the third and present chapel, Edmonton Congregational church, built on the west side of Fore Street opposite Sebastopol Road. Built in yellow brick and pebbledash, with a stone cross and metal spire, it consists of a dual-purpose main hall and sanctuary, with later additions. The congregation was formed by the amalgamation of Lower Edmonton with Edmonton and Tottenham chapel.[88]

Queen's Road Congregational chapel, another mission church belonging to Edmonton and Tottenham chapel, was erected soon after 1860 on the east side of Queen's Road, just south of its junction with Town Road.[89] A brick and slated building with accommodation for 300, it was put up for sale in 1872.[90]

Palmers Green Congregational church[91] originated in meetings held in 1907 in a cottage in Hazelwood Lane. Avondale hall in Hoppers Road was hired in May 1909 and four months later a church hall was erected in Fox Lane. A church on the adjoining site at the junction of Fox Lane with Burford Gardens was opened in 1914.[92] It is a red-brick building with stone dressings, built in a late Gothic style to the design of George Baines and Son of Clement's Inn.[93] A temporary hall, Burford hall, was added at the back in 1922 and the church was extended in 1929.

BAPTISTS. Ebenezer chapel, a small brick building on the south side of Claremont Street, Upper Edmonton, was built and registered by Calvinistic Independents in 1818.[94] In 1851 there were 150 sittings and an average attendance of 90 at the morning and evening services.[95] On census Sunday 1903, when it was used by Strict Baptists, it was attended by 30 people in the morning and 43 in the evening.[96] It was rebuilt in 1958[97] but had closed by 1972.

Providence chapel was erected in 1825 in Vicar's Moor Lane by John Udall the elder, a member of a Winchmore Hill family which used its grocer's shop as a front for the sale of contraband goods. The chapel was registered by Independents,[98] and the Udallite sect which worshipped there called itself Independent in 1851 and Calvinistic in 1866.[99] By 1867, however, it was described as Baptist[1] and in 1926 as Strict Baptist.[2] The original chapel had 60 sittings and an attendance on census Sunday 1851 of 38 in the morning and 33 in the afternoon. The chapel was rebuilt in 1888[3] in yellow brick with red brick dressings in the Gothic style. Attendance on census Sunday 1903 was 24 in the morning and 31 in the afternoon.

Lower Edmonton Baptist chapel was built in Lower Fore Street by Particular or Calvinistic Baptists in 1861. It stood with a British school near the junction with New Road, in the area later called the Broadway.[4] A gallery, lecture rooms, and vestries were added in 1885 and there were 400 sittings in 1908.[5] On census Sunday 1903 the chapel was attended by 151 people in the morning

[79] *Kelly's Dirs. Mdx.* (1882, 1886, 1937); *Kelly's Dir. Tottenham* (1897–8).
[80] Guildhall MS. 9580/2.
[81] Round, *Southgate and Winchmore Hill*, 39; *The Times*, 31 Jan. 1890.
[82] Guildhall MS. 9580/2.
[83] C 54/12684 mm. 24–30; Robinson, *Edmonton*, 185; see above.
[84] *Lond. Gaz.* 19 July 1839, p. 1437. See p. 185.
[85] *Kelly's Dir. Tottenham* (1893–4); Fisk, *Edmonton*, 90.
[86] G.R.O. Worship Reg. no. 720. The records of Lower Edmonton Congregational church (1852–86) are at the Greater Lond. Rec. Off. (County Hall) N/C/65.
[87] Fisk, *Edmonton*, 174; photograph *penes* Edmonton Publ. Libr.
[88] G.R.O. Worship Reg. nos. 27683, 67173; ex inf. Mr. L. J. Brockett (1972).
[89] C 54/15556 no. 10.

[90] Fisk, *Edmonton*, 90; sales parts. (1872) *penes* Edmonton Publ. Libr.
[91] Unless otherwise stated, this account is based upon *Palmers Green Congreg. Church, Jubilee Story, 1907–57* (pamphlet).
[92] G.R.O. Worship Reg. nos. 44246, 46313.
[93] *Building News*, cvii. 461.
[94] Guildhall MS. 9580/5; C 54/9751 no. 9.
[95] H.O. 129/137/3/1/7.
[96] G.R.O. Worship Reg. nos. 61945, 67247.
[97] Photographs *penes* Edmonton Publ. Libr.
[98] Guildhall MS. 9580/6, f. 9; C 54/15850 no. 4.
[99] H.O. 129/137/3/1/11; *Green's Dir. Stoke Newington etc.* (1866); Regnart, *Winchmore Hill*, 24, 75.
[1] O.S. Map 1/2,500, Mdx. VII. 10 (1867 edn.).
[2] G.R.O. Worship Reg. no. 50170.
[3] Foundation stone.
[4] C 54/15914 no. 11; G.R.O. Worship Reg. no. 11782.
[5] *Kelly's Dir. Mdx.* (1908).

and 387 in the evening. A freehold site was purchased in 1913 to give further accommodation.[6] The chapel, built in yellow and grey brick in the Gothic style, could seat 450 in 1972.[7] The Lower Edmonton Baptist chapel was endowed with several charities. After a sale of property in 1897 £442 stock was invested, although by 1921 the Lower Edmonton Baptist poor fund consisted of only £200 stock. Thomas and Sarah Frances Row, by wills proved 1935 and 1936, each bequeathed £200 stock to the minister for distribution among the poor. The income from the total £600 was £15 in 1966. Sarah Row also devised her home to be sold and the proceeds devoted by the minister to providing homes rent-free for two old couples. The income in 1966 was £5.[8]

New Southgate Baptist chapel,[9] originally Colney Hatch chapel, was opened by Particular Baptists at the corner of High Road and Grove Road in 1865.[10] It was a brick building with seating for 310 people,[11] built in the Romanesque style. It was used as a Sunday school after 1901 when a new church, with seating for 750,[12] was built in red brick with stone dressings in a Gothic style on the opposite side of Grove Road.[13] It was the largest Baptist church in 1903, attended on census Sunday by 342 people in the morning and 355 in the evening. Both buildings were damaged during the Second World War but the church was repaired in 1952 and the hall was rebuilt in 1958. The church could seat 420 in 1972.[14]

The chapel in Palmers Green[15] grew out of a mission started in 1878 by John Knight in cottages in Hazelwood Lane. On census Sunday 1903 the mission was attended by 29 people in the morning and 36 in the evening. In 1905 a chapel was built on a slope on the west side of Green Lanes near Deadman's bridge.[16] The chapel, of brick with a plaster and wood facing, stood on pillars over a hall and was enlarged by the addition of a new hall in 1969. There was seating for 325 in 1972.[17]

Oakwood Park chapel[18] derived from earlier chapels in Chase Side, Southgate. Local Baptists, encouraged by the preacher, Charles Hadden Spurgeon, bought a site in Chase Road in 1884, where they erected a corrugated iron building, and in 1894 moved to the former Congregational chapel in Chase Side.[19] Attendance on census Sunday 1903 was 87 in the morning and 110 in the evening. The chapel, a brick building, was demolished in 1936 after the congregation had moved to Merrivale in Oakwood Park.[20] The site had

been given by a builder, C. W. B. Simmonds, and a new chapel, of red brick with stone dressings and originally called Oakwood Park Free church, was opened in 1935.[21] After the Second World War, a hall was built next to the church, which seated 350 in 1964.[22]

St. George's chapel, a stock-brick building in a Gothic style in Russell Road, Bowes Park, was founded in 1896.[23] It was registered by Baptists in 1897[24] but had passed to the Methodists by 1903.

Winchmore Hill chapel[25] originated in the union of local Baptists worshipping in a private house with a congregation which had used the 17th-century Glasshouse Yard (Islington) church. A builder, Edmondson, gave a site at the junction of Compton Road with Green Lanes, where a chapel was opened in 1907.[26] The building, in red brick with stone dressings, was designed in the late Gothic style by W. Hayne. A hall was added in 1966 and the chapel seated 425 in 1972.[27]

South Road chapel in New Southgate was registered by the Old Baptist Union from 1926 until 1954.[28]

A Baptist mission hall opened at Marsh Side between 1886 and 1893 but had closed by 1896.[29]

METHODISTS.[30] Lower Fore Street (W) chapel[31] originated in a group of Wesleyans who met in a room in Bury Street in 1826.[32] In 1829 they erected a plain brick chapel with 110 sittings on the eastern side of Lower Fore Street, where the average congregation was said to be 70 in 1851.[33] In 1860 the foundation stone was laid of a chapel for 250, on the same side of the street,[34] designed in brick with stone dressings by Charles Laws. The old chapel was demolished and in 1864 Sunday school buildings were erected behind the new one. On census Sunday 1903 the attendance was 179 in the morning and 138 in the afternoon. In 1911 a new Central hall with accommodation for 1,250 was opened south of the chapel.[35] The chapel was demolished in 1929, when new Sunday-school buildings were erected,[36] and the Central hall in 1971, after which date services were held in the Sunday school.[37]

Winchmore Hill (W) chapel[38] is the third Methodist chapel in the area. From 1847 until 1866 the Wesleyans worshipped in a chapel at the southern end of the village. The chapel, which accommodated 80 people, was attended on census Sunday 1851 by 30 in the morning, 40 in the afternoon, and 40 in the evening.[39] The foundation stone of a second chapel was laid in 1880 west of Green Lanes, on ground

---

[6] Fisk, *Edmonton*, 170–1.

[7] *Baptist Handbk.* (1972).

[8] Char. Com. files; *Endowed Chars.* (*Mdx.*), H.C. 306, pp. 6–7 (1899), lxx.

[9] Unless otherwise stated, this account is based upon *New Southgate Baptist Church, 1863–1963* (pamphlet).

[10] G.R.O. Worship Reg. no. 17148; C 54/16401 no. 3.

[11] *Kelly's Dir. Mdx.* (1890).

[12] Ibid. (1908).

[13] G.R.O. Worship Reg. no. 38928.

[14] *Baptist Handbk.* (1972).

[15] Unless otherwise stated, ex inf. the minister (1972).

[16] G.R.O. Worship Reg. no. 41865.

[17] *Baptist Handbk.* (1972).

[18] Unless otherwise stated, ex inf. the minister (1972).

[19] G.R.O. Worship Reg. no. 38136.

[20] Newby, *Old Southgate*, 59.

[21] G.R.O. Worship Reg. no. 56363.

[22] *Baptist Handbk.* (1972).

[23] Datestone on bldg.; *Kelly's Dir. Mdx.* (1908).

[24] G.R.O. Worship Reg. no. 35874.

[25] Unless otherwise stated, ex inf. the minister (1972).

[26] G.R.O. Worship Reg. no. 43171; datestone on bldg.

[27] *Baptist Handbk.* (1972).

[28] G.R.O. Worship Reg. no. 50272.

[29] *Kelly's Dirs. Tottenham* (1893–4, 1896–7); *Kelly's Dir. Mdx.* (1886).

[30] In the following account the letters (W) and (P) denote former Wesleyan and Primitive Methodist chs.

[31] Unless otherwise stated, this account is based upon Fisk, *Edmonton*, 171–3.

[32] Guildhall MS. 9580/6, f. 104.

[33] Ibid. f. 270; C 54/10960 no. 21.

[34] The site was acquired in 1853: C 54/14580 no. 6.

[35] M.R.O., Acc. 1104.   [36] *Kelly's Dir. Mdx.* (1933).

[37] Ex inf. the minister (1972).

[38] Unless otherwise stated, ex inf. Mr. D. Barnes (Trustees' treasurer, 1972).

[39] Guildhall MS. 9580/8, f. 290; G.R.O. Worship Reg. no. 5774.

adjoining Eaton Park.[40] On census Sunday 1903 the attendance was 50 in the morning and 54 in the evening. A third chapel, of red and yellow brick with stone dressings and accommodating 700, opened in 1912 next to the second chapel, which continued in use as a church hall.

A room at no. 1 Snells Park (P) was registered for worship by Primitive Methodists from 1854 until 1866 when they moved to White Hart Lane (Tottenham).[41]

New Southgate (W) chapel[42] traced its origins to meetings held in a mission room in Palmers Green Road from 1886 until 1896.[43] In 1898 the Wesleyans opened a chapel in High (formerly Betstyle) Road.[44] Built in red brick with stone dressings in a Gothic style, it has accommodation for 300 people and five schoolrooms. It held the largest Methodist congregations on census Sunday 1903, 189 people in the morning and 170 in the evening.

The chapel at the Bourne (W),[45] which replaced an earlier chapel at Chase Side, originated in 1885 when Wesleyans met in a cottage at no. 1 Ada Villas, Chelmsford Road. They later met in a shop and marquee in Chase Side and in an iron building formerly used as a Congregational Sunday school. In 1891 they erected an iron chapel in Chase Side, west of the Baptist chapel,[46] which on census Sunday 1903 was attended by 52 people in the morning and 58 in the evening. The iron chapel was sold to St. Andrew's church, Southgate, as a church hall in 1929 and the congregation moved to a new chapel and Sunday school, built of red brick with stone dressings at the corner of the Bourne and Queen Elizabeth's Drive in 1929.[47] A new Sunday school was used from 1937.

Springfield Road (P) chapel was erected at the corner of Springfield Road and Cross Road in New Southgate between 1892 and 1896[48] and registered by Primitive Methodists from 1908 until 1936.[49] It was attended by 22 people in the morning and 39 in the evening on census Sunday 1903.

The Ripon Road (P) chapel, at the junction of Ripon and Hertford roads, grew out of Primitive Methodist meetings held in a mission house in St. Mary's Terrace from 1900 until 1902.[50] The iron chapel was built in 1902 and attended on census Sunday 1903 by 82 people in the morning and 85 in the evening. It was officially closed in 1964.[51]

Bush Hill Park chapel (P)[52] originated in meetings held by Primitive Methodists in a house in Wellington Road in 1903. In 1905 they erected Emmanuel assembly hall, a plain red-brick building with stone dressings, at the corner of Wellington and Edenbridge roads.[53] A red-brick chapel was erected on adjoining land in 1940[54] and a small hall was added after the Second World War.

St. George's chapel (W) in Russell Road, Bowes Park, had been taken over from the Baptists before census Sunday 1903, when it was attended by 88 people in the morning and 85 in the evening. The Methodists may have continued to rent the chapel[55] until 1934, when it passed to the Brethren,[56] but it is more probable that it became an undenominational mission after Bowes Park chapel opened in 1907.

Trinity-at-Bowes chapel[57] was built on the site of Bowes Park (W) chapel at the corner of Bowes and Palmerston roads in 1973. Bowes Park chapel, a redbrick and stone building with accommodation for 950, was built in 1907 and adjoining Sunday schools with 9 rooms were erected in 1909.[58] In 1969 Bowes Park amalgamated with Trinity chapel, Wood Green, to form the church of Trinity-at-Bowes. The old chapel was demolished in 1972.

Grange Park chapel[59] in 1938 replaced an earlier chapel on the corner between Old Park Ridings and Park Drive. The site had previously formed part of an orchard and the first chapel, erected in 1921,[60] was often called 'the church in the orchard'. The new building, designed by C. H. Brightiff and described as the best of its kind in the county,[61] was enlarged between 1970 and 1973.

Oakwood chapel[62] originated in meetings held in a shop in Bramley Road from 1939 until the opening of a hall in Westgate Avenue in 1950.[63] From 1939 Laing's estate office had been used for some church activities and in 1953 it was purchased under the name of Lonsdale hall, to serve as a youth centre until its sale in 1963. A chapel was built next to the hall in 1959 and new buildings for church activities were erected near by in 1964.

BRETHREN. Belmont hall mission room opened on the south side of Bounces Road between 1882 and 1886[64] and was attended by 6 people in the morning and 71 in the evening on census Sunday 1903. It closed when Croyland Road gospel hall, a plain redbrick building, opened in 1926.[65]

St. Matthias mission hall in Victoria Road was taken over from the Church of England between 1917 and 1922[66] and used by the Brethren until after 1938.[67]

St. George's chapel in Russell Road, Bowes Park, previously used by Baptists and Methodists, passed to the Brethren in 1934 and was acquired from them in 1955 by Elim Pentecostalists.[68]

Bury Street chapel originated in meetings over a shop in Bury Street Parade in 1938. Brethren planned a hall in Bury Street in 1939, a temporary

[40] G.R.O. Worship Reg. no. 25391.
[41] Ibid. 2583; Fisk, *Edmonton*, 76.
[42] Unless otherwise stated, this account is based upon information supplied by the minister (1972).
[43] G.R.O. Worship Reg. no. 29616.
[44] Ibid. 30636, 37136; datestone on bldg.
[45] Unless otherwise stated, this account is based upon *Southgate (The Bourne) Methodist Church* (pamphlet).
[46] G.R.O. Worship Reg. no. 32920.
[47] Ibid. 52253.
[48] *Kelly's Dir. Barnet* (1892–3).
[49] G.R.O. Worship Reg. no. 43122.
[50] Ibid. 37832.
[51] Ibid. 39067; *Kelly's Dir. Mdx.* (1926).
[52] Unless otherwise stated, ex inf. the minister (1972).
[53] G.R.O. Worship Reg. no. 41428.
[54] Ibid. 59241.
[55] *Kelly's Dir. Mdx.* (1908).

[56] See below.
[57] Unless otherwise stated, ex inf. the minister (1972).
[58] G.R.O. Worship Reg. nos. 42794, 43478.
[59] Unless otherwise stated, ex inf. the minister (1972).
[60] G.R.O. Worship Reg. no. 48166.
[61] Robbins, *Mdx.* 561.
[62] Unless otherwise stated, this account is based on *Oakwood Methodist Church Silver Jubilee, 1939–64* (pamphlet).
[63] G.R.O. Worship Reg. no. 58598.
[64] *Kelly's Dirs. Mdx.* (1882, 1886); *Kelly's Dirs. Tottenham* (1893–4, 1922–3).
[65] *Kelly's Dir. Mdx.* (1926); G.R.O. Worship Reg. no. 50505.
[66] *Kelly's Dir. Mdx.* (1917); *Kelly's Dir. Tottenham* (1922).
[67] O.S. Map 1/2,500, Mdx. VII. 15 (1938 edn.).
[68] G.R.O. Worship Reg. no. 55048.

hut was erected after the Second World War, and in 1951 a permanent brick chapel was opened.[69]

Amberly hall in Fox Lane, Palmers Green, was registered in 1946 by Brethren who had been at Wood Green since 1937.[70]

SALVATION ARMY. New Southgate hall[71] originated in meetings held by the Salvation Army in two small houses at the southern end of Palmers Road, opposite the Beehive inn, in 1886. A red-brick citadel on the southern side of Garfield Road replaced the earlier centre, which since 1888[72] had been designated a barracks, in 1895.[73] On census Sunday 1903 it was attended by 34 people in the morning and 103 in the evening.

Edmonton citadel corps in Fore Street first met in the North Middlesex hall in Upper Fore Street in 1889. Although the registration of the hall was not cancelled until 1896,[74] the corps moved to its main centre, the citadel in Fore Street, where there was accommodation for 550 people, in 1892.[75] On census Sunday 1903 it was attended by 145 people in the morning and 437 in the evening.

Other halls were registered by the Salvation Army at no. 95 Fore Street from 1908 until 1914[76] and at no. 338 Hertford Road from 1909 until 1910.[77]

OTHER DENOMINATIONS. The meeting-house in Meeting House Lane, Upper Edmonton, was used by the Countess of Huntingdon's Connexion between c. 1819 and c. 1839.[78]

Christ Church in Coach and Horses Lane was registered by 'Episcopalian' dissenters from 1853 until 1896.[79]

Lower Edmonton chapel was registered by Evangelical Protestant dissenters from 1854 until 1866.[80]

Upper Edmonton Free church[81] originated in undenominational mission meetings held in the 1880s by Christopher King, a former clown, in a hall behind a shop in Fore Street and later in the Angel assembly rooms. After King's departure the congregation, in conjunction with the Gospel Union, erected a temporary iron hall for 400 people on leased land at the junction of Langhedge Lane and Grove Street in 1889.[82] The hall, listed among Congregational missions in 1903,[83] was replaced in 1912 by an iron Sunday-school building[84] and in 1913 by a brick people's tabernacle, designed by Frank Bethell.[85] In 1952 a new Sunday school replaced the old one, which had been destroyed by fire in 1939.

The London City Mission opened Hyde mission hall on the east side of Hyde Lane (later Victoria Road), north of its junction with Chauncey Street in 1888.[86] On census Sunday 1903 it was attended by 66 people in the evening.[87] It was taken over by the Church of England, as St. Matthias mission room, in 1905 and later by the Brethren. The London City Mission opened another Hyde mission hall at no. 26 Sunnyside, south of the original hall, in 1906.[88] It was still there in 1937.[89]

An evangelical mission hall had been erected on the north side of Statham Grove, off Bull Lane, by 1890. It was attended on census Sunday 1903 by 49 people in the morning and 140 in the evening and was still there in 1937.[90]

St. George's Presbyterian church[91] originated in meetings in Avondale hall of a group which had moved to Palmers Green from Wood Green. In 1914 a brick and stone church in a Gothic style opened in Fox Lane.[92] A church hall for the Sunday school was opened at the back in 1927.

Tanners End Free church, on the south side of Statham Grove, began as a mission hall for un-designated Christians in 1913.[93] Known as Tanners End mission in 1937,[94] its name was changed to Tanners End Free church in 1948.[95]

Edmonton Spiritualist National church,[96] originally Tottenham and Edmonton Spiritualist church,[97] grew out of meetings held at Beech hall near Cedars Road in Lower Edmonton and also in Tottenham and Stoke Newington in the early 20th century. The chapel, a brick building consisting of a hall and ante-room with accommodation for 175 people, opened in Linnell Road in 1929. It was enlarged after 1945 and in 1972 accommodated a total of 230 people. The Temple of the Trinity Lodge for Spiritual Healing[98] grew out of meetings held by the National Christian Spiritualist church in High Road, Wood Green, from 1938. In 1941 the group moved to no. 95 Green Lanes, Edmonton,[99] a former branch of Lloyds Bank, where it bought the freehold in 1972.

Lower Edmonton mission, held in rooms at no. 436 Hertford Road, was registered by un-designated Christians in 1929.[1]

A Pentecostal mission room in Cowper Road, off Upper Fore Street, opened between 1926 and 1933[2] and survived in 1938.[3]

Elim Pentecostal church, originally St. George's chapel in Russell Road, Bowes Park, was taken over from the Brethren in 1955.[4]

There was a Seventh Day Adventist hall at no. 18 Bounces Road in 1937.[5] Advent church, a plain

[69] Ibid. 58349, 64278; ex inf. the secretary (1972).
[70] G.R.O. Worship Reg. nos. 57673, 61300; Borough of Southgate, *Official Guide* [1963].
[71] Unless otherwise stated, ex inf. the secretary (1972).
[72] G.R.O. Worship Reg. no. 30958.
[73] Ibid. 35006.
[74] Ibid. 31711.
[75] Ibid. 33434.
[76] Ibid. 43092.
[77] Ibid. 43579.
[78] *St. James, Upper Edmonton Monthly Paper*, Aug. 1888 *penes* St. James's church.
[79] G.R.O. Worship Reg. no. 721.
[80] Ibid. 5997.
[81] Unless otherwise stated, this account is based on *People's Tabernacle, Grove Street, 1888–1938* (pamphlet) and ex inf. the secretary (1972).
[82] G.R.O. Worship Reg. no. 31367.
[83] See above.
[84] G.R.O. Worship Reg. no. 45461.
[85] Ibid. 45734; datestone on bldg.
[86] Ex inf. Mr. D. O. Pam (1974).
[87] Mudie-Smith, *Religious Life of London*, 401.

[88] G.R.O. Worship Reg. no. 41547.
[89] *Kelly's Dir. Mdx.* (1937).
[90] *Kelly's Dirs. Mdx.* (1890, 1908, 1937).
[91] Unless otherwise stated, this account is based on *St. George's Presbyterian Church, Palmers Green* (pamphlet).
[92] G.R.O. Worship Reg. no. 45941.
[93] Ibid. 45569.
[94] *Kelly's Dir. Mdx.* (1937).
[95] G.R.O. Worship Reg. no. 62116.
[96] Unless otherwise stated, this account is based upon information supplied by the minister (1972) and upon *The Weekly Herald*, 25 Oct. 1929.
[97] G.R.O. Worship Reg. no. 53311.
[98] Unless otherwise stated, ex inf. the secretary (1972).
[99] G.R.O. Worship Reg. nos. 59520, 59965.
[1] Ibid. 51964.
[2] *Kelly's Dirs. Mdx.* (1926, 1933).
[3] O.S. Map 1/2,500, Mdx. VII. 15 (1938 edn.).
[4] G.R.O. Worship Reg. no. 55048.
[5] *Kelly's Dir. Mdx.* (1937).

yellow-brick building in Cuckoo Hall Lane, was registered by Seventh Day Adventists in 1939.[6]

In 1939 Christian Scientists registered the rear of no. 131 Palmerston Road, Bowes Park.[7]

In 1952 members of the overcrowded Enfield congregation of Jehovah's Witnesses purchased a former club building, no. 303 Galliard Road, which they registered as Kingdom hall. The building was enlarged in 1970–1 to seat 150 people and the average attendance at meetings in 1972 was 125.[8]

JUDAISM.[9] It was not until the 1930s, long after the opening of a Jewish school[10] and a Federation cemetery,[11] that Jews began moving into Old and New Southgate. Palmers Green and Southgate synagogue was registered for worship at no. 131 Palmerston Road in 1933.[12] It was affiliated to the United Synagogue and in 1936 became a District synagogue on the congregation's move to a new building in Brownlow Road,[13] which was severely damaged during the war and replaced in 1957.[14]

Southgate and District Progressive (formerly Liberal) synagogue originated in services held in members' houses in 1943. From 1944 until 1954 services were held in the community hall in Southgate. A house at no. 75 Chase Road was acquired in 1954 and used for worship until a new synagogue was erected in the grounds in 1959.[15]

Cockfosters and North Southgate District synagogue, a member of the United Synagogue, was founded as an offshoot of Palmers Green synagogue in 1948. A synagogue was built in Old Farm Avenue, Southgate, in 1953 and consecrated in 1954. A new community hall and classrooms were opened in 1965.[16] The synagogue served about 1,200 families in 1972, mainly from Cockfosters.[17]

Southgate and District Reform synagogue and communal centre was opened at the junction of Queens Avenue and Farm Road in 1963.

A Jewish youth centre, Southgate Habonim, originated in 1962 as a branch of Stamford Hill Habonim. It met in a British Legion hall in Nursery Road, Southgate, and afterwards as a small group in private houses. Nos. 375 and 377 Bowes Road were purchased in 1966 and demolished in 1969, when a wooden meeting-place or moadon was erected on the site.[18]

EDUCATION.[19] There was a schoolmaster in Edmonton in 1583.[20] In 1606 Henry Smith of London left a £2 annual rent-charge on premises in Silver Street towards freeing poor boys and paying the master until the school was wholly free.[21] William Pulley was the schoolmaster in 1616[22] and the master of the 'common school-house' in Edmonton was left money by will proved 1623.[23] Latymer school was established under the will of Edward Latymer dated 1624[24] and although there is no evidence that a school was built then, John Wilde by will proved 1665 left £4 to the schoolmaster of the 'new school of Edmonton'.[25] By will proved 1679 Thomas Style granted an annual rent-charge of £20 to be paid to a schoolmaster chosen by the vestry to teach 20 poor boys Latin grammar. At first there were apparently schoolmasters for both Latymer's and Style's charities but in 1739 a school-house next to the alms-houses in Church Street[26] was purchased, possibly the one mentioned by Henry Smith or John Wilde, and in 1742 all the educational charities were amalgamated. Benjamin Hare, who was nominated schoolmaster in 1680,[27] was followed by Thomas Hare in 1724 and Zachariah Hare in 1737. The Adams family were headmasters from 1781 until 1868.

Latymer school catered only for boys but in 1778 a girls' charity school was started in Edmonton[28] and in 1783 Mrs. Elizabeth Cowling left £1,454 in trust for the education and clothing of poor children in Southgate ward. Apparently no separate Cowling school was founded and by 1823 £43 a year from Mrs. Cowling's gift was applied to clothing 9 boys and 9 girls.[29]

Christopher Taylor conducted a Quaker school in Edmonton until c. 1682, when it was taken over by George Keith, and Bridget Austell had one in Southgate before she moved to Tottenham in 1689.[30] William Le Hunt started a school at Edmonton c. 1707 which was described in 1716 as a large popish seminary for young men to be sent to foreign seminaries.[31] The Children's Friend Sunday school at Chase Side, an Independent school, was in existence by 1805,[32] a school was kept at Southgate by the Quaker Josiah Forster before he moved to Tottenham in 1810, and a Sunday school attached to Tottenham and Edmonton Congregational church was started in Fore Street in 1822.[33] By 1819 there were three dissenting Sunday schools, teaching 67 children, and two Anglican Sunday schools, one in Edmonton with 120 children and one at Southgate with 130. In addition 81 boys were educated at Latymer school, 72 girls at the girls' charity school, and 136 children at Walker's school. The

---

[6] G.R.O. Worship Reg. nos. 58946, 60856.

[7] Ibid. 59006.

[8] Ibid. 63696; ex inf. the presiding overseer (1972).

[9] Except where otherwise stated, this section is based upon *Jewish Yr. Bks.*

[10] See p. 202.

[11] See p. 180.

[12] G.R.O. Worship Reg. no. 54314.

[13] Ibid. no. 56649; O.S. Map 1/2,500, Mdx. VII. 14 (1936 edn.).

[14] *Formation of Palmers Green and Southgate Dist. Synagogue* [pamphlet hist.].

[15] *Southgate and Dist. Liberal Synagogue, 25th Anniversary* [pamphlet].

[16] Datestone on bldg.

[17] Ex inf. the rabbi.

[18] Ex inf. the sec.

[19] Except where otherwise stated, this account is based on G. W. Sturges, *Schs. of Edmonton Hund.*; *Public Elem. Schs. 1906* [Cd. 3510], H.C. (1907), lxiii; *Bd. of Educ.,*

List 21 (H.M.S.O. 1919–38); Ed. 7/86–88; inf. from heads of schs. (1973).

[20] Guildhall MS. 9537/5.

[21] Robinson, *Edmonton*, 143.

[22] M.R.O., Acc. 241/18.

[23] Prob. 11/141 (P.C.C. 20 Swann, will of Sir John Weld).

[24] *V.C.H. Mdx.* i. 305.

[25] Prob. 11/316 (P.C.C. 9 Hyde, will of John Wilde).

[26] See plan in M.R.O., M.C.C./A/Pl. 1.

[27] Guildhall MS. 10116A file 1.   [28] See below.

[29] *9th Rep. Com. Char.* 178.

[30] *Short Jnl. and Itinerant Jnls. of George Fox,* ed. N. Penney, 324, 338; *Jnl. of George Fox,* ed. N. Penney, i. 55, 410; ii. 455.

[31] E. S. Worrall, *The Confessor Wm. Le Hunt, Priest and Schoolmaster of Enfield and Edmonton* (Edmonton Hund. Hist. Soc., n.d.).

[32] Guildhall MS. 9580/2.

[33] Fisk, *Edmonton,* 89.

poor were then said to be 'very desirous' of education and increasingly able to pay for it.[34]

By 1833 13 day-schools and two day- and Sunday schools were attended by 777 children and 10 boarding-schools by 460 children. Most of the day-schools were probably dame schools, apart from Southgate National school for girls, which had been founded since 1819.[35] The National Society soon extended its activities until by 1846 there were 9 schools, attended by 827 children. The number, with an infants' school capable of accommodating 150 children, was then deemed sufficient.[36] Other National schools opened in 1851 and 1866 and the Anglican monopoly was challenged only by a school at Southgate, probably small, which was kept by the Baptist Robert Blagden from c. 1839 until after 1851,[37] by a British school opened in 1861, and by a Wesleyan Sunday school in Fore Street established in 1873. Millfield House in Silver Street was opened by Strand union in 1849 but was for orphans from London.[38] In 1870 there were 21 schools, 12 of them connected with the Church of England or the National Society, 2 with the British Society, and 4 with no religious affiliation. They consisted of 7 public schools attended by 594 children, 7 private schools attended by 440, 6 'adventure' schools attended by 76, and one school in the course of being supplied.[39]

A school board was formed compulsorily in 1880.[40] Three temporary board schools were opened in 1881 and the first permanent school was opened in 1882. By 1904 the board had established another eight permanent schools and one temporary school. Four Church of England schools were opened in the same period. Under the Act of 1902 Edmonton became a Part III authority and an education committee replaced the school board in Edmonton U.D. In Southgate education became the responsibility of the county council.[41]

Edmonton's schools became severely overcrowded before the First World War but the education committee, mostly for financial reasons, was slow to provide new ones. A Roman Catholic elementary school was opened in 1912 and four elementary schools were opened by Edmonton between 1928 and 1937. Efforts were made to implement the Hadow Report and reorganize elementary schools into senior and junior schools. Apart from the central school which was opened in 1919, all six secondary schools opened in Edmonton before 1945 were founded between 1927 and 1932. Southgate, under the county education authority, acquired its schools earlier, although there were hopes in 1909 that the ban on classes of more than 60 pupils might be circumvented by allowing one teacher to take two classes.[42] One elementary council school opened in 1908, two in 1914, and one in 1936. Secondary schools were founded in 1910 and 1919 and five between 1927 and 1938.

All the secondary schools, except two, became secondary modern schools after the 1944 Act. Six new secondary modern schools were opened after the Second World War, although some were closed in 1960. Seven new primary schools were opened, mostly in the early 1950s.

In 1965 both Southgate and Edmonton became part of Enfield L.B., which in 1967 produced a scheme for comprehensive education. After initial opposition the scheme was put into effect and all the secondary public schools in the area, except Latymer Upper school which had Voluntary status, were reorganized. Nearly all the new comprehensive schools extended their curricula and many acquired extra accommodation. Some schools, notably in Southgate, took children from the ages of 11 to 18 and others were organized on the two-tier system, with lower schools for children up to the age of fourteen.

Elementary Schools founded before 1880. Edmonton girls' charity school[43] was established by public subscription in 1778. Subscribers of £1 1s. a year became annual governors and donors of £10 10s. became governors for life. Governors had the right to present children to the school. Legacies and gifts totalled £3,381 by 1818, the largest being those of James Vere (£300 in 1780), George Stanbridge (£1,030 in 1782), and Mrs. Worsfold (£500 in 1817). Income was augmented by the sale of needlework, by charity sermons, and after 1891 by government grants.

The foundation stone of a new school was laid in 1784 on land offered by Obadiah Legrew, who in 1793 pulled down the school-house and rebuilt it on his copyhold estate near by. The building, extended in 1827, survives on the south side of Church Street near the junction with Fore Street and consists of a simple yellow-brick structure with red-brick dressings. In the centre is a statue of a charity girl and the legend 'A structure of Hope founded in Faith on the basis of Charity'. Pupils, aged between 7 and 12 or sometimes 14, were clothed and educated, although the main purpose was to fit them for domestic service. The National system was introduced in 1815. Numbers, which rose from 12 in 1778 to 30 in 1798 and 72 in 1819[44] and 1833,[45] fell to 60 in 1846[46] and 43 in 1863. They rose again to 69 in 1903 but the school, unable to fulfil the terms of its foundation and comply with the 1902 Act, closed in 1904. The investments of the charity accumulated until 1913 when they were transferred to the Girls' Special Instruction Foundation, established by a Scheme of the Board of Education.

St. Paul's Church of England school at Winchmore Hill[47] originated by 1813 and possibly

[34] *Educ. of Poor Digest*, p. 536.
[35] *Educ. Enquiry Abstract*, 89.
[36] Nat. Soc. *Church Schs. Inquiry, 1846–7*, Mdx. 4–5.
[37] Robson, *Lond. Dir.* (1839); *Pigot's Dir. Mdx.* (1840); H.O. 107/1703 pp. 142 sqq.
[38] *V.C.H. Mdx.* i. 229; H.O. 107/1703 pp. 56 sqq.; *Kelly's Dir. Mdx.* (1908); O.S. Map 1/2,500, Mdx. VII. 15 (1867, 1914 edns.).
[39] *Returns relating to Elem. Educ.* H.C. 201, pp. 570–1 (1871), lv.
[40] *Lond. Gaz.* 20 July 1880, p. 4042; *Kelly's Dir. Mdx.* (1890).

[41] *Kelly's Dir. Mdx.* (1908); Mdx. Cnty. Council, *Primary and Secondary Educ. in Mdx. 1900–65*.
[42] *Recorder for Palmers Green, Winchmore Hill and Southgate*, Oct. 1909 *penes* Broomfield Mus.
[43] Unless otherwise stated, the account of this school is based upon E. Hoare, *Edmonton Girls Charity Sch. 1778–1904* (Edmonton Hund. Hist. Soc., n.d.).
[44] *Educ. of Poor Digest*, 536.
[45] *Educ. Enquiry Abstract*, 89.
[46] Nat. Soc. *Church Schs. Inquiry, 1846–7*, Mdx. 4–5.
[47] Unless otherwise stated, the account of this school is based upon E. W. Spalding, *Looking Forward* (pamphlet hist. of St. Paul's church).

as early as 1785[48] in a one-roomed weatherboarded cottage in Church Hill, which was still there in 1972. In 1846 the school was attended on weekdays and Sundays by a total of 32 boys and 49 girls. It was affiliated to the National Society and supported by subscriptions and pence.[49] In 1859 the foundation stone of a larger school was laid on a site next to the church given by John Donnithorne Taylor. The second school, usually known as Winchmore Hill National school, could accommodate 220 boys, 150 girls, and 51 infants in 1908.[50] Attendance rose from 84 in 1870[51] to 220 in 1906. By 1958 the building had become dilapidated, the children moved to St. Paul's hall and in 1960 the foundation stone of a third school was laid in Ringwood Way. The new school was financed by a government grant, the diocese of London, and the parish, especially by an association of friends of the school. In 1973 there were 345 infants and juniors on the roll.

In 1810 John Walker established a boys' school on part of his estate at the corner of Powys Lane. It was a plain single-storey brick building with a thatched roof.[52] As the Walker charity school it was owned by the Walker family, from whose endowment it received £70 in 1968. Originally run on Lancasterian lines, to teach the children of 'the surrounding peasantry' reading, writing, and arithmetic,[53] it had become a Church of England school, Southgate boys', by 1868 when it applied for a parliamentary grant. Attendance was 140 in 1833[54] and 65 in 1868. A fund for rebuilding was started in 1869 but it was not until 1887 that the school moved to Chase Road and the Powys Lane premises closed.[55] The numbers rose to 170 in 1906. Southgate boys' Church of England school was reorganized as a junior mixed school after the closure of the girls' school in 1933 and was amalgamated with the infants' school in 1937. As St. Andrew's school it expanded in 1964, when new buildings were opened, and in 1973 had 269 juniors and infants on the roll.[56]

Edmonton National, later All Saints, school next to the path from Church Street was erected in 1818 and conveyed to trustees in 1822. It was governed by a committee appointed by subscribers, supported by endowment, subscriptions, and pence, and attended in 1846 by 96 boys and 67 girls in two classrooms.[57] An infants' school was added in 1863 and in 1864 there were 50 boys, 24 girls, and 30 infants. In 1871 the juniors and infants were divided into separate departments. The school was enlarged in 1888 and attended in 1890 by 160 girls and 206 infants.[58] It was enlarged again in 1898 and rebuilt in

1901,[59] attendance rising to 962 in 1906. There were 215 infants and 138 juniors on the roll in 1973.

A day school in Southgate, supported by subscriptions and pence, was attended by 70 girls in 1833.[60] It apparently occupied a small upper room at the opposite end of the village from the boys' school[61] until 1836 when the Walkers of Arnos Grove built a school for girls at Southgate Green. An infants' school, managed by the incumbent and a committee of 'ladies', was established in the same building, later known as the Walker memorial hall, in 1840. By 1846 the girls' school was affiliated to National Society and attended by 74 children.[62] It was extended in the early 1880s and the infants moved to a new school in 1896.[63] There were 203 girls in 1906 but only 22 in 1933, when the school was closed and the pupils transferred to the boys' school in Chase Road.

St. John's school was a Sunday and day school for girls attached to St. John's chapel in Meeting House Lane.[64] In 1846 it consisted of one schoolroom attended by 56 girls and was supported by subscriptions and pence.[65] It was presumably closed when St. James's church and school superseded St. John's.[66]

By will proved 1847 John Snell left 1 a. as the site for a Church of England school for the poor.[67] A school for boys, affiliated to the National Society, opened by St. James's church in 1851. Girls' and infants' departments were added in 1871 and there were further enlargements in 1879, 1885, and 1893.[68] In 1906 752 children attended the school. It was rebuilt in 1963[69] and had 263 children on the roll in 1973.

An infants' school opened in Southgate with about 100 children in 1865.[70] By 1890 there were two infants' schools, one called Farm Road or the Chase school, accommodating 60 children and attended by 32, and the other at Chase Side, accommodating 40 and attended by 30.[71] The two schools were replaced in 1895 by Southgate Church of England infants' school, which was built next to the boys' school in Chase Road and financed by a government grant, an endowment, and voluntary contributions. It was attended by 147 children in 1906 and by 63 in 1919. In 1937 the school amalgamated with the junior mixed school, originally the boys' school.

Lower Edmonton British school was built adjoining the Baptist chapel in Lower Fore Street in 1861.[72] It was receiving a parliamentary grant by 1870, when it was attended by 71 children,[73] but numbers had dropped to 44 in 1875, the year of

[48] Plaque on bldg.
[49] Nat. Soc. *Church Schs. Inquiry, 1846–7*, Mdx. 4–5.
[50] *Kelly's Dir. Mdx.* (1908).
[51] *Rep. of Educ. Cttee. of Council, 1870* [C. 406], p. 504, H.C. (1871), xxii.
[52] *9th Rep. Com. Char.* H.C. 258, p. 178 (1823), ix; Newby, *Old Southgate*, 77; photograph (1884) *penes* Broomfield Mus.; O.S. Map 1/2,500, Mdx. VII. 14 (1867 edn.).
[53] *9th Rep. Com. Char.* H.C. 258, p. 178 (1823), ix.
[54] *Educ. Enquiry Abstract*, 89.
[55] Newby, *Old Southgate*, 77.
[56] Ex inf. Miss G. Morris (1973).
[57] Nat. Soc. *Church Schs. Inquiry, 1846–7*, Mdx. 4–5.
[58] *Kelly's Dir. Mdx.* (1890).
[59] Ibid. (1908).
[60] *Educ. Enquiry Abstract*, 89.

[61] Round, *Southgate and Winchmore Hill*, 41.
[62] Nat. Soc. *Church Schs. Inquiry, 1846–7*, Mdx. 4–5.
[63] Newby, *Old Southgate*, 83.
[64] *St. James, Upper Edmonton Monthly Paper*, Aug. 1888 *penes* St. James's church.
[65] Nat. Soc. *Church Schs. Inquiry, 1846–7*, Mdx. 4–5.
[66] See p. 185.
[67] Conveyance by Snell's trustees to vicar and church-wardens, 1849 *penes* St. James's church.
[68] *Kelly's Dir. Mdx.* (1890, 1908).
[69] Datestone in bldg.
[70] Ex inf. Miss G. Morris (1973).
[71] *Kelly's Dir. Mdx.* (1890); *Rep. of Educ. Cttee. of Council, 1888* [C. 5804–I], p. 607, H.C. (1889), xxix.
[72] C 54/15914 no. 11; see p. 192.
[73] *Rep. of Educ. Cttee. of Council, 1870* [C. 406], p. 496, H.C. (1871), xxii.

closure.[74] It subsequently became a Sunday school attached to the chapel.[75]

Tile Kiln Lane National school was founded by deed in 1866 and regulated by a Charity Commission Scheme of 1890.[76] Originally an infants' school,[77] it was attended in 1878 by 66 children[78] and in 1893, when it was described as a mixed school, by 119.[79] It was replaced by St. Michael's National school, Bowes Park, in 1896.[80]

Elementary Schools founded between 1880 and 1903. Temporary board schools for boys, girls, and infants opened in 1881. The boys occupied Elm House, a former private school in Fore Street near the junction with Brettenham Road, until 1882. The girls used the Wesleyan Sunday school in Fore Street until 1893[81] and the infants used the mission room in Dyson's Road.

The first permanent board school opened in Brettenham Road in 1882 with boys from Elm House. There were boys', girls', and infants' departments until after the Second World War, when the boys and girls were amalgamated as a junior mixed school. The yellow-brick building was enlarged in 1885, 1887, 1889, and 1892[82] and numbers rose from 892 in 1888[83] to 1,235 in 1906, thereafter dropping until 1973, when there were 301 in the junior school and 250 in the infants'.

Garfield Road board school in New Southgate opened in 1883 with departments for boys, girls, and infants and, after 1936, the first nursery class in Middlesex. Numbers rose from 418 in 1888[84] to 1,211 in 1893[85] but fell to 539 in 1919 and 308 in 1973.

St. Aldhelm's National infants' school was built in Windmill Road in 1883 for 240 children[86] and attended in 1888 by 90 infants.[87] It had 133 boys in 1893[88] and was later superseded by Silver Street board school.

Lower Latymer school was created out of Latymer school by a Charity Commissioners' Scheme of 1868. It was endowed and attended by fee-paying boys aged 7 to 14. A government grant was made in 1884[89] and a separate building was erected in 1901 in Maldon Road. It was reorganized into a Church of England junior boys' school in 1947, granted Aided status in 1961, and modernized in 1962. The school was attended by 269 boys in 1906, 300 in 1919, and 209 in 1973. It closed in that year, when the buildings passed to All Saints school.[90]

Croyland Road board school opened in 1884 for 200 boys, 100 girls, and 261 infants. The school was enlarged in 1889 and 1891 and again, when an upper standard school opened, in 1901.[91] From

1901 until its closure in 1921 the junior mixed department used the original school building. When the senior school closed in 1959 the juniors moved into the former seniors' building and the infants into the juniors' building. Numbers in the four departments increased from 841 in 1888[92] to 2,295 in 1906, declining to 1,239 in 1919. There were 221 infants and 317 juniors on the roll in 1973.

St. Michael's National school, later St. Michael-at-Bowes Church of England primary school, opened in Tottenhall Road in 1896 with accommodation for 377 children in mixed and infants' departments. Attendance was 182 in 1899,[93] 198 in 1906, and 219 in 1919. The school was rebuilt in 1972 and had 280 children on the roll in 1973.

Raynham Road board school opened in 1896 for boys, girls, and infants. The departments were housed on different floors of a large yellow-brick building with red dressings, typical of the architecture of the Edmonton board. A second building erected in 1901 was used as a higher grade school until 1937, when the infants moved there. The girls' department of Edmonton central school was housed at Raynham Road from 1920 until 1921.[94] The total attendance was 1,038 in 1896, 1,743 in 1906, and 1,575 in 1919. In 1973 there were 278 children on the roll at the junior school and 260, including some in a new nursery unit, at the infants'.

St. Peter's temporary board school opened in Bounces Road in 1898. It was a junior mixed school, attended in 1899 by 142 children[95] and superseded by Eldon Road school.

Eldon Road board school opened in 1899. The infants were housed in one building and the boys', girls', and junior mixed departments on separate floors in an adjoining building. Eldon Road school was attended in 1908 by 2,313 children, of whom 537 were juniors and 625 infants.[96] The total dropped to 1,853 in 1919 and in 1973 there were 501 on the roll at the junior school and 462, including 60 at nursery classes, on the roll at the infants'.

Silver Street board school, later Huxley primary school, opened in 1901 on part of the former Huxley estate.[97] The building had boys', girls', and infants' departments on separate floors. The girls were transferred to Hazelbury school in 1931, the infants' school closed in 1957,[98] and the junior boys' school closed in 1972. Total attendance at Silver Street was 1,514 in 1906 and 1,244 in 1919.

Bowes Road board school opened in 1901 with boys, girls, and infants on separate floors. Senior and junior schools were created in 1937. The school was attended by 794 boys, girls, and infants in 1906 and by 761 in 1919. In 1973 there were 284 children on

[74] Ibid. *1875* [C. 1265–I], p. 369, H.C. (1876), xxiv; *1876* [C. 1513–I], p. 586, H.C. (1877), xxiii.
[75] O.S. Map 1/2,500, Mdx. VII. 11 (1867, 1914 edns.).
[76] *Endowed Chars. (Mdx.)*, H.C. 306, pp. 8–9 (1899), lxx.
[77] O.S. Map 1/2,500, Mdx. VII. 14 (1867 edn.).
[78] *Rep. of Educ. Cttee. of Council, 1878* [C. 2342–I], p. 958, H.C. (1878–9), xxiii.
[79] *Returns of Schs. 1893* [C. 7529], p. 420, H.C. (1894), lxv.
[80] See below.
[81] Log book *penes* Edmonton Publ. Libr.
[82] *Kelly's Dirs. Mdx.* (1890, 1908).
[83] *Rep. of Educ. Cttee. of Council, 1888* [C. 5804–I], p. 600, H.C. (1889), xxix.
[84] Ibid.
[85] *Returns of Schs. 1893* [C. 7529], p. 426, H.C. (1894), lxv.
[86] *Kelly's Dir. Mdx.* (1890).
[87] *Rep. of Educ. Cttee. of Council, 1888* [C. 5804–I], p. 600, H.C. (1889), xxix.
[88] *Returns of Schs. 1893* [C. 7529], p. 420, H.C. (1894), lxv.
[89] *V.C.H. Mdx.* i. 305.
[90] Ex inf. Mr. D. O. Pam (1974).
[91] *Kelly's Dirs. Mdx.* (1890, 1908).
[92] *Rep. of Educ. Cttee. of Council, 1888* [C. 5804–I], p. 600, H.C. (1889), xxix.
[93] *Returns of Schs. 1899* [Cd. 315], p. 572, H.C. (1900), lxv(2).
[94] See below.
[95] *Returns of Schs. 1899* [Cd. 315], p. 580, H.C. (1900), lxv(2).
[96] *Kelly's Dir. Mdx.* (1908).
[97] M.R.O., Acc. 815/6/11.
[98] G. W. Sturges, *The Silver Link*, 17, 39.

the roll at the infants' school and 440 at the junior school.

Houndsfield Road board school opened in 1903 with departments for boys, girls, and mixed juniors on different floors in one building and for infants in a second building. It was reorganized for boys, girls, and infants in 1926 and became a junior mixed and infants' school in 1931. A new wing was added to the juniors' building in 1935. The schools were attended by a total of 1,003 children in 1906 and 1,084 in 1919. There were 311 children on the roll at the junior school in 1973 and 305 infants, including 60 in the nursery class.

Montagu Road board school opened in 1904 with accommodation for 300 boys, 300 girls, 300 juniors, and 460 infants.[99] The school was attended by 737 children in 1906 and by 999 in 1919. It was re-organized for boys, girls, and infants in 1925 and total attendance had dropped to 241 by 1927. The infants' department was abolished and the school became a secondary modern under the 1944 Act.

Elementary Schools founded between 1903 and 1945. St. Edmund's Roman Catholic school opened in Hertford Road in 1912. It received a government grant and consisted of mixed and infants' departments until 1952, when it became a joint junior and infants' primary school. There were extensions in 1969 and numbers rose from 273 in 1919 to 314 in 1973.

Raglan school, the first to be founded by Edmonton's education committee, opened in Bush Hill Park in 1928. Infants were admitted in 1929 and a separate infants' school was built in 1934. Extensions were later made to both junior and infants' schools, where the total attendance was 571 in 1932. In 1973 there were 695 juniors and 485 infants on the roll.

Hazelbury council school consisted of three parallel buildings in Haselbury Road. The infants' school opened in the southernmost building in 1930, the junior girls' in the central building in 1931, and the senior girls' in the northernmost building. In 1972 the junior girls amalgamated with Huxley junior boys to form Hazelbury junior mixed school, in the recently vacated secondary school building. The infants moved into the former junior school building, leaving the southern building to house a progress centre. In 1932 952 children attended the three departments. In 1973 there were 506 juniors and 369 infants on the roll.

Galliard council school opened in 1937 and consisted of two buildings, for mixed juniors and infants, on the east side of Galliard Road. Later extensions to the infants' school included the addition of a nursery. The total attendance in 1938 was 568. In 1973 there were 279 juniors and 287 infants on the roll.

Oakthorpe council school opened in 1937 in Tile Kiln Lane, where junior mixed and infants' schools shared one building. The two departments were attended by 511 children in 1938. Two classrooms were added to the junior school in 1939 and in 1973 there were 308 enrolled at the junior school and 218 at the infants'.

Hazelwood Lane school was erected in 1908 by Middlesex C.C., the education authority for Southgate, as a mixed and infants' school in one department with accommodation for 600 children.[1] A second building was erected in 1911 for the 350 juniors and infants, leaving the original building to older children. Reorganization into junior mixed and infants' schools took place in 1933. New buildings were added in 1971 and the school, which had been attended by 711 seniors, juniors, and infants in 1919, had 490 juniors and 305 infants on the roll in 1973.

Winchmore council school opened in Highfield Road in 1914 as a mixed and infants' school. Under reorganization in accordance with the Hadow Report seniors occupied the first floor and juniors and infants the ground floor of the same building until the seniors moved to a new site in 1956. The school was attended by 297 children in 1919. In 1973 there were 426 juniors and 250 infants on the roll.

Tottenhall infants' school was built in 1914 by Middlesex C.C. next to St. Michael-at-Bowes school but served as a hospital during the First World War and officially opened as an infants' school only in 1924. It was attended by 164 children in 1927 and had 240 infants on the roll in 1973.

De Bohun primary school in Green Road, Southgate, opened in 1936 and divided, in 1937, into junior mixed and infants' departments. From 1955 juniors occupied the first floor and infants the ground floor of the school. In 1973 there were 324 juniors, who also had an annexe, and 289 infants, including 60 nursery children, on the roll.

Primary Schools founded after 1945. Cuckoo Hall primary school opened in 1948 with junior and infants' departments in adjoining buildings. There were 265 juniors and 244 infants on the roll in 1973.[2]

Wilbury primary school opened in 1953 with infants on the ground floor and juniors on the first floor of the same building. There were 315 juniors and 230 infants on the roll in 1973.

Walker primary school for infants and juniors opened in Waterfall Road in 1953. There were 414 children on the roll in 1973.

Eversley primary school, the last school founded with separate juniors' and infants' departments, opened in Chase Road in 1954 and moved to Chaseville Park Road in 1957. There were 379 juniors and 235 infants, housed in adjacent buildings, on the roll in 1973.

Firs Farm primary school opened in 1954. Additions were made in 1967 and there were 330 children on the roll in 1973.

St. Monica's Roman Catholic school opened in Cannon Road, Southgate, in 1954. It was later extended and had 439 children on the roll in 1973.

Fleecefield primary school opened in Brettenham Road in 1957. There were 260 children on the roll in 1973.

Our Lady of Lourdes Roman Catholic school opened in the Limes Avenue, New Southgate, in 1971. There were 250 children on the roll in 1973.

[99] *Kelly's Dir. Mdx.* (1908).
[1] *Architect,* lxxix. 113.

[2] Officially opened in 1952: pamphlet *penes* Edmonton Publ. Libr., Ep. 370.

Secondary and senior schools founded before 1967.
Apart from Latymer school, divided into an upper and lower school in 1868,[3] the first source of public secondary education was St. Barnabas parochial school, opened in 1882 as an upper grade school attached to the mission church at the corner of Hertford Road and Bury Street. It accommodated 200 children and closed in 1902.[4]

Edmonton central school was founded by Edmonton's education committee in 1919, housing 80 boys at Croyland Road board school and 80 girls at Brettenham Road and from 1920 at Raynham Road. In 1922 the central school became a grammar school, called Edmonton county school, and from 1927 both boys and girls used the technical institute in Church Street. In 1931 a new building designed by W. T. Curtis, on a site next to Great Cambridge Road, was opened with accommodation for 600. It was much altered in 1962 and further extended in 1968.[5]

A mixed selective central school, Edmonton higher grade school, opened in 1927 in the former infants' department at Raynham Road, which had recently been vacated by Edmonton county school. The school opened with 78 boys and 82 girls aged from 11 to 15, who followed a partly commercial and technical curriculum. In 1937 they moved to new premises with accommodation for 400 at the corner of Wilbury Way and Bull Lane. More emphasis was laid on commercial and technical subjects, numbers increased to 305 with the addition of classes for 16-year olds, and a new teaching block was added in 1967.

In accordance with the Hadow Report Edmonton's education committee opened secondary departments at the following board schools between 1927 and 1932: Brettenham Road for 270 senior girls, Montagu Road for 270 senior boys, Eldon Road for 500 senior boys and 500 senior girls, Silver Street for 320 senior boys, and Hazelbury for 480 senior girls. Brettenham Road closed after the 1944 Act, when the others became secondary modern schools. Montagu Road closed in 1963 and the rest survived until the reorganization of 1968.[6]

Mixed secondary modern schools were created after the 1944 Act at Houndsfield in 1947, Cuckoo Hall in 1949,[7] and Croyland, Raynham, and Raglan schools by 1949. Croyland and Raglan secondary modern schools closed in 1959 and Rowantree opened in 1960 in Little Bury Street.

Southgate acquired secondary schools a decade earlier than Edmonton. Broomfield House opened in 1907 and was attended by 163 boys in 1909. They were transferred to Southgate county school, a mixed grammar school for 600 children, which opened in 1910. It was housed in Fox Lane until it moved to a new building in Sussex Way, Cockfosters, in 1960.

A second mixed grammar school was opened with 90 pupils at Tottenhall Road in 1919. It moved to Southgate House in 1924 when it became known as Minchenden school. There were considerable

extensions in 1930 and 1947 and from 1960 until 1967 part of the Fox Lane school was used as an annexe.[8]

Senior mixed departments were organized by 1919 at Garfield Road, for 404 pupils until 1927–32, and Hazelwood Lane, for 600 until 1932–6. A secondary mixed department for 400 opened at Winchmore Hill council school between 1932 and 1936. It became a secondary modern school after the 1944 Act and moved to the other side of Highfield Road in 1956.

Oakwood school in Chase Road opened with departments for juniors and seniors in 1933. It had accommodation for 400 senior boys and girls and from 1956, when the junior department closed, it was exclusively a secondary modern school. There were major extensions in 1965–6. Arnos Grove school in Wilmer Way opened in 1938 and was extended in 1948, 1957, 1964, and 1966.

Comprehensive schools founded since 1967.[9] Under the comprehensive scheme drawn up by Enfield L.B. in 1967 Huxley county secondary school, which had changed its name from Silver Street senior school in 1955, was closed. Its pupils were transferred to Edmonton higher grade school at Wilbury Way, which became an all-age comprehensive school to serve south Edmonton. After some controversy the school was temporarily closed in 1968 and re-opened as part of the two-tier system which was adopted throughout the former borough of Edmonton.

The school at Wilbury Way was renamed Weir Hall and became an upper school, with Raynham and Hazelbury as lower schools. In 1972, however, all three schools were replaced by Aylward school, whose younger pupils used a new building in Silver Street and the vacated premises of Huxley school while the seniors were accommodated in the former Weir Hall premises. In 1973 Aylward school, which had 339 children enrolled in the upper and 761 in the lower school, was linked with Brettenham, Hazelbury, Raynham, Wilbury, and St. James's Church of England primary schools.

Edmonton school, created in 1967, consisted of a lower school for those aged 11 to 14 in the former Rowantree buildings, which were extended, and an upper school for those aged 14 to 18 in the former Edmonton county school. The two buildings housed approximately 1,250 pupils drawn from Galliard, Raglan, All Saints Church of England, and Lower Latymer primary schools.

Eldon and Houndsfield secondary modern schools reopened in 1968 as lower schools providing comprehensive education for children aged 11 to 14 who then moved on to Mandeville (formerly Cuckoo Hall secondary) school, which became an upper school. In 1973 there were 350 children on the roll at Houndsfield and 400 at Mandeville.[10] The schools were linked to Eldon, Croyland, Cuckoo Hall, Fleecefield, Houndsfield, and St. Edmund's Roman Catholic primary schools.

---

[3] The upper sch. became a co-educational grammar sch. in 1910: *V.C.H. Mdx.* i. 305.
[4] *Kelly's Dir. Mdx.* (1890); *Kelly's Dirs. Enfield* (1901–2, 1902–3).   [5] *The Times*, 30 Nov. 1931.
[6] Mdx. Cnty. Council, *Lists of Educ. Services* (1963–4).
[7] Official opening 1952: pamphlet *penes* Edmonton Publ. Libr., Ep. 370.

[8] *Minchenden School Golden Anniversary, 1919–69* (pamphlet *penes* Edmonton Publ. Libr.).
[9] Unless otherwise stated, based upon lists supplied by the education department of Enfield L.B. (1973) and inf. from heads of schs. (1973).
[10] The headmaster of Eldon refused to give the numbers for his school (1973).

Within the former borough of Southgate Arnos and Winchmore secondary modern schools became all-age comprehensive schools, with approximately 800 and 970 children on their rolls in 1973. Arnos school, which was extended in 1967, 1969, and 1972, was linked with Bowes, Garfield, Oakthorpe, Our Lady of Lourdes Roman Catholic, and St. Michael's Church of England primary schools. Winchmore was linked with Firs Farm, Winchmore, and St. Paul's Church of England primary schools.

Southgate school was formed by the amalgamation of Oakwood and Southgate county grammar schools. The lower school, with 730 children aged 11 to 14 on the roll, used the former Oakwood buildings in 1973, while the upper school, in the county grammar school buildings in Sussex Way, had 580 pupils. The schools were linked with De Bohun and Eversley primary schools in Southgate and Grange Park and Hadley Wood in Enfield.

Minchenden grammar school formed the nucleus of Minchenden comprehensive schools. The lower school, with 480 pupils enrolled in 1973, used the Fox Lane premises which had served as an annexe for the grammar school. The grammar school itself in High Street became the upper school, with 863 pupils on the roll in 1973.

Special schools. A centre for the instruction of deaf children was started at Bush Hill Park school in 1899 and there was a special class for the partially blind at Montagu Road school from 1925 until 1935.[11] Halliwick, originally Bush Hill House, was bought in 1911 by the Girls Cripples' Home and taken over in 1926 by the Church of England Children's Society. It was run as a special school for cripples and in 1949 accommodated 60 girls.[12] From 1919 until 1947 Edmonton's education committee were joint managers with Enfield of Durants special school.[13]

Hazelbury open air school was opened by Edmonton B.C. in 1938 next to the other Hazelbury schools. It was planned for 170 mainly tubercular children but later catered for other delicate children, especially asthmatics. It took over part of the former Hazelbury secondary modern school in 1972 and had 139 children aged 5 to 16 on the roll in 1973.

Oaktree school, a special day school for the educationally sub-normal, was opened in Chase Side in 1965 and had 147 children on the roll in 1973.

Technical Education. Middlesex C.C. was providing technical education at the Edmonton centre in Pymmes Park House in 1908[14] and in 1912 opened Edmonton technical institute on the site formerly occupied by Latymer school.[15] In 1932 the junior technical school for girls, which had opened

in Tottenham in 1914, moved to Edmonton technical institute, where it was renamed the Edmonton School for the Needle Trades and accommodated girls aged over 13.[16] It closed in 1964.[17]

Southgate technical college was formed in 1962 with classes at Southgate county grammar school in Fox Lane. The main college building in High Street opened in 1963 and extensions were built between 1969 and 1971 to replace church halls, although a centre at Montagu Road school was still being used in 1974. A total of 6,629 students attended the college during the session of 1971–2.[18]

Private schools. During the 19th century, especially in its early and middle years, Edmonton was noted for its private schools.[19] In 1833 there were 8 small day-schools, of which two dated from 1819 and 1820 respectively, which were run at the parents' expense and attended by a total of 117 children. There were 10 boarding-schools, three of them opened since 1818, attended by 282 boys and 178 girls.[20]

By 1851[21] there were 85 teachers in Edmonton, including 13 governesses and one private tutor, and 392 children at 13 boarding-schools. The largest boarding-school was College House in Upper Fore Street, next to the Bell inn, which was attended by 93 boys and run by the White family from before 1840[22] until 1887 when it moved to Eastbourne.[23] A little farther north Edmonton House, attended by 30 boys, was a Jewish school which was opened by H. N. Solomon c. 1840 and closed c. 1880.[24] On the opposite side of Fore Street Elm House school was attended by 39 boys. It belonged to Dr. John Ireland, who advertised its 10 a. of cricket-ground and charged 30–40 guineas a year,[25] and in 1881 was taken over as a temporary board school. Also in Fore Street was Priory school with 24 boys and, just north of the junction with Silver Street, Eagle House academy, with 19 girls. Eagle House, still a genteel girls' school c. 1885, was pulled down in 1913.[26] There were 30 boys at Tile Kilns and 34 at Bridport Hall, a large house which had been opened as a boarding-school before 1840.[27]

The largest boarding-schools in Southgate in 1851 were Eagle Hall and College House. Eagle Hall in High Street had been opened in 1783 for the sons of the local gentry by Isaac Hunt, father of Leigh and tutor to the duke of Chandos. The school, which was run for many years by the Rumsey family, who extended it c. 1829,[28] had 45 boarders in 1851 and prepared boys for the civil service, the universities, the law, and medicine in 1872.[29] It was still open in 1880[30] but seems to have closed by 1890.[31] College House, which also had 45 boys in 1851, was in Chase Side and probably connected

[11] Log book *penes* Edmonton Publ. Libr.
[12] Borough of Edmonton, *Official Guide* [1963].
[13] Mins. of Cttee. *penes* Edmonton Publ. Libr. For Durants school, s.v. Enfield.
[14] *Kelly's Dir. Mdx.* (1908).
[15] Datestone on bldg.; M.R.O., M.C.C./A/Pl. 1–3.
[16] O.S. Map 1/2,500, Mdx. VII. 11 (1914, 1935, and 1939 edns.).
[17] Ex inf. Mr. D. O. Pam (1973).
[18] Southgate Technical College, *Annual Report, 1971–2*; ex inf. the principal (1973); prospectus (1974).
[19] *V.C.H. Mdx.* i. 253.
[20] *Educ. Enquiry Abstract*, 89.
[21] H.O. 107/1703.

[22] *Pigot's Dir. Mdx.* (1840). See plate facing p. 176.
[23] *V.C.H. Mdx.* i. 274; O.S. Map 1/2,500, Mdx. VII. 15 (1867 edn.).
[24] *V.C.H. Mdx.* i. 263; O.S. Map 1/2,500, Mdx. VII. 15 (1867 edn.).
[25] O.S. Map 1/2,500, Mdx. VII. 15 (1867 edn.). See p. 199.
[26] Fisk, *Edmonton*, 73; O.S. Map 1/2,500, Mdx. VII. 15 (1867 edn.).
[27] *Pigot's Dir. Mdx.* (1840); Griffin, *Old Tottenham and Edmonton*, 101.
[28] Round, *Southgate and Winchmore Hill*, 34; *Home Cnties. Mag.* xi. 181.
[29] *V.C.H. Mdx.* i. 271.   [30] M.R.O., Acc. 98/12.
[31] *Kelly's Dir. Mdx.* (1890).

with the neighbouring Independent chapel.[32] It had been founded before 1828 and was still open in 1867.[33]

The other boarding-schools of 1851, Hydeside House for boys and three girls' schools in Silver Street, were very small and mostly short-lived, although two of them had existed in 1840.[34] There were also many day-schools, also short-lived and probably small, particularly near Fore Street.[35]

Many other large houses were used as private schools. Palmers Green academy, a boys' boarding-school, offered classics, languages, writing, arithmetic, merchants' accounts, geography, and astronomy in 1797.[36] Shortly before its demolition in 1818, the old Weir Hall was used as a boarding-school[37] and the subsequent house of that name was a college for boys in 1914.[38] There was a girls' boarding-school at Southgate House in 1828 and a boys' boarding school at Manor House, Church Street, in 1840.[39] Prospect House in Church Street, a day-school in 1851,[40] was run in 1861 by a member of the medical profession who offered botany, chemistry, and some medicine as well as the more usual subjects.[41] Edmonton grammar school, a large building in Church (Bridport) Road near St. James's church, existed from c. 1860 until 1878.[42]

In 1870 old Edmonton had 7 private schools, attended by 268 boys and 172 girls, and 6 'adventure' schools, attended by 38 boys and 38 girls.[43] By 1890, after the building of the railway and the spread of suburban housing, there were only 6 private schools, although the population had quadrupled since 1851. There were, however, 13 private schools in the rest of the old parish, mainly in New Southgate, Bowes Park, and Winchmore Hill,[44] areas which retained the rural attractions and large vacant houses previously possessed by Edmonton. Among these schools were Belmont House, Pollocks Grove, and Glenwood House in Winchmore Hill,[45] Millbridge in Church Street, and Mayfield in High Street, Southgate. Millbridge and Mayfield survived in 1908,[46] when there were 19 private schools, of which only four were in old Edmonton. Bowes Park had 6 and Palmers Green four. Bush Hill House was used as a high-class girls' boarding-school from 1904 until 1911 and Winchmore Hill collegiate school was founded in 1906 with accommodation for 130 boys and was still open in 1949. Avondale college, a boarding-school for 100 girls, existed at Wade's Hill, Winchmore Hill, in 1908.[47]

Franklin House, a boys' preparatory school which had opened in Wood Green by 1897, moved to Frankfort House in Palmerston Road in 1901, changed its name in 1917, extended the buildings in 1921, and had 138 boys on the roll in 1973. Palmers Green high school opened as a private day-school in Green Lanes, Palmers Green, in 1905 and moved to a new building in Hoppers Road, Winchmore Hill, in 1918. There were extensions in 1958, 1962, and 1970 and there were 280 girls on the roll in 1973. Former pupils included the actress Flora Robson and the poet Stevie Smith.

The nuns of St. Angela's Providence convent at Wood Green, who had started teaching there in 1905, later transferred their primary department to a school acquired from the Ursuline sisters in Oakthorpe Road, Palmers Green.[48] There were 120 children on the roll in 1973, when a new Roman Catholic comprehensive school was planned. Salcombe school opened in Avenue Road, Southgate, in 1919. A large classroom was added in 1924, more houses were acquired in Chase Side in 1942 and 1945, and a hall was built in 1969. The school, for junior boys and girls, had 140 children on the roll in 1973. Keble preparatory school for boys opened in St. John's hall, Hoppers Road, in 1929. It moved to the Elms in Wade's Hill in 1930 and a new school building was erected in 1935 and extended in 1949. There were 218 boys on the roll in 1973. The Benedictine nuns of the Regina Pacis convent in Priory Close, Southgate, ran a junior school by 1967[49] and had some 120 children on the roll in 1973.

CHARITIES FOR THE POOR.[50] In 1278 Walden abbey undertook to pay £1 a year out of the rectory to feed 30 paupers in Edmonton but payments apparently ceased at the Dissolution.[51] Sir Christopher Askew, alderman of London, by will proved 1539, left £100 for 'best full white herrings' to be distributed among the poor of Edmonton each Lent.[52] His son Richard said that the charity had already lapsed by 1551, because of the high price of herrings.[53]

During the 17th century important charities were founded for schools, which are dealt with above, and for alms-houses. By 1819 there were 20 charities in Edmonton, mostly for the poor or to augment the existing education and alms-house charities. They were administered as the Edmonton charities by trustees consisting of the vicar and churchwardens

[32] The deacon of the chapel was Matthew Thomson, the schoolmaster of College House: H.O. 107/1703 p. 100 sqq.; H.O. 129/137/3/10.
[33] O.S. Map 1/2,500, Mdx. VII. 9 (1867 edn.).
[34] *Pigot's Dir. Mdx.* (1840). And see headmaster of Hydeside House's address to boys, 1842 *penes* Edmonton Publ. Libr.
[35] *Pigot's Dir. Mdx.* (1840); *Green's Dir. Stoke Newington etc.* (1866). Day-schools are not listed in the census returns.
[36] *V.C.H. Mdx.* i. 247.
[37] J. Dugdale, *New British Traveller*, iii. 485.
[38] Fisk, *Edmonton*, 141.
[39] *Pigot's Dir. Mdx.* (1840).
[40] H.O. 107/1703 pp. 212 sqq.
[41] *V.C.H. Mdx.* i. 272.
[42] M.R.O., MR/LMD 3/14; sales particulars (1878) *penes* Edmonton Publ. Libr.; O.S. Map 1/2,500, Mdx. VII. 15 (1867 edn.).
[43] *Returns relating to Elem. Educ.* H.C. 201, pp. 570–1 (1871), lv.

[44] *Kelly's Dir. Mdx.* (1890).
[45] Regnart, *Winchmore Hill*, 5, 38–9.
[46] *Kelly's Dir. Mdx.* (1908).
[47] Ibid.; Regnart, *Winchmore Hill*, 74; *Recorder for Palmers Green, Winchmore Hill and Southgate*, Sept. 1909 *penes* Broomfield Mus.
[48] See p. 373.
[49] *Cath. Dir.* (1967).
[50] Except where otherwise stated, the section is based on Char. Com. files and material supplied by the clerk of Edmonton United chars. (1973); *9th Rep. Com. Char.* H.C. 258, pp. 178–87 (1823), ix; *Analytical Digest of Reps. from 1832*, H.C. 115, pp. 418–19 (1835), xi; *Gen. Digest of Endowed Chars.* H.C. 433, pp. 14–15 (1867–8), lii, pt. 1; *Endowed Chars. (Mdx.)*, H.C. 306, pp. 6–9 (1899), lxx; *Acct. of Edmonton Par. Chars.* (1819), reps. and procs. of Edmonton par. chars. investigation cttee. (1849) *penes* Edmonton Publ. Libr. (E360).
[51] *Valor Eccl.* (Rec. Com.), vi, p. xiii.
[52] Prob. 11/27 (P.C.C. F30 Dyngeley).
[53] Prob. 11/34 (P.C.C. F31 Bucke).

and 11 prominent inhabitants.[54] A committee of the vestry, appointed in 1848, alleged that 11 charities should not be administered by the trustees but by the parish or by the vicar and churchwardens, that the funds of the various charities were amalgamated, and that there was misappropriation, particularly in the case of Latymer's charity, which accounted for £500 out of the total annual income of £900. The trustees denied the charges and by a Charity Commission Scheme of 1866 were authorized to administer together 23 charities, although excluding the Latymer charity. The 23 charities were those of Alston, Cade, Chaplin, Colfe, Elliott, Hallam, Huxley, Jackson, Lewitt, Maule, Pitt, Rogers, Skip, Smith, Stanbridge, Edmund and Sarah Slaughter, Style, Tatem, Uvedale, Wilde of Edmonton, Wilde of Barking, and Wyatt.

In 1889 another parochial committee reported that money, particularly for apprenticing, was not being properly applied and in 1891 it proposed a new Scheme. It was not until 1899, however, that the Charity Commission established a new board of trustees, consisting of the vicar, 5 representatives of Edmonton U.D.C. and 4 of Southgate U.D.C., and 8 co-opted members. There were to be two groups of charities—the United charities of Judith Alston and others and the Ecclesiastical charities. The Ecclesiastical charities consisted of Maule's charity and the ecclesiastical provisions of the charities of Hallam, Rogers, and Wilde of Edmonton, producing a total annual income of £143. The United charities consisted of the remaining charities in the 1866 Scheme, together with those of Baker, Bellis, Board, John and Henry Field, Jifkins, Larman, Whitbread, and part of Knight's and Rowley's charities. The total stock amounted to £9,933 and the annual income to £469.

By a Scheme of 1902 the United charities were divided into three branches: educational, which consisted of £20 a year from Style's and £8 a year from Wilde of Edmonton's charities; apprenticing, consisting of £10 a year from Style's, £6 a year from Wilde of Edmonton's charities, and the relevant portion of Chaplin's charity; and alms-houses and pensioners, to which all the other income was applied. The educational branch was abstracted from the United charities by a Scheme of 1905, which transformed it into the Educational Foundations of John Wilde of Edmonton and Thomas Style. Knight's charity and the Oswin fund were added to the United charities in 1914 and 1928 respectively. By a Scheme of 1965 pensioners were omitted from the third branch of the United charities, all the money going to the alms-houses. The income of the United charities in 1964 was £1,760, of which £228 was paid to alms-people. In 1973 the income was £1,100, which was wholly applied to the upkeep of the alms-houses. By 1973 the apprenticing branch of the charity was dormant, virtually no applications being made for it.

Several charities were founded during the 19th century for the benefit of Southgate parish, especially by the Walker family, and in 1906 the Southgate relief committee, which included the vicar and churchwardens of Christ Church, was formed to administer them. In 1973 the committee administered £120 income from the charities of John Julian, Frederick Walker, Vyell E. Walker, and Russell Walker, and the relevant portions of Sophia Walker's charity and the Weld Chapel trust.[55]

THE UNITED CHARITIES. *Alms-house charities.* In 1662 John Wilde of Edmonton, had 'lately' built three alms-houses next to the churchyard in Church Street. By will proved 1665 he conveyed houses and 25 a., mostly of common-field land, to trustees to apply the profits to several charities, including £4 a year for the inmates of the alms-houses.[56] By 1867 £7 was being paid by Wilde's charity to the alms-houses.

Thomas Style (d. 1679) built two alms-houses adjoining the churchyard for 6 poor men and 6 poor women of Edmonton. In 1679 he endowed the alms-houses with part of a rent-charge of £66 on Dephams estate, of which £1 16s. a year was to be spent on repairs and £33 16s. a year on weekly payments of 1s. 1d. each to the almspeople.

John Lewitt of Palmers Green, by will dated 1771, bequeathed £800 stock yielding £24 a year which was distributed among the 12 inmates of Style's alms-houses. George Stanbridge of Edmonton, by will dated 1780, bequeathed £500 stock to the trustees of Wilde's and Style's alms-houses, who in 1823 distributed the income of £16 10s. amongst the 15 alms-people. Other charities for the benefit of the 15 inmates were those of Sarah Huxley, daughter of Thomas Huxley of Weir Hall, who bequeathed £1,000 yielding £38 a year by will dated 1800; Miss Catherine Tatem of Edmonton, who bequeathed £50 stock yielding £1 10s. by will dated 1812; Thomas Elliott, clock-maker of Edmonton, who by will dated 1824 bequeathed £450 stock, which in 1899 yielded £12; John Pitt, who bequeathed £100 stock yielding £3 a year by will dated 1826;[57] Edmund Slaughter of Edmonton, who by will proved 1832 bequeathed £500 stock, yielding £14 in 1899;[58] and William Skip of Edmonton, who left £100 stock yielding £3 a year subject to the repair of his vault, by will dated 1836. In 1861 Thomas Knight of Edmonton endowed the 15 alms-houses with £500 stock producing £13 15s. and in 1879 Hannah Whitbread gave £607 stock yielding £18, to maintain the buildings or benefit the inmates.

Several charities provided for benefits in kind. By will dated 1820 Sarah Slaughter directed that the interest on £50 stock was to be spent on Christmas dinner for the 15 alms-people. The interest was £1 10s. in 1867. Ann Larman, by will proved 1867, bequeathed £105 stock yielding £3 a year to buy coal for the inmates of Style's alms-houses. In 1892 George Bellis left £103 stock yielding £3 to buy coal for the 15 alms-people. By will proved 1892 Thomas William Rowley bequeathed £500 stock producing £14 to provide bread and coal for the 15 alms-people but by a Scheme of 1893 the money was to supplement their stipends.

The alms-people, in 1851 6 men and 9 women, mostly widows,[59] were chosen by the vestry until 1899 when full control passed to the trustees. The alms-houses were in disrepair in the 1740s

---

[54] Robinson, *Edmonton*, 142–78.
[55] Ex inf. the sec., Southgate relief cttee. (1973).
[56] Prob. 11/316 (P.C.C. 9 Hyde, will of John Wilde).
[57] Subject to the repair of his vault and tombstone.
[58] C 54/10899 nos. 3–4.
[59] H.O. 107/1703 p. 195.

and Style's alms-houses were rebuilt in 1754 and again in 1903 to the designs of H. W. Dobb. Nearly all the stock was sold in 1960 to modernize the buildings but the Ministry of Housing made a grant for the Charity Commissioners to reinvest.

In 1851 Thomas Knight gave two cottages which he had recently erected in Church Lane in trust to the Edmonton benefit society, for two old and handicapped members of the society or their widows.[60] The cottages, which Knight endowed with £50 stock yielding £1 5s. a year, were administered as part of the United charities under a Scheme of 1914. There were four widows in Knight's alms-houses in 1933 but in 1960 the cottages were demolished and six garages, each let at 15s. a week, were built on the site.

Pensioners' charities. Henry Cade of Edmonton, yeoman, in 1578 gave a rent-charge of 6s. 8d. from a house, later the Cock public house, and 1 a. on the west of Hertford Road for the use of the poor. In 1823 it was added to the sacrament money and paid to the poor 'from time to time'.

By will proved 1579[61] Richard Rogers the elder, a London goldsmith who lived in Edmonton, left all his freehold property in Edmonton and Tottenham in trust to pay, *inter alia*,[62] 1s. a week in bread and money to 6 of the poorest people of Edmonton and 13s. 4d. to the poor on the anniversary of his death. Rogers's nephew Richard Rogers the younger, Comptroller of the Mint, by will dated 1636, left a rent-charge of £2 to provide 6d. a week in money or bread for 6 poor people and 10s. 8d. for distribution among the poor on the first Sunday in August. Edward Rogers of Edmonton, son of Richard the younger, left a further rent-charge of £1 9s. 4d. by will proved 1659, to be distributed, *inter alia*, as 6d. a week in bread to poor parishioners. In 1823 the total income of the Rogers charities, which were always distributed together, was £7 1s. 4d., from rent-charges on freehold estates in Fore Street, Church Street, and the marsh. Of this £5 4s. was paid in bread to 12 poor people every Sunday and £1 4s. to the poor on the first Sunday in August. The rent-charges were redeemed in 1934 and 1964.

By will dated 1614 John Wilde of Barking (Essex) gave a rent-charge of £2 a year upon premises in Fore Street, to buy twopenny-loaves for the poor of Edmonton each quarter. The rent-charge was redeemed in 1934.

Jasper Hallam, leatherseller of London, by will dated 1625, left £3 6s. 8d. out of a rent-charge on Bury farm to provide £2 worth of bread for the poor every Sunday in Lent and 6s. 8d. for a Lenten meal for the poor town-born people of Edmonton. The rent-charge was redeemed in 1903.

Among property devised by the Revd. Abraham Colfe to the Leathersellers' Company of London for charitable purposes, by will dated 1656, was 5 a. in Edmonton. A rent-charge of 8s. 8d. from part of the property on the east of Lower Fore Street was to buy two penny loaves each Sunday for two of the 'godliest and poorest' householders of Edmonton.[63] By 1823 the money was applied by the churchwardens in occasional charity to the poor.

By indenture and will dated 1677 Judith, widow of Penning Alston, grocer of London, conveyed copyhold property in trust to pay annuities and thereafter to provide £4 quarterly payments to the poor of Edmonton and £1 a year each to 16 other poor people. The property, in 1677 a house, 9 a. of common-field arable, and 2 a. of marsh-land, was exchanged at inclosure for a house and 7 a. at Tanners End and 5 a. of marsh-land. In 1819 the profits of £28 were distributed in quarterly payments of £1 to the poor and in £1 payments on 1 January to 20 poor annuitants. By 1867 the quarterly payments were given in bread and £78 was given in money. The marsh-land was sold in 1907 and the land at Tanners End in 1914 and 1928; the purchase money was invested for the benefit of the United charities.

Catherine Jackson, of the family which owned Broomfield, left £100 in trust for the poor of Southgate by will dated 1687. The poor received £5 a year until the capital, together with money from Maule's and Latymer's charities, was used to purchase land in Hammersmith. The rent therefrom was apportioned among the three charities, £3 10s. being allotted to Jackson's charity from 1768 and paid in bread or 5s. doles to the poor of Southgate. The rent had risen to £7 10s. by 1899 and was given to Southgate widows in 1902.[64] The land at Hammersmith was sold in 1913 and the money invested.

By will proved 1771 John Lewitt[65] bequeathed £100 stock, the interest on which was spent in bread for the poor. By will dated 1780 George Stanbridge bequeathed £400 stock, the interest to provide bread for the poor between Michaelmas and Lady Day. By 1823 £12 was distributed in bread. Margaret Uvedale (d. 1814), widow of Rear-Admiral Samuel Uvedale, bequeathed £300 stock by will dated 1813.[66] The income was to maintain the vault of the family of William Washbourne, vicar of Edmonton, and to relieve the aged poor of Church Street ward on Christmas day. By 1819 there was £37 10s. interest, of which £2 10s. was spent on the vault and £35 distributed in £1 annuities.

By will proved 1828 John Field bequeathed £1,000 stock and by will proved 1836 Henry Field bequeathed £500 stock, to supply bread and coals for the poor. The interest from their combined charities was £45 in 1867. By will proved 1844 William Baker bequeathed £100 stock yielding £3 interest, to be paid to the elderly poor subject to the repair of a grave. By will proved 1858 Ann Jifkins left £47 stock, the interest to be used for repairing her husband's tomb and distributed to the poor of Church Street ward on Christmas day. By will proved 1878 Edward Board bequeathed £928 stock yielding £25 a year to provide money and clothing for 20 aged poor, with preference for natives or old residents of Edmonton and for those engaged in agriculture. The Oswin fund, founded by Mrs. Sarah Eleanor Browne by will proved 1901, consisted of £654 stock and £31 annuities.

Apprenticing charities. By will proved 1665, John Wilde of Edmonton left £6 a year for apprenticing two sons of two poor widows of Edmonton to some trade in the City of London.

[60] C 54/14336 no. 3.   [61] Prob. 11/61 (P.C.C. 22 Baker).
[62] See Eccl. chars. above, p. 182.
[63] *10th Rep. Com. Char.* H.C. 103, p. 261 (1824), xiii.

[64] Mason, *Story of Southgate*, 46.
[65] For Lewitt's benefaction to the alms-hos., see above.
[66] Robinson, *Edmonton*, 91–2.

In 1679 Thomas Style gave £10 a year to apprentice one or two poor boys within the parish.

In 1724 Francis Chaplin and his wife Joyce conveyed the moiety of 6½ a. of marsh-land to be used after their deaths for the repair of Chaplin's vault in the church and for apprenticing a poor boy from Edmonton. Through neglect at inclosure the land was apportioned to others and only ½ a. at Jeremy's Green and £30 were allotted to the charity. By 1823 two cottages had been built and the rent of £3 3s. was applied in apprenticing one boy, although the trustees were criticized in 1849 for retaining the money or granting too little. The land was sold and the money invested in 1905. In 1933 it produced £17 a year.

Ecclesiastical charities.[67] By will dated 1714 Thomas Maule bequeathed £100 for the benefit of 10 poor church-going widows. In 1737 the money, with money from Jackson's and Latymer's charities, was used to buy land in Hammersmith, the rent from which was divided among the charities. Until *c.* 1819 the £3 a year apportioned to Maule's charity was given to three inmates of Wilde's alms-houses but thereafter it was given to 10 poor widows who regularly attended church. When the Ecclesiastical charities were instituted in 1899, Maule's charity produced £7 10s. a year. The land was sold in 1913 and by 1962 the income from Maule's charity had risen to £43, of which 15 poor widows received 10s. each and the remainder was paid into the sick and poor fund.

SOUTHGATE CHARITIES.[68] The charity of Sir John Weld of Arnolds (d. 1623) provided for payments of £13 6s. 8d. to 6 poor kindred and £2 12s. in bread to 12 poor widows of Southgate every Sunday.[69] By 1867 £31 4s. a year was distributed in bread and in 1973 the bread portion of the charity was administered by the Southgate relief committee.

Mrs. Sophia Walker, by will proved 1865, bequeathed £596 stock for educational and other charitable objects in Southgate. In 1899 £2 15s., the interest on £101 stock, was spent on medical or nursing needs. In 1973 the income was divided among the Southgate relief committee, Christ Church Sunday school, and St. Andrew's day school.

By will proved 1892 John Julian left £1,000 stock to provide £1 each for 20 poor widows of Christ Church parish in the week before Christmas and to divide the remaining interest in bread for the poor. In 1962 the income was £25, administered by Southgate relief committee.

Four of the Walker brothers made bequests for the benefit of the poor of Southgate. Frederick Walker, by will proved 1890, Vyell Edward Walker, by will proved 1906, and Russell Walker, by will proved 1907, each left £1,000 stock. In 1962 the income was £34, £33, and £33 respectively, administered by the Southgate relief committee. Isaac Donnithorne Walker left £500, which yielded £15 in 1962 and which the vicar of Southgate still administered for the poor of Southgate village in 1973.

By will dated 1826 Elizabeth Martin bequeathed

£498 stock, the interest to be distributed to the poor of Christ Church. In 1970 the charity produced £12 which was given by the vicar in money and Christmas gifts to old age pensioners.

John Woolnough, by will proved 1939, left money to Southgate corporation to provide Christmas dinners and coal for old people. Trustees were appointed by a Scheme of 1961 and in 1973 the income was under £250.

OTHER CHARITIES FOR THE POOR. There was a group of charities for medical and nursing purposes: Elizabeth Whitehead bequeathed £116 stock yielding £3 4s. in 1800, Mrs. Frances Smith bequeathed £272 yielding £7 9s. 8d. in 1811, and Edmund Slaughter bequeathed £107 stock yielding £2 19s in 1831. By 1872 there was also a lying-in charity, of which the origin is unknown, which in 1899 consisted of £150 stock yielding £4 2s. 4d. By a Scheme of 1940 its administration passed to the trustees of the United charities.

Mrs. Esther Doe, by deed in 1863 and by will in 1872, left houses and stock yielding an annual income of £447 which was to be spent on the alms-houses.

The Bush prize fund, founded in 1869, provided £10 a year from £250 stock to be used for apprenticing children.

George Ringrose, by will proved 1885, left £92 stock producing £2 11s. to be spent in coal, bread, and money for the deserving poor of Edmonton. The income in 1966 was £2 6s. 4d.

Isaac Padman, by will dated 1818, left £500 to be invested, the income to be applied to the religious and 'respectable' poor of Winchmore Hill. By a Scheme of 1893 the income of £24 a year was to be applied in nursing, provident clubs, clothes, or temporary relief to the residents of the ecclesiastical district of Winchmore Hill, the rest of Edmonton parish, and Enfield or any adjoining parish. In 1965 the income was £20, which the ministers of Winchmore Hill Congregational church and Christ Church Congregational church, Enfield, distributed in coal, bedding, and clothes.

By will proved 1880 Peregrine Hogg Purvis of Winchmore Hill left £2,000 to the vicar and churchwardens of St. Paul, Winchmore Hill, the interest to be distributed annually before Christmas in £1-gifts to 50 poor inhabitants of Winchmore Hill, irrespective of creed but with preference to residents in Highfield Row. In 1966 the income was £53. He also left £100 stock, producing £2 15s. in 1899, to nonconformist bodies, £200 stock producing £5 10s. for church purposes, and £200 stock producing £5 10s. for education.

Elizabeth Winsdale, by will proved 1887, left £500 for the sick poor of the parish of St. James, Upper Edmonton. The sum was invested and produced £13 a year in 1964. In addition to his bequest to the alms-houses Thomas William Rowley, by will proved 1892, bequeathed £200 stock yielding £5 10s. a year to the poor of St. James's parish. Edward Chapman, by will proved 1902, bequeathed £250, the income to provide coal for the poor of St. James's at Christmas. In 1969 the income of some £7 was spent on coal for 3 persons. Maria

---

[67] Most of the Ecclesiastical chars. have been treated above, p. 182.

[68] Recent inf. supplied by the sec., Southgate relief cttee. (1973).
[69] Prob. 11/141 (P.C.C. 20 Swann); see p. 184.

Linzell, by will proved 1920, bequeathed £50 to augment offertories for the poor, defray the cost of church work, or benefit the parish charities of St. James's. The income was £3 in 1964.

By will proved 1937 Frances Isabella Hammond

bequeathed £300 to maintain a tomb in St. Mary's, Edmonton, any residue to benefit the sick and poor of the parish. The income in 1966 was £10, spent on groceries and other necessities.

ENFIELD

ENFIELD[1] contained 12,460 a. in 1831, when it was the largest parish in Middlesex after Harrow with Pinner.[2] Enfield 'Town', as it came to be called,[3] grew up on the edge of Enfield Chase over a mile west of the main road from London to Ware, which entered the parish about 8 miles from London at Ponders End.[4] The eastern part of the parish was for long the most thickly populated, with road- and river-side settlements at Ponders End, Enfield Highway, Enfield Wash, and Enfield Lock, and the 19th-century Royal Small Arms factory which produced the Lee-Enfield rifle. Before the inclosure of the Chase under the Act of 1777[5] the parish covered 14,779 a.[6] but for the purposes of this article the boundaries are those established in 1779, when the Act came into effect.[7]

From 1779 the parish formed a rectangle measuring 8 miles from east to west and 3 from north to south. It was bounded on the north by Cheshunt and Northaw (Herts.), on the west by South Mimms and Monken Hadley in Middlesex and East Barnet (Herts.), and on the south by Edmonton. The eastern boundary was formed by the river Lea and the Mar dyke, which bordered Essex, and was alone in following natural features.[8] A tract between World's End Lane and the South Lodge estate was transferred to Enfield from Edmonton between 1858 and 1871.[9] Two detached pieces of land in Monken Hadley, totalling 54 a., remained part of Enfield after the division of the Chase; they are treated under Monken Hadley to which they were transferred in 1882 and 1894.[10] Further boundary revisions reduced the total acreage to 12,601 a. in 1901. In 1924 26 a. near Potters Bar (South Mimms) were transferred to South Mimms R.D. and in 1926 a narrow strip of land along World's End Lane was transferred to Southgate U.D. Between 1931 and 1951 the area of Enfield U.D., roughly conterminous with the old parish, dropped from 12,574 a. to 12,339 a. after changes which included the transfer to Southgate U.D. of a tongue of land projecting south from Cockfosters on either side of Cockfosters Road.[11] Enfield joined Edmonton to form the London Borough of Enfield in 1965.[12]

The western part of the parish, reaching 363 ft. above sea level near New Cottage farm, is formed of London Clay, with a strip of pebble gravel running along the northern part of the Ridgeway; there are

patches of pebble gravel at Clay Hill and near Potters Bar and Monken Hadley, while the southern end of the Ridgeway runs through glacial gravel to boulder clay. Glacial deposits also occur at Cockfosters and near Trent Park and South Lodge. From the centre of the parish, where there are some steep hills, the ground slopes eastward towards the Lea through clay and an extensive area of terrace gravel and then through brickearth. The brickearth gives way to flood plain gravel between ½ mile and 1 mile west of the Lea and to alluvium in the riverside marshes.[13]

From the hills in the west flow several tributaries of the Lea. Maiden's brook, called the Wash brook in 1826,[14] rises at Potters Bar, meets Cuffley brook from Hertfordshire near Clay Hill, and joins the Lea about a mile south of the northern parish boundary. The lower part of Maiden's brook was still navigable in 1824, when the vestry appointed a committee to investigate the state of wharfing in Turkey Street.[15] Salmon's brook rises near Roundhedge Hill in the north-west of the parish and runs south-eastward through a valley, entering Edmonton south of Enfield Town at Bush Hill; it has two tributaries, the Leeging Beech gutter, which rises in the grounds of Trent Park, and Merryhills brook farther south, which rises near Cockfosters. A third stream, Pymme's brook, rises near the suburb of Hadley Wood and runs south into Monken Hadley, after passing through two large artificial ponds, the southernmost of which was recorded in 1656 as New Pond.[16] The ponds had assumed their modern shape by 1686.[17]

The New River was cut through the parish from north to south and opened in 1613.[18] The original course closely followed the 100 ft. contour line but was straightened in 1859 and again c. 1890, when it was channelled in three mains to Bush Hill park. In 1974 portions of the old course remained in Whitewebbs park and around Enfield Town and the river was carried over Maiden's brook by an aqueduct east of Maiden's bridge. Another aqueduct of cast iron in Flash Road, carrying the old stream over Cuffley brook, was built in 1820–1 when a diversion was made necessary after the portion of the river west of Flash Road had been bought by Edward Harman of Claysmore[19] and converted into an artificial lake, which survives in the grounds of

[1] The article was written in 1972. Any references to later years are dated. The help of Mr. A. H. Hall in commenting on the article is gratefully acknowledged.
[2] Census, 1831.
[3] See below, p. 214.
[4] O.S. Map 6″, Mdx. VII. NE. (1868 edn.).
[5] Enfield Chase Act, 17 Geo. III, c.17.
[6] W. Robinson, Hist. and Antiquities of Enfield (1823 edn.), i. 2.
[7] Parts of the Chase were transferred to Edmonton, Monken Hadley, and South Mimms; see pp. 130, 260, 271.
[8] O.S. Maps 6″, Mdx. I. SE.; II. SE., SW.; V. NE.; VII. NE., NW. (1868 and later edns.).

[9] J. Tuff, Hist. Notices of Enfield (1858), map facing frontispiece; Census, 1871.
[10] See p. 260.
[11] Census, 1891–1951.
[12] See p. 243.
[13] Geol. Surv. Map 1″, drift, sheet 256 (1951 edn.).
[14] Rep. on Bridges in Mdx.
[15] Vestry min. bk. (1823–39) penes Enfield L.B.
[16] M.P.C. 50A (D.L. 31/50A).
[17] D.L. 42/126.
[18] The para. is based on Enfield Arch. Soc., Industrial Arch. in Enfield (1971), pp. 27–31. See also above, p. 131.
[19] See p. 216.

Wildwood. Before 1820 the river passed under Cuffley brook in a trough or 'flash', rebuilt by Robert Mylne in 1775, parts of which survive. The ornamental aspect of the river was praised in 1823[20] and proposals to drain the superfluous old course *c.* 1890 were defeated by public agitation.[21]

The southern part of the eastern parish boundary was formed by the Mar dyke, a cut running west of the Lea through the marshes into Edmonton. Another cut, the mill river, left the Lea in the north-eastern corner of the parish and ran south, to join the Mar dyke at the south-eastern boundary. It was built to supply medieval mills[22] and was mentioned in the later 16th century, when a lock had been constructed between Wild and Mill marshes.[23] In 1572 the mill river was said to be of greater size than the main river[24] but an Act was passed to make the Lea itself navigable as far as Ware (Herts.) in 1571 and the work was completed by 1576.[25]

The old river was effectively superseded after improvements to the mill river under an Act of 1767.[26] Work began on the Enfield Cut of the Lea Navigation in 1769 and on the southern extension, called the Edmonton Cut, in 1770. Enfield Lock was constructed on the site of the old mill river lock and a surveyor's house was built in 1792, on the site of the later British Waterways' depot. An increase in traffic led to the construction of a second lock, at Ponders End, in 1793. Near by an early-19th-century dock was being used in 1832 for barges travelling between London and Hertfordshire;[27] a new double lock was built in 1959.[28] A third lock, at Rammey marsh in the extreme north of the parish, was built by 1867.[29] The old course of the Lea was submerged by King George's reservoir (446 a.), opened in 1913.[30]

Enfield won intermittent notoriety in the 18th century. Dick Turpin, whose grandfather reputedly had lived at Clay Hill, was said to lurk in new Camlet Moat on the Chase.[31] From 1753 until 1755 36 pamphlets and 14 prints were published on Elizabeth Canning, a servant girl convicted of perjury after claiming to have been abducted and robbed at Enfield Wash.[32] In 1779 sightseers were attracted by Thomas Hill Everett, the outsize baby son of the manager of the mills by the Lea, who lived at Scotland Green; the child was then exhibited in London, where it died in 1780.[33]

Natives[34] included the author Henry Baker (1734–66), Isaac D'Israeli (1766–1848), born in a house on the site of Enfield Town railway station which later became a private school attended by John Keats,[35] the civil engineer Sir Joseph Bazalgette (1819–91), and the poet and bibliographer of angling

Thomas Westwood (1814–88), whose father, a former haberdasher, was described by his friend Charles Lamb as 'a star among the minor gentry'. Gerard Legh (d. 1563), writer on heraldry, owed his education to Robert Wroth of Durants and the romance writer Robert Paltock (1697–1767) spent his early years in Enfield. Richard Brownlow (1553–1638), chief prothonotary of the Common Pleas,[36] and Sir George Wharton, Bt. (1617–81) died in their houses at Enfield and Edward Stephens (d. 1706), pamphleteer, was buried in the parish. Among other residents were John Hadley (1682–1744), mathematician and scientific mechanist, John Cartwright (1740–1824), political reformer and friend of Thomas Holt White of Chase Lodge,[37] William Saunders (1743–1817), physician, buried in the parish church, Sir Nathaniel Dance (1748–1827), commander under the East India Company, Mary Linwood (1755–1845), composer and needlework artist,[38] Thomas Smart (1776–1867),[39] musician, and Leitch Ritchie (?1800–65), novelist.[40] The critic Walter Pater (1839–94) spent his early years at a house in Baker Street, called Yarra House in 1911 and afterwards demolished.[41] William Booth (1829–1912), founder of the Salvation Army, moved to no. 33 Lancaster Avenue, Hadley Wood, in 1889[42] and Sir Herbert Gresley (1894–1941), locomotive engineer, lived at Camlet House, Hadley Wood, in the 1920s.[43] Other notable residents are mentioned elsewhere in the article.

William Henry van Nassau van Zuylesteyn, who married a daughter of Sir Henry Wroth of Durants, in 1695 was created Lord Enfield, Viscount Tunbridge, and earl of Rochford, which titles were held by his descendants until the honours became extinct in 1830.[44] After John Byng, Lord Strafford of Harmondsworth, was created Viscount Enfield and earl of Strafford in 1847,[45] Viscount Enfield became the courtesy title of the earl of Strafford's eldest son.[46]

COMMUNICATIONS. Ermine Street, mentioned in the reign of Edward I,[47] apparently entered the parish south of Enfield Town and passed east of Forty Hill and Bull's Cross.[48] Together with the other main roads it formed a rough grid pattern of highways from London crossed by routes leading westward from the Lea. The main north–south route, later known as Hertford Road, may have been the high street of Enfield mentioned in 1260.[49] It bisected the land between the Chase and the Lea, running slightly west of the marshes along the river. The road was placed under the new Stamford Hill turnpike trust in 1713[50] and taken over by the

[20] Robinson, *Enfield*, i. 25.
[21] M. Briggs, *Mdx. Old and New*, 60.
[22] See p. 236.
[23] Hatfield C.P.M. II/53.
[24] B.M. Harl. MS. 1579, f. 155; Robinson, *Enfield*, i. 36.
[25] D. O. Pam, *Tudor Enfield, The Maltmen and the Lea Navigation* (Edmonton Hund. Hist. Soc. n.d.), 7–8; see above, p. 130.
[26] The para. is based on Enfield Arch. Soc., *Ind. Arch. in Enfield*, 36–8.
[27] *Pigot's Com. Dir.* (1832–4).
[28] New Enfield Hist. (TS. chapters of unpub. hist. at Enfield libr.).
[29] O.S. Map 6", Mdx. III. SW. (1868 edn.).
[30] V. N. Allemandy, *Enfield Past and Present*, 61, 63.
[31] *D.N.B.*; C. W. Whitaker, *Enfield*, 149.
[32] Robinson, *Enfield*, ii. 132–51.
[33] Ibid. 152–4; *Gent. Mag.* i. 126.

[34] Except where otherwise stated, the para. is based on *D.N.B.*
[35] Robbins, *Mdx.* 250; see p. 257.
[36] C 142/492/107.   [37] Tuff, *Enfield*, 60.
[38] Ibid. 62.
[39] Whitaker, *Enfield*, 300.
[40] Tuff, *Enfield*, 62.
[41] Whitaker, *Enfield*, 122–3; *D.N.B.*
[42] Nancy Clark, *Hadley Wood*, 109.
[43] *Who Was Who*, 1941–50; Clark, *Hadley Wood*, 61.
[44] *Complete Peerage*, xi. 53–5.   [45] Ibid. xii(1), 334.
[46] Debrett, *Peerage* (1973–4), 1065.
[47] Lysons, *Environs*, ii. 312.
[48] Whitaker, *Enfield*, 15.
[49] *Sel. Cases of Proc. without Writ* (Selden Soc. lx), p. 40.
[50] D. O. Pam, *Stamford Hill, Green Lanes Turnpike Trust* (Edmonton Hund. Hist. Soc. 1963), i. 1–3.

commissioners for the metropolitan turnpike roads in 1826.[51] A short realignment north of Enfield Highway had taken place by 1830,[52] the new stretch passing east of what was henceforth known as Old Road. Hertford Road crossed Maiden's brook by a ford at Enfield Wash,[53] where a footbridge existed by 1675.[54] In 1772 another wooden bridge was built by the turnpike trustees but in 1814 the state of both bridge and road was very bad[55] and in 1820 the bridge, which was intended to take carriages when the brook was in flood, fell down.[56] A new wooden footbridge was built by the county in 1821[57] and a carriage bridge by the parish soon after 1827.[58]

A less important north–south route ran farther west, entering the parish at Bush Hill, passing east of Enfield church and market-place, and proceeding north-eastward over Forty Hill to Bull's Cross near the Hertfordshire boundary. It was called the highway from Bull's Cross to Enfield church in 1512[59] but sections of the road later acquired separate names; south of Enfield Town it was London Road and from the town to Forty Hill it formed Silver Street and Baker Street, the latter name occurring in 1572.[60] North of Forty Hill the road dipped to cross Maiden's brook by Maiden's bridge, mentioned in 1572[61] but impassable by 1759.[62] A new single-arched bridge was built in 1795[63] and was repaired in the early 1970s.[64] A northern continuation of the road from Bull's Cross into Cheshunt was called Hillocks Lane in 1754[65] but in 1972 was only a private drive to Theobalds Park. In the 18th century the Stamford Hill turnpike trust took over London Road as far north as Enfield Town.[66] The entrance to the town from the south was said to be very narrow and dangerous in 1823, when improvements were proposed.[67]

A third northerly route, through the western part of the parish, crossed the Chase from Cockfosters to Potters Bar. In 1656 it apparently ended abruptly a little beyond West Lodge[68] but its northward continuation was shown in 1777.[69] The southern stretch was known as Cockfosters Road and the northern part as Southgate Road in 1972.

Several roads ran from east to west on either side of Hertford Road. The southernmost, from the Lea to London Road, crossed Hertford Road at Ponders End and formed the main link between Ponders End and Enfield Town until c. 1800.[70] Its western section was known in 1572[71] as Bungeys or Bungers Lane

but by 1823 was more generally called Brick or Red Lane; it was said to have been nearly impassable in the later 18th century and in 1823 to have been a private road of William Mellish.[72] It was renamed Lincoln Road between 1868 and 1897.[73] South Street, the stretch east of Hertford Road, was mentioned in 1548.[74] In 1868 it ended by the mill later known as Wright's flour mill[75] but by 1897 it had been extended, as Valley Road, to cross the Lea at Ponders End lock.[76]

North of Bungeys Lane Farm Road ran westward from Ponders End and continued as a footpath to Enfield Town, until in 1803 it was extended west across Southbury field to the town as a public road.[77] It became known as Nags Head Road but by 1896 had been renamed Southbury Road, the name Nags Head Road being transferred to a new road running eastward from the junction of Southbury and Hertford roads toward the Lea.[78] Southbury Road was widened to take trams in 1909–10.[79] By 1972 Nags Head Road had been extended on a bridge over the Lea Navigation to meet Lea Valley Road, forming part of a major east-west arterial route.

Green Street, farther north, was so named in 1471.[80] At its eastern end it split into Stockingswater and Millmarsh lanes, both of which led to the Lea. Millmarsh Lane crossed the mill river by a bridge, mentioned in 1472,[81] which came to be identified with Raddington bridge, whose profits had been used by Baldwin Raddington, lord of the manor, to endow a charity in 1397.[82] The bridge was ruinous in 1655[83] and after collapsing in 1801[84] it was not rebuilt, the vestry having decided that it was the responsibility of the trustees of the Lea Navigation.

Carterhatch and Hoe lanes, north of Green Street, ran westward from Hertford Road to Forty Hill. One of them may have been the king's highway from Horsepool (Enfield Highway) to the Chase mentioned in 1366;[85] both were recorded in 1572.[86] Turkey Street, farther north, was recorded in 1427[87] and ran from Enfield Wash to a point south of Bull's Cross. Its eastern part skirted Maiden's brook, which it crossed by a bridge near the site of Turkey Street railway station. A bridge existed in 1759[88] and was replaced in 1791 by one of three arches, of brick and stone, which was repaired in 1809 but was said to be dilapidated in 1826.[89] A lane running eastward from Enfield Wash to the Lea was called Norris Lane in 1577,[90] Marsh Lane in 1754,[91] Welches Lane

[51] Ibid. ii. 29.
[52] Vestry min. bks. (1823–39) penes Enfield L.B., pp. 231–2.
[53] Robinson, Enfield, i. 38. The ford was probably the 'wash' mentioned in John Gilpin, which Cowper mistakenly placed in Edmonton.
[54] Ogilby, Road Bk. (c. 1677); Rep. on Bridges in Mdx. 103.
[55] Pam, Stamford Hill, Green Lanes Turnpike Trust, i. 17; ii. 27.
[56] Robinson, Enfield, i. 37 n.
[57] Rep. on Bridges in Mdx. 104.
[58] Vestry min. bk. (1807–22), p. 511.
[59] M.R.O., Acc. 813/1.
[60] D.L. 43/7/5.
[61] Ibid.
[62] M.R.O., D.R.O. 4/1/7.
[63] Rep. on Bridges in Mdx. 103.
[64] Ex inf. Mr. A. H. Hall.
[65] Rocque, Map of Mdx. (1754).
[66] L.J. xix. 571a.
[67] Robinson, Enfield, i. 46.
[68] M.P.C. 50A (D.L. 31/50A).
[69] Map of Enfield Chase (1777) in Robinson, Enfield, i, facing p. 208.

[70] Robinson, Enfield, i. 72; Trinity Coll. Cambridge, Estate MSS., Enfield survey and map (1754).
[71] D.L. 43/7/5.
[72] Robinson, Enfield, i. 71–2.
[73] O.S. Maps 6″, Mdx. VII. NE. (1868 and 1897 edns.).
[74] Cal. Pat. 1548–9, 37.
[75] O.S. Map 6″, Mdx. VII. NE. (1868 edn.).
[76] Ibid. (1897 edn.).
[77] M.R.O., Enfield Incl. Award (1803).
[78] O.S. Map 6″, Mdx. VII. NE. (1868 and 1897 edns.).
[79] Whitaker, Enfield, 173.
[80] Cal. Close, 1468–76, 220.
[81] Pam, Tudor Enfield, 3.
[82] See below, p. 245; Robinson, Enfield, ii. 161.
[83] M.R.O., Cal. Mdx. Sess. Bks. (1652–7), pp. 106–7.
[84] Vestry min. bk. (1797–1807) penes Enfield L.B.
[85] M.R.O., Acc. 903/139.
[86] D.L. 43/7/5; see below, p. 213.
[87] M.R.O., Acc. 903/124.
[88] M.R.O., D.R.O. 4/1/7.
[89] Rep. on Bridges in Mdx. 103.
[90] D.L. 43/7/5.
[91] Trinity Coll. Cambridge, Estate MSS., Enfield survey and map.

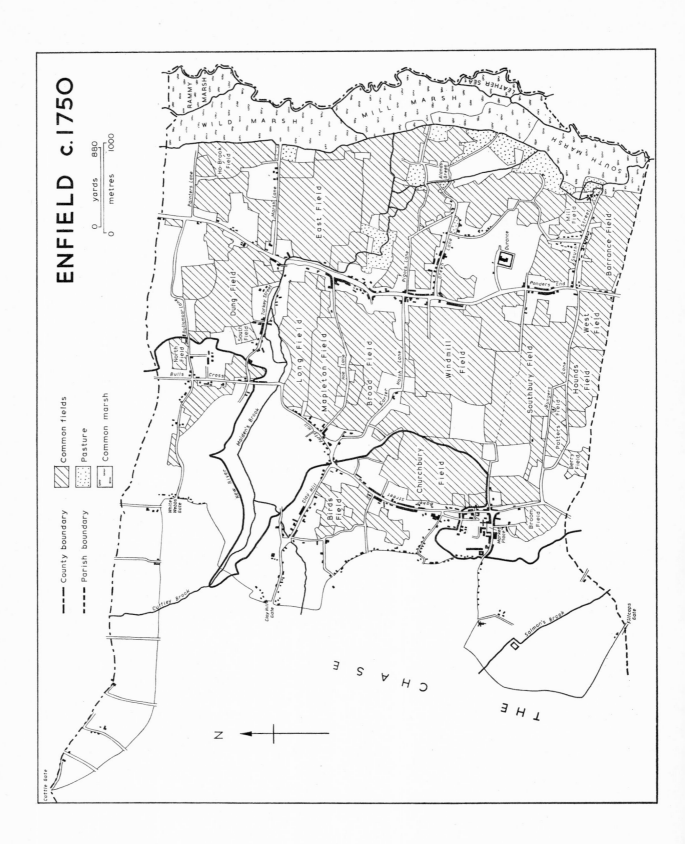

ENFIELD c.1750

County boundary
Parish boundary

Common fields
Pasture
Common marsh

RAMMY MARSH
WILD MARSH
MILL MARSH
LEATHER SEAL
SOUTH MARSH

Ho-Brook Field
Painters Lane
Marsh Lane
East Field
Alonds Green
Mill Field
South Street
Durance
Ponders End
Barrance Field

Dung Field
Bullsmoor Lane
Turkey Street
South Field
Long Field
Mapleton Field
Pigots Lane
Green Lane
Windmill Field
Southbury Field
West Field
Hounds Field

North Field
Bulls Cross
Clay Hill
Hoe Lane
Broad Field
Horse Match Lane
Churchbury Field
Bull Lane
Buggers Lane
Potters Field
Berry Field

White Webbs Gate
New River
Maiden's Brook
Mill Pond
Birds Field
Baker Street
Broom Field
Moated Place

Cuffley Brook
Clay Hill Gate
Salmon's Brook
Flitcaps Gate

THE CHASE

Cattle Gate

N

0 yards 880
0 metres 1000

210

in 1823,[92] and Ordnance Road by 1897.[93] The building of the Royal Small Arms factory *c.* 1804[94] led to an increase of traffic and in 1818 the Board of Ordnance unsuccessfully indicted the parish for failing to repair the road.[95] Part of the road was diverted in 1865.[96] The northernmost of the east-west cross routes, Bullsmoor (or Belsmoor) and Painters lanes, were both recorded in 1572.[97] Painters Lane in 1972 was a path leading to the Lea.

The chief road running west from the route linking Bull's Cross to Enfield Town was that which led from the town to Enfield Chase. Later known as Church Street, it entered the Chase at Park Gate, which in 1658 stood slightly east of the bridge over the New River.[98] Thence in 1658 a track ran north alongside the modern Chase Green, its southernmost portion forming the path which came to be called Gentleman's Row. Having crossed the New River, it ran north-west across the Chase to the top of Holtwhite's Hill where it met Parsonage Lane, so called in 1572,[99] which later stopped at Chase Side. The western part of the road, with the other major roads through those parts of the Chase allotted to Enfield, was made public in 1803[1] and renamed Holtwhite's Hill between 1868 and 1897.[2] Another road ran westward from Baker Street to join Holtwhite's Hill at the summit. The road was simply New Road in 1754[3] but its western part had become Lavender Hill by 1868, presumably after the lavender formerly grown there;[4] the eastern part was called New Lane in 1867 and Lancaster Road by 1898.[5] Chase Side, running northward from Chase Green to New Lane (Lavender Hill), probably existed as Woodside in 1572[6] and received its modern name after 1803.[7]

From the junction at the top of Holtwhite's Hill the Ridgeway ran north-west across the Chase in 1658.[8] Near the western boundary it joined the road running north from Cockfosters and as Camlet Way, mentioned in 1658 and named after an ancient site called Camlet Moat,[9] continued westward into Monken Hadley. The stretch of the Ridgeway east of Cockfosters Road had been renamed Hadley Road by 1803, at which date the Ridgeway itself continued north-westward to Potters Bar.[10] The Act of 1777 ordered that the Ridgeway be extended south-eastward to Enfield Town[11] and in 1778 work was in progress.[12] A committee of the vestry reported in 1807 that the roads built under the inclosure Acts were unusable[13] and in the mid 19th century the Ridgeway was said to be a muddy track;[14] later, however, it became part of the busiest east-west route in the parish. At the top of Windmill Hill, so called in 1868,[15] the extended Ridgeway met a road running from Enfield to East Barnet, known as Merryhill Way in 1658[16] and East Barnet Road in 1803.[17] From east to west it was called Slades Hill, Enfield Road, and Bramley Road in 1974.

From Forty Hill a road which ran westward was known as Bridge Street in 1572[18] and Clay Hill Lane in 1754.[19] It crossed Maiden's brook by a bridge which needed repair in 1759[20] and was rebuilt, with one arch, in 1803.[21] Beyond Clay Hill it continued north as Theobalds Park Road, first mentioned in 1803,[22] to the former park in Cheshunt (Herts.),[23] near whose boundary it met a road from Bull's Cross. In 1572 the eastern part of the road from Bull's Cross was called Rome Street and the rest White Webbs Lane,[24] a name later extended to the whole length. West of the junction with Theobalds Park Road, White Webbs Lane continued as Cattle Gate Lane to the boundary with Northaw (Herts.). Like East Lodge Lane, which ran south-westward to connect it with the Ridgeway near East Lodge, it was made into a public road at inclosure in 1803.[25] The most northerly of the east-west routes in Enfield, Coopers Lane, which followed the boundary from Cattle Gate to Potters Bar, also became a public way in 1803.

The most important addition to the early-19th-century road-pattern was Great Cambridge Road, built in 1923–4 and widened in the 1960s.[26] It follows a straight line from south to north, bisecting the area between Hertford Road and the route through Enfield Town to Bull's Cross.

A coach called the Enfield Fly left Enfield for London on weekdays in 1783, returning in the afternoons,[27] and by 1791 coaches ran twice daily to Holborn, Bishopsgate Street, and Aldersgate Street.[28] In 1832 there were four coaches a day from Enfield Town to London, as well as coaches from Enfield Highway to Ware and Hertford.[29] Omnibuses served Forty Hill and Clay Hill in 1862[30] and a horse tram service from Stamford Hill through Tottenham and Edmonton was extended to Ponders End in 1882. Horses were replaced by steam locomotives in 1885 but in 1891 horse traction was resumed.[31] In 1890 trams ran every quarter hour from Ponders End to Finsbury Park.[32] The service was electrified in 1905 and in 1908 was extended along Hertford Road to

[92] Robinson, *Enfield*, i. 70.
[93] O.S. Maps 6″, Mdx. II. SE. (1897 edn.).
[94] See p. 238.
[95] Vestry min. bk. (1807–22).
[96] M.R.O., S.R. 5226/32/2 Oct. 1865.
[97] D.L. 43/7/5.
[98] M.P.C. 50A (D.L. 31/50A).
[99] D.L. 43/7/5.
[1] M.R.O., Enfield Incl. Award and Map. The Enclosure Act, 41 Geo. III, c. 143, was finally put into effect in 1806: Robinson, *Enfield*, ii. 294.
[2] O.S. Map 6″, Mdx. VII. NW. (1868 and 1897 edns.).
[3] Trinity Coll. Cambridge, Estate MSS., Enfield survey and map.
[4] O.S. Map 6″, Mdx. VII. NE. (1867 edn.); see p. 234.
[5] O.S. Map 6″, Mdx. VII. NE. (1898 edn.).
[6] D.L. 43/7/5.
[7] M.R.O., Enfield Incl. Award and Map.
[8] M.P.C. 50A (D.L. 31/50A).
[9] See p. 260.
[10] M.R.O., Enfield Incl. Award and Map.
[11] 17 Geo. III, c. 17, s. 48.
[12] M.R.O., D.R.O. 4/2/11.

[13] Vestry min. bk. (1797–1807) *penes* Enfield L.B.
[14] Whitaker, *Enfield*, 251.
[15] O.S. Map 6″, Mdx. VII. NE. (1868 edn.). For the windmill, see p. 236.
[16] M.P.C. 50A (D.L. 31/50A).
[17] M.R.O., Enfield Incl. Award and Map.
[18] D.L. 43/7/5.
[19] Trinity Coll. Cambridge, Estate MSS., Enfield survey and map.
[20] M.R.O., D.R.O. 4/1/7.
[21] *Rep. on Bridges in Mdx.* 102.
[22] M.R.O., Enfield Incl. Award and Map.
[23] *V.C.H. Herts.* iii. 447–50.
[24] D.L. 43/7/5.
[25] M.R.O., Enfield Incl. Award and Map.
[26] Ex inf. Mr. A. H. Hall; see p. 223.
[27] Robbins, *Mdx.* 243; M.R.O., Hist. Notes 30/10/64.
[28] *Universal British Dir.* iii. 81.
[29] *Pigot's Com. Dir.* (1832–4).
[30] *Kelly's Dir. Mdx.* (1862). Except where otherwise stated the rest of the para. is based on New Enfield Hist.
[31] See above, p. 137.
[32] *Kelly's Dir. Mdx.* (1890).

Waltham Cross (Herts.). In 1909 a service along London Road to Enfield Town was introduced and about two years later trams began running to the town along Southbury Road. From 1912 they ran through from Enfield Town to Tottenham Court Road and a year or so later from Ponders End, Enfield Highway, and Waltham Cross to Smithfield.[33] They were replaced by trolley-buses in 1938 and they in turn by motor-buses in 1961.[34]

The Northern and Eastern (later the Great Eastern) Railway opened its main line along the Lea valley in 1840[35] and a station was built in South Street to serve Ponders End.[36] Ordnance Factory station in Ordnance Road was opened in 1855 and in 1886 was renamed Enfield Lock.[37] A third station, Brimsdown, was opened at the end of Green Street in 1884.[38] Services at first were infrequent and the distance of the stations from the largest centre of population, Enfield Town, prompted the promotion of a branch line from Water Lane, Edmonton (later Angel Road). An Act was passed in 1846[39] and in 1849 the line was opened to a terminus in Nags Head Lane (near Southbury Road).[40] In 1859 there were ten trains a day in each direction, the journey from Enfield Town to London taking 45 minutes, while on the Cambridge main line ten trains called at Ponders End in each direction, of which four stopped additionally at Ordnance Factory station.[41] The service to Enfield Town greatly improved after the opening of a line from Bethnal Green to Lower Edmonton in 1872, although some trains continued to use the longer route via Angel Road until 1939.[42] The first Enfield Town station, a 17th-century house which had served as a private school,[43] was replaced in 1872. Workmen's trains ran from 1874, with a return fare to London of 2d., and in 1891 five left Enfield Town daily before 6.30 a.m.[44] By 1901 trains from Enfield Town to London were half-hourly, except at rush hours, and in 1920 a faster service was introduced.[45]

In 1891 the G.E.R. opened a new line through the parish from Lower Edmonton to Cheshunt, with stations in Southbury Road and Turkey Street, the second of which was called Forty Hill.[46] Trains ran to White Hart Lane (Tottenham), where passengers had to change. The expected suburban growth did not take place, partly because of the lack of through trains to London, and the line was closed to passengers in 1909 after the introduction of electric trams along Hertford Road. It was reopened from 1915 to 1919 for workers in local munitions factories, with an extra station in Carterhatch Lane, but thereafter until 1961 was used only by a daily freight train. When suburban services to Liverpool Street were electrified in 1961, however, the line was again opened with half-hourly electric trains to Bishops

Stortford (Herts.) calling at the two older stations, which were renamed Southbury and Turkey Street. The branch to Enfield Town was also electrified in 1961, a new station was built, and the journey to London reduced to 29 minutes with trains leaving every 20 minutes except at rush hours.[47] Electric trains also ran along the main line through Ponders End at half-hourly intervals from 1970.

The Great Northern Railway built its main line north from London through the western part of the parish in 1850, but Enfield had no station when the line which later ran from King's Cross was opened from a temporary station in Maiden Lane in 1852.[48] In 1885, however, a station was opened in Camlet Way to serve the new Hadley Wood estate, with twelve trains a day to London.[49] In 1972 there was a half hourly service, with extra trains at rush hours. A branch from the main line at Wood Green through Enfield to rejoin the main line at Hertford was approved in 1865 but the line was not opened until 1871 and did not proceed farther north than the Enfield terminus in Windmill Hill.[50] In 1887 37 trains a day left Enfield for King's Cross,[51] while some ran to Broad Street and others until 1907 to Woolwich and Victoria.[52] The plan to extend the railway to Hertford was revived in 1897 and the line was opened in 1910 as far as Cuffley (Herts.), with new stations at Grange Park, Gordon Hill, and Crews Hill; the old terminus was turned into a goods depot and a new station (called Enfield Chase) was built to the east, at the foot of Windmill Hill.[53] The extension involved the building of a fourteen-arched brick viaduct, called Rendlesham viaduct, over the valley of Maiden's brook between Gordon Hill and Crews Hill stations.[54] Trains ran at half-hourly intervals and more frequently at rush hours in 1972, although for some time several of them terminated at Gordon Hill.[55]

The last railway to be built was the Cockfosters extension of London Transport's Piccadilly line, opened in 1933.[56] It penetrated only the south-western corner of the old parish, where its terminus was constructed in Cockfosters Road. The station, an impressive building of reinforced concrete and glass by Charles Holden,[57] served as a railhead for motor-bus services to expanding suburban districts.

GROWTH BEFORE 1850. An oval camp in Hadley wood, covering 15 a. and from 1850 bisected by the main line of the G.N.R., is evidence of prehistoric settlement in the thickly wooded western part of the parish.[58] Farther east there were probably Bronze- and Iron-age dwellings near the Lea at Ponders End and some houses were built west of the Roman Ermine Street, especially in the region of Bush Hill Park.[59] Other Roman finds were at a moated site

33 Whitaker, *Enfield*, 173; ex inf. Mr. H. V. Borley.
34 New Enfield Hist.
35 C. J. Allen, *Gt. Eastern Rly.* (1968 edn.), 11.
36 Enfield Arch. Soc., *Ind. Arch. in Enfield*, 40.
37 Ex inf. Mr. H. V. Borley.
38 *Ind. Arch. in Enfield*, 41.
39 Tuff, *Enfield*, 188.
40 Allen, *Gt. Eastern Rly.* 235.
41 *Meyer's Enfield Observer*, Jan. 1859.
42 N. P. White, *Regional Hist. of Rlys. in Gt. Britain*, iii. 173-4.
43 See p. 257.   44 White, op. cit. 175.
45 Allen, *Gt. Eastern Rly.* 186.
46 The para. is based on Allen, *Gt. Eastern Rly.* 66-7, and *Mdx. Quarterly*, N.S. xiv. 4-5.

47 Allen, *Gt. Eastern Rly.* 229.
48 Grinling, *Gt. Northern Rly.* (1966 edn.), 90, 126.
49 Clark, *Hadley Wood*, 37, 58. For the estate, see below, p. 221.
50 Grinling, *Gt. Northern Rly.* 231, 261.
51 *Bradshaw's Rly. Guide* (Aug. 1887).
52 Grinling, *Gt. Northern Rly.* 458.
53 *Ind. Arch. in Enfield*, 40.
54 Ibid. 42.
55 Grinling, *Gt. Northern Rly.* 461.
56 C. E. Lee, *Sixty Yrs. of the Piccadilly*, 22.
57 Robbins, *Mdx.* 185.
58 *T.L.M.A.S.* x. 98-9.
59 *V.C.H. Mdx.* i. 50-1, 57, 65, 69-70.

south of Queen's Road, called Oldbury Moat and later filled in,[60] and at another site, of uncertain date, by Salmon's brook on the modern Enfield golf course.[61]

A church probably existed by 1086,[62] near the *feld* or clearing which gave its name to Enfield.[63] Most of the parish seems at that date to have been covered by woodland, part of which already had been inclosed as a park.[64] The park was probably the area known in 1324 as the Frith or inner park[65] and was later called the Old Park, to distinguish it from the much larger Enfield Chase. In 1650 the Old Park occupied 553 a. south-west of Enfield Town and its eastern edge ran from Park Gate to the Edmonton boundary. It was divided into meadows between 1661 and 1686.[66]

By 1223 the park, inclosed within a paling, had been extended almost to the northern parish boundary at Cattle gate (*porta de Catthal*).[67] This new outer park was called the Chase in 1326[68] but later was sometimes called Enfield wood.[69] In 1572 it covered the entire western half of the parish and was entered from the east by four gates: Park, Parsonage Lane, Phipps Hatch, and Mores Hatch.[70] Two more gates, at the end of New Lane (later Lavender Hill) and at Whitewebbs, led into the Chase from the east in 1656, when there were entrances from the north at Cattle, Hook, and Coopers Lane gates, from the west at Potters Bar and Monken Hadley, and from the south at Bourne gate, Southgate, and Hammonds Hook gate.[71] Carterhatch Lane seems to preserve the name of an earlier gate, suggesting that the Chase may once have stretched east of the boundary recorded in 1572.[72] In 1611 500 a. in the north-east of the Chase were inclosed within the park of Theobalds (Herts.)[73] and in 1650 the total area was estimated at 7,904 a.[74] In 1658 the eastern boundary of the Chase was marked by the western and northern limits of the Old Park as far as Park gate, west of the church. Thence it followed the later Gentleman's Row, Chase Side, and Brigadier Hill, crossing Maiden's brook and running along the line of Flash Road and around the eastern edge of the modern Whitewebbs estate. Turning west, it followed Whitewebbs and Theobalds Park roads to meet the county boundary at Cattle gate.[75] There were no further changes until the Chase was split up in 1779,[76] an attempt to do so during the Interregnum having been thwarted by the Restoration.[77]

Apart from three lodges, built for keepers but

converted into gentlemen's seats,[78] the Chase was virtually uninhabited. In 1593 it contained only deer,[79] whose number by 1724 had been reduced by poachers.[80] In 1676 the diarist John Evelyn was impressed that so large a tract near London should have no building except the three lodges, 'the rest a solitary desert yet stored with no less than 3,000 deer'.[81] Accusations of witchcraft between 1591 and 1615 probably arose from suspicious gatherings in the Chase,[82] where a chapel had been found equipped for black masses.[83] Plotters were said to be hiding in the woods in 1666[84] and gangs of robbers to lurk there in 1742.[85]

Medieval settlement was concentrated in the eastern part of the parish, between the wooded heights of Enfield Chase and the marshes by the Lea. Common arable fields were first recorded in the 13th century[86] and by 1572 they occupied well over half of the cultivated land, mostly in the low-lying area east of the road through Enfield Town to Forty Hill and Bull's Cross.[87] Immediately adjoining the Lea were the common marshes, used for grazing.[88] The three northernmost, Rammey, Wild, and Mill marshes, were all so named by the 14th century.[89] To the south were Leathersey, mentioned in 1484,[90] and South marsh, mentioned in 1419.[91] Inclosures in the 16th century were mainly on the fringe of the central common field area:[92] near Enfield Town, west of Baker Street, east of Ponders End, and in the north-east of the parish near Painters Lane. After further inclosures an Act was passed in 1801 and put into effect in 1803, covering the whole of the parish east of the former Chase, together with that part of the Chase which had been allotted to the parish in 1777.[93]

With a few exceptions, including the manor-houses in the east of the parish, medieval settlement was on the main routes from north to south. In 1572 most people lived in villages or hamlets along the road through Enfield Town near the Chase or along Hertford Road, which ran on flat, lower ground,[94] while the intervening fields remained almost uninhabited until the end of the 19th century.[95] Many unauthorized cottages were erected c. 1600: in 1605 over 60 were said to have been built during the previous 50 years[96] and more had appeared by 1618.[97] There were 562 houses in 1664, 200 of them in Enfield Green ward which contained Enfield Town. The four other wards or quarters which then served as local government units were Bull's Cross, with 144 houses, Green Street (otherwise Horsepool

[60] Ibid. ii. 5; Whitaker, *Enfield*, 174.
[61] *V.C.H. Mdx.* ii. 2–3, 5.
[62] Ibid. i. 126.
[63] Possibly 'Eana's open space': *P.N. Mdx.* (E.P.N.S.), 71.
[64] *V.C.H. Mdx.* i. 126.
[65] *Cal. Close*, 1323–7, 217–18. [66] See p. 230.
[67] *Cur. Reg. R.* xi. 18; D.L. 25/20.
[68] *Cal. Close*, 1323–7, 439–40. For the admin. hist. of the Chase see *V.C.H. Mdx.* ii. 226–30.
[69] M.R.O., Acc. 312/4.
[70] D.L. 43/7/5.
[71] M.P.C. 145 (D.L. 31/175).
[72] *P.N. Mdx.* (E.P.N.S.), 72.
[73] *Cal. S.P. Dom.* 1611–18, 81.
[74] E 317/Mdx./17.
[75] M.P.C. 50A (D.L. 31/50A).
[76] See above, p. 207.
[77] *V.C.H. Mdx.* ii. 228–9; see below, p. 231.
[78] See p. 231.
[79] Norden, *Speculum Britanniae* (1723 edn.), 26.

[80] Daniel Defoe, *Tour through Eng. and Wales* (Everyman edn.), ii. 3.
[81] *Diary of John Evelyn*, ed. E. S. de Beer, iv. 92.
[82] *Mdx. Cnty. Recs.* i. 196, 237; ii. 57–8, 79–80, 116.
[83] Ford, *Enfield*, 126–7.
[84] *Cal. S.P. Dom.* 1665–6, 195.
[85] Hist. MSS. Com. 53 *Bath*, i, p. 270.
[86] *P.N. Mdx.* (E.P.N.S.), 213; see below, p. 233.
[87] D.L. 43/7/5.
[88] See p. 233.
[89] D.L. 43/7/1.
[90] *P.N. Mdx.* (E.P.N.S.), 213.
[91] S.C. 6/915/26.
[92] D.L. 43/7/5.
[93] Enfield Incl. Act, 41 Geo. III, c. 143.
[94] D.L. 43/7/5.
[95] Cf. Rocque, *Map of Mdx.* (1754); Enfield Incl. Map (1803); O.S. Maps 6", Mdx. I. SE.; II. SE., SW.; VI. NE.; VII. NE., NW. (1868 and 1897 edns.).
[96] D.L. 43/7/6.
[97] S.C. 2/118/55.

Stones or Enfield Highway), with 100, Ponders End, with 58, and Parsonage, with 50.[98] By 1801 the total number of houses had nearly doubled, to 993, and by 1851 it had reached 1,891.[99]

Many rich maltmen lived in Enfield in the 15th and 16th centuries, before local prosperity was undermined by the Act of 1571 for improving the Lea.[1] Large houses were also built, at least from the 16th century, for families attracted by Enfield's accessibility from London and its royal connexions. In 1664 nine houses had 10 hearths or more.[2] The parish continued to be a fashionable place of residence in the 18th century and in 1832 was noted for its many handsome seats, most of them in or around Enfield Town and the roads to its north.[3]

Enfield Town, so called from the 17th century, was named from a green south of the parish church.[4] A market and fairs were granted in 1303, houses overlooked the green in 1364,[5] and Whitelocks Lane led there in 1511.[6] South of the green was the manor-house later known as Enfield Palace,[7] while near by other large 16th-century houses included the Vine, mentioned in 1562.[8] The Greyhound inn stood on the eastern side of the green in 1596;[9] as an early-17th-century brick building with 'Dutch' gables it afterwards served as a vestry hall and magistrates' court but was demolished in 1897.[10] The old King's Head, demolished soon after 1897,[11] had been built on the north side of the green by 1670[12] and the George stood on the south side in 1666.[13] There was a school-house west of the churchyard in 1572[14] and it survived as a red-brick building, part of Enfield grammar school, in 1972.[15] Much property was destroyed by fire in 1657.[16]

Enfield Town began to assume its modern layout after a market-place had been established in 1632 on the site of the Vine.[17] In 1670 it contained a market house, a market cross, a weigh-house, 6 shops on the west side, and 24 stalls in the market-place.[18] A pump existed by 1764.[19] Although Enfield was described in 1806 as the skeleton of a market town,[20] the early-19th-century market-place was shown as a busy square, with many buildings used as shops.[21] The wooden octagonal market house was replaced in 1826 by a stone Gothic cross,[22] parts of which were moved to the grounds of Myddelton House in 1904, when an octagonal market building on Corinthian columns was erected to the designs of Sydney W. Cranfield.[23] Most of the older buildings in the square were demolished in the later 19th century.

By 1656 Enfield Town had spread westward along

Church Lane as far as the Chase, northward along Silver Street, and southward along London Road.[24] Most of the larger houses of the 16th and 17th centuries, like Redlingtons, mentioned in 1641, were later demolished,[25] although some survived in Church Street into the 19th century. Burleigh House was built c. 1700 west of the market-place but replaced soon after 1913 by a cinema, with shops along the street frontage of the grounds.[26] Chaseside House, a large stuccoed building on the south side of Church Street, was erected c. 1830 by James Farrer Steadman on the site of an earlier house and later also made way for shops.[27] The Rising Sun inn stood near by in 1752[28] and was replaced by shops in 1933.[29] The area enclosed by Church Street, Silver Street, and the New River was never completely built up; in 1754 most of it was still covered by private grounds and orchards[30] and in 1972, apart from some rows of 19th-century cottages and late-19th-century houses, it was largely devoted to schools' sports grounds.

There were houses on the boundary of the Chase, north of Park gate, in 1572.[31] One belonged to Sir Francis Wroth and another, that of a Mr. Fortescue, may have occupied the site of the large timber-framed Fortescue Hall, which bore the date 1608 and was demolished in 1816.[32] Among smaller timber-framed houses of the 16th and 17th centuries was one where Charles Lamb, the writer, came to live in 1825.[33] In 1972 the house, no. 17, had an 18th-century plastered façade. Some brick houses were built near by in the 18th century when the path facing the Chase became known as Gentleman's Row. They include the former Little Park, to the south, a large building with a pedimented centre and later wings, in 1974 occupied by the council, and, at the northern end of the row, Archway House, a pedimented building in grey brick of c. 1750, through which an arch leads to Love's Row (later Holly Walk). Gentleman's Row faces Chase Green, a remnant of the Chase preserved as an open space when the parish was inclosed in 1803.

North of Gentleman's Row building was sparse until the end of the 18th century. Some houses on the edge of the Chase included a cottage called Wolfes in 1572[34] and another called Goddards in 1608.[35] By 1656 more houses had been built[36] and by 1686 the area was known as Chase Side.[37] Ivy House was built there, by a pond at the corner of Parsonage Lane, in the early 18th century and demolished after a fire c. 1900.[38] On the inclosure of

[98] M.R.O., MR/TH/5. The distribution of housing in 1664 corresponds with the population figures for 1642; see below, p. 218.
[99] *Census*, 1801, 1851.
[1] Pam, *Tudor Enfield*, 3, 7–8.
[2] M.R.O., MR/TH/5.
[3] Pigot, *Com. Dir.* (1832–4).
[4] e.g. M.R.O., MR/TH/5.
[5] M.R.O., Acc. 903/41.
[6] Ibid. /19b.   [7] See p. 225.
[8] M.R.O., Acc. 903/2.
[9] Ibid. /50.
[10] *Mdx. & Herts. N. & Q.* iii. 27; see below, p. 221.
[11] *Mdx. & Herts. N. & Q.* iii. 28.
[12] M.R.O., Acc. 903/32; see p. 221.
[13] C 5/633/40.
[14] D.L. 43/7/5.
[15] Except where otherwise stated, all buildings of the 17th cent. and later were of brick.
[16] *Cal. S.P. Dom.* 1657–8, 329.
[17] M.R.O., Acc. 903/20; see p. 237.

[18] M.R.O., Acc. 903/32.
[19] Ibid. /38.
[20] Camden, *Britannia*, ed. Gough, ii. 107.
[21] Prints *penes* Enfield libr.
[22] Robinson, *Enfield*, i. 8–9; Tuff, *Enfield*, 28–9.
[23] Whitaker, *Enfield*, 194.
[24] M.P.C. 145.
[25] M.R.O., Acc. 16/5, f.5.
[26] Whitaker, *Enfield*, 223; M.R.O., Acc. 1084/1.
[27] Ford, *Enfield*, 33–4; Whitaker, *Enfield*, 224.
[28] M.R.O., L.V. 7/29.
[29] Photograph *penes* Enfield libr.
[30] Rocque, *Map of Mdx.* (1754).
[31] D.L. 43/7/5.
[32] Robinson, *Enfield*, i. 252–3.
[33] Whitaker, *Enfield*, 308.
[34] D.L. 43/7/5.
[35] Trinity Coll. Cambridge, Estate MSS., box 43.
[36] M.P.C. 145.
[37] D.L. 42/126.
[38] Photograph *penes* Enfield libr.

the Chase in 1779 Chase Side became a through road and buildings, including an Independent chapel and the surviving no. 60, were built on its western side to face older ones on the east.[39] Early-19th-century houses include two more of Charles Lamb's homes: the Poplars, 1827–29, and Westwood Cottage, 1829–33.[40] Gloucester Place, a terrace on the western side of the road, is dated 1823 and other cottages on the opposite side are of about the same date. West of Chase Side Gordon House was built on the Chase near the top of Gordon Hill. It was named after an early occupant, Lord George Gordon (1751–93), instigator of the Gordon Riots,[41] later belonged to Sir Thomas Hallifax (1721–89), Lord Mayor of London and a founder of the bank which became Glyn, Mills & Co.,[42] and was demolished c. 1860.[43] Chase Lodge, to the south, was built after the inclosure of the Chase. It belonged in 1834 to T. Cotton,[44] then to Thomas Holt White, a commentator on Shakespeare, after whom Holtwhite's Hill is named,[45] and was demolished shortly before 1911.[46]

Farther north buildings clustered at the junction of Chase Side and New Lane (later Lancaster Road) in 1656[47] and by 1754 stretched intermittently from Parsonage Lane northward to Phipps Hatch gate.[48] Some small 18th- and early-19th-century houses and shops survive in Chase Side and its northern continuation, Brigadier Hill. The Holly Bush inn was recorded in 1752[49] and a large weatherboarded house at the bottom of Brigadier Hill is 18th-century. Other large houses farther up the hill, including the Cedars, Brigadier House, and Warwick House,[50] have been demolished.

Another ribbon of building ran northward from the eastern end of the town, along Silver Street and Baker Street where the Rectory, the Vicarage, and the first manor-house of Worcesters stood in the 16th century, with several smaller dwellings.[51] Houses called Blakes and Mortimers Farm stood near by, while in Parsonage Lane there was another called Bates in 1608. A house called Woodcock Hall existed in 1656[52] and towards the northern end of Baker Street there was a stone cross.[53] The five-bay front of Enfield Court (later part of Enfield grammar school), at the northern end of Silver Street, was built in the late 17th century but afterwards greatly extended; a riding house was added in 1858 and the south wing rebuilt in 1864 by Col. Alfred Plantagenet Somerset.[54] A chapel was built on the eastern side of Baker Street in 1689[55] and houses extended on both sides of the road from the town north to New Lane by 1754.[56] More houses were built in the later 18th century, including three in Baker Street in 1774[57] and two which were built speculatively by John Copeley in 1786.[58]

Eighteenth-century survivals in Silver Street include White Lodge, a striking weatherboarded building with a symmetrical façade and classical doorcase. From 1862 until 1895 it was the home of Joseph Whitaker, founder of *Whitaker's Almanack*.[59] No. 90, with a hipped roof, was built c. 1700, and nos. 60 and 62, a pair south of White Lodge, in the later 18th century. John Sherwen (1749–1826), the physician and archaeologist who is said to have grown the first rhubarb in England, had a house in Silver Street from the 1770s.[60] Baker Street, with the exception of nos. 174 and 278, with their mansard roofs, has lost its 18th-century appearance. Large houses which survived until the 20th century included Fox Hall, north of the Rectory, Lee House, used as a school in the 19th century under the name of Gothic Hall, and Holmwood and Pattensweir, adjacent 18th-century buildings at the corner of Clay Hill.[61] Pettins Ware, recorded in 1686,[62] had been a name for the northern end of Baker Street at the junction of the road leading to Clay Hill. In 1719 Henry Gough, M.P., a director of the East India Company,[63] bought a house there to which c. 1779 his son Richard, antiquary (1735–1809), added a library with a Gothic window and fireplace designed by James Essex.[64] Richard Gough left his topographical material, including two volumes of notes on Enfield,[65] to the Bodleian Library, Oxford, and in 1806 recalled many pleasing hours of research in his native parish.[66] His house, which became known as Gough Park, was demolished in 1899.[67] John Abernethy (1764–1831), surgeon and teacher, and James Rennell (1742–1830), geographer, both retired to houses in Baker Street.[68] The Hop Poles inn at the corner of Lancaster Road was built in 1909 on the site of a weatherboarded building.[69]

Forty Green, near Gough Park, formed a triangular open space at the junction of Baker Street, Carterhatch Lane, and Forty Hill. Richard atte Forteye held an estate in Enfield in the 14th century[70] and houses bordered the green in 1572.[71] Sir Samuel Starling lived in one called Garretts Place in 1635[72] and the White House stood there, together with some shops, in 1686.[73] The area around Forty Green and Forty Hill became fashionable in the 18th century. Brigadier Hall was built on the south side of the green by William Bridger, a former Lord Mayor of London, between 1764 and 1779[74] and Adelaide House was built to the west shortly before 1828.[75] Both have been demolished

[39] See p. 250.
[40] Whitaker, *Enfield*, 233, 312, 321–2, 334.
[41] Whitaker, *Enfield*, 296.
[42] *D.N.B.*; F. G. Hilton Price, *Handbk. of Lond. Bankers*, 66.
[43] Whitaker, *Enfield*, 292.
[44] C. F. Partington, *Nat. Hist. and Views of Lond. and Environs*, ii, facing p. 45.
[45] Ford, *Enfield*, 56.
[46] Whitaker, *Enfield*, 244.   [47] Date on house.
[48] Rocque, *Map of Mdx.* (1754).
[49] M.R.O., L.V. 7/29.
[50] Whitaker, *Enfield*, 238–42.
[51] D.L. 43/7/5.
[52] M.R.O., Acc. 16/8.
[53] Trinity Coll. Cambridge, Estate MSS., box 43.
[54] Ford, *Enfield*, 95.
[55] See p. 250.
[56] Rocque, *Map of Mdx.* (1754).
[57] M.R.O., Acc. 98/22.
[58] M.R.O., Acc. 801/43.
[59] Whitaker, *Enfield*, 112.
[60] *D.N.B.*; J. G. L. Burnby, *John Sherwen and Drug Cultivation in Enfield* (Edmonton Hund. Hist. Soc. 1973).
[61] Whitaker, *Enfield*, 113–26.
[62] D.L. 42/126.
[63] M.R.O., Acc. 531/19; Robinson, *Enfield*, i. 259.
[64] Colvin, *Dict. of Architects*, 200.
[65] Bodl. MS. Gough Mdx. 8–9.
[66] Camden, *Britannia*, ed. Gough, ii. 107.
[67] Whitaker, *Enfield*, 126.
[68] Ibid. 295, 297.
[69] *Enfield Gaz.* 21 Aug. 1970; Whitaker, *Enfield*, 122.
[70] D.L. 43/7/1.
[71] D.L. 43/7/5.   [72] D.L. 42/125.
[73] D.L. 42/126.
[74] M.R.O., Acc. 371/5–6; Ford, *Enfield*, 97.
[75] M.R.O., Acc. 371/88; Whitaker, *Enfield*, 127.

but the Hermitage, dated 1704, survives, with a terrace on the west side of the green called Cottage Place, built in 1833.

On Forty Hill there were houses in 1572[76] near the Little Park, which was first recorded in 1543 as the park of Elsing Hall.[77] The park was later incorporated into the Forty Hall estate and by 1656 had been turned into farmland. The large 16th- or early-17th-century Dower House survives within the Forty Hall estate, where Forty Hall itself was built near the site of an older dwelling between 1629 and 1636,[78] and several houses were erected on the eastern side of the hill in the 18th century, opposite the Forty Hall grounds. Worcester Lodge, of c. 1700, is at the corner of Goat Lane, at the other corner of which the Goat inn stood in 1911[79] before its replacement by an inn of the same name at Forty Green. Elsynge House, with Venetian windows on the ground floor, was built farther north in the late 18th century and the Elms, a large stuccoed house, in the early 19th. Sparrow Hall, at the top of Forty Hill, dates from c. 1787[80] and Clock House, near by, has a late-19th-century façade.[81] George Birkbeck (1776–1841), the founder of mechanics' institutions, lived at Forty Hill after 1824.[82] A church was built in 1835.[83]

Clay Hill existed in 1572 as a small settlement near the bridge over Maiden's brook west of Forty Green.[84] The name presumably derived from a tenement there called Clays and perhaps from William atte Cleye, who was resident in the parish in 1274.[85] The hamlet was reached by a road running from Forty Green through land inclosed by the mid 18th century[86] to enter the Chase at Mores Hatch gate, near the site of St. John's church and the Fallow Buck inn. The area by the bridge later became known as Bull Beggars' Hole.[87] Clay Hill consisted in the 18th century of houses scattered along the road on either side of the bridge for almost a mile.[88] The Rose and Crown, by the bridge in 1686,[89] and the timber-framed Fallow Buck, on the hill to the west, are the oldest surviving buildings. Bramley House, a large 18th-century house east of the bridge, was known as Great Pipers[90] in the 18th century and in 1972 served as a mental hospital. The adjacent Little Pipers, an early-19th-century *cottage orné* with bargeboarded gables, preserves the name of a tenement mentioned, with Great Pipers, in 1572.[91] The Firs, farther east, is 18th-century. Claysmore, a plain stuccoed house in wooded grounds west of the bridge, was built in the early 19th century,[92] extended with a picture gallery designed by John Hill, a local builder, and later

demolished.[93] James Whatman Bosanquet (1804–77), the Biblical chronologist, lived there and was active in local affairs, financing the building of the near-by St. John's church.[94] In 1972 the road which climbed the hill from the bridge to the church was still lined by the gardens of large 18th- and 19th-century houses, although some of the houses themselves, like the early-19th-century Hill Lodge,[95] had disappeared. The Italianate Clay Hill House survived, as did Clay Hill Lodge to the west and Wildwood to the north.

Buildings were scattered on the edge of the Chase near Mores Hatch gate and Whitewebbs in 1572[96] and formed a small group at Whitewebbs in 1656.[97] The King and Tinker inn and some houses still stand alone by the old boundary of the Chase near White Webbs House, which was built on the former Chase to the south.[98] The land north of Whitewebbs Road was inclosed within Theobalds Park in 1611 and later turned over to farming. It can be distinguished from the Chase itself by its old farmhouses, the most noteworthy being the Glasgow Stud farm-house, a 17th-century gabled building with an elaborately carved contemporary fireplace.[99] White Webbs farm-house, 18th-century and with a hipped roof, stands about ½ mile farther east.

Cockfosters, mentioned in 1524,[1] was the only hamlet in the western part of the parish before the inclosure of the Chase. The settlement was isolated on the edge of the woodland about half way along the road between Southgate (Edmonton) and Potters Bar (South Mimms). Edmund Kendall of Lincoln's Inn lived in a house called Cockfosters in 1613[2] and there was a small group of houses in 1754, the largest of which was Buckskin Hall[3] on the East Barnet boundary west of the later Chalk Lane. Renamed Dacre Lodge,[4] in 1884 it was a plain stuccoed building reputedly on the site of a hunting box of James I[5] and after a fire in 1895 it was rebuilt.[6] Norrysbury, to the north, was said in 1890 to stand near the site of Norris Farm, an outlying part of Elsing manor.[7] The only large house within the tongue of the parish which projected south of Cockfosters was Mount Pleasant, or Belmont, on the East Barnet boundary on the site of the residence of the antiquarian Lord William Howard (1563–1640).[8] The Cock inn existed in 1798[9] and a church from 1839 but mid-19th-century Cockfosters was still a remote hamlet.[10]

The hamlet of Bull's Cross, Bedelescrosse in 1465,[11] grew up by the cross roads east of Whitewebbs. Its chief buildings were the manor-houses of Goldbeaters and Honeylands[12] and a house called

[76] D.L. 43/7/5.
[77] See p. 226.
[78] See p. 227.
[79] Whitaker, *Enfield*, 133.
[80] M.R.O., Acc. 262/1/36b.
[81] Whitaker, *Enfield*, 139.
[82] Ibid. 299.
[83] See p. 247.
[84] D.L. 43/7/5.
[85] *P.N. Mdx.* (E.P.N.S.), 73.
[86] Rocque, *Map of Mdx.* (1754).
[87] Whitaker, *Enfield*, 149.
[88] Rocque, *Map of Mdx.* (1754); Enfield Incl. Map.
[89] D.L. 42/126.
[90] Robinson, *Enfield*, ii. 254.
[91] D.L. 43/7/5.
[92] Ford, *Enfield*, 57.
[93] Tuff, *Enfield*, 34, 62.
[94] *D.N.B.*; Whitaker, *Enfield*, 303–4; see below, p. 248.

[95] Pevsner, *Mdx.* 52.
[96] D.L. 43/7/5.
[97] M.P.C. 145.
[98] See p. 230.
[99] Min. of Town and Country Planning, List of Bldgs. (1949).
[1] *P.N. Mdx.* (E.P.N.S.), 73.
[2] *Mdx. Sess. Recs.* i. 172.
[3] Trinity Coll. Cambridge, Estate MSS., Enfield survey and map.
[4] Whitaker, *Enfield*, 265 and n; O.S. Map 6″, Mdx. VII. NW. (1897 edn.).
[5] B.M. Maps 137 a.2(10).
[6] *Kelly's Dir. Mdx.* (1908).   [7] Ibid. (1890).
[8] *D.N.B.*; Whitaker, *Enfield*, 285.
[9] Bodl. MS. Top. Mdx. b.1, f. 91.
[10] Thorne, *Environs*, i. 185.
[11] M.R.O., Acc. 903/125.
[12] See pp. 228–9.

the Dairy House, described as very ancient *c.* 1656, whose site is unknown.[13] There were two new cottages at Honeylane corner in 1572 and other houses along the later Bullsmoor Lane.[14] The Pied Bull, a timber-framed inn surviving in 1974, existed in 1752[15] and Bullsmoor Place, the house of Col. Thomas Boddam, in 1800.[16] The hamlet consisted in 1972 of a few scattered houses and terraced cottages surrounded by agricultural land. Another cluster of houses grew up about ¼ mile farther south, at the junction of Bull's Cross with Turkey Street. Bowling Green House, on the west side of the road, was conveyed to Daniel Parker, a London pewterer, in 1678[17] but had been demolished by 1823.[18] Myddelton House, in 1972 the headquarters of the Lee Valley regional park authority, was built on an adjoining site in 1818 by Henry Carington Bowles to the designs of Messrs. Ferry and Wallen of Spital Square (Stepney)[19] and extended before 1873.[20] On the east side of the road are Winterton Lodge, an early-19th-century stuccoed building later divided into three, and Garnault, a mid-19th-century Italianate house. Some 19th-century cottages and a late-17th-century house form an extension of the hamlet along the road sloping down to Maiden's brook, which acts as a natural boundary between Bull's Cross and Forty Hill to the south.

Turkey Street ran eastward across open fields from the wooded hills around Forty Hill and Bull's Cross to Hertford Road. Along the street was one of the main pre-19th-century settlements, containing ten houses in 1572, two of them new and another belonging to a London brewer.[21] A house called Sweeting existed in 1658[22] and the Plough inn, later rebuilt, by 1752.[23] In 1754 the cottages in Turkey Street formed a group near the inn, a little to the east of the bridge over the New River.[24] In the mid 19th century the only substantial house was the 18th-century Roselands, belonging to the Jones family,[25] whose grounds from 1968 were occupied by the upper school of St. Ignatius's college. In 1972 a row of small houses of *c.* 1800, the central pair with a mansard roof, survived on the south side of the street amid extensive modern building.

The hamlet of Enfield Wash grew up at the eastern end of Turkey Street, where Hertford Road forded Maiden's brook.[26] Grove House, in large grounds near the junction with Turkey Street, was built in the 18th century[27] and demolished between 1920 and 1935.[28] It was visited by the artist Thomas Rowlandson (1756–1827), a close friend of the owner Matthew Michell, a London banker.[29]

Freezy Water farm, commemorated in the name of a modern district, lay to the north in 1768.[30] Enfield Wash was so named in 1675[31] but more commonly known as Horsepool Stones until the 18th century,[32] by which time it marked the northernmost end of a line of houses scattered along Hertford Road for about 1½ mile.[33]

Enfield Highway, south of Enfield Wash, by 1754 was the name of a settlement where houses stood closely together along Hertford Road, between Hoe Lane and Green Street.[34] The hamlet was called Cocksmiths End in 1572[35] and again in 1658, when it contained a house called Drakes.[36] It extended eastward towards the marshes along Green Street, where thirteen houses were recorded in 1572,[37] and included a house called Mitchells in 1742.[38]

The north-east part of Enfield parish, in contrast to the hillier country west of the open fields, possessed few large houses. In 1658 traffic along Hertford Road was served by the Chequers inn at Horsepool Stones and the Four Swans at Cocksmiths End[39] and in 1752 by the Sun and Woolpack, the Fox and Crown, the Bell, the Red Lion, and the Black Horse,[40] all later rebuilt. St. James's church, the façade of the Bell, and some villas in Hertford Road, among them nos. 372, 472–4, and 651, survive from the early 19th century amidst later suburban housing.

Ponders End stood on Hertford Road about ½ mile south of Enfield Highway, separated from it by the old manorial lands of Durants and Suffolks. Probably the name derived from John Ponder (fl. 1373), whose own family may have held land on the border of Enfield and Edmonton *c.* 1200.[41] In 1572 the settlement contained a mansion belonging to Richard Gaywood of London, a new cottage in Bungeys Lane (later Lincoln Road), and some houses along South Street, which led eastward towards the Lea.[42] A large 16th-century house called Lincoln House was reputedly the residence of William Wickham, bishop of Lincoln and later of Winchester, from 1577 to 1594[43] and of Henry Fiennes, earl of Lincoln (d. 1616).[44] The house was much altered in the early 19th century[45] and was severely damaged by fire before 1873.[46] In 1972 an early-19th-century stuccoed villa called Lincoln House stood on the corner of Lincoln Road. Eagle House, later demolished, was built near by *c.* 1750 by Richard Darby of Gray's Inn.[47] The Goat, Two Brewers, and White Hart inns existed in 1752.[48] A hamlet called Scotland was mentioned in 1607[49] and there were some houses at Scotland Green, a little to the

[13] M.R.O., Acc. 16/8.
[14] D.L. 43/7/5.
[15] M.R.O., L.V. 7/29.
[16] Sales parts. *penes* Enfield libr.
[17] M.R.O., Acc. 39/1023–4.
[18] Robinson, *Enfield*, i. 269.
[19] Ibid. 270.
[20] Ford, *Enfield*, illus. facing p. 76.
[21] D.L. 43/7/5.
[22] M.R.O., Acc. 16/4.   [23] M.R.O., L.V. 7/29.
[24] Rocque, *Map of Mdx.* (1754).
[25] Ford, *Enfield*, 88–9; O.S. Map 6", Mdx. II. SE. (1868 edn.).
[26] *P.N. Mdx.* (E.P.N.S.), 73. For the ford, see above, p. 209.
[27] Sales parts. *penes* Enfield libr.; Trinity Coll. Cambridge, Estate MSS., Enfield survey and map.
[28] O.S. Map 6", Mdx. II. SE. (1920 and 1935 edns.).
[29] J. Hayes, *Rowlandson, Watercolours and Drawings*, 11, 20, 23.

[30] Bodl. MS. Gough Mdx. 9, f. 18v.
[31] *P.N. Mdx.* (E.P.N.S.), 73.
[32] e.g. D.L. 43/7/5; M.R.O., Acc. 133, f. 48.
[33] Rocque, *Map of Mdx.* (1754); Enfield Incl. Map.
[34] Rocque, *Map of Mdx.* (1754).
[35] D.L. 43/7/5.
[36] M.R.O., Acc. 16/4.
[37] D.L. 43/7/5.
[38] M.R.O., Acc. 133, f. 59.
[39] M.R.O., Acc. 16/4.
[40] M.R.O., L.V. 7/29.
[41] *P.N. Mdx.* (E.P.N.S.), 74.
[42] D.L. 43/7/5.
[43] *D.N.B.*; Whitaker, *Enfield*, 157–8.
[44] Lysons, *Environs*, ii. 304–5.
[45] Robinson, *Enfield*, i. 252.
[46] Ford, *Enfield*, 97.
[47] Whitaker, *Enfield*, 159.
[48] M.R.O., L.V. 7/29.
[49] M.R.O., Acc. 16/5, f. 2.

north of South Street, in 1754.[50] Romantic drawings of derelict cottages at Scotland Green, with others at Bull's Cross and Green Street, were published by J. T. Smith of Edmonton in 1797.[51]

The hamlets along Hertford Road marked the eastern limit of settlement until the 19th century. A few farmhouses stood alone amid the open fields, with the moated manor-houses of Durants and Elsing,[52] but there were no buildings on the marshy ground by the Lea, apart from those connected with river traffic, like the flour mill at the end of South Street[53] and the Swan and Pike inn farther north at Enfield Lock. An arms factory which was opened at Enfield Lock c. 1804 had cottages for 2 foremen and 60 workers by 1828[54] but did not lead to rapid growth until its own enlargement, as the Royal Small Arms factory, in 1854.[55]

The western half of the parish, comprising the former Chase, also remained very thinly populated before 1830. Some small encroachments made in the 18th century and earlier, notably by main roads near Monken Hadley and Potters Bar, were said in 1767 to be of little value, consisting only of labourers' wooden cottages on small plots.[56] Inclosure did not radically alter the pattern of settlement within the former Chase but it wrought great changes on the landscape: scarcely any trees were left by 1823[57] and the remaining patches of woodland were largely confined to the estates of Trent Park and other seats which had been built after inclosure. New buildings included the farm-houses of Holly Hill and Ferny-hill farms, which survive, Home Villa[58] and other early-19th-century villas on the Ridgeway, and isolated houses like Owls Hall at Crews Hill. A small hamlet grew up at the junction of the Ridgeway and East Lodge Lane. By 1819 it was called Botany Bay, probably to emphasize its remoteness,[59] and by 1868 it consisted of a few brick cottages and a farm-house.[60]

Despite the emptiness of the Chase, Enfield until the later 19th century contained more inhabitants than Edmonton or Tottenham. In 1547 the parish had 1,000 communicants[61] and in 1642 the pro-testation oath was taken by 496 adult males.[62] In 1676 there were 1,489 conformists, 1 papist, and 10 other nonconformists.[63] The population increased from 5,581 in 1801 to 6,636 in 1811 and 8,227 in 1821 but thereafter rose less steeply to reach 9,453 by 1851.[64] Enfield Town ward or quarter was the most populous in 1642, with 179 adult males, followed by Bull's Cross with 112, Horsepool Stones (otherwise Green Street or Enfield Highway) with 97, Ponders End with 65, and Parsonage with 43.[65] By 1811, when there were only four divisions, as many as 3,055 persons were in Enfield Town, which

included Baker Street, Clay Hill, and the eastern edge of Chase Side; 1,698 lived in Green Street and Ponders End ward, in the south-east of the parish, 1,048 in Chase and 835 in Bull's Cross wards.[66]

GROWTH AFTER 1850. The opening of the branch line to Enfield Town in 1849 led to several proposals for new housing. Residents, however, proved hard to attract and in the 1850s the population of the old parish, excluding Forty Hill and Enfield Highway, declined from 6,990 to 6,543, although the number of houses rose.[67] Slow progress was made by the National Freehold Land Co., the first to draw up a plan, which bought market gardens west of London Road in 1852 and offered free season tickets to London to the purchasers of 'first and second rate' houses.[68] Four streets were laid out and named Essex, Cecil, Raleigh, and Sydney roads, to advertise the Elizabethan associations of the area. The land was divided into 462 plots and in 1854 proposed prices ranged from £400 for detached houses in London Road to £100 for terraced cottages in Raleigh Road.[69] The estate was called Enfield New Town in 1859,[70] when two rows of cottages were built in Raleigh Road,[71] but in Sydney Road plots remained available in 1865[72] and houses were still under construction in 1874.[73] When completed, the estate consisted mainly of detached houses in London Road, semi-detached villas in Cecil, Essex, and Sydney Roads, and terraces farther west in Raleigh Road.

Other new building near Enfield Town was similarly delayed. The Conservative Land Society bought a small estate on the south side of Southbury Road by Oldbury Moat c. 1854 and laid out Burleigh, Queen's, and Stanley roads. An offer of free season tickets was fruitless, by 1868 only two houses had been built,[74] and in 1897 the streets had still to be completed.[75] Meanwhile the North London Society bought Gordon House, demolished it, and laid out roads. Nothing had been built by 1858[76] but there were houses in Halifax and Gordon roads by 1868.[77] An extension of the estate was planned in the 1880s[78] and houses were being built in Gordon Hill, on the site of Gordon House itself, in 1894.[79] On the Bridgen Hall estate, at the foot of Forty Hill, Ridler, Bridgenhall, Morley, and St. George's roads had been laid out by 1866,[80] when 63 plots were offered for sale,[81] but the roads were not fully built up until after the First World War.[82]

Growth in the eastern part of the parish in the 1850s was stimulated both by factories and by the opening in 1840 of a station in South Street to serve Ponders End. The Royal Small Arms factory was

[50] Rocque, *Map of Mdx.* (1754).
[51] J. T. Smith, *Remarks on Rural Scenery* (1797).
[52] Bodl. MS. Gough Mdx. 8, f. 36v.; see p. 226.
[53] See p. 236.
[54] *Jnl. Soc. Army Hist. Research*, xii. 199.
[55] See below, p. 238.
[56] Lease bk. *penes* Duchy of Lanc. Office; see pp. 261, 278.
[57] Robinson, *Enfield*, i. 224.
[58] Sales parts. *penes* Enfield libr.
[59] *P.N. Mdx.* (E.P.N.S.), 74–5.
[60] O.S. Map 6", Mdx. II. SW. (1868 edn.).
[61] E 301/34/184.   [62] H.L., Mdx. Protestation Rets.
[63] Wm. Salt Libr., Stafford, Salt MS. 33, p. 40.
[64] *Census*, 1801–51.   [65] H.L., Mdx. Protestation Rets.
[66] *Census*, 1811. The ward boundaries are described in Tuff, *Enfield*, 33.

[67] *Census*, 1851–61.
[68] Tuff, *Enfield*, 211.
[69] M.R.O., Acc. 525/5.
[70] *Meyer's Enfield Observer*, 1 Feb. 1859.
[71] Dates on Rose and Laura cottages.
[72] Sales parts. *penes* Enfield libr.
[73] Date on Home Villas.
[74] Tuff, *Enfield*, 212; O.S. Map 6", Mdx. VII NE. (1868 edn.).
[75] O.S. Map 6", Mdx. VII. NE. (1897 edn.).
[76] Tuff, *Enfield*, 212.
[77] O.S. Map 6", Mdx. VII. NE. (1868 edn.).
[78] Whitaker, *Enfield*, 91.
[79] Ex inf. Enfield L.B., Land Charges Dept.
[80] O.S. Map 1/2,500, Mdx. VII. 3 (1866 edn.).
[81] Sales parts. *penes* Enfield libr.
[82] O.S. Maps 6", Mdx. VII. NE. (1897 and later edns.).

enlarged in 1854 while in South Street Baylis's crape works employed nearly 200 people by 1858.[83] The population of the ecclesiastical district of St. James, Enfield Highway, which included Ponders End and Enfield Wash, trebled from 1,534 in 1851 to 4,954 in 1861, the increase being attributed to expansion at the small arms factory. By 1871, when the factory's work-force had again increased and a jute factory had opened at Ponders End, the population had risen to 8,027.[84]

An estate attached to Ponders End mill (later Wright's flour mill) was put up for sale in 1853 and some land west of Ponders End station divided into building lots.[85] Alma, Napier, and New roads were laid out there and by 1868 terraced housing stretched down one side of New Road. Farther north more people settled at Enfield Highway and Enfield Wash, both along Hertford Road and new branch roads. The houses included cottages built in East Road in 1859 and Amelia and Alpha cottages, dated 1859, and Rose Cottages, dated 1867, in Hertford Road. By 1868 there were houses in Jasper, St. James's, and Grove roads.[86]

East of Enfield Wash, between the railway and the Lea, builders catered largely for employees at the Royal Small Arms factory. A terrace called Government Row was constructed on the east bank of the Lea Navigation in the shadow of the factory, while farther west in Ordnance Road officers were accommodated in large, semi-detached stuccoed houses.[87] Near by both Medcalf Road, laid out in 1861,[88] and Warwick Road were lined with terraces by 1865.[89] The area near the factory acquired a character and life of its own, isolated from the rest of the parish and with its own church, school,[90] and two public houses, the Greyhound and the Royal Small Arms.

North of Enfield Wash the 33-acre Putney Lodge estate was conveyed by James Bennett to the British Land Co. in 1867. Mandeville, Totteridge, and Putney roads had been laid out by 1867, when 296 building plots were for sale,[91] and 6-roomed houses were offered in 1869, when the proximity of the Royal Small Arms factory was stressed.[92] Plots were still available in 1893[93] but the estate was almost completely built up by 1897.[94] In 1887 the Standard Freehold Land Co. of Woolwich (Kent) sold plots in Standard Road, near Enfield Lock (formerly Ordnance Factory) station; they were bought by a builder from Kilburn[95] and the street had been built up by 1897.[96] A large tract south of Ordnance Road was acquired for building after the sale of Woodham Connop's lands in eastern Enfield in 1869 but little building took place until the 20th century.[97]

Building began to spread rapidly northward from Enfield Town in the 1870s. Houses were under construction around Lancaster (formerly New) Road in 1869, when Woodham Connop's land near by was offered for sale.[98] The popularity of the area was enhanced by the opening of the G.N.R.'s branch to Enfield in 1871, the shortening of the G.E.R.'s route from Enfield Town to London in 1872, and the introduction of cheap fares. In St. Andrew's parish, excluding the new parishes of St. John, Clay Hill, and Christ Church, Cockfosters, the population rose from 5,087 in 1871 to 11,033 in 1891.[99] The Birkbeck Freehold Land Society bought some of the Connops' land north of Lancaster Road and by 1887 had laid out ten streets, including Birkbeck Road and Morley Hill, with kerbed footpaths and full drainage. The estate, initially called 'New Enfield', was about a mile from each of the railway stations in Enfield Town but in 1897 many of the plots remained empty, despite the society's earlier claim that there was a demand for cottage property.[1] More houses were built near the Birkbeck estate at the end of the 19th century, also for the working or lower middle class. By 1896 Rosemary and Primrose avenues had been laid out to the east, and Gloucester, Brodie, and Burlington roads to the west. More streets, with similar terraces, were built on both sides of Lancaster Road between 1896 and 1913.[2] Park farm, stretching north from Phipps Hatch Lane to Clay Hill, was advertised for building in 1909, when Gordon Hill station on the G.N.R.'s Hertford extension was shortly to be opened.[3] The estate, however, was acquired by Enfield U.D.C. and opened as a public park in 1911.[4]

Bush Hill Park, south of Enfield Town, was offered for sale in 1871.[5] The land, advertised as suited for small houses and close to railway stations,[6] was bought by the Bush Hill Park Co., whose fortunes were said in 1911 to have fluctuated.[7] When the estate eventually was built, it was not socially homogeneous; west of the Enfield Town railway line there were detached houses, many of them gabled and tile-hung, in large gardens along tree-lined streets, while to the east terraces in straight lines followed the pattern set by the land societies' estates elsewhere in Enfield. Housing spread rapidly after the opening of the G.E.R.'s Bush Hill Park station in 1880.[8] Main Avenue east of the station, and the streets leading off it to the north, had been built up by 1897,[9] Millais Road in 1899, Poynter Road in 1901–3, and Landseer Road in 1903.[10] West of the railway houses stood in Wellington, Village, and Private roads by 1897;[11] no. 8 Private Road, designed by Arthur H. Mackmurdo c. 1883, is notable for its flat roof and other advanced architectural features.[12]

Building on former Chase land near Windmill Hill and the Ridgeway was also encouraged by the

[83] See p. 238.
[84] Census, 1851–71.
[85] M.R.O., Acc. 311/44.
[86] O.S. Maps 6", Mdx. VII. NE.; II. SE. (1868 edn.).
[87] Enfield Arch. Soc., Ind. Arch. in Enfield, 12.
[88] Date plaque at entrance to street.
[89] M.R.O., Acc. 704/3, /5, /9.
[90] Ind. Arch. in Enfield, 12; Jnl. Soc. Army Hist. Res. xii. 203 (plan); see below, pp. 238, 249, 254.
[91] M.R.O., Acc. 704/9, /19.
[92] Ibid., Acc. 686/1–4.   [93] Ibid., Acc. 704/10.
[94] O.S. Map 6", Mdx. II. SE. (1897 edn.).
[95] M.R.O., Acc. 704/9.
[96] O.S. Map 6", Mdx. II. SE. (1897 edn.).
[97] M.R.O., Acc. 704/10; see below, p. 222.
[98] M.R.O., Acc. 727/168.

[99] Census, 1871–91.
[1] Sales parts. penes Enfield libr.; O.S. Map 6", Mdx. VII. NE. (1897 edn.).
[2] O.S. Maps 1/2,500, Mdx. VII. 3 (1896 and 1913 edns.); ex inf. Enfield L.B., Land Charges Dept.
[3] M.R.O., Acc. 704/15.
[4] See p. 244.
[5] The house and most of the estate were in Edmonton. See p. 161.
[6] Sales parts. penes Enfield libr.
[7] Whitaker, Enfield, 90–1.
[8] The station was in Edmonton; see below, p. 136.
[9] O.S. Map 6", Mdx. VII. NE. (1897 edn.).
[10] Ex. inf. Enfield L.B., Land Charges Dept.
[11] O.S. Map 6", Mdx. VII. NE. (1897 edn.).
[12] Pevsner, Pioneers of Modern Design (Pelican Bks.), 156.

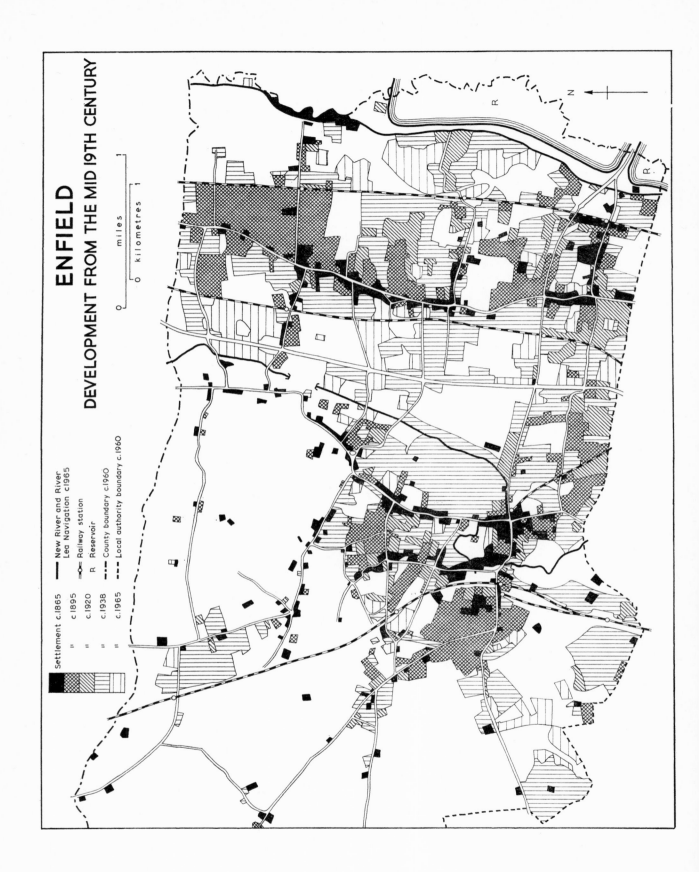

ENFIELD
DEVELOPMENT FROM THE MID 19TH CENTURY

Settlement c.1865
" c.1895
" c.1920
" c.1938
" c.1965

New River and River
Lea Navigation c1965
Railway station
R   Reservoir
County boundary c.1960
Local authority boundary c.1960

miles
kilometres

opening of the G.N.R. station in Enfield in 1871. As in the western part of Bush Hill Park, the houses were mainly for middle-class commuters. The most ambitious plan was that begun in 1879 by A. Culloden Rowan, who constructed Bycullah, Rowan-tree, and Culloden roads on the 54-acre estate of Bycullah Park, a house north of Windmill Hill built in the mid 19th century by J. R. Riddell, a retired Indian Army officer.[13] Detached and semi-detached houses of two types were proposed, one with Gothic porches and the other with tile-hanging and mock timber framing; prospective buyers were told that care had been taken to preserve trees, that the views were good, and the drainage was thorough.[14] Despite the provision of social facilities centred round an 'Athenaeum', progress was so slow that simpler houses were eventually built.[15] By 1897 the estate was complete[16] and in 1972 it preserved a distinct 'garden suburb' appearance, although blocks of flats had replaced many of the original houses. Chase Green Avenue, built in 1880,[17] joined the Bycullah estate to Chase Side.

In the Ridgeway some houses were built in 1882[18] and farther west, in Slades Hill, building land had been advertised in 1879.[19] By 1897 some of the largest houses in the parish, with fine views westward over farm-land, lined the Ridgeway as far as the junction with Holtwhite's Hill.[20] Claypatch, illustrated in 1899,[21] was built to the designs of Sydney W. Cranfield and Ridgemount to those of A. N. Hart,[22] who also designed ornate, tile-hung houses at the top of Windmill Hill in partnership with P. L. Waterhouse.[23] At the southern end of the Ridgeway Uplands Park Road had been built on part of the glebe land by 1896[24] and there were also houses in the adjacent Chase Ridings by 1897. Drapers Road, leading from the Ridgeway to Holtwhite's Hill, had been laid out by 1897, when plots were advertised,[25] although little building took place until c. 1922–5.[26] The demand for villas was said to be unlimited and two short streets at the foot of Holtwhite's Hill, Holtwhite's Avenue and Trinity Street, the second on land owned by Trinity College, Cambridge, were soon filled with terraced houses.[27]

At Hadley Wood, in the extreme west of the parish, growth was linked with the opening of a station on the G.N.R.'s main line in 1885. Charles Jack, tenant of the Beech Hill estate, leased some land north of Camlet Way in 1884 and laid out Crescent East, which had 15 large semi-detached houses by 1888, and Crescent West. Lancaster Avenue had been laid out by 1901 and in 1914 there were about 100 houses in the area, including some along Camlet Way itself.[28] An abortive plan to build

on the grounds of Beech Hill Park was put forward in 1899.[29] Hadley Wood thereafter remained an isolated upper-middle-class neighbourhood, separated by open country from more populous suburbs.

The estate of Chase Park, near Enfield Town, was offered as good building land in 1879, the vendors emphasizing its potential for building. Shirley and Station roads, adjoining the G.N.R. (later Enfield Chase) station, had been divided into lots for building by 1880[30] and were soon lined with terraces but most of the estate was still open in 1897.[31] Along Old Park Avenue, leading southward across the former Enfield Old Park, detached and semi-detached houses with gables and mock timber framing were being built c. 1900.[32] At its southern end similar houses were built in the Chine, the Grangeway, and Old Park Ridings after the opening of the G.N.R.'s Grange Park station in 1910.[33] The area was described as a nascent suburb in 1911.[34]

The centre of Enfield Town began to assume its modern, urban appearance at the end of the 19th century. A row of shops at the corner of London Road, designed by J. S. Moye, was said in 1878 to have greatly enhanced the southern entrance to the town.[35] The Nags Head inn (later demolished) was built shortly before 1883 to designs by Ernest Shum of Bedford as part of a scheme for improving the approach to the station.[36] Lloyds Bank had moved into larger premises in the market-place, designed by Alexander Stenning, by 1893[37] and a new London and Provincial (later Barclays) Bank, of red brick and profusely adorned in the Jacobean manner, was built on the site of the Greyhound in 1897.[38] The King's Head was replaced by a gabled, tile-hung building in 1899[39] and the George had been rebuilt, to incorporate some of the original materials, by 1911.[40] Most of the older shops were also rebuilt c. 1900 and new ones built included Town Parade in Silver Street, dated 1906. The western side of the market-place remained comparatively unchanged until the sale of Burleigh House, 'the finest undeveloped area . . . in the district', in 1913[41] and the south side until the construction of Pearson's department store on the site of the manor-house (Enfield Palace) in 1928.[42] In Church Street the former frontage of Burleigh House was covered with shops, with a cinema to the rear. Farther west Little Park Gardens was laid out after Little Park had been sold to Enfield local board in 1888[43] and newly built houses there were for sale in 1899.[44] Chaseside House, on the opposite side of Church Street, was sold in 1901, after a plan for building on the northern part of the grounds had already been produced.[45] Houses were later built along a western

[13] Whitaker, *Enfield*, 91, 249; poster *penes* Enfield libr.
[14] Poster *penes* Enfield libr.
[15] Whitaker, *Enfield*, 250–1.
[16] O.S. Map 6″, Mdx. VII. NW. (1897 edn.).
[17] Whitaker, *Enfield*, 251.
[18] Ibid. 91.
[19] Sales parts. *penes* Enfield libr.
[20] O.S. Map 6″, Mdx. VII. NW. (1897 edn.).
[21] *Building News*, lxxvii. 361.
[22] Whitaker, *Enfield*, 253–4.
[23] *Building News*, lxxxix. 44; *Builder*, lxxxviii. 518.
[24] M.R.O., Acc. 387/71–2.
[25] O.S. Maps 6″, Mdx. VII. NW. (1897 edn.); sales parts. *penes* Enfield libr.
[26] Ex inf. Enfield L.B., Land Charges Dept.
[27] Sales parts. *penes* Enfield libr.; Trinity Coll. Cambridge, Estate MSS., box 43.

[28] Clark, *Hadley Wood*, 37, 42–3.
[29] Ibid. 42–4.
[30] Sales parts. *penes* Enfield libr.
[31] O.S. Maps 6″, Mdx. VII. NE., NW. (1897 edn.).
[32] Date on houses; *Building News*, lxxix. 501.
[33] Ex inf. Enfield L.B., Land Charges Dept.
[34] Whitaker, *Enfield*, 245.
[35] *Architect*, xx. 114.   [36] Ibid. xxix. 195.
[37] *Building News*, lxv. 269.
[38] Date on building.
[39] Date on building.
[40] Whitaker, *Enfield*, 182.
[41] M.R.O., Acc. 1084/3.
[42] Enfield L.B., *Official Guide* [1970].
[43] See p. 243.
[44] Sales parts. *penes* Enfield libr.
[45] Whitaker, *Enfield*, 225; sales parts. *penes* Enfield libr.

continuation of Cecil Road and shops along Church Street. This southern part of the estate became Enfield Town park, opened in 1903 as the first of several public parks proposed by the U.D.C.[46]

With the exception of the new Bush Hill Park estate, the land on the east side of Enfield Town station was still largely devoted to farming and market gardening in 1897.[47] There was extensive building on both sides of Southbury Road, however, immediately before the First World War, while south of Southbury Road a recreation ground was opened on former market gardens. Housing here preceded the extension of tram services to Enfield Town along Southbury Road in 1911; terraces were being built in Cecil Avenue and Halstead Road in 1901, in Clive Road in 1904, and in Sketty Road from 1903 to 1910.[48] By 1920 the built-up area had reached its easternmost limit at Clive Road.[49]

Growth in the eastern part of the parish before the First World War was less residential than around Enfield Town. Market gardens and other old sources of local employment continued to flourish, while large new industries began to attract a working-class population. Ponders End, which in 1876 retained something of its old gentility,[50] grew rapidly after the opening of the Ediswan electric light factory in 1886. There were some houses in Aden and Suez roads, near the factory, in 1896[51] but few others were built on the marshes east of the G.E.R. line and in 1972 the area was almost entirely industrial.

Most of the new housing at Ponders End was west of the main railway line, to take advantage of the opening of the G.E.R.'s line from Lower Edmonton to Cheshunt in 1891 and the extension of trams along Hertford Road in 1907. New shops, chapels, and halls replaced the weatherboarded and mansard-roofed cottages which had formerly lined Hertford Road, both at Ponders End and farther north at Enfield Highway and Enfield Wash. The first houses in Nags Head Road, on land formerly owned by the Connop family, were built c. 1891 and terraces were also constructed in 1897 and 1907.[52] New houses in Garfield Road were advertised in 1892 as near to Churchbury station, with its excellent service for workmen.[53] Houses were built in Lincoln Road in 1893[54] and Allens, Orchard, and Church roads on the former Allen's farm at the corner of South Street and Hertford Road were planned in 1897, after an earlier scheme had failed.[55] Some houses were built c. 1900 but most of the sites remained vacant until c. 1930.[56] Plots at the eastern end of Nags Head Road were advertised in 1904, when there was said to be a great demand for artisans' houses in the area.[57] By 1914 building had spread north from Nags Head Road to Durants Road, on the former Durants manor house estate, with building plots in King Edward's and Alexandra roads being offered by the

Enfield and District Freehold Land Society.[58] In 1906 the Enfield, Waltham and Cheshunt Building Society planned Southfield, Clarence, and Northfield roads, south of Lincoln Road; some of the land was bought by the General Freehold Land Co. and the streets had largely been built up by 1910.[59] Farther west houses appeared in Norfolk, Suffolk, and Oxford roads c. 1907–8.[60] In 1914 nurseries and market gardens still separated Ponders End from both Enfield Town and Enfield Highway.[61] Larger estates were built in the north-east of the parish at Enfield Wash and Enfield Lock, near the small arms factory.

The General Freehold Land Co. was selling plots formerly owned by the Connop family in Chesterfield Road, south of Ordnance Road, in 1898 and houses were built there and in Beaconsfield, Catisfield, and neighbouring roads from c. 1899 until the First World War.[62] North of Ordnance Road the Rosary estate was mentioned in 1891[63] and there were some houses in Catherine Road in 1897. Forest, Ashton, and Park Roads had been laid out by 1897[64] and two years later the Canning Town, Silvertown and Victoria Dock Freehold Land and Building Co. was selling plots in Forest Road, although none of the roads was fully built up until the period between the World Wars.[65] The United Counties Land, Building and Investment Society acquired an estate near the former Freezy Water farm, west of Hertford Road, in 1881, and laid out Holly, Oakhurst, and Holmwood Roads; several houses had appeared by 1897[66] but there, too, plots remained empty until the 1930s.

Brimsdown station, on the G.E.R. main line, was opened in 1884. There was a scattering of new houses in Green Street and the newly-laid-out Brimsdown Avenue, Osborne Road, and Mayfield Road by 1897,[67] although the roads were not completely built up until after the First World War. Farther west the British Land Co. acquired a small estate east of Hertford Road and was selling plots in Elmore and Riley roads in 1892.[68] Land was also being sold in Connop Road in 1891 and in Albany Road in 1897 and 1901.[69] When houses were planned in Albany and St. Stephen's roads in 1901 Enfield Highway was described as a rapidly increasing district, with a keen demand for artisans' houses and a good service of workmens' trains from Enfield Lock station.[70] To cater for the increased population the U.D.C. opened Albany park in 1902 and Durants park in 1903.

Between 1921 and 1931 the rate of building slackened and the total population rose by only 11·9 per cent, after increases of 20–30 per cent in the twenty years before the First World War.[71] The rate again increased in the 1930s, especially at Enfield Highway, where extensive council housing was

[46] Whitaker, *Enfield*, 225.
[47] O.S. Map 6", Mdx. VII. NE. (1897 edn.).
[48] Ex. inf. Enfield L.B., Land Charges Dept.
[49] O.S. Map 6", Mdx. VII. NE. (1920 edn.).
[50] Thorne, *Environs*, i. 181.
[51] O.S. Map 1/2,500, Mdx. VII. 8 (1896 edn.).
[52] M.R.O., Acc. 704/10; dates on houses.
[53] M.R.O., Acc. 808. The rly. line was closed in 1909: see above, p. 212.
[54] Date on house.
[55] M.R.O., Acc. 179; Acc. 220/2–4.
[56] Ex inf. Enfield L.B., Land Charges Dept.
[57] M.R.O., Acc. 704/15.
[58] Ibid., /16.

[59] Ibid., 704/15; ex inf. Enfield L.B., Land Charges Dept.
[60] Ex inf. Enfield L.B., Land Charges Dept.; O.S. Map 6", Mdx. VII. NE. (1920 edn.).
[61] O.S. Map 6", Mdx. VII. NE. (1920 edn.).
[62] M.R.O., Acc. 704/15; ex inf. Enfield L.B., Land Charges Dept.
[63] M.R.O., Acc. 704/15.
[64] O.S. Map 6", Mdx. II. SE. (1897 edn.).
[65] M.R.O., Acc. 704/15.   [66] Ibid., /14–15.
[67] O.S. Map 6", Mdx. VII. NE. (1897 edn.).
[68] M.R.O., Acc. 704/10–11.
[69] Ibid., /11, /15.   [70] Ibid., /15.
[71] *Census*, 1891–1931.

undertaken. The two largest estates were south of Carterhatch Lane, around Central Avenue, and north of Brimsdown railway station over an area bounded by Bell Lane, Brimsdown Avenue, Croft Road, and Redlands Road. In Hertford Road itself shopping parades replaced earlier, smaller, houses and shops near St. James's church. Residential building on the market gardens was encouraged by the growth of heavy industry along the Lea in Brimsdown, which had been foreshadowed by the opening of the power station there in 1907.[72]

The opening of Great Cambridge Road through the parish in 1923–4 stimulated much private building. East of the road 21 estates, for 2,500 houses, were approved between 1931 and 1937[73] and building continued until 1939.[74] Most of it was carried out by firms from outside Enfield like Newman Eyre of Romford (Essex), who built the 286 houses on the Aylands estate (Ayland, Larmans, Balmoral, and Windsor roads) at Enfield Wash after 1933, and Thomas Blade of Romford, who built the Longfield estate at Enfield Highway (Longfield, Winnington, and Dell roads and the Loning), with 284 houses and 4 shops after 1934. Local builders included Enfield Highway Co-Operative Society, whose Unity estate consisted of 104 houses in Meadway and Crossway after 1934, and Oatlands Estates of Carterhatch Lane, who planned 136 houses in Carterhatch Road, Leyland Avenue, and Sharon Road in 1932. An Enfield architect, Frank Lee, designed the Westmoor estate at Brimsdown in 1937. Private and municipal building radically changed eastern Enfield in the period between the World Wars; by 1939 market gardening had been considerably reduced and the formerly distinct settlements of Ponders End, Enfield Highway, and Enfield Wash had coalesced.[75]

By contrast the old division between Enfield Town and the eastern part of the parish was maintained, since on much of the land along Great Cambridge Road market gardens gave way to industry, playing fields, and schools. Few council houses were built around Enfield Town, where the main area of growth was between Baker Street and the New River. Newman Eyre was allowed to put up 594 houses on 50 a. east of Churchbury Lane in 1934 and another 286 houses to the north in 1935, while E. N. Stephens of Willesden obtained permission for 279 houses on former vicarage glebe land to the south. The grounds of the Rectory, on the other side of Baker Street, had been sold in 1926 and Monastery Gardens built on the site. To the south-west, near Grange Park station, 472 houses and seven new roads comprising the Uplands estate were built by Marshall Estates after 1933.[76]

The south-western corner of the parish changed after the extension of the Piccadilly line in 1933. Cockfosters, in 1911 still described as a charming little village,[77] appeared more suburban with the building of a shopping parade near its new station. Near Oakwood station the South Lodge estate was developed by John Laing & Co. after 1935[78] and

housing covered much of the neighbourhood by 1939.[79] Farther north growth was limited to the Hadley Wood area. By 1929 there were houses, mainly detached, in Wagon Road, as well as along Cockfosters Road on the edge of the Beech Hill estate. Although most of Beech Hill Park became a golf course in 1920 the Greenwood estate, to the west, was sold in 1925 and by 1939 had been covered with about 300 houses. Building spread after the Second World War. Greenbrook Avenue was laid out in 1948 and Covert Way in 1958; Duchy and Kingwell roads were laid out in 1954–5 and Broadgates Avenue was built in 1957.[80]

The loss of the rural character of the former Chase was predicted in 1911, on the building of the G.N.R.'s Hertford extension,[81] and again in 1934, after the Piccadilly line reached Cockfosters.[82] Such fears proved unfounded, largely because of the absence of fast roads and Underground railways from most of the hilly western half of the parish. Suburban building in the former Chase during the 1930s was limited to its southern fringe, to Hadley Wood, and a small estate of 102 houses at Crews Hill built after 1931,[83] while elsewhere farm-land survived. Moreover large areas were acquired as golf courses after the First World War, including those at Crews Hill, bought from Trinity College, Cambridge, after 1915, and others at Bush Hill Park and on the Old Park estate. Crews Hill course, with the Trent Park and Beech Hill estates and a large tract of farm-land south-west of the Ridgeway, by 1934 had been included in a North Middlesex 'green girdle' proposed by the county council.[84] Later they became part of the wider Green Belt, with other portions of the former Chase, and in 1937 Middlesex also bought the bulk of the duchy of Lancaster's estates in the parish, covering 2,000 a., to add to the Belt.[85] Other rural areas, notably the White Webbs and Forty Hall estates, were acquired by the U.D.C. as parks after the Second World War, as was Trent Park.

Growth since the Second World War, restricted by Green Belt legislation, has largely been confined to rebuilding by the council and infilling by private firms. Private builders were particularly active on former nursery-land in the east part of the parish, near Enfield Wash and Ponders End. Prefabricated bungalows were built west of Bull's Cross by the U.D.C. after 1945[86] and later replaced by permanent houses, forming a large estate on both sides of Great Cambridge Road, with a small shopping centre in Kempe Road. Another council estate was built east of Hertford Road at Enfield Highway, around Addison Road, in the 1950s and a later one was built north of Hoe Lane, around Meyer Gardens and Pentrich Avenue. Tower-blocks of flats were erected by Enfield L.B. in the late 1960s on the sites of older terraces west of Ponders End station, at the corner of Hertford and Ordnance roads, in Holbrook Close off Goat Lane, and at the western end of Bell Lane, Enfield Highway. Another large estate of flats was built on the Hundred Acres, a piece of land

[72] See p. 243.
[73] Development files *penes* Enfield L.B.
[74] O.S. Maps 1/2,500, Mdx. VII. 4 (1936 and 1939 edns.).
[75] O.S. Map 1/2,500, Mdx. VII. 4 (1939 edn.).
[76] Development files *penes* Enfield L.B.
[77] Whitaker, *Enfield*, 261.
[78] Development files *penes* Enfield L.B.

[79] O.S. Map 1/2,500, Mdx. VII. 4 (1939 edn.).
[80] Clark, *Hadley Wood*, 45–6, 48–9.
[81] Whitaker, *Enfield*, 272–3.
[82] Briggs, *Mdx. Old and New*, 61.
[83] Development files *penes* Enfield L.B.
[84] Briggs, *Mdx. Old and New*, 61.
[85] Ex inf. Duchy of Lanc. office.
[86] Boro. of Enfield, *Official Guide* [1955].

belonging to the parish in Lavender Hill, in the late 1960s.[87] Another council estate, at Bush Hill Park, was begun after the demolition of Fifth, Sixth, and Seventh avenues in 1974, and many expensive private flats replaced older houses along the Ridgeway.[88]

The sky-line of Enfield Town was greatly changed by the construction of Tower Point, an eleven-storeyed office block covering most of the eastern side of Sydney Road, in the late 1960s and by a tower which was being added to the new civic centre in Silver Street in 1974. Despite such changes and heavy traffic along Church Street, the centre of Enfield retains a remarkable number of old buildings, walled gardens, and leafy walks. Beyond the church and grammar school on the north side of the market-place playing fields, bordered by the New River, form an open space in the heart of the town. From the cross-roads a few yards east of the market-place Silver Street leads northward past a few dignified houses, including the Vicarage amid ancient trees, while Southbury Road heads eastward beside gardens along the New River. At the western end of the main shopping area Church Street crosses the New River by the foot of Windmill Hill. South of the bridge the river separates Town park from Bush Hill Park golf course, a green tract stretching to Bush Hill on the old Edmonton boundary. North of the bridge it passes between Gentleman's Row and Chase Green gardens, where houses, cottages, and foot-paths recall Enfield as it was in the late 18th and early 19th centuries.

The population of the parish rose from 9,453 in 1851 to 12,424 in 1861, 16,054 in 1871, and 19,104 in 1881, and then more rapidly to 31,803 in 1891, 42,738 in 1901, and 56,338 in 1911. It had reached 60,738 in 1921, 67,874 in 1931, and a peak of 110,465 in 1951, but was only 109,542 in 1961.[89]

MANORS. The manor of *ENFIELD* was held by Ansgar the staller in 1066 and by Geoffrey de Mandeville in 1086.[90] It passed to Geoffrey's son William, to his grandson Geoffrey, earl of Essex (d. 1144), and then in turn to the earl's sons Ernulf, Geoffrey, earl of Essex (d. 1166), and William, earl of Essex (d. 1189). William was succeeded by his aunt Beatrice de Say, but in 1190 his lands were granted to Geoffrey fitz Piers, who had married her grand-daughter Beatrice and who was created earl of Essex in 1199.[91] Geoffrey was succeeded in 1213 by his son Geoffrey, who took the name Mandeville and was in possession of Enfield, as part of the honor of Mandeville, in 1214.[92] The younger Geoffrey was succeeded in 1216 by his brother William, who died,

also without issue, in 1227.[93] William's widow Christine was granted the manor in 1227, when she married Raymond de Burgh,[94] but died childless in 1232, whereupon seisin was granted to Roger of Dauntsey, second husband of William de Mandeville's last surviving sister Maud, countess of Hereford, pending the decision in a suit for their divorce.[95] Livery of Maud's lands was finally granted to Roger of Dauntsey shortly before his wife's death in 1236, after which it was granted to Maud's son and heir, Humphrey de Bohun, earl of Hereford and Essex.[96]

Humphrey de Bohun, to whom the manor was confirmed in 1266,[97] was succeeded in 1275 by his grandson Humphrey,[98] whose son and namesake succeeded in 1298. In 1299 the manor was held in chief, as of the honor of Mandeville, as $\frac{1}{4}$ knight's fee,[99] and in 1302 it was included in a settlement on the earl's marriage to Edward I's daughter Elizabeth.[1] In 1322 Humphrey was succeeded by his son John (d. 1336), during whose minority the manor was held by the king and, after 1325, by the bishop of Exeter.[2] John was succeeded by his brother Humphrey (d. 1361),[3] whose nephew and successor Humphrey came of age in 1363.[4] Humphrey died in 1373 without male issue and the manor was assigned in dower to his widow Joan (d. 1419).[5] After her death[6] it was in the hands of Henry V,[7] whose father, as earl of Derby, in 1384 had married Mary, younger daughter and coheir of Humphrey, last de Bohun earl of Hereford.[8] By a final partition of Earl Humphrey's estates between the descendants of his daughters in 1421, the manor was assigned in purparty to the king,[9] who in 1422 granted it to Queen Catherine in dower.[10]

After 1421 the manor remained with the duchy of Lancaster, except during the Interregnum.[11] Enfield was successively granted in dower during the 15th century to Margaret of Anjou, wife of Henry VI, and Elizabeth Woodville, wife of Edward IV.[12] In 1550 it was granted by Edward VI to his sister Elizabeth for life.[13] It was leased in 1484[14] and often thereafter; the lease was acquired in 1742 by James Brydges, duke of Chandos (d. 1744), and remained in his family until 1795.[15]

A capital messuage with a dovecot existed in 1299[16] and the earl of Hereford was licensed in 1347 to crenellate his manor-house.[17] A house called the manor of Camelot, presumably at Camlet Moat in Enfield Chase, was demolished in 1440 to raise money for repairs to Hertford castle; apart from the foundations of a bridge over the moat, no trace of the building has been discovered.[18] Another house, called the manor-house, was leased in 1439, when rooms over and near the gateway were reserved for

87 *The Times*, 8 Feb. 1966.
88 Ex inf. Mr. A. H. Hall.
89 *Census*, 1851–1961.
90 *V.C.H. Mdx.* i. 126.
91 *Complete Peerage*, v. 115–24.
92 Ibid. 126; *Cur. Reg. R.* vii. 110–11.
93 *Complete Peerage*, v. 130–2.
94 Ibid. 133 n.; *Rot. Litt. Claus.* (Rec. Com.), ii. 179.
95 *Close R.* 1231–4, 81, 85, 96; *Complete Peerage*, v. 134.
96 *Complete Peerage*, v. 134; vi. 460.
97 *Cal. Pat.* 1258–66, 543.
98 For the descent of the earldom of Hereford from 1275 until 1373, see *Complete Peerage*, vi. 462–73.
99 *Cal. Inq. p.m.* iii, p. 424.
1 *Cal. Chart. R.* 1300–26, 33.
2 *Cal. Fine R.* 1319–27, 365.

3 *Cal. Inq. p.m.* viii, p. 25.
4 Ibid. 473; *Cal. Inq. p.m.* xi, p. 366.
5 *Cal. Close*, 1369–74, 496.
6 *Feud. Aids*, vi. 486; *Complete Peerage*, vi. 474.
7 S.C. 6/915/26.
8 *Complete Peerage*, vi. 477.
9 *Rot. Parl.* iv. 136.
10 D.L. 42/18.
11 *Cal. Treas. Bks.* 1660–7, 53.
12 S.C. 6/1093/14; /1094/8.
13 *Cal. Pat.* 1549–51, 240.
14 D.L. 42/20.
15 Duchy of Lanc. office, index to enrolment bks.
16 *Cal. Inq. p.m.* iii, p. 424.
17 *Cal. Pat.* 1345–8, 450.
18 D.L. 42/18 f. 148v.; *Hist. of King's Works*, ii. 680 n.

the king.[19] Henry VIII stayed at Enfield, presumably at the manor-house, in 1520 and 1527,[20] but later royal visits seem to have been to Elsing Hall, the manor-house of Worcesters, which came into the hands of the duchy of Lancaster in 1539.[21] In 1572 the manor-house, which stood by Enfield Green near the modern market-place, was occupied by John Taylor, together with a moated house called Lockstones Hall,[22] and in 1582 it was leased to Henry Middlemore.[23] It seems to have been the building known after the end of the 18th century as Enfield Palace, a two-storeyed gabled structure of the 16th century with a central block and wings, whose walls were decorated with the initials E.R. (for Elizabeth I or Edward VI).[24] Although the manor-house was leased in 1635, with most of the demesne, to Sir Thomas Trevor (1586–1656), judge,[25] part of it was used as a private school from c. 1670 until the late 19th century.[26] In 1787 a pond, extensive gardens, and part of the palace yard survived.[27] The house had been greatly reduced in size by 1792 and later was partly refaced[28] but the interior retained 'vestiges of former splendour' in 1823.[29] The building was shut in with shops and houses in 1876[30] and was demolished in 1928, having served as a post office and later as a Conservative club, to make way for an extension to Pearson's department store.[31] A panelled room, however, was re-erected in an annexe to no. 5, Gentleman's Row; it contains an elaborate plaster ceiling and a stone fireplace of high quality, both enriched with Tudor emblems.[32]

Property in Enfield held by William de Plessis at the end of the 12th century[33] was probably that conveyed in 1232 by Roger of Dauntsey to his son Richard.[34] Richard de Plessis held ¼ knight's fee of the manor of Enfield in 1235[35] and died in 1289,[36] whereupon his estate was divided between his sisters Aveline, wife of John Durant, and Emme, wife of John Heron.[37] After Aveline's death in 1312[38] her property passed in turn to her son Richard (d. 1333),[39] Richard's son Thomas (d. 1349),[40] and Thomas's daughter Maud, who had married John Wroth by 1353.[41] By 1376 she was again married, to Sir Baldwin Raddington,[42] and in 1381 the manor of

DURANTS PLACE, known subsequently as *DURANTS*, was conveyed to Raddington,[43] at whose death in 1401 it reverted to William, son of John and Maud Wroth.[44] The other portion of Richard de Plessis's lands passed from his daughter Emme to her husband John Heron (d. 1326)[45] and then to his son John, who died without issue in 1335.[46] In 1336 it was divided between Margaret, sister of the younger John Heron, and John Garton, his nephew,[47] a London mercer, who died seised of both portions in 1362,[48] when he was succeeded by his son John. In 1412 John Garton of London held lands in Enfield worth £10,[49] which had been consolidated with the manor of Durants by the end of the 15th century.[50] Meanwhile William Wroth's lands descended in 1408 to his son William (d. 1444) and then to his grandson John (d. 1480).[51]

John Wroth's son and namesake died in 1517 seised of Durants, which had been settled on his eldest surviving son Robert, later attorney-general of the duchy of Lancaster.[52] From Robert the manor passed in 1535[53] to his son Thomas, later Sir Thomas, Wroth (1516–73), the politician, and then to Sir Thomas's son Robert (?1540–1606), who was knighted in 1597.[54] Sir Robert's son, another Sir Robert, of Loughton (Essex) succeeded him and died in 1614, leaving an infant son who died in 1616. John, the younger Sir Robert's brother, died in 1642[55] seised of both moieties of Durants, one of which had been quitclaimed to him by Sir Thomas and Sir Peter Wroth in 1634. John's brother and heir Henry was succeeded in 1652 by his younger son and namesake,[56] later Sir Henry (d. 1671), a royalist and patron of Thomas Fuller.[57] Durants was sold by Sir Henry's trustees in 1672 to Sir Thomas Stringer, the holder in 1686,[58] whose son William in 1723 conveyed it to Richard Darby,[59] who in 1735 gave it to his daughter Margaret, wife of William Underwood.[60] Underwood conveyed it in 1744 to Samuel Child[61] of Osterley Park, Heston (d. 1752); he was succeeded by his son Francis (d. 1763), whose brother Robert conveyed Durants to Robert Dent in 1774.[62] It was conveyed by Dent in that year to John Dawes, by Dawes to Sands Chapman in 1787, and by Chapman to Newell Connop of Penton

---

[19] *V.C.H. Mdx.* ii. 76.
[20] *L. & P. Hen. VIII*, iii, pp. 403, 1543; iv (2), p. 1476.
[21] See below.
[22] D.L. 43/7/5.
[23] Lysons, *Environs*, ii. 284.
[24] Guildhall Libr., print coll.
[25] D.L. 42/125; *D.N.B.*
[26] See p. 257.
[27] M.R.O., Acc. 801/43.
[28] *Ambulator*, 10th edn. (1807), 108; Lysons, *Environs*, ii and plate. An inscription over the door of the room preserved in Gentleman's Row (see below) reads: 'Altered by T. Callaway 1791'.
[29] Robinson, *Enfield*, i, 119 and frontispiece.
[30] Thorne, *Environs*, 175.
[31] Robbins, *Mdx.* 246; Briggs, *Mdx. Old and New*, 66; Whitaker, *Enfield*, 191.
[32] Hist. Mon. Com. *Mdx.* 22–3 and plates 40, 59; Pevsner, *Mdx.* 51.
[33] *Cur. Reg. R.* xiv. 423.
[34] C.P. 25(1)/146/8/95.
[35] *Bk. of Fees*, i. 474.
[36] *Cal. Inq. p.m.* ii, p. 442.
[37] *Cal. Close*, 1288–96, 49–50; *Cal. Inq. p.m.* iii, p. 58.
[38] *Cal. Inq. p.m.* v, p. 192.
[39] Ibid. vii, p. 360.
[40] Ibid. ix, p. 311.
[41] Ibid. x, p. 111–2.

[42] C.P. 25(1)/151/74 no. 533.
[43] C.P. 25(1)/151/76 no. 47.
[44] C 137/171/17.
[45] *Cal. Inq. p.m.* vi, p. 467.
[46] Ibid. vii, p. 462.
[47] *Cal. Close*, 1333–7, 561–3.
[48] *Cal. Inq. p.m.* xi, p. 266; *Cal. Close*, 1339–41, 469.
[49] *Feud. Aids*, vi. 491.
[50] D.L. 30/72/893.
[51] C 140/74/28; Robinson, *Enfield*, i. 144.
[52] C 142/32/31; *Sel. Cases in Star Cha.* (Selden Soc. xxv), p. 202 n.; R. Somerville, *Duchy of Lancaster*, i. 408, 606.
[53] Prob. 11/25 (P.C.C. 36 Hogen, will of Robert Wroth); C 142/57/7.
[54] Robinson, *Enfield*, i. 146; *D.N.B.*; D. O. Pam, *Protestant Gentlemen. The Wroths of Durants Arbour* (Edmonton Hund. Hist. Soc. 1973).
[55] *V.C.H. Essex*, iv. 119.
[56] W. C. Waller, 'Wroth of Loughton Hall', *Trans. Essex Arch. Soc.* N.S. viii. 181, 347–8; C.P. 25(2)/574/1652 Trin. Mdx.
[57] *D.N.B.*
[58] C 6/295/41.
[59] C.P. 25(2)/1037/9 Geo. I Trin.
[60] Robinson, *Enfield*, i. 150.
[61] C.P. 25(2)/1166/18 Geo. II Hil.; *V.C.H. Mdx.* iii. 109.
[62] M.R.O., Acc. 133, p. 79; Lysons, *Environs*, ii. 301.

in Crediton (Devon) in 1793.[63] Newell Connop died in 1831, leaving the manor to his son Woodham (d. 1868),[64] whose widow Emily was lady of the manor in 1874.[65] The manor was later sold to Sir William Jaffray, Bt., of Skilts in Studley (Warws.), in whose name a court was held in 1891; rights were said to be extinct in 1911.[66]

Newell Connop greatly enlarged the Durants estate from 150 a. near the manor-house. In 1787 he bought 285 a. around Enfield Highway and Ponders End, which formerly had belonged to Eliab Breton of Forty Hall,[67] and c. 1792 he bought 462 a. of common-field land in the same area from Charles Bowles.[68] In 1804 he purchased 168 a. from John Blackburn of Bush Hill, Edmonton, bringing his total estate in Enfield to 1,226 a., most of it in the south-east part of the parish.[69] Later purchases included Bury farm, 149 a., in 1818.[70] On Newell Connop's death his estates were divided among his family[71] and on Woodham's death many were sold, with the manor.[72] The copyhold lands in the 18th and 19th centuries consisted of cottages and small parcels in the south of the parish, mostly near Ponders End.[73]

Durants manor-house, a large moated building around a courtyard, stood east of Hertford Road and north of Ponders End. There was a ruined dovecot near by in 1362.[74] After a fire at the end of the 18th century a small farm-house was built on part of the site.[75] The rest of the old structure, including the gate-house, was demolished in 1910.[76]

John, son of Henry of Enfield, held property in 1298, which became the nucleus of the manor of *WORCESTERS*, sometimes called *WORCESTERS AND ELSING HALL*.[77] John of Enfield's son John held land in 1329[78] and died in 1349 seised of 34 a. held in chief as of the honor of Mandeville and 313 a. held of the earl of Hereford.[79] The younger John of Enfield's widow Margaret had married again by 1352[80] and in 1373 Francis, John's son, quitclaimed property in Enfield and Edmonton to Margaret and her second husband John Wroth, citizen of London,[81] who in 1396[82] was succeeded by his son Sir John Wroth (d. 1407).[83] In 1408 the estate was committed to Sir John Tiptoft during the minority of Sir John Wroth's son and namesake[84] but in 1412 John Wroth died seised of the manor, called Wroth's Place.[85] It passed to his sister Elizabeth, wife of Sir William Palton, who in 1413 was succeeded by her cousin Sir John, later Lord, Tiptoft (d. 1443).[86] Tiptoft's son John, later earl of Worcester, was executed in

1470 and his grandson Edward died childless in 1485, whereupon the manor, then called Tiptofts, passed to Philippe Grimston, daughter of John, Lord Tiptoft (d. 1443), and widow of Thomas, Lord Ros (d. 1464), whose son Edmund, Lord Ros, died at Enfield in 1508. The manor passed to Ros's sister Isabel and her husband Sir Thomas Lovell, Speaker of the House of Commons, who had been given custody of the Ros estates in 1492, when Lord Ros was declared insane.[87] Sir Thomas died in 1524, having settled the manor on Thomas Manners (d. 1543), Lord Ros and later earl of Rutland.[88] In 1539 Lord Rutland exchanged the manor, then called Worcesters, with the king for the monastery of Croxton Kerrial (Leics.).[89]

The manor was granted in 1550 to Princess Elizabeth for life.[90] In 1602, as queen, she gave it to trustees for Robert Cecil (d. 1612), later earl of Salisbury.[91] Robert's son William, earl of Salisbury, conveyed it in 1616 to Sir Nicholas Raynton (d. 1646),[92] a haberdasher who became lord mayor of London in 1632. The manor passed to Nicholas's grandson Nicholas (d. 1696), who left it to his daughter Mary, wife of John Wolstenholme, later a baronet (d. 1708). John was succeeded by his sons Nicholas (d. 1716) and William (d. 1723) and then by his daughter Elizabeth, who married Eliab Breton of Norton (Northants.). Breton died in 1785 and in 1787 the manor was purchased from his executors by Edmund Armstrong.[93] When Armstrong died in 1799, it was bought by James Meyer (d. 1826).[94] He was succeeded by his nephew Christian Paul Meyer, whose son James died in 1894; the manor was sold in 1895 to Henry Carrington Bowles Bowles of Myddelton House, whose son Col. H. F. Bowles held it in 1911.[95]

Sir Nicholas Raynton's estate in 1656 included 50 a. surrounding the new manor-house of Forty Hall, 70 a. around the older Enfield House, 427 a. in the common fields,[96] and the former New Park and warren, containing 375 a. Eliab Breton held as many as 1,536 a. in the parish, spreading westward from Forty Hill to Enfield Highway and to the marshes by the Lea,[97] but the lands were split up after his death. James Meyer added 120 a., purchased from Joseph Mellish, to the manor and Forty Hall c. 1800.[98] In 1873 the Forty Hall estate was a compact block of 280 a.;[99] in 1951, when it was bought, with the house, by Enfield U.D.C., it contained 265 a.[1] Some small pieces of copyhold land belonging to Worcesters manor survived in

[63] Lysons, *Environs*, ii. 301; Whitaker, *Enfield*, 43.
[64] M.R.O., Acc. 801/1101–2; Acc. 727/169.
[65] M.R.O., Acc. 133, p. 361.
[66] Ibid. p. 412; Whitaker, *Enfield*, 43–4.
[67] M.R.O., Acc. 801/43.
[68] Ibid. /78–9; see below.
[69] M.R.O., Acc. 801/275; /279; /1046.
[70] Ibid. /1219.
[71] Ibid. /1097–1105.
[72] M.R.O., Acc. 727/168.
[73] M.R.O., Acc. 133.
[74] *Cal. Inq. p.m.* xi, p. 266.
[75] Robinson, *Enfield*, i. 153–7; Guildhall Libr., drawing in illus. edn. of Lysons, *Environs*, ii.
[76] Whitaker, *Enfield*, 161.
[77] *Cal. Pat.* 1292–1301, 354.
[78] Ibid. 1327–30, 410.
[79] *Cal. Inq. p.m.* ix, pp. 169–70.
[80] *Cal. Close*, 1349–54, 445.   [81] Ibid. 1369–74, 546.
[82] C 136/95/19(4).
[83] *Cal. Inq. p.m.* (Rec. Com.), iii. 30g.

[84] *Cal. Fine R.* 1405–13, 97.
[85] C 137/86/25.
[86] *Cal. Fine R.* 1413–22, 43; *Cal. Inq. p.m.* (Rec. Com.), iv. 6, 213; *Complete Peerage*, xii(1), 746.
[87] D.L. 41/42/62; Robinson, *Enfield*, i. 126–7; *D.N.B.*; *Complete Peerage*, xi. 106–7; xii(2), 846.
[88] C 142/41/79.
[89] C 54/419/6; *L. & P. Hen. VIII*, xiv(1), p. 256.
[90] *Cal. Pat.* 1549–51, 240.
[91] M.R.O., Acc. 16/9; D.L. 41/42/62.
[92] Ford, *Enfield*, 70.
[93] Lysons, *Environs*, ii. 296–7; Robinson, *Enfield*, i, pedigree facing p. 140. Sales parts. for Worcesters and Goldbeaters, 1787, are in M.R.O., Acc. 801/43–4.
[94] Lysons, *Environs* (Suppl.), 139.
[95] Whitaker, *Enfield*, 42, 137.
[96] M.R.O., Acc. 16/8.
[97] M.R.O., Acc. 262/1/36b.
[98] Robinson, *Enfield*, i. 235–9.
[99] Ford, *Enfield*, 72.
[1] Boro. of Enfield, *Official Guide* [1962].

1855 at Clay Hill, at Enfield Town, in Baker Street, and near the Ridgeway,[2] but they were enfranchised before the First World War.

The first known manor-house of Worcesters stood in or near Baker Street and survived in 1656;[3] it may have been the capital messuage mentioned in 1412.[4] Queen Margaret of Scotland stayed for two nights in 1516 at Sir Thomas Lovell's house, called Elsing Hall and later Enfield House,[5] which then served as the manor-house of Worcesters and where Lovell lived in splendour.[6] It stood north-east of the later Forty Hall and was said to have been built by John Tiptoft, earl of Worcester,[7] although there were extensive repairs in 1541[8] by James Needham, Clerk of the King's Works, in 1542 in preparation for a Christmas visit by Prince Edward and his sisters, and again under Elizabeth I.[9] The building was of brick, at least in part, and arranged around two courtyards.[10] In 1568 the rooms included a library[11] and there were subsequent references to a hall and a chapel.[12] Elizabeth I stayed at Enfield, presumably at Elsing Hall, in 1561, 1564, 1568, and 1572,[13] and the house remained in the hands of the Crown when Worcesters manor was alienated in 1602. By 1597, however, it was unsound[14] and in 1608 there was a warrant to demolish it and to use the materials for proposed extensions to James I's house at Theobalds (Herts.).[15] Part of the building remained, including the gatehouse and hall,[16] and from 1616 to 1623 Philip Herbert, earl of Montgomery and later of Pembroke (d. 1650), lived there as keeper.[17] The house was conveyed to him in 1641,[18] but in 1656 it was in the hands of Nicholas Raynton.[19] It was demolished, probably soon afterwards, and its site remained hidden until it was excavated in 1963–6.[20]

Forty Hall, which became the manor-house of Worcesters in the 17th century, was built on the site of an earlier house by Sir Nicholas Raynton between 1629 and 1636,[21] but its appearance was much altered c. 1708[22] by the Wolstenholmes. It is a three-storeyed building of restrained classical design, with a square plan and a hipped roof. Early-17th-century features include moulded plaster ceilings, panelling, fireplaces, and the hall screen. The exterior brickwork must have been renewed early in the 18th century, when the present windows were introduced and the roofline was altered. Then and later in the century there was some replanning of the interior necessitating new fittings and decoration, most notably in the entrance hall where the panelling is decorated with plaster cartouches.[23] The centre of the east front and the staircase were remodelled c. 1900. The extensive out-buildings north-west of the house include a large rusticated brick gateway in the Artisan-Mannerist style of the 1630s. In 1787 the innermost courtyard comprised coach houses, stables, barns, a brewhouse and a mill house, while the outer court contained farm buildings. There were pleasure grounds of 12 a. and a park of 159 a.[24] The gabled main lodge was built to the designs of Sydney W. Cranfield after 1903.[25] Conspirators in the Rye House Plot were said to have been concealed in the house by Nicholas Raynton in 1683.[26] Forty Hall, with its grounds, was bought by Enfield U.D.C. in 1951, opened to the public as a museum in 1955, and restored in 1962, when the outbuildings were converted into an exhibition gallery and reception rooms.[27]

Ellis of Suffolk held a house and land in Enfield in 1307,[28] which may have been the nucleus of the manor of SUFFOLKS or COLT'S FARM conveyed, with lands in Essex, by John Norton to Thomas Colt and others in 1459.[29] The manor, called Nortons, was forfeited in 1460 and granted to Henry Fillongley[30] but in 1475 it passed from Joan, widow of Thomas Colt, to her son John.[31] Henry, son of George Colt, held the manor in 1556.[32] George Colt conveyed it in 1578 or 1579 to Sir Robert Wroth of Durants, whose son Robert was seised of it in 1608.[33] John Wroth held the manor in 1635 but in 1686 it was in the hands of Joshua Galliard,[34] in whose family it descended until Mary, daughter of Pierce Galliard, married Charles Bowles of East Sheen (Surr.). In 1792 Bowles sold the manor to Newell Connop, with 462 a. in the common fields and marshes,[35] whereupon the manorial estates, near Ponders End[36] and doubtless including part of the field called Suffolks, were integrated with Connop's lands.[37] Suffolks manor-house probably stood near Suffolks Orchard at Enfield Highway. The site of a farm called Suffolks, on the western side of Hertford Road, was recorded in 1572[38] and a 'desirable residence' was built on Suffolks Orchard shortly before 1869.[39]

The manor of ELSING or NORRIS FARM seems to have originated in a knight's fee in Enfield and Sawbridgeworth (Herts.), held in 1372 by Jordan of Elsing of the earl of Hereford.[40] The fee was held in the mid 15th century by Christine Norris.[41] In 1464 the estate, described as the manor

[2] M.R.O., Acc. 16/16.
[3] M.R.O., Acc. 16/4; /8.　　　　　[4] C 137/86/25.
[5] L. & P. Hen. VIII, ii(1), p. 533.
[6] Hist. MSS. Com. 24, Rutland, iv, pp. 260–2. Lovell's funeral cortège set out for Haliwell priory from Enfield: L. & P. Hen. VIII, iv(1), p. 150.
[7] Norden, Spec. Brit. 19.
[8] Bodl. MS. Rawl. D. 781, ff. 188–207; B.M. Add. MS. 10109, ff. 116–22.
[9] E 351/3200–3203; E 351/3211–3216; E 351/3326 m. 10.
[10] Hist. MSS. Com. 24, Rutland, iv, pp. 282; Enfield Arch. Soc., Site of Elsynge Hall (Research Report i), 13.
[11] Bodl. MS. Rawl. A. 195c, ff. 243v.–251v.
[12] E 351/3215–6.
[13] E. K. Chambers, Elizabethan Stage, iv. 78, 81, 84, 88.
[14] Hist. MSS. Com. 9, Hatfield House, vii, p. 458.
[15] Cal. S.P. Dom. 1603–10, 419.
[16] E 351/3244.
[17] Cal. S.P. Dom. 1611–18, 392, 512; 1619–23, 481; Lysons, Environs, ii. 318–9.
[18] D.L. 42/24.
[19] M.R.O., Acc. 16/8.

[20] Enfield Arch. Soc. Society News, xv (1964), 4.
[21] M.R.O., Acc. 16/8; Hist. Mon. Com. Mdx. 23–4 and plates 61–4; a lead pipe is dated 1629.
[22] Rainwater-head.
[23] Robinson, Enfield, i. 237.
[24] M.R.O., Acc. 801/43.
[25] Building News, lxxxv. 67.
[26] Cal. S.P. Dom. 1683, 263, 339, 349; 1683–4, 48, 282.
[27] Ex inf. Enfield Libr.
[28] C.P. 25(1)/148/38 no. 353.
[29] C.P. 25(1)/293/73 no. 434.
[30] Cal. Pat. 1452–61, 583.　　　　　[31] C 140/531/34.
[32] C.P. 25(2)/83/711/2 & 3 P. & M. East.
[33] C 2/Jas.I/W.16/59.
[34] D.L. 42/125; /126.
[35] Lysons, Environs, ii. 302–3; M.R.O., Acc. 801/78–9.
[36] Lysons, Environs, ii. 303.
[37] See above.
[38] D.L. 43/7/5.
[39] M.R.O., Acc. 727/168.
[40] Cal. Inq. p.m. xiii, p. 143.
[41] Feud. Aids, vi. 583.

of Elsing, was conveyed by John Wood to William Kele, clerk,[42] and in 1521 it was conveyed, as the manor of Norris, by Cecily Sudeby, daughter and heir of Edmund Norris, to John Wilford (d. 1544) and others.[43] John Wilford's son Stephen died in 1567 seised of two thirds of the manor,[44] the remaining third having passed to the Hunsdon family and being held in 1643 by Henry Hunsdon.[45] In 1686 Hunsdon's portion was apparently mortgaged[46] and soon afterwards it ceased to be regarded as a manor. The larger part passed to Stephen Wilford's son John, who held it in 1568, to John's son William in 1605,[47] to John Wilford by 1635, and George, son of Edward Wilford, by 1686.[48] Richard Wilford conveyed the manor in 1707 to John Cotton, who sold it in 1734 to Robert Mackeris (d. 1735).[49] Mackeris devised the manor to his widow Priscilla, who married Thomas Sexton, James Jones, and thirdly James Fenwick, whose son Thomas James Fenwick held the property in 1793.[50] On Thomas James Fenwick's bankruptcy his assignees conveyed the estate in 1804 to Newell Connop, lord of Durants,[51] from whom it descended to Woodham Connop, although a portion was held in 1811 by the heirs of Sarah Pinnock.[52] Part, known as Plantation or Welches farm, was conveyed in 1878 by William Woodham Connop to William Smith of Westbourne Terrace (Paddington), who in 1893 left it to his sons Philip, Arthur, and Henry.[53] In 1911 the farm, containing 120 a., was held by Howard Smith of Ford House, Wolverhampton, and Henry Herbert Smith of Calne (Wilts.); manorial rights were then said to have been extinct for many years.[54]

The manor-house of Norris Farm, mentioned in 1572,[55] was behind a moat in Welches Lane (later Ordnance Road), where Plantation Farm stood in the 19th and 20th centuries. In 1972 the site was covered by a housing estate. A timber-framed house called Norris Farm, probably the old manor-house, was demolished in 1786 and replaced by a plain brick farmhouse,[56] later also demolished. The manorial lands lay in the eastern part of the parish, near Enfield Lock, at Ponders End, and in the common marshes, although there was an outlying portion, separated from the main estate in the 16th century, at Monken Hadley.[57] After inclosure in 1806 the estate was conterminous with Plantation farm, which contained 120 a. in 1911.[58]

Ellis of Honeyland held land in Enfield in 1275,[59] which may later have become part of the manor of *HONEYLANDS and PENTRICHES* or *CAPELS*, which in 1486 was sold by Jane, wife of Sir Thomas Lewknor and widow of Sir John Yonge, to Sir William Capel.[60] In 1546 Sir Giles, Sir Henry, and Edward Capel surrendered the manor to the

Crown[61] and in 1562 Elizabeth I granted it to William Horne, who sold it in the same year to John Tamworth. In 1575 it was in the hands of Thomas Sydney, from whom it was acquired by Sir Thomas Knolles.[62] Knolles conveyed it in 1600 to Sir Robert Wroth of Durants,[63] for whom courts were held in 1611. Courts were held from 1626 to 1632 in the name of William Pennefather, who sold the manor in 1638 to William Avery, who held it until 1694. William Eyre and John Avery were holding courts in 1696 and Norton Avery from 1698 to 1721. In 1724 the manor was sold to Charles Eyre, who held courts until 1745, but Robert Jacomb was lord in 1751 and remained so until 1783, when he conveyed it to William Hart, who conveyed it in 1793 to Rawson Hart Boddam, a former governor of Bombay.[64] The manor was acquired between 1811 and 1815 by James Meyer of Forty Hall and its descent thereafter followed that of Worcesters until 1894, when it was inherited by Meyer's two daughters, Katharine and Mary Colvin Meyer, who were ladies of the manor in 1901.[65] Manorial rights were extinguished soon afterwards. It was claimed in 1794 that the manor was fully independent and free of quit-rents to the manor of Enfield.[66]

The manor-house of Honeylands was leased by the queen to Robert Wroth in 1562[67] and had grounds of 17 a. in 1572.[68] It stood near Bull's Cross and seems to have been demolished in the late 18th century by Robert Jacomb, who built Capel House near North field. Jacomb's house was itself demolished after 1793 by Rawson Hart Boddam, who transferred the name Capel House to his own residence, which had been built north of Bullsmoor Lane[69] by Alexander Hamilton (d. 1761).[70] The new manor-house was 'greatly improved' by Boddam but was sold after his death and in 1823 lay empty.[71] It was purchased in 1840 by James Warren, whose nephew James died there in 1904.[72] From 1971, as Capel Manor, it served as a management centre for Enfield college of technology. Capel Manor is a plain two-storeyed brick building with a frontage which has been extended at each end. A lodge in Bullsmoor Lane is dated 1876. The lands of Honeylands manor were scattered in the common fields and marshes of the north-eastern part of the parish. In 1546 some manorial land lay in Cheshunt (Herts.)[73] and in 1794 the demesne was said to be near the Pied Bull at Bull's Cross.[74] Rawson Hart Boddam held some 200 a. near Capel House but the estate was divided after his death[75] and in 1840 it totalled only 31 a.[76] In 1855 there were a few small parcels of copyhold land at Enfield Wash, at Whitewebbs, in Turkey Street, and in Cheshunt.[77]

The rectorial estate of Enfield, held by the abbots

42 C.P. 25(1)/152/96 no. 7.
43 C.P. 25(2)/27/179/24.
44 C 142/145/60. 45 C 142/698/61.
46 D.L. 42/126.
47 C 60/384/27; C 60/443/65.
48 D.L. 42/125; D.L. 42/126.
49 Lysons, *Environs*, ii. 334.
50 M.R.O., Acc. 801/305. 51 Ibid. /296; /298–9.
52 Lysons, *Environs* (Suppl.), 139.
53 M.R.O., Acc. 704/box 12.
54 Whitaker, *Enfield*, 45–7. 55 D.L. 43/7/5.
56 Robinson, *Enfield*, i. 160–1.
57 M.R.O., Acc. 801/283; Robinson, *Enfield*, i. 159; see above.
58 Whitaker, *Enfield*, 45.
59 C.P. 25(1)/148/26/30.
60 *Cal. Close*, 1485–1500, 35.
61 C.P. 25(2)/52/381 Hen. VIII Trin. no. 38.
62 Lysons, *Environs*, ii. 303.
63 C.P. 25(2)/262/42 Eliz. Hil.
64 Lysons, *Environs*, ii. 303; M.R.O., Acc. 16/1.
65 M.R.O., Acc. 16/1.
66 Ibid.
67 E 310/19/95 f. 50. 68 D.L. 43/7/5.
69 Robinson, *Enfield*, i. 164–5.
70 Ibid. 257; *European Mag.* xlv 1804), 38.
71 Robinson, *Enfield*, i. 257–8.
72 Ford, *Enfield*, 94; Whitaker, *Enfield*, 48.
73 E 318/box 7/238. 74 M.R.O., Acc. 16/1.
75 Robinson, *Enfield*, i. 258.
76 Ford, *Enfield*, 94.
77 M.R.O., Acc. 16/16.

of Walden, was assessed at 63 marks in the mid 13th century[78] and £40 in 1291.[79] It was granted to Sir Thomas Audley, later Lord Audley of Walden, at the Dissolution in 1538,[80] surrendered to the Crown in 1542,[81] and granted to Trinity College, Cambridge, in 1546.[82] The estate, called *RECTORY* manor in 1580, consisted in 1608 of land and houses near Baker Street and Parsonage Lane and the site of the manor, presumably the rectory house, known as Surlow.[83] In 1650 there were 37 a., apart from the rectory house and grounds, and the great tithes were worth £230 a year.[84] When tithes were extinguished in the Chase under the Act of 1777, Trinity College and the vicar received 519 a., mostly west of the duchy lands between the Ridgeway and the road from Enfield Town to East Barnet. In 1803 the college acquired an additional 498 a. between the Ridgeway and Crews Hill, of which 68 a. were soon sold, out of Enfield parish's allotment from the Chase and 535 a. farther east, stretching from Forty Hill to the eastern boundary.[85] Part of the estate was built on at the end of the 19th century and more later became Crews Hill golf course.[86] Rectory manor was said to survive in 1911[87] but the last piece of land, the garden of the rectory house, was sold in 1926.[88]

Both the land and the great tithes were leased out in 1650.[89] The estate was leased in 1721 to Joseph Gascoigne Nightingale, whose daughter and heir married Wilmot Vaughan, earl of Lisburne, the lessee from 1754.[90] Thereafter the Vaughans leased the rectory estate until 1882, when Trinity College assumed direct management.[91] The rectory house, at the corner of Baker Street and Parsonage Lane, was described in 1823 as ancient and of good size.[92] It was two-storeyed, with an early-19th-century garden front of 7 bays, and was demolished in 1928.[93]

The so-called manor of *GOLDBEATERS*, with a house and lands, was conveyed in 1515 by Roger Bendbow to the bishop of London, Sir Thomas Lovell, and others,[94] probably on behalf of the hospital of the Savoy, which held the manor in 1535.[95] At the temporary suppression of the hospital in 1553 the estate, no longer called a manor, was given to the new hospital of Bridewell (London)[96] but in 1572 it was held by Robert Huicke (d. ?1581), Elizabeth I's physician,[97] who lived at Whitewebbs. The land later became part of Bull's Cross farm, totalling 119 a., which belonged to Eliab Breton and was sold after his death, together with the former

manor-house of Goldbeaters, to Joseph Mellish of Bush Hill, Edmonton.[98] On Joseph Mellish's death the farm passed to his nephews John and William Mellish, who sold part of it to Christopher Strothoffe (d. 1801).[99] Strothoffe's widow Elizabeth held it in 1811[1] and later left it to her nephew Richard Glover, who sold the former manor-house to Arthur Windus (d. 1818); in 1823 it belonged to Hester Windus but much of the farm had been absorbed into the Forty Hall estate.[2] The old manor-house stood in the hamlet of Bull's Cross west of the road leading to Enfield Town[3] and was described as ancient in 1656.[4] It had been demolished by 1787, when Christopher Strothoffe was leasing a house at Bull's Cross from the executors of Eliab Breton and was said to have spent a large sum on his estate.[5] The house at Bull's Cross called the Manor House, which belonged in 1911 to Gen. Sir John French (1852–1925), later field-marshal and earl of Ypres, had no connexion with Goldbeaters.[6]

OTHER ESTATES. In 1271 Thorney abbey (Cambs.) acquired from Walter atte Hatch an estate called the chamberlain's fee,[7] which possibly took its name from Richard the chamberlain, whose widow held land in Enfield in 1268.[8] In 1275 the abbey bought land from St. Bartholomew's priory, Smithfield.[9] A house was built by Abbot William of Yaxley and enlarged by his successor William Clopton, who rebuilt its ruined chapel.[10] Rights of pasture in Enfield Chase were confirmed to Thorney by Humphrey de Bohun, earl of Hereford and Essex, in 1348.[11] The abbots' house was leased out at the Dissolution, together with a grove to its south and Rough, Chapel, and Mores Hatch groves.[12] The house was granted in 1540 to Thomas Wroth[13] and in 1635 some of the former abbey's lands, called Cranes, were held by John Wroth of Durants, while 44 a. near Mores Hatch gate were held by William Pennefather.[14] Crane's farm remained part of the Durants estate and in 1795 was held by Newell Connop.[15]

St. Bartholomew's priory, having sold its arable in Enfield to Thorney in 1275, was left with small scattered pieces of pasture, some of which in 1306 lay in Wild marsh.[16] In 1547 a meadow and garden belonging to the priory were granted to the Corporation of London[17] and in 1705 a house and garden in the parish were held by the governors of St. Bartholomew's hospital.[18]

[78] *Val. of Norw.*, ed. Lunt, 359.
[79] *Tax. Eccl.* (Rec. Com.), 17.
[80] *L. & P. Hen. VIII*, xviii(1), p. 410.
[81] E 305/C 58.
[82] *L. & P. Hen. VIII*, xxi(2), p. 342.
[83] Trinity Coll. Cambridge, Estate MSS. box 43 (ct. bk.).
[84] *Home Cnties. Mag.* i. 317–18.
[85] Enfield Chase Act, 17 Geo. III, c.17; M.R.O., Enfield Incl. Award and Map; Robinson, *Enfield*, ii. 352.
[86] See above, p. 223.
[87] Whitaker, *Enfield*, 51.
[88] *Kelly's Dir. Enfield* (1931).
[89] *Home Cnties. Mag.* i. 317–18.
[90] Robinson, *Enfield*, i. 286; Ford, *Enfield*, 296–7.
[91] Ford, *Enfield*, 297.
[92] Robinson, *Enfield*, i. 287–8.
[93] Enfield libr., photographic coll.
[94] C.P. 25(2)/27/178/26.
[95] *Valor Eccl.* (Rec. Com.), i. 358; *V.C.H. Lond.* i. 548.
[96] *Cal. Pat.* 1553, 283–4.

[97] D.L. 43/7/4; Robinson, *Enfield*, i7. 9; *D.N.B.*
[98] Robinson, *Enfield*, i. 241. Sales pas'rts for Worcester and Goldbeaters are in M.R.O., Acc. 801/43–4.
[99] Robinson, *Enfield*, i. 242.
[1] Lysons, *Environs* (Suppl.), 139.
[2] Robinson, *Enfield*, i. 167, 242.
[3] M.R.O., Acc. 801/43.
[4] M.R.O., Acc. 16/8.
[5] See p. 226.
[6] Whitaker, *Enfield*, 49; *D.N.B.*
[7] Camb. Univ. Libr., Add. MS. 3021, ff. 363v.–4, 368.
[8] D.L. 25/18.
[9] Camb. Univ. Libr., Add. MS. 3021, f. 359.
[10] Ibid. ff. 449, 460v.
[11] *Cal. Pat.* 1348–50, 31.   [12] S.C. 12/36/22.
[13] *L. & P. Hen. VIII*, xv, p. 348.
[14] D.L. 42/125.
[15] D.L. 42/126; Lysons, *Environs*, ii. 304.
[16] Webb, *Recs. of St. Barts.* i. 341.
[17] *L. & P. Hen. VIII*, xxi(2), p. 415.
[18] C 78/1502 no. 5.

In 1274 the hospital of St. Mary without Bishopsgate held land in the parish of Adam Durant.[19] In 1338 John Banbury of Hackney gave 33 a. in Hackney and Enfield to the hospital,[20] which in 1538 held 10 a. in Enfield.[21]

William the treasurer (*bursarius*) and others gave land to the priory of Haliwell, Shoreditch, in 1282.[22] Sir Robert Wroth leased 9 a. in Mill marsh from the priory in 1532[23] and John Wroth was granted the land in 1544.[24]

The priory of St. John of Jerusalem held property in the parish *c.* 1324.[25] In 1536 it consisted of 7 a. in Littlefordsey,[26] which were granted in 1544 to John Wroth of Durants.[27]

The Old Park, called the inner park or Frith in 1324,[28] descended with the Chase but was in a neglected state in 1635[29] and was granted *c.* 1650 to Parliamentarian soldiers in lieu of pay.[30] In 1650 it covered 553 a., of which 74 a. were in Edmonton, and contained a brick lodge and an inclosure called the hop garden.[31] The estate was still described as a park in 1661, when it was granted by the duchy to George Monck, duke of Albemarle,[32] but it had been converted to farm-land by 1686.[33] After the death of Christopher Monck, duke of Albemarle (d. 1688), it was granted in 1689 to William Bentinck, earl of Portland (d. 1709),[34] but in 1709 it was held by Christopher Monck's widow Elizabeth, dowager duchess of Montagu (d. 1734),[35] and in 1736, when it had been reduced to 230 a., by Grace, Countess Granville, a kinswoman of the Moncks, who sold it to Samuel Clayton.[36] The estate was augmented in 1779 by 30 a. allotted for loss of common rights in the Chase.[37] In 1823 Old Park was held by Samuel Clayton, nephew of John Clayton,[38] and in 1825 it was bought by Mrs. Winchester Lewis, who had sold a large part by 1834 when she retained Old Park House and 59 a., most of it in Edmonton.[39] In 1873 the estate belonged to Edward Ford, son-in-law of Mrs. Lewis and co-author of a history of Enfield,[40] from whom it passed to his son John Walker Ford, who sold it before 1910.[41] In 1921[42] the house and 125 a. were held by Bush Hill Park golf club.

Old Park House, in 1973 the club-house of Bush Hill Park golf club, was said in 1873 to be comparatively modern and to include only a small part of the lodge mentioned in 1650.[43] The oldest part of the house is a red-brick block of the late 18th century. On the east side are additions in a Tudor style of *c.* 1850 and on the north further additions of the late 19th century, probably replacing the last fragments of the 17th-century house. The grounds contain the remains of a Grecian temple, which stood there in 1910,[44] and an earthwork.[45]

Chase Park estate originated in 34 a. on the eastern side of Old Park near Enfield Town, which were bought from Samuel Clayton by Thomas Cotton in 1811. The land was sold in 1822 to a Mr. Browning, who conveyed it in 1832 to his son-in-law William Carr, the purchaser of a further 56 a. of Old Park from Mrs. Lewis in 1832. His estate was sold in 1859 to Francis Adams,[46] whose devisees offered it for sale in 1879.[47] Some of the land was later absorbed in Town park, created in 1902, and much of the rest became part of Bush Hill golf course. Chase Park, a plain stuccoed house built by Browning,[48] stood empty in 1908[49] and was demolished soon afterwards.

A new tenement at Whitewebbs was acquired by Agnes and Stephen Wilford in 1543.[50] Robert Huicke the physician,[51] who held land in Enfield by 1555,[52] in 1570 was granted a conduit in the Chase to supply water to his mansion called Whitewebbs.[53] The house was associated with the Gunpowder Plot[54] and was held in 1635, with 10 a. called Colleges, by Dr. Samuel Ward, the divine.[55] It was claimed by a Dr. Bockenham in 1653 and afterwards acquired by Michel Garnault. When Daniel Garnault died in 1809 the estate, some 31 a., passed to his sister Ann, who married Henry Bowles of Myddelton House, Bull's Cross, the owner in 1823. The house, which had stood near Myddelton House, was demolished *c.* 1790.[56]

An estate of 134 a. called Whitewebbs farm belonged to Eliab Breton of Forty Hall, after whose death it was bought by Dr. Abraham Wilkinson, who received 68 a. in the former Chase under the Act of 1801.[57] In 1873 it belonged to Wilkinson's grandson, Henry Wilkinson (d. 1887),[58] owner of a notable collection of paintings and *objets d'art*.[59] The estate was later purchased by Enfield U.D.C. as a public park, which in 1955 totalled 232 a.[60] The core of the existing house called White Webbs was built by Abraham Wilkinson in 1791; it was lengthened and greatly enlarged in the mid 19th century and was again altered in the 1870s to the designs of Charles Stuart Robertson, who gave it its French Renaissance exterior.[61] The house, in 1973 an old people's home, is a large two-storeyed building with a low tower over the entrance and one-storeyed wings.

[19] C.P. 25(1)/148/26/30.
[20] *Cal. Pat.* 1338–40, 14.
[21] S.C. 6/Hen. VIII/2396 m. 94.
[22] C.P. 25(1)/148/29/115.
[23] S.C. 6/Hen. VIII/2396 m. 117.
[24] *L. & P. Hen. VIII*, xix(2), p. 187.
[25] *Cal. Inq. ad quod damnum* (Rec. Com.), 280.
[26] S.C. 6/Hen. VIII/2402 m. 32.
[27] *L. & P. Hen. VIII*, xix(2), p. 187.
[28] See above, p. 213.
[29] D.L. 42/125; see p. 213.
[30] E 320/L 45; *Cal. S.P. Dom.* 1655, 391.
[31] E 317/Mdx./18; *T.L.M.A.S.* x. 431–3.
[32] C 66/2961 no. 35.
[33] D.L. 42/126.
[34] *D.N.B.*; Lysons, *Environs*, ii. 291; D.L. 42/24.
[35] C 7/282/75; *Complete Peerage*, ix. 107.
[36] Ford, *Enfield*, 30–1; *Complete Peerage*, ii. 20; vi. 89.
[37] 17 Geo. III, c. 17, s.7.
[38] Robinson, *Enfield*, i. 122.
[39] Ford, *Enfield*, 31; map dated 1834 *penes* Enfield libr.
[40] Ford, *Enfield*, 31.

[41] *Home Cnties. Mag.* xii. 260.
[42] *Kelly's Dir. Enfield* (1921).
[43] Ford, *Enfield*, 31.
[44] *Home Cnties. Mag.* xii. 260–1.
[45] *V.C.H. Mdx.* i. 50–1.
[46] Ford, *Enfield*, 32.
[47] Sales parts. *penes* Enfield libr.
[48] Ford, *Enfield*, 32.
[49] *Kelly's Dir. Mdx.* (1908).
[50] *L. & P. Hen. VIII*, xviii(1), p. 262.   [51] *D.N.B.*
[52] C.P. 25(2)/74/629 no. 33.
[53] Bodl. MS. Gough Mdx. 8, f. 35.
[54] See p. 249.
[55] D.L. 42/125; *D.N.B.*
[56] Robinson, *Enfield*, i. 243–7.
[57] Ibid. i. 247–8. Sales parts. for Whitewebbs farm, 1787, are in M.R.O., Acc. 801/45.
[58] Ford, *Enfield*, 83.
[59] Thorne, *Environs*, i. 178.
[60] Boro. of Enfield, *Official Guide* [1955].
[61] Ford, *Enfield*, 84; N. Hirshman, TS. hist. of Enfield hos. *penes* Enfield libr.

The first estates formed out of Enfield Chase were those leased out with the three lodges. Two of the dwellings, Bull's Lodge and Augustine's Lodge, were recorded in 1593.[62] There were three lodges in 1635, occupied by the under-keepers of the north, south, and east bailiwicks of the Chase,[63] and in 1650 the inclosed land around them totalled 181 a.[64] In 1686 88 a. were attached to West Lodge, 66 a. to South Lodge, and 38 a. to East Lodge.[65] The West Lodge estate remained the largest: it was augmented in 1742 by 98 a. on the east and south sides, leased separately by James Brydges, duke of Chandos,[66] and in 1889 it amounted to 189 a.[67] The South Lodge estate was enlarged in the 18th century and contained 115 a. in 1841, when 34 a. formed a park around the house,[68] while the East Lodge estate contained 114 a. in 1845.[69] All three estates continued to be leased out by the duchy after the inclosure of the rest of the Chase in 1779. South Lodge was sold to John Laing & Son, building contractors, in 1935 and the other two to the county council in 1937 as part of the Green Belt.[70]

In 1650 the lodges were named after the under-keepers who lived there. Potter's Lodge, in the middle of the Chase and evidently the largest and newest, was a three-storeyed brick building, worth thrice as much as either of the other two; Norris's and Dighton's lodges were one-storeyed buildings of timber and 'Flemish walls', with attic rooms.[71] During the Interregnum the lodges were occupied by army officers[72] and after the Restoration they were leased to high officers of the Chase or to outsiders as country retreats. West Lodge was occupied from c. 1680 by Henry Coventry, Lord Coventry (1619–86), a former secretary of state and chief ranger of the Chase.[73] John Evelyn in 1676 thought it very pretty and commodious, with fine gardens and artificial ponds.[74] It was later leased by James Brydges, duke of Chandos (d. 1744), another chief ranger and lessee of Enfield manor, who employed Edward Shepherd to refront the house between 1730 and 1732 and later sub-let it.[75] At the end of the 18th century West Lodge was a plain three-storeyed brick building with a seven-bay front and rusticated quoins, apparently unaltered since 1732.[76] The house was leased to a farmer in 1808, when the gardens were overgrown,[77] and in 1832 it was demolished by a new lessee, Archibald Paris.[78] It was replaced by a plain stuccoed building, used as a hotel in 1973.

The lease of South Lodge was bought by William Pitt, later earl of Chatham, in 1747. In 1748 the house was rebuilt and the surrounding fields were made into a park with ornamental lakes, a temple to Pan, a pyramid, and a bridge. Pitt sold the lease in 1755, claiming that he had never stayed at South Lodge for more than a week.[79] After a period of neglect the estate was restored at the end of the 18th century by Thomas Skinner, alderman of London.[80] The house was then a three-storeyed stuccoed building, with a canted bay window at the centre of the garden front.[81] It was demolished after the sale of the surrounding land in 1935.

East Lodge, said to have been a hunting seat of Charles I,[82] was rebuilt in 1668 by the lessee Charles, Lord Gerard, later earl of Macclesfield (d. 1694).[83] The lodge or its successor was afterwards leased by Alexander Wedderburn, Lord Chancellor and later earl of Rosslyn (d. 1805), and known as the Red Lodge, to distinguish it from the near-by White Lodge, a two-storeyed stuccoed house, built in the late 18th century and leased with the Red Lodge.[84] In 1808 the Red Lodge was in very poor repair after long disuse[85] and before 1823 it was demolished.[86] The White Lodge was demolished by G. J. Graham before 1873 and was replaced by the modern East Lodge.[87]

When the Chase was divided, 3,219 a., together with the lands around the three lodges, remained with the duchy of Lancaster.[88] The duchy was empowered to sell up to 250 a.[89] and in 1777 152 a. north of Cockfosters were bought by Francis Russell, secretary of the duchy court, who built a house called Beech Hill Park south of Camlet Way.[90] In 1781 the estate was enlarged by 106 a. on its west and south sides[91] but in 1790 it was sold to William Franks of Mount Pleasant, Cockfosters, whose executors sold it in 1800 to Archibald Paris.[92] The land was sold c. 1858 to Charles Jack (d. 1896), whose sons offered it for sale in 1901.[93] It was purchased in 1920 by the Economic Insurance Co., which leased the greater part of it to Hadley Wood golf club.[94] Beech Hill Park, in 1973 the club-house of Hadley Wood golf club, was built before 1786;[95] it is a plain stuccoed building of two storeys, with a main front of seven bays, the central three of which are flanked by giant Doric pilasters. Wings were added in the 19th century. The landscaped grounds were described in 1796 as truly picturesque.[96]

Archibald Paris of Beech Hill held many lands of the duchy of Lancaster. In 1799 he took over the leases of Suits Hill and Greenwood, west of Beech

[62] Norden, *Spec. Brit.* 15–16.
[63] D.L. 42/125.
[64] E 317/Mdx./20; *T.L.M.A.S.* x. 434.
[65] M.P.C. 107 (D.L. 31/134).
[66] Lease bk. 1765, ff. 124–127v, *penes* Duchy of Lanc. office.
[67] Sales parts. *penes* Barnet Mus.
[68] M.P.C. 175 (D.L. 31/216).
[69] M.P.C. 136 (D.L. 31/162).
[70] Ex inf. Duchy of Lancaster office.
[71] E 317/Mdx./20; *T.L.M.A.S.* x. 434.
[72] M.P.C. 50A (D.L. 31/50A).
[73] Hist. MSS. Com. 36, *Ormonde*, v. 331, 393; *Cal. Treas. Bks.* 1679–80, 503; *D.N.B.*
[74] *Diary of John Evelyn*, ed. E. S. de Beer, iv. 92.
[75] Baker, *Chandos*, 387–9.
[76] Guildhall Libr., illus. edn. of Lysons, *Environs*, ii.
[77] Survey of duchy estates, vol. 1, *penes* Duchy of Lanc. office.
[78] Ford, *Enfield*, 49.
[79] B. Williams, *Life of Pitt*, i. 262.

[80] *Ambulator* (4th edn.), 209.
[81] Guildhall Libr., illus. edn. of Lysons, *Environs*, ii.
[82] Lysons, *Environs*, ii. 289.
[83] *Cal. Treas. Bks.* 1667–8, 496; *Cal. S.P. Dom.* 1668–9, 585.
[84] Robinson, *Enfield*, i. 226–7; Guildhall Libr., illus. edn. of Lysons, *Environs*, ii.
[85] Survey of duchy estates, vol. 1, *penes* Duchy of Lanc. office.
[86] Robinson, *Enfield*, i. 227.
[87] Ford, *Enfield*, 50.   [88] 17 Geo. III, c. 17.
[89] Ibid. ss. 37–8.
[90] Lysons, *Environs*, iv. 624; Enfield lease bk. *penes* Duchy of Lanc. office.
[91] Ex inf. Duchy of Lanc. office.
[92] N. Hirshman, TS. Hist. of Enfield hos. *penes* Enfield libr.
[93] Ibid.; Whitaker, *Enfield*, 266; sales parts. *penes* Enfield libr.
[94] Hirshman, Hist. of Enfield hos.
[95] *European Mag.* May 1796.   [96] Ibid.

Hill, and of Monkey mead, to the north, and in 1829 he leased 1,338 a. of duchy land. The leases were assigned in 1833 and 1838 to Sir Edward Barnes, a former governor of Ceylon, who lived at Greenwood, west of Beech Hill Park.[97] Greenwood House, with 107 a., was sold by the duchy in 1925 and the house was demolished in 1967.[98] Monkey Mead farm was leased in 1857 by Charles Jack, who later began to build on the Hadley Wood estate.[99] The estate's trustees ceased to hold the lease in 1941 and the freeholds were later sold off piecemeal by the duchy.[1]

The Trent Place estate originated in 250 a. north of West Lodge, which were leased in 1779[2] to Sir Richard Jebb, Bt. (1729–87), the physician.[3] Jebb built a villa called Trent Place after the Italian town where he had cured the duke of Gloucester of a serious illness.[4] In 1787 the estate contained 385 a., of which 300 a. were park land.[5] After passing through several hands[6] the lease was assigned in 1833 to David Bevan of Mount Pleasant, Cockfosters, who assigned it in 1837 to his son Robert Cooper Lee Bevan (d. 1890).[7] In 1857 the Trent Place estate contained 475 a., while Bevan leased another 93 a. called Clay Pit Hill farm to the north-west and 114 a. at Cockfosters to the south.[8] His son Francis Augustus Bevan bought 57 a. south of the main estate from the duchy of Lancaster in 1892.[9] From 1909 most of the property was leased by Sir Edward Sassoon, Bt.,[10] whose son Philip (1888–1939), later Under-Secretary for Air and First Commissioner of Works, purchased it from the duchy in 1922,[11] when it totalled 570 a. Sir Philip Sassoon devised the land to a cousin, Mrs. David Gubbay, who sold it soon after the Second World War as part of the Green Belt.[12]

The first Trent Place was a 'compact villa' of brick, with a portico and a curved central portion.[13] Sir William Chambers carried out unspecified alterations for Sir Richard Jebb[14] and Francis Repton was said to have beautified the house and its grounds, which contained a lake, for John Cumming, the occupier in 1816.[15] The house was enlarged by Robert Bevan before 1873[16] and again by his son in 1894.[17] In 1926 Sir Philip Sassoon began extensive changes, seemingly to his own designs, refacing the outside with red brick and stone dressings from the demolished Devonshire House in Piccadilly, removing a 19th-century north tower, building terraces, and redecorating the interiors. The result was a dignified mansion in the early-18th-century manner, with the roof hidden behind a balustraded cornice.

The orangery, completed shortly before 1931, was designed by Col. Reginald Cooper.[18] In the 1930s Trent Place was noted for its exotic furnishings and for Sassoon's lavish entertainments, patronized by royalty.[19] The house later became a teachers' training college and the grounds a park.[20]

North Lodge was built on duchy land after the inclosure of the Chase and in 1791 was occupied by Thomas James.[21] In 1857 the estate contained 328 a. and was leased to Charles King, who was also tenant of the adjoining New Cottage farm.[22] North Lodge was included in the sale of land for the Green Belt in 1937.[23] The house is two-storeyed, of brick, with a front of five bays and a pedimented centrepiece. It has been used by the county council as a remand home since 1941 and has been renamed Kilvinton Hall.[24]

The remaining duchy land in Enfield was split up and leased out at the inclosure of the Chase. In 1867 the largest farms were New Cottage (209 a.), Holly Hill (373 a.), Sloper's Pond (100 a.), Plumridge (301 a.), North Lodge (382 a.), and Monkey Mead (222 a.).[25] In 1937 2,002 a., including most of the farms, were sold by the duchy to Middlesex C.C. as part of the Green Belt.[26]

The eastern part of the Chase, 1,733 a., was allotted to the parish of Enfield under the Act of 1777 and was divided and inclosed in 1803, when the largest portion went to Trinity College.[27] Other allotments included 98 a. south of Cattle gate to William Mellish, who was also awarded 314 a. from lands lying east of the former Chase, between Ponders End and Enfield Town.[28]

ECONOMIC HISTORY.

AGRICULTURE. In 1086 Enfield was assessed at 30 hides, of which 14 were in demesne. There was meadow for 24 ploughs, pasture for the cattle of the vill, a mill, a park, and woodland for 2,000 pigs. The manor was valued at £50, as it had been T.R.E., although it was worth only £20 when Geoffrey de Mandeville received it. There were 4 ploughs on the demesne and the villeins had 16 ploughs. The tenants included a villein on one hide, 3 villeins each on $\frac{1}{2}$ hide, a priest on one virgate, 17 villeins each on one virgate, 36 villeins each on $\frac{1}{2}$ virgate, 20 bordars on one hide and one virgate, 7 cottars on 23 a., and 5 cottars on 7 a. There were also 18 cottars and 6 serfs.[29]

In 1289 Durants comprised 294 a. of arable, 27 a. of meadow, and 27 a. of pasture,[30] while farther west in 1336 the demesne of Enfield contained 420 a. of

[97] Clark, *Hadley Wood*, 33–4.
[98] Ibid. 45.
[99] Plans of Enfield estates (1857) *penes* Duchy of Lanc. office; see above, p. 221.
[1] Clark, *Hadley Wood*, 46.
[2] Plan of estates in Enfield (1782) *penes* Duchy of Lanc. office.
[3] *D.N.B.*
[4] *Ambulator* (4th edn.), 233.
[5] Sales parts. *penes* Enfield libr.
[6] Lysons, *Environs*, ii. 291.
[7] Index to enrolment bks. *penes* Duchy of Lanc. office; *Mdx. Quarterly*, N.S. x. 12.
[8] Plans of Enfield estates (1857) *penes* Duchy of Lanc. office.
[9] Ex inf. Duchy of Lanc. office.
[10] *Mdx. Quarterly*, N.S. x. 12.
[11] Ex inf. Duchy of Lanc. office; *D.N.B.*
[12] *Mdx. Quarterly*, N.S. x. 12.
[13] Sales parts. (1787) *penes* Enfield libr.
[14] Colvin, *Dict. of Architects*, 135.
[15] Brewer, *Beauties of Eng. and Wales*, x(5), 734; *Country Life*, lxix. 40.
[16] Ford, *Enfield*, plate facing p. 53.
[17] *Home Cnties. Mag.* xii. 264.
[18] *Country Life*, lxix. 43–6.
[19] *Chips: Diaries of Sir Hen. Channon*, ed. R. Rhodes James (Penguin edn.), 39, 250.
[20] See below, pp. 244, 257.
[21] *Univ. Brit. Dir.* [?1795], 85.
[22] Plan of Enfield estates *penes* Duchy of Lanc. office.
[23] See below.
[24] Index to enrolments (post 1921) *penes* Duchy of Lanc. office.
[25] Plans of Enfield estates (1857) *penes* Duchy of Lanc. office.
[26] Ex inf. Duchy of Lanc. office.
[27] See p. 229.
[28] M.R.O., Enfield Incl. Act.
[29] *V.C.H. Mdx.* i. 126.
[30] *Cal. Inq. p.m.* ii, p. 442.

arable, 63 a. of meadow, and 39 a. of pasture.[31] Livestock seized by the sheriff on Enfield manor in 1327 amounted to 130 oxen, 154 cows, 160 steers, 101 heifers, and 1,680 sheep.[32] By 1487, moreover, pasture on both Sir Thomas Lovell's estates of Elsing and Lowdes was worth more than twice as much as the arable land.[33]

In 1289 freemen owed 86 customary works every August on the Durants manor[34] and unspecified villein services were also recorded.[35] On Enfield manor there were freemen, copyholders, cottars, and molmen in the mid 14th century.[36] Services were still performed by 22 molmen in 1419,[37] although by 1324 labour had been hired on the Enfield demesne for carting corn and mowing hay.[38] In 1419 the molmen, who apparently owed more services than the cottars, performed hoeing, carting, and autumn boon-works; other works, however, which included the carrying of corn, were being sold.[39] In 1439, when the demesne was leased, the molmen's works were being sold at $3\frac{1}{4}d.$ apiece but customary weeding, mowing, and reaping works were still specified.[40]

Most of the parish east of the Chase was divided into large open arable fields, with common marshes along the Lea. Broad field was mentioned in 1228 and East field in 1275.[41] By 1572 there were 38 common fields, mostly east of Enfield Town and Forty Hill[42] but some, inclosed before the mid 18th century,[43] extending westward towards the Chase. The fields varied greatly in size: in 1572 the largest, Broad field, covered 272 a., while the smallest, Moat field, contained only 9 a. North field (213 a.) covered much of the area north of Bullsmoor Lane and West field (104 a.) lay on the western side of the road to Enfield Town and Edmonton. South-west of it, near Mores Hatch gate to the Chase, lay Ferney field (207 a.). Between Bullsmoor Lane and Turkey Street the largest fields were South field and Dung field, both of them 60 a., while the area between Turkey Street and Hoe Lane was occupied by Long field (151 a.) and Mapleton field (95 a.). East of Hertford Road the largest field was East field (171 a.), with Holdbrook or Ho-Brook field to the north. The centre of the parish, between Baker Street and Hertford Road, also contained large common fields, which included Broad field (272 a.) from Hoe Lane to Carterhatch Lane and, farther south, Windmill field (263 a.), Churchbury field (189 a.), and Southbury field (237 a.). By 1754 several fields had been divided and there were 2,891 a. of inclosed to 2,747 a. of open-field land.[44]

The strips in the fields were called journeys in 1686 and were divided from one another by 'bulks'.[45] Each manor had some demesne land in the common fields. In 1584 the Elsing demesne contained 260 a. in the common fields and only 20 a. of inclosures[46] and in 1635 the Enfield demesne contained 78 a. of inclosed land to 432 a. of arable and 95 a. of meadow in the common fields, all leased to William Bowyer; another 48 a. were leased to John Wroth and 87 a. to John Wilford.[47] In 1686 all the Enfield demesne lands were leased by Nicholas Raynton.[48] On Durants manor the inclosure of demesne land occurred earlier; by 1649 only 7 a. of the demesne was open field land.[49] In the early 16th century discontent was caused by inclosures on Durants manor,[50] although later the practice became concentrated in the area immediately east of the Chase. In 1572 small inclosures were recorded in all parts of the parish.[51] In 1635 Sir Nicholas Raynton was said to have recently inclosed 17 a.[52] and in 1656 the former Little Park, part of Raynton's estate, consisted chiefly of inclosed meadow.[53] The disparking of the Old Park in the 17th century[54] further added to the amount of inclosed land in the parish.

Enfield inhabitants claimed rights of grazing in the Chase, mentioned in 1372[55] and set out in detail in 1542,[56] as well as in the common fields and marshes. In the late 16th century the common fields were being opened to grazing while they lay fallow,[57] in 1593 the marshes were said to have been turned into good pasture,[58] and in 1657 some of them were being opened as Lammas lands.[59] Threats to grazing rights often caused violence, as in 1475 when people from Enfield led the opposition to Sir Richard Charlton, lord of Dephams in Edmonton,[60] or c. 1493,[61] when they pulled down fences belonging to his successor Sir Thomas Bourchier and claimed sanction of the duchy of Lancaster court.[62] The men of Enfield were not always welcome in Edmonton, where c. 1563 the commoners blocked the entrance to the marshes and kept mares there to exclude cattle from Enfield.[63] In Enfield itself John Wroth of Durants was accused in 1514 of inclosing 40 a. and barring cattle from his fields in open seasons[64] and in 1548 four men were imprisoned after a riot directed at Sir Thomas Wroth.[65] Sir Robert Wroth was said in 1589 to have been the greatest incloser of common fields in the parish.[66] John Taylor, farmer of Enfield manor, was amerced c. 1566 for allegedly inclosing 52 a. of waste land[67] but was found guiltless by the duchy court, which concluded that some Enfield tenants had hoped to force him to let them farm his lands.[68]

Much of the trouble seems to have arisen from a

[31] Ibid. viii, p. 25; Robinson, *Enfield*, i. 96.
[32] *Cal. Mem. R.* 1326–7, p. 115.
[33] Belvoir Castle, Roos 965 [minister's acct.].
[34] *Cal. Inq. p.m.* ii, p. 442.
[35] *Cal. Close*, 1288–96, 13.
[36] D.L. 43/7/1.
[37] S.C. 6/915/26.
[38] S.C. 6/1146/20.
[39] S.C. 6/915/26; *V.C.H. Mdx.* ii. 64–5.
[40] *V.C.H. Mdx.* ii. 76; D.L. 29/42/825.
[41] *P.N. Mdx.* (E.P.N.S.), 213.
[42] D.L. 43/7/5.
[43] Trinity Coll. Cambridge, Estate MSS., Enfield survey and map.
[44] D.L. 43/7/5; Trinity Coll. Cambridge, Estate MSS., Enfield survey and map.
[45] C 6/295/41.   [46] D.L. 1/131/w6.
[47] D.L. 42/125.
[48] D.L. 42/126.

[49] C 6/295/41.
[50] See below.
[51] D.L. 43/7/5.
[52] D.L. 42/125.
[53] M.R.O., Acc. 16/8.
[54] See p. 230.
[55] *Cal. Inq. p.m.* xiii, p. 133.
[56] B.M. Harl. MS. 368, ff. 104–6; *V.C.H. Mdx.* ii. 226–7.
[57] D.L. 1/131/w6.
[58] Norden, *Spec. Brit.* 19.
[59] E 317/Mdx./19.   [60] See p. 167.
[61] D.L. 1/1/E5.
[62] D.L. 1/19/E1.
[63] D.L. 1/46/M7.
[64] D.L. 1/19/E1.
[65] *Acts. of P.C.* 1547–50, 219.
[66] B.M. Lansd. MS. 59, no. 30, f. 59.
[67] D.L. 1/74/T2.
[68] D.L. 44/206.

rise in the population.[69] The Chase was said to be overcharged *c.* 1572[70] and William Kympton, lord of Monken Hadley, was accused of keeping too many animals there in 1580, 1581, and 1587.[71] John Wilford, lord of Elsing, declared in 1584 that a recent increase in the number of houses and inclosures had burdened the common fields with too many cattle; he had therefore inclosed 8 a. near his manor-house, whereupon his fences had been destroyed.[72] Distress was compounded by Enfield's decline as an entrepôt for the malt trade after the construction of the Lea Navigation[73] and in 1589 a group of inhabitants complained to the queen of their impoverishment.[74] Their move may have been linked to a petition in that year to Lord Burghley, seeking the release of 24 women who had been indicted for breaking down fences.[75] In 1613 fences on Elsing manor were again demolished[76] and as late as 1719 one William Jakings claimed that he had been reduced to poverty by resisting the unlawful inclosure of common fields.[77]

By 1754[78] there were 1,646 a. of inclosed pasture, including the land around the Chase lodges, and 1,245 a. of inclosed arable; the common arable fields totalled 2,747 a. and there were 794 a. of common meadow, mostly in the marshes. Some of the inclosed arable land produced a second yearly crop of turnips, while the Forty Hall estate, which was completely inclosed, yielded large quantities of hay as well as wheat. In 1769[79] hay farming predominated in the mainly inclosed area west of the road from Enfield Town to Bull's Cross, where 900 a. bore hay, 400 a. spring corn, and 100 a. wheat, while 380 a. were 'fed lands'. By contrast farther east between the road from Enfield Town to Bull's Cross and Hertford Road there were 350 a. of hay, 700 a. of wheat and spring corn, 350 a. of spring grain, and only 150 a. of 'fed lands'. The common marshes by the Lea also yielded much hay, which was in demand for winter feeding for the large numbers of cattle on the Chase. In 1769 2,330 a. in Enfield were used for growing wheat or spring corn and 2,150 a. for hay; 790 a. were 'fed lands' and 1,020 a. lay fallow. The best arable land in the late 18th century was said to be in Churchbury field.[80] A three-course rotation was in use in the common arable fields in 1796, with wheat followed by spring corn and a third year of fallow, when the fields lay open to the parishioners' animals.[81] The marshes were open to cattle from Lammas until early April, after which a crop of hay was sown.[82]

When the Chase was inclosed in 1779, the duchy's allotment was set aside as farm-land, while 1,532 a.

on its eastern side were allotted to Enfield as a common pasture for householders with premises worth more than £6 a year; sheep were excluded and in 1796 there were said to be 614 head of cattle there.[83] Proposals to inclose the allotment, with the common fields in the rest of the parish, were opposed by many who feared the impoverishment of hundreds of cottagers[84] but supported by the chief landowners. In 1793 Abraham Wilkinson of White Webbs considered agriculture to be sadly restricted and claimed that the common field land by the New River, which lay fallow every third year, could after inclosure be turned into valuable meadows.[85] An Act for inclosing the parish was passed in 1803, when there were 2,891 a. of inclosed and 3,540 a. of un-inclosed land outside the former Chase.[86]

There was a pound at Chase Side which had disappeared by 1686,[87] and one near the boundary of the Old Park in 1692.[88] A new pound was built in 1804[89] and apparently survived at the northern end of Chase Green in 1868.[90]

Apple-growing for cider was said in 1823 to have once been important, although no orchards survived.[91] Lavender was grown on 16 a. near Baker Street in the early 19th century[92] and was commemorated in the western end of New Lane, Lavender Hill. Fifteen market gardeners were recorded in 1862, most of them near Enfield Highway but some in Baker Street.[93] In 1867 there were several orchards at Enfield Highway[94] and in 1869 market gardens accounted for much of the Connop estate in the eastern part of the parish.[95] After inclosure the farms near the Lea continued to be split between arable and pasture, although fields formed out of the former common were very large in comparison with those farther west; one of Trinity College's farms at Brimsdown had fields of 44 a. and 60 a. in 1855.[96] Market gardens encroached increasingly on the farm-land between Hertford Road and the Lea during the later 19th century,[97] until by 1900 Enfield was said to be the main parish for market gardening in northern Middlesex and the second in the whole county.[98] Tomatoes and cucumbers were the main crops,[99] although flowers were also grown, and glass-houses covered several hundred acres.[1] By 1920, with the expansion of industry and suburban housing, some of the market gardens around Ponders End and Enfield Highway had disappeared. New nurseries had opened in the extreme north-east at Freezy Water and farther west at Crews Hill[2] but in 1934 those around Great Cambridge Road were giving way to factories, schools, and houses.[3] In 1947 commercial horticulture accounted for 536 a., of

[69] See p. 213.
[70] D.L. 44/206.
[71] D.L. 1/115/A27; D.L. 1/119/A30; D.L. 1/148/S32.
[72] D.L. 1/131/W6.
[73] See p. 237.
[74] B.M. Lansd. MS. 60, no. 38.
[75] Ibid. 59, no. 30, f. 59; no. 31, f. 61; *Mdx. Cnty. Recs.* i. 187–8.
[76] *Mdx. Sess. Recs.* N.S. i. 22.
[77] Trinity Coll. Cambridge, Estate MSS., box 43(e).
[78] Trinity Coll. Cambridge, Estate MSS., Enfield survey and map.
[79] Bodl. MS. Gough Mdx. 8, f. 52.
[80] Ibid. f. 96v.
[81] Middleton, *View*, 529.
[82] Ibid. 219.
[83] Middleton, *View*, 116–17.
[84] Bodl. MS. Gough Mdx. 8, f. 54.
[85] Middleton, *View*, 528–9.

[86] M.R.O., Enfield Incl. Award and Map.
[87] Robinson, *Enfield*, ii. 256.
[88] M.R.O., Acc. 903/142.
[89] Vestry order bk. (1797–1807), 298, *penes* Enfield L.B.
[90] O.S. Map 6″, Mdx. VII. NE. (1868 edn.).
[91] Robinson, *Enfield*, i. 20.
[92] Tuff, *Enfield*, 15.
[93] *Kelly's Dir. Mdx.* (1862).
[94] O.S. Map 1/2,500, Mdx. VII. 4 (1867 edn.).
[95] M.R.O., Acc. 727/168.
[96] Trinity Coll. Cambridge, Estate MSS., box 43 (D.1).
[97] O.S. Maps 6″, Mdx. VII. NE.; II. SE. (1863 and 1897 edns.); *Jnl. Royal Agric. Soc.* 3rd ser. ix (1898), 527.
[98] Bennett, *Horticultural Industries of Mdx.* 15, 20.
[99] Ibid. 11.
[1] *Jnl. Royal Agric. Soc.* 3rd ser. ix. 522–7.
[2] O.S. Maps 6″, Mdx. VII. NE.; II. SE., SW. (1920 edn.); *Kelly's Dir. Enfield* (1921).
[3] Briggs, *Mdx. Old and New*, 64.

which 85 a. were under glass,[4] and market gardens and nurseries were limited to the extreme north and north-east parts of the parish. They continued to dwindle until in 1966 there was only one large-scale concern, Theobalds Park farm, near Crews Hill, which covered 140 a. and produced vegetables for the London markets.[5] Several smaller nurseries survived around Crews Hill Road in 1974.

The western part of Enfield remained more agricultural. Initial attempts to cultivate the Chase after its inclosure were largely unsuccessful because of the poor soil, a mixture of gravel and heavy clay, and the inexperience of the farmers.[6] In 1787 Thomas Bulkeley was said to have failed to sell lands, which he had leased in the Chase, in lots of 30 or 40 a. to Londoners for country residences.[7] By 1796, however, only about 1,200 a. of the duchy's allotment remained in an unimproved state.[8] Some of the lessees, like Abraham Wilkinson, applied chalk and lime to the soil[9] but others, like J. Wigston of Trent Place, thought the land better suited for stock farming and retained many of the old trees to provide settings for their mansions.[10] By 1823 the Chase had been almost completely converted to tillage[11] and c. 1850 most of its farms were said to be profitable,[12] although problems of cultivation persisted. In 1855 one of Trinity College's farms was in a bad state, whereas another on the former Chase was well manured and bore some root crops as well as wheat and dairy produce.[13]

Farm-land amounted to 9,234 a. in 1887[14] and covered over 8,000 a., two-thirds of the parish, in 1911.[15] It included most of the former Chase, which was later preserved in the Green Belt with the result that there were still 4,761 a. devoted to agriculture in 1937. The farm-land was mainly under grass, 6,494 a. in 1887 and 4,195 a. in 1937, and supplied much hay for London in the 1880s and 1890s.[16] Later pasture became more important: in 1921 Plumridge and Ridgway farms were dairy farms[17] and by 1937 nearly two-thirds of the grassland was used for grazing. Numbers of livestock remained high: there were 1,343 cattle, 1,040 sheep, and 681 pigs in 1887 and 1,245 cattle, 1,686 sheep, and 1,266 pigs in 1937. Green and root crops were more widespread than corn: potatoes and cabbages covered over 700 a. in 1887 and over 560 a. in 1917, although the acreage of potatoes had fallen to 33 by 1937.

A return to arable farming began after the Second World War, partly because of the shortage of labour. Of 4,803 a. of farm-land in 1957, only 1,868 were under grass, mostly for grazing. Corn, however, had

so expanded that 467 a. produced wheat, 584 a. barley, and 350 a. mixed crops for threshing.[18] Stock farms included Glasgow Stud farm at Crews Hill, occupied by the British Bloodstock Agency.[19]

WOODS. Enfield had woodland for 2,000 pigs in 1086.[20] Shingles from trees in the Chase were used to roof the palace of Westminster in 1220,[21] 120 oaks were felled for work at Westminster in 1546,[22] and more oaks were taken for repairs to Sir William Cecil's house at Hatfield (Herts.) in 1567.[23] Enfield's inhabitants maintained a right to collect firewood from the Chase: in 1650 they claimed 'decayed and dotard trees' at 2s. a load, free brushwood on St. George's day, brushwood at 8d. a load for the rest of the year, and free rotten wood.[24]

The woodland was guarded as jealously as were grazing rights. In 1536 the ranger and keepers were accused of illegally felling trees in the Chase.[25] In 1575 an order was made for better preservation of deer and timber[26] but in 1583 Enfield men accused the earl of Southampton, farmer and woodward of the Chase, of destroying the wood.[27] Illegal felling seems to have increased[28] until in 1603 a group of women assembled at Whitewebbs to urge that wood from the Chase should be burnt in the king's house at Enfield or given to the poor.[29] In 1604 trees were cut down to build bridges over the Lea.[30] Meanwhile security in the Chase grew less effective. A keeper was killed by a poacher in 1578[31] and in 1594 deer were escaping through gaps in the fence.[32] In 1605 the king complained that the Chase 'hard by our ordinary residence' was shamefully neglected and that the poor were brought to misery by new tenants and encroachers.[33] There were so many sheep that deer escaped in search of food,[34] while the destruction of woodland and especially of large oak trees, according to Sir Vincent Skinner, who lived at Enfield, was far beyond anything known.[35]

The inclosure of 120 a. of the Chase within Theobalds Park in 1611[36] took place without disturbance and tenants were compensated for loss of rights.[37] In 1635, however, the duchy's tenants of Enfield claimed that a decision to forbid the pasture of their sheep in the Chase, because of the threat to the deer, had left them no means of manuring their arable land.[38] The ruling against pasture of sheep seems to have been ignored, as it was not mentioned in 1650,[39] but the destruction of woodland and deer, after apparently coming to an end, increased again during the Civil War. In 1642 several men were imprisoned for killing deer on a large scale[40] and in 1643 another four were imprisoned for selling

[4] Bennett, *Horticult. Ind. of Mdx.* 38.
[5] New Enfield Hist.
[6] Middleton, *View*, 119, 124; Lysons, *Environs*, ii. 288.
[7] Lease bk. *penes* Duchy of Lanc. office.
[8] Middleton, *View*, 522.
[9] Ibid. 525, 528.
[10] Ibid. 530, 533.
[11] Robinson, *Enfield*, i. 224.
[12] Tuff, *Enfield*, 87.
[13] Trinity Coll. Cambridge, Estate MSS., box 43 (D.1).
[14] Except where otherwise stated the para. is based on M.A.F. 68/136; M.A.F. 68/1105; M.A.F. 68/1675; M.A.F. 68/2815; M.A.F. 68/3837.
[15] Whitaker, *Enfield*, 351.
[16] New Enfield Hist.
[17] *Kelly's Dir. Enfield* (1921).
[18] M.A.F. 68/4576.
[19] Boro. of Enfield, *Official Guide* [1955].
[20] *V.C.H. Mdx.* i. 126.
[21] *Rot. Litt. Claus.* (Rec. Com.), i. 416b.
[22] *L. & P. Hen. VIII*, xxi(1), p. 474.
[23] D.L. 42/23.
[24] *T.L.M.A.S.* x. 436-7.
[25] *L. & P. Hen. VIII*, addenda (1), pp. 397-8.
[26] B.M. Lansd. MS. 105, no. 12.
[27] D.L. 1/131/S24.
[28] D.L. 1/170/S4; D.L. 1/200/A42; D.L. 1/206/A6.
[29] *Cal. S.P. Dom.* 1603-10, 13.
[30] Ibid. 150.
[31] Hist. MSS. Com. 9, *Hatfield House*, xiii, pp. 155-6.
[32] Ibid. p. 523.
[33] Ibid. xvii. p. 473.
[34] Ibid. pp. 318-9.
[35] Ibid. p. 116.
[36] *Cal. S.P. Dom.* 1611-18, 81.
[37] Ibid. 158.
[38] D.L. 42/125.
[39] *T.L.M.A.S.* x. 436.
[40] *L.J.* v. 597a, 609a.

wood.[41] While searching for stolen wood in 1643, the woodward and constables were attacked by some 50 people at Winchmore Hill.[42] In 1654 the destruction of wood in the Chase was said to have cost £2,000.[43]

Parliament decided to sell the Chase in 1652[44] but inclosure did not take place until after a survey in 1658, under which 1,522 a. was granted to the parishioners of Enfield in compensation.[45] In 1659 men from Enfield and neighbouring parishes claimed that their allotment was too small and began pulling down newly-erected fences, for which they were acquitted at quarter sessions. Soon afterwards between 160 and 250 local men clashed with soldiers who were protecting the purchasers of the Chase lands[46] and two troops of horse were called in.[47] Both the purchasers and the local inhabitants subsequently petitioned Parliament to redress their grievances.[48]

The Chase was restored to the Crown in 1660 and restocking with deer began in 1662.[49] An order in 1660 tried to stop the parishioners from illegally cutting down trees[50] and attempts were made to remove the 200–300 people who had built cottages there during the Interregnum.[51] Poaching increased[52] and as the Chase became less frequently used for royal hunting, its officers and their lessees assumed greater local importance. In 1697 Sir Basil Firebrace, ranger and master of the game, was accused of profiteering on the sale of timber[53] and in 1701 the felling of trees was forbidden.[54] Sir Basil's successor, James Brydges, duke of Chandos, attempted to end poaching and introduced Scottish cattle[55] but trespassing and felling continued[56] and in 1777 the Chase was described by Arthur Young as 'a scandal to the government'.[57] When inclosure took place in 1779, the deer were removed to Luton Hoo (Beds.),[58] although many of the trees survived in park-land.[59]

MILLS. A mill rendered 10s. in 1086.[60] Geoffrey de Mandeville, earl of Essex (d. 1144), granted a mill to the abbot of Walden[61] and Roger de Canteloup held a water-mill and stank in 1234–5.[62] Fulling and corn mills were held by Richard de Plessis under the abbot in 1289 and later descended with Durants manor;[63] in 1362 one of them, leased to John Garton, would not grind for want of millstones.[64] An unspecified water-mill was held by Humphrey de Bohun, earl of Hereford, in 1363.[65] The Durants

mills were probably on or near the sites of the two water-mills which were held by Sir Robert Wroth, lord of Durants, in 1614.[66]

One of Wroth's mills was presumably Enfield mill, which stood in South marsh and in the late 16th century was a two-storeyed building with a tiled roof.[67] At the end of the mill river, it was held in 1635 by John Wroth[68] and described in 1754 as a corn mill.[69] It was replaced c. 1789 by a new building, much of which is probably preserved in Wright's flour mill near Ponders End railway station.[70] The mill is large and weatherboarded, with an adjoining brick house. In 1853 it contained seven pairs of millstones and could grind 500 sacks of flour weekly; there was storage for 1,000 qr. of wheat and barges of 60 tons could be drawn up alongside it.[71] A new plant opened in 1961, to increase production to 300 tons a week,[72] and in 1971 produced both flour and animal food stuffs.[73]

The Wroth family's other mill apparently stood near Enfield lock and gave its name to Mill marsh. A Mill Street was mentioned in 1393.[74] In 1653 the Ordnance officers were to treat with John and Henry Wroth about the use of their mill near the lock for making gunpowder[75] but there was no reference to gunpowder after 1664[76] and the mill may have closed by the 18th century.

John of Enfield held a mill in 1329,[77] which may have been the water-mill granted with the manor of Worcesters to Princess Elizabeth in 1550.[78] Its location is unknown. Another water-mill, by New pond in the Chase, was held of the Crown by John Witherings in 1635 but had been demolished by 1686.[79] Henry Frowyk held a windmill in Enfield in 1284,[80] perhaps near the site of Hadley windmill on the edge of the Chase.[81] In 1635 Hadley mill was one of two windmills in Enfield manor. The other, on Windmill Hill west of Enfield Town, was in good repair;[82] it later became known as Enfield mill and was disused by 1897,[83] shortly before its demolition.

A leather mill stood north of Wright's flour mill in 1754[84] but had disappeared before 1845;[85] it may have been the mill for dressing skins which was recorded in 1831.[86] A paper mill on the marshes near Brimsdown in 1776[87] seems to have been short-lived, as was a fulling mill on the Lea mentioned in 1805.[88] Two flour mills mentioned in 1866, one at Fernyhill

[41] Hist. MSS. Com. 4, *5th Rep., Hse. of Lords*, p. 109.
[42] *L.J.* vi. 328b.
[43] *Cal. S.P. Dom.* 1654, 168.
[44] *C.J.* vii. 222.
[45] E 317/Mdx. /17A–17R; M.P.C. 50A (D.L. 31/50A).
[46] *Bloody News from Enfield* (1659); *Relation of Cruelties... upon the inhabitants of Enfield* (1659); *Relation of a Riotous Insurrection ... of the Inhabitants of Enfield* (1659).
[47] *Cal. S.P. Dom.* 1658–9, 363–4.
[48] *C.J.* vii. 721–2.
[49] *Cal. S.P. Dom.* 1661–2, 241.
[50] *L.J.* xi. 53a.
[51] *Cal. S.P. Dom.* 1660–1, 394.
[52] M.R.O., Cal. Mdx. Sess. Bks. (1673–9), 59–60.
[53] Clark, *Hadley Wood*, 20–1.
[54] *Cal. S.P. Dom.* 1700–2, 322.
[55] Baker, *Chandos*, 391; Clark, *Hadley Wood*, 22–3.
[56] e.g. M.R.O., Cal. Mdx. Sess. Bks. (1748–50), 27; *Home Cnties. Mag.* xii. 258.
[57] Whitaker, *Enfield*, 272.
[58] Tuff, *Enfield*, 86.
[59] See p. 235.
[60] *V.C.H. Mdx.* i. 126.
[61] *Cal. Chart. R.* 1226–57, 337.
[62] J.I. 1/536 rot. 1.
[63] *Cal. Inq. p.m.* ii, p. 442; vii, p. 492.
[64] Ibid. xi, p. 266.

[65] Ibid. xi, p. 366.
[66] C2/Jas. I/W17/6.
[67] Hatfield C.P.M. II/53.
[68] D.L. 42/125.
[69] Trinity Coll. Cambridge, Estate MSS., Enfield survey and map.
[70] *Ind. Arch. in Enfield*, 6.
[71] M.R.O., Acc. 311/44.
[72] Boro. of Enfield, *Official Guide* [1962].
[73] *Ind. Arch. in Enfield*, 7.
[74] M.R.O., Acc. 903/143.
[75] *Cal. S.P. Dom.* 1652–3, 399.
[76] M.R.O., MR/TH/5, m. 10d.
[77] *Cal. Pat.* 1327–30, 410.
[78] Ibid. 1549–51, 240.
[79] D.L. 42/125–6.
[80] C.P. 25(1)/148/30/132.
[81] See pp. 266, 283.
[82] D.L. 42/125; M.P.C. 145 (D.L. 31/175).
[83] O.S. Map 6", Mdx. VII. NW. (1897 edn.).
[84] Trinity Coll. Cambridge, Estate MSS., Enfield survey and map.
[85] M.R.O., Acc. 311/38.
[86] Lewis, *Topog. Dict.* ii. 135.
[87] A. H. Shorter, *Paper Mills and Paper Makers in Eng.* 213; *Ind. Arch. in Enfield*, 6.
[88] O.S. Map 1", Mdx. Sheet 1 (1805 edn.).

farm north of Cockfosters and the other, which was powered by steam, in Turkey Street, had both disappeared by 1896.[89]

MARKETS AND FAIRS. In 1303 the king granted Humphrey de Bohun a weekly market at Enfield and two annual fairs of three days, to be held at the feasts of St. Andrew (30 Nov.) and of the Assumption (15 Aug.).[90] The fair formerly held on the feast of the Assumption was later transferred to 23 September[91] and described in 1823 as a 'mere holiday'.[92] It flourished in 1858[93] but was suppressed as a source of immorality in 1869.[94] The St. Andrew's day fair became a cheese fair and by 1823 was used only for the sale of old horses and cattle.[95] It was still held in 1908.[96]

The Beggar's Bush fairs founded at Southgate in 1614[97] were held at the top of Clay Hill in 1771 but later restored to Southgate.[98] Labourers still met annually at Easter and Whitsun for rustic sports near the Holly Bush inn, south of Clay Hill, in 1823.[99]

In 1585 a Sunday meat market by the church gate was vehemently opposed by the clergy, who invited preachers to condemn it and later petitioned Lord Burghley for its closure.[1] In 1586 some parishioners requested its retention, claiming that the curate, Leonard Thickpenny, had overturned a stall and threatened to beat the butcher.[2] They apparently failed but in 1618 James I granted a Saturday market, with a court of pie-powder, to Sir Nicholas Salter and others and stipulated that the profits be reserved for the poor.[3] The market was held south of the church, on the site of a house called the Vine which was bought by the parish in 1632.[4] The poor were suffering from its decline by the end of the century, because of the high prices of food elsewhere,[5] and, despite two attempts to revive it, it was moribund in 1823.[6] It was later successfully revived and was held on its old site each Saturday in 1971 and twice weekly from 1974.[7]

TRADE AND INDUSTRY. A maltman was recorded in 1393[8] and by the late 15th century several men[9] processed malt from Royston and Ware (Herts.) and sent it by road to London. Some families, including the Hunsdons and Cordells, thereby grew rich and left large bequests to the parish church.[10] Enfield's importance may have stemmed partly from its inhabitants' freedom from paying tolls, a privilege confirmed in 1543 after several Enfield maltmen had had their sacks distrained in London.[11] The opening of the Lea Navigation in 1576 diverted traffic from the road to the river, bypassing Enfield.[12] In 1581 a group of maltmen, encouraged by Robert Wroth who owned mills on the river,[13] cut the banks and drove stakes into the watercourse, for which several offenders were imprisoned.[14] Despite petitions to Lord Burghley[15] the trade through Enfield declined and by 1593 the passage of barges from Ware to London had also decreased.[16] Maltmen still lived in Enfield in 1615[17] but their business died out soon afterwards.

Enfield tanners were first mentioned in 1469[18] and the tanning of hides from London was considered an important local trade in 1662.[19] A tan yard stood in Church field in 1658[20] and another in Green Street in 1686.[21] One tannery remained, in Silver Street,[22] in 1828 and was described as extensive in 1831.[23] There was a factory for making paper in Chase Side c. 1800, but it had disappeared by 1823.[24]

Brick-, tile-, and lime-kilns were supplied with fuel from the Chase c. 1490.[25] There was a tile-kiln near Potters Bar in 1656,[26] perhaps the kiln which survived at Hadley Wood into the 19th century,[27] and a brick clamp in Church field in 1658.[28] Digging for bricks was carried out in the Chase in 1688[29] and Brick Kiln field, on the site of Enfield Town station, was so named by 1785.[30] The expansion of brick-making in the 19th century, however, took place in the eastern part of the parish; in 1823 there was a brick-field in Lincoln Road[31] and by 1868[32] there were brick-fields and clay mills there and in Southbury Road and Old Road, Enfield Highway. In 1971 the only surviving brick-works was Gabriel's in Hoe Lane, opened soon after 1930 and specializing in red facing-bricks, some of them hand-made.[33]

There was a brewery in 1696[34] and at the end of the 18th century Hill's brew-house in Green Street was supplying five ale-houses in Forty Hill.[35] Two breweries existed in 1832.[36] One of them, the Stag brewery by the New River at Chase Side, was taken over as a works for dyeing cotton in 1856[37] but became a brewery once more in the 1880s and closed

[89] O.S. Maps 1/2,500, Mdx. II. 16; VII. 1 (1867 and 1896 edns.).
[90] Cal. Chart. R. 1300–26, 35.
[91] Univ. Brit. Dir. [?1795], 81.
[92] Robinson, Enfield, i. 10.   [93] Tuff, Enfield, 29.
[94] Ford, Enfield, 103–5.
[95] Robinson, Enfield, i. 10.
[96] Kelly's Dir. Mdx. (1908).
[97] See p. 169.
[98] Bodl. MS. Gough Mdx. 9, f. 5v.; Robinson, Enfield, i. 10.
[99] Robinson, Enfield, i. 11.
[1] B.M. Lansd. MS. 43, no. 60; Edmonton Hund. Notes and Queries (Edmonton Hund. Hist. Soc. 1970), ii.
[2] B.M. Lansd. MS. 43, no. 18, ff. 37–8.
[3] C 66/2179/10. The charter was in the possession of the trustees of Enfield parochial charities in 1974.
[4] M.R.O., Acc. 903/20. For the market-place, see p. 214.
[5] Bodl. MS. Top. Mdx. b.1, f. 53.
[6] Robinson, Enfield, i. 8–9.
[7] Ex inf. Mr. A. H. Hall.
[8] M.R.O., Acc. 903/143.
[9] Cal. Close, 1454–61, 34, 45, 305.
[10] Pam, Tudor Enfield, 3–4.
[11] Hist. MSS. Com. 7, 8th Rep. I, Corp. of Pontefract, p 271.

[12] Pam, op. cit. 7.
[13] See p. 236.
[14] Pam, op. cit. 9.
[15] B.M. Lansd. MS. 32, no. 40; 38, nos. 32, 35.
[16] Norden, Spec. Brit. 11.
[17] Mdx. Sess. Recs. ii. 228.
[18] Cal. Close, 1468–76, 76; Mdx. Sess. Recs. i. 217.
[19] T. Fuller, Worthies of England (1840 edn.), ii. 312.
[20] M.R.O., Acc. 16/4.
[21] D.L. 42/126.
[22] Enfield Arch. Soc., Ind. Arch. in Enfield, 2.
[23] Lewis, Topographical Dict. ii. 135.
[24] Robinson, Enfield, i. 19.
[25] Belvoir Castle, A/C. 272.
[26] M.P.C. 145 (D.L. 31/175).
[27] Ind. Arch. in Enfield, 2.
[28] M.R.O., Acc. 16/4.
[29] D.L. 41/16/12.
[30] Map of Eliab Breton's estate penes Enfield libr.
[31] Robinson, Enfield, i. 71 n.
[32] O.S. Map 6", Mdx. VII. NE. (1868 edn.).
[33] Ind. Arch. in Enfield, 23.
[34] C.P. 25(2)/854/8 Wm. III (Mdx.).
[35] Bodl. MS. Gough Mdx. 9, f. 20.
[36] Pigot's Com. Dir. (1832–4).
[37] Tuff, Enfield, 209.

soon after 1890.[38] The Cannon brewery, opposite the junction of Baker Street and Lancaster Road, had been built by 1868[39] but had disappeared by 1890.[40] Ponders End brewery adjoined the White Hart inn in 1869[41] and closed in the early 20th century.[42]

Tradesmen c. 1795 included two hairdressers, a milliner, a watch-maker, two peruke-makers, an upholsterer, a bookseller and stationer, and a writing master,[43] while in 1832 they included an auctioneer, two chemists, five linen drapers, two straw-hat makers, a bookbinder, three toy dealers, a coach-maker and a wine dealer.[44] As suburban housing spread, shopping centres grew up at Ponders End, Enfield Highway, Enfield Lock and, later, at Cockfosters, but the main centre has always been Enfield Town. The most prominent store there, Pearson's, was founded in 1903 and moved into its modern premises on the site of Enfield manor-house in 1928; in 1970 it employed over 400 people.[45]

The loss of Enfield market was said in 1832 to have injured the town's trade;[46] tanning had virtually ceased and there were only two factories, one for funeral crape and the other for small arms. The crape factory, opened at the corner of South Street and Scotland Green Road by Messrs. Grout and Baylis of Norwich in 1809, had nearly 200 employees by 1858, most of them from Ponders End.[47] It was closed in 1894 and taken over by the United Flexible Metallic Tubing Co., which still occupied the site and some of the original buildings in 1971.[48]

In 1804 it was proposed to build a small arms factory near the old water-mill at Enfield Lock,[49] downstream from the Royal Gunpowder factory at Waltham Holy Cross (Essex).[50] The assembling of muskets apparently started soon afterwards, before 32 a. were bought by the Board of Ordnance and plans, one of them by the elder John Rennie, were produced in 1813 and 1814.[51] The making of barrels was transferred from Lewisham to Enfield c. 1816, 'lock' and 'finishing' sections followed, and in 1853 the first Enfield rifle was issued. In 1854, when the Board of Ordnance took over the full production of its own small arms, the factory was rebuilt on a much larger scale. American machinery was installed and in 1861 the workforce numbered 1,700. In 1974 the factory covered 55 a., its area having been halved since the Second World War, and employed some 1,200 people. The chapel, in the 14th-century Gothic style, was never consecrated and was demolished in 1928.[52] The original brick factory buildings, around a quadrangle with a clock tower,[53] were still largely complete but the canal basin which served the factory had been filled in.

Other large-scale industries were limited to the eastern side of the parish, initially because of access to the Lea. Most of the early factories were at Ponders End, where the London Jute Works opened in 1865 and closed in 1882.[54] The presence of the jute factory influenced the establishment of the Corticene Floor Covering Co.'s works farther south, in the modern Wharf Road, in the 1870s; the factory had a wharf on the Lea, to handle cork and jute for making linoleum, and closed c. 1930 but some of its buildings survived in 1972.[55] By 1882 there was also a matting factory in South Street, a colour manufacturer in Derby Road, and a steam dye-works at a house in South Street called Bylocks Hall.[56] In 1904 Bylocks Hall was the registered office of the Paternoster Printing Co.[57]

The Edison Swan United Electric Light Co. (Ediswan) took over the site of the London Jute Works in 1886[58] and employed 650 persons there by 1890.[59] In 1904 the first thermionic radio valve was produced in a laboratory there, in 1916 the factory became the first in Britain to produce radio valves commercially, and in 1936 the first television tube factory in the country was opened on the site. The factory was afterwards sold by Thorn Electrical Industries, whereupon the buildings were demolished.[60] Ashby's Plating Works opened near by in Colmore Road in 1900 and still carried out electroplating, metal polishing, and stove enamelling in 1970.[61] In Aden Road there was a paper factory by 1921[62] and a slicing machine works by 1937.[63] The Enfield Tool Manufacturing Co., which in 1970 formed part of the Plessey Co., opened a factory in Alma Road c. 1935.[64] Barton's Forge and Iron Works opened a factory in Alexandra Road in 1943 and began specializing in the heat treatment of metals in 1947, while Chanter and Harding, sheet metal workers, opened a factory in the same road in 1947 and Enfield Plastics, toolmakers and producers of plastic injection mouldings, opened one in 1966.[65]

After 1900 the eastern part of the parish began to attract London firms seeking more space. Thomas Morson and Co., manufacturing chemists, moved from Fleet Market to a site adjoining the Corticene linoleum factory in 1901. The opening of the North Metropolitan Electric Power Supply Co.'s power station at Brimsdown in 1907[66] stimulated the growth of heavy engineering on the west bank of the Lea, which continued in the period between the World Wars and gave modern Enfield its distinctive character as an industrial centre. The Ruberoid Co. began manufacturing roofing materials at Brimsdown in 1910 and the Enfield Electric Cable Manufacturing Co., later Enfield Standard Power Cables, opened a factory farther north in 1913.[67] The Imperial Lamp

[38] Kelly's Dir. Mdx. (1890); Ind. Arch. in Enfield, 14.
[39] O.S. Map 6″, Mdx. VII. NE. (1867 edn.).
[40] Kelly's Dir. Mdx. (1890).
[41] Meyer's Enfield Observer, 1 Jan. 1869; M.R.O., Acc. 107/93.
[42] O.S. Maps 6″, Mdx. VII. NE. (1896 and 1920 edns.).
[43] Univ. Brit. Dir. [?1795], 83–5.
[44] Pigot's Com. Dir. (1832–4).
[45] Enfield L.B., Official Guide [1970].
[46] Pigot's Com. Dir. (1832–4).
[47] Ind. Arch. in Enfield, 14; Tuff, Enfield, 208–9; Lewis, Topog. Dict. (1831), ii. 135.
[48] Ind. Arch. in Enfield, 16.
[49] Except where otherwise stated the para. is based on Jnl. Soc. Army Hist. Res. xii. 197–212; Ind. Arch. in Enfield, 8–12; and inf. supplied by the dir.
[50] V.C.H. Essex, v. 164.
[51] M.P.H. 366, 583, 764 (W.O. 78/1461, /1871, /2589).

Presumably it was the new buildings, not the factory itself, which opened in 1816: Lewis, Topographical Dict. ii. 135.
[52] Photographs penes Royal Small Arms factory.
[53] See plate facing p. 240.
[54] Ind. Arch. in Enfield, 3.
[55] Ibid. 13, 18–19.
[56] Kelly's Dir. Mdx. (1882).
[57] M.R.O., Acc. 678/37A.
[58] Ind. Arch. in Enfield, 20.
[59] Kelly's Dir. Mdx. (1890).
[60] Ind. Arch. in Enfield, 20–2.
[61] Enfield L.B., Official Guide [1970].
[62] Kelly's Dir. Enfield (1921).
[63] Kelly's Dir. Mdx. (1937).
[64] Boro. of Enfield, Official Guide [1962].
[65] Enfield L.B., Official Guide [1970].
[66] Ind. Arch. in Enfield, 4; see below, p. 243.
[67] Enfield L.B., Official Guide [1970].

Works and the Brimsdown Lead Works were also established by 1913;[68] in 1971 the lamp works were occupied by Thorn A.E.I. Radio Valves & Tubes. By 1921 there were also factories in Stockingswater Lane for electric smelting and for making metallic cartridges.[69] Enfield Rolling Mills followed in 1924 and Brimsdown Castings in 1928; in 1970 the former were the largest British manufacturers of brass, copper, phosphor bronze, zinc, and aluminium.[70] By 1932 most sites by the Lea had been filled and factories were appearing farther west, near Brimsdown station.[71] Industry then spread northward to include Lockfield Avenue, which in 1971 contained the factories of Moulded Rubber Products, Padley Stainless Steels, Scripto Pens, and Sterling Vitreous Enamels.

Several firms were established west of Hertford Road at Ponders End after 1918, many of them on the sites of former nurseries. E. & E. Kaye opened a factory for copper wire in Queensway in 1922,[72] Stadium Ltd., manufacturers of plastics for the motor industry, began production near by in 1930, and H. D. Murray opened a machine-tool factory in 1936.[73] By 1937 there were factories for making accumulators, wireless apparatus, metal window-frames, and shop fittings in Queensway, and there were cabinet-makers in Lincoln Road,[74] where Reeves & Sons had opened a factory for painters' materials c. 1925.[75] Other factories in Queensway in 1938 included those of the Standard Fuse Co. and the British Electric Resistance Co.[76]

Industrialization west of the railway from Lower Edmonton to Cheshunt awaited the building of Great Cambridge Road in 1923–4. Belling & Lee opened a factory for electrical components in 1925[77] and later took over Bridge works, Southbury Road. By 1938, when Sangamo Weston began making electrical wire switches and meters,[78] factories lined the eastern side of Great Cambridge Road to the north of Southbury Road.[79] Standard Telephones and Cables later established their data equipment and systems division, formed in 1959, on a near-by site.[80] Some of the factories were later acquired by Thorn Electrical Industries, who occupied Cambridge House and in 1957 built the Sylvania-Thorn laboratories for research into colour television near the Ferguson Radio Co.'s works.[81]

The industrial pattern of Enfield has changed little since the Second World War. Firms established since 1945 have included the Diecasting Tool and Engineering Co., which opened a factory in Ordnance Road in 1955,[82] Conway Stewart & Co., pen manufacturers, and Gor-Ray, skirt manufacturers, both in Great Cambridge Road, International Flavors and Fragrances, in Crown Road, and Tricity Cookers in Mollison Avenue.[83]

SOCIAL LIFE. The town of Enfield was presented at quarter sessions for playing unlawful games c. 1555,[84] perhaps the year when 11 persons were accused of playing dice, cards, and bowls.[85] Major highways and the proximity of the Chase seem to have contributed to disorder in the 16th and 17th centuries, when there were several complaints of illegal gatherings and games.[86] Complaints were also made in 1675 of the excessive number of alehouses in the parish.[87]

There was a rabbit warren of 8 a. near Forty Hall in 1656.[88] Izaak Walton fished in Enfield, presumably on the Lea,[89] and in 1635 there were fisheries at Rammey Reach and on the Old Pond in the Chase.[90] There were frequent complaints of illegal hunting on the Chase[91] and in 1675 the use of guns in particular was condemned.[92] Efforts were made to halt the destruction of game and fish in Honeylands manor in 1787.[93]

Despite an attempt in 1632 to publicize medicinal baths at Enfield House,[94] no permanent spa was established. A bowling alley near Turkey Street in 1656[95] seems to have given its name to Bowling Green House, near the site of the later Myddelton House.[96] Part of a field north of the King's Head inn in Enfield Town was a bowling green by 1762 and was still one in 1851.[97]

Horse races were started on the marshes at the end of Green Street in 1788 and revived in 1816 near the later Wright's flour mill;[98] racing afterwards took place near Enfield Lock but had died out long before 1858.[99] The races drew disreputable crowds: 20,000 people gathered in 1801 to see a boxing match which was eventually banned, whereupon they were dispersed by local volunteer associations and the Hertfordshire Yeomanry Cavalry.[1] Racing was revived in 1870 by the owner of Bycullah Park, who ran well attended steeplechases in his grounds during Easter week until 1878.[2]

The first friendly society, the United society, began to meet in the Sun and Woolpack inn, Enfield Wash, in 1794, when extra branches were also formed at the King's Arms and the Black Horse.[3] In the same year the Amicable Union society began to meet in the Goat, Forty Hill, and the Society of Good Fellowship in the Falcon, South Street.[4] The

[68] O.S. Map 1/2,500, Mdx. VII. 4 (1913 edn.).
[69] Kelly's Dir. Enfield (1921).
[70] Boro. of Enfield, Official Guide [1962]; Enfield L.B., Official Guide [1970].
[71] Smith, 'Industrialization of Grtr. Lond.' 49.
[72] Boro. of Enfield, Official Guide [1962].
[73] Enfield L.B., Official Guide [1970].
[74] Kelly's Dir. Mdx. (1937).
[75] Boro. of Enfield, Official Guide [1962].
[76] O.S. Map 6", Mdx. VII. NE. (1938 edn.).
[77] Boro. of Enfield, Official Guide [1962]; Robbins, Mdx. 243.
[78] Boro. of Enfield, Official Guide [1962].
[79] O.S. Map 6", Mdx. VII. NE. (1938 edn.).
[80] Enfield L.B., Official Guide [1962].
[81] Architectural Rev. cxix. 54; cxxi. 197.
[82] Boro. of Enfield, Official Guide [1962].
[83] Enfield L.B., Official Guide [1970].
[84] M.R.O., Acc. 275/507.
[85] Hist. MSS. Com. 39, 15th Rep. II, Misc. Papers, p. 258.

[86] e.g. Mdx. Cnty. Recs. ii. 81; M.R.O., Cal. Mdx. Sess. Bks. (1652–7), 93–4, 156.
[87] Ibid. (1673–9), 59–60.
[88] M.R.O., Acc. 16/8.
[89] V.C.H. Mdx. ii. 269.
[90] D.L. 42/125.
[91] e.g. Cal. Treas. Bks. 1679–80, p. 503.
[92] M.R.O., Cal. Mdx. Sess. Bks. (1673–9), 59–60.
[93] Bodl. MS. Top. Mdx. b.1, f. 71.
[94] Tuff, Enfield, 37n.
[95] M.R.O., Acc. 16/8.
[96] See p. 217.
[97] M.R.O., Acc. 903/88–90.
[98] Robinson, Enfield, i. 23–4.
[99] Tuff, Enfield, 30.
[1] Ford, Enfield, 108–9.
[2] Whitaker, Enfield, 89, 250.
[3] FS. 1/419/618; FS. 1/574; FS. 1/604.
[4] FS. 1/565; FS. 1/584.

Amicable society met at the New Inn at Coopers Lane gate from 1796 and the United Benefit society at the Three Horseshoes from 1800.[5] Among early-19th-century societies was the United Sisters' friendly society for women, at the King's Head from 1810 to 1820.[6] After 1812[7] there were no new registrations until that of the Enfield benefit society in 1838, meeting in the free school, Enfield Town, and subsequently in the temperance hall.[8] Several new societies, all of which used inns, were founded in the next 20 years.[9]

There was a savings bank and a penny club in 1826[10] and another successful bank was established in 1839 to promote saving among the middle and poorer classes.[11] The Enfield coal club, which operated from the temperance hall, was established in 1841[12] and the Enfield literary and scientific institution, a mechanics' institute, existed by 1851.[13] The Enfield young men's mutual improvement society was meeting in the infants' school in Baker Street in 1859.[14] The Enfield ladies' visiting society was founded in 1828, to give occasional relief in kind and help to suppress mendicity.[15] The Enfield philanthropic institution was founded in 1836 and survived in 1911.[16]

Attempts were made to make Enfield a local social centre after 1800. A subscription assembly was held for three nights in the assembly rooms by the King's Head in 1801, families paying two guineas and receiving tea and coffee.[17] The assembly rooms were used in 1858 for public meetings, large vestry meetings, lectures, and entertainments.[18] Enfield cricket club existed by 1814[19] and held practices twice a week in 1857,[20] when the Society of Enfield Archers first met in Chase Side.[21] In 1830 Charles Lamb wrote that people in Enfield did not look like country folk and that they had a circulating library.[22] Another library was established in 1850 by J. H. Meyers 'for the principal families'.[23] Meyers also founded the monthly *Meyers' Enfield Observer*, which first appeared in 1859 and continued in 1971 as the weekly *Enfield Observer*. The weekly *Middlesex Observer* had been founded by 1890[24] and the weekly *Enfield Chronicle* and the monthly *Enfield Illustrated Magazine* were published in 1899.[25]

Rural pastimes persisted. A maypole was erected annually until the mid 19th century, although the practice had ceased by 1859.[26] The North Middlesex and South Hertfordshire farmers' club, formed in 1853, met monthly at the King's Head and arranged annual ploughing matches and agricultural shows.[27]

The Enfield Chase staghounds were established by Col. Sir Alfred Somerset in 1885; in 1899 the kennels were moved from his house, Enfield Court, to Barnet (Herts.)[28] and soon after the First World War the hunt was disbanded.[29] A hunt called the Enfield Chase foxhounds held point-to-points in 1955.[30]

Many societies were formed in the late 19th century. A temperance hall was opened in Brigadier Hill in 1859[31] and St. Andrew's temperance club existed in 1890.[32] Enfield musical society was founded in 1862 and a Conservative society, a freemasons' lodge, and a working men's institute were all active in 1869.[33] A co-operative society was founded at Enfield Lock by workers in the Royal Small Arms factory in 1872; it later became Enfield Highway co-operative society, taking over other similar societies in Enfield Town[34] and Hoddesdon (Herts.).[35] Parish tea meetings were advertised in 1889,[36] the Walker church institute, Sydney Road, was built in 1889,[37] and a Church of England working men's club was meeting in Silver Street in 1890.[38] E. A. Bowles of Forty Hall arranged lectures and concerts in the local elementary school in the late 19th century.[39] A church institute was built in Napier Road, Ponders End, in 1893[40] and another was opened to serve the new suburbs north of Lancaster Road in 1896; a coffee tavern, working men's club, and library were provided, together with a hall for temperance meetings.[41] St. Mark's institute, Bush Hill Park, was built in 1907 and also accommodated temperance organizations.[42] By 1890 there was a Constitutional club meeting in London Road, a Radical club in Lancaster Road, a Conservative working men's club at Enfield Wash, and Conservative, Liberal, and Radical clubs at Ponders End.[43] Working men's clubs had been founded at Cockfosters and Bush Hill Park by 1898.[44]

An anonymous writer in 1905 considered Enfield suburban to the core, citing the pretentiousness of the literary union but praising the dramatic society.[45] A tennis club was founded at Hadley Wood c. 1895 and assumed a prominent place in local social life.[46] Bush Hill Park golf club was founded in 1896 and later acquired its 18-hole course in Enfield Old Park. Enfield golf club was established with a course south of Windmill Hill in 1902, Crews Hill golf club was founded in 1915,[47] and Hadley Wood golf club at Beech Hill Park in 1922.[48]

By 1921 the Ponders End electric theatre was open in Hertford Road and the Queens Hall cinema in

[5] FS. 1/809; FS. 1/1130.
[6] FS. 1/1310.
[7] FS. 1/1101; FS. 1/1309; FS. 1/1421.
[8] FS. 1/464; FS. 1/2304.
[9] FS. 1/2305; FS. 1/2447; FS. 1/3173; FS. 1/3240.
[10] Robinson, *Enfield*, ii. 131.
[11] Tuff, *Enfield*, 216.
[12] FS. 1/2454.
[13] T. Kelly, *George Birkbeck*, 314.
[14] *Meyers' Enfield Observer*, Jan. 1859.
[15] Tuff, *Enfield*, 220.
[16] Ibid. 218; Whitaker, *Enfield*, 82.
[17] Bodl. MS. Top. Mdx. b.1, f. 109.
[18] Tuff, *Enfield*, 223.
[19] Boro. of Enfield, *Official Guide* [1955].
[20] Tuff, *Enfield*, 215.
[21] Ibid.
[22] Whitaker, *Enfield*, 82n.
[23] Tuff, *Enfield*, 216.
[24] *Kelly's Dir. Mdx.* (1890).
[25] *Willing's Press Guide* (1899).
[26] *Meyers' Enfield Observer*, May 1859.
[27] Tuff, *Enfield*, 214.
[28] *V.C.H. Mdx.* ii. 262.
[29] Briggs, *Mdx. Old and New*, 63.
[30] Boro. of Enfield, *Official Guide* [1955].
[31] *Meyers' Enfield Observer*, May 1859.
[32] *Kelly's Dir. Mdx.* (1890).
[33] *Meyers' Enfield Observer*, Jan. 1869.
[34] Existing in 1890: *Kelly's Dir. Mdx.* (1890).
[35] New Enfield Hist.
[36] *Meyers' Enfield Observer*, Mar. 1869.
[37] Whitaker, *Enfield*, 184.
[38] *Kelly's Dir. Mdx.* (1890).
[39] F. Wilson, *Memories of Forty Hill*, 10.
[40] *Kelly's Dir. Mdx.* (1908).
[41] *Kelly's Dir. Tottenham* (1898-9).
[42] *Kelly's Dir. Enfield* (1921).
[43] *Kelly's Dir. Mdx.* (1890). [44] Ibid. (1890, 1898).
[45] *Enfield Tatler*, Mar. 1905, p. 35.
[46] Clark, *Hadley Wood*, 93.
[47] *Kelly's Dir. Mdx.* (1931).
[48] Clark, *Hadley Wood*, 45.

TOTTENHAM: THE FLOUR MILLS *c.* 1800

ENFIELD: THE ROYAL SMALL ARMS FACTORY *c.* 1972
The canal basin, since filled in, is in the foreground

Hendon: cottages at Mill Hill

South Mimms: Blanche Farm

Great Stanmore: nos. 57–65 the Broadway

Little Stanmore: nos. 97–101 Edgware High Street

VERNACULAR BUILDING

London Road.[49] The Rialto picture theatre opened in the 1920s, providing a tea room and lounge.[50] There were four cinemas in 1955[51] including the Plaza, Ponders End, which was taken over by Enfield B.C. in 1956 and renamed the Howard hall, to be used for plays and receptions.[52] Choral, literary, musical and dramatic groups also existed.[53] The Hadley Wood association was founded in 1964 to provide social facilities in its part of the parish.[54]

LOCAL GOVERNMENT. In 1294 Humphrey de Bohun, earl of Hereford and Essex, successfully claimed view of frankpledge and infangthief in his manor of Enfield from time immemorial. The abbot of Walden also sustained his claim to certain rights in Enfield, including view of frankpledge and the assizes of bread and of ale, although he admitted that he had never had a pillory or tumbril and that the earl's bailiffs had always taken amercements of blood and of hue and cry.[55] The abbots' rights derived from a grant of 1248 by the earl's grandfather[56] and their estate became Rectory manor, for which a court leet was being held in the 18th century.[57] Courts were being held for Enfield manor in 1324[58] and a court leet met annually after Michaelmas in 1363.[59] Court rolls, however, survive only from 1618 to 1649 and from 1705 to 1850, during which period the lord exercised view of frankpledge and the two assizes.[60] In 1823 courts leet and baron met twice a year at the Rose and Crown, Enfield Highway, having formerly been held in a barn and then at the King's Head.[61]

Thomas Durant claimed view of frankpledge in the mid 14th century[62] on the estate which later became the manor of Durants, for which a court book records courts baron from 1689 to 1905.[63] A court book for the manor of Honeylands and Pentriches records courts baron from 1509 to 1909 and courts leet with view of frankpledge in 1785 and 1786.[64] Courts for the manor later known as Worcesters were being held in 1412[65] and court rolls survive from 1599 to 1732, with an abstract from 1599 to 1759;[66] in 1823 courts baron were still held at irregular intervals.[67]

By 1618 Enfield manorial court appointed a constable, two capital pledges (later called headboroughs), and a bread-weigher and ale-taster annually for each of the four wards or quarters of the parish: Enfield Green, later called Enfield Town, Bull's Cross, Ponders End, and Horsepool Stones, later known as Green Street.[68] Quasi-criminal jurisdiction was no longer exercised in the 17th century but there were several presentments over fencing, ditching, and pasturing animals, while the court continued to mete out fines for offences connected with the Chase.[69] In 1823 the officials chosen at the court leet were a constable, two headboroughs, a brander, and an aleconner for the Town quarter, a constable, a headborough, and a brander for Bull's Cross quarter, and two headboroughs, a brander, and a hayward for Green Street and Ponders End, which by then had amalgamated.[70] The office of aleconner had been revived in 1813, when 20 shopkeepers were fined and 150 publicans' pots were destroyed.[71] The proceeds from the fines were invested and in 1885, when the office of aleconner had again lapsed, a Charity Commissioners' Scheme directed that the annual income of £5 be spent on maintaining Chase Green.[72] The last manorial court was held in 1925.[73]

A pillory stood in the market place in 1646.[74] Stocks were mentioned in 1682[75] and still existed east of the market place in 1876, by which date the pillory had disappeared.[76] A cage at Enfield Highway, with stocks attached, was dilapidated by 1833;[77] it was superseded by a building which may have been the lock-up which stood on the south of Brick Lane, near the junction with the Hertford road, in 1868.[78] A watch-house at Enfield Town replaced an older one in 1784[79] and in turn was replaced in 1830 by a watch-house east of the market place, with a beadle's house attached, which had been paid for out of King James's charity.[80] The Enfield association was formed to preserve public order in 1794, when 14 people volunteered as special constables.[81] In 1798 the association met twice a week in order to police the parish and in 1805 it was offering rewards for information which would lead to arrests.[82]

There were three churchwardens in 1481[83] and four in 1580.[84] In 1691 each of the four wards had a churchwarden but in 1696 Green Street and Ponders End wards were amalgamated. The churchwarden for Enfield Green or Town ward was appointed by the vicar, the others by the vestry.[85] Vestry meetings were held monthly in 1616[86] and were recorded in order books which survive from 1671 to 1744 and from 1797.[87] Meetings took place in a room at the church and were still monthly in the early 19th century, when they were usually chaired by the vicar; prominent local landowners often attended and numbers rarely fell below eight, sometimes rising to twenty or more.[88]

[49] Kelly's Dir. Enfield (1921).
[50] Enfield U.D.C., Official Guide [n.d.].
[51] Boro. of Enfield, Official Guide [1955].
[52] Ibid. [1962].
[53] Ibid. [1955].
[54] Clark, Hadley Wood, 103.
[55] Plac. de Quo Warr. (Rec. Com.), 479.
[56] Cal. Chart. R. 1226-57, 337.
[57] Lysons, Environs, ii. 311.
[58] S.C. 6/1146/20.
[59] Cal. Inq. p.m. xi, p. 366.
[60] S.C. 2/188/55-64; D.L. 30/99/1371.
[61] Robinson, Enfield, i. 97-8.
[62] D.L. 43/7/1.
[63] M.R.O., Acc. 133.   [64] M.R.O., Acc. 16/1.
[65] C 137/227/25.
[66] M.R.O., Acc. 16/5; Acc. 276/8.
[67] Robinson, Enfield, i. 141.
[68] S.C. 2/118/55.
[69] D.L. 30/99/1371.

[70] Robinson, Enfield, i. 97-8.
[71] P. Hardy, Hints for . . . the Inhabitants of Enfield, 39-41.
[72] Weld, Enfield Charities, 28.
[73] Boro. of Enfield, Official Guide [1955].
[74] M.R.O., Cal. Mdx. Sess. Bks. (1644-52), 63.
[75] Ibid. (1679-82), 147.
[76] Thorne, Environs, i. 179.
[77] Vestry order bk. (1823-39), 321-3 penes Enfield L.B.
[78] O.S. Map 6", Mdx. VII. NE. (1868 edn.).
[79] M.R.O., D.R.O. 4/3/18.
[80] Vestry order bk. (1823-39), 197, 227.
[81] Bodl. MS. Top. Mdx. b.1, ff. 80-1.
[82] Ibid. ff. 85, 137.
[83] M.R.O., Acc. 903/123.
[84] Guildhall MS. 9537/4.
[85] Ford, Enfield, 306.
[86] Mdx. Sess. Recs. iv. 4.
[87] Penes Enfield L.B. at Enfield civic centre.
[88] Vestry order bks. (1797-1807), passim.

A parish clerk was mentioned in 1524[89] and an overseer of the poor was appointed annually in 1580 for each of the four wards.[90] An irregular series of overseers' accounts survives from 1750 to 1834 and poor-rate books exist from 1740 to 1842.[91] During the early 18th century a constable had special responsibility for vagrants[92] and in 1750 there was a beadle for Bull's Cross quarter.[93] In 1807 the beadle, who was paid, had responsibility for the whole parish[94] but in 1827 two paid assistants were appointed and given uniforms.[95] An assistant beadle for St. James's, Enfield Highway, was appointed in 1836.[96] Other officials included a sexton in 1807,[97] a crier in 1798,[98] and a salaried apothecary and surgeon in 1807.[99]

In 1630 Robert Curtis was paid for setting the poor to work.[1] A workhouse at Chase Side was leased from 1719[2] and bought in 1740.[3] It had been extended to include a school-room[4] by 1788 and a pest-house by 1802.[5] The workhouse contained 60 inmates in 1826, when its state was said to be 'tolerable',[6] but in 1827 it made way for a new brick building, also at Chase Side,[7] which later became Edmonton union school.[8] The poor were farmed out in 1765 to a contractor who would feed and clothe the workhouse inmates and relieve the out-poor when required by the overseers; all paupers were to wear uniform and be badged.[9] In 1778 poor-relief was said to be costly and complaints were made about non-parishioners in the workhouse.[10] In 1802 a committee was set up to manage the workhouse, which was to be inspected weekly, and new rules were devised.[11] Conditions were still deplored in 1806, when 'rags and idleness' were prevalent,[12] but had improved by 1813.[13] From 1806 poor boys and girls from the workhouse were sent to work at a silk factory at Sewardstone (Essex).[14]

There seem to have been no parish houses.[15] Several charities helped to lighten the burden of poor-relief, while common rights may have lessened the demand for relief before inclosure. Thereafter poor-rates could be supplemented by rents from the parish's allotment out of the Chase and by the sale of timber.[16] In 1775–6 £1,022 was raised from the poor-rates, of which £857 was spent on the poor,[17] and in 1831 the rates brought in £4,118.[18] Subscriptions were raised for a lying-in fund, to employ a midwife, in 1797[19] and to supply cheap bread

in 1799.[20] The Enfield philanthropic institution was established in 1836 to relieve the deserving poor.[21]

In 1784 there was a complaint of confusion at the vestry meetings[22] and in 1802, after financial irregularities, the vicar was made treasurer and the vestry clerk collector of rents, gifts, and poor-rates. Accounts thenceforth were to be audited annually, the overseers were to answer to a committee, and attempts were made to limit expenditure at inns. In 1803 the churchwarden for the Town quarter was censured for profiteering over supplies to the workhouse and in 1806 the overseers were ordered to collect the poor-rates more rigorously. By 1806, however, it was claimed that the parish was out of debt[23] and in 1808 its management of the poor was said to have improved greatly.[24] In 1821 a select vestry was established, meeting weekly or fortnightly at the workhouse to supervise poor-relief.[25] In 1834 the vicar stated that it contained gentlemen, farmers, and tradesmen, and had worked very advantageously.[26]

A surveyor of the highways was mentioned in 1705[27] and by the end of the 18th century there was a surveyor for each ward. Highway-rate books survive from 1801 to 1828.[28] A paid 'general surveyor' for the whole parish, except the former Chase, was finally appointed in 1824[29] but the surveyors' accounts were so unsatisfactory in 1833 that they raised fears of a return to the system of unpaid surveyors.[30] Under the inclosure Act of 1777 the king's allotment, the lodges, and the allotments to Trinity College, Cambridge, and the vicar of Enfield became in 1778 a separate highway district, called Enfield Chase district, with two surveyors appointed by the duchy of Lancaster.[31]

After strong objections from the vestry, which claimed that the parish was more populous than any of the thirty poor-law unions already formed and that the poor would suffer in too large a unit, Enfield joined Edmonton union in 1836,[32] whereupon the workhouse at Chase Side became the union school.[33] A highway board was formed in 1841 under the Highway Act of 1835,[34] and a local board of health, under the Public Health Act of 1848, in 1850.[35] Enfield became an urban district under the Local Government Act of 1894, with three councillors elected for each of four wards: Town, Chase and

[89] L. & P. Hen. VIII, iv(1), p. 150.
[90] Guildhall MS. 9537/4.
[91] M.R.O., D.R.O. 4/23; ibid. /1–308.
[92] M.R.O., Cal. Mdx. Sess. Bks. (1722–7), 257–8.
[93] M.R.O., D.R.O. 4/23/1.
[94] Vestry order bk. (1797–1807), 435.
[95] Ibid. (1823–39), 129.
[96] Ibid. 432.
[97] Ibid. (1807–22), 13, 98.
[98] Ibid. (1797–1807), 68.
[99] Ibid. (1807–22), 8.
[1] M.R.O., D.R.O. 4/1/1A.
[2] Vestry order bk. (1690–1744).
[3] Robinson, Enfield, ii. 113.
[4] M.R.O., D.R.O. 4/3/18.
[5] Vestry order bk. (1797–1807), 167.
[6] Robinson, Enfield, ii. 113.
[7] Whitaker, Enfield, 351.
[8] See p. 254.
[9] M.R.O., D.R.O. 4/2/10.
[10] Ibid.
[11] Vestry order bk. (1797–1807), 218–9.
[12] Ibid. 383–93.
[13] P. Hardy, Hints for . . . the Inhabitants of Enfield, 6.
[14] Vestry order bk. (1797–1807), 426.

[15] M.R.O., D.R.O. 4/1–308.
[16] See below, p. 259.
[17] Rep. Cttee. on Rets. by Overseers, 1776, 396.
[18] Rep. Com. Poor Laws, H.C. 44, p. 93f (1834), xxxv.
[19] Robinson, Enfield, ii. 130.
[20] Vestry order bk. (1797–1807), 100–2.
[21] Tuff, Enfield, 218.
[22] M.R.O., D.R.O. 4/22.
[23] Vestry order bk. (1797–1807), 202–5, 239–41, 383–93, 427–8.
[24] Ibid. (1807–22), 44.
[25] Whitaker, Enfield, 341; M.R.O., D.R.O. 4/22.
[26] Rep. Com. Poor Laws, H.C. 44, p. 93f (1834), xxxv.
[27] M.R.O., Cal. Mdx. Sess. Bks. (1722–7), 257–8.
[28] M.R.O., D.R.O. 4/387–425.
[29] Vestry order bk. (1797–1807), 74–5; ibid. (1823–39), 63–4.
[30] Ibid. 332–3.
[31] 17 Geo. III, c. 17, s. 45.
[32] Vestry order bk. (1823–39), 419–21; S. I. Richardson, Edmonton Poor Law Union (Edmonton Hund. Hist. Soc.), 11.
[33] See p. 254.
[34] 5 & 6 Wm. IV, c. 50; vestry order bk. (1840–52), 6.
[35] Lond. Gaz. 21 June 1850, p. 1747.

Bull's Cross, Ordnance, and Green Street and Ponders End.[36] Bush Hill Park ward and Hadley Wood and Cockfosters ward were added before 1911.[37] Enfield U.D. was incorporated in 1955, by which date it was the second largest urban district in the country, with a population exceeding those of 39 of the 83 county boroughs.[38] The borough had 10 wards: Bush Hill Park, Cambridge Road, Chase, Enfield Wash, Green Street, Ordnance, Ponders End, Town, West, and Willow,[39] each electing three councillors. In 1965 the borough became part of Enfield L.B., under the London Government Act of 1963.

URBAN DISTRICT (LATER BOROUGH) OF ENFIELD. *Or, an enfield rampant gules; on a chief vert a bar wavy argent charged with a barrulet wavy azure*
[Granted 1946]

as council offices.[40] Land for a new town hall in Church Street was purchased in 1902[41] but the U.D.C. remained at Little Park until 1961, when the first part of a new civic centre in Silver Street, designed by Eric G. Boughton, was opened.[42] The uncompleted building was the administrative centre of Enfield L.B. in 1971, when the old offices in Little Park served as the health department. In 1972 work began on extensions to the civic centre, also designed by Boughton and including an eleven-storeyed tower block.[43]

LONDON BOROUGH OF ENFIELD. *Or, on a fess wavy vert, a bar wavy argent charged with a barrulet wavy azure, over all an enfield rampant gules*
[Granted 1965]

The Labour party dominated Enfield B.C. and at first, by a narrow majority, controlled the new London Borough. Conservatives gained control in 1968 and retained it, with a much smaller majority, in 1971.[44]

PUBLIC SERVICES. A private conduit served Whitewebbs in 1569[45] and the brick conduit-house

survived in 1873.[46] Under the inclosure Act of 1777 a water-pipe was provided from Sir Thomas Hallifax's conduit on the Chase for the inhabitants of Enfield[47] and in 1847 a parish pump in the market place was replaced.[48] A water-works undertaking was set up in 1850[49] and in 1854 the local board opened a works in Alma Road, Ponders End, with a small reservoir in Southbury Road and a larger one at the top of Holtwhite's Hill, where a water-tower was built in 1887;[50] a pumping station in Hadley Road was built in 1902 and a water-tower in the Ridgeway in 1913–14. In 1904 responsibility for the water supply was transferred from Enfield U.D. to the Metropolitan Water Board.[51] The board built pumping stations near the northern and south-western ends of King George's reservoir, opened in 1913, and on Rammey marsh.[52]

In 1825 water from Windmill Hill flowed through a sewer at Chase Green,[53] which in 1835 was replaced by a brick drain disgorging into the 'parish drain'.[54] The local board proposed a drainage system in 1854 and built a sewage works by 1857 but, after a dispute, was forbidden to use a watercourse which ran from the works through Edmonton parish.[55] A sewage farm was built in 1877 on Cuckoo Hill farm, Edmonton, and enlarged by 1911 to cover 110 a.[56] The sewage works were purchased by the county council in 1938[57] and modernized in 1939.[58] By 1962 some of the sewage from the parish was being purified at the East Middlesex sewage works at Deephams Farm, Edmonton.[59]

Some influential inhabitants resolved in 1850 to establish a gas company in Enfield, where a gas-works had been built in Sydney Road by 1858.[60] Another works was opened south of Ponders End railway station in 1859.[61] In 1879 the Ponders End Gas Co. was amalgamated with the Enfield Gas Co.[62] and in 1911 the combined undertaking was transferred to the Tottenham and Edmonton Gas Light and Coke Co.[63] The works in Sydney Road were still in use in 1908[64] but in 1921 most of the parish was supplied with gas from works in Edmonton, although Hadley Wood and Cockfosters were served by the Barnet and District Gas and Water Co.[65] The gas-works at Ponders End were closed in 1970.[66] An Act of 1898 gave the Enfield Gas Co. powers to supply the parish with electricity.[67] The North Metropolitan Electric Power Supply Co. opened a power station at Brimsdown in 1907[68] and was empowered to supply electricity to the parish in 1922.[69] The power station was extended from 1924, when 41 a. were acquired from Trinity College, Cambridge,[70] until 1955 and employed some 700 persons c. 1960. Thereafter the workforce contracted

[36] Whitaker, *Enfield*, 342.
[37] *Census*, 1911.
[38] Boro. of Enfield, *Official Guide* [1955]; New Enfield Hist.
[39] *Census* (1961).
[40] Tuff, *Enfield*, 217; Whitaker, *Enfield*, 344.
[41] Whitaker, *Enfield*, 344.
[42] I. Nairn, *Modern Buildings in Lond.* 79.
[43] Ex inf. the town clerk and chief executive.
[44] Election results in *The Times*, e.g. 9 May 1958, 9 May 1964, 10 May 1968, 14 May 1971.
[45] Robinson, *Enfield*, i. 245.
[46] Ford, *Enfield*, 83.   [47] 17 Geo. III, c. 17.
[48] Vestry order bk. (1840–52), 172.
[49] Whitaker, *Enfield*, 345.
[50] *Ind. Arch. in Enfield*, 31–3.   [51] 2 Edw. VII, c. 41.
[52] O.S. Maps 6", Mdx. III. SW.; VII. NE.; VIII. NW. (1920 edn.).

[53] Vestry order bk. (1823–39), 85.
[54] Ibid. 374.
[55] New Enfield Hist.
[56] Whitaker, *Enfield*, 344.
[57] New Enfield Hist.
[58] Boro. of Enfield, *Official Guide* [1955].
[59] Ibid. [1962]; see above, p. 180.
[60] Tuff, *Enfield*, 210.
[61] *Ind. Arch. in Enfield*, 3.
[62] 42 & 43 Vic. c. 159.
[63] 1 & 2 Geo. V, c. 42.
[64] *Kelly's Dir. Mdx.* (1908).
[65] *Kelly's Dir. Enfield* (1921).
[66] Enfield libr., photographic coll.
[67] 61 & 62 Vic. c. 57, s. 46.
[68] *Ind. Arch. in Enfield*, 4.
[69] 12 & 13 Geo. V, c. 77.
[70] Trinity Coll. Cambridge, Estate MSS., box 43(s).

to 250 by 1974, when most of Enfield L.B. and adjacent areas in Essex were still supplied from Brimsdown.[71]

There was a pest-house for plague victims in the Chase, near Enfield Town, in 1658.[72] In 1875 a cottage hospital with 5 beds was opened in Chase Side, supported by voluntary contributions.[73] It was extended in 1888[74] and again after the First World War, when it was renamed Enfield War Memorial hospital; in 1939 there were 39 beds. In 1948 the new Enfield group hospital management committee took over the hospital, which had 46 patients in 1971.[75]

Enfield and Edmonton isolation hospital was established in 1891 in huts at the southern end of World's End Lane. The first brick-built ward was opened in 1899. Some non-infectious cases were received during the Second World War and the hospital subsequently became a general hospital, where a maternity unit was opened in 1963. In 1948 the hospital came under Enfield management committee and was renamed South Lodge hospital. It was united with the nearby Highlands hospital, Edmonton, in 1968.[76]

Bramley House, Clay Hill, was being used as a mental home in 1921 and was formally established by the county council as a mental deficiency institution in 1930. In 1948 it came under the control of South Ockendon management committee and in 1971 catered for some 70 high grade mentally handicapped female patients.[77]

A home for old people was established in 1938 in the former Chase Farm schools,[78] which were extended by two new wards. In 1939 it was turned into an emergency hospital with 800 beds and in 1948 it was placed under Enfield management committee as a general hospital. By 1971 the number of beds had been reduced to under 400 and work had begun on a new building.[79]

The old union workhouse school at Chase Side, in whose grounds an infirmary for 40 children had been built in 1855,[80] became the infirmary of Edmonton union in 1886.[81] It was a public assistance institution containing about 100 chronic sick, 100 healthy adults, and 50 mentally handicapped boys by 1939, when it was extended to take another 200 patients. In 1948 the institution came under Enfield management committee and was renamed St. Michael's hospital. In 1971 it catered for the elderly and had 310 patients, mostly women.[82]

A parish fire-engine, in the care of a paid keeper, was housed by the church porch in 1805.[83] In 1843 a new engine-house was built on the eastern side of the King's Head.[84] A volunteer fire brigade existed

in 1869[85] at Ponders End, where the fire station was purchased by Enfield local board in 1891.[86] In 1971 there were two fire stations in the parish, in Carterhatch Lane and in Holtwhite's Hill.

The watch-house which had been built in 1830 served as a police station in 1868.[87] It was superseded in 1873 by a new station in London Road, which itself was replaced in the 1960s by one at no. 41 Baker Street.[88] Stations had also been opened in Enfield Highway and Enfield Lock by 1890.[89] There was a police station in Ponders End High Street in 1971,[90] when the old watch-house survived as part of an office.

A burial board was set up in 1871 and a 9-acre cemetery at the top of Brigadier Hill was opened in 1872 on part of the Hundred Acres belonging to the parish.[91] The cemetery was enlarged by 3 a. in 1897.[92] Enfield crematorium, Great Cambridge Road, was opened in 1938 by Tottenham and Wood Green burial board; the brick buildings, with a central tower flanked by two chapels, were designed by Sir Guy Dawber, Wilson and Fox.[93]

The first public open space in Enfield was Chase Green, containing 12 a., which was left uninclosed under the Act of 1806 and later placed under the management of the vicar, churchwardens, and overseers. Culloden Rowan gave £500 for its upkeep c. 1880 and in 1898 it was transferred to Enfield U.D.C.[94] The following pieces of land were bought by the U.D.C. as public open spaces: Town park (23 a.), Albany park, Enfield Lock (18 a.), both opened in 1902; Durants park, Enfield Highway (34 a.), opened in 1903; Hilly fields, Clay Hill (62 a.), opened in 1911; and Bush Hill Park recreation ground (27 a.).[95] Ponders End recreation ground (8 a.) was purchased in 1920 and 1925.[96] Enfield playing fields, 128 a. north of Southbury Road, were open by 1938.[97] The Forty Hall estate (265 a.) was acquired in 1951 and Forty Hall was opened as a museum. In 1971 Whitewebbs park (232 a.) was also a public park, administered by Enfield L.B.,[98] and Trent Park was administered by the G.L.C.[99]

The Public Libraries Act of 1855 was adopted in 1892 and a lending library opened in 1894 in part of the local board offices in Little Park.[1] In 1912 the library moved to a new red brick building with stone dressings in Cecil Road, financed by Andrew Carnegie.[2] By 1908 there were branch libraries at Ponders End and Enfield Wash[3] and in 1910 a new building at Enfield Highway was opened with a gift from Carnegie.[4] In 1971 there were additional branch libraries in Kemp Road, Enfield Road, Fourth Avenue, and Ponders End High Street.

[71] Ex inf. the station superintendent. See plate facing p. 177.
[72] M.P.C. 50A (D.L. 31/50A).
[73] Kelly's Dir. Mdx. (1890); ex inf. the hospital sec.
[74] Whitaker, Enfield, 92.
[75] Ex inf. the hospital sec.
[76] Ex inf. the sec., Highlands hosp.
[77] Ex inf. the sec., South Ockendon hosp. group.
[78] See p. 254.
[79] Ex inf. the sec., Chase Farm hosp.
[80] Tuff, Enfield, 227.
[81] Whitaker, Enfield, 234.
[82] Ex inf. the sec.
[83] Vestry order bk. (1797–1807), 360; Robinson, Enfield, ii. 4.
[84] Vestry order bk. (1840–52), 23.
[85] Meyers' Enfield Observer, 1 Jan. 1869.
[86] Whitaker, Enfield, 345.

[87] Tuff, Enfield, 218.
[88] Ford, Enfield, 111.
[89] Kelly's Dir. Mdx. (1890).
[90] Enfield L.B., Official Guide [1970].
[91] Ford, Enfield, 287; Kelly's Dir. Mdx. (1890).
[92] Whitaker, Enfield, 242.
[93] Builder, clxx. 305.
[94] Char. Com. files.
[95] Kelly's Dir. Enfield (1921).
[96] Ibid. (1931).
[97] O.S. Map 6″, Mdx. VII. NE. (1938 edn.).
[98] Enfield L.B., Official Guide [1970].
[99] Ex inf. Mr. A. H. Hall.
[1] Kelly's Dir. Mdx. (1908); Boro. of Enfield, Official Guide [1955].
[2] Enfield U.D., Official Guide [c. 1921].
[3] Kelly's Dir. Mdx. (1908).
[4] Kelly's Dir. Enfield (1921).

Public baths were opened in Newbury Avenue, Enfield Lock, in 1893.[5] An open-air swimming pool in Southbury Road was opened in 1933.[6]

There were 1,746 council houses in Enfield by 1939. A further 347 prefabricated bungalows were built by the U.D.C. after 1945 on Manor farm, Great Cambridge Road, and near Enfield Town and 1,795 other houses and flats between 1945 and 1955.[7]

CHURCHES. There was a priest at Enfield in 1086.[8] At about that date Geoffrey de Mandeville gave a portion of the tithes, with pannage in the park and woods, to his newly-founded priory at Hurley (Berks.). His grandson Geoffrey, earl of Essex (d. 1144), gave the monks an annual rent of 100s. in exchange for the tithes of Enfield and Edmonton, which henceforth were to support the churches there.[9] In 1136, however, the church at Enfield was granted to the earl's foundation at Walden (Essex),[10] although Hurley retained its rights of pannage in the Chase and the tithe of nuts there until 1258, when they were exchanged with Walden for the church of Streatley (Berks.).[11] A single church served the parish until 1831.[12]

The Enfield church was appropriated by Walden before the end of the 13th century[13] and a vicarage was ordained before 1254.[14] In 1538, at the Dissolution, the rectory and advowson of Enfield were granted to Sir Thomas Audley, later Lord Audley of Walden,[15] who surrendered them in 1542 to the king.[16] In 1548 they were given to Trinity College, Cambridge,[17] with whom they remained. Vicars were appointed by the abbots of Walden until 1540, when Lord Audley presented; the Crown presented in 1550 and Trinity College in 1556, as on all subsequent occasions except 1579, when the archbishop of Canterbury presented by lapse.[18]

Godfrey de Beston gave a house adjoining the churchyard, which he had purchased from Richard de Plessis, to Bartholomew, vicar of Enfield, between 1272 and 1289; a garden was later granted by Richard de Plessis.[19] In 1291 the vicarage was valued at £6[20] and in 1535 at £26.[21] In 1649 the vicarial glebe consisted of the vicarage house with barns and outhouses, two orchards, a close of pasture, and 2 a. in the common fields, and was worth £8 a year; the small tithes, together with dues and oblations, amounted to £50 a year.[22] When the Chase was inclosed the vicar received 90 a. in lieu of tithes and Trinity College, Cambridge, as patron, was empowered to add another 160 a. out of its own allot-ment on condition that the vicar should always resign his college fellowship on accepting the living.[23] The estate, later known as Vicarage farm, was settled upon the benefice in 1778.[24] Under the inclosure Act of 1801 a further 362 a. was granted to the vicarage in lieu of tithes in the rest of the parish, including 175 a. between the Hadley and East Barnet roads, 47 a. near Crew's Hill, and 118 a. in the common marshes and north of Turkey Street; 3 a. was given in place of the glebe land in Churchbury field.[25] In 1835 the net annual income of the vicarage was £1,174[26] but the income from glebe lands had fallen by 1870.[27] The vicarage house, a timber-framed building on the western side of Silver Street, appeared very old in 1795.[28] It was given a stuccoed garden front of two storeys and five bays in 1801, when other alterations were carried out,[29] and was completely cased in brick in 1845.[30] After further alterations it was still occupied by the vicar in 1972.

Baldwin Raddington, lord of Durants, was licensed in 1397 to endow a chantry with property, including Raddington bridge, worth £10 a year. One or two priests were to celebrate mass daily in Enfield church for the founder[31] but apparently they had ceased to do so before the Reformation. Edward Causton, vicar of Enfield, was licensed in 1471 to found a chantry at St. Mary's altar in the parish church for the souls of Robert Blossom (d. 1418) and his wife Agnes.[32] The chantry was endowed with land worth 10 marks a year at South Benfleet, Hadleigh, and Thundersley (Essex), including the manor of Poynetts in South Benfleet, and in 1548 it supported a priest at Enfield.[33] The lands were granted in 1548 to Walter Farre and Ralph Standish of London[34] but later formed part of the endowment of Enfield grammar school and the parochial charities.[35]

The brotherhood of Our Lady at Enfield was mentioned in 1464, when Walter Ford left 13s. 4d. for an obit.[36] In 1484 John Ford gave a close and 3 a. to support a brotherhood priest and Maud Hammond later gave a tenement in South Street to maintain the priest and for an obit. The brotherhood was also endowed with 4 a. by Thomas Aylward, a tenement by one Rotherham, and two crofts[37] and 1 a. by Hugh Ford, all for the performance of obits. The income of the brotherhood c. 1500 was £3 13s.; it owned the church house with a croft, which had been bought by the parishioners, and supported two priests, one of whom was expected to sing.[38] Its land may have included the tenement at the 'steeple end' of the parish church and the meadow called Prounces

[5] Whitaker, Enfield, 345.
[6] Boro. of Enfield, Official Guide [1955].
[7] Ibid.
[8] V.C.H. Mdx. i. 126.
[9] Dugdale, Mon. iii. 435.
[10] Dugdale, Mon. iv. 149; Regesta Regum Anglo-Normannorum, iii, ed. H. A. Cronne and R. H. C. Davis, p. 332.
[11] Dugdale, Mon. iii. 435–6.
[12] See below.
[13] B.M. Cott. MS. Vesp. E. vi, f. 6.
[14] Val. of Norw., ed. Lunt, 359.
[15] L. & P. Hen. VIII, xiii(1), p. 410.
[16] E 305/C 58.
[17] L. & P. Hen. VIII, xxi(2), p. 342.
[18] Hennessy, Novum Repertorium, 149.
[19] B.M. Harl. MS. 3697; Ford, Enfield, 302.
[20] Tax. Eccl. (Rec. Com.), 17.
[21] Valor Eccl. (Rec. Com.), i. 433.
[22] Home Cnties. Mag. i. 318.

[23] Act for Dividing Enfield Chase, 17 Geo. III, c. 17, ss. 15–18.
[24] Trinity Coll. Cambridge, Estate MSS, box 43.
[25] Robinson, Enfield, ii. 297–8.
[26] Rep. Com. Eccl. Revs. [C. 67], pp. 644–5, H.C. (1835), xxii.
[27] Ford, Enfield, 301.
[28] Lysons, Environs, ii. 312.
[29] Robinson, Enfield, i. 293–4.
[30] Ford, Enfield, 302.
[31] Cal. Pat. 1396–9, 115; Lysons, Environs, ii. 313.
[32] Lysons, Environs, ii. 314; V.C.H. Mdx. i. 294.
[33] Hennessy, Novum Repertorium, 148.
[34] Cal. Pat. 1548–9, 74.
[35] V.C.H. Mdx. i. 294; see below, p. 258.
[36] D. Pam, Late Mediaeval Religion in Edmonton, Enfield and Tottenham (Edmonton Hund. Hist. Soc., 1968), p. 10.
[37] Ford, Enfield, 131–3; Hennessy, Novum Repertorium, 148.
[38] Ford, Enfield, 133–4.

which, with 2 a. of wood, were granted in 1549 to John Hulson and Bartholomew Brokesby of London.[39] Walter Baldwin, at an unknown date, gave 3 a. of meadow for a light before St. Mary's altar.[40] Some chantry land in Enfield was granted in 1549 to John Bellowe of Grimsby (Lincs.) and Edward Streitbury of London,[41] and other lands belonging to obits were granted to John Holson and William Pendrede.[42]

There is no record of pluralism either before or after the Reformation.[43] Thomas Thompson, vicar 1505 to 1540, and Henry Lockwood, vicar 1540–5, were both masters of Christ's College, Cambridge. Thompson opposed early reformers, who may have been encouraged by Sir Thomas Wroth, lord of Durants and an ardent Protestant;[44] in 1539 Thomas Cromwell was told that the vicar had called the English Bible 'the book of Arthur Cobler' and its readers heretics, who had been seduced by a 'green learning that will fade away'.[45] Thomas Sedgwick (fl. 1550–65), who became vicar in 1556, was a Romanist who had been Lady Margaret professor of divinity at Cambridge University, 1554–6, and later became regius professor there; he resigned the living in 1557.[46] There was an assistant curate in the parish in 1548. In 1631 Henry Loft of Enfield endowed a lectureship at the parish church, where the lecturer, appointed by the vestry, was to preach on Sunday afternoons.[47] A lecturer was still being appointed in the late 19th century.[48] William Roberts, vicar from 1616, is said to have been ejected from the benefice in 1642;[49] a successor, Walter Bridges, was 'an able and painful preacher' in 1649.[50] Daniel Manning, vicar from 1659, was ejected at the Restoration and died in the parish in 1666.[51]

In 1685 it was ordered that the communion table be railed in.[52] There were two services each Sunday in the parish church in the early 18th century, when communion was celebrated monthly and at festivals.[53] In 1766 prayers were being read in the church on three weekdays by the lecturer, who was also master of the grammar school.[54] In 1873 communion was being celebrated weekly at 8 a.m.; the other Sunday services were Matins and Evensong, with an extra Sunday evening service at which all seats were free.[55] An assistant curate was appointed frequently after the end of the 18th century;[56] in 1823 his stipend, £100 a year, was fixed by private agreement.[57] In 1849 the vestry opposed changes in the fittings of the church which might affect its Protestant character.[58] There was a dispute about ritualism in 1859, when J. W. Bosanquet of Claysmore formed a 'Protestant Association' to combat alleged popish practices in the new church of St. John, Clay Hill; accusations were later also levelled against the services in Enfield parish church.[59] William Maclagan (1826–1910), later archbishop of York, was curate from 1865 to 1869 and is said to have brought about a spiritual revival in the parish.[60]

The church of ST. ANDREW stands at the northern end of the market-place, at the centre of Enfield Town.[61] It is a rectangular building with aisled nave and chancel, a western tower, and a south porch. Most of the fabric of the church is 14th- or 15th-century, much restored, and the south aisle dates from 1824. The walls of the older parts are of ragstone, flint rubble, and brick, with Reigate stone dressings; the south aisle is of brick. The east end of the chancel is of the 13th century, the west tower is probably a century earlier, and their relative positions suggest an early medieval church of considerable length. In the 14th century the chancel arch was rebuilt and arcades were constructed along both sides of the nave and chancel, implying aisles and side chapels. The walls of the north aisle and chapel were rebuilt early in the 16th century, probably to give greater width; at about the same time the south aisle and chapel were also rebuilt and a clerestory was added to the nave. A timber-framed south porch, with muniment room above,[62] may not be of much later date. John Barley, by will dated 1500, left money towards the rebuilding of the north chapel, where he asked to be buried, and also to the building of the new south chapel and to a new high altar.[63] Carved stones between the clerestory windows seem to represent the badges of Sir Thomas Lovell, of Elsing Hall (d. 1524); in 1522–3 Sir Thomas spent £11 on glass for the clerestory windows and for carvings of badges and coats of arms in the church[64] and in 1531 his widow, Eleanor, spent £3 on a window there.[65] A staircase turret to the former rood-loft projects from the north wall. The chapel at the east end of the south aisle may have served Raddington's chantry.[66] There were seven altars besides the high altar shortly before the Reformation, the most important of which were St. Mary's in the north and St. James's in the south chapel.[67]

The roof and floor of the chancel were in a poor state in 1685.[68] The church was 'beautified' in 1705[69] and repaired in 1771; a medieval doom painting on wood, over the chancel arch, was removed when the arch was widened in 1779 and later was apparently destroyed.[70] The fabric was again decayed in 1787;[71] Mr. Leverton of Great Queen Street was appointed to repair it in 1789.[72] More repairs were carried out

[39] Cal. Pat. 1548–9, 229–30. The meadow called Prounces may later have become part of the endowment of Prounces charity; see below, p. 258.
[40] Hennessy, Novum Repertorium, 148.
[41] Cal. Pat. 1548–9, 210.
[42] E 315/68 p. 365.
[43] Hennessy, Novum Repertorium, pp. lxxxii–lxxxiii.
[44] V.C.H. Mdx. ii. 31; D.N.B.
[45] L. & P. Hen. VIII, xiv(2), p. 349.
[46] D.N.B.
[47] Robinson, Enfield, i. 301.
[48] Ford, Enfield, 306.
[49] Walker Revised, ed. Matthews, 261.
[50] Home Cnties. Mag. i. 318.
[51] Calamy Revised, ed. Matthews, 336.
[52] Guildhall MS. 9537/20, f. 73.
[53] Guildhall MS. 9550.
[54] Ibid. 9558, f. 432.
[55] Ford, Enfield, 306.
[56] Guildhall MS. 9557, f. 30.
[57] Robinson, Enfield, i. 300.
[58] Vestry order bk. (1840–52), p. 248.
[59] Meyers' Enfield Observer, 1 Feb. 1859, 1 Dec. 1859; for St. John, Clay Hill, see below.
[60] D.N.B.; Whitaker, Enfield, 85.
[61] Section based on Hist. Mon. Com. Mdx. 20–22.
[62] See plate facing p. 81.
[63] Pam, Late Mediaeval Religion, 10.
[64] Hist. MSS. Com. 24, Rutland, iv, p. 265.
[65] Ibid. 269.
[66] Enfield par. ch., Guide (1968), 9, 11; Robinson, Enfield, ii. 162, suggested that the chapel was in the north aisle.
[67] Pam, Late Mediaeval Religion, 12.
[68] Guildhall MS. 9537/20, f. 73.
[69] Bodl. MS. Rawl. B. 389b, f. 23.
[70] Robinson, Enfield, ii. 6, 8–9.
[71] Bodl. MS. Gough Mdx. 8, f. 44.
[72] Ibid. ff. 46, 50.

in 1810, under the supervision of Edmund Lapidge,[73] and in 1819 a new gallery was built in the north aisle.[74] In 1824 the south aisle was replaced by a larger brick one with three-light Perpendicular windows and a gallery designed by William Lochner.[75] Despite the vestry's earlier opposition,[76] the medieval sedilia were restored in 1852, the pews were altered under the supervision of J. P. St. Aubyn in 1853,[77] and the choir was moved into the chancel. The church was reroofed in 1866–7 and a choir vestry built.[78] At another restoration in 1908 the galleries were shortened and a chapel dedicated to St. John was established at the eastern end of the south aisle.[79]

There was a 'pair of organs' in the church in 1552.[80] By will dated 1751 Mary Nicholl left £900 to the parish to buy an organ and to pay an organist;[81] the organ was built in 1752, probably by Robert Bridge, and the large and impressive wooden case survives, although the organ itself has been completely rebuilt. The organ was returned to its original position in the west gallery in 1952, after being removed in 1885 to the east end of the south aisle and in 1908 to a corresponding position in the north aisle.[82] Other fittings include a wooden bread shelf of c. 1630 in the north chapel. The pulpit and eagle lectern were presented to the church in 1866–7.[83] The east window was largely obscured at the beginning of the 19th century by a large oak altarpiece, which rendered the chancel 'gloomy and dark'; the window was slightly enlarged before 1823 and stained glass was inserted[84] but in 1834 the vestry ordered the churchwardens to open it up and to replace the reredos with a less massive Gothic screen,[85] itself replaced by a marble reredos in 1901. The window's existing stained glass and Decorated tracery date from c. 1873.[86]

Among the brasses is a figured plate to William Smith (d. 1592) and his wife Joan. An altar-tomb bears the finest brass in Middlesex,[87] to Joyce, Lady Tiptoft (d. 1446), beneath a canopy of c. 1530. Other monuments include kneeling figures commemorating Robert Deycrowe (d. 1586), Robert Middlemore (d. 1610), and Francis Evrington (d. 1614); a cartouche flanked by Mannerist figures of Faith and Charity, commemorating Martha Palmer (d. 1617); a large wall monument in the north chapel to Sir Nicholas Raynton (d. 1646), with stiff, recumbent figures of him and his wife; and a standing wall monument to Thomas Stringer (d. 1706) with a bust under a tent-like canopy, against a slab remounted by a broken pediment.

The plate includes two flagons dated 1786, four cups, four patens, and a pewter alms-dish.[88] There are eight bells: (i) and (ii) 1808, Mears; (iii), (vi), (vii), (viii) 1724, Richard Phelps; (iv) and (v) recast

late 19th century. The sanctus bell, the earliest work of William Wightman, is dated 1680.[89] The registers are complete from 1550.[90]

The church of *ST. JAMES*, Enfield Highway, was built as a chapel of ease in 1831 to the designs of William Lochner on ground south of Green Street given by Woodham Connop.[91] In 1834 a district was assigned to the church, consisting of that part of the parish of Enfield east of the Hertford road, and thereafter the living, which was in the gift of the vicar of Enfield, was described as a perpetual curacy.[92] The church is a plain aisled building of stock brick, in Commissioners' Gothic, with a western tower and battlemented exterior. A chancel in the Early English style was added in 1864.[93] There were galleries round three sides of the nave by the end of the century. The north and south galleries had been removed by 1967, when a fire seriously damaged the east end of the church. At the rebuilding the chancel arch was removed and a plain sanctuary was built in continuation of the nave.[94]

JESUS CHURCH, Forty Hill, was built in 1835 at the expense of Christian Paul Meyer of Forty Hall, who endowed it with £4,000 and 7 a.; a further 7 a. was given by Trinity College, Cambridge, in 1871.[95] The church became a perpetual curacy in 1845, with a district formed out of the parish of St. Andrew.[96] The patronage has always been vested in the vicar of Enfield.[97] The church, which was designed by Thomas Ashwell in imitation of Holy Trinity, Tottenham,[98] is a plain aisled grey-brick building with lancet windows and turrets at the west end. A south-east vestry was added in 1889 and the chancel, in the Perpendicular style, was built in 1926 to the designs of A. E. Henderson.[99]

CHRIST CHURCH, Cockfosters, was built at the expense of Robert Cooper Lee Bevan of Trent Park in 1839.[1] The benefice, a perpetual curacy, was in the gift of the founder and remained with the Bevan family; in 1970 the advowson, which was held by trustees, was styled a vicarage.[2] The church, originally a plain building of stock brick, with lancet windows and a tower with a short spire, was designed by Henry Edward Kendall. In 1898 the orientation was reversed when a north aisle, transeptal chapels, chancel, and vestries were added by Sir Arthur Blomfield. A new vestry and boiler-house were added c. 1970. A church house was opened in 1933. Services at the church have always been Evangelical in character.

Services for the hamlet of Clay Hill were held before 1847 in a building fitted up as a private chapel by Edward Harman of Claysmore. In 1847 the new owner of Claysmore, James Whatman Bosanquet, in co-operation with the vicar of Enfield, established a Sunday afternoon service in the chapel,[3] which was

[73] M.R.O., D.R.O. 4/22.
[74] Robinson, *Enfield*, ii. 7.
[75] Vestry order bk. (1823–39), p. 49.
[76] Ibid. (1840–52), p. 248.
[77] Tuff, *Enfield*, 110–1.   [78] Ford, *Enfield*, 273.
[79] Whitaker, *Enfield*, 201–3.
[80] E 315/498 f. 23.
[81] *9th Rep. Com. Char.* H.C. 258, p. 208 (1823), ix.
[82] Enfield par. ch., *Guide*, 19.
[83] Ford, *Enfield*, 273.
[84] Robinson, *Enfield*, ii. 4–5.
[85] Vestry order bk. (1823–39), p. 344.
[86] Ford, *Enfield*, 273; Enfield par. ch., *Guide*, 7.
[87] *T.L.M.A.S.* xix. 156–67.
[88] Freshfield, *Communion Plate*, 16.

[89] *T.L.M.A.S.* xvii. 138–9.
[90] In 1973 the regs. were kept in the ch.
[91] Ford, *Enfield*, 313; Colvin, *Dictionary of Architects*, 369.
[92] Hennessy, *Novum Repertorium*, 150; *Lond. Gaz.* 22 July 1834, p. 1373.
[93] Ford, *Enfield*, 313.
[94] Enfield libr., photographic coll.
[95] Ford, *Enfield*, 314.
[96] *Lond. Gaz.* 26 Dec. 1845, p. 7317.
[97] Hennessy, *Novum Repertorium*, 151.
[98] Pevsner, *Mdx.* 53.
[99] *T.L.M.A.S.* xviii(2), no. 51.
[1] Section based on *125th Anniversary Booklet* (1964).
[2] *Lond. Dioc. Bk.* (1970).
[3] Ford, *Enfield*, 57–8.

attended by an average of 65 persons in 1851.[4] In 1858 the permanent church of *ST. JOHN*, Clay Hill, was built as a chapel of ease to Enfield parish church and financed by the sale of glebe land to the New River Co.; it was consecrated in 1865.[5] A district, formed out of the parish of St. Andrew and the district of Jesus Church, Forty Hill, was assigned to the new church in 1867.[6] The benefice, which has always been in the gift of the vicar of Enfield, was initially styled a perpetual curacy but a vicarage from 1875.[7] The church, a small Gothic building of polychrome brick inside and out, with a nave, chancel, south porch, and western turret, was designed by J. P. St. Aubyn.[8] Early manifestations of Tractarianism were opposed by James Whatman Bosanquet, who complained of 'mysterious mutterings' and ceremonies 'revolting to the feelings of every good Protestant', as a result of which the church was closed for a period in 1859 by the bishop of London.[9] The vicarage house, in materials similar to those of the church, was also designed by St. Aubyn.[10]

A schoolroom near the junction of Chase Side and Gordon Hill was licensed for services in 1871.[11] The permanent church of *ST. MICHAEL* was built in 1873 on land given by George Batters of Brigadier Hall and, as a chapel of ease, was served by clergy from Enfield parish church.[12] A parish was formed in 1931 and in 1970 the living was described as a vicarage, in the gift of the vicar of Enfield.[13] The church, which was designed by R. H. Carpenter,[14] was left unfinished in 1874 because of lack of funds; it is a ragstone building in a 14th-century style, consisting of a three-bay aisled nave, a north transept, and a vaulted apsidal chancel, arranged in the Tractarian manner, with exposed brick walls. The interior is spacious. The temporary west wall was replaced in 1963 by a new stone wall with a narthex.

The church of *ST. MATTHEW*, at the corner of South Street and Church Road, Ponders End, was built in 1877–8 as a chapel of ease to St. James, Enfield Highway.[15] Incumbents have always been appointed by the vicar of Enfield[16] and the living was described as a vicarage in 1907.[17] The nave and north aisle of the present church survive from the original building, which was designed by H. J. Paull; the chancel was added in 1900 to the designs of J. E. K. and J. P. Cutts.[18] The church is a plain Gothic building of Kentish ragstone.

The church of *ST. MARY MAGDALENE*, at the corner of Windmill Hill and Ridgeway, was opened in 1883 and financed by Georgiana Hannah Twells of Chaseside House, as a memorial to her husband Philip Twells, M.P. (d. 1880).[19] A district, taken from St. Andrew's parish, was assigned in 1884.[20] The first incumbent, who was styled vicar after 1885, was appointed by Mrs. Twells;[21] in 1908 and 1947 the advowson was in the hands of P. T. Marshall[22] and by 1951 it was exercised by the bishop of London.[23] The church, designed by William Butterfield in a 14th-century style,[24] is a large building of Kentish ragstone consisting of an aisled nave and a lower chancel, with a western tower and prominent spire. The lofty interior, an unusually plain example of the architect's work, has windows filled with stained glass of different dates and the chancel covered with paintings by Charles Buckeridge, dated 1897, and by N. H. Westlake, dated 1899; a wooden screen separating nave from chancel was built in 1898, while a south chapel was added in 1907–8. The adjacent vicarage, in 1974 no longer used for the purpose, was designed by Butterfield, while the church hall was built to the designs of C. W. Reeves in 1894.[25]

An iron mission-room was built in Fourth Avenue, Bush Hill Park, by the vicar of Enfield in 1885 and served by clergy from the parish church.[26] The permanent church of *ST. MARK*, on the corner of Main Avenue and St. Mark's Road, was consecrated in 1893 as a chapel of ease to Enfield parish church. A parish was formed in 1903 and the vicar appointed by the bishop of London, with whom the patronage has remained.[27] The church, a spacious aisled building with nave, chancel, and north and south chapels, was designed by J. E. K. and J. P. Cutts in a plain Early English style and built of red brick with stone dressings; it was not completed until 1915 and an intended north-west spire was never built. A church institute was built in 1907. Since 1910 the church has maintained an Anglo-Catholic form of worship.

There was a mission church dedicated to St. Luke in Acacia Road in 1890.[28] The permanent church of *ST. LUKE*, Browning Road, was later built on the site of Brigadier House, partly at the expense of the Revd. V. T. Macy, and was consecrated in 1900; the nave was added in 1908.[29] A parish was formed in 1900 out of the parish of St. John, Clay Hill,[30] and in 1970 the patronage of the living, a vicarage, was in the hands of the bishop of London.[31] The church is a large red brick building in the early Gothic style, designed by James Brooks;[32] it contains an aisled nave and chancel of the same height, with lower north and south transepts and a pointed turret over the east end of the nave.

In 1898 there was an iron church in Hertford Road, Enfield Highway,[33] which was still in use as a

[4] H.O. 129/137/4/1/2.
[5] Ford, *Enfield*, 315.
[6] *Lond. Gaz.* 22 Mar. 1867, p. 1847.
[7] Hennessy, *Novum Repertorium*, 151.
[8] *T.L.M.A.S.* xviii(2), no. 54.
[9] *Meyers' Enfield Observer*, 1 Feb. 1859, 1 July 1859.
[10] Thorne, *Environs*, i. 181.
[11] Section based on inf. supplied by the vicar, St. Michael, Chase Side.
[12] Ford, *Enfield*, 316.
[13] *Lond. Dioc. Bk.* (1970).
[14] *T.L.M.A.S.* xviii(2), no. 59.
[15] *Kelly's Dir. Mdx.* (1882).
[16] Hennessy, *Novum Repertorium*, 151; *Lond. Dioc. Bk.* (1970).
[17] *Crockford* (1907).
[18] *T.L.M.A.S.* xviii(2), no. 58.

[19] H. R. Clutton, *St. Mary Magdalene, Enfield* (1971), 5.
[20] *37th Rep. Eccl. Com.* [C. 4323], p. 55, H.C. (1884–5), xxi.
[21] Hennessy, *Novum Repertorium*, 151.
[22] *Kelly's Dir. Mdx.* (1908); *Crockford* (1947).
[23] *Crockford* (1951–2).
[24] Pevsner, *Mdx.* 51.
[25] Clutton, *St. Mary Magdalene*, 21.
[26] Section based on St. Mark's church, *Jubilee Booklet* (1943).
[27] *Kelly's Dir. Mdx.* (1908); *Lond. Dioc. Bk.* (1970).
[28] *Kelly's Dir. Mdx.* (1890).
[29] Whitaker, *Enfield*, 241–2; *Kelly's Dir. Mdx.* (1908).
[30] *Kelly's Dir. Mdx.* (1908).
[31] *Lond. Dioc. Bk.* (1970).
[32] *Building News*, lxxv. 391.
[33] *Kelly's Dir. Tottenham* (1898–9).

hall in 1973. An ecclesiastical district, taken from the parishes of Jesus Church, Forty Hill, and St. James, Enfield Highway, was annexed to the church in 1901[34] and the permanent church of *ST. GEORGE*, Enfield Wash, was begun in 1900 and completed in 1906.[35] In 1908 the living was described as a vicarage, in the gift of the bishop of London, with whom it has remained.[36] The church is a large, gaunt, red-brick building in the early Gothic style, designed by J. E. K. and J. P. Cutts; it contains an aisled nave and chancel and the base of a south-west tower which was not completed.[37]

Sunday evening services were held *c.* 1900–10 in a wooden hut in the grounds of St. Ronan's, Hadley Wood.[38] In 1911 a small church room in Camlet Way was built of rusticated concrete blocks to the designs of A. E. Kingwell and licensed for services. In 1936 a small chancel was added and the building was consecrated as the church of *ST. PAUL*, Hadley Wood. The church has always been a chapel of ease to Christ Church, Cockfosters, but has had a resident curate since 1912 and has been managed by its own church committee since 1930.

The church of *ST. PETER AND ST. PAUL*, Ordnance Road, was built in 1928 to replace a garrison chapel in the Royal Small Arms factory, Enfield Lock, which existed in 1882[39] and was closed in 1921.[40] The new church, a plain brick building, was a chapel of ease to St. James, Enfield Highway. It was damaged by bombs in the Second World War and later demolished; a new church was built to the east, from the designs of Romilly Craze, and consecrated in 1969. The church is a brick building of simple plan with tall three-light windows, a western narthex and baptistery, and a south-western tower; in 1969 it became the mother church of a new parish formed out of the parish of St. James, Enfield Highway.

In the late 1920s services were held in a hall until the church of *ST. PETER*, Grange Park, was built at the corner of Vera Avenue and Langham Gardens in 1941. A new parish was assigned from that of St. Paul, Winchmore Hill, which previously had served the district, and St. Andrew, Enfield, and the bishop of London became patron. The church, built of grey brick to the designs of C. A. Farey, consists of apsidal chancel, transepts, and aisled nave. Among many fittings from older churches, damaged during the Second World War, is the marble font from St. Catherine's, Hammersmith, previously in St. Catherine Coleman, London (demolished 1926). The bell, 1785, is from St. John's, Drury Lane.[41]

The mission church of *ST. GILES*, Bullsmoor Lane, was built in 1954 to serve the northern part of the parish of Jesus Church, Forty Hill. The plain brick building with a wooden bell-turret serves as both church and hall, and in 1971 the church was served by a priest-in-charge.[42]

ROMAN CATHOLICISM. John Towneley, a recusant who was probably the man of that name from Towneley (Lancs.), was living in Enfield between 1586 and 1591.[43] He seems to have left before 1605, when Enfield acquired some notoriety in connexion with the Gunpowder Plot. White Webbs was acquired *c.* 1600 by Henry Garnet, a Jesuit priest, and was used as a refuge for up to 14 other priests. The composer William Byrd played the organ there at masses which were attended by members of the nobility[44] and in 1605 the house was visited by Robert Catesby and Thomas Winter, two of the Gunpowder plotters.[45] After the discovery of the plot Popish books and relics were discovered in the house, which contained trap doors and concealed passages.[46]

There were intermittent convictions of Enfield men for recusancy between 1617 and 1640, and again between 1679 and 1684.[47] In 1706 there were two known papist families in the parish, one at Scotland Green and the other at Forty Hill,[48] and in 1766 there were three reputed Roman Catholics.[49] There were still a few at the end of the 18th century[50] but no place of worship was provided until 1862, when a mission chapel was founded in Cecil Road.[51] A permanent parish church, dedicated to Our Lady of Mount Carmel and St. George, was opened on an adjacent site in 1901 and the former mission church became a school in 1905. The church was destroyed by a land mine in 1940, whereupon services were held in the assembly hall of St. George's school, Gordon Road, until a large church in London Road was opened in 1958. The new church is of yellow brick, with a basilican plan and some Florentine Renaissance details, designed by John E. Sterrett and B. D. Kaye.[52]

There was a Roman Catholic chapel in Alma Road, Ponders End, in 1896[53] which was served in 1908 by priests from Lower Edmonton.[54] A parish was formed in 1912 and in 1921 the present church of St. Mary, Nags Head Road, a plain stone building in the Perpendicular style, was opened.[55]

The Crusade of Rescue and the Sisters of Charity took over a building in Holtwhite's Hill for use as an orphanage in 1890.[56] The chapel was registered for worship as the church of Our Lady of Walsingham and the English Martyrs in 1964.[57] The Sisters of the Holy Trinity of Nazareth first came to Enfield in 1902, and in 1907 took over a house in London Road, which has since been extended.[58] Soon afterwards they built another house, called the Loreto convent, in Durants Road, Ponders End.

[34] *Kelly's Dir. Mdx.* (1908).
[35] *T.L.M.A.S.* xviii(2), no. 52.
[36] *Kelly's Dir. Mdx.* (1908); *Lond. Dioc. Bk.* (1970).
[37] *T.L.M.A.S.* xviii(2), no. 52; see above, pl. facing p. 80.
[38] Section based on Christ Church, Cockfosters, *125th Anniversary Booklet* (1964).
[39] *Kelly's Dir. Mdx.* (1882).
[40] Section based on inf. supplied by the vicar; see p. 238.
[41] *T.L.M.A.S.* xviii(2), no. 60; ex inf. the vicar.
[42] Ex inf. the priest-in-charge.
[43] *Cath. Rec. Soc.* lvii, p. xxx; *Cal. S.P. Dom.* 1591–4, 149.
[44] P. Caraman, *Henry Garnet*, 264, 317.
[45] *Essex Recusant*, viii. 104; *Cal. S.P. Dom.* 1603–10, 292.
[46] *Cal. S.P. Dom.* 1603–10, 250.
[47] *Mdx. Cnty. Recs.* ii. 131, 134; iii. 20, 144; iv. 132, 141, 243; *Cath. Rec. Soc.* xxx. 265.
[48] Guildhall MS. 9800A.
[49] Ibid. 9558, f. 432.
[50] Ibid. 9557, f. 30.
[51] *Cath. Dir.* (1901).
[52] Ex inf. the parish priest, Our Lady of Mount Carmel and St. George.
[53] O.S. Map, 1/2,500, Mdx. VII. 8 (1896 edn.).
[54] *Kelly's Dir. Mdx.* (1908).
[55] *Cath. Dir.* (1969).
[56] See p. 257.
[57] G.R.O., Worship Reg. no. 69774.
[58] Ex. inf. the parish priest, Our Lady of Mount Carmel and St. George.

PROTESTANT NONCONFORMITY. John Chishul (d. 1672), a Congregationalist, established a school in Enfield after his expulsion from the rectory of Tiverton (Devon) in 1660.[59] In 1672 John Sheffield (d. 1680), the ejected rector of St. Swithin, London Stone, was licensed to preach in Enfield,[60] where in 1672 a house belonging to John Hocklie was licensed for Presbyterian worship.[61] Congregationalists began meeting in Baker Street in 1687 and built the first nonconformist chapel in the parish in 1689.[62] Quakers met from 1667 and later acquired a meeting-house on the eastern side of Baker Street; their meetings ceased in 1794 and the house was afterwards turned into two dwellings.[63] A Baptist, Joseph Maisters (d. 1717), was licensed to preach in Baker Street in 1689[64] but his congregation does not seem to have survived him. William Parnell was found guilty in 1685 of holding unlawful conventicles in his house.[65]

Quakers and Congregationalists were the only nonconformists to flourish in the early 18th century. Congregationalists began meeting at Ponders End in 1745 and later built a permanent church, perhaps giving rise to a comment in 1766 that there were many dissenters in the parish.[66] In 1780 a second Congregationalist chapel was built in Chase Side and served from the countess of Huntingdon's college at Cheshunt (Herts.). Another chapel was built near by, after a schism in 1791, and united with the older church in 1871.[67] Six places of worship, most of them temporary, were registered by Congregationalists at Ponders End and Enfield Highway between 1797 and 1816;[68] small chapels at Whitewebbs and Botany Bay, serving remoter areas, were opened later in the 19th century.

There was a Methodist chapel in 1790, when it was said that Methodists had greatly increased,[69] and a short-lived Wesleyan chapel in Turkey Street in 1824.[70] Wesleyans reappeared in Baker Street in 1844,[71] at Ponders End in 1849, and at Enfield Wash in 1859. Primitive Methodists acquired a barn at Chase Side, in 1852, where services were 'conducted and visited by but a few persons of the labouring classes'.[72] Baptist chapels recorded in 1816 and 1824[73] seem to have been short-lived, as was a Particular Baptist church in Baker Street opened in 1861. In 1868, however, new Baptist churches were built at Enfield Town and in Totteridge Road, Enfield Wash. Strict Baptists, in Turkey Street by 1852,[74] later established chapels at Enfield Wash and at Ponders End. Brethren were worshipping in 1873 in a room facing Chase Green.[75] Other sects in the late 19th century included the Mormons, whose first chapel, at Ponders End, was opened in 1865, and the Salvation Army, who opened their first hall, at Enfield Wash, in 1883.

In 1862 there were 10 nonconformist chapels, 6 of them Congregationalist, 3 Wesleyan Methodist, and one Primitive Methodist.[76] By 1900 all the larger sects were represented except the Presbyterians, who began worshipping at Enfield Town in 1902 and opened a church in 1907. Protestant nonconformists accounted for more than two-fifths of one Sunday's 15,015 worshippers in 1903, Anglicans totalling 8,123 and Roman Catholics 404. The most numerous were Congregationalists with 2,738 worshippers, followed by Methodists with 1,312 and Brethren with 601.[77] Nonconformist churches were built in the period between the World Wars to serve new housing estates at Cockfosters and in the eastern part of the parish but their total numbers fell after the Second World War as some older buildings, notably at Enfield Town, were closed. In 1970 there were 4 Baptist, 5 Congregational, and 4 Methodist churches, one Presbyterian church, and 13 churches or halls belonging to other denominations.

CONGREGATIONALISTS. Baker Street meeting-house originated in a group established by Obadiah Hughes (d. 1705), a minister from Plymouth, which used a barn in 1687 and acquired new premises in 1689. A new chapel was built in 1702 and altered in 1752, 1771, and 1848. Schoolrooms were added in 1860 and a larger chapel, to seat 500, was built in 1862.[78] From 1924 until 1933 the chapel was used as a Salvation Army hall.[79] In 1933 it was taken over by Baptists and renamed Emmanuel Baptist church.[80]

Ponders End Congregationalists met in 1745 in a house at Scotland Green belonging to Lady Collutt. A plain chapel with round-headed windows was built in High Street in 1757 and a church hall was built in 1908 and enlarged in 1922.[81] The chapel, which seated 600,[82] was damaged by bombs in 1940 and was later demolished, whereupon the congregation moved to the church hall. In 1959 a brick church and adjoining hall, designed by Ernest W. Banfield & Son, were opened and the older hall was demolished.[83] Congregationalists also met in South Street from 1856 until 1866.[84]

In Chase Side Zion or the Old Independent chapel, seating 210, was built in 1780 at the expense of Peter Dupont, a retired London innkeeper. In 1791 the congregation split over the appointment of a minister who was later expelled for bigamy and Chase Side chapel was erected immediately north of Zion chapel. The new chapel, although considered socially superior,[85] was badly built and replaced by a larger one in 1832.[86] In 1871 the two congregations re-united[87] and in 1875 Christ Church was built on the site of Zion chapel. Christ Church, a large cruciform building of brick faced with Kentish rag, was designed in the Decorated style by J. Tarring &

[59] *Calamy Revised*, ed. Matthews, 115.
[60] Ibid. 436.
[61] *Cal. S.P. Dom.* 1672, 237.
[62] *Calamy Revised*, ed. Matthews, 282; Ford, *Enfield*, 331; see below.
[63] W. Beck and T. F. Ball, *Lond. Friends' Meetings*, 301; Robinson, *Enfield*, ii. 127.
[64] *Calamy Revised*, ed. Matthews, 333.
[65] *Mdx. Cnty. Recs.* iv. 286.
[66] Guildhall MS. 9554, f. 432.
[67] See below.
[68] Guildhall MS. 9580/1–4.
[69] Ibid. 9558, f. 432.
[70] Ibid. 9580/6, f. 73.
[71] Ibid. /8, f. 207.
[72] Tuff, *Enfield*, 115.

[73] Guildhall MS. 9580/5.
[74] C 54/14410/6, pt. 88.
[75] Ford, *Enfield*, 334.
[76] *Kelly's Dir. Mdx.* (1862).
[77] Mudie-Smith, *Rel. Life*, 397.
[78] G. W. Knight, *Nonconf. Churches in Enfield* (Edmonton Hund. Hist. Soc. 1973), 4; and see below, plate facing p. 321.
[79] G.R.O. Worship Reg. no. 49265.
[80] Knight, op. cit. 4; see below.
[81] *200th Anniversary Booklet* (1946).
[82] Knight, op. cit. 4.
[83] Ex inf. the sec.
[84] G.R.O. Worship Reg. no. 7716.
[85] Knight, op. cit. 4–5.
[86] Tuff, *Enfield*, 113–4.
[87] Knight, op. cit. 6.

Sons.[88] The old Chase Side chapel survived in 1911 as a lecture hall[89] but was later demolished.

At Enfield Highway a chapel seating 130 was built c. 1820[90] and replaced in 1854 by a building with a schoolroom attached, on the western side of Hertford Road and south of the junction with Hoe Lane.[91] A new church opened in 1896, closed in 1924,[92] and subsequently became a co-operative hall.[93]

At Whitewebbs a building was used by Congregationalists in 1832[94] and a chapel near the King and Tinker inn was registered in 1861 by the Countess of Huntingdon's Connexion and closed in 1959.[95] In 1873 it was served by students from Cheshunt College (Herts.)[96] and in 1921 by Christ Church, Chase Side.[97]

At Botany Bay services were held in 1851 in a small chapel, seating 66.[98] The chapel, like that at Whitewebbs, had links with the Countess of Huntingdon's Connexion, although it was usually described as Independent. It was closed in 1896.[99]

At Lancaster Road an iron church was used from 1880[1] until a permanent building was opened by Christ Church in 1885. In 1909 a Congregational institute was built near by in Armfield Road and services were held there, while the building in Lancaster Road became a hall. In 1917 the congregation separated from Christ Church, under the name of Armfield Road Congregational church, but in 1937 the building in Lancaster Road was reoccupied and enlarged and in 1938 it was rededicated as Lancaster Road Congregational church.[2] The church is a plain brick building with a rose window and a short spire at the western end.

Bush Hill Park church began as a Baptist mission in the later Wheatsheaf hall, Main Avenue, in 1881. It was taken over by Congregationalists, who from 1887 met in the new Avenue hall, Sixth Avenue. The modern church in Main Avenue was erected in 1910, largely at the expense of George Spicer, and was later given the additional name of the George Spicer memorial church. Avenue hall was sold in 1936.[3]

At Cockfosters a church in Freston Gardens was built in 1939 with proceeds from the sale of Finsbury Park Congregational church (Hornsey). In 1958 a hall, Freston hall, was built.[4]

METHODISTS.[5] Enfield Methodist (W) church originated in meetings in a wooden hut in a garden in Baker Street in 1845, services previously having been held in a room in Bonnett's Yard, Baker Street.[6] In 1864 a brick church in Cecil Road was opened, with seating for 250, and 1889 it was replaced by a ragstone Gothic building, with a spire, at the western end of Church Street.[7] The church in Cecil Road was later used by St. Andrew's National school.[8] In 1919 the new church was gutted by fire and immediately rebuilt, with stained-glass memorial windows. The church hall was built in 1914.[9]

Ponders End (W) church began when a chapel, of unknown location, was built in 1849.[10] In 1892 another chapel was built at the eastern end of South Street[11] and in 1931 the modern brick church was built on the western side of High Street.[12] Another chapel, in Alma Road, existed from 1882 to 1898.[13]

Ordnance Road (W) church was founded in 1859, when a small brick chapel was opened in Grove Road. In 1879 it was replaced by an iron building in Ordnance Road, which was itself replaced by a brick chapel and schoolroom in 1904. A new red-brick church, of cruciform plan, was built and opened in 1957. It stands south of the church built in 1904, which in 1973 served as the church hall.[14]

Chase Side (P) church began with meetings on the green in 1851. A barn near the Holly Bush was taken over in 1852 and a new brick chapel and schoolroom to its south were opened in 1858.[15] The congregation moved in 1894 to another brick chapel on the opposite side of Chase Side, which was closed in 1957.[16] The chapel then became a Salvation Army hall[17] and the congregation united with Enfield Methodist (formerly Wesleyan) church.[18]

St. John's church, Great Cambridge Road, was erected in 1960 as a dual-purpose building, five years after services had started in a hut.[19]

STRICT BAPTISTS. Ebenezer chapel, Baker Street, was registered by Particular Baptists in 1861 but closed in 1866.[20]

Providence chapel was built in Alma Road, Enfield Wash, in 1863 by Strict Baptists who had formerly worshipped in Baker Street and in Grove Road.[21] The building, known as Enfield Highway Baptist chapel, was replaced in 1875 by the Providence chapel, Putney Road,[22] which seated 40 and survived in 1973.[23]

BAPTISTS. Enfield Baptist church was founded with help from C. H. Spurgeon in 1867, when services were held in a room over the Rising Sun, Church Street. An iron chapel in London Road was opened later in that year, and Enfield Baptist tabernacle, an impressive classical building of brick with stone dressings, was opened in London Road

---

[88] *Builder*, xxxiii. 1131. All three chapels are illus. in Knight, op. cit., plates facing p. 6.
[89] Whitaker, *Enfield*, 230.
[90] Knight, op. cit. 7.
[91] Ford, *Enfield*, 333; O.S. Map 6″, Mdx. VIII. NE. (1868 edn.).
[92] G.R.O., Worship Reg. no. 35358.
[93] Totteridge Road Bapt. ch., *Centenary Booklet* (1968).
[94] Guildhall MS. 9580/7, f. 62.
[95] G.R.O., Worship Reg. no. 11694.
[96] Ford, *Enfield*, 334.
[97] *Kelly's Dir. Enfield* (1921).
[98] Knight, op. cit. 7.
[99] G.R.O., Worship Reg. no. 11695.
[1] Knight, op. cit. 7.
[2] *75th Anniversary Booklet* (1960).
[3] Knight, op. cit. 7; ex inf. the minister.
[4] Ex inf. the minister.

[5] In the foll. accounts the letters (W) and (P) denote former Wesleyan and Primitive Methodist chs.
[6] Guildhall MS. 9580/8, ff. 131, 207.
[7] Knight, op. cit. 10.   [8] See p. 254.
[9] Knight, op. cit. 10; ex inf. the chapel steward.
[10] H.O. 129/137/4/1/6.
[11] G.R.O., Worship Reg. no. 35715.
[12] Boro. of Enfield, *Official Guide* [1955].
[13] Ibid.
[14] Knight, op. cit. 10; G.R.O., Worship Reg. no. 66318.
[15] Knight, op. cit. 10–11.
[16] G.R.O., Worship Reg. no. 34662.
[17] Ibid. 66348.
[18] Ex inf. the chapel steward, Enfield Meth. ch.
[19] Boro. of Enfield, *Official Guide* [1962].
[20] G.R.O., Worship Reg. nos. 41429, 14546.
[21] Ibid. 15944; ex inf. Mr. S. T. Hill.
[22] Ex inf. Mr. S. T. Hill.
[23] Knight, op. cit. 9.

in 1875. Membership at first was for Particular Baptists, although open communion was permitted.[24] A lecture hall which formed part of the tabernacle was enlarged in 1882 and the site of the National school was bought as a Sunday school hall in 1890.[25] The tabernacle was sold in 1925 and in 1926 a plain brick church was opened in Cecil Road,[26] where there was seating for 400 in 1972.[27]

Emmanuel Baptist church, formerly the Congregationalist chapel in Baker Street, was registered by the Old Baptist Union in 1933 and still used in 1973.[28]

Totteridge Road church was opened with help from Spurgeon in 1868 for members who had met in Enfield Highway Congregational church and previously at Waltham Cross (Herts.). Although originally described as Particular Baptists, the congregation has always permitted open communion and belonged to the Baptist Union. A larger brick church was built in front of the older one in 1871 and seated 450 in 1972. The original building became a hall, which was replaced in 1933.[29]

Eden chapel originated in a chapel which existed in Napier Road, Ponders End, from 1880 to 1892, when it was replaced by one in South Street.[30] Eden chapel itself, a small brick building in Nags Head Road, was registered in 1898[31] but was derelict in 1971.

Suffolks church originated in a Sunday school started in 1934 by Enfield Baptist church to serve the new housing estates of eastern Enfield. Land in Carterhatch Lane was purchased in 1938 and the church, a plain brick structure with seating for 250, was built in 1957.[32]

SALVATION ARMY. Halls in South Street, Ponders End, and Grove Road, Enfield Wash, were registered in 1885; the first closed in 1896 and the second in 1903.[33] A hall in Seventh Avenue, Bush Hill Park, was registered in 1902 and replaced in 1926.[34] In 1971 Salvationists also used a hall in Chase Side, acquired from the Primitive Methodists in 1957.[35] Other halls temporarily occupied by the Army have been in Ordnance Road (1910–12), Lancaster Road (1911–57), South Street, Ponders End (1912–54), and Baker Street (1924–33).[36]

PRESBYTERIANS. A lecture hall at the western end of Church Street was built in 1902 and used for services until 1907, when the church of St. Paul was opened. The church, a ragstone building in the 13th-century Gothic style, was designed by William Wallace and was originally intended to have a spire.[37] It could seat c. 500 in 1973.[38]

OTHER DENOMINATIONS. Mormons held services in a house in Alma Road, Ponders End, from 1865 until 1876.[39] In 1882 a group of anti-polygamy Mormons opened a chapel in Baker Street, which was closed in 1896.[40] Another group, called the Reorganized Latter-Day Saints, in 1912 registered a house in Baker Street[41] and in 1929[42] built a small brick church in Lancaster Road, which was used in 1971.

Alma Hope chapel, New Road, Ponders End, existed from 1875 to 1896.[43] A mission hall in Alma Road near by was registered for worship in 1879 by the Ponders End mission and closed in 1896.[44]

Protestant dissenters registered a chapel at Botany Bay in 1882 and closed it in 1897.[45] In 1971 there was an undenominational chapel in East Lodge Lane, Botany Bay.

Enfield Town Evangelical Free church, Cecil Road, was built in 1897. It was severely damaged in the Second World War and replaced in 1956 by a plain brick building, with seating for 250.[46]

An iron room in Coopers Lane, on the boundary near Potters Bar, was registered by Brethren in 1897 and closed in 1961.[47]

A mission hall in Shirley Road existed in 1898.[48] It was registered by unspecified Christians in 1901 and replaced by the modern brick building, Shirley Road Gospel hall, in 1960.[49] Enfield Highway Gospel hall, Hertford Road, was registered by Brethren in 1903[50] and was still used in 1971. Brethren also registered a gospel hall in Leighton Road, Bush Hill Park, in 1910,[51] where they remained in 1971, and worshipped at the Causeway hall by 1927.[52] They registered a meeting room in Chase Side in 1921[53] and Primrose hall, Lavender Road, in 1926[54] but no longer used either place in 1971.

Jehovah's Witnesses registered a garage at no. 179 Baker Street, formerly the nonconformist school of industry,[55] as a Kingdom hall in 1940.[56] They moved to a new hall, seating 200, at no. 191c Baker Street in 1970.[57]

The Assemblies of God registered Waldron hall, Genotin Road, in 1947 but ceased to use it in 1964.[58] From 1949 they also worshipped in a new brick chapel in Lincoln Road,[59] which in 1971 was styled Lincoln Road Pentecostal chapel.

The Beacon of Light Christian Spiritualist church, at no. 331 Carterhatch Lane, was registered in 1949[60] and still used in 1971.

[24] Ex inf. the minister.
[25] Knight, op. cit. 8.
[26] *Centenary Booklet* (1967).
[27] *Baptist Handbk.* (1972).
[28] G.R.O., Worship Reg. no. 54538; Knight, op. cit. 4.
[29] *Centenary Booklet* (1968); Knight, op. cit. 9; *Baptist Handbk.* (1972).
[30] G.R.O., Worship Reg. nos. 25014, 33353.
[31] Ibid. 36389.
[32] *Enfield Bapt. Ch. Centenary Booklet* (1967); *Baptist Handbk.* (1972).
[33] G.R.O., Worship Reg. nos. 28356, 28863.
[34] Ibid. 38830, 50271.
[35] Ibid. 66348; see above.
[36] G.R.O., Worship Reg. nos. 44517, 44659, 45214, 49265.
[37] *Semi-jubilee Booklet* (1927).
[38] Ex inf. the minister.
[39] G.R.O., Worship Reg. no. 16718.
[40] Ibid. 26684.
[41] Ibid. 45398.
[42] Date on building.
[43] G.R.O., Worship Reg. no. 22178.
[44] Ibid. 24815.
[45] Ibid. 26342.
[46] Dates on building; ex inf. the minister.
[47] G.R.O., Worship Reg. no. 35999.
[48] *Kelly's Dir. Tottenham* (1898–9).
[49] G.R.O., Worship Reg. nos. 38706, 67617.
[50] Ibid. 40032.
[51] Ibid. 44543.
[52] *Kelly's Dir. Barnet* (1927).
[53] G.R.O., Worship Reg. no. 48132.
[54] Ibid. 50472.
[55] *Kelly's Dir. Mdx.* (1862).
[56] G.R.O., Worship Reg. no. 59315.
[57] Ex inf. Mr. D. S. Taylor.
[58] G.R.O., Worship Reg. no. 61734.
[59] Ibid. 62496.
[60] Ibid. 62499.

An unsectarian mission room at Brigadier Hill existed in 1898.[61] In 1951 Brigadier hall was registered by undesignated Christians[62] and in 1970 it was replaced by a two-storeyed brick and weatherboarded building, combining the Brigadier Free church with a youth centre.[63]

The London City Mission held services in Baker Street in 1873.[64] In 1955 the mission registered a plain brick hall in Turkey Street.[65]

A room at no. 23 Heene Road was registered by unspecified Christians in 1969.[66]

JUDAISM. Enfield and Winchmore Hill synagogue, an affiliated member of the United Synagogue, was established at no. 53 Wellington Road, Bush Hill Park, in 1950.[67]

EDUCATION. A school-house which stood east of the churchyard in 1572[68] may have housed Enfield grammar school until the erection of the surviving building c. 1586.[69] Several private schools were established in the 17th and 18th centuries,[70] when the grammar school alone seems to have catered for the poor. Mary Turpin, by will dated 1775, left £200 to teach three poor girls reading, writing, and needlework.[71] In 1787 a school for poor boys and girls was opened in premises in Baker Street which had once formed part of the Old Fighting Cock alehouse; the school, which was supported by voluntary subscriptions, had declined by 1826[72] and disappeared soon afterwards. Its closure may have resulted from the opening of two schools of industry for girls, the first in 1800 by Anglicans and the second in 1806 by nonconformists. An infants' school was opened in 1824 and another, by nonconformists, in 1830.[73] The second school was at Ponders End, where a part-time factory school was also opened in 1830[74] and closed with the jute factory in 1882, by which time it had over 150 pupils.[75]

A National school opened at Enfield Highway in 1833 and was followed by several similar schools both for Enfield Town and the remoter areas, including Forty Hill and Cockfosters. Nonconformists opened a British school, at Chase Side, in 1838 and Roman Catholics opened their first school, at Ponders End, in 1888. The government financed a school at the Royal Small Arms factory from 1846 and a short-lived ragged school in Baker Street offered rudimentary education to 'the poorest of the poor' on Sunday afternoons and some evenings in 1859.[76] With those exceptions primary education remained an Anglican monopoly until the foundation of a school board, which occurred in 1894.[77] In 1893 all but three of the 17 schools receiving Parliamentary grants were controlled by the Church of England.[78]

Five schools were built by Enfield school board before 1900. One, at Bush Hill Park, was condemned as extravagant in the local press, which accused the board of trying to destroy the voluntary schools as well as robbing the ratepayers.[79] The board ceased to exist when Enfield became a Part III authority under the Education Act of 1902.[80] Four more schools were established by the U.D.C. before 1914 but only two entirely new schools were built in the period between the World Wars;[81] in 1938 the local authority controlled 19 schools.[82] Enfield became an excepted district under the 1944 Education Act[83] and at the end of the Second World War the education committee embarked on an extensive building programme: between 1945 and 1965, seven primary and four secondary schools were built and another four secondary schools were extended.[84] In 1965 responsibility passed to Enfield L.B. and in 1967 a comprehensive system of secondary education was introduced.

By 1964 there were three grammar schools: Enfield (boys), the county school (girls), and Ambrose Fleming (boys). Of the nine secondary modern schools, four shared their premises with primary schools: Bush Hill Park (mixed), George Spicer central (mixed), Ponders End (girls), and Suffolks (mixed).[85] All four schools lost their secondary departments under the comprehensive reorganization. In 1970 Enfield L.B. controlled 9 secondary and 28 primary schools and one special school within the ancient parish.

Elementary schools founded before 1903.[86] An Anglican school of industry for girls was opened in 1800 in premises in the churchyard belonging to Prounce's charity and once known as the Old Coffee House.[87] The school, supported by voluntary contributions and managed by a committee of ladies, provided free clothing for 30 of its pupils. In 1876 new accommodation was found in a red-brick Tudor style building in Silver Street but in 1909 the school closed and the premises were divided between a home for district nurses and a preparatory school.[88]

A nonconformist school for 50 girls was established in 1806 in Baker Street.[89] The school, supported by voluntary subscriptions and collections at local chapels, supplied free clothing for 40 of the girls.[90]

[61] *Kelly's Dir. Tottenham* (1898–9).
[62] G.R.O., Worship Reg. no. 63062.
[63] Ibid. 72179.
[64] Ford, *Enfield*, 334.
[65] G.R.O., Worship Reg. no. 65075.
[66] Ibid. 71959.
[67] *Jewish Yr. Bk.* (1950 and later edns.).
[68] D.L. 43/7/5.
[69] *V.C.H. Mdx.* i. 294.
[70] See below.
[71] *9th Rep. Com. Char.* 194.
[72] Robinson, *Enfield*, ii. 128.
[73] *Educ. Enquiry Abstract*, 89–90.
[74] *V.C.H. Mdx.* i. 214 n.
[75] New Enfield Hist.
[76] *Meyers' Enfield Observer*, 1 Aug. 1859.
[77] Whitaker, *Enfield*, 4.
[78] *Returns of Schs. 1893* [C. 7529], pp. 236, 420, H.C. (1894), lxv.

[79] Mdx. C.C., *Primary & Secondary Educ. in Mdx. 1900–1965*, 25.   [80] Ibid. 26.
[81] Suffolks, opened 1934, and Albany, opened 1939.
[82] *Bd. of Educ.*, *List 21* (H.M.S.O. 1938).
[83] Mdx. C.C., *Educ. in Mdx. 1900–1965*, 41.
[84] Ibid. 57.
[85] Mdx. C.C. educ. cttee. *List of Schs. 1957*.
[86] In the foll. accounts of individual schools, attendance figures for 1893 are from *Returns of Schs. 1893* [C. 7529], p. 420, H.C. (1894), lxv; figs. for 1906 are from *Public Elem. Schs. 1906* [Cd. 3510], p. 455, H.C. (1907), lxiii; and those for 1919 from *Bd. of Educ.*, *List 21* (H.M.S.O. 1919). Except where otherwise stated, figs. for 1971–4 have been supplied by the headmaster or headmistress.
[87] Ford, *Enfield*, 327; *Digest of Rets. on Educ. of Poor*, H.C. 224, p. 536 (1819), ix(1).
[88] Whitaker, *Enfield*, 111; date on building.
[89] Tuff, *Enfield*, 191; *Educ. of Poor Digest*, 536.
[90] Robinson, *Enfield*, ii. 129.

In 1838, with the founding of Chase Side British school, the building was converted into an infants' school[91] which by 1911 had long been closed. The premises, which later served as a garage[92] and a hall for Jehovah's Witnesses,[93] were derelict in 1971.

St. James's National school, Enfield Highway, was founded in 1833. Brick buildings, containing schoolrooms for boys and girls, opened in the triangle formed by Old and Hertford roads in 1834[94] and held 90 pupils in 1853. An infants' department in a separate building was opened in 1841, with 45 pupils, and a new boys' school was opened in 1872 on a site nearer St. James's church.[95] The total attendance was 659 in 1893 and 440 in 1919. In 1970 the school, which had Voluntary Aided status, occupied premises in Frederick Crescent and had 274 juniors and infants on the roll.

Edmonton union school opened in the former workhouse in Chase Side after Enfield joined the poor law union in 1836. It was extended in 1839,[96] an infirmary was built in its grounds in 1844,[97] and a new workhouse school for 500 children was opened at Chase Farm on the Ridgeway in 1886.[98] Chase Farm school was later converted into an old people's home and, in 1939, into Chase Farm hospital.[99]

Chase Side British school, a brick building with separate schoolrooms for boys and girls, was opened in 1838 by local Congregationalists with an attendance of 158.[1] There were 320 boys, girls, and infants in 1893. In 1895 the school became a board school and in 1901 the pupils were transferred to the new Chase Side board school in Trinity Road;[2] the old building survived in 1971 as a depot for United Dairies.

St. Andrew's or Enfield National school opened in 1839 in a detached brick building in London Road, with separate schoolrooms for boys and girls.[3] Evening classes for adults were being held there in 1858.[4] An extra classroom and an infants' schoolroom were added in 1868[5] and separate boys' accommodation was opened in Sydney Road in 1879, the older building continuing in use by girls and infants.[6] The total attendance was 606 in 1893 and 264 in 1919. In 1891 the girls moved to the former Wesleyan church at the corner of Cecil and Sydney roads,[7] which they left in 1926 on the opening of a new junior and infants' school in Sydney Road.[8] St. Andrew's school, which was Voluntary Aided, moved to no. 116 Churchbury Lane in 1972 and had 339 children enrolled in 1974. The former girls' school served in 1971 as the parish hall of St. Andrew's church.

Trent Church of England school was founded for girls and infants of Cockfosters in 1838 by R. C. L. Bevan of Trent Park, on land near Christ Church but within the parish of East Barnet (Herts.).[9] A boys' school, built by subscription, was opened near by in Cockfosters Road, Enfield, in 1859[10] and had attendances of 67 in 1893 and 76 in 1919. The boys' school closed in 1938[11] on its amalgamation with the girls' and was later demolished. The old girls' school was rebuilt in 1957.[12]

St. Matthew's National school for infants, Ponders End, opened in South Street in 1840.[13] In 1873 it was described as a mixed school for 120 children[14] and in 1882 the infants, numbering about 100, were moved to rented premises ¼ mile away.[15] In 1906 junior girls and infants were reunited in South Street, where there was an attendance of 291 in 1919. In 1970 the school, which was Voluntary Aided, remained in the building of 1840 and had 103 infants enrolled.

The Royal Small Arms factory school, financed by the government, opened within the factory for juniors and infants in 1846.[16] A separate infants' school was built in 1870, when evening as well as day classes were being held.[17] In 1893 there was a total attendance of 501 but by 1899 the pupils had been transferred to the new Chesterfield Road board school.[18] The original building then became a police station guarding the entrance to the factory.[19]

Love's Row Church of England infants' school originated in one of two infants' schools opened in rented premises by the vicar of Enfield c. 1847.[20] One of the schools occupied a detached building formerly used by dissenters in Love's Row, Enfield Town, in 1873[21] but disappeared soon afterwards, presumably being merged with Gordon Lane infants' school.[22]

Maiden's bridge infants' school opened in a small red-brick building north of Maiden's bridge, Bull's Cross, in 1848.[23] It was built and supported by James Meyer of Forty Hall[24] and never received a government grant. It survived in 1897[25] but seems to have disappeared when an infants' department was added to Forty Hill Church of England school before 1907.[26] The building was being used in 1971 as a Scouts' hut.

Forty Hill National school, with separate departments for boys and girls, opened in a red-brick Italianate building south of Maiden's bridge in 1851.[27] The school was enlarged in 1868[28] and was attended by 157 children in 1893 and 128 in 1919. Further additions were made after the Second World

[91] Tuff, *Enfield*, 191.
[92] Whitaker, *Enfield*, 122.
[93] See p. 252.
[94] Ed. 7/88; O.S. Map 6", Mdx. VII. NE. (1868 edn.).
[95] Ford, *Enfield*, 328.
[96] Richardson, *Edmonton Union*, 29.
[97] Tuff, *Enfield*, 227.
[98] *Kelly's Dir. Mdx.* (1890).
[99] See p. 244.
[1] Ed. 7/88.
[2] R. W. Taylor, *Hist. of a School*, 14–16.
[3] Ed. 7/88.
[4] Tuff, *Enfield*, 192.
[5] Ford, *Enfield*, 327.
[6] *Kelly's Dir. Mdx.* (1890).
[7] Date on building; ex inf. the chapel steward, Enfield Meth. ch.
[8] *Board of Educ., List 21* (H.M.S.O. 1927).
[9] Ed. 7/88.
[10] Ford, *Enfield*, 328; O.S. Map 6", Mdx. VII. NW. (1896 edn.).
[11] *Bd. of Educ., List 21* (H.M.S.O. 1938).
[12] Christ Church, Cockfosters, *125th Anniversary Booklet* (1964).
[13] Date on building.
[14] Ford, *Enfield*, 328.
[15] Ed. 7/88.
[16] *Kelly's Dir. Mdx.* (1890); Ford, *Enfield*, 328.
[17] *Kelly's Dir. Mdx.* (1870).
[18] *Returns of Schs. 1899* [Cd. 315], p. 572, H.C. (1900), lxv(2).
[19] Enfield Arch. Soc., *Society News*, xxx (1968).
[20] Ed. 7/88.
[21] Ford, *Enfield*, 327.
[22] See below.
[23] Date on building.
[24] Ford, *Enfield*, 328.
[25] O.S. Map 6", Mdx. II. SE. (1897 edn.).
[26] *Publ. Elem. Schs. 1906*, 455.
[27] Ed. 7/88.
[28] Ford, *Enfield*, 328.

Aiar. In 1974 the school, which was Voluntary Wded, had 125 infants and juniors.

St. John's National school, Clay Hill, opened in a wooden schoolroom for juniors and infants in 1858.[29] The school was rebuilt in 1888[30] and attended by 82 children in 1893 and 40 in 1919. It was extended in 1968 and had 54 juniors and infants by 1971.[31]

St. Michael's Church of England school may have originated in an infants' school which existed in Chase Side in 1858.[32] In 1865 another infants' school, consisting of one room for c. 50 pupils, opened in Chase Side south of the Holly Bush inn, possibly as a replacement of the earlier school.[33] In 1870 the school, described as St. Michael's, Holly Bush, school and catering for both infants and juniors, moved to a larger building.[34] A new infants' school was built at the foot of Gordon Hill in 1877, a school for boys opened at the foot of Brigadier Hill in 1882, and a girls' school, later St. Michael's church hall, opened in 1889. The total attendance was 489 in 1893 and 442 in 1919. The three schools were amalgamated in 1939 and housed in the boys' school, which was extended in 1959 and 1970. The old infants' school was demolished in 1950.[35]

St. Andrew's Church of England infants' school, Gordon Lane, opened with 45 infants in 1872 on a site given by Trinity College, Cambridge.[36] The school seems to have replaced an earlier one on the western side of Baker Street.[37] It had attendances of 144 in 1893 and 58 in 1919 and closed in 1923.[38]

Ordnance Road Church of England infants' school opened in a schoolroom with accommodation for 80 in 1875.[39] Attendance had risen to 180 by 1893 but the school closed between 1899 and 1906,[40] on the building of Chesterfield Road board school.

Bush Hill Park National school, Main Avenue, opened in 1882 in a schoolroom and a classroom belonging to the trustees of the Bishop of London's Fund.[41] There were 259 infants in 1893 and 147 juniors and infants in 1919. The school closed in 1937.[42]

St. Mary's Roman Catholic school for infants and juniors opened in Alma Road, Ponders End, in 1888. It adjoined St. Mary's church and consisted of a schoolroom and a classroom.[43] Attendance was 128 in 1893 and 121 in 1919. The school moved to a new building in Durants Road in 1928.[44] It was reconstructed after the Second World War and was a Voluntary Aided school, with 259 infants and juniors, in 1974.

St. Luke's Church of England infants' school opened in 1893 in a new building adjacent to St. Luke's church.[45] The school, attended by 89 children in 1906, had closed by 1919.[46]

Elementary schools founded between 1894 and 1903.[47] Botany Bay board school opened as a temporary school in 1895 in temporary accommodation, which was replaced by a permanent building in East Lodge Lane in 1914. There were attendances of 31 boys and girls in 1906 and 24 in 1919. The school roll numbered 60 infants and juniors in 1974.

Bush Hill Park board school opened in 1896 and was extended in 1908. It was attended by 1,427 juniors and infants in 1906 and by 1,262 in 1919. There were 453 children enrolled at the junior school and c. 300 at the infants' in 1974.

Alma Road board school, Ponders End, opened in 1897. It was attended by 1,107 juniors and infants in 1906 and by 827 in 1919. There were 341 children enrolled at the junior school and 249 at the infants' in 1974.

Chesterfield Road board school, Enfield Lock, also opened in 1897. It was attended by 1,697 juniors and infants in 1906 and by 1,219 in 1919. There were 620 children enrolled at the junior school and 360 at the infants' in 1974.

Chase Side board school, Trinity Street, opened in 1901. It was attended by 1,020 juniors and infants in 1906 and by 753 in 1919. There were 530 juniors and infants on the roll in 1974.

St. George's Church of England infants' school, Enfield Wash, was built by 1906. It contained 164 pupils in 1906 and 77 in 1919. The school was Voluntary Aided, with 167 infants enrolled, in 1974.

Elementary schools founded between 1903 and 1945.[48] St. George's Roman Catholic school, Cecil Road, opened in 1903 and was rebuilt in 1939.[49] It had 45 boys and girls in 1906 and 48 in 1919. The school was Voluntary Aided, with 394 infants and juniors on the roll in 1974.

Southbury Road council school opened in Swansea Road in 1905 and had 966 juniors and infants in 1919. There were 320 enrolled at the junior school, which also used an annexe in Glyn Road, and 184 at the infants' in 1974.

Eastfield Road council school opened in 1909 and had 406 juniors and infants in 1919. There were 439 enrolled at the junior school and 235 at the infants' in 1974.

Lavender Road council school opened in 1910 and had 918 juniors and infants in 1919. There were 476 enrolled at the junior school and 345 at the infants' in 1974.

The George Spicer council school, Southbury Road, opened in 1912. There were 805 juniors and juniors in 1919 and 460 in 1974.

Suffolks council school, Brick Lane, opened in 1934.[50] In 1974, when one wing was occupied by Bishop Stopford's school, there were 270 juniors and infants enrolled.

[29] Ed. 7/88.
[30] *Kelly's Dir. Mdx.* (1890).
[31] Ex inf. the headmistress.   [32] Tuff, *Enfield*, 192.
[33] Ed. 7/88; O.S. Map 6″, Mdx. VII. NE. (1868 edn.).
[34] Ford, *Enfield*, 327.
[35] Ex inf. the headmistress.
[36] Ed. 7/88; Ford, *Enfield*, 327.
[37] O.S. Map 6″, Mdx. VII. NE. (1868 edn.); the school may have been one of those opened by the vicar c. 1847: Ed. 7/88.
[38] *Bd. of Educ., List 21* (H.M.S.O. 1927).
[39] Ed. 7/88.
[40] *Returns of Schs. 1899* [Cd. 315], p. 572, H.C. (1900), lxv.

[41] Ed. 7/88.
[42] *Bd. of Educ., List 21* (H.M.S.O. 1938).
[43] Ed. 7/88.
[44] *Bd. of Educ., List 21* (H.M.S.O. 1932).
[45] Ed. 7/88.
[46] *Bd. of Educ., List 21* (H.M.S.O. 1919).
[47] See p. 253 n. 86 and Ed. 7/88.
[48] Except where otherwise stated, the foll. two sections are based on Ed. 7/88, and on inf. supplied by Enfield L.B. Educ. Dept. and by the headmasters and headmistresses.
[49] Ex inf. the par. priest, Our Lady of Mount Carmel and St. George.
[50] *Bd. of Educ., List 21* (H.M.S.O. 1934).

Brimsdown council school, East Street, opened in 1939. There were 500 enrolled at the junior school and 263 at the infants', both in Green Street, in 1974.

Merryhills council school, Bincote Road, opened in 1940 with accommodation for 280 juniors and infants. There were more than 600 pupils by 1949, before the opening of Grange Park school, but numbers had fallen to 379 by 1971.

Primary schools founded after 1945. Carterhatch school, Carterhatch Lane, opened in 1949. In 1974 there was a junior school, with 220 on the roll, and an infants', with 265.

Prince of Wales school, Salisbury Road, opened in 1950. The junior school had 284 pupils in 1971 and the infants' school had 195 in 1974.

Grange Park school, World's End Lane, opened in 1951. In 1971 there was a junior school, with 268 pupils, and an infants', with 228.

Honilands school, Lovell Road, opened in 1953 to serve the near-by council estate. The junior school had 240 pupils in 1971 and the infants' 229 in 1974.

Worcesters school, Goat Lane, opened in 1954. In 1971 the junior school had 240 pupils and the infants' 200.

Capel Manor school, Bullsmoor Lane, opened in 1958. There were 259 juniors and infants on the roll in 1974.

Hadley Wood school, Courtleigh Avenue, opened in 1965. There were *c*. 175 juniors and infants on the roll in 1974.

Secondary and senior schools. Apart from Enfield grammar[51] school the first source of public secondary education was Enfield upper grade school, opened in 1891 as a private school for girls.[52] It was also attended by infants and fees were still charged in 1906, although it was then listed among other schools receiving public support. Attendance was 143 in 1906 and 124 in 1919. The school closed in 1926.[53]

Enfield county school for girls opened in 1909 in Holly Walk, sharing a large red-brick building with a pupil-teachers' centre and a technical institute. An extension, connected with the older block, was built after the Second World War. In 1967 the school combined with Chace girls' secondary school to form Enfield Chace comprehensive school.

Ponders End junior technical, subsequently Enfield secondary technical and later Ambrose Fleming, school opened in High Street, Ponders End, in 1911. It moved to Enfield technical college,[54] Queensway, in 1941 and was renamed in 1944 and again in 1959. The school moved to Collinwood Avenue in 1962 and became an all-age comprehensive school in 1967. It had 1,000 boys and girls in 1971.

George Spicer selective central school opened in Southbury Road, adjoining the junior school,[55] and survived until its replacement by Kingsmead comprehensive school.

Albany secondary modern schools for boys and girls opened in 1939 in Bell Lane, in a brick building

designed by Frank Lee.[56] It later became an all-age mixed comprehensive school, with 990 pupils in 1974.

Chace secondary modern school for girls had opened in Rosemary Avenue by 1957.[57] It was later absorbed into Enfield Chace comprehensive school.

Chace secondary modern school for boys opened in Churchbury Lane in 1956.[58] It became a junior comprehensive in 1967 and an all-age comprehensive school in 1970. There were 840 pupils in 1971.

Cardinal Allen Roman Catholic mixed secondary modern school opened in Enfield Road in 1962.[59] It had Voluntary Special Agreement status and made way for St. Ignatius's college in 1968.

Comprehensive schools founded since 1967.[60] Enfield Chace school was formed in 1967 out of Enfield county and Chace girls' secondary schools. From 1971 the buildings in Rosemary Avenue housed girls aged 11–13, while older girls attended Holly Walk. There was a total of 1,200 pupils in 1974.

Kingsmead school opened in Southbury Road in 1967, replacing George Spicer central, Bush Hill Park, and Ponders End (girls') schools. A sixth-form block was added in 1970 and there were *c*. 950 pupils in 1971.

Bishop Stopford's school, an Aided comprehensive, was founded in 1967 when premises in Brick Lane were acquired from Enfield L.B. by the diocese of London. There were *c*. 900 boys and girls in 1974.

Holy Family school was founded as a Roman Catholic Aided comprehensive, whose upper tier used a former private school run by sisters of the Holy Family in London Road while the juniors temporarily used part of Bush Hill Park's premises in Main Avenue. There were *c*. 425 girls on the roll in 1974.

St. Ignatius's college, a Roman Catholic Aided grammar school, moved from Tottenham[61] in 1968, on its conversion into a two-tier comprehensive school. The upper school occupied new buildings in Turkey Street, where there were *c*. 725 boys in 1971, and the lower, with 420 boys in 1974, took over the Cardinal Allen school in Enfield Road.

Special school.[62] Edmonton and Enfield joint special school, later Durants school, opened in 1920 under a joint committee of the two councils. It was a day-school for 90 educationally sub-normal children and occupied Nassau House, Enfield Highway, which in 1939 was replaced by a building designed by Frank Lee as the first of its kind in southern England.[63] Accommodation was extended to take 160 children in 1949, Stapleton House was afterwards acquired at Potters Bar, and by 1955 the roll had risen to 220. A new wing was added to Durants in 1963 and the Stapleton House annexe was closed on the establishment of Oaktree school, Edmonton, in 1965.

Enfield college of technology.[64] In 1901 Sir Joseph Wilson Swan bought a house in the High Street,

[51] *V.C.H. Mdx.* i. 294.
[52] Ed. 7/88.
[53] *Bd. of Educ., List 21* (H.M.S.O. 1927).
[54] See below.
[55] Mdx. C.C. educ. cttee. *List of Schs.* (1957).
[56] *Builder*, clvi. 1227.
[57] Mdx. C.C. educ. cttee. *List of Schs.* (1957).
[58] R. W. Taylor, *Hist. of a School*, 27.

[59] Ex inf. the par. priest, Our Lady of Mount Carmel and St. George.
[60] The foll. section is based on inf. supplied by the headmasters and headmistresses.   [61] See p. 373.
[62] Section based on inf. supplied by the headmaster.
[63] *Builder*, clvi. 801.
[64] Section based on inf. supplied by the senior tutor librarian, Enfield tech. coll.

Wrotham Park from the south-west. The stables are shown to the left

Dancers Hill House: the Saloon and the North Front

SOUTH MIMMS

Monken Hadley: the Green

Tottenham: nos. 5 and 6 Bruce Grove

South Mimms: the Gateway to Dyrham Park

Ponders End, which, as the Ediswan institute, was used for evening classes and social activities by workers at the Ediswan factory. The building was purchased by the county council in 1905 and replaced in 1911 by the technical institute, which also housed the newly-founded Ponders End junior technical school[65] and where evening classes continued. The institute was extended in 1924 and larger buildings on a 39-acre site in Queensway were begun in 1938. Classes began in the uncompleted new building, known as Enfield technical college, in 1941, after the older premises had been damaged by bombs. In 1959 the college gained recognition from London University for courses leading to external degrees in engineering and in 1962 it took over the entire building in Queensway on the technical school's move to Collinwood Avenue. The college was reorganized in 1967 into faculties of arts and technology. In 1971, when there were 1,300 students on full-time or sandwich courses and 900 part-time students, a new tutorial block was opened and Capel Manor, Bull's Cross, acquired as a management centre. The old technical institute in Ponders End High Street was rebuilt after the Second World War and in 1971 housed the science block of the technical college. The college has been designated as one of the constituents of a new polytechnic, to include Hendon technical college and Hornsey school of art.

Trent Park college. A residential emergency teachers' training college for men opened in 1949 in Trent Place[66] and became a permanent training college for men and women specializing in art, music, and drama in 1950.[67] Ludgrove Hall, Cockfosters,[68] was later acquired as a hostel.

Private schools. Some London merchants were sending their children to be 'nursed and put to school' at Enfield c. 1636.[69] John Chishul (d. 1672), an ejected Congregationalist minister, kept a school there after the Restoration[70] and Dr. Robert Uvedale, master of the grammar school, opened a private boarding school in Enfield manor-house c. 1670.[71] Later known as the Palace school, it was attended by the chemist George Fownes (1815–49)[72] and closed in 1896.[73] There was a flourishing academy for Presbyterians at Forty Hill in the 18th century, run by the Revd. Andrew Kinross[74] and numbering some aristocratic pupils.[75] Another nonconformist, the Revd. John Ryland, opened a school in the late 18th-century house in Nags Head Road, Enfield Town, which later became the first Enfield Town railway station; John Keats, the poet, was educated there under Ryland's successor, John Clarke,[76] as were his friends the writers Charles Cowden Clarke (1787–1877) and Edward Holmes (1797–1859).[77]

Isaac D'Israeli was said to have attended a school at Ponders End run by a Scotsman named Morison.[78] The mathematician Charles Babbage (1792–1871) and the novelist Captain Frederick Marryat (1792–1848) attended a school run by the Revd. Stephen Freeman in a house in Baker Street later known as Holmwood.[79]

In 1832 Enfield had 12 boarding schools, five private day-schools, and one preparatory school;[80] in 1858, apart from the Palace school, there were two old-established schools for girls at Chase Side and Ponders End and boys' schools at Enfield Highway, in Silver Street, and in Gothic Hall, Baker Street.[81] An independent school for girls was opened in St. Ronan's, Hadley Wood, in 1897 and closed in 1939.[82] The number of private schools in the parish fell during the 20th century. Survivors in 1970 included Clark's grammar school, Bycullah Road, and Enfield preparatory school, London Road.[83]

A gaunt brick school building at the top of Holtwhite's Hill was erected in 1885 by the Revd. R. H. Wix.[84] It was taken over as an orphanage by the Roman Catholic sisters of Charity in 1890 and later extended. In 1971 the building, which was run by the Crusade of Rescue together with the sisters, served as a hostel for families.[85] The sisters of the Holy Family of Nazareth established a private school adjoining their convent in London Road soon after moving there in 1907. The school became part of a new comprehensive school under the reorganization of secondary education in 1967.[86]

CHARITIES FOR THE POOR.[87]

A hospital, mentioned in 1568[88] and again in 1605,[89] apparently had no connexion with later alms-houses. The unused balances of five charities were combined in 1805 to purchase £700 stock, the income of which was distributed in bread to the poor. The charities, however, continued to be administered separately until 1888, when seven of the more important were consolidated as the Enfield parochial charities, the bulk of whose income was to provide pensions for unrelieved parishioners. In 1904 £800 stock was appropriated for education and in 1905 a further 18 charities[90] were included among the Enfield parochial charities. In 1968 the income of the combined charities was £11,779 and the expenditure £12,484, of which £6,226 was spent on pensions, grants, and fuel, £298 on the alms-houses, and £3,960 on maintaining the market-place and other properties, the rents and profits from which accounted for most of the income. There was a balance in hand of £16,627.

The first alms-houses were built in Turkey Street by Anne Crowe, who, by will dated 1763, left £500

[65] See above.
[66] New Enfield Hist.
[67] C. Radcliff, *Mdx.* [nd], 191–2.   [68] See p. 265.
[69] *Cal. S.P. Dom.* 1635–6, 523.
[70] *Calamy Revised*, ed. Matthews, 115.
[71] Brewer, *Beauties of England and Wales*, x(5), 723.
[72] Whitaker, *Enfield*, 458.
[73] *V.C.H. Mdx.* i. 243.
[74] Ibid. 248.
[75] Hist. MSS. Com. 34, *14th Rep. III, Roxburghe*, p. 49.
[76] *V.C.H. Mdx.* i. 249; Whitaker, *Enfield*, 176.
[77] Robbins, *Mdx.* 250; *D.N.B.*
[78] Whitaker, *Enfield*, 298.
[79] Whitaker, *Enfield*, 125.
[80] *Pigot's Com. Dir.* (1832–4).

[81] Tuff, *Enfield*, 192.
[82] Clark, *Hadley Wood*, 79, 81.
[83] Enfield L.B., *Information Handbk.* (1970).
[84] Whitaker, *Enfield*, 244–5.
[85] *Westminster Yr. Bk.* (1969); ex inf. the par. priest, Our Lady of Mount Carmel and St. George.
[86] Ex inf. the par. priest, Our Lady of Mount Carmel and St. George; see above.
[87] Except where otherwise stated, the section is based on *9th Rep. Com. Char.* 187–208; H. C. Weld, *Enfield Charities* (1895); and Char. Com. files.
[88] Hist. MSS. Com. 6, *7th Rep.*, W. M. Molyneux, p. 621.
[89] Hist. MSS. Com. 9, *Hatfield House*, xvii, p. 97.
[90] Including Sir Nicholas Raynton's char. for apprenticing.

stock in trust to repair them and to buy coal for the inmates. A further £200 stock was bequeathed by the Revd. C. W. Bollaerts, by will proved 1863. The modern alms-houses, four two-roomed apartments in a red-brick single-storeyed range with a steeply-pitched roof and tall chimneys, were built at the expense of H. C. B. Bowles of Myddelton House in 1893, partly on land given by him. In 1960 the charity had an income of no more than £18 a year and by a Scheme of 1961 it became one of the Enfield parochial charities.

Charles Wright in 1848 settled alms-houses which he had built at Enfield Highway in trust for the benefit of six aged widows who had lived for at least a year at Enfield Wash, Enfield Highway, Green Street, South Street, or Ponders End.[91] He also gave a rent-charge on houses in the parish of St. Luke, Old Street, to provide each widow with £10 a year and a ton of coal at Christmas. The charity became one of the Enfield parochial charities in 1905 and the property in St. Luke's parish had been sold for investment by 1964. Wright's alms-houses consisted of a plain brick building, with a central pediment dated 1847, in 1972.

In 1516 the parish bought a house called Prounces, probably that occupied by John Prouns in 1399, with its adjacent grounds.[92] Enfield grammar school was built next to the house soon after 1586[93] and in 1623, when the estate was settled in trust, the house was reserved as a schoolmaster's residence. The rest of the property was leased out and the rents were applied for unspecified charitable purposes within the parish. The King's Head inn, south of the school, was later built on ground belonging to the charity and in 1793 a building called the old coffee house, later the church school of industry, occupied the site of Prounces, another house having been found for the schoolmaster. The charity was allotted 2 a. on Enfield Chase in 1806, under the Inclosure Act of 1801. The school and the schoolmaster's house were included in a Scheme governing the grammar school in 1874, while the remaining endowments, consisting of the King's Head and 2 a. adjoining it with an annual income of £63, were transferred in 1888 to the Enfield parochial charities.

By deed of 1558 £6 13s. 4d. a year from land called Poynetts at South Benfleet and Hadleigh (Essex), formerly the endowment of a chantry in Enfield parish church,[94] was set aside for the schoolmaster at Enfield, the remaining profits being devoted to the poor.[95] The land was conveyed to trustees in 1621, when the schoolmaster's salary was raised to £20. By the early 19th century the profits seem to have been devoted entirely to the upkeep of the grammar school, although they were administered as part of a general fund which combined the incomes of several other charities for the poor, a procedure which led to much confusion.[96] There is no evidence that the income from Poynetts was subsequently devoted to the poor. In 1816 it was invested in land.

Thomas Wilson of London, brewer, by will dated 1590, left the profits of three houses in Whitechapel as pensions to six poor men of Enfield. In 1614 the property was settled in trust. One of the houses was sold in 1803 for £1,260 and the purchase money invested in stock. In 1888, when the charity became one of the Enfield parochial charities, its annual income was £210 from the rents of nos. 2–3 Whitechapel High Street and £68 from £2,281 stock. The remaining houses were sold in 1960.

Jasper Nicholl left £50 to the poor of Enfield, with which his executors bought the Bull and Bell at Horsepool Stones, together with 3 a. in Long and East fields in 1612. The estate was farmed for £3 a year and the lease bought by the parish in 1620. In 1823 the annual income was £32, of which £25 was used to relieve two aged women and to provide bread. In 1861 the land was leased for building and Jasper Road was constructed. In 1888, when the charity became one of the Enfield parochial charities, its annual income was £60, derived mainly from rents in Jasper Road. Some of the remaining land was sold to Enfield U.D.C. in 1913.

When Enfield market was established in 1618[97] the profits were reserved for the poor. In 1632 the parish purchased a building called the Vine at Enfield Green as a market-house, the rents of which swelled the income of the charity. The house was later replaced by a market cross.[98] Under the inclosure award of 1806 3 a. on the former Chase was allotted to the market-place charity, whose income was combined with that of Prounce's charity and paid before 1814 to the master of Enfield grammar school. In 1823, however, £20 of the two charities' total income of £36 was being paid as a pension to a widow; £12 came from the market-place charity and consisted of the rents of five houses on the western side of the market-place. The houses were demolished after 1847[99] and in 1888, when the charity became one of the Enfield parochial charities, its annual income was £9 10s., from market tolls and dues and the rent of the Chase allotment. By the mid 20th century the parochial charities were drawing much of their income from the market, including £912 in 1968 for the rents of stalls and another large sum from car-parking fees in the market-place.

John David, by will dated 1620, devised the house later known as the Greyhound inn, on the east side of Enfield Green (afterwards the market-place), for four poor widows. Five houses were built north of the Greyhound and were replaced soon after 1788 by a terrace. The charity was allotted 4 a. on the Chase in 1806 and the annual income was £41 in 1823. The charity became one of the Enfield parochial charities in 1888, when the income was £180. The Greyhound, which had long ceased to be an inn, was leased in 1893 to the London and Provincial Bank, which built a bank on its site in 1899 and paid a ground rent of £120 per annum to the parochial charities.

James I was said to have given £200 to Enfield as compensation for inclosing part of the Chase within Theobalds Park. With that sum the parishioners bought 30 a. called Marshes and Devizes at North Mimms (Herts.), which were settled in trust in 1622, and devoted the profits to any general use concerning Enfield or its poor. The estate was sold under an Act of 1808[1] for £1,740, which was invested in stock. In 1816 the trustees, together with those of Poynett's

91 Tuff, *Enfield*, 117.
92 Tuff, *Enfield*, 119.
93 *V.C.H. Mdx.* i. 294–5.
94 See p. 245.
95 Tuff, *Enfield*, 132.
96 Robinson, *Enfield*, ii. 174, 177.
97 See p. 237.
98 See p. 214.
99 Vestry min. bk. (1840–52), 139–40.
1 48 Geo. III, c. 156.

charity, purchased the 184-acre Edwards Hall estate at Eastwood (Essex), of which 95 a. south of the road from Rayleigh to Southend were considered as the endowment of King James's charity and the rest as that of Poynett's charity.[2] The annual rent of the southern part of the estate amounted to £40 in 1888, when King James's charity became one of the Enfield parochial charities. The property, later known as Lower Edwards Hall farm, was sold in 1922 and the purchase money, £3,562, invested in stock.

George Cock of St. James's, Clerkenwell, by will dated 1635, left £30 from which the income was to buy bread for the poor. A house and close at Clay Hill were purchased and in 1806 the charity was allotted 1 a. out of the former Chase. In 1829 the premises at Clay Hill were exchanged for a building used as the vestry clerk's office at Enfield Town and in 1905, when the charity became one of the Enfield parochial charities, the rents from the building accounted for most of the annual income of £67.

William Billings, by will dated 1659, gave a rent-charge of £1 on lands in Enfield and a house at Clay Hill for clothing poor children. By will dated 1666 Ann Osborne of St. Saviour's, Southwark, gave the parish of Enfield £100 to buy lands, which would provide an income for poor widows and the education of one or more orphans. In 1672 her bequest was used to purchase the lands subject to the rent-charge of £1 under Billings's will. The combined charity was awarded 3 a. on the Chase under the award of 1806 but the rest of the lands were sold in 1816 and 1888 and the proceeds invested in stock. In 1888, when the charity became one of the Enfield parochial charities, its income was £29. The allotment from the Chase, fronting Lower Gordon Road, was exchanged in 1886 for an adjoining plot, which was sold for £2,500 in 1897, when the proceeds were invested.

Elizabeth Anne Eaton, by will dated 1806, gave her estate at Enfield to be divided between six poor widows. Since the will was imperfect and in default of heirs, the property escheated to the lords of the manors of Enfield and Worcesters. James Meyer, lord of Worcesters, sold the 14 a. in his manor, invested the proceeds together with £390 from his own funds in £2,000 stock, and appointed trustees to divide the income among the six widows. By a Scheme of 1955 the charity, whose annual income was £60, was included with the Enfield parochial charities.

Thomas Wroth,[3] after a decision of the duchy of Lancaster court in 1547, gave a rent-charge of £1 7s. 6d.[4] for unspecified charitable purposes, as compensation for inclosing 55 a. in Stonards field. The money was later spent on bread for the poor. Robert Rampston, by will dated 1585, gave a rent-charge of £2 on his lands, later known as Strood Hall farm, in Little Canfield, Little Easton, and Great Dunmow (Essex), for the relief of the poor. William Smith, by will dated 1592, gave a rent-charge of £4 on his lands in Enfield for distribution among the poor. John Deycrowe, by will dated 1627, gave a rent-charge of £4 on property in Green Street for the relief of the poor. The rent-charge was

redeemed c. 1895 and the proceeds were invested in stock. Henry Loft, by will dated 1631, gave rent-charges of £12 for the relief of six poor widows, £4 for clothing the poor, and £4 for a lecturer at the parish church,[5] charged upon his lands in Enfield and Chigwell (Essex). Thomas Pigot, by will dated 1681, gave a rent-charge of 10s. on his property in Enfield to provide bread for the poor of Ponders End. The charity was lost by 1823. Richard Darby, by will dated 1735, gave £100 to be distributed among the poor of Ponders End. In 1776 the accumulated funds were invested in £333 stock, which in 1905 produced £8 a year. Mary Nicholl, by will dated 1751, gave the interest on £50 to buy bread for the poor. In 1905 the income of the charity was £1 from £53 stock. Frederick Maurer, by will dated 1772, gave £50 to the poor. Stock worth £57 was bought and in 1813 augmented by a further £43 stock purchased from the accumulated balances of other charities administered by the vicar and churchwardens. In 1905 the charity had an income of £2 10s.

When the Chase was divided under the Act of 1777, Enfield parish was allotted 200 a. west of Chase Side, which it inclosed and leased out in aid of the land tax and poor-rates. After half had been sold to redeem land tax in 1800 the remainder, called the Hundred Acres, continued to be administered by the churchwardens as trustees. Its rents supplemented the poor-rates until it was gradually sold during the 20th century, when the proceeds were invested in stock which was worth £131,324 in 1962. The annual income was c. £6,000 in 1970, when, following the formation of Enfield L.B., it was allowed to accumulate pending a decision of the Charity Commissioners.[6] Proceeds from the sale of timber on the Enfield allotment of the Chase also supplemented the poor-rates; by 1801 £2,668 had been raised and invested[7] and in 1895 the parish derived an annual income of £416 from £15,132 stock.[8]

Joseph Ellsom, by will dated 1797, gave the interest on £200 to two poor widows or spinsters over the age of 60. The residue of his estate, which amounted to £313, was also invested and the proceeds were devoted to the relief of two more widows. In 1905 the income of the charity was £16, derived from £640 stock. Thomas Dickason, by will dated 1813, gave the interest on £200 to the poor, with preference to the widows of householders. In 1905 the income of the charity was £7 from £285 stock. Frances Claxton, by will dated 1817, gave £333 stock for the upkeep of her grave, with the residue for the relief of a widow aged at least 60. In 1905 the income of the charity was £8. John Francis Mesturas, by will dated 1817, gave £50 to the poor. In 1905 the income of the charity was £1 from £50 stock. Avice Kelham (d. 1841), by will dated 1829, gave the interest on £1,000 stock to provide coal for aged widows. In 1905 the income of the charity was £25. Ann Gough, by codicil dated 1830, gave £200 to the poor. The sum was invested in £220 stock, which produced £5 10s. a year in 1905. Thomas Weston gave money at an unknown date in the 19th century, the income from which was

[2] See above.
[3] Except where otherwise stated, the foll. were all included among the Enfield parochial chars. in 1905.
[4] 6d. for each acre inclosed.
[5] See p. 246.
[6] Char. Com. files; ex inf. Mr. A. H. Hall.
[7] Vestry order bk. (1797–1807), 143.
[8] Weld, Enfield Chars. 41.

to augment Thomas Dickason's gift. In 1905 the income of 9s. 8d. was derived from £20 stock.

Joseph Smith, by will proved 1870, left the proceeds from the sale of his pictures and other effects for the benefit of two poor communicants of Enfield parish church, two of Enfield Baptist chapel, and two of the Congregational church in Baker Street. The bequest did not take effect until the death of Smith's niece in 1905. In 1967 the income of the charity, which was not administered by the Enfield parochial charities, was £4 from £71 stock.

William Clark, by will proved 1881, left money to buy clothing for poor widows. His charity became one of the Enfield parochial charities under a Scheme of 1929. In 1960 the income was £16 from £625 stock. Georgiana Hannah Twells, by will proved

1899, gave the interest on £1,000 for clothes and blankets for the poor of the ecclesiastical district of St. Mary Magdalene each winter. The charity, which remained separate, in 1966 had an income of £25, derived from £1,060 stock. James Foote Clunie, by will proved 1910, gave his house, Handsworth Lodge, London Road, to be sold on the death of his wife to provide coal and general relief for the poor. In 1960 the income of the charity, which was administered by the Enfield parochial charities, was £8 from £279 stock. Eliza Peel, by will proved 1911, gave the interest on £100 to maintain her family's graves, with the surplus to provide clothing for four widows. The charity, which was not one of the Enfield parochial charities, had an income in 1966 of £4 from £124 stock.

MONKEN HADLEY

MONKEN HADLEY[1] lay in north-east Middlesex about 12 miles from London and at the south-western corner of Enfield Chase, north of the market town of Chipping Barnet (Herts.).[2] The name Hadley was first recorded c. 1136, when a hermitage there belonged to the abbey of Walden (Essex). Hadley was sometimes said to lie within Edmonton[3] but in practice was a separate parish by c. 1175.[4] It was sometimes called Monkenchurch until the end of the 15th century.[5]

The 19th-century parish was shaped like a narrow wedge, bounded on the west by South Mimms, on the north by Enfield, and on the south by Chipping Barnet and East Barnet (Herts.); the Great North Road ran across its western, and shortest, side. Before the division of Enfield Chase the parish was said to contain 340 a.[6] but that was probably too low an estimate, since no more than 240 a. were allotted from the Chase under the Act of 1777[7] and the total acreage in 1871 was 641.[8] In 1866 the southern boundary followed the county boundary for over 2 miles from the Great North Road at no. 142 High Street, Barnet, to the hamlet of Cockfosters. The western boundary ran northward from Barnet for about ½ mile along the western side of Hadley Green to a point adjoining the modern Old Fold Manor golf club house.[9] From there the northern boundary ran south-eastward to Cockfosters, crossing the Great North Road by the Windmill inn and forming for most of its length a straight line dividing Hadley Common from the rest of the former Enfield Chase.[10] A narrow leg of land about ½ mile long, projecting northward near the parish church, was allotted to Monken Hadley as glebe land in 1779,[11] dividing 46 a. at the extreme south-western corner of Enfield from its parent parish. A further 8 a. at the southern end of the leg of land, around Mount House and its grounds,

remained a detached portion of Enfield until in 1882 they were transferred to Monken Hadley.[12] The isolated 46 a. of Enfield were transferred in 1894, increasing the size of Monken Hadley to 695 a.[13]

In 1889 Monken Hadley was transferred to the administrative county of Hertfordshire[14] and in 1894 it was divided into the civil parishes of Hadley, 27 a. in the south-west under Barnet U.D.C., and Monken Hadley, 668 a. under East Barnet Valley U.D.C.[15] From 1965 both civil parishes formed part of Barnet L.B.[16] The article, except where otherwise stated, deals with the area covered by the civil parishes in 1894.

The western part of the parish lies over 400 ft. above sea level on a plateau of pebble gravel; the soil to the east is London Clay.[17] The ground slopes from the western plateau to the valley of Pymme's brook, 200 ft. above sea level, whence it rises again towards Cockfosters. Pymme's brook cuts across the eastern end of the parish for ¼ mile.

Notable inhabitants not mentioned elsewhere in this article included Arthur Jackson (1593–1666), divine, Sir Robert Atkyns (1647–1711), historian of Gloucestershire, John Monro (1715–91), physician, Hester Chapone (1727–1801), essayist, and Frances Trollope (1780–1863), novelist and mother of Anthony Trollope.[18]

In the 18th century the Great North Road from Barnet was the only major route through Monken Hadley. A road led north-eastward from the Great North Road past the church and across Enfield Chase, where it was called Camlet Way,[19] and a short road, called Dury Road after a late-18th-century family,[20] skirted the northern side of Hadley Green. A track, in 1971 a bridle way, ran along the south side of Hadley Common to Cockfosters, following for most of its length the boundary hedge which

[1] The article was written in 1971. Any references to later years are dated.
[2] O.S. Maps 1/2,500, Mdx. VI. 3, 4 (1866 and later edns.).
[3] Dugdale, Mon. iv. 148–9.
[4] B.M. Harl. MS. 3697, f. 39.
[5] P.N. Herts. (E.P.N.S.), 75.
[6] Lysons, Environs, ii. 517.
[7] Act for Dividing Enfield Chase, 17 Geo. III, c. 17; the division did not take effect until 1779: Robinson, Enfield, i. 216.
[8] Census, 1871; the figure of 2,530 a., given in the 1831 Census, possibly includes Enfield Chase.

[9] In South Mimms. See p. 283.
[10] Robinson, Enfield, i, map facing p. 208.
[11] See p. 268.
[12] Census, 1891.
[13] Ibid. 1901.
[14] M.R.O., Reps. of Local Inqs. (1889–97).
[15] Ibid.
[16] Lond. Govt. Act, 1963, c. 33.
[17] Geol. Surv. Map 1″, drift, sheet 256 (1951 edn.).
[18] D.N.B.; Walford, Greater Lond. 329.
[19] See p. 211.
[20] F. C. Cass, Monken Hadley (1880), 199.

marked the southern limit of Enfield Chase[21] and crossing Pymme's brook by a wooden bridge,[22] which was replaced in 1827 by a brick one.[23] The western part of the track, later called Hadley Wood Road, was metalled in the late 19th century. In 1798 the Great North Road through Hadley and South Mimms was 'insufferably bad'.[24] Apart from the many coaches which regularly passed through,[25] the village itself was served by coaches which left the Old Bell, Holborn, twice daily c. 1836,[26] while in 1845 four coaches in the opposite direction left the Two Brewers on weekday mornings and another left in the early evening.[27] The main line of the Great Northern Railway was cut across the eastern corner of the parish in 1850.[28] There have been no major alterations to the pattern of communications in the 20th century: in 1971 the Great North Road alone carried public transport, with London Transport motor-buses and Green Line coaches providing links with Barnet, Hatfield, and central London.

The hermitage, established c. 1136 within the park later called Enfield Chase, was the first recorded settlement.[29] The village of Hadley, whose name implies a clearing,[30] apparently grew up near by at the edge of the Chase. It stood on the gravel-topped plateau at the western end of the parish and doubtless was influenced by the Great North Road and the growth of Chipping Barnet.[31] There is no evidence that there were open fields.

Hadley Common, containing 190 a., was allotted to Monken Hadley in 1779 in lieu of the parishioners' rights in Enfield Chase.[32] It was sometimes called Hadley Wood or the New Common and was managed after 1777 by curators appointed by the vestry. Preservation of the woodland was regarded in 1789 as very important:[33] trees were planted, new gates were provided in 1824,[34] and in 1876 parishioners still pastured their animals there.[35] From 1799 the surveyors of the highways acted as curators, assisted by a deputy.[36] In 1971 Hadley Common, which was managed by trustees, stretched from the church to the easternmost tip of the parish at Cockfosters, thickly wooded and little affected by the spread of suburban London to its borders.

Hadley Green or the Old Common, a flat, badly-drained open area of 24 a. crossed by the Great North Road, was never part of Enfield Chase. There was a William atte Green among the inhabitants of Hadley in 1345.[37] In 1777 the vestry tried to prevent soil, gravel, and turf from being taken from the

green,[38] while attempts at inclosure were later encouraged by the lord of the manor, Peter Moore, who planted a semicircle of trees on it and made a ha-ha around it. The vestry won an action against him in King's Bench in 1815 and finally secured the green as an open space after a further action in 1818.[39]

Some timber-framed cottages from Hadley Green, which were removed in 1936 to the Abbey folk park, New Barnet (Herts.), contain 15th-century features.[40] The manor-house was built, probably in the 16th century, on the eastern side of the green,[41] and in 1971 a cottage on the south side of Hadley Common also survived from the 16th century.[42] In the mid 17th century Monken Hadley village clustered around the parish church and spread eastward along the edge of Enfield Chase, as well as to the south and west by the sides of the green. By 1656 several houses had been built along the southern edge of the common[43] and by 1754 they formed a continuous line from Barnet High Street along the eastern side of Hadley Green and beyond the parish church.[44]

Hadley had wealthy residents by 1664, when 8 houses had ten or more hearths.[45] Growth was encouraged by the proximity of the Great North Road, several large brick houses being built in the 18th and 19th centuries, some of them by speculators.[46] In 1798 Monken Hadley's small, genteel houses illustrated the fact that near London poor soil at the summit of a hill generally commanded a better price than rich soil in a valley.[47] The village had many gentry c. 1814.[48] Building since that date has done little to alter its appearance or its social composition.

South of Hadley Green, small houses and cottages had spread northward from Chipping Barnet by 1754.[49] In 1866 that corner of the parish contained terraced houses along the main road and neighbouring courts and alleys, like May Payne's Place.[50] Population declined in the early 20th century,[51] when some of the older houses were demolished, but rose again as a result of building east of the main road in Hadley Ridge, East View, and Wyburn Avenue. The White Bear, at the extreme south-western corner of the parish, in Barnet High Street, existed in 1624[52] but was demolished in 1831 and replaced by a building which later became a chemist's shop.[53] The inn was one of four in the parish in 1752;[54] by 1803 the number had been reduced to two.[55]

The area called Hadley Highstone, north of

[21] D.L. 42/125.
[22] *Rep. on Bridges in Mdx.* 99.
[23] Hadley vestry min. bk. (1820–32) *penes* Barnet Mus.
[24] Middleton, *View*, 395.
[25] *Pigot's Com. Dir.* (1832–4), s.v. Chipping Barnet.
[26] *Mdx. & Herts. N. & Q.* iv (1898), 105.
[27] *P.O. Dir. Mdx.* (1845).
[28] C. H. Grinling, *Hist. of Gt. Northern Rly.* 90. Hadley Wood stn. was in Enfield. See above, p. 212.
[29] *Cal. Chart. R.* 1226–57, 337; *V.C.H. Mdx.* ii. 225–6; see below, p. 263. The site of the hermitage is unknown. Geoffrey de Mandeville (d. 1144) mentioned 'brothers' at Hadley: see below, p. 267.
[30] *P.N. Herts.* (E.P.N.S.), 75.
[31] A market at Chipping Barnet was granted in 1199: *V.C.H. Herts.* ii. 330.
[32] Act for Dividing Enfield Chase, 17 Geo. III, c. 17.
[33] Hadley vestry min. bk. (1757–94) *penes* Barnet Mus.
[34] Vestry min. bk. (1757–94).
[35] Thorne, *Environs*, i. 266; see below, p. 265.
[36] M.R.O., D.R.O. 17/B1/1.

[37] *P.N. Herts.* (E.P.N.S.), 75.
[38] Vestry min. bk. (1757–94).
[39] M.R.O., D.R.O. 17/B1/1.
[40] *T.L.M.A.S.* xiii. 495.   [41] See p. 264.
[42] The cottage adjoining Hurst Cott.: Min. of Town & Country Planning, List of Bldgs. (1948).
[43] M.P.C. 145.
[44] Rocque, *Map of Mdx.* (1754).
[45] M.R.O., MR/TH/5.
[46] e.g. the Elms, Monkenholt. See below.
[47] Middleton, *View*, 24.
[48] Hughson, *British Metropolis and its Neighbourhood*, vi. 138.
[49] Rocque, *Map of Mdx.* (1754).
[50] O.S. Maps 1/2,500, Mdx. VI. 3, 4 (1866 edn.).
[51] See above. The area lay within Hadley civil par.
[52] C 142/408/125.
[53] W. Marcham, 'Hist. Notes on Hadley Par.' (TS *penes* Barnet Mus.), 3.
[54] M.R.O., L.V. 7/29.
[55] Ibid. 10/111.

Hadley Green on either side of the Great North Road, formed part of Enfield parish until 1894. Small houses were built on the eastern side of the road before 1754, on encroachment from Enfield Chase.[56] The Two Brewers inn existed in 1752[57] and the Windmill in 1803,[58] but they were rebuilt c. 1930 and c. 1900 respectively. A third inn, the William IV, retained some early weatherboarded buildings in 1971, when the Great North Road was lined mainly by 19th-century yellow-brick terraces, interspersed with larger houses dated between 1887 and 1908.[59]

The numerous 18th- and 19th-century houses contributed to the designation of much of the parish in 1968 as a conservation area under the Civic Amenities Act.[60] Most of the bigger ones face the green and the common.[61] Between the two tracts of open space, houses, some of them with high brick walls, are scattered along the winding road leading to the church, an area which has changed little since 1816 when it was praised for its picturesque aspect.[62] Houses on the eastern side of Hadley Green include, at the southern end, the Grange and Ossulston House, the latter with a rusticated surround to the semicircular-headed doorway. They were built soon after 1764 by John Horton, a sugar refiner, on the site of the Rose and Crown inn and conveyed in 1786 to William Makepeace Thackeray,[63] grandfather of the novelist and brother-in-law of Peter Moore.[64] North of Ossulston House, beyond two small stuccoed cottages, stood the Elms, Mercers, and the building known in the 19th century as the Manor House,[65] all of which were destroyed by bombs c. 1944.[66] The Elms was erected in 1770 by John Tate, a Barnet builder, on land leased from Thomas Lewis, builder, of Theobalds Road (Holborn).[67] To the north lie Hadley House,[68] in extensive grounds, and Fairholt, a stuccoed mid-18th-century house with a central pediment and a pedimented doorcase. Monkenholt, farther north, a similar stuccoed building but with a bow front, was built soon after 1767 by Thomas Lewis on land leased from the lord of the manor, John Pinney.[69] Lewis may also have built Hollybush, to the north,[70] which adjoins a smaller early-18th-century house. Livingstone Cottage and the adjoining Monken Cottage, between Monkenholt and Hollybush House, are mid-18th-century buildings of urban appearance. Livingstone Cottage was the residence, 1857–8, of Dr. David Livingstone, who wrote *Missionary Travels and Researches in South Africa* there;[71] later residents included James Agate (1877–1947), the dramatic critic.[72] Grandon, at the north-east corner of the green, next to Wilbraham's alms-houses,[73] is early-18th-century.

In 1625 a house stood on or near the site of Hadley Bourne (formerly Dury House), which with its pedimented wooden doorcase seems to have been built soon after the property was sold in 1725 to Percival Chandler, a London fishmonger.[74] To the west in Dury Road are Stoberry Lodge, an early-19th-century stuccoed villa, and, beyond, no. 29, formerly Thorndon Friars, built shortly before 1740 on land belonging to the Chandlers.[75] Between Thorndon Friars and the Great North Road smaller dwellings, several of them weatherboarded and pantiled, line both sides of the road. They include a pair of early-19th-century cottages with barge-boarded gables, shutters, and a loggia of Gothic arches.

The largest house in the road leading from Hadley Green to the church was the Priory, demolished after 1953,[76] a 16th-century building, which was given an elaborate stuccoed Gothic front c. 1800.[77] The house belonged c. 1800 to the Revd. David Garrow,[78] whose son, the lawyer Sir William Garrow (1760–1840), was born there.[79] In 1971 the site was occupied by neo-Georgian houses called the Cedars and Little Pipers. Hadley Grove, lying well back from the road to the east, was a large late-18th-century house rebuilt in the early 20th century in the neo-Georgian manner, to the designs of H. A. Welch.[80] Beacon House, next to the church, is smaller and seems to contain parts of the building conveyed by Thomas Fletcher to the parish in 1616;[81] it was enlarged and refronted in the 18th century, when it belonged to the Shewell family.[82] White Lodge, on the opposite side of the road, dates from before 1711[83] and contains an elaborately covered early-18th-century doorcase, but has been substantially altered.[84] Hadley Lodge, by the gate at the entrance to Hadley Common, is an 18th-century stuccoed house incorporating some earlier features, with a slate mansard roof and a porch supported on five Ionic columns.

The only large residence north of the church is Mount House, a richly detailed red-brick building, with a pedimented centrepiece and a carved doorcase flanked by Ionic half-columns. It was built in the early 18th century on a hill near the windmill,[85] on ground inclosed from Enfield Chase,[86] and remained within Enfield parish until 1882.[87] Residents have included Joseph Henry Green (1791–1863), surgeon and author.[88] South of the common, Lemmons, formerly Gladsmuir House, stands on the site of a house belonging to Henry Bellamy in 1584;[89] the building, with a Doric porch, an extension to the east, and a room enriched with late-18th-century medallions, has been much altered

[56] D.L. 31/171.
[57] M.R.O., L.V. 7/26.
[58] Ibid. 10/111.
[59] e.g. Warwick Terrace, 1908.
[60] Barnet L.B., *Monken Hadley Conservation Area* (1970), 1.
[61] See plate facing p. 257.
[62] Brewer, *Beauties of Eng. and Wales*, x (5), 741.
[63] M.L.R. 1764/3/90, /91; 1786/3/46. See p. 264.
[64] Cass, *Hadley*, 76.   [65] See p. 264.
[66] Photographs *penes* Barnet Mus.
[67] M.L.R. 1784/2/315.   [68] See p. 264.
[69] M.L.R. 1768/1/575.
[70] Marcham, 'Notes', 13–14.
[71] Barnet L.B., *Official Guide* [1967]; plaque on house.
[72] Marcham, 'Notes' 14.
[73] See p. 270.

[74] Marcham, 'Notes', 5; M.L.R. 1739/2/59.
[75] M.L.R. 1740/4/858, /859.
[76] Pevsner, *Herts.* 169.
[77] Guildhall Libr., illus. edn. of Lysons, *Environs*; photographs *penes* Barnet Mus.
[78] Cass, *Hadley*, 183; Garrow had bought the house in 1760.
[79] D.N.B.
[80] Pevsner, *Herts.* 169.
[81] See p. 270.
[82] Marcham, 'Notes', 9.
[83] M.L.R. 1711/1/100.
[84] Marcham, 'Notes', 11.
[85] See p. 266.
[86] M.L.R. 1735/4/150, /151.   [87] See above.
[88] D.N.B.; Walford, *Greater Lond.* 329.
[89] Prob. 11/67 (P.C.C. 12 Watson).

since it was built by the Quilter family, which owned the property from 1736 to 1909.[90] It was owned by the author Kingsley Amis in 1972,[91] when the poet laureate Cecil Day-Lewis died there.[92] Hurst Cottage, to the east, is a stuccoed, early-18th-century house. The Chase, farther east, has an early-19th-century façade. Beyond stands Hadley Hurst, a tall brick house with a hipped roof and a wooden eaves cornice; the central doorway is surmounted by a curved broken pediment in the baroque manner, while the interior contains panelled rooms, with fire-places of Palladian design. The house was built shortly before 1707[93] on land which had belonged to Henry Bellamy.[94] Its extensive stable buildings have been turned into separate dwellings but the landscaped grounds survive.

Apart from four isolated houses — Ludgrove, the Blue House, Folly Farm, and Capons House — on the edge of Enfield Chase, the eastern part of the parish remained almost completely free of building until the British Land Co. bought the Woodcock farm, or Capons House, estate in 1868.[95] Woodville, Hadley, Clifford, Latimer, and Tudor roads were subsequently laid out as a northward extension of New Barnet, where a railway station was opened on the Great Northern main line in 1852.[96] Building spread northward to the Crescent, where some large brick houses included Monkenhurst, of ecclesiastical appearance and with a pyramid-capped tower, built in 1881 to the designs of Peter Dollar.[97] More suburban building took place farther east after the Second World War, stimulated by the opening in 1933 of the northern terminus of the Piccadilly line at Cockfosters, in Enfield parish.[98]

The battle of Barnet, fought at Hadley and South Mimms in 1471,[99] probably started on Hadley Green or the western part of Hadley Common and perhaps spread east of the church and down the slopes towards Chipping Barnet.[1] A commemorative obelisk was erected in 1740 by Sir Jeremy Sambrook of Bush Hill Park, Edmonton, and North Mimms (Herts.).[2] It stood on the western boundary and later was moved into South Mimms[3] but there is no evidence that it marked the spot where Warwick fell. The obelisk gave the name Hadley Highstone to the group of cottages built to the south.

There were 180 communicants in the parish in 1547.[4] Ninety-one adult males took the protestation oath in 1642,[5] 74 persons were chargeable and 22 were not chargeable for hearth tax in 1664,[6] and 227

persons were recorded in 1676.[7] Numbers were not affected by the inclusion of Hadley Common: in 1801 there were 584 inhabitants, in 1811 718, and in 1821 926.[8] The rate of increase then slowed down and in 1891 there were 1,302 inhabitants. The population of the civil parishes of Hadley and Monken Hadley together totalled 1,776 in 1931, that of Hadley having declined from 541 to 253 since 1891. In 1951 the population of the two civil parishes was 4,423.[9]

MANOR AND OTHER ESTATES. The hermitage of Hadley was included in the grant of lands made by Geoffrey de Mandeville, earl of Essex (d. 1144), to Walden abbey (Essex) in 1136.[10] The grant was confirmed in 1248[11] and the abbot claimed jurisdiction in Hadley in 1294[12] but the manor of *HADLEY* or *MONKEN HADLEY*, forming a division of Edmonton manor,[13] was not mentioned by name until the early 16th century.[14] In 1538, on the dissolution of the abbey, it was granted to the Lord Chancellor Sir Thomas, later Lord, Audley (1488–1544),[15] who was licensed in 1540 to alienate it to Francis Goodere of Hadley.[16] Goodere conveyed it in 1545 to William, later Sir William, Stanford (1509–58), a justice of the Common Pleas.[17] William's son Robert conveyed the manor in 1569 to Thomas Smallwood,[18] who in 1571 conveyed it for life to Robert's mother, Alice, and her second husband Roger Carew.[19] On Alice's death in 1573 Robert Stanford conveyed the manor to William Kympton, merchant tailor of London,[20] who settled it in 1582 on his son Robert.[21] Robert Kympton sold it in 1621 to Thomas Emerson of Hadley and Nicholas Hawes of London,[22] together with a capital messuage, 5 a., and another 30 a. already in Emerson's occupation. Emerson died in 1624[23] and in 1627 his son and namesake conveyed the manor to Michael Grigg,[24] who sold it in 1647 to John Langham, alderman of London.[25]

By 1651 the manor had passed into the possession of John Masters, who conveyed it to William Ashton (d. 1651).[26] William's widow Mary, who married Sir Edward Turnor (d. 1676),[27] Speaker and Chief Baron,[28] held a life-interest apparently until her death in 1701.[29] The reversion was held successively by John Hayes and his sons John (d. 1670) and Simon (d. 1692),[30] from whom it passed under a mortgage of 1684 to Vere Booth of Adderbury

[90] Barnet Mus., L 11, 17–18; M.L.R. 1909/25/961. The house had an estate of 23 a. in 1778: M.R.O., Acc. 549/Bundle 18.
[91] *Who's Who* (1972).
[92] *The Times*, 23 May 1972.
[93] C 54/4963/5.
[94] Prob. 11/67 (P.C.C. 12 Watson).
[95] See p. 265; O.S. Maps, 1/2,500, Mdx. VI. 3, 4 (1866 edn.).
[96] Grinling, *Gt. Northern Rly.* 126.
[97] Marcham, 'Notes'.   [98] See p. 212.
[99] *V.C.H. Mdx.* ii. 27–8.
[1] *V.C.H. Herts.* ii. 329; Cass, *Hadley*, 9–17.
[2] *V.C.H. Herts.* ii. 329.
[3] See p. 276.
[4] Hennessy, *Novum Repertorium*, 184.
[5] H.L., Mdx. Protestation Rets.
[6] M.R.O., MR/TH/5.
[7] William Salt Libr., Stafford, Salt MS. 33, p. 40.
[8] *Census*, 1801 and later edns.
[9] The parish was split among different wards in the 1961 census.

[10] B.M. Cott. MS. Vesp. E. vi, f. 26.
[11] *Cal. Chart. R.* 1226–57, 337.
[12] *Plac. de Quo. Warr.* (Rec. Com.), 479; see above, p. 176.
[13] See p. 128.
[14] *Valor Eccl.* (Rec. Com.), vi, p. xii.
[15] *L. & P. Hen. VIII*, xiii (1), pp. 212, 410; *D.N.B.*
[16] *L. & P. Hen. VIII*, xv, p. 292.
[17] Ibid. xx(1), p. 59; *D.N.B.*
[18] *Cal. Pat.* 1566–9, 408.
[19] Ibid. 179.
[20] Cass, *Hadley*, 51; C 66/1120 m. 11.
[21] C 66/1218 m. 12.
[22] C 54/2470 no. 14.
[23] Cass, *Hadley*, 61.
[24] C 54/2687 no. 5.
[25] C 54/3379.
[26] C.P. 25(2)/574/1650 Hil.; Cass, *Hadley*, 64.
[27] Cass, *Hadley*, 65.
[28] *D.N.B.*
[29] Barnet Mus., Hadley vestry min. bk. (1672–1712); Cass, *Hadley*, 66–8.
[30] Prob. 11/306 (P.C.C. 179 May); Cass, *Hadley*, 66.

(Oxon.).[31] By will proved 1718[32] Booth devised the manor to his brother George (d. 1726), whose executrix Hester Pinney[33] conveyed the manor in 1737 to her nephew Azariah Pinney of Bettiscombe (Dors.).[34] Azariah died in 1759, leaving it to his cousin John Frederick Pinney, a West Indies planter (d. 1762).[35] J. F. Pinney devised the manor to his cousin John Pinney, whose son John Pinney of Blackdown (Dors.) sold it in 1791 to the Radical politician Peter Moore (1753–1828), who fled the country on losing his fortune in 1825.[36] The manor was conveyed in 1830 by Peter's nephew Stephen Moore to trustees,[37] who conveyed it in 1832 to John Bonus Child of Hadley[38] (d. 1832).[39] Child's widow Frances held the manor until her death in 1855, after which it was sold to Henry Hyde of Ely Place, Holborn[40] (d. 1877), whose widow Julia, by will proved 1887, ordered it to be sold.[41] It was purchased in 1890 by Emily and Rhoda Wyburn[42] and in 1934, on Rhoda's death, by East Barnet U.D.C.[43]

The manorial estate consisted in 1621 of the manor-house and 50 a., 30 a. of which was in hand, along with several houses in the village.[44] Most of the land was leased in 1724 to Percival Chandler[45] and in 1737 the lord retained no more than 14 a.[46] After the house and the last of the land had been sold in 1795 to Sir Charles Pole, Bt., as trustee for Eleazor Philip Salomans,[47] the lordship consisted merely of rights over Hadley Green.[48] Frances Child (d. 1855) held 37 a. east of Hadley Green, including some land which had formerly been part of the manorial estate.[49] Her estate remained intact until it was bought, together with the manor, by East Barnet U.D.C., who incorporated most of it into the open space called King George's field.[50]

The manor-house at Hadley, recorded in 1544–5,[51] had 27 hearths in 1664, when Margaret Hayes was living there.[52] It was described as the old manor-house in 1724[53] and seems to have been replaced soon afterwards by a large red-brick building, with a main front of five bays and two storeys surmounted by a pediment. The house, on the east of Hadley Green, received a three-storeyed addition to the south, probably later in the 18th century. Soon after its sale in 1795[54] it acquired the name Hadley House. The residence known as the Manor House in the 19th century stood farther south, also on the east side of Hadley Green. It was a plain 18th-century building of three storeys, stuccoed, with a Doric porch. It belonged in 1746 to Thomas Chandler[55] and was occupied in the later 18th century by William Makepeace Thackeray.[56] After its purchase in 1829 by John Bonus Child[57] it remained the seat of successive lords of the manor until 1934. It was destroyed by a bomb in 1944.[58]

The estate in the eastern part of the parish known as Ludgrove or Ludgrave farm passed from John Lightgrave, a London goldsmith, to his son John, who in 1423 quitclaimed it to trustees.[59] A house called Ludgrave was held c. 1523 by Thomas Green and Laurence Foxley,[60] and in 1542, with 30 a. of land and 18 a. of wood, it was conveyed by John Marsh, server of the king's chamber, to the Crown, as part of an exchange.[61] The Crown granted the estate in 1553 to William Herbert, earl of Pembroke,[62] who conveyed it to Thomas Highgate of Hayes in 1560.[63] Highgate died seised of the property in 1576,[64] and it later came into the hands of William Becher, haberdasher of London, who conveyed it in 1596 to John Quarles, draper.[65] It was sold in 1611 by Cornelius Fish and others to Sir Roger Wilbraham, Master of Requests.[66] Sir Roger's daughter and heir, Mary, married Sir Thomas Pelham and their son Sir John Pelham sold the estate in 1663 to Ambrose Brunskill of Hadley and Northaw (Herts.), who died in 1670.[67] Ludgrove passed to Brunskill's eldest daughter, Jane, who married Thomas Walton, and then successively to Walton's elder son Ambrose and his younger son John,[68] who was living at the Blue House, on the estate, in 1686.[69] In 1714 John Walton's widow Mary conveyed the estate, consisting of Ludgrove farm with 66 a. in Hadley and 26 a. in East Barnet (Herts.), Blue House farm with 102 a. in Hadley and East Barnet, and a brick house called Cockfosters, to Ephraim Beauchamp of Tottenham.[70] Beauchamp's widow Lettice conveyed it in 1730 in trust for William Beauchamp, later Sir William Beauchamp-Proctor, Bt., Ephraim Beauchamp's grandson.[71] The estate subsequently came into the possession of Vice-Admiral Temple West (1713–1757),[72] after whose death it passed to his second son Col. Temple West, who died in 1783.[73] Col. West's widow Jane was in possession of Ludgraves or Blue House farm in 1796.[74] It was sold on the death of her son C. H. West to Archibald Paris of Beech Hill, Enfield, who held it in 1811.[75] In 1880 it was in the

[31] Cass, *Hadley*, 67–8.
[32] Prob. 11/562 (P.C.C. 24 Tenison).
[33] Prob. 11/610 (P.C.C. 139 Plymouth).
[34] Cass, *Hadley*, 70.
[35] Prob. 11/857 (P.C.C. 252 Lynch); Cass, *Hadley*, 71–2.
[36] Cass, *Hadley*, 72–3; *D.N.B.*
[37] M.L.R. 1831/6/376.
[38] M.L.R. 1832/1/687.
[39] Cass, *Hadley*, 76.
[40] Ibid. 76.
[41] M.R.O., Acc. 370/14, /17.
[42] M.L.R. 1890/16/630.
[43] Marcham, 'Notes', 22.
[44] C 54/2470 no. 14.
[45] Cass, *Hadley*, 69.
[46] Ibid. 70.
[47] M.L.R. 1795/4/201.
[48] Cass, *Hadley*, 72.
[49] M.L.R. 1857/12/520.
[50] Marcham, 'Notes', 21.
[51] C 54/438 no. 18.
[52] M.R.O., MR/TH/5.
[53] Cass, *Hadley*, 69.

[54] M.L.R. 1795/4/201.
[55] Ibid. 1747/2/829.
[56] Cass, *Hadley*, 76.
[57] M.L.R. 1829/2/770.
[58] Marcham, 'Notes', 21.
[59] *Cal. Close*, 1422–9, 56, 58.
[60] C 1/487 no. 28.
[61] E 305/C. 53.
[62] *Cal. Pat.* 1554, 170.
[63] Ibid. 1560–3, 53.
[64] C 142/174/40.
[65] C 54/1314 no. 487.
[66] C 54/2088 no. 33.
[67] Prob. 11/334 (P.C.C. 146 Penn).
[68] C 78/1441 no. 13.
[69] D.L. 43/7/10. Blue Ho. was mentioned in 1635: D.L. 42/125.
[70] M.L.R. 1714/2/102.
[71] Ibid. 1730/5/279; G.E.C. *Baronetage*, v. 88.
[72] *D.N.B.*; Cass, *Hadley*, 36.
[73] Cass, *Hadley*, 36.
[74] Lysons, *Environs*, ii. 518–19.
[75] Lysons, *Environs*, Suppl. 176.

possession of R. C. L. Bevan of Trent Place, Enfield.[76]

In spite of a statement by Lysons,[77] there is no evidence that the Ludgrove estate was a manor. Ludgrove House, in 1596 a 'very fair house' in a valley near Enfield Chase,[78] had 17 hearths in 1672,[79] when it was used as a school.[80] No trace of the building survives. The later Ludgrove Hall, belonging to Trent Park college, Enfield, is at Cockfosters, perhaps on the site of the former Blue House. It is a plain early-19th-century stuccoed building, with a large late-19th-century red-brick extension to the south and a still later addition of c. 1900, with a mansard roof, to the north, adjoining the Cockfosters–Hadley bridle-path. Some buildings which survived in 1971 may have belonged to Blue House farm-house, which was situated east of Ludgrove in 1896.[81]

Capons House, east of Hadley village, belonged in 1635 to Dr. Brett[82] and in 1686 to William Nicholl.[83] In 1741 it was held by Samuel Nicholl of Hillingdon[84] and in 1766 by John Nicholl of Scalm Park (Yorks.), who conveyed it in the same year to Robert Pardoe of Lincoln's Inn.[85] The estate, 28 a. in 1766, was in the hands of Sir Culling Smith, Bt., formerly of Hadley Grove and Hadley Hurst, in 1807.[86] The adjacent Bonnyes farm was conveyed in 1613 by Henry Goodere to Francis Kirtland of Holborn, tailor.[87] The farm-house, which had served as a workhouse,[88] was conveyed in 1778, together with 24 a., to Sir Culling Smith,[89] and, with Capons House, was conveyed by him in 1807 to Charles Cottrell of Hadley (d. 1829).[90] In 1836 Cottrell's nephew Charles Herbert Cottrell of Brighton (Suss.) conveyed the combined estates, which together formed Woodcock or Capons House farm, containing 42 a. in Hadley and 15 a. in Chipping Barnet (Herts.), to Samuel Strong of Hadley.[91] Strong sold them in 1868 to the British Land Co., which covered the area with suburban houses.[92]

There was a new house built by Thomas Turpin on the site of the later Folly Farm, between Capons House and Ludgrove, in 1686.[93] It came in the late 18th century to Francis Barroneau of New Lodge, South Mimms (d. 1814), whose widow Elizabeth (d. 1846) devised the surrounding estate of 67 a. to her nephew the Revd. Robert Francis Wilson.[94] Robert's son Thomas Percival Wilson conveyed it in 1904 in trust for Edward Hanson Freshfield,[95] who conveyed the farm in 1913, when it consisted of 53 a., to E. H. Lefroy and the Revd. F. L. Deane.[96] They sold 22 a. of it in 1919 to S. Maw & Sons,[97] from whom it passed in 1936 to East Barnet U.D.C.[98]

ECONOMIC AND SOCIAL HISTORY. The Ludgrove estate, in the eastern part of the parish, had been fully inclosed by 1553[99] and all the agricultural land had been inclosed by 1754.[1] Out of the 340 a. in Monken Hadley 300 a. were meadow or pasture shortly before the extension of the parish boundaries in 1779.[2] Glebe farm, however, which formed part of the allotment from the Chase in 1779, was chiefly arable: in 1848 only seven of its 53 a. were meadow[3] and in 1853 few cattle were pastured.[4] Glebe, Woodcock, and Gothic farms existed in 1866[5] and Hadley farm, at Hadley Highstone, was described as a dairy farm in 1913.[6] Some of the fields south of Hadley Common gave way to suburban housing after the sale of part of Woodcock, or Capons House, farm in 1868,[7] but a little farm-land survived in 1971.

In addition to Hadley Green the parishioners also enjoyed common rights in Enfield Chase. There were frequent disputes, as in 1581 when proceedings were taken against William Kympton, lord of the manor, for letting his sheep graze to the detriment of the poor and the Chase.[8] Parishioners were often condemned in the 16th and 17th centuries for poaching within the Chase, and their own claims were periodically threatened. During the Interregnum Monken Hadley joined Edmonton and South Mimms in petitioning to retain the right to pasture animals and take wood,[9] and in 1703 several inhabitants contributed to a fund for defending the rights of common.[10] After Hadley Common had been granted to the parish in 1779 to replace common rights over the whole Chase,[11] the curators made a small annual profit from the sale of bushes and faggots. Any attempt to clear and till the land, as happened elsewhere in the former Chase, was resisted, although in 1789 there were so many new trees that some had to be felled.[12] In 1799 the vestry imposed new rules, later amended, for the management of Hadley Common: a maximum of 150 loads of bushes or 10 a. of underwood was to be sold each year, while each occupier of more than 3 a. in the parish was allowed to keep cattle, according to a prescribed stint, but not to graze horses, pigs, bulls, or sheep.[13] A new pound was built there in 1799 but a replacement was requested, from the lord, in 1835. A common keeper was appointed in 1826[14] and cattle were still being grazed on Hadley Common in 1876.[15] The practice died out as Londoners began to resort there and in 1970 the area was used solely for recreation.[16] Grazing also continued on Hadley Green, which the vestry likewise preserved as an

[76] Cass, *Hadley*, 36.
[77] Lysons, *Environs*, ii. 518.
[78] Norden, *Spec. Brit.* 36.
[79] M.R.O., MR/TH/22.
[80] See p. 269.
[81] O.S. Map 6", Mdx. VII. NW. (1896 edn.).
[82] D.L. 42/125.
[83] D.L. 43/7/10.
[84] M.L.R. 1741/4/199, /200.
[85] Ibid. 1766/6/421.
[86] Ibid. 1808/1/20; Cass, *Hadley*, 111, 172.
[87] C 54/2133 no. 33.
[88] See p. 267.
[89] M.L.R. 1778/1/291.
[90] Ibid. 1808/1/20; Cass, *Hadley*, 113.
[91] M.L.R. 1836/5/490.
[92] Barnet Mus., L 11, p. 180.
[93] D.L. 43/7/10.
[94] M.L.R. 1859/15/80, /81; Cass, *Hadley*, 174.
[95] Barnet Mus., L 11, p. 151.

[96] M.L.R. 1913/11/111.
[97] Ibid. 1919/15/652.
[98] Barnet Mus., L 11, p. 152.
[99] *Cal. Pat.* 1553, 170; see above, p. 264.
[1] J. Rocque, *Map of Mdx.* (1754).
[2] Lysons, *Environs*, ii. 517.
[3] M.R.O., TA/M'HAD.
[4] Sale parts. *penes* Barnet Mus.
[5] O.S. Maps 1/2,500, Mdx. VI. 3, 4 (1866 edn.).
[6] *Kelly's Dir. Herts.* (1913–14).
[7] See above.
[8] D.L. 1/115/A27.
[9] *T.L.M.A.S.* x. 293; E 317/Mdx. 17A; see p. 236.
[10] Hadley vestry min. bk. (1672–1712) *penes* Barnet Mus.
[11] Ibid. (1757–94); see above, p. 261.
[12] Vestry min. bk. (1757–94).
[13] M.R.O., D.R.O. 17/B1/1.
[14] Vestry min. bks. *penes* Barnet Mus.
[15] Thorne, *Environs*, i. 266.
[16] Barnet L.B., *Monken Hadley Conservation Area*, 12.

open space.[17] In 1827 the constables were ordered to prevent bathing in the ponds,[18] which in 1970 were used only for angling.[19]

Maltmen were living in the parish in 1447 and 1449,[20] and there was a tile-kiln in 1573.[21] Inhabitants c. 1615 included tailors, carpenters, oatmealmen, and weavers.[22] A brewery was established in 1700[23] and in 1795 it moved to a site by the Great North Road, at the northern end of Hadley Green,[24] where it was rebuilt as a four-storeyed yellow-brick building in 1890.[25] Retail trades have long been concentrated in the south-western corner of the parish, on the outskirts of Chipping Barnet, which contained most of Monken Hadley's butchers, carpenters, grocers, and shoemakers c. 1832.[26] There were several shops, a post office, and a dairy at Hadley Highstone and by the green in 1908[27] but most had disappeared by 1971, when Chipping Barnet was the nearest shopping centre.

In 1635 a windmill stood a few yards inside what was then part of Enfield parish, by the Great North Road, a little north of the modern Dury Road.[28] It disappeared between 1740 and 1777 but presumably gave its name to Mill Corner and the Windmill inn.[29] Another windmill stood on Beacon Hill, near the site of Mount House, in 1629[30] but had gone by 1735.[31] Both mills were within Enfield Chase and were held of Enfield manor. A third windmill was erected on Hadley Green west of the Great North Road in 1821.[32] It was replaced in 1827 by a mill which later came into private ownership[33] and which disappeared between 1866 and 1897.[34]

Londoners owned land in Monken Hadley at least from the early 15th century[35] and later settled there in large numbers.[36] By the 20th century there were many wealthy residents and, in contrast to neighbouring parishes, neither new factories nor large housing estates. In 1961 self-employed business and professional persons formed a third of the population of Hadley ward in East Barnet U.D.[37] and they, together with most other inhabitants of the old parish, worked outside the boundaries.

A piece of ground near Hadley served as a bowling alley in 1658[38] and in 1748 there was a coffee house near the windmill by the Great North Road.[39] There was a rifle range on the south-western slopes of the parish in 1866.[40] An iron building was erected in 1896 at Hadley Highstone to serve as a reading room[41] and in 1971, renamed Hadley memorial hall, constituted a meeting-place for local societies.

LOCAL GOVERNMENT. The abbot of Walden,

after claiming view of frankpledge and the assizes of bread and ale in Hadley, Mimms, Edmonton, and Enfield in 1294, altered his plea to claim the rights in Enfield alone.[42] Hadley was part, probably originally a tithing, of Edmonton manor.[43] Officers for Hadley were elected at the court leet for Edmonton, held in Whitsun week. Two ale-tasters were recorded only in 1661, the date of Edmonton's first extant court book,[44] but a constable was elected regularly until 1740, after which date Hadley was not mentioned.[45] A signer of beasts was appointed in 1682[46] and regularly from 1703, although the office was sometimes combined with that of constable.[47]

Vestry minute books survive from 1672 to 1914;[48] there are also churchwardens' accounts from 1717 to 1821 and, with a few gaps, overseers' accounts from 1678 to 1835, and parish rate books from 1757 to 1852.[49] The vestry met about four times a year in the late 17th century and from 1722 it normally met monthly in the church.[50] Incumbents, although present at more than half of the meetings, presided irregularly in the 18th century and more frequently in the 19th. From the mid 18th century leading residents seem to have wielded considerable influence; at the end of the century members of the Thackeray, Day, Quilter, Cottrell, and Smith families were all frequent attenders. A vestry clerk was first recorded in 1733.[51]

There were two churchwardens and two overseers in 1580[52] but by 1677 each office was held by one man only.[53] In 1689 the vestry successfully claimed that the incumbent, as a donee, could not appoint the churchwarden.[54] The number of overseers was restored to two c. 1775 and sometimes four were appointed.[55] There were two constables in 1614 and subsequent years[56] but by 1661 there was only one, appointed by the vestry. A headborough was appointed by the vestry from 1696 onwards. There were two or more surveyors of the highways from 1677 and statute duty was still in force in 1828. In 1734 the surveyors were warned to be more careful in collecting rates. A pauper was made a salaried street-keeper in 1826 but his office was abolished in 1835.[57]

Large areas of common land, together with several charities and two sets of alms-houses, reduced the necessity for parish relief, although after 1799 use of the common was restricted to those who paid land tax.[58] A workhouse was opened in rented premises in 1738, when 3 paupers were moved there and it was agreed that all persons receiving alms from the parish should be badged. From 1799 male inmates were enjoined to wear yellow stockings and the

[17] See p. 261.
[18] Vestry min. bk. (1820–32).
[19] Monken Hadley Conservation Area, 5.
[20] Cal. Close, 1447–54, 34–5, 142–3.
[21] Cass, Hadley, 52.
[22] Mdx. Sess. Recs. i. 9, 18, 54, 298, 344.
[23] Date on later brewery.   [24] M.L.R. 1802/4/274.
[25] Plans penes Barnet Mus.
[26] Pigot's Com. Dir. (1832–4).
[27] Kelly's Dir. Herts. (1908).   [28] D.L. 42/125.
[29] M.L.R. 1740/4/878, 859; Barnet Mus., L 11, p. 91.
[30] C 54/2850/20.
[31] M.L.R. 1735/4/150–1.
[32] Vestry min. bk. (1820–32).
[33] Kelly's Dir. Mdx. (1845).
[34] O.S. Maps 1/2,500, Mdx. VI. 3 (1866 edn.); 6", Mdx. VI. NE. (1897 edn.).
[35] Cal. Close, 1405–9, 250.   [36] See p. 261.
[37] Census, 1961.   [38] E 317/Mdx. 17A.

[39] M.L.R. 1748/3/76.
[40] O.S. Map 1/2,500, Mdx. VI. 4 (1866 edn.).
[41] Kelly's Dir. Herts. (1908).
[42] Plac. de Quo Warr. (Rec. Com.), 479.
[43] M.R.O., Acc. 695/42, f. 1.
[44] Ibid. /15, f. 1.   [45] Ibid /15–19.
[46] Ibid. /16, f. 17.
[47] Ibid. /17, ff. 50 v., 147 et seq.
[48] At Barnet Mus., apart from the books for 1794–1820 and 1832–1914, which are at the M.R.O., D.R.O. 17/B1/1, /2.
[49] Accts. and rate bks. at Barnet Mus.
[50] Vestry min. bks. (1672–1712), (1714–31).
[51] Ibid. (1714–31).   [52] Guildhall MS. 9537/4.
[53] Vestry min. bk. (1672–1712).
[54] Ibid.   [55] Ibid. (1757–94).
[56] Mdx. Sess. Recs. i. 445; iii. 232; iv. 152, 202, 281.
[57] Vestry min. bks.
[58] M.R.O., D.R.O. 17/B1/1.

women to wear uniform blue clothes. The poor were farmed from 1740 until 1768, when the parish took over direct management of both workhouse and out-poor, moving the workhouse to a building which had served as a foundling hospital.[59] The first workhouse may have been Bonnyes Farm, which was used as such before 1778; the second perhaps stood on the edge of Hadley Common, near Latimer's Elm between Hadley and Cockfosters.[60] The reorganization of 1768 adversely affected the paupers, whose diet was increased by half in 1776 after complaints that it had been severely cut. In 1780 the vestry blamed conditions in the workhouse on the mistress, who, however, was not dismissed and in 1787 was given charge of the new Sunday school. A salaried parish doctor was appointed in 1782.[61] In 1775–6 £185 was raised by poor-rates, of which £142 was spent on the poor.[62]

From the late 18th century the wealthier householders made attempts, largely unsuccessful, to reduce parish expenditure. Doles of bread were introduced in 1796 and tickets for cheap rice, potatoes, and cured herrings in 1801. A salaried assistant overseer was appointed in 1820[63] and a windmill was built for the parish in 1821, to provide both employment and cheap flour.[64] In 1823 the out-poor were ordered to attend the vestry every quarter and were relieved partly with doles of flour, and the diet in the workhouse was restricted. From 1827 the workhouse was again farmed and in 1832 the system was said to be fully satisfactory. Monken Hadley became part of Barnet poor law union in 1835, whereupon the parish workhouse was closed.[65]

A whipping-post and cucking-stool were supplied in 1677[66] and the constable in 1693 had to furnish the names of persons who were deficient in watching for thieves. Two paid watchmen were appointed in 1786 and parishioners subscribed to the newly formed Barnet association for the prosecution of burglary and robbery in 1792.[67] The employment of night watchmen was revived in 1820, after a lapse, and a third man carried out a day patrol in 1826. New stocks were erected in 1787; they were placed near the pound in 1788, rebuilt in 1827, and in 1866 stood on Hadley Green west of the Great North Road.[68]

In 1863 Monken Hadley became part of Barnet local board district[69] and in 1875 most of the parish came under the jurisdiction of East Barnet Valley urban sanitary district,[70] later East Barnet Valley U.D. and subsequently East Barnet U.D.; that part of the parish which adjoined Chipping Barnet, however, became part of Barnet urban sanitary district, later Barnet U.D.[71] The parish was trans-

ferred in 1889 to Hertfordshire administrative county and from 1894 the part in East Barnet Valley U.D. became Monken Hadley civil parish, while that within Barnet U.D. became Hadley civil parish.[72] Both civil parishes became part of Barnet L.B. in 1965, when they were transferred from Hertfordshire to Greater London.[73]

CHURCH. Brothers living according to rule at Hadley were mentioned by Geoffrey de Mandeville, earl of Essex (d. 1144).[74] He also granted a hermitage in the park of Hadley to Walden abbey (Essex) c. 1136.[75] When the bishop of London confirmed Walden in its ecclesiastical possessions c. 1175 Hadley was listed among the parochial churches.[76] No vicarage was constituted at Monken Hadley, where the curacy was described as a donative in the early 18th century[77] but later apparently became presentative. In 1777, with the inclosure of Enfield Chase, the parish was made subject to the jurisdiction of the bishop, except for induction, institution, and the payment of visitation fees.[78]

Medieval incumbents were presumably appointed by the abbots of Walden.[79] The church was not mentioned in the earliest grants of the manor after the Dissolution but it was conveyed, with the manor, by Francis Goodere to William Stanford in 1545[80] and descended with the manor until 1786, when the advowson was purchased by William Baker.[81] Incumbents apparently were appointed by the lords, although the bishop of London collated in 1565 and the Committee for Plundered Ministers in 1644.[82] William Baker (d. 1824) devised the advowson in trust for his son William Robert Baker, an infant, but in 1827 it was conveyed to the incumbent J. R. Thackeray (d. 1831), who left it to his son R. W. Thackeray, rector of Hunsdon (Herts.). It was sold in 1846 to the Revd. George Proctor and in 1857 to Frederick Cass of Little Grove, East Barnet (Herts.). In 1861 Cass left the advowson to his son and namesake, who, as incumbent, was styled rector in 1880.[83] In 1908 the living was in the gift of F. C. G. Cass,[84] rector 1891–1900,[85] and in 1927 of Miss Cass-Tewart; in 1928, however, it belonged to F. N. Dove, in 1930 to W. W. Dove,[86] and in 1970 to A. N. Dove.[87]

The benefice was valued at 40s. in the mid 13th century[88] and at 4 marks in 1291[89] but it was excluded from later taxations and its value was not subsequently recorded until 1649, when it was estimated at around £30 a year.[90] In 1690 it was worth more than £40 a year.[91] Tithes are not mentioned before 1580, when the incumbent was

[59] Vestry min. bks.
[60] Cass, Hadley, 9.
[61] Vestry min. bks.
[62] Rep. Cttee. on Rets. by Overseers, 1776, 396.
[63] M.R.O., D.R.O. 17/B1/1.
[64] Vestry min. bk. (1820–32).
[65] Ibid.; Poor Law Com. 1st Rep. 250.
[66] Except where otherwise stated, the para. is based on vestry min. bks. (1672–1712) sqq.
[67] Mdx. & Herts. N. & Q. iv. 32–5.
[68] O.S. Map 1/2,500, Mdx. VI. 3 (1866 edn.).
[69] Lond. Gaz. 25 Sept. 1863, p. 4649; 2 Oct. 1863, p. 4745.
[70] 37 & 38 Vic. c. 152.   [71] Census, 1881.
[72] M.R.O., Reps. of Local Inqs. (1889–97).
[73] Lond. Govt. Act, 1963, c. 33.
[74] Dugdale, Mon. iii. 435.
[75] Ibid. iv. 148–9; V.C.H. Mdx. ii. 19.

[76] B.M. Harl. MS. 3697, f. 39.
[77] Newcourt, Repertorium, i. 621.
[78] Act for Dividing Enfield Chase, 17 Geo. III, c. 17. See p. 260.
[79] Hennessy, Novum Repertorium, 184. Appointments by the Crown from 1295 and by the abbot of Westminster in 1328 were for Hadleigh (Essex).
[80] C.P. 25(2)/27/185 no. 42.
[81] Lysons, Environs, ii. 523.
[82] Hennessy, Novum Repertorium, 184.
[83] Cass, Hadley, 80–1.
[84] Kelly's Dir. Herts. (1908).   [85] Clergy List (1905).
[86] Kelly's Dirs. Barnet (1927, 1928, 1939).
[87] Lond. Dioc. Bk. (1970).
[88] Val. of Norw., ed. Lunt, 360.
[89] Tax. Eccl. (Rec. Com.), 17.
[90] Home Cnties. Mag. i. 318.
[91] Mdx. Cnty. Recs. Sess. Bks. 1689–1709, 15.

expected to pay the lord of the manor 26s. 8d. and receive back 6s. 8d. for his tithes.[92] When Enfield Chase was inclosed in 1779, 50 a. of Hadley's allotment lying north of Camlet Way, later called Glebe farm, was assigned to the incumbent in place of tithes in Hadley, although Hadley Common and Glebe farm, which had formed part of Enfield Chase, continued to pay great tithes to Trinity College, Cambridge, which held Enfield rectory, and small tithes to the vicar of Enfield.[93] Part of Glebe farm was sold in 1799 to redeem land tax[94] and in 1835 the income of the benefice was £199 net, derived solely from the profits of Glebe farm.[95] In 1848 the tithes of the land which had been part of Enfield Chase were commuted, the great tithes for £8 and the small tithes for £11.[96]

A 'vicarage house' was leased in 1573[97] but William Kympton, lord of the manor, built a new house for the incumbent about five years later.[98] It had apparently been alienated by 1627, since it was then in the possession of Francis Atkinson, a layman,[99] and in 1657, when it was conveyed to Justinian Pagitt, it was divided into two tenements, neither of them occupied by the incumbent.[1] In 1666 William Tompson, curate of Hadley, was living in a house belonging to Edward Nicholl[2] and in 1678[3] Justinian Pagitt conveyed the old 'vicarage house' to trustees as residences for the incumbent, for alms-people, and for the parish clerk.[4] The rectory house, as it was then called, was enlarged c. 1788 by joining two of the alms-houses to it;[5] it was rebuilt in 1824, again enlarged after 1846,[6] and conveyed to the Ecclesiastical Commissioners in 1901.[7] The parish clerk's house, a small stuccoed building later called Gate House, was built in the early 19th century and afterwards given Gothic windows and barge-boarded gables. In 1958 the house became part of the endowment of the new Pagitt ecclesiastical charity.[8]

Bernard Carrier, appointed to the benefice in 1580, was described in 1588 by the lord of the manor as an honest and learned preacher.[9] Ely Turner, his successor, was ejected in 1644[10] and had not been replaced by 1649.[11] Most subsequent incumbents until the early 19th century were pluralists but all seem to have been resident. Robert Taylor, curate 1673–94 and 1695–1717, from 1681 held the livings of East Barnet and Chipping Barnet (Herts.);[12] in 1689 he had a dispute with the vestry over the appointment of the churchwarden[13] and in 1694 he resigned. Mary Turnor, who held a life-interest in the manor, then appointed her own nominee[14] but Taylor was reinstated in 1695. John Pennant, curate

1732–70, was rector of Compton Martin (Som.) and chaplain to Princess Augusta, George III's mother.[15] His successor John Burrows, curate until his death in 1786, was from 1773 rector of St. Clement Danes; he belonged to the literary coterie of Hester Chapone, who praised his preaching.[16] In 1782 Burrows appointed as assistant curate his relative Charles Jeffryes Cottrell,[17] later of Hadley Lodge, who succeeded him and held Monken Hadley with a succession of other livings until his own death in 1819.[18] Frederick Charles Cass, who became rector in 1860, published scholarly local histories.

Two obits were being observed in 1547, one instituted by Thomas Hall and the other by John Turner, who gave 5s. a year out of a tenement in the parish for the purpose.[19] In 1784 a beadle was appointed by the vestry, after church services had been repeatedly interrupted by children.[20] A Sunday school for boys was instituted in 1787 and was endowed with £333 stock in 1796 by David Garrow, curate, who specified that pupils should be taught psalm-singing and church music; there was a paid superintendent and numbers were limited to 20.[21] In 1810 two Sunday services were held, with prayers twice weekly during Lent; the sacrament was administered four times a year, when there were between 50 and 60 communicants.[22] In 1851 morning congregations averaged 200 and afternoon congregations 250.[23]

The church of *ST. MARY THE VIRGIN*, said in 1504 to be dedicated to St. Mary and St. James,[24] was rebuilt c. 1494,[25] presumably on the site of an older building whose nave may be preserved in the later plan. It occupies a prominent position on the edge of Hadley Common and is a cruciform building in the Perpendicular style with aisled nave, chancel, transepts, north vestry, western tower, and south porch, and is of brown flint with stone dressings. The late-15th-century rebuilding probably began with the chancel and transeptal chapels, dedicated to St. Anne and St. Catherine,[26] followed by the tower. The aisles, which are connected to the nave by two-bay arcades and flank the tower, were probably not added until the 16th century. If there was formerly a chancel arch it had been removed by that time. Thomas Emerson (d. 1624), lord of the manor, completely refurnished the interior and plastered the ceilings.[27] In 1680 Henry Coventry, later Lord Coventry, built a gallery in the north aisle[28] and in 1725 another one was built by Percival Chandler, for which purpose the north aisle wall was raised. In 1729 the south aisle wall was heightened and two

[92] Cass, *Hadley*, 82.
[93] Ibid. 18; 17 Geo. III, c. 17.
[94] Cass, *Hadley*, 18.
[95] *Rep. Com. Eccl. Revenues*, 649.
[96] M.R.O., TA/M'HAD.
[97] C 66/1120 m. 11.
[98] Cass, *Hadley*, 80.
[99] C 54/2717 no. 2.
[1] Cass, *Hadley*, 201–2.
[2] Vestry min. bk. (1672–1712).
[3] *9th Rep. Com. Char.* 212.
[4] See p. 270.
[5] *9th Rep. Com. Char.* 213.
[6] Cass, *Hadley*, 80.
[7] Char. Com. files.
[8] Ibid. A stable east of the church became known as the church ho. in the 19th cent.: *Christ Ch. Barnet Review* (1928), 265.
[9] Cass, *Hadley*, 80, 82.
[10] *Walker Revised*, ed. Matthews, 262.

[11] *Home Cnties. Mag.* i. 318.
[12] Cass, *Hadley*, 95.
[13] See p. 266.
[14] Vestry min. bk. (1672–1712).
[15] Cass, *Hadley*, 102.
[16] Ibid. 105–6.   [17] Ibid. 104.
[18] Ibid. 111.
[19] Hennessy, *Novum Repertorium*, 184.
[20] Vestry min. bk. (1757–94).
[21] M.R.O., D.R.O. 17/B1/1; Cass, *Hadley*, 183.
[22] Guildhall MS. 9558, f. 442. St. James was the dedication of Walden abbey.
[23] H.O. 129/136/2/1/1.
[24] Prob. 11/14 (P.C.C. 12 Holgrave, will of John Goodere).
[25] Date on tower.
[26] Prob. 11/14 (P.C.C. 12 Holgrave); Prob. 11/12 (P.C.C. 17 Moone).
[27] Cass, *Hadley*, 60.
[28] Vestry min. bk. (1672–1712).

new windows were inserted[29] and in 1757 a round-headed window was built in the north aisle. Another gallery was erected in 1776 by the curate David Garrow to accommodate the poor.[30] Another gallery and more pews were built in 1810.[31]

In 1848 G. E. Street replaced the old interior[32] with one which is redolent of early Tractarianism. The pulpit, galleries, and plastered ceiling were removed, the stonework was repointed, the aisle walls were moved some 18 inches outwards,[33] and the chancel floor, which had been below that of the nave, was raised a step above it.[34] An organ was later installed, together with open pews, a new pulpit, and stained glass in all the windows. In 1855 the south porch was rebuilt,[35] in 1888 a vestry was added north of the chancel, and in 1958 the south transept was furnished by Barrington Baker as a chapel dedicated, as it had been before the Reformation, to St. Catherine.[36]

The plain late-15th-century font has a modern cover. At the top of the stair-turret at the south-western corner of the tower is a copper beacon, replacing one blown down in 1779, which may have served to guide travellers across Enfield Chase.[37] The windows in the south wall of the chancel and the south transept are by Wailes, those in the transept with coats of arms by Willement, and the memorial windows in the aisles are by Clayton and Bell.[38] Some glass, including that in the east window, was destroyed in the Second World War.[39]

The oldest brass, dated 1442, to Philip and Margaret Green and Margaret Somercotes, survives from the earlier building. Others include those to Walter Turner and his wife,[40] dated 1494, Walter Turner and his family, 1500, Thomas Goodere and his wife, 1518, and William Gale and his family, 1614. A brass to John Goodere (d. 1504) is in the Rectory.[41] A wall monument to Sir Roger Wilbraham (d. 1616), by the elder Nicholas Stone,[42] contains notable busts of Wilbraham and his wife, above kneeling effigies of their daughters, and one to Henry Carew (d. 1626) and his mother Alice Stanford (d. 1573) contains a painted portrait of the son within an oval surround. A marble cartouche in the baroque manner, by William Stanton,[43] commemorates Elizabeth (d. 1678), widow of Mutton Davies and daughter of Sir Thomas Wilbraham. Later memorials include a draped marble slab surmounted by an urn, by Richard Westmacott the younger,[44] commemorating Catherine Pennant (d. 1797), niece of the curate John Pennant. There are also several monuments to members of the Barroneau, Ince, Moore, Quilter, Cottrell, and Smith families. In the churchyard are monuments of the Monro, Garrow, and Hopegood families.[45]

There is a small bell, with no inscription, and there are six large bells: (i), (ii), and (v) late-19th-century; (iii) 1702; (iv) 1711; (vi) 1714, C. W. Waylett.[46] A notable collection of church plate includes a gilt cup dated 1562, with a paten cover dated 1657; a silver gilt standing cup and cover of coconut-shell shape, the cover surmounted by a female figure, dated 1586; a silver gilt flagon, dated 1609, shaped like a coffee pot and with the spout in the form of a dragon's head; an elaborate silver gilt cup of 1610, with a cover surmounted by a spire, and a similar but larger cup, dated 1615; a paten dated 1618; and two alms-dishes, one dated 1723 and the other 1847. Several of the items were presented by Thomas Emerson.[47] The registers begin in 1619 but those of births and deaths are complete only from 1732 and there is a gap in the marriage registers from 1746 to 1755.

NONCONFORMITY. Some members of the Bellamy family who owned land in the parish in the late 16th century were recusants.[48] Ralph Noble, yeoman, was indicted for recusancy in 1581[49] and Anne Berrowe in 1640.[50] Eleven residents, presumably papists, were accused of not attending church in 1674.[51] There were said to be three papists in the parish in 1676[52] and one in 1706.[53] The Sisters of St. Martha established a convent at Hadley Bourne in 1948[54] but there was no Roman Catholic church in 1971.

There were 17 dissenters in 1676.[55] A Wesleyan group, established by 1760,[56] met later in the building in Barnet High Street now used as Barnet Baptist tabernacle. The chapel was occupied by Wesleyans until 1891[57] but registered in 1893 by Baptists,[58] whose congregation existed by 1845.[59] It is stuccoed, with round-arched windows, and has been much altered externally. Methodists also worshipped in Hadley chapel, Hadley Common, from 1861 to 1892.[60]

William Lloyd registered the schoolroom of his house as a place of worship for Independents in 1808[61] but in 1810 there were said to be only two dissenters in the parish, apart from Methodists,[62] and no permanent Independent chapel was established. A building at Hadley Green in the possession of Henry Williams was registered by unspecified Protestants in 1819.[63] Barnet Baptist tabernacle was the only nonconformist place of worship in 1971.

EDUCATION. Francis Atkinson (d. 1665) established an academy for gentlemen's sons at Ludgrove in the mid 17th century, under his son-in-law

[29] Ibid. (1714–31).
[30] Ibid. (1757–94).
[31] M.R.O., D.R.O. 17/B1/1.
[32] A drawing of the interior in the early 19th cent. is in Cass, *Hadley*, facing p. 116.
[33] Cass, *Hadley*, 117.
[34] St. Mary's ch. *Guide Bk.* (1955).
[35] Cass, *Hadley*, 117.   [36] *Guide Bk.* (1955).
[37] Lysons, *Environs*, ii. 519; *Mdx. & Herts. N. & Q.* iii. 213.
[38] Cass, *Hadley*, 126–7.   [39] *Guide Bk.* (1955).
[40] Prob. 11/10 (P.C.C. 21 Vox).
[41] *T.L.M.A.S.* xx. 179–89.
[42] Pevsner, *Herts.* 168.
[43] Gunnis, *Dict. of Sculptors*, 368.   [44] Ibid. 425.
[45] Cass, *Hadley*, 181–6.
[46] *T.L.M.A.S.* xvii. 140.
[47] Freshfield, *Communion Plate*, 20–1.
[48] Cass, *Hadley*, 136.
[49] *Mdx. County Recs.* i. 133.   [50] Ibid. iii. 153.
[51] Ibid. iv. 56–7.
[52] William Salt Libr., Stafford, Salt MS. 33, p. 40.
[53] Guildhall MS. 9800A.
[54] Ex inf. the headmistress, St. Martha's Convent sr. sch.
[55] William Salt Libr., Stafford, Salt MS. 33, p. 40.
[56] See p. 303; C 54/6689/6 pt. 5.
[57] For the later chapel in S. Mimms see p. 303.
[58] G.R.O., Worship Reg. no. 33787.
[59] *Kelly's Dir. Mdx.* (1845).
[60] G.R.O., Worship Reg. no. 11564.
[61] Guildhall MS. 9580/3.   [62] Ibid. 9558, f. 442.
[63] Ibid. 9580/5.

Joshua Poole (fl. 1632–46) of Clare Hall, Cambridge.[64] Atkinson's brother-in-law Gregory Lovell later took over the school, which seems to have closed soon after 1679.[65] Another boys' school was being run by David Garrow in 1747.[66]

A girls' school was set up in 1737 and financed by subscriptions. Books and spinning-wheels were bought in 1738 and in 1742 Andrew Hopegood bequeathed £4 a year for clothing and educating 12 girls of the parish.[67] The school was also left £30 by Thomas Shewell in 1770, £10 by John Shewell in 1772, and £10 by Judith Shewell in 1773.[68] It was re-established as a charity school in 1780 and a new school-house was built in 1800, when it became a school of industry;[69] in 1814, when it was run according to Dr. Bell's method, 20 girls received £1 a year for clothes and were educated free, while another 30 paid 2d. a week.[70] The school was associated with Hadley National school in 1832.

Poor boys were first taught at the Sunday school in 1787.[71] A day school for 20 boys was opened by a nonconformist in 1799 and supported by subscriptions; when the founder died it came under Anglican management and was run according to the National system by the superintendent of the Sunday school. There were about 80 pupils in 1819, of whom 20 were clothed and educated free while the rest paid 2d. a week. A day school for 60 girls, of whom 43 came from outside Hadley, existed in 1819, when the poor were said not to lack the means of education.[72] There were five schools in 1833, including one day and boarding school for 31 girls, run by Baptists.[73]

The two National schools were removed in 1832 to new premises on Hadley Common, near the entrance to Mount House, where, although under the same roof, they were still managed separately.[74] In 1871 there were 19 boys and 31 girls at the schools,[75] which received a government grant in 1878.[76] By 1893 the schools had been amalgamated as Monken Hadley National mixed school, with an attendance of 86.[77] In 1908 the school was managed, together with the infants' school and Highstone school, by the Hadley grouped schools committee.[78] It later became a junior mixed and infants' school and in 1943 was rebuilt on the same site.[79] There were 98 children on the roll in 1974.[80]

Monken Hadley Church of England infants' school was established before 1863 in a building on Hadley Green belonging to George Pooley, the upper storey of which was the schoolmistress's residence. It had the same management as the National schools and in 1875 there were 35 pupils.[81] The school received a government grant in 1878[82] but was closed in 1922, when there were 30 pupils.[83]

A schoolroom was opened before 1866 in premises north of the Windmill inn at Hadley Highstone, rented by the vicar of Christ Church, Barnet.[84] The school, which had 40 girls and infants in 1874,[85] closed between 1908 and 1919.[86]

The Sisters of St. Martha moved the senior girls from their independent school in Wood Street, Barnet, to Mount House in 1947. Mount House was enlarged in 1960 and 1968 and was attended by some 300 girls in 1974, of whom 35 boarded with the nuns at Hadley Bourne.[87]

CHARITIES FOR THE POOR.[88] Sir Roger Wilbraham built alms-houses for six poor women at the north-eastern corner of Hadley Green in 1612. They were endowed with the rents and profits of two houses in the parish of St. John, Clerkenwell. A total of £1,180 stock was added to the endowment between 1791 and 1819, as a result of benefactions by Samuel Whitbread, George Burrows, Mrs. Mary Horton, Sir Culling Smith, and the Revd. C. J. Cottrell, and in 1880 the income of the charity was £157, derived from the interest on £3,102 stock and the rent of no. 56 St. John's Square, Clerkenwell.[89] The alms-houses, a single-storeyed row of six red-brick cottages, were extended at the back in 1815.

In 1616 Thomas Fletcher bequeathed to the poor of Monken Hadley a rent-charge of £4, which in 1966 was paid by the occupiers of Beacon House, west of the church. A Scheme of 1910 united the charity with that of Thomas Browning, which had been founded by will proved 1804 and endowed with £260 stock, and produced £7 a year in 1966. In 1966 the income of Browning's and Fletcher's charities was applied to the general benefit of the poor or of other residents selected by the trustees.

In 1626 Thomas Emerson conveyed land in Monken Hadley in trust for the benefit of the parishioners. The rent of £8 supplied coal for the poor at 1s. a bushel but in 1809 the trustees resolved to spend it on coal for the church stove. The charity came to an end soon after the parish joined the Barnet union in 1835, when the house was sold to contribute towards the union workhouse.[90]

In 1678 Justinian Pagitt conveyed the old 'vicarage house' in trust, to provide residences for the incumbent, the parish clerk,[91] and six poor couples or single women. From 1788 two of the alms-houses were leased to the incumbent to raise money for the repair of the other four. After some £200 had been raised by subscription, the alms-houses were replaced c. 1822 by four new houses on an adjoining part of the Rectory garden, the rector taking the old

64 D.N.B.; Cass, Hadley, 27–8.
65 Cal. S.P. Dom. 1678–80, 78.
66 Cass, Hadley, 183.
67 Acct. bk. penes Barnet Mus.; Cass, Hadley, 185–6.
68 Lysons, Environs, ii. 526.
69 Ibid. Suppl. 177.
70 Brewer, Beauties of Eng. and Wales. x(5), 747.
71 See p. 268.
72 Educ. of Poor Digest, 539.
73 Educ. Enquiry Abstract, 106.
74 Ed. 7/86.
75 Returns Rel. to Elem. Educ. H.C. 201, pp. 570–1 (1871), lv.
76 Rep. of Educ. Cttee. of Council, 1878–9 [C.2342–I], p. 948, H.C. (1878–9), xxiii.
77 Returns of Schs. 1893 [C.7529], p. 422, H.C. (1894), lxv.

78 Kelly's Dir. Mdx. (1908).
79 Char. Com. files.
80 Ex inf. the headmistress.
81 Ed. 7/86.
82 Rep. of Educ. Cttee. of Council, 1878–9, p. 948.
83 Bd. of Educ., List 21 (H.M.S.O. 1927), 130.
84 O.S. Maps 1/2,500, Mdx. VI. 3 (1866 edn.); the school was in the detached portion of Enfield par.
85 Ed. 7/86.
86 Kelly's Dir. Mdx. (1908); Bd. of Educ., List 21 (H.M.S.O. 1919), pp. 130–1.
87 Ex inf. the headmistress, St. Martha's Convent sr. sch.
88 Except where otherwise stated, the section is based on 9th Rep. Com. Char. 210–14, and Char. Com. files.
89 Cass, Hadley, 163.
90 Ibid. 62–3.
91 See p. 268.

site in exchange. Two more alms-houses were added to the south end of the building in 1848 and the balance of the funds was invested in £86 stock. Pagitt's alms-houses consist of a two-storeyed brick building east of the church; the frontage is faced with knapped flint and pierced by Gothic doors and windows.

By will proved 1883 George Pooley left the income on £2,500 stock for distribution among the Pagitt alms-people. His endowment was united with

the Pagitt charity in 1884 and afterwards was further augmented by bequests from Charles Hemery and others. By a Scheme of 1958 the monetary endowments of £2,856 were established as the Pagitt alms-house charity, to maintain the alms-houses, while the parish clerk's house formed part of the new Pagitt ecclesiastical charity. In 1967 the income of the alms-house charity was £321, which included interest on £250 granted by the Jesus Hospital charity, Chipping Barnet (Herts.).

SOUTH MIMMS

SOUTH MIMMS[1] parish occupied the most northerly part of Middlesex. Its main centre of population in the north-west lay some 14 miles from London.[2] South Mimms was first recorded in 1253,[3] the 'south' being added to distinguish it from the village of North Mimms in Herts. The parish contained the modern urban district of Potters Bar and a portion of High Barnet, also known as West Barnet or Mimms Side, which later became part of the London Borough of Barnet. South Mimms was until 1781 roughly the shape of an inverted triangle, bounded on the north by Northaw and North Mimms, on the west by Ridge, on the south by Chipping Barnet (all in Herts.), and on the east by Enfield and Monken Hadley. The former eastern boundary stretched from Summer Pool, or Sugar Well, to Ganwick Corner and was defined by Gannick Bank; it passed thence to Potters Bar.[4]

For the purpose of this article the boundaries are those established in 1781, when 1,062 a. were allotted[5] under the Act for dividing Enfield Chase (1777).[6] In 1871 the area was 6,386 a.[7] and the boundaries, except the eastern one, followed those of the county. The short southern boundary passed along the earthwork known as Grim's Dyke; it ran from the corner of Galley Lane, keeping north of Wood Street and including most of Union Street, to a point between Chipping Barnet church and the Rising Sun in Barnet High Street. The western boundary ran north from Chipping Barnet along Galley Lane, while the northern boundary ran eastward through Mimmshall wood, keeping to the south of the Causeway, Potters Bar. The eastern boundary, formed at the division of Enfield Chase,[8] ran from a little to the south of Union Street along the western edge of Hadley Green to Old Fold Manor golf club house, where it turned south-eastward, rejoining the Great North Road for a few yards, and thence running north-eastward, crossing Wagon and Southgate roads and joining the northern boundary at Coopers Lane Road.

In 1889 76 a. at Mimms Side which had been in Barnet local board district, together with 9 a. ad-

ministered by East Barnet Valley local board, were transferred to the administrative county of Hertford. Under the Local Government Act of 1894 South Mimms was divided into two civil parishes, the greater northern part coming under the jurisdiction of South Mimms R.D. and the 76 a. in Barnet U.D. becoming South Mimms U.D. The 9 a. which formed part of East Barnet Valley U.D. were added to Monken Hadley and in 1896 an additional 199 a. were transferred from South Mimms R.D. to South Mimms U.D.[9] In 1924 South Mimms R.D. gained 26 a. near Potters Bar, including the Causeway and Coopers Lane, from Enfield U.D.[10] and in 1926 part of South Mimms R.D. was exchanged for part of the parish of Ridge (Barnet R.D.).[11] In 1965 Potters Bar U.D.C., which had superseded South Mimms R.D., was added to the administrative county of Hertford and South Mimms U.D. was transferred from Hertfordshire to the London Borough of Barnet.[12]

The soil[13] is mainly London Clay. Beneath the clay lies a thick layer of chalk, which is exposed to the west of the Barnet by-pass and also in the valley of Mimmshall brook, where, resting on it, is a narrow band of Reading Beds. On the highest land are patches of pebble gravel, rarely more than 10 ft. thick. They cover a narrow ridge from Barnet to Bentley Heath, a wider area along Potters Bar High Street to Little Heath, and parts of Mimmshall wood, Dugdale Hill, and Dyrham Park. Other drift deposits include boulder clay in the north and north-east and alluvium fill in the valley of Mimmshall brook.

The ground[14] in the north-west, except for Mimmshall wood, is c. 250 ft. It rises very gradually from South Mimms village to the centre of the parish, where there are some steep hills. From Baker Street there is an abrupt ascent to a flat ridge of c. 400–420 ft., which runs from Barnet to Potters Bar along the Great North Road. The ridge forms part of the South Hertfordshire plateau and is a watershed between the drainage to Mimmshall brook on the west and the tributaries of the river Lea on the east.[15]

[1] The article was written in 1972–3. Any references to later years are dated. The help of Mrs. H. M. Baker in making material available and commenting on the article is gratefully acknowledged.
[2] Except where otherwise stated, the rest of the para. and the following para. are based on O.S. Maps 6", Mdx. I. NW., NE., SW., and VI. NW., NE. (1864 and later editions).
[3] P.N. Mdx. (E.P.N.S.), 76.
[4] J. Rocque, Map of Mdx. (1754); F. C. Cass, South Mimms, 2.
[5] M.R.O., D.R.O. 5/H1/1 (S. Mimms Incl. Award, 1781).

[6] 17 Geo. III, c. 17.
[7] Census, 1871.
[8] M.R.O., F 84/6b.
[9] M.R.O., Reps of Local Inqs. (1889–97), 17, 24, 29.
[10] Story of Potters Bar and South Mimms, ed. K. R. Davis, 96.
[11] Kelly's Dir. Barnet (1927).
[12] Lond. Govt. Act, 1963, c. 33.
[13] The para. is based on Geol. Surv. Map 1", drift, sheet 256 (1951 edn.); Story of Potters Bar, 15–21.
[14] The para. is based on O.S. Maps 6", Mdx. I. NW., NE., SW., SE., and VI. NW., NE. (1864 edn.).
[15] Story of Potters Bar, 19.

The main water-course[16] is Mimmshall brook which rises near Stirling Corner and flows north-east in a broad vale through Dyrham Park. Turning, it flows due north, and, except when full, disappears into swallow holes beyond the parish boundary. Holmshill brook, Clare Hall brook, and the Catherine Bourne are tributaries from the west, and the Barnet Ditches, Kitts End stream, Wrotham Park stream, Bentley Heath brook, and Potters Bar brook from the east. Potters Bar brook rises north of Ganwick Corner, passing under the railway line and flowing along the east side of the embankment to Darkes Lane bridge, whence it runs under the pavement, eventually emerging to cross Potters Bar golf course and join Mimmshall brook west of Warrengate Farm.

Most notable people connected with the parish were owners or lessees of large houses, or incumbents who are mentioned below. Some residents held minor offices at court, including Thomas Danyell, described in 1478 as a valet to the king.[17] Mary Turnor (*née* Ewer), wife of the judge Sir Edward Turnor[18] (1617–76), occupied property in South Mimms.[19] James Catnach (d. 1841), publisher, came to London in 1813 and bought the former White Lion at Dancers Hill in 1836.[20]

Considerable traces of a Roman road, linking London with Hatfield and Stevenage (Herts.), have been found north of Potters Bar; Cockfosters Road perhaps represents it farther south.[21] The main medieval roads ran north-south, to Barnet, and were crossed by east-west routes. The Great North Road ran along the eastern boundary[22] and occasioned many bequests in the later Middle Ages.[23] By the early 18th century it had been moved farther eastward, into the Chase, and that section between Hadley windmill and Ganwick Corner had been turnpiked.[24] Despite many Acts for its repair,[25] the road was still 'insufferably bad' in 1798.[26]

Just within the southern boundary, at Hadley Highstone, a road ran north-west to St. Albans[27] from the Great North Road. Mentioned *c.* 1220,[28] the old road to St. Albans followed a tortuous course through Kitts End, Dancers Hill, and Mimms Wash. It entered South Mimms village by Greyhound Lane, served as the main street, crossed a water-splash, and proceeded towards Mimmshall wood and Ridge Hill.[29] It was often flooded and in

need of repair,[30] an Act for its improvement being passed in 1714.[31] According to Defoe in 1725, the work was so well done that 'the bottom is not only repaired, but the narrow places are widened, hills levelled, bottoms raised, and the ascents and descents made easy'.[32] Nevertheless in 1727 seven travellers were said to have died upon the road, one of them from drowning.[33] Further Acts for its repair were passed in 1735 and 1750.[34] It was superseded in the early 19th century by a road constructed by Thomas Telford as part of a plan to improve communications with Holyhead. The section of road from Barnet to South Mimms, completed *c.* 1828,[35] followed a fairly straight line to Ridge Hill, cutting through South Mimms village at an angle and by-passing the old main street.[36]

Farther east Southgate Road, a continuation of Cockfosters Road,[37] ran northwards from Cockfosters to Potters Bar. It was constructed between *c.* 1607[38] and 1777.[39] Part of the western boundary of the parish was marked by Galley Lane, so called in 1475.[40] During the Middle Ages a track in the extreme north led eastward from South Mimms castle, through Darkes, to the Chase. Parts of it survive as a footpath from Billy Lows Lane, across Potters Bar golf course, to the castle.[41] Another west-east route was Mutton Lane, in existence by 1473,[42] where possibly the moot of Edmonton hundred had met,[43] and in 1594 extending from Mimms Hall to the Chase.[44] Farther south the Great North Road and the old road to St. Albans had been linked by a road passing along the later northern edge of Wrotham Park. It was known as Ryverstrete Lane in 1479[45] (Reeves Street in 1604),[46] as Green Dragon Lane in 1750,[47] and afterwards as Dancers Hill Road. Roads running north from Dancers Hill Road towards Wyllyotts included Baker Street (formerly Old Street),[48] which joined Darkes Lane, Bentley Heath Lane, recorded in 1479 as Alen Street,[49] and Sawyers Lane, first mentioned in 1475.[50] Various minor roads led from Potters Bar to Enfield Chase: Quakers Lane (1452),[51] and New Lane, later called Billy Lows Lane after the occupier of a cottage there (1425).[52] By 1754[53] the village of South Mimms was linked to Dyrham Park by Blanche Lane, while Bridgefoot and Dugdale Hill lanes (Updell Hill) connected Potters Bar with the Bridgefoot estate. Wagon Road,

[16] The para. is based on O.S. Maps 6″, Mdx. I; VI. NW., NE. (1864 edn.); *Story of Potters Bar*, 20.
[17] Glouc. Co. Rec. Off. T 195/A/2.
[18] Hatfield C.F.E.P. (Gen.) 106/8; *D.N.B.* See p. 268.
[19] M.R.O., MR/TH/22.
[20] *D.N.B.*; *Herts. Countryside*, July 1969, no. 123.
[21] I. D. Margary, *Rom. Roads* (1967), 201.
[22] Hatfield C.P.M. Suppl. 22 (Country between Hatfield and Lond. 1607–8).
[23] e.g. Cass, *South Mimms*, 5, 77.
[24] M.P.C. 143; M.R. 667; Turnpike Act 7 Geo. I, c. 18.
[25] e.g. *L.J.* xxiii. 579; xxvi. 334; xxxii. 513.
[26] Middleton, *View*, 395.
[27] J. Ogilby, *Map of Mdx.* (c. 1677). The road is sometimes regarded as a branch of the Great North Road: Potters Bar, *Official Guide* [1972].
[28] *Cartulary of St. Barts. Hosp.* ed. N. J. M. Kerling (1973).
[29] F. Brittain, *South Mymms*, 85; J. Rocque, *Map of Mdx.* (1754).
[30] e.g. Hatfield C.F.E.P. (Ct. Roll) 14/28, f. 1; Prob. 11/14 (P.C.C. 18 Holgrave, will of Roger Wright); Prob. 11/1 (P.C.C. 13 Rous, will of Thos. Frowyk).

[31] Brittain, *South Mymms*, 85.
[32] *Story of Potters Bar*, 85.
[33] Cass, *South Mimms*, 6.
[34] Brittain, *South Mymms*, 85.
[35] Potters Bar, *Official Guide* [1972].
[36] O.S. Maps 6″, Mdx. I. NW., SW., SE.; VI. NE. (1864 edn.).
[37] See p. 209.
[38] Hatfield C.P.M. Suppl. 22.
[39] Robinson, *Enfield*, i, map facing p. 208.
[40] B.M. Add. Ch. 8142.
[41] *Story of Potters Bar*, 82.
[42] Hatfield C.F.E.P. (Ct. Roll) 14/27, f. 9.
[43] *T.L.M.A.S.* xvi. 149.
[44] M.R.O., F. 58A (Map of Wyllyotts by Ralph Treswell).
[45] *Cal. Close*, 1476–85, 160.
[46] Hatfield C.F.E.P. (Ct. Roll) 28/20.
[47] M.L.R. 1750/3/690.
[48] Hatfield C.F.E.P. (Deeds) 280/10.
[49] *Cal. Close*, 1476–85, 159.
[50] B.M. Add. Ch. 8142.
[51] Hatfield C.F.E.P. (Ct. Roll) 14/27, f. 4v.
[52] E 40/2622; *Story of Potters Bar*, 60.
[53] The para. is based on Rocque, *Map of Mdx.* (1754).

which joined the Southgate road, existed by 1781, and communication with Enfield had been improved by the construction of the Ridgeway.[54]

By 1730 that section of the Great North Road running from Ganwick Corner along Potters Bar High Street, across Morven and up Colliers Lane,[55] had been turnpiked,[56] after which it was much improved.[57] The route from Potters Bar to Hatfield was further improved in 1802, when Hatfield Road was built from the site of the war memorial to Little Heath, with a toll bar at the northern end of High Street, near the Green Man.[58]

The extension of the parks at Dyrham and Wrotham affected several public highways. In 1736 the earl of Albemarle closed two roads across Dyrham Park; part of the road known as Trotters Bottom replaced what became the carriage drive and another diversion was made west of the estate.[59] Green Dragon Lane, which ran from several cottages owned by the Byngs to North Lodge at the entrance to Wrotham, was diverted farther north in 1815[60] The need for a straight road from the bottom of South Mimms churchyard to Mimms Hall which would avoid Water Lane was recognized in 1863.[61] Most of the land for the making of the road was provided by the marquess of Salisbury and it became known as Cecil Road.[62]

In the 20th century several major roads have been cut through the parish. The Great North Way, or Barnet bypass, was constructed in 1927 for three-lane traffic but converted to dual carriageways in 1965; a flyover was built in 1962 to take Cecil Road over it. In 1963 the South Mimms bypass was built to divert traffic on Telford's road to the west of South Mimms village. In 1973 work had begun on the D-ring road which was planned to run eastward across the parish to Enfield.[63]

Among early bridges were Walebridge (1345), Fynchenellys (1452), and Blountesbridge (1473).[64] A ford north-east of the church across Mimmshall brook[65] may have been the Longford mentioned in 1473.[66] Farther south stood a footbridge, recorded as Highbridge in 1489,[67] under which Mimmshall brook flowed into Wash Lane.[68] The bridge was repairable by the lord of the manor in 1661[69] and was again in need of repair in 1706[70] and 1812.[71] North of Highbridge the brook spread across the low ground of Mimms Wash and Water Lane, where it could still impede travellers after the building of a three-arched, brick road-bridge in 1772.[72] Dyrham Park Road bridge, two-arched and of brick,[73] was erected across Trotters Bottom by the lord of Dyrhams to replace the parish bridge inclosed in his park in 1736.[74] Farther east, on the old road to St.

Albans (later Kitts End Road) was the bridge known in the late 18th century as Margery bridge.[75] In 1861 the vestry built a bridge at Mimms Hall Bottom.[76]

In 1637 a coach from London to St. Albans passed twice weekly through the parish.[77] By c. 1832 several coaches ran daily from Potters Bar to Hatfield and one ran every week-day to Luton (Beds.), Wellingborough (Northants.), and St. Albans.[78] Before the making of Telford's road coaches had been forced to travel at 5 m.p.h. but by 1836 they were running from London to South Mimms in 1 hour 40 minutes. Services declined with the coming of the railway to Potters Bar, although horse-drawn carriages operated from the station.

From 1912 a motor-bus ran from Golders Green via South Mimms to St. Albans. Between 1913 and 1916, and intermittently from 1919 to 1925, a Sunday service from Golders Green to Hatfield called at Potters Bar High Street. The London terminus was changed to Aldwych in 1926 but the service was soon withdrawn in favour of one which ran via the Barnet bypass. Barnet, an omnibus terminus from c. 1880, had been served by electric trams from 1907. In 1930 a motor-bus route was extended from Victoria station to Potters Bar station via Wood Green, and a local private firm started a peak hour service from Charing Cross to Brookmans Park, via Golders Green and Barnet, which operated until 1933. A subsidiary of the London General Omnibus Co., the Overground Co., which in 1930 had built the Potters Bar garage, in 1932 extended to Potters Bar its route from Victoria to Hadley Highstone. With the growth of Potters Bar motor-bus services quickly expanded, providing connexions with Chingford (Essex), Hitchin (Herts.), Enfield and St. Albans, and Hertford. Quicker services over longer distances were operated by Green Line coaches and Messrs. Birch Bros. The routes have changed little since 1939.

The main line of the G.N.R. was cut through Potters Bar in 1850, when an unfinished station was opened in Darkes Lane.[79] In 1850 eight trains a day ran from Potters Bar to London and five in the other direction. By 1861 there were ten trains from London and fourteen from Potters Bar,[80] the time from King's Cross varying from 31 to 40 minutes.[81] Most of the suburban trains were extended to Farringdon Street with[82] the opening of the Metropolitan Railway in 1863 and to Moorgate Street from 1869. From 1872 the G.N.R.'s line from Finchley to High Barnet served the south part of the parish; in 1940 the branch was linked to the Northern line tube. In 1875 a spur was constructed from Finsbury Park to Canonbury, providing a quicker

[54] M.R.O., F/84/6b.
[55] Rocque, *Map of Mdx.* (1754).
[56] *Story of Potters Bar,* 85–6.
[57] *L.J.* xxiii. 579; xxxii. 513; xxxv. 350; Herts. Rec. Off., Tp. 116, 117.
[58] *Story of Potters Bar,* 86.
[59] M.R.O., S.B. 934, pp. 43–5.
[60] Ibid. S.R. 3923/157.   [61] Ibid. D.R.O. 5/C1/4.
[62] O.S. Maps 6", Mdx. I. NW., NE. (1864 edn.).
[63] *Story of Potters Bar,* 84, 86–7, 90–3.
[64] Hatfield C.F.E.P. (Ct. Roll) 14/27, ff. 1, 5, 11.
[65] *Rep. on Bridges in Mdx.* 97.
[66] Hatfield C.F.E.P. (Ct. Roll) 14/27, f. 11.
[67] Ibid. 14/28, f. 1.
[68] Prob. 11/14 (P.C.C. 18 Holgrave, will of Roger Wright).
[69] Hatfield C.F.E.P. (Legal) 104/3.
[70] Hatfield C.F.E.P. (Ct. Bk. 1702–31), 15.
[71] M.R.O., D.R.O. 5/C1/1.
[72] Herts. Rec. Off., Tp. 143, pp. 31, 149, 154–7, 163; *Rep. on Bridges in Mdx.* 98; M.R.O., D.R.O. 5/C1/1.
[73] *Rep. on Bridges in Mdx.* 98.
[74] M.R.O., S.B. 934, pp. 43–5.
[75] Hatfield C.F.E.P. (Ct. Bk. 1774–1802), p. 310.
[76] M.R.O., D.R.O. 5/C1/4.
[77] Except where otherwise stated, the foll. two paras. are based on *Story of Potters Bar,* 84, 86–7, 90–3.
[78] Pigot, *Com. Dir.* (1832–4).
[79] B.T.C. Per. 34/17, p. 116.
[80] *Story of Potters Bar,* 88, 90.
[81] B.T.C. TT. 3/34.
[82] Except where otherwise stated, the rest of the section is based on C. H. Grinling, *Hist. of Gt. Northern Rly.* (1966 edn.), 126, 201, 257, 280, 303, 415; H. P. White, *Regional Hist. of Rlys. of Gt. Brit.* iii. 160; *Story of Potters Bar,* 88–90.

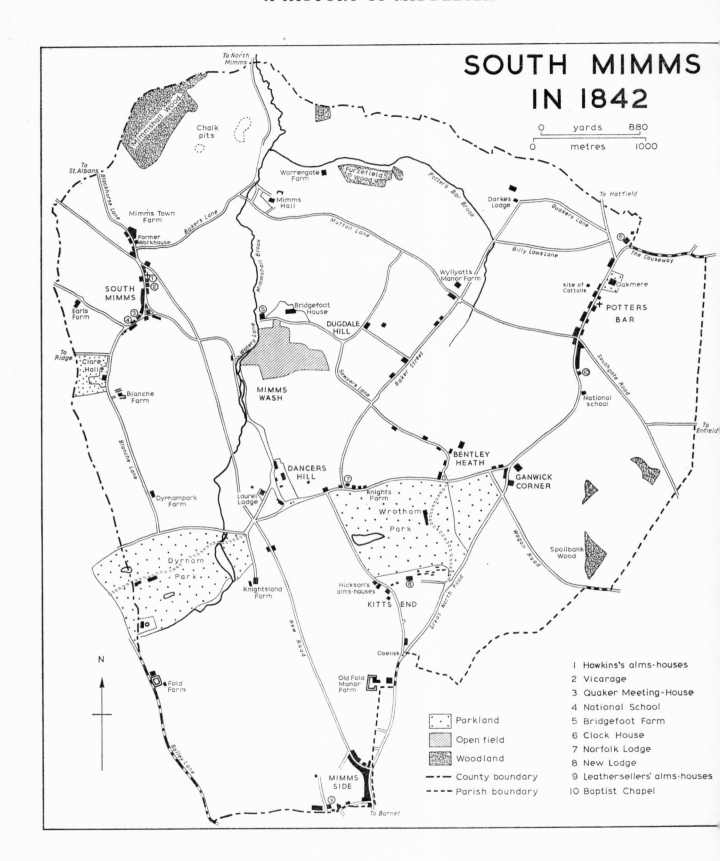

SOUTH MIMMS
IN 1842

0 yards 880

0 metres 1000

1 Howkins's alms-houses
2 Vicarage
3 Quaker Meeting-House
4 National School
5 Bridgefoot Farm
6 Clock House
7 Norfolk Lodge
8 New Lodge
9 Leathersellers' alms-houses
10 Baptist Chapel

Parkland

Open field

Woodland

— · — County boundary

— — — Parish boundary

service from Potters Bar to the City; trains at first were operated by the North London Railway and after 1923 by the L.M.S.R. Potters Bar inhabitants complained that neither waiting rooms nor platforms were large enough in 1885[83] and extensive alterations to the old station at Potters Bar[84] were carried out in 1954.[85] Although the G.N.R. track was quadrupled to New Barnet in 1892, the widening of the Potters Bar section was not completed until 1959. In 1973 diesel trains ran half-hourly to and from Kings Cross.[86] Further rail facilities for the southern part of the parish were provided when the Cockfosters extension of the Piccadilly line was opened in 1933.[87]

The broad pattern of settlement and communications remained virtually the same until the 19th century. The divisions within the parish are perpetuated in the modern districts of Potters Bar (including the village of South Mimms) and Barnet, part of which lies in Barnet L.B.

Early settlement seems to have avoided the wooded slopes of London Clay and to have sought the gravel-capped ridge, with its well-water, and also the shelter of the Mimmshall brook valley, where the soil could more easily be worked. Roman settlement along the high ground at Parkfield, Potters Bar, is indicated by finds of tiles, a small tile-kiln, and pottery of the 1st century A.D.[88] The early importance of the extreme north-west is shown by the building there of both a castle, on the site of what appears to have been a Saxon settlement,[89] and South Mimms manor-house. In the 13th century the manor-house, together with its mill, stood north of the main village, perhaps because increasing traffic, particularly after the establishment of Barnet market, made the route to St. Albans a more attractive position. Settlement centred upon the church and by c. 1220 there was a sprinkling of tenements along the roads leading towards it.[90]

Another village grew up in the north-east, at Potters Bar. Although the name is not recorded until 1381,[91] the first part is presumably derived from the 13th-century family of Le Pottere. The 'bar' is said to have been one of the gates of Enfield Chase,[92] although in 1594 it is shown well away from the boundary.[93] By c. 1200 the site of Cattalls had been established at the north end of High Street, along the gravel-capped ridge. The manor-house of Wyllyotts stood on the west side of Darkes Lane and to its south at Mutton Lane cross-roads was the manorial pound. Scattered tenements lay north of the house, several along tracks leading to the Chase. The moated site of Darkes, recorded in 1490, was linked to the manor-house by Darkes Lane and with other

small tenements which lay along New Lane and the Causeway. Tenements belonging to the Moss family, such as Long Croft recorded by 1432,[94] stood north and south of New Lane, and houses at Tottenhalls and at the Clock House site were held by Simon Flexmore. Near the manor-house in the southern part of Potters Bar[95] lay several small tofts. Geffrons, recorded as early as 1278,[96] stood west of the Barnet road and south of a pathway which ran parallel to Mutton Lane and led from Goodwin Stile to Darkes Lane.[97] By 1455 Geffrons and a toft called Bovyngdons, also known as Pounses,[98] had passed to Sir John Fortescue;[99] they formed part of the manor of South Mimms in the 16th century.[1] Growth in the areas bordering on Enfield Chase and around the church is reflected in the election of aleconners for those two districts in 1345.[2]

By the 13th century Old Fold manor, with its well-defined moat,[3] was an important centre on the edge of Hadley Green. The manorial mill, standing on one of the highest points in the parish, was recorded in the 13th century and Old Fold park was early formed.[4] Blanche Farm in the west of the parish was recorded in 1420. To its south an earthwork and enclosure probably mark the early site of Dyrham Park manor-house. Farther west, adjoining Galley Lane and south of Fold Farm, is a small moated enclosure, with traces of brickwork. Another concentration of population in medieval times was in the middle of the parish at Dancers Hill, along the old road to St. Albans. By the 15th century many of the fields and property there were known as Mandeville or variants of Mandeville and belonged to the manor of South Mimms.[5] In 1489 several lanes led to small crofts and cottages in the area.[6]

In medieval times, however, there were large tracts of woodland or waste. Waste-land lay south of the village of South Mimms[7] and most of the area south of Dancers Hill Road was also originally common land, with two large gravel pits which later became fishponds.[8] The north-east part of the modern Wrotham Park was formerly Bentley Heath. Farther west lay the waste known in 1479 as Kitts End Heath,[9] and to the south was Kitts End Green. On part of the green was a cottage, with a moat[10] of which one side remains, known in the early 17th century as the hermitage and said to have been a chapel to which the dead had been taken after the battle of Barnet.[11] The battle had been fought on the borders of South Mimms and Monken Hadley in 1471[12] and a chapel was afterwards built on the plain about half a mile from Barnet; in the late 16th century the chapel served as a dwelling.[13] By the mid 17th century the hermitage had come into the hands of John Howkins,[14] a local landowner and

[83] B.T.C. GN. 7/6/10.
[84] Ibid. Historical relics (1952 photo. of stn.).
[85] Arch. Rev. cxix. 175.
[86] Potters Bar, Official Guide [1972].   [87] See p. 212.
[88] Story of Potters Bar, 23.
[89] See p. 282.
[90] Cart. of St. Barts. Hosp. no. 1222.
[91] Guildhall MS. 6809.
[92] P.N. Mdx. (E.P.N.S.), 77.
[93] M.R.O., F. 85A, on which the foll. section is based.
[94] Guildhall MS. 6809.
[95] B.M. Add. Ch. 19907.
[96] C.P. 25(1)1/148/27/52.
[97] Guildhall MS. 6809; B.M. Add. Ch. 19907.
[98] C.P. 25(2)1/61/475/5 Edw. VI Mich.; B.M. Add. Ch. 19907.

[99] C.P. 25(1)1/152/94/165.
[1] Hatfield C.F.E.P. (Ct. Roll) 23/16.
[2] Ibid. 14/27, f. 1.
[3] V.C.H. Mdx. ii. 9.
[4] Hist. MSS. Com. 24, Rutland, iv, p. 262; J.I. 1/540 m. 3d.
[5] Barnet and Dist. Loc. Hist. Soc. Bull. xvii.
[6] Hatfield C.F.E.P. (Ct. Roll) 14/28, f. 1.
[7] Ibid. (Deeds) 147/2.
[8] Ibid. 162/21.
[9] Cal. Close, 1476–85, 160.
[10] M.R.O., F. 84/6b.
[11] Hatfield C.F.E.P. (Gen.) 66/7.
[12] V.C.H. Mdx. ii. 27–8; T.L.M.A.S. vi. 1; see p. 268.
[13] J. Stow, Annales . . . of England (1615 edn.), 423.
[14] Hatfield C.F.E.P. (Deeds) 162/21.

benefactor, who in 1651 planned to rebuild it.[15] In the 18th century it was incorporated in Francis Barroneau's estate of New Lodge. To the north-east lay an area called Dead Man's Bottom, perhaps also associated with the battle. A commemorative obelisk was erected on the line of the Gannick Bank in 1740 but in 1842 was moved to its present site south of Wrotham Park.[16]

In the 16th and 17th centuries several cottages were erected on the waste at Kitts End and encroachments were made on the Chase.[17] More notable was the construction of country residences by prosperous Londoners, some of whom are commemorated in the parish church. The Elizabethan manor-house of Durhams occupied the site of the later building and to its east in a hollow lay the farm-house of Knightsland. In the centre of the parish in Dancers Hill Road stood a house called Richards and to the north, on the site of the later Bentley Heath farm-lands, was the house known as Gannock, which existed by 1627. Farther north a house which later formed part of the Bridgefoot estate was recorded in 1567 and the 'capital messuage' at Cattalls Grove, Potters Bar, was built in 1596. Apart from Knightsland most of the the 16th-century dwellings have been demolished. A residence called Knights, about half-way between the southern end of Baker Street and Bentley Heath on the north side of Green Dragon Lane,[18] belonged to John Adderley (d. 1652)[19] and afterwards to Col. William Webb, Surveyor-General of Woods.[20] When the lane (later Dancers Hill Road) was diverted in 1815, the house was pulled down and the gardens, which lay near the site of the Byng mausoleum, were incorporated in Wrotham Park.[21] Wicks Place at Dancers Hill was owned by John Nicholl of Hendon Hall in 1709, when it formed part of a settlement made on the marriage of his son John to Mary Pym; the property included several cottages and 29 a. of land. The house was bought in 1808 by Henry Heyman, who renamed it Laurel Cottage, and afterwards passed to the Trotters of Dyrham Park, who called it Laurel Lodge. It housed soldiers during the Second World War and was demolished in the late 1950s.[22] In c. 1670 a copyhold house called Ottways Garden, later known as Bridgefoot Farm, stood on part of the Bridgefoot estate. Seventeenth-century barns are recorded at Knightsland, Bridgefoot Farm, and Fold Farm.[23] A striking feature was the rebuilding or enlarging of several existing houses. Most of the fabric of Blanche Farm dated from c. 1600 and both the north part of Mimms Hall and the west part of Wyllyotts from the 16th century. The timber-framed house at Fold Farm was built in the 17th century on property which had belonged to the Cockett family in the later 16th century[24] and had passed to Thomas Ravenscroft,[25]

a governor of Queen Elizabeth's grammar school and a benefactor of Chipping Barnet.[26]

In the 16th and 17th centuries the main area of settlement was still South Mimms village, which assumed a roughly triangular shape.[27] The church has been considerably enlarged in the 15th and 16th centuries, while buildings clustered to the north and south of it.[28] By the early 17th century several buildings had been erected on both sides of Blackhorse Lane. Sparrow Farm was built on its west side c. 1500 and later converted into three cottages. Its upper storey probably once projected on the east side of the middle block, whose upper floor appears to have been open to the roof; it was of three bays, with double-chamfered wall-posts supporting cambered tie-beams with curved braces. The end blocks probably formed the original cross-wings.[29] To the north-east lay a group which in the early 17th century seems to have comprised the rectory house, South Mimms poorhouse, Shenley poorhouse, and the later Black Horse inn. Fields stretched around, including the rectorial land known as Waldens.[30] North of the church and occupying a central position on the St. Albans road stood the White Hart inn and between the church and the small vicarage-house were the five Howkins's alms-houses, erected in 1652 to the annoyance of some neighbouring inhabitants.[31] A few widely scattered houses south of the church also formed part of the village.[32] Two other inns existed briefly: the Prince's Arms, which later formed part of the Clare Hall estate, was recorded in 1683,[33] and the Red Bull, adjoining Chantry mead, in 1714.[34]

In contrast to the village of South Mimms, Potters Bar until the 18th century seems to have remained a hamlet of small crofts. Many of the dwellings were probably made of wood, and there are frequent references to 'moving a cottage'.[35] Two wooden houses survived in High Street until c. 1950 and others existed in the Causeway. In c. 1580, however, a brick house, with two storeys and attics, was erected in High Street; it was known as Goodwin Stile in the later 17th century, when it belonged to James Hickson of the Brewers' Company of London, and later as Ladbrooke Farm and stood until c. 1911. Two inns were also built along the Hatfield section of the Great North Road: the Swan with Two Necks, called the New Inn in 1658, and the Green Man, recorded in 1672.[36]

By 1658 a large hamlet was spreading along the old St. Albans road at Kitts End. Cottages lay scattered around the area later occupied by Home farm. The Bull's Head inn was first recorded in 1523[37] and six alms-houses, built by James Hickson on the slope descending to Dancers Hill, stood there from 1687 to 1856. In the southern part of the parish, at Barnet, shops and cottages had been erected by 1553.[38]

[15] Ibid. 87/5.
[16] M.P.C. 144; Brittain, *South Mymms*, 19.
[17] Cass, *South Mimms*, 2; M.R.O., F. 57.
[18] M.R.O., F. 57.
[19] Prob. 11/220 (P.C.C. 18 Bowyer).
[20] M.R.O., Acc. 526/47.
[21] Ibid. S.R. 3923/157.
[22] *Barnet and Dist. Loc. Hist. Soc. Bull.* xvii.
[23] Hist. Mon. Com. *Mdx.* 95–6.
[24] Cass, *South Mimms*, 35.
[25] Prob. 11/159 (P.C.C. 30 St. John).
[26] *V.C.H. Herts.* ii. 333; Brittain, *South Mymms*, 36; Cass, *South Mimms*, 36.

[27] Hatfield C.P.M. Suppl. 22.
[28] Ibid.; Ogilby, *Map of Mdx.* (c. 1677).
[29] Hist. Mon. Com. *Mdx.* 96.
[30] M.R.O., D.R.O. 5/F1/1.
[31] Ibid.
[32] Hatfield C.P.M. Suppl. 22.
[33] M.R.O., Acc. 172/3.
[34] M.L.R. 1714/5/66–7.
[35] Guildhall MS. 5454.
[36] *Story of Potters Bar*, 57, 60, 62–3.
[37] Prob. 11/23 (P.C.C. 18 Porch, will of Hen. Frowyk).
[38] *Cal. Pat.* 1553, 119–20.

Several inns catered for the many travellers using the Great North Road: the Robin Hood, held of the manor of Barnet, was recorded in 1659,[39] although its location is uncertain, and the Blue Bell in 1668.[40] The Hart's Horns, next to the Bell and seemingly on the corner of the later Union Street, was mentioned in 1553[41] and stood west of the Great North Road;[42] it was converted into shops in 1929.[43]

Despite the growth of villages and hamlets much of the parish was still open in the late 17th and early 18th centuries.[44] Two highwaymen were buried in South Mimms churchyard[45] and the two major roads also brought vagrants and other unwanted fugitives[46] from plague-stricken London. In 1665 'above one hundred and more, which died of the plague in the same year' were buried at South Mimms.[47]

In 1754[48] most inhabitants were still living along the Great North Road and the road to St. Albans, mainly in South Mimms village and at Kitts End. South Mimms village seems to have spread along Blackhorse Lane, although spaces remained between the houses. South of the church buildings lined the western edge of the road but few had been erected on the other side. Several brick cottages, some of which later became shops, had been built at the southern end of the village in Blanche Lane and Greyhound Lane. At Kitts End houses lay scattered along the road to St. Albans (Kitts End Road), whence they spread eastward towards the Chase. Most of them were small cottages. often divided into two or more tenements. In 1728 eight such cottages, together with 11 a. of land, were sold by William Pratt to Thomas Reynolds, the owner of Pinchbank,[49] and c. 1750 at least ten copyhold cottages at Kitts End were held by Admiral Byng.[50] The hamlet was said to have eight inns in 1756,[51] although two, the Windmill and the Two Brewers, were in Enfield Chase, adjoining Monken Hadley.[52] The largest inn was the White Lion which had beds for twelve men and stabling for forty-three horses. It stood near the Hermitage and probably close to the Two Sawyers and the Angel (formerly known as the Chequers). South of the old road through Kitts End stood the Crown, which in 1767 took the name of the Angel after the older inn had been pulled down.[53] Farther south was the weatherboarded Bull's Head,[54] which for a short time was called the Three Compasses,[55] and between Gannick Bank and the Great North Road stood the Maypole.[56] A group near the White Lion included two wash-houses to the inn[57] and beyond was a house which was probably

that licensed in 1732 as the Bunch of Grapes.[58] North of the hamlet stood Pinchbank, at one time known as Strangeways.

Houses were dotted along both sides of Dancers Hill Road, which contained Stonard's house and copyhold land called Angels,[59] the rent-charge on which supported Howkins's alms-houses. At the junction of Wash Lane and Dancer Hill Road, known as Cuckold Corner, there were various tenements in the late 17th century.[60] By 1712 they included a cottage, a shop, and other buildings,[61] one of which was licensed as the White Lion in 1726.[62] Another small cottage and a smithy had been added by 1732.[63] East of Cuckold Corner and opposite the end of Kitts End Road stood an inn called Mandeville, recorded in 1623 and renamed the Green Dragon by 1635;[64] it was sold to George Byng in 1768[65] and by 1842 had moved to a new site on Telford's road.[66] East of Wash and Water lanes were groups of buildings belonging to two farms.[67] In 1712 George Howes, the occupier of the copyhold farm which lay south of Aldwick, had pulled down part of a mansion in Water Lane.[68]

The growth of South Mimms village, Kitts End, and Dancers Hill in the 18th century reflects increasing traffic along the two major roads. While the rural character of South Mimms village was frequently noted, the roads possessed many inns, offering comfort rather than elegance.[69] At High Street, Barnet, 18th-century inns included the Roebuck, which was later replaced by the Rising Sun, and the Green Man, in 1753 the meeting-place for beating the bounds of the parish and later said to have been much frequented by Sir Robert Peel. Others were the King of Prussia (changed to King George in 1914) and the Green Dragon, which was converted into shops in 1928.[70] Scattered inns faced the St. Albans road as it passed through Kitts End and Dancers Hill. At Mimms Wash stood the Five Bells[71] and the Badger, which was part of the Bridgefoot estate.[72] The approach to South Mimms village was marked by another concentration of inns. They included the Black Horse and the Queen's Head in Blackhorse Lane and the Cross Keys, where the post office was housed in 1845 between the church and the White Hart.[73] The Greyhound, formerly the Dog and Badger,[74] stood until 1918, and the Live and Let Live was licensed until 1907, when it was replaced by a garage, and the Black Bull until 1909. Towards Ridge Hill stood the Red Lion, formerly the Sun, which lost its licence in 1931, and to its north the Plough, licensed until 1907.[75]

[39] C 6/18/65.
[40] M.R.O., Acc. 548/39.
[41] Cal. Pat. 1553, 119–20.
[42] M.R.O., S.R. 4543/33.
[43] Brittain, South Mymms, 88.
[44] e.g. Mdx. Sess. Recs. i. 35–6; Mdx. Cnty. Recs. iii. 19.
[45] Brittain, South Mymms, 45.   [46] See p. 295.
[47] Brittain, South Mymms, 42.
[48] Except where otherwise stated, the following acct. is based on Rocque, Map of Mdx. (1754).
[49] M.L.R. 1728/1/62–64.
[50] Barnet and Dist. Loc. Hist. Soc. Bull. xvi.
[51] W.O. 30/49.   [52] See p. 262.
[53] W.O. 30/49; M.R.O., L.V. 3/96, 5/2, 6/2, 7/36, 8/51; M.L.R. 1771/2/226.
[54] Illus. in Barnet and Dist. Loc. Hist. Soc. Bull. xvi.
[55] Hatfield C.F.E.P. (S. Mimms) 1/20; M.R.O., L.V. 6/10, 8/62.
[56] M.R. 667.
[57] Hatfield C.F.E.P. (Ct. Bks.) iii. 1774–1802.
[58] M.R.O., L.V. 6/10.

[59] M.L.R. 1750/3/690; 1713/6/128–31.
[60] S.C. 2/227/83; B.M. Stowe 847, p. 64.
[61] Hatfield C.F.E.P. (Ct. Bks.) i. 1702–31, p. 53; Herts. Rec. Office D/ETr/T.18.
[62] M.R.O., L.V. 5/2.
[63] Hatfield C.F.E.P. (Ct. Bks.) ii. 1732–73, p. 20; Herts. Rec. Office D/Etr/T.20.
[64] C 142/733/14; Herts. Rec. Office D/ETr/T.25.
[65] As part of the Dancers Hill estate; see p. 285.
[66] M.R.O., TA/S. Mimms.
[67] Herts. Rec. Office D/ETr/T.25.
[68] Hatfield C.F.E.P. (Ct. Bks.) i. 1702–31, p. 53.
[69] Brewer, Beauties of Eng. and Wales, x(5), 748.
[70] M.R.O., L.V. 7/29, 8/62; Brittain, South Mymms, 88.
[71] Hatfield C.F.E.P. (Ct. Bks.) i. 1702–31, pp. 206–7.
[72] Ibid. iii. 1774–1802, pp. 126–7.
[73] Brittain, South Mymms, 87; M.R.O., L.V. 7/29.
[74] Hatfield C.F.E.P. (Ct. Bks.) v. 1824–72.
[75] Brittain, South Mymms, 87–9; M.R.O., L.V. 7/29, 10/111.

Improvements to the Great North Road between Ganwick Corner and Lemsfordmills (Herts.)[76] led to some growth at Potters Bar. A third inn, the Robin Hood and Little John, was built in High Street, and to its south on a new site stood the Swan with Two Necks which had been renamed the White Horse.[77] Several inns were also erected along the road from Ganwick Corner to the Causeway. The Duke of York at Ganwick Corner was licensed in 1752 and known for a short time as the White Horse.[78] Adjacent to the Southgate road, the Lion was formed in 1761 out of two cottages.[79] The Red Lion, in the grounds of Morven and mentioned in 1686,[80] served a group of timber cottages which stood at the northern end of High Street; access was impeded after the construction of Hatfield Road in 1802 and the site was leased to the owner of Morven in 1856.[81] North of Mutton Lane timber houses lined both sides of the Hatfield–London Road[82] and by the late 18th century both Methodists and Baptists had begun to meet in barns near by.

In the 18th century the parish was still notable for the number of seats occupied by Londoners. The improved turnpike road brought Potters Bar within easy reach of the City and new houses included Wrotham Park, Bridgefoot House, Dancers Hill House, Easy Lodge (later known as Parkfield), Salisbury House, and Blake Hall, as well as the rebuilt Dyrham Park. Whereas several houses still exist and the sites of others are known, no trace remains of Blake Hall; it is sometimes shown on the site of the later Elm Court in Mutton Lane but in 1754 it was marked farther west on the south side of the road.[83] Near South Mimms village the estate of Clare Hall was also formed in the early 18th century. The most imposing seat at Kitts End was New Lodge, which was built in 1767 by Thomas Nuthall, ranger of Enfield Chase and later Treasury Solicitor; it had spacious grounds, with a paddock of 13 a. formed out of common land south of the house.[84] The Thackeray family lived at Kitts End in the later 18th century, before moving to Monken Hadley manor-house.[85] William Makepeace Thackeray, an officer in the Bengal civil service, was residing there in 1780 and in the following year his son Richmond Thackeray, father of the novelist, was baptized at South Mimms church.[86]

Several farm-houses were built or altered during the 18th century. Bridgefoot farm-house was built c. 1750, weatherboarded barns were erected at Earls and Bentley Heath farms, additions were made to Fold Farm, and the whole of Knightsland was cased in brick.[87]

With the establishment of mansions in spacious parks humbler housing tended to be confined to the main roads. In 1770 there were said to have been thirty encroachments into Enfield Chase at Potters Bar,[88] but most new buildings there and at Mimms Green were timber-built cottages and barns on small plots.[89] Cottages, barns, several shops, including a wheelwright's, and what later became a school-house were built on Mimms Green.[90] In 1769 encroachments included a cottage and an inn called the Maypole on the edge of the Chase, between Gannick Bank and the new line of the Great North Road.[91] The property then belonged to Thomas Nuthall and eventually passed to George Byng in 1782.[92]

In 1781 the common lands at Bentley Heath and Kitts End were added to the South Mimms allotment of the Chase and the whole was inclosed.[93] There was no radical change in the pattern of settlement, for by 1864 the neighbourhood was still very sparsely populated,[94] but the landscape was greatly affected by allotments to the large estates, notably Wrotham, New Lodge, and Old Fold manor.[95] Kitts End Green was divided into seven portions, all of which, except that belonging to Turpin Bastick, were incorporated in the grounds of New Lodge. Francis Barroneau, the owner, also bought the Hermitage and other cottages from Lord Salisbury and in 1786 closed the road through the hamlet of Kitts End, since it ran between the paddock and the south front of his house.[96] New Lodge, standing in finely wooded grounds, was apparently a stuccoed building with side wings.[97] Joseph Farington, the Academician and diarist, stayed there in 1806 and was informed by Barroneau that a genteel establishment at that time could not be formed for much less than £10,000.[98] Adjacent to the hamlet of Potters Bar lay 108 a. from the Chase which formed part of the estate of Oakmere.[99] A house was built on land farther west and the grounds were landscaped.

The main change in the early 19th century was the reconstruction of the road from London to St. Albans, which diverted traffic from Kitts End, Dancers Hill, and the main street of South Mimms village itself. As a result 'the innkeepers and other frontagers relegated . . . to a stagnant backwater'[1] became impoverished, although the White Hart in South Mimms village had merely to acquire a new front in order to face the Telford road. The Cross Keys in South Mimms village[2] and the Angel and the Bull's Head at Kitts End were among the inns that disappeared.[3] The White Lion and near-by smithy at Dancers Hill reverted to private use, the smithy being pulled down in 1875.[4] The hamlet of Kitts End quickly decayed. Most of the properties and lands on the west side of the old Kitts End Road

[76] See p. 273.
[77] *Story of Potters Bar*, 62–3, 66; M.R.O., F. 56.
[78] M.R.O., L.V. 10/111; *Story of Potters Bar*, 66.
[79] *Story of Potters Bar*, 67.
[80] Guildhall MS. 5481 (will of Jas. Hickson).
[81] *Story of Potters Bar*, 67; M.R.O., F. 56.
[82] M.R.O., F. 115; Rocque, *Map of Mdx.* (1754).
[83] *Story of Potters Bar*, 67; Rocque, *Map of Mdx.* (1754).
[84] *Barnet and Dist. Loc. Hist. Soc. Bull.* xvi; see p. 279.
[85] See p. 264.   [86] Brittain, *South Mymms*, 63.
[87] Hist. Mon. Com. *Mdx.* 95–6; Min. of Town and Country Planning, List of Bldgs. (1948).
[88] Lease bk. 1767 *penes* Duchy of Lanc. office, ff. 14v.–17v.
[89] Hatfield C.F.E.P. (Ct. Bks.) i. 1702–31; ii. 1732–73; M.R.O., F. 56.

[90] Hatfield C.F.E.P. (Ct. Bks.) ii. 1732–73; iii. 1774–1802.
[91] M.P.C. 143; M.R. 667.
[92] Lease bk. 1767 *penes* Duchy of Lanc. office, ff. 18v.–19; *Barnet and Dist. Loc. Hist. Soc. Bull.* xvi.
[93] See p. 290.
[94] O.S. Map 6", Mdx. I. SE. (1864 edn.).
[95] M.R.O., F. 84/6b.
[96] *Barnet and Dist. Loc. Hist. Soc. Bull.* xvi.
[97] Guildhall Pr. W/SOU(1).
[98] Brittain, *South Mymms*, 63.
[99] M.R.O., F. 84/6b.
[1] C. G. Harper, *The Holyhead Road*, 93.
[2] See p. 277.
[3] *Barnet and Dist. Loc. Hist. Soc. Bull.* xvi.
[4] Ibid. xvii.

were bought by the Byngs of Wrotham Park, who replaced them with estate cottages. The Hickson alms-houses were moved from Kitts End to South Mimms village in 1856. A few years later New Lodge was demolished and its grounds were added to Wrotham Park. By the 1860s the old hamlet of Kitts End had been absorbed into the park, which then occupied a large triangle of land.[5]

Apart from the National school erected in 1834 very little building took place in South Mimms village, whose population declined between 1851 and 1861. There were 174 houses in 1871 but by 1901 the number had increased only to 200.[6] Many cottages fell into disrepair and were described in 1895 as insalubrious.[7] By the late 19th century an annual fair enjoyed only a lingering existence and the village was considered to be suitable for an isolation hospital.

Steady growth at Potters Bar in the early 19th century is evidenced by the building of a church, chapels, and a school. By 1851 the district of St. John's contained 187 houses and had a population of 992. The construction of the G.N.R. did not, however, lead to rapid change; the population dropped to 959 in 1861 and rose only to 1,691 in 1901, a much slower rate of growth than in the southern part of the parish.[8] Meanwhile several inns opened near the workmen's temporary camps in Dove Lane and Mutton Lane. The Railroad inn (or the Beer Engine House) in Mutton Lane lost its licence in 1906 and afterwards became known as Limerick House, the local headquarters of the British Red Cross Society. The Old Station hotel, opened in Darkes Lane c. 1880, was rebuilt c. 1938 and renamed the Potters Bar.[9] Two London speculators, George Singer and Robert Vickery, in 1855 became copyhold tenants of c. 30 a. of the manor of Wyllyotts and the next day purchased the enfranchisement, planning to develop the Osborne Park estate in the north of Potters Bar by laying out over 200 plots. Little, however, was actually built, apart from the Builder's Arms in Heath Road, some cottages and shops in Church Road, and a few houses in Osborne and Heath roads, one of which presumably later became Lochinver school. Other 19th-century building was mainly confined to large houses, notably Morven, Mount Grace in Church Road, and a few in Wagon Road and Baker Street, and to cottages on the south side of the Southgate road.[10] Morven was erected on the site of the 16th-century Clock House, replacing a house built there by the Hammonds in c. 1750. Its occupier in 1856, Mrs. Catherine Lee, obtained a 99-year lease of part of the site from the Brewers' Company of London.

The fastest growth, however, was around Barnet, which was still an important thoroughfare and, especially after 1872, linked by good rail services to London. Union Street, adjacent to High Street, was laid out c. 1835[11] and the boundary stone marking the division between the parishes of South Mimms and Chipping Barnet was placed 198 yards from the eastern end of it.[12] In 1838 six alms-houses were built by Richard Thornton, former master of the Leathersellers' Company of London, on land in Union street which had been acquired by the company in 1603.[13] Six more alms-houses were founded in 1850 and a lodge was erected c. 1860, when accommodation was limited to the aged poor of the company. A single-storeyed northern block was built in 1866 for seven inmates from John Hasilwood's alms-houses at St. Helen's, Bishopsgate (London), and a chapel was added in 1931. In 1966 the two-storeyed east and west blocks were rebuilt and in 1972 the Leathersellers' alms-houses, of light stone and in the Gothic style, formed three sides of a quadrangle around a garden.

By the 1850s there were many inns, shops, and schools near by in Union Street, especially along its northern side, and in High Street.[14] A Roman Catholic church was built in High Street in 1850 and replaced by one in Union Street in 1865, to which several schools were attached.[15] Christ Church and its schoolrooms were built in New Road in 1844–5 and within a decade buildings had spread along both sides of the road as far as the church: they included commercial premises, 'an academy', and the 18th-century White Lion.[16] By 1871 Christ Church parish contained 342 houses in which lived 1,598 persons, nearly 50 per cent of the total population of South Mimms. Twenty years later there were 699 houses in the Barnet portion of the old parish, compared with 180 in South Mimms village and 328 in Potters Bar.[17] In 1864 Alston and Stapylton roads and the Avenue had been laid out but contained only a few buildings.[18] Expansion[19] within the next thirty years consisted mainly of filling the gaps between Alston and Stapylton roads. Strafford, Carnarvon, and Salisbury roads, and the Drive had all been built by 1897, with Marriott and Ravenscroft Park roads to the west. More buildings were erected along Union Street, those on the south side standing especially close together. In addition to residential housing the Albion was opened in Union Street[20] and the Sebright Arms in Alston Road. Schools lined Salisbury and Strafford roads, mission rooms appeared in Alston Road and shops in Calvert Road,[21] until 1901 there were 942 houses in the area.[22] Afterwards the rate of growth slowed down, although building continued north of Alston Road, where a dental manufacturing works had been established.[23] By 1906 premises at nos. 95 and 97 High Street were occupied by Barclays Bank and more shops and coffee rooms had been opened.[24] In the later 19th and early 20th century several military battalions had barracks in Union Street, Stapylton Road, and Salisbury Road.[25]

[5] Ibid. xvi.
[6] Census, 1851, 1861, 1871, 1901.
[7] Brittain, South Mymms, 134–5.
[8] Census, 1851, 1861, 1901.
[9] Story of Potters Bar, 73; M.R.O., Hist. Notes 7.9.55.
[10] Story of Potters Bar, 74, 67; O.S. Maps 6", Mdx. I. SE. (1897 edn.).
[11] Cass, South Mymms, 21.
[12] M.R.O., S.R. 4543/33.
[13] The rest of the para. is based on City of Lond. Livery Cos. [C. 4073–IV], p. 194, H.C. (1884), xxxix (v), and inf. supplied by the clerk of the company.
[14] Kelly's Dirs. Herts. (1851, 1855).	[15] Ibid. (1902).

[16] Kelly's Dirs. Herts. (1851, 1855); Craven & Co. Dir. (1854).
[17] Census, 1871, 1891.
[18] O.S. Map 6", Mdx. VI. NE. (1864 edn.).
[19] Except where otherwise stated, the following para. is based on O.S. Map 6", Mdx. VI. NE. (1897 edn.); Kelly's Dirs. Herts. (1878, 1882); Kelly's Dir. Barnet (1889–90).
[20] Kelly's Dir. Barnet (1892–3).
[21] Ibid. (1889–90).	[22] Census, 1901.
[23] Kelly's Dir. Barnet (1906); O.S. Map 6", Mdx. VI. NE. (1897 edn.).
[24] Kelly's Dir. Barnet (1906).
[25] Ibid. (1894–5, 1906, 1909–10).

In Potters Bar many large houses were built between 1850 and the First World War.[26] Banister Fletcher designed some detached houses in the Avenue,[27] 'of an economic character',[28] with cement-covered walls, steeply-pitched roofs, and tile-hung gables.[29] Plans to extend St. John's church had to be abandoned, largely because of opposition from the owners of family vaults.[30] Settlement, however, still tended to be concentrated along High Street, with very few buildings on the former Chase, apart from those belonging to Chase Farm.[31] By the early 20th century there was only a sprinkling of houses at the northern end of Darkes Lane, where a wooden hut was apparently the first shop in the 1930s.[32] In 1902 36 a. belonging to Wyllyotts manor at Dugdale Hill was sold to Lord Salisbury and in 1919 South Mimms R.D.C. bought 3 a. in Mutton Lane for a depot, although they failed to purchase Wyllyotts manor-house from the Brewers' Company of London.[34]

There was a lack of humbler housing despite some building in 1901 in Blanche Lane.[35] Three years later in both South Mimms village and Potters Bar the poor suffered from much overcrowding and high rents.[36] Six cottages were erected at Mimms End by E. L. Hamilton in 1914 and the R.D.C. built twelve more in 1915 on land adjoining the St. Albans road, part of which was occupied by a sewage disposal works. The twelve cottages, together with another ten built there in 1921, to be known as the Cecil Cottages.[37] In the 1920s, however, there was still much insanitary housing in South Mimms village and the vicar offered to sell a small piece of glebeland on the condition that only workers' homes should be built there.[38] In 1929 the council built 120 houses in Mutton Lane but in 1930 the chairman stated that four cottages which had been condemned forty years before were still occupied. By 1939 344 council houses had been built, mostly along Mutton Lane and on the Cranborne estate in the north-west part of Potters Bar. Private houses, mainly detached, were still under construction north-west of Potters Bar station in the Avenue, Heath Drive, and Mount Grace Road.[40]

New housing in the 1930s[41] consisted mainly of bungalows in the area between High Street and Darkes Lane, and around Baker Street. Residential roads, many of them closes, appeared on both sides of Baker Street, while between the Walk and Byng Drive blocks of flats were erected in Strafford Gate. Some building took place in the grounds of former mansions: in 1938 a school was built on land once belonging to Parkfield, and in 1937 and 1949 houses were erected on part of the Oakmere estate. The spread of housing in the western part of Potters Bar led to the building there of Cranborne school in 1933 and the establishment of a mission, from which developed the parish of King Charles the Martyr.

The first multiple stores appeared in High Street c. 1930 but the main shopping parade developed in the southern half of Darkes Lane. As early as 1895 a room had been rented by Messrs. Sharples, Lucas Tuke and Co., later amalgamated with Barclays Bank, who provided a one-hour banking service two days a week. A post office, first established at the Green Man, transferred to the premises later used by Barclays and afterwards moved to the Barnet road. In 1935 a sorting office was built in Darkes Lane and in 1963 a Crown post office was opened next to it. A telephone exchange was opened in 1903 at a private house in Hatfield Road but moved in 1930 to a large building at the corner of Billy Lows Lane, where new premises were built in 1972.

While housing spread west of High Street towards South Mimms village, it was not until the 1950s that there was much growth east of the road. Outside authorities eventually bought 80 a. there for council housing: in 1952 Edmonton B.C. compulsorily purchased land adjoining Mutton Lane and Barnet Road, while Tottenham B.C. acted similarly over land behind the Causeway and Tempest Avenue. The Torrington estate, a large private estate between Tottenham's property and the Causeway, was completed in the 1960s. Near-by estates, Trewenna and Bear Wood, were still under construction in 1973. There was also considerable building in the southern end of Potters Bar, which included old peoples' houses in Byers Close. High density building after 1950 gave rise to many maisonettes, including those in Rosary Court and on the Mutton Lane estate. Five-storeyed offices were erected in 1963 in High Street and a year later an eight-storeyed office block was built in Darkes Lane, opposite the station. A similar block was erected in Mutton Lane on land sold by the Congregational church.

Despite the spate of building the network of houses and roads in Potters Bar is broken up by large open spaces. On either side of High Street lie the parklands of Oakmere and Parkfield, with King George's field to the west and, beyond that, Potters Bar golf course. The area is fringed by woodland and residential roads are tree-lined. In 1973 there were striking contrasts between the suburban avenues covering the north-east of the parish in Potters Bar, the old village in the north-west, and 19th-century housing in Barnet. Much of the parish was still open, with farm-land mainly in the centre and some patches of woodland.

Although bounded by motorways, the village of South Mimms has retained a rural air. It is dominated by the church, with its bold tower and 'perfect village cemetery'[42] which stands west of Telford's road and south of Hickson's alms-houses.[43] To the south are the modern vicarage house (called 'the Rectory'), with its old garden wall and gateposts, and the glebeland. Blackhorse Lane, north of the church, contains three red-brick 18th-century cottages. North-east of council housing in the same road

[26] Story of Potters Bar, 74.
[27] Bldg. News, lxxxvii. 11.
[28] Bldg. News, xcix. 357.
[29] Pevsner, Mdx. 134.
[30] Story of Potters Bar, 74.
[31] O.S. Map 6", Mdx. I. SE. (1897, 1920 edns.).
[32] Story of Potters Bar, 74.
[33] Hatfield C.F.E.P. (S. Mimms) 2/84.
[34] Ibid. (S. Mimms) 4/127.   [35] Dates on bldgs.
[36] Brittain, South Mymms, 144.

[37] Ibid. 145; Story of Potters Bar, 112.
[38] Hatfield C.F.E.P. (S. Mimms) 3/121.
[39] Brittain, South Mymms, 145.
[40] Story of Potters Bar, 112, 76.
[41] Except where otherwise stated, the following acct. is based on Story of Potters Bar, 76–9, 112.
[42] Ambulator, 12th edn. (1820), 225.
[43] Except where otherwise stated, the following 9 paras. are based on Hist. Mon. Com. Mdx. 95–6, and Min. of Town and Country Planning, List of Bldgs. (1948).

stands the Black Horse inn, red-brick and with an early-18th-century exterior. To its south, at the junction of the old and new St. Albans roads, is the timber-framed White Hart, late-17th-century but much altered and containing some 18th-century plaster panelling on the first floor and a plaster ceiling. The upper village has several 18th-century houses along Greyhound and Blanche lanes, among 19th-century grey-brick cottages and neo-Georgian 20th-century houses. South of the Rectory in Blanche Lane stand the 'Village Stores', an 18th-century red-brick cottage, and the Post Office Stores, early-18th-century and of whitewashed brick, with some timber-framing at the rear. At the corner of Blanche and Greyhound lanes stands the White House, a Regency building. In Greyhound Lane is Cedar House, red-brick and of the 18th century, with modern additions on the west; it has bow windows on either side of the door and two venetian windows on the first floor.

West of South Mimms village stands Earls Farm with its modern house and 18th-century weather-boarded barns. Blanche Lane leads southward past Clare Hall hospital, mainly huts to the north of a red-brick house almost opposite Blanche Farm. Its grounds contain a lake and examples of 19th-century landscape gardening. A new farm-house has been erected at Blanche Farm on the site of an earlier building. In contrast to the western fringes of the village, the eastern parts illustrate 20th-century growth. Beyond a garden centre at Bignell's Corner at the end of Greyhound Lane stand the modern Middlesex Arms and the Esso Motor hotel.

Fields stretch across the centre of the parish, interspersed by farm-buildings and several large houses. South-east of South Mimms village stands the mid-18th-century red-brick farm-house at Bridgefoot next to three 17th-century barns, one of five and the other two of three bays, weatherboarded and with pantiled roofs. North-east of the farm the modern Bridgefoot House has replaced the 18th-century residence. Farther south-east in Bentley Heath Lane and near Elm Farm is the 17th-century house belonging to Bentley Heath Farm, of brown brick and with a stuccoed doorcase. There are two 18th-century barns, of seven and four bays respectively. West of the corner of Bentley Heath Lane and Dancers Hill Road, at which stands Trinity chapel, are several 18th- and 19th-century buildings, including Norfolk Lodge, and some cottages erected by 1875 by the Trotters of Dyrham Park on the site of the former smithy and cottage.[44] At the north end of Dancers Hill, along Wash Lane, is the stuccoed Dancers Hill House, long and narrow. To its north is the L-shaped house of Dancers Hill Farm, a stuccoed building with a green slate roof; the north façade has a flat rusticated doorcase and the west façade has a ground floor semicircular bay, above which are three-light semicircular windows. Two inns in the centre of the parish possess 18th-century buildings. West of the St. Albans road and south of Wash Farm is the whitewashed brick building of the Green Dragon, which previously had stood opposite Kitts End Road since at least the early 17th century. At Ganwick Corner, south of Potters Bar, stands the Duke of York, 18th-century and red-brick, with many later additions.

The area south of Dancers Hill Road is dominated by two large estates: Dyrham Park and Wrotham Park. Dyrham Park, in 1973 used by a private golf club, is surrounded by lodges and arched gateways. The long mansion stands in wooded grounds, which contain several lakes. To the east the ground rises steeply to the finely timbered park of Wrotham, overlooked by its imposing house and incorporating several lakes and the scattered remains of stone buildings. North and east of the park in Bentley Heath Lane, Dancers Hill Road, and the Great North Road, lie several groups of estate cottages, bearing the letter 'S' and erected by George Byng, earl of Strafford (d. 1886).

Scattered among the fields at the southern end of the parish are several old farm-buildings. Near the entrance to Dyrham Park is the 16th-century Knightsland Farm and on the east side of St. Albans Road is a 17th-century barn of half H-shaped plan. South-west of Knightsland, on the boundary in Galley Lane, is Fold Farm, with moat. The L-shaped farm-house, timber-framed and faced with brick, was built in the 17th century but later extended; 17th-century barns to its north and east have been much altered. East of Wrotham stretch fields, diversified by patches of woodland.

Just beyond the southern tip of Wrotham Park lies the area known as Hadley Highstone, whose northern part lies within South Mimms. Old Fold Lane and Taylors Lane, west of the Great North Road, are lined by cottages and terraces, some of them stuccoed and mostly 19th-century. To the north stands the former childrens' hospital and, farther north, Kitts End Lodge, a red-brick building in the Gothic style. West of Hadley Green the Byng Road playing fields and Old Fold Manor golf course are patches of green fringing the suburbia of High Barnet. West of Barnet High Street houses, mainly 19th-century, line a network of roads, whose character is varied by the grounds and Tudor-style buildings of Queen Elizabeth's grammar school and the Leathersellers' alms-houses. There are few old buildings in the neighbourhood, apart from some small 18th-century cottages and houses in St. Albans Road, among them the White Lion.

Barnet High Street is lined with 20th-century shop fronts, which in many cases conceal earlier structures.

Among the 20th-century housing, industrial estates, and shopping centres in Potters Bar, are some old survivals, most of them along the Great North Road (High Street). The Green Man, at the northern end of High Street, is timbered and plastered and apparently 17th-century, although 'much altered' by 1937. To its south stands the White Horse, a long low building of the early 18th century, plastered, with a Victorian verandah and bay windows. At the junction of High Street with the Southgate road is the Lion, a late-18th-century stuccoed building with later additions. Salisbury House, which became a private school in the 19th century, stands on the east side of High Street. A two-storeyed, red-brick house of the 18th century, it has a wooden doorcase and parapet wall, and an extension. Farther north-east is the Victorian mansion Oakmere House, with its wooded grounds, which include 3 a. of ornamental water.[45] Between

[44] Barnet and Dist. Loc. Hist. Soc. Bull. xvii.

[45] Potters Bar, Official Guide [1972]; Kelly's Dir. Mdx. (1902).

High Street and the Causeway stands another Victorian house, Morven Park; it was acquired by the National Trust *c.* 1930 and almost half of its grounds lie outside the parish. The corner of the Causeway and Hatfield Road is dominated by the white and gold war memorial, designed in 1920 by C. F. A. Voysey.[46] To the south-west, in Darkes Lane, the timber-framed structure of Wyllyotts manor-house stands next to modern council offices and adjacent to the railway station, industrial estate, and main shopping parade.

The extreme north-west of the parish, where early settlement had focused, consists mainly of farm-land, through which several major roads pass. The few scattered buildings, all east of the road, include Warrengate Farm and the small 16th-century L-shaped manor-house at Mimms Hall. To the west, fields stretch out towards Mimmshall wood, crossed by public footpaths.

There were 340 communicants in 1547[47] and 292 adult males who took the protestation oath in 1641.[48] In 1676 480 conformists and 20 nonconformists were recorded.[49] The population seems to have fluctuated in the 17th century, with outbreaks of plague in 1603, 1623–5, and 1665. Numbers increased during the 18th century, although smallpox contributed to a rise in infant mortality,[50] and rose steadily from 1,698 in 1801 to 3,238 in 1861. From 1871 to 1901 the population more than doubled, largely because of building around Barnet. The rise levelled off after 1911, only to increase again in 1931, when South Mimms R.D. contained 5,720 persons, at a density of 0.93 persons an acre, and South Mimms U.D. had 5,501 persons at a density of 20.2 persons an acre. Between 1931 and 1951 the population increased by 100 per cent; the number of persons in South Mimms U.D. (i.e. High Barnet) was 4,481, compared with 17,172 persons in Potters Bar U.D. In 1961 Potters Bar U.D. contained 23,376 persons.[51]

MANORS. In 1086 South Mimms was held by Geoffrey de Mandeville as a berewick of the manor of Edmonton, and in the time of King Edward it had belonged to Ansgar the staller.[52] The overlordship of *SOUTH MIMMS* manor followed the descent of Enfield.[53] The manor seems to have been subinfeudated in 1140–4, when Geoffrey de Mandeville, earl of Essex (d. 1144), granted half of it to Hugh of Eu.[54] By 1210–12 the whole manor was in the hands of Ernulf de Mandeville, probably a descendant of Geoffrey's eldest son, Ernulf, who held it of the honor of Mandeville for one knight's

fee.[55] Ernulf seems to have been deprived of his holding, for in 1216 the manor was granted by King John to Henry the Teuton.[56] Ernulf's son, another Ernulf,[57] had regained possession by 1235–6[58] and from him it apparently passed to his brother Hugh.[59] It was later in the possession of the Lewknor family, who seem to have been connected with the Mandevilles, for in 1268 Sir Roger Lewknor held a Suffolk manor of Hugh de Mandeville.[60] Sir Roger was succeeded in 1295 by his son Thomas,[61] whose heir Thomas secured a grant of free warren in South Mimms in 1313.[62] The first recorded lease of the manor was by Thomas's son, Roger, to John de Byllyngdon in 1394 for 20 years.[63] The manor remained in the Lewknor family until 1483, when Sir Thomas Lewknor was attainted and his lands granted to Robert Scrope.[64] In 1484 Lewknor was pardoned[65] and his lands were restored in 1485.[66]

It is uncertain when the manor was transferred from the Lewknor family to the Windsors. In 1503 the manor court was held in the name of Edmund Dudley, and other feoffees, to the use of Dudley's brother-in-law Andrew Windsor, later Lord Windsor (d. 1543).[67] In 1519, however, Roger Lewknor, who was said to be seised in fee of the manor, leased it to Sir Andrew and George Windsor, during the life of Sir Thomas West and others. In 1525 Sir Edward Neville, who was Sir Andrew's son-in-law and said to be the sole surviving trustee, released the manor to Roger Corbett and Henry Draper. In 1530 South Mimms was conveyed by Draper to Sir Edward Neville, William Windsor, and others.[68] In 1542 it was claimed by Anne Knyvett, a daughter of Roger Lewknor, and her husband John Vaughan,[69] from whom it was eventually conveyed in 1567 to Edward, Lord Windsor (d. 1575).[70] The manor descended in the Windsor family until 1606 when Henry Howard, earl of Northampton, and other executors of Henry, Lord Windsor (d. 1605), sold it to Robert Cecil, earl of Salisbury (d. 1612).[71] The manorial estate has remained largely intact in the hands of the Cecil family.

A castle assumed to have been built by Geoffrey de Mandeville, earl of Essex (d. 1144), on his manor of Mimms *c.* 1141, was discovered in 1918.[72] Excavations in 1960–7 revealed a simple but well-appointed motte-and-bailey castle, with a structure beneath the bailey bank which may have been the church granted to Walden in 1136 or may represent earlier manorial buildings. The castle seems to have been sacked by King Stephen's forces but pottery finds indicate the later domestic use of the bailey, probably in connexion with the working of the adjacent chalk pits.[73] A manor-house was first recorded

[46] Pevsner, *Mdx.* 134; National Trust, *Rep.* (1966), 69.
[47] E 301/34/117.
[48] Hse. of Lords, Mdx. Protestation Rets.
[49] William Salt Libr., Stafford, Salt MS. 33, p. 40.
[50] Brittain, *South Mymms*, 30.
[51] *Census*, 1801–1961.
[52] *V.C.H. Mdx.* i. 126.
[53] See p. 224.
[54] 'Original Charters of Herbert and Gervase, Abbots of Westminster (1121–57)', ed. P. Chaplais, *Medieval Miscellany for D. M. Stenton* (P.R.S. N.S. xxxvi), 96.
[55] *Red Bk. Exch.* (Rolls Ser.), ii. 283.
[56] *Rot. Litt. Claus.* (Rec. Com.), i. 250.
[57] *Cur. Reg. R.* viii. 110.
[58] *Bk. of Fees*, i. 474.
[59] Herts. Rec. Off., D/ETr/Tl no. 166; *Cartulary of St. Barts. Hosp.* no. 1223.

[60] *Story of Potters Bar*, 34.
[61] *Cal. Inq. p.m.* iii, pp. 179–80.
[62] *Cal. Chart. R.* 1300–26, 201.
[63] Hatfield C.F.E.P. (Deeds) 219/8.
[64] B.M. Harl. MS. 433 pp. 47b, 122; *Cal. Pat.* 1476–85, 376.
[65] *Cal. Pat.* 1476–85, 435.
[66] *Rot. Parl.* (Rec. Com.), vi. 273.
[67] Hatfield C.F.E.P. (Ct. Roll) 14/28, f. 6v.; *Hist. of Parl. Biogs. 1439–1509*, p. 285.
[68] Hatfield C.F.E.P. (Legal) 28/8; ex inf. Hist. Parl.
[69] Hatfield C.F.E.P. (Legal) 9/1; (Deeds) 143/2.
[70] C.P. 25(2)259/9 Eliz. East.
[71] Hatfield C.F.E.P. (Deeds) 143/20.
[72] *T.L.M.A.S.* xiii. 175, 464.
[73] J. P. C. Kent, 'Excavations at the . . . Castle of S. Mimms', *Barnet and Dist. Loc. Hist. Soc. Bull.* xv.

in 1268.[74] There was a capital messuage with a dove-cot in 1336[75] and by the 15th century the house had become known as 'Mimmehall'.[76] The early building probably stood on or near the site of Warrengate farm-house,[77] whereas the modern Mimms Hall stands farther south in what was formerly Windmill field.[78] The northern part of the house, a hall with cross-wings, was built in the early 16th century, and afterwards encased in brick. It was extended in the 17th century on the east and south, and later was much altered. Some of the original timber-framing, with tie-beams and wall-posts, is visible and fragments of the moat remain.[79]

The manor of *OLD FOLD* emerged from the capital manor. It was bought from Ernulf de Mande-ville by the Frowyks, who were prosperous London merchants, shortly after 1271[80] and it descended in the direct male line of the family until 1527. In 1308 Henry Frowyk was kidnapped by Thomas Lewknor, lord of South Mimms, William Pouns, a local land-owner,[81] his son Richard, and John of Felstead, parson of Hadley. Henry was married to William Pouns's daughter, Margaret, for which act the Frowyks subsequently obtained financial redress, on the grounds that Henry was a minor in the wardship of his mother Agnes.[82] Henry died in 1377, having outlived his son Thomas. His grandson Henry married Alice Cornwall, whose second husband Thomas Charlton had the manor in 1397,[83] apparently during the minority of Thomas, Henry and Alice's son. Thomas Frowyk was the husband of Elizabeth Aske, heir to the manor of Weld or Newberries in Shenley (Herts.).[84] His son and heir Henry married Joan Lewknor[85] but was sued for debt by Sir Roger Lewknor and committed to prison.[86] Accordingly Henry sold the manor of Weld and lands in Shenley, Aldenham, and St. Albans (Herts.) in 1473[87] and sold the manor of Durhams and land in London to his cousin Thomas Frowyk of Gunnersbury two years later,[88] although he retained Old Fold. His successors seem not to have paid the rent for Old Fold which was due to the manor of South Mimms, and in 1501 Henry's grandson and namesake was distrained for the non-payment for many years.[89] The younger Henry married Anne, daughter and co-heir of Robert Knollys, who brought the manor of North Mimms (Herts.) into the Frowyk family. Henry's son Thomas married Mary, daughter of Sir William Sandys, and died without issue.[90] By will proved in 1527, Henry therefore left his estates to his daughter Elizabeth and the children of her first husband John Coningsby.[91] It was not until

1547, however, that Elizabeth recovered Old Fold from John Palmer and his wife Mary, whose first husband had been Thomas Frowyk.[92] In 1551 Elizabeth and her husband William Dodds conveyed the manor to Thomas White.[93] It was eventually re-gained by Elizabeth's son, Sir Henry Coningsby, who, by will dated 1590, left it to his eldest son Ralph.[94] In 1639 when the manor extended beyond South Mimms and into the parishes of Enfield, Monken Hadley, and Chipping Barnet, it was sold by Thomas Coningsby to Thomas Allen of Finch-ley.[95] In 1841 the Revd. E. P. Cooper, whose father had inherited the Allen estates in 1830, sold the manor to George Byng of Wrotham Park.[96] Part of the estate was subsequently purchased by the Middlesex C.C.[97] and 124 a. were used from 1910 by Old Fold Manor golf club.[98]

Old Fold was said to comprise 132½ a. in the late 13th century.[99] At the inclosure of Enfield Chase in 1777 almost 37 a. were added to it[1] and in 1836 the estate, which included Old Fold House and land, Old Fold farm, Wales farm, and Pimlico House, consisted of 516 a.[2] The site of a manor-house, mentioned in 1310,[3] is marked by three sides of a moat alongside the headquarters of Old Fold Manor golf club.[4] Old Fold Manor House is an 18th-century house. Next to it stands the golf club house: two former cottages which are connected by an early-19th-century gateway with four columns and a parapet decorated with Soanian incised line ornament.[5]

The manor of *DEREHAMS* or *DURHAMS* was also a derivative of the capital manor.[6] It derives its name from John Durham, who in 1340 acquired half a house and 324 a. in South Mimms, together with land in Ridge, from Thomas de la Pannetrye.[7] He was granted the remaining interest in the property by Margery, wife of Richard Pouns, in 1341.[8] John Durham's daughter and heir, Margaret, married Thomas, son of Henry Frowyk of Old Fold, and after Durham's death in 1368[9] the manor descended with Old Fold[10] until its sale in 1473 to Thomas Frowyk of Gunnersbury (d. 1485).[11] The manor passed to Thomas's second son, Sir Thomas Frowyk (d. 1506),[12] Chief Justice of Common Pleas, whose daughter Frideswide became the first wife of Sir Thomas Cheyney, treasurer of the royal household. By will proved 1559 Cheyney left Durhams to his three granddaughters, Anne and Alice Kempe and the wife of William Cromer.[13] The manor was in the hands of Thomas Kempe in 1567,[14] and by 1578 it had passed to William Lee[15] who was still in

[74] C 132/35/12.
[75] C 135/47/11.   [76] *P.N. Mdx.* (E.P.N.S.), 78.
[77] Brittain, *South Mymms*, 11.
[78] Hatfield C.F.E.P. (Gen.) 62/5.
[79] Hist. Mon. Com. *Mdx.* 95.
[80] Lysons, *Mdx. Parishes*, 228; J.I. 1/540 rot. 3v.
[81] C.P. 25(1)/148/37/320; and see p. 275.
[82] *Year Bk.* 2 & 3 Edw. II (Selden Soc. xix), 162.
[83] Cass, *South Mimms*, 25.
[84] Brittain, *South Mymms*, 17; *V.C.H. Herts.* ii. 270.
[85] *Mdx. Pedigrees*, ed. R. Mundy, 90.
[86] *Cal. Pat.* 1476–85, 8.
[87] *Cal. Close*, 1476–85, 12.
[88] *Cal. Close*, 1468–76, 351–2.
[89] Hatfield C.F.E.P. (Ct. Roll) 14/28, f. 4v.
[90] Cass, *South Mimms*, 102, 111.
[91] *Story of Potters Bar*, 41.
[92] C.P. 25(2)/61/473/1 Edw. VI Hil.
[93] C.P. 25(2)/61/475/5 Edw. VI Mich.
[94] Prob. 11/77 (P.C.C. 5 Sainberbe).

[95] M.R.O., Acc. 351/683. For the descent of the manor in the Allen family see M.R.O., Acc. 351/715–717.
[96] M.R.O., Acc. 351/719; *Story of Potters Bar*, 45.
[97] *Story of Potters Bar*, 115.
[98] Ex inf. the secretary.
[99] *Yr. Bk.* 2 & 3 Edw. II (Selden Soc. xix), 162.
[1] M.P.C. 220.
[2] M.L.R. 1836/7/709, 710.
[3] *Yr. Bk.* 2 & 3 Edw. II (Selden Soc. xix), 162.
[4] *Story of Potters Bar*, 38.
[5] Pevsner, *Herts.* 168.
[6] *Cal. Inq. p.m. Hen. VII*, i, p. 74.
[7] C.P. 25(1)/287/40/287.
[8] C.P. 25(1)/150/58/141.
[9] *Story of Potters Bar*, 38.   [10] See above.
[11] *Cal. Close*, 1468–76, 351–2.
[12] *Cal. Inq. p.m. Hen. VII*, i, p. 74.
[13] Cass, *South Mimms*, 30.
[14] Hatfield C.F.E.P. (Ct. Roll) 23/16.
[15] Prob. 11/61 (P.C.C. 13 Bakon, will of Hen. Taylor).

possession in 1591.[16] In 1593 it was held by John Layce,[17] a London clothworker, whose heir was his son, Sir Rowland.[18] In 1602 the manor was sold by Henry Fleetwood to Clement, later Sir Clement, Scudamore (d. 1616), and Clement his son, later also knighted.[19] Sir Clement Scudamore the younger died in 1633, leaving his son and namesake a minor.[20] By 1653 Durhams belonged to John Austen,[21] whose grandson, John Austen, M.P. for Middlesex, sold the manor in 1733 to Anne, wife of William Anne van Keppel, earl of Albemarle (d. 1754). In 1773 Durhams was sold by their son William Keppel to Christopher Bethell, from whose executors it was purchased in 1798 by John Trotter,[22] an army contractor.[23] The manor was subsequently held by four generations of Trotters, until its sale to the Middlesex and Hertfordshire county councils in 1938.[24] The grounds have since been used as a private golf course.[25]

In 1506 the manor, which extended into Hertfordshire, included a house and 350 a.[26] The original manor-house may have stood beside Galley Lane, where a complete moat survives next to Fold Farm.[27] Another possible site is said to have been farther east, where there is an earthwork and enclosure.[28] The Elizabethan house, apparently on or near the site of the present building,[29] was destroyed by fire c. 1806 and replaced soon afterwards[30] by a large villa[31] known as Dyrham Park with a Tuscan entrance portico on the north, a semicircular bow on the south, and deep eaves. Some late-18th-century fittings in the north-west service-wing may survive from a wing in a similar relationship to the earlier house. There have been many alterations, the most recent being those to adapt the interior for use as a club house. In the mid 18th century the park had a predominantly formal layout with double avenues and a canal. Late in the century it was enlarged on the east and a costly new gateway[32] was provided to the New Road. The park was redesigned in a less formal manner c. 1822[33] and nothing remained of the avenues in 1973.

WYLLYOTTS manor derives its name from a family,[34] although it was not called a manor in 1349 when held by Robert and John Wyliot.[35] By 1478 the manor had come into the possession of the Lewknors, for in that year it was devised by Sir Roger Lewknor to his younger son, Roger.[36] In 1479 it was held by Henry Kyghley and Thomas Bartelot, who had married into the Lewknor family

and who were presumably trustees,[37] and was said to comprise 80 a. arable, 44 a. pasture, and 48 a. woodland.[38] From Roger Lewknor, styled lord of the manor of South Mimms and Wyllyotts in 1504, Wyllyotts passed to his son Edmund,[39] whose son Thomas and wife Bridget sold it in 1562 to William Dodds of North Mimms and his wife Catherine, reserving an annual rent-charge which was sold in 1568 to William Larke. The manor was sold by Dodds to William Stanford of Perry Hall (Staffs.) in 1575 and conveyed by Stanford in 1594 to his cousin Robert Taylor and his wife Elizabeth,[40] who in 1601 bought Larke's rent-charge.[41] Taylor enlarged Wyllyotts by the purchase of lands, including Cattalls and Smythies, which had formerly belonged to South Mimms manor. In 1603 he sold Wyllyotts to Sir Roger Aston,[42] who in 1605 conveyed it to Robert Honeywood of Hoxton,[43] from whom it passed in 1607 to Eleanor Hyde, widow, and John Wylde, her cousin and heir. In 1619 Sir John Wylde conveyed the manor to Henry Featherstone, from whom it was purchased in 1623 by Walter Lee, merchant tailor of London, who in 1629 conveyed it to his nephew, Walter Lee the younger. On Walter's bankruptcy his assignees sold Wyllyotts in 1650 to Alexander Wilding,[44] who in turn sold it in 1651 to Stephen Ewer and Bret Netter,[45] probably as trustees for James Hickson of the Brewers' Company of London, to whom they conveyed it later that year.[46] Hickson, by will proved 1689, devised the manor, including the 'chief manor house', to the Brewers' Company,[47] for the upkeep of his almshouses.[48] In 1925 the manor-house was purchased from the Brewers' Company by A. Hugh Seabrook. It was sold to Potters Bar U.D.C. in 1937.[49] In 1973 the council had leased it to a firm of restaurant owners.[50]

The manor-house of Wyllyotts stands a little to the west of Potters Bar station.[51] A house existed there in 1581 and was said in 1664 to have been enlarged or rebuilt by Walter Lee, haberdasher of London.[52] The existing house, which is timber-framed, is probably of c. 1800 but incorporates some re-used older material;[53] it was stuccoed prior to an extensive restoration for A. H. Seabrook. The adjacent aisled barn is incomplete but is probably part of one of the buildings shown on the site in 1594,[54] when it would have been newly built.

Under the Act for dividing Enfield Chase (1777), the South Mimms allotment of 1,026 a. 3 p. was to

[16] *Mdx. Cnty. Recs.* i. 202.
[17] Norden, *Spec. Brit.* 18.
[18] *Story of Potters Bar*, 45.
[19] C.P. 43/78 rot. 6; Prob. 11/128 (P.C.C. 76 Cope, will of Sir Clement Scudamore the elder); Shaw, *Knights*, ii. 185.
[20] C 142/468/100.
[21] C 5/387/9.
[22] Cass, *South Mimms*, 34–5.
[23] D.N.B.
[24] *Story of Potters Bar*, 48.
[25] Potters Bar, *Official Guide* [1972].
[26] *Story of Potters Bar*, 48.
[27] Brittain, *South Mymms*, 16. The moat, however, seems more likely to have been part of Fold Farm: see above, p. 275.
[28] Brittain, *South Mymms*, 16.
[29] *Story of Potters Bar*, 48.
[30] *Ambulator*, 12th edn. (1820), 85.
[31] Except where otherwise stated, the foll. description is based on Pevsner, *Mdx.* 39–40.
[32] *Ambulator*, 10th edn. (1807), 100.
[33] Herts. Rec. Off., D/ETr/Pl–4.

[34] *Cal. Pat.* 1345–48, 39; Guildhall MS. 6809; Hatfield C.F.E.P. (Ct. Roll) 14/27, f. 1.
[35] *Cal. Close*, 1349–54, 85.
[36] Prob. 11/7 (P.C.C. 1 Logg).
[37] Cass, *South Mimms*, 38.
[38] Lysons, *Mdx. Parishes*, 228.
[39] *Story of Potters Bar*, 58.
[40] Guildhall MS. 5885.
[41] C.P. 25(2)/173/43 Eliz. Hil.
[42] Guildhall MS. 5885.
[43] Guildhall MS. 5521.
[44] Lysons, *Mdx. Parishes*, 229.
[45] C.P. 25(2)/574/1651 Trin./Mdx.
[46] Guildhall MS. 5884.
[47] *Story of Potters Bar*, 59.
[48] See p. 307.
[49] *Story of Potters Bar*, 59, 103.
[50] Ex inf. the clerk, Potters Bar U.D.C.
[51] Para based on inf. of R.C.H.M. (Eng.).
[52] Guildhall MS. 6813 [charters of 1581 and 1664].
[53] Robbins, *Mdx.* plate 32.
[54] M.R.O., F. 58A.

become the manor of *NEW MIMMS*.[55] The creation of a new manor, while unusual, was to oblige a local landowner, who intended to lease it 'for the purpose of protecting and supplying his table with game'. The lease, however, did not take effect.[56]

The reputed manor of *MANDEVILLE*[57] originated in lands called Mandevilles Oak, Mandevilles, Great Mandevilles, and Mandefield, which lay on Dancers Hill and formed part of the manor of South Mimms. The tradition of a manor persisted in the 18th century, when a list of claims on Enfield Chase, which alluded to rights supposedly granted by Hugh de Mandeville to the holders of Old Fold and Durhams, included an uncompleted draft by the lord of Mandeville. A manor was first recorded in 1575, when it was owned by Jasper Annesley and his wife Joan, who two years later conveyed it to Henry Isham, a London mercer.[58] Isham already possessed three small properties which later formed part of the estate: the field known as Roundabout, or Mandevilles, Ripley Grove and Welks field, which John Annesley had sold to John Walker in 1542, and a house called Dancers Hill with 6 a., which had been sold in 1558 to Christopher Troughton by William Dodds and his wife Elizabeth. In 1596 Mandeville was sold by Gregory Isham to Richard Ketterick, who added some copyhold lands bought from the lord of South Mimms. In 1635 it passed from the Ketterick family to Thomas Harrison, a collector of ship-money, and, like Ketterick, a governor of Barnet grammar school. Financial difficulties forced Harrison to sell the larger part of the estate in 1674 to Sir Henry Blount, whose grandson Henry sold it to Thomas Andrews in 1700. Four years later the property was conveyed to David Hechstetter, a Hamburg merchant, whose son David succeeded in 1721 and reunited it in 1748 with lands which he had bought from the heirs of Richard Harrison. Two years later he leased Dancers Hill House with 10 a. to Charles Ross, a Westminster builder, for eighty years. On Hechstetter's death in 1757 the lands passed to his wife Charlotte for life, with remainder to his nephews, but in 1768 Charlotte Hechstetter broke the entail and sold the property, comprising in all 158 a.,[59] to the trustees of George Byng. Charles Ross, as lessee, was followed by his nephew William Gowan in 1770 and afterwards by a succession of other lessees, until in 1842 the tenant was Thomas White, who farmed most of the lands to the east of Wash Lane.

A house at Dancers Hill is recorded in 1558. It was inhabited in turn by the Kettericks and by the Harrisons, who apparently added a bowling green, and in 1748 was described as the old manor-house, although during Ross's lease it became known as the mansion house. It was considerably altered in 1856 by John Chapman, a builder who used old materials.

The core of the existing house is a small Palladian villa which was probably built by Charles Ross. It was of three storeys and had on the principal floor a saloon, at one end of which was an open loggia behind a portico, flanked by three smaller rooms with a staircase in the fourth corner. It was a tall house in relation to its plan and it appears that in the early 19th century an earth bank was raised on three sides to disguise the basement, when the entrance was moved from the south front to the north.[60] Balancing extensions to east and west were added c. 1860, when the attic floor was completely remodelled, and shortly afterwards a further extension was made to the east. The original house was of brick but it was later stuccoed, probably to disguise the alterations. The 18th-century gardens included an avenue on the north, of which traces remain. A less formal garden was made on the south in the 19th century.

OTHER ESTATES. When Geoffrey de Mandeville, earl of Essex (d. 1144), founded the abbey of Walden (Essex) c. 1140, he included in its endowment the church of and lands in South Mimms.[61] South Mimms, however, had probably been included in the grant of tithes and pannage made by the earl's grandfather Geoffrey to Hurley priory (Berks.), a cell of Westminster, c. 1086.[62] After the earl had granted Hurley an annual rent of £5 in lieu of all tithes except tithes of pannage,[63] Hurley retained its portion at South Mimms until 1255, when it agreed to exchange it with Walden for the church of Streatley (Berks.).[64] A dispute with Westminster occurred c. 1150, when the abbey seized Walden's revenues and granted nine marks a year from South Mimms church to Absalom, a priest.[65] In 1221–2 an agreement was reached between Hurley and Cathale priory (Herts.) concerning the division of tithes produced from the land which Ernulf de Mandeville had granted to Cathale.[66]

South Mimms rectory was surrendered by Walden in 1538 and granted to Sir Thomas Audley,[67] who in 1540 was licensed to alienate it to Francis Goodere.[68] In 1545 Goodere granted it, together with the manor of Monken Hadley, to William Stanford,[69] who in the same year conveyed the rectory[70] to Sir Thomas Wriothesley, Lord Chancellor (d. 1550), who in turn surrendered it to the Crown.[71] In 1546 the king granted it to John Veysey, bishop of Exeter, in exchange for the manor of Faringdon (Hants).[72] Veysey conveyed it to Thomas Fisher in 1548.[73] By 1552 the rectory was in the possession of Sir William Cavendish, who exchanged it with the king,[74] and in 1558 it was granted to Edmund Bonner, bishop of London.[75] After Bonner's deprivation Elizabeth I leased it for 21 years to James Conyers in 1576[76] and it was afterwards held on lease by William

[55] 17 Geo. III, c. xvii.
[56] Bk. of Surveys I (1783) *penes* Duchy of Lanc. office.
[57] Except where otherwise stated, this section is based on H. M. Baker, 'Dancers Hill and the Manor of Mandeville', *Barnet and Dist. Loc. Hist. Soc. Bull.* xvii (Nov. 1973).
[58] *Cat. Anct. D.* v, A 12483.
[59] M.L.R. 1768/7/47, 1769/1/483, 1/484.
[60] Proposals for the addition of wings in 1789 to the design of Ric. Pace of Burford do not appear to have been executed: Colvin, *Dict. of Architects*, 427.
[61] *Regesta Regum Anglo-Normannorum*, iii. pp. 332–3.
[62] W.A.M. 2001.   [63] Ibid. 2182.
[64] F. T. Wethered, *Lands and Tythes of Hurley Priory*, 36.
[65] C. H. Emson, 'Bk. of the Foundation of Walden Abbey', *Essex Review*, xlvi. 84.
[66] W.A.M. 2185; see p. 286.
[67] *L. & P. Hen. VIII*, xiii(1), p. 212.
[68] Ibid. xv, p. 292.
[69] Ibid. xx(1), p. 59.
[70] Hatfield C.P. 143; 148, f. 202.
[71] *D.N.B.*; *L. & P. Hen. VIII*, xx(1), p. 333.
[72] Ibid. xxi(i), p. 248.
[73] *Cal. Pat.* 1548–9, 403.
[74] Ibid. 1550–53, 288.
[75] Ibid. 1557–8, 400.
[76] C 66/1152.

Roberts[77] and by John Parrott and his wife Agnes.[78] In 1607 James I granted it to William Harrison and Thomas Bulbeck,[79] by whom it was sold in the same year to Robert Cecil, earl of Salisbury.[80] Thereafter it descended with the manor.

About 1190 the rectorial estate comprised 18 a. of arable land adjoining the church, from which rents of 5s. 4d. a year were paid to Walden.[81] The rectory was valued at 12 marks c. 1247[82] and at £14 13s. 4d. in 1291.[83] In Elizabethan times the estate lay in the Kings Grove,[84] adjacent to woodland called Parsonage bushes.[85] In 1650, when it was farmed by Stephen Ewer, the 'parsonage' was worth £160 and consisted of 20 a., a small cottage, and a barn, together with the great tithes.[86] The rectorial tithes were extinguished in 1841 and an annual rent-charge of £744 was awarded to the marquess of Salisbury.[87]

The rectory was leased to the Ewer family for most of the 17th century.[88] The parsonage house had to be kept in good repair by the lessees in 1688[89] and was last recorded in 1715.[90] It probably stood in the row of tenements held by the Ewers in Blackhorse Lane, since land to the east was described as rectorial land known as Waldens.[91] In 1842 Parsonage or Tithe farm extended over an area to the north of the Black Horse inn.[92]

Among other religious houses holding land in South Mimms, St. Bartholomew's hospital, Smithfield, acquired property near the church between 1220 and 1230. The estate consisted of land granted by Gunulf de Mandeville;[93] 3 a. and another house and tenement formerly held by William Suthmymmes, clerk, both given by Ernulf de Mandeville;[94] and 16 a. conveyed by John Feron.[95] A grange belonging to the hospital was leased to Richard Heyn c. 1250, on condition that he should store both corn and a plough which was needed for sowing the land held of St. Bartholomew's for life by Robert, vicar of South Mimms.[96]

In 1542 lands in South Mimms, worth 4s. 6d. a year,[97] which formerly belonged to Sopwell priory (Herts.), were granted in tail male to Richard (later Sir Richard) Lee.[98] He was survived by his daughter Mary who married Humphrey Coningsby, son of John Coningsby and Elizabeth Frowyk.[99]

Ernulf de Mandeville endowed the Augustinian priory of Cathale (Herts.) c. 1220 with land near the northern end of High Street, Potters Bar.[1] Although Cathale's possessions were transferred to Cheshunt priory in 1240,[2] its name persisted through the Potters Bar lands, which were known as 'Cattalls' or 'Cutholes'.[3] Cheshunt seems to have sold the property, for in 1425 three grocers of London, William Beveridge, Edmund Twyne, and John Parker, granted 'a croft and grove called Cathale' to John Daniel of Edmonton and John Canon of London.[4] The estate later belonged to the guild or brotherhood at Barnet, and in 1548 was bought by Richard Audley and John Reed.[5] It was sold by Henry Goodere to Robert Taylor, lord of Wyllyotts, in 1596[6] and acquired in turn by Sir Roger Aston and Robert Honeywood.[7] From Honeywood it passed to the Flexmores,[8] remaining with them until 1741 when Mary Dakin (née Flexmore) divided it among several relatives, of one whom, John Greenhill, later reunited the lands.[9] In 1773–4 part of the estate was sold to the trustees of George Byng and the remaining part to Richard Plaistow, a neighbouring landowner.[10]

Cattall House, designed for Robert Taylor by John Thorpe,[11] had been demolished by 1745.[12] Plaistow in c. 1770 built Easy Lodge on land to the south-east.[13] His family[14] sold the estate in 1835 to Charles Marryat, who renamed the house Cedar Lodge. It was known at Parkfield by 1859 and, with 62 a.,[15] was in the hands of Col. W. L. Carpenter, who leased it to Henry Parker. In 1877 Parker purchased the freehold, and, after his death in 1892, the house was leased successively to Henry Burt, chairman of Middlesex C.C., to Sir Lionel Fletcher, a shipping magnate, then for a house of prayer and as a girls' school. In 1934 Parker's daughter Mary sold the estate, part of which was acquired as an open space (Parkfield) by Potters Bar U.D.C. The house was demolished in 1936, and blocks of flats, called Parkside, were later erected on the site.[16]

Between 1439 and 1447 Thomas Frowyk founded a chantry chapel[17] and endowed it with lands that had been held by his family before 1387.[18] The estate comprised lands called Gannok (120 a.) at Bentley Heath, Old House field (14 a.) near Mobbs Hole, Dyrham Park, and 14 a. of woodland in 1547, when it was sold to the king's physician, Walter Cromer, and his wife Alice.[19] In 1555 Gannok, Old House field, and Chantry mead were given in custody to Thomas Hewys, one of the queen's physicians, who had married Cromer's widow, Alice.[20] In 1561

77 E 134/34 Eliz. Trin. 1.
78 Guildhall MS. 9171/18.
79 Hatfield C.F.E.P. (Deeds) 213/14.
80 Ibid. (Deeds) 213/13.
81 W.A.M. 168.
82 St. Paul's MS. W.D. 9, f. 85v.
83 Tax. Eccl. (Rec. Com.), 17.
84 Hatfield C.F.E.P. (Deeds) 280/10.
85 Ibid. (Gen.) 62/5.
86 Home Cnties. Mag. i. 317.
87 M.R.O., TA/S. Mimms.
88 Hatfield C.F.E.P. (Deeds) 76/15, 146/14, 127/23.
89 Ibid. (Legal) 173/6.
90 Ibid. (S. Mimms) 1/4.
91 See p. 295.
92 M.R.O., TA/S. Mimms.
93 Cartulary of St. Barts. Hosp. no. 1222.
94 Ibid. nos. 1220, 1221.
95 Ibid. no. 1219.
96 Ibid. no. 1225.
97 Dugdale, Monasticon, iii. 366.
98 L. & P. Hen. VIII, xvii, p. 161.
99 Cass, South Mimms, 67.
1 W.A.M. 2185.

2 V.C.H. Herts. iv. 426.
3 Story of Potters Bar, 53.
4 E 40/2622.
5 Cal. Pat. 1548–9, 78.
6 Guildhall MSS. 5885, 5521.
7 Guildhall MSS. 5521, 5885.
8 Mdx. Pedigrees, ed. R. Mundy, 176.
9 M.L.R. 1741/4/399.
10 M.L.R. 1773/5/393–4; 1776/1/41–2.
11 J. Summerson, John Thorpe (Walpole Soc. xl), 102–3, pl. 105.
12 Guildhall MS. 5521.
13 M.L.R. 1771/4/481–2.
14 Except where otherwise stated, the rest of the para. is based on Story of Potters Bar, 67–8, and Barnet Mus. 2144, pp. 3, 19, 113 [TS. coll. by H. J. Butcher, 1950].
15 Potters Bar and S. Mimms, Catalogue of an Exhibition (1959), p. 91.
16 Potters Bar, Official Guide [1972].
17 See p. 299.
18 Guildhall MS. 6809.
19 L. & P. Hen. VIII, xxi(2), p. 410; Newcourt, Repertorium, 727.
20 Cal. Pat. 1554–5, 279.

Thomas Cromer, Walter's son, conveyed the entire estate to Thomas Blackwell,[21] who in the same year conveyed the chantry house, with its garden and orchard, and Chantry mead (6 a.) to Thomas Nowell and his wife Agnes, and Old House field, then comprising 30 a., to Nicholas and Thomas Parrott.[22]

John Parrott (d. 1595) left Gannok and two parts of Old House field to his wife Agnes and a third part of Old House field to his son Thomas.[23] Gannok later passed to Sir Edmund Bowyer (d. 1627).[24] It was inherited by Sir William Smyth, who in 1779 married Anne, daughter of John Wyndham Bowyer, and was subsequently purchased by the Byngs of Wrotham Park.[25]

Chantry mead, lying in South Mimms village, was sold by John Foster, a London armourer, to Brian Kynaston and his wife Anne in 1597. Brian died in 1616, devising the property to John Broad, who later became Anne's second husband.[26] By the later 17th century the land was in the possession of the Hodges family, who were Quakers. A Quaker meeting-house later stood on part of the site.[27]

The house at Gannok is described in 1877 as having been 'demolished within living memory',[28] but some of its fishponds remain. The estate has given its name to Ganwick (formerly Galley) Corner.[29]

The estate called Darkes, which lay in the north of the parish, was possibly connected in the later 14th century with John Derk, a collier.[30] In 1490 John Fortescue sold it to a kinsman, Sir John Fortescue M.P. of Ponsbourne (Herts.), who died in 1500.[31] Henry Fortescue conveyed the property, then comprising 150 a., to William Stanford in 1553.[32] By 1604 the Stanfords had sold it,[33] together with the advowson of South Mimms vicarage,[34] to Thomas Marsh, clerk to the Court of Star Chamber.[35] Thereafter it descended with the advowson of the vicarage[36] until 1796, when it was purchased by John Hunter from the trustees of William Parker Hammond. The estate, consisting of 230 a.,[37] was later sold by Thomas Hunter to Thomas Willson (d. 1817)[38] and was still held by the Willson family in 1842, although leased out to Richard Stevens.[39] In 1973 part of the estate was occupied by Potters Bar golf club.[40] A moated house stood on the west side of Darkes Lane in 1594.[41] It was pulled down in 1830 and replaced by Darkes Farm, which was demolished c. 1956.[42]

The estate called Blanches,[43] in the western part of the parish, belonged to John Durham in the later 14th century. By 1575 it had become part of the property of Sir Robert Stanford of Perry Hall (now in Birmingham),[44] who by 1596 had sold it to Henry (later Sir Henry) Boteler (d. c. 1608). In 1603 Boteler assigned the estate to trustees for his second son Henry and in 1614 Blanches passed from Henry to a younger brother, Ralph, a merchant tailor of London. By 1618 Ralph had sold Blanche farm to Edward North, later serjeant-at-arms to Charles I, after whose death in 1650 it passed to his son Edward. It was held by John, son of Edward North the younger, in 1658 and afterwards by John's sisters, Mary and Sarah. They sold the farm in 1670 to James Ware of Hampstead, who, by will of 1671, divided it equally between his daughters, Grace, Sarah, and Mary. By 1711 Grace had purchased the other shares and in 1719 she settled two-thirds of the estate on her daughter Elizabeth and her future husband Thomas Knapp, a London merchant. The remaining third passed to a second daughter Grace in 1729, when she married Jeremiah Batley. By 1758 the estate seems to have been re-united under Rebecca Knapp, sister of Thomas Knapp. In the early 19th century Blanche farm was held by Rebecca Pocock, from whom it passed in 1837 to Louisa Edgell of London, whose family retained it until 1912 when Mrs. Jane Naper sold it to Captain Horace Kemble. Seven months later he sold the estate to Mrs. Trotter of Dyrham Park. In 1938 the entire Dyrham Park estate, including Blanche farm, was sold by Captain Frederick Trotter and in 1965 it passed to the G.L.C.[45]

The house, demolished in 1969, was a timber-framed structure, dating in part from the early 15th century. The ground storey had been largely re-built in brick but the original fenestration had been retained and on the west front were four lights with moulded wooden mullions. Two rooms on the upper floor had been lined with early-18th-century panelling. The house was surrounded by a moat, of which the north and south sides survive.

Knightsland, sometimes called 'Nicelands',[46] situated to the east of Dyrham Park, was in the possession of Richard Gardiner in the earlier 16th century.[47] In 1618 the estate, consisting of 120 a., was owned by William Crowley, who left it in tail male to his three sons.[48] In 1653 Henry Crowley sold Knightsland to William Godfrey (d. 1657).[49] It later passed to the Nicholls, who held it until 1716 when John Nicholl sold the property, then comprising 150 a., to Paul Jervis.[50] Jervis, by will dated 1718, left the estate to his wife Dorothy,[51] who afterwards married the Revd. James Knight and died in 1721, leaving Knightsland to her brother, Edward Peach,[52] who sold it to Admiral John Byng in 1752.[53] It has since remained in the hands of the Byng family and has been successively leased to Thomas Hill, the

[21] Ibid. 1560–63, 205.
[22] Ibid. 369.
[23] Guildhall MS. 9171.
[24] Wards 5/30/434.
[25] Cass, South Mimms, 23.
[26] C 142/376/124.
[27] See p. 302.
[28] Cass, op. cit. 23.
[29] Story of Potters Bar, 42.
[30] Story of Potters Bar, 56.
[31] Ibid.; Cal. Close, 1485–1500, 142.
[32] C.P. 25(2)/83/709 1 Mary Mich.
[33] Guildhall MS. 5884.
[34] C.P. 25(2)/173/45 Eliz. Hil.
[35] Story of Potters Bar, 56.
[36] See p. 298.
[37] M.L.R. 1804/6/403.
[38] Prob. 11/1597 (P.C.C. 553 Effingham).

[39] M.R.O., TA/S. Mimms.
[40] See p. 294.
[41] M.R.O., F. 58A.
[42] Story of Potters Bar, 56; for a plan of Darkes Farm in c. 1839, see M.R.O., Acc. 262/1(c).
[43] The following two paras. are based on inf. supplied by G.L.C. Hist. Buildings Div. and on Hist. Mon. Com. Mdx. 95.
[44] V.C.H. Warws. vii. 71.
[45] See pp. 284, 296.
[46] M.R.O., TA/S. Mimms.
[47] Herts. Rec. Off., 3AR 70r.
[48] Prob. 11/132 (P.C.C. 98 Meade); C 142/377/80.
[49] B.M. Add. Ch. 17814.
[50] M.L.R. 1716/1/174.
[51] Prob. 11/565 (P.C.C. 179 Tenison).
[52] M.L.R. 1737/2/442–443.
[53] Ibid. 1752/1/439.

Osmonds (until 1866), the Southwells (1867–86), the Durrants (1887–95), and to the Mossmans (since 1896).[54]

The house[55] has a west cross-wing, possibly early-16th-century, containing the service room, and a long hall-range of the latter part of the same century. Presumably it formerly extended farther east to provide space for a parlour. In the principal room on the first floor of the hall-range there is a late-16th-century painting of the Prodigal Son[56] and there are pattern paintings of similar date in another bedroom. One room in the cross-wing is lined with reset linen-fold panelling of the early 16th century, said to have been put in by John Byng c. 1750.[57] He was probably also responsible for casing much of the original timber-framing of the walls with brick and for reconstructing the roof.

Mimms Hall farm, which formed part of the demesne of South Mimms manor, was leased for 20 years to Freeman and Rayner in 1504[58] and for ten years to Thomas Smith in 1525.[59] It was occupied by the Burr family in the late 16th century, although there were several disputes over the tenancy.[60] Leases, usually for 21 years, were made to George Bayne (1597),[61] Thomas Conyers (1607),[62] A. Bigg (1624),[63] J. Clark (1647),[64] Edward Roberts (1681),[65] Elizabeth Roberts (1717),[66] and Thomas Kympton (1762).[67] In 1790 Mimms Hall was still occupied by the Kympton family,[68] and in 1808 the estate comprised 492 a.[69] The Farr family lived there in the 1830s and Thomas White was the tenant in 1841. From 1846 to 1924 it was leased to the Giddens family and in the 1930s to F. Woodall.[70]

Warrengate farm, another demesne farm, originated in the lands leased by Henry, Lord Windsor, to John Parrott in 1594.[71] They were leased to M. Barker and R. Wyllshere in 1597[72] but were in the occupation of John Grey and one Ketteridge in 1598.[73] Some of the lands were still held by the Ketteridge family in 1636.[74] The estate, comprising 241½ a., was leased for 21 years to Ralph Clarke in 1669,[75] and in 1681, when it was enlarged by a further 30 a., the lease was made to Richard Carrington.[76] Benjamin Gage became the tenant in 1760[77] and was still in possession in 1790.[78] The lease was held by Edward Whalley in 1841[79] and in

the late 19th and early 20th centuries by the Field family.[80]

In the later 16th century Robert Mayhew possessed a tenement and 60 a. which later formed part of the Bridgefoot estate.[81] His family, originating in Shoreditch, had been granted lands in South Mimms in 1420.[82] In addition to the Mayhews' 60 a., other Bridgefoot lands c. 1606 were held by Roger Hodsden (30 a.) and Richard Flexmore (6 a.).[83] Susan Mayhew married Christopher Colson in 1607[84] and was in possession in 1641.[85] By 1653 the estate of 96 a. was owned by John Colson[86] and c. 1670 Colson sold it to James Ware, a vintner of London,[87] who in 1672 left it to his three daughters.[88] By 1714 Ware's son-in-law, Daniel Luddington of the Middle Temple, was in possession of the estate, to which had been added the Badger in Wash Lane and land called 'Monsieurs'. About 1717 it was bought from the Luddingtons by Edward Vincent,[89] whose family still held 151 a. in 1842.[90] Bridgefoot passed from the Vincents to S. O. Percival in 1848, who sold it to C. H. Cock in 1872.[91] After Cock's death in 1903 it was bought by the Byngs, who leased it out.[92] Lord Herbert Scott was the tenant there in the early 20th century.[93]

About 1670 the estate incorporated a house called Ottways Garden, which in 1680 was alternatively known as Bridgefoot Farm,[94] a name which survives in a building at the bottom of Bridgefoot Lane. The Vincents built Bridgefoot House farther east in the mid 18th century; it was of yellow-brick and stone dressings, with a slate mansard roof, a parapet and central pediment, and semicircular-headed windows.[95] The house was replaced in the mid 20th century by a red-brick building.

Green Dragon Lane farm, near Dancers Hill, originated in a house and land called Richards and Coxlands, which were held by the Catcher family in the 1560s.[96] In 1595 the estate was conveyed by them to Ambrose Roystone,[97] who was still in possession in 1605.[98] By 1662 Coxlands was in the hands of James Fletcher, and it descended in the Fletcher family.[99] In 1720 the estate, 81 a.,[1] belonged to James Brydges, duke of Chandos,[2] from whom it passed in 1744 to his surviving son, Henry. An Act of 1746 authorized Henry to sell much of his property[3]

54 M.R.O., TA/S. Mimms; Brittain, *South Mymms*, 53–4.
55 Hist. Mon. Com. *Mdx.* 95–6.
56 *The Times*, 6th Aug. 1935.
57 Brittain, *South Mymms*, 53 and plate facing p. 42.
58 Hatfield C.F.E.P. (Deeds) 219/9.
59 Ibid. (Deeds) 219/13.
60 Ibid. (Legal) 28/8; 213/1; 33/17; (Box) T/28.
61 Ibid. (Deeds) 153/2.
62 Ibid. 89/7.
63 Ibid. 162/20.
64 Ibid. 127/18.
65 Ibid. (Legal) 126/7.
66 Ibid. (S. Mimms) 1/5.
67 Ibid. (Deeds) 87/12.
68 M.L.R. 1790/8/122.
69 Ibid. 1808/1/179.
70 Brittain, *South Mymms*, 11; M.R.O., TA/S. Mimms.
71 Hatfield C.F.E.P. (Deeds) 200/9.
72 Ibid. 147/2.
73 Ibid. (Gen.) 136/2.
74 Ibid. (Deeds) 162/14.
75 Ibid. 127/15.
76 Ibid. (Legal) 126/7.
77 Ibid. (S. Mimms) 1/7.
78 M.L.R. 1790/8/122.
79 M.R.O., TA/S. Mimms.
80 Hatfield C.F.E.P. (S. Mimms) 4/124; Brittain, *South Mymms*, 141.
81 Hatfield C.F.E.P. (Ct. Roll) 23/16; (Deeds) 280/10.
82 C.P. 25(1)/152/87/30.
83 Hatfield C.F.E.P. (Deeds) 280/10.
84 M.R.O., D.R.O. 5/A1/1.   85 E 179/253/8.
86 Hatfield C.F.E.P. (Accts.) 47/15.
87 E 179/253/22.
88 Prob. 11/339 (P.C.C. 67 Eure).
89 Herts. Rec. Off., D/ETr/T.14; Hatfield C.F.E.P. (S. Mimms Ct. Bk.) i, 106.
90 M.R.O., TA/S. Mimms.
91 Hatfield C.F.E.P. (S. Mimms Ct. Bk.), v, p. 261; ibid. p. 479.
92 Brittain, *South Mymms*, 63.
93 *Kelly's Dir. Mdx.* (1910).
94 Herts. Rec. Off., D/ETr/T.14.
95 Min. of Town and Country Planning, list of buildings (1948); Guildhall Pr. W/SOU(1).
96 Hatfield C.F.E.P. (Ct. Roll) 23/16; Req. 2/180/15.
97 Guildhall MS. 5455.
98 Ibid. MS. 5885.
99 Hatfield C.F.E.P. (Gen.) 106/13; Guildhall MS. 5884.
1 M.R.O., Acc. 262/72/1.
2 Guildhall MS. 5884.
3 Guildhall MS. 5454; see p. 115.

and in 1747 Green Dragon Lane farm was bought by Robert Vincent,[4] whose family sold it to the Byngs in 1838.[5] Norfolk Lodge, of white brick with stone dressings, replaced the old farm-house c. 1863.[6]

In 1592 Harrow School held land called Denhams in South Mimms and Boltons in North Mimms.[7] In 1560 the lands had belonged to Gilbert Gerard,[8] a friend of John Lyon, the founder of the school.[9] Denhams comprised some 42 a. adjacent to Darkes Lodge[10] and by an Act of 1797 was exchanged with John Hunter,[11] the owner of Darkes.[12]

The Clare Hall or Clay Hall estate originated in c. 40 a. acquired piecemeal between 1730 and 1745 by Thomas Roberts, a linen-draper. The property included the Prince's Arms, with 4 a. called Marriotts, and fields called Upper Reeves, Pond Reeves, and Rushy Reeves (30 a.). Roberts died bankrupt c. 1747 and his widow Anna sold the estate to Temple West,[13] who served under Admiral John Byng at Minorca.[14] After West's death in 1757 Clare Hall passed to his son, who sold it to James Barwick in 1779. From the Barwicks it descended in 1797 to Catherine Sharp[15] who was still in possession in 1842.[16] By 1874 the estate was in the hands of Edward Wright,[17] a stockbroker.[18] On his death in 1886 it passed to Theresa Southwell, Louisa Limes, Mary Morgan, and Henrietta Williams,[19] who founded St. Monica's priory there.[20] In 1896 Clare Hall, comprising c. 70 a., became a private smallpox hospital.[21]

Although described as newly-erected c. 1745,[22] the house in 1973 appeared to be largely late-18th-century, with various 19th-century additions. It is a plain red-brick building.[23] The street wall and gate contain cherub-heads and knots on the buttresses, said to have come from the Wren church of St. Antholin (City of London.)[24]

Wrotham Park,[25] lying south of Potters Bar, consisted of the land purchased by Admiral John Byng in 1750. Totalling 150 a., the estate then comprised a house known as Pinchbank, Sheepcotes, an inn called the Chequers (renamed the Angel by 1750), and several other farms. Pinchbank and its abutments (80 a.) were first recorded in 1310 when it was said that Reynold Frowyk (d. 1300) had held them of Roger Lewknor.[26] In 1479 the lands were granted by Henry Frowyk of Old Fold to John Goodere of Hadley as part of a marriage settlement. William Stanford obtained the manor of Monken Hadley and land at Kitts End from the Gooderes in 1544, and his son Robert sold the manor and land at Pinchbank to William Kympton in 1574. Pinchbank and the rest of the lands later passed to John Howkins (d. 1678).

In 1713 another branch of the Howkins family sold them to Thomas Reynolds, a director of the South Seas Co., who changed the name of the house from Pinchbank to Strangeways and whose son Francis sold the estate to Admiral Byng.[27] Byng built a new 'stareabout pile'[28] to the north-west of Pinchbank by 1754 and called it Wrotham Park, after Wrotham (Kent), the Byngs' original home. On the admiral's execution in 1757 the estate passed to his nephew, George Byng, M.P., and later to his son George. In 1847 it descended to General Sir John Byng, who had been created earl of Strafford,[29] and thereafter it remained a Byng seat.

At the inclosure of Enfield Chase 56 a. were allotted to Wrotham Park, which in 1859 was further enlarged by the purchase of the New Lodge estate.[30] Thereafter Wrotham Park (c. 286 a.)[31] occupied a triangle of land, bounded by Kitts End Road, Dancers Hill Road, and the Great North Road.

Wrotham Park[32] is situated on the edge of a small valley and the principal front has fine views to the south-west across its park-land and beyond. The house was built on a virgin site in the early 1750s to the design of Isaac Ware and has been described as his best work. As first built it had a central block of two storeys fronted by an Ionic portico which is approached by curving staircases. Short wings of one storey linked the block to terminal pavilions with canted bay fronts and domed roofs. The original plan did not provide as much accommodation as its overall size might have suggested and some internal rearrangement had already taken place by 1771. Then c. 1810 an upper storey was added to the wings and in 1854 they were extended eastward to line up with the central portion of that front, which probably received its projecting porch at the same time. The house was severely damaged by fire in 1883 and in the course of reconstruction an extra storey was added to the central block and shallow bays replaced the original venetian windows of the main front. The plan of the principal rooms was to a large extent restored but the existing decoration is much plainer than it must once have been.

The early-19th-century stables are a short distance north of the house and were joined to it in 1854 by a low service court. The landscaped park, formed when the house was begun, extends in all directions. Against the west front a terraced lawn was laid out in the 19th century and to the north-west there is a Victorian garden with an iron-framed orangery of simple Gothic design. The south lodges are early-19th-century, the lodge to the north is later.

Oakmere,[33] on the eastern side of High Street,

[4] Guildhall MS. 5454.
[5] Hatfield C.F.E.P. (S. Mimms) 2/51.
[6] Herts. Rec. Off., D/ETr/T.18.
[7] M.R.O., Acc. 398/22.
[8] C.P. 25(2)/259/2 Eliz. East.
[9] See V.C.H. Mdx. i. 299.
[10] Guildhall MS. 5521.
[11] M.R.O., Acc. 398/22.
[12] See p. 287.
[13] M.R.O., Acc. 172/3.
[14] D.N.B.
[15] Hatfield C.F.E.P. (Ct. Bk.) iii, 1774–1802.
[16] M.R.O., TA/S. Mimms.
[17] Ret. of Owners of Land [C. 1097], H.C. (1874), lxii(1).
[18] Brittain, South Mymms, 145.
[19] Hatfield C.F.E.P. (Ct. Bk.) vii, 1873–1913.
[20] See p. 302.

[21] F. A. H. Simmonds, Hist. of Clare Hall Hosp. 10; see p. 297.
[22] M.R.O., Acc. 172/3.
[23] Guildhall Pr. W/SOU(1).
[24] Pevsner, Mdx. 143.
[25] Unless otherwise stated, the acct. is based upon Barnet & Dist. Loc. Hist. Soc. Bulletin, xvi (Nov. 1970).
[26] Year Bk. 2 & 3 Edw. II (Selden Soc. xix), 162.
[27] See D.N.B.
[28] Torrington Diaries, ed. C. B. Andrews (1938), iv. 149.
[29] D.N.B.
[30] See p. 278.
[31] Kelly's Dir. Mdx. (1908).
[32] The foll. three paras. are based on Country Life, xl. 404–9, 458–66 and illus.; see also above, plate facing p. 256.
[33] Except where otherwise stated, the foll. two paras. are based on Story of Potters Bar, 69.

Potters Bar, originated in the 108 a. of the former Chase allotted to James Cecil, earl of Salisbury, under the inclosure award of 1781.[34] In 1787 the land was sold to John Hunt of Gobions, Brookhams Park, who gave it to his niece, Amelia Chauncy, on her marriage to Col. W. L. Carpenter, Deputy Adjutant-General in Bombay. In 1861 the estate belonged to Carpenter's daughter Margaret and her husband Horatio Kemble, from whom it passed to their son, Lt.-Col. Horace Kemble (d. 1935). He leased the property to the Lofts family, c. 1890–1915, and then to Mrs. William Forbes until her death in 1936. Kemble sold most of Oakmere in 1920, retaining the house and grounds, which were subsequently purchased by Potters Bar U.D.C. in 1937.

Oakmere House was built in 1840 on the site of small encroachments into the Chase, to the west of Lord Salisbury's allotment.[35] The house is in the Italianate style and retains the external alterations made by Horatio Kemble in the 1860s. Since 1937 it has been used for education offices, a Citizens' Advice Bureau, and various local functions.

ECONOMIC HISTORY. AGRICULTURE. In 1086 South Mimms was not separately assessed but was included in the manor of Edmonton.[36] It seems likely that most of it was covered by forest until the 12th century and that the manorial lands were gradually extended by assarting. By 1268 there were ten virgates in villeinage.[37] It was said in 1295 that the villeins were tallaged at the lord's will, but that they had never paid more than 6d. yearly. The free tenants owed quit-rents totalling £6 19s. 6d. and the copyhold rents amounted to 26s. 8d. The customary tenants owed 806 days' work at ½d. and 606 days' work were due in harvest at 1d. a day.[38] The rents and customary services were still the same in 1349, when the manor consisted of 400 a. of arable, 15 a. of meadow, 15 a. of wood, and 15 a. of fresh land (terra frisca).[39]

The demesne was leased at least from 1394[40] and by the 1590s had become divided into four main parcels:[41] Mimms Hall farm,[42] Warrengate farm,[43] lands called Tapperdel and Dennysmead,[44] and a farm of c. 57 a., the largest part of which was 30 a. called Long field.[45] It was usually leased for 21 years,[46] although the woods were sometimes leased separately for 30 years.[47] There were 68 tenants on the capital manor c. 1600, of whom about two-thirds were copyholders. Quit-rents had fallen from the mid 14th century to £4 1s. 2d. and copyhold rents

had risen to £8 17s. 6d.,[48] while in 1688 free and customary rents amounted to £26 13s. 10d.[49] A few copyholds were enfranchised during the lordship and at the instigation of Henry, Lord Windsor (d. 1605),[50] but most took place in the late 19th century.[51]

Arable farming predominated in the later 13th century, accounting for 400 a. or 90 per cent of the demesne of South Mimms manor.[52] Nearly 47 per cent of the demesne of Wyllyotts manor in 1479 consisted of arable, slightly over 25 per cent was pasture, and the rest was woodland.[53] Dairies at Old Fold and Durhams were mentioned in 1442.[54] and such names as Old Fold, Shepecotefeld (1375), and Shepherds' Dell[55] indicate sheep-farming; in 1340 one-ninth of wool and lambs was paid by Henry Frowyk of Old Fold.[56] Between 1613 and 1617 twenty inhabitants of South Mimms were licensed as badgers or kidders.[57] There was a rabbit warren on the demesne of South Mimms manor by 1313 and another in the northern part of Old Fold by 1442.[58]

A common field called Aldwick, south of Bridgefoot House and adjoining Mimms Wash,[59] was so named by 1437.[60] There were frequent disputes over the field, as in 1454 between Richard Style, farmer of the demesne of South Mimms manor, and the tenants who had put their beasts to graze in Aldwick. Style had not repaired the gate and hedge at the adjoining Tapperdelgate field and impounded the beasts which strayed there from the common.[61] During the 18th century there were several presentments for growing wheat at Aldwick when it should have been left fallow.[62] According to manorial custom arable lands were to lie fallow every third year, and barley could not be sown after the wheat crop without letting the land lie as pasture for one year.[63] In the late 18th century the rotation of crops on the clay was summer fallow, followed by wheat, then beans, pease, or oats and summer fallow; on the better soil it was turnips on the summer fallows, barley with broad clover, clover fed or mown, wheat on clover lay, with one ploughing.[64] In 1842 Aldwick was still divided into strips and described as a common field.[65]

Large pieces of waste at Bentley Heath and Kitts End amounted to some 300 a.,[66] while land at the southern end of South Mimms village originally formed Mimms Green.[67] The common land at Kitts End Green, containing two fishponds which were formerly gravel pits, by 1781 had been divided into seven allotments,[68] the waste at Bentley Heath and Kitts End having been added to the South Mimms

[34] M.R.O., F. 84/6b.
[35] Ibid.
[36] V.C.H. Mdx. i. 126.
[37] C 132/35/12.
[38] C 133/72/4.
[39] Lysons, Mdx. Parishes, 227.
[40] See p. 282.
[41] Hatfield C.F.E.P. (Gen.) 136/2.
[42] See p. 288.
[43] See p. 288.
[44] Hatfield C.F.E.P. (Deeds) 186/4, 127/22.
[45] Ibid. (Accts.) 111/17.
[46] e.g. ibid. (Legal) 126/7; (Deeds) 1/7.
[47] e.g. ibid. (Deeds) 1/7.
[48] Ibid. (Accts.) 12/36.
[49] Ibid. (Accts.) 65/15.
[50] Hatfield C.F.E.P. (Gen.) 66/7.
[51] e.g. M.A.F. 9/185/10305; M.A.F. 9/185/11559; M.A.F. 9/185/14118; M.A.F. 9/185/18774; M.A.F. 9/185/19577.

[52] C 133/72/4.
[53] Lysons, Mdx. Parishes, 228.
[54] Cass, South Mimms, 86.
[55] P.N. Mdx. (E.P.N.S.), 213.
[56] Inq. Non. (Rec. Com.), 195.
[57] Mdx. Sess. Recs. i. 256–7, 449; ii. 294; iii. 69; iv. 25–6, 159, 285.
[58] Cass, South Mimms, 85.
[59] Brittain, South Mymms, 90.
[60] Hatfield C.F.E.P. (Ct. Roll) 14/27, f. 4.
[61] Ibid. f. 2.
[62] Hatfield C.F.E.P. (Ct. Bk.) i, 1702–31, p. 25; (Ct. Bk.) ii, 1732–73, p. 2.
[63] Ibid. (Legal) 126/7.
[64] V.C.H. Mdx. ii. 208.
[65] M.R.O., TA/S. Mimms.
[66] Hatfield C.P. (Legal) 90/4.
[67] e.g. Hatfield C.F.E.P. (Ct. Bk.) iii, 1774–1802, p. 354.
[68] H. M. Baker, Barnet and Dist. Loc. Hist. Soc. Bull. xvi.

allotment of the Chase.[69] In 1849 following upon an investigation into common rights it was ruled that the ratepayers might pasture their beasts on the common during the whole of the fallow year until Michaelmas, and every other year after the crops were removed until Candlemas following. Until 1829 it had been customary to have two crops and one fallow, and between 1829 and 1849 three crops and a fallow.[70] By 1864 it seems that the claim to common rights had been extinguished by purchase, for in that year it was stated that the parish had no right to interfere with the inclosure of waste land at Mimms Wash and Bentley Heath.[71]

Freeholders of the manor of South Mimms had enjoyed common pasture for their cattle at all seasons and pannage for their pigs in mast time within the borders of Enfield Chase. They also had the right to take bushes from the Chase, although in return they had to maintain the fences of their ingrounds bordering on the Chase.[72] Similar rights were enjoyed by the tenants of Old Fold,[73] by virtue of which that manor was awarded an allotment in the Chase in 1777.[74] The inhabitants of South Mimms frequently complained about their loss of rights, especially during the Interregnum[75] when the government proposed to sell the Chase in lots. Despite restocking at the Restoration, the parishioners of South Mimms in 1686 broke down the fence that ran from Hadley windmill to Potters Bar.[76] Apart from concerted attacks various inroads were made into the Chase and much wood was destroyed.[77] In 1762 a blacksmith of Potters Bar was imprisoned for destroying several young beech trees and also sentenced to monthly floggings in Enfield market place.[78] In 1770 the duchy allowed several occupiers in Wyllyotts manor to take leases of the encroachments that they had made upon the Chase.[79] With the inclosure of the Chase in 1777, South Mimms was allotted 1,026 a. 3p. (excluding the 36 a. given to Old Fold) in a long sweep stretching from its Herts. boundary to Hatfield.[80] In contrast to most of the Enfield allotments, which remained uncultivated, the South Mimms allotments were soon tilled.[81] Byng was said to have a farm as his portion of the allotment, which might 'challenge some of the best land in the kingdom for the "burthen" it produces and for the peculiar good husbandry which is bestowed on it'.[82]

By c. 1606 565 a., or almost 69 per cent, of the demesne of South Mimms manor was arable and pasture, 30 a. was meadow, and 228 a. woodland. The annual yield from much of the arable was low, as oats had been grown there year after year without at any time leaving the land fallow. A low value was also given for the meadow, since it was all

upland.[83] By c. 1800 arable covered less than 42 per cent of the parish, the greater part of the farm-land supplying hay which was sold in London.[84] In 1867 permanent grass accounted for 79 per cent, or 4,371 a. out of a total of 5,485 a. under cultivation,[85] and by 1897 it had increased by another 412 a.[86] By 1971 arable had shrunk to a mere 10 per cent out of 5,003 a. of farm-land. Fields used for grazing, however, had expanded to cover 1,607 a.[87] and by 1937 they exceeded the amount of grass for mowing.[88] By 1957, when there were still 3,857 a. of farm-land, the proportion of arable had increased to almost 33 per cent, the rest being meadow.[89]

Corn, chiefly oats, was grown on 36 per cent of the arable in 1801. Peas were the largest green crop, covering 108 a., while beans were grown on 87 a., turnips or rape on 62 a., and potatoes on 9 a.[90] By 1867, when corn accounted for 41 per cent of the arable, wheat had become more important than oats, and there were fewer green than root crops.[91] Seventy years later no beans or peas were grown and root crops had declined, while corn gradually assumed greater importance.[92] In 1957 there were 1,335 a. of corn, of which barley covered 437 a., wheat 351 a., and oats 220 a. The increase in barley was presumably associated with the keeping of beef cattle.[93]

Sheep were the main livestock in 1867, when 1,947 were kept; numbers fell to 1,266 in 1897 but rose again to 1,767 in 1917. Cows, particularly dairy cows, increased from 253 in 1867 to 1,059 in 1917, until by 1957 there were as many as 1,134, compared with 851 sheep. In 1867 554 pigs were kept but the number afterwards declined, only to rise rapidly again to 858 in 1937 and to 1,988 in 1957. Horses reached their highest number of 270 in 1917, falling to 28 in 1957. The most numerous livestock in 1957 were fowls, when there were as many as 4,983.[94]

In 1867 there were 58 agricultural holdings and in 1917 there were 65, of which 37 were less than 50 a. and only one was over 300 a. Of the 5,003 a. of farm-land in 1917 115 a. were owned and 3,888 a. rented.[95] In 1973 there were 12 farms, most of them leased from the G.L.C. or from the Wrotham Park estate.[96] Of the larger farms Fold farm in Galley Lane comprised 168 a. and was a dairy farm with 200 cows; farther north Blanche farm, comprising 230 a., was also used mainly for dairy-farming, with 180 cows; c. 133 a. at Knightsland farm were used for crops. Horses were kept at Wrotham Park, Elm, and Bridgefoot farms.

WOODS. Foresters were recorded in the 14th and 15th centuries.[97] Woodland made up no more than

[69] M.R.O., Acc. 262/1/134.
[70] M.R.O., D.R.O. 5/C1/4 (vestry min. bk. 1846–88), 2 Mar. 1849.
[71] Ibid. Dec. 1864.
[72] D.L. 1/121/E5; Hatfield C.F.E.P. (Legal) 33/21; C.P. (Legal) 90/4.
[73] D.L. 1/54/F7; M.R.O., Acc. 351/660.
[74] M.R.O., MR/DE S. Mimms (1781).
[75] T.L.M.A.S. x. 293.
[76] Brittain, South Mymms, 61–2.
[77] e.g. D.L. 1/170/S4.
[78] Brittain, South Mymms, 62.
[79] Entry bk. 24 May 1770 penes Duchy of Lanc. office.
[80] M.R.O., MR/DE S. Mimms.
[81] V.C.H. Mdx. ii. 210.
[82] Middleton, View, 522.

[83] Hatfield C.F.E.P. (Gen.) 66/7.
[84] H.O. 67/16.
[85] M.A.F. 68/136.
[86] M.A.F. 68/1675.
[87] M.A.F. 68/2815.
[88] M.A.F. 68/3837.
[89] M.A.F. 68/4576.
[90] H.O. 67/16.
[91] M.A.F. 68/136.
[92] M.A.F. 68/3837.
[93] M.A.F. 68/4576.
[94] M.A.F. 68/136; M.A.F. 68/1675; M.A.F. 68/2815; M.A.F. 68/3837; M.A.F. 68/4576.
[95] M.A.F. 68/136; M.A.F. 68/2815.
[96] The rest of the para. is based on inf. supplied by the occupiers.
[97] C.P. 25(1)/152/87/30; Guildhall MS. 6809.

3 per cent of the 445 a. in demesne of South Mimms manor in 1349[98] but by 1598 it was calculated as 240 a., forming some 29 per cent of the 829 a. in demesne. Woods comprised the 109 a. of Osgarsland, the 68 a. of Tothill, the 31 a. of Parsonage bushes, as well as Moor grove, Cherrytree grove, and Kings close which together covered 31 a.[99] In 1340 the manor of Durhams possessed 20 a. of woodland among its 324 a. in South Mimms,[1] and c. 28 per cent of Wyllyotts manor was wooded in 1479.[2] In 1442 the two main areas of woodland on the manor of Old Fold were said to be in the west and in the north at Heron grove adjoining the rabbit warren.[3]

Woods and underwoods were often reserved in late-16th- and early-17th-century leases,[4] although tenants of South Mimms manor were granted hedge-bote in Enfield Chase.[5] The right to fell wood at certain periods was sold by the lord of South Mimms, provided that sufficient storers were left.[6] In the early 17th century the right was enjoyed by F. Page, an officer in the king's woodyards, to whom the wood-grounds of the demesne had been leased for 30 years.[7] Woods tended to be leased or sold separately[8] and were frequently inclosed in the 17th century.[9] They were often leased out in the late 17th and 18th centuries, mostly to tenants of the farmlands, although the lord reserved timber, young saplings, and pollard trees.[10]

There were many presentments from medieval times for illegally taking wood.[11] On the demesne of Wyllyotts oaks were felled in Halfpenny grove in 1594 so that it might be converted to meadow or pasture.[12] In 1620 woodland was said to comprise 12 per cent of the known area of the parish.[13] By 1842 woods made up 97 a., or under 2 per cent, of South Mimms, and comprised chiefly Wrotham and Dyrham Parks, and Mimmshall, Furzefield, Pilvage, Chase, Fir, and Spoilbank woods.[14]

MILLS. Isabel Frowyk held a windmill in South Mimms in 1289. It probably stood between Old Fold and Christ Church.[15] A mill was among the appurtenances of Old Fold held by the Frowyks in 1310,[16] and among those leased in 1639 to Thomas Allen.[17]

There was a windmill on the demesne of South Mimms in 1295[18] and probably by c. 1220, when Gervase and Arnold, millers of South Mimms, are mentioned.[19] It was recorded again in 1336[20] and in 1349 was said to be worth 13s. 4d.[21] It presumably stood near the site of the manor-house in Windmill field.[22]

A third mill, of unspecified type, was included in 1668 among the outbuildings of the Blue Bell Inn, Mimms Side.[23] A mill also figured among the property of Steven Bowman in 1628.[24] Later it was apparently forfeited as deodand but granted to William Bowman by the earl of Salisbury in 1668.[25]

MARKETS AND FAIRS. A market at Barnet, granted by King John to the monks of St. Albans in 1199 and held on Thursdays,[26] also served South Mimms. It was originally held in Barnet but by 1889 it had been moved to South Mimms to a site in St. Albans Road.[27] In 1967 the market was privately managed and had become a stall market held twice weekly.[28]

A fair, mainly for pleasure, was held on Whit Tuesday on South Mimms Green.[29] It was apparently discontinued soon after 1899.[30] Two annual fairs, each lasting three days, were held at Barnet.[31] The April fair, which was a cattle and horse fair, had died out before the end of the 19th century,[32] but the September fair, 'for cattle and pleasure',[33] continued to flourish, being condemned by schoolmasters at South Mimms and Potters Bar.[34] In 1967 the September fair was still held and had been combined with a horse fair.[35]

TRADE AND INDUSTRY. Apart from a blacksmith mentioned c. 1220,[36] some of the earliest known tradesmen were maltmen, recorded in 1417 and again in 1420, 1423, and 1447.[37] Others included wheelwrights in 1420 and 1485[38] and upholsterers in 1588.[39] In the 17th century residents included an upholsterer, plasterer, shoemaker, tanner, tailor, cordwainer, carpenters, brewers, and oatmeal makers.[40]

Chalk pits in the north-west of the parish seem to have been in use from medieval times and, in the 1960s, were worked by the Barnet Lime Co.[41] Charcoal-burning gave rise to the name Colliers Lane (recorded in 1453),[42] and a collier is first mentioned in 1382.[43] Page, lessee of the demesne woods of South Mimms manor, was a charcoal-burner c.

[98] Lysons, *Mdx. Parishes*, 227.
[99] Hatfield C.F.E.P. (Gen.) 136/2.
[1] C.P. 25(1)/287/40/287.
[2] Lysons, *Mdx. Parishes*, 228.
[3] Cass, *South Mimms*, 85.
[4] e.g. M.R.O., Acc. 349/45; Hatfield C.F.E.P. (Deeds) 162/14, 153/2.
[5] Hatfield C.P. (Legal) 90/4.   [6] Ibid. (Gen.) 66/7.
[7] Ibid. (Gen.) 66/7; (Deeds) 1/7.
[8] Ibid. (Legal) 38/2; (Deeds) 169/17; (Gen.) 42/19, 18/29.
[9] Ibid. (Deeds) 127/15; 127/18.
[10] Ibid. (Legal) 126/7; (Deeds) 87/12; 127/15.
[11] Ibid. (Ct. Roll) 14/27, ff. 1, 7; (Ct. Bk.) ii, 1723–73, p. 294; B.M. Add. Ch. 8142, p. 2.
[12] M.R.O., F. 58A.
[13] Hatfield C.F.E.P. (Bills) 113/5.
[14] M.R.O., TA/S. Mimms.
[15] Brittain, *South Mymms*, 14.
[16] *Yr. Bk.* 2 & 3 Edw. II (Seld. Soc. xix), 162.
[17] M.R.O., Acc. 351/683.   [18] C 133/72/4.
[19] *Cartulary of St. Barts. Hosp.* no. 1222.
[20] C 135/47/11.
[21] Lysons, *Mdx. Parishes*, 227.
[22] Windmill field is on the plan of the manorial demesne, Hatfield C.F.E.P. (Gen.) 62/5.
[23] M.R.O., Acc. 548/39.
[24] Hatfield C.F.E.P. Box D/7.
[25] Ibid. C.P. (Legal) 90/4.
[26] *Rot. Chart.* (Rec. Com.), 11; see also *V.C.H. Herts.* ii. 330.
[27] *Kelly's Dir. Barnet* (1889–90).
[28] Barnet L.B., *Official Guide* [1967].
[29] Brittain, *South Mymms*, 121, 132; Hatfield C.F.E.P. (S. Mimms) 3/123.
[30] Hatfield C.F.E.P. (S. Mimms) 3/123.
[31] *V.C.H. Herts.* ii. 330.
[32] Brittain, *South Mymms*, 121.
[33] Pigot, *Com. Dir.* (1832–4).
[34] M.R.O., MCC/E P.B. 1869; D.R.O. 5/G1/1, p. 17.
[35] Barnet L.B., *Official Guide* [1967].
[36] *Cartulary of St. Barts. Hosp.* no. 1222.
[37] *Cal. Close*, 1413–19, 437; 1419–22, 67; 1422–29, 134; 1447–54, 34.
[38] Ibid. 1419–22, 68; 1476–85, 412.
[39] *Mdx. Cnty. Recs.* i. 175.
[40] *Mdx. Sess. Recs.* i. 128–9; iii. 242; iv. 10; Prob. 11/286, 292, 294 (P.C.C. 6, 333, 437 Pell); Prob. 11/276 (P.C.C. 245 Weeton). Hatfield C.F.E.P. (Gen.) 116/7; 106/7.
[41] *Barnet and Dist. Local Hist. Soc. Bull.* xv.
[42] Hatfield C.F.E.P. (Ct. Roll) 14/27, f. 4v.
[43] *Story of Potters Bar*, 56.

1606[44] and several other colliers are recorded in the 17th century.[45] There were gravel pits at Kitts End, Bentley Heath, and in what later became Oakmere Park.[46] Fuel for making bricks seems to have come from Enfield Chase and, from the fabric of Ladbrooke farm-house, it seems that the industry was in existence in Elizabethan times.[47] A 7-acre brickyard lay north of the site of St. John's school, Potters Bar, in 1658[48] and a kiln (probably for bricks) was among the goods of William Bowman in 1668.[49] Several bricklayers are recorded in the early 17th century[50] and a cottage built on the Chase was called the Brick Kiln in 1781.[51] Two fields in the north of the parish belonging to Darkes and to Warrengate farm were both known as Brick Kiln field.[52] A cottage, standing on the corner of Kitts End Green and known by 1881 as Basketts Lot, was formerly described as Silk Weavers Hall.[53]

In 1801 South Mimms contained 99 farm workers and as many as 95 tradesmen or craftsmen. Almost 89 per cent of the population fell within neither category. By 1831, when numbers had increased by only 15 per cent, 298 families were employed in agriculture, 113 in trade or manufacturing, and 32 in other occupations, most of them in domestic service.[54]

In the mid 19th century, when most inhabitants were still engaged in agriculture,[55] tradesmen and craftsmen lived mainly in High Street, Barnet, although there were some in High Street, Potters Bar, and in South Mimms village. The presence of several wheelwrights, harness makers, coach makers, blacksmiths, and saddlers was a consequence of traffic along the Great North Road. Specialized tradesmen included a white-smith and bell-hanger, a bird-preserver, a straw-bonnet maker, and a hurdle-maker.[56] In the late 19th century there were commercial premises in several Barnet streets including two chandlers' shops and a hay dealer's in Calvert Road, and grocers and an umbrella maker's in Union Street.[57] A dental factory had been established in Alston Road by 1897[58] and was still there in 1914. Several laundries were started in Barnet in the early 20th century in Queen's, New, and Sebright roads. There were still craftsmen connected with horse traffic, as well as several gamekeepers and gardeners employed at the large residences.[59]

The building of the G.N.R. line between King's Cross and York c. 1850 eventually led to the growth of Darkes Lane, Potters Bar, as a shopping and industrial centre. After the Second World War an industrial estate was built adjacent to the railway goods yard and in 1973 was occupied by 14 firms.

They included Amalgamated Plastics Leaside Works, Kemlows Diecasting Products, and other light engineering works. The Progress Press has been in Station Close since 1966 and practises offset lithography.[60] In 1973 18 firms were occupying sites on both sides of Cranborne Road in the north of the parish. Among them was a branch of W. Harold Perry, the largest Ford main dealers, which opened in Potters Bar in 1959 and by 1973 employed 80 persons.[61] Other comparatively large firms included C. P. Roberts & Co., Declon Foam Plastics, and J. & L. Randall, toy manufacturers. Knight Strip Metals, after thirteen years in Station Close, in 1973 moved into a warehouse and factory at Knuway House, Cranborne Road, where it made high-precision metal foils and strip and supplied many aircraft parts.[62] Other light engineering firms occupied sites in St. Albans Road and High Street, Potters Bar. In 1973 considerable building was being carried out in Potters Bar, and a new factory, Hoval Boilers, employing 86 people, had been erected in Mutton Lane, on land owned by the Unilever Pension Trust of Blackfriars, London.

SOCIAL LIFE. There were frequent complaints of illegal hunting both in the South Mimms warren and in Enfield Chase.[63] The lords of South Mimms and Old Fold manors claimed hunting rights in the Chase,[64] which were confirmed in 1563 for Ralph Waller, the tenant of Old Fold.[65] The Enfield Chase Staghounds met in South Mimms until c. 1918 and the Old Berkeley hunted there until the foundation of Major Smith-Bosanquet's Hunt in 1908.[66] Many boys were kept away from school in the 1880s and 1890s in order to beat the woods for shooting parties.[67]

There were 28 licensed victuallers in 1715,[68] about the same number throughout the 18th century,[69] and 20 in 1820.[70] Vicars in the late 19th century criticized the prevalence of drunkenness: P. F. Hammond refused the pot of beer offered him at the church door in 1889[71] and his successor, W. H. Wood, urged that the number of public houses should be reduced. In 1894, besides beershops, there were eight public houses in South Mimms village, serving a population of 250.[72] In 1876 a branch of the Church of England temperance society was formed in South Mimms and by 1885 it had over 170 members.[73] The licence of the Queen's Head was withdrawn in 1892 and that of the Greyhound, restored in 1894, in 1918.[74] Many tea rooms and coffee taverns were opened, especially in High Street,

44 Hatfield C.F.E.P. (Gen.) 66/7.
45 M.R.O., MJSP 1617/1.
46 Hatfield C.F.E.P. (Ct. Bk.) vii; Barnet and Dist. Loc. Hist. Soc. Bull. xvi.
47 See p. 276.
48 M.R.O., F. 57.
49 Hatfield C.P. (Legal) 90/4.
50 Mdx. Sess. Recs. iv. 263; Hatfield C.F.E.P. (Gen.) 116/7.
51 M.R.O., F. 84/6b.
52 Hatfield C.F.E.P. (S. Mimms) 2/58; M.R.O., F. 58A.
53 Hatfield C.F.E.P. (Ct. Bk.) vii.
54 Census, 1801, 1831.
55 Ibid. 1851.
56 Kelly's Dirs. Essex, Herts., Mdx. (1845, 1851, 1855).
57 Kelly's Dirs. Barnet (1889–90, 1893–4).
58 O.S. Map 6", Mdx. VI. NE. (1897 edn.).
59 Kelly's Dirs. Mdx. (1902, 1906, 1910); Kelly's Dir.

Herts. (1902); Kelly's Dirs. Barnet (1906, 1909–10, 1913–14).
60 Ex inf. Mr. J. V. Rout.
61 Ex inf. Mr. J. D. Hunter.
62 Ex inf. Mr. B. W. Knight.
63 Hatfield C.F.E.P. (Ct. Roll) 14/28, f. 4; D.L. 1/170/54.
64 Hatfield C.F.E.P. (Legal) 33/21; M.R.O., Acc. 351/660.
65 D.L. 1/54/F7.
66 Brittain, South Mymms, 122.
67 M.R.O., D.R.O. 5/G1/1 (sch. log bk. 1870–95), 209, 214.
68 M.R.O., L.V. 3/1.
69 Ibid. 3/96; 5/2; 5/20; 6/2; 7/36; 8/62.
70 Ibid. 20/1.
71 Brittain, South Mymms, 115.
72 Ibid. 133–4.
73 Ibid. 115–16.
74 Ibid. 134.

Barnet, in the late 19th century.[75] In 1907 the Plough in South Mimms village became the Plough tea rooms.[76]

The Amicable Union society met at the Cross Keys, South Mimms, between 1801 and 1808[77] and another friendly society at the Red Lion in 1815.[78] At Potters Bar in the 1830s the New Friendly society met at the White Horse.[79] and another society at the Robin Hood and Little John.[80] The United Society of South Mimms, which met at the Bull, Potters Bar, in 1807, owned the former workhouse from 1836 until 1869.[81] The local lodge (Court Cecil) of the Ancient Order of Foresters was founded in 1867.[82]

In the late 19th century local fairs were well-attended and in 1876 a foresters' fête was held in the village.[83] Although the holiday formerly given on May Day was abolished in 1871, school attendances on that day were still very low during the 1880s.[84] In 1891 oak apples were worn as button holes on May 29th, as they still were in the 1930s.[85]

Potters Bar village institute was built in 1893 by public subscription in memory of Henry Parker of Parkfield, and contained a hall seating 200 persons, a reading room, lending library, and billiard room. Club premises were added to the institute by E. C. Mott and a cricket club was started.[86] The hall was later purchased by the Potters Bar branch of the British Legion and used as their headquarters.[87] The Hyde institute and reading rooms, built in 1904, although outside the boundaries, were intended to serve South Mimms residents within a two-mile radius of Chipping Barnet parish church.[88] Local organizations founded in the late 19th century included the South Mimms choral society (c. 1890), the Young Men's friendly society (1891), and the Horticultural society (1891).[89] Other horticultural societies were started[90] and in 1969 a 10-acre field in St. Albans Road was rented by the Brookdale garden community association and divided into 75 plots, for recreation and organic cultivation.[91]

In 1973 Old Fold Manor golf club, founded in 1910, had a course of 124 a.[92] and Potters Bar golf club, formed in 1923, had 140 a.[93] There was also a private golf club at Dyrham Park.[94] The Ritz cinema opened in Darkes Lane in 1934[95] but was pulled down in 1967–8.[96]

LOCAL GOVERNMENT. In 1294 a jury upheld Roger Lewknor, lord of South Mimms, in his claim to exercise view of frankpledge, tumbrel, waif,

judgement of robbers, the assizes of bread and ale, and free warren. The abbot of Walden also claimed view of frankpledge and the assizes of bread and ale in South Mimms but later withdrew his claim.[97] In 1345 Roger Lewknor exercised view of frankpledge on Thursday in Whitsun[98] and presumably similar courts were held between 1345 and 1451. Court rolls survive, with some gaps, from 1451[99] and court books run from 1702 to 1913.[1] Until the early 17th century[2] a view of frankpledge, occasionally called a court leet, and a court baron were normally held on Thursday in Whitsun week. For most of the 17th century a view of frankpledge and a court baron were usually held in April, but sometimes an additional court baron was held in February, May, June, or July. Throughout the 18th century there was a view with a general court baron in April, and by the late 18th century normally at least one special court baron a year. After 1824 views lapsed and general courts baron were usually held several times a year. They met at Mimms Hall until 1875 and subsequently at the White Hart.

Aleconners are mentioned at the view of frankpledge held in 1345. A constable was elected in 1452, two constables were appointed in 1455, and three headboroughs in 1475. By 1610 the manorial officials consisted of two constables, four headboroughs, and two aleconners. From 1639 until 1777 two beast-markers in Enfield Chase were elected annually. Constables, headboroughs, and aleconners continued to be appointed by the manorial courts until 1824. From the 17th century most of the courts' business related to land transactions, although attempts were also made to limit vagrancy by fining tenants who took in strangers.

No details survive about courts on the manors of Durhams and Old Fold. Copies of a few early 17th-century proceedings and court books from 1727 to 1926 exist for the manor of Wyllyotts;[3] earlier rolls have been lost although an index from 1440 to 1757 survives,[4] as well as a custumal compiled c. 1700.[5] For most of the 18th century there was at least one court baron, in September. It usually met at the Cross Keys in the 18th century, and subsequently at the White Hart or White Horse. The bulk of the business at the court baron consisted of management of the commons and waste.[6]

The South Mimms manorial pound, recorded in 1598,[7] still stood near the Greyhound inn in 1864.[8] The Wyllyotts pound was situated at the Mutton Lane crossroads in 1594.[9] Instruments of punish-

[75] Kelly's Dirs. Mdx. (1894, 1898); Kelly's Dir. Barnet (1889–90).
[76] Brittain, South Mymms, 89.
[77] F.S. 1/897.
[78] F.S. 1/1362.
[79] F.S. 1/2140.
[80] F.S. 1/1935.
[81] F.S. 1/1211; F.S. 1/1683; Brittain, South Mymms, 94.
[82] F.S. 1/4601.
[83] Brittain, South Mymms, 121; M.R.O., D.R.O. 5/G1/1 (sch. log bk. 1870–95), 120.
[84] M.R.O., D.R.O. 5/G1/1 (sch. log bk. 1870–95), 11.
[85] Brittain, South Mymms, 132.
[86] Char. Com. file; Kelly's Dir. Mdx. (1908).
[87] Potters Bar, Official Guide [1972].
[88] Kelly's Dir. Barnet (1927).
[89] Brittain, South Mymms, 128.
[90] Kelly's Dir. Mdx. (1902).
[91] Char. Com. file.
[92] Ex inf. the sec.

[93] Ex inf. the sec.
[94] Potters Bar, Official Guide [1972].
[95] Story of Potters Bar, 76.
[96] Ex inf. Mrs. H. M. Baker.
[97] Plac. de Quo Warr. (Rec. Com.), 478–9.
[98] Hatfield C.F.E.P. (Ct. Roll) 14/27, f. 1.
[99] Ibid. ff. 2–12; 14/28, ff. 1–12; Ct. Rolls 19/10, 14/25, 28/20, 23/12, 23/13, 23/16, 27/13; Gen. 105/1, 2, 116/4, 7, 115/11, 120/2, 10, 136/1, 186/7, 32/6, 8, 9; Legal 24/2; Deeds 68/5; Accts. 106/17; B.M. Add. Ch. 8142; Stowe 847, 848; S.C. 2/227/82; Req. 2/286/72, /35/101.
[1] Hatfield C.F.E.P. (Ct. Bks.) i–vii.
[2] Except where otherwise stated the foll. paras. are based on ct. rolls and ct. bks: see above.
[3] Guildhall MS. 5454/1–9.
[4] Ibid. 5455.
[5] Ibid. 5456.
[6] Ibid. 5454/1–9.
[7] Hatfield C.F.E.P. (Gen.) 136/2.
[8] O.S. Map 6", Mdx. I. SW. (1864 edn.).
[9] M.R.O., F. 58/A.

ment were provided by the lord of South Mimms manor but in 1489 there was neither a gallows nor a cucking-stool,[10] and no pillory in 1501.[11]

Two churchwardens were mentioned in 1580.[12] The earliest surviving minute book of the parish dates only from 1727.[13] It covers eight years and is concerned solely with the parish workhouse. Vestry minute books survive from 1752,[14] with a gap between 1839 and 1846, and churchwardens' accounts from 1854.[15] The vestry minute book for 1752–1806[16] records only the two meetings held at Easter and September or December each year, at one of which the appointment of the manorial officials was approved and at the other churchwardens and overseers were elected. The vestry generally met on the first Wednesday in the month at the beginning of the 19th century, often seventeen or eighteen times a year between 1812 and 1834, and usually four or five times a year in the 1860s. Meetings were held at first in the Cross Keys, the Bull, the White Hart, and the Green Dragon. From 1804 they usually met in the church or in the vestry room at the workhouse. The vicar or assistant curate often took the chair but in their absence a leading landowner, such as George Byng, presided. Attendance fluctuated from about 7 or 8 in the late 18th century to 2 or 3 in 1808–10, and to 65 in March 1831. Meetings had to be adjourned in 1821 and 1823 as only parish officers were present. The vestry, apparently open, was dominated by the big landowners, although regular attenders included bricklayers, carpenters, and innkeepers.[17] Efforts were made to control the parish officers: in 1800 the overseer was ordered to justify his bill and the surveyor of the highways was to be summoned before two justices for having failed to account to the vestry.

The vicar and vestry each elected a churchwarden. From c. 1776 until c. 1843 it was usual for the people's warden to serve as vicar's warden in the following year. Some churchwardens held office for long periods: Henry Taylor served from 1840 until 1865 and Zachariah French from 1867 until 1903. In 1679 John Wells, high constable of Edmonton hundred, was chosen overseer of South Mimms but quarter sessions ordered his discharge, considering it impossible to perform both offices satisfactorily.[18] From 1724 there were usually two overseers, who, on relinquishing their posts, sometimes became churchwardens. Most overseers were gentlemen, although a few were tradesmen, and in the 19th century many held office for four or five years. Their accounts run from 1806 until 1828.[19] Surveyors of the highways were mentioned in 1752[20] and their accounts date from 1833.[21] Two surveyors, often substantial landowners, were generally appointed each year but by 1770 the number had risen to ten.

A salaried surveyor of the whole parish was appointed in 1793. In 1772 the parish was divided between Mimms Town, Kitts End, and Potters Bar for road-repairing. Mimms Hall was added as a fourth division in 1783 but replaced by Dyrham Lane in 1793 and by Mimms Side, Barnet, in 1798. A highway rate of 4d. in the £ was levied by the vestry in 1799 and thereafter the rate fluctuated from 3d. to 6d.[22] The[23] constables' expenses were paid by the vestry in 1800, although it was not until 1826 that the vestry itself appointed either constables or head-boroughs. It was decided in 1812 that a beadle should be chosen annually, paid, and clothed, and in 1802 a salary was voted to the vestry clerk. The church clerk was paid in 1805 and his duties combined with that of sexton in 1822.

The poor-rate, 4d. in 1675–6,[24] was levied twice a year by 1727.[25] In 1775–6 out of £392 raised £358 was spent on the poor.[26] Vagrancy was a special problem, for in 1730 it was said that the two great roads from London and the proximity of Enfield Chase were responsible for a large number of idle people from other parishes.[27] In 1714 the constable was given an allowance of £40 a year by the county authorities for passing vagrants.[28] Frequent petitions were made by the constables for vagrant money and were usually granted until 1740,[29] when the court allowed only 75 per cent of the amounts claimed for 1737–40.[30] During the 18th century[31] the vestry often paid paupers to move, as in 1727 when they gave 6s. to a sick man, thinking it 'proper to give him something to be rid of him'. The demand for outdoor relief increased at the end of the 18th century, and the vestry in 1799 decided to raise £450 by subscriptions in order to reduce the price of bread. In the following year wages were supplemented from the rates on a sliding scale. In 1807 the cost of outdoor relief was £31 but by 1813 it had risen to £329 and by 1817 43 persons received outdoor relief. Although numbers fell in the 1820s, distress was still apparent from the many fines for turnip-stealing. The parish continued to give occasional relief to discharged soldiers and seamen. From 1817 it employed the able-bodied poor on the roads but by 1825 single men were denied work on the roads and wages for married men fell. In 1832 the vestry considered providing further employment for the poor by renting a piece of land from Lord Salisbury.

In 1637 a house on the east side of Blackhorse Lane, standing in a block which comprised the rectory and Shenley poorhouse, had been bought by the parish with £85 given for the poor. The profits were either to be distributed twice a year to the most needy parishioners or to be used for apprenticing orphans or poor children.[32] In the later 18th century poor people were accommodated in a parish house

[10] Hatfield C.F.E.P. (Ct. Roll) 14/28, f. 1.
[11] Ibid. f. 5v.
[12] Guildhall MS. 9537/4.
[13] M.R.O., D.R.O. 5/D4/1.
[14] Ibid. 5/C3/1; 5/C1/1–4. A fuller min. bk. from 1750 to 1778, now lost, was consulted by Brittain, South Mymms.
[15] M.R.O., D.R.O. 5/B1/1.
[16] The following paras. are based on the vestry min. bks. and churchwardens' accts.: see above.
[17] As listed in Pigot, Com. Dir. (1832–4).
[18] M.R.O., Cal. Mdx. Sess. Bks., 1679–82, 49.
[19] M.R.O., D.R.O. 5/D1/1; 5/D1/1, 2.
[20] Ibid. 5/C3/1.
[21] Ibid. 5/E2/1–17.
[22] Ibid. 5/C3/1; 5/C1/1–4.

[23] Except where stated the foll. two paras. are based on the vestry min. bks.
[24] M.R.O., Cal. Mdx. Sess. Bks., 1673–79, 40.
[25] In addition to the vestry min. bks. there is a parish receipt and payment bk., 1840–51: M.R.O., D.R.O. 5/D1/3.
[26] Rep. Cttee. on Rets. by Overseers, 1776, 396, 627.
[27] M.R.O., D.R.O. 5/D4/1.
[28] M.R.O., Cal. Mdx. Sess. Bks., 1710–14, 45.
[29] Ibid. 1739–41, 47–49.
[30] M.R.O., MJ/OC iv, ff. 186–186v.
[31] The rest of the para. is based on M.R.O., D.R.O. 5/D4/1; 5/C3/1; 5/C1/1–3; 5/D4/2 (reg. of poor in workhouse and out-pensioners, 1816–27); Brittain, South Mymms, 77.
[32] M.R.O., D.R.O. 5/F1/1.

at the obelisk, Hadley Side,[33] probably that later known as Silk Weavers' Hall,[34] and in another house at Dugdale Hill.[35] In 1724 it was decided to repair and use as a workhouse the property which had been bought in 1637.[36] Between 1727 and 1734 the trustees met occasionally at Kitts End, but more usually in the workhouse itself, where outbuildings were to be converted in 1729 in order to provide additional accommodation. In 1730 a widow was paid to teach the other inmates to spin and to 'keep them constantly to it' but in the following year the trustees found the wheels standing idle; accordingly smoking in the spinning-room was banned and, instead, tobacco was to be distributed monthly by the master.[37] In 1754 all persons in the workhouse were to be badged and in 1755 any troublesome inmate was to be confined to the village cage.[38]

In 1776 the workhouse was said to accommodate 55 persons,[39] and the average number rose from 32 in 1816 to 52 in 1817 and remained at c. 30 in the 1820s.[40] In 1801 the spinning-room had 22 jersey wheels and three linen-spinning wheels.[41] The poor were farmed out[42] for a fixed sum, £360 in 1778[43] and £570 in 1801 but lower in 1814 than in 1778. The vestry had to investigate the conduct of the workhouse-master in 1728 and 1810, and dismissed the master for drunkenness in 1832.[44] In 1812 the vestry itself decided to assume responsibility for the indoor poor but a fortnight later it reverted to the old system. From 1814 the contractor also had to relieve the out-poor.

Vaccination against smallpox was given to the poor in 1768 and the children in the workhouse were vaccinated in 1775.[45] From 1801 a parish doctor was paid to attend the poor in South Mimms, Barnet, Hadley, and Ridge. The vestry complained of negligence in 1825 but he was re-appointed in 1830 after a contested election and his salary raised. In 1832 care of the poor was given to two doctors, one of whom was to visit the workhouse each month.

In 1626 a whipping-post and cucking-stool were to be erected at Kitts End.[46] A cage for prisoners, mentioned in 1755, stood by the church gate; a better site was sought in 1812 but the old cage remained until 1847.[47] In 1792 South Mimms joined the Barnet association, which was formed to prosecute theft and to which fifteen parishioners subscribed,[48] and in 1823 a bill was paid for watching the church 22 nights.[49] Stocks were erected in Potters Bar in 1801 but were broken down by the inhabitants. A reward was offered for information and in 1816 the vestry dealt with several persons who had caused a riot there.[50]

In 1835 the parish became part of the Barnet poor law union. The workhouse was sold in 1836 to the United Society of South Mimms and the inmates were transferred to the new workhouse at Barnet.[51]

The vestry did not confine itself to church affairs after 1835. It often discussed the water supply and in 1887 it complained about the increased police rate and questioned the necessity of having twenty-two policemen at Potters Bar. A sanitary inspector was appointed in 1859, at an annual salary, but was warned not to incur any extra expenses. In 1849 three inspectors were appointed under the Lighting and Watching Act of 1834 and in 1859 another one was appointed under the Nuisance Removal Act. The parish protested in 1879 against the proposed union of Friern Barnet and South Mimms as Barnet highway district, arguing that the roads were well maintained at moderate cost by the surveyors chosen in vestry. In 1886 the vestry complained that the expenditure of the rural sanitary authority was about the same as when the parish had been double its present size, population, and rateable value.[52]

In 1863 part of the parish known as Mimms, or Barnet, Side was transferred to Barnet local board, and in 1889 that area, together with 9 a. in the district of East Barnet Valley local board, became part of the administrative county of Hertford. The greater part of the parish was included in Barnet rural sanitary district in 1872 and in 1894 became South Mimms R.D. Under the Local Government Act of 1894 the part of the parish in Barnet U.D. became South Mimms U.D. and that part in East Barnet Valley U.D. was added to Monken Hadley. In 1896 a further 199 a. was transferred from South Mimms R.D. to South Mimms U.D., and from Middlesex to Hertfordshire.[53] In 1934 South Mimms R.D. became Potters Bar U.D. and was divided into the Potters Bar ward and South Mimms and Bentley Heath ward, returning six and three members respectively. In 1953 there were three wards, returning fifteen members, and by 1959 the number of wards had increased to five.[54] Oakmere House was used by the district education sub-committee and Wyllyotts Manor was bought by Potters Bar U.D.C. in 1937 to house the departments of the surveyor, treasurer, and public health inspector.[55] New council offices were subsequently built alongside the manor-house. In 1965 Potters Bar U.D. was transferred to the administrative county of Hertford and South Mimms U.D. became part of Barnet L.B. and was transferred from Hertfordshire to Greater London.[56] In 1974 Potters Bar was merged with other authorities to form the district council of Hertsmere.

PUBLIC SERVICES. Until the introduction of a piped supply in the late 19th century water was derived almost wholly from shallow wells.[57] There was a parish pump at the upper end of the village in

[33] Brittain, South Mymms, 59.
[34] Silk Weavers' Hall, or Bastick's Lot, is shown near the obelisk: M.R.O., F. 84/6b; see p. 278.
[35] Brittain, South Mymms, 59–60.
[36] M.R.O., D.R.O. 5/C2/2.
[37] Ibid. 5/D4/1.
[38] Brittain, South Mymms, 58.
[39] Rep. Cttee. on Rets. by Overseers, 1776, 396.
[40] M.R.O., D.R.O. 5/D4/2.
[41] Ibid. 5/C1/1.
[42] Except where stated, the foll. two paras. are based on vestry min. bks.
[43] Brittain, South Mymms, 70.
[44] Ibid. 92–3.
[45] Ibid. 49.
[46] Mdx. Sess. Recs. iii. 6–7.
[47] Brittain, South Mymms, 58, 59; M.R.O., D.R.O. 5/C1/1–4.
[48] Mdx. and Herts. N. and Q. iv. 32–5.
[49] Brittain, South Mymms, 78.
[50] M.R.O., D.R.O. 5/C1/1–2.
[51] Ibid. 5/C1/3; Story of Potters Bar, 106–7; 1st Rep. Poor Law Com. H.C. 500, App. D, p. 250 (1835), xxxv.
[52] M.R.O., D.R.O. 5/C1/3–4; 3 & 4 Wm. IV, c. 90.
[53] M.R.O., Reps. of Local Inqs. 1889–97, 17, 24, 29; Story of Potters Bar, 110; Brittain, South Mymms, 116.
[54] Potters Bar, Official Guide [1972].
[55] Story of Potters Bar, 103.
[56] Lond. Govt. Act, 1963, c. 33.
[57] Story of Potters Bar, 110; O.S. Map 6", Mdx. I. SE. (1864 edn.).

1828 but none at the lower end in 1859, when the vestry accepted the offer of a leading resident to convey water from a spring or pond, apparently free of charge.[58] Contamination of the drinking water was blamed for outbreaks of cholera in 1854 and diphtheria in 1884–5 and, as the rural sanitary authority had done nothing about the water supply 'beyond the preparation of a report', special vestry meetings were held in 1885. It was finally agreed that the Barnet Water Co., which served Barnet Side, should extend its mains to South Mimms. The laying-on of water in 1888 was unpopular with some parishioners, however, for it had resulted in one local farmer raising the rents of his cottages.[59] The company derived its water from wells sunk in the chalk at Barnet and Potters Bar[60] until 1904, when other wells were sunk outside the parish. Pumping from the Potters Bar well had ceased by c. 1948. The Barnet Water Co. was absorbed into the Lee Valley Water Co. in 1960.[61]

The absence of a proper sewerage system contributed to the frequent attacks of diphtheria in the 19th century. In 1877 the local medical officer of health reported that sewage from Potters Bar overflowed from cesspools into ditches. Following a second report in 1884 a special committee was appointed, only to clash with property owners who feared unnecessary expense. The South Mimms drainage district was created in 1887 but did not include Potters Bar, which escaped contributing to the special rate.[62] In 1891 Barnet rural sanitary authority built a sewage disposal works and constructed sewers on c. 11 a. adjoining St. Albans Road which it had purchased from the Brewers' Company of London. A sewage farm was established on c. 22 a. at the northern end of Cranborne Road in 1899 and most of the houses near by had been connected by 1907. Sewers were laid in Mutton Lane in 1925 and Grimsdyke was joined up with Potters Bar sewage farm in 1929–30, thereby ending differential rates in the parish for the cost of sewerage. With the increase in population in the 1930s the two disposal works became inadequate, whereupon Potters Bar joined the Colne Valley sewerage board (renamed the West Hertfordshire main drainage authority in 1959), to whose new central sewage disposal works the Potters Bar sewers were connected in 1957. The authority, however, took only a limited amount of soil sewage, leaving Potters Bar U.D.C. to dispose of any excess as well as surface water.[63]

The vestry resolved in 1850 to levy a 6d. rate in order to bring gas lighting to Barnet Side.[64] The Potters Bar Gas and Coke Co. was incorporated in 1869 and the Barnet Consumers' Gas Co. in 1871; the combined undertaking was amalgamated with the East Barnet Gas and Coke Co. in 1872 to form the Barnet District Gas and Water Co. In 1896 the council refused to provide street lighting in South Mimms village. In 1925 the North Metropolitan Electric Power Supply Co. opened a transformer station in Hatfield Road, Potters Bar. Some private

houses and the church of St. Giles were supplied with electricity, several gas street-lamps were adapted for electricity in Potters Bar, and two electric lamps were placed in South Mimms village. Gas for domestic purposes was supplied from 1930.[65]

The parish of South Mimms was added to the Metropolitan Police District in 1840.[66] South Mimms police station was built in Blackhorse Lane in 1847 and married quarters were added in 1908. Potters Bar police station in the Causeway dates from 1891 and has replaced the Potters Bar or Southgate station which existed in 1883.[67]

Chipping Barnet had a fire engine which in 1859 could be used by South Mimms. From 1925 South Mimms, Barnet, and Enfield jointly paid for the engine. In 1939 Potters Bar built its own fire and ambulance station on land in Mutton Lane, given by Mr. H. W. Tilbury. Control of the station passed to Middlesex in 1948, Potters Bar being grouped in a division with Southgate and Wood Green. By 1969 it had been joined with Hatfield and Welwyn Garden City in the eastern division of Hertfordshire.[68]

A cottage hospital with a dispensary, supported by voluntary subscriptions, was established in Richmond Road, Potters Bar, in 1884.[69] In 1939 it moved to new buildings alongside Mutton Lane, erected and equipped by means of a loan from the Charity Commissioners. Known as the Potters Bar and District hospital, it is a general practitioners' hospital with 56 beds, controlled by the Barnet group hospital management committee.[70]

The private smallpox hospital[71] that opened at Clare Hall in 1896 was first established in 1746 at Clerkenwell, transferring to King's Cross in 1793 and to Highgate Hill in 1850, before moving to South Mimms. The hospital, a brick building for 33 patients, was erected north of the mansion, on the corner of Blanche and Cross Oaks lanes. The villagers protested at its siting and thought that contagion was carried from the hospital to the village.[72] With the increased incidence of smallpox in Middlesex c. 1901, temporary accommodation of wood and iron, consisting of 16 large and 16 small wards, was added. In 1905 management passed to the Middlesex Districts joint smallpox hospital board but by 1911, as smallpox had declined, the hospital began to receive tuberculous patients. By 1929, when it passed into the control of the county council, there were c. 184 beds, to which an X-ray department and small operating theatre were added in 1937. During the Second World War Clare Hall became an emergency hospital, with huts of brick and asbestos to provide extra accommodation, but by 1942 all 540 beds had to be reserved for tuberculous patients. In 1948 it was transferred to the North West Metropolitan regional hospital board and became a thoracic hospital. In 1972 it was scheduled to close.[73]

In 1908 there was a convalescent home in connexion with the British Lying-in hospital for poor married women, but it had only one resident in 1911

[58] M.R.O., D.R.O. 5/C1/2, /4.
[59] Brittain, South Mymms, 106–7, 114, 135.
[60] Kelly's Dir. Mdx. (1908).
[61] Story of Potters Bar, 119.
[62] Ibid. 110; Brittain, South Mymms, 114–15.
[63] Story of Potters Bar, 111.
[64] M.R.O., D.R.O. 5/C1/4.
[65] Story of Potters Bar, 119; Brittain, South Mymms, 146.
[66] Lond. Gaz. 13 Oct. 1840, 2250.

[67] Story of Potters Bar, 109.
[68] Ibid. 117.
[69] Ibid. 116.
[70] Char. Com. file; ex inf. the hosp. sec.
[71] Except where otherwise stated, the para. is based on F. A. M. Simmonds, 'Hist. of Clare Hall Hosp.' [pamphlet (1962) penes Barnet Mus.].
[72] Clare Hall, sales parts. 1851 penes Barnet Mus.
[73] Ex inf. the hosp. sec.

and was no longer recorded by 1914.[74] Another convalescent home at no. 7 Alston Road, probably run by nonconformists,[75] had 6 residents in 1891. In 1894–5 it was known as the West Barnet convalescent home, but it was not mentioned after that date.[76] The Children's Home hospital at Hadley Highstone was built in 1911 and a year later had beds for 20 children. By 1933 it appears to have closed.[77] The building has since been used as a private old peoples' home.

In 1912 a voluntary library was established at St. John's, Potters Bar. Cranborne library opened in 1939 and another branch of the Hertfordshire county library was established at the Elms, High Street, in 1965.[78]

There is a cemetery in Mutton Lane, at the entrance to which stands a wooden porch dated 1909. In 1972[79] almost four-fifths of the area of the parish constituted open space. Between 1934 and 1937 Potters Bar U.D.C. acquired 114 a.; Parkfield (24 a.) was purchased in 1934 with the help of Middlesex C.C. and a school was built on part of it. In 1935 40 a. were acquired at Furzefield, stretching from Mutton Lane to Cranborne Road sewage farm; 18 a. have been developed as a sports centre, which includes a covered swimming pool. In the following year a further 25 a. north of the sewage farm were acquired. In 1937 25 a. at Oakmere Park were bought but later that year and in 1949 part of the land was sold for housing and in 1957 more was sold for a car park. Potters Bar U.D.C. also contributed to the purchase of Dyrham Park and of Old Fold Manor golf course and land near Southgate Road and the Ridgeway.

CHURCHES. A church at South Mimms was first mentioned c. 1140, when it was included in Geoffrey de Mandeville's grant to his new foundation at Walden (Essex).[80] The appropriation to Walden abbey was confirmed between 1163 and 1172[81] and a vicarage had been ordained before 1180–3.[82] Walden retained the rectory and the advowson of the vicarage until the Dissolution.

In 1538 the advowson had been granted to Sir Thomas Audley,[83] although later that year Joanna, widow of Thomas Goodere, presented *pro ista vice*.[84] Audley was licensed in 1540 to alienate it to Francis Goodere,[85] and in 1545 Francis Goodere granted it to William Stanford.[86] The advowson became separated from the rectory later in the same year[87] and in 1569–71 was settled by William's son and heir Robert, together with the manor and chapel of Monken Hadley,[88] on Alice Stanford and her second husband Roger Carew for life, with remainder to Robert.[89] By grant of a turn Owen Jones had presented in 1570 and John Parrott in 1586.[90] William Stanford granted the advowson in 1603 to Thomas Marsh,[91] whose heirs held it until 1712, although they exercised the right only thrice, George Fane presenting in 1663 and John Wray in 1666.[92] Edward Marsh, by will dated 1700, left the advowson to his wife Grace, with remainder, in default of any issue of his own, to William Parker and other sons by Grace's previous marriage to Dr. William Parker. From 1712 the patronage was held by the Parker family,[93] although the Crown, owing to the lunacy of William Parker, presented in 1766, 1769, twice in 1770, and in 1773.[94] The trustees of William Parker Hammond[95] presented in 1790 and 1806,[96] and thereafter the advowson was retained by the Hammond family until 1915, when it was bought by E. L. Hamilton.[97] In 1958 it was devised to the bishop of London.[98]

In c. 1190 the vicar was paying one mark a year to the monks of Walden in return for the oblations and small tithes of the parish.[99] The vicarage was valued at four marks c. 1247,[1] at five marks in 1291,[2] and by 1535 had risen to £12 3s. 4d.[3] By 1547 an unknown person had given 12 a. of land to the church.[4] In 1649 the living comprised the vicarage house, with the churchyard adjoining and one pightle of c. ½ a., and the small tithes, together worth £30.[5] The vicarial tithes, paid at the rate of 3d. in the £, were worth £20 in 1731, although payment was two years in arrears.[6] With the inclosure of Enfield Chase, the vicar was allotted 27 a. adjoining the road leading from Ganwick Corner to Southgate, which he exchanged with Edward Vincent for 7 a. south of the churchyard and vicarage house.[7] During the 19th century most of the glebe was leased and by 1835 the annual gross income of the vicarage was £336.[8] In 1841 a rent-charge of £595 was allotted to the vicar in lieu of small tithes, and the great and small tithes arising from the glebe lands were commuted to rent-charges of £1 6s. to be paid to Lord Salisbury, the impropriate rector, and 10s. 6d. to the vicar, whenever the lands were not occupied by the vicar. The glebe covered 9 a. in 1842, and consisted of the vicarage house, the churchyard, and meadow land in Blackhorse and Blanche lanes.[9] After some of the glebe had been added to the burial ground,[10] it was estimated in 1887 that there were 7 a.[11]

A vicarage house was first mentioned in 1361.[12]

[74] *Kelly's Dirs. Mdx.* (1908, 1910, 1912, 1914); *Census*, 1911.
[75] The house was registered for undenominational worship in 1893: see p. 303.
[76] *Kelly's Dirs. Barnet* (1892–3, 1894–5); *Census*, 1891.
[77] *Kelly's Dirs. Mdx.* (1912, 1933); *Census*, 1911.
[78] *Story of Potters Bar*, 130.
[79] The foll. para. is based on *Story of Potters Bar*, 48, 115; Potters Bar, *Official Guide* [1972].
[80] See p. 282.
[81] *Letters and Charts. of Gilbert Foliot*, ed. A. Morey & Z. N. Brooke, 474–5.
[82] Ibid. 475–6.
[83] *L. & P. Hen. VIII*, xiii(1), p. 212.
[84] F. C. Cass, *Monken Hadley*, 48.
[85] *L. & P. Hen. VIII*, xv, p. 292.
[86] Ibid. xx(1), p. 59.
[87] Ibid. p. 532.
[88] *Cal. Pat.* 1566–9, 408.
[89] Ibid. 179.
[90] Hennessy, *Novum Repertorium*, 342.

[91] C.P. 25(2)/173/45 Eliz. Hil.
[92] Hennessy, *Novum Repertorium*, 342.
[93] Cass, *South Mimms*, 41.
[94] Hennessy, op. cit. 342.
[95] M.R.O., Acc. 389/15.
[96] Hennessy, op. cit. 343.
[97] Brittain, *South Mymms*, 26.
[98] *Story of Potters Bar*, 41.
[99] *Essex Rev.* xlvi. 168.
[1] St. Paul's MS., W.D.9, f. 85v.
[2] *Tax. Eccl.* (Rec. Com.), 17.
[3] *Valor Eccl.* (Rec. Com.), i. 433.   [4] E 301/34/117.
[5] *Home Cnties. Mag.* i. 317.
[6] M.R.O., D.R.O. 5/C2/2.
[7] M.R.O., D.R.O. 5/H1/1(1781).
[8] *Rep. Com. Eccl. Revenues*, 665.
[9] M.R.O., TA/S. Mimms.
[10] M.R.O., D.R.O. 5/C1/4.
[11] *Return of Glebe Lands*, H.C. 307, p. 90 (1887), lxiv.
[12] *Cal. Pat.* 1358–61, 545.

The modern building, of red brick, has an 18th-century garden-wall and gateposts. In 1951 plans were drawn up for two houses to be built on the glebe land, for the use of the curate and verger.[13]

Between 1439 and 1447 Thomas Frowyk founded a chantry chapel for his own and his parents' souls. It opened out of the north side of the chancel of the parish church[14] and was endowed with 148 a.[15] After its suppression in 1547[16] the lands were granted to the king's physician, Walter Cromer.[17]

Provisions for lamps for the altar of St. Mary in the church accompanied grants of land to St. Bartholomew's hospital in the early 13th century.[18] John Hassell, vicar, in 1413 left 6s. 8d. for a St. Catherine's light.[19] None of the gifts of money and livestock recorded in 1547 was of more than four kine.[20] Henry Ewer (d. 1641) gave a yearly rent-charge of 10s. out of a house, in 1973 the site of the Black Horse,[21] for a sermon on Good Friday and John Bradshaw (d. 1698) endowed a Christmas 'bread service' which was still held in 1973.[22]

Most of the early vicars seem to have been resident, although several were pluralists: John Barrow (1468–1471) was also vicar of Sawbridgeworth (Herts.) and John Brikenden (1554–58) also held an Essex living. Thomas Willeford seems frequently to have visited Rome until 1385, when he was forbidden to travel abroad to prosecute suits prejudicial to the Crown.[23] William Foster was examined in scriptures in 1586 and retained the living for another 32 years.[24] William Tuttey, vicar from 1643, had left the parish by 1645 and was ejected at the Restoration as a Presbyterian.[25] 'Silver-tongued Batt',[26] vicar c. 1644–5, was popular[27] but under his successor, the episcopalian George Pierce, it was said in 1650 that the parish had long lacked a 'pious' preacher.[28] During Pierce's incumbency Ely Turner, an ejected minister from Monken Hadley, officiated at baptisms.[29] Arnold Spencer, who presumably succeeded Pierce, was deprived in 1662.[30] Vincent Hodgkin, vicar 1667–87, for four years combined the living with that of Hertingfordbury (Herts.) In 1677 three men, including John Nicholl of Knightsland, protested during Hodgkin's sermon and were afterwards imprisoned for brawling.[31] Several 18th- and 19th-century vicars were pluralists: John Jacob (1724–31) was vicar of Ridge from 1725, John Heathfield (1773–90) held the living of Northaw, both P. A. Hammond (1790–1806) and his younger brother, F. T. Hammond (1806–12), held South Mimms and Widford (Herts.) simultaneously, and G. F. Bates (1812–41) held West Malling (Kent).[32] Edward Evanson, vicar 1766–70 and later rector of

Tewkesbury, wrote several tracts which caused his prosecution for heresy, although he was acquitted on a technical flaw, and eventually became a Unitarian minister.[33]

High church practices have been a feature since the coming of C. Thompson, vicar 1852–70. In 1854 the vestry rejected a plan for restoration by G. E. Street on the grounds that it was too popish. P. F. Hammond (1870–89) was attacked for 'sacerdotalism' in the local press but W. H. Wood (1889–98) introduced more ritualism and redecorated the church with the approval of most of the parishioners.[34] His successor A. Hay (1898–1954), who set up a Calvary in the churchyard and further altered the interior of the church,[35] substituted Mass for Matins in 1910. A parish hall, with reading-rooms and a library, was built in 1891.[36]

There were two services each Sunday in the early 18th century, when communion was celebrated between three and five times a year.[37] By 1790 communion was celebrated four times a year, and there were 40 communicants.[38] Assistant curates were appointed frequently from the late 18th century.

The church continued to serve the whole of South Mimms until 1836, when the parish of St. John, Potters Bar, was created. Christ Church, Barnet, built in 1845, became a separate parish in 1884. St. John's was replaced as the parish church of Potters Bar by that of St. Mary the Virgin and All Saints in 1915, and development in the western part of Potters Bar led to the creation of the parish of King Charles the Martyr.[39]

The church of *ST. GILES*[40] lies toward the west side of the parish and has a chancel with north vestry and chapel, nave with north aisle and south porch, and west tower. Except for the north aisle and chapel, which are partly of brick, the walls are of flint rubble with stone dressings.

The chancel, or at least its western part, is of the 13th century; the east end may be an extension of the earlier 14th century, the date of the east window. It is not structurally divided from the nave which appears to have been rebuilt at the end of the 14th century, the date of the windows and doorway in the south wall. The three-stage tower was added c. 1450 and has a western doorway and an external stair turret. The north chapel and aisle, with their arcades of two and four bays, were built in the early 16th century[41] and the latter was apparently complete by 1526,[42] when the stained glass windows depicting its donors were in place.[43] The whole church appears to have been richly provided with stained glass of the

[13] M.R.O., D.R.O. 5/A9/2.
[14] Brittain, *South Mymms*, 17.
[15] See p. 286.
[16] Brittain, *South Mymms*, 17, 26.
[17] See p. 286.
[18] *Cartulary of St. Barts. Hosp.* nos. 1220, 1227.
[19] Brittain, *South Mymms*, 26.
[20] E 301/34/117.
[21] Brittain, *South Mymms*, 87.
[22] See p. 307.
[23] Brittain, *South Mymms*, 151–2.
[24] Guildhall MS. 9537/6.
[25] *Calamy Revised*, ed. Matthews, 499.
[26] A. Gordon, *Freedom after Ejection*, 209.
[27] *Calamy Revised*, 37.
[28] *Home Cnties. Mag.* i. 317.
[29] *Walker Revised*, ed. Matthews, 262.
[30] Hennessy, *Novum Repertorium*, 342.
[31] Brittain, *South Mymms*, 42.

[32] Ibid. 152.
[33] Ibid. 60; *D.N.B.*
[34] Brittain, op. cit. 143, 103–6, 109–13, 127–31.
[35] See below, p. 300.
[36] Brittain, op. cit. 127.
[37] Guildhall MS. 9550.
[38] Ibid. MS. 9557.
[39] See below, p. 301.
[40] Except where otherwise stated, the architectural description of the church is based on Hist. Mon. Com. *Mdx.* 93–5; Pevsner, *Mdx.* 142–3; *Par. Ch. of St. Giles South Mymms. A Little Guide.*
[41] Henry Frowyk, by will dated 1523, left £20 to the building of a north aisle or chapel: Prob. 11/22 (P.C.C. 18 Porch).
[42] Date on some of the windows.
[43] Missing names of donors are supplied by an inventory of 1621: *Gent. Mag. Eng. Topography*, viii. (1896), 265–8.

medieval period. The chapel, which may be a little older than the aisle, is enclosed by wooden screens which are decorated with the leopard's head badge of Frowyk. There was formerly a late medieval rood screen.

The chancel was out of repair in 1685, when it was ordered that the communion table be railed in.[44] By the 18th century[45] all the medieval glass, except the lower part of four panels in the north aisle, had gone and the chancel, nave, and aisle had flat plaster ceilings. Then the walls and the screens of the Frowyk chapel were all whitewashed. There was a gallery for children at the west end, extending some way along both sides of the nave, and there were box pews, a lofty pulpit, and a reading desk. The royal arms were 'placed where the rood had been'. Externally the south porch was of classical design and the tower was covered in ivy.

The lead roof of the nave was replaced by slates in 1823 and the gabled roof of the chantry by a flat leaded roof and a battlement before 1849. In 1846 a flint-and-brick wall was built at the west end of the church and Lord Salisbury, as lay rector, was asked to repair the chancel. In 1848 he still had not done so and the vestry resolved on legal proceedings. By 1852 the church had fallen into greater disrepair but the vestry, after rejecting G. E. Street's plans, decided merely to repair the pavement and to patch the windows. The chancel-roof and communion rails were in bad condition in 1861, when another dispute occurred with the lay rector, and minor repairs were done in 1864 and 1868. By 1876 the fabric was causing concern and the vestry accordingly appointed Street to carry out a complete restoration. The church was re-opened in 1878, after the plaster had been stripped from the exterior, a south porch built, and a battlement added to the south wall to give height to the nave. Inside, the lath-and-plaster ceilings were taken out but the timber roof of the aisle was preserved; whitewash and white paint were removed, the box-pews were replaced by oak ones based on the design of two which had survived from the 16th century, and a stone pulpit and an oak rood-loft were installed. No stained glass had been introduced into the church since 1541, but in 1889 the central light of the east window was filled with Munich glass and in 1894 more stained glass was inserted. Much decoration was carried out over the next 20 years, including the further addition of stained glass, the display of plate and paintings, the hanging of Stations of the Cross in 1908, and the placing of a crucifix in the rood loft in 1910.

In 1552 the church possessed a pair of organs.[46] A barrel-organ had been introduced in 1813, although the innovation was not welcomed by all the parishioners, and a new organ built in the chantry in 1889.[47] The square bowl-font dates from the 13th century and has 14th-century panelling on the pier.

Its cover, designed by Sir Ninian Comper in 1938, is supported on four gilt pillars. Other fittings include a 13th-century piscina, a 13th- or 14th-century chest, and two 16th-century linen-fold bench ends.[48]

The notable collection of monuments includes 15th- to 18th-century brasses to members of the Frowyk, Ewer, Harrison, Hodsden, and Ketterick families, including one commemorating Thomas Frowyk (d. 1448), his wife, and nineteen children. Wall-monuments include an early-17th-century memorial, with a death's-head and carrying the arms of the Nowell family,[49] and memorials to William Adams by Thomas Denman and Mary Dakin by William Spratt.[50] There are 17th-century floor-slabs to the families of Norbury, Marsh, Howkins, Adderley, and Ewer, and a canopied altar-tomb with some Renaissance features, perhaps that of Henry Frowyk (d. 1527). In the north chapel there is a canopied tomb in an earlier style bearing the arms of Frowyk impaled with those of Throckmorton, Aske, Knollys, and Lewknor, and with an effigy of a man in armour adorned with the Frowyk leopard's head; it is probably that of Henry's son Thomas, who died by 1527.[51] The churchyard contains a large monument to Sir John Austen, M.P. (d. 1742).[52]

By 1552 the church had 4 bells, as well as a sanctus bell and 2 hand-bells.[53] In 1778 the bells, whether the same ones or not, were rehung but in 1812 they were replaced by a new peal of six.[54] Two of the bells were recast in 1893[55] and the whole peal rehung. A church clock was repaired in 1802 and a new one given by George Byng in 1812.[56] The plate includes three 17th-century brass alms-dishes which are probably Dutch or Flemish. The Georgian altar-plate was recast in 1890 and consists of a flagon, cup, paten, and spoon.[57] The registers date from 1558 and are complete.[58]

The church of *ST. JOHN THE BAPTIST*, Potters Bar, was opened in 1835 as a chapel of ease, on a site in High Street given by Lt. Col. W. L. Carpenter of Oakmere House. Most of the building funds were contributed by George Byng of Wrotham Park,[59] who made the first presentation, the patronage afterwards being vested in the bishop of London.[60] Before the District Church Tithes Act Amendment Act of 1868 the vicar was sometimes described as a perpetual curate.[61] A grant from Queen Anne's Bounty covered most of the cost of building a vicarage house west of High Street, on former waste of Wyllyotts manor acquired by George Byng.[62] The first incumbent, H. G. Watkins, who held the cure for 53 years,[63] was governor of 5 London hospitals[64] as well as founder of 2 schools in Potters Bar.[65] The church, built in 'Ranger's Patent Stone', was designed by Edmund Blore[66] in a Norman style and consisted of a semicircular apsidal chancel, a nave, and a western tower containing one

[44] Guildhall MS. 9537/20.
[45] The following two paras. are based on Brittain, *South Mymms*, 80–1, 103–6, 110–113, 131, 140–2.
[46] E 315/498/29.
[47] Brittain, *South Mymms*, 81–2, 138.
[48] *T.L.M.A.S.* xviii(2), no. 136.
[49] R. M. Robbins, 'Rawlinson's notes on Mdx. Churches', *Lond. & Mdx. Historian*, i. 2–5.
[50] R. Gunnis, *Dict. of Brit. Sculptors*, 127, 364.
[51] Brittain, *South Mymms*, 21; Cass, *South Mimms*, 66.
[52] Robbins, *Mdx.* 312.
[53] E 315/498/29.
[54] Brittain, op. cit. 79.

[55] *T.L.M.A.S.* xviii(2), no. 136.
[56] Brittain, op. cit. 80, 128.
[57] Freshfield, *Communion Plate*, 40.
[58] M.R.O., D.R.O. 5/A1/1.
[59] *Story of Potters Bar*, 72; Brittain, op. cit. 97.
[60] Hennessy, *Novum Repertorium*, 343.
[61] Crockford, *Clergy List for 1859*.
[62] M.R.O., Acc. 1083/7; Barnet Mus. 2144, p. 102.
[63] Hennessy, *Novum Repertorium*, 344.
[64] *Par. Ch. of Potters Bar — St. Mary the Virgin and All Saints. Jubilee Yr. 1915–65* [pamphlet].
[65] See p. 304.
[66] *T.L.M.A.S.* xviii(2), no. 139.

bell. Internally the building was a simple, white-washed rectangle with a flat ceiling, plain glass, box pews, and a western choir gallery, all centred on a three-decker pulpit.[67] The church had many monuments to members of the Byng family, who were buried there until a mausoleum was built in Wrotham Park in 1880.[68] In 1908 the church had 250 seatings, of which one-third were free.[69] A fire damaged the roof in 1911[70] and in the following year a fund was inaugurated for the erection of a new church,[71] whither the font, stone pulpit, and organ were transferred.[72]

The church of *ST. MARY THE VIRGIN AND ALL SAINTS*,[73] which replaced St. John's, was erected in 1915 on the opposite side of the road to the old church, on land given by J. Hart. The church, designed by J. S. Alder, was built of freestone in the 14th-century style, and comprised choir, two side-chapels, nave, clerestory, and one bell.[74] The altar cross in the Lady chapel is made from the metal of a Zeppelin that was brought down in Potters Bar in 1916.[75] The new building, with its large windows, raised sanctuary with marble paving, and stone altar under a baldachin, was in marked contrast to St. John's, which had been designed solely as a preaching-house. The completion of the building, without the tower that had originally been planned, was carried out in 1967.[76] The original vicarage, built for the incumbents of St. John's, was replaced by one on an adjacent site in the Walk c. 1928.

CHRIST CHURCH,[77] Barnet, was built principally at the cost of Captain Trotter of Dyrham Park, who purchased part of Four Acre field from George Byng in 1844. There he erected a minister's house and a school in which services were held. The church, opened as a chapel of ease in 1845, was consecrated in 1852. A conventional district was assigned to it in 1853 and a separate ecclesiastical parish created in 1884. The living was endowed by Trotter with £1,000 and was a perpetual curacy until 1898, when the full rights of a vicar were granted to the incumbent. The parsonage was enlarged 1851–4, and in 1896 a plot of land (1 a.) was purchased as glebe from Lord Strafford. Canon Mowbray Trotter gave the land surrounding the church c. 1904, whereupon the Ecclesiastical Commissioners increased the benefice income by £350. In 1919 the patronage of the living passed from the Trotter family to the Church Patronage Society. A house was acquired for assistant curates and in 1900 a burial ground was added, partly through a gift by Mrs. Llewellyn, sister of Canon Trotter.[78] The first incumbent, Alfred Moritz Myers (1845–52), was a converted Jew. His successor William Pennefather[79] became a friend of David Livingstone, who attended the church while staying in Hadley Green in 1857–8.

The church, of flint with stone dressings, was designed by G. G. (later Sir Gilbert) Scott in the Early English style, and consisted of chancel, nave of three bays, south aisle, south porch, and turret containing one bell.[80] A north aisle was added in 1855, of approximately equal proportions to the nave, and a gallery was installed at the west end of the new part of the building to accommodate orphans of the Crimean War. The organ was renovated in 1882 and eventually replaced in 1914. Alterations, including taking out the pews, reducing the length of the gallery, and removing the external wall which cut short the north aisle, culminated in panelling the east end in 1929. The Pennefather Memorial hall was erected in 1907, after 2,500 guineas had been left in trust to the church by Leopold Taylor.[81]

TRINITY CHAPEL at Bentley Heath was designed by S. S. Teulon[82] and erected by George Byng, earl of Strafford (d. 1886), in 1866.[83] It is of red brick with patterns of white and black and some stone dressings, and consists of a chancel with north vestry, nave with wooden south porch, and apsidal baptistery. The memorial to George Byng, formerly in St. John's, was moved there.[84] Although the chapel was built for the Byng family, the public were admitted to services. In 1973 it was seldom used.

The mission church of *ST. MICHAEL AND ALL ANGELS* in Church Road, Potters Bar, was erected in 1874 at the sole cost of Watkins, vicar of St. John's. A corrugated iron building, it seated 160[85] but was burned down c. 1942 and not replaced.[86]

In 1937[87] the London Diocesan Home Mission founded the Cranborne mission[88] to serve the new housing estates in the western part of Potters Bar. The Revd. E. Etherington was the first missioner, holding services in his own house and later in a garage. The church hall was built in 1938 and used for worship until in 1941 the permanent church of *KING CHARLES THE MARTYR* was built, with money from the Royal Martyr Church Union, on a site at the corner of Dugdale Hill Lane and Mutton Lane given by Viscount Cranborne (later marquess of Salisbury). In 1949 the district was made a separate parish. The living was a perpetual curacy in the patronage of the bishop of London.[89] The church, designed by F. C. Eden and R. Marchant in the 17th-century vernacular style, is red-brick and comprises a chancel with vestry, aisled nave and south porch, and apsidal baptistery. Fittings include a font, choir-stalls, and pulpit in the 17th-century style.

ROMAN CATHOLICISM. In the investigation that followed the capture of Edmund Campion in 1581, a resident of South Mimms, one Griffin, was among those suspected of aiding Jesuits.[90] By 1676 there were said to be no papists in the parish[91] but five years later Charles Malgrave of South Mimms was presented for recusancy.[92]

[67] Plates in *Par. Ch. of Potters Bar*.
[68] Brittain, *South Mymms*, 97.
[69] *Kelly's Dir. Essex, Herts. and Mdx.* (1908).
[70] *Par. Ch. of Potters Bar*.   [71] Char. Com. files.
[72] *Par. Ch. of Potters Bar*.
[73] Except where stated, section based on *Par. Ch. of Potters Bar*.
[74] *Kelly's Dir. Essex, Herts. and Mdx.* (1933).
[75] *T.L.M.A.S.* xviii(2), no. 138.
[76] Ex inf. the vicar.
[77] Except where stated, the section is based on R. G. G. Hooper, *Story of One Hundred Yrs.* [pamphlet].
[78] Char. Com. files.

[79] Brittain, *South Mymms*, 100.
[80] *Kelly's Dir. Essex, Herts. and Mdx.* (1890).
[81] Char. Com. files.
[82] Pevsner, *Mdx.* 27.
[83] *Kelly's Dir. Essex, Herts. and Mdx.* (1890).
[84] Potters Bar, *Official Guide* [1972].
[85] *Kelly's Dir. Essex, Herts. and Mdx.* (1890).
[86] *Story of Potters Bar*, 74.
[87] The para. is based on inf. given by the vicar.
[88] *Crockford* (1947).   [89] Ibid. (1951–2).
[90] *Acts of P.C.* 1581–2, 164.
[91] William Salt Libr., Stafford, Salt MS. 33, p. 40.
[92] *Mdx. Cnty. Recs.* iv. 151.

A mission was started at High Barnet in 1849[93] by Dr. Faa di Bruno, the General of the Pious Society of Missions, helped by four Passionists from the Hyde between 1850 and 1855.[94] A large Italianate church was built in High Street in 1850[95] but proved unsuitable for the climate and had to be pulled down.[96] Until part of the modern church was opened in 1865, services were held in the schoolroom. St. Gregory's chapel was added in 1870, the eastern part of the nave and Lady chapel in 1878, and the west end was completed in 1931.[97] The church is a brick building in the Gothic style seating 300.

Between 1867 and 1886 the Southwell family used the large attic at Knightsland as a Roman Catholic chapel.[98] A sister of W. H. Southwell was the superior of the Roman Catholic nunnery which, under the name of St. Monica's priory, used Clare Hall between 1886 and 1896.[99]

In 1920 a room at Wyllyotts manor was placed at the disposal of Roman Catholics by Mr. Beckett, whose son conducted services there. In 1922 Sir Nicholas Grattan Doyle provided a chapel in Boundary House, the chapel furnishings later being transferred to Hillside in Barnet Road, which the Spanish Vincentians had acquired in 1922 as a college for training missionaries. In 1925 the Vincentians built a temporary church at Hillside, which was destroyed by enemy action in 1945. Services were afterwards held in their community chapel and hall, until in 1950 the order was relieved of pastoral duties and the brick church of Our Lady of the Assumption was built in Mutton Lane. The Vincentians themselves built a brick church in Southgate Road in 1960;[1] dedicated to St. Vincent de Paul and Ste. Louise de Marillac, it was opened to the public and from 1969 has served a new parish in east Potters Bar.[2]

About 1922 Irish Dominican sisters established a convent in Church Road, whose chapel local Roman Catholics could attend. The convent was closed in 1937 and the building demolished in 1956.[3] In 1972 maisonettes called Rosary Court stood on its site.

PROTESTANT NONCONFORMITY. William Tuttey, vicar of South Mimms in 1642, was ejected[4] from Totteridge in 1661, but continued active in the area and was preaching at Chipping Barnet c. 1669.[5] Timothy Batt, who had been vicar c. 1644–5[6] and who was ejected from Creech (Som.) at the Restoration, revisited South Mimms in 1685 where he was received with great affection.[7] His successor, George Pierce, a royalist sympathizer, was unacceptable to the 'well-affected' members of his parish in 1649.[8]

By 1676 there were twenty nonconformists[9] and by c. 1700 there were meeting-houses for both Anabaptists and Quakers.[10] The Anabaptists seem to have been active until 1739,[11] after which there is no further reference to their church. Quakers at South Mimms had been visited in 1677 by George Fox,[12] who returned in 1678 to attend a meeting in the house of Samuel Hodges.[13] In 1682 Hodges refused to pay a fine for allowing a 'seditious conventicle' to be held in his house. The parish constable, Richard Mason, was ordered to distrain him, but he declined to execute the warrant and was himself tried.[14] In 1686 Hodges sold land known as Chantry mead to William Wyld, of High Barnet, for the use of Friends. A meeting-house was built on part of the land in 1697 and the remainder of the property was used as a burial ground. Membership increased c. 1707 as a group of Quakers who had formerly met at John Hickman's house at Kitts End joined the South Mimms meeting. More land was purchased in 1737 to enlarge the burial ground.[15] After the death in 1768 of Ezekiel Lofty, who had been the leading Quaker in the parish,[16] the meeting declined. By 1771 worshippers met only three times a year, in 1773 half-yearly, and in 1787 the meeting was discontinued. The land was sold for £120 in 1818.[17] Quakers were still meeting for worship, however, in 1842 in a house adjoining Chantry mead and next to the site of the National school.[18]

By the end of the 18th century other nonconformist bodies were active in the parish, mostly at Potters Bar and Barnet Side, both areas being some three miles from the parish church. Many parishioners probably drifted into nonconformity rather than attend church in Monken Hadley or Chipping Barnet.[19]

A small group of Baptists began to worship in a barn at Potters Bar in 1788.[20] In 1789 they built a permanent church,[21] where the first sermon was given by the celebrated preacher Rowland Hill,[22] of the Surrey Chapel in London. The church joined the Hertfordshire Association of Baptist Churches in 1804. A new church was built in 1869, when the membership was about 50,[23] and was registered for worship on behalf of the Particular Baptists.[24] The building, in the Romanesque style, was extended in 1884, the Spurgeon hall and Primary room being added.[25] It was re-named Ware hall in 1964 when the present church was built in Barnet Road.[26] An unlocated place of worship was registered by Baptists in Union Street in 1878, but the registration was cancelled in 1895.[27] Another group of Baptists acquired a room for worship in South Mimms in 1894.[28] Five years later, supported by several

[93] Brittain, *South Mymms*, 102.
[94] Ex inf. Father Sylvester Palmer; *Kelly's Dir. Mdx.* (1855). The ch. is dedic. to St. Mary and St. Gregory.
[95] *Catholic Dir.* (1851).
[96] Brittain, op. cit. 102.
[97] *Kelly's Dir. Barnet* (1932).
[98] Brittain, op. cit. 53.
[99] Ibid. 145.
[1] *Story of Potters Bar*, 77–8.
[2] *Catholic Dir.* (1970).
[3] *Story of Potters Bar*, 77.
[4] See p. 299.
[5] *Calamy Revised*, ed. Matthews, 499.
[6] See p 299.
[7] *Calamy Revised*, 37.
[8] *Walker Revised*, ed. Matthews, 121.
[9] William Salt Libr., Stafford, Salt MS. 33, p. 40.
[10] M.R.O., MR/RO 5, m. 27 (1690–98).

[11] W. T. Whitley, *Baptists of Lond.* (1928), 122.
[12] *Short Jnl. and Itinerary Jnls. of Geo. Fox*, ed. N. Penney, 232.
[13] Ibid. 269–70.
[14] *Mdx. Cnty. Recs.* iv. 183.
[15] W. Beck and T. F. Ball, *Lond. Friends' Meetings*, 298.
[16] Brittain, *South Mymms*, 83.
[17] Beck and Ball, *Lond. Friends' Meetings*, 298.
[18] M.R.O., TA/S. Mimms.
[19] *Home Cnties. Mag.* i. 317.
[20] Brittain, op. cit. 84.
[21] Ex inf. the sec., Potters Bar Baptist ch.
[22] Brittain, *South Mymms*, 84.   [23] Ex inf. the sec.
[24] G.R.O. Worship Reg. no. 21923.
[25] Ex inf. the sec.
[26] *Baptist Handbk.* (1972), 163.
[27] G.R.O. Worship Reg. no. 23918.
[28] *Barnet Press*, 13 Oct. 1894.

parishioners who resented ritualism at St. Giles, they planned to erect a Protestant Free church on the village green. Objections were made however, to the proposed siting of the chapel and it was never built.[29]

By 1760 Wesleyans were worshipping in a cottage[30] which, although often said to be in South Mimms,[31] stood on the Monken Hadley side of the boundary in High Street.[32] In 1891 the congregation moved from the chapel, which had replaced the cottage, to a new chapel[33] that stood a few yards to the south within South Mimms parish. The new chapel was opened in 1892 and registered for worship,[34] the old chapel being sold to the Baptists. In 1937 the Wyburn hall was opened as an extension to the main Wesley hall. The church, damaged in the Second World War,[35] is built of stone in the Decorated style, with turrets at the western end.

In the late 18th century Methodists were meeting in a barn at Darkes Farm.[36] There is no further record of their activity in Potters Bar until the 1880s. A chapel was built in Hatfield Road in 1883, and a new hall was erected and opened in 1933. Methodists worshipped there until the present red-brick chapel was built in Baker Street in 1941. A new hall was erected alongside the chapel in 1955. The chapel itself was altered and enlarged in 1959 and was renamed St. John's Methodist church. In 1972 it ran a mission Sunday school on a housing estate.[37]

In 1810 the house of William Franklin was certified for worship, but no denomination was given.[38] In 1826 the house of William Earnfield was licensed for a group of dissenters, led by their minister, Richard Cooper.[39] A house belonging to William Stephens was registered for Independents in 1838.[40] In 1851 a minister resident at Mill Hill served a church in South Mimms which was said to have been built in 1813.[41]

Captain John Trotter, inspired by the evangelical assistant curate of Christ Church, William Pennefather, started to hold evening services c. 1845 in a building in Blanche Lane which later became a post office. In 1849 the London City Mission appointed a missioner, who was to include Ridge and Shenley in his district. A mission hall was built next to the old site in 1915,[42] and it was still used for worship in 1932.[43] Later the Conservative Association met there but in the early 1950s it was acquired by the London Baptist Property Board and used for Sunday services and a Sunday school until 1969, after which only the Sunday school continued to meet.[44]

The Salvation Army met in the town hall, Union Street, in 1883[45] and in temporary premises in Salisbury Road,[46] until a permanent citadel was opened in Salisbury Road in 1891.[47] The building was registered for worship in 1892[48] and a hall was acquired for young people in 1918.[49] Salvation Army barracks were opened in Station Road, Potters Bar, in 1897, but the corps had collapsed by 1903.[50]

An 'iron room' in Alston Road was registered for undenominational worship from 1893 until 1913.[51] The room was used by the Church of Christ in 1920[52] and by the Assemblies of God from 1955.[53]

From 1884 Plymouth Brethren met in a room in Salisbury Road,[54] until they registered the Salisbury chapel for worship in 1894.[55] A second group began to hold meetings in the house of Robert Simmonds, no. 15 Union Street, in 1930.[56]

The Barnet Brotherhood and Sisterhood (P.S.A.) started to meet c. 1914 in a brick building in Union Street, the front of which had been opened c. 1888 as the Barnet reading room. From 1918 to 1968 the premises were occupied by the Ministry of Labour and the P.S.A. was admitted only on Sundays. In 1972 the P.S.A. had full use of all the rooms, except the upstairs hall which was occupied by a Christian Mobile Group.[57]

Plans[58] were made to build a Congregational church in Potters Bar by Miss E. H. Alder, supported by the Misses F. C. Carpenter and R. M. Scott, in 1926. Land in Darkes Lane was bought in 1931 and a brick church opened there three years later. A Sunday school was started in 1935. Plans for a larger church in Mutton Lane, on a site given by Mr. H. W. Tilbury in 1938, were abandoned after the outbreak of war. An additional hall was erected in 1953. The land in Mutton Lane was sold in 1963 and the proceeds used to build a new church in Darkes Lane, next to the original one. It was finished in 1966.[59]

Services were held by the Y.W.C.A. at no. 1A Union Street between 1892 and 1919[60] in the building formerly used as Barnet free school.[61] The building was afterwards used as a furniture store[62] but from 1941 Christian Spiritualists have held services there.[63] Another group were meeting at Potters Bar Spiritualist church, Hill Rise, in 1972.[64]

In 1938 the Cranborne Gospel mission was founded by the local Free Church Council to provide a Sunday school for the housing estates in western Potters Bar. Meetings were first held in Cranborne school and afterwards at Elm Court, Mutton Lane. In 1968 the church became affiliated to the Fellowship of Independent Evangelical Churches, and changed its name to Potters Bar Evangelical Free church. Although meetings were still held in Elm Court in 1972, the church was negotiating the lease

[29] Hatfield C.F.E.P. (S. Mimms) 3/123.
[30] *High Barnet Methodist Ch. 1770–1970* [bicentenary booklet], 8.
[31] *Ret. of churches, chapels . . .* , H.C. 401 (1832), 1; *Baptist Handbk.* (1972), 155.
[32] See p. 269.
[33] *High Barnet Meth. Ch.* 9.
[34] G.R.O. Worship Reg. no. 33236.
[35] *High Barnet Meth. Ch.* 9, 12.
[36] Brittain, op. cit. 96.
[37] Ex inf. the minister.
[38] Guildhall MS. 9580/3.
[39] Ibid. 9580/6.
[40] Ibid. 9580/7.
[41] H.O. 129/136/1/4/9.
[42] Brittain, *South Mymms*, 101.
[43] *Kelly's Dir. Barnet* (1932).
[44] Ex inf. the sec., High Barnet Baptist ch.
[45] G.R.O. Worship Reg. no. 27548.

[46] Ibid. 30463.
[47] Plaque on building.
[48] G.R.O. Worship Reg. no. 33089.
[49] Ibid. 47189.
[50] Ibid. 36154.   [51] Ibid. 33956.
[52] *Kelly's Dir. Barnet* (1920–21).
[53] G.R.O. Worship Reg. no. 64845.
[54] Ibid. 27813.
[55] Ibid. 34558; *Free Church Dir.* (1968/9).
[56] *Kelly's Dir. Barnet* (1930).
[57] Ex inf. the Revd. Mark Reeves.
[58] The para. is based on *Potters Bar Congreg. Church, 1934–66.*
[59] *Congreg. Yr. Bk.* (1971–2).
[60] *Kelly's Dir. Barnet* (1892–3, 1919–20).
[61] See p. 305.
[62] *Kelly's Dir. Barnet* (1919–20).
[63] G.R.O. Worship Reg. no. 59718.
[64] Potters Bar, *Official Guide* [1972].

of a plot of land from Potters Bar U.D.C. and hoped to have its own building.[65]

The Potters Bar congregation of Jehovah's Witnesses started in 1957 with a group of voluntary ministers from Barnet. Meetings were held successively at Elm Court, Oakmere House, Potters Bar hotel, and the village hall in Cotton Road until 1970, when it was decided to share a Kingdom hall with the Barnet congregation.[66]

The modern group of Quakers began to meet in Potters Bar in 1957. They have no permanent meeting-house but have used the Red Cross Headquarters in Mutton Lane and in 1972 were worshipping in the committee room of the church of King Charles the Martyr.[67]

The Christian meeting-place, 7 Exchange Buildings, St. Albans Road, was registered for undenominational worship in 1964,[68] but was no longer being used for that purpose in 1972. Other meeting-places of unknown denomination are the Assembly hall in Union Street, and the meeting room at 17 Union Street, which was registered in 1964.[69]

JUDAISM. The Potters Bar Jewish Community was founded in 1940. Its members worshipped in temporary premises until 1968, when a permanent synagogue, affiliated to the United Synagogue, was built at Brookmans Park. In 1971 fifty families were said to be connected with the synagogue.[70] The Potters Bar Jewish centre, in Tavistock Close, governed by a trust deed of 1966,[71] provides for the advancement of the Jewish religion, the education of Jewish children, and the relief of poor and aged Jews.

EDUCATION. There was a schoolmaster at South Mimms in 1580.[72] In 1752 the vestry appointed a man to teach children at a school held in the church[73] but there was still no endowed school in 1800, when the education of the poor was financed by voluntary subscriptions.[74] In 1816 a Sunday school accommodated c. 70 children[75] and in 1819 it contained 155 children, some of whom were partly clothed by subscriptions. In addition four unendowed day schools provided for 185 children by 1819: 14 or 15 poor girls were clothed and educated in a school founded by Mrs. Byng of Wrotham Park; a school at South Mimms and Potters Bar contained 100 children; a school at Bentley Heath accommodated 30; and another at Barnet and Hadley contained 40.[76] In 1833 there were ten day schools, one for 20 girls paid for by Mrs. Byng and the other nine containing 166 boys and 74 girls at the charge of their parents; 3 Sunday schools, accommodating 99 boys and 80

girls, were all supported by voluntary contributions.[77]

Although plans for a National school were made c. 1816[78] it was not until 1834 that one was started. A permanent brick building, consisting of a mixed schoolroom and an infants' classroom, separated by the teachers' residence, was erected in Blanche Lane in 1836.[79] The school received a parliamentary grant of £75 in 1837[80] and was afterwards financed by voluntary contributions, school pence, and, from 1870, regular parliamentary grants. In 1857 a master and a mistress had charge of 93 children and an evening school was run in connexion with the day school.[81] Matthew Arnold commented adversely in 1871–3, but was pleased after the school's enlargement in 1874, while still critical of the examination work.[82] By 1878–9 the teaching in the infants' class earned high praise,[83] although irregular attendance continued to hamper progress in the junior school.[84] In 1884 the school was rebuilt for 180 children[85] and by 1893, with an average attendance of 115,[86] it was described as a well-ordered country school doing creditable work.[87] It later became known as St. Giles's Church of England school and in 1958 moved to new premises closer to the church. In 1972 it was attended by 121 pupils.[88]

A National school, later known as St. John's Church of England school, was built at the expense of the first incumbent of St. John's in Potters Bar in 1839,[89] on land in Barnet Road given by George Byng. It was a brick building, consisting of a schoolroom for boys, girls, and infants, and a teacher's house, where the parlour was occasionally used as a classroom. It was maintained by voluntary contributions and school pence and, after 1870, regular parliamentary grants. There were 41 pupils in 1839, taught by a master and mistress, and 77 in 1857.[90] The infants were transferred to their own school on vicarage land in 1862,[91] described as a 'succursal' of the National school[92] but in practice a separate institution, erected and governed by the incumbent. The schoolroom and teacher's house formed one building which was surrounded by a playground. The children were taught plain needlework, and the average attendance in 1878 was 46. The school was maintained by voluntary contributions, which were supplemented by the founder, and by school pence.[93] On the founder's death in 1890 the infants' school was placed under the same management as the junior school, and, with rising attendance, was in constant financial difficulty. After subsidence under the old premises the juniors moved in 1872 to Southgate Road, where land had been given by Mrs. Kemble. The new school, incorporating houses for a master and mistress, was built with a little help from the National Society.[94] The average at-

[65] Ex inf. Mr. W. Rutherford.
[66] The para. is based on inf. supplied by the presiding overseer.
[67] Ex inf. Mrs. M. Brazier.
[68] G.R.O. Worship Reg. no. 69557.
[69] Ibid. 69770.
[70] *Jewish Yr. Bk.* (1971). The bldg. is in Herts.
[71] Char. Com. files.
[72] Guildhall MS. 9537/4.
[73] Brittain, *South Mymms*, 118.
[74] Lysons, *Mdx. Parishes*, 238.
[75] Brewer, *Beauties of Eng. and Wales*, x(5), 756.
[76] *Educ. of Poor Digest*, 539.
[77] *Educ. Enquiry Abstract*, 576.
[78] Brewer, op. cit. 756.
[79] Ed. 7/86; O.S. Maps 6", Mdx. I. SW. (1864 edn.).

[80] *Mins. of Educ. Cttee. of Council, 1854–5* [1926], p. 202, H.C. (1854–5), xlii.
[81] Ed. 7/86.   [82] Brittain, *South Mymms*, 119–21.
[83] *Rep. of Educ. Cttee. of Council, 1878–9* [C. 2342–I]. p. 749, H.C. (1878–9), xxiii.
[84] Brittain, op. cit. 121–4.
[85] *Kelly's Dir. Essex, Herts. and Mdx.* (1890).
[86] *Returns of Schs. 1893* [C. 7529], p. 424, H.C. (1894), lxv.
[87] Brittain, op. cit. 125.   [88] Ex inf. the headmaster.
[89] *Story of Potters Bar*, 121–2.
[90] Brittain, op. cit. 98; Ed. 7/86.
[91] *Story of Potters Bar*, 122.
[92] *Rep. of Educ. Cttee. of Council, 1878–9*, p. 746.
[93] Ed. 7/86.
[94] *Story of Potters Bar*, 124–5; *Kelly's Dir. Mdx.* (1882).

tendance in 1872 was 65[95] and 117 by 1888.[96] The building was enlarged in 1893.[97]

Christ Church Parochial or National school was established in 1844 in St. Albans Road, the year before Christ Church itself was built on an adjoining site. The first classrooms (in 1972 the headquarters of the Barnet Division of the British Red Cross Society) were taken over for the girls when new premises for the boys were built in Alston Road in 1880.[98] In 1892 a separate infants' department was added on land given by Lord Strafford (d. 1898) adjacent to the original school, to replace a temporary iron room which had been condemned. The schools were erected without aid from the National Society, although from 1893 grants were received from the Society, in addition to a parliamentary maintenance grant which had been paid since 1872. In 1876 92 children were attending the schools[99] and by 1893 the average attendance had risen to 462.[1] In 1952 the girls joined the boys in Alston Road, where the infants were also accommodated, under a separate head. The infants moved to a two-classroom building in Byng Road in 1962 whither the juniors followed in 1968, after three more class-rooms had been added.[2]

A British school existed in Union Street, Barnet, from c. 1854 to 1866. It was served by a master and mistress and was attended by an average of 80 boys and 50 girls.[3]

By 1870 four schools in South Mimms were connected with the Church of England or the National Society, while one school had no religious ties. There were two public schools accommodating 172 children, two private voluntary schools with 187 children, and one private 'adventure' school with 21 children. Two other establishments omitted to make returns.[4] One of the schools recorded was presumably the Barnet ragged or free school which had been founded in 1856; it was given new buildings in 1872,[5] probably no. 1A Union Street,[6] which was later used by the Y.W.C.A.[7] and from 1941 by Christian Spiritualists.[8]

A fifth Church of England school was erected by Lord Strafford (d. 1886) at Bentley Heath in 1876, to accommodate 50 infants. Average attendance was 40 in 1890[9] but had fallen to 15 in 1904–5[10] and to 9 in 1906.[11] The school was closed in 1914.[12]

The five Anglican schools accommodated c. 1,352 children in 1904–5.[13] Under the 1902 Act control of education in South Mimms passed to Middlesex

C.C., except for the Barnet portion of the parish, containing the Christ Church schools, which was transferred to Hertfordshire C.C.[14] In 1910 Hertfordshire C.C. opened a senior and junior mixed school in Byng Road,[15] which in 1918–19 was attended by 178 seniors and 166 juniors.[16]

St. John's Church of England infants' school was handed over to Middlesex C.C. by 1919[17] and St. John's junior mixed in 1920.[18] Under the recommendations of the Hadow Report, St. John's schools were reorganized in 1933, the High Street school becoming a senior mixed school and the Southgate Road building accommodating juniors and infants. Cranborne junior mixed and infants' School opened as one school in that year[19] but was reorganized as two schools in 1936 and was then extended.[20] The seniors moved from High Street to a new building at Parkfield in 1938, when the juniors and infants transferred to the senior school[21] which was renamed Ladbrooke, after the farm which one stood beside it.[22] St. John's was retained as a separate infants' school.

By the 1944 Education Act Potters Bar (including South Mimms) was controlled by a district education sub-committee.[23] Grammar and technical education had to be obtained in Enfield, Southgate, or Wood Green until 1948, when Parkfield secondary modern school was changed into a comprehensive school.[24] More classrooms were built and, in order to meet the full secondary requirements of South Mimms and Potters Bar, new buildings were erected at Mount Grace, where first-year secondary children moved in 1952.[25] In 1954 Ladbrooke juniors moved to Parkfield, leaving Ladbrooke to the infants' school.[26] Mount Grace comprehensive school was officially opened at the same time. The growth of local housing estates led to the building of a new science block in Church Road and extensions to Parkfield. Mount Grace became organized as a lower school in the Walk (formerly Parkfield), housing first-and second-year pupils, and a main school in Church Road, for third- to sixth-form boys and girls.[27] In 1972 there were c. 1,500 children.[28] In 1973 building had started on Owen's school, in Sawyers Lane, and some pupils had been transferred there from Islington.[29]

More primary education was provided with the opening of Oakmere schools in 1958[30] and Sunny-bank schools in 1960.[31] Oakmere infants' school opened with 176 children, of whom 131 were

[95] *Rep. of Educ. Cttee. of Council, 1873* [C. 812], p. 460, H.C. (1873), xxiv.
[96] *Rep. of Educ. Cttee. of Council, 1888* [C. 5804–I], p. 607, H.C. (1889), xxix.
[97] *Kelly's Dir. Mdx.* (1908).
[98] *Barnet Press*, 23 Feb. 1962 [cutting in Nat. Soc. files].
[99] Nat. Soc. files.
[1] *Returns of Schs. 1893*, p. 424.
[2] Ex inf. the headmaster.
[3] *Craven & Co.'s Dir. Beds. and Herts.* (1854); *Kelly's Dir. Herts.* (1866).
[4] *Returns relating to Elem. Educ.* H.C. 201, p. 242 (1871), lv.
[5] Ed. 7/87.
[6] Plaque on building states that it was erected in 1872.
[7] *Kelly's Dir. Barnet* (1892–3).
[8] See p. 303.
[9] *Kelly's Dir. Essex, Herts., Mdx.* (1890).
[10] *Public Elem. Schs. 1906* [Cd. 3510], p. 449, H.C. (1907), lxiii.
[11] *Voluntary Schs. Rets.* H.C. 178–xx, p. 30 (1906), lxxxviii.

[12] Ed. 7/87.
[13] *Pub. Elem. Schs. 1906*, 449.
[14] *Kelly's Dir. Essex, Herts., Mdx.* (1908).
[15] Ex inf. the headmaster, Foulds jnr. mixed and infts. sch.
[16] *Bd. of Educ., List 21* (H.M.S.O., 1919).
[17] Ibid.
[18] Potters Bar, *Official Guide* [1972].
[19] M.R.O., Hist. Notes 1.5.59.
[20] Ex inf. the sec., Cranborne jnr. sch.
[21] M.R.O., Hist. Notes 1.5.59.
[22] Ex inf. the headmaster.
[23] Sturges, *Schs. of Edmonton Hund.* 218.
[24] Ibid. 99, 109.
[25] *Mount Grace Sch. Hist. and Buildings* [sch. pamphlet].
[26] M.R.O., Hist. Notes, 1.5.59.
[27] *Mount Grace Sch.*
[28] Ex inf. the sec.
[29] For the previous hist. of the school see *V.C.H. Mdx.* i. 310–11.
[30] Ex inf. Mr. B. Warren.
[31] *Story of Potters Bar*, 129.

transferred from Ladbrooke school. Three classrooms were added in 1961 and there were 230 children by 1972. Oakmere junior school opened with 196 children transferred from Parkfield junior school. Five classrooms were built in 1964 and by 1972 the school accommodated 321 children. In 1960 the rest of Parkfield junior school transferred to the new Sunnybank junior school, whereupon Parkfield became Mount Grace lower school.[32] Post-war extensions were made to Cranborne infants' school, which, with Cranborne junior school, contained 741 pupils in 1974.[33] At various times hutted accommodation has supplemented the permanent buildings at Ladbrooke primary school, which by 1972 had a roll of c. 320.[34]

In 1965 the Potters Bar and South Mimms portion of the parish became part of the mid-Hertfordshire division, while responsibility for education in the southern part of the parish, which contained Foulds junior mixed and infants' school, Christ Church Church of England school, and Queen Elizabeth's boys' grammar school, passed to Barnet L.B.[35] Foulds school, formerly Byng Road council school, had been extended in 1918 but became a junior school only in 1954. In 1972 it was attended by 298 pupils.[36] Christ Church remained Voluntary Aided, with 202 children.[37] Queen Elizabeth's grammar school for boys,[38] founded in 1573 and situated south of the boundary in Wood Street, moved in 1932 to a new building in the scholastic Tudor style in Queen's Road, within South Mimms parish.[39] It was reorganized as a comprehensive school in 1971.[40]

A private boarding school for boys, later called an 'academy',[41] existed at Salisbury House, Potters Bar, in 1805.[42] In 1819 there were six dame-schools[43] and in 1823–4 Thomas Haigh ran a boys' classical academy at South Mimms.[44] A dame-school that was frequently criticized by the masters of the South Mimms National school[45] eventually closed in 1883.[46] In Potters Bar twelve children were admitted to the National school between 1875 and 1877 from Mrs. Disney's school, although there is no further record of her teaching.[47] In the later 19th century there were various private schools but they were usually short-lived.[48] There are several private day schools of fairly recent growth: Anthorne, in Quaker's Lane, incorporating Potters Bar high school, opened in 1932[49] and caters mainly for girls wishing to train for ballet and drama, although boys attend the preparatory and kindergarten departments;[50] Linden school was opened in Ladbrooke Drive in 1932 for boys and girls from 3 to 11 years of age and in 1966 was occupying premises in Byng Drive for 65 pupils;[51] Lochinver House school was founded in 1947, extended in 1970, and attended by 220 boys aged 5 to 13 in 1972.[52]

Roman Catholic schools have existed since 1866, when St. Andrew's school was built in Union Street, Barnet. It was a boarding school, conducted by the fathers of the Institute of St. Andrew, and was attended by c. 100 boys in 1890.[53] Boys were frequently transferred at the age of 14 to St. Joseph's House, where they were apprenticed to a trade,[54] and by 1905 the school had its own press, where pupils could learn printing.[55] The fathers also ran St. Pancras's school, which was started in 1874[56] to give a full middle-class education to c. 60 boys. In 1890 the average attendance was 40.[57] By 1896–7 St. Andrew's school had been transferred to Brunswick House,[58] Wood Street, outside the parish, and in 1911–12 St. Pancras's school also moved there.[59] A Roman Catholic school also existed at nos. 3–5 Union Street from c. 1889 to 1911.[60] St. Catherine's, a boarding school for poor girls, was run on the same lines as St. Andrew's school[61] and had an average attendance of 25 in 1886,[62] after which it is not recorded.

Another Roman Catholic school, also called St. Catherine's, was established in Stapylton Road in 1909[63] to accommodate 58 infants and juniors. It was attended by 55 children in 1918–19[64] and by 71 in 1938.[65] A larger school was built in 1961 in Vale Drive,[66] outside the parish, but the school has an annexe within the boundary, in Union Street.[67] Pope Paul Roman Catholic school was erected at Great Slades, off Baker Street, in 1967 and was attended by 187 children in 1972.[68]

CHARITIES.[69] In 1652 John Howkins built five alms-houses for poor women on land between the church and the vicarage house.[70] By will dated 1677 he left a rent-charge of £5 a year out of property at Wrotham Park for quarterly payments to the almspeople but he did not provide for the upkeep of the houses, which fell upon the parish. In 1811 Francis Barroneau left £100 stock, the interest to be distributed half-yearly among the inmates, and in 1844 Elizabeth Barroneau bequeathed £50 stock on simi-

[32] Ex inf. Mr. B. Warren.
[33] Ex inf. the headmistresses.
[34] Ex inf. the headmaster.
[35] See p. 296.
[36] Ex inf. the headmaster.
[37] Ex inf. the headmaster.
[38] V.C.H. Herts. ii. 79–81.
[39] Kelly's Dir. Essex, Herts., Mdx. (1933).
[40] Ex inf. Barnet L.B., chief educ. offr.
[41] Kelly's Dir. Mdx. (1855).
[42] Story of Potters Bar, 21.
[43] Educ. of Poor Digest, 539.
[44] Pigot, Lond. and Prov. Dir. (1823–4).
[45] M.R.O., D.R.O. 5/G1/1 (log bk. 1870–95), 113, 121, 127.
[46] Ibid. 245.
[47] Story of Potters Bar, 125.
[48] Kelly's Dirs. Mdx. (1862, 1866, 1870, 1874, 1878, 1886, 1898); Kelly's Dir. Barnet (1892–3).
[49] Sturges, op. cit. 181.
[50] Potters Bar, Official Guide [1972].
[51] Sturges, op. cit. 181; Story of Potters Bar, 130.
[52] Ex inf. the headmaster.
[53] Kelly's Dir. Essex, Herts. and Mdx. (1890).
[54] Catholic Dir. (1878).
[55] Ibid. (1905).
[56] Ibid. (1874).
[57] Ibid. (1900); Kelly's Dir. Essex, Herts. and Mdx. (1890).
[58] Kelly's Dir. Barnet (1896–7).
[59] Ibid. (1911–12).
[60] Ibid. (1889–1900, 1910–11).
[61] Catholic Dir. (1878).
[62] Kelly's Dir. Herts. (1886).
[63] Ex inf. the headmaster.
[64] Bd. of Educ., List 21 (H.M.S.O., 1919).
[65] Ibid. (1938).
[66] Ex inf. the headmaster.
[67] Kelly's Dir. Barnet (1969).
[68] Ex inf. the headmaster.
[69] Except where otherwise stated, the following section is based on Char. Com. files; 8th Rep. Com. Char. H.C. 13(1823), viii; 9th Rep. Com. Char.
[70] Brittain, South Mymms, 41.

lar terms. In 1837 Mrs. Kerney left £200 to provide bread and coal for widows in the alms-houses and George Pooley, by will proved 1883, left £2,500, the income on which was to be paid in doles. Before 1928 an unknown donor had given £24 and F. Abraham made a gift to Howkins's alms-houses which in 1899 was represented by £32 stock.[71] The buildings gradually fell into decay and were demolished, the site being sold in 1928 and the rent-charge of £5 redeemed in 1939 for £224 stock.

John Bradshaw (d. 1698) left £3 a year, charged upon lands in South Mimms and Enfield Chase, to provide 20s. for the vicar of South Mimms for preaching a sermon on Christmas Eve and 40s. for bread to be distributed among poor parishioners. The property was later conveyed to Paul Jervis[72] (d. 1718) and became part of the City Parochial Foundation. In 1895 the trustees of Bradshaw's charity applied for the redemption of the annuity and £120 stock was transferred from the central fund to the credit of the charity.

George Ferne Bates, vicar of South Mimms, by will proved 1841, left £250, the interest to provide coals for the poor. Thomas Maling Nicholson, a later vicar, by will proved 1852, gave £100 for the same purpose.

Under a Scheme of 1941 the gifts of Howkins, the Barroneaus, Kerney, Pooley, the unknown donor, Abraham, Bradshaw, Bates, and Nicholson were consolidated as the South Mimms parochial charities. The Scheme provided that the charities should be managed under that title, although each should retain its own identity. The annual income of £77 7s. 8d. from Howkins's and the six other related charities was to be applied in pensions of between 6s. 6d. and 10s. a week to poor women of good character who had resided in the parish for at least two years. One of the pensioners was to be a widow and called 'the Kerney pensioner'. The annual income of £8 15s. from the charities of Bates and Nicholson was to be spent on coal for poor persons living in South Mimms and not in receipt of poor law relief, as selected by the trustees. The £3 from Bradshaw's charity was to provide 20s. to the vicar as before and 40s. in cash or bread for distribution among parishioners attending the 'Bread Service'.

James Hickson, of the Brewers' Company of London, by will dated 1686, devised in trust his manor of Wyllyotts and other lands at South Mimms for the endowment of six alms-houses which he had built at Kitts End. The endowment provided for the upkeep of the property and payments to the alms-people, each of whom was to receive £4 and a load of firewood every year, and a gown every second year. The company, on the recommendation of the vicar, churchwardens, and overseers, were to select alms-people from the poor inhabitants of South Mimms. The alms-houses were rebuilt by the company in 1750 and c. 1800 they were inhabited by six widows who each received £6 a year, a further £1 instead of the firewood, and a gown of grey cloth every second year. There was an additional payment of 10s. 6d. to each widow at Christmas. Six new alms-houses were built in grey brick in 1856, on a site where the Cross Keys inn had formerly stood.[73] The old alms-houses, each consisting of a single room and a coalshed, were in poor conditions in 1867, when they were leased out.[74]

Hickson's endowment was augmented by the gift of John Neiman, who, by will dated 1802, left £700 stock subject to a life interest, to provide weekly payments to the almspeople. The charity became payable in 1820 and after legacy duty £644 stock was transferred to the company, raising the total income of each widow by 1823 to £10 14s. 10d. The two charities were combined by the Charity Commissioners in 1894. By 1961 the total payment of allowances and gifts to inmates had risen to £457.

George Pooley, by will dated 1883, left £10,300, later invested in stock, the interest to be applied to poor persons of Monken Hadley and part of South Mimms. The charity, called the George and Mary Ann Pooley trust, is governed by Schemes of 1884, 1899, 1904, and 1924, the first of which provides that the income shall benefit 15 poor persons who have resided in the parishes of Monken Hadley and South Mimms (including the ecclesiastical districts of Christ Church and St. John's, Potters Bar) for not less than two years, preference to be given to those who have been reduced by misfortune from better circumstances. By 1962 the annual income was £270 and in 1971 twenty quarterly payments of £4 10s. were made to each of the fifteen pensioners, less nine payments not made owing to temporary vacancies.

TOTTENHAM

TOTTENHAM[1] parish contained 4,680 a. in 1831.[2] Its shape was roughly that of a trapezium, divided from north to south by the Roman and medieval way later called High Road, with a westerly projection from the north-west corner around Wood Green. High Road, along which most early settlement took place, entered the parish nearly 3½ miles from London and continued northward for more than 2 miles; the centre of Wood Green lay about 6 miles from London.[3] Tottenham, which occurs in Domesday Book, was often known as Tottenham High Cross, from the medieval wayside cross in High Road.[4] Wood Green, recorded in 1445,[5] existed as a separate local government unit from 1888 until 1965.[6] The two districts are widely known as the respective homes of Tottenham Hotspur football club and of the Alexandra Palace.[7] From the late 19th century the south-western corner of Tottenham

[71] Endowed Chars. (Lond.), H.C. 306, p. 20 (1899), lxx.
[72] Guildhall, St. Sepulchre's Chars. Box 135.
[73] Kelly's Dir. Mdx. (1867).
[74] Barnet Mus. 2144, p. 7.
[1] The article was written in 1973. Any references to later years are dated. The help of Mr. Ian Murray in making material available and commenting on the article is gratefully acknowledged.

[2] Census, 1831.
[3] Except where otherwise stated, the rest of the para. and the foll. two paras. are based on O.S. Maps 6", Mdx.XII. (1863–9 and later edns.).
[4] P.N. Mdx. (E.P.N.S.), 78.
[5] Tottenham Man. Rolls (1318–1503), transl. W. McB. Marcham, 76.
[6] See pp. 344–5.   [7] See pp. 340–1.

contained part of the new suburb of Harringay.[8]

The parish abutted Essex along the river Lea on the east, Edmonton on the north, Friern Barnet on the west, Hornsey on the west and south, and Stoke Newington and Hackney on the south. From the north-east corner of the parish the boundary ran from the river across High Road and westward to the later junction of Bowes and North Circular roads. Thence it followed North Circular Road before turning southward along Alexandra Park Road and eastward, north-east of Muswell Avenue and Muswell Hill, to take in Alexandra Park. North-west of Ducketts Common it again turned south, keeping roughly parallel to Green Lanes until it passed the site of Harringay Arena, where it turned east and ran to the Lea along Eade Road and slightly to the south of Vartry and Craven Park roads.

In 1888 Tottenham was divided from Wood Green by a line running due south from Devonshire (formerly Clay) Hill to meet White Hart Lane near its later junction with Roundway and thence south-westward along Westbury Avenue to Ducketts Common. Boundaries thereafter changed very little: a parcel of farm-land was transferred from Wood Green to Southgate local board district in 1892,[9] a small exchange was made between Tottenham and Hackney under an order of 1907, and in 1934 Tottenham surrendered less than 1 a. to Hornsey and 3 a. to Wood Green and received 1 a. from each authority.[10] In 1951 Tottenham covered 3,012 a. and Wood Green 1,606 a.[11] Both boroughs were amalgamated with Hornsey in 1965 to form the London Borough of Haringey.[12]

The soil bordering the Lea is alluvium, which in the north reaches almost as far as the first railway line and farther west, beyond the line, in the south. Brickearth stretches south from Edmonton between the railway and High Road, although a strip of Flood Plain Gravel runs along the northern part of the road itself as far as Lordship Lane. Brickearth also lies north of White Hart Lane as far west as Devonshire Hill and occurs in patches, surrounded by Taplow Gravel, at Bruce Castle and part of Church Lane. The remainder of the parish is predominantly London Clay, with a little Boyn Hill Gravel west and south-west of Devonshire Hill and some glacial gravel on the site of Alexandra Palace.[13]

The eastern part of Tottenham is low-lying and flat.[14] Nowhere east of High Road does the ground reach 50 ft. above sea-level, except around the high cross (the Tottenham Hill of Izaak Walton's *Compleat Angler*) and at the descent from Stamford Hill in the south, where the road enters the parish at 75 ft. Tottenham west of High Road is mostly over 50 ft. in the north, save along the course of the Moselle, but is lower in the south save around Downhills Park, part of which lies at 100 ft. and

along the boundary. Wood Green is more undulating, with the 100-ft. contour running southwestward from the Edmonton boundary at Devonshire Hill Lane. Near Bounds Green the land rises to 200 ft. above Wood Green tunnel, near Bounds Green, and farther south a ridge from Hampstead crosses the border of Muswell Hill (Hornsey) to reach 300 ft. at the site of the Alexandra Palace.

The Moselle stream, so called from colloquial forms of Muswell Hill,[15] flows across the boundary into Wood Green north of Hornsey station.[16] The course runs north-eastward to Lordship Lane, which it follows before meandering in one curve to the south and another to the north, reaching High Road by the junction with White Hart Lane. Thence it flows along High Road to a point near Scotland Green, where it turns eastward to the marshes and the Lea. It there forms a straight stretch known by 1408[17] and in 1619 as Garbell ditch[18] and 200 years later as Carbuncle ditch.[19] In 1619 a watercourse later called Stonebridge stream crossed the parish in the south, between the later West Green and St. Ann's roads. A ditch ran from Garbell ditch near the High Road as far as the Hale in 1619 and survived in a shortened form in 1818.[20]

The New River, opened in 1613, was cut across high ground in the north-west of the parish.[21] It followed a very crooked course, dictated by the contours, entering from Edmonton west of Wood Green High Road, turning back to recross the boundary a little to the east, and re-entering the parish at Clay Hill, near the later Great Cambridge Road; thence it ran south-westward, with a south-easterly bulge at Wood Green, before turning south by Wood Green Common and making for Hornsey.[22] A shorter course was later adopted, whereby the New River went underground at Myddleton Road and re-emerged west of Wood Green Common; from the mid 19th century it has run through a reservoir abutting the border with Hornsey.[23]

While the river Lea itself formed the eastern boundary, the Garbell ditch drained into an artificial cut to the west,[24] an extension of Pymme's brook which ran southward through the marshes from Edmonton and, as the mill stream, joined the main river below Tottenham mills. Watercourses connecting the two formed several islands in the marshes in 1619. In 1767 the vestry unsuccessfully opposed legislation which led to the construction of a straight cut from Edmonton, the River Lea Navigation,[25] which met Pymme's brook at Stonebridge lock. The Act of 1767[26] provided that the mill stream, below the lock, should serve as an extension to the Lea Navigation although rights of passage were not formally secured until 1779;[27] the new cut was later continued west of the stream to Ferry Lane, where Tottenham lock was constructed, to rejoin the old

[8] *P.N. Mdx.* (E.P.N.S.), 123.
[9] M.R.O., *Reps. of Local Inqs. 1889–97*, 570.
[10] *Census*, 1911, 1931 (pt. ii).
[11] Ibid. 1951.
[12] See p. 345.
[13] Geol. Surv. Map 1″, drift, sheet 256 (1951 edn.).
[14] The para. is based on O.S. Maps 6″, TQ 29 SE., 39 SW., 39 SE., 38 NW., and 38 NE. (1962–8 edn.).
[15] *P.N. Mdx.* (E.P.N.S.), 4.
[16] Except where otherwise stated, the para. is based on O.S. Maps 6″, Mdx. XII. (1863–9 edn.).
[17] *P.N. Mdx.* (E.P.N.S.), 80.
[18] W. Robinson, *Hist. and Antiquities of . . . Tottenham High Cross* (1840 edn.), map of 1619. The original map,

which cannot be traced, was made for a survey of the manorial lands of Richard Sackville, earl of Dorset, in 1619. The field bk. which accompanied the Dorset survey is in M.R.O., Acc. 695/9.
[19] Robinson, *Tottenham*, map of 1818.
[20] Ibid. maps of 1619 and 1818.
[21] Ibid. i. 32.
[22] Ibid. maps of 1619 and 1818.
[23] O.S. Maps 6″, Mdx. XII. NW. (1863–9 edn.).
[24] Except where otherwise stated, the para. is based on Robinson, *Tottenham*, i. 19–31, and maps of 1619 and 1818.
[25] Bruce Castle Mus., D/PT/2A/3, f. 52.
[26] River Lea Navigation Act, 7 Geo. III, c. 51.
[27] Ibid. 19 Geo. III, c. 58.

river south of the mills. To the east, the original course of the Lea has been obscured by further cuts and the opening under an Act of 1897 of Banbury reservoir, in the extreme north-east, and Lockwood reservoir, across the centre of the eastern parish boundary.[28]

Three springs are mentioned by William Bedwell, vicar of Tottenham from 1607 to 1632 and author of the first local history,[29] although one of them, Muswell ('mossy spring' or 'well'), was in Hornsey.[30] St. Loy's well lay near High Road, north-west of the cross, presumably close to the obscure chapel of St. Loy also mentioned by Bedwell, and Bishop's well issued from a hillock south of the Moselle opposite the vicarage house. Both were known for their curative properties before Bedwell's time and were still so noted in the early 19th century,[31] when they were cleansed. By 1876 St. Loy's well, close to the railway line, was in a neglected state and Bishop's well had been drained on the incorporation of Well field into Tottenham cemetery. Dunstan's well, in Tottenham wood, was recognizable from 1619 until the 1860s.[32]

Most of Tottenham's distinguished residents, including pupils at its private schools, are mentioned elsewhere in the article.[33] The author Dr. Edward Simpson (1578–1651) was born in the parish, where his father was vicar, the rabbinical scholar Hugh Broughton (1549–1612) died there, at the house of a draper named Benet, and William Strode (?1599–1645), one of the 'five members', also died at Tottenham. John Hoadly (1678–1746), archbishop of Armagh, was native, as were the physician Dr. Thomas Hodgkin (1766–1845), the missionary John Williams (1796–1839), the botanist John Joseph Bennett (1801–76), and the lithographer Douglas Morison (1814–47). Sir Michael Foster (1689–1763), a justice of the King's Bench, lived at Grove House,[34] John Hindle (1761–96), the composer, had property in the parish after 1789, and Charles Erdman Petersdorff (1800–86), the legal writer, was the son of a London furrier who lived also at Ivy House. The Quaker poet Bernard Barton (1784–1849), spent part of his childhood at Tottenham, where he described his grandfather's large residence.[35] The *Legend of St. Loy* and *Tottenham* were the first poems published by John Abraham Heraud (1799–1887), who often visited his father at Tottenham.[36] The author and bookseller William Hone (1780–1842) retired from London to Church Road and died in High Road two years later.[37]

The aeronaut Henry Tracey Coxwell (1819–1900) practised as a dentist at no. 689 High Road and made several ballooning ascents from Tottenham Green.[38] The radical politician Charles Bradlaugh (1833–91) attended vestry meetings while a resident

of Northumberland Park in the 1860s.[39] Sir Charles Reed, M.P. chairman of the London school board, died at Earlsmead, in High Road, in 1881.[40] Mrs. Charlotte Eliza Lawson (1832–1906), who, as Mrs. J. H. Riddell, depicted the neighbourhood of West Green in some of her novels, lived for a time in Hanger Lane.[41] The author Ted Willis, created a life peer in 1963,[42] was born and educated in Tottenham which he described in his autobiography.[43] Robert Craigmyle Morrison (1881–1953), a local councillor and M.P., was created Lord Morrison of Tottenham in 1945.[44]

COMMUNICATIONS. From medieval times the parish has been crossed by main thoroughfares from London, themselves connected by roads leading from the high ground in the west towards the Lea.[45] Ermine Street, from London to Lincoln, skirted the Lea valley, although early local historians followed Camden in believing that the Romans had branched off at Kingsland and taken a more westerly route along Green Lanes; according to that view, it was not until John's reign that the men of Ware (Herts.) diverted the road to lower ground, on a course parallel to the Lea.[46] It was later established that Ermine Street for the most part kept to the line of High Road northward from Stamford Hill as far as Bruce Grove; thence the Roman route headed due north close to the line of Pembury Road and across the Moselle to Snells Park (Edmonton), while the later High Road diverged slightly eastward, to avoid flooding, before rejoining the old route at Snells Park.

Much of the modern road pattern had been established by 1619.[47] High Road ran northward in the east and Green Lanes, dividing at the later junction of Wood Green High Road and Bounds Green Road, in the west; between them routes corresponding to the later White Hart and Lordship lanes and West Green and St. Ann's roads crossed the middle of the parish. The western part of White Hart Lane was then called Apeland Street as far as the parsonage house, whence a lane later marked by Devonshire Hill Lane led to the Edmonton border at Clay Hill. Most of Lordship Lane, from Chapmans Green to High Road, was called Berry Lane, although its modern name was recorded in 1526.[48] West Green Road had no name between Ducketts Common and West Green, whence it continued to High Road as Blackhope or Blackup Lane, with Philip or High Cross Lane as a north-easterly branch. St. Ann's Road was marked by Chisley Lane, called Hanger Lane from the 18th century. Wolves Lane, recorded in 1397,[49] headed north across the boundary from Apeland Street, a lane (later Snakes Lane) linked Apeland Street with Berry Lane at Chapmans

[28] See p. 346.
[29] Bedwell's 'Brief Description' is printed in W. J. Roe, *Ancient Tottenham*, 95–119.
[30] *P.N. Mdx.* (E.P.N.S.), 124. Except where otherwise stated, the rest of the para. is based on Robinson, *Tottenham*, i. 16–19; F. Fisk, *Hist. Tottenham*, ser. i. 123–4.
[31] T. Cox, *Magna Britannia* (1724 edn.), iii. 35; *Pigot's Com. Dir.* (1832–4).
[32] O.S. Map 6″, Mdx. XII. NW. (1863–9 edn.).
[33] Except where otherwise stated, the foll. two paras. are based on *D.N.B.* and supplts.
[34] Robinson, *Tottenham*, i. 117.
[35] Thorne, *Environs*, ii. 623–4.
[36] Fisk, *Tottenham*, ii. 278.
[37] Ibid. 287.

[38] Fisk, *Tottenham*, ii. 271.
[39] Ibid. 261.   [40] Ibid. 298.
[41] Ibid. 299.
[42] *Who's Who*, *1971*, 3415.
[43] *Whatever Happened to Tom Mix* (1970).
[44] *Who Was Who*, *1951–60*, 791.
[45] Except where otherwise stated, the para. is based on Roe, *Ancient Tottenham*, 67–70.
[46] W. Camden, *Britannia*, transl. P. Holland (1610 edn.), 407.
[47] Except where otherwise stated, the para. is based on Robinson, *Tottenham*, map of 1619.
[48] *Tottenham Man. Rolls* (*1510–31*), transl. W. McB. Marcham, 188.
[49] *P.N. Mdx.* (E.P.N.S.), 78.

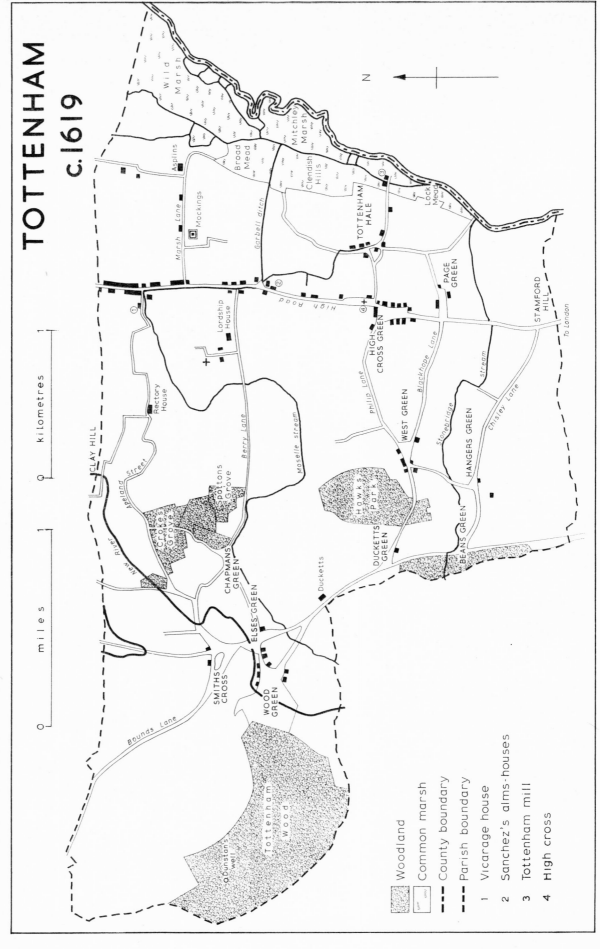

TOTTENHAM c.1619

N

Wild Marsh

Mitchley Marsh

Broad Mead

Asplins

Clendish Hills

Marsh Lane

Mockings

Garbell ditch

Lock Mead

TOTTENHAM HALE

Lordship House

High Road

PAGE GREEN

STAMFORD HILL

To London

CLAY HILL

Rectory House

Apeland Street

Berry Lane

Moselle stream

HIGH CROSS GREEN

Philip Lane

WEST GREEN

Blackhope Lane

Stonebridge

Stream

HANGERS GREEN

Chisley Lane

New River

Crokes Grove

Pottons Grove

CHAPMANS GREEN

ELSES GREEN

Ducketts

Hawks Park

DUCKETTS GREEN

BEANS GREEN

SMITHS CROSS

WOOD GREEN

Bounds Lane

oDunstans well

Tottenham Wood

kilometres

miles

Woodland

Common marsh

County boundary

Parish boundary

1 Vicarage house

2 Sanchez's alms-houses

3 Tottenham mill

4 High cross

Green, and a forerunner of Black Boy Lane linked West Green with Hanger Lane. Eastward from High Road branched Marsh (later Park) Lane, recorded in 1467, High Cross Lane, leading to the Hale, and Broad Lane.[50] From the Hale one lane headed north-east into the marshes and another, slightly south of the modern Ferry Lane, led to Tottenham mills. There was also a way from Broad Lane to the Lea, along the line of Markfield Road.

The network of roads changed little in the next 200 years, save around Bruce Castle and the neighbouring stretch of High Road. Church Lane, which had merely connected Lordship Lane with the parish church in 1619, was extended north and east, as Church Road, to meet High Road in 1810 and was crossed at right angles by Love Lane in 1818,[51] while Bruce Grove had been constructed north-west from High Road to the entrance to Bruce Castle in the 1790s.[52] High Road itself was said to be part of the worst road near London in 1713, when it was placed under the new Stamford Hill turnpike trust.[53] A toll-house was built on Stamford Hill and was still used for meetings of the trustees after a new gate had been erected to the north, in order to prevent traffic from evading payment by using Hanger Lane.[54] The trustees, as they had been empowered to do in 1713, also set up a subsidiary gate where Hornsey (later Turnpike) Lane joined Green Lanes, although they did not become responsible for maintaining Green Lanes until 1789. The commissioners for the metropolitan turnpike roads superseded the trustees in 1826.[55]

Seven Sisters Road, to improve access from Islington and so from the west end of London, was driven north-eastward across open country to reach Tottenham High Road in 1833.[56] Thereafter, for nearly a century, roads were built as a result of the spread of housing rather than to ease the flow of traffic. Northumberland Park in the 1860s was the forerunner of scores of residential avenues, to which were later added roads serving local factories. It was not until the 1920s that a major north-south route was driven through the centre of the parish. Lordship Lane was then linked with West Green and Belmont roads by Downhills Way and with White Hart Lane by Roundway. From Roundway, Great Cambridge Road headed north across Edmonton.[57]

In 1619 High Road crossed the Moselle by Lordship bridge, where the stream turned eastward as Garbell ditch. It also crossed Stonebridge stream at the foot of Stamford Hill by Mark or Stone bridge,[58] presumably the bridge in the king's highway which had been ruinous in 1555.[59] William Bedwell stated that both bridges were of stone and that the only similar one was Blackup bridge at Page Green.[60] In 1826 Lordship bridge comprised a single-arched

culvert of brick, close to a dam with flood-gates which the turnpike trustees had built. At that time High Road also crossed a single-arched brick bridge to the north, opposite Marsh Lane, which was maintained by the parish.[61] Stone bridge, enlarged by the metropolitan roads commissioners, was described as the only proper bridge bearing High Road in 1840, the others being mere sewers or culverts.[62] It gave its name to the 19th-century Stonebridge House, which by the 1890s had given way to Stonebridge Road.[63]

A bridge in Berry (later Lordship) Lane was held to be the joint responsibility of the lords of the four Tottenham manors in 1397.[64] In 1619 the Moselle was bridged where it passed under Lordship Lane, west of the church, and under Green Lanes near Wood Green; there was also at least one bridge over the New River at Wood Green and one carrying Black Boy Lane over Stonebridge stream in the south. By the early 19th century there were six bridges over the meandering New River, all of them maintained by the New River Co. Tottenham mills were reached by a bridge over the mill stream in 1619, when King's bridge, beyond them, led across the old Lea to Walthamstow. East, West, and Centre bridges were built there after the digging of the Lea Navigation cut; in 1826 tolls were collected at the eastern and western bridges, which, like the central one, were maintained by the proprietors.[65] Presumably there was also a ferry in the mid 19th century, giving rise to the Ferry Boat inn and the name Ferry Lane.[66] Under an Act of 1869 tolls at the mills were abolished and the roads made public.[67] In 1915 the bridges were replaced by a new one, leading eastward to Forest Road, Walthamstow.[68]

Several bridges crossed the ditches which intersected the marsh-land. In 1619 one bridge led from Broad mead to Wild marsh and another to Clendish Hills, while a third linked Clendish Hills with Mitchley marsh.[69] The first was of stone, which had needed repair in 1523, and was still so marked in Bedwell's time, although not singled out by him. Mitchley bridge, recorded from 1519, was of timber; every freeholder and copyholder had to pay towards its upkeep in 1572, when the lord was to supply materials.[70]

Tottenham High Road afforded relatively good communications with London. Coaches started from the Swan, the Red Lion, the Ship, and other inns throughout the day in 1832–47[71] and omnibuses both to the City and to Oxford Street had been licensed by 1839.[72] The first railway, reaching London by a circuitous route that was twice as long as the road journey, offered little competition to the coaches,[73] which left every 15 minutes in 1845.[74] When later on railways became the main passenger

[50] Ibid.
[51] Robinson, *Tottenham*, i. 96 and maps of 1619 and 1818.
[52] Ibid. i. 95.
[53] D.O. Pam, *Stamford Hill, Green Lanes Turnpike Trust*, i. (Edmonton Hund. Hist. Soc. 1963), 2–3.
[54] Fisk, *Tottenham*, i. 43.
[55] Pam, op. cit. ii. (1965), 4, 24, 29.
[56] Robinson, *Tottenham*, i. 45–6.
[57] O.S. Maps 6", Mdx. XII. SE., NE., NW., and SW. (1863–9 and later edns.); *The Times*, 7 May 1925.
[58] Robinson, *Tottenham*, map of 1619.
[59] *Tottenham Man. Rolls* (*1547–58*), transl. W. McB. Marcham, 112. [60] Robinson, *Tottenham*, i. 42.
[61] *Rep. on Bridges in Mdx.* 112–14.
[62] Robinson, *Tottenham*, i. 42–3.

[63] O.S. Map 6", Mdx. XII. NE. (1863–9 and 1894–6 edns.).
[64] *Tottenham Man. Rolls* (*1377–99*), transl. R. Oram, 297.
[65] Robinson, *Tottenham*, map of 1619; *Rep. on Bridges in Mdx.* 112–14.
[66] O.S. Map 6", Mdx. XII. NE. (1863–9 edn.).
[67] Kew and other bridges Act, 32 & 33 Vic. c. 19 (Local).
[68] Plaque on bridge.
[69] Robinson, *Tottenham*, map of 1619.
[70] *Tottenham Man. Rolls* (*1510–31*), 131, 177; ibid. (*1558–82*), transl. W. McB. Marcham, 129.
[71] *Pigot's Com. Dir.* (1832–4).
[72] T. C. Barker and M. Robbins, *Hist. Lond. Transport*, i. 402. [73] G. H. Lake, *Rlys. of Tottenham*, 11.
[74] *P.O. Dir. Six Home Cnties.* (1845).

carriers, omnibuses connected the stations with various points along High Road. In 1860 there was a service from Park station to the junction of Northumberland Park with High Road and thence to the Angel, Edmonton,[75] and in 1871 omnibuses began to ply to the Angel from the new South Tottenham station.[76]

A single tram-line from Stamford Hill to Edmonton, with 8 passing places in Tottenham, was opened by the North London Tramways Co. in 1881.[77] A south-westerly extension along Seven Sisters Road and through Manor House to join the North Metropolitan at Finsbury Park was added in 1885 and followed by a branch from Manor House to Wood Green two years later.[78] Merryweather steam trams, unpopular for their dirt and noise,[79] were introduced by the North London Co. under a seven-year licence in 1885; they were also ordered for the Wood Green line,[80] running every ten minutes from Wood Green High Road to Finsbury Park station.[81] In 1891 control passed to the North Metropolitan Co., which reverted to horse-power[82] and in 1892 laid double lines along Tottenham High Road.[83]

The Metropolitan Electric Tramways Co. introduced a service from Finsbury Park to the corner of Seven Sisters and High roads in 1904; electric trams were taken along High Road to Lordship Lane later in the same year and connected Stamford Hill with Silver Street, Edmonton, in 1905.[84] Wood Green became the northern terminus of one of the company's radial routes, through Finsbury Park,[85] when a depot at Jolly Butchers Hill was opened in 1904, on a site previously leased to the North London Tramways Co.[86] M.E.T. trams linked Wood Green with Bruce Grove, Tottenham, from 1904, Hornsey and Alexandra Park from 1905, and Bounds Green from 1906, before the route from Finsbury Park was extended towards Enfield. They also ran between Tottenham Hale and Walthamstow from 1906.[87]

Trolley-buses arrived in 1936, passing through Tottenham Hale to link Walthamstow with the Underground railway at Manor House station. Many trams, including those running along High Road from Stamford Hill to Enfield, were replaced by trolley-buses in 1938,[88] when the depot at Wood Green was converted.[89] Tottenham garage, near the High Cross, was opened in 1913 to hold motor-buses of the Tramways (M.E.T.) Omnibus Co., a subsidiary of Metropolitan Electric Tramways, which itself was associated with the London General Omnibus Co.[90] Between 1911 and 1914 motor-bus services were introduced to link both Tottenham and Wood Green with the west end and southern suburbs of London.[91] Trolley-buses were superseded by six new motor-bus routes in 1961,[92] when the Wood Green garage was again converted.[93]

In 1840 the Northern and Eastern Railway Co. opened its line from Stratford (Essex) to Broxbourne (Herts.),[94] running through the east of the parish with a station called Tottenham (later Tottenham Hale) and, from 1842, another called Marsh Lane (later Park, later Northumberland Park). Trains were allowed to run beyond Stratford to the Bishopsgate terminus of the Eastern Counties Railway Co., which leased the whole line from 1844 and itself became part of the Great Eastern Co. in 1862, although the Northern and Eastern Co. retained its separate identity for another 40 years. The line was not well situated for residents, being nearer the river than High Road and providing an expensive journey to the City. Tottenham station, in open country north of Ferry Lane, was used by Queen Victoria and Prince Albert when they visited Cambridge in state in 1847. Before the building of the Tottenham and Hampstead Junction Railway a large cattle-dock adjoined Tottenham station, where livestock was taken off the trains and herded over High Road towards the Metropolitan Cattle Market at Holloway.

The Tottenham and Hampstead Junction Railway, authorized in 1862, opened in 1868. It was linked to the G.E.R. line by North Junction, and later also by South and West junctions, south of Tottenham station, and crossed the south of the parish towards Crouch Hill. Although destined to be an important link between the systems of the L.N.E.R. and the L.M.S.R., the line at first served no stations within Tottenham itself. South Tottenham station, at the foot of Stamford Hill, was opened in 1871, Harringay Park (later Harringay Stadium) in 1880, and St. Ann's Road, between the two, in 1882. The line was taken over by the Tottenham and Hampstead Joint Committee, representing the Midland and the Great Eastern companies, in 1902.

In 1872 a better London service was provided by the opening of the Great Eastern's line from Bethnal Green to Edmonton, which soon ran from a new terminus at Liverpool Street. The line was raised to cross the Tottenham and Hampstead railway at right-angles and passed through three new stations close to High Road: Seven Sisters, Bruce Grove, and White Hart Lane.

Meanwhile, in the north-west, the Great Northern Railway had opened its line from Maiden Lane (afterwards from King's Cross) to Hatfield in 1850 and provided a station at Wood Green in 1859.[95] A branch line from Wood Green through Southgate to Enfield was opened in 1871, with a station near the boundary at Bowes Park in 1880.[96] Another G.N.R. branch, from the Finsbury Park to High Barnet line through Hornsey, was opened between Highgate and Alexandra Palace in 1873. That part of the line which crossed Alexandra Park was paid for by the owners of the palace and was not acquired by the G.N.R. until 1911.[97]

A direct rail link between east and west was

[75] Tottenham and Edmonton Advertiser, time-table facing p. 100.
[76] New Mdx. Cnty. Pictorial, no. 4, N.S. p. 15.
[77] Fisk, Tottenham, i. 143.
[78] Barker and Robbins, op. cit. i. 267.
[79] Fisk, Tottenham, i. 143.
[80] Barker and Robbins, op. cit. i. 267, 294.
[81] Kelly's Dir. Essex, Herts. and Mdx. (1890).
[82] Barker and Robbins, op. cit. i. 267.
[83] Fisk, Tottenham, i. 144.
[84] Ibid.
[85] A. A. Jackson, Semi-Detached London, 27.
[86] Ex inf. the press offr. L.T.E.

[87] Jackson, op. cit. 329–30.
[88] Bruce Castle Mus., 871, 875 [newspaper cuttings and timetables.]
[89] Ex inf. L.T.E. [90] Idem.
[91] Jackson, op. cit. 334.
[92] Kelly's Dir. Mdx. (1926); Bruce Castle Mus., 875.
[93] Ex inf. L.T.E.
[94] Except where otherwise stated, the foll. six paras. are based on G. H. Lake, Rlys. of Tottenham, passim.
[95] C. H. Grinling, Hist. of Gt. Northern Rly. (1966 edn.), 90, 124, 257.
[96] Ibid. 261.
[97] Ibid. 293, 264.

achieved only in 1878, when the G.E.R. opened a line from South Tottenham to Palace Gates, a little north-west of Wood Green station. Intermediate stations, also opened in 1878, were at West Green and at Green Lanes (renamed Green Lanes and Noel Park in 1884, Noel Park and Wood Green in 1902). Palace Gates was linked to Bowes Park, on the Enfield line, in 1930.

The railway companies opened no new stations after 1882, although from 1894 the Tottenham and Forest Gate line led from South Tottenham across the Lea to south-east Essex. In 1945 South Tottenham had an exceptionally long goods yard, mainly for coal, and there were other goods yards at Tottenham Hale, White Hart Lane, and West Green; extensive marshalling yards stretched from Northumberland Park almost half way to Tottenham Hale and rolling stock was kept at Palace Gates. All the 19th-century stations remained open save St. Ann's Road, which was closed in 1942. The Alexandra Palace line survived until 1954[98] and the Palace Gates line until 1963.[99]

Underground stations at Turnpike Lane, Wood Green, and Bounds Green, designed in an advanced style by Charles Holden,[1] were opened by the London Electric Railway on an extension of the Piccadilly line in 1932. The line reached Cockfosters in 1933, when it was taken over by the London Passenger Transport Board.[2] Tottenham itself remained without an underground service until the opening in 1968 of the first section of the London Transport Board's Victoria line, from Walthamstow to Highbury and Islington, with stations at Seven Sisters and Tottenham Hale.[3]

GROWTH BEFORE 1850. An Anglo-Saxon settlement, otherwise unrecorded, is indicated by the reference to Tottenham, 'Totta's ham',[4] in Domesday Book.[5] Presumably it bordered the Roman road, the medieval Tottenham street, along which most of the population was concentrated until the 19th century. Eastward lay rich pastures on the marshes by the river Lea,[6] while to the west stretched poorer soil, with woods whose bounds were gradually pushed back towards Muswell Hill in the course of the Middle Ages.[7]

The existence of a weir by 1086 and of a mill by 1254[8] suggest early habitations at the Hale (later Tottenham Hale), midway between High Road and Mill mead, although the name first occurs only in 1318, in a reference to John of the Hale.[9] The manor-house of Tottenham, described in 1254,[10] may have stood west of High Road, close to the church recorded by 1134 and the later site of Bruce Castle. After the division of the manor in 1254 there were prob-

ably three manor-houses; in addition the farmstead of the 14th-century sub-manor of Mockings was marked by a moat on the south side of Marsh (later Park) Lane, between High Road and the marshes. A rectangular 'homestead moat' was shown in the 19th century in the park of Downhills but was not recorded earlier.[11] The hospital of St. Lawrence at Clayhanger, once assumed to have been in Clayhanger parish (Devon), probably stood at Clay Hill, mid-way along the border with Edmonton;[12] it was recorded only from 1229 to 1264 and is not known to have been connected with the equally obscure 15th-century hospital of St. Loy, which itself seems to have disappeared before the Reformation.[13] Chapels, of unknown date, were later said to have stood by a hermitage close to High Road[14] and St. Loy's well.[15]

Accessibility from London led many citizens and religious houses to acquire property in Tottenham from the time of Ughtred of London, who by 1152 held land which afterwards passed to the nuns of Clerkenwell.[16] The Black Death is not known to have changed the pattern of settlement, although many deaths were presented: in 1348 on the manor of Daubeneys 15 copyhold tenements fell vacant and 10 reverted to the lord, presumably because the heirs had died.[17] Despite the plague the late 14th century saw considerable pressure of population on the land.[18]

The centre of Tottenham village, in so far as the roadside settlement possessed one, was marked by the high cross and by a green, the modern Tottenham Green, immediately south.[19] The cross, crowning a slight rise in High Road, was once associated with the funeral cortège of Eleanor of Castile[20] but was later found to have been no more than a wayside cross, first mentioned in 1409.[21] It stood on a mound and was of wood capped with lead c. 1580, some twenty years before its replacement at the expense of Owen Wood, dean of Armagh, who lived on the east side of the green.[22] Wood provided a plain octagonal brick column of 4 stages, surmounted by a weather-vane. The cross was stuccoed and ornamented in the Gothic style in 1809, since which date its appearance has not changed.[23]

Except along High Road and at the Hale medieval settlement took place around a number of greens. In the west assarting had permitted the building of a farmstead called Ducketts, north of the later Ducketts Common, by 1293.[24] Page Green, mentioned in 1348, stretched eastward from High Road a little way south of Tottenham Green, along Broad Lane towards a crossing of the Lea below Tottenham mill; the Page family, recorded from 1319,[25] still held land there in 1395.[26] West Green, midway along the

[98] H. P. White, *Regional Hist. of Rlys. of Gt. Britain*, iii. 165.
[99] Ibid. 176.
[1] Pevsner, *Mdx.* 175.
[2] C. E. Lee, *Sixty Years of the Piccadilly*, 22.
[3] *Whitaker's Almanack* (1970), 1020.
[4] *P.N. Mdx.* (E.P.N.S.), 78.
[5] *V.C.H. Mdx.* i. 129.
[6] See p. 334.
[7] See p. 336.
[8] See p. 336.
[9] *Tottenham Man. Rolls* (*1318–1503*), 11.
[10] See p. 327.
[11] Hist. Mon. Com. *Mdx.* 121; O.S. Maps 6″, Mdx. XII. NE. (1863–9 edn.).
[12] F. Roth, *Engl. Austin Friars*, i. 264–5.

[13] *V.C.H. Mdx.* i. 153; D. Knowles and R. N. Hadcock, *Med. Rel. Hos.* (1971 edn.), 318, 353. See p. 331.
[14] See p. 314.   [15] See p. 309.
[16] See p. 330.
[17] *Tottenham Man. Rolls* (*1318–1503*), pp. vii, 48–9.
[18] *T.L.M.A.S.* xxiv. 205.
[19] Except where otherwise stated, the para. is based on Robinson, *Tottenham*, i. 91–2.
[20] e.g. T. Cox, *Magna Britannia*, iii (1724), 35.
[21] *P.N. Mdx.* (E.P.N.S.), 80.
[22] W. J. Roe, *Tottenham, Edmonton and Enfield Hist. Note Bk.* 33.
[23] See plate facing p. 64.
[24] See p. 330.
[25] *Tottenham Man. Rolls* (*1318–1503*), 40, 12.
[26] Ibid. (*1377–99*), 147.

lane linking High Road opposite Page Green with Green Lanes at Ducketts, was mentioned in 1384. Beans Green, south of Ducketts at the junction of Green Lanes with Hanger Lane, was recorded in 1393 and Chapmans Green, where Lordship Lane later met Snakes Lane, in 1381,[27] but there were probably no hamlets at either place during the Middle Ages.

By the late 14th century traffic through Tottenham was in places impeded by residents, to judge from fines on tenants who had erected 'levesells' or bowers on the king's highway.[28] As many as 6 inns were recorded in 1455–6, all of them probably in High Road.[29] Many were large timber-framed buildings, of which the last remains survived until the 19th century.[30] Brick-making, the only medieval industry of note, also flourished in 1430.[31] A tenement called the hermitage was recorded in 1455–6.[32] Henry VIII, when greeting his sister Margaret at Bruce Castle, made a payment to the hermit of Tottenham in 1517.[33]

Tottenham itself became well known, presumably because of the many travellers who passed that way. Although it had no fair, a mid-15th-century satire on chivalry called the *Tournament of Tottenham* describes a rustic joust which was held there, attended by 'all the men of the country, of Islington, of Highgate, and Hackney'.[34] The expression 'Tottenham shall turn French', signifying something that could not possibly happen, was quoted by many local historians from the time of William Bedwell but used as early as 1536 by Thomas Howard, duke of Norfolk, when assuring Thomas Cromwell of his loyalty.[35]

Wards, recorded from 1515, were probably created on the basis of population; if their boundaries were those later described by Bedwell, three-quarters of the inhabitants lived in Lower, Middle, or High Cross ward, each of which contained sections of High Road, and the remainder in Wood Green ward, covering the western half of the parish.[36]

The early 16th century also saw considerable extensions to the parish church,[37] followed from 1514 by the complete rebuilding of Bruces manor-house (the core of the modern Bruce Castle), on a scale fit to receive royalty.[38] At the Reformation the hermitage became a private residence[39] and the division of monastic lands further increased the influx of outsiders, many of whom provided themselves with fine houses.[40] Alms-people were accommodated in cottages by the churchyard, under a charity established by George Henningham (d. 1536) and a range of alms-houses, endowed by Balthasar Sanchez, was built in High Road south of Scotland Green in 1600.[41] In the early 18th century it was thought that the alms-houses occupied the site of the offertory of St. Loy,[42] described by Bedwell as a poorhouse.[43]

In 1619[44] most parishioners still lived along High Road, mainly around the green at the high cross, farther north near the junction with Berry (later Lordship) Lane, and along the stretch from Marsh (later Park) Lane to the Edmonton boundary. The hermitage stood in High Road between Page and High Cross greens. There were many places where farm-land bordered the road, which had no houses on either side between Stamford Hill and Tottenham Green or along the west side for some distance north of the cross. Buildings stood closest together to the north of Marsh Lane, providing a contrast with the deserted portion of High Road in the extreme south of the parish.

East of High Road there were four houses at Page Green, more at the Hale, and a few along Marsh Lane as far as Asplins Farm, slightly east of the modern Northumberland Park railway station. Roses were grown along Marsh Lane, and elsewhere in the parish,[45] but the marshes themselves lay deserted, save for Tottenham mills, where both flour and leather were made. West of High Road, Berry or Lordship Lane led to the manor-house, the church, and a near-by farm, and Apeland Street (later White Hart Lane) led to the vicarage and rectory houses. Eight buildings around West Green constituted the only hamlet amidst the farm-land in the centre of Tottenham.

Much woodland survived in groves interspersed with fields in the western third of the parish. There were isolated houses at Hangers Green, where Black Boy Lane joined Hanger Lane, and at Ducketts Green, but there was none at Beans or Chapmans greens. The sole hamlet was Wood Green, where four houses occupied plots beside the New River and others faced the green itself, which was backed by the slopes of Tottenham wood. Close by, a little to the east, there were a few dwellings where Green Lanes joined Lordship Lane at Elses Green and White Hart Lane at Smiths Cross. There was also a farm at Clay Hill.[46]

A notable feature from the 16th century was the number of large houses, most of them leased to Londoners as country retreats. The Black House, in High Road opposite White Hart Lane, was said by Bedwell to boast an inscription recording that Henry VIII stayed there as George Henningham's guest.[47] Awlfield Farm, next to the church, was described as a fair tenement in 1585, as was the moated manor-house of Mockings,[48] although neither was among the grander buildings in 1619. By far the most imposing were the 'lordship house' or Bruce Castle and the parsonage house, together with Mattisons, the seat of Sir Julius Caesar, on the far side of Tottenham wood and in reality in Hornsey parish. Several spacious houses bordered High Cross or Tottenham Green, while others stood at Tottenham Hale or farther north, along High Road; Ducketts farm-house was termed a mansion and Asplins farm-house was large, as were Willoughbies

[27] *Tottenham Man. Rolls (1377–99)*, 29, 134, 203.
[28] *Tottenham Man. Rolls (1377–99)*, 192, 204.
[29] Bruce Castle Mus., MR/76 (TS. transl. pp. 32–3).
[30] Robinson, *Tottenham*, i. 61–4.
[31] See p. 337.
[32] Bruce Castle Mus., MR/7 (TS. transl. p. 23).
[33] *L. & P. Hen. VIII*, ii (2), 1473; see p. 327.
[34] *Oxford Bk. of Light Verse*, ed. W. H. Auden, 41.
[35] *L. & P. Hen. VIII*, xi, p. 102.
[36] See p. 343.
[37] See p. 351.
[38] See p. 327.

[39] *L. & P. Hen. VIII*, xx(2), 452; Bruce Castle Mus., MR/121.
[40] See below.
[41] See p. 377.
[42] Oldfield and Dyson, *Hist. Tottenham*, 15–16.
[43] W. J. Roe, *Ancient Tottenham*, 118.
[44] The foll. three paras. are based on Robinson, *Tottenham*, map of 1619.
[45] See p. 335.
[46] Bruce Castle Mus., MR/121.
[47] Roe, *Ancient Tottenham*, 118.
[48] Bruce Castle Mus., MR/121.

along a lane to its north, and Crokes farm-house, belonging to Sir Edward Barkham, at the south corner of White Hart Lane and High Road.[49] The Black House survived as Rydley, belonging to Alderman William Gore and perhaps already a summer retreat for Sir John Coke, the secretary of state, who was to stay there regularly between 1625 and 1640.[50] Rydley was considered sumptuous, as was a newly built house of Nathaniel Martin. On the north side of Wood Green another fine house belonged to Ambrose Wheeler.[51] It was partly an interest in benefactions made by the Barkhams, Wheelers, and other wealthy families which prompted William Bedwell to write his 'Brief Description' in 1631[52] and which later led Henry Hare, Lord Coleraine (d. 1708), to compose his 'History and antiquities of the town and church of Tottenham', a work expanded by his grandson and namesake.[53]

Bedwell singled out three local wonders, all of them arboreal. The chief one was a walnut tree, which flourished without growing bigger and was popularly associated with the burning of an unknown Protestant. It stood, encircled by elms, at the eastern end of Page Green beside High Road, where trees were shown in 1619. Bedwell, who supplied no name, made it clear that interest centred on the walnut itself,[54] which survived in 1724.[55] The clump was known as the Seven Sisters by 1732, when the lord's licence was sought for the lower boughs to be lopped.[56] Although the walnut had died by 1790[57] the clump survived or was renewed, to give its name to the new road in 1833 and,[58] like the high cross, to a locality.

The construction of the New River and the wholesale felling of trees were deplored by Bedwell,[59] who saw that they greatly changed the appearance of the western part of the parish. A residence built south of the church by Joseph Fenton, in modern times called the Priory and converted into the vicarage house, survives as an example of the activities of wealthy Londoners.[60] Other examples were the mansion used by Sir John Coke where, according to Bedwell, the former Black House served as outbuildings,[61] and a large house on the north side of Tottenham Green owned by Sir Abraham Reynardson,[62] who restored it in 1647 and lived there after his deposition as lord mayor of London in 1649.[63] In 1664 there were at least 15 large houses assessed at more than 10 hearths, headed by Sir Hugh Smithson's with 22 and Sir Edward Barkham's with 21. The population was still fairly evenly distributed between the wards. Lower ward contained 56 houses, Middle 57, and High Cross 72; there were 58 houses in Wood Green ward, where no building was assessed at more than 8 hearths.[64]

In 1631 Bedwell found the air wholesome and

temperate and described the marshes as pleasant meadows, sometimes flooded but too remote to be dangerous.[65] Such praises were repeated in 1724[66] and, combined with easy access from London, may explain why Tottenham attracted many private schools. At least two select academies preceded the endowment in 1686 of a local grammar school for boys, which also had to compete with institutions run by the Society of Friends. The Friends, who were to provide the district with many distinguished names during the next two centuries, opened their first permanent meeting-house in High Road in 1714.[67]

While building continued during the late 17th and 18th centuries, the pattern of development remained essentially that of 1619.[68] Defoe, in the 1720s, was struck by the many new houses along the main road from London to Enfield, notably in Tottenham and Edmonton where they seemed to form 'one continued street'.[69] In reality builders tended to concentrate on those stretches of High Road which were already popular: around Tottenham Green, the high cross, and northward, especially along the eastern side. Apart from some houses on the boundary at Stamford Hill, the southern stretch remained empty as far as Page Green in 1754, when there was also open country on the west side of High Road between Lordship and White Hart lanes. North of the cross building had become almost continuous along the east side of High Road by 1800 and most of the gaps on either side had been filled by the grounds of big houses. South of Page Green, however, the road still passed through fields, presumably because of damp ground near Stonebridge stream. The open approach and the juxtaposition of large and humble dwellings perhaps explain a comment that Tottenham village, with an unpleasantly flat situation, chiefly comprised one long street of straggling and unequal houses, with little rural charm.[70]

Small settlements away from High Road attracted little attention in the 18th century. Tottenham Hale, which possessed an inn and which was marked separately in 1754, remained the one hamlet of any size; although comparatively close, in 1818 it had yet to be connected with High Road by building along High Cross Lane. East of the Hale there stood only the mill on the Lea and, far to the north, a few buildings in Marsh and Willoughby lanes. In the centre of the parish West Green still comprised no more than half a dozen houses in 1800. North of it stretched the largest park in Tottenham, around Mount Pleasant, which had been built on the site of an early-18th-century residence, Downhills House.[71] Wood Green was the only settlement named in the west in 1754, and was still very small in 1818. Its houses were widely scattered, some facing the green

[49] Robinson, *Tottenham*, map of 1619.
[50] *Cal. S.P. Dom.* 1625, 61; 1638, 487.
[51] M.R.O., Acc. 695/9, ff. 35, 46, 60.
[52] See p. 309 and note.
[53] Bodl. MS. Gough Mdx. 5. The hist. was printed at the end of H. G. Oldfield and R. R. Dyson, *Hist. and Antiquities of Tottenham High Cross* (1790); a second edn., by Dyson alone, was pub. in 1792.
[54] Roe, op. cit. 115; Robinson, *Tottenham*, map of 1619.
[55] Cox, *Magna Brit.* iii. 35.
[56] M.R.O., Acc. 695/1, f. 428v.
[57] Oldfield and Dyson, op. cit. 6.
[58] See p. 311.
[59] Roe, *Ancient Tottenham*, 107–8.
[60] See p. 350.

[61] Roe, op. cit. 118.
[62] *D.N.B.*
[63] Robinson, *Tottenham*, i. 102–3 and plate.
[64] M.R.O., MR/TH/5, ff. 5–7.
[65] Roe, *Ancient Tottenham*, 104.
[66] Cox, *Magna Brit.* iii. 34.
[67] See p. 358.
[68] Except where otherwise stated, the foll. five paras. are based on J. Rocque, *Map of Mdx.* (1754); T. Milne, *Plan . . . of Lond. and Westminster, circumjacent towns and parishes* (1800); and Robinson, *Tottenham*, map of 1818.
[69] Daniel Defoe, *Tour thro' Eng. and Wales* (Everyman edn.), ii. 2.
[70] Brewer, *Beauties of Eng. and Wales*, x(5), 697.
[71] See p. 332.

itself, known as Wood Green common, others to the north where Green Lanes ascended Jolly Butchers (later Clay Bush) Hill, and a few to the east along Lordship Lane. On the slopes farther west, the woods had dwindled to a few groves among ploughed fields by 1800. There were no houses save Nightingale Hall, on the south side of Bounds Green Lane by 1754, two buildings in the extreme north-west, facing the long strip which was Bounds Green itself, and Tottenham Wood Farm near the top of Muswell Hill.

Most visitors, finding nothing of great note, discussed the antiquities and proverbs mentioned by Bedwell. Such character as the parish possessed still came from the substantial merchants' homes. Defoe considered them 'unequalled in their degree, . . . generally belonging to the middle sort of mankind, grown wealthy by trade, and who still taste of London'; many owners, dividing their time between the City and the country, were immensely rich. He singled out one villa, the first to strike a traveller from London, newly built by a former goldsmith called Wanley;[72] although small, its architecture and gardens made it the most beautiful house in the entire region.[73] Such houses stood mainly around Tottenham Green or along the west side of High Road.

Much costly new building, alteration, and landscaping took place c. 1800.[74] Near Stamford Hill, on the east side of High Road, Markfield House was built by William Hobson, a Quaker building contractor,[75] who acquired neighbouring farm-land to make an estate of 37 a. by 1840. At the Seven Sisters, on the corner of High Road and Page Green, an earlier house was replaced c. 1800 by a villa which was afterwards bought by Hobson and occupied by the first minister of Holy Trinity chapel. Cottages on the south side of Page Green were replaced c. 1806 by the residence of William Row, set in 12 a. of grounds laid out by Humphry Repton and considered one of the finest in the parish.[76] Row also bought a neighbouring villa at the eastern end of Page Green, built at about the same date and later called the Hurst. On the north side of Tottenham Green Reynardson's house made way for two villas c. 1810 and on the west side Grove House, a boarding school from the mid 18th century, was greatly altered. Dean Wood's house by the high cross was divided and in 1820 three villas were built where a pond had been filled in at the corner of High Road and High Cross Lane. Farther north, at the corner of Lordship Lane, stood a house possibly dating from before 1700 but refaced in the Palladian manner and provided with curved flanking colonnades c. 1740, when it had been owned by a London merchant named Philip de la Haize. It passed to a City draper, Samuel Salte, and was enlarged by his brother William, in whose day it was called the Corridor and for whom the gardens were landscaped by Repton. William Salte, noted for his lavish but informal hos-

pitality, entertained the dukes of Cambridge and Sussex there in 1808.[77] Alterations were also carried out at the early-17th-century Asplins farm-house, which received a three-storeyed façade c. 1750,[78] and, in the 1820s, at the near-by Willoughby House.

In the late 18th and early 19th centuries the spread of villas along some of the lanes branching off High Road was more noticeable than the growth of separate hamlets. The most uniform building, made possible by the break-up of the manorial estate in 1789, took place along the new road called Bruce Grove; superior, semi-detached houses, soon associated with rich Quaker families,[79] lined part of its south-western side by 1800. At the north-western end of the row the residence later called Elmhurst had been built by 1818 and on the south side of Lordship Lane Elmslea faced the park of Bruce Castle by 1843.[80] Building also took place along the north side of White Hart Lane: in 1816 it boasted several capacious villas, probably including Moselle House and Moselle Villa near the vicarage, and the new Tottenham Terrace, whose only defect was thought to be that the dwellings stood too close together.[81] The same row contained Trafalgar House, from 1821 the home of the topographer and local historian William Robinson,[82] who acquired many neighbouring properties.[83] Farther west the lane passed between Rectory Farm, on the north, and the park of the rectory house, then called the Moated House. Beyond lay open country, apart from a farm afterwards called Tent Farm on the site of the late-19th-century potteries.

Rich parishioners left their mark in many charitable institutions, nearly all of them housed along High Road. The Blue Coat school was built in 1735, Reynardson's alms-houses were opened in 1737, and the Pound or Phesaunt's alms-houses, after demolition of the old structures around the churchyard, a few years later. Close to High Street, in Marsh Lane, a workhouse was built in 1783. The Green Coat school of industry was established in 1792, followed by Lancasterian schools in 1812 and 1815. While Quakers continued at their meeting-house, other nonconformists used private rooms from the 1790s until the first permanent chapel was built, for Methodists, in 1818. Roman Catholics worshipped in Queen Street, close to the Edmonton boundary, from 1793.

The residential nature of most new building gave late-18th-century Tottenham the appearance of an extended, semi-rural suburb rather than a town. Industry, apart from brick-making, was virtually confined to riverside mills until the construction of a lace-factory in 1810 and a silk-factory five years later, a tanyard in the grounds of White Hall having proved short-lived.[84] The factories, near High Road in Love and Factory lanes respectively, passed through several hands before 1837, when one of them became a rubber mill, whose owners soon faced lawsuits for causing pollution.[85] There were no

[72] Perhaps Geo. Wanley, elected to the livery in 1712: W. T. Prideaux, *List . . . of the Worshipful Co. of Goldsmiths*, 51. [73] Defoe, op. cit. ii. 2.

[74] Except where otherwise stated, the houses are described in Robinson, *Tottenham*, i. 107–32, where many are illustrated. [75] Robbins, *Mdx.* 346.

[76] Water-colour, 1806, in J. Harris, *Georgian Country Hos.*, plate 2.

[77] Brewer, *Beauties of Eng. and Wales*, x(5), 700; Fisk, *Tottenham*, i. 100.

[78] Hist. Mon. Com. *Mdx.* 123.

[79] Robinson, *Tottenham*, i. 96.

[80] Tottenham Rent-Charge 1843, Bruce Castle Mus., D/PT/102A, p. 49.

[81] Brewer, *Beauties of Eng. and Wales*, x(5), 700.

[82] *D.N.B.*; A. Abrahams, *Life and Works of Wm. Robinson*, 11.

[83] Bruce Castle Mus., D/PT/102A, pp. 103–6.

[84] Oldfield and Dyson, op. cit.

[85] See p. 337.

other businesses of any size, except breweries, in the mid 19th century. Meanwhile private schools continued to benefit from the relatively healthy air; among them were establishments opened in 1827 at Bruce Castle and in the following year at Grove House, both of which became nationally known. As late as 1859 the authoress Mrs. J. H. Riddell described Tottenham as a very quiet and secluded town, where fortunes could be made by enterprising traders or craftsmen who secured the patronage of the local gentry. West Green, where she lived, might be a hundred miles from London and did not take easily to strangers from Tottenham itself.[86]

A doubling of the population between 1811 and 1851 was reflected in many new schools and chapels and in the first modern Anglican church, built at Tottenham Green in 1830.[87] The opening of a railway station in 1840 and of a church at Wood Green in 1844 presaged the establishment of a local board in 1848 and a transformation of the old parish when the social standing of much housing along High Road would be lowered and the contrast between concentrated development there and open country to the west would be ended. In 1840, however, it was still possible for William Robinson to claim that the pattern of settlement did not differ greatly from that of 1619. All but a few of the inhabitants lived in or near High Road. Tottenham Hale was a village with with an inn and some 125 houses, containing over 600 people. Around West Green there were about 18 houses, some of them considered respectable family residences, and at Wood Green Common there were only ten.[88]

Tottenham had 355 communicants in 1547.[89] The protestation oath was taken by 252 adult males in 1641–2[90] and there were 87 conformists and 43 nonconformists in 1676.[91] Some 119 houses were recorded in 1619[92] and 243 in 1664.[93] By 1801 there were 3,629 inhabitants, whose numbers rose steadily over the following decades to reach 6,937 in 1831 and 9,120 in 1851. The population remained fairly evenly distributed between the three wards covering High Road: Lower, Middle, and High Cross wards contained 1,612, 1,343, and 1,187 persons respectively in 1811 and 3,165, 2,273, and 2,413 in 1851. Wood Green ward, which included West Green, contained 429, less than a tenth of the total, in 1811 and 1,269, less than a seventh, in 1851.[94]

GROWTH AFTER 1850. The arrival of the Northern and Eastern railway in 1840 did not markedly improve communications with London, nor did new centres of population arise around the first stations, east of Tottenham Hale and near Asplins Farm.[95] The situation of the stations, however, was responsible for buildings spreading eastward from High Road. By 1863 Tottenham Hale had been joined to the village around the high cross by buildings along the south side of High Cross Lane, while terraces lined part of the new Somerset and Chesnut roads a little to the north; Stamford and Markfield roads had been laid out east of Page Green, where 84 small building plots had been offered for sale ten years earlier,[96] although a stretch of Broad Lane still approached Tottenham Hale through fields. Farther north near Park station there were houses along part of Marsh and Willoughby lanes, where St. Paul's church had been built and Willoughby House had been demolished in 1858,[97] and many middle-class villas along a new link between the railway and High Road, called Northumberland Park. Tottenham, on a map, no longer appeared as a ribbon of settlement.

Several plans for further railways were canvassed in the 1840s and 1850s.[98] The prospect of better communications and public services, rather than the state of those already enjoyed, probably stimulated development in the 1850s, when the population rose by more than 4,000.[99] A new cemetery, amid fields north of the parish church, was consecrated in 1857, one year before the Drapers' Company of London bought the Elms opposite the high cross as the site for a boys' school and alms-houses. Tottenham's change from a select residential neighbourhood into a crowded, lower-middle- and working-class suburb was hastened from 1858, when the City merchants and gentry who hitherto had dominated the local board were replaced by men who worked locally, notably doctors and builders, and who saw the district as ready for development.[1] Hasty building, allowing the population to rise by nearly 10,000 in the 1860s,[2] brought many crises over water supply and sewerage, for which Tottenham became notorious.

By the mid 1860s there was no open country along either side of High Road north of Tottenham Green, although many residences still stood in their own grounds. Between Seven Sisters and Hanger Lane (later St. Ann's Road) the only buildings were Stonebridge House on the west, Markfield House on the east, and a bridge carrying the Tottenham and Hampstead Junction railway. Housing was densest in the north, along lanes and alleys close to High Road south of White Hart Lane, with small terraced dwellings in William, Moselle, and Whitehall streets, formerly occupied by White Hall, as well as in Love Lane and Church Road. Development along the roads leading to the G.E.R. stations was partly balanced by housing along the chief roads to the west: Hanger Lane, West Green Road, Philip Lane, Lordship Lane, containing Bruce Terrace, and White Hart Lane. Only along the south side of Philip Lane, however, did it reach as far as another village, West Green.

In the eastern part of the parish most of the premises along High Road still backed on open country north of Tottenham Hale and south of Marsh Lane. Beyond the railway line the marshes contained little

[86] Mrs. J. H. Riddell, *Above Suspicion*, i, 3, 35, 29, 36.
[87] *Educ. Enquiry Abstract*, 582.
[88] Robinson, *Tottenham*, i. 58, 66, 71.
[89] E 301/34/163.
[90] H.L., Mdx. Protestation Rets.
[91] William Salt Libr., Stafford, Salt MS. 33, p. 40.
[92] *Local Pop. Studies Mag.* no. 2, 31.
[93] M.R.O., MR/TH/5.
[94] *Census*, 1801–51.
[95] Except where otherwise stated, the foll. ten paras. of

the section are based on O.S. Maps 6", Mdx. XII. (1863–9 edn.).
[96] Bruce Castle Mus., Tottenham sales of property, i (1851–90), no. 3.
[97] Fisk, *Tottenham*, ii. 229.
[98] G. H. Lake, *Rlys. of Tottenham*, 14.
[99] See p. 324.
[1] 'Public Health in Tottenham, 1850–72' [survey by students of Lond. Sch. of Hygiene and Trop. Medicine, inc. as app. to rep. of med. offr. of health 1951], *penes* Bruce Castle Mus., 18–21.   [2] See p. 324.

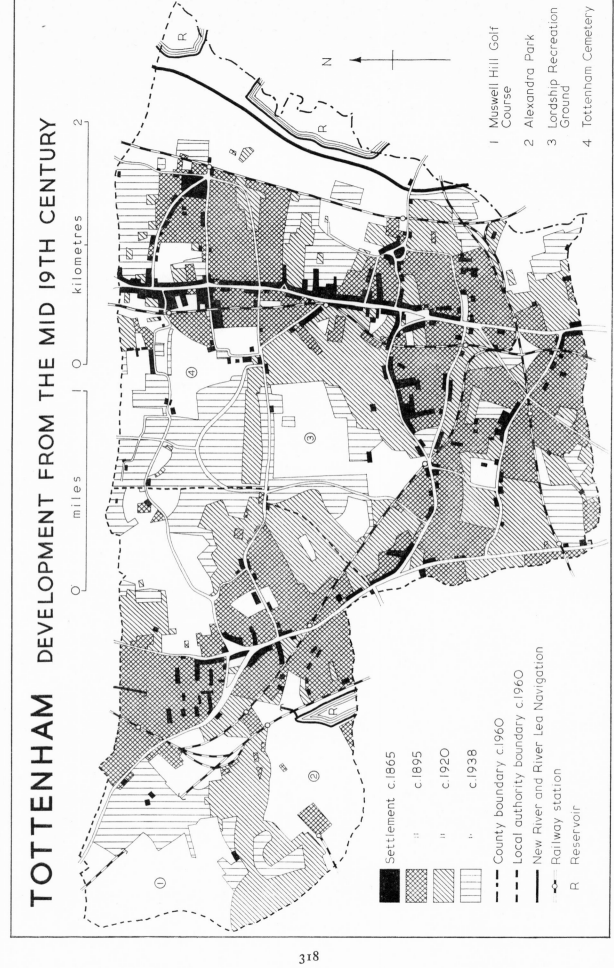

TOTTENHAM   DEVELOPMENT FROM THE MID 19TH CENTURY

Settlement c.1865
"   c.1895
"   c.1920
"   c.1938

County boundary c.1960
Local authority boundary c.1960
New River and River Lea Navigation
Railway station
R   Reservoir

1 Muswell Hill Golf Course
2 Alexandra Park
3 Lordship Recreation Ground
4 Tottenham Cemetery

N

miles

kilometres

apart from Ferry Lane, leading past Tottenham lock to the recently gutted mills, and from Stonebridge lock, Asplins Farm, and a new rifle range in the extreme north-east. The centre of the parish was also rural, from Downhills park northward to Clay Hill. Beyond a group of houses around Bruce Castle, Lordship Lane ran through fields which stretched to Chapmans Green, the sole buildings being those of Broadwater and Grainger's farms. West of Tottenham Park, White Hart Lane similarly passed nothing except Tent Farm and a few cottages, while the lane to the north led past Clayhill (later Devonshire Hill) Lodge and River House, across the New River to Clayhill Farm on the boundary.

South of Downhills changes proceeded more rapidly. Farm-land still stretched westward from High Road to Green Lanes, along the course of Stonebridge stream, and, in places, bordered West Green Road and Hanger Lane, but there were clear signs that the entire length of West Green Road would soon be lined with houses. West Green itself retained some large dwellings, including West Green House, West Green Lodge, Woodlands, and Gothic House, and possessed a school and chapel. It was linked with High Cross not only along Philip Lane but by terraced housing in the new Clyde Road, where 36 a. of meadow had been offered for building in 1851;[3] Philip Lane and West Green Road were connected by Summerhill Road, where terraces had been built in 1856 and 1859, and by Bathurst (later Lawrence) Road, which contained a floor-cloth factory. To the west Stanley Street (later Road) and some neighbouring roads had been laid out, between the old village centre and the junction of West Green Road with Green Lanes. A few houses had been built south of the junction and others stretched northward, facing Ducketts Common, as far as Ducketts farm-house, then called Dovecote House.

Less than a half a mile south of West Green, a new centre was arising around St. Ann's church, consecrated in 1861. The church, together with its vicarage house, model cottages dated 1858, and schools, had been paid for chiefly by Fowler Newsam, who lived in High Road at Stamford Hill. It served the Chestnuts and St. John's, Suffolk, Oak, and York lodges, near by, and other large residences in the south part of the parish: the Retreat and the Hermitage, amid fields bordering Hermitage Road, Woodberry Lodge, Albion Lodge, Gothic House, and Barnfield House, farther east in Hanger Lane, and several mansions at Stamford Hill, where Coleraine House, the Shrubbery, and Sherborough House all stood on the Tottenham side of the boundary. Newsam's choice of a rural site had been attacked by those who felt that a church was more urgently needed at West Green or Tottenham Hale.[4] By the mid 1860s, however, the new parish was already losing its exclusive air; the Avenue and South Grove had been laid out near the church, the Tottenham and Hampstead Junction railway cut across both Hermitage Road and Hanger Lane,

and the tile-works still existed in the extreme south-west.

Even more rapid growth took place at Wood Green, where the church built in 1844 was found to be far too small by 1863. A direct railway to London, foreshadowed by the G.N.R. line in 1850 and achieved with the opening of a station ten years later, combined with undulating, still partly wooded, country to make the area attractive to large institutions, as well as to speculators planning a new middle-class suburb. Wood Green was 'as charming a spot as its sylvan name implies' in 1847, when the foundation stone of the Fishmongers' and Poulterers' institution was laid immediately north of the church.[5] The institution, an asylum for 12 married couples, was opened in 1850. It was designed by Mee and William Webb as an imposing two-storeyed[6] range in the Tudor style, with a central turreted gateway. South of the church the Printers' alms-houses, another two-storeyed Tudor range designed by Webb, were founded in 1849 for 12 couples and opened in 1856. In 1871 two more wings doubled the accommodation, and twenty years later an extension was opened by the duchess of Albany, marking the first royal visit to Wood Green.[7] The Royal Masonic institution opened its boys' school in Lordship House, Lordship Lane, in 1857 and replaced it with a large new building, later the Home and Colonial training college, in 1865. In that year land in Nightingale Road was provided for John Fuller's alms-houses, after the original site in Shoreditch had been sold.[8] Wood Green's first elementary school was opened in 1859 and its first chapel was built, by Congregationalists, in 1864.

Wood Green began to grow neither around the old common nor the new station, but north of the church in the triangle between Green Lanes and Bounds Green Lane. Commerce, Nightingale, Finsbury, Truro, and Clarence roads were all laid out there in the mid 1860s. South-east of Wood Green common, Caxton and Mayes roads were also laid out and near the Hornsey boundary a tobacco factory and reservoir bordered the railway. Cherson House, Wood Green House, and other large residences still overlooked the New River near the common. To the east, along Lordship Lane, Elm Lodge stood with a few cottages at the former Chapmans Green. To the north-east Green Lanes ran past the entrance lodge of Chitts Hill House, which stood with a farm-house in some 31 a. in 1843, when it belonged to Mary Overend;[9] Mrs. Overend still lived there in 1862[10] and Samuel Page in 1867.[11] In contrast with the rows of villas leading off the north side of Bounds Green Lane, building on the south side was confined to a group opposite the church and to Nightingale Hall opposite Commerce Road. Nightingale Hall, with grounds and farm-land totalling 72 a., was occupied by Thomas Pearson in 1843;[12] it passed in 1864 from Pearson to his widow,[13] afterwards Mrs. Pearson Kidd, who lived there for another 30 years.[14] Farther west the only buildings were at Bounds Green, which possessed some cottages, a tavern, and

[3] Bruce Castle Mus., Tottenham sales, i, no. 2.
[4] See p. 352.   [5] *Illus. Lond. News*, 26 June 1847.
[6] A. H. Eason, *Fishmongers' and Poulterers' Inst.* 42–3, and Bruce Castle Mus., 988 [newspaper cuttings].
[7] *Printers' Pension, Almsho. and Orphan Asylum Corp. Souvenir* [centenary booklet] and Bruce Castle Mus. 988 [newspaper cuttings].

[8] Char. Com. files.
[9] Bruce Castle Mus., D/PT/102A/3, p. 96.
[10] *P.O. Dir. Mdx.* (1862).
[11] *Kelly's Dir. Mdx.* (1867).
[12] Bruce Castle Mus., D/PT/102A/3, pp. 162–3.
[13] M.R.O., Acc. 1016/358, /360.
[14] *St. Mic. Wood Grn. 1844–1944* [centenary booklet], 11.

a brick-works, and at Tottenham Wood Farm, which was approached by a lane from Muswell Hill in Hornsey. The first Alexandra Palace was not built until 1873, although a pleasure ground along the Hornsey boundary was opened ten years earlier.

Building in the 1860s mostly took place in the hitherto neglected parts west of Tottenham High Road, particularly around West Green and at Wood Green. While the total population rose by nearly 10,000, Wood Green ward alone saw an increase of some 5,500.[15] By 1869 residents at Wood Green were demanding their own local board[16] and it was clear that their new suburb, enjoying a separate rail link with London, had a future of its own.[17] Inevitably development thereafter spread around High Road in the east of the parish, the railway lines in the south, and Wood Green in the west, leaving farm-land in the centre and north which was not touched until the 20th century.

The crucial factor in the sudden growth of the eastern part of Tottenham was the arrival of the G.E.R., ultimately running from Liverpool Street to Enfield, in 1872. The line itself destroyed most of the rural advantages still enjoyed by large houses on or near the west side of High Road, including those in Bruce Grove. More important, the issue of cheap early morning tickets to London, which was strenuously opposed in local newspapers, attracted thousands of working-class immigrants and finally ended Tottenham's reputation for health and gentility.[18] By 1876 housing stretched almost continuously along the two miles from Stamford Hill to Edmonton; much of it was considered commonplace and some of it wretched, although here and there wrought-iron gates or walls with overhanging trees recalled more stately days.[19]

The opening of stations on the Tottenham and Hampstead Junction line, beginning with South Tottenham in 1871, and the construction of the G.E.R. line through West Green in 1878, hastened the spread of building over the south of the parish. By 1875 villas around St. Ann's had been built on ground recently deemed an irreclaimable morass and West Green had been transformed: 'the old village is still there, but it is huddled up against Streets, and Villas, and Places, and all the other devices of modern investors.'[20] In consequence the population of the parish more than doubled during the 1870s, when the urgent demand for elementary education frustrated determined local efforts to avoid a school board, and had reached 97,174 by 1891.[21] The effects of the influx were recognized in 1888, when Tottenham, with West Green, was separated from Wood Green. Their differing characters were described in 1894: Tottenham ,the most populous of all London's outlying districts, was mainly given over to the lower middle class, notably City clerks and warehousemen, whereas Wood Green had many well-to-do residents.[22] For much of the area, including the southern part of Wood Green, the assessment was

flattering; standardized stock-brick terraces formed a working-class railway suburb, where houses stood 40 to an acre, 'with back gardens distinctly minimal and front gardens merely nominal'.[23]

Much building covered the sites of former mansions. Lordship Hall, on the south corner of High Road and Lordship Lane, was demolished for road-widening in 1867. William Salte's house, auctioned after his death in 1817 and empty in 1870, made way for the shopping parade known as Criterion Buildings, dated 1880, and for Ruskin, Cedar, and Pembury roads. Soon afterwards Bruce Castle and Birkbeck roads were built up[24] on land which had been auctioned with Fair Lawn, on the north corner of Lordship Lane, in 1875.[25] Farther south in High Road the parade called Grove Terrace, opposite Page Green, was also built in 1880[26] and Suffield Lodge, at the south corner of West Green Road, was offered as building land in the same year. The Rows' residence at Page Green was also sold for housing with 11½ a. in 1880, as were Markfield House with 80 a. in 1879 and 90 plots on the near-by Earlsmead estate in 1882.[27] Properties auctioned at West Green included West Green House in 1884 and the Woodlands in 1888. The British Land Co. bought Downhills in 1881 and the neighbouring Mount Pleasant estate was offered as 135 building lots along Mount Pleasant Road in 1890.[28]

Sometimes a large private house was adapted to serve an institution, as when Avenue House on Tottenham Green was acquired by the Evangelical Protestant Deaconesses' institution (later the Prince of Wales's general hospital) in 1868, when Elmslea was bought by the Drapers' Company of London for Thomas Corney's school in the same year, or when Suffolk Lodge became a priory for the Servite sisters in 1871. On part of the Elmslea estate, facing Bruce Grove, the Drapers' Company built alms-houses in 1869 to replace those at Bow belonging to the Jolles, Pemel, and Edmanson trusts; most of the dwellings were assigned to Edmanson's charity for sail-makers from which the whole group became known as the Sailmakers' alms-houses.[29] Alderman Staines's alms-houses were built in Beaufoy Road in 1868 on their removal from the Barbican, London. After the last three inmates had been pensioned off in 1899 the property was leased out by the trustees of the Cripplegate Foundation, who had taken over Staines's charity, until its acquisition by Haringey in 1965.[30] St. Katharine's college, for women teachers, was opened in 1878 by the S.P.C.K. in the Ferns, a large house north of Fair Lawn;[31] in 1880 it moved to former glebe land in White Hart Lane, where a three-storeyed building, later extended, was built in the style of William and Mary to the designs of A. W. Blomfield.[32]

Although most of Wood Green became a middle-class suburb, c. 100 a. of the farm-land of Ducketts, adjoining West Green, was bought in 1882 by the Artizans', Labourers', and General Dwellings Co.

[15] Census, 1861, 1871.   [16] Fisk, Tottenham, ii. 88.
[17] Urban Development of Haringey Area (Haringey L.B., Local Hist. Occasional Papers no. 1), 5.
[18] Ibid. 3–5; Lake, Rlys. of Tottenham, 20–1.
[19] Thorne, Environs, ii. 621.
[20] Mrs. J. H. Riddell, Above Suspicion, 2.
[21] Census, 1871–91; see p. 324.
[22] Urban Develop. of Haringey, 6–7.
[23] A. A. Jackson, Semi-Det. Lond. 22.
[24] Fisk, Tottenham, i. 100.

[25] Bruce Castle Mus., Tottenham sales, i, no. 21.
[26] Date on building.
[27] Bruce Castle Mus., Tottenham sales, i, nos. 44, 47, 53; Fisk, Tottenham, ii. 224.
[28] Bruce Castle Mus., 927; Tottenham sales, i, nos. 65, 82.
[29] Kelly's Dir. Essex, Herts. and Mdx. (1890); ex inf. the clerk, Drapers' Co. of Lond.
[30] Ex inf. Edmonton Hund. Hist. Soc.
[31] Sturges, Schs. of Edmonton Hund. 124.
[32] Builder, xli. 185.

Enfield: Chase Farm School *c.* 1890

Tottenham: Bruce Castle in 1686

TOTTENHAM: HOLY TRINITY CHURCH *c.* 1830

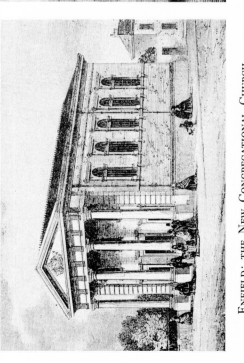

HENDON: THE CONGREGATIONAL CHURCH,
BRENT STREET *c.* 1855

ENFIELD: THE NEW CONGREGATIONAL CHURCH,
BAKER STREET *c.* 1862

(from 1952 the Artizans' and General Properties Co.).[33] The company, founded by clerks and working men in 1867 and later with the earl of Shaftesbury as president, had already carried out similar schemes at Battersea, Queen's Park, and elsewhere. In 1883 work began on the Noel Park estate, which was named after the chairman, Ernest Noel, M.P., and had some 7,000 inhabitants within three years.[34] The first residents found that cheap tickets were available only for early trains, although the G.N.R. Co. conceded some half-price fares in 1886. Construction therefore outran lettings, causing work to be suspended for a time in 1887. Although not finally completed until 1929, most of Noel Park had been built by 1907, when its 2,000-odd dwellings formed the largest group belonging to the company, itself London's biggest provider of working-class housing from 1890 until it was overtaken by the L.C.C. The estate, from which public houses were excluded, contained the Empire theatre, shops, and several roads named after directors of the company, including Ashley Crescent, Pelham Road, and Farrant, Hewitt, and Lymington avenues.

By the mid 1890s neither Tottenham Hale, West Green, nor St. Ann's could be distinguished as separate hamlets.[35] The last open spaces along Tottenham High Road had gone, with terraced streets on the sites of Stonebridge House and Markfield House, although a few old residences bordered High Road at Stamford Hill. At Page Green the Hurst alone survived as a large house, until its auction in 1893.[36] Building covered almost the whole area between High Road and the G.E.R. line, although there were nursery gardens south of Tottenham Hale and in the extreme north, beyond Northumberland Park; the only fields were in the south-east, near the sewage works, around Down Lane south of the Carbuncle ditch, and along the Edmonton boundary. Between the railway and the Lea, however, the marshes had been little affected, apart from the Longwater pumping station. In the extreme south building stretched westward across Seven Sisters Road to Tiverton Road and was about to cover the south-western corner, where Vale Road had been planned and the Hermitage and the Retreat had gone. From 1892 the North-Eastern fever hospital (later St. Ann's) stood in 19 a. on the south side of St. Ann's Road opposite the Chestnuts, which itself was for sale in 1895.[37] Housing stretched in a broad belt across the parish, filling most of the land between St. Ann's Road, West Green Road, and Philip Lane. About 1890 development started on the Haringey House estate, extending from Hornsey into south-western Tottenham, where by 1900 'practically a new town' had arisen, with over 1,800 houses and shops. In that year the residents, generally better off than those of St. Ann's or West Green, secured the creation of their own ward, Harringay.[38] By contrast the centre of the old parish, in 1894 the north-western quarter of the new Tottenham U.D., was still open. The Avenue had been

built from Bruce Grove, where Elmhurst was the first of the old residences to disappear, in 1896,[39] but the park of Bruce Castle and Tottenham cemetery helped to restrict building westward from High Road. From Downhills farm-land stretched across Lordship and White Hart lanes to Edmonton.

Wood Green by the mid 1890s was joined by buildings both to Southgate and to Hornsey. Near the Southgate boundary, around Whittington and Marlborough roads, the National Liberal Land Co. had auctioned many plots on the Bowes Park estate between 1880 and 1890.[40] Building along part of the south side of Bounds Green Lane was prevented by the survival of Nightingale Hall until c. 1896, when it made way for a bicycle track, which was soon replaced by Braemar Avenue and neighbouring roads.[41] Chitts Hill House also survived, although Woodside Road and parallel avenues had already been planned to cover its grounds. Westbury Avenue separated Wood Green in the south-east from Tottenham, and Granville Road had been laid out in plots as far as the boundary. There were fields, however, between Westbury Avenue and Noel Park, which ended at Gladstone Avenue, and in the north-east along White Hart Lane. The western part of Wood Green remained open, largely because Alexandra Palace stood in 180 a. of park-land with Muswell Hill golf club, established in 1894, as its neighbour to the north.

Both Tottenham and Wood Green grew ever more populous until the First World War, total numbers reaching 136,744 by 1901 and 186,787 by 1911. Much the higher density was achieved in Tottenham, with 34 persons an acre in 1901 and over 45 persons in 1911.[42] Although growth had started with families leaving London, whither householders travelled to work, it was inevitable that some of the land near the marshes or the railways, cheap but undesirable for housing, should be used for factories.[43] Firms began to move from London, the first large company being the furniture-makers Harris Lebus in 1900, and soon provided much local employment. By 1914 there were three main pockets of industry: in the extreme south around Vale Road, around Tottenham Hale, and north of Northumberland Park.[44] New buildings along High Road included extensive offices for the Tottenham and Edmonton Gas Light & Coke Co. in 1901, the Jewish home and hospital in 1903, Windsor Parade on the north corner of Dowsett Road in 1907, and a parade opposite Bruce Grove in 1907–8. A music-hall was built on land of the Drapers' Company in 1908 and a skating-rink next door in 1909. The factories, offices, and shops, together with the railways and their yards, gave much of Tottenham an urban rather than a suburban appearance. To keep pace with the change the U.D.C. began to acquire open spaces, beginning with Bruce Castle park in 1892, and replaced the houses on the west side of Tottenham Green with an imposing row of civic buildings.

[33] Except where otherwise stated, the para. is based on *Artizans Centenary, 1867–1967*, and on inf. supplied by Mr. F. W. J. Adams.
[34] *The Lion* [newsheet of St. Mark, Noel Pk.], 3–17 Sept. 1972.
[35] Except where otherwise stated, the foll. two paras. are based on O.S. Maps 6", Mdx. XII. (1894–6 edn.).
[36] Bruce Castle Mus., Tottenham sales, ii (1891–1900), no. 8.
[37] Ibid. no. 31.
[38] M.R.O., *Reps. of Local Inqs. 1895–1907* [unpag.].
[39] Fisk, *Tottenham*, i. 75.
[40] Bruce Castle Mus., Tottenham sales, i, nos. 46, 48, 86.
[41] *St. Mic. Wood Grn. 1844–1944*, 11.
[42] *Census*, 1901, 1911.
[43] *Urban Develop. of Haringey*, 4.
[44] See p. 338.

Wood Green possessed few factories and those were mainly close to the railway line and confined, like working-class housing, to the south part. Institutions were still attracted there: in 1904 Shoreditch council, which already owned Fuller's alms-houses, built St. Leonard's House and Porter's and Walter's alms-houses nearby in Nightingale Road.[45] Wood Green U.D.C. followed a similar policy to Tottenham but, with so much open space and a wealthier population, had less need to spend money. From 1907 its most imposing civic building was the library, while for the town hall a converted residence was still used. There was a density of little more than 21 persons an acre in 1901 and 30 in 1911.[46]

The north part of Tottenham began to be connected with Wood Green in 1901, when the L.C.C., despite local opposition,[47] bought some 225 a. of farm-land with the intention of housing 42,500 persons. The land, most of it in Tottenham U.D. but extending into Wood Green and Edmonton, lay in two blocks, of which the larger comprised 179 a. along the north side of Lordship Lane. By 1910 Tower Gardens had been laid out and 48 a. had been covered with 3- to 5-roomed terraced houses.[48] Immediately to the east the Peabody Donation Fund completed 154 terraced cottages in 1907. Since much of the district was already working-class, the L.C.C. was empowered to allow private firms to build more expensive houses on part of its land in 1912.[49]

The open country which existed in the 1890s had been much reduced by 1920.[50] In Tottenham some waste ground in the extreme south-east and a recreation ground at Down Lane (renamed Park View Road) constituted the only areas between High Road and the G.E.R. line that had not been built up, while the patches of industry were clearly marked by factories. The L.C.C. estate stretched westward to the Wood Green boundary, forming a belt between Tower Gardens Road and Risley Avenue, and houses also extended south-eastward from Wood Green's Noel Park estate as far as Boundary Road, in Tottenham. The central wedge of farm-land had thus been cut in two, leaving the fields of Broadwater farm from Downhills to Lordship Lane, together with more fields stretching from Risley Avenue across White Hart Lane northward into Edmonton and north-westward into Wood Green. The western part of Wood Green U.D. was still largely open, although Alexandra Park was separated from Muswell Hill golf course by housing between Albert and Alexandra Park roads and by similar housing which stretched from Muswell Hill to Grosvenor Road and the Avenue.

Farm-land finally vanished in the years between the World Wars. During that period the population continued to rise, giving Tottenham a density of over 52 persons an acre in 1931.[51] The L.C.C. pressed ahead with its plans, finishing 7 blocks around Topham Square in 1924[52] and more than doubling the number of its tenants, to over 10,000, between 1919 and 1938.[53] Much of the Broadwater Farm

estate along the Moselle was saved by the U.D.C. from building and opened as Lordship recreation ground in 1932, although new housing bordered it to the south along the Avenue and Higham, Wilmot, and Walpole roads. North of White Hart Lane the secne was transformed. Great Cambridge Road brought traffic from Edmonton, which was diverted around the L.C.C. estate along Roundway, and the rest of the countryside was covered with suburban avenues, interspersed with allotments and recreation grounds. Most of the roads north of Risley Avenue had been laid out by 1938; those where houses were planned or under construction included Gospatrick and Henningham roads, belonging to the L.C.C., Compton Crescent, Acacia, Laburnum and Oak avenues, and Creighton Road. Residents were served by new shopping parades, a hall and library built in 1935, and St. John the Baptist's church, near the junction of White Hart Lane with Great Cambridge Road.

Elsewhere in Tottenham building was confined to filling in those areas which had not been reserved for recreation. East of High Road, housing in 1938 stretched farther along Carew and other roads to leave no empty sites around Down Lane recreation ground. Lockmead and Riverside roads were laid out in the extreme south-east and factories built or planned from Northumberland Park as far as the Edmonton boundary in the north-east. Industry also spread beyond the G.E.R. line, along the edge of the marshes: the works of Keith Blackman were built north-east of Tottenham Hale in 1938 and the old farm-house of Asplins was hemmed in by factories, which were under construction along both sides of Garman Road. At West Green a space at the junction of Philip Lane and West Green Road was filled with housing along Mansfield Avenue and neighbouring roads to the west. In the extreme south-west land bordering the railway and Harringay Park station was covered by Harringay Stadium and Arena. Overcrowding was worst in the southern part of the borough, from Stamford Hill to Harringay, with a density of more than 97 persons an acre in Chestnuts ward.[54]

In the north-east part of Wood Green allotments and playing fields preserved some open land along White Hart Lane in 1938. Housing crept closer to the potteries, however, along Devonshire Hill Lane by the Edmonton boundary and along Perth Road and the Crossway to the south. In the north-west, building covered most of the ground from Bounds Green Lane to the G.N.R. line and reached the edge of Muswell Hill golf course south-west of the railway tunnel, on land belonging to the Church Commissioners as part of the Tottenham Rectory estate.[55] Durnsford Road and neighbouring avenues, from Bidwell Gardens and Crescent Rise northward to Cline Road, had been laid out by 1938.

Many estates in the period between the World Wars were the work of the local authorities. In 1920 Tottenham U.D. planned 636 houses around Rectory Farm and Devonshire Hill and also rather

45 *Kelly's Dir. Wood Grn. and Southgate* (1934).
46 *Census*, 1901, 1911.
47 Fisk, *Tottenham*, ii. 195–6.
48 *Architectural Rev.* xviii (1910) and Bruce Castle Mus., 925 [cuttings].
49 Jackson, *Semi-Det. Lond.* 57–8.
50 Except where otherwise stated, the foll. four paras. are
based on O.S. Maps 6″, Mdx. XII. (1920 edn. and 1938 revision).
51 *Census*, 1931.
52 *Builder*, 13 Mar. 1925.
53 Jackson, op. cit. 94.
54 *Census*, 1931.
55 Church. Com. 15495A [map].

fewer at Bromley Road, on land belonging to the parochial charities.[56] Over 800 dwellings were built, to which another 300 houses and flats were added in the 1930s when the Weir Hall estate was laid out to the east of Great Cambridge Road on the Edmonton side of the boundary.[57] In Scotland Green and Parkhurst Road, Tottenham, old cottages were replaced by 36 small homes, which had been completed by 1941.[58] Wood Green in 1933 had two council estates, in White Hart Lane and Durnsford Road, together comprising 244 houses.[59] Soon afterwards a few more were built, in Perth Road.[60]

Many old features disappeared with piecemeal rebuilding along Tottenham High Road in the 1920s and 1930s. They included Phesaunt's and Sanchez's alms-houses, the shopping parade called Sanchez House being built in 1923,[61] and many villas in front of Tottenham Hotspurs' football ground, where a large stand was built in 1934. Inmates of the last parochial alms-houses, Reynardson's, left in 1938, after a parade had been built in front of the Wesleyans' oldest chapel, south of the junction with Bruce Grove. Most of those 17th- and 18th-century buildings which survived in 1937 stood north of Bruce Grove and on the east side of High Road.[62]

Municipal building increased after the Second World War, most of it on older sites and some of it on bombed premises. Temporary bungalows were built and in 1946 plans were made to re-house nearly 300 persons in the war-damaged Asplins, Manor, and Chalgrove roads.[63] Properties requisitioned during the war were maintained by Tottenham B.C., which in 1955 still had charge of 1,900 such family units. By that date there was virtually no new land left for housing in the borough and the council was preparing to build an estate of 300 dwellings at Potters Bar.[64] Wood Green by 1952 had more than doubled its permanent accommodation, with new houses in Durnsford Road, Tunnel Gardens, and Park Grove, 58 flats near by in Bounds Green Road and others elsewhere, including 56 in Vincent Road.[65]

During the 1950s and 1960s industry remained in the areas where it was already established; factory estates were opened off High Road and later at Bounds Green, and by 1966 an electricity transformer station on the marshes vied in size with the near-by gas-works, in Edmonton.[66] Slum-clearance and road-widening were helped by a fall in the population, despite the settlement of many coloured immigrants in south Tottenham. Much of the densest flow of traffic was borne by Tottenham High Road, south of Bruce Grove,[67] although Wood Green High Road was overcrowded owing to its growing popularity with shoppers; by 1961 total trade turn-over in Wood Green High Road was more than thrice that of the shops around Bruce Grove.[68] The only considerable housing development on new land was the Broadwater Farm estate, where blocks of flats east of Lordship recreation ground were finished in the early 1970s.[69] Much sub-standard property was compulsorily purchased by Haringey L.B., which also acquired the old Palace Gates railway line, closed in 1963, for housing. The council bought the 2,175 properties on the Noel Park estate in 1966[70] and, despite the sale of the former marshes to the Lee Valley regional park authority, was by far the largest landowner within the old parish in 1974.

Large-scale municipal rebuilding was planned in 1974, most of it in the south and east parts of Tottenham. Work was in progress between High Cross and Tottenham Hale, where houses had been demolished from Scales Road to Colsterworth Road, in patches on each side of Broad Lane, on land around the railway crossing between Seven Sisters and High roads, and on more westerly sites bordering Seven Sisters, St. Ann's, and West Green roads. Farther north off High Road, rebuilding was taking place around Stirling Road, south of Lansdowne Road, and around Tenterden Road, north-east of Bruce Castle park. New housing had been completed along Clyde Road, parallel with Philip Lane, and between Durban Road and the Edmonton boundary.

The reorganization of local government in 1965 stimulated proposals to redevelop the heart of Wood Green, both as the centre of the new London Borough and as a shopping district.[71] Already, in 1958, Wood Green B.C. had opened a new town hall, as part of a larger civic scheme, on the site of the Fishmongers' institution, while the years from 1961 to 1966 saw a rise in retail sales which left no rival shopping centre in north London nearer than Ealing or Ilford. Haringey council accordingly decided to discard earlier projects, to exploit the closure of the Palace Gates railway and, in conjunction with private firms, to carry out a comprehensive plan covering sites from the town hall southward to Turnpike Lane. Provision would be made for new shops, an arts and recreation centre around the Odeon cinema, student hostels, offices, factories, and much new housing. As part of the project the municipal library was demolished in 1973 and Woodall House was acquired from the Eastern Gas Board in 1974. By 1974 a few new buildings within the area had already been completed; they included the Post Office's sector switching centre, a block at the south corner of Bounds Green Road and High Road.

As a result of rebuilding much of Victorian Tottenham and Wood Green was transformed after the Second World War. In 1973 very little survived from before the mid 19th century, although the open spaces of the Lea Valley authority and the timbered slopes around Alexandra Palace were reminders that travellers once saw Tottenham as a roadside village, in low-lying farm-land, with wooded heights to the west. Tottenham High Road itself was a busy street, with few imposing buildings, often congested both by shoppers and by through-traffic. The Seven Sisters, replanted by 1876[72] and again by 1909,[73] had

[56] Fisk, *Tottenham*, ii. 335.
[57] Tottenham, *Official Guide* [1955–6].
[58] *Builder*, clxi. 97.
[59] Wood Green, *Incorporation Brochure* [1933].
[60] Wood Green, *Official Guide* [1958].
[61] Date on building.
[62] Hist. Mon. Com. *Mdx.* 123.   [63] *Builder*, clxx. 165.
[64] Tottenham, *Official Guide* [1955–6].
[65] *Wood Grn. Dir.* (1952–3).
[66] O.S. Map 1/1,250, TQ 3591 SW. (1966 revn.).

[67] Haringey L.B., *Structure Plan, Transport* (1970), 4–5.
[68] Ibid. *Shopping*, 3.
[69] The rest of the para. and the foll. para. are based on a land ownership map and inf. supplied by Haringey L.B., Town Planning Dept.
[70] *Artizans Centenary, 1867–1967*, 43.
[71] The para. is based on notes and map of the Haringey central area plan, supplied by Haringey L.B.
[72] Thorne, *Environs*, ii. 622.
[73] Couchman, *Reminiscences of Tottenham*, 10.

disappeared with rebuilding at Page Green. Trees still sheltered a public garden at Tottenham or High Cross Green and the high cross itself, restored in 1929,[74] stood on the east side of the road.

Mid-19th-century houses flank the main block of the Prince of Wales's general hospital, facing Tottenham Green.[75] Holy Trinity church, with its Sunday school dated 1847, stands on the north side of the green, while the early-20th-century municipal range lines the west. Farther north several timber-framed houses which survived on the east side of High Road in 1937 have since disappeared: nos. 824–6, 830–6, 864, and 884–890A. On the west side nos. 855 and 857 have gone, as has Brook House, which in 1951 stood on the site of B.R.S. parcels depot by the Edmonton boundary. The oldest buildings are Dial House, no. 790, perhaps dating from the early 17th century but remodelled and bearing a sundial dated 1691, and nos. 859–63, where a range of c. 1700 has been converted into shops. Dial House stands empty next to a mid-18th-century range, Percy House, whose wrought-iron gate and stone pillars of c. 1700 are the last relics of the genteel garden fronts which once faced High Road. Other residences include no. 581, a three-storeyed detached house of the late 18th century, nos. 583–5, a semi-detached pair of slightly earlier date, and nos. 695–7, early-19th-century houses next to the Baptist chapel, which was built in 1825; at Scotland Green a mid-19th-century house is used by the Y.M.C.A. A few other late-18th- and early-19th century structures can be seen above modern shop fronts.

A row of stately semi-detached yellow-brick residences of the early 19th century extends from the railway along the south-western side of Bruce Grove, where most of them serve as offices and some have been restored. Three sides of a spacious quadrangle and part of the north-east side of Bruce Grove near the junction with Lordship Lane are lined by the two-storey ranges of the 44 Sailmakers' alms-houses; they are of stock brick with stone dressings, with a chapel in the central range and a lodge at the south end. The future of the alms-houses, the last to survive in Tottenham or Wood Green, was uncertain in 1974. The junction itself is overlooked by Bruce Castle, in a corner of its park. Church Lane, close to the western wing of the mansion, leads northward from Lordship Lane past Parkside preparatory school, the much altered early-19th-century home of Albert Hill, and the walled garden of the early-17th-century Priory towards the parish church. Thence the lane turns east and north to join Church Road, the northern limit of the park, at Prospect Place, where there are five pairs of semi-detached brick cottages dated 1822. Beyond the churchyard and north-west of the park Tottenham cemetery provides a stretch of green as far as White Hart Lane. Heavy traffic uses Lordship Lane and skirts the L.C.C. estate west of Church Lane, yet tall trees and old buildings form a comparatively peaceful enclave between Bruce Castle and the church.

The demolition of Asplins farm-house, which survived in 1951, has left few other pre-Victorian buildings. The Ferry Boat inn, east of Tottenham Hale, has a stuccoed 18th-century façade of c. 1800. Bruce Terrace, a modest yellow-brick row, stands neglected by the railway line in Lordship Lane; it was built by an early-19th-century iron-founder, Thomas Finney, and some of the houses retain iron steps which were laid at the gate-ways instead of stone slabs.[76] Wood Green has nothing of comparable date, except a row of small brick houses on the south side of Bounds Green Lane, preserved in the plans for a new town centre. The former town hall, re-named Woodside House, is a three-storeyed brick building, with a southerly extension; it stands in its park, a solitary reminder of Wood Green's spacious mid-19th-century residences.

The residential avenues which cover the centre of the old parish contain little of note, except the older housing estates. At Noel Park the red-brick terraced houses, with small gardens, represent the Artizans', Labourers', and General Dwellings Co.'s original aim to supply working-class families with individual homes. They were designed by Rowland Plumbe, who proposed five classes of house.[77] Slight variations in porches and other details, together with taller buildings at the corners and rows of trees, help to soften the long, straight roads, which are laid out in a grid-pattern.[78] In Lordship Lane the Peabody Trust's cottages are terraces of stock brick, with red-brick dressings, in short tree-lined roads. The L.C.C.'s first houses, mainly two-storeyed terraces south of Risley Avenue, were designed by the council's superintending architect, W. E. Riley. They are of stock or red brick, some of them gabled and slate-hung, in a style employed at Hampstead Garden Suburb.[79] They contrast with flats and houses north of Risley Avenue, designed after the First World War by G. Topham Forrest, who was much influenced by Belgian municipal schemes.[80]

The population of the old parish more than doubled in the two decades after 1851, reaching 13,240 in 1861 and 22,869 in 1871.[81] It had doubled again, to 46,456, by 1881 and yet again, to 97,174, by 1891. Thereafter the rate of increase slowed down, bringing the total to 102,541 in Tottenham U.D. and 34,233 in Wood Green U.D. ten years later. Tottenham had 137,418 inhabitants in 1911, 146,711 in 1921, and 157,772 in 1931, while in Wood Green numbers rose more slowly from 49,369 to 50,707 and, in 1931, to 54,181. As in neighbouring areas, the population fell during and after the Second World War: the figures for Tottenham and Wood Green respectively were 126,929 and 52,228 in 1951 and 113,249 and 47,945 in 1961.

MANORS. Waltheof, son of Siward of Northumbria, held Tottenham, probably from 1065 when he became earl of Huntingdon on the banishment of Tostig.[82] In 1086, ten years after Waltheof's execution, Tottenham was held by his widow Countess Judith, daughter of William the Conqueror's sister

---

[74] Roe, *Ancient Tottenham*, 12.
[75] Except where otherwise stated, the foll. three paras. are based on Hist. Mon. Com. *Mdx.* 121–3, and Pevsner, *Mdx.* 157, 175.
[76] Couchman, *Reminiscences of Tottenham*, 54.
[77] Bruce Castle Mus., vestry plan 87.

[78] Pevsner, *Mdx.* 175; Jackson, *Semi–Det. Lond.* 57.
[79] *Architectural Rev.* xviii.
[80] Pevsner, *Mdx.* 157; *Builder*, cxxxviii. 416–17.
[81] The para. is based on *Census*, 1851–1961.
[82] For the descent of the earldom of Huntingdon until 1237 see *Complete Peerage*, vi. 638–47.

Adelize.[83] Presumably it passed with Huntingdon through Maud, daughter of Waltheof and Judith, to her successive husbands Simon de St. Liz (d. c. 1111) and David of Scotland, each of whom received the earldom. David, who succeeded in 1124 as King David I, resigned Huntingdon in 1136 to his son Henry (d. 1152), who made a grant of lands in Tottenham.[84] Huntingdon had passed to Simon de St. Liz (II), born of Maud's first marriage and a supporter of King Stephen, by 1146, but in 1157 it was restored to Henry's son, King Malcolm IV (d. 1165). Further grants in Tottenham were made by Malcolm and by his brother and successor William the Lion,[85] who forfeited his English honors in 1174, when Huntingdon was vested in Simon de St. Liz (II)'s son and namesake. On the death of Simon de St. Liz (III) in 1184 the earldom was restored to William, who resigned it to his brother David in the following year. David, deprived c. 1215 but restored in 1218, was succeeded in 1219 by his son John the Scot, whereupon the manor of *TOTTENHAM*, with that of Kempston (Beds.), was assigned to his widow Maud, daughter of Hugh (II), earl of Chester (d. 1181).[86] John was created earl of Chester in 1232 and died without issue in 1237, when the two manors were granted to his widow Helen, as the customary dower of a countess of Huntingdon.[87] In 1238 they were granted again to Helen and to her second husband, Robert de Quincy.[88]

On the death of John's widow in 1253 the manor, as part of his honor of Huntingdon, passed to the descendants of his married sisters and coheirs.[89] Margaret, the eldest, had become the wife of Alan, lord of Galloway, and mother of Devorgild, wife of John de Balliol, while Isabel, the second, had married Robert de Bruce, lord of Annandale; both sisters, as great-granddaughters of David I, transmitted Scottish royal blood to their children. A third sister, Ada, had married Henry de Hastings.[90] In 1254 Tottenham was therefore divided into three,[91] probably by sharing out the tenants rather than dividing the land.[92] The three manors, all held in chief, thereafter descended separately until they were reunited by John Gedney in the early 15th century.[93]

One third of Earl John's Tottenham lands, which became the manor of *BALLIOLS* or *DAUBENEYS*, passed to Devorgild de Balliol, who in 1281 granted them to her son John.[94] They were forfeited after John's abdication as king of Scotland in 1296 and were leased out during pleasure in 1299, first to William Persone[95] and then to Edward I's nephew

John of Brittany, later earl of Richmond,[96] who secured a grant for himself and his heirs in 1308.[97] When John died childless in 1334,[98] his Tottenham lands were bestowed for life on Sir William Daubeney,[99] who likewise secured a grant for his heirs three years later.[1] An exchange of Daubeney's share of Tottenham for the earl of Pembroke's share of Kempston, licensed in 1342, apparently was not put into effect, since Balliols was entailed by Daubeney in 1344.[2] When Sir William died in 1360 the manor passed to his son Giles Daubeney,[3] who in 1382 was licensed to convey it to the London draper John of Northampton, otherwise Comberton.[4] Two years later, after John of Northampton's forfeiture, it was granted for life to John Beauchamp of Holt,[5] later Lord Beauchamp of Kidderminster, on whose own forfeiture in 1388 it reverted to the Crown.[6] A grant to William Brightbrook and others in 1389 was cancelled later in the same year because of the claims of John of Northampton,[7] who had regained it by 1392 and who was succeeded by his son James in 1397.[8] On James's death in 1409 it passed to William Comberton, son of John Comberton and grandson of William, who had been John of Northampton's elder brother,[9] and in 1412 it was held during William's minority by Thomas Burton, a London grocer.[10] In 1421 Daubeneys was inherited by William's brother Richard Comberton[11] and by 1426 it had been conveyed to Richard Chippenham and others, who still held it in 1433.[12] Thereafter it was reunited with the other subdivisions of the manor which had been acquired by John Gedney, a London draper, who died seised of them in 1449.[13]

The manor of *BRUCES* arose from that part of Tottenham allotted in 1254 to Sir Robert de Bruce, son of Earl John's sister Isabel. It was vested in Sir Robert's son Richard, who died before his father, and on Sir Robert's own death in 1295 descended to another son and namesake. In 1304 it passed from the younger Robert to his son Robert de Bruce, earl of Carrick, who forfeited his English estates on becoming king of Scotland two years later.[14] Bruce's Tottenham lands were thereafter kept in hand for some time and farmed out for short fixed periods or during the king's pleasure; they were committed to Gertuch Honest at an unknown date, to Roger de Wateville in 1311,[15] to John of Elsfield in 1312,[16] to the royal clerk Adam de Herewinton in 1315, to David de Betoigne in 1317,[17] and, in the same year, to Walter of Shobdon, steward of the queen's household.[18] By 1335 a third of the estate had been granted to Richard Spigurnel,[19] from whom it passed to John de Mocking to become the manor of Mockings.[20]

[83] *V.C.H. Mdx.* i. 129.   [84] See p. 330.
[85] *Cart. of St. Mary, Clerkenwell*, pp. 15–16.
[86] *Rot. Litt. Claus.* (Rec. Com.), i. 395.
[87] *Close R. 1234–7*, 467.
[88] Ibid. 1237–42, 24.
[89] Ibid. 1251–3, 412.
[90] *Complete Peerage* s.v. Chester, Hastings, and Balliol.
[91] *Cal. Inq. p.m.* i, p. 82.
[92] *Tottenham Man. Rolls (1377–99)*, p. iv.
[93] See below.
[94] *Cal. Close, 1279–88*, 125.
[95] *Cal. Fine R. 1272–1307*, 411.
[96] *Cal. Pat. 1301–7*, 471.
[97] *Cal. Chart. R. 1300–26*, 122.
[98] *Cal. Inq. p.m.* vi, p. 428.
[99] *Cal. Close, 1333–7*, 199.
[1] *Cal. Pat. 1334–8*, 401.
[2] Ibid. 1340–3, 426; 1343–5, 322.

[3] *Cal. Inq. p.m.* xiv, p. 24.
[4] R. Bird, *Turbulent Lond. of Ric. II*, 7–8.
[5] *Cal. Pat. 1381–5*, 210, 493.
[6] Ibid. 1388–92, 80.
[7] *Cal. Close 1389–92*, 22.
[8] *Tottenham Man. Rolls (1377–99)*, 119, 158.
[9] C 137/73/44.   [10] *Feud. Aids*, vi. 491.
[11] C 139/14/7.
[12] *Cal. Pat. 1422–9*, 349; 1429–36, 327.
[13] C 139/134/18.
[14] *Cal. Inq. p.m.* i, pp. 82, 377; iv. 141; *Complete Peerage* s.v. Brus.
[15] *Cal. Fine R. 1307–19*, 109.
[16] *Cal. Close, 1323–7*, 435.
[17] *Cal. Fine R. 1307–19*, 251, 322.
[18] *Cal. Pat. 1313–17*, 669.
[19] Ibid. 1334–8, 118.
[20] See below.

The rest of Bruces was granted, perhaps at the same time, to Sir Thomas Heath, who was lord by 1341[21] and remained so until his death in 1374.[22] Edmund of Cheshunt, the king's falconer, received Bruces for life in 1374 and in fee two years later.[23] Courts were held for him, as Edmund Fauconer, until 1397, when he was succeeded by his son Robert,[24] who in 1398 conveyed the manor to John Walden and others.[25] John, brother of Roger Walden, archbishop of Canterbury, died in 1417[26] and a year later the profits were granted to his wife Idony, who had been enfeoffed jointly with him[27] and who died in 1425.[28] Bruces afterwards was taken into the king's hands, since some of Walden's trustees had acted without licence, but in 1427 it was released to John Gedney, to whom it had been left in reversion.[29]

The third part of Earl John's estate passed to Sir Henry de Hastings, son of his sister Ada, and became the manor of *HASTINGS* or *PEMBROKES*.[30] Sir Henry was imprisoned with Simon de Montfort's supporters in 1266, when part of his Tottenham lands was assigned to his wife Joan, the rest having been given to John de Balliol.[31] Tottenham had been restored to Henry by 1268, when he pledged it as security to Balliol, and was assigned to Joan as her dower in 1269.[32] Thereafter it descended to Henry's son John, Lord Hastings, from whom Hugh de Kendale, received a grant for life in 1292,[33] to John's son and namesake in 1313, and to the younger John's six-year old son Laurence in 1325. Laurence, earl of Pembroke from 1339, died in 1348 and was succeeded by his infant son John, earl of Pembroke,[34] whose death in 1375 was followed by a grant of Pembrokes to his widow, Anne, as her dower.[35] It passed in 1384 to her eleven-year old son John[36] and on his death in 1389 to his kinsman Reynold, Lord Grey of Ruthin.[37] John's widow Philippa (d. 1401), who had married Richard Fitz Alan, earl of Arundel, was granted the manor as her dower in 1397, after Grey had conveyed it in reversion to John Walden, his brother Roger, and others.[38] Pembrokes, like Bruces, was thereafter held by John Walden,[39] his widow Idony, and by trustees who had conveyed it to John Gedney by 1427.[40]

The third part of Bruces which became the manor of *MOCKINGS* was granted to Richard Spigurnel for life before 1335, when he received a further grant in tail.[41] In 1340 Spigurnel confirmed the conveyance of a third of a third of the manor of Tottenham to John de Mocking, of Somerset, and his wife Nichole,[42] who held it of the earldom of Pembroke.

After the deaths of John in 1347 and Nichole in the following year the lands passed to their son Nicholas, who died in 1360 leaving his sisters Margaret, wife of Roger Shipbroke, and Idony, wife of Simon Benington, as coheirs.[43] The death of Idony in 1361 and of her son John of Abingdon in 1363 brought her moiety to the Shipbrokes,[44] who within a few months conveyed the whole estate to Helming Leget and his wife Margery, Nicholas Mocking's widow.[45] In 1397 it passed to Helming's son and namesake and in 1427 to his grandson Thomas, who mortgaged it to John Gedney.[46] The estate was first called the manor of Mockings in 1427, when Thomas's aunt Elizabeth Leget quitclaimed her rights to Gedney.[47]

From John Gedney's time the manor of Tottenham remained united, although it was normally described collectively as the manors of Pembrokes, Bruces, Daubeneys, and Mockings. All four parts were vested by Gedney in Thomas Staunton, mercer, and other trustees, who in 1459 were licensed to grant them to Gedney's widow Joan for life, with remainder to Richard Turnaunt, husband of her late daughter Elizabeth, and his wife Joan.[48] On Joan Gedney's death in 1462[49] they passed to the Turnaunts, who again vested them in Thomas Staunton and others in 1464.[50] Turnaunt died seised of the manors in 1486, when they passed to his daughter Thomasine, grand-daughter of Joan Gedney and wife of Sir John Risley.[51] In 1507 a recovery was executed and the lands vested for life in Risley, with remainder to the bishop of Winchester and other feoffees on behalf of the king.[52] Risley, who survived Thomasine, died childless in 1511 or 1512, whereupon the lands passed to the Crown.[53]

The manors of Tottenham, with all Risley's property in Tottenham, Edmonton, and Enfield, were granted in tail to Sir William Compton in 1513.[54] On his death in 1528 they passed to his son Peter, a minor,[55] who in 1549 was succeeded by his posthumous son Henry, later Lord Compton (d. 1589).[56] Anne, Henry's second wife, presumably held Tottenham as her dower; she married Robert Sackville in 1592 and afterwards conveyed the manors to her stepson William, Lord Compton, later earl of Northampton, who sold or mortgaged them to Thomas Sutton and Thomas Wheeler. In 1604 Wheeler sold the manors to Thomas Sackville, earl of Dorset, who was succeeded by his son Robert Sackville in 1608. They descended to Richard, Robert's son and Anne's stepson, in 1609 and to Richard's brother Edward in 1624.[57] In the follow-

---

[21] *Tottenham Man. Rolls (1318–1503)*, 29.
[22] *Cal. Inq. p.m.* xiv, p. 35.
[23] *Cal. Pat.* 1374–7, 26, 398.
[24] *Tottenham Man. Rolls (1377–99)*, i, 88.
[25] *Cal. Close*, 1396–9, 423, 427.
[26] E. A. Webb, *Recs. of St. Barts.* i. 192, 535.
[27] *Cal. Close*, 1413–19, 463.
[28] Prob. 11/3 (P.C.C.6 Luffenam).
[29] *Cal. Close*, 1422–9, 286–7.
[30] *Cal. Inq. p.m.* i, p. 82; *Complete Peerage* s.v. Hastings.
[31] *Cal. Pat.* 1258–66, 557.
[32] *Cal. Close*, 1264–8, 561; 1268–72, 40.
[33] *Cal. Chart. R.* 1257–1300, 421.
[34] *Cal. Inq. p.m.* v, p. 230; vi, p. 385; ix, p. 113; xiv, p. 149.
[35] *Cal. Pat.* 1374–7, 195.
[36] C 136/36/67.
[37] *Complete Peerage*, vi. 155.
[38] *Cal. Close*, 1396–9, 179; 1399–1402, 227–8.
[39] *Feud. Aids*, vi. 491.

[40] *Cal. Close*, 1413–19, 463; 1422–9, 286–7. See above.
[41] *Cal. Pat.* 1334–8, 118.
[42] M.R.O., Acc. 1068/1.
[43] *Cal. Inq. p.m.* ix, pp. 13, 88; x, pp. 504, 506.
[44] Ibid. xi, pp. 31, 221.
[45] Ibid. xiii, p. 164; *Cal. Pat.* 1367–70, 322.
[46] M.R.O., Acc. 1068, intro. in catalogue.
[47] M.R.O., Acc. 1068/13.
[48] *Cal. Pat.* 1452–61, 474.   [49] C 140/8/21.
[50] *Cal. Pat.* 1461–7, 325–6.
[51] *Cal. Pat.* 1484–5, 228–9; *Cal. Inq. p.m. Hen. VII*, i, pp. 80–1.
[52] *Cal. Close*, 1500–9, 284.
[53] Prob. 11/17 (P.C.C. 8 Fetiplace).
[54] *L. & P. Hen. VIII*, i(2), p. 939.
[55] C 142/147/64.
[56] C 142/72/43; *Complete Peerage*, s.v. Compton, says that Henry was born in 1539.
[57] Oldfield and Dyson, *Hist. Tottenham*, 20; *Complete Peerage*, s.v. Dorset; C 142/405/153.

ing year they were sold, to pay Richard's debts, and in 1626 conveyed to trustees to the use of Hugh Hare, Lord Coleraine.[58]

From 1626 the four manors of Tottenham descended for over a century in the Hare family. In 1682 they passed from Hugh, Lord Coleraine, to his son Henry, chief author of the history of Tottenham, and in 1708 from Henry, Lord Coleraine, to his grandson and namesake, on whose death without legitimate issue in 1749 the peerage became extinct. The younger Henry, Lord Coleraine, by will of 1746, left all his lands in Middlesex to Henrietta Rose Peregrina Duplessis, a child born to him in Italy in 1745 by Rose Duplessis, the daughter of a French clergyman.[59] The younger Rose was recognized as lady of the manors from 1749 until 1755[60] but was then debarred, as an alien, while Lord Coleraine's heirs at law remained excluded by his will. The manors therefore escheated to the Crown until in 1763,[61] partly through the interest of Chauncey Townsend, M.P., a private Act was passed authorizing their grant to the trustees of Rose, who had married his son James Townsend.[62] They passed in 1787 from James to his son Henry Hare Townsend,[63] who auctioned most of the lands in 1789[64] and sold the lordships in 1792 to Thomas Smith of Gray's Inn. In 1805 they were conveyed by Smith to Sir William Curtis, Bt., M.P., of Cullands Grove (Southgate), a former lord mayor of London.[65] Thereafter they descended in the Curtis family, which also held the lordship of Edmonton.[66]

Tottenham had a manor-house, with a hall and other rooms, granges, fish-ponds, and garden, in 1254.[67] The 'Lordship House', so called in 1619 when it had already given its name to Lordship Lane,[68] was originally the manor-house of Bruces, retained in the hands of Joan Gedney in 1455–6.[69] It was reconstructed on or near its old site by Sir William Compton,[70] better known as builder of the mansion at Compton Wynyates (Warws.),[71] and had presumably been completed by c. 1516, when Queen Margaret of Scotland stayed there to be greeted by her brother, Henry VIII.[72] Nothing remains of Sir William's work at Tottenham except perhaps the red-brick, two-storey circular tower, of unknown purpose, which stands to the south-west of the house. The rest was rebuilt as a typical late Elizabethan country residence,[73] presumably after Norden had noted it in 1593 as Lord Compton's 'proper ancient house'.[74] Together with its outbuildings, including a dovecot, orchards, and gardens, the manor-house covered some 5 a. in 1585, when it remained in the lord's hand.[75] It was depicted, with the older tower, as a substantial building

on the map made for the earl of Dorset in 1619, at which date the grounds comprised some 9 a.; to the north-west, mid-way between the mansion and the church, lay a tenement called the wash-house, which, with the manor-house itself, Lordsmead, and other nearby lands, formed a compact estate of 86 a. which had been leased for 21 years to Sir Thomas Penistone, Bt.[76] Bruce Castle, as the mansion was later called, presumably again served as the lord's residence when Lord Coleraine carried out alterations c. 1684.[77] Further building work was effected in the 18th century by both the Hare and Townsend families.[78] The mansion was bought in at the auction of Henry Hare Townsend's property in 1789[79] but sold in 1792 to Thomas Smith, who lived at Grove House and finally separated Bruce Castle from the lordship by selling the estate to Ayton Lee. Bruce Castle passed from Ayton to his cousin Richard Lee, a London banker, and c. 1804 was bought by the politician and philanthropist John Eardley (later Eardley-Wilmot), who offered it with 46 a. at auction in 1813 and soon afterwards sold it to John Ede, a City merchant. Ede in 1827 sold the mansion with 15 a. to the Hill brothers for use as a school.[80] After the school's closure in 1891 Bruce Castle was bought by the local board, which opened the grounds as a public park in the following year. Tottenham U.D.C. installed its public health offices at Bruce Castle in 1903 and maintained a local museum there from 1906 until the First World War. It was then used for welfare offices until the return of the museum in 1927, followed by the installation of a collection on postal history. In 1969 Bruce Castle, which continued to house the postal and other exhibits, was officially reopened as the regimental museum of the Middlesex Regiment.[81]

Bruce Castle,[82] a three-storeyed building of red-brick with stone dressings, stands south-south-east of the parish church, at the corner of a timbered park and facing south to the junction of Bruce Grove with Lordship Lane. The original E-shaped Elizabethan mansion, greatly altered in plan and detail, is visible chiefly in the semi-octagonal bays at either end of the south front. The main porch, projecting from the middle of the front, is of two storeys, with stone pilasters, cornices, and rusticated quoins, and dates from shortly before 1686. It is surmounted by a wooden balustrade and a three-stage clock-tower with further balustrades, terminating in a cupola. The north front is of early-18th-century brick, with a pediment containing the Hare arms. The east side comprises one of two wings added later in the century by James Townsend, who also replaced the south gables with a parapet and renewed all the

[58] B.M. Lansd. MS. 827, ff. 125–6; M.R.O., Acc. 695/1, f. 1.

[59] Oldfield and Dyson, op. cit. 33–7, 48–56; *Complete Peerage*, s.v. Coleraine.

[60] M.R.O., Acc. 695/1, ff. 491v.–498r.

[61] Oldfield and Dyson, op. cit. 83–4.

[62] Estate Acts, 3 Geo. III, c. 45; *Hist. of Parlt. 1754–90*, iii. 537.   [63] Oldfield and Dyson, op. cit. 84.

[64] Robinson, *Tottenham*, i, Appx. I, 3–19; orig. sales partics. in M.R.O., Acc. 1016/475.

[65] Robinson, *Tottenham*, i. 171.

[66] M.R.O., Acc. 695/2, /3, /4; see p. 150.

[67] *Cal. Inq. Misc.* i, p. 69.

[68] Robinson, *Tottenham*, map of 1619; see p. 309.

[69] Bruce Castle Mus., MR/76 [TS. transl. p. 21].

[70] Bruce Castle Mus., 927 BRU [official programme, 1969].

[71] *V.C.H. Warws.* v. 60.

[72] *L. & P. Hen. VIII*, ii(1), p. 533.

[73] Hist. Mon. Com. *Mdx.* 121–2; Pevsner, *Mdx.* 156.

[74] John Norden, *Speculum Britanniae* (1723 edn.), 41.

[75] Bruce Castle Mus., MR/121.

[76] Robinson, *Tottenham*, map of 1619; M.R.O., Acc. 695/9, ff. 6–7 [survey, 1619].

[77] See plate facing p. 320.

[78] See below.

[79] M.R.O., Acc. 1016/475.

[80] Robinson, *Tottenham*, i. 218–19; M. Weiner, *John Eardley-Wilmot* (Edmonton Hund. Hist. Soc. 1971).

[81] Bruce Castle Mus., 927 BRU [newspaper cuttings and programme]; see pp. 341–2.

[82] Except where otherwise stated, the para. is based on Hist. Mon. Com. *Mdx.* 121–2 and Pevsner, *Mdx.* 156.

windows. Since the demolition of Townsend's west wing and of stables and coach-houses to the north by John Ede, Bruce Castle has enjoyed something close to its modern appearance[83] from the south; the plainer north front has a Victorian addition at the west end. The interior contains a late 17th-century staircase and an ornate fireplace of marble and carved wood, which was perhaps brought from Italy by the third Lord Coleraine.

The manor-house of Mockings, on the south side of Marsh (later Park) Lane, was retained by Joan Gedney in 1455–6[84] but had been leased to Alice Marsh, widow, in 1585.[85] It was a comparatively modest building, with a moat and some 4 a. of grounds, in 1619, when it was leased with other demesne lands to John Burrough.[86] Mockings was a 'neat' dwelling, leased with farm buildings and 68 a. to Edwin Paine, when offered for sale in 1789.[87] It was bought by Thomas Smith and retained its moat and drawbridge in 1792, but was sold in 1803 to a Mr. Cooper, who demolished the house. The moat survived in 1840[88] and was still partly visible, south-east of St. Paul's church, in the 1860s.[89]

The rectorial estate of Tottenham was held by the Augustinian canons of Holy Trinity, Aldgate, from the 12th century until the surrender of their house in 1532. Apart from the church itself, given by King David I of Scotland before the death of the first prior in 1147,[90] the canons received many small properties from the time of Otes of Tottenham, who in 1182 sold them 5 a. in Appeland and Langland and who soon afterwards gave them a further 2 a. in Langland.[91] The rectory was assessed at 30 marks in the mid 13th century[92] and at £14 in 1291.[93] In 1534, two years after the priory's surrender, all Holy Trinity's possessions in Edmonton and Tottenham were granted to Sir Thomas Audley.[94] They had returned to the Crown by 1538, when they were granted to William, Lord Howard, and his wife Margaret,[95] who exchanged them with the king in 1541.[96] In 1543 174 a. of wood, which had been leased out by Holy Trinity, were granted separately by the Crown.[97] Courts for Tottenham RECTORY manor were held for the king from 1541 until 1544 and thereafter for the chapter of St. Paul's,[98] who, by virtue of their manor of Bowes, were already landowners in the parish[99] and who were granted the rectory in 1544.[1] Thereafter the manor remained with St. Paul's for three centuries, except during the Interregnum when the lessee, Stephen Beale, was recorded as lord between 1651 and 1659.[2] When the

tithes were commuted for £1,685 10s. in 1844, £885 was awarded to the chapter and their lessee.[3] Thirty years later manorial rights passed to the Ecclesiastical Commissioners.[4]

Both the land and the great tithes were normally leased out. A 40-year lease from 1525 was granted by Holy Trinity to Dr. Thomas Bentley and a 60-year lease from 1585 was granted by St. Paul's to Anthony Cole.[5] In 1622 the lease was left by Humphrey Westwood, a London goldsmith, to his son and namesake,[6] who held it in 1650[7] shortly before the estate's sequestration and purchase, together with the lordship, by Stephen Beale. After the Restoration Beale was retained as lessee by St. Paul's, his son Joshua succeeding in 1667[8] and receiving new 21-year leases in 1700 and 1707.[9] The Beales' interest passed to the Hobbys, through the marriage of Stephen's daughter Mary (d. 1708), and to the Jermyns, through the marriage of Margaret Maria Hobby (d. 1735);[10] leases were granted to the administrator of the estate of Stephen Jermyn, a lunatic, in 1788 and to his coheirs Harriet, wife of Henry Eyre, and Mary Udney, widow, in 1796.[11] Henry Piper Sperling, who bought the lease in 1797, conveyed the house and 26 a. to William Wright and later, in 1819, leased out the great tithes to Thomas Tuck.[12] In 1866 the bulk of the rectory estate, excluding the house and 30 a. adjoining it, was leased by St. Paul's to the Revd. John Sperling. In 1878 it comprised c. 125 a., of which 58 a. were in Tottenham, chiefly between the northern boundary and White Hart Lane, north of the rectory house, or between the lane and the Moselle, to the east. Other parts lay along the boundary, around Tile Kiln farm in Edmonton, and in the marshes of both parishes. At that date the Ecclesiastical Commissioners held a total of 208 a. in Tottenham, most of it in the extreme north-west and belonging to the manor of Bowes.[13] The freehold interest was finally sold in 1958.[14]

The parsonage house occupied a slight eminence on the south side of White Hart Lane, north-west of the church, from which it was separated by the Moselle stream.[15] It seems to have been a very large building in 1619[16] and was noted by Bedwell,[17] but the story that it stood on the site of Pembrokes manor-house, itself mentioned in 1455–6,[18] was not recorded until the late 18th century. The house was then said to have been rebuilt in local brick by one Soames,[19] presumably a tenant of the Westwoods. Stephen Beale was assessed on 13 hearths when he occupied the parsonage in 1664.[20] It was called the

[83] Views from the south, dated 1686 and 1840, are in Robinson, *Tottenham*, i, plates facing pp. 217, 219.
[84] Bruce Castle Mus., MR/76 [TS. transl. p. 31].
[85] Bruce Castle Mus., MR/121.
[86] Robinson, *Tottenham*, map of 1619; M.R.O., Acc. 695/9, f. 20.
[87] M.R.O., Acc. 1016/475.
[88] Robinson, *Tottenham*, i. 253–4.
[89] O.S. Maps 6", Mdx. XII. NE. (1863–9 edn.).
[90] *Cartulary of Holy Trin. Aldgate* (Lond. Rec. Soc.), 3, 229.
[91] *Cat. Anct. D.* iv, A 7277; ii, A 2553.
[92] *Val. of Norw.*, ed. Lunt, 359.
[93] *Tax. Eccl.* (Rec. Com.), 17.
[94] S.C. 6/Hen. VIII/2357 m. 1.
[95] *L. & P. Hen. VIII*, xiii(1), p. 242.
[96] Ibid. xvi, p. 458.
[97] Ibid. xviii(2), p. 142; xix(1), p. 495.
[98] St. Paul's MSS., box B 48.
[99] *Feud. Aids*, vi. 487; see p. 151.
[1] *L. & P. Hen. VIII*, xix(1), p. 495.

[2] St. Paul's MSS., box B 50.
[3] Church Com. S.4, f. 345.
[4] Bruce Castle Mus., D/MR/A/6.
[5] Robinson, *Tottenham*, i. 222.
[6] Prob. 11/139 (P.C.C. 139 Savile).
[7] *Home Cnties. Mag.* i. 319.
[8] Prob. 11/323 (P.C.C. 16 Carr).
[9] Guildhall Libr., uncat. Church Com. deed 169141.
[10] Robinson, *Tottenham*, i. 223; ii. 59, 62.
[11] Guildhall Libr., Church Com. deed 169141.
[12] Robinson, *Tottenham*, i. 223–4.
[13] Church Com. S.4 [survey]; 15495A [map].
[14] See p. 152.
[15] O.S. Map 6", Mdx. XII. NE. (1863–9 edn.).
[16] Robinson, *Tottenham*, map of 1619.
[17] W. J. Roe, *Ancient Tottenham*, 108.
[18] Bruce Castle Mus., MR/76 [TS. transl. p. 20].
[19] Oldfield and Dyson, *Hist. Tottenham*, 24. It was later said to have been built in 1896; see Fisk, *Tottenham*, i. 134.
[20] M.R.O., MR/TH/5.

Moated House in 1797[21] and was praised as a handsome and well situated residence when held by Henry Sperling, who had filled in the moat by 1816.[22] Sperling's sale of the lease separated the house and grounds from the rest of the rectory estate. The chapter leased it in 1819 to William Wright, after whose death it was acquired by J. Rawlings of the Middle Temple.[23] When Rawlings was resident in 1843 the grounds were called Tottenham Park,[24] a name applied to the house itself in the 1860s during the occupation of Maj. William James Gillam,[25] who had a curious cottage, designed by Philip Webb, erected to remind him of one where he had lain wounded in the Crimean War.[26] The mansion, in good repair when auctioned in 1896,[27] was deserted by 1905 and pulled down before 1913, when the estate was offered for sale as building land.[28]

The so-called manor of *DUCKETTS*, once thought to have been Dovecotes,[29] derived its name from the Duckett (Duket) family, a London dynasty of the 12th and 13th centuries. James of Steventon conveyed rents and arable at Woodleigh to John Renger, clerk, in 1256–7 and later quitclaimed all his lands there to Laurence Duckett and his wife Maud.[30] Laurence, a London citizen and perhaps the goldsmith murdered in 1284, also acquired a house at Tottenham from Richard de la Piere c. 1260[31] and witnessed several grants of land there to Holy Trinity priory.[32] In 1293 William le Brun quitclaimed his rights in a house and lands in Tottenham and Harringay, lately held by his kinsman and namesake, to Laurence, son of Laurence Duckett.[33] John, son of Laurence Duckett, leased all his late father's lands in Tottenham to William Furneys, pepperer of London, and his wife Cecily in 1314,[34] as well as 12 a. in Michley marsh to John de Denum in 1325 and 25 a. to John de Mocking, fishmonger, in 1326.[35] The inherited lands and the reversion of those in Michley were sold by John Duckett to Matthew Palmer in 1331.[36] By 1334 the estate, called the manor of Duckett, had been acquired from Palmer by the king's tent-maker John of Yaxley,[37] who also acquired John de Mocking's interest[38] and in 1345 conveyed it to Sir John Stanford,[39] a justice of the Common Pleas,[40] to whom Thomas Duckett quitclaimed his rights to the property in 1346.[41] From 1360 the estate was leased out by William of Brightley,[42] Sir John's cousin and heir, whose widow

Joan in 1388 released all her dower rights there to John Doget otherwise Butterwick and his wife Alice,[43] who had acquired the lease.[44] From Doget, who himself leased out the manor in 1389, Ducketts descended to his heir William Rote, whose widow Elizabeth granted it to Richard Sturgeon,[45] holder of Duckettsland in 1455–6,[46] and others. Sturgeon, having built the chapel of St. Mary and St. Michael at St. Bartholomew's hospital, vested the estate in Nicholas Bayley, one of his executors,[47] who was to convey it to the hospital for the support of a chantry priest. The land was surrendered to St. Bartholomew's by Bayley and other trustees in 1464,[48] after the master had accused Bayley of felling the timber for his own profit.[49] In 1520 St. Bartholomew's leased out the house and most of the lands to John Watson, a London brewer,[50] and in 1535, after John Brereton had been made master, William Brereton became the lessee. Brereton's lease was forfeited on his attainder in 1536 and granted by the king to Thomas Heneage,[51] from whom it passed to Robert Heneage.

In 1547 the manor of Ducketts was separated from most of the hospital's lands, which went to the City of London,[52] and bought by Richard Cecil of Burghley,[53] who soon afterwards sold it to Sir Edward, later Lord, North.[54] In 1554, when Ducketts comprised 3 houses and 700 a., Lord North conveyed it to William Parker, a London draper,[55] whose son William conveyed it in 1576 to feoffees, from whom it passed in 1580 to John Dudley of Stoke Newington.[56] Sir Francis Popham[57] held Ducketts in 1619[58] and sold it twenty years later to Sir Edmund Scott of Lambeth,[59] who was succeeded by his brother Sir Stephen Scott of Cheshunt (Herts.). In 1660 Stephen's son John sold the manor to Dr. Edmund Trench (d. 1689),[60] whose son Samuel died in possession in 1741. Most of the estate then passed to Samuel's daughter Sarah and her husband, John Berney of Bracon Hall (Norf.), while a smaller part, forming Grainger's farm, passed to the antiquary Richard Muilman Trench Chiswell,[61] grandson of Edmund Trench's niece Mary. A year after Chiswells' suicide in 1797 his portion was sold to Michael and John Phillips, whose family had been tenants for over twenty years and still owned Graingers in 1851. Meanwhile John Berney's share passed in 1800 to his widow and afterwards to Thomas Trench Berney,

[21] Robinson, *Tottenham*, i, Appx. I.
[22] Brewer, *Beauties of Eng. and Wales*, x(5), 699; Robinson, op. cit. i, plate facing p. 222.
[23] Robinson, op. cit. i. 224–5.
[24] Bruce Castle Mus., D/PT/102A/3, p. 37.
[25] *P.O. Dir. Mdx.* (1862), 586; O.S. Map 6″, Mdx. XII. NE. (1863–9 edn.).
[26] Victoria and Albert Mus., Dept. of Prints and Drawings, E. 1341916.
[27] Bruce Castle Mus., Tottenham sales, ii, no. 19.
[28] Fisk, *Tottenham*, i. 134–6.
[29] Robinson, *Tottenham*, i. 241.
[30] St. Barts. Hosp., medieval deeds 918, 950. Photocopies of many of the deeds concerning Ducketts are at Bruce Castle Mus.
[31] St. Barts. Hosp., med. deeds 952.
[32] *Cat. Anct. D.* ii, A 2351, A 2535, A 2537.
[33] C.P. 40/100 carte rot. 150.
[34] St. Barts. Hosp., med. deeds 955, 956.
[35] Ibid. 957–61.   [36] Ibid. 963–6.
[37] St. Barts. Hosp., Add. deeds 107.
[38] St Barts. Hosp., med. deeds 974.
[39] C.P. 25(1)/150/60 no. 192.
[40] E. Foss, *Judges of England*, iii. 512.
[41] C.P. 25(1)/150/61 no. 202.

[42] St. Barts. Hosp., med. deeds 979–80.
[43] *Cal. Close*, 1385–9, 484.
[44] St. Barts. Hosp., med. deeds 991.
[45] Ibid. 966, 999.
[46] Bruce Castle Mus., MR/76 [TS. transl. p. 10].
[47] Prob. 11/4 (P.C.C. 9 Stokton).
[48] *Cart. of St. Barts. Hosp.* ed. N. J. M. Kerling, nos. 1113–1123.
[49] Robinson, *Tottenham*, i. 247–9.
[50] C 1/485/21; C 1/580/20.
[51] *L. & P. Hen. VIII*, vii(1), p. 157.
[52] Ibid. xxi(2), p. 416.
[53] *Cal. Pat.* 1547–8, 241.
[54] Inf. supplied by Mr. C. J. C. Harris from deeds of the Berney fam. of Hockering Ho. in the Norf. and Norwich Rec. Office.
[55] C.P. 25(2)/74 no. 629.
[56] Berney fam. deeds.   [57] *D.N.B.*
[58] M.R.O., Acc. 695/9, f. 124.
[59] Except where otherwise stated, the rest of the para. and the foll. para. are based on inf. supplied by Mr. C. J. C. Harris, based on Berney fam. deeds, Tottenham man. rolls, land-tax assessments, and poor-rate bks.
[60] *Calamy Revised*, ed. Matthews, 492.
[61] *D.N.B.*

who sold it in 1840 to Alfred Jones. Berney's land covered *c.* 138 a. in 1821 and stretched from the farm-house north-east to Lordship Lane, being bounded on the north-west by the Moselle and along the east by fields which had been detached to form Grainger's farm.[62] Most of Ducketts was bought in 1862 by Thomas Clark, who built twelve houses south of the farm-house but retained the rest until 1881.

The mansion- or farm-house of Ducketts stood on the east side of the later Wood Green High Road, north of the site of Turnpike Lane station. It included a gatehouse, a moat, and farm buildings in 1520[63] and retained its moat until the 1860s, when the building was called Dovecote House.[64] Although it was normally occupied by lessees after it passed from the Ducketts, Alfred Jones lived there in the 1840s and Thomas Clark in the 1870s. The last occupant was recorded in 1881, shortly before most of the land was taken for the Noel Park estate. Grainger's farm-house, built between 1818 and 1844[65] on the south side of Lordship Lane, survived until the 1890s.[66]

Nicholas Twyford repeatedly failed to do fealty at courts of Bruces manor between 1380 and 1383. It is not known whether Nicholas was the London gold-smith of that name who supported John of North-ampton nor if he was connected with a John Twyford who held of Daubeneys in the 1390s.[67] John Twyford held property in Tottenham worth 100*s.* a year in 1412[68] and was in dispute with John Walden in 1414–15.[69] William Drayton held several parcels of the tenement called Twyford forty years later, when tenants of the so-called manor of *TWYFORDS* were listed with those of other sub-divisions of Tottenham manor.[70] Sir John Elrington, treasurer of the king's household,[71] died in 1482–3 seised of Middlesex property including 3 houses and 80 a. in Tottenham, most of which passed to his eldest son Simon. The Tottenham lands, involved with others in disputes between Sir John's brother, widow, and children, presumably comprised part of Twyfords.[72] Richard Turnaunt named Twyfords along with his other manors in 1486[73] but Simon Elrington's son Thomas died seised of the manor of Twyford and 380 a., held of Sir William Compton, in 1523, when he was succeeded by his 2-year old son and namesake.[74] It was later acquired by John Cayzer or Keyser, who in his will of 1556 empowered his brother Nicholas, a London vintner, to sell Twyfords and other property to meet bequests to his children.[75] The manor was normally called

Twyfords or Martins from 1599, when John Boulton died seised of it.[76] John's son Simon left lands within the manor, near Hanger Lane, to his son Abraham in 1618.[77] In the following year it was held by Matthew de Questor,[78] who shared with his son and namesake the office of postmaster for foreign parts and who enfeoffed trustees in 1623 on his son's marriage to Mary Fitzherbert.[79] In 1624 the younger Matthew died[80] and in 1641 Twyfords was conveyed by Mary Lewyn, presumably his widow, and her husband William to Henry Browne. The estate included 3 houses in 1641,[81] after which date it ceased to be called a manor.

OTHER ESTATES. One of Tottenham's largest monastic estates was that held by the Augustinian canonesses of St. Mary, Clerkenwell. Henry of Scotland (d. 1152) gave Ughtred of London 140 a. in the 'hanger'[82] of Tottenham, together with half of a water-meadow which Ingram, chancellor of Scotland and bishop of Glasgow, had held, the right to take 4 tree-trunks a year, and pannage for 10 pigs. In 1160–3 Henry's son Malcolm IV of Scotland con-firmed a grant of the same property to Robert, son of Swein of Northampton, who between 1165 and 1176 gave it to St. Mary's priory. Robert's gift re-ceived confirmation, by 1176, from Henry II and from Malcolm's successor William the Lion.[83] The nuns thereafter retained the estate, as well as that of Muswell in Hornsey, until the Dissolution.[84] It was claimed that they held of the manor of Bruces[85] but the prioress withheld fealty from Sir Thomas Heath in the 1340s[86] and was frequently a defaulter at courts later in the century.[87] The property included a house in 1345[88] and 3 crofts called Oatfields, land in a field called Great Hanger, and woods and mea-dow in Snaresmead by 1455–6.[89] Great Hanger and Oatfields were leased out on the eve of the Dis-solution,[90] as were 11 a. in Tottenham marsh and closes in Snaresmead and Thistlefield.[91] After Sir William Kingston had bought the reversion of the lease of Great Hanger and Oatfields, it was granted to his stepson Edmund Jerningham in 1540.[92] On Jerningham's death in 1546 the lands passed to his step-brother Sir Anthony Kingston,[93] who surren-dered part of Great Hanger (140 a.) to Henry Jerningham and Oatfields to Edward Pate,[94] to whom Jerningham surrendered Great Hanger later in the same year.[95] In 1553 Pate conveyed Oatfields to William Parker, a London draper,[96] and his 140 a.

[62] Robinson, *Tottenham*, i, Appx. I, p. 33 and map of 1821.
[63] C 1/485/21; C 1/580/20.
[64] O.S. Map 6″, Mdx. XII. NW. (1863–9 edn.).
[65] Robinson, *Tottenham*, map of 1818; Bruce Castle Mus., Tithe Award map.
[66] O.S. Map 6″, Mdx. XII. NW. (1894–6 edn.).
[67] e.g. Tottenham Man. Rolls (*1377–99*), 13–14, 22–3, 247, 249, 313.
[68] *Feud. Aids*, vi. 491.
[69] C 146/9646.
[70] Bruce Castle Mus., MR/76 (TS. transl.).
[71] A. R. Myers, *Household of Edw. IV*, 33–4, 290.
[72] Prob. 11/7 (P.C.C. 8 Logg); C 1/125/58–62.
[73] Prob. 11/7 (P.C.C. 25 Logg).
[74] C 142/81/229.
[75] C 142/110/120.
[76] C 142/377/51.
[77] Prob. 11/131 (P.C.C. 18 Meade).
[78] M.R.O., Acc. 695/9.
[79] C 2/Jas. I/C8/14.

[80] C 142/441/10.
[81] C.P. 25(2)/528/16 Chas. I Hil.
[82] From *hangra*, 'wooded slope': *P.N. Mdx.* (E.P.N.S.), 79, 91.
[83] *Cartulary of St. Mary, Clerkenwell* (Camden 3rd ser. lxxi), pp. 11, 14–18. Most of the charters are transl. in Robinson, *Tottenham*, i. 257–60.
[84] J. F. Connolly and J. Harvey Bloom, *An Island of Clerkenwell*, 7–8, 11.
[85] Bruce Castle Mus., MR/76 [TS. transl. pp. 1–3].
[86] *Year Bk.* 19 Edw. III (Rolls Ser.), 411.
[87] Tottenham Man. Rolls (*1318–77*), 27, 33, 50.
[88] *Year Bk.* 19 Edw. III, 411.
[89] Bruce Castle Mus., MR/76 [TS. transl. pp. 1–3].
[90] *L. &. P. Hen. VIII*, xv, p. 166.
[91] S.C. 6/Hen. VIII/2396 m. 100.
[92] *L. & P. Hen. VIII*, xv, p. 166.
[93] C 142/75/1.
[94] *L. & P. Hen. VIII*, xxi(1), p. 251.
[95] Ibid. xxi(2), p. 247.
[96] *Cal. Pat.* 1553, 272.

in Great Hanger to Augustine Hinde, alderman,[97] who was succeeded in 1554 by his infant son Rowland.[98] Thereafter the former monastic lands remained split up; most of them were granted in 1560 to Michael Lock, a London mercer,[99] and Oatfields was conveyed by Parker to Thomas More, another mercer, in 1561.[1] Oatfields, Snaresmead, and Thistle-field formed part of the freehold estate of Edward Barkham in 1619.[2]

The London Charterhouse possessed an estate called Bounds and Woodleigh, on the borders of Tottenham and Edmonton, which originated in lands held by Thomas, son of John Bonde or le Bounde. Thomas acquired a house and land in Edmonton from Alice King in 1337–8[3] and conveyed them, with other lands inherited from his father in both parishes, to his brother Simon in 1342. They passed in turn to Gilbert Fox in 1357–8, to William Fordham in 1360–1, to James Walsh and Gilbert Neel and then to John Ollescamp, a London fuller, in 1364, and from Ollescamp to John Cambridge, a fishmonger, in 1371.[4] Cambridge, who also acquired Arnolds and other lands,[5] vested the property in William Wal-worth and others, from whom it passed to the king, who in 1378 granted it to the Carthusians.[6] The prior, a frequent defaulter at the courts of Daubeneys in the late 14th century,[7] held c. 126 a. of woods and 20 a. of other lands in 1463; the woods included Bounds wood and Austredding in Tottenham and greater and lesser woods called Arnolds (the modern Arnos Grove) in Edmonton, while the fields lay entirely in Tottenham.[8] In 1543, five years after the priory's suppression, Charterhouse wood was granted to Sir John, later Lord, Williams and Sir Edward, later Lord, North. At that date it comprised 60 a. west of Bounds Green, adjoining the Edmon-ton property of the chapter of St. Paul's at Bowes Heath.[9] Sir Edward's son Roger, Lord North, con-veyed the woods to Sir Thomas Wroth in 1565.[10]

The hospital of St. Mary without Bishopsgate had a small property, worth 26s. 8d. a year in 1412.[11] At that time it presumably included the hospital of St. Loy, recorded in 1409, built or restored by Thomas Billington and conveyed by him to the London house.[12] John Pertrishe was said to hold the 'hospitill with garden' as a copyhold of Pembrokes in 1455–6[13] and the hospital of St. Loy itself disappeared at some date after 1484.[14] St Mary's none the less retained the site in Tottenham until the Dissolution, since its former 5-acre pasture called the Spital-house was granted to Sir Ralph Sadler in 1550.[15] Lands in the common marsh of Tottenham had also been held by St. Mary's in 1468–9.[16]

Kilburn priory had lands in Tottenham by 1455–6, when the prioress, as a free tenant of Pembrokes, held two parcels amounting to 6 a. at Wood Green and Woodridings.[17] In 1514 the nuns had a close at Woodridings called Dores pightle and in 1528 they also had a meadow in Wild Marsh.[18] Their lands were leased to John Wheeler for 10s. a year in 1535–6[19] and their former closes of Baker's field and Dores pightle were sold by the Crown to Henry Audley and John Cordell in 1544.[20]

The priory of St. Bartholomew, Smithfield, was said to have lands in Tottenham worth 10s. a year in 1291.[21] Presumably they included the property in Tottenham and Edmonton which was leased for 31 years to George Henningham for 6s. 8d. a year in 1511.[22] Lands belonging to the knights of St. John of Jerusalem in Edmonton and neighbouring parishes, leased out in 1536, included 3 a. in Tot-tenham Broadmead.[23]

After the Reformation 174 a. of wood in Tot-tenham and Edmonton became separated from the other lands which had belonged to Holy Trinity. The woods, which the priory had leased separately to Nicholas Gray,[24] were sold in 1543 to John Tawe and Edward Taylor,[25] who in 1545 conveyed 164 a. to John Grimston.[26] One third was conveyed by Grimston in 1546 to Nicholas Askew and his wife Alice,[27] who in 1551 surrendered 24 a. to John Eccleston, a London grocer.[28] By 1553 Eccleston had been succeeded by his son John, a minor,[29] pre-sumably the man of that name who occupied a tene-ment called the Blue House in 1585.[30]

The family of William Coombe, a free tenant of Mockings in 1467, probably gave its name to the estate called Coombes Croft.[31] William's house on the south side of Marsh (later Park) Lane was pre-sumably the close of some 4 a. called Coombes Croft, of which Sir William Lock, alderman of London, died seised in 1551. Michael Lock, mercer, did homage for Coombes Croft with other lands in Tottenham in 1576[32] and Thomas Lock of Merton (Surr.) conveyed them in 1634 to Thomas Wilcocks and Tobias Massye, who settled them in trust for the poor.[33] Thereafter Coombes Croft formed part of the Tottenham charity estates until its sale to the urban district council in 1920. Part of Coombes Croft house, which had been built as a workhouse in the 18th century,[34] was opened as a public library in 1925, after the rest had been demolished to make way for Bromley Road.

The estate of Stone Leas, a name recorded in 1467,[35] lay south of Coombes Croft and on the same side of High Road. Stone Leas comprised a house,

97 Ibid. 1553–4, 361.
98 Ibid. 1554–5, 78.
99 Ibid. 1558–60, 438–9.
1 Ibid. 1560–3, 200.
2 M.R.O., Acc. 695/5, ff. 50–1.
3 E 326/5168.
4 E 315/34 no. 96.
5 L.R. 2/61 ff. 145–6.
6 Cal. Pat. 1377–81, 242; Cal. Close, 1381–5, 158–9.
7 Tottenham Man. Rolls (1377–99), passim.
8 L.R. 2/61 ff. 146v.–147v.
9 L. & P. Hen. VIII, xviii(1), p. 132.
10 Cal. Pat. 1563–6, 197.
11 Feud. Aids, vi. 487.
12 Oldfield and Dyson, Hist. Tottenham, 15–16.
13 Bruce Castle Mus., MR/76 [TS. transl. p. 10].
14 V.C.H. Mdx. i. 153.
15 Cal. Pat. 1549–51, 268.
16 S.C. 6/1108/18.

17 Bruce Castle Mus., MR/76 [TS. transl. pp. 11–12].
18 Tottenham Man. Rolls (1510–31), 41, 214.
19 S.C. 6/Hen. VIII/2345 m. 12.
20 L. & P. Hen. VIII, xix(2), p. 194.
21 Tax. Eccl. (Rec. Com.), 13.
22 E 303/9/268.
23 S.C. 6/Hen. VIII/2402 m. 32; see p. 155.
24 L. &.P Hen. VIII, xix(1), p. 495.
25 Ibid. xviii(2), p. 142.
26 Ibid. xix(2), p. 59.   27 Ibid. xxi(1), p. 582.
28 Cal. Pat. 1550–3, 59.
29 Ibid. 1553, 6.
30 Bruce Castle Mus., MR/121.
31 Except where otherwise stated, the para. is based on Coombes Croft Branch Libr. [pamphlet, 1925].
32 Bruce Castle Mus., D/PT/7F/13.
33 Ibid./14; see p. 378.
34 See p. 343.
35 P.N. Mdx. (E.P.N.S.), 78.

A HISTORY OF MIDDLESEX

courtyard, and 71 a. in 1585, by which date it had been sold in fee farm to Nicholas Backhouse and was held by Samuel Backhouse.[36] By 1599 it was in the hands of Balthasar Sanchez, who set aside a plot for his alms-houses and in 1601 provided that repairs and pensions should be paid for out of the rest of the estate, which was left to his brother-in-law Christopher Scurrow.[37] It had passed from Scurrow to Bridget, widow of John Moyse, a grocer of London, by 1619, when Bridget surrendered the ½ a. covered by the alms-houses to trustees.[38] Stone Leas later passed to the Scales family, being owned by John Scales in 1826[39] and 1840[40] and by Edward Scales in 1845.[41]

The largest freehold estate in 1619 belonged to Edward Barkham, alderman of London, who held 174 a. in addition to 65 a. of copyhold land. The freehold included Crokes farm,[42] which was presumably named after John Croke, a London alderman who held land in Tottenham late of John Drayton by 1455–6 and who left property there to his son and namesake in 1477.[43] Lionel, son of William Dalby, sold it with some London property to Edward Barkham,[44] whose family thereby became responsible for maintaining Dalby's charity.[45] In 1619 the farm-house was a substantial house opposite the vicarage, with land stretching south along High Road from White Hart Lane to a point opposite Marsh Lane, while Crokes grove survived as some 29 a. of woodland north of Chapmans Green.[46] Barkham, who was knighted and became lord mayor of London, was succeeded in 1634 by his eldest son Sir Edward Barkham, Bt., of Tottenham and of South Acre (Norf.),[47] but settled Crokes farm on a younger son, Robert Barkham of Wainfleet St. Mary[48] (Lincs.), later also knighted. Sir Robert, by will proved 1661, ordered that his mansion in Tottenham should be sold for the benefit of his second son and namesake,[49] but it may have been acquired by the testator's brother Sir Edward, who was assessed on 21 hearths in 1664.[50] In 1667 Sir Edward left the Tottenham house to his second son, William,[51] who later inherited the Norfolk estates and died in 1695, when the title became extinct. Edward, son of Sir Robert Barkham of Wainfleet St. Mary, also secured a baronetcy, which passed to his son Robert and then to his childless grandson Edward, who was buried at Tottenham in 1711. Part of Crokes farm presumably comprised the three tenements near the corner of White Hart Lane which were left to the parish by Mrs. Jane Barkham in 1724.[52] The main property, however, was acquired by Ephraim Beauchamp (d. 1728),[53] whose son

Thomas (d. 1724) married Anne, daughter of William Proctor of Epsom (Surr.) and whose grandson William took the surname Beauchamp-Proctor on becoming a baronet in 1744.[54] The house, rebuilt, was known as White Hall for some years before 1790, when Sir William's son, Sir Thomas Beauchamp-Proctor, sold his estates in Tottenham.[55] A Mr. Abrahams from Houndsditch bought the mansion and built a tanyard and offices, which were removed by his successor Mr. Andrews. White Hall then passed to Henry Hunt, to William May Simmonds, and in 1827 to Charles Soames,[56] the occupier of some 6 a. in 1843.[57] In Soames's time an entrance from High Road replaced the old one from White Hart Lane; the mansion, a three-storeyed pedimented building with single-storey wings, was screened by trees from High Road and faced south across a lake.[58] It had given its name to Whitehall Street by the 1860s, when the lake had gone and most of the ground had been built over,[59] and was still discernible, although much altered, in 1913.[60]

Demesne land called Downhills, perhaps the le Downe recorded in 1467,[61] gave its name to Downhills House, later Mount Pleasant House. The land lay in the centre of the parish between Lordship Lane and Philip Lane and had been divided by 1585, when 10 a. were leased out at will;[62] in 1619 several closes of pasture at Downhills, totalling 65 a. were leased to three tenants.[63] The newly built Downhills House, approached by a drive along the line of the later Downhills Park Road, was leased out from 1728, together with Broadwater farm in Lordship Lane. A new three-storeyed mansion, of brick with a pediment and two low wings, had been built by 1789, when it was occupied by Rowland Stephenson, a banker, who let the farm to the Phillips family.[64] Mount Pleasant, as the house was then called, was withdrawn from auction when Henry Hare Townsend broke up the manorial estate in that year; it was again withdrawn after Stephenson's death in 1808, when the mansion was offered with 81 a. and the farm-house with 119 a.[65] Henry Hare Townsend, who had remained the owner, himself lived at Mount Pleasant from 1823 until his death in 1826, after which it was leased out by his son the Revd. Chauncey Townsend, the poet.[66] The mansion, separated from most of the farm-lands, was renamed Downhills, occupied in 1855 by John Lawford[67] and sold in 1881 to the British Land Co. It was demolished after its purchase in 1902 by Tottenham U.D.C., which used the surrounding land as Downhills recreation ground.[68] A second Mount Pleasant had been built to the east by 1865[69] and was

[36] Bruce Castle Mus., MR/121.
[37] See p. 377.
[38] Bruce Castle Mus., D/PT/7A/1.
[39] 14th Rep. Com. Char. 159.
[40] Robinson, Tottenham, ii. 255.
[41] Bruce Castle Mus., 988 [drawing of tablet over alms-ho.].
[42] M.R.O., Acc. 695/9, ff. 25–7, 51–2.
[43] Bruce Castle Mus., MR/71; Prob. 11/7 (P.C.C. 4 Logg).
[44] C 142/512/1.
[45] See p. 378.
[46] Robinson, Tottenham, map of 1619.
[47] G.E.C. Baronetage, i. 219.
[48] C 142/512/1.
[49] Prob. 11/305 (P.C.C. 106 May).
[50] M.R.O., MR/TH/5.
[51] Prob. 11/324 (P.C.C. 102 Carr).
[52] G.E.C. Baronetage, i. 219; iii. 222.

[53] Robinson, Tottenham, i. 126.
[54] Burke, Peerage (1959), 176.
[55] Oldfield and Dyson, Hist. Tottenham, 104.
[56] Robinson, Tottenham, i. 124.
[57] Bruce Castle Mus., D/PT/102A/3, p. 142.
[58] Robinson, Tottenham, i, plate facing p. 124.
[59] O.S. Map 6", Mdx. XII. NE. (1863–9 edn.).
[60] Fisk, Tottenham, i. 98.
[61] P.N. Mdx. (E.P.N.S.), 80.
[62] Bruce Castle Mus., MR/121.
[63] M.R.O., Acc. 695/9, ff. 14–16; Robinson, Tottenham, map of 1619.
[64] M.R.O., Acc. 1016/475; Bruce Castle Mus., watercolour on display.
[65] M.R.O., Acc. 1016/476.
[66] Robinson, Tottenham, i. 117; D.N.B.
[67] Kelly's Dir. Mdx. (1855).
[68] Ex inf. chief supt. of parks, Haringey L.B.
[69] O.S. Map 6", Mdx. XII. NE. (1863–9 edn.).

332

offered for sale with its own estate as 135 building lots, bordering the later Mount Pleasant Road, in 1890.[70]

Although most of the lands and the medieval manor-house of Willoughbies were in Edmonton,[71] a house called Willoughbies had been built on the Tottenham side of the boundary by 1619.[72] After the sale of the Edmonton portion of the original estate in 1717 Lucy Beteress, who married John Bowry in 1725, retained the property in Tottenham. It was heavily encumbered with mortgages and annuities and in 1735, under an Act of 1731,[73] trustees sold the house and a small amount of land to Robert Turner, whose heirs sold it in 1757 to Daniel Booth.[74] He conveyed Willoughby House in 1764 to Hananel Mendes Da Costa of London,[75] who sold it to Stephen Briggs in 1773.[76] Andrew Jordaine acquired it in 1779, Richard Welch and then William Wilson in 1792, and Archibald Bryson by 1800. Bryson's son and namesake inherited it in 1807 and sold it to William Hyde in 1812. On Hyde's bankruptcy the estate, by that time little more than 11 a., was bought in 1821 by a Mr. Smale,[77] presumably the Henry Lewis Smale who lived there in 1843.[78] The house and grounds, on the west side of Willoughby Lane, were improved by Smale and survived, with villas on either side, in the 1860s.[79]

ECONOMIC HISTORY.

AGRICULTURE. In 1086 Tottenham was assessed at 5 hides and Countess Judith had a further 2 carucates in demesne. There was meadow for 10 ploughs, pasture for the cattle of the vill, a weir, and woodland for 500 pigs. The value had fallen from £26 T.R.E. to £10 when the countess received it, presumably after Earl Waltheof's execution in 1076, but had afterwards risen to £25 15s. and 3 ounces of gold. The lady had 2 ploughs on the demesne and her tenants had 12 ploughs. The tenants included 6 villeins on 6 virgates, 24 villeins each on ½ virgate, and 12 bordars each on 5 a., in all accounting for 20 virgates, as well as a priest on ½ hide and 17 cottars. There were 2 Frenchmen on 1 hide and 3 virgates, and 4 serfs.[80]

Tottenham, with rich grass-land along the Lea and poorer clay to the west, was probably always better suited to livestock than to crops.[81] In 1254, on the eve of the manor's division, meadow was valued at 5s. 4¼d. an acre and pasture at 3s. 3d., whereas the best arable, on the demesne, was worth only 4½d.[82] At that date there were 527 a. of demesne arable, 40 villein holdings each of a 32-acre virgate, 92 a. of meadow, and 16 a. of pasture. The number of Domesday virgates had doubled, presumably from assarts, but the total of 1,915 a. covered less than half of the parish; the rest was made up of woods of unknown extent and the lands of free tenants, who paid £4 10s. 4d. in quit-rents.

Isolated accounts for the three manors in the early 14th century give a total acreage reduced by less than one eighth from that of 1254 but show 14 per cent less demesne arable. In 1304 Bruces had 110 a. in demesne, part of which was leased out by 1318; 60 a. were leased out 30 years later and 108 a. by 1399. On the larger manor of Balliols or Daubeneys, with 171 a. in demesne in 1334, tenants leased 162 a. by 1389–90, although John of Northampton briefly tried to resume direct cultivation in 1392. After John Gedney had reunited the manors, the demesne was farmed by one individual and later by three or four tenants. In 1585 Henry, Lord Compton, retained the manor-house (later Bruce Castle) and a mere 38 a. apart from woodland, letting some 475 a. of the demesne on long leases and 150 a. at will.[83] In 1619 the woods alone remained in hand.[84]

In the 14th century holdings were relatively numerous for so much indifferent land. The manors probably contained over 100 unfree tenants in the 1340s and as many, with at least 20 free tenants, fifty years later. Their numbers suggest that pressure from a rising population was relieved only briefly by the Black Death. Most holdings were small, the median size on Pembrokes being 7½ a. c. 1343, although a few were considerable: John atte Marsh held 41 a., nearly a tenth of the villein land on Pembrokes, c. 1343, when his family in all held some 92 a., and Thomas Harding held some 55 a. in 1368. Of the 20 villein land holdings on Pembrokes, perhaps 15 were held by families bearing the name of their tenement at the beginning of the 14th century, 11 were so held c. 1343, and 7 in 1368. It therefore seems that the subdivision of the original whole or half virgates did not begin much before 1300.

Copyhold lands customarily were inherited by the youngest son or, in default of male issue, were divided among daughters. The practice, known as Borough English, was recorded in the 15th,[85] 17th,[86] and early 19th centuries, and was still observed in 1771.[87] A heriot was due only from owners of cattle and admission was granted at the age of 14.[88] Copyholds might not be sublet for more than a year and a day without permission.[89] By the late 14th century, however, numerous property transactions had produced an active free market in land, subject merely to the lord's licence.

After 1368 the number of very small tenants fell and that of tenants with 15–30 a. increased. By 1459 large holdings included those of St. Mary's, Clerkenwell, with 260 a., St. Paul's, with at least 220 a., and John Drayton, with more than 180 a. Many of those who bought both free and copyhold lands, and so helped to break up the old virgate holdings, were rich Londoners. The Marsh family itself was among those which made way: a 24-acre tenement held by John atte Marsh in 1368 passed in turn to his son

[70] Bruce Castle Mus., 927.   [71] See p. 152.
[72] Robinson, *Tottenham*, map of 1619.
[73] Bowry Estates Act, 4 Geo. II, c. 28 (Priv. Act).
[74] M.L.R. 1757/4/363–5.
[75] M.L.R. 1764/3/372–4.
[76] M.L.R. 1773/3/517–8.
[77] Robinson, *Tottenham*, i. 111–12.
[78] Bruce Castle Mus., D/PT/102A/3, p. 141.
[79] Robinson, *Tottenham*, i. 113; O.S. Map 6″, Mdx. XII. NE. (1863–9 edn.).
[80] *V.C.H. Mdx.* i. 129.
[81] Except where otherwise stated, the following 8 paras.

are based on D. Moss and I. Murray, 'Land and Labour in 14th cent. Tottenham', *T.L.M.A.S.* xxiv. 199–220, and 'A 15th-cent. Mdx. Terrier', *T.L.M.A.S.* xxv. 285–94.
[82] C 132/16/7. The extent is largely transl. in Robinson, *Tottenham*, i. 163–4.
[83] Bruce Castle Mus., MR/121.   [84] See p. 336.
[85] A custumal of 1457–8 is transl. in Robinson, *Tottenham*, i. 186–96.
[86] M.R.O., Acc. 695/9 f. 146.
[87] M.R.O., Acc. 695/14.
[88] M.R.O., Acc. 695/9 f. 142.
[89] Robinson, *Tottenham*, i. 190.

Thomas and then to a daughter of Gilbert atte Marsh, who, with her husband Richard, sold it to a London girdler named Thomas Purnell.

Nothing certain is known of the original common fields. There was no simple division of each main field in 1254, which would have fragmented the tenants' allegiance, and probably no geographical division for the same reason; perhaps the tenants themselves were shared out, later divided allegiances being attributable to purchases or indirect inheritance.[90] It has sometimes been assumed that common fields never existed, since almost the whole parish, in contrast to Edmonton, had been inclosed by 1619.[91] The large amounts of demesne leased out in the 14th century presumably were farmed in severalty. On the other hand references to crops and services suggest a three-course rotation and many land transactions reveal widely scattered strips; references to inclosed land, moreover, were comparatively rare, while attempted inclosures included one by James Northampton concerning land 'common every third year'. The many fields recorded from that time offer little guidance, since most were small ones which had resulted from assarting. Those most often mentioned were South field, also called St. Loys field in 1619,[92] when it was north of High Cross Lane, and Home field, both of which may have been open fields surviving as part of an enlarged and complicated pattern. In all, it seems that common agriculture persisted in the late 14th century, side by side with a growing tendency towards farming in severalty.

Manorial officers in the late 14th century included a steward, reeve, and woodward. Both Bruces and Daubeneys produced a considerable surplus of faggots, hay, and pasture, which was sold for the lord; demesne animals were not recorded and neither meat nor dairy produce was sold. Services on Pembrokes in the middle of the century were not heavy: 37 winter and 31 summer works were required for a virgate and the villeins' ploughing accounted for a mere 45 a., implying that most of the demesne was already leased out or worked by hired labour. There were apparently no payments in kind. In addition to the 20 villein holdings, on which varying amounts of services had been commuted, there were 8 molmen, paying much higher rents but performing lighter services, and 9 cottars, who owed rents and minute works.

A comparatively mild regime did not prevent unrest. In 1351 offenders against the Statute of Labourers were forcibly rescued from custody[93] and at the beginning of Richard II's reign services went unperformed, the entire homage of Daubeneys being in mercy in 1378-9. Things were 'taken away from the mill' in 1380-1 and mysterious payments to a priest 'coming with a certain sign' were erased from the accounts, perhaps because they indicated sympathy with the Peasants' Revolt. John of Northampton in 1392-3 tried to reverse the general trend by restoring services and sowing former grass-land

on the demesne, which secured a high yield. By 1394-5 his accounts were in deficit, perhaps because tenants withheld their rent, and the reaction was over. Daubeneys was spared in 1399, when Henry of Lancaster's army seized all the hay from the grange of Bruces, presumably in revenge for the Waldens' close association, through Archbishop Roger Walden, with Richard II. Pembrokes may have been similarly despoiled, for in 1403 a commission of oyer and terminer was set up after the Waldens' tenants had refused their services.[94]

Hay-making or cutmead, on the lord's land in the marshes, was among the last services to be abandoned. Works owed by every tenant on the reunited manors were specified in 1478-9[95] and the obligation to mow and to stack in the lord's grange was recorded in 1619.[96] The lord held 172 a. in the marshes in 1585, keeping 21 a. in hand and leasing out 76 a. for long terms and 75 a. from year to year.[97]

Tottenham marsh had been divided into six by 1585: Wild marsh, Michley, and Mill mead lay east of the Mill stream, Broad mead, Clendish Hills, and Lock mead to the west. The marshes were made up of shots, each comprising several parcels.[98] In 1619 Wild marsh contained 72 parcels, Michley 41, Mill mead 13, Broad mead 11, Clendish Hills 33, and Lock mead 7, a total of 177 parcels covering some 303 a. In addition there were 8 parcels in the 20-acre Hale field and 8 in the 45-acre Downfield, both of which adjoined Clendish Hills.[99]

A hayward for the marshes was normally chosen every year at the manorial court, together with two cattle-markers and two drivers for all the common lands.[1] A tenant might claim pasturage in summer for as many beasts as he could support on his own lands in winter.[2] In the mid 19th century the right was said to extend to every resident landholder, while a householder occupying property assessed at less than £10 for the poor-rate was entitled to pasture 2 head. The marshes then were normally open to the commons from 12 August until 5 April and known as the Lammas lands. The hayward, who had taken over the duties of the markers, branded all livestock entitled to common pasturage, supervised their driving, and patrolled the commons, in order to detect surcharging and turn away or impound hogs and other unauthorized beasts.[3] There was a 'pound garden' at the north corner of Lordship Lane and High Road in 1619.[4] A pound-keeper was recorded from 1766,[5] the pound being in High Road close to Pheasaunt's alms-houses, until its removal in 1840 to Tottenham Hale, where it was rebuilt in 1883 and finally condemned in 1922.[6] The lord's agent appointed one man to the posts of pound- and marsh-keeper and common driver as late as 1891, nine years before the Lammas lands were vested in Tottenham U.D.C.[7]

In 1585, when most of the demesne was leased out, by far the most substantial tenant was Richard Martin, a goldsmith and future lord mayor of London,[8] who held c. 279 a., including 50 a. at will.[9]

[90] Tottenham Man. Rolls (1377-99), iv.
[91] Ibid. (1318-77), xi-xii.
[92] Robinson, Tottenham, map of 1619.
[93] Cal. Pat. 1350-4, 158.
[94] Ibid. 1401-5, 361.
[95] Bruce Castle Mus., MR/94.
[96] M.R.O., Acc. 695/9 f. 150.
[97] Bruce Castle Mus., MR/121.   [98] Ibid.
[99] M.R.O., Acc. 695/9 ff. 125-39.

[1] e.g. M.R.O., Acc. 695/1 f. 20v.
[2] M.R.O., Acc. 695/9 f. 140.
[3] M.R.O., Acc. 1016/470, /471.
[4] M.R.O., Acc. 695/9 f. 17.
[5] M.R.O., Acc. 695/1 f. 554.
[6] Fisk, Tottenham, ii. 44, 341.
[7] M.R.O., Acc. 1016/472, /473.
[8] D.N.B.
[9] Bruce Castle Mus., MR/121.

In 1619 the whole demesne, apart from the woodland, was divided among 18 tenants.[10] Nearly all enjoyed new leases for 21 years, the chief tenants being Joseph Fenton with 179 a., John Burrough with 139 a., Sir Thomas Penistone with 86 a., Thomas Adams with 85 a., and Edward Barkham with 66 a. The largest freeholders were Barkham with 174 a., Ambrose Wheeler with 141 a., Edward Osborne with 82 a., Bridget Moyse with 78 a., Lady Heybourne with 75 a., and the heirs of Michael Lock, with 71 a. The chief copyholders were Elizabeth Candler, with 345 a., Anthony Crewe with 80 a., Thomas Bolton with 63 a., and Erasmus Greenway with 62 a. London merchants predominated: Fenton was a barber-surgeon, Barkham an alderman, Crewe a mercer, as Lock had been,[11] and Greenway a grocer; Bridget Moyse was the widow of John Moyse, also a grocer, and Elizabeth Candler the widow of Richard Candler, a mercer, and related both to the Locks and the Heybournes.[12] Other residents connected with the City included William Gore, an alderman, with a 'sumptuously built' freehold house in High Road, Sir James Price in the right of his wife Joan, widow of John Ballett, a goldsmith, and Thomas Goddard, son and namesake of an ironmonger. Only 4 small wastehold parcels were recorded, although in 1656 many unauthorized cottages were ordered to be pulled down.[13]

Most of the arable in 1619 was on newly-cleared woodland in the north-west, between the Moselle and the New River, or along Stonebridge stream or to the west of the marshes. The centre of the parish, like the marshland, was chiefly meadow.[14] Much the same pattern persisted in 1800, when the largest block of arable lay around the remnants of Tottenham wood.[15] Three quarters of the parish was grass-land and 440 a., little more than a tenth, was arable.[16]

Grass-land dwindled faster than arable in the late 19th century. Corn and green crops accounted for 338 a. in 1870, almost the same acreage in 1890, 298 a. in 1900, and 161 a. in 1910, while grass-land shrank from 1,943 a. to 1,268 a., 1,173 a., and, in 1910, to 720 a. Corn itself was grown on barely one quarter of the arable in 1870 and on one third in 1890, when wheat was the main crop, and on a mere 17 a. in 1900. The chief green crops in 1870 were vetches on 85 a., followed by mangolds, potatoes, and swedes or turnips; potatoes formed the largest crop in 1890, on 67 a., cabbages in 1900, on 50 a., and potatoes again in 1910, on 70 a. Most of the grass-land was mown annually in the 1870s and 1880s but by 1910 grazing predominated. The number of cattle fell steadily from 611 in 1870 to 110 in 1910; sheep, numbering c. 300 in 1870, had almost disappeared by the end of the century but increased

to 176 by 1910, while the number of pigs similarly declined, only to rise again to 315; there were 103 horses in 1870, 149 by 1900, and 31 in 1910.[17]

In 1619 roses were grown on land in Marsh Lane belonging to Asplins farm and on two neighbouring crofts, as well as south-east of High Cross green, opposite the east end of the parsonage grounds, and on larger rose-fields by the New River north-west of Serles green.[18] The Asplins farm site, 6 a. called Hencroft, was marked as 'now converted into a garden of roses',[19] implying the recent expansion of a considerable business, presumably to supply apothecaries with petals.[20] Although roses were not recorded again, the Asplins lands lay very close to those of William Coleman (c. 1743–1808), who had a local nursery by 1777. Coleman held some 60 a. at the end of the 18th century, half lying west of High Road on each side of Church Road, where Nursery Street and Nursery Court survive, and half bordering Marsh Lane in a block later marked by Lansdowne, Sutherland, Chalgrove, and Shelbourne roads. William's widow Ann and son George (d. 1822) continued his Tottenham nursery, presumably from the 'Old Nursery' in Marsh Lane after 22 a. west of High Road had been auctioned in 1810.[21] Sarah Coleman, probably George's widow, ran the business until 1833, while Charles Coleman worked a smaller area in Church Road.[22] There were also market gardens on the north side of Marsh Lane and along Willoughby Lane c. 1800.[23] All had gone by the 1860s, when there was a Whitehouse nursery west of Church farm. Whitehouse nursery existed in the 1890s, as did Tottenham nursery south of Paxton Road and 8 other nurseries in the neighbourhood of Park Road and Northumberland Park, as well as two south of Tottenham Hale. A nursery survived off Trulock Road and another off the later Tariff Road in 1920.[24]

The total amount of agricultural land decreased from 2,280 a. in 1870 to 1,604 a. in 1890, 1,495 a. in 1900 (of which 513 a. were in Wood Green), and 881 a. in 1910. In 1870 there were 85 agricultural holdings, in 1910 twenty-one.[25] Among the last farms were Graingers farm in the 1890s, Devonshire Hill (formerly Clayhill), Rectory, Broadwater, and Whitebraid Hall farms, all of which existed in 1920,[26] and Asplins farm, which survived in 1933.[27]

Allotments, worked by members of a society in the mid 19th century,[28] were first provided by Tottenham U.D.C. at Downhills and elsewhere during the First World War.[29] In 1920 Tottenham had allotments near the Edmonton boundary, both on the marshes and north of White Hart Lane, and Wood Green had sites north and south of White Hart Lane and by the railway south-east of Durnsford Road.[30] In the 1930s Tottenham U.D.C. permitted the temporary use of marshland north of Ferry Lane,[31]

[10] Except where otherwise stated, the para. is based on M.R.O., Acc. 695/9.   [11] See p. 331.
[12] Prob. 11/125 (P.C.C. 24 Rudd, will of Ric. Candler), /141 (P.C.C. 4 Swann, will of Eliz. Candler); Robinson, *Tottenham*, ii. 41–3.   [13] M.R.O., Acc. 695/1 f. 88.
[14] Ex inf. the archivist, Haringey L.B.
[15] T. Milne, *Plan of . . . London and Westminster, circumjacent towns and parishes* (1800).
[16] Middleton, *View*, table facing p. 560.
[17] M.A.F. 68/250, /1276, /1846, /2416.
[18] Robinson, *Tottenham*, map of 1619.
[19] M.R.O., Acc. 695/9 f. 65.
[20] Ex inf. Mr. J. H. Harvey.
[21] Partics. in Robinson, *Tottenham*, i. 26–30.

[22] J. H. Harvey, 'Nurseries on Milne's Land-Use Map', *T.L.M.A.S.* xxiv. 193–4.
[23] Milne, *Plan* (1800).
[24] O.S. Maps 6", Mdx. XII. NE., NW. (1863–9, 1894–6, and 1920 edns.).
[25] M.A.F. 68/250; M.A.F. 68/1276; M.A.F. 68/1846; M.A.F. 68/2416.
[26] O.S. Maps 6", Mdx. XII. NE., NW. (1894–6 and 1920 edns.).
[27] *Kelly's Dir. Mdx.* (1933).   [28] See p. 339.
[29] Ex inf. Chief Supt. of Parks, Haringey L.B.
[30] O.S. Maps 6", Mdx. XII. NE., NW. (1920 edn.).
[31] D. H. Smith, 'Industrialization of Greater Lond.' (Lond. Univ. Ph.D thesis, 1932), 59–60.

acquired 8 a. as a permanent site in Marsh Lane[32] and set aside 10 a. on the new White Hart Lane estate.[33] Allotments in the 1960s included sites in Marsh, Willoughby, Devonshire Hill, and White Hart lanes, on the White Hart Lane estate, along the Moselle, and, at Wood Green, near Durnsford Road and on the edge of Muswell Hill golf course.[34]

WOODS. Countess Judith held woodland for 500 pigs in 1086.[35] Presumably the woods were divided equally in 1254: they accounted for 100 a. on the manor of Robert de Bruce and 110 a. on that of John de Hastings in the early 14th century,[36] for 400 a. on the reunited manors of Sir John Risley,[37] and 500 a. on those of Sir William Compton.[38] Tottenham wood was leased out separately in 1530,[39] when in the king's hands through the minority of Peter Compton, and Holy Trinity priory likewise made a separate lease of 174 a.[40] Sales by the Crown later separated most of the woodland which had been held by religious houses from the rest of the former monastic estates.[41]

There were well over 500 a. on the demesne in 1585. Tottenham wood covered 425 a. in the extreme west of the parish and Hawks park,[42] recorded in 1455–6,[43] covered 72 a. east of Ducketts, on the north side of West Green Lane (later West Green Road). Spottons or the Little Lords grove comprised 18 a. on the north side of Lordship Lane. Lords grove, c. 9 a. a little to the east of Spottons grove and bordering Chapmans Green, was not mentioned, while a second Lords grove, on the south side of West Green Lane opposite Hawks park, was said to have been sold to Richard Martin, alderman of London and a substantial tenant. Probably the timber alone had been sold to Martin, as it had at Spottons grove, since both the tracts called Lords grove belonged to the demesne in 1619. Two recent fellings had taken place at Hawks park, which was well stored with young trees, and Spottons, which had been poorly stocked. Conditions were worst in Tottenham wood, where no timber trees had survived the felling of 90 a. in the previous year; there had been little replenishment with staddles and the ground was choked with varied undergrowth.[44]

The same woods remained in the lord's hand in 1619, although Tottenham wood had been reduced to 388 a. and the total acreage to 501 a. Tottenham wood contained 4,660 timber trees awaiting sale, Hawks park had 888, Spottons grove 248, and each Lords grove had about 100. There was little wood-land outside the demesne, apart from a block adjoining Spottons and Lords groves to the north and including the 27 a. of Crokes Grove held by Edward Barkham, a parcel at Wood Green held by Ambrose Wheeler, and strips along the Moselle by Ducketts land and south of Ducketts Green.[45]

Inroads continued, perhaps more rapidly, after 1619, leading William Bedwell to complain of the daily reduction in the timber.[46] In 1754 Tottenham wood still crowned the western heights[47] but most of it had been cleared by 1789, when it was auctioned as a separate estate with the rest of Henry Townsend's property.[48] Tottenham Wood farm-house had been built by 1818 and was surrounded by some 400 a., of which 11 a. made up the last remnants of the parish's woodland in 1840.[49] The farm was sold to the builders of the first Alexandra Palace after the death of Thomas Rhodes in 1856[50] but the farmhouse or its successor still stood, as Tottenham Wood House, north of the junction of the new Albert and Alexandra Park roads, in the 1890s.[51]

MILLS. A water-mill was divided with the rest of the manor in 1254 and included the right to fish in an adjacent pond in the early 14th century.[52] The head of water may have been provided by a weir which had been held by Countess Judith in 1086.[53] In 1374 Sir Thomas Heath's share of the mill was ruinous.[54] The mill was farmed, apparently by the year, in 1470–1,[55] the common miller was fined for excessive tolls in 1530,[56] and a tenant was fined for refusing to take his corn there in 1558.[57] It was leased out with 12 a. of near-by meadow in 1585[58] and stood next to a leather mill in 1619, when both were known as Tottenham mills. The mills stood on the west side of Mill mead, approached from the Hale by a lane slightly south of the later Ferry Lane; they included a new tile-hung tenement and two oyster-beds in Mill mead.[59]

In 1656 the lord was presented for making gunpowder in place of flour.[60] A paper-mill alone seems to have existed from c. 1680; it was insured in 1735 by Israel Johannot, one of a well-known family of French paper-makers, and in 1757 and 1761 by Thomas Cooke, perhaps the man who was rewarded by the Royal Society of Arts for making paper with copper plates.[61] In 1770 it was let to Edward Wyburd,[62] who converted it into a corn-mill, which was burned down in 1788.[63] Corn- and oil-mills, on opposite sides of the road, were at once erected and were sold to John Cook soon after the general auction of the Townsend estates. In the 1790s the corn-mill itself[64] was said to pay for the rent, enabling Wyburd

32 Ex inf. Chief Supt. of Parks.
33 Bruce Castle Mus., 961 [cutting].
34 O.S. Maps TQ 29 SE., 39 SW. (1962–8 edn.).
35 V.C.H. Mdx. i. 129.
36 Cal. Inq. p.m. iv, p. 141; v, p. 230.
37 Cal. Pat. 1494–1509, 535.
38 C 142/47/64.
39 L. & P. Hen. VIII, iv(3), p. 2857.
40 Ibid. xix(1), p. 495.
41 See p. 331.
42 Bruce Castle Mus., MR/121.
43 Bruce Castle Mus., MR/76 (TS. transl. p. 9).
44 Bruce Castle Mus., MR/121.
45 M.R.O., Acc. 695/9, ff. 2–5 and Robinson, Tottenham, map of 1619.
46 W. J. Roe, Ancient Tottenham, 107.
47 Rocque, Map of Mdx. (1754).
48 M.R.O., Acc. 1016/475.
49 Robinson, Tottenham, i. 50–55 and map of 1818.

50 Fisk, Tottenham, ii. 182.
51 O.S. Maps 6″, Mdx. XII. NW. (1863–9 and later edns.).
52 Cal. Inq. p.m. vii, p. 428; ix, p. 113.
53 V.C.H. Mdx. i. 129.
54 Cal. Inq. p.m. xiv, p. 35.
55 Bruce Castle Mus., MR/90.
56 Tottenham Man. Rolls (1510–31), 243.
57 Ibid. (1547–58), 151.
58 Bruce Castle Mus., MR/121.
59 M.R.O., Acc. 695/9, ff. 27–9; Robinson, Tottenham, map of 1619.
60 M.R.O., Acc. 695/1, f. 88.
61 A. H. Shorter, Paper Mills and Paper Making in Eng., 48, 86, 213.
62 M.R.O., Acc. 1016/475; Shorter, op. cit. 213.
63 Except where otherwise stated, the rest of the section is based on Robinson, Tottenham, i. 136–7.
64 See plate facing p. 240.

TOTTENHAM: THE GEORGE AND VULTURE c. 1800

HENDON: THE GOLDERS GREEN HIPPODROME IN 1914

Wood Green: the First Alexandra Palace as projected in 1871

Hendon Aerodrome from the West *c.* 1930
The Northern line to Edgware is in the foreground

to sublet the oil business. In 1824 there was a coal-wharf at the mills,[65] which were occupied by Messrs. Curtoys and Mathew as successors to Charles Pratt, who had bought Wyburd's interest. The freehold was bought from Cook by the New River Co. in 1836. The mills, badly damaged by flooding in 1817, were not rebuilt after a fire c. 1860,[66] although their ruins survived in 1920.[67]

Some 57 a. were offered with the mills in 1789 and were still attached to them in 1840: the buildings, with inclosed grass-land and part of Tottenham Hale field, covered c. 15 a., while 21 parcels in the marshes made up the remainder. The River Lea Navigation Act of 1779 safeguarded the flow to the mills and approved annual payments which were already being made to James Townsend.[68] In 1790 lessees received £50 a year from the River Lea Co., as well as tolls levied at the bridge,[69] and in 1810 they were also paid by landowners in Mitchley marsh, who had to cross the mills' lands after the parish declined to rebuild a bridge to the marsh from Down Lane.

TRADE AND INDUSTRY. Brick-making flourished by 1435–6, when 28,500 'breeks' were sold. The date was an early one for the use of the term, which evidently included tiles, and for such activity so far inland. Over 100,000 bricks were sold over three years, to John Drayton and other local landowners, and to men from Edmonton, Enfield, and London. It is possible that sales thereafter increased so much that details were not entered on the bailiff's accounts,[70] for the only other 15th-century reference to the working of clay or brickearth is the occupation of Perkyn the Potter, hero of the *Tournament of Tottenham*.[71] Brickearth, which lay close to the parish church as well as east of High Road, was exploited by Sir William Compton for rebuilding Bruce Castle, but few bricks were made, or at any rate used, locally later in the 16th century.[72] Brickearth was exploited around High Cross and elsewhere in 1631[73] and digging by High Road was licensed in 1704.[74] The industry flourished during 19th-century building when brick-makers also used clinker from domestic fires;[75] three brick-makers recorded in 1832–4 were still in business in 1845 and included one in Green Lanes who, with a builder, was the only manufacturer in Wood Green ward.[76] In 1818 there was a brick-field on the Rectory estate, close to the Edmonton boundary,[77] and in 1843 Nathaniel Lee owned a tile-works with at least 13 cottages in the extreme south-west of the parish, near the site of Harringay Stadium.[78] The tile-kilns survived in the 1860s, with a brick-field immediately

east of Tottenham cemetery and a brick-works between the railway tunnel and Bounds Green Road. By the 1890s both works were potteries; in addition the Tottenham and White Hart Lane potteries were near together, north of White Hart Lane, and a brick-works operated in the south, between Vale and Seven Sisters roads. All the potteries save the one at Harringay survived in 1920, when the Bounds Green works made glazed bricks and tiles,[79] and those in White Hart Lane still made horticultural pottery in 1934.[80]

Of 178 male residents whose occupations were recorded between 1574 and 1592, 119 or some two-thirds worked on the land. Another 12 were in household service, accounting for 7 per cent of the total and perhaps an underestimate of the fluctuating domestic servant population. There were 11 men engaged in the clothing and 6 in the building trades, 9 'moniers', who may have made tradesmen's tokens, and 6 blacksmiths, at least 4 of them in business at the same time. Presumably it was the need to cater for travellers and the presence of rich Londoners which produced so many families not engaged in agriculture.[81]

Tottenham, despite its 19th-century growth, had little industry before the 1890s.[82] By 1801 twice as many persons were engaged in trade or manufacture as agriculture, yet 30 years later nearly all the men in the first category were shopkeepers or craftsmen, catering for the well-to-do.[83] In 1824 they included, among commoner tradespeople, 2 auctioneers, 3 chemists, 5 straw-hat makers, a bookseller, and a perfumer and hairdresser; a pawnbroker, a furrier, and an umbrella-maker existed by 1845.[84]

Apart from Tottenham mills, with their paper-making and other businesses, and a short-lived tannery at White Hall,[85] the first factory was one built for lace-making by William Herbert of Nottingham in 1810. It comprised two four-storeyed ranges in Love Lane, on part of the site of Coleman's nursery, where Herbert employed some 140 persons before his retirement to Nottingham in 1837. He was succeeded by crape manufacturers, John and James Baylis[86] and afterwards Messrs. Le Gros, Thompson & Bird, who moved to Norwich after a fire in 1860.[87] Another early factory, for winding silk, was built by Louis Frébout in 1815 and gave rise to Factory Lane. From c. 1820 it was leased for lace-making by Messrs. Lacy & Fisher, who had some 300 employees. In 1837 it was taken over by the new London Caoutchouc Co.,[88] which had been empowered to maintain imports of India rubber and promote its use[89] and which was later known as William Warne & Co.,[90] from a partner who died in 1861. The

---

[65] *Pigot's Gen Dir.* (1824), 74.

[66] Mrs. J. W. Couchman, *Reminiscences of Tottenham*, 16.

[67] O.S. Map 6″, Mdx. XII. NE. (1920 edn.).

[68] See p. 308.

[69] Oldfield and Dyson, *Hist. Tottenham*, 38–9.

[70] F. H. Fenton, *Some Recent Work on Tottenham Man. Rolls* (Edmonton Hund. Hist. Soc. 1961), 12. The entries are transcribed in D. Avery, *Poverty and Philanthropy in Tottenham* (ibid. 1963), 21.

[71] *Oxford Bk. of Light Verse*, ed. W. H. Auden, 42.

[72] *Tottenham Man. Rolls* (*1510–31*), p. v.

[73] Roe, *Ancient Tottenham*, 104.

[74] M.R.O., Acc. 564/76.   [75] Fisk, *Tottenham*, ii. 185.

[76] *Pigot's Com. Dir. Six Home Cnties.* (1832–4); *P.O. Dir. Six Home Cnties.* (1845).

[77] Robinson, *Tottenham*, map of 1818.

[78] Bruce Castle Mus., D/PT/102A/3, p. 185, and Tottenham Tithe Apportionment Map.

[79] O.S. Maps 6″, Mdx. XII. SE., NE., and NW. (1863–9 and later edns.).

[80] Tottenham, *Official Guide* [1934].

[81] The figures are taken from the burial regs.: D. Avery, 'Male Occupations in a rural Mdx. par.' *Local Pop. Studies Mag. and Newsletter*, ii. 29–35.

[82] D. H. Smith, 'Recent Industrialization of Greater Lond.' (Lond. Univ. Ph.D. thesis, 1932), 47.

[83] *Census*, 1801–31; *Pigot's Com. Dir.* (1832–4).

[84] *Pigot's Gen Dir.* (1824); *P.O. Dir.* (1845).

[85] See pp. 336, 332.

[86] Robinson, *Tottenham*, i. 68–9; Bruce Castle Mus., D/PT/102A/3, pp. 24, 67.

[87] Mrs. J. W. Couchman, *Reminiscences of Tottenham*, 53.

[88] Robinson, *Tottenham*, i. 66–8.

[89] Lond. Caoutchouc Co. Act, 7 Wm. IV & I Vic. c. 132 (Local and Personal).

[90] *Kelly's Dir. Essex, Herts. and Mdx.* (1890).

rubber mills were extended after one of the four-storeyed blocks had been burned down in 1839 and included a 160-feet high stack, demolished in 1903. Part of the site was sold in 1904 to the Society of Licensed Victuallers, who built Dowsett Road, but the company continued to make rubber solution and a wide range of articles in Tottenham until it completed a move to Barking after the First World War.[91]

There were 2 local brewers in 1824 and 5, including Jeremiah Freeman and son, in 1845.[92] Frederick Freeman and John Fullagar owned Tottenham Brewery and Gripper Bros. owned the Bell Brewery in 1862.[93] Both firms survived in 1890, when Otto Vollmann managed the Tottenham Lager Beer Brewery and Ice Factory[94] for a German company which had bought Grove House on the closure of the school.[95] Grippers' premises were bought by Whitbread & Co. in 1896 and turned into a bottling depot in the same year, although some of the older brewery buildings, on the east side of High Road south of Park Lane, were still used in 1924.[96] Fremlin Bros. had a bottling depot and stores at no. 20 White Hart Lane from c. 1908 until the 1950s.[97]

A floor-cloth factory in Bathurst (later Laurence) Road and a tobacco-works south of Wood Green Common, both recorded in the 1860s, were apparently short-lived.[98] At the beginning of the 20th century there were still no large factories in Tottenham, apart from that of Harris Lebus,[99] furniture-makers who in 1900 acquired 13½ a. for their Finsbury works on former nursery-land south of Ferry Lane.[1] Although other firms were to follow at Tottenham Hale, Lebus remained exceptional until the 1930s in having a site east of the railway line there, presumably chosen for the carriage of timber by water.[2] Wood Green meanwhile was developing as a preponderantly residential suburb: there was a tobacco factory on the Hornsey border, south of the gas works, in the 1860s[3] and later arrivals included the confectioners Barratt & Co., who moved from Islington to a former piano factory in Mayes Road in 1880.[4]

Industry had begun to concentrate in three areas before the First World War:[5] in the east at Tottenham Hale, in the north-east from Northumberland Park towards Edmonton, and in the extreme south half way along the old boundary with Stoke Newington. Factories at the Hale, served by Tottenham station, were mostly between Broad Lane and the railway, along Fountayne and Fawley roads, and included those of Millington & Sons, manufacturing stationers, from 1903[6] and of Gestetner Duplicators from 1906; by 1920 a few more firms, including the Eagle Pencil Co., had opened north of Ferry Lane,

in wartime buildings along Ashley Road. Factories in the north-east, served by Park (later Northumberland Park) station, sprang up first along Tariff Road, where Kolok, founded in 1904, were making carbons and ribbons at their Rochester works from 1913.[7] Also in the north-east, alone on the marsh-land save for the Longwater pumping station, English Abrasives bought the site of their London Emery works in 1902 and moved there from Clerkenwell in 1904.[8] Off High Road a wide variety of family businesses, including Kolok, started in and around Paxton Road; Edward Barber & Co., water-fittings manufacturers, who opened their non-ferrous sand foundry and finishing shop in 1908, were the last to come there and were the oldest survivors by 1973.[9] In the south industry occupied a more constricted area of former waste ground between Vale and Eade roads, where Maynard's, the confectioners, moved from Stamford Hill in 1906.[10] In the north-west the Standard Bottle Co. started to make glass containers at Bounds Green in 1921 and continued there until 1971, the year after its acquisition by Heenan Beddow.[11]

The spread of housing over the centre of the parish between the World Wars left little room for new concentrations of industry, except along the north side of White Hart Lane near the potteries.[12] Newcomers there included Wonder Bakery, a new firm which opened in 1937.[13] In Queen Street, close to the Edmonton boundary, L. Lazarus & Son had a large furniture factory by 1935; in 1950 it was acquired by Sparklets, a subsidiary of the British Oxygen Co.[14] Building continued in the extreme north-east, where by 1951 Brantwood Road and its factories had been extended eastward to Willoughby Lane, and started in the north-west along Cline Road, Bounds Green. Factories were also erected on sites or gardens of older buildings on both sides of Tottenham High Road near Edmonton, those on the east stretching beyond Tottenham Hotspurs' football ground as far as Lansdowne Road. By 1959 some 40 firms occupied the Wingate trading estate, which had then recently replaced a plate-glass manufacturer's at nos. 784–792 High Road.

In the south-east Keith Blackman, fan manufacturers, moved in 1938 to a 10½ a. riverside site, approached from Ferry Lane by the new Mill Mead Road.[15] Harris Lebus built a large depot on adjoining land, immediately east of the railway, in 1956 and owned some 36 a. in 1970, when its entire Finsbury works was sold to the G.L.C. The buildings on the south side of Ferry Lane were then demolished, while the depot on the north was used by the G.L.C. for supplies.[16] Gestetner (see below), too,

[91] Fisk, *Tottenham*, ii. 200.
[92] *Pigot's Gen. Dir.* (1824); *P.O. Dir.* (1845).
[93] *P.O. Dir. Mdx.* (1862); *Tottenham and Edmonton Advertiser*, 1025.
[94] *Kelly's Dir.* (1890).
[95] *Biog. Cat. Lond. Friends' Inst.* (1888), 836; see p. 376.
[96] Ex inf. Whitbread & Co. Ltd.
[97] *Kelly's Dir.* (1908); *P.O. Dir. Lond.* (1952).
[98] O.S. Maps 6", Mdx. XII. NE., NW. (1863–9 edn.).
[99] Smith, 'Industrialization of Grtr. Lond.' 47.
[1] *Urban Develop. of Haringey Area* (Haringey L.B., Local Hist. Occasional Papers, 1973), 4.
[2] Smith, op. cit. 57.
[3] O.S. Maps 6", Mdx. XII. NW. (1863–9 edn.).
[4] Ex inf. Barratt & Co. Ltd.
[5] Except where otherwise stated, the para. is based on

Smith, op. cit. 57–8; O.S. Maps 6", Mdx. XII. NE., NW. (1920 edn.); *Haringey Guide* [1972].
[6] J. Evans, *The Endless Web*, 185.
[7] Ex inf. Kolok Div., Ozalid Co. Ltd.
[8] Ex inf. Engl. Abrasives Ltd.
[9] Ex inf. Edw. Barber & Co.
[10] Ex inf. Maynards Ltd.
[11] Ex inf. Heenan Spark Ltd.
[12] Except where otherwise stated, the foll. two paras. are based on O.S. Maps 6", Mdx. XII. NE., NW. (1920 edn.); 1/25,000, TQ 38, 39 (1951–2 edn.); 6", TQ 39 SE., SW., TQ 38 NW. (1968 edn.); *P.O. Dirs. Lond.* (1952–70).
[13] Ex inf. Wonder Bakery, Wood Green.
[14] O.S. Map 1/2,500, Mdx. XII. 3 (1935 revn.); *P.O. Dir. Lond.* (1949); ex inf. British Oxygen Co. Ltd.
[15] *Builder*, clvii. 110; ex inf. Keith Blackman Ltd.
[16] Ex inf. Harris Lebus Ltd.

expanded, opening a plant in Brantwood Road in 1965, a research centre off Fountayne Road in 1967, a despatch centre at the Fawley Road plant in 1970, and an adjacent training centre in 1972.[17] In the following year John Dickinson & Co., which had merged with Millington & Sons (see above) in 1918, transferred its London warehouse to the enlarged Basildon works, formerly Crown works, in Fountayne Road.[18] At Bounds Green an industrial estate which was established in the mid 1960s housed 39 firms in 1970;[19] building work there was still in progress in 1973.

In 1973 Tottenham contained many engineering and light industrial firms whose names were household words.[20] Gestetner, the largest duplicator manufacturers in the world, had some 3,000 employees at their Tottenham plants. John Dickinson & Co. employed c. 900 in making stationery at their Basildon works, Keith Blackman employed 750, and Barratt & Co. (from 1966 a member of the Geo. Bassett group) c. 700. Other firms with work-forces of several hundred included Kolok (from 1963 a division of Ozalid Ltd.), Maynard's, with 590, Charrington & Co., with 500 at a bottling and keg store in Brantwood Road, English Abrasives Ltd. and Wonder Bakery (a branch of Spillers-French Baking) with 450 each, Cannon Rubber, with over 360 at Ashley Road and High Road, and Whitbread's, with c. 250 at their bottling depot. London Transport had a staff, including bus crews, of c. 710 at its Tottenham garage and 420 at its Wood Green garage.[21]

SOCIAL LIFE. Throughout the early 16th century the manorial court levied fines for illegal games, which included cards and dice, from 1517, and bowls, from 1528. Hunting over the lord's manor was also punished by fines.[22] In 1567 the butts were defective and it was ordered that new ones should be set up near the high cross.[23]

Many half-timbered buildings which survived in the 19th century were thought to have been medieval inns.[24] In 1455–6 mention was made of the Hart, the Tabard, the Crown, the George, the Bell, and the Swan.[25] Two inn-keepers were accused of obstructing the highway before their houses with ale-booths and benches in 1517[26] and another landlord was ordered to take down his sign for refusing hospitality to strangers in 1560.[27] The Swan at High Cross was often illustrated in Izaak Walton's *Compleat Angler* as the 'sweet shady arbour' where Piscator took his friend Venator, although the author's 17th-century riverside haunts can no longer be identified.[28]

There were 15 inns licensed in 1716[29] and 22 in 1759. Those in 1759 included two called the White Hart, one on the east side of High Road and one at

Tottenham Hale, and the George and Vulture.[30] The White Hart in High Road had taken the place of an earlier inn called the Horns, presumably the Hart's Horn of 1585,[31] which stood nearly opposite at the north corner of White Hart Lane and was divided before its partial demolition in 1824. The George and Vulture, in High Road almost facing the later junction with Bruce Grove, contained a banqueting room and a bowling green, popular with Londoners;[32] the old building had become a school by c. 1807 and was pulled down in 1829, although the banqueting room had been restored by 1840.[33] A new George and Vulture, almost facing Bruce Grove; survived in 1890, when there were 19 public houses in Tottenham and 8 in Wood Green.[34]

Local benefactors, often incumbents or rich Quakers, supported many societies in the early 19th century. The Charitable bank, the first district bank to offer a safe deposit for small savings of 1s. and upwards, was established in 1804 by Mrs. Powell, of the Chestnuts, with the vicar among its 9 trustees; it was renamed the Savings bank in 1829, opening weekly at the grammar school, and increased the number of its depositors from 111 to 517 within ten years.[35] Thrift was also encouraged by the Provident District society, formed in 1829, whose liberal subscribers enabled it to add 6d. to every 1s. saved; the society had four women visitors, one for each district of the parish, and also distributed bread tickets to casual beggars.

Tottenham penny club, founded in 1811, provided clothing from subscriptions of 1d. a week which matched those made by poor children. A Church of England clothing club also existed by 1843 and there was a charity for lying-in women by 1832.[36] A ladies' bible association distributed cheap bibles from 1818 and a local branch of the Society for the Propagation of the Gospel opened in 1839. Tottenham temperance society first met at the Wesleyan chapel in 1831; members adopted total abstinence in 1836 and thereafter used the Lancasterian boys' school, where inn-keepers fomented a riot in 1838, or the girls' school.

Early friendly societies included the True British society, at the Plough inn from 1796 until 1815, the True Britons' benefit society at the White Hart from 1809, and the Friendly Brothers' benefit society from 1816.[37] Garden allotments behind the workhouse were let by the vestry to some 40 families shortly before the establishment of the poor law union, after which the practice was continued by the trustees of the parochial charities. An allotment society was formed in 1843, with the vicar as president; part of the glebe in White Hart Lane was divided into plots and there were plans to acquire land at High Cross and the Hale. The movement owed much to James Dean, an engineer concerned with social problems, who was also active in the

[17] Ex inf. Gestetner Ltd.
[18] Ex inf. John Dickinson & Co. Ltd.
[19] P.O. Dirs. Lond.
[20] The section is based on inf. supplied by the cos.
[21] Ex inf. L.T.E.
[22] Tottenham Man. Rolls (*1510–31*), 25–6, 99, 126, 221 et seq.
[23] Ibid. (*1558–82*), 84.
[24] Robinson, *Tottenham*, i. 61–4.
[25] Bruce Castle Mus., MR/76 (TS. transl. pp. 32–3).
[26] Tottenham Man. Rolls (*1510–31*), 98.
[27] Ibid. (*1558–82*), 17.

[28] Fisk, *Tottenham*, ii. 331–3. See plate facing p. 64.
[29] M.R.O., L.V. 3/1.
[30] M.R.O., L.V. 7/36.
[31] Bruce Castle Mus., MR/121.
[32] See plate facing p. 336.
[33] Robinson, *Tottenham*, i. 61–6.
[34] *Kelly's Dir. Essex, Herts. and Mdx.* (1890).
[35] Except where otherwise stated, the foll. two paras. are based on Robinson, *Tottenham*, ii. 281–94, 311–12, and [J. Dean] *Tottenham and its Institutions in 1843*, 29–31.
[36] *Pigot's Com. Dir.* (1832–4).
[37] F.S.1/836; F.S.1/1253; F.S.1/1497.

Stoke Newington, Tottenham and Hackney Accumulating Fund society, founded in the same year to promote savings by the lower middle class and help with house purchases.[38]

In 1829 former pupils of the Lancasterian school formed a library, which afterwards lost support but was revived in 1834 as the Tottenham and Edmonton mechanics' library. It was called the Tottenham and Edmonton mechanics' literary and scientific institution by 1840, when some 140 subscribers could use 500 books at the school and also hear lectures there.[39] After a second decline it reopened as Tottenham public library in the new lecture hall, where it finally closed in 1879.[40] The Church of England in 1840 had a lending library of S.P.C.K. publications at the house of the parish clerk.[41] The first public lecture hall was built by William Janson on the west side of High Road, north of Bruce Grove.[42] It was used by Presbyterians and then by Congregationalists in the 1860s and was renamed Bruce Grove hall c. 1880, when the Brethren began to worship there.[43] After 1903 it became the Conservative club and later served the Klinger clothing company and, in 1923, the Ministry of Labour;[44] it survived in 1939.[45]

Tottenham attracted many Sunday visitors by 1860, when there were complaints of young men from London lounging offensively in the churchyard and impeding worshippers.[46] Swimming in the Lea, once a poor man's pastime, had become so popular that in the summer of 1861 over 100 persons a day bathed at a place called the May Bush, where they paid for the use of a field.[47] The Ferry Boat inn was popular in the 1870s, when it had a boat-house and tea-gardens,[48] and survived in 1973.

A want of amenities was deplored in the press in 1873, particularly the poor state of the literary institution and the lack of baths, clubs, and recreation grounds.[49] The Y.M.C.A. had opened a branch in High Road in 1872,[50] however, and many groups provided social evenings: Tottenham choral society had existed since c. 1860, when there had also been an Edmonton and Tottenham Tonic Sol-Fa club; the lecture hall had been used for some years by the Pickwick histrionic club, which aimed to 'amuse and elevate the working classes'; and the Tuesday Evening Entertainments and the Tottenham and Edmonton working men's temperance society, presumably the former temperance association, also held concerts. Church halls or chapels served for many events, including St. Paul's penny readings in the 1870s; St. John's literary society functioned by 1873,[51] Coleraine Park literary society by 1880,[52] and Tottenham musical society by 1883. Debates were held at the Tottenham House of Commons, which

in 1883 moved from High Cross to a larger room at the Red House in High Road.[53]

A local militia, the Tottenham Loyal Association, had been formed in 1792 and lasted for about four years.[54] In 1859 prominent residents subscribed towards a volunteer unit, which was raised in 1860 as the 33rd Mdx. (Tottenham) Volunteer Rifle Corps.[55] The corps paraded at the National school in Park Lane until a near-by drill-hall, formerly part of the Coombes Croft estate,[56] was ready in 1863. A rifle range of 1,000 yards[57] was opened in 1861 on Wild marsh, between Pymme's brook and the Lea. The butts, close to the Edmonton boundary, were burnt down three times[58] but still used in the 1890s.[59] Under reorganization, started in 1877, the corps became the Tottenham detachment ('G' Company) of the 3rd Middlesex Rifle Volunteers, although with control of its own finances, and from 1907 it formed a territorial battalion of the Middlesex Regiment. The hall and drill-ground in Park Lane still belonged to Tottenham (U.D.) charity in 1968.[60]

From 1873 Wood Green has possessed a famous amusement centre, the Alexandra Palace, crowning Muswell Hill. In 1860 representatives of the Great Northern Palace Co. explained their plans at Tottenham's lecture hall[61] and in 1863 a pleasure ground was opened as a commercial venture.[62] The first palace, built of materials from the buildings of the International Exhibition at South Kensington in 1862, was burnt down within a few days of its opening.[63] The second, designed for Lucas Bros. by John Johnson, was opened on the same site in 1875 and, like its predecessor, intended as north London's counterpart of the Crystal Palace. It was a sprawling brick building of nearly 8 a., with two glass-domed conservatories among the many halls and galleries extending east and west of the great hall, which contained Europe's largest concert organ, by Henry Willis.[64] In 1900, after contributions from the local authorities towards their purchase, the park and palace were vested in trustees representing the county council and the urban districts of Hornsey, Wood Green, Islington, Tottenham, Friern Barnet, Finchley, Stoke Newington, Finsbury, and Edmonton.[65] The trustees were allowed to charge for admission on bank holidays in 1903 and to raise money by holding exhibitions in 1913.[66]

The 'Ally Pally', as it came to be called, was used for refugees and prisoners of war from 1914 to 1918 and for evacuees and as a furniture store in the Second World War. At other times plays, exhibitions, lectures, dinners, dances, and skating all took place in the palace itself; the 180-acre park contained a banqueting hall, a swimming pool and an athletics

[38] Tottenham and its Institutions, 1–23.
[39] Robinson, Tottenham, ii. 294–7.
[40] Fisk, Tottenham, ii. 194.
[41] Robinson, Tottenham, ii. 312.
[42] Fisk, Tottenham, ii. 194.
[43] See pp. 361–2.
[44] Fisk, Tottenham, ii. 195.
[45] Bruce Castle Mus., 942 [cutting].
[46] Tottenham and Edmonton Advertiser, 115.
[47] Ibid. 126, 203.
[48] Thorne, Environs, ii. 625.
[49] Tottenham and Edmonton Advertiser, 2997.
[50] Ibid. 2810.
[51] Ibid. 115–16, 3026, 3059.
[52] Coventry's Weekly Advertiser, 24 Dec. 1880.
[53] Weekly Advertiser, 12 Jan., 16 Feb. 1883.
[54] V.C.H. Mdx. ii. 59.

[55] Except where otherwise stated, the para. is based on TS. notes penes Bruce Castle Mus.
[56] Char. Com. files.
[57] O.S. Map 6", Mdx. XII. NE. (1863–9 edn.).
[58] Fisk, Tottenham, ii. 341.
[59] O.S. Map 6", Mdx. XII. NE. (1894–6 edn.).
[60] Char. Com. files.
[61] Tottenham and Edmonton Advertiser, 120.
[62] Except where otherwise stated, the foll. two paras. are based on booklets pub. by the trustees penes Bruce Castle Mus.
[63] See plate facing p. 337.
[64] Builder, xxxi. 687.
[65] Alex. Pk. and Pal. (Public Purposes) Act, 63 & 64 Vic. c. 259 (Local Act).
[66] Ibid. 3 Ed. VII, c. 179 (Local Act); Bruce Castle Mus., 960/1.

ground, as well as the most central race-course in the London area, where meetings were held from 1888.[67] Memorable events included descents by parachute in 1888, organ recitals to audiences of up to 12,000, concerts with international artists, and in 1936 the world's first television service, transmitted from the south-east corner of the palace by the B.B.C., which had a lease of studios there until 1977. In 1966 control passed to the G.L.C., which sold the Willis organ and pulled down the grandstand on the race-course. In 1973 the future of the buildings was in doubt.[68]

Tottenham and Edmonton cricket club, founded by 1860, was apparently the first of several such clubs; one at Alexandra Park, started c. 1874, claimed to have the finest ground in north London, some 2 a. larger than Lords. The marshes near Willoughby Lane became popular with sporting groups, among them Park athletic club, which held annual events there in the 1870s.[69] In 1882 members of Hotspur cricket club, so called from its links with the Northumberland Park area, decided to keep in touch during the winter by forming their own football team, with the same name.[70]

Hotspur football club, one of many local groups, started with a grant from the cricket club and at first consisted largely of boys from St. John's middle class school.[71] In 1883 the club was reformed and in 1884 it was renamed Tottenham Hotspur, to avoid confusion with a London team. Matches took place on the marshes until 1888, when a field off Northumberland Park was shared with another club and admission fees were charged. A wooden grandstand, to seat 100, was built in 1894, professionalism was adopted in 1895, and the club reorganized as a limited liability company in 1898. A more central pitch was leased from Messrs. Charrington in 1899, with accommodation for 10,000, and soon afterwards bought and enlarged; it lay behind the White Hart inn and, although east of High Road, became known as the White Hart Lane ground. Tottenham Hotspur thereafter enjoyed periods of national prestige, winning the Football Association Challenge Cup in 1901 and again twenty years later, when it was still the only professional club in the south of England to have triumphed in a final of the Cup Tie. Larger crowds necessitated improvements to the ground: the East stand, seating 5,000, replaced an older structure in 1910, roofs were later built for spectators along the north and south, and villas to the west made way for a double-decker stand in 1934, bringing the total accommodation to 78,000. In 1951 Hotspurs were champions in the first division of the Football League and in 1961 they became the first team since 1897 to win both the league championship and the F.A. Cup. Further victories in the Cup Tie in 1962 and 1967 helped to earn them a world-wide reputation.[72]

Muswell Hill golf club, with a course of 18 holes north-west of Alexandra Park, was established as a London club in 1894.[73] A club-house near the corner of Rhodes Avenue served 500 members in 1934;[74] numbers were about the same in 1973, when the course covered nearly 100 a. bordering Alexandra Park Road.[75] Employees at the gasworks, over the Edmonton boundary, formed Tottenham gas club in 1908 and built a club-house east of Willoughby Lane as a war memorial in 1924. The club had some 14 a. of sports grounds and over 1,300 members in 1973.[76] The Greyhound Racing Association built a track near Harringay station, with a stand and terraces for 50,000 spectators, in 1927.[77] Harringay Arena, a covered stadium for ice-hockey and similar games, was opened immediately to the south-west in 1936; it was designed by Oscar Faber as a plain brick octagonal building, with steel trusses for the roof and a capacity of 11,000.[78]

Forster hall, opened for the Blue Ribbon Gospel Temperance Movement in 1885, was regularly used from the first by Tottenham orchestral society. It was advertised as the People's Palace by the Walturdaw Animated Picture Co. in 1907 and continued as a cinema until 1923. The Tottenham Palace, designed by Eylson and Long,[79] was built as a music hall in 1908 on the Drapers' Company's land north of Tottenham high school, where a skating rink was constructed in 1909;[80] the last stage performances in the hall took place in 1924, by which time the rink had become the Canadian Rink cinema; thereafter films were shown at the Tottenham Palace until its conversion to a bingo-hall c. 1970, while the former rink served as a dance-hall.[81] Another music-hall, the Wood Green Empire, still offered live shows in 1918 but was used only for television rehearsals in 1964.[82] Bruce Grove cinema, planned, with a dance hall, by the Tottenham Cinema and Entertainment Co. in 1920 on a site in Bruce Grove,[83] was still used for films in 1964 but served as a bingo and social club in 1970. The Imperial (later Essoldo) cinema, West Green Road, was an early purpose-built cinema, one of the few to survive in the 1960s, when it was used by Atlas Lighting Ltd. Other cinemas included the Gaumont, a large building of the 1930s, the Palladium, Wood Green High Road, demolished by 1964, the Corner, Seven Sisters Road, the Mayfair, Tottenham High Road, the Coliseum, Green Lanes, and the Central, Station Road, all converted to other uses by 1964, and the Rex, Station Road, converted by 1970. The Florida, Tottenham High Road, closed down after 1970,[84] leaving the Odeon, Wood Green High Road, and the ABC (formerly the Ritz), close to Turnpike Lane station, as the only cinemas open in 1973.

Tottenham U.D. opened a museum at the Chestnuts in 1905 and transferred it to Bruce Castle in 1906. After closure during the First World War the museum re-opened temporarily in the central library, before returning to Bruce Castle in 1927.

[67] V.C.H. Mdx. ii. 265.   [68] The Times, 9 May 1973.
[69] Tottenham and Edmonton Advertiser, 114, 165, 2774, 3180.
[70] G. Wagstaffe Simmons, Tottenham Hotspur Football Club, 15; J. Holland, Spurs, 23.
[71] Except where otherwise stated, the para. is based on Simmons, op. cit. and Holland, op. cit. passim.
[72] Whitaker's Almanack (1962); ibid. (1963); ibid. (1968).
[73] V.C.H. Mdx. ii. 279–80.
[74] Kelly's Dir. Wood Grn. and Southgate (1934).
[75] Ex inf. the sec.

[76] Ex inf. the personnel director, Eastern Gas.
[77] Bruce Castle Mus., 963 [cuttings].
[78] Bruce Castle Mus., 965 [cuttings].
[79] Evg. Standard, 2 Aug. 1973.
[80] Ex inf. the clerk, Drapers' Co. of Lond.
[81] Bruce Castle Mus., 994 [TS. notes]; Kelly's Dir. Lond. (1970).
[82] Mdx. Local Hist. Council Bull. xviii. 7.
[83] Bruce Castle Mus., 994 [prospectus].
[84] Mdx. Local Hist. Council Bull. xviii. 1–21; P.O. Dirs. Lond. (1959, 1964, 1970).

From 1928 the museum also housed a collection illustrating postal history, lent by the Union of Post Office Workers.[85] Mementoes of the Middlesex Regiment were added in 1969.[86]

Tottenham local board adopted the Baths and Washhouses Act in 1893, when slipper baths were already provided commercially at High Cross.[87] In 1904 work started on Tottenham central baths, next to the new fire station, where slipper baths and two swimming baths were installed. Slipper baths were also opened at Conway Road in 1926 and, with public laundries, at Tiverton and Bromley roads in 1932. An open-air swimming bath was built near Stonebridge lock[88] and, in 1937, a 'lido' was opened.[89] At Wood Green a covered swimming bath in Western Road was opened in 1911; there was an open-air pool in Alexandra Park[90] and in 1934 another one was opened in Durnsford Road.[91]

A mid-19th-century local newspaper, *Paul Pry*, circulated for a short time *c.* 1839.[92] The *Tottenham and Edmonton Advertiser* was established in 1855, presumably by George Coventry, the owner and printer in 1862.[93] It acted as a monthly forum for local views and outlived all its weekly rivals except the *Tottenham and Edmonton Weekly Herald*, started in 1861 by George Cowing and acquired in 1864 by his manager, Edwin Herbert Crusha. Faced with competition from the *Herald*, the older publication became *Coventry's Weekly Advertiser* in 1880 and was called simply the *Weekly Advertiser* from 1881, when it claimed to be the oldest suburban paper in Middlesex. In 1883 it was taken over by Crusha, who by 1890 had also founded the *Wood Green Weekly Herald*. Both the *Tottenham and Edmonton Weekly Herald* and the *Wood Green Weekly Herald* were published in 1973. More short-lived newspapers included the *North London Echo and Wood Green Chronicle*, published in 1890,[94] the *Tottenham Chronicle*, the *Star*, the *Stamford Hill Times*, and the *Weekly Standard*.

LOCAL GOVERNMENT. MANORIAL GOVERNMENT. Separate courts were held for Daubeneys, Bruces, and Pembrokes and, at least from 1422–3, for Mockings[95] until 1429, after which date a single court served all the manors.[96] Records survive for most years, although not equally fully for all the subdivisions, from 1318, when a court was held for Daubeneys, to 1920.[97] In the 14th century there was usually a view of frankpledge around Whitsun and at least one other court, in the autumn;[98] in the 17th century the view, called a court leet in the 1650s,

was held immediately before a court baron in the autumn, with at least one court at another season.[99] The last view took place in 1847 and the last court baron met in 1870,[1] although transactions were recorded for another 50 years. Courts met in the 1650s at the White Hart inn[2] and from 1807, if not earlier, at the Plough.[3]

In 1294 view of frankpledge, infangthief, outfangthief, and tumbrils were claimed by Hugh de Kendale as grantee for life of the manor of Hastings (later Pembrokes). The same rights, as well as the assizes of bread and ale, gallows, and waifs and strays, were claimed by John de Balliol, king of Scotland, for the manor of Balliols (later Daubeneys), and by Robert de Bruce for his manor of Bruces.[4] Headboroughs were chosen at the view of frankpledge in 1319, the assizes of bread and ale were held regularly from the mid 14th century,[5] and constables were chosen by 1394.[6] All the 13th-century liberties were enjoyed by Richard Turnaunt at his death in 1486, as well as fines of outlawry and the right of free warren.[7]

There was a pillory in High Road in 1455–68[8] but by 1526 Tottenham had neither stocks, a cucking stool nor a pillory, and also lacked weights and measures for the assizes. The lord had supplied none of them three years later, except apparently a cucking stool, with which a woman was threatened in 1530.[9] During the 17th and most of the 18th centuries 2 aleconners and 4 constables, one for each ward, were chosen annually at the manorial court, as were a hayward, 2 common drivers, and 2 markers of cattle to protect the common lands.[10] From the mid 18th century there was some competition between the rights of the court and those of the vestry, which first appointed a constable in 1750.[11] Courts were concerned almost entirely with property transactions from 1780, yet parishioners demanded that a manorial court should consider public nuisances in 1797;[12] after the lord had named the constables in 1806 the vestry asked to be told of his intentions in future,[13] as late as 1844 it complained of great inconvenience arising from the court's failure to provide parish officers and in 1847 it approved the appointments which at last had been made.[14]

Perquisites of court were included in the grant of Tottenham Rectory manor, late of Holy Trinity priory, to Sir Thomas Audley.[15] A court was held in 1536[16] and courts baron, recorded from 1541, were held for the king and then for the chapter of St. Paul's and, in the 1650s, for Stephen Beale. They dealt with the election of homagers and property

[85] Tottenham, *Official Guide* [1934].
[86] Bruce Castle Mus., 927 BRU.
[87] Bruce Castle Mus., 932 [TS. notes].
[88] Tottenham, *Official Guide* [1934].
[89] Bruce Castle Mus., 965 [cutting].
[90] *Kelly's Dir. Wood Grn. and Southgate* (1934).
[91] Ibid. (1938).
[92] See p. 175. Except where otherwise stated, the para. is based on Couchman, *Reminiscences of Tottenham*, 73; Fisk, *Tottenham*, ii. 226; and copies of the *Advertiser* and the *Herald penes* Bruce Castle Mus.
[93] *P.O. Dir. Mdx.* (1862).
[94] *Kelly's Dir. Mdx.* (1890).
[95] Bruce Castle Mus., MR/37.
[96] Bruce Castle Mus. MR/33, m. 7.
[97] Court rolls 1318–1732 are at Bruce Castle Mus.; copies of ct. rolls 1626–1920 and ct. bks. 1733–1852 are at M.R.O., Acc. 695. Transcripts of the 14th-cent. and most of the 16th-cent. rolls have been pub. by the boro. of Tottenham,

libraries and mus. dept. The collection is described in the first vol., *Tottenham Manorial Rolls* (1377–99), intro.
[98] *Tottenham Man. Rolls* (1318–77); ibid. (1377–99).
[99] M.R.O., Acc. 695/1.
[1] Ibid. /3, ff. 4, 332.
[2] Ibid. /1, ff. 67, 84.
[3] Ibid. /2, f. 141.
[4] *Plac. de Quo Warr.* (Rec. Com.), 476.
[5] *Tottenham Man. Rolls* (1318–77), 4, 41.
[6] Ibid. (1377–99), 265.   [7] C 142/2/19.
[8] Bruce Castle Mus., MR/71.
[9] *Tottenham Man. Rolls* (1510–31), 194, 234, 242.
[10] M.R.O., Acc. 695/1.
[11] E. Hoare, *Eighteenth-cent. Tottenham: Par. and Vestry* (Edmonton Hund. Hist. Soc. 1971), 8–9.
[12] Bruce Castle Mus., D/PT/2A/5, ff. 58, 60.
[13] Ibid. /6, f. 55.
[14] Ibid. /7, ff. 418, 550–1.   [15] See p. 328.
[16] S.C.6/Hen. VIII/2357 m. 1d.

transactions, meeting nearly every summer and, at least from 1694, normally following courts for the St. Paul's manors in Edmonton. The last session was in 1863, although business which took place out of court was recorded until 1905.[17]

PARISH GOVERNMENT TO 1837. The division of the parish into wards can be traced to 1515 when, in the manorial court, two constables were chosen for High Street, one for High Cross, and one for Wood Green.[18] In 1565 there was a constable for the Hale and High Cross and in 1566 one for the Nether End quarter and another for the Middle quarter. Four wards were represented from 1577,[19] with boundaries presumably based on population: in William Bedwell's time Nether (afterwards Lower), Middle, and High Cross wards covered the eastern part of the parish from north to south, with a combined acreage roughly equal to that of Wood Green ward, which covered the rest.[20]

There were two churchwardens by 1577[21] and isolated accounts of the upper churchwarden survive from the time of Charles I.[22] The earliest records of a vestry, the minute books, date only from 1676[23] and consecutive churchwardens' accounts from 1732.[24] Meetings were held at the vestry house, which Lord Coleraine first offered to rebuild in 1688.[25] The average attendance was 12 in the 1690s and again at the end of the 18th century, but it was no more than 5 in the 1740s. The vicar or his curate often presided and occasional attenders included Henry, Lord Coleraine (d. 1708), Hugh Smithson, Henry, Lord Coleraine (d. 1749), and James Townsend, who served as a churchwarden.

A churchwarden served one year as lower and a second year as upper churchwarden until 1776, when the vicar asserted a right to fill one of the offices. Exemptions could be obtained from this and from other duties, fines being doubled to £10 in 1733. Four collectors, called overseers from the early 18th century, were nominated for approval by quarter sessions. Other salaried appointments were those of a sexton, vestry clerk, and beadle, mentioned respectively in 1691, 1696, and 1730. Surveyors of the highways existed by 1654,[26] two being chosen at quarter sessions from a list submitted by the vestry. Offices later multiplied: the vestry clerk became assistant overseer in 1756 and the beadle performed a similar function from 1798 before the appointment of a full-time salaried official was recommended in 1818, while a salaried assistant surveyor was provided from 1772 until 1798, when the number of surveyors was doubled. Constables, first nominated by the vestry in 1750, had one assistant for the whole parish from 1798 and two by 1805.

Inhabitants were listed according to wards both for church-rates, by 1628,[27] and poor-rates, by 1637.[28] Eighteenth-century poor-rates were normally fixed four times a year and varied considerably,

from 2d. in the £ in 1742 to 18d. in 1763. Any person who rented a house worth £5 a year or more was made liable to poor-rates from 1775. In 1775-6, out of £763 raised, £694 was spent on the poor.[29] Expenditure rose to £2,140 in 1816, £3,133 in 1819, and £4,065 in 1821,[30] but had fallen to £2,242 in 1836-7, the last year when Tottenham maintained its own poor.[31] The parish's income was augmented by fines, pew-rents, and, above all, by charities and sums for the waste-land; from 1833, after criticism of the accounts, the income from the waste-lands and parish estates was paid into a separate fund, with its own treasurer.

Poor-relief, in the form of clothing and small payments, was given by the churchwardens at the vicar's direction in 1628.[32] In 1681 a parish child was supported and in 1682 the vestry ordered that all regular pensioners should be paid by the collector for Wood Green ward, whose colleagues were to hand over their sums for disbursement by the churchwardens: 12 regular pensions, mostly of 2s. a week, were authorized in 1687 and 14 in 1695. Landowners were forbidden to employ strangers between Michaelmas and Lady Day from 1699, in order to provide work for the poor. Ten years later all pensioners had their goods listed and in 1721 they were ordered to wear badges. Casual payments continued to be made both by churchwardens and overseers after the opening of a workhouse; regulations for the workhouse in 1789 laid down that out-relief should be discouraged as much as possible, but considerable casual payments made the overseers' accounts confusing in 1833.

From 1730 to 1744 the poor were housed in rented premises under successive salaried masters the vestry paying the whole cost. From 1744 the poor were farmed until in 1763 a workhouse was built on part of Coombes Croft, Marsh Lane. Thereafter the vestry alternated between direct management and farming out, the contractor receiving either an annual salary, a fixed price per head, or a combination of the two. Under the regulations drawn up in 1789 and substantially reissued in 1818, a committee of 24 guardians was to meet monthly at the workhouse, 4 members were to carry out weekly inspections, and suitable ladies might give their advice; the master and mistress were always to be resident, inmates could keep 2d. in the shilling of their earnings, and children should be taught to read. The workhouse held 44 persons in 1775-6 and was too small by 1818, when 7 Tottenham paupers had recently been kept in other parishes. A proposal to form a select vestry, under the Sturges Bourne Act,[33] was rejected in 1819 and 1825 but adopted in 1833, when 14 members were elected.

The vestry contributed towards a robbery committee for Edmonton hundred in 1692 and built a parish cage in 1743. It agreed to raise a special rate in 1774 for the trustees of the Stamford Hill turnpike

[17] Ct. rolls 1541-1690 are at St. Paul's MSS., boxes B 48, 50; ct. bks. from 1694 are at Bruce Castle, D/MR/A/1-7.
[18] *Tottenham Man. Rolls (1510-31)*, 56.
[19] Ibid. *(1558-82)*, 65, 75, 145.
[20] W. J. Roe, *Ancient Tottenham*, 105.
[21] Guildhall MS. 9537/4.
[22] Bruce Castle Mus., D/PT/1A/2-5; the earliest acct., 1628, is uncat.
[23] Bruce Castle Mus., D/PT/2A/1-13 (1676-1933).
[24] Ibid. /1A/13 (1732-66), /14-16 (1829-96).
[25] Except where otherwise stated, the rest of the sub-

section is based on Hoare, *18th-cent. Tottenham*, and on the vestry min. bks. (see n. 23 above).
[26] Bruce Castle Mus., D/PT/6A.
[27] Bruce Castle Mus., uncat. acct.
[28] Bruce Castle Mus., D/PT/1A/3.
[29] *Rep. Cttee. on Rets. by Overseers, 1776*, 397.
[30] *Rep. Sel. Cttee. on Poor Rate Returns*, H.C. 748, p. 99 (1821).
[31] *Poor Law Com. 3rd Rep.* H.C. 546, App. D, p. 109 (1837).
[32] Bruce Castle Mus., uncat. acct.   [33] 59 Geo. III, c. 12.

trust, who would light and watch Tottenham High Road during the winter months. In 1800 the cage was replaced by a watch-house near the Blue Coat school, with a keeper from 1821 to 1827. An association to protect property was formed in 1828, earlier nightly patrols having been reduced from lack of funds;[34] a salaried street-keeper and constable was appointed separately from the watch-house keeper in that year and made a full-time official, under the overseers, in 1830. The vestry declined to seek the introduction of the new police in 1830 and to take over the watching of the turnpike roads in 1831. It adopted the Lighting and Watching Act in 1833 but failed to reappoint the inspectors after three years, leaving private subscribers to support a temporary constabulary.[35] A board of surveyors was set up in 1835 under the General Highways Act.[36]

From 1795 an engineer was chosen with other officers at Easter. In 1809 the vestry adopted the City of London's practice of offering graduated rewards to the first machines to reach a fire. It also empowered the engineer to hire up to 20 helpers and, in 1821, ordered him to exercise the machine four times a year. It is not certain whether the first engine-house stood next to the watch-house, as it certainly did after the two had been placed in the same man's charge.

A special rate, mainly to pay for nursing, was levied because of an epidemic in 1637.[37] Medical services were paid for in 1697 and a surgeon for the poor received an annual salary, with more for dislocations and fractures, from 1739. The workhouse at Coombes Croft does not seem to have been supplemented with a pest-house, as was demanded by the master in 1775, two years after admissions had temporarily been stopped because of fever. In 1785 it was decided to choose one of two local surgeons alternately at Easter and in 1791 to pay him more for maternity cases. Reimbursement for giving free innoculations was approved in 1798. In 1831 the surgeon was required to submit all expenses weekly to the overseers, as in Edmonton, and relieved of some work by the appointment of a parish midwife. A board of health, formed under the threat of a cholera outbreak, functioned for about a year from the end of 1831;[38] it acted at first without parochial authority, until extra members were added by the vestry.

LOCAL GOVERNMENT AFTER 1837. Tottenham joined Hampstead, Hornsey, Edmonton, Enfield, Cheshunt (Herts.) and Waltham Abbey (Essex) in the new Edmonton poor law union in 1837. The parish workhouse was then closed and the inmates were transferred to the Edmonton building, pending the establishment of a workhouse for the union.[39]

Although the temporary board of health had been disbanded after the cholera epidemic in 1832, the vestry, faced with a steady rise in population acquiesced in surrendering most of its powers after the establishment of Edmonton union.[40] Inclusion within the area of the Metropolitan Police was sought three years before Tottenham achieved it, with neighbouring parishes, in 1840.[41] Lighting inspectors were appointed after the adoption of the Turnpike Lighting Act in 1841. The parish was among the first to petition for the establishment of a local board under the Public Health Act of 1848 and was empowered to elect a body of 9 members in 1850.[42]

Tottenham local board of health, which soon superseded the surveyors as the highway authority, took over lighting under the Public Health Act of 1858 and in 1859 became responsible for fire-fighting. Membership was raised to 12 in 1871 and to 18 in 1887, when the rise in population west of High Road led to the division of the district into 6 wards: High Cross, Middle, Lower, Wood Green, West Green, and St. Ann's.[43] Despite the board's initial zeal its measures were repeatedly overtaken by the population growth and so incurred fierce local criticism. In 1858 control finally passed from City men to local interests, whose pursuit of rapid building and consequent trouble over sewerage brought the board's reputation to a low point by 1871: in that year, quarrelsome and almost penniless, it was accused in the *Herald* of having ruined everything and everybody. Conditions thereafter improved, largely under the stimulus of a local pressure group, Tottenham Sanitary Association, which was formed in 1873 and promoted its own candidates at elections.[44] The board occupied two rooms in Somerset Road, where the grammar school later had a playground, until the beginning of 1874, when it moved to Coombes Croft House after accepting a 21-years' lease.[45]

As early as 1869 the new middle-class residents of Wood Green demanded their own administration.[46] In 1888 the Tottenham Local Board (Division of District) Act[47] made Wood Green ward a separate district. Tottenham was left with some 65,000 people, while 23,000 were placed under the new authority.[48] The two local boards became urban district councils under the Local Government Act of 1894. Borough status was granted to Wood Green in 1933 and to Tottenham in the following year.[49]

BOROUGH OF TOTTENHAM. *Gules, a saltire couped or; on a chief indented or, a helmet sable between two billets azure, each charged with an estoile or*

[Granted 1934]

[34] Robinson, *Tottenham*, i. 74–5.
[35] Ibid.
[36] 'Public Health in Tottenham, 1850–72' [survey by students of Lond. Sch. of Hygiene and Trop. Medicine, inc. as appx. to rep. of med. offr. of health 1951, *penes* Bruce Castle Mus.], 3.
[37] Bruce Castle Mus., D/PT/1A/3.
[38] The bd.'s min. bk. is in Bruce Castle Mus., D/PT/2D.
[39] S. I. Richardson, *Edmonton Poor Law Union, 1837–54* (Edmonton Hund. Hist. Soc.), 11, 24.
[40] Except where otherwise stated, the foll. two paras. are based on 'Public Health in Tottenham', *passim*.

[41] Bruce Castle Mus., D/PT/2A/8, f. 119; *Lond. Gaz.* 13 Oct. 1840, p. 2250.
[42] *Lond. Gaz.* 12 Feb. 1850, p. 393.
[43] M.R.O., *Reps. of Local Inquiries, 1889–94*, 579.
[44] C. H. Cooper, 'Urban Growth in Tottenham, 1870–94' [TS. thesis *penes* Bruce Castle Mus.].
[45] Bruce Castle Mus., 932 [TS. notes].
[46] Fisk, *Tottenham*, ii. 88.
[47] 51 & 52 Vic. c. 187 (Local Act).
[48] M.R.O., *Reps. of Local Inqs. 1889–94*, 579.
[49] *Kelly's Dir. Wood Grn. and Southgate* (1934); Tottenham, *Official Guide* [1934].

Tottenham local board was left with 5 wards and 15 members in 1888.[50] A proposal to double the membership was resisted in 1893, when the county council complained that the local boundaries did not agree with parliamentary or county electoral divisions, which were themselves brought into line with the wards in 1897. All members retired every third year until 1900, when one member was permitted to retire annually in each ward. By that date middle-class residents on the newly developed land around Haringey House, resenting their inclusion in pre-dominantly working-class wards, were seeking to be transferred from Tottenham U.D. to Hornsey. Harringay ward was therefore created in 1901,[51] out of parts of West Green and St. Ann's, and the urban district council was enlarged to 18 members. Membership was raised to 30 in 1905 and to 40 in 1925. Reorganization in the 1920s affected all the wards except West Green and raised the number from 6 to 8: Bruce Grove and Stoneleigh, Chestnuts, Green Lanes, Park and Coleraine, Stamford Hill, Town Hall, West Green, and White Hart Lane. By 1951 further changes had produced 11 wards: Bruce Grove and Central, Chestnuts, Coleraine, Green Lanes, High Cross and Stoneleigh, Park, Seven Sisters, Stamford Hill, Town Hall, West Green, and White Hart Lane. Throughout the existence of Tottenham B.C. the Labour party had a large majority.[52]

Tottenham town hall was opened in 1905,[53] on the west side of the Green, where Eaton House, Wilton House, the Ferns, and Hatfield House had been acquired as the site for a group of civic buildings. The hall, of red brick with stone dressings, was designed in a baroque style by A. S. Taylor and A. R. Jennett.[54] It was flanked to north and south by the new central baths and the central fire station, plainer buildings but of similar materials. In 1913 the opening of Tottenham county school next to the baths completed a range which formed an imposing municipal centre. The town hall, which remained the seat of local government until the absorption of Tottenham into Haringey, was used for social services, health, and housing offices in 1972.[55]

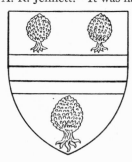

BOROUGH OF WOOD GREEN. *Or, on a fess azure between three yew trees eradicated proper a barrulet argent*
[Granted 1933]

At Wood Green the local board and the U.D.C. began with 12 members.[56] In 1910 membership was raised to 18 and the district was divided into 5 wards: Alexandra Park, Bowes Park, Central, Noel Park, and Town Hall. There were 23 members from 1919 until 1933, when the charter dissolved Bowes Park and Central wards, leaving the remaining three to return 6 members each to a council which also included 6 aldermen.[57]

LONDON BOROUGH OF HARINGEY. *Sable, eight rays issuing from the fess point throughout or*
[Granted 1965]

Opponents of the Labour party dominated the borough council until 1950, when Labour gained control from the Independents.[58] Earlham Grove House in Wood Green High Road was occupied by the board in 1890[59] and acquired, with nearly 11 a., in 1893. The offices were extended in 1913[60] and served as the town hall until the first stage of a new scheme was finished in 1958. The new town hall, facing High Road south of Trinity Road, was designed by Sir John Brown and A. E. Henson, whose original plans had been approved 20 years earlier.[61] It served as the civic centre of Haringey in 1972.

In 1965, under the London Government Act of 1963, Tottenham joined Wood Green and Hornsey to form the London Borough of Haringey.[62] The new council, of 10 aldermen and 60 councillors representing 20 wards, met at the civic centre in Wood Green. Administration was reorganized by the appointment of a chief executive and town clerk and of directors of educational, financial, public, social, and technical services. In 1972 the chief executive and town clerk, with the directors of finance and public services, were at Wood Green and the education offices were in Somerset Road, while social services were administered from Tottenham town hall and technical services from Hornsey town hall. Haringey has been Labour controlled except between 1968 and 1971, when the Conservatives had a majority.[63]

PUBLIC SERVICES. A new fire engine was ordered by the vestry in 1838, after it had been found impossible to hire one by the year, the old system of rewards was abandoned in 1844, and expenses were paid out of the waste-land fund.[64] Tottenham volunteer fire brigade was set up by public subscription in 1870 and moved from the old engine-house to Coombes Croft in 1876. There was one manual engine, with a fire-escape and curricle, in 1892, when the entire staff was dismissed for insubordination.[65] The brigade became the first in England to adopt petrol motor traction in 1903, when Harringay fire station was opened in Conway Road and equipped

[50] Except where otherwise stated, the para. is based on *Reps. of Local Inqs. 1889–94, 1895–1907*; Bruce Castle Mus., 932; and *Census, 1891–1951*.
[51] *Census*, 1901.
[52] Election results in *The Times*, e.g. 2 Nov. 1934, 14 May 1949.
[53] Except where otherwise stated, the para. is based on Tottenham, *Official Guide* [1934].
[54] *Builder*, xc. 409–10.
[55] *Haringey A–Z* (1972).
[56] *Kelly's Dir. Essex, Herts. & Mdx.* (1890), 1276.
[57] Wood Green, *Incorporation Brochure* [1933].

[58] Election results in *The Times*, e.g. 3 Nov. 1936, 12 May 1950.
[59] *Kelly's Dir. Essex, Herts. & Mdx.* (1890), 1276.
[60] *Kelly's Dir. Wood Grn.* (1934).
[61] *Builder*, cliv. 1237; cxciv. 1074.
[62] Except where otherwise stated, the para. is based on *Haringey Guide* [1972] and *Haringey A–Z* [1972].
[63] Election results in *The Times*, e.g. 9 May 1964, 10 May 1968.
[64] Bruce Castle Mus., D/PT/2A/7 ff. 149, 155, 335, 406.
[65] Bruce Castle Mus., 932 [TS. notes].

with a combined chemical fire engine, hose tender, fire-escape, and motor.[66] The central fire station, next to the town hall, was opened in 1905.[67] Wood Green had its own fire service, with an engine-house in High Road, by 1901 and a station in Bounds Green Road from 1914.[68] Both brigades became part of the national fire service in the Second World War and later part of the Middlesex fire brigade,[69] itself absorbed in 1965 into the enlarged London fire brigade. In 1973 the old central fire station was used for ambulances and Tottenham was served by the G.L.C.'s station in St. Loys Road.[70]

Despite Tottenham's vaunted springs[71] the general quality of its water was poor until soft water could be found by sinking wells over 100 ft. deep, through the clay, towards the end of the 18th century. In 1840 supplies still came from a well and pump on the Green, given by Thomas Smith when lord of the manor, from wells sunk at Page Green by the Row family, from a well and fountain erected opposite the Bell and Hare by the vestry, and from a well by the Plough at Tottenham Hale.[72] A government inspector, favouring the petition for the formation of a local board, assumed that Tottenham would be able to tap an inexhaustible amount of water between the clay and the chalk.[73]

Tottenham local board claimed to have ensured a full water supply to all built-up areas in 1853[74] but was forced to extend its works at the Hale in 1856 and thereafter drew on the sewage-enriched marshlands, to the detriment of public health until its blunder was exposed in 1873. The underground supply faltered in 1864 and was always intermittent from 1867, whereupon the wealthy made their own arrangements with the great water companies, while others resorted to carriers, cisterns, and private wells. The board undertook to make adequate provision in 1872,[75] ignored an inspector's advice to turn to the companies, and in 1876 installed a pump at the works, giving Tottenham purer water than any of its neighbours and permitting the closure of the pump on the Green in 1883.[76] In that year work began on a tower next to a reservoir in the charity estates' Hill Pond field at Downhills.[77] In 1892 the board, while still relying much on wells and on its works at the Hale and at Downhills,[78] opened Longwater pumping station on the edge of Wild marsh. Since 1880, however, the district had become partly dependent on the New River Co., which itself was responsible for Wood Green, and on the East London Waterworks Co., since the two companies virtually monopolized the flow from the Lea.[79] The New River Co. had constructed a reservoir and filter beds south of Wood Green station by the 1860s[80] and the East London Co. had covered part of Tottenham marshes with Banbury and Lockwood reservoirs, authorized in 1897, by 1904. In that year the companies, together with the over-burdened

municipal undertaking, were absorbed by the new Metropolitan Water Board, which thereafter supplied the entire area.[81]

Sewerage was the worst problem arising from Tottenham's mid-19th-century expansion. In 1843 the riverside lands were generally malarial and by 1848 some 800 houses discharged their waste into the Moselle alone. The local board built a works at Markfield Road, Page Green, contracted for treatment with a manure manufacturer, and in the mid 1850s was as proud of its sewerage as of its water system. After the contractor's death in 1858 sewage was dissipated into the land around Page Green, to the anger of residents, and discharged into the Lea; the River Lea Trustees obtained a suspended injunction in 1865 and Tottenham was accused of killing nearly 4,000 persons by polluting the East London Co.'s water supply in 1866. Meanwhile the Moselle and other streams were increasingly contaminated from higher neighbourhoods, proposals for a joint Lea Valley drainage scheme were stifled by parochialism, and in 1869 the court of Chancery refused further suspensions of its ban on dispersing untreated sewage. The board, deadlocked between supporters and opponents of plans to pipe waste to a costly irrigation works in Walthamstow, saw Tottenhams' death-rate rise to 21.4 per thousand in 1871, worse than in any save the poorest parts of eastern London. Improvements began with the provision of a pipe along Lordship Lane from Wood Green in 1872, cleansing of the Moselle after Hornsey had constructed its own sewer, and an agreement with the Chemical Manure Co. for treatment of sewage. After the separation of Wood Green the Markfield Road works became the responsibility of a joint committee[82] and under an Act of 1891 the sewage of both authorities was passed on from Tottenham to the Northern High Level sewer in Hackney, part of the L.C.C.'s main drainage system, for disposal.[83] A beam engine, installed at Markfield Road in 1886 and used occasionally until the final closure of the works in 1964, was to be restored in 1973.[84]

A refuse destructor was established by Tottenham U.D.C. on 4 a. immediately north of Down Lane recreation ground in 1903.[85] Its furnaces still served as Haringey L.B.'s cleansing headquarters in 1972. Wood Green possessed a modern destructor in Western Road in 1933.[86]

There was said to be gas-lighting by 1833 and some 60 gas-lamps lit the entire length of Tottenham High Road in 1840, when fuel was provided by the Imperial Gas Co. at Haggerston. After 1847 supplies came from the new Tottenham and Edmonton Gas Light & Coke Co., which acquired works in Edmonton.[87] After absorbing neighbouring undertakings, the firm became known as the Tottenham District Light, Heat, & Power Co. in 1914 and as the Tottenham & District Gas Co. in 1928.[88] It opened

[66] Bruce Castle Mus., 933 [correspondence, 1954].
[67] Tottenham, *Official Guide* [1934].
[68] *Kelly's Dir. Wood Grn.* (1901–2); ibid. (1934).
[69] Char. Com. files.
[70] *Haringey A–Z* [1972]. [71] See p. 309.
[72] Robinson, *Tottenham*, i. 5, 8, 11.
[73] 'Pub. Health in Tottenham, 1850–72', 8.
[74] Except where otherwise stated, the foll. two paras. are based on 'Pub. Health in Tottenham, 1850–72' and 'Urban Growth in Tottenham, 1870–94' *penes* Bruce Castle Mus. [75] *Lond. Gaz.* 23 Feb. 1872, p. 722.
[76] Tottenham, *Official Guide* [1934].
[77] Fisk, *Tottenham*, ii. 201.

[78] *Kelly's Dir. Essex, Herts. & Mdx.* (1890).
[79] L. J. Flowerdew and G. C. Berry, *London's Water Supply 1903–53*, 85, 156.
[80] O.S. Map 6", Mdx. XII. NW. (1863–9 edn.).
[81] *London's Water Supply*, 15, 86.
[82] M.R.O., *Reps. of Local Inqs. 1889–94*, 579.
[83] Tottenham and Wood Green Sewerage Act, 54 & 55 Vic. c. 205 (Local Act).
[84] Enfield Archaeol. Soc. *Society News*, no. 39.
[85] Tottenham, *Official Guide* [1934].
[86] Wood Green, *Incorporation Brochure* [1933].
[87] Fisk, *Tottenham*, ii. 211.
[88] M.R.O., Acc. 1153/I.

imposing showrooms at the corner of High Road and Lordship Lane in 1901[89] and later moved its chief offices to the former Royal Masonic school at Wood Green, which was renamed Woodall House and occupied by the company's successor, the Eastern Gas Board, in 1972. An Act of 1898, empowered the Tottenham and Edmonton Gas Light & Coke Co. to provide electricity, which afterwards became the responsibility of the North Metropolitan Electric Power Supply Co.[90]

Tottenham and Edmonton general dispensary was opened by public subscription at no. 746 High Road in 1864. Services at first were provided free but a small weekly charge for membership was later introduced,[91] to supplement collections made at local churches.[92] There were 941 members, nearly half of them representing families, in 1907. In 1910 the trustees were authorized to rebuild the premises, which remained in use in 1938, when membership was 404.[93]

The Prince of Wales's general hospital originated in the Evangelical Protestant Deaconesses' institution and training hospital,[94] founded by Dr. Laseron with help from John Morley of Upper Clapton and his brother Samuel. Avenue House, on the south-east side of the Green, was converted and opened, with a new hospital block, in 1868; the old house was replaced in 1881 and further extensions included the John Morley wing, opened in 1887. The institution had 14 offshoots, including two hospitals in Ireland, at the time of Laseron's death in 1894, whereupon subscriptions declined. Under a Charity Commissioners' Scheme effective from 1899 the voluntary deaconesses surrendered control to a committee and were replaced by paid, certificated nurses; to mark the change from a training centre to a general hospital for the district, the institution was renamed Tottenham hospital. Further additions were made and, to emphasize that it served a wide area, the name was again changed to the Prince of Wales's general hospital in 1907.[95] After adjoining property had been bought in 1917, additions included a building for out-patients, opened in 1932, and a new home for 55 nurses.[96] In 1972 the hospital lay within the North-East Metropolitan region and was administered by Tottenham hospital management committee. It had 200 beds and dealt with acute cases.[97]

St. Ann's general hospital was opened, as the North Eastern fever hospital, by the Metropolitan Asylums Board in 1892.[98] The hospital, which had been established against strong local opposition,[99] originated in temporary buildings erected during a scarlet fever epidemic and occupying 19 a. on the south side of St. Ann's Road. Permanent blocks were completed in 1900 and 548 beds were planned in 1901, by which time the site had been enlarged to 33 a.[1] The L.C.C. took over responsibility in 1930

and replaced the remaining huts before the Second World War. In 1948 St. Ann's assumed its modern name, on becoming a general hospital. In 1973, when it was under the Tottenham management committee, it occupied 28 a. and had 586 beds.[2]

Wood Green and Southgate hospital was opened in 1895 as the Passmore Edwards cottage hospital,[3] paid for largely by Passmore Edwards himself. It stood in Bounds Green Road, on ground bought from the Ecclesiastical Commissioners, and was designed as a small brick, tile-hung building,[4] with 8 beds for patients from Wood Green, Hornsey, and Southgate. There were 25 beds from 1904 and 52 from 1922, but plans for a complete rebuilding were ended by the Second World War. The hospital, renamed in the late 1930s,[5] became part of the Northern group in 1948 and part of the Barnet group in 1963. After further modernization it had 45 beds in 1973.

In 1972 the Bearsted Memorial hospital, Lordship Lane, had 38 beds for maternity cases. Tottenham hospital management committee also administered medical centres in Park Lane, opened in 1941, and Lordship Lane, the Woodberry Down health centre in Green Lanes, a centre for spastics at the Vale school, and a cardiology unit at the Blanche Nevile school for the deaf.[6]

The Alexandra maternity home was founded during the Second World War by Dr. R. R. P. Garrow, medical officer of health for Hornsey, in a private nursing home in Alexandra Park Road. The home was afterwards acquired by the county council and later extended to contain 25 beds. It was administered by the North London group hospital management committee in 1972, when there were 25 beds, and closed during that year, when negotiations started for its transfer to Haringey L.B.[7]

The Jewish Home and Hospital at Tottenham was not founded for local residents. It opened in 1889 as the Home and Hospital for Jewish Incurables and occupied houses in Hackney and afterwards in Walthamstow, offering care and religious facilities to poor immigrant Jews. In 1899 a committee was formed under Stuart Samuel, M.P. (later Sir Stuart Samuel, Bt.), which bought land in Tottenham High Road where part of a three-storeyed, red-brick building was opened in 1903. The new home included a concert hall and was designed for 80 patients, with men on the ground floor and women overhead. An extension for 34 beds and a synagogue were completed in 1914, the synagogue being consecrated after the First World War. A nurses' home was opened in 1938 and a new block in 1964.[8] The institution had 114 patients in 1972.[9]

In 1908 the Metropolitan Police had stations at no. 398 Tottenham High Road and in St. Ann's Road and built a new one at no. 347 Wood Green High Road.[10] All three were still in use in 1972,

[89] Fisk, *Tottenham*, ii. 212.
[90] 61 & 62 Vic. c. 161 (Local Act); Tottenham, *Official Guide* [1934].
[91] Fisk, *Tottenham*, ii. 223.
[92] *Kelly's Dir. Essex, Herts. & Mdx.* (1890).
[93] Tottenham and Edmonton Gen. Disp. annual reps. [Char. Com. files].
[94] Except where otherwise stated, the para. is based on Fisk, *Tottenham*, ii. 188–93.
[95] Tottenham, *Official Guide* [1934].   [96] Ibid.
[97] *Hosp. Yr. Bk.* (1972).
[98] Except where otherwise stated, the para. is based on inf. supplied by the hosp. sec.

[99] Fisk, *Tottenham*, ii. 36–7.
[1] *Builder*, lxxx. 519.
[2] *Hosp. Yr. Bk.* (1972).
[3] Except where otherwise stated, the section is based on inf. supplied by the hosp. sec.
[4] *Building News*, lxvii. 285.
[5] *Kelly's Dirs. Wood Grn.* (1934, 1938).
[6] *Hosp. Yr. Bk.* (1972).
[7] Ibid; ex inf. the sec. and Dr. J. Helen Garrow.
[8] Ex inf. the admin. director.
[9] Ibid.; *Jewish Yr. Bk.* (1972).
[10] *Kelly's Dir. Essex, Herts. & Mdx.* (1908); date on building.

although the main Tottenham station was rebuilt in 1913.[11] Tottenham court house, a neo-Georgian building by W. T. Curtiss, was opened in 1937 on the site of Elmslea.[12]

A burial board, formed in 1854,[13] continued to serve the whole parish from offices at no. 586 High Road after Wood Green became a separate local board district. Five acres north of the church, bounded by the Moselle, were opened as a burial ground in 1858, 3 a. having been consecrated in 1857. Two chapels were built, of Kentish rag with Bath stone dressings, for Anglican and nonconformist services.[14] The ground was later enlarged southward almost as far as the churchyard and north-westward over Tottenham Park to White Hart Lane.[15] Burials there included that of the architect William Butterfield (d. 1900), who restored the parish church and whose sister lived at Tottenham.[16] In 1933 the board bought land for a crematorium at Enfield and after the Second World War it converted the unused north-western corner of the cemetery, including the lake which had belonged to Tottenham Park, into a garden of rest. Tottenham cemetery, owned by Haringey L.B., covered 57 a. in 1972.[17] A mortuary had been opened in Park Lane by 1890.[18]

The Public Libraries Act, rejected by the ratepayers of Tottenham in 1889, was adopted for both Tottenham and Wood Green in 1891. In Tottenham temporary reading rooms were opened at Eaton House where the town hall was later built, in 1892. A new central library, on the site of Stanstead House on the west side of High Road, opposite the High Cross, was opened in 1896 and later extended. Reading rooms at the Chestnuts, St. Ann's Road, were opened in 1900 and soon converted into a lending library, which moved to the education offices in Philip Lane in 1917 and, as West Green library, was permanently accommodated in Vincent Road from 1931. A second branch library was opened in Coombes Croft House in 1925 and a third, St. Ann's, was established in 1931 in Cissbury Road.[19] Devonshire Hill branch library, Compton Crescent, was built in 1935.[20] There was also a reading room at Bruce Castle from 1907 until 1916.[21] At Wood Green a public library was opened at the town hall in 1892 and a reading room at no. 86 High Road in 1895. A central library, built at the junction of Station and High roads with a donation from Andrew Carnegie, opened in 1907.[22]

Between 1892 and 1931 Tottenham U.D.C. acquired 356 a. for public recreation.[23] The first park, 20 a. of grounds adjoining Bruce Castle, was opened in 1892 and the second, the 13-acre Chestnuts recreation ground, was bought in 1898. An Act

of 1900 vested the Lammas Lands in the council,[24] which had acquired 122 a. in the Marshes between the Great Eastern railway and the river Lea by 1905, when a further 25 a. east of the river were conveyed by the Metropolitan Water Board. Immediately west of the railway the 19½-acre Down field, most of it formerly Lammas Land, was acquired in 1902 and later became Down Lane recreation ground. Downhills Park was purchased in 1902 and, with a further 4 a., totalled some 30 a. in 1905. Additions after the First World War included an ornamental garden in Seven Sisters Road, given by T. A. Mason in 1925, the 10-acre Belmont recreation ground, bought in the same year, and the 18-acre Markfield recreation ground in the south-east, bordering the Lea. The largest addition comprised 54 a. between Lordship Lane and Higham Road, bought from the Townsend trustees in 1926, opened as Lordship recreation ground in 1932, and augmented by the gift of a further 43½ a. Tottenham, Page, and West greens, Ducketts Common, and other remnants of common land made up a further 15 a.

The spread of housing estates over the centre of Tottenham in the 1930s left little room for new open spaces. In 1972 the Markfield sewage pumping station was being converted into Haringey's first adventure playground for children.[25] Tottenham marshes were sold to the Lee Valley regional park authority, which took control in 1973, leaving Lordship recreation ground as the largest public space in the old parish.

Wood Green U.D. had less need to buy open spaces, since the district contained 154 a. of the 173 a. which made up Alexandra Park in 1908. In that year the council bought 26 a. next to Wood Green town hall, part of which formed Town Hall, later Woodside, park. A further 42½ a. consisted of small pieces of waste land, most of which, including the 6 a. of Wood Green Common, had been laid out for recreation.[26] In 1933 the borough contained 342 a. of open space and directly controlled 186 a.; the New River playing fields accounted for 30 a., the White Hart Lane and Albert Road recreation grounds for 18 a. and 17 a. respectively and the new Perth Road field for 11 a.[27]

CHURCHES. In 1086 a priest held ½ hide at Tottenham.[28] By 1134 King David I of Scotland had given the church of Tottenham to the Augustinian canons of Holy Trinity, Aldgate.[29] The grant was confirmed between 1163 and 1174[30] and again in 1201.[31] A vicarage was endowed by William of Sainte-Mère-Eglise,[32] bishop of London from 1198

[11] *Building News*, civ. 305.
[12] Bruce Castle Mus., 935 [pamphlet].
[13] Bruce Castle Mus., 983 [newspaper cutting].
[14] *Kelly's Dir. Essex, Herts. & Mdx.* (1890).
[15] Fisk, *Tottenham*, ii. 145–6.
[16] P. Thompson, *Wm. Butterfield*, 433.
[17] Ex inf. Haringey L.B., cemeteries and crematorium supt.
[18] *Kelly's Dir. Essex, Herts. & Mdx.* (1890).
[19] Tottenham, *Official Guide* [1934].
[20] Date on building.
[21] Coombes Croft branch libr. [pamphlet, 1925].
[22] Wood Green, *Incorp. Brochure* [1933].
[23] Except where otherwise stated, the para. is based on Tottenham, *Official Guide* [1934] and on inf. supplied by the chief supt. of parks, Haringey L.B.

[24] Tottenham U.D.C. Act, 63 & 64 Vic. c. 284 (Local Act).
[25] *Haringey Guide* [1972].
[26] *Kelly's Dir. Essex, Herts. & Mdx.* (1908), 427.
[27] Wood Green, *Incorp. Brochure* [1933].
[28] *V.C.H. Mdx.* i. 129.
[29] *Cart. of Holy Trin. Aldgate* (Lond. Rec. Soc. vii), 3, 229. David announced the grant to Gilbert the Universal, bishop of London from 1128 to 1134.
[30] *Letters and charters of Gilbert Foliot*, ed. A. Morey and Z. N. Brooke, 450.
[31] *Letters of Pope Innocent III*, ed. C. R. and M. G. Cheney, p. 46.
[32] Hennessy, *Novum Repertorium*, 427. King David's grant and later confirmations are in B.M. Cott. Ch. xiii, nos. 11–14.

to 1221, and thereafter a vicar served the whole parish until the creation of the district chapelry of Holy Trinity in the early 19th century.[33]

Priors of Holy Trinity presented all the known vicars from 1327 until the early 16th century. The patronage was exercised by John Lawrence on behalf of John Jekyll in 1510 and by William Redman and Robert Heynes, by grant of a turn, in 1525, but Holy Trinity again presented in 1526.[34] After the Dissolution the king granted the advowson, together with the rectory estate, successively to Sir Thomas Audley, to William, Lord Howard, and, in 1544, to the chapter of St. Paul's.[35] The vicar was presented in 1551 by John Cook and thereafter by St. Paul's[36] until the Interregnum, when Sir Edward Barkham and others 'approved' the minister.[37] The chapter regained the patronage at the Restoration and retained it in 1972.[38]

One half of the tithes of grain at Tottenham was granted by Simon de St. Liz (I) in 1107 to his newly founded priory of St. Andrew, Northampton,[39] which was confirmed in its right as late as 1329[40] but apparently had lost it by 1535.[41] William of Sainte-Mère-Eglise endowed the vicar with small tithes and with a pension of 20s. from the canon's treasury, in return for a quit-rent.[42] The vicarage was never wealthy. It was assessed at 5 marks in the mid 13th century[43] and had risen to £5 in 1291;[44] it was taxed at a mere 16 marks in 1428[45] and was valued at £14 in 1535.[46] The minister occupied or leased out property worth £17 a year in 1650, by which date the small tithes, owing to the remissness of the parishioners, were estimated at no more than £30.[47] In the 1660s Dr. Edward Spark complained to St. Paul's that his predecessor William Wimpew had refused any augmentation, that Stephen Beale as farmer of the rectory was obstructive, and that he himself had only £58 18s. 8d. a year, of which £38 18s. 8d. came from tithes.[48] By 1700 lessees of St. Paul's were paying £10 yearly to augment the benefice,[49] which was estimated to be worth £100 in the early and mid 18th century[50] and £300 in 1810, when the vicar received £175 in small tithes, £100 in fees and augmentations, £10 from the farmer of the rectory, and Easter offerings.[51] The net income was £978 in 1835.[52] When all the tithes were commuted for £1,685 10s. in 1844, the vicar was awarded a rent-charge of £800.[53]

On the endowment of the vicarage 2 a. was set aside for the vicar's house.[54] In 1455–6 the glebe comprised the site of the house with 4 a., an additional 7 a. lately belonging to the rectory, and a small grove.[55] The same land was probably held by William Bedwell, who reckoned that it covered 10 or 11 a., including 1–2 a. at Wood Green;[56] in his time the vicarage house stood next to an orchard, with pasture called Vicarage croft to the north-west, and the slip at Wood Green contained a cottage by the New River.[57] In 1799 the Wood Green property was sold, to redeem the land-tax, and in 1810 the vicar had only his close of pasture adjoining one acre around the house.[58] The pasture was still glebe in 1844, by which time the grounds of the house had been extended to cover more than 8 a.,[59] but all were apparently sold when a new house was bought in the 1860s.[60]

The first recorded vicarage house stood in 1610 on the north side of White Hart Lane, close to the junction with High Road.[61] Bedwell, then in occupation, considered it a small thing, of less note than the glebeland,[62] and Edward Sparke, pleading poverty, complained that the buildings were ruinous.[63] The house had been refaced by 1810, when the White Hart Lane front was of brick with sash windows while the other sides were tile-hung and described as ancient; it was then of two floors, the upper one having 7 bedrooms, and a garret.[64] In the 1860s the vicar moved from White Hart Lane to no. 776 High Road,[65] an old house which remained the Vicarage until the purchase of the Priory[66] in 1905.[67] The oldest part of the original Vicarage was pulled down in 1873[68] and the rest was used by the stationmaster at White Hart Lane in 1913, when the premises in High Road served as the Working Men's Tariff Reform club.[69]

The Priory, so called by the 1860s because it was thought to occupy the site of a residence of the priors of Holy Trinity,[70] apparently replaced Awlfield farmhouse,[71] which stood immediately south of the church in 1619. In that year the farm was leased out with demesne lands totalling 179 a. to Joseph Fenton, a barber-surgeon of London and the most substantial of the demesne tenants.[72] Thereafter the farm was presumably leased, as in 1785, until in 1789 the house and 132 a. were bought by the tenant, Edwin Paine.[73] The estate stretched westward across the

[33] See p. 351.
[34] Hennessy, *Novum Repertorium*, 427–8.
[35] For Tottenham Rectory manor, see p. 328.
[36] Hennessy, op. cit. 428.
[37] *Home Cnties. Mag.* i. 319.
[38] Hennessy, op. cit. 428; *Crockford* (1971–2).
[39] *Regesta Regum Anglo-Normannorum*, ii, ed. C. Johnson and H. A. Cronne, pp. 69–70.
[40] *Cal. Chart. R.* 1327–41, 119.
[41] *Valor Eccl.* (Rec. Com.), iv. 313.
[42] Newcourt, *Repertorium*, i. 754.
[43] *Val. of Norw.*, ed. Lunt, 359.
[44] *Tax. Eccl.* (Rec. Com.), 17, 20.
[45] *Feud. Aids*, iii. 377.
[46] *Valor Eccl.* (Rec. Com.), i. 433.
[47] *Home Cnties. Mag.* i. 319.
[48] St. Paul's MSS., Box A 58.
[49] Guildhall Libr., uncat. Church Com. deed 169141.
[50] Guildhall MSS. 9550, 9556–7.
[51] Guildhall MS. 9628/5.
[52] *Rep. Com. Eccl. Revenues*, 674–5.
[53] Church Com. S 4, f. 345.
[54] Hennessy, *Novum Repertorium*, 427.
[55] Bruce Castle Mus., MR/76 [TS. transl. pp. 12, 18, 20].

[56] W. J. Roe, *Ancient Tottenham*, 108.
[57] Guildhall MS. 9628/5; Robinson, *Tottenham*, map of 1619.
[58] Guildhall MS. 9628/5. The Wood Green land was still marked as glebe in 1818: Robinson, *Tottenham*, map of 1818.
[59] Bruce Castle Mus., D/PT/102A/13.
[60] See below.
[61] Guildhall MS. 9628/5; Robinson, *Tottenham*, map of 1619.
[62] Roe, *Ancient Tottenham*, 108.
[63] St. Paul's MSS., Box A 58.
[64] Guildhall MS. 9628/5; Robinson, *Tottenham*, ii, plate facing p. 92.
[65] Bruce Castle Mus., Tottenham sales iii (1902–13), no. 16.
[66] Fisk, *Tottenham*, i. 133.
[67] Bruce Castle Mus., 983 [cutting from *Country Life*].
[68] *Tottenham and Edmonton Advertiser*, 2899.
[69] Fisk, *Tottenham*, i. 134.
[70] Fisk, *Tottenham*, i. 138.
[71] Bruce Castle Mus., MR/121.
[72] M.R.O., Acc. 695/9, ff. 8–10; Robinson, *Tottenham*, map of 1619.
[73] M.R.O., Acc. 1016/475.

Moselle, along the north side of Lordship Lane, thirty years later[74] and was sometimes known as Church farm.[75] After its acquisition by the L.C.C., the Priory was saved from demolition by the Revd. Denton Jones, since whose time it has served as the vicarage-house.[76]

In 1973 the Priory,[77] a two-storeyed building with cellar and attics, was largely screened from Church Lane by a brick wall, containing an early-18th-century wrought iron gate from the old Vicarage in High Road.[78] The north wing is partly timber-framed and it probably survives from an earlier hall and cross-wing house which Joseph Fenton remodelled. Fenton's name and rebus occur in the plaster-work of the hall ceiling and on panelling in a bedroom, with the dates 1620 and 1621. More alterations took place in the early 18th century, when the framed projection of the south wing was removed and the main front was renewed in brick and provided with a wooden doorcase. Inside an elaborate wooden overmantel was put into the hall and a new staircase was built behind the main range. During the 19th century there were extensions to the south wing and when the house was converted into a vicarage further alterations were made at the back and to the fittings.

A chantry was founded under the will of John Drayton, dated 1456, a goldsmith who left his lands in reversion to St. Paul's for the support of two priests to say masses at Roger Walden's tomb in the cathedral and St. Katharine's altar in Tottenham church severally. Masses were also to be celebrated twice weekly at the chapel of St. Ann called the Hermitage.[79] Drayton's chantry was worth £6 13s. 4d. a year in 1535[80] but was not included with other properties valued in 1547. William Courtman otherwise Clark, a London vintner, by will proved 1528, left land in trust, the rent from which primarily was to pay for Easter expenses, including bread and wine at communion; the residue was to go to Courtman's heir for 20 years and thereafter to the poor.[81] In 1547, when Courtman's benefaction was somewhat differently defined, 66s. a year was also paid by the keepers of 33 cows which had been given by various benefactors for the support of a chantry priest.[82] The lands left by Courtman were sold by the Crown, with many others, to Thomas Bourchier and Henry Tanner in 1548.[83]

Edward Mariner, vicar 1474–83, was licensed to hold Tottenham with one other living in 1478.[84] Dr. Geoffrey Wharton, a canon of St. Paul's, resigned the living after a year in 1526 on becoming archdeacon of London.[85] William Bedwell, vicar

1607–32 and author of the first local history, was an Arabic scholar and one of the Westminster translators of the Bible.[86] William Wimpew, displaced from 1644 until the Restoration,[87] also secured a prebend of Lincoln in 1664.[88] Dr. Edward Sparke, who continued as vicar of Walthamstow for a short time after his institution to Tottenham in 1666, was a royal chaplain and theological writer.[89] Samuel Pratt, appointed in 1693, became minister of the Savoy and a canon of Windsor in 1697 and dean of Rochester in 1706; he resigned Tottenham in favour of his son Daniel in 1707.[90] Thomas Comyn, vicar 1771–98, was second chaplain of the Royal Hospital, Chelsea, from 1782 and chaplain there from 1787.[91] Thomas Newcome, vicar 1824–51, was also rector of Shenley (Herts.).[92] The living was often bestowed as a reward by St. Paul's: John Husband, vicar 1714–38, his successor Christopher Morrison, and William John Hall, vicar 1851–62, were minor canons and Alexander Wilson, vicar 1870–98, was a canon.[93] There was a resident assistant curate in the time of Samuel Pratt[94] and, if not earlier, from the time of John Husband, who himself stayed in the parish from Easter until Michaelmas.[95] John Rotheram (1725–89), the theologian, was curate from 1757 to 1766.[96] The curate's stipend was recorded in 1774, 1807,[97] and 1835.[98]

In 1650 Tottenham was said to be served by an able minister, William Bates, and to possess a church which could conveniently hold all the worshippers.[99] Edward Sparke, however, declared that ignorance and faction threatened unless his parishioners should become as concerned for their souls as for their bodies; he had vainly suggested that the congregation should support an evening sermon with £40 a year, of which half should go to himself and half to a reader, which would still be below the rate of the meanest lecturer.[1] In 1685, when Sparke was still vicar, it was ordered that the communion table should be placed under the east window and railed in, as formerly.[2] Sparke's successor, Samuel Pratt, first allowed the vestry to choose a lecturer in 1693.[3] Attacks on Pratt, perhaps as a pluralist, were condemned in 1695 by the vestry, which hinted at dissenters' malice and declared that the parish could never desire to be better served than by the vicar and his assistant curate.[4] When John Husband was vicar, services were held twice on Sundays and the sacraments were administered once a month and on three feast days.[5] In the 1770s there were still two Sunday services, as well as a monthly communion attended by 50–60 people. Two Sunday schools had been started by 1790.[6] In 1851 there were attendances of

74 Robinson, *Tottenham*, map of 1818.
75 O.S. Map 6″, Mdx. XII. NE. (1863–9 edn.).
76 Fisk, *Tottenham*, i. 138.
77 The para. is based on Hist. Mon. Com. *Mdx.* 122 and plates 40, 169, 184; Pevsner, *Mdx.* 157; and Bruce Castle Mus., 983 [cutting from *Country Life*].
78 Fisk, *Tottenham*, ii. 151.
79 Robinson, *Tottenham*, ii. 3–4.
80 *Valor Eccl.* (Rec. Com.), i. 434.
81 Prob. 11/22 (P.C.C. 35 Porch).
82 E 301/34/163.
83 *Cal. Pat.* 1547–8, 411, 413.
84 *Cal. Papal Regs.* xiii. 587.
85 Le Neve, *Fasti, 1300–1541, St. Paul's, Lond.* 9, 45.
86 *D.N.B.*
87 Matthews, *Walker Revised*, 262.
88 Le Neve, *Fasti*, ed. T. D. Hardy, ii. 118.
89 *D.N.B.*

90 R. Somerville, *The Savoy*, 248.
91 C. G. T. Dean, *Royal Hosp. Chelsea*, 309–10.
92 *Alumni Cantab.* pt. 3, iv. 534.
93 Hennessy, *Nov. Repertorium*, 428 and notes.
94 Bruce Castle Mus., D/PT/2A/1, ff. 32, 56.
95 Guildhall MS. 9550. Several curates are listed in Robinson, *Tottenham*, ii. 110.
96 *D.N.B.*
97 Guildhall MS. 9557.
98 *Rep. Com. Eccl. Revs.* 674–5.
99 *Home Cnties. Mag.* i. 319.
1 St. Paul's MSS., Box A 58.
2 Guildhall MS. 9537/20.
3 Bruce Castle Mus., D/PT/2A/1, f. 52; Robinson, *Tottenham*, ii. 111.
4 Bruce Castle Mus., D/PT/2A/1, f. 56.
5 Guildhall MS. 9550.
6 Ibid. 9557.

613, including 161 children from Sunday school, in the morning and 525, including 150 children, in the evening.[7]

The church of All Saints now called *ALL HALLOWS* was so dedicated by the 15th century.[8] It stands on the west side of Church Lane, separated from housing to the east and north by Bruce Castle's grounds and Tottenham cemetery and to the south by the Priory. The building, after many alterations, comprises a chancel with north-east vestries and north and south transepts, an aisled nave of 6 bays, a south porch, and a 4-stage west tower.[9] A contrast of textures and colours is provided by the materials: flint rubble, ragstone, varied brickwork, and dressings of stone. By the end of the 14th century the surviving tower and arcades suggest a building with an aisled nave of 4 bays and a chancel with north and south chapels. During the 15th century both aisles were rebuilt, probably to a greater width, and that on the south side was continued beyond the rood screen into the rebuilt chapel. The two-storey south porch, of red brick with dark diapering and stone dressings, was added *c.* 1500. A north-east vestry over a burial vault for the Hare family was erected in 1696; a circular structure with a leaded dome surmounted by an obelisk, it was demolished in 1875 on the reorganization of Lord Coleraine's charity.[10] The fourth stage of the tower, in brick and battlemented, was added during the 18th century. At a restoration in 1816 the church was probably again extended eastward, by one bay, and the north aisle was rebuilt in yellowish-brown brick. A further restoration in 1875 included the addition of a chancel, transepts, and vestries to the east; the work, by William Butterfield, was carried out in a Geometrical style but in materials similar to those of the porch. The many changes and slight 20th-century war damage have left few of the architectural details unaffected, although much original stonework has been reset. A western gallery for children was altered to accommodate more parishioners in 1741, when a new children's gallery was built over the south-west door. A north gallery, for the use of nine subscribers and their households, was added in 1821. All three galleries were subsequently removed, the first being the north one *c.*1862.[11]

Fittings include French glass of *c.* 1600,[12] presented in 1807 by John Eardley and later moved from the chancel to the north aisle, and an early-17th-century communion table. There is a brass inscription to Geoffrey Walkeden (d. 1599) and there are figured brasses to Elizabeth Burrough (d. 1616) and Margaret Irby (d. 1640). An imposing marble wall-monument displays the kneeling figures of Richard Candler (d. 1602), his son-in-law Sir Ferdinando

Heybourne (d. 1618), and their wives, and another portrays Sir John Melton and his wife (d. 1640).[13] A third, in black and white marble, of three stages and advanced in style, has busts by Edward Marshall of Sir Robert Barkham, his wife Mary (d. 1644), and their 12 children. Other monuments include a slab to Bridget Moyse (d. 1626) and, in the churchyard, headstones commemorating Rebecca Angell (d. 1682) and Mary Hobby (d. 1708), as well as many table-tombs of the early 19th century.

The church possessed 4 bells in 1552[14] and a great bell, weighing 2,011 lb., which was recast in 1612. Presumably they were the 5 bells which were recast in 1696, when a sixth was added. In 1972 the tower held 8 bells: (i) and (ii) 1881;[15] (iii) to (viii) 1696, Philip Wightman. A sanctus bell mentioned in 1552 may have been the one replaced in 1801, when Dr. Humphrey Jackson gave a French bell of 1663, said to have been taken from the Quebec garrison in 1759. A chalice and some other pieces, kept in private houses, were said in 1552 to be the only valuables to have survived two burglaries.[16] Communion vessels were again stolen in 1818[17] and in 1897 there was no plate dating from before the late 19th century.[18] The registers date from 1558 and are complete.[19]

HOLY TRINITY chapel, on the north side of Tottenham Green, was built 1828–30 out of public subscriptions and a Parliamentary grant.[20] A district chapelry, taken from the parent parish, was assigned in 1844[21] and perpetual curates were thereafter appointed by the vicar of Tottenham.[22] There was seating for about 800 but attendance was poor in 1851[23] and was denounced as scandalous for so respectable a community in 1879, when many letters to the local newspapers attacked the vicar, W. C. Howell, for using the Gregorian chant.[24] The church was designed in yellow stock brick with stone dressings by James Savage. It is a plain building, comprising a nave, sanctuary, and aisles; when new it was highly praised, although the crocketed pinnacles were condemned as Perpendicular blemishes on an otherwise austere work in the Early English style.[25] A school, between the church and High Road, was built in 1847.[26]

A chapel of ease, dedicated to *ST. MICHAEL*, was consecrated at Wood Green in 1844.[27] It was paid for by subscriptions and a grant from the Church Building Society and could seat 200, although attendances of no more than 48 in the morning and 85 in the evening were recorded in 1851, when there was no Sunday school.[28] The building, when erected, stood amid fields in the fork between Bounds Green Lane and Green Lanes (later Bounds Green Road and High Road). G. G.

[7] H.O. 129/137/2/3/3.
[8] Fisk, *Tottenham*, ii. 20.
[9] Except where otherwise stated, the rest of the para. and the following two paras. are based on Hist. Mon. Com. *Mdx.* 119–21; Robinson, *Tottenham*, ii. 5–17, 40–80; and Pevsner, *Mdx.* 155–6.
[10] See p. 379. Lord Coleraine's addition, an 'eyesore' according to Robinson, is shown in a painting of the church from the north by John Constable, *c.* 1830: Robbins, *Mdx.* plate 1.
[11] Guildhall MS. 9532/13, f. 329.
[12] Hist. Mon. Com. *Mdx.* plate 179.
[13] Ibid. plate 180.
[14] *T.L.M.A.S.* xvii. 41.
[15] Ibid. xviii(2), no. 167.
[16] E 315/498f. 26.

[17] Bruce Castle Mus., D/PT/2A/7, f. 80.
[18] Freshfield, *Communion Plate*, 52.
[19] The registers from 1558 to 1896 are in M.R.O., D.R.O. 15/A1/1–31.
[20] Bruce Castle Mus., 984/1; Robinson, *Tottenham*, ii. 134–7; M. H. Post, *Six Hundred New Churches*, 158–9.
[21] *Lond. Gaz.* 10 Dec. 1844, pp. 5115–16.
[22] Hennessy, *Novum Repertorium*, 429.
[23] H.O. 129/137/2/1/2.
[24] Bruce Castle Mus., 984/1.
[25] *Gent. Mag.* ci(2), 11–13 and frontispiece.
[26] Inscription on building; see p. 367.
[27] Except where otherwise stated, the following two paras. are based on *St. Mic. Wood Grn. 1844–1944* [centenary booklet] and TS. notes *penes* the vicar.
[28] H.O. 129/137/2/4/4.

(later Sir Gilbert) Scott and W. B. Moffat designed it, in Kentish rag and Brownhill stone, in the Decorated style. It consisted of an aisleless nave and a short chancel. Damage from subsidence caused temporary closure in the 1850s and presumably prompted a complaint in the press in 1863 that Wood Green, with its rapidly growing population, was served by 'a little crippled church on crutches'. In 1865 the building was reconstructed in an early Decorated style, with an aisled nave designed by Henry Curzon. A new chancel, also by Curzon, was built in 1869–70, a south-east tower was added in 1873–4, largely at the cost of Samuel Page of Chitts Hill, and a spire in 1887.[29] St. Michael's became a district chapelry, taken from the parent parish, in 1866, with the vicar of Tottenham as patron.[30] A church hall, designed by J. S. Alder, was built on the south side of Bounds Green Road in 1911.[31]

In 1973 the church, which had seating for c. 450,[32] was unusual in being served by a vicar and three assistant curates and in having charge of two mission churches. The church of St. John, Brook Road, was dedicated in 1898 and the iron church of the Good Shepherd, formerly at Neasden, was erected in Berwick Road in 1916.

In north Tottenham services were held in an iron building, on the site later occupied by no. 125 Northumberland Park, from 1855 until land for a permanent church in Park Lane was given by Miss Jemima Holt, of Marie House, High Road.[33] The church of ST. PAUL was begun in 1858[34] and consecrated in 1859,[35] when a district chapelry was assigned out of All Hallows parish,[36] with the vicar of Tottenham as patron.[37] Much of the money was raised by the first incumbent, D. J. Harrison.[38] The building, of Kentish ragstone, was designed in a Decorated style by William Mumford. It consisted of aisled nave, sanctuary, north and south transepts, west gallery, and north-west tower with spire,[39] and could seat 750. The fabric had been little altered by 1972 but in 1973 it was demolished, with the near-by vicarage, to make way for a new church, hall, and flats.[40]

Assistant curates from Holy Trinity held Sunday afternoon services at the Hermitage school, opened in 1858 on the north side of Hanger Lane (later St. Ann's Road).[41] A few yards farther east the church of ST. ANN was founded in 1860 and dedicated in 1861, whereupon a district was assigned from Holy Trinity parish. Both school and church were chiefly paid for by Fowler Newsam, a City merchant who lived in High Road opposite the junction with St. Ann's Road, on behalf of his daughter Mrs. E. M. Robins, whose house was on the site of the later St. Ann's hospital. Fowler Newsam became the first patron and was succeeded by Mrs. Robins (d. 1895), who in 1891 devised the patronage to the chapter of St. Paul's.[42] Of the 625 sittings only 100 were free. The church was attended by rich businessmen's

families, which led a newspaper correspondent to complain in 1872 that an iron church in West Green or Tottenham Hale would have been more beneficial than Newsam's lavishly favoured St. Ann's, in rural surroundings and catering largely for outsiders. The building cost as much as £11,000, with a vicarage to the north-east (demolished 1962), and was much praised for the richness of its detail, both internal and external.[43] It was designed by Thomas Talbot Bury in the Decorated style, of brick, faced with Kentish ragstone and with dressings of Bath stone, and comprised an aisled nave, north and south transepts, apsidal chancel, and south-west tower and spire. A single vestry served both clergy and choir until 1897, when a separate one for the choir was consecrated; the original vestry was converted into a memorial chapel in 1921, when a new clergy vestry was added. The steeple, damaged in the Second World War, was repaired in 1954–5, and other parts of the fabric were restored in 1958 and 1961. Fittings included an organ on which Mendelssohn had played at Crosby Hall (City of London), whence it was brought by Mr. and Mrs. Robins. There was seating for about 480 in 1972.

A rise in the working-class population of south Tottenham led to the hire of rooms as a soup kitchen before the opening of the Newsam Memorial House, with a resident mission woman, on the south side of St. Ann's Road. A hall was added at the back, with help from the Bishop of London's Fund, and dedicated in 1914; it was pulled down in the 1960s, when a new parish hall was built north of the church. The same fund contributed to a parish hall in Braemar Road, opened as the Mission of the Good Shepherd in 1906 and bombed in the Second World War. It also helped to build a hall in Blackboy Lane, dedicated as St. Andrew's church in 1908 and thereafter served by a curate-in-charge until the Second World War; St. Andrew's was used as the headquarters of the Church company of the Boys' Brigade from 1947 until it was burned down in 1970.

In the populous Stamford Hill area an iron church, dedicated to ST. JOHN THE DIVINE, was opened in Franklin Street in 1880. It was replaced by a church in Vartry Road six years later, when a parish was created out of St. Ann's, whose vicar became the patron. Lord Amherst gave the site and the Bishop of London's Fund contributed. The church, of red brick with stone dressings, was designed by S. W. Grant in the Early English style; it had seating for 650 and consisted of aisled nave, chancel, north-east sacristy, and south-east organ-chamber. A mission house was opened in Harefield Road in 1891 and a parish room was built in 1894.[44] Despite repairs to the church itself in 1953[45] the fabric became so dilapidated that from the late 1960s 120–150 worshippers met in a large hut within the nave. In 1973 it was planned to demolish the church,

[29] Bruce Castle Mus., 984/1; T.L.M.A.S. xviii(2), no. 229.
[30] Lond. Gaz. 6 Feb. 1866, p. 649, 20 Oct. 1874, p. 4770.
[31] Inscription on building.
[32] Ex inf. the vicar.
[33] Fisk, Tottenham, ii. 248–9; Hennessy, Novum Repertorium, 429.
[34] Inscription on church.
[35] Fisk, op. cit. ii. 249.
[36] Lond. Gaz. 10 June 1859, pp. 2276–7.
[37] Hennessy, Novum Repertorium, 429.

[38] Ex inf. the par. priest.
[39] T.L.M.A.S. xviii(2), no. 176.
[40] Ex inf. the par. priest.
[41] Except where otherwise stated, the following three paras. are based on St. Ann's Ch. Stamford Hill, 1861–1961 [centenary booklet] and inf. supplied by the vicar.
[42] 44th Rep. Eccl. Com. [C. 6616], p. 46, H.C. (1892), xxvii.
[43] Bruce Castle Mus., 984/1 [newspaper cuttings].
[44] Fisk, Tottenham, ii. 245.
[45] T.L.M.A.S. xviii (2), no. 173.

with its adjoining clergy-house and hall, and to rebuild on part of the old site.[46]

Services were started by a mission from Marlborough College (Wilts.) at the new Coleraine Park board school in 1881. The church of *ST. MARY THE VIRGIN* was consecrated in 1887, Marlborough College having contributed over one third of the cost of the site, on the south side of Lansdowne Road, and of the building.[47] A consolidated chapelry, taken from the parishes of All Hallows, Holy Trinity, and St. Paul, was created in 1888,[48] with the bishop of London as patron.[49] The church, designed by J. E. K. Cutts, was of red brick with stone dressings, in the Early English style; it seated 720 and comprised a western vestry, an aisled nave, an apsidal chancel with the altar raised unusually high, a north-east chapel, and a south-east organ-chamber.[50] A mission hall in Mitchley Road, Stoneleigh South, was opened in the 1890s and later halls were built in Kemble[51] and Lansdowne roads. The Kemble hall was used by the parish in 1973, when the other halls were leased out.[52]

At West Green, where residents hitherto had been faced with a difficult journey to St. Ann's, services began in the Willow Walk school in 1882.[53] Two years later an iron church, which had served the parishioners of All Souls', Clapton, was erected, with help from the London Diocesan Home Mission, on land in West Green Road leased from W. Hodson of Downhills. In 1888 the permanent *CHRIST CHURCH* was consecrated, at the junction of Stanmore and Waldeck roads, and in 1889 a consolidated chapelry was formed out of Holy Trinity, All Hallows, St. Michael's, and St. Ann's,[54] with the vicar of Holy Trinity as patron.[55] The church was designed by Hodson and Whitehead, of red brick with some stone dressings, in the Early English style. It seated 700 and comprised an aisled nave and a chancel; the roof was relaid with pantiles after the Second World War. The iron building was retained for Sunday school classes until 1893, when a parish hall was opened in Waldeck Road, where successive vicarage houses later separated it from the parish church.

In 1884, a year after work had started on the Noel Park estate, services and Sunday school classes were held over a shop in Park Road South, later no. 9 Lymington Avenue.[56] A site for a church at the centre of the estate had already been bought by Richard Foster and extended, to include a hall and vicarage, by the Bishop of London's Fund; money also had been raised in Shrewsbury to erect a mission hall, which would be supported by the Shropshire Mission to East London. The hall was dedicated in 1885 and the church of *ST. MARK* consecrated in

1889, when a district was assigned from St. Michael's, Wood Green,[57] with the bishop of London as patron.[58] In 1902–3 St. Mark's had the largest Anglican attendance in the parish, with a congregation twice that of any other church in Wood Green.[59] The church, of red brick, seated 850 and consisted of aisled nave, transepts, chancel, north-east chapel, and south-east vestry; it was designed by Rowland Plumbe in Venetian Gothic and was intended to have a lofty bell-tower. The mission hall was retained for parish meetings and formed, with the church and vicarage, an island site between Gladstone and Lymington avenues.

A mission hall, holding 250, was built by the Drapers' Company of London in 1884 to serve the poor and populous area between Page Green and Tottenham Hale. A permanent building was planned ten years later but was not consecrated, as the church of *ST. PETER*, Broad Lane, until 1900,[60] when a district chapelry was formed out of Holy Trinity parish.[61] The bishop of London became patron.[62] The church, of red-brick with stone dressings, was designed in an early Gothic style by J. S. Alder; it seated 800 and consisted of aisled nave, transepts, chancel, and south-east chapel. The building was restored after war damage in 1955[63] but closed c. 1970.[64] It awaited demolition in 1973, when the parish was divided between the churches of Holy Trinity and St. Bartholomew.[65]

The detached portion of the parish of St. James, Clerkenwell, which lay to the north-east of Muswell Hill in Hornsey parish, became a mission district in 1899.[66] For a year services were held at the Norwegian House, a wooden building, formerly used as a restaurant in the grounds of Alexandra Palace, which stood near the junction of Alexandra Park Road and the Avenue. The iron church of *ST. ANDREW*, a little to the east on land which had been bought by the Bishop of London's Fund, was dedicated in 1900, when a new parish was created out of the outlying portion of Clerkenwell and part of St. Michael's, Wood Green, with the bishop of London as patron.[67] A permanent church of red brick with stone dressings, designed by J. S. Alder in a Decorated style, was consecrated in 1903; it seated 800 and was not orientated. It consisted of aisled nave, transepts, chancel, south-east chapel, and western spire. A hall, to the west, was opened in 1923 and was used for worship after the church had been gutted by an incendiary bomb in 1944. St. Andrew's was dedicated again in 1957, having been remodelled by R. S. Morris to incorporate the shell of its predecessor. The new church seated 414 and was set back from the road, with a bellcot instead of a spire; it contained a bronze tablet which was all

[46] Ex inf. the par. priest.
[47] Fisk, *Tottenham*, ii. 247–8.
[48] *Lond. Gaz.* 23 Nov. 1888, pp. 6417–18.
[49] Hennessy, *Novum Repertorium*, 429.
[50] *T.L.M.A.S.* xviii(2), no. 175; Bruce Castle Mus., 984/1 [newspaper cutting and photos.].
[51] Fisk, *Tottenham*, ii. 248.
[52] Ex inf. the vicar.
[53] Except where otherwise stated, the para. is based on *Christ Ch. West Green* [75th anniv. booklet] and Bruce Castle Mus. 984/1 [newspaper cuttings].
[54] *Lond. Gaz.* 30 July 1889, pp. 4085–6.
[55] Hennessy, *Novum Repertorium*, 428.
[56] Except where otherwise stated, the para. is based on *The Lion* [newsheet of St. Mark, Noel Pk.], 3–17 Sept. 1972.

[57] *43rd Rep. Eccl. Com.* [C. 6294], p. 46, H.C. (1890–1), xxvi.
[58] *Clergy List* (1892).
[59] Mudie-Smith, *Rel. Life*, 402.
[60] Fisk, *Tottenham*, ii. 250; *Building News*, lxvii. 891.
[61] *53rd. Rep. Eccl. Com.* [Cd. 497], p. 57, H.C. (1901), xviii.
[62] *Crockford* (1905).
[63] Fisk, *Tottenham*, ii. 250; *T.L.M.A.S.* xviii(2), no. 177.
[64] Ex inf. the vicar, St. Barts. Stamford Hill.
[65] *Holy Trin. Par. Mag.* Oct. 1973.
[66] Except where otherwise stated, the para. is based on H. E. Boisseau, *Hist. of St. Andrew's Ch. 1899–1950* and *St. Andrew's Ch.* [rededication leaflet, 1957].
[67] *54th Rep. Eccl. Com.* [Cd. 1001], p. 64, H.C. (1902), xxii.

that survived of a memorial to the first vicar by Sir Ninian Comper, which had been placed above the altar in 1938.

A red-brick hall, dedicated to St. Alban, was built on the east side of Stonebridge Road in 1899.[68] It became a parish hall[69] after the church of *ST. BARTHOLOMEW*, Stamford Hill, had been built on the north side of Craven Park Road in 1904, with funds from the sale of the City church of St. Bartholomew, Moor Lane, London (demolished 1902),[70] which itself had replaced St. Bartholomew by the Exchange, London. A consolidated chapelry from St. Ann's, Hanger Lane, and St. Thomas's, Stamford Hill, was created in 1905[71] and the patronage was vested in the Crown.[72] The church, of red brick with stone dressings, was designed by W. D. Caroë in the Perpendicular style; it comprised aisled nave, north and south aisles and transepts, chancel with a crypt chapel and vestries underneath, south-east chapel, and west gallery. The 17th-century pulpit sides and font-cover, attributed to Grinling Gibbons, came from St. Bartholomew by the Exchange, as did the font itself and the later altar-rails.[73] The plate included several early Victorian pieces from St. Bartholomew's, Moor Lane.

The corrugated iron church of *ST. SAVIOUR*,[74] at the highest point reached by Palace Gates (later Alexandra Park) Road, was dedicated in 1900. It accommodated 300 and was used for services until the consecration of part of its successor in 1904, shortly before a district chapelry was formed out of St. Michael's, Wood Green,[75] with the bishop of London as patron.[76] The iron building then became a parish hall and was moved farther south in 1907, to make way for the west end of the permanent church, which was completed two years later. The new church, designed by J. S. Alder, was of red brick with stone dressings, in the Decorated style, and was not orientated; seating 700, it consisted of aisled nave with transepts, apsidal chancel, and north-east chapel. In 1926 a memorial hall was opened, on an adjacent site to the west which had been bought five years earlier.

The mission church of St. Peter, in the charge of St. Michael-at-Bowes (Southgate), was established in 1883, on the corner of Bounds Green and Brownlow roads.[77] A brick building in the Early English style, with chancel and nave, it later became the church of *ST. GABRIEL* and was turned into a parish hall in 1906, on the consecration of part of a new church on the south side of Bounds Green Road. In that year a consolidated chapelry was formed out of St. Michael's, Wood Green, St. Michael-at-Bowes, and St. Paul's, New Southgate.[78] The new church, designed by E. B. Carter, was of red brick with stone dressings, in a late Gothic

style, and was not orientated; after the 'east' end had been consecrated in 1915, it accommodated 600 and consisted of undivided aisled nave and chancel and south-east chapel, all plastered internally. Fittings included a 19th-century pulpit, lectern, and choir-stalls from St. Paul, Great Portland Street, and an ancient processional cross, of Russian design but unknown origin, which had been given to St. Peter's mission. A church hall to the west, on the corner of Durnsford Road, was opened in 1937.

In 1899 the London Diocesan Home Mission established a district which was served by an iron church in Philip Lane. A permanent church, dedicated to *ST. PHILIP THE APOSTLE*, was founded in 1906 on the east corner of Clonmell Road and Philip Lane.[79] A consolidated chapelry, from the parishes of Holy Trinity and Christ Church, was formed in 1907,[80] and the bishop of London became patron of the living.[81] The new church, of red brick with stone dressings, was designed by J. P. Cutts in the Perpendicular style; it was not orientated and consisted of an aisled nave, a chancel, which was finished in 1911, and a south-east chapel, and seated 800. There were plans for a north-west tower, of which only the first stage was completed. The organ came from St. Philip, Clerkenwell.[82] A yellow-brick church hall was built to the west, near Spur Road.

In 1902 the London Diocesan Home Mission established a district at Chitts Hill, with an iron church near the top of Wolves Lane to serve the new housing estates on the slope to the south. A permanent church, dedicated to *ST. CUTHBERT*, was consecrated in 1907,[83] when a consolidated chapelry was created out of the parishes of All Hallows and St. Michael, Wood Green, the patron being the Church Pastoral Aid Society.[84] The church, of red brick with stone dressings, was designed by J. S. Alder in a Decorated style; its west end was completed in 1930, leaving a church shorter than the one originally planned and consisting of an aisled nave with arcades of stone, chancel, north-east chapel,[85] and transeptal vestry and organ-chamber. There was seating for *c*. 300 in 1973. A hall was built to the east in 1923 and, although intended to be temporary, was remodelled in 1965.[86]

Services for residents around Walpole Road were held in a priest's house from 1908 and afterwards in an iron church, until the consecration of *ST. BENET FINK* in 1912. The new church was designed by J. S. Alder and paid for by funds from the sale of the City church of St. Peter-le-Poer, London (demolished 1908) which itself had replaced St. Benet Fink, London (demolished 1844).[87] A consolidated chapelry, taken from the parishes of All Hallows, Christ Church, and St. Mark, was formed in 1912,[88] and the patronage was vested in the chapter of St.

[68] Inscription on building.
[69] Ex inf. the vicar.
[70] *Builder*, xl. 380.
[71] *58th Rep. Eccl. Com.* [Cd. 2859], p. 66, H.C. (1906), xxvi.
[72] *Crockford* (1907).
[73] *T.L.M.A.S.* xviii(2), no. 171.
[74] Except where otherwise stated, the para. is based on *St. Saviour's Ch., 50 Yrs. of Progress* [booklet, 1950].
[75] *57th Rep. Eccl. Com.* [Cd. 2411], p. 56, H.C. (1905), xxiii.
[76] *Crockford* (1907).
[77] Except where otherwise stated, the para. is based on *St. Gabriel's Ch. . . . Diamond Jubilee 1905–65* [souvenir brochure].

[78] *59th Rep. Eccl. Com.* [Cd. 3377], p. 60, H.C. (1907), xx.
[79] Fisk, *Tottenham*, ii. 251.
[80] *60th Rep. Eccl. Com.* [Cd. 3953], p. 54, H.C. (1908), xxiv.
[81] *Crockford* (1915).
[82] Fisk, *Tottenham*, ii. 251; *T.L.M.A.S.* xviii(2), no. 178.
[83] *St. Cuthbert's . . . Jubilee Brochure, 1907–57.*
[84] *60th Rep. Eccl. Com.* [Cd. 3953], p. 54, H.C. (1908), xxiv.
[85] *T.L.M.A.S.* xviii(2), no. 231.
[86] Ex inf. the vicar.
[87] Fisk, *Tottenham*, ii. 243.
[88] *66th Rep. Eccl. Com.* [Cd. 7301], p. 59, H.C. (1914), xxv.

Paul's.[89] The new church, near the junction of Walpole Road and Lordship Lane, was built of brick with stone dressings, and was not orientated; it had seating for 750, and consisted of aisled nave, double transepts, chancel, and chapel. The rosewood organ case came from St. Peter-le-Poer, as did the communion plate.[90] A brick hall was built to the north-west c. 1924.[91]

The mission church of St. Hilda, on the corner of White Hart Lane and Great Cambridge Road,[92] was established by the London Diocesan Home Mission in 1926. It was replaced in 1939 by the church of *ST. JOHN THE BAPTIST*, Great Cambridge Road, designed by Messrs. Seely and Paget and largely paid for by the sale of St. John the Baptist, Great Marlborough Street (demolished 1937).[93] The church, which has an aisled nave, chancel, and north-west chapel, is of red brick and concrete, with some copper cladding and tiled roofs. The complex west front, centred on a semi-circular portico enclosing a statue of the Baptist, conceals a shed-like main building. A pantile-roofed hall was built behind the church, in Acacia Avenue.[94] The patron was the rector of St. James's, Piccadilly, London, who had earlier been patron of the Great Marlborough Street church.[95]

ROMAN CATHOLICISM. Recusants from Tottenham were indicted for a decade after 1583, numbers reaching as many as ten in 1592.[96] The most prominent were William Vaux, Lord Vaux of Harrowden, freed from the Fleet after harbouring Edmund Campion, and his sons Henry and George.[97] Vaux, although confined to a house which he rented in Hackney, was often described as of Tottenham and was apparently the centre of a circle which extended into that parish.[98] Papists said to be resident included two gentlemen, Andrew Mallory and Ferdinando Parris, and their wives. After further indictments in 1608 and 1640,[99] no Roman Catholics were recorded until the end of the 18th century.

French émigrés under Father, later Cardinal, Cheverus[1] opened a chapel in Queen Street in 1793, thereby starting the revival of Roman Catholic worship on the northern fringe of London.[2] Bishop John Douglas, vicar apostolic of the London district, estimated that nearly 100 people attended in 1796,[3] the year of Cheverus's departure for America. The chapel, dedicated to St. Francis de Sales, was rebuilt in Chapel Place, White Hart Lane, in 1826 and reopened in 1827, when a school was established near by.[4] In 1840 the congregation, normally small, was swollen every summer by Irish workers; in 1851 the average attendance was estimated at 200 in the morning and 100 in the evening.[5] From the 1860s Archbishop, later Cardinal, Manning preached annually at the chapel, in aid of the school.[6] Services were transferred in 1882 to a new school in Brereton Road, where a partition between schoolroom and chapel was removed on Sundays;[7] the old chapel was then sold, although the building survived, as a blouse factory, for at least 30 years.[8] In 1895 another church of St. Francis de Sales, designed some 7 years earlier by J. and B. Sinnott of Liverpool,[9] was opened between the school and High Road, at the south corner of Brereton Road.[10] In 1972 it was a yellow-brick building, decorated with red bricks and stone dressings, in the Gothic style; work on a new sanctuary and entrance had been completed in 1967, and there was seating for 500.

At Wood Green the church of St. Paul was established in Station Road in 1882[11] and certified in 1884.[12] A new brick church, designed by E. Goldie in the Romanesque style,[13] was registered in 1904[14] and in turn gave way to a striking building designed by John Rochford, of Sheffield, which was opened in 1971. The building, of white roughcast and brick, has seating for 600; it is roughly triangular, with a side-chapel and a corridor-porch containing glass from the old church, and adjoins a parish hall.[15]

In the south Jesuits established a college at Stamford Hill in 1894[16] and registered the chapel of St. Ignatius, on the west side of High Road, in 1896.[17] The chapel, designed by Benedict Williamson,[18] was replaced in 1903[19] by a massive structure which served both the parish and the college.[20] The new church, also by Williamson, was built of greyish-purple brick with stone dressings in the style of a Spanish Romanesque cathedral. It is cruciform in plan, with a choir and aisled nave supported by flying buttresses and two towers facing High Road.[21]

Roman Catholics at West Green worshipped either at Wood Green or Stamford Hill until 1927, when they opened a wooden church at no. 370 West Green Road.[22] The building was enlarged in 1953 and moved a few yards to the west in 1958 to make way for the brick and concrete church of St. John Vianney, which was opened in 1959 and consecrated in 1964. The new church held 480 people in 1972, when the old wooden church served as a parish hall.[23]

The chapel of St. Bede, at the corner of Compton Crescent and White Hart Lane, was built and registered,[24] as part of a private school, in 1938. After closure during the Second World War the school was reopened by Jesuits and later made an

[89] *Crockford* (1915).
[90] *T.L.M.A.S.* xviii(2), no. 172; Fisk, *Tottenham*, ii. 243.
[91] Ex inf. the vicar.
[92] *Crockford* (1926).
[93] Bruce Castle Mus., 984/1 [newspaper cuttings].
[94] *T.L.M.A.S.* xviii(2), no. 174.
[95] *Crockford* (1907, 1969–70).
[96] *Mdx. Cnty. Recs.* i. 144, 209.
[97] *Complete Peerage*, s.v. Vaux.
[98] G. Anstruther, *Vaux of Harrowden*, 149.
[99] *Mdx. Cnty. Recs.* i. 144, 167, 173, 209; ii. 35; iii. 153, 158.
[1] *Dictionnaire de Biographie Française*, viii. 1090.
[2] Except where otherwise stated, the para. is based on Robinson, *Tottenham*, ii. 300–1, and on inf. supplied by Revd. V. McCarthy, rural dean.
[3] W. M. Brady, *Episcopal Succession*, iii. 180.
[4] See p. 367.
[5] H.O. 129/137/2/1/7.

[6] Bruce Castle Mus., 984/3 [newspaper cutting, 1875].
[7] G.R.O. Worship Reg. no. 26023; Ed. 7/88 (inc. plan).
[8] Fisk, *Tottenham*, i. 128.
[9] *Architect*, xl. 293; *Building News*, lxix. 556.
[10] G.R.O. Worship Reg. no. 35066.
[11] *Catholic Dir.* (1970).
[12] G.R.O. Worship Reg. no. 27661.
[13] *Builder*, lxxxv. 316.
[14] G.R.O. Worship Reg. no. 40682.
[15] Ex inf. the par. priest.
[16] *Catholic Dir.* (1970).
[17] G.R.O. Worship Reg. no. 35218.
[18] *Building News*, ci. 403.
[19] G.R.O. Worship Reg. no. 39677.
[20] See p. 372.
[21] *Building News*, ci. 403.
[22] G.R.O. Worship Reg. no. 50808.
[23] Ex inf. the par. priest.
[24] G.R.O. Worship Reg. no. 58067.

annexe to St. Thomas More's secondary school. No classes were held there in 1972, when the building, a plain yellow-brick hall, was used solely for Sunday Mass and served from St. Francis de Sales.[25]

At the suggestion of Cardinal Manning a group of Servite Sisters settled in Suffolk Lodge, on the south side of St. Ann's Road, in 1871. The house, which formed the nucleus of St. Mary's Priory, was re-fronted in 1876 and the neighbouring Priory Villa and Leamington House were acquired in 1878. A chapel was begun in 1880 and opened in 1883; it was enlarged in 1906, when the priory too was extended, with an eastern wing. In 1972 there were 42 sisters, some of whom taught at St. Mary's school and others farther afield; the community also included nurses, retired sisters, and novices.[26]

Marist Sisters opened a convent next to the church of St. Francis de Sales in 1888. The convent, which for a time contained an orphanage and a school, closed between 1913 and 1922.[27]

In 1903 the Daughters of Providence, from France, acquired their first English premises by leasing a house in Ruskin Road, Tottenham. Encouraged by the Revd. John Nicholson, of St. Paul's, Wood Green, they moved to Broseley Villas, Bounds Green Road, and opened a school there in 1905. They moved again in 1907, to two large houses in Stuart Crescent, where they later rented two more houses and in 1921 they bought the Brabançonne, a house in spacious grounds at the corner of Wood Green High Road and Earlham Grove, as a senior school. On the building of a new school in 1926, the Brabançonne became a convent house for the nuns.[28]

PROTESTANT NONCONFORMITY. Two former vicars of Tottenham, Gaspar Hickes and William Bates, were expelled from their livings at St. Dunstan-in-the-West, London, and Landrake (Cornw.) in 1662. At least two other ejected ministers settled in the parish,[29] perhaps attracted there by a body of dissenters which numbered 43 in 1676.[30]

Most of the early sectaries were probably Quakers, who were strong in eastern Middlesex.[31] In 1689 Bridget Austell moved her school from Southgate to Tottenham High Cross, where George Fox often stayed during the following fifteen months. Fox preached at large meetings and attributed the size of one to the attendance of many Londoners.[32] By 1712 there were two Quaker boarding schools and the number of Friends was increasing, partly, it was claimed, because of intemperate attacks by the vicar and others upon the former Anglican divine, Richard Claridge, who kept one of the schools and refused to pay tithe.[33] After a succession of houses

had been licensed for worship,[34] the site for a permanent meeting-house was bought, with help from the Six Weeks' Meeting, in 1714. Quakers continued to flourish during the 18th century, when Tottenham gradually replaced Enfield as the centre for the monthly meeting.[35] Their meeting-house was apparently the only fixed place of worship for non-conformists in the parish until the 1790s and they remained the largest sect, with some eminent members, although by 1810 they were said to be diminishing.[36] During the 19th century there was never more than one meeting-place, which in 1840 drew part of its attendance from outside the parish.

Independents were prominent in the general revival of nonconformity in the late 18th century. They were licensed to use a house near the Black Bull in 1791 and one at Tottenham Hale in 1798. Another house at Tottenham Hale, no. 6 Down Row, was registered in 1828 and an outbuilding near the tile-kilns in Green Lanes was registered in 1849.[37] Thereafter places certified by Independents became known as Congregational churches.[38]

Wesleyan Methodists,[39] who arrived between 1766 and 1790,[40] registered a place of worship in 1795. Their numbers rose but slowly, despite the opening of a Sunday school, the building of a larger chapel near Bruce Grove in 1818, and an influx of Wesleyans from Nottingham to work in a new silk-factory.[41] Attendance figures in 1851 showed that growth had remained modest, perhaps because of competition from the Baptists and other stricter sects.

Baptists[42] in 1823 were served by itinerant preachers at a private house. In 1825, with help from Miss Dermer of Coleraine House and Joseph Fletcher of Bruce Grove, a large chapel was built in High Road. Thereafter expansion was rapid: Baptists certified no. 2 Brook Place in 1830[43] and Fletcher, on behalf of 'Calvinists' or 'Evangelicals', certified a building at West Green in 1837, as well as rooms at Wood Green in the same year,[44] at William Place in 1838, at Scotland Green and Queen Street Terrace in 1839,[45] and at the Lancasterian school in 1851.[46] Meanwhile Particular Baptists had registered a building in High Road in 1824.[47] Despite the number of places of worship for Baptists, attendance at Tottenham Baptist church alone in 1851 was more than double that at the Wesleyan services.

The Brethren[48] began to meet in Stoneley South in 1838, shortly before a chapel in Brook Street was opened by the brothers Robert and John Eliot Howard. The Brethren were strengthened by secessions from the Society of Friends and in 1840 both sects were singled out, with the Wesleyans and Baptists, as the principal nonconformists in the parish.[49] Guided by the Howards, Brook Street chapel played an important part in the Brethren

[25] Ex inf. Revd. V. McCarthy.
[26] Ex inf. Sister M. Cuthbert, O.S.M.
[27] Fisk, *Tottenham*, i. 128; *Kelly's Dir. Mdx.* (1890, 1908); see p. 376.
[28] Ex inf. Sister Mary Agnes; *Daughters of Providence* [booklet, 1953].
[29] *Calamy Revised*, ed. Matthews, 35, 43, 260, 291.
[30] William Salt Libr. Stafford, Salt MS. 33, p. 40.
[31] W. Beck and T. F. Ball, *Lond. Friends' Meetings*, 295.
[32] *Short Jnl. and Itinerary Jnls. of Geo. Fox*, ed. N. Penney, 200, 207, 214–15, 217, 220–1.
[33] J. Besse, *Life and Posthumous Works of Ric. Claridge* (1726), 198–294; see p. 375.
[34] For fuller details on the Soc. of Friends, see p. 358.
[35] Beck and Ball, op. cit. 301.
[36] Guildhall MSS. 9557, 9558.
[37] Ibid. 9580/1, /2, /6, /9.
[38] G.R.O. Worship Reg. nos. 16170, 18781.
[39] See p. 358.
[40] Guildhall MS. 9558.
[41] *St. Mark's Meth. Ch. 1867–1967* [centenary booklet].
[42] See p. 360.
[43] Guildhall MS. 9580/6 f. 286.
[44] Ibid. 9580/7 ff. 255, 286.
[45] Ibid. 9580/8 ff. 12, 41–2, 53.
[46] Ibid. 9580/9 f. 103.
[47] Ibid. 9580/5.
[48] See p. 361.
[49] Robinson, *Tottenham*, ii. 302.

movement, as did the congregations at Clapton and Hackney, and included several distinguished members in the late 19th century.

Undesignated dissenters registered houses at Tottenham in 1807 and at Tottenham Hale, where Robert Martin styled himself minister, in 1820.[50] They also registered rooms at Wood Green in 1829 and in White Hart Lane in 1835 and a house at Tottenham Terrace in 1844.[51] Such places were the forerunners of many halls and lodgings which became places of worship, often briefly, in the late 19th and 20th centuries.

As the population increased rapidly from the 1860s, the larger sects began to expand, opening new chapels and often rebuilding existing ones.[52] In 1867 Wesleyan Methodists replaced their chapel with a larger one and in 1871, in the newly suburban Wood Green, they began the first of 50 churches to be promoted by a building fund for the London area.[53] In the 1870s it was noted in local newspapers that Wesleyans, like Presbyterians, erected unusually grand churches, since they could call on outsiders to contribute.[54] Chapels were registered in south Tottenham in 1882 and near Alexandra Park in 1891. Finsbury Park and Wood Green became an independent circuit, formed out of Highbury, in 1875, and when St. George's chapel, Bowes Park (Edmonton), was bought by the Methodists in 1901, it was entrusted to Trinity chapel, Wood Green.[55] Tottenham meanwhile became the head of a large circuit, stretching from Seven Sisters Road to as far north as Cheshunt (Herts.) in 1896, and was credited with one of the most active communities in north London, despite a lack of wealthy residents.[56] Primitive Methodists, after registering rooms in 1854 and 1861, opened four chapels between 1872 and 1900: in Northumberland Park, in West Green Road, in Station Road, Wood Green, and in St. John's Road, south Tottenham. In 1903 Wesleyan Methodists alone formed the second largest nonconformist group in Tottenham with a total Sunday attendance of 1,287, and the largest in Wood Green, with an attendance of 1,487.[57] United Methodist churches were registered in High Road, south Tottenham, in 1909 and the Avenue, Bruce Grove, in 1910.

Baptists, too, spread from Tottenham High Road over the rest of the parish.[58] A group which was meeting at West Green by 1862 opened a chapel in 1865 and became responsible in the 1880s for missions in Dagmar Road (Hornsey) and Avenue Road. Meanwhile Wood Green Baptist church was founded by a group formed in 1865 and, in the extreme south, Woodberry Down church opened in 1883. A second church at Wood Green arose from meetings begun in 1892 by Baptists from Hornsey, who in 1902 found a permanent home in Westbury Avenue. A third church, registered in Palace Road by seceders from Wood Green Baptist church, proved short-lived. Strict Baptists began to assemble

near the high cross in 1884 and moved to Napier Road in 1887. Another group, meeting by 1886, registered a chapel in Park Ridings, Wood Green, in 1892, seventeen years before seceders opened a chapel in Eldon Road, off Lordship Lane. Baptists formed Tottenham's largest sect in 1903, with a total Sunday attendance of 1,559.[59]

Although earlier meetings of Independents had died out, Congregationalists established themselves in both Wood Green and Tottenham.[60] Wood Green Congregational church was registered in 1864, by a group formed in 1861, and in Tottenham High Road, previously served by Edmonton, services began in 1866, two years before the opening of High Cross Congregational church. Ambitious building plans at first brought financial crises and changes of minister, Wood Green in 1873 being held up in the press as an example of the dangers of too small a pastorate; both churches, however, were popular and ultimately successful. In the south a mission hall in St. Ann's Road was opened in 1880 under the direction of a large church at Stamford Hill. The southwest was served by Harringay church and the northwest by Bowes Park church, both registered in 1902, and the extreme west by Alexandra Park church, opened in 1907. Presbyterians,[61] who had appeared by 1863, registered a church in Tottenham High Road in 1866 and a flourishing one at Wood Green in 1879.

The number of places registered for nonconformist worship rose steadily between 1850 and the First World War: four between 1852 and 1859, eight in the 1860s, nine in the 1870s, 12 in the 1880s, 13 in the 1890s, and 31 from 1900 until 1915.[62] In 1903 over half of one Sunday's 16,863 worshippers in Tottenham were nonconformists, Anglicans accounting for only 5,076 and Roman Catholics for 2,273; among Wood Green's 11,580 worshippers the nonconformist proportion was still higher, for 3,260 were Anglican and no more than 822 Roman Catholic. Tottenham, however, had a very poor record of attendance in general; its ratio of 1 in 6.06 was the lowest in outer London, below that of Stepney and comparable with that of Battersea or Shoreditch.[63]

The Salvation Army appeared in 1884 and was quickly followed by more groups of Brethren.[64] In 1903 the Salvation Army drew total Sunday attendances of 1,128 in Tottenham, where it had the third largest nonconformist congregation, and 1,012 in Wood Green, where it had the fourth largest.[65] Wood Green attracted many sects previously unrepresented in the area, the better-known ones including Unitarians from 1894, the Catholic Apostolic Church from 1906, and Welsh Calvinistic Methodists by 1915. A building at Downhills, West Green, registered in 1883, proved to be the forerunner of many halls opened by undesignated Christians. West Green hall was built in 1901 and run by the Robins Mission, itself later absorbed by the interdenominational London City Mission

[50] Guildhall MSS. 9580/3, /5.
[51] G.R.O. Worship Returns, Lond. dioc. nos. 1642, 1877, 2188.
[52] See below.
[53] Inscription on building.
[54] Bruce Castle Mus., 984/52, /55, /57 [newspaper cuttings].
[55] J. G. Beauchamp, Trin. Wesl. Ch. Wood Green, 1872–1922 [jubilee souvenir].
[56] Bruce Castle Mus., 984/55 [newspaper cuttings].

[57] Mudie-Smith, Rel. Life, 403, 406.
[58] See below.
[59] Mudie-Smith, Rel. Life, 403, 406.
[60] See p. 361.   [61] See p. 362.
[62] The figures, based on G.R.O. Worship Reg., include a few places that were registered more than once.
[63] Mudie-Smith, Rel. Life, 18, 339–40, 403, 406.
[64] For the halls mentioned in the following three paras. see below.
[65] Mudie-Smith, Rel. Life, 403, 406.

which opened its first Tottenham meeting-place in 1912. Quakers began meeting at Wood Green in 1904 but at Tottenham numbers declined during the later 19th century, in contrast to the trend among nonconformists in general and among Quakers elsewhere.

After the First World War most of the established denominations concentrated on improving their existing premises, although the building of the White Hart Lane estate brought the Wesleyans to Gospatrick Road in 1931. The London City Mission continued its work, with three new halls in 1930, and took over the Robins Mission's rebuilt West Green hall in 1938.[66] Spiritualists, who were to flourish during the Second World War, were again recorded from 1926, and newcomers included the Elim Foursquare Gospel Alliance by 1929 and Jehovah's Witnesses by 1938. In the 1930s the movement of many inhabitants to more modern suburbs eventually led to the closure of Tottenham's Presbyterian church.

Since 1945 many of the older churches have been rebuilt or altered to accommodate smaller numbers, while others have closed. Wood Green's Presbyterians amalgamated with nearby Congregationalists in 1950, preceding the general union of their denominations by 22 years. Congregationalists also gave up the oldest nonconformist church in Wood Green a few years later and the Unitarians closed their premises in 1966. Methodists, after rebuilding St. Mark's, sold three churches between 1969 and 1971. The London City Mission opened a new hall in 1951 but the most striking progress was made by newcomers, often American based, or, in the 1960s, by sects which appealed to West Indian immigrants; they included Jehovah's Witnesses, Seventh Day Adventists, Assemblies of God, and several Pentecostal groups.

SOCIETY OF FRIENDS. Tottenham meeting-house, the first permanent meeting-place for dissenters in the parish, was built in 1714,[67] although the project had been considered in 1706.[68] Various houses had previously been licensed for worship: one of Francis Clare near the pound in 1698,[69] one belonging to Richard Claridge in 1707 and 1712, and one belonging to Alice Hayes in 1714.[70] The meeting-house occupied a plot with a frontage of 50 ft. along High Road, immediately north of Sanchez's alms-houses, and was enlarged in 1777. Prominent local Quakers included Thomas Shillitoe (1754–1836), an evangelist who travelled much abroad, Mrs. Priscilla Wakefield (1750–1820), author, philanthropist, and one of the first promoters of savings banks,[71] and the

Forster family, particularly active in education.[72] Part of an adjoining orchard was bought from Shillitoe in 1803, as an addition to the burial ground, and building repairs in the 1820s were followed by substantial reconstruction in 1833,[73] which raised the number of seats to 600. About 60 Tottenham families attended in 1840, as well as Quakers from neighbouring parishes.[74] The meeting-house was registered in 1854 as no. 594 High Road[75] and further altered in 1880; a schoolroom was built over a verandah along its main front and railings replaced a wall which had screened it from the road.[76] Attendance figures, however, declined from 156 in the morning and 101 in the afternoon in 1851,[77] to 27 and 78 in 1903[78] and to an average of 32 in October 1914.[79] New first-floor premises on the same site, behind offices and over a supermarket, were opened in 1962. They were designed in yellow brick by H. M. Lidbetter and comprised a roof-top forecourt, schoolrooms, and a kitchen, as well as a large room for worship.[80]

At Wood Green, small meetings were held in Bradley hall, Station Road, from 1904 until 1922.[81]

METHODISTS.[82] St. Mark's (W) church originated in Wesleyans' erection of a place of worship, opposite the George and Vulture, which they registered in 1795.[83] A Sunday school was opened a few years later[84] but there were no more than 37 declared Wesleyans by 1810,[85] when services were thinly attended.[86] A new building was paid for by voluntary subscriptions and registered in 1818, when the membership was 64. It stood behind a burial ground on the east side of High Road, nearly opposite Bruce Grove, and had over 400 seats, although attendance averaged only 150 in the morning and 160 in the evening on Census Sunday in 1851.[87] A larger chapel, dedicated to St. Mark, was opened in 1867, whereupon the old building, to which a hall and classrooms had recently been added, was used solely as a Sunday school until 1880. It was then put to commercial uses and the burial ground built over. In 1904 it was almost completely burnt down. The new chapel (later church) of St. Mark, occupying land on the west side of High Road acquired from the Forster family, was built of undressed stone in 'modernized Gothic', with a tower and steeple. Extensive school buildings were put up at the rear in 1880. Over 500 people attended both Sunday morning and evening services at St. Mark's in 1903. After the steeple had been found unsafe in 1937, shops were built along High Road, with an entrance to the church in the middle of the parade beneath a square tower. During the Second World War land-mines

[66] Char. Com. files.
[67] W. Beck and T. F. Ball, *Lond. Friends' Meetings*, 303.
[68] Soc. of Friends, Friends' Ho. libr., Six Weeks Meeting min. bk. 1704–10, f. 88.
[69] *Mdx. Cnty. Recs. Sess. Bks. 1689–1709*, 193; Beck and Ball, op. cit. 302.
[70] Guildhall MS. 9579.
[71] *D.N.B.*
[72] See p. 375.
[73] Beck and Ball, op. cit. 303–4.
[74] Robinson, *Tottenham*, ii. 297.
[75] G.R.O. Worship Reg. no. 4765.
[76] Print, *c.* 1850, and TS. notes in Bruce Castle Mus., 984/51; photo, 1905, in Friends' Ho. libr.
[77] H.O. 129/137/2/1/8.
[78] All attendance figs. for 1903 come from R. Mudie-Smith, *Rel. Life of Lond.* 402–3 (Wood Green), 404–6 (Tottenham).

[79] Friends' Ho. libr. *Census of Attendance at Meetings* [1914].
[80] *The Friend*, cxx. 744.
[81] G.R.O. Worship Reg. no. 43337; Friends' Ho. libr., Meeting Recs. 9–11; Mudie-Smith, *Rel. Life*, 405.
[82] In the following account the letters (W), (P), and (U) denote former Wesleyan, Primitive, and United Methodist chs.
[83] Guildhall MS. 9580/1.
[84] The sch. was opened in 1797 according to *St. Mark's Meth. Ch. 1867–1967* [centenary booklet], which, however, also says that the first services were held in a barn in 1813.
[85] Except where otherwise stated, the rest of the para. is based on Fisk, *Tottenham*, i. 137, *St. Mark's Meth. Ch. 1867–1967*, and Bruce Castle Mus., 985/55 [newspaper cuttings.].
[86] Guildhall MS. 9558.
[87] H.O. 129/137/2/1/5.

almost destroyed the schools and damaged the church, where the seating was reduced from 750 in 1940 to 662 by 1960.[88] New schoolrooms were opened in 1956 and a reconstructed church, of yellow brick, was opened in 1963. St. Mark's had seating for 244 in 1973.[89]

Trinity (W) church, Wood Green,[90] arose from open-air services which had begun in 1864. In 1868 worshippers occupied a mission room in Finsbury Road and in 1869 they acquired a site on the north side of Southgate (later Trinity) Road, where Trinity chapel was dedicated in 1872. The building was designed by the Revd. J. N. Johnson, a steward of the Highbury circuit; it was of greyish brick with stone dressings, in the Early English style, and prompted a press comment that at Wood Green the Wesleyan chapel looked like a church and the church like a chapel.[91] Seating was increased in 1880, when a new school was built at the rear, and in 1900 three halls were opened. In 1903, with nearly 700 worshippers on Sunday morning and 800 in the evening, there was a larger attendance than at any other nonconformist church in Tottenham or Wood Green. The former Baptist chapel of St. George, Bowes Park (Edmonton), was placed under the care of Trinity church, which contributed to its purchase by the Methodists in 1901.[92] Trinity church itself was sold to the Greek Orthodox Church in 1970.[93]

Northumberland Park (P) church, on the north side of the road almost opposite Worcester Avenue, was founded in 1870[94] and registered in 1872.[95] The building was of greyish-yellow brick, with red-granite pillars by the main door, in a mixture of Byzantine and later styles. Sunday attendances of 101 and 139 were recorded in 1903. It was used by Methodists until its sale to the Calvary Church of God in Christ in 1971.[96]

West Green Road (P) church presumably began as a temporary building, registered in 1877 but no longer used by Primitive Methodists in 1896.[97] A new chapel of yellow brick, with red-brick dressings, on the south side of West Green Road opposite Belmont Road, was founded in 1888[98] and registered in 1894.[99] It had Sunday attendances of 122 and 76 in 1903. The building, which seated 176, was sold in 1969 and used by immigrants as the Derby Hall Christian Assembly room in 1972.[1]

Stonebridge Road (W) church, south Tottenham, a red-brick chapel at the corner of Stonebridge and Highwalk roads, was built and registered in 1882.[2] Sunday attendances of fewer than 100 were recorded

in 1903. Sale of the premises was sanctioned in 1936.[3] The building was registered as St. Andrew's Collegiate church by undesignated Christians in 1954 and was bought by the Church of God in 1967.[4]

Station Road (P) church, Wood Green, was registered in 1882 and had attendances of 44 and 62 in 1903. It was replaced by the Bourne temple, registered in 1908 but no longer used in 1939.[5]

Earlsmead (U) church originated in meetings over a shop in St. Ann's Road, which led to the building of Earlsmead Bible Christian hall, registered in High Road in 1886.[6] Later the hall was also used by Methodists, calling themselves Gospel Christians, from the nearby Westerfield Road hall.[7] The congregation, after joining the United Methodist Free Churches, opened a second chapel in High Road in 1909, whereupon the old one became a schoolroom. Earlsmead United Methodist church was recertified, as Central hall, in 1935.[8] It had seating for 750 and was closed in 1953.[9]

The Avenue (W) church, Alexandra Park, was registered in 1891 but had closed by 1912.[10]

St. John's Road (P) church, south Tottenham, was registered in 1900 and had Sunday attendances of 88 and 106 in 1903. It had closed by 1950.[11]

Miller Memorial (U) church[12] was constituted in 1904, although members met in private houses until the erection of a corrugated iron building in 1905. Three or four years later an appeal was launched for a permanent church in memory of the Revd. Ira Miller, late president of the London Church Extension Committee, and the Revd. Marmaduke Miller, editor of the *Connexional Magazine*. There were ambitious plans for a building in the Renaissance style, with a horseshoe-shaped chapel to seat 800 and nine Sunday school classrooms, at the corner of the Avenue and Mount Pleasant Road. Eventually a stone church in the Gothic style, seating 350,[13] was begun on that site in 1925[14] and registered in 1926.[15] The foundation of a neighbouring church hall, in the Avenue, was laid in 1957.[16]

The Welsh Calvinistic Methodist church, Wood Green, was registered in 1915.[17] The premises, on the north-west side of Palace Road, had previously been used by Baptists.[18] In 1972 they comprised a small building, of brick with stone dressings, and an adjoining hall at the back.

Gospatrick Road (W) church was registered in 1931, four years after Methodists from St. Mark's began to hold services on the White Hart Lane

[88] Ex inf. Meth. Dept. for Chapel Affairs.
[89] Ex inf. the superintendent minister, Tottenham and Stoke Newington circuit.
[90] Except where otherwise stated, the para. is based on J. G. Beauchamp, *Trin. Wesl. Ch. Wood Green, 1872–1922* [jubilee souvenir].
[91] Bruce Castle Mus., 984/57 [newspaper cutting].
[92] G.R.O. Worship Reg. no. 42794.
[93] Ex inf. Meth. Dept. for Chapel Affairs.
[94] Inscription on building.
[95] G.R.O. Worship Reg. no. 21029.
[96] Ex inf. Meth. Dept. for Chapel Affairs.
[97] G.R.O. Worship Reg. no. 23501.
[98] Inscription on building.
[99] G.R.O. Worship Reg. no. 34439.
[1] Ex inf. Meth. Dept. for Chapel Affairs and the superintendent minister, Tottenham and Stoke Newington circuit.
[2] G.R.O. Worship Reg. no. 26579.
[3] Ex inf. Meth. Dept. for Chapel Affairs.

[4] G.R.O. Worship Reg. no. 64673; ex inf. the minister, Church of God.
[5] G.R.O. Worship Reg. nos. 26213, 43323.
[6] Fisk, *Tottenham*, ii. 242; G.R.O. Worship Reg. no. 29365.
[7] See p. 360.
[8] Fisk, *Tottenham*, ii. 242; G.R.O. Worship Reg. nos. 43662, 55914.
[9] Ex inf. the superintendent minister, Tottenham and Stoke Newington circuit.
[10] G.R.O. Worship Reg. no. 32663.   [11] Ibid. 37906.
[12] Except where otherwise stated, the para. is based on Bruce Castle Mus., 984/55 (Miller Mem. Ch. Appeal booklet).
[13] Ex inf. the superintendent minister, Tottenham and Stoke Newington circuit.
[14] Inscription on building.
[15] G.R.O. Worship Reg. no. 50400.
[16] Inscription on building.
[17] G.R.O. Worship Reg. no. 46585.   [18] See p. 361.

estate.[19] The church stood east of the junction with Deyncourt Road and in 1972 was a small brown brick building, seating 200,[20] with a hall at the rear.

BAPTISTS. Tottenham Baptist church,[21] on the west side of High Road, was built by Joseph Fletcher and other subscribers in 1825 and opened in 1826. Previously Baptists had met at the house of Thomas Harwood, near the White Hart, before moving to a coach-house belonging to Miss Dermer. Land for the permanent church was also provided by Miss Dermer, who gave an additional plot for a Sunday school and a minister's house in 1830. The church, a substantial brick building with a porch flanked by Doric columns, was designed by J. Clark.[22] Despite its size, side-galleries increased the accommodation to 900 in 1836. Some 800 Baptists were said to worship there in 1840,[23] although by 1851 the average congregation was 400–500[24] and in 1903, after several other churches had opened, the Sunday attendances were 319 and 353. Further internal alterations, necessitating temporary closure, were carried out in 1875–6; the Sunday school was rebuilt in 1889 and the church itself became the first public building in Tottenham to be lit by electricity in 1907. Tottenham Baptist church, with its seating reduced to 700,[25] was the parish's oldest surviving place of worship, apart from All Saints, in 1972.

West Green Baptist church[26] originated in services which George N. Watson was holding on the Downhills estate by 1862. A permanent site on the east of Blacksop Lane (later Dorset Road), at the junction with West Green Road, was bought in 1864. Salem chapel, built with financial help from Watson, was opened in 1865 but attendance fell on Watson's retirement and the church was reorganized, as Union chapel, in 1869. At about that time an adjoining plot was bought for a Sunday school, although the first classes were held in a room at the corner of Dagmar Road, where a mission operated in the 1880s to serve the nearby Woodberry estate. Classes were held in the church itself shortly before 1886, when the iron Dorset hall was set up to accommodate a Sunday school and mission in Avenue Road. There were Sunday attendances of 141 and 250 in 1903. Despite the hall's closure in 1913, it was not until 1924 that a new Dorset hall was opened, at the rear of the church. Another hall, the Dorset Memorial hall, was opened in 1953. The church itself, a Gothic building of yellow brick with stone dressings, was damaged by fire in 1877; repairs were carried out in 1932 and a glass porch was added in 1968.[27] There was seating for 450 worshippers in 1972.[28]

Wood Green, later Braemar Avenue, Baptist church[29] arose from meetings at private houses, including that of a Mr. Cassini in Finsbury Road,

from 1865, two years before James Pugh had charge of a church in Nightingale Road. After reorganizations under the same minister. land was bought and a church was opened, as Wood Green Baptist chapel, on the west side of Finsbury Road in 1876.[30] Sunday attendances of 153 and 208 were recorded in 1903. The congregation was linked with a mission in Station Road from 1886 until 1907, when both bodies moved to Braemar Avenue. Meanwhile several members had seceded from Wood Green in 1904, to re-form in Palace Road,[31] whereupon the Finsbury Road premises were sold to the Catholic Apostolic Church.[32] In 1908 a new church was opened at the corner of Braemar Avenue and Bounds Green Road and in 1914 Palace Road was reunited with the Wood Green membership, which later changed its name to Braemar Avenue Baptist church. The building, designed by George Baines and Son,[33] was of red brick with white stone dressings; a hall at the back was extended in the 1950s. There was seating for 500 in 1972.

Woodberry Down, the first Baptist church to serve south Tottenham, was built with help from the congregation at Hackney Downs and opened in 1883. The church, on the south corner of Vartry and Seven Sisters roads, was designed by Paull and Bonella as an imposing red-brick building dressed in Bath stone, with rounded staircase turrets at the west end and a central ventilating turret. Rooms were added to the east end in 1912 and the seats were reduced from over 900 to 750 after internal reconstruction in 1954.[34]

Shaftesbury hall, Carlton Road, Bowes Park, was registered in 1885. It had attendances of 78 and 103 in 1903 and was still used by Baptists in 1937 but had been closed by 1954.[35]

Westerfield hall,[36] a former G.P.O. sorting office in Westerfield Road near Seven Sisters station, was registered in 1887 by Gospel Christians.[37] When the congregation started to use Earlsmead hall,[38] the building in Westerfield Road was leased for Baptist worship by a Mr. Eastty, who acted as lay pastor until his retirement. Sunday attendances of 19 and 89 were recorded in 1903. Members were affiliated to Tottenham Baptist church from 1900 but continued to meet at Westerfield Road, where there was seating for 200,[39] until the Second World War. A few Sunday school classes were held after the war before the premises were sold, whereupon the children moved to West Green.

Westbury Avenue church originated in meetings of Baptists from Campsbourne Road (Hornsey) in Turnpike Lane in 1891. They formed a church two years later and moved to Dovecote hall in 1895 and to a new chapel at the junction of Westbury Avenue with Willingdon Road in 1902. There were Sunday

[19] St. Mark's Meth. Ch. 1867–1967; G.R.O. Worship Reg. no. 53122.
[20] Ex inf. the superintendent minister, Tottenham and Stoke Newington circuit.
[21] Except where otherwise stated, the para. is based on Fisk, Tottenham, i. 152, and W. P. West, Tottenham Bapt. Ch. 1827–1952.
[22] Print, 1827, in Bruce Castle Mus., 984/53.
[23] Robinson, Tottenham, ii. 300.
[24] H.O. 129/137/2/3/6.   [25] Bapt. Handbk. (1972).
[26] Except where otherwise stated, the para. is based on Hist. West Green Bapt. Ch. 1868–1968 [centenary booklet].
[27] Ex inf. the sec.
[28] Bapt. Handbk. (1972).
[29] Except where otherwise stated, the para. is based on

W. T. Whitley, Baptists of Lond. 204 and inf. supplied by the sec.
[30] G.R.O. Worship Reg. nos. 19481, 23103.
[31] See p. 361.
[32] See p. 363.
[33] Inscription on building.
[34] Ex inf. the sec.
[35] G.R.O. Worship Reg. no. 29045; Kelly's Dir. Mdx. (1937).
[36] Except where otherwise stated, the para. is based on West, Tottenham Bapt. Ch. 17–18.
[37] Reg. incorrectly as Westfield hall: G.R.O. Worship Reg. no. 30306.
[38] See p. 359.
[39] Whitley, op. cit. 235, 297.

attendances of 119 and 145 in 1903. The chapel was rebuilt, with a hall, in 1930, when the seating capacity was raised from 250 to 300.[40]

Palace Road, Wood Green, contained a small chapel which was registered in 1907[41] by Bowes Park Baptist church, a group which had seceded from Wood Green three years before. The congregation rejoined Wood Green Baptist church in 1914,[42] whereupon the building in Palace Road passed to Welsh Methodists.[43]

STRICT BAPTISTS. Ebenezer Strict Baptist chapel, Napier Road, traced its origins to meetings held at Welbourne hall, near the high cross, in 1884. Worshippers moved to a site in the fork between Napier and Ranelagh roads, north of Philip Lane, in 1887. Ebenezer chapel, registered there in 1898, had Sunday attendances of 65 and 93 in 1903 and seating for 300 twenty-five years later. In 1972 it was a low yellow-brick building, with red-brick decoration.[44]

Park Ridings Strict Baptist chapel, Wood Green, arose from meetings at no. 9 Dovecote Villas in 1886. Two years later worshippers formed a church and in 1892 they registered an iron building on the east side of Park Ridings,[45] where Sunday attendances numbered 71 and 81 in 1903. A new red-brick chapel, seating 250,[46] was begun in 1922 and registered in 1923. It was again registered as the undenominational Wood Green Evangelical church in 1971[47] and used as such in 1972, when a brick and stone hall stood at the corner of Mayes Road and Hornsey Park Road.

Eldon Road Strict Baptist church, Wood Green, was the creation of seceders from Park Ridings, who opened a new church at Dovecote hall, a wooden building in West Green High Road, in 1909. Sunday school classes were also held there until the congregation moved for 14 months to Noel Park school and in 1911 opened an iron church on the west side of Eldon Road. With aid from the sale of Bassett Street Strict Baptist church, Kentish Town, the site was extended and a new church, with a school hall at the rear, was opened in 1936. An additional school hall was opened nearby in 1955.[48] The church, of brick with stone dressings, had seating for 220 in 1972.[49]

BRETHREN.[50] Brook Street chapel was opened in 1839 by Robert Howard and his brother John Eliot Howard, the naturalist,[51] a year after Brethren had begun meeting at the house of Mrs. Sands in Stoneley South. The Howards, who belonged to the chemical manufacturing firm of Howard & Sons, had seceded from the Society of Friends and were

joined in 1839 by their father Luke,[52] the meteorologist. The chapel was thriving in 1840, when it supported a Sunday school;[53] it was attended by about 140 in the morning and 120 in the evening on Census Sunday in 1851,[54] two years after the congregation's Tottenham Statement had rejected the exclusive doctrines of J. N. Darby. Well-known attenders included the zoologist Philip Henry Gosse,[55] who was married from Robert Howard's house in 1848 and was later portrayed by Edmund Gosse in *Father and Son*, the philanthropist Thomas Barnardo, baptized at Brook Street in 1862 at the age of 17,[56] and James Hudson Taylor, promoter of the China Inland Mission. From about 1880 until 1903 assemblies took place in a lecture hall which the Brethren renamed Bruce Grove hall, on the opposite side of High Road, while Sunday school classes were held in the chapel. A schoolroom was built at the back of the chapel to mark its jubilee and an adjoining room for youth-work was put up in 1955. In 1972 the chapel itself was a low yellow-brick building, modernized inside but with its original seating capacity of 200.

Ten worshippers, described as Brethren, attended a 'place of exhortation' at West Green infants' school in 1851.[57] Others, sometimes calling themselves 'open' or Christian Brethren, registered the 'Rest' mission rooms, Station Road, Wood Green, in 1885 (closed by 1960), Wellesley hall, High Road, West Green in 1893, Lordship hall, Lordship Lane, in 1910 (closed by 1954),[58] Woodberry hall, St. John's Road (opened by 1899, closed by 1971),[59] Ringslade hall, nos. 3 and 5 Ringslade Road, Wood Green, in 1928, and a room at 597 Seven Sisters Road in 1931.[60]

CONGREGATIONALISTS. Wood Green Congregational church was registered in 1864,[61] three years after meetings had started in schoolrooms nearby. The building, the first permanent nonconformist church to serve the new houses of Wood Green, was estimated to hold 500 and in 1873 was criticized as too large;[62] in 1903 it had Sunday attendances of 267 and 195. It was classical in style, with round-headed doors and windows, pilasters, and a pedimented front facing Lordship Lane at the corner of Redvers Road. The congregation was united with Harringay Congregational church in 1964, whereupon Wood Green church was acquired by the local authority as an arts centre.[63]

High Cross church[64] was founded largely through the efforts of William John Eales, a wealthy merchant of Bruce Grove and a member of Edmonton Congregational church. Besides hiring a lecture hall for

[40] Ibid. 213, 303; ex inf. Miss B. V. Dainton.
[41] G.R.O. Worship Reg. no. 42190.
[42] Ex inf. the sec. Braemar Ave. Bapt. ch.
[43] See p. 359.
[44] Whitley, *Baptists of Lond.* 232, 297; G.R.O. Worship Reg. no. 36498.
[45] Whitley, op. cit. 239; G.R.O. Worship Reg. no. 33414.
[46] Whitley, op. cit. 303.
[47] Inscription on building; G.R.O. Worship Reg. no. 48790.
[48] *From Dovecote Hall to Eldon Road* [jubilee booklet], 5-10, 14.
[49] *Bapt. Handbk.* (1972).
[50] Except where otherwise stated, the para. is based on Fisk, *Tottenham*, ii. 239; F. R. Coad, *Hist. of the Brethren Movement*, 76-7, 159, 174-5, 222, 301; and on inf. supplied by Mr. H. C. Hitchcock.

[51] *D.N.B.*
[52] Ibid.
[53] Robinson, *Tottenham*, ii. 302.
[54] H.O. 129/137/2/1/9.
[55] *D.N.B.*
[56] Bruce Castle Mus., 985/54 (TS. hist.).
[57] H.O. 129/137/2/4/10.
[58] G.R.O. Worship Reg. nos. 28653, 33655, 44179.
[59] *Kelly's Dir. Stamford Hill and Tottenham* (1899-1900); G.R.O. Worship Reg. no. 49875.
[60] G.R.O. Worship Reg. nos. 51406, 52997.
[61] G.R.O. Worship Reg. no. 16170.
[62] Bruce Castle Mus., 984/57 [newspaper cutting].
[63] Ex inf. Mr. D. C. Prowting.
[64] Except where otherwise stated, the para. is based on D. C. Prowting, *From the Beginning* [High Cross Congreg. ch. centenary booklet, 1966].

services in 1866 Eales was instrumental in enrolling members for a new church in 1867, in starting a Sunday school, and in erecting a church on the east side of High Road opposite High Cross Green. The building was opened in 1868 but its ambitious design, to seat 600, burdened the trustees with debt for over 50 years and contributed to frequent changes of minister in the late 19th century. Sunday school attendance nonetheless rose, necessitating extra classes in the institute in Philip Lane in the 1890s when the church also operated a mission at Page Green.[65] In 1903 there were Sunday attendances of 343 and 704 at the church and 60 and 86 at the mission. Adjoining property along High Road was bought in 1907 and exchanged in 1919 for land behind the church, where two temporary halls were put up. A brick memorial hall was opened there in 1929, after the earlier buildings, one of them later known as the John Williams hall, had been moved. The church itself, a Gothic structure of stone with some ornamental brickwork, was altered internally in the late 1930s. Services were held in the John Williams hall during repairs to the main front after the Second World War and in the memorial hall during work on the ceiling in 1958; the entrance was reconstructed, to provide a vestibule, in 1966. There was seating for 900 worshippers in 1972.[66]

St. Ann's Road mission station was opened in 1878 by members of Stamford Hill Congregational church, Clapton Common. There were 150 sittings in 1895 and 300 in 1951.[67]

Harringay Congregational church[68] originated in a Sunday school started in 1891 in Falkland hall, an upstairs room behind a shop at the south corner of Falkland Road and Green Lanes. Land was bought at the junction of Allison Road with Green Lanes and an iron building was opened there in 1894. It was replaced by a permanent church, opened in 1902, and by a new hall and schoolrooms, built as a three-storey block in Allison Road in 1912. There were Sunday attendances of 341 and 406 in 1903. The church, of red brick with stone dressings and in the Gothic style, underwent major internal reconstruction in 1970, when the seating capacity was reduced from about 650 to 220. All three halls, collectively known as Allison hall, were retained by the church in 1972, although the bottom one had been leased to the government since 1947. In 1969 Harringay Congregational church united with Hornsey Church of Christ. The Hornsey premises, in Wightman Road, were sold and the new church became known as Harringay United church.

Bowes Park Congregational church began as a hall and schoolrooms, registered in 1902, at the corner of Arcadian Gardens and Wood Green High Road. A large red-brick church with stone dressings, adjoining the hall, was founded in 1909 and registered in 1912.[69] After the congregation had united

with that of St. James's Presbyterian church in 1950, the premises became those of the United Church of St. James-at-Bowes.

Alexandra Park (Whitefield Memorial) church[70] was founded by Congregationalists who first met at the house of Dr. Mailer in Alexandra Park Road. Many, before moving to the new suburb, had worshipped at the Whitefield tabernacle, Leonard Street, Finsbury. A building east of the corner with Albert Road was opened in 1907 and members of the Finsbury tabernacle automatically became members of the new church, which at first was called Whitefield tabernacle but was recertified as Alexandra Park Congregational church in 1922.[71] The church, of red brick with stone dressings, had seating for 550 in 1972.[72] A two-storey brick hall was built on the north side in 1932 and a lower hall was added to the back in 1965. Numerous benefactions for the Finsbury tabernacle were transferred to the minister and deacons of Alexandra Park congregation. Eleven charities, regulated in 1958 as the charities of Maria Godfrey and others, produced a gross income of £315 in 1971, when £164 was distributed among four needy parishioners.[73]

PRESBYTERIANS. St. John's church, High Road, north Tottenham, was registered in 1866, three years after services had started in a lecture hall.[74] The building, designed by W. G. Habershon and Pite, had seats for 450. By 1876 St. John's had opened a mission hall in Coleraine Park, which remained in use until 1915 and, as a Sunday school, until 1917.[75] There were Sunday attendances of 137 and 170 at the church and 29 and 57 at the mission in 1903. After the First World War the removal of many members to the outer suburbs reduced the active congregation to about 40 by 1939, when the church was accordingly closed.[76]

St. James's church, Wood Green, was formed in 1875, when the Presbyterian Church of England took over an iron chapel which had been used for four years by the Church of Scotland.[77] There were about 100 members in 1877, when work started on a church in Green Lanes. The new building, of red-brick dressed with Bath stone, was noted for its grandeur. It seated 400 worshippers, apart from those in the galleries, but was soon extended to take 700; in 1902 it had the fourth largest congregation within the London Presbytery[78] and in 1903 Sunday attendances were 585 and 465. In 1950 members united with Bowes Park Congregational church, whose premises they used as the United Church of St. James-at-Bowes.[79] The former Presbyterian church afterwards served as a warehouse and survived in 1974.[80]

THE SALVATION ARMY. In 1884 the army registered an iron hall at Bruce Grove and barracks in

[65] *Congreg. Yr. Bk.* (1895).
[66] Ibid. (1971–2).
[67] Ibid. (1895, 1951).
[68] The para. is based on *Harringay Congreg. Ch.* [booklet, 1932] and inf. supplied by the sec.
[69] G.R.O. Worship Reg. nos. 39000, 45172; inscriptions on buildings.
[70] Except where otherwise stated, the para. is based on *Alexandra Pk. Congreg. Ch.* [booklet, 1970] and inf. supplied by the sec.
[71] G.R.O. Worship Reg. nos. 43416, 48387.
[72] *Congreg. Yr. Bk.* (1971–2).

[73] Char. Com. files. The early hist. of the charities is reserved for treatment in the article on Finsbury.
[74] G.R.O. Worship Reg. no. 17369; Fisk, *Tottenham*, ii. 246.
[75] Ex inf. the librarian, Utd. Reformed Ch. Hist. Soc.; G.R.O. Worship Reg. nos. 23475, 38194.
[76] *Tottenham and Edmonton Weekly Herald*, 27 Jan. 1939.
[77] Ex inf. the librarian, Utd. Reformed Ch. Hist. Soc.
[78] Bruce Castle Mus., 984/52 [newspaper cutting]; *In Memoriam Rev. Duncan Macrae* [pamphlet, 1906].
[79] Presb. Ch. of Engld. *Official Handbk.* (1966–7).
[80] Ex inf. Mr. D. C. Prowting.

Finsbury Road, Wood Green, both of which meeting places had been given up by 1896.[81] The Wood Green citadel, a two-storeyed red-brick hall at the corner of Mayes and Alexandra Park roads, was registered in 1890. It remained open in 1972, as did a similar hall begun in 1891[82] and registered in 1895 for the Tottenham citadel corps at Page Green. From 1900 the army in north Tottenham used Elm hall, in Church Road, before opening a yellow-brick hall on the corner of High Road and Paxton Road in 1908.[83] A fourth hall still used in 1972 was also opened in 1908, at Terront Road, West Green.[84] By 1929 the army had a hall in Perth Road, Wood Green, which had been given up by 1954.[85]

LUTHERAN CHURCH. A group of German bakers settled near south Tottenham during the late 19th century and secured a pastor from the Lutheran Church, Missouri, U.S.A. Holy Trinity, a combined church and school building, was dedicated at no. 53 Antill Road in 1901,[86] registered by Lutherans of the unaltered Augsburg Confession in 1923, and re-registered by the Evangelical Lutheran Church of England in 1948.[87] A porch, vestry, and chancel were added in 1935 but the original seating capacity of 90 remained unchanged in 1972, when the church was a simple red-brick building, with a Dutch gable. A temporary hall was dedicated in 1949 and a permanent hall opened 20 years later.[88]

OTHER DENOMINATIONS AND UNSPECIFIED MISSIONS. The Free Church of England registered St. John Wycliffe's, Tottenham Green, in 1853 but used it only for about eleven years.[89]

A building at Downhills, West Green, belonging to William Tucker, was registered by undesignated Christians from 1861 until 1896 and again, as Downhills hall, from 1896 until 1907.[90]

The Free English Church registered no. 15 Houghton Road, near Seven Sisters station, in 1882 but was no longer there in 1896.[91]

A gospel hall in Southgate Road, Wood Green, was registered by unspecified Christians from 1872 to 1913. A hall at Bruce Grove which was registered by the Gospel Temperance Mission from 1883 until 1896[92] may have been the iron building where the Blue Ribbon Gospel Temperance Mission started its work in 1882. The Blue Ribbon Movement later built Forster hall in Forster Road,[93] registered from 1885 until 1896. Christians who registered a room at no. 1A Woodlands Park Road in 1900 moved to a hall in Clarence Road, West Green, in 1905.[94]

Unitarians formed a congregation at Wood Green in 1890.[95] Four years later they registered Unity hall in Newnham Road, where a new church and hall

were registered in 1902.[96] After the closure of Unity church in 1966, members assembled with the Unitarian Fellowship of Enfield and Barnet at Cockfosters.[97]

The Catholic Apostolic Church, which previously had used premises in Gloucester Road, Holloway, registered the former Baptist church in Finsbury Road in 1906.[98] The church, a brick building with a south-east turret, was vacant by 1965, when it was acquired from trustees by the Greek Orthodox community.[99]

The Robins Mission administered West Green hall, built in 1901 and later bought by the president of the mission, James Hillyer, who helped to pay for its reconstruction as a two-storeyed building in 1930. Hillyer, by will proved 1938, settled the hall on trustees whom he enjoined not to permit High Church practices; he also left £250 a year towards the missioner's salary, £50 a year for repairs, and dividends to be distributed annually in gifts of 10s. among members aged over 70. The property and its endowment were vested in the London City Mission by a Scheme of 1940.[1]

The London City Mission registered its first hall, in Tebworth Road, in 1912. Trafalgar mission hall in Queen Street, off White Hart Lane, was registered in 1930 and replaced by Trafalgar Memorial hall in 1941. A new hall in High Cross Road was also registered in 1930, as was Shaftesbury Memorial hall in Fladbury Road, and a mission in Siddons Road started in 1951. All, except Shaftesbury Memorial hall, were still undenominational meeting-places in 1971.[2]

Spiritualists met at Wyvern House, no. 193 High Road, in 1903, when 46 attended a Sunday evening service. In 1926 they registered Bradley hall, Bradley Park Road, Wood Green, and in 1932 moved to a room in Stuart House, River Park Road, which they had left by 1954.[3] Tottenham and Edmonton Spiritualist church opened in 1929 in Edmonton,[4] whither the Temple of the Trinity for Spiritual Healing moved after three years at no. 371 High Road, Wood Green, in 1941. The Sanctuary of St. Andrew, registered at no. 65 Duckett Road in 1942, had closed by 1964.[5] Wood Green Spiritualist church, unconnected with any earlier group but affiliated to the Spiritualist National Union, was opened in 1953; services were held in a private house, at the corner of Maryland Road and High Road, which could seat 120 in 1972.[6] Spiritualists forming the Mount Zion Church of God began to meet at Crowland Road junior school in 1965[7] and registered no. 192 High Road in 1967.[8]

The Elim Foursquare Gospel Alliance registered Elim hall, a rented room on the first floor of no. 614 High Road, Tottenham, in 1929,[9] soon after

[81] G.R.O. Worship Reg. nos. 28074, 27794.
[82] Date on building.
[83] G.R.O. Worship Reg. nos. 32404, 34578, 37828, 43029.
[84] Ibid. 43230; date on building.
[85] G.R.O. Worship Reg. no. 51757.
[86] Ex inf. the minister.
[87] G.R.O. Worship Reg. nos. 48824, 62136.
[88] Ex inf. the minister.
[89] G.R.O. Worship Reg. no. 952.
[90] Ibid. 14469, 35359.
[91] Ibid. 26105.
[92] Ibid. 20986, 26885.
[93] Fisk, Tottenham, ii. 187–8.
[94] G.R.O. Worship Reg. nos. 29048, 37663, 40852.

[95] Gen. Assembly of Unit. and Free Christian Chs. Dir. (1972–3).
[96] G.R.O. Worship Reg. nos. 34437, 38809.
[97] Unit. Dir. (1972–3).
[98] G.R.O. Worship Reg. nos. 32291, 41895.
[99] Ex inf. Gregorios, bishop of Tropaeou.
[1] Char. Com. files.
[2] G.R.O. Worship Reg. nos. 45516, 52373, 52446, 59716, 64673.
[3] Ibid. 50294, 53671.   [4] See p. 195.
[5] G.R.O. Worship Reg. nos. 59520, 59965, 60291.
[6] Ex inf. the president.
[7] Ex inf. the minister.
[8] G.R.O. Worship Reg. no. 71007.
[9] Ibid. no. 51724.

Pentecostal meetings had started there. It was replaced by Brook hall, Brook Road, Wood Green, which remained in use from *c.* 1930 until 1955, when worshippers moved to Russell Road (Edmonton).[10]

Jehovah's Witnesses registered the first floor of nos. 6 and 8 Westbury Avenue as a Kingdom hall in 1938 and met there until 1953. A hall in Wingmore Road was registered in 1959 and used until 1970. Jehovah's Witnesses still owned the building in 1972, when they were seeking a larger one in the area. Meetings were held at the Adult School hall, Commerce Road, for ten years until 1972, when the congregation had temporarily to share a Kingdom hall which had been opened at no. 5 Glenwood Road in 1970.[11]

The Tottenham Assembly of the Church of God, soon renamed the Redemption Church of God, registered premises in the Crescent in 1962.[12] Ten years later the church occupied a small, part roughcast, hall next to no. 1 the Crescent.

The Church of God acquired the former St. Andrew's Collegiate church, previously a Methodist chapel, in Stonebridge Road in 1967.[13]

The Calvary Church of God in Christ (U.K.) bought the former Methodist church in Northumberland Park in 1971.[14] There was seating for 250 in 1973.[15]

Seventh Day Adventists worshipped in a corrugated iron hall at the corner of Northcott Avenue and Bounds Green Road in 1972.[16]

The New Testament Church of God, whose general headquarters were at Cleveland, Tennessee (U.S.A.), worshipped at no. 628 High Road, a 19th-century house near Scotland Green belonging to the Y.W.C.A., in 1972.[17]

Pentecostal meetings were popular among West Indian immigrants from the 1960s. The groups were often short-lived and, despite their name, were not registered among the Pentecostal churches.[18] In 1972 they included assemblies at Coleraine Park primary school, Downhills school, and Woodlands Park junior school.[19]

GREEK ORTHODOX CHURCHES.[20] Services were held in the Anglican church of St. Mark, Noel Park, from the beginning of 1965 until the former Catholic Apostolic church in Finsbury Avenue was leased later that year. The church, after repairs and internal alterations, still served the Greek Orthodox community of St. Barnabas, Wood Green, in 1972.

Rising numbers led to the purchase of the Methodists' Trinity chapel, Trinity Road, in 1970 and to its elevation to the status of a cathedral under an assistant bishop, of Tropaeou. By 1972, when there were estimated to be 25,000 to 30,000 Greek Ortho-

dox Christians in north London, the Wood Green community had evening and Sunday schools, as well as women's and youth organizations.

JUDAISM. Small meetings were held at a private house in Tottenham Hale until brewers' premises at no. 366 High Road, near the corner of Somerset Road, were occupied by Tottenham Hebrew congregation in 1904.[21] Members of the synagogue came to be affiliated to the Federation of Synagogues.[22] The building could seat 300 in 1972, when there was a separate hall for religious instruction.[23]

Jews in south Tottenham worshipped in private homes and occasionally at Craven Park Road school from 1934 until the opening of a brick building behind no. 111 Crowland Road in 1938. Classrooms were added in 1954 and a communal hall was built in 1961. There was seating for 440 at South Tottenham District synagogue, a member of the United Synagogue,[24] in 1972.[25]

Edmonton and Tottenham Hebrew congregation arose from meetings which were held at no. 53 Lansdowne Road several years before the ground floor of a Victorian house, no. 41 Lansdowne Road, was converted for worship in 1934. The synagogue, whose members came to be affiliated to the United Synagogue four years later, was enlarged in 1956, to bring the seating to about 200, and an adjoining hall and annexe were built in 1964.[26]

EDUCATION.[27] A schoolmaster was recorded from 1580[28] until 1599 and another in 1615.[29] William Bedwell noted, as hearsay, that property at Page Green had been given to maintain a free school, which may mean that Tottenham grammar school existed by 1631, but in 1732, when Nicholas Reynardson's alms-houses were established under his will of 1685, a grammar school was said to have been built since the date of the will. There is no sign that Reynardson's provision for teaching 20 poor children ever became effective.[30] Apart from some free tuition given by Richard Claridge[31] the grammar school, endowed or re-endowed in 1686, alone catered for the poor until the opening of the Blue and the Green Coat schools, girls' charity schools founded respectively *c.* 1735 and in 1792.[32]

Education for the poor was claimed to be adequate in 1819, when Tottenham, with a population of some 5,000, had places for 60 boys at the grammar school, for 40 girls at each of the charity schools, and 100 boys and 100 girls at two recently established Lancasterian schools.[33] By 1835 a further 65 children attended a Roman Catholic school.[34] Churches led in the expansion of public elementary

[10] Ex inf. the sec.-general, Elim Pentecostal Church.
[11] G.R.O. Worship Reg. nos. 58194, 67350, 71293, 72080; ex inf. the branch manager, Watch Tower Bible and Tract Soc. of Pennsylvania.
[12] G.R.O. Worship Reg. no. 68508.
[13] Ex inf. the minister.
[14] Ex inf. Meth. Dept. for Chapel Affairs.
[15] Ex inf. the superintendent minister, Tottenham and Stoke Newington circuit.
[16] Notice by building.   [17] Ex inf. the minister.
[18] Ex inf. Pentecostal Ch. Enquiry.
[19] Ex inf. Haringey L.B., pub. relations offr.
[20] The section is based on inf. supplied by Gregorios, bishop of Tropaeou.
[21] Ex inf. the sec.

[22] *Jewish Yr. Bk.* (1972).
[23] Ex inf. the sec.   [24] Ex inf. Rabbi S. Halstuk.
[25] *Jewish Yr. Bk.* (1972).
[26] Ex inf. the sec.
[27] Except where otherwise stated, the foll. nine paras. are based on G. W. Sturges, *Schs. of Edmonton hund.* and *Willingly to Sch.* (Haringey L.B. Archives Cttee. cat. of exhib. 1970).
[28] Guildhall MS. 9537/4.
[29] *Mdx. Sess. Recs.* ii. 229.
[30] *14th Rep. Com. Char.* H.C. 382, p. 161 (1826), xii.
[31] See p. 356.
[32] For individual schs. see below.
[33] *Educ. of Poor Digest*, 555.
[34] *Educ. Enquiry Abstract*, 582.

education until a rapidly rising working-class population in the 1870s outran their efforts.

The Education Act of 1870, largely the work of W. E. Forster, who had been privately educated in Tottenham, aroused strong local controversy. The vicar of St. Paul's and Fowler Newsam led opposition to the foundation of a school board, with unanimous support from the press. Vigorous fund-raising permitted improvements to the grammar and Blue Coat schools and to most Church establishments,[35] but the doubling of the population between 1870 and 1880 created a deficiency of over 2,000 places. In 1879 the Education Department ordered a local board to be set up.[36]

Tottenham school board occupied hired offices at Coombes Croft until 1900, when it moved to a permanent site in Philip Lane.[37] It remained responsible for the whole ancient parish, although Wood Green became a separate local board district in 1888. Temporary classrooms were rented at once and the first of ten planned new schools, at Coleraine Park, was ready in 1881. The board schools, with boys, girls, and infants on separate floors, had provided over 5,000 new places by 1891. In 1895 there was some demand for the London school board to take over, since the parents of nearly all Tottenham's board school pupils worked in the City, whereupon the local body claimed that its new schools cost £12 a place, compared with £18–£20 for the London school board.[38] The worst overcrowding in 1898 was around Page Green, in the south-east around Stamford Hill, at West Green, and at Noel Park, but in all areas the position had improved within ten years. By 1902, at the end of its existence, the school board had founded 15 new schools, many of them with over 1,500 pupils, and had opened Tottenham's first special school, for the deaf.

In 1903 Tottenham and Wood Green became separate Part III authorities, responsible for elementary education, under the Act of 1902. The education committees of the two councils continued the building programme of the school board, 7 new schools being opened in Tottenham between 1906 and 1912. Poor children had first received school meals at Wood Green, where the penny dinners committee fed 225 on its first day in 1885. At Tottenham, out of 1,187 pupils examined, 979 were found to be undernourished in 1906, a year before the passage of the Education (Provision of Meals) Act, which the committee adopted in 1908. The introduction of medical inspections in schools led to the treatment of over 2,000 extra cases at the Prince of Wales's hospital alone in 1910. An eye clinic was opened in 1911 and dental clinics were started in 1914.[39]

Public secondary education remained the preserve of the old grammar school until 1901, when, in anticipation of the Act of 1902, Tottenham county school was opened as the first co-educational school of its kind in Middlesex. Tottenham high school for girls, owned by the Drapers' Company, was taken over by Middlesex C.C. in 1909 and, like the county school, modelled on the grammar school. All

Tottenham's secondary education was then provided by those three schools and by the Roman Catholic St. Ignatius's college, which received public grants from 1906. Wood Green's needs had been partly met in 1884 by the opening of Higher Grade schools; from 1910 they competed with a new secondary school in Glendale Avenue, and eventually they were replaced by Trinity county school. Technical education, started in 1892 under the Technical Instruction Act of 1889, developed quickly after the opening of Tottenham polytechnic in 1897.

Under the Act of 1918 Tottenham's education committee opened Downhills, Down Lane, and Risley Avenue as selective central schools, despite the Labour party's opposition on the grounds that such schools, between elementary and secondary, would retard the introduction of a general secondary system.[40] It was not until 1937 that the first nursery school was opened, in Vale Road. Resources were spent mainly on reorganizing elementary schools into senior and junior schools, on the lines of the Hadow Report, and on reducing the size of classes. Although most buildings had been finished by 1912, with classrooms to hold 70 or 80, rapid progress was made under a ten-year plan of 1935: the new Rowland Hill school, made necessary by development around Lordship Lane, was opened in 1938 and 10 old schools had been modernized by 1939.[41]

Under the Act of 1944, Tottenham became an 'excepted district', while Wood Green formed an educational division of the county. Tottenham administered 16,000 children in 1946, when the last all-age county schools disappeared with the reorganization of Bruce Grove, Stamford Hill, and Crowland Road schools.[42] Since the southern part was so densely built up, it was predicted that all the larger schemes, for older pupils, would be carried out in the north.[43] Primary schools themselves were divided, until by 1949 Tottenham had 15 infants' and 14 junior schools, in addition to two junior mixed and infants' schools awaiting reorganization, while Wood Green had 5 infants' and 5 junior schools; there were also 6 Voluntary primary schools in Tottenham and two in Wood Green. Tottenham had 12 secondary modern schools and Wood Green three. Grammar-school education was still provided by four schools in Tottenham and one in Wood Green, while the work of the old polytechnic was continued by Tottenham technical college.

From 1965 education in both Tottenham and Wood Green was the responsibility of Haringey L.B. In 1972 the two former boroughs contained 21 schools for juniors, 21 for infants, and 10 (mostly denominational) for juniors and infants together, as well as 3 nursery schools, 4 special schools, and a school for maladjusted pupils. Secondary education was reorganized from 1967 in order to create comprehensive schools for pupils aged 11 to 18. By 1972 the county secondary schools had been grouped into 7 comprehensive units. Of 5 Voluntary Aided or Controlled schools in that year, the Somerset school contained the old grammar school, St. Katharine's was shortly to be expanded into a Church of England

[35] Nat. Soc. files.
[36] *Lond. Gaz.* 14 Nov. 1879, p. 6425.
[37] Bruce Castle Mus., 951 [TS. notes].
[38] Ibid. 959.
[39] Tottenham educ. cttee. *Annual Rep. of Med. Inspection Dept.* (1910–14).

[40] H. C. Davis, *Three Doz. Yrs., Hist. of Downhills Sel. Cent. Sch.* 6, 10.
[41] Bruce Castle Mus., *Boro. of Tottenham Devel. Plan for Educ. 1946*, 8.
[42] Bruce Castle Mus., *Boro. of Tottenham educ. cttee. min. bk. 1945–6*, 8–9. [43] Ibid. 7–9.

comprehensive, and the upper and lower St. Thomas More schools were to form a single Roman Catholic comprehensive; the fifth school, St. Angela's Roman Catholic, was about to move to Edmonton.[44]

Elementary schools founded before 1879.[45] The Blue Coat school[46] was established by local subscribers c. 1735, as the first school in Edmonton hundred to offer primary education other than of a dame school type to the poor. Presumably it always stood on the east side of High Road at Scotland Green, where Thomas Smith conveyed land to trustees in 1797 and where it was rebuilt in 1833.[47] The new building, in the Jacobean style, contained a schoolroom for 80 children and adjoined a mistress's house. About 40 girls, aged 7 to 14, were clothed and educated in 1833; numbers had risen to 60 by 1840, when a further 10 received instruction alone. A committee of subscribers under the vicar nominated pupils and appointed weekly visitors. The income came mainly from subscriptions, an annual charity sermon, and the girls' needlework.[48] Investments were worth £1,500 in 1840; Thomas Barber, by will proved 1844, left £250 to the school, whose funds had reached £2,000 by 1857.[49] Part of the stock was sold in 1876, after the parish had given the trustees the site of an adjoining watch-house; the blue uniform was thereupon discontinued and the accommodation enlarged to take 120 pupils, as part of the campaign against a school board. The school was converted into Tottenham middle class girls' school in 1886, whereupon modest fees were charged until their abolition by the local education committee in 1903. Attendance for a time remained well below capacity: 56 in 1888,[50] 77 ten years later, when a parliamentary grant was being paid, and 112 by 1906. Places were said to be in heavy demand in 1927,[51] when the premises were condemned as too small, but in 1930 the pupils were moved to All Hallows school. The 19th-century building, converted into shops, survived in 1973.

The Green Coat school,[52] called for many years the School of Industry, was founded in 1792 through the efforts of Mrs. Priscilla Wakefield. It occupied land given by Thomas Smith on the east side of High Road, next to Phesaunt's alms-houses at the corner of Stoneley South, and included a house for the mistress.[53] The curriculum, the sources of income, and the management were similar to those of the Blue school, save that by 1840 funds amounted to c. £700 and the pupils attended Holy Trinity chapel rather than the parish church. There were

then 40 girls, aged 8 to 14, each of whom received a guinea on leaving and triennial awards for staying in the same employment. Thomas Barber left stock worth £250 by will proved 1844[54] and a parliamentary grant was being paid by 1862,[55] when a new building was erected behind the grammar school in Somerset Road. Plans to take fee-payers, who would not receive the green and white clothing,[56] were presumably realized after the move: in 1864, 30 out of 72 pupils did not wear the uniform. Enlargements allowed numbers to rise to 173 by 1898, whereafter attendance varied little until the addition of new classrooms in 1939. The school ceased to be described as a school of industry c. 1907, when it became formally attached to Holy Trinity church. From 1952 it was housed in two buildings, the infants having moved into the old Holy Trinity school by Tottenham Green, and from 1955 it became mixed throughout, boys being admitted from the infants' department. Attendance at the Green Coat school, the oldest in Tottenham, rose to 254 in the 1960s but had declined, after rebuilding around Somerset Road, to 226 by 1972.

A Lancasterian school for boys[57] opened in a barn on the west side of High Road in 1812 and moved in 1822 to a new brick building, accommodating c. 180 with a master's house adjoining, on the south side of Church Road. There were 141 boys in 1820 and 172 in 1840. Management was by a committee of local subscribers, at one time including Albert Hill and members of the Forster family. Pupils were taught under the regulations of the British School Society[58] and were publicly examined yearly. The income came from school pence, supplemented by voluntary contributions and, by 1862, annual parliamentary grants.[59] Two classrooms were added in 1850,[60] enabling attendance to rise to 225 in 1864. Numbers were no more than 169 in 1882,[61] five years before control passed to Tottenham school board, which put up a new building to hold over 1,200 boys, girls, and infants.[62] The building was enlarged to take over 1,700 children from 1905, although attendance was only 1,240 in 1919. The Lancasterian school, divided into junior mixed and infants' schools in 1939, still occupied premises in King's Road in 1973, when there were 350 juniors and 215 infants enrolled.

A girls' Lancasterian school was established in 1815, in a building adjoining a mistress's house at the corner of High Road and Reform Row. Its committee was subject to the managers of the boys' school. The income came from school pence, subscriptions, and small profits from the girls' needlework;[63] in 1840 the girls' school relied on the surplus

44 Ex inf. Haringey L.B., chief educ. offr.
45 In the foll. accounts of individual schools, attendance figs. for 1898 are from *Schs. in Receipt of Parl. Grants 1898–9* [C. 9454], p. 170, H.C. (1899), lxxiv; figs. for 1906 are from *Public Elem. Schs. 1906* [Cd. 3510], pp. 458, 462, H.C. (1907), lxiii; and those for 1919 from *Bd. of Educ., List 21* (H.M.S.O. 1919). Except where otherwise stated, figs. for 1973 have been supplied by the headmaster or headmistress.
46 Except where otherwise stated, the para. is based on Robinson, *Tottenham*, ii. 304–5, Sturges, *Schs.* 155–6, and *Willingly to Sch.* 10.
47 Robinson, *Tottenham*, ii, plate facing p. 304.
48 *Educ. Enquiry Abstract*, 582.
49 Char. Com. files; Ed. 7/87.
50 *Rep. of Educ. Cttee. of Council, 1888* [C. 5804–1], p. 607, H.C. (1889), xxix.
51 Nat. Soc. files.
52 Except where otherwise stated the para. is based on

Robinson, *Tottenham*, ii. 306–7, Sturges, *Schs.* 150–1, *Willingly to Sch.* 11, and inf. supplied by the headmaster.
53 Robinson, *Tottenham*, ii, plate facing p. 306.
54 Char. Com. files.
55 *Rep. of Educ. Cttee. of Council, 1862–3* [3171], p. 455, H.C. (1863), xlvii.
56 Ed. 7/88.
57 Except where otherwise stated, the foll. two paras. are based on Robinson, *Tottenham*, 308–11, Sturges, *Schs.* 158, and *Willingly to Sch.* 18–21.
58 Ed. 7/88.
59 *Rep. of Educ. Cttee. of Council, 1862–3*, p. 455.
60 Ed. 7/88.
61 *Schs. Aided by Parl. Grants, 1882* [C. 3706–1], p. 703, H.C. (1883), xxv.
62 Ed. 7/88; *Schs. in Receipt of Parl. Grants, 1898–9* [C. 9454], p. 170, H.C. (1899), lxxiv.
63 Ed. 7/87.

from the boys' school funds. Attendance was 79 in 1821 and 117 in 1864. After 1887 the school was absorbed into the Lancasterian board school.[64] The building was pulled down c. 1900.

St. Francis de Sales Roman Catholic school originated in a school for boys, girls, and infants opened in 1827 close to the new church in Chapel Place. It had 65 pupils, a master, and a mistress in 1835.[65] A new schoolroom was built in 1858 and enlarged in 1873,[66] four years before classes moved to Brereton Road,[67] where a new building was finished in 1882.[68] At that date school pence, paid by those who could afford to do so, were supplemented by a parliamentary grant.[69] The building comprised a schoolroom, partitioned off from the chapel on weekdays, and a classroom; a separate boys' department was opened in 1885 and an additional schoolroom, for an infants' department, was finished in 1886.[70] The enlarged school had 349 pupils by 1905, but attendance fell to 287 in 1919 and 252 in 1938.[71] The former Marist convent's school was taken over after 1945 and extended in 1958 and 1969. Separate junior and infants' schools were created in 1971; there were 270 juniors and 216 infants in 1972.

West Green British mixed school opened in 1834, in a new building, leased from John Eliot Howard, on the south side of West Green Road. It contained a single schoolroom, although in the 1860s an adjoining room, perhaps part of the mistress's house, was sometimes used. The income came mainly from voluntary contributions and school pence. The school was not recorded after 1872 and presumably was superseded by West Green board school.[72]

All Hallows boys' school, also known as Tottenham National school, opened in 1841 on the south side of Marsh (later Park) Lane, near High Road. The site was leased to the vicar of Tottenham and others by trustees for the Coombes Croft estate.[73] There was a schoolroom for 124 and a house for the master, who in 1848 had an assistant. Attendance was usually low, 55 in 1852[74] and 87 in 1859, until a particularly bad inspector's report in 1871 led to the master's dismissal. The income came from voluntary contributions, augmented by school pence, in 1848; an annual grant was paid from 1862.[75] Formal union with the National Society took place in 1875, in return for help in adding a classroom for 70 pupils. Accommodation was increased to 135 places by 1882,[76] 168 by 1898, and 238 by 1906; thereafter it remained the same for over 30 years, although attendance, which had been full at the turn of the century, fell in the period between the World Wars.[77] All Hallows became a junior girls' and infants'

school after the Second World War[78] and was granted Voluntary Aided status in 1952.[79] In 1971 it was amalgamated with St. Paul's National school to form St. Paul's and All Hallows junior and infants' schools, next door to each other in new buildings on the north side of Park Lane. In 1972 there were 313 infants, most of whom went on to the junior school.[80]

High Cross or Trinity district infants' school opened in 1848 in a building east of the church. The school, later called Holy Trinity school, was linked with the National Society and derived its income mainly from voluntary contributions and school pence before the payment of an annual grant from 1862.[81] There were 76 pupils in 1865 and, perhaps after enlargements, almost a full complement of 105 twenty years later.[82] Numbers thereafter varied very little until the building was condemned in 1924. Land to the south of the church, formerly part of the vicarage garden, was acquired in 1932 and a new school for 120 infants was opened there in that year.[83] The original building, dated 1847, survived in 1972.[84]

Edmonton and Tottenham ragged and industrial school was founded by Dr. Michael Laseron, a German-born convert from Judaism, in 1858. The building, close to Laseron's house in Snells Park, Edmonton, comprised one schoolroom for boys and girls and another for infants. It was vested in Anglican trustees and the income came entirely from voluntary contributions[85] until Thomas Knight left stock worth £331 in 1861. A larger building in Union Row, on the Tottenham side of the boundary, was opened in 1862 by Lord Shaftesbury, as the Ragged and Industrial Home, and in 1865 a wing was added, where orphans could learn printing. The school was furnished with desks by the parish, in efforts to avoid a school board, and moved to Pembroke House in High Road c. 1878, when the old building was auctioned. It closed c. 1890 and Knight's endowment was divided between Edmonton and Tottenham school boards.[86]

The Hermitage school[87] for boys, girls, and infants, later St. Ann's girls' school, opened in 1858 as the first of three schools connected with St. Ann's church and, like the church itself, largely paid for by Fowler Newsam. The building, including a teacher's house, stood on the north side of Hanger Lane, later St. Ann's Road. The school was in union with the National Society and the income, from voluntary contributions and pence, was supplemented by Newsam's family,[88] although an annual grant was made from 1862;[89] Newsam's daughter Mrs. Robins left £1,000 to the school, by will proved 1895.[90] The establishment of St. Ann's

[64] Fisk, *Tottenham*, ii. 173.
[65] *Educ. Enquiry Abstract*, 582.
[66] Ed. 7/87.
[67] Ex inf. the headmaster, St. Francis de Sales jr. sch.
[68] Ed. 7/88.
[69] *Schs. Aided by Parl. Grants, 1882*, p. 703.
[70] Ed. 7/88.
[71] *Bd. of Educ., List 21* (H.M.S.O. 1938).
[72] Ed. 7/87; Ed. 7/88.
[73] Except where otherwise stated, the para. is based on Nat. Soc. files, *Willingly to Sch.* 20, and Ed. 7/88.
[74] *Mins. of Educ. Cttee. of Council, 1852-3* [1623], p. 414, H.C. (1853), lxxix (1).
[75] *Rep. of Educ. Cttee. of Council, 1862-3*, p. 455.
[76] *Schs. Aided by Parl. Grants, 1882*, p. 703.
[77] *Bd. of Educ., List 21* (H.M.S.O. 1919, 1938).
[78] Sturges, *Schs.* 173.
[79] Tottenham educ. cttee. min. bk. 1952-3, 158.

[80] Ex inf. the headmistress, St. Paul's and All Hallows inf. sch.
[81] Ed. 7/88; *Rep. of Educ. Cttee. of Council, 1862-3*, p. 455.
[82] *Rep. of Educ. Cttee. of Council, 1865-6* [3666], p. 560, H.C. (1866), xxvii; *Schs. Aided by Parl. Grants, 1882*, p. 703.
[83] Nat. Soc. files; *Bd. of Educ., List 21* (H.M.S.O. 1919, 1936).   [84] Inscription on building.
[85] Ed. 7/87; Fisk, *Tottenham*, ii. 293-4.
[86] Sturges, *Schs.* 196-8; *Willingly to Sch.* 11-12; Nat. Soc. files (Willow Walk); Char. Com. files; Bruce Castle Mus., Tottenham sales, i. no. 37.
[87] Except where otherwise stated, the para. is based on *St. Ann's Ch. Sch. 1858-1958* [centenary booklet].
[88] Ed. 7/88.
[89] *Rep. of Educ. Cttee. of Council, 1862-3*, p. 455.
[90] Char. Com. files.

boys' school in 1863 and of a new infants' school in 1871 left girls alone at the old Hermitage school. Attendance at the girls' and infants' schools combined rose from 74 in 1865 to 95 in 1870[91] and 287 (18 more than the recognized accommodation) in 1882,[92] but fell to 228 by 1898 and remained at that level twenty years later. Despite rapidly increasing numbers of poor children, in 1870 Matthew Arnold considered the three St. Ann's schools the best in Tottenham and in 1890 they were excused annual inspections by the Education Department. There were long waiting lists in 1918, but the buildings were soon afterwards blacklisted by the Board of Education.[93] Reorganization into a senior school and a junior mixed and infants' school took place in 1934, the seniors using St. Ann's memorial hall until their school's closure in 1939, the juniors and infants taking over all the old school buildings. Additional accommodation was begun in 1958, whereupon the girls' old school became Robins building and the boys' Newsam building, while the original structure retained its name as Hermitage infants' school. St. Ann's school, which was granted Voluntary Aided status in 1951, had 235 children on the roll in 1973.[94]

St. Michael's National school,[95] Wood Green, began c. 1856[96] as a Sunday school in a new building a few yards west of the church. Infants' day classes started in 1859 and the school was enlarged in 1863,[97] ten years before public subscriptions and the gift of a site by Mrs. Bella Goff Pearson of Nightingale Hall led to the opening of a new school for the older children,[98] with separate rooms for boys and girls. The expanded St. Michael's, answering the threat of a school board, was supported by a parliamentary grant, voluntary contributions, and pence in 1874.[99] Matthew Arnold praised it in 1879, and attendance rose from 375 in 1893[1] to 420 in 1898 but fell to 399 in 1919. Boys and girls were placed under a single head from 1908 and were joined by the infants, who had continued to occupy the original premises, in the Second World War. There were 240 children on the roll in 1973.

All Hallows infant's school, founded to provide for infants near the old parish church and in the new populous district of St. Paul's, began in 1862 or 1863 in a room rented by the vicar at the back of Beech House.[2] In 1871 voluntary contributions and school pence supported a certificated mistress. The school, still using private premises, was reconstituted in that year but was not recorded thereafter.[3]

St. Ann's boys' school[4] was built and opened in 1863, chiefly at the expense of Fowler Newsam. It stood north of Hermitage school and was opened as a single classroom for 80. The school was intended for boys who had left Hermitage at 8 or 9 and who could otherwise go only to West Green; being in union with the National Society, it was at first often called Stamford Hill National school. A certificated master was supported by voluntary contributions, school pence, a charity sermon,[5] and, by 1865, a parliamentary grant; in addition the school received £1,200 under Mrs. Robins's will.[6] In the late 19th century it shared the high reputation of St. Ann's girls' and infants' schools. Attendance rose to 95 in 1870 and 121, slightly more than the recognized accommodation, in 1882;[7] in 1898 it was 127, after enlargement to take 145, and in 1919, after further extensions, it was 151. The boys' school was amalgamated with the other St. Ann's schools in in 1934.[8]

Tottenham Wesleyan infants' school opened in 1864, in a schoolroom and two classrooms, under a certificated mistress, and was supported by school pence, voluntary contributions,[9] and, from 1865, a parliamentary grant. The average attendance was 35 in 1865 and 58 in 1870.[10] The school seems to have closed before 1881.[11]

Trinity school, Willow Walk, began when the vicar of Holy Trinity rented premises at West Green c. 1866. In 1873 the building was below standard, when Fowler Newsam offered a new site,[12] but it was enlarged and re-equipped by opponents of a school board.[13] An average of 59 boys, girls, and infants attended in 1878, and 87 in 1882.[14] The vicar's support ceased in 1883[15] but the local board took over the school in 1884.[16] Willow Walk had closed by 1888,[17] presumably because of the opening of West Green board school.

St. Paul's National school[18] for girls and infants opened in 1870, after the vicar had leased a site in Park Lane from the trustees of the Tottenham charity estates. It consisted at first of one schoolroom, used also for Sunday school, adjoining a mistress's house.[19] An additional classroom was built in 1875 and a parliamentary grant was obtained; attendance thereupon rose to 162 in 1878[20] and to 330, slightly more than the official maximum, in 1898. The accommodation had been increased to 351 by 1906 but reduced to 264 by 1919. St. Paul's became a junior mixed and infants' school after the Second World War[21] and was granted Aided status

91 Rep. of Educ. Cttee. of Council, 1865–6, p. 560; 1870–1 [C. 406], p. 503, H.C. (1871), xxii.
92 Schs. Aided by Parl. Grants, 1882.
93 Nat. Soc. files.
94 Tottenham educ. cttee. min. bk. 1951–2, 150; ex inf. the headmaster.
95 Except where otherwise stated, the para. is based on St. Mics. Ch. of Engl. Primary Sch. [centenary booklet 1960].
96 Ed. 7/88.
97 Ibid.
98 Schs. of Tottenham [cat. 1936].
99 Ed. 7/88.
1 Returns of Schs. 1893 [C. 7529], p. 424, H.C. (1894), lxv.
2 Nat. Soc. files.
3 Ed. 7/88.
4 Except where otherwise stated, the para. is based on St. Ann's Ch. Sch. 1858–1958 and Nat. Soc. files.
5 Ed. 7/88.
6 Char. Com. files.
7 Rep. of Educ. Cttee. of Council, 1870–1 [C. 406], p. 503, H.C. (1871), xxii; Schs. Aided by Parl. Grants, 1882, p. 703.
8 See above.
9 Ed. 7/87.
10 Schs. Aided by Parl. Grants, 1865–6, p. 560; Rep. of Educ. Cttee. of Council, 1870–1, p. 503.
11 Ed. 7/87.
12 Nat. Soc. files.
13 Ed. 7/87.
14 Rep. of Educ. Cttee. of Council, 1878–9 [C. 2342–1], p. 958, H.C. (1878–9), xxiii; Schs. Aided by Parl. Grants, 1882, p. 703.
15 Schs. of Tottenham [cat. 1936].
16 Ed. 7/87.
17 Rep. of Educ. Cttee. of Council, 1888–9 [C. 5804–1], p. 607, H.C. (1889), xxix.
18 Except where otherwise stated, the para. is based on Nat. Soc. files.
19 Ed. 7/88.
20 Rep. of Educ. Cttee. of Council, 1878–9, p. 958.
21 Sturges, Schs. 173.

in 1952.[22] It was amalgamated with the former All Hallows boys' school in 1971, to form St. Paul's and All Hallows junior and infants' schools, in new premises on the north side of Park Lane. The old buildings, bought by Haringey L.B., were used by the housing department in 1972.[23]

A new Hermitage school, for infants only,[24] opened in 1871. The chief benefactor, Fowler Newsam, referred to it as his own infants' school in 1873, when he secured a National Society grant for its enlargement. Attendance figures were included with those for the nearby girls' establishment, which was supervised by the same committee. By will proved 1895 Newsam's daughter Mrs. Robins left £800 to the infants' school.[25] After reorganization in 1934 the school formed part of the junior school, although the building retained its name as Hermitage infants' school.

Tottenham Elementary school for boys opened in 1876, in a schoolroom and two smaller classrooms built 15 years earlier. Its foundation was probably a belated move by the churches in the campaign against a school board: the premises were rented from the Wesleyans, the chairman of the governors was a Presbyterian minister, and the secretary was the vicar of St. Paul's.[26] A parliamentary grant was paid in 1878, when the average attendance was 195.[27] The school was closed on or shortly after the establishment of the school board in 1879.

Love Lane infants' school was probably opened by the Society for Promoting Christian Knowledge in 1879,[28] a year after the society founded its Tottenham training college (later St. Katharine's college.)[29] Pupils were transferred to the college's new practising school in 1880, whereupon the premises in Love Lane were hired as a boys' school by the local board.[30]

Elementary schools founded between 1879 and 1903. Tottenham Practising National school was built and opened in 1880 by the S.P.C.K. after the society's training college had moved into new buildings in White Hart Lane. The school was designed both for infants transferred from Love Lane and for upper grade girls.[31] A parliamentary grant was obtained and the total accommodation raised from 435 in 1882 to 486 in 1898, while attendance rose from 355[32] to 398. When the training college changed its name the school became known as St. Katharine's practising school. In 1906, the girls' department was overcrowded and the infants' not quite full. St. Katharine's became a senior girls' school *c.* 1937, providing only secondary education.[33]

Wood Green board school originated in separate boys', girls', and infants' schools, opened 'to supply temporarily the great educational deficiency'. In 1880 the boys met in premises belonging to Wood Green Congregational church, the girls in rooms belonging to the Baptists, and the infants in a temperance hall. A new building was opened in White Hart Lane in 1884.[34] It held 1,256 boys, girls, and infants in 1898 and, as White Hart Lane county school, 1,170 in 1919. After older children had been transferred, new buildings were erected in Earlham Grove and eventually renamed Earlham junior and infants' schools.[35]

West Green board school began in 1881 as a temporary school for 115 boys and moved to a slightly larger iron hall, leased from Primitive Methodists, three years later. In 1886 the boys, together with girls and infants from Willow Walk, moved to a school for some 1,200 pupils in Woodlands Park Road. The new building was similar to Wood Green board school[36] but places were in greater demand, for in 1889 the main hall had to be divided by curtains to provide extra classrooms.[37] West Green was the second most overcrowded school in the old parish in 1898, with 1,239 places for 1,448 pupils, and in 1906, by which time the number of excess pupils had fallen by one quarter. One of the first English experiments in a freer teaching method known as the Dalton plan was begun in the boys' department in 1921 by A. J. Lynch, the author of several works on education.[38] Unlike other county primary schools West Green was not reorganized into separate junior and infants' establishments.[39] In 1972 it still occupied its 19th-century buildings as a junior mixed and infants' school, with 390 pupils on the roll.

Coleraine Park board school, the first of its kind to be purpose-built in Tottenham,[40] opened in 1881, with accommodation for 1,152 boys, girls, and infants.[41] The school was nearly full in 1898 and had 50 pupils too many in 1906 but by 1919 attendance was 100 short of the reduced number of places, 1,092. Separate junior schools for boys and girls were established in 1928, after senior pupils had left, and merged in 1945. Junior and infants' schools, with 417 and 243 pupils on their respective rolls, continued to share the 19th-century building in 1973.

Bruce Grove board school was established, presumably in rented accommodation, by early 1882, when there was one school for 210 boys and another for 184 girls.[42] In 1894 a permanent building for 1,564 boys, girls, and infants opened in Sperling Road.[43] Attendance rose to 1,686 by 1906 but had fallen to 1,124 by 1919. Separate junior and infants' schools were formed in 1946 and shared the original building in 1972, when the infants also used nearby prefabricated classrooms. In that year there were 493 pupils at the junior school and 312 at the infants' school.

Stamford Hill board school in Burghley Road, where a few boys were already being taught,[44] opened for girls and infants in 1882. There were 1,415 pupils in 1888, three years before the opening

---

[22] *Tottenham educ. cttee. min. bk. 1952–3,* 95.
[23] Ex inf. the headmistress; see p. 352.
[24] Except where otherwise stated, the para. is based on *St. Ann's Ch. Sch. 1858–1958* and Nat. Soc. files.
[25] Char. Com. files.
[26] Ed. 7/87; *Schs. of Tottenham,* 29.
[27] *Rep. of Educ. Cttee. of Council, 1878,* p. 958.
[28] Ex inf. the headmistress, St. Katharine's sr. sch.
[29] See below.
[30] Ed. 7/87.
[31] Ed. 7/88.
[32] *Schs. Aided by Parl. Grants, 1882,* p. 703.

[33] See p. 373.
[34] Ed. 7/87; Ed. 7/88.
[35] Mdx. C.C. educ. cttee. *List 1957*; see below.
[36] Schs. of Tottenham [cat. 1936]; Ed. 7/88.
[37] *Willingly to Sch.* 26.
[38] A. J. Lynch, *Rise and Progress of the Dalton Plan,* 133–4.
[39] Sturges *Schs.* 176.
[40] *Willingly to Sch.* 25.
[41] Ed. 7/88; *Schs. Aided by Parl. Grants, 1882,* p. 703.
[42] *Schs. Aided by Parl. Grants, 1882,* p. 703.
[43] Ed. 7/87; *Schs. in Receipt of Parl. Grts. 1898,* p. 170.
[44] *Schs. Aided by Parl. Grants, 1882,* p. 703.

of a separate building for infants. Overcrowding, stimulated by the abolition of weekly pence, reached a peak *c.* 1898, when Stamford Hill had nearly 100 pupils too many, despite being the largest school in Tottenham, with 1,711 places.[45] Pressure had eased by 1906 and accommodation had been reduced to 1,655 by 1919. In 1946 the school was divided into junior mixed and infant's schools, which occupied the old premises in 1972. At that date the juniors' roll numbered 300 and the infants' 180.

Page Green board school for boys, girls, and infants opened in Broad Lane in 1882.[46] It rapidly became overcrowded with the ending of school pence in 1891[47] and had 1,814 pupils in 1893[48] but by 1898, with the establishment of Earlsmead school, attendance had been brought down to little more than the number of places, 1,656. The accommodation thereafter was reduced, to 1,536 by 1906 and 1,465 by 1919. The infants' department closed in 1933,[49] after which Page Green became a mixed secondary modern school.[50] In 1972 the 19th-century buildings were shared by Hornsey College of Art and the new Welbourne primary school.[51]

St. Paul's Roman Catholic school, Wood Green, opened in 1884 in a newly erected iron church in Station Road. A one-storey brick schoolhouse was built behind the church in 1885[52] and the school's income, from pence and voluntary contributions,[53] was supplemented by a parliamentary grant in 1887.[54] The accommodation, initially for 80 boys, girls, and infants,[55] had increased to 223 places by 1898 and 339 by 1906, but had fallen to 280 in 1919. Under a seven-year programme, starting in 1960, the school was completely rebuilt. There were 249 infants and juniors on the roll in 1972.[56]

Noel Park board school opened in Gladstone Avenue in 1889, three years after the board first rented infants' accommodation attached to Wood Green Congregational church.[57] The new building had room for 1,524 boys, girls, and infants in 1898 but an average attendance of 1,803 made it the most overcrowded of all the board's schools. Numbers had been brought down to 1,481 by 1906 and 1,258 by 1919. In 1972 the 19th-century building was still occupied by Noel Park junior and Noel Park infants' schools, which had 552 and 352 pupils respectively.

Bounds Green board school originated in 1888 with infants' classes in the iron Shaftesbury hall in Carlton Road. In 1895 Bowes Park infants' board school, as it was called, was superseded by a new school in Bounds Green Road, where juniors occupied one building and infants another.[58] The infants' department quickly won a high reputation and often gained remission of government inspection, parents being invited to view classes in progress.[59] Bounds Green school had 1,295 places and 1,089 pupils in 1906 but by 1919 there were 1,271 places and only 983 pupils. Seniors were transferred in 1939, after which date the premises were occupied by separate junior mixed and infants' schools; in 1972 there were 472 juniors and in 1973 the number of infants was expected to rise from 295 to 330.[60]

Seven Sisters board school[61] opened in 1889 on an island site bounded by Seaford, Rosslyn, and Braemar roads. There was accommodation for 1,639 boys, girls, and infants in 1898, when the average attendance was 1,843. Numbers had fallen to 1,677 by 1906 but bad overcrowding persisted in 1911, when one girls' class numbered 88 and another 120; in 1919 there were only 1,351 pupils. Older children were transferred in 1934, leaving the building to juniors and infants, who, forming separate schools, still occupied it in 1972. The infants also acquired temporary classrooms in Greenfield Road in 1967 and a new hall there in 1969, and from 1970 some of the juniors were taught in the former Culvert Road school in South Grove. There were 580 children at the junior school and 514 at the infants' school in 1972.

Union Row board school, with accommodation for 400 boys, was opened in 1890, probably as a temporary school. It was less than half full in 1893 and had closed by 1898.[62]

Downhills board school opened in a new building in Philip Lane in 1893, with 1,543 places. It was attended by 1,403 boys, girls, and infants in 1898 and by 1,620 eight years later. In 1913 senior pupils were moved to another new building,[63] where they were later absorbed into Downhills selective central school.[64] The various Downhills school buildings formed the largest such complex in Tottenham in 1919, with 2,293 places. In 1973 the old structure was shared between a junior school, with 370 pupils, and an infants', with 300 pupils.

Alexandra board school, Western Road, Wood Green, began with mixed juniors' and infants' classes in a new iron building in 1894. The accommodation was 569 and the average attendance 311 in 1898. Juniors and infants were provided with separate buildings on the same site three years later.[65] Alexandra school had 1,038 places in 1906, when it was almost full, and 1,209 in 1919, when attendance had sunk to 897. Senior pupils were moved to Bounds Green, Lordship Lane, or Noel Park in 1947. Separate junior and infants' schools, with 230 and 210 pupils on their respective rolls. remained on the premises in 1972.[66]

St. Ignatius's Roman Catholic elementary school was opened by Jesuits in 1895 in a former outbuilding of Burleigh House, adjoining a site which had been bought for St. Ignatius's college in 1894. It did not receive a public grant until 1906 but thereafter expanded rapidly,[67] in a new building shared with the college and accommodating 465 by 1919. In

[45] Ex inf. the headmistresses, Stamford Hill jr. and inf. schs.; *Rep. of Educ. Cttee. of Council, 1888–9*, p. 608.
[46] Ed. 7/88.
[47] *Willingly to Sch.* 25.
[48] *Returns of Schs. 1893*, p. 428.
[49] *Bd. of Educ., List 21* (H.M.S.O. 1936).
[50] Sturges, *Schs.* 105.
[51] Ex inf. the headmistress, Welbourne prim. sch.
[52] Ex inf. the headmaster.
[53] Ed. 7/88.
[54] *Rep. of Educ. Cttee. of Council, 1888–9*, p. 608.
[55] Ed. 7/88.
[56] Ex inf. the headmaster.   [57] Ed. 7/88.
[58] Ed. 7/87; Ed. 7/88.

[59] *Willingly to Sch.* 26–7.
[60] Ex inf. the headmaster, Bounds Grn. jnr. sch., and the headmistress, Bounds Grn. infts. sch.
[61] The para. is based on *Seven Sisters Sch.* [Diamond Jub. booklet, 1949] and inf. supplied by the headmaster, Seven Sisters' jr. sch., and the headmistress, Seven Sisters inf. sch.
[62] *Kelly's Dir. Mdx.* (1890); *Returns of Schs. 1893*, p. 428.
[63] Ed. 7/88.
[64] H. C. Davis, *Three Doz. Yrs.* [hist. of Downhills sel. cent. sch.], 7.   [65] Ed. 7/88.
[66] Ex inf. the headmaster, Alexandra jr. sch., and the headmistress, Alexandra inf. sch.
[67] Sturges, *Schs.* 113–15; Ed. 7/88.

1952 it was reorganized as a junior mixed and infants' school, when older pupils moved to St. Thomas More's, and acquired Aided status.[68] There were 405 juniors and infants on the roll in 1973, when the infants were taught in a new building.

Earlsmead board school, with 1,125 places, opened in Broad Lane in 1897.[69] It had 38 pupils too many in 1906 but obviated overcrowding at Page Green.[70] The number of places had been reduced to 1,093 by 1919. The premises were later shared by separate junior and infants' schools, which amalgamated in 1973 and contained 350 children in 1974.[71]

Gladstone Avenue temporary board school opened in 1898 or 1899 as a junior mixed school. Its new building, leased from the Bishop of London's Fund, accommodated 320. Staff and pupils moved to Lordship Lane council school in 1906.[72]

Woodlands Park board school, St. Ann's Road, opened in 1900[73] to accommodate 1,500 juniors and infants. It was overcrowded in 1906, with 1,678 pupils, and the number of places had been reduced to 1,457 by 1919. In 1972 separate buildings on the same site were used by junior and infants' schools, with 490 and 310 pupils respectively.

Elementary schools founded between 1903 and 1945. Tottenham U.D. education committee established the following schools. Forster Road mixed school opened in 1905, in premises leased from St. Mark's Wesleyan church and accommodating 256 children. It closed in 1907 but reopened on the same site in 1910, to relieve pressure on the Bruce Grove and Parkhurst Road schools.[74] The school had ceased to function by 1919.

Belmont Road school opened in temporary quarters in 1906 and moved to a new building in 1908.[75] There was accommodation for 1,636 children in 1919 and for 1,458 in 1938.[76] Reorganization had created separate secondary modern, junior, and infants' schools by 1949.[77] A new Belmont junior school, the first primary school to be completed in Tottenham after the Second World War, opened in Rusper Road in 1955,[78] while senior pupils and infants remained on the old site in Downhills Park Road. By 1963 the infants also had moved to Rusper Road,[79] where they occupied their own buildings in 1972. At that date 435 children attended the junior school and 310 the infants'.

Parkhurst Road school, built and opened in 1907, when the first Forster Road school closed,[80] had 1,260 places but only 896 pupils in 1919. Senior children later formed boys and girls' secondary modern schools, afterwards amalgamated.[81] In 1972 Parkhurst infants' school survived in the old buildings, with 258 full-time pupils on the roll.[82]

Crowland Road school opened in 1911, to relieve overcrowding at Earlsmead, Seven Sisters, Stamford Hill, and Page Green schools.[83] Between the World Wars there were 1,420 places, occupied by 1,012 children in 1919 and by 769 in 1938.[84] Crowland secondary modern school was formed in 1946.[85] In 1972 juniors and infants continued to occupy separate buildings on the old site, with 320 juniors and 226 infants on their respective rolls.

Down Lane school opened in Park View Road in 1911.[86] Under the Education Act of 1918 part of it was turned into a selective central school for girls,[87] although juniors and infants remained on the premises, where there were 1,636 places in 1919. Separate junior and infants' schools were created in 1940, the infants' closing some 20 years later. In 1967, on the reorganization of secondary education and consequent closure of the former central school, the juniors moved to Parkhurst Road, where there were 313 children enrolled in 1972.[88]

Coombes Croft temporary council school opened in 1912 in part of the premises formerly leased as council offices and later for grammar school pupils from the Tottenham charity estates.[89] The school, for junior boys drawn from the Lancasterian school, had 96 places in 1919. It was closed in 1924.[90]

Woodberry Down temporary council school opened in 1913 in premises leased from Woodberry Down Baptist church. The school, intended to relieve pressure at Stamford Hill, had 224 places in 1919 and closed in 1926.[91]

Risley Avenue school, the Roundway, opened in 1913 with 1,894 places, to take pupils from the Lancasterian, Bruce Grove, and Belmont Road schools.[92] Under the Act of 1918 part of it became a selective central school for boys until 1928, when the boys moved to Down Lane.[93] Until 1967 senior girls shared the building with junior mixed and infants' schools, which had 451, including 28 from the Blanche Nevile school, and 390 children on their respective rolls in 1972.[94]

Culvert Road, later South Grove, school opened in a new building in 1913, when pupils were moved there from Woodlands Park, Seven Sisters, West Green, and Downhills schools.[95] Between the World Wars the accommodation was reduced from 1,520 to 1,225 places.[96] During the 1920s the staff for a time included Stephen Critten, later known as the novelist Neil Bell, and the pupils included Edward Willis, later the author Lord Willis.[97] Separate boys' and girls' secondary schools and an infants' school were afterwards formed, the infants' closing c. 1963. After the absorption of the secondary schools into a comprehensive establishment, the whole building became an annexe of Hornsey College of Art until

[68] *Tottenham educ. cttee. min. bk. 1951–2*, 334; *1952–3*, 95.
[69] Ed. 7/88.
[70] *Willingly to Sch.* 26.
[71] Ex inf. the sec., Earlsmead jr. mixed and inf. sch.
[72] Ed. 7/88.
[73] Ibid.
[74] Ed. 7/87; Ed. 7/88.
[75] Ed. 7/88.
[76] *Bd. of Educ., List 21* (H.M.S.O. 1938).
[77] Sturges, *Schs.* 105, 173, 175.
[78] Bruce Castle Mus., 959 [programme, 1955].
[79] Mdx. C.C. educ. cttee. *List of Schs. 1957*; *List of Educ. Svces. 1963.*
[80] Ed. 7/88.
[81] Sturges, *Schs.* 105; Mdx. C.C. educ. cttee. *List . . . 1957.*
[82] Ex inf. the headmistress.
[83] Ed. 7/88.

[84] *Bd. of Educ., List 21* (H.M.S.O. 1938).
[85] *Tottenham educ. cttee. min. bk. 1945–6*, 9.
[86] Sturges, *Schs.* 214.
[87] H. C. Davis, *Three Doz. Yrs.* 6.
[88] Mdx. C.C. educ. cttee. *List . . . 1957, 1963*; ex inf. the headmaster.
[89] Ed. 7/88; *Coombes Croft branch libr.* [pamphlet, 1925].
[90] *Bd. of Educ., List 21* (H.M.S.O. 1927).
[91] Ed. 7/88; *Bd. of Educ., List 21* (H.M.S.O. 1932).
[92] Ed. 7/88.
[93] Davis, op. cit. 6, 16.
[94] Ex inf. the headmaster, Risley Ave. jr. sch., and the headmistress, Risley Ave. inf. sch.
[95] Ed. 7/88.
[96] *Bd. of Educ., List 21* (H.M.S.O. 1919, 1938).
[97] *Willingly to Sch.* 27.

Seven Sisters junior school took over the upper floor in 1970.[98]

Allison Road school opened in 1913 in premises leased from Harringay Congregational church for Tottenham infants who previously had attended schools in Hornsey. The school, which had 200 places, closed during or immediately after the Second World War.[99]

Amherst Park temporary council school opened on the same day as the schools in Culvert and Allison roads in a building leased from Amherst Park Wesleyan church. It accommodated 250 boys, taken from Stamford Hill school, and closed in 1925.

Devonshire Hill school, Weir Hall Road, opened in 1926 with places for 760 juniors and infants from the Lancasterian and Risley Avenue schools. It occupied the same site in 1972, when there were 550 children on the roll.

Wood Green education committee established the following schools. Lordship Lane school opened in 1906, superseding the temporary school in Gladstone Avenue. By 1912 four temporary classrooms had been added to the main building, intended for infants only, and in 1919 there were 1,120 places.[1] Separate boys' secondary, junior mixed, and infants' schools were later formed.[2] Both junior and infants' schools remained on the site in 1972, when there were 477 juniors and 342 infants.

Muswell Hill temporary council school, for juniors and infants, opened in Albert Road in 1908 and closed in 1920. There was accommodation for 360 in 1919.[3]

Rhodes Avenue school opened in 1930, with accommodation for 434 juniors and infants.[4] In 1952 a separate infants' school was established on the same site. There were 294 pupils enrolled at the junior school and 200 at the infants' school in 1972.[5]

White Hart Lane New school, called Earlham school since 1968, opened in Earlham Grove in 1939. Infants and juniors shared the same building. By 1973 the infants' school, intended for less than 200, had 270 pupils, while the junior school had 441.[6]

Primary schools founded after 1945.[7] St. Mary's Priory junior and infants' schools opened on the priory's land in Hermitage Road in 1966. They were run by the Servite sisters and had 315 and 220 children on their rolls in 1972.

Broadwater Farm primary school, in the newly built Adams Road, was founded in 1970 by Haringey L.B. to serve the Broadwater Farm estate. There were 206 infants and juniors in 1972.

Tiverton primary school was opened by Haringey in 1970 in Pulford Road, where it served the surrounding new estate. There were 116 juniors and 134 infants in 1972.

St. Martin of Porres Catholic school opened in 1972 in Blake Road, as a second primary school to serve the parish of St. Paul, Wood Green, for an estimated 245 children in 1973.

Welbourne primary school was opened by Haringey in 1972, to serve the area that was being rebuilt between High Road, Broad Lane, and Chesnut Road. Classes began in part of the former Page Green school, which was shared with the teachers' training department of Hornsey College of Art.

Secondary and senior schools founded before 1967. Apart from Tottenham grammar school[8] the first source of public secondary education was the Higher Grade board school at Wood Green. It was intended for pupils who wished to stay on after passing the 7th standard of an elementary school, and, although administered under the Elementary Code, catered for those who would otherwise have had to travel to the grammar school.[9] Separate boys' and girls' establishments opened in 1884, using premises rented from the Wesleyans and Presbyterians. By 1898 both schools were overcowded: the boys', in Trinity Road, had 226 places and 286 pupils, and the girls', in Naas Road (later Canning Crescent), had 144 places and double that number of pupils. In 1899 both boys and girls moved to a new building in Bounds Green Road, where there was room for 900 in 1906 and 1,040 in 1919. Fees, originally 9d. a week, were 6d. a week from 1899, when each sex could compete for 100 free places.[10] Wood Green Higher Grade school closed on being taken over by the Middlesex education committee in 1921 but reopened as Trinity county grammar school.[11]

Tottenham county school was established by Middlesex C.C. at Grove House in 1901[12] and was the first secondary school founded by the council in expectation of the following year's Education Act. As one of the earliest co-educational secondary schools in the country it was fiercely criticized. For twelve years accommodation was shared with Tottenham polytechnic, for which Grove House had originally been acquired, while numbers rose from 80 to c. 400. In 1913 the school moved into a new building, for 450 pupils, on the Green; numbers had reached 543 by 1936 and 658 by 1953, a year before extra space was found in High Cross memorial hall. New buildings at Selby Road, Devonshire Hill, next to the playing fields, were started in 1961 and occupied in 1963. Tottenham county school closed in 1967, when its premises were taken over by Tottenham school.[13] In 1973 the building on the Green was occupied by the Moselle school.

St. Ignatius's college was founded in 1894, when Jesuits bought Morecambe Lodge, Stamford Hill. Private secondary education was provided there for Roman Catholic boys until a new building, which also housed mixed elementary pupils, was brought into use from 1907. A public grant was first paid in 1906 and increased in 1908, on condition that 25 per

[98] Mdx. C.C. educ. cttee. *List . . . 1963*; ex inf. the headmaster, Seven Sister jr. sch.
[99] The foll. three paras. are based on Ed. 7/88 and *Bd. of Educ., List 21* (H.M.S.O. 1919, 1927, 1938).
[1] Ed. 7/88.
[2] Sturges, *Schs.* 105, 173, 176.
[3] Ed. 7/88; *Bd. of Educ., List 21* (H.M.S.O. 1932).
[4] *Bd. of Educ., List 21* (H.M.S.O. 1932).
[5] Ex inf. the headmistresses.
[6] Ex inf. the headmistresses.

[7] The foll. five paras. are based on inf. supplied by the headmasters and headmistresses.
[8] *V.C.H. Mdx.* i. 314. The school ceased to exist on the reorganization of secondary educ. in 1967.
[9] Sturges, *Schs.* 98, 106.
[10] Ed. 7/88.
[11] Sturges, *Schs.* 99.
[12] Except where otherwise stated, the para. is based on *Tottenham County Sch. Chron.* Dec. 1963, pp. 1–3, and *Willingly to Sch.* 31.
[13] Ex inf. the headmaster, Tottenham sch.

cent of the places should be free.[14] The school, granted Aided status in 1950,[15] moved to Enfield in 1968.[16]

Tottenham high school[17] for girls was established in 1885 by the Church Schools Co., which had leased the premises in High Road formerly occupied by the Drapers' college for boys. The Drapers' Company itself took over the school in 1887, managing it as a day school with over 100 pupils and charging 3 or 4 guineas a term. Government was through a committee including local members until 1891 and then through the Drapers' own education committee until 1909, when Middlesex C.C. took over. The council bought the property in 1921. A new building was erected on the south side facing High Road in 1926. There were c. 500 pupils by 1949,[18] eighteen years before the school's absorption into High Cross comprehensive school.[19]

Glendale, originally Wood Green, county school was established by Middlesex C.C. as a mixed grammar school in 1910.[20] The school was amalgamated with Trinity county school to form Wood Green county grammar school in 1962. It then moved from Glendale Avenue to White Hart Lane, leaving its old premises for Woodside school. Under the comprehensive scheme of 1967 the buildings in Glendale Avenue were assigned to St. Thomas More upper school and the new ones in White Hart Lane to Wood Green comprehensive school.[21]

Downhills selective central school was opened by Tottenham education committee in 1919, under powers conferred by the Act of 1918.[22] The central school offered a curriculum like that of the grammar schools to mixed pupils from the age of eleven. It occupied part of the old Downhills board school's buildings in Philip Lane and was redesigned as a secondary modern establishment between 1957 and 1963.

Down Lane selective central school was opened under the Act of 1918 to provide a largely commercial or technical curriculum for girls. In 1928 the boys from Risley Avenue were transferred to Down Lane, which later became a secondary modern school.

Risley Avenue central school was the third of its kind established by Tottenham education committee. It was a boys' school with a curriculum like that at Down Lane and was closed in 1928.

Trinity county school, Bounds Green Road, was opened as a mixed grammar school, after the county council had taken over the Higher Grade school in 1921.[23] On its amalgamation with Glendale school in 1962 it moved to White Hart Lane, whereupon the old buildings were taken over by Parkwood school.[24]

St. Katharine's Church of England school became a girls' secondary modern school c. 1937, having previously, as St. Katharine's practising school, been an all-age school.[25] In 1962 it moved from buildings forming part of the training college complex to new accommodation near-by, entered from Pretoria Road. The school became comprehensive in 1967, retaining the Voluntary Aided status which it had enjoyed since 1952.[26]

Rowland Hill secondary modern school opened in Lordship Lane in 1938, with 539 boys and staff drawn mainly from Risley Avenue, Devonshire Hill, and the Lancasterian schools. Its foundation, contemplated since the closure of Risley Avenue central school, had been made necessary by the higher leaving age and the growth of council estates in north Tottenham.[27]

St. Angela's Providence Convent school began as a private school in Bounds Green Road in 1905. It acquired the Brabançonne in Earlham Grove, Wood Green, in 1921 and moved into a new school behind the Brabançonne in 1926.[28] The Daughters of Providence took over the Ursuline sisters' direct grant school in Oakthorpe Road, Palmers Green (Southgate), in 1932; most of the seniors from Palmers Green moved in 1933 to Wood Green, where St. Angela's continued as a direct grant day school until 1945, while infants and juniors moved from Wood Green to Palmers Green. St. Angela's, Wood Green, became a 'transitionally assisted' grammar school in 1945 and Voluntary Aided in 1950, when it had 280 girls. In 1972 it was intended that the 410 pupils from Wood Green would transfer to a Roman Catholic comprehensive school at Palmers Green.[29]

St. Thomas More Roman Catholic school opened in 1952, fourteen years after work had begun on the buildings, in Holcombe Road. It remained a mixed Voluntary Special Agreement school until 1968, when the roll numbered 540, and was then reorganized on a two-tier comprehensive basis.[30]

Under the reorganization started in 1934, the following secondary modern schools were created in Tottenham out of existing elementary schools, part of whose premises they continued to use:[31] Belmont (mixed); Crowland (mixed), closed between 1949 and 1957;[32] Page Green (mixed), closed between 1957 and 1963; Parkhurst (mixed); Risley Avenue (girls); South Grove (boys); South Grove (girls). The following were formed in Wood Green: Bounds Green (mixed); Lordship Lane (boys), closed between 1957 and 1963; Noel Park (girls), closed between 1957 and 1963.

The following secondary modern schools were established after 1945: Markfield (mixed), Gladesmore Road, Tottenham; Cecil Rhodes (mixed), Rhodes Avenue, Wood Green (1959);[33] Parkwood (girls) (1963), Bounds Green Road, Wood Green, replacing Noel Park; Woodside (boys) (1962),

[14] Sturges, Schs. 113–14.
[15] Tottenham educ. cttee. min. bk. 1949–50, p. 317.
[16] See p. 256.
[17] Except where otherwise stated, the para. is based on M. W. Baines, Short Hist. Tottenham High Sch. 21–2, 26–7, 32.
[18] Sturges, Schs. 95.
[19] Ex inf. the headmistress, High Cross sch.
[20] Sturges, Schs. 98.
[21] Ex inf. Dr. A. D. H. Fishlock, headmaster of Wood Green sch.
[22] The foll. three paras. are based on H. C. Davis, Three Dozen Yrs. 6–7, and Mdx. C.C. educ. cttee. Lists 1957, 1963.
[23] Sturges, Schs. 99.

[24] Ex inf. Dr. A. D. H. Fishlock.
[25] Bd. of Educ., List 21 (H.M.S.O. 1936, 1938).
[26] Ex inf. the headmistress; Tottenham educ. cttee. min. bk. 1952–3, 158.
[27] Schs. of Tottenham [catalogue 1936]; Rowland Hill, 1938–48 [pamphlet].
[28] Ex inf. Sister Mary Agnes; Daughters of Providence [booklet, 1953]. See p. 356.
[29] Sturges, Schs. 115–16; ex inf. the headmistress, St. Angela's Providence Convent sch.
[30] Ex inf. the headmasters.
[31] Except where otherwise stated, the two foll. paras. are based on Mdx. C.C. educ. cttee. Lists . . . 1957, 1963.
[32] Sturges, Schs. 105.
[33] Ex inf. the headmistress, Alexandra Park sch.

Glendale Avenue, Wood Green, replacing Lordship Lane.

Comprehensive schools founded since 1967.[34] Alexandra Park opened as a mixed school in 1967. The lower school took over a building in Park Road which had been erected for Bounds Green school in 1965, while the upper school occupied the former Cecil Rhodes school's premises. A library and other extensions had been built on the Rhodes Avenue site by 1973, when there were plans to increase the number of pupils to 1,320 within two years.

The Drayton school opened in Gladesmore Road in 1967, occupying a senior school which had been built in 1910, an extension added in 1938, and a new secondary modern school which had opened in 1957. The Grovelands extension was built in 1969 and further rooms were planned for 1973. There were 990 boys and girls enrolled in 1972.

High Cross school opened in 1967, in the premises formerly used by Tottenham high school, in High Road, and by Down Lane central school. There were *c.* 1,050 girls on the roll in 1972.

St. Katharine's Church of England School became comprehensive in 1967 but retained its Voluntary Aided status. There were 406 girls on the roll in 1972.

The Somerset school was formed in 1967 by the amalgamation of Tottenham grammar and Rowland Hill schools. The grammar school's Voluntary Controlled status was retained, with foundation governors in addition to those appointed by the local authority. The upper school took over the buildings in White Hart Lane which had been erected for the grammar school in 1938 and enlarged in 1960, while the lower school, for first- and second-year boys, occupied the former Rowland Hill school. Extensions included a library at the lower school in 1970 and sixth-form rooms. There were 1,022 boys enrolled in 1972[35].

Tottenham school opened as a mixed school in 1967 in the old Tottenham county school's buildings in Selby Road. A sixth-form centre and a sports hall had been added by 1972, when there were 1,038 pupils on the roll.

Wood Green comprehensive school was formed in 1967 with boys from Wood Green county grammar and Woodside schools and some girls from Parkwood school. The upper tier occupied the former grammar school's buildings in White Hart Lane, to which additions had been made by 1972, while the lower tier used the Glendale Avenue premises of the former Woodside school. The number on the roll was 1,210 in 1973, when extensions were planned to accommodate all the pupils on the White Hart Lane site.

St. Thomas More upper school was formed in 1968, when it became part of a Roman Catholic comprehensive school and moved from the former St. Thomas More secondary modern school into the premises previously occupied by Trinity grammar school. There were 420 pupils on the roll in 1972.

St. Thomas More lower school remained in Holcombe Road on becoming the lower tier of the new comprehensive school in 1968. It contained 540 children, aged 11 to 14, in 1972, when there were plans for their eventual rehousing, together with those of the upper school, at Wood Green.[36]

The William Forster school, which replaced Downhills secondary school, opened in a new building in Langham Road in 1970, to mark the centenary of Forster's Education Act. There were 1,230 pupils on the roll in 1973.

Northumberland Park opened as a mixed school in the former Tottenham county school's premises in 1972. A move to Trulock Road was then planned for 1974 and numbers were expected to rise to 1,320 by 1977.

Special and nursery schools.[37] The Blanche Nevile school began as the Cedars school for deaf children in 1895, when Tottenham school board took over a house in Philip Lane. Pupils from Edmonton were admitted and the school soon moved to two larger houses, which were replaced in 1924. Extensions allowed numbers to rise to *c.* 70 by 1949.[38] In 1972 there were 151 children, 64 of them severely deaf and receiving education at the school.

The Vale school was opened by Tottenham education committee in Vale Road in 1928. It was intended for 70 physically handicapped children, including those suffering from heart trouble, and was taken over by the county council when enlargement became necessary.[39] In 1972 there were 86 pupils enrolled.

Moselle school, Haringey's first school for the educationally subnormal, opened in 1970 in part of the former Tottenham county school on the Green, where there was room for 75 children. In 1973 it was planned to move to premises for 150.

William Harvey school for the mentally subnormal opened in 1970 in new buildings in Adams Road. There were 108 children, aged 3 to 16, on the roll in 1973.

The New Day school or White Hart Lane old school, for maladjusted pupils, temporarily occupied the premises of the former White Hart Lane county school in 1972.

Vale Road nursery school, the first of its kind founded by Tottenham education committee, opened in 1937; there were 75 places, filled part-time by 150 infants, in 1972. Additional nursery space was provided during the Second World War at Pembury House, Lansdowne Road, and at Rowland Hill school, both of which afterwards became separate nursery schools, with 116 and 90 full- and part-time infants in 1972. Nursery classes were added to most infants' schools after the Second World War.

Tottenham technical college. Classes in art, science, and technical subjects began at Grove House in 1892, five years before the building was bought by Middlesex C.C. to form Tottenham polytechnic.[40] Evening attendance rose to 1,191 by 1911, although work was limited to small art classes during the day, chiefly because the premises were shared with Tottenham county school from 1901 until 1913. A large block, the oldest part of the college to survive in

---

[34] Except where otherwise stated, the foll. eleven paras. are based on inf. supplied by the headmasters and headmistresses.

[35] *Somerset sch.* [prospectus, 1972].

[36] Ex inf. Haringey L.B., chief educ. offr.

[37] Except where otherwise stated, the foll. six paras. are based on inf. supplied by the headmasters and headmistresses.

[38] Sturges, *Schs.* 184–5.

[39] Ibid. 187–8.

[40] *Willingly to Sch.* 33.

1972, was built to the south in 1910 and Grove House itself was replaced by a new main building between 1936 and 1939, when the polytechnic was renamed Tottenham technical college. A large extension at the rear was opened in 1955[41] and an annexe acquired behind Montagu Road school (Edmonton) in 1963; the college left Montagu Road in 1972,[42] by which date another annexe had been opened at South Grove.[43] By 1936 there were three departments: a junior technical school for 200 boys aged 13–16, a similar commercial school for 100 boys and girls, and evening classes for 1,400 students.[44] The junior schools were phased out soon after 1960, although the college expanded to comprise five departments and some 4,000 students, only 500 of whom were evening attenders, by 1972. In that year there were plans to change the name to Tottenham college of technology.[45]

Private schools. Until the spread of working-class housing in the 1870s Tottenham was noted for its private schools. largely patronized by London families. As early as c. 1670 Mark Lewis advertised a 'gymnasium', specializing in languages, and in 1673 Mrs. Bathsua Makin, formerly tutor to Charles I's daughter Elizabeth, announced a wide curriculum in her prospectus for a girls' school.[46] A boarding establishment was also kept by the scholar William Baxter (1650–1723), nephew of Richard Baxter; three of William's children were baptized at the parish church between 1695 and 1700, before he left to become headmaster of the Mercers' school, London.[47]

There were two Quaker schools by 1712. One had been started five years earlier by Richard Claridge, who took about 20 boarders in addition to local boys. Claridge taught some of his pupils free, maintaining that they were neglected by the grammar school, and survived the denunciations of its master and the vicar, as well as an action at law brought by Lord Coleraine's widow and Hugh Smithson.[48] Claridge moved to London but others claimed to continue his school in a building adjoining the Old Ship inn, later called Sunnyside, until its demolition in 1910.[49]

The Forster family's long connexion with Tottenham began in 1752 when Josiah Forster (d. 1763), a Coventry schoolmaster, converted Sir Abraham Reynardson's house on the Green into a boys' boarding school[50] offering commercial and technical subjects. Josiah was followed by his son-in-law Thomas Coar, a former assistant of Archdeacon Paley and author of *A Grammar of the English Tongue.* Coar retired in 1810, leaving the school to his nephew Josiah Forster, who previously

had taught in Southgate and who soon moved to the near-by Eagle House, where Coar's daughters Deborah and Fanny also ran a boys' preparatory school of good repute. Josiah Forster retired in 1810 and the Coar sisters left in 1841, after Forster's school had passed to Dr. Andrew Price, who specialized in foreign boarders. Eagle House school,[51] which later catered more for nonconformist day-boys, survived until the building was burned down c. 1884.[52]

The opening of Bruce Castle,[53] destined to be Tottenham's best-known school, was announced in 1827 by the Hill family, after their purchase of the mansion with 15 a. from John Ede. The Hills, already well known for their methods used at Hazelwood, in Edgbaston (Warws.), probably wanted to anticipate the foundation of a similar school near London by Jeremy Bentham, Lord Brougham, and other radical admirers. A partnership of four brothers managed the new school, with Rowland Hill as headmaster until 1833, when Hazelwood was closed, after the transfer of many pupils to Tottenham, and Rowland's brother Arthur took over. Bruce Castle was modelled on Hazelwood in its wide syllabus, relaxed discipline, and stress on self-government by the boys, as propounded by the Hills in 1833.[54] Financially it was a greater success, printing its own magazine, the *Brucian,*[55] from 1839 and winning high praise in the 1840s,[56] when Charles Dickens admired its methods as 'the only recognition of education as a broad system of moral and intellectual philosophy that I have ever seen in practice'.[57] Under Arthur Hill Bruce Castle gradually became more conventional until most of its pupils attended the parish church. Arthur was followed by his son George Norman Birkbeck Hill,[58] whose succession by the Revd. William Almack ended the family's connexion in 1877. Almack closed Bruce Castle in 1891 and soon afterwards the local authority bought it as a museum.

Grove House school[59] opened in 1829 in the former home of Thomas Smith, which had been bought by Quakers in 1828 as a boarding school for c. 25 boys. It was presumably founded because of the retirement of Josiah Forster, who was one of the trustees. Charging fees of c. £100 a year, it was in reputation second only to Bruce Castle, which it resembled in its spacious surroundings,[60] its advanced curriculum, and the absence of corporal punishment. After a fall in attendance during the 1850s, it was enlarged by the headmaster Arthur Robert Abbott, who supervised 46 boarders and 4 assistant masters in 1868. Abbott virtually took control on becoming the lessee in 1871 and accepted

[41] Tottenham Tech. Coll. *Students' Handbk.* [1972].
[42] Mdx. C.C. educ. cttee. *Lists . . . 1963, 1964; Southgate Tech. Coll. Ann. Reps. 1971–2.*
[43] Ex inf. the registrar.
[44] Tottenham educ. cttee. *Educ. Week Handbk.* [1956].
[45] Ex inf. the registrar.
[46] *Willingly to Sch.* 12; *V.C.H. Mdx.* i. 243, 252.
[47] *D.N.B.*; Fisk, *Tottenham,* ii. 257–8.
[48] *Willingly to Sch.* 13; J. Besse, *Life of . . . Ric. Claridge,* 198, 202, 216–26.
[49] Sturges, *Schs.* 73; Fisk, *Tottenham,* i. 106–7, 116.
[50] Except where otherwise stated, the para. is based on *Willingly to Sch.* 13, Sturges, *Schs.* 74, and T. Compton, *Recollections of Tottenham Friends and the Forster family,* 9–14, 57–9.
[51] Engraving, 1854, in Bruce Castle Mus.
[52] Bruce Castle Mus., Tottenham sales, i, no. 59.

[53] Except where otherwise stated, the para. is based on *Willingly to Sch.* 16–18, and J. L. Dobson, 'Hill fam. and Educ. Change', *Durham Research Rev.* ii (10) (1959); iii (11) (1960); iii (12) (1961). Additional refs. are cited in *V.C.H. Mdx.* i. 256 n. 78.
[54] *Sketch of the System . . . at the Schs. of Bruce Castle, Tottenham, and Hazelwood, near Birmingham* (1833).
[55] A major source, in the absence of many admin. recs.; copies in Bruce Castle Mus.
[56] e.g. Chambers's *Edinburgh Jnl.* (1843), vol. xii, no. 599, 22 Jly. 1843, pp. 213–15.
[57] *Dickensian,* li(4) (1955), 175.   [58] *D.N.B.*
[59] Except where otherwise stated, the para. is based on S. W. Brown, *Leighton Park,* 6–25; *Willingly to Sch.* 13–14; Sturges, *Schs.* 75; and TS. notes *penes* Bruce Castle Mus.
[60] Lithograph, 1842, *penes* Bruce Castle Mus.

non-Quakers from 1873. He bought the school in 1877, after taking Anglican orders, and closed it abruptly a few months later, although Quaker families connected with Grove House were to contribute towards its successor, founded at Leighton Park, Reading, in 1889. From 1886 until 1889 part of the premises was leased by the Drapers' Company, as a temporary home for Bancroft's school in the course of its move from Mile End to Woodford (Essex).[61] Old boys of Grove House who achieved eminence included W. E. Forster (1818–86), Dr. Daniel Tuke (1827–95), Lord Lister (1827–1912), Sir Robert Fowler (1828–91), Alfred Waterhouse (1830–1905), Sir Edward Tylor (1832–1907), Joseph Henry Shorthouse (1834–1903),[62] and Joseph Albert Pease (1860–1943), who, as President of the Board of Education, returned in 1912 to open a new building for Tottenham county school, which had previously used the former Grove House.[63]

The Royal Masonic school, Wood Green, occupied the site of Lordship House and 10 a. bought in 1856. It was opened in 1857 for c. 70 sons of poor or deceased freemasons and, encouraged by the Queen's patronage, was well supported by subscriptions. The first building was replaced in 1865[64] by a larger one of stone, designed by Edwin Pearce and J. B. Wilson and Son in the Gothic style.[65] In 1878 there were 211 pupils, twenty of them admitted by purchase or presentation.[66] Twenty years later the managers moved the school to Bushey (Herts.) and sold the Wood Green site to the Home and Colonial School Society for a training college.[67] The building was renamed Woodall House after its sale to the Tottenham and District Gas Co. in the 1930s and acquired by Haringey from the Eastern Gas Board in 1974.[68]

The Drapers' college was built on land bought in 1858, when the Company was about to move its alms-houses from the City. The school was designed for 50 freemen's sons, boarders aged 8–15, to be brought up on Anglican principles. The boys were housed in part of a north-south block, set well back from the west side of High Road and reached by paths flanking rows of alms-houses to north and south. After buying extra land the Company closed the school in 1885, only to reopen it as a girls' high school in 1887.[69]

Elmslea, Lordship Lane, was bought by the Drapers' Company in 1869 and opened for fatherless Anglican girls three years later, with £36,000 left by a former master, Thomas Corney (d. 1866). The inmates, whose number rose from 24 to 40, were aged 7–18 and were taught at Elmslea until the opening of Tottenham High school. After Elmslea's

closure in 1930, the Tottenham magistrates' court-house was built on the site.[70]

High Cross college, on land afterwards occupied by Rawlinson Terrace, offered a broad curriculum by the 1860s and lasted until 1881. In 1879 it prepared boys of any age for the public schools or government examinations.[71]

Apart from the schools already mentioned as many as 14 small private institutions were listed in 1832. Two, kept by the Misses Wilson at the Elms and by Miss Hague in High Road, survived in the same hands in 1845, while Wood Green had but one short-lived private school in 1839. Genteel academies presumably helped to support the professors of music, dancing, and writing who lived at Tottenham in 1845.[72] Later girls' schools included Moselle House, in High Road opposite Park Road from 1869 to 1872, Felix House, opened in 1857 and apparently closed in the early 1880s, and Hope Cottage, West Green Road, which was exceptionally expensive, according to its prospectus.[73] Girls also boarded with the Servite Sisters and others with the Marist Sisters, who conducted a small school and an orphanage in 1890 but no longer did so in 1908.[74]

Among some 40 private schools existing c. 1880 were Wellesley House, West Green, where boys were prepared for public schools, St. John's middle class school, founded in 1868 and with a few boarders among its 80–90 boys, and the Grammar School, Nightingale House, Wood Green, where boys were coached for the universities and public examinations. Tottenham college, one of the largest establishments, took many foreign pupils and printed brochures in French; it first occupied the Cedars and later a 12-acre site at the corner of Selby Road, White Hart Lane, where it had closed by 1923.[75]

The number of private schools declined from the late 19th century. Clark's College opened a branch at the Hollies, Stuart Crescent, Wood Green, in 1909; it still offered a general education and commercial training to over 100 pupils in 1949 and closed in the 1960s.[76] An Anglo-German school existed in Antill Road in 1910, presumably for the children of German immigrants who established a Lutheran church there.[77] As late as 1949 small preparatory schools included Norton school in Tottenham and Elmsly school in Wood Green.[78] Parkside preparatory school opened in 1920 in Church Lane, in the former home of Rowland Hill's nephew, Albert Hill; there were 73 boys and girls, aged 5–11, in 1973.[79]

CHARITIES FOR THE POOR.[80] Neglect of

[61] *Bancroft's Sch. 1737–1937*, ed. D. C. R. Francombe and D. E. Coult, 53–72.
[62] *D.N.B.*; *V.C.H. Mdx.* i. 261.
[63] *Tottenham County Sch. Chron.* Dec. 1963.
[64] Ex inf. the headmaster, Royal Masonic Sch., Bushey, and the sec., Royal Masonic Inst. for Boys; Sturges, *Schs.* 76. [65] *Builder*, xiii. 86.
[66] F. S. de Carteret-Bisson, *Our Schs. and Colls.* i. 717.
[67] Sturges, *Schs.* 76; *Willingly to Sch.* 16.
[68] Ex inf. Haringey L.B. town planning dept.
[69] M. W. Baines, *Short Hist. Tottenham High Sch.* 7–13, 21.
[70] Ibid. 18–19; A. H. Johnson, *Hist. of Drapers' of Lond.* iii. 481.
[71] Prospectus *penes* Bruce Castle Mus.; Bisson, op. cit. i. 885, lii.
[72] Pigot, *Com. Dir.* (1832–4), (1839); *P.O. Dir. Home Counties* (1845).

[73] *Willingly to Sch.* 15; prospectuses for most of the schools are in Bruce Castle Mus.
[74] Bisson, op. cit. ii. 623; Fisk, *Tottenham*, i. 128; *Kelly's Dirs. Mdx.* (1890, 1908).
[75] Bisson, op. cit. i. 713, 885; *Willingly to Sch.* 15; Fisk, *Tottenham*, ii. 176–7.
[76] Sturges, *Schs.* 118–19; *P.O. Dirs. Lond.* (1964, 1970).
[77] *Kelly's Dir. Tottenham and Edmonton* (1909–10).
[78] Sturges, *Schs.* 182.
[79] Ex inf. the principal.
[80] Except where otherwise stated, the section is based on Char. Com. files; D. Avery, *Poverty and Philanthropy in Tottenham in the 16th and 17th cents.* (Edmonton Hund. Hist. Soc. 1963), 5; *14th Rep. Com. Char.* H.C. 382, pp. 157–69 (1826), xii; *Gen. Digest Endowed Chars.* H.C. 433, pp. 68–9 (1867–8), lii(1); *Endowed Chars. Mdx.* H.C. 306, pp. 24–5 (1899), lxx.

several charities was revealed in William Bedwell's description of 1631 and, more explicitly, in the history compiled mainly by Henry Hare, Lord Coleraine (d. 1708). In Bedwell's time the gift of herrings from William Dalby[81] had been discontinued and a then recent bequest of 40s. a year from Humphrey Westwood out of the profits of the rectory[82] had never been honoured. As early as 1634 three legacies had been used to buy property which became known as the charity estates; these lands had been improved but to no public benefit, according to Lord Coleraine, who also condemned the abatement of other sums due to the poor.[83] Similar maladministration, all the graver for the additional gifts made in the 18th and early 19th centuries, was discovered by the Brougham commissioners in 1825, when the estates were treated as common parish property and the rents, with several other payments, went into a general account. After the threat of legal action the charities were regulated by a succession of Schemes, until by 1893 an inspector could commend the unusual amount of local interest, which would make forthcoming reorganization relatively easy.

In 1896 the administrative division of the ancient parish led to the consolidation of most of its charities in two groups, one called the Alms-houses and the other the General charities. Together they were placed under two bodies, headed by the vicars of All Saints, Tottenham, and St. Michael's, Wood Green, and each with 5 of its 9 trustees appointed by the respective district council. The bodies were jointly to choose an estate committee, with 4 representatives from Tottenham and 2 from Wood Green, which would let and maintain all the property, paying stipends of 6s. to 10s. a week to the inmates of the three sets of parochial alms-houses; two-thirds of the remaining income was to go to the trustees for Tottenham and one third to those from Wood Green, for distribution in pensions and for the general benefit of the poor. Two out of every three alms-people were to be chosen by the Tottenham trustees and the remainder by those from Wood Green.

Under a further Scheme of 1917 most of the property and the funds were divided between the two local authorities, as the Tottenham (U.D.) charity and the Wood Green (U.D.) charity, while a small part of the land managed by the estate committee was left to a new Estate charity representing both councils, which shared its income as before. Tottenham took over the alms-houses and stock worth £9,620, while Wood Green received a few houses and £6,371.

In 1967–8 the Tottenham (U.D.) charity had an income of £2,660, most of it paid out in pensions of 8s. a week; £841, nearly a third of its revenue, came from ground-rents. The Wood Green (U.D.) charity, on the other hand, disposed of most of its property in the early 1960s, investing the proceeds in the borough's own stock; the last ground rents were sold in 1965 and the income rose to £8,362 in 1970–1.

THE TOTTENHAM (U.D.) AND WOOD GREEN (U.D.) CHARITIES. *Alms-house charities.* Phesaunt's, later also called the Pound, alms-houses originally comprised three tenements on the east side of the churchyard. They were founded for three poor widows by George Henningham (d.1536) according to a brass formerly in the church,[84] on which Bedwell presumably based his statement that they had been built by a Mr. Phesaunt.[85] Lord Coleraine, c. 1705, complained that one of the alms-houses had become an alehouse.[86] The houses were demolished by the vestry c. 1744 and rebuilt on the east side of High Road, between the pound and the site later occupied by the Green school.[87] The vestry, which filled the vacancies, increased the accommodation to seven in 1847.[88] The Old and New Pound alms-houses, as thenceforth they were usually called, were considered cramped and inconvenient in 1893. After their inmates had chosen to move to Reynardson's alms-houses rather than to receive bigger pensions, the sale of Phesaunt's alms-houses was sanctioned in 1925.

Phesaunt's alms-people benefited from several 19th-century bequests. Charles Saunders, by will dated 1817, left £300 stock from which each widow was supplied with 3 threepenny loaves a week until 1823, when distribution was temporarily stopped by a law-suit. Elizabeth Saunders, by will dated 1818, augmented the gift by consols worth nearly £223, on which half the income was spent on bread and half in cash. Pensions were further augmented out of part of the income of the charity estates from 1828, £200 from Richard Mountford (d.1833), £4 a head from William Odell, by will dated 1842, £500 from Thomas Barber, by will dated 1844, £500 from Caroline Dawson, by will dated 1879, and £320 net from James Saul, by will proved 1890. Residents in the three newer alms-houses also received the income from Jane Barkham's gift,[89] the interest on £204 stock bequeathed by George Gasson in 1866, and £210 given by Sarah and Mary Dawson in 1881.

Sanchez's alms-houses,[90] for 8 old men or women of Tottenham, were founded by Balthasar Sanchez, a naturalized Spaniard who had been confectioner to King Philip II of Spain before moving from London to the George and Vulture inn in High Road. By will dated 1599 Sanchez set aside 7 a. at Stone Leas for alms-houses, which were to be built and endowed with money from his estate. In the event he himself completed the building work in 1600 and, by a codicil of 1601, left the 7 a., apart from the site of the alms-houses, together with the sums previously intended as an endowment and all other lands attached to Stone Leas, to his brother-in-law and executor Christopher Scurrow; in return Scurrow and all future owners of Stone Leas became responsible for repairing the alms-houses and paying each inmate £2 a year in quarterly sums, with 15s. every second year for a frieze gown. The vicar, churchwardens, and four other feoffees were to fill and regulate the alms-houses and visit them on St. Bartholomew's day.

[81] See below.
[82] Prob. 11/139 (P.C.C. 139 Savile).
[83] Oldfield and Dyson, *Hist. Tottenham*, 15–29.
[84] Robinson, *Tottenham*, ii. 266.
[85] Roe, op. cit. 118. Henningham's daughter Margaret married Jasper Phesaunt: Prob. 11/27 (P.C.C. 13 Dyngeley).
[86] Fisk, *Tottenham*, ii. 125.
[87] Robinson, op. cit. ii, plate facing p. 306.
[88] Bruce Castle Mus., *Tottenham Chars. 1888* [rep. by cttee. of vestry].
[89] See below.
[90] A 19th-cent. min. bk. and other recs. from 1619 to 1895 are in Bruce Castle Mus., D/PT/7A/1–11.

The alms-houses consisted of a row of 8 single-room tenements, each with its garden, built of brick and with an inscription beneath a central gable.[91] They were the oldest such buildings in Tottenham from the mid 18th century and in 1825 were habitable but damp and inconvenient from the raising of the road level. Despite work carried out by successive owners of Stone Leas, complete rebuilding was urged as early as 1868. The Stone Leas estate redeemed its liability for repairs in 1902 and sale of the alms-houses was sanctioned in 1919; six years later they were demolished to make way for Burgess's Stores.[92]

Sanchez's alms-people benefited from the interest on £1,400 stock from Thomas Cooke, by his will dated 1810; after litigation 2s. a week was paid to each inmate in 1825. Pensions were later augmented out of £100 from Mrs. Sarah Beachcroft, by will dated 1834, part of the rent from the charity estates, £500 from Caroline Dawson, by will dated 1879, and £320 net from James Saul, by will proved 1890.

Reynardson's alms-houses[93] for 6 men and 6 women were to be built and maintained with £2,000 from the estate of Nicholas Reynardson, by his will dated 1685. A chapel was to be provided for daily prayers and the instruction of 20 poor children, the minister or teacher was to have £20 a year and a black gown at Christmas, and each alms-person was to receive £4 a year in quarterly payments, with a black gown. Reynardson's executors, with the vicar and churchwardens, were to add to their number to make 12 trustees, who would manage the charity. The provisions were confirmed by a Scheme of 1730, after the death of Reynardson's widow, save that the master of the free school was to read the prayers for £10 a year. The alms-houses, accommodating 8 persons, were opened in 1737. In 1825 there were 5 men and 3 women, chosen under the mistaken impression that inmates should enjoy no other parish relief and each receiving coals worth 20s. a year in lieu of a gown. Prayers were then read twice weekly in winter by the assistant curate for £6, although by 1851 they were read only on Thursdays.[94]

The alms-houses, next to the free school, comprised a brick row of 8 two-storeyed apartments, with a central chapel bearing an inscription over its doorway.[95] In 1825 they were in poor repair, since the income was inadequate, but work was carried out in 1828 and 60 years later they were thought satisfactory. They were portrayed, in a kindly light, in *Children of Gibeon* (1886), Sir Walter Besant's novel on east London life.[96] Sale of the alms-houses was authorized in 1938, when the last inmates moved to two houses belonging to the Drapers' Company in Bruce Grove, but an auction in 1939 was unsuccessful. The site was requisitioned for allotments in the Second World War and a sale was finally effected in 1951.

Pensions for Reynardson's alms-people were first augmented when Dr. Matthew Clarke, by will dated 1777, left the reversion of £600 in trust, which supplied an income from stock worth £966 from 1788. Mrs. Sarah Dickinson, by will of unknown date, left money to buy stock worth £200, which was vested in trustees in 1803. Thomas Cooke, by will dated 1810, left the interest on £1,400 stock, Richard Mountford (d. 1833) left £100 in trust for the inmates and a similar sum for the officiating minister, John Marshall, by will dated 1838, left the reversion of dividends on stock which was worth £793 in 1880, and James Saul, by will proved 1890, left £320 net. Repairs were assisted by £50 given in trust by Isaac Guillemard in 1798 and £20 left by Sarah Beachcroft, by will dated 1834. Reynardson's alms-houses were the best endowed in Tottenham, with funds worth £4,469 in 1863 and £5,825 in 1896.

The charity estates.[97] Balthasar Sanchez, in addition to endowing his alms-houses, left £100 in trust to provide bread for the poor. Dame Mary Woodhouse, by will proved in 1609, left £30 in trust for ten poor persons,[98] and Anne, countess of Dorset (d. 1618), gave £50. In 1634 all three sums were used to buy a house, the 5-acre close of Coombes Croft, the 5½-acre Hill Pond field at Downhills, and other property of Thomas Lock, which thereupon was vested in the vicar and other trustees to form the Tottenham charity estates. Lord Coleraine, c. 1705, complained that the property was neglected[99] and commissioners in 1825 noted that, apart from the weekly bread-dole, the profits were not applied directly to charitable uses. The lands, which were leased out by a committee of the vestry, nonetheless had gained in value: the house, divided by 1725 when it had been called the Three Conies, had become the Bell and Hare inn, a workhouse and infirmary had been built on part of Coombes Croft,[1] and further houses had been bought in 1807 with part of the accumulated income. Under an Order of 1828 the 4 women in Phesaunt's alms-houses were each to have 4s. a week from the charity estates; a Scheme of 1833 allowed the sum to be raised to 6s. and another of 1842 awarded 2s. a week to Sanchez's alms-people. Hill Pond field was leased to the local board as the site for a reservoir in 1853,[2] several houses along High Road were bought in 1862 with surplus funds, and a site in Park Lane was leased out for St. Paul's National school in 1869. The Coombes Croft estate was developed under a building lease granted in 1882 to C. J. Childs and by 1888 the charity had a net annual income of £260. The trustees of the Tottenham (U.D.) charity were authorized to sell the house and grounds of Coombes Croft in 1920 and Hill Pond field four years later but they retained property in Park Lane, Bromley, and High roads, including a drill hall and St. Paul's school, in 1967–8.

Other distributive charities. William Dalby, a fishmonger of London whose will was proved in 1593,[3] ordered that barrels of herrings should be distributed in Lent among the poor. Although Bedwell reported that nothing was provided,[4] Lord Coleraine recalled having seen a tablet in the church valuing the fish at

[91] Robinson, *Tottenham*, ii. 255 and plate facing p. 214.
[92] W. J. Roe, *Tottenham, Edmonton and Enfield Hist. Notebk.* 123.
[93] Mins. and accts. of the trustees from 1734 to 1869 are in Bruce Castle Mus., D/PT/7C/1–2.
[94] H.O. 129/137/2/1/1.
[95] Robinson, *Tottenham*, ii. 265 and plate facing p. 257.
[96] Bruce Castle Mus., 988 [newspaper cutting].

[97] Recs. of the lands and the charity from 1484 to 1916 are in Bruce Castle Mus., D/PT/7F/1–57.
[98] Prob. 11/113 (P.C.C. 47 Dorset).
[99] Oldfield and Dyson, op. cit. 22.
[1] See p. 343.
[2] Bruce Castle Mus., D/PT/7F/25; /26.
[3] Prob. 11/82 (P.C.C. 84 Neville).
[4] Roe, *Ancient Tottenham*, 118.

£10. According to Coleraine Sir Edward Barkham, who acquired Dalby's property in Tottenham and the City, had agreed to pay 50s. a year but Sir William Barkham, after the Great Fire, had secured an abatement to 34s. 8d.[5] A rent-charge of £2 2s., on houses in Cheapside, was paid by 1825 and still paid 60 years later.

Thomas Wheeler, by will proved 1611, left 12 pennyworth of bread for the vicar and churchwardens to distribute every Sunday, preferably in 1d. loaves, to the poor of Tottenham and especially those of Wood Green.[6] Accordingly £2 12s. a year was thereafter charged on his former property in the parish.

Sir Robert Barkham, by indenture of 1648,[7] secured a burial place in fee in the church. In return he assigned a rent-charge on land near Blackhope Lane, which was to provide 10s. a year for the poor and 2s. for the sexton. Payments ceased in 1782, perhaps because of an imperfect instrument which in 1825 was thought to make it hard to secure enforcement.

Lucy, Lady Coleraine, by will dated 1680, left £100 on which the interest was to be distributed by the vicar, overseers, and churchwardens at Christmas.

Mrs. Jane Barkham, by will dated 1724, left three tenements on the west side of High Road north of White Hart Lane, from which the rent was to benefit the poor. The houses were replaced by two others, leased out for 61 years in 1764 and still retained, as nos. 809 and 811 High Road, in 1896. The annual rent, £6 16s., had been assigned to supporting the inmates of the New Pound alms-houses by 1863.

Mrs. Barbara Skinner, by will dated 1759, left £100 to furnish clothing and other necessities for the poor. Richard Toll, by will dated 1767, left £100 stock, on which the dividends were to provide bread. Philip de la Haize, by will dated 1768, left the interest on £100. William Wood, in the same year, bequeathed a turnpike bill for £100, on which the interest was to provide bread. Stock representing the four bequests, with that of Lucy, Lady Coleraine, was valued at £740 in 1786. The sum was later reduced by sale but was raised to £525 when John Ardesoif, by will dated 1789, left £100 for a bread dole. All six benefactions, representing stock worth £629 in 1825 and £939 in 1863, continued to be listed together until the reorganization which led to the establishment of Tottenham (U.D.) charity.

Mrs. Mary Tyler, by will dated 1802 and a codicil of 1804, left the interest on £50 for bread. Richard Patmore, by will dated 1816, left the interest on £100 for bread. Both sums were sold and jointly reinvested in 1824. John Field, by will dated 1820, left the reversion of £1,000 after the deaths of his son and daughter to provide bread and coals, together with a further £500. Mrs. Field, by will of unknown date but before 1863, augmented the charity with £500 stock for coals. In 1868 the total income amounted to £45, distributed in tickets for coals to some 15 persons. William Wallis, by will dated 1825, left the interest on £100, which was distributed in bread at the churches of All Saints, Holy Trinity, and St. Michael in 1868. Daniel Silver, by will of c. 1833, left the interest on £100, which in 1868 was distributed like Wallis's legacy.

Richard Mountford (d. 1833), in addition to his alms-house bequests, left £100 to the churchwardens for a bread dole. Thomas Barber, by will proved 1844, in addition to his gift to Phesaunt's alms-houses, left £500 for bread and clothing. Henry Scambler, by will proved 1845, left the interest on £1,000 for half-yearly payments to 3 poor persons, who would be chosen by the householders. In 1868 elections took place at the lecture hall and were criticized as noisy and inconvenient in an inspector's report. Robert James Seagoe, by will proved 1851, left £100 stock to the churchwardens. The sexton was to receive 5s. a year, Park Lane National school was to have 10s., and the residue was to provide bread for the poor. From 1896 sums due to the school were paid into a separate account, in the name of Seagoe's educational foundation. John Priest, by will of unknown date but before 1863, left stock worth £90 to provide coals.

Lord Coleraine's charity.[8] Henry, Lord Coleraine, by will dated 1702, left £100 for the purchase of land, the income from which was to be used in the first instance to maintain a vault and vestry which he had built in the church and thereafter at the vestry's discretion. His widow Elizabeth added £40 to help buy 4 a. at Drayner's Grove, which was settled in trust in 1710. The land was exchanged for 6 a. opposite Duckett's farm, Hornsey, in 1792 and an additional plot with two houses in Fortis Green Road was allotted under the Inclosure Act for Finchley Common. The profits went into parish funds in 1825, when the income far exceeded the repair costs, and part of the surplus was paid towards the demolition of the Coleraine vault and the reinterment of the family fifty years later. A building lease was granted from 1886 for the field at Ducketts Green, where Coleraine Terrace and neighbouring roads had been laid out within five years. The increasing value of Lord Coleraine's lands, applied to no public purpose, was one of the main reasons for reorganizing the parochial charities in 1896.

OTHER CHARITIES FOR THE POOR. Mary Overend of Chitts Hill, by indenture dated 1859, conveyed stock worth £1,250 to four trustees, including Josiah Forster. The trustees, who were to be members of the Society of Friends, were to distribute the income in sums not exceeding £5 among old or sick residents of Tottenham, especially widows or those needing help with their rent. Under a Scheme of 1960 the managers of Josiah Forster's trust were placed in charge of Mary Overend's charity, which in 1966 had stock worth £1,670 and paid out £57 10s. in gifts.

Josiah Forster's trust was established in 1862, when Forster and his wife conveyed four cottages and £500 stock to W. E. Forster, M.P., and others, who should belong to the Tottenham Monthly Meeting. The cottages had then recently been built by the grantor on land inclosed out of an orchard on the north side of Philip Lane. They were to be maintained by the trustees, who should choose the inmates from Tottenham inhabitants, not necessarily Quakers, giving preference to widows or spinsters

[5] Oldfield and Dyson, op. cit. 23.
[6] Prob. 11/118 (P.C.C. 79 Wood).
[7] Bruce Castle Mus., D/PT/7E.

[8] Recs of Drayners Grove and Ld. Coleraine's char. from 1658 to 1855 are in Bruce Castle Mus., D/PT/7B/1–21.

aged at least 55. Each resident was to have ½ ton of coal a year but was expected to have enough personal resources to ensure some degree of comfort. Under a Scheme of 1955 Friends Trusts Ltd. became custodian trustees and six members of the Devonshire House and Tottenham Monthly Meeting became managing trustees. Residents could be required to pay up to 5s. a week towards the upkeep of the cottages, which had recently been repaired, in 1960 and up to 15s. in 1967. In 1970 assets consisted of the four cottages, nos. 88, 90, 92, and 94 Philip Lane, and stock worth £1,672, producing an income of £40.

Bayly's charity comprised stock worth £90 in 1867, when the income of £2 14s. was distributed. In 1886, when the stock was transferred to the Official Trustees, its origins were unknown: J. W. Robins stated that he had regularly handed over the dividends to the vicar of Holy Trinity, whose predecessor, George Twining Brewster, declared that the charity had existed on his own arrival in Tottenham some 40 years earlier. In the early 1950s £2 5s. was shared among five recipients annually at Christmas.

The Revd. E. R. Larken of Burton by Lincoln (Lincs.), by will proved 1895, left £140 in memory of his sister to the vicar and churchwardens of Tottenham, who were to spend the interest on the poor. By 1899 £114 had been invested in stock. In the early 1950s there was an income of nearly £8 a year but no money was distributed.

The Wilson fund was endowed by Alexander Wilson, vicar of Tottenham, whose will was proved in 1898. Proceeds from the sale of his real and the residue of his personal estate were to be invested by the next incumbent, who should distribute the income twice yearly among poor communicants. Accordingly £8,491 was invested in 1898. In the 1950s the fund's income was £227 and by 1972 it had reached £1,000[9] a year, paid out by the vicar in pensions and gifts.

Mrs. Sophia Parry, by will proved 1901, left the proceeds from the sale of her real and the residue of her personal estate to the vicar and churchwardens of St. Ann's, on behalf of the poor. Stock worth £1,000 and £677 was transferred to the Official Trustees in 1903. In 1966 the Charity Commissioners approved the practice of devoting the income of £41 18s. 4d. towards the stipend of the parish sister, a social worker serving St. Ann's and neighbouring parishes.

[9] Ex inf. the vicar.

INDEX

NOTE: An italic page-number denotes an illustration on that page or facing it.

Among the abbreviations used in the index, sometimes with the addition of an *s* to indicate plurality, the following may need elucidation: agric., agriculture; Alb., Albert; alms-ho., alms-house; And., Andrew; Ant., Anthony; Art., Arthur; bt., baronet; Bart., Bartholomew; Benj., Benjamin; bp., bishop; bd., board; boro., borough; Bros., Brothers; bldr., builder; bldg., building; Capt., Captain; Cath., Catherine; Cathm., Catholicism; chars., charities; Chas., Charles; Chris., Christopher; chs., churches; Coll., College; Col., Colonel; cttee., committee; co., company; ctss., countess; ct., court; Dan., Daniel; dau., daughter; dom., domestic; Edm., Edmund; educ., education; Edw., Edward; Eliz., Elizabeth; Ern., Ernest; fam., family; Fran., Francis; Fred., Frederick; gdning., gardening; Gen., General; Geof., Geoffrey; geol., geology; Geo., George; Gilb., Gilbert; Hen., Henry; Herb., Herbert; hosp., hospital; ho., house; ind., industry; Jas., James; Jos., Joseph; jr., junior; Kath., Katharine; Laur., Laurence; libr., library; Lond., London; ld., lord; man., manor; mchss., marchioness; Marg., Margaret; mkt., market; m., married; Mat., Matthew; Mic., Michael; mus., museum; Nat., Nathaniel; Nic., Nicholas; nonconf., nonconformity; par., parish; Pet., Peter; Phil., Philip; pop., population; pub., public; *q.v., quod vide*; rly., railway; Reg., Reginald; Revd., Reverend; Ric., Richard; Rob., Robert; Rog., Roger; Rom., Roman; Sam., Samuel; sch., school; sr., senior; svces., services; Sim., Simon; soc., social *or* society; s., son; sta., station; Steph., Stephen; Thos., Thomas; Vct., Viscount; Wal., Walter; wid., widow; w., wife; Wm., William; wkho., workhouse; wks., works

CORRIGENDA TO VOLUMES I, II, AND IV

Earlier lists of corrigenda will be found in Volumes I, III, and IV.

Vol. I, page 2, line 14, *for* 'Dollis Brook and Pymmes Brook, draining to the Lea.' *read* 'Pymmes Brook, draining to the Lea, and Dollis Brook.'
,, ,, 65, line 2, *for* 'evironmental' *read* 'environmental'
,, ,, 175, note 91, *for* 'Ibid.' *read* '*Cal. Chart. R.* 1327–41,'
,, ,, 314*b*, line 7 from end, *for* '1933' *read* '1938'
,, ,, 362*a*, s.v. Ossulstone, *for* '65–76' *read* '65–7'
Vol. II, page 398*a*, *for* '1608' *read* '1618'
Vol. IV, page ix, *after* 'Gore Hundred' *delete* '(*part*)'
,, ,, 24*b*, line 6, *for* '1796' *read* '1794'
,, ,, 27, note 3, *after* 'p.' *add* '35'
,, ,, 30*b*, line 30, *for* '1796' *read* '1794'
,, ,, 36*a*, line 9 from end, *for* 'Buryges' *read* 'Burgeys'
,, ,, 41*b*, line 1, *for* '1796' *read* '1794'
,, ,, 63*b*, line 13, *for* 'completed by 1796' *read* 'officially opened in 1794'
,, ,, 63, note 76, *delete whole footnote and substitute* '*Aris's Birmingham Gaz.* 17 Nov. 1794.'
,, ,, 64*a*, line 22, *after* 'west' *insert* 'as far as Taplow'
,, ,, 66*b*, lines 7–8, *delete from* 'For' *to* 'but'
,, ,, 66*b*, line 8, *delete* 'later'
,, ,, 79*a*, line 7 from end, *for* '1796' *read* '1794'
,, ,, 80*a*, line 5, *for* '1796' *read* '1794'
,, ,, 80*a*, line 31, *for* 'has' *read* 'had'
,, ,, 81*a*, line 39, *for* '1796' *read* '1794'
,, ,, 81*a*, line 6 from end, *for* 'Barclays' *read* 'Barclay'
,, ,, 81*b*, line 37, *for* 'Keane' *read* 'Kean'
,, ,, 90*b*, lines 33–4, *for* 'Flanders Green' *read* 'Flaunden'
,, ,, 100*b*, lines 13–15 from end, *for* 'the Metropolitan line, which had hitherto terminated at Harrow, was extended' *read* 'a branch from the Metropolitan line at Harrow was built'
,, ,, 105*a*, line 30, *for* 'At the beginning of the 20th century' *read* 'In 1876'
,, ,, 110*a*, line 29, *for* 'north-west corner' *read* 'west'
,, ,, 113*a*, note 52, *for* 'E. J. D. Obson' *read* 'E. J. Dobson'
,, ,, 115*a*, lines 11, 13, 15, and 19 from end, *for* 'Morton' *read* 'Norton'
,, ,, 115*a*, line 9 from end, *for* 'Morton's' *read* 'Norton's'
,, ,, 128, note 23, *for* '*T.L.M.A.S.* vii' *read* '*T.L.M.A.S.* xiii'
,, ,, 132*a* line 37, *for* '1932' *read* '1908'
,, ,, 132, note 72, *after* 'Executive' *delete full point and add* 'and on A. E. Bennet and H. V. Borley, *Lond. Transport Rlys.* (amended 1967), 22–24 and notes 164–6'
,, ,, 135, note 46, *for* '*T.L.M.A.S.* vii' *read* '*T.L.M.A.S.* xiii'
,, ,, 139, note 82, *for* '*T.L.M.A.S.* vii' *read* '*T.L.M.A.S.* xiii'
,, ,, 143*a*, lines 20–1, *delete from* 'There was' *to* '1547,⁸⁷' *and for* 'but the' *read* '. The'
,, ,, 143*a*, line 23, *for* '⁸⁸' *read* '⁸⁷' *and for* '⁸⁹' *read* '⁸⁸'
,, ,, 143*a*, line 26, *for* 'Wood, in' *read* 'Wood,⁸⁹ in'
,, ,, 143, note 87, *delete whole footnote*
,, ,, 143, note 88, *for* '88' *read* '87'
,, ,, 143, note 89, *for* '89' *read* '88'
,, ,, 143, note 90, *for* '90' *read* '89' *and for* '261/1; King's' *read* '261/1. ⁹⁰ King's'
,, ,, 144*a*, line 15, *for* 'six bells,' *read* 'eight bells, six of'
,, ,, 144*a*, line 21, *delete* 'a silver flagon of before 1685²⁴'
,, ,, 144*a*, line 22, *for* '²⁵' *read* '²⁴'. *Thereafter insert* 'There was once a flagon of before 1685²⁵'
,, ,, 144, note 22, *before* 'Par.' *insert* '*T.L.M.A.S.* xviii(2), no. 140;'
,, ,, 144, note 24, *for* '24' *read* '25'
,, ,, 144, note 25, *for* '25' *read* '24'
,, ,, 152*b*, line 27, *for* 'branch of' *read* 'branch from'
,, ,, 170*a*, note 7, *for* 'W. R. Grimes' *read* 'W. F. Grimes'
,, ,, 172*b*, line 18 from end, *for* 'geminga' *read* 'gumeninga'
,, ,, 180*b*, line 1 from end, *for* 'Hatch End' *read* 'Pinner'
,, ,, 188*b*, line 6 from end, *for* '1910' *read* '1908'
,, ,, 188, note 2, *for* '80' *read* '18'
,, ,, 188, note 17, line 1, *before* 'Land' *insert* 'A. E. Bennett and H. V. Borley, *Lond. Transport Rlys.* 22;'
,, ,, 195*a*, note 21, *for* 'Perkins' *read* 'Perkin'
,, ,, 198*b*, line 19 from end, *for* 'in 1845' *read* 'by 1844'
,, ,, 198*b*, line 4 from end, *for* '1886' *read* '1885'
,, ,, 198, note 38, *for* '320' *read* '80'
,, ,, 199*a*, lines 3–5, *after* 'in' *delete rest of sentence and substitute* '1915, Northwick Park in 1923, and Preston Road halt (a station from 1932) in 1908.'
,, ,, 199*a*, line 6, *for* 'c. 1929' *read* 'in 1913'
,, ,, 199*a*, lines 13–19, *delete from* 'The line' *to* 'Hill' *and substitute* 'In 1910 the service was extended by the Metropolitan line to Rayners Lane, where a halt on the Uxbridge branch line had been opened in 1906. Metropolitan District line stations were opened in 1903 at Alperton (originally Perivale-Alperton), Sudbury Town, and Sudbury Hill.'
,, ,, 199*a*, line 26, *for* 'Greenford to Neasden' *read* 'Neasden to High Wycombe'
,, ,, 199*a*, lines 28–30, *delete from* 'and at' *to* '1910' *and substitute* ', at Wembley Hill, and at South Harrow (later Sudbury Hill).'
,, ,, 199, note 40, *before* 'Wemb.' *insert* 'A. E. Bennett and H. V. Borley, *Lond. Transport Rlys.* 21–22, 24, 28;'
,, ,, 199, note 41, *after* '48' *delete full point and add* '; Bennett and Borley, op. cit. 21–22, 28, and map facing p. 32.'
,, ,, 199, note 42, *delete whole footnote and substitute* 'Sommerfield, op. cit. 38; H. P. White, *Regional Hist. of Rlys. of Gt. Britain*, iii. 143.'
,, ,, 207*b*, line 31, *for* 'in 1933' *read* 'by 1932'
,, ,, 207, note 71, *delete whole footnote and substitute* 'Robbins, *Middlesex*, 330.'

Vol. IV, page 245*b*, lines 8–9, *delete whole sentence and substitute* 'The Brent, which had been straightened, continued to form the boundary between Wembley and Willesden.'

,,	,,	257, note 40, *for* '781' *read* '78'
,,	,,	258, note 62, *for* '8' *read* '80'
,,	,,	272*c*, s.v. Buryges, *for* 'Buryges' *read* 'Burgeys'
,,	,,	275*c*, s.v. Flanders Green, *for* 'Flanders Green' *read* 'Flaunden'
,,	,,	279*b*, s.v. Keane, *for* 'Keane' *read* 'Kean'
,,	,,	281*a*, s.v. Morton, *delete from* 'Cath.' *to* 'John (d. 1523), 115;' *and substitute* 'John, 210–11;'
,,	,,	281*c*, s.v. Norton, *before* 'fam.' *insert* 'Cath., w. of John (fl. 1517), m. 2 Thos. Roberts, 115; Chris., 115; Edith, *see* Ruislip; John (fl. 1517), 115; John (d. 1523), 115;'
,,	,,	283*c*, s.v. Roberts, *for* 'Morton' *read* 'Norton'
,,	,,	284*a*, s.v. Ruislip, Edith, *for* 'Morton' *read* 'Norton'